W9-DCD-118

**Readings
in Labor Economics
and Labor Relations**

WITHDRAWN
University of
Illinois Library
at Urbana-Champaign

Readings
in Labor Economics
and Labor Relations

Edited by

RICHARD L. ROWAN

The Wharton School
University of Pennsylvania

 Third Edition   1976

RICHARD D. IRWIN, INC.   Homewood, Illinois   60430
Irwin-Dorsey International   Arundel, Sussex   BN18 9AB
Irwin-Dorsey Limited   Georgetown, Ontario   L7G 4B3

© RICHARD D. IRWIN, INC., 1968, 1972, and 1976

All rights reserved. No part of this publication may be reproduced, stored in a retrieval system, or transmitted, in any form or by any means, electronic, mechanical, photocopying, recording, or otherwise, without the prior written permission of the publisher.

Third Edition

First Printing, March 1976

ISBN 0-256-01829-4
Library of Congress Catalog Card No. 75–35095
Printed in the United States of America

331.08
R78r
1976
cop.5

Institute of Labor

Preface

The general lack of readily available supplementary reading resources to meet the needs of students who take labor courses readily available creates the need for this book of readings in labor economics and labor relations. It is hoped that professors and students in the labor field will find it helpful in the areas of labor history, labor economics, collective bargaining, and industrial relations. Supplementation of basic texts has been the major criterion in the selection of articles. Particular emphasis has been placed on making available articles that libraries cannot stock in quantities, and an attempt has been made to select judiciously from both the classics and the current literature.

The book is organized in such a way that it can be used as an integrated whole, or any one section may be used to enhance the student's understanding in a particular area. Brief introductory remarks are provided for each section of the volume to give some assistance to the reader. An explanatory note highlighting the major points dealt with by the author in each essay enables one to determine the relative use of the material quickly and rather easily.

Permission from authors and publishers to reprint materials in this volume is acknowledged with sincere appreciation. Their kind cooperation has meant that a much finer book could be prepared than would have been possible otherwise.

I would like to thank Mark Blondman, my student assistant, who performed many details in a good-natured and efficient manner. He served as an excellent critic of the materials to be included, always reminding me that my function was not to impress the pros in the field but rather to provide an understandable and useful set of readings for the students. I am also constantly aware of the encouragement and inspiration provided by Marilyn, John, and Jennifer Rowan.

In the final analysis, the success of the book depends on the excellence of the articles selected; this, of course, means that the editor has a special sense of indebtedness to the authors whose research, analysis, and opinions are herein made available.

February 1976   RICHARD L. ROWAN

v

Contents

part three
THE STRUCTURE AND GOVERNMENT OF UNIONS

part four
COLLECTIVE BARGAINING

part one

An Introduction to Labor Economics and
Labor Relations
A. Human Resources in a Free Society

The two articles in this section contain general statements pertaining to the world or society in which industrial relations operates. They should be read together to give the student a broad perspective for understanding the particular labor problems and issues raised in the remaining articles in the book.

The development of human resources is a vital element in a free society, and the manner in which it is accomplished determines the quality of life. If the institutional forms—unions, corporations, governments—develop hardening of the arteries at any point in the maturation process, creativity is stifled, motivation is subdued, and human advancement is curtailed. Within this context, John W. Gardner poses the question: "Suppose one tried to imagine a society that would be relatively immune to decay—an ever-renewing society. What would it be like? What would be the ingredients that provided the immunity?" In part, the answer lies in the ability of a society to experiment, depart from the conventional, recognize challenges, and resolve conflict in an orderly manner.

A study of the field of labor and industrial relations may begin with a consideration of the points raised by Gardner. Are unions and corpo-rations willing to experiment with new solutions to challenging problems? Can conflict continue to be resolved with the traditional strike mechanism? Are the institutional forms capable of change in order that they may continue to renew themselves?

In order to better understand what the process of industrialization means to the relationship of various groups in a society, the authors of the second article, supported by the Ford Foundation, conducted research in some 35 countries to examine interrelationships between labor, management, and the government. Their study led to an interesting and important set of conclusions for those who wish to understand what may be the impact on labor and management under different forms of industrialization. In their article, the reader is made aware that labor problems in an industrial society are very similar regardless of the prevailing form of government. "As industrialization advances, the forces making for uniformity among different societies become stronger than those perpetuating diversity." Industrial relations problems are comparable from one country to another whether or not the economic order is oriented toward capitalism or socialism.

1. The Ever-Renewing Society: Is It Possible? Does Science Hold the Sought-For Pattern?*

Every few years the archeologists unearth another ancient civilization that flourished for a time and then died. The modern mind, acutely conscious of the sweep of history and chronically apprehensive, is quick to ask, "Is it our turn now?"

Rather than debate that overworked topic, I am going to ask another kind of question: Suppose one tried to imagine a society that would be relatively immune to decay—an ever-renewing society. What would it be like? What would be the ingredients that provided the immunity?

The skeptic may ask whether any society should last forever, even ours. It is not a crucial question. If longevity were the only virtue of the continuously renewing society, the whole exercise might turn out to be numbingly dull. But a society that has learned the secret of continuous renewal will be a more interesting and a more vital society—not in some distant future but in the present.

To accomplish renewal, we need to understand what prevents it.

When we talk about revitalizing a society, we tend to put exclusive emphasis on finding new ideas. But there is usually no shortage of new ideas; the problem is to get a hearing for them. And that means breaking through the crusty rigidity and stubborn complacency of the status quo. The aging society develops elaborate defenses against new ideas—"mind-forged manacles," in William Blake's vivid phrase.

The development of resistance to new ideas is a familiar process in the individual. The infant is a model of openness to new experience—receptive, curious, eager, unafraid, willing to try anything. As the years pass these priceless qualities fade. He becomes more cautious, less eager, and accumulates deeply rooted habits and fixed attitudes.

The same process may be observed in organizations. The young organization is willing to experiment with a variety of ways to solve its problems. It is not bowed by the weight of tradition. It rushes in where angels fear to tread. As it matures it develops settled policies and habitual modes of solving problems. In doing so, it becomes more efficient, but also less flexible, less willing to look freshly at each day's experience. Its increasingly fixed routines and practices are congealed in an elaborate body of written rules. In the final state of organizational senility there is a rule or precedent for everything. Someone has said that the last act of a dying organization is to get out a new and enlarged edition of the rule book.

And written rules are the least of the problems. In mature societies and organizations there grows a choking underbrush of customs and precedents. There comes to be an accepted way to do everything. Eccentric experimentation and radical departures from past practice are ruled out. The more pervasive this conventionality, the less likely is the innovator to flourish. Sir Henry Bessemer, inventor of the Bessemer process for steelmaking, said,

I had an immense advantage over many others dealing with the problem inasmuch as I had no fixed ideas derived from long-established practice to control and bias my mind, and did not suffer from the general belief that whatever is, is right.

* Reproduced with permission of the author and publisher from *Saturday Review,* January 5, 1963. Copyright 1963 Saturday Review, Inc.

† John W. Gardner is a former Secretary of Health, Education, and Welfare and is currently Chairman of Common Cause, Washington, D.C.

As a society becomes more concerned with precedent and custom, it comes to care more about how things are done and less about whether they are done. The man who wins acclaim is not the one who "gets things done" but the one who has an ingrained knowledge of the rules and accepted practices. Whether he accomplishes anything is less important than whether he conducts himself in an "appropriate" manner.

The body of custom, convention, and "reputable" standards exercises such an oppressive effect on creative minds that new developments in a field often originate outside the area of respectable practice. The break with traditional art was not fostered within the Academy. Jazz did not spring from the bosom of the respectable music world. The land grant colleges, possibly the most impressive innovation in the history of American higher education, did not spring from the inner circle of higher education as it then existed. Motels, the most significant development in innkeeping of this generation, were at first regarded with scorn by reputable hotel people.

Vested interests constitute another problem for the aging society. Certain things remain unchanged for the simple reason that changing them would jeopardize the rights, privileges, or advantages of specific individuals. Many established ways of doing things are held in place not by logic nor even by habit but by the enormous restraining force of vested interests. The phrase "vested interests" has been associated with individuals or organizations of wealth and power, but the vested interests of workers may be as strong as those of the top executives.

The more democratic an organization (or society), the more clearly it will reflect the interests of its members. So a democratic group may be particularly susceptible to the rigidifying force of vested interest.

Still another reason for the loss of vitality and momentum in a society is a lowered level of motivation. It is not always easy to say why motivation deteriorates. Perhaps people stop believing in the things they once believed in—the things that gave meaning to their efforts. Perhaps they grow soft from easy living. Perhaps they fall into the decadent habit of imagining that intense effort is somehow unsophisticated, that dedication is naive, that ambition is a bit crude. Or perhaps a rule-ridden society has bottled up their energy, or channeled it into all the tiny rivulets of conformity.

One may argue, as Toynbee does, that a society needs challenge. It is true. But societies differ notably in their capacity to see the challenge that exists. No society has ever so mastered the environment and itself that no challenge remained; but a good many have gone to sleep because they failed to understand the challenge that was undeniably there.

So much for the factors that contribute to loss of vitality in a society. What can be done about them?

Many of the qualities crucial to a society's continued vitality are qualities of youth: vigor, flexibility, enthusiasm, readiness to learn. This could lead us to imagine that the critical question is how to stay young. But youth implies immaturity. And though everyone wants to be youthful, no one wants to be immature.

Every society must mature; but much depends on how the maturation takes place. A society whose maturing consists simply of acquiring more firmly established ways of doing things is headed for the graveyard—even if it learns to do those things with greater and greater skill. In the ever-renewing society, what matures is a system of framework within which continuous innovation, renewal, and rebirth can occur.

Concern with decay and renewal in societies must give due emphasis both to continuity and change. The scientist in his laboratory may seem to be the personification of innovation and change, yet he functions effectively because of certain deeply established continuities in his life. As a scientist, he is living out a tradition several centuries old in its modern incarnation, thousands of years old in its deeper roots. And every move he makes reflects skills, attitudes, and habits of mind that were years in the making. He is part of an enduring tradition and a firmly established intellectual system; but it is a tradition and a system designed to accomplish its own continuous renewal.

The free society is not the only kind that can accomplish change. A totalitarian regime coming to power on the heels of a revolution may be well fitted to accomplish one great burst of change. But in the long run its spurt of energy is not only in danger of dying out but of being replaced by deadly rigidity. Compared to the free society, it is not well fitted for continuous renewal.

One crucial respect in which the ever-renewing society parts company with all totalitarianism is in pluralism. The ever-renewing society is willing to entertain diverse views. There are many sources of initiative rather than one. Power is widely dispersed rather than tightly held. There are multiple channels through which the individual may gain information and express his views.

It would be hard to overemphasize the importance of pluralism in keeping a society alive. The ever-renewing society is not convinced that it enjoys eternal youth. It knows that it is forever growing old and must look to its seed beds. If a society is dominated by one official point of view, the tentative beginnings of a new point of view may be a matter of devastating strain and conflict. In a pluralistic society, where there are already various points of view, the emergence of another is hardly noticed. In an open society freedom of communication insures that the new ideas will be brought into confrontation with the old.

Perhaps the most important characteristic of an ever-renewing system is that it has built-in provisions for vigorous criticism. It protects the dissenter and the nonconformist. It knows that from the ranks of the critics come not only cranks and troublemakers but saviors and innovators. And since the spirit that welcomes nonconformity is a fragile thing, the ever-renewing society does not depend on that spirit alone. It devises explicit legal and constitutional arrangements to protect the critic.

And that brings us to another requirement for the continuously renewing society. It must have some capacity to resolve conflicts, both internal and external. Without such capacity, society either will be destroyed or will dissipate its energies in the maintenance of fiercely entrenched feuds. The peace that it seeks is not a state of passivity and uneventfulness. It knows that without the ebb and flow of conflict and tension progress will not be made in eradicating old evils or opening new frontiers; but it is committed to the orderly "management of tensions." Thus in its internal affairs it deliberately makes possible certain kinds of conflict, e.g., by protecting dissenters and assuring them a hearing; but it creates a framework of rules which will assure that the conflict is resolved in an orderly fashion. It devises institutional arrangements that provide a harmless outlet for minor tensions and resolve some of the worst tensions before they reach the point of explosion.

In the last analysis, no society will be capable of continuous renewal unless it produces the kind of men who can further that process. It will need innovative men and men with the capacity for self-renewal.

An awareness of this need is now being expressed in the popularity of the word creativity.

It is more than a word today, it is an incantation. It is a kind of psychic wonder drug, powerful and presumably painless; and everyone wants a prescription. But the fact that the word has become a slogan should not make us antagonistic to the thing itself. What is implied in the word creativity, rightly conceived, is something that the continuously renewing society needs very much.

Only a handful of men and women in any population will achieve the highest levels of creativity and innovation. But a good many can be moderately creative, and even more can show some spark of creativity at some time in their lives. The number of men and women who exhibit some measure of creativity, and the extent to which they exhibit it, may depend very much on the climate in which they find themselves.

From all that we know of the creative individual—and we now know a good deal—he thrives on freedom. Recent research shows that he is not the capricious and disorderly spirit some romantics have imagined him to be. He may be quite conventional with respect to all the trivial customs and niceties of life. But in the area of his creative work he must be free to believe or doubt, agree or disagree. He must be free to ask the unsettling questions and free to come up with disturbing answers.

When Alexander the Great visited Diogenes and asked whether he could do anything for the famed teacher, Diogenes replied, "Only stand out of my light." Perhaps some day we shall know how to heighten creativity. Until then, one of the best things we can do for creative men and women is to stand out of their light.

No one knows why some individuals seem capable to self-renewal while others do not. The people interested in adult education have struggled heroically to increase the opportunities for self-development, and they have succeeded marvelously. Now they had better turn to the thing that is really blocking self-development—the individual's own intricately designed, self-constructed prison, or to put it another way, the individual's incapacity for self-renewal.

It is not unusual to find that the major changes in life—marriage, a move to a new city, a new job, or a national emergency—reveal to us quite suddenly how much we had been imprisoned by the comfortable web we had woven around ourselves. Unlike the jailbird, we don't know that we have been imprisoned until after we have broken out. It was a common experience during World War II that men and women who had been forced to break the pattern of their lives often discovered within themselves resources and abilities they had not known to exist.

When we have learned to accomplish such self-renewal without wars and other culturally expensive disasters, we shall have discovered one of the most important secrets a society can learn, a secret that will unlock new resources of vitality throughout the society. And we shall have done something to avert the hardening of the arteries that attacks so many societies. Men who have lost their adaptiveness naturally resist change. The most stubborn protector of his own vested interest is the man who has lost the capacity for self-renewal.

What are the characteristics of the self-renewing man, and what might we do to foster those characteristics? Though we are far from understanding these matters, we have a few pieces of the puzzle.

1. The self-renewing man is versatile and adaptive. He is not trapped in the techniques, procedures, or routines of the moment. He is not the victim of fixed habits and attitudes. He is not imprisoned by extreme specialization. This last point is so important (and so easily misunderstood) that we must deal with it cautiously. Specialization is a universal feature of biological functioning, dramatically observable in insect societies and in the structure and functioning of the cells that make up a living organism. In humans, it is not peculiar to the modern age. Division of labor is older than recorded history. So specialization as such is no cause for alarm. But specialization today has extended far beyond anything we knew in the past; and this presents two difficulties. First, there are tasks that cannot be performed by men too far gone in specialism —leadership and management, certain kinds of innovation, communication, teaching, and many of the responsibilities of child-rearing and citizenship. Second, the highly specialized person often loses the adaptability so essential today. He may not be able to reorient himself when technological change makes his specialty obsolete.

In a rapidly changing world, versatility is a priceless asset, and the self-renewing man has not lost that vitally important attribute. He may be a specialist, but he has also retained the capacity to function as a generalist. Within limits he has even retained the capacity to change specialties.

We are beginning to understand how to educate for versatility and renewal, but we must deepen that understanding. If we indoctrinate the young person in an elaborate set of fixed beliefs, we are insuring his early obsolescence. The alternative is to develop skills, attitudes, habits of mind, and the kinds of knowledge and understanding that will be the instruments of continuous change and growth on the part of the young person.

This suggests a standard in terms of which we may judge the effectiveness of all education— and so judged, much education today is monumentally ineffective. All too often we are giving young people cut flowers when we should be teaching them to grow their own plants. We are stuffing their heads with the products of earlier innovation rather than teaching them how to innovate. We think of the mind as a storehouse to be filled rather than as an instrument to be used.

2. The self-renewing man is highly motivated and respects the sources of his own energy and motivation. He knows how important it is to believe in what he is doing. He knows how important it is to pursue the things about which he has deep conviction. Enthusiasm for the task to be accomplished lifts him out of the ruts of habit and customary procedure. Drive and conviction give him the courage to risk failure. (One of the reasons mature people stop learning is that they become less and less willing to risk failure.) And not only does he respond to challenge; he sees challenge where others fail to see it.

But the society does not always find these attributes easy to live with. Drive and conviction can be a nuisance. The enthusiast annoys people by pushing ideas a little too hard. He makes mistakes because he is too eager. He lacks the cool, detached urbanity of the ideal organization man. But the ever-renewing society sees high motivation as a precious asset and allows wide latitude to the enthusiast. It does more than that—much more. It puts a strong emphasis on standards, on excellence, on high performance. It fosters a climate in which dedication, enthusiasm and drive are not only welcomed but expected. It does not accept the "sophisticated" view that zeal is somehow unworthy of cultivated people.

3. For the self-renewing man the development of his own potentialities and the process of self-discovery never end. It is a sad but unarguable fact that most human beings go through life only partially aware of the full range of their abilities. In our own society we could do much more than we now do to encourage self-development. We could, for example, drop the increasingly silly fiction that education is for youngsters, and devise arrangements suitable for lifelong learning. An even more important task is to remove the obstacles to individual fulfillment. This means doing away with the gross inequalities of opportunity imposed on some of our citizens by race prejudice and economic hardship. It means a continuous and effective operation of "talent salvage" to assist young people to achieve the promise they have within them.

But the development of one's talent is only part, perhaps the easiest part, of self-development. Another part is self-knowledge. The maxim "know thyself"—so ancient, so deceptively simple, so difficult to follow—has gained in richness of meaning as we learn more about man's nature. Modern research in psychology and psychiatry has shown the extent to which mental health is bound up in a reasonably objective view of the self, in accessibility of the self to consciousness, and in acceptance of the self. And we have learned how crucial is the young person's search for identity.

Josh Billings said, "It is not only the most difficult thing to know one's self but the most inconvenient." It is a lifelong process, and formal education is only a part of the process—though an important part. Consider the comment of Learned Hand in his discussion of liberty: "By enlightenment men gain insight into their own being, and that is what frees them."

The ever-renewing society will be a free society. It will understand that the only stability possible today is stability in motion. It will foster a climate in which the seedlings of new ideas can survive and the deadwood of obsolete ideas be hacked out. Above all, it will recognize that its capacity for renewal depends on the individuals who make it up. It will foster innovative, versatile, and self-renewing men and women and give them room to breathe.

2. Industrialism and Industrial Man*

Clark Kerr, Frederick H. Harbison, John T. Dunlop, and Charles A. Myers†

Over five years ago the four of us wrote an article for the *International Labour Review* entitled "The Labour Problem in Economic Development: A Framework for Reappraisal."[1] In that article we suggested an "alternate framework" to replace the "traditional analysis" of labour problems in modern industrial society. We argued that it is "the process of industrialisation" rather than "capitalism" which gives rise to labour problems, that industrial systems differ according to the nature and effectiveness of enterprise organisations and of the elites that direct them, and that "one universal response" to industrialisation is "protest" on the part of the labour force as it is fitted into the new social structure. Then, as now, we sought to go beyond the mere description of individual countries; we sought a system of ideas upon which to make generalisations concerning all industrialising societies at all stages of their development.

In the course of the past five years we have learned much from our own studies and travels as well as from those of our colleagues in the Inter-University Study of Labour Problems in Economic Development. The four of us have ourselves travelled on all five continents. The Inter-University Study has sponsored over 40 projects involving research in over 35 countries; and a total of 73 persons of 11 different nationalities have been involved in some phase of its work. Persons associated with the Inter-University Study

have to date published 14 books and 23 articles, and another 10 to 12 monographs are already in the advanced stages of preparation. On the basis of our own study and that of our colleagues, we have presented in a forthcoming volume our new formulation of labour problems in economic development, and in this article we shall summarise a few of our basic ideas and findings.[2]

We project a future, still long distant, with a world-wide society of "pluralistic industrialism," in which managers and the managed may still carry on their endless tug of war, in which the contest between the forces of uniformity and diversity will continue, but in which persuasion, pressure, and manipulation will take the place of the open industrial conflict of the earlier stages of development.

In this new formulation, moreover, we have been forced to alter considerably some of our earlier concepts. We have become convinced, for example, that "protest" is not such a dominant aspect of industrialisation as we once thought. Indeed, labour protest is on the decline even as industrialisation around the world proceeds at an ever faster pace. Thus, instead of concentrating on protest, we have turned our attention to the inevitable "structuring" of the managers and the managed in the course of industrialisation and to the complex "web of rules" which binds men together in new chains of subordination and creates a network of rights, obligations, and functions of workers, technicians, and managers in the hierarchy of far-flung private and governmental organisations.

This article, as well as the book upon which it

* Copyright © International Labour Office, Geneva (Switzerland). Reprinted from the *International Labour Review*, Vol. 82, No. 3, September 1960, pp. 1–15, by permission.

† At the time of writing, the authors were professors at the University of California, Princeton, Harvard, and MIT, respectively.

[1] *International Labour Review*, Vol. 71, No. 3, March 1955.

[2] Clark Kerr, Frederick H. Harbison, John T. Dunlop, and Charles A. Myers, *Industrialism and Industrial Man* (Cambridge, Mass.: Harvard University Press, 1960).

is based, is a partial summary of our views at this time. But it by no means constitutes our "final judgment," for we are committed to pressing our inquiry forward into new areas.

THE LOGIC OF INDUSTRIALISM

Industrialisation has been abroad in the world for only about two centuries. One hundred years ago only England had crossed the great divide on the road toward the industrial society. Today, in the middle of the 20th century, perhaps a third of the world's population lives in countries which are at least partially industrialised. The remaining two-thirds of the world's peoples, spurred by the revolution of rising aspirations, are in the throes of initiating the march toward industrialism. Probably by the middle of the 21st century industrialisation will have swept away most pre-industrial forms of society, except possibly for a few odd backwaters. This is the great transformation in the history of mankind on this planet—more basic, more rapid, and more universal than anything that has gone before. The industrial society knows no national boundaries; it is destined to be a world-wide society.

What then are the common characteristics and imperatives which are inherent in this universal society toward which all peoples are marching? First, the industrial society is associated with a level of technology far in advance of that of earlier societies. The science and technology of industrialism is based upon research organisations: universities, research institutions, laboratories, and specialised departments of enterprise. In this society it is axiomatic that the frontiers of knowledge are limitless. Industrial society is also characterised by vast investments in plant, equipment, and machinery which demand the accumulation of capital on a massive scale.

Secondly, the industrial system demands in its labour force a wide range of professions and skills. Indeed, the creation of high-level manpower is one of the major problems encountered in the transition to industrialism. And, since science and technology generate continuous change, new skills and occupations are constantly replacing the old. Thus, industrialism requires an educational system functionally related to the skills and professions imperative to its technology. The variety of skills, responsibilities, and employment conditions at the work place creates a new ordering or structuring of society. There are successive levels of authority of managers and the managed as well as extensive specialisation of functions at various levels in the industrial hierarchy. And, as part of this structuring process, the working forces are governed by a web of rules which prescribes such things as hiring, compensation, layoffs, promotions, shift changes, transfers, retirements, and discipline in the work place.

Thirdly, industrialism is associated with sizeable organisations. It is mainly an urban society. It is necessarily characterised by large governmental organisations. And the production of goods and services becomes ever more concentrated in the hands of large enterprises, whether they be private or public. In other words, industrial society is "the organisation society."

Fourthly, the industrial society, in order to survive, must develop a "consensus" which relates individuals and groups to each other and provides a common body of ideas, beliefs, and value judgments. The working force, for example, must be dedicated to hard work, and its individuals must assume responsibility for performance of assigned tasks and norms. Regardless of how this is achieved the industrial society must secure a pace of work and a personal responsibility exercised by individual workers and managers unknown in economic activity in traditional societies.

These, in brief, are the common features of the industrial society. Every case of industrialisation, however, may not be expected to be identical. There are different roads to industrialism, and the choice of these roads is made by an elite minority which in effect organises and leads the march toward the new society.

For purposes of analysis we have delineated five ideal types of elite which may under varying circumstances and depending upon the pre-industrial society assume leadership in the industrialisation process. Each of these elites has a strategy by which it seeks to order the surrounding society in a consistent manner.

The dynastic elite is drawn from the old military or landed aristocracy, and it is held together by a common allegiance to the established order. It cherishes the virtues and the institutions of the past—the family, the national State, private property, and the notion that people born into one class are sentenced by predestination to remain there. It organises a paternal industrial society, with a paternalistic State, paternalistic employers, and the idea of dependent workers, who are loyal to their superiors and beholden to them for their welfare and leadership. This elite, though in some cases moving slowly along the road, often organises a relatively smooth passage from the traditional to the industrial society. It was prominent in the industrialisation of Japan and in the early stages of industrial development in Germany.

The members of the second elite are drawn from a rising middle class. Its ideology is economically individualistic and politically egalitarian. Its creed is opportunity for the individual, laissez faire as a policy of government, with decentralisation of decision-making power. This elite takes progress for granted, relying on the free interplay of market forces to promote the common good. It can perhaps best be identified with capitalism in the early stages of the Industrial Revolution in England and its subsequent spread to the United States.

The third elite may be characterised as the revolutionary intellectuals. It sweeps aside both the dynastic elite and the rising middle class. The revolutionary intellectuals, self-identified for the task of leadership by their support of what they claim to be a scientific and superior theory of history, set out to pour new wine into entirely new bottles. Their principal new bottle is the monolithic, centralised State. The prime movers of this society demand a rapid forced march toward industrialism, and they mould education, art, literature, and labour organisations to their single-minded purpose.

Next are the colonial administrators who have been, in the past at least, the originators of industrialisation in some of the underdeveloped countries of the world. Their concern, however, is less with the countries they rule and more with the interests and the requirements of the home countries. For this reason they face an almost impossible task. They are not only exponents of a new system of production; they are also members of an external or alien society. Inevitably, with the march of time, they are dislodged peacefully or overthrown violently.

The fifth elite is composed of the new nationalist leaders and their followers in the emerging nations of the world. They may be drawn from the leadership of prior independence movements, military leaders, or persons who were sent abroad to be educated. The members of this group are in a hurry—to deliver and to deliver fast. They are sparked by nationalism, but in itself nationalism is more of a sentiment than a rational system of thought. They are prone to seize upon any or all means to build rapidly the political and economic structures of their countries. They have no single philosophy of economic progress; but they have before them the choice of different roads—that travelled by the middle class, that of the dynastic elite, and that of the revolutionary intellectuals. As late starters on the march towards industrialism they can pick and choose both technology and organisational arrangements to effect the transition. The drive of these new nationalist leaders is well illustrated by these words of Gamal Abdel Nasser: "We shall march forward as one people who have vowed to proceed on a holy march of industrialising."

To be sure, these "ideal types" seldom appear in a pure form; they abstract from reality. The industrialising elite in any particular country characteristically is a mixture of several of these types, but as analytical devices they give a structure to the task of understanding the different forms of industrialisation; they help to explain the strategies involved and the patterns of management-labour relations which emerge.

Each of the industrialising elites develops a strategy toward the changes to be made in the culture of the traditional societies. The critical elements in the cultural environment are the family system, class and race, religious and ethical valuations, legal concepts, and the concept of the national State. Some elements of the pre-existing culture are more resistant than others to the penetration of industrialisation; some elites, such as for example the dynastic, place higher priority on preserving the traditional values. In modern times the elites encounter resistance to change, but concurrently they are assisted by strong aspirations for rapid improvement in living standards. The strategy and success of the different industrialising elites are thus affected in part by the strength and rigidity of the pre-industrial culture and in part by the revolution of rising aspirations. But in the end the new culture of industrialism successfully penetrates and changes the old order.

The elites are also confronted by a number of other constraints, no matter what strategy they elect on the road to the industrial society. First, there are the economic limitations in the short period. These include the availability of capital, the natural resources of the country, its stage of educational development, the level and rate of increase of population, and the capacity to engage in export trade. Secondly, the chronological date at which a country embarks on the industrialising process makes a difference in the course of growth. There are advantages and disadvantages in an early as compared with a late start. Both the timing of the initial thrust of industrialisation and the level of development from which a country starts are likely to shape the magnitude of the effort confronting the elites and the policies adopted to start the journey.

Finally, the industrialising elites are required to make a series of major decisions within the cultural and economic constraints just mentioned. Among the more important questioned posed are these: How fast shall the society be industrialised? How shall the requisite capital formation be secured? What shall be the priorities in development projects? What shall be the characteristics of the educational system and the means of training managers, technicians, and workers? How self-sufficient or integrated shall the country be with the world economy? And shall it be the conscious aim of public policy to limit the increase in population? Taken as a group, the answers to these questions describe a programme and a time schedule for an industrialising elite.

A detailed analysis of the strategies of the different elites in decision-making along the road of industrialisation lies beyond the scope of this article.[3] In general, however, the dynastic elite is prone to be content with a less strenuous pace; it offers continuity between the old and the new. The rising middle class is apt to rely upon the market and upon elected governments to determine the pace of industrialisation; it offers individual choice. The revolutionary intellectuals rely upon the single-party State as the engine of development; they offer a harsh but high-velocity industrialisation. The colonial administrators gear the pace to the needs and interests of the mother country; but they are doomed to extinction. The new nationalist leaders encounter perhaps the most serious problems in setting the pace. The aspirations of their masses have been stimulated to expect immediate and substantial results from national independence, while the political uncertainties of a new State complicate the problems of accumulating the necessary human and material capital from both within and beyond the national borders.

Given the economic and cultural limitations listed above, the faster the pace of industrialisation the greater is the need to restrict consumption in order to accumulate capital, the more necessary is the resort to direct control by the government, the more drastic is the required reorganisation in agriculture associated with the development of an industrial labour force, the more likely is the resort to a rigid ideology and compulsion in motivating the work force, and the more centralised must be the web of rules to govern the work place. In determining the pace and the rationale of industrialisation, some elites

are more consistently ruthless and determined than others.

In summary, the imperatives of industrialisation cause the industrialising elites to overcome certain constraints and to achieve certain objectives which are the same in all societies undergoing transformation. The approaches which they take to these constraints and objectives explain in large measure the diversity among industrialising economies. Using this system of thought, or logic of industrialism, an examination will now be made of the extent and nature of the labour problems which are likely to arise during the development process.

THE MANAGERS AND THE MANAGED

The labour problems of industrialising societies have their origin in the structuring of relationships between the managers and the managed. They both give rise to and emanate from the web of rules which links men together in the new society. They are related to the power, position, and policies of the managers of enterprises whether public or private; to the development of the industrial working forces; to the impact of industrialisation on the worker and his response thereto; and to the making of the rules by workers, managers, and the State. Each of these aspects will now be examined briefly.

The Managers of Enterprise

The managers of enterprises, public and private, and their technical and professional subordinates are part of every industrialising elite. Management is a hierarchy of functions and people. It includes entrepreneurs, managers, administrators, engineers, and professional specialists who hold the top positions in enterprises. So defined, management is crucial to the success of any industrialisation effort. It may be viewed from three perspectives: as an economic resource, as a class, and as a system of authority within the enterprise.

As an economic resource, management becomes more important with the advance of industrialisation. The number of persons in the managerial ranks increases both absolutely and relatively in the economy. This is the inevitable consequence of larger capital outlays, the pace of innovation, the use of more modern machinery, the growth of markets, and the increasing complexity of advancing industrial societies. The accumulation of managerial resources, moreover, requires ever-increasing outlays for technical and

---

[3] See Kerr et al., *Industrialism and Industrial Man*, chap. 5, for fuller discussion.

managerial education, and forces educational institutions to become more functionally oriented to the training of skilled technicians, engineers, scientists, and administrators.

As a class, management becomes more of a profession as industrialisation progresses. In the early stages of development, where enterprises may be new or very small, access to the managerial ranks may be largely dependent on family relationships in some societies, or political connections in others. But as the managerial class must inevitably grow larger it becomes less arbitrarily exclusive. As industrial society lays ever more stress upon scientific discovery, technological innovation, and economic progress, patrimonial and political managers are swept aside by the professionals.

As a system of authority, management becomes less dictatorial in its labour policies. In all societies, of course, management cherishes the prerogatives of a rule maker. But others, such as the State and the labour unions, also seek and gain a voice in the rule-making process. As industrialisation advances, they tend to limit, to regulate, or sometimes even to displace the unilateral authority of management over the labour force. As a consequence, dictatorial or paternalistic direction gives way to a kind of constitutional management in which the rules of employment are based upon laws, decisions of governments, collective contracts, or agreements. In a few situations employer-employee relationships within the firm may develop along democratic lines with joint participation.

The differences in management are related to the stage of industrial development and also to the elites which assume leadership in the society. The dynastic elite, for example, tends to perpetuate a family-oriented and paternalistic managerial system, whereas the middle-class elite introduces a professionalised managerial class more quickly. The revolutionary intellectuals try to prolong the life of political management, while the new nationalist leaders may encourage the development of any or all kinds of management as the occasion demands.

Yet, despite the fact that the ranks of professional management are destined to expand in all industrialising societies, the managerial class has neither the capacity nor the will to become the dominant ruling group. The managers are characteristically the agents of stockholders, of state bureaucracies, or in some cases of workers' councils. Since they are preoccupied with the internal affairs of enterprise, which become ever more complex, the members of the managerial class are prone to become conformists rather than leaders in the larger affairs of society.[4]

The Development of the Industrial Labour Force

Most countries have human resources which are available for industrial employment, but no country is endowed with persons possessing the habits, skills, and "know-how" necessary for industrial development. Thus, the industrialising elites, and particularly the managers of enterprises, are required to build a large and diversified industrial labour force. This involves four interrelated processes: recruitment, commitment, upgrading, and security.

Recruitment is the first step in development of the industrial labour force. It is the process of selecting, hiring, and assigning persons to jobs. Commitment is a longer and more intricate process. It consists of achieving the workers' permanent attachment to and acceptance of industrial employment as a way of life. Upgrading is the process of building the skills, the work habits, and the incentives for productive employment. It involves the training and the energising of the working force. Security includes the various facilities which may be necessary to provide worker security both on and off the job.

From our studies and those of others we have concluded that recruitment, commitment, and upgrading of labour forces can be achieved reasonably well in any industrialising society. Industrial man is a product not of a particular climate or ancestry but rather of persistent effort and investment. Despite the allegations to the contrary, man everywhere is adaptable to the industrial system.

The more difficult and persistent problem is that would-be workers are more often pounding on the gates to be let inside the factory system. Surplus labour and chronic redundancy is the more common problem of most of the underdeveloped countries, even in the early stages of industrialisation. Population keeps expanding more rapidly than industrial employment; urban areas become overcrowded; underemployment persists in the rural areas even as industrialisation advances. The rate of population increase tends to fall only after living standards have risen substantially, and this takes time even in those countries making a rapid march toward industrialism.

[4] A comprehensive analysis of management is presented in another book in the Inter-University series: Frederick Harbison and Charles A. Myers, *Management in the Industrial World, an International Analysis*.

The newly industrialising countries, therefore, are faced with a dilemma—where and how to hold surplus labour. If held on the land, disguised unemployment mounts; if held within the factories, productive efficiency is impaired; if held outside the factories in overcrowded urban areas, the strain on community resources becomes intolerable. Only employment on massive, labour-intensive public works, roads, or irrigation systems seems to offer an answer. Certainly, in the face of mounting pressures of population, industrialisation on its own offers no cure.

Here again the elites adopt somewhat different strategies in developing and managing industrial labour forces. The dynastic elite will rely more heavily on paternalistic devices to commit the worker to industrial enterprise; the middle class will depend upon the labour market; the revolutionary intellectuals will get commitment by ideological appeals, direction of employment, and differential incentives. The dynastic elite is likely to require the employers to provide jobs for all permanent members of the industrial working force but is unconcerned with employment problems outside the factory gates. The middle-class elite relies upon the forces of the product market to provide jobs in the long run. The revolutionary intellectuals either refuse to admit the existence of mass unemployment or mobilise a redundant labour force on public works projects. And the nationalist leaders tend to adopt any or all means which appear to offer the most satisfactory solution for the time being.

The Response of the Worker to Industrialisation

Industrialisation redesigns and restructures its human raw materials, whatever the source. Thus, the development of an industrial work force necessarily involves the destruction of old ways of life and the acceptance of the new imperatives of the industrial work community. While the worker is in the end malleable, his metamorphosis gives rise to many forms of protest.

Characteristically, the partially committed labour force may express protest through excessive absenteeism, turnover, theft, sabotage, and spontaneous or sporadic work stoppages. The committed labour force is more likely to organise industry-wide strikes and formal political activity, while day-to-day grievances are presented through disputes machinery or labour courts, largely without stoppages. Marx saw the intensity of protest increasing in the course of capitalist development. We hold a contrary view. Our studies reveal that protest tends to reach its peak relatively early in the transformation and to decline in its overt manifestations as industrialisation reaches the more advanced stages. Incipient protest is moderated, channelled, and redirected in the advanced industrial society.

The elites, of course, must cope with the problem of worker protest, and here again they adopt different policies toward the formation of labour organisations which possess potential economic and political power. And in each society the emerging labour organisations adapt themselves rather distinctively to the prevailing environment. The labour organisations in the dynastic society remain "foreign" to the elite; in the middle-class society, they tend to conform to the product market structure. The revolutionary intellectuals regard labour organisations as instruments of and subservient to the State. The colonial administrators find labour organisations always in opposition, forever pressing relentlessly for national independence. And the labour organisations under the new nationalist leaders are often beset with conflicting and divided loyalties, sometimes conforming to and on other occasions bringing pressure against the new regime.

Most labour organisations, and particularly those in the newly industrialising countries, pose thorny issues for the elites. First, they lay claim to higher wages, while the elites may be preoccupied with capital formation. Secondly, they may strike at a time when work stoppages will be detrimental to production. Thirdly, they of necessity demand redress of worker grievances and complaints, while the nationalist leaders, in particular, may be intent upon achieving better discipline, a faster rate of work, and more output. Finally, labour organisations are prone to seek independence and freedom as institutions, while the elites are more concerned with making them politically subservient or insuring that they will be politically neutral or powerless.

Labour organisations, in summary, are essentially reflections of the societies in which they develop. The universal responses of workers to industrialisation, and the nature of expressions of their protest, are increasingly moulded to conform and contribute to the strategy of the industrialising elites. Though the leaders of labour seldom rise to dominating positions in a society, they are persons who always warrant recognition.

The Rule Makers and the Rules

Industrialisation creates industrial workers, managers, and government agencies. All three are necessarily involved in industrial relations. And, just as industrialisation brings about different economic systems, so does it necessarily develop different "industrial relations systems." Again, according to the nature of the elites and to the stage of development, every industrial relations system fulfils at least three major functions. First, it defines the relative rights and responsibilities of workers, managers, and the State, and establishes the power relationships between them. Secondly, it channels and controls the responses of workers and managers to the dislocations, frustrations, and insecurities inherent in the industrialising process. And thirdly, it establishes the network of rules, both substantive and procedural, which govern the work place and the work community. Industrial relations systems reflect the persistent themes of uniformity and diversity which have been referred to in this analysis. In our book we have described in some detail the factors accounting for this uniformity and diversity, and we have also pointed out how specific rules are dependent upon the stage of development and the nature of the industrialising elites.[5] These rules govern such things as recruitment and commitment, levels of compensation, the wage structure, and procedures for settlement of disputes.

In effect, therefore, the industrial relations system provides the structure and the machinery for the functional relationship between the managers and the managed in any industrialising society. As a system it is related to the economic system with which it operates. Industrial relations systems, therefore, can be logically analysed and usefully compared. They are not unique, isolated institutional arrangements with particular significance only to a particular country. It is thus manifestly possible and desirable to compare labour problems in one country with those in another, and our analytical framework, we feel, offers a method for doing this.

THE ROAD AHEAD

As industrialisation advances, the forces making for uniformity among different societies become stronger than those perpetuating diversity. With the passage of time, each developing nation moves further from its pre-industrial stage and from its original industrial leaders. As they bring in new recruits from different strata, the various elites become less distinct. The ideological differences tend to fade; the cultural patterns of the world intermingle and merge. The once vast ideological differences between capitalism and communism give way to more pragmatic considerations in the operation of industrial society. Increasingly, the elites all appear in the same light.

The trend toward greater uniformity is attributable to a variety of pressures. Technology in itself is a unifying force. The thrust of progress also serves the cause of uniformity, and gradually there is less difference between the various categories of workers and industries in each country. Education brings about a new equality with the elimination of illiteracy and the development of skills. The State everywhere becomes ever larger and more important. Larger-scale enterprises are common hallmarks of all advanced industrial societies. Finally, the compulsion to compare helps to achieve uniformity. The pressures for progress and participation in a new economic order are enhanced by the world-wide character of industrialisation, by international trade, by travel, by modern means of communication, and by global exchange of ideas.

The road ahead leads to what we call "pluralistic industrialism." The fully developed industrial society in our view will be one in which the struggle between uniformity and diversity continues, a society which is centralising and decentralising at the same time, a dynamic society which, while marked by complex and conflicting pressures, develops a common cultural consensus.

In this pluralistic industrial society the State will not wither away. It will handle the conflict among the differing power elements in the society; it will control collusion by producers against consumers; and it will establish the relationship between members and their organisations. The managers of enterprise, whether public or private, will be professionals, technically trained and carefully selected for their tasks. They will be bureaucratic managers, if private, and managerial bureaucrats, if public. The distinction between managers will be based more upon the size and scope of their enterprises than upon the ownership of the means of production. Occupational and professional associations will range alongside the State and large-scale enterprise as centres of power and influence. And uniting the State, the enterprises, and the occupational associations will be a great web of rules established by all three entities, but particularly by the first.

In this society conflict will persist, but it will take the form of bureaucratic skirmishes rather

---

[5] For an even more extended discussion, see John T. Dunlop, *Industrial Relations Systems.*

than class war. Groups will jockey for position over the setting of jurisdictions, the authority to make decisions, the forming of alliances, and the granting or withdrawal of support or effort. The great battles of conflicting parties will be replaced by a myriad of minor contests over comparative details. Labour organisations will cease to be parts of class movements urging programmes of total reform and become more purely pressure groups representing the occupational interests of their members.

In this emerging world-wide society industrial man will be subject to great pressures of conformity imposed not alone by enterprise management but also by the State and by his occupational association. For most people any true scope for the independent spirit on the job will be missing. But, outside his working life, industrial man may enjoy more freedom than in most earlier forms of society. Politically he can have influence.

He will enjoy higher living standards, greater leisure, and more education. And, along with the bureaucratic conservatism of economic life, there may be a new Bohemianism in other aspects of man's existence which can give rise to a new search for individuality and a new meaning to liberty.

Technology need not, as Marx thought, reach into every corner of society. Indeed, the conformity to technology may bring a new dedication to individuality. This is the two-sided face of pluralistic industrialism that makes it a split personality looking in two directions at the same time. Utopia, of course, never arrives, but industrial man the world over will probably acquire greater freedom in his personal life at the cost of greater conformity in his working life. Industrialism can and will bring about for him a better existence.

B. Characteristics of the Labor Force

This section deals primarily with projections concerning the labor force to 1980, the concept of the labor force, and trends in the composition of the labor force. Students will notice that the materials presented here are drawn mainly from government publications. The *Monthly Labor Review*, published by the U.S. Department of Labor, is an excellent source of information, and every student in labor relations should become acquainted with it. In addition, the various bulletins published by the Bureau of Labor Statistics provide extensive data for those concerned with labor problems.

The first article in this section elaborates on employment trends to 1980. "General trends and growth factors that are expected to affect industry employment in a services economy . . . through the 1970s are described . . . for the major industry groups." Implications of the projections are discussed in a concluding part of the article. The second article discusses some of the problems involved with collecting unemployment data. Calame provides a good understanding of the way the survey is conducted that yields the unemployment statistic. He explains why some

critics have become skeptical of the unemployment rate.

The last three articles in this section deal with particular aspects of the labor force: discouraged workers, moonlighters, and women. In the past few decades, focus has been placed on the "hidden unemployed" or "discouraged workers" within the context of the labor supply concept. Discouraged workers are "those persons who want work but are not looking for a job because of a belief that their search would be in vain." Flaim discusses the problems of identifying and measuring "discouraged workers."

Those who hold more than one job in the labor force—moonlighters—constitute between 3 and 4 million people. Vera C. Perrella discusses the "reasons for moonlighting, degree of attachment to moonlighting, personal characteristics of multiple jobholders, and occupations, industries, and hours worked on primary and secondary jobs." In addition, the author indicates some of the social and economic aspects of moonlighting.

Women workers constitute a growing portion of the labor force. Waldman and McEaddy examine, by industry and occupation, the status of women in the labor force.

3. Employment Trends: Projections and Implications*

U.S. Department of Labor

The kind and level of manpower requirements of the 1970s are intertwined with the nature of the industrial changes that seem likely to occur over the decade.

General trends and growth factors that are expected to affect industry employment in a services economy (with 3 percent unemployment) through the 1970s are described below for the major industry groups. (See Chart 1.)

Service-Producing Industries

The most dramatic change in industry employment in recent years has been the employment shift towards service-producing industries. Shortly after the turn of this century, only three in every ten workers were in service industries. By 1950, the weight had shifted to just over five in every ten in service industries; by 1968 the proportion had inched to six in every ten. In 1980, close to seven in every ten workers—or 68 million—are projected to be in service industries. (See Table 1.)

Transportation, Communications, and Public Utilities. Employment in this group of industries is expected to increase to close to 5 million in 1980, up from 4.5 million in 1968. Despite this small employment gain, its share of total employment will decline from 5.6 percent in 1968 to 5 percent.

Transportation employment has been dominated by the long, slow decline in railroad employment during the postwar period. Even though employment in trucking and air transportation has expanded, the decline in railroad employment has been severe enough to cause an overall

decline in the average for all transportation industries. But a turnaround is expected: trucking and air transportation will increase fast enough to offset whatever further small railroad declines occur; an overall slow gain in employment is projected.

Public utilities and communications are highly productive service industries. Hence, even though the services provided by these industries are expected to expand significantly—output has the highest projected rate of increase through the 1970s among all nonfarm industries—employment will increase only moderately to 1980 and will decline as a proportion of total employment.

Trade. The largest of the service industries, wholesale and retail trade, is interwoven throughout the economic system in a network of wholesale and retail establishments. Trade employment changes are expected to parallel those of the whole economy and with trade's relative share —one fifth—of total employment remaining about the same in 1980. Employment, however, will rise from 16.6 million in 1968 to 20.5 million in 1980.

Retail trade employment will expand most rapidly in general merchandise stores and eating and drinking establishments. Technological developments such as vending machines, other self-service gadgets, and electronic computers for inventory control and billing will tend to retard employment growth.

Wholesale trade employment will increase more rapidly than that of retail trade. Employment in motor vehicles, automotive equipment, and machinery equipment and supply will be among the faster growing areas.

Finance, Insurance, and Real Estate. Employment in these industries is expected to increase at about the same rate as total employ-

* From U.S. Department of Labor, Bureau of Labor Statistics, *The U.S. Economy in 1980*, Bulletin 1673, 1970.

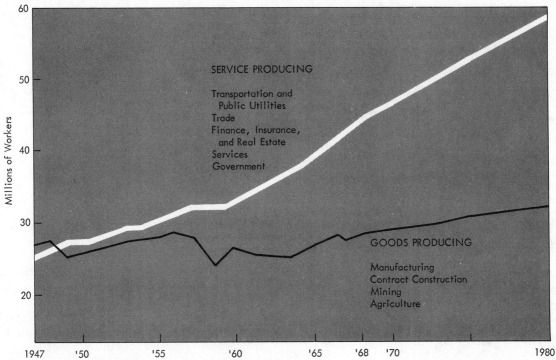

*Wage and salary workers only, except in agriculture which includes self-employed and unpaid family workers.

ment each year through the 1970s and to account for only a slightly larger share—4.7 percent—of total employment in 1980 than in 1968. Employment, however, will rise from 3.7 million in 1968 to 4.6 million in 1980.

Banking employment is expected to grow at a slower pace than in the last decade, as advancing automation eliminates many clerical functions. Electronic data processing equipment also is expected to slow employment growth in the security dealers and exchanges sector, a rapid growth area. Increase in the size of firms may also limit employment gains.

Although restrained somewhat by the computerization of recordkeeping functions, insurance employment will continue to grow at about the same pace as during the 1960s because of the steadily rising population.

Real estate employment will grow at a slightly faster pace than in the past decade; it is little affected by technological advances but highly responsive to the rising number of family formations.

Services.   These industries, including private household employment, will increase their share

of total employment by 1980, rising from 18.7 percent in 1968 to about 21 percent in 1980 and at a faster rate than total employment. Employment will rise to 21 million in 1980, up from 15 million in 1968.

Employment growth in this heterogeneous group of service industries, which include personal, business, health, and educational services, will be related to a substantial increase in population, a rapid rise in personal disposable income, expanding economic activity, and a growing demand for medical, educational, and other services. The output of these labor-intensive industries is less affected by technological change than many other industries, hence their employment growth is not restrained very much by productivity advances.

Within the services division, employment growth is expected in all major industries between 1968 and 1980, ranging from 14 percent for motion picture employment to almost 100 percent for miscellaneous business services. Growth in business services is expected to be particularly rapid as firms rely increasingly on advertising services to sell their products; on

TABLE 1   Changes in Total and Wage and Salary Employment by Industry Sector, 1965 and 1968 (actual) and 1980 (projected for services and durable goods economies) (in thousands)

| | 1965 | | 1968 | | 1980 Services Economy 3-Percent Unemployment | | 1980 Services Economy 4-Percent Unemployment | | 1980 Durables Economy 3-Percent Unemployment | | 1980 Durables Economy 4-Percent Unemployment | |
Industry Sector	Total Employment	Wage and Salary Employment	Total Employment*	Wage and Salary Employment*	Total Employment	Wage and Salary Employment*	Total Employment	Wage and Salary Employment*	Total Employment	Wage and Salary Employment*	Total Employment	Wage and Salary Employment*
Goods Producing												
Total	27,786	26,401	28,975	27,657	31,618	30,115	31,200	22,809	32,515	31,112	32,286	30,795
Manufacturing	18,454	18,062	20,125	19,768	22,358	21,935	22,133	21,712	23,240	22,817	23,005	22,584
Agriculture, forestry, and fisheries	4,671	4,521	4,154	4,012	3,188	3,030	3,156	3,000	3,192	3,034	3,160	3,004
Construction	3,994	3,186	4,050	3,257	5,482	4,600	5,427	4,553	5,595	4,713	5,539	4,665
Mining	667	632	646	610	590	550	584	544	588	548	582	542
Service Producing												
Total	46,782	41,367	51,813	46,449	67,982	62,085	67,300	61,465	66,785	60,885	66,114	60,279
Services industries	13,722	11,501	15,113	12,826	21,080	18,660	20,867	18,474	20,585	18,165	20,376	17,983
Trade	15,352	12,716	16,604	14,081	20,487	17,625	20,282	17,450	20,501	17,639	20,236	17,464
Transportation, communications, and public utilities	4,250	4,036	4,524	4,313	4,976	4,740	4,926	4,692	4,961	4,725	4,911	4,677
Finance, insurance, and real estate	3,367	3,023	3,726	3,383	4,639	4,260	4,593	4,217	4,538	4,159	4,493	4,117
Government	10,091	10,091	11,846	11,846	16,800	16,800	16,632	16,632	16,200	16,200	16,038	16,038

* Except for agriculture which includes self-employed and unpaid family workers.

accounting, auditing, bookkeeping, and computing services to handle their recordkeeping; on contract firms to provide maintenance service; and on audit bureaus and collecting agencies to cope with mushrooming consumer credit.

Government. Employment has grown faster in government than in any other sector in the economy. From 1960–68 employment grew at the rate of 4.5 percent a year, nearly 2½ times the rate for total employment. The sharp rise in recent years has been stimulated, however, by the needs of the Viet Nam war as well as by the rapid growth in population, the increasing proportion of young and old persons in the population who require more services, and the general growth in demand for more and better government services. Employment is projected to rise more slowly through the 1970s—at 2.9 percent a year—reaching 16.8 million in 1980, up from 11.8 million in 1968. Employment among federal government workers will rise only slightly, but state and local employment will continue to expand rapidly.

Although the rate of increase in state and local government employment will be higher compared with almost any other sector, the growth will be slower than during the 1960s, mainly because of an anticipated easing in the rate of growth for educational services, which account for roughly half of total employment in state and local governments.

Goods-Producing Industries

Despite a steadily rising total output of goods to unprecedented levels through the 1970s, the goods-producing industries encompass the only major industries in which employment is expected to decline—mining and agriculture—and one industry—manufacturing—for which employment growth is expected to be slower than during the 1960s. Only one goods producer, construction, is expected to show a quickened pace of employment growth through the 1970s. This modest employment expansion, overall, for goods-producing industries, in the face of an overall healthy increase in output, reflects, of course, their rising productivity.

Altogether, the goods-producing industries employed 29 million workers in 1968 and are expected to increase to 31.6 million by 1980. However, their share of total employment will drop to less than a third by 1980 from about 36 percent in 1968.

Agriculture. Large increases in productivity, small gains in output, and a continuing concentration of employment on large farms will result in further decline, about 1 million, in agricultural employment between 1968–80. The agricultural share of total employment will also decline from 5.1 percent in 1968 to 3.2 percent in 1980.

Mining. Employment has been declining for many years because of above average gains in productivity and decreased demand, particularly for coal. Mining is projected to have the lowest rate of increase in output among all nonfarm industries. Continued employment declines are projected through the 1970s although at a reduced rate because of some resurgence in the demand for coal. Employment will be less than 600,000 by 1980.

Future employment growth will be limited by the increasing use of new and improved labor-saving devices and techniques, such as continuous mining machinery systems and more efficient exploration and recovery techniques in crude oil and natural gas extraction.

Construction. This industry may benefit from intensive application of existing technology that would increase the output per man-hour. Already, prefabricated panels and shells for houses show promise of more widespread use. At the same time the national housing goal for the decade 1968–78 calls for the construction of 20 million new housing units in the private market and the production of 6 million new and rehabilitated units with public assistance in one form or another. This will spur growth in the construction industry, which is expected to grow at 2.5 percent a year in the 1970s, nearly twice its growth rate during the 1960s. Additional demand will come from an expansion in state and local government needs, particularly for highway construction and new and rehabilitated housing units, and from expanding investment in industrial plants. Employment will rise from 4 million in 1968 to nearly 5.5 million by 1980.

Manufacturing. Still the biggest industry, manufacturing is expected to remain as the largest single source of jobs in the economy. Manpower requirements in manufacturing, however, are expected to increase at a slower pace, at 0.9 percent a year, than that experienced during the 1960s, chiefly because the recent increases in employment in industries heavily oriented toward defense—ordnance, communications equipment, electronic components, aircraft and parts, and shipbuilding—are not expected to continue at the same pace in the 1970s. Employment, however, will rise from 20 million in 1968 to 22.4 million in 1980.

In general, manpower requirements will continue to increase faster in durable goods manufacturing than in nondurable goods industries. Growth in the durable goods sector will be accelerated by the significantly increased demand for building materials for housing construction. As in the past, changes in employment in individual manufacturing industries are expected to vary widely, depending on the impact of technology as well as shifts in demand. The increasing application of technological innovations to manufacturing processes is expected to continue to reduce unit labor requirements in manufacturing. Major technological developments that will continue to limit growth in manufacturing employment include numerical control of machine tools, new metal processing methods, machinery improvements, improved materials handling (including layout), new and improved raw materials and products, instrumentation and automatic controls, and electronic computers.

How the Employment Projections Differ

Employment projections for a durable goods economy, even though weighted more heavily toward the production of goods, still produce an economy weighted more toward the service sector than the present one. The rate at which employment shifts away from the goods-producing part of the economy, however, is slower in the durable goods projection than in the services projection.

Durable goods manufacturing accounts for about 1 percent more of total employment under the assumptions upon which the durable goods economy projections in 1980 are based than under the assumptions used for the services economy projections. Employment in the nondurable goods industries, however, is only modestly changed between the two structures of the economy. Transportation and trade are both roughly the same; manufacturing is slightly higher; services and government, slightly lower. In both types of economy, manufacturing shows a declining proportion of total employment while services and government show increasing proportions of total employment.

Occupational Employment

Industry changes during the 1970s will have a strong influence on occupations—which ones will grow and which will contract. Each industry in the economy requires a specific mix of occupations. As industries react to changes in final demand and in relation to each other, the relative importance of particular occupations also changes.

Beyond the effect of interindustry relation-

ships, industry occupational structures are also affected by internal changes within industries. Just as technological advances that increase worker productivity have significantly affected employment and output, these advances significantly affected the occupational structure of the work force. As a result of technological innovations, new occupations have emerged; others have expanded, contracted, or even disappeared; and the content and skill requirements of a great many occupations have been altered. But technology and final demand are not the only factors affecting occupational shifts. Changes can occur as a result of revised work rules, new directions in government policy, and severe shortages that force substitutions in the kinds of workers hired (Table 2).

Several long-term occupational trends are expected to continue:

White-collar occupations, the fastest growing occupational group over the past 50 years, will continue in that mode. This group, which surpassed employment in blue-collar occupations for the first time in 1956, will account for about half of all employed workers (50.8 percent) by 1980. Employment in these occupations will rise from 35.6 million in 1968 to 48.3 million in 1980.

Blue-collar occupations, a slow growing occupational group, will account for almost one third (32.7 percent) of the work force by 1980, down from 36.3 percent in 1968. Employment, however, will rise from 27.5 million in 1968 to 31.1 million in 1980. Many occupations within the group, particularly in the skilled craft and foremen category, require years of specialized training.

TABLE 2 Average Annual Rate of Employment Change, by Major Occupational Group, 1960–68 (actual) and 1968–80 (projected for a services economy with 3-percent unemployment)

Occupational Group	1960–68	1968–80
Total......................	1.8	1.9
White-collar workers...............	2.8	2.6
Professional, technical, and kindred......................	4.1	3.4
Managers, officials, and proprietors......................	1.2	1.7
Clerical........................	3.5	2.5
Sales........................	1.2	2.2
Blue-collar workers.................	1.7	1.0
Craftsmen and foremen........	2.0	1.7
Operatives.....................	2.0	0.8
Nonfarm laborers..............	—	−0.1
Service workers.....................	2.0	2.8
Farm workers.......................	−5.1	−3.4

Farm workers will continue to decline—from 4.6 percent of the work force in 1968 to 2.7 percent in 1980—as machines take over many more of the production processes on the farm. Employment will also shrink from 3.5 million in 1968 to 2.6 million in 1980.

Service occupations will continue to expand through the 1970s increasing by two fifths, which is more than one and a half times the expansion for all occupations combined. Employment will rise to 13.1 million in 1980, up from 9.4 million in 1968.

Net Occupational Openings

Projections of occupational requirements, which encompass the total employed civilian work force, indicate that the total openings arising from occupational growth and replacement needs will be about 48 million between 1968–80, or about 4 million jobs to be filled every year throughout the period. Although the inflow to the labor force through the 1970s matches the overall number of net job openings[1]—transfers between occupations cancel out—this balance in no way suggests a perfect fit between entry requirements and worker qualifications. Such a match depends on the future education and training of young people, the degree of flexibility workers show in adapting to changing requirements and employers utilize in adapting hiring standards to the available labor force. Average annual openings by detailed occupation may identify those areas where opportunities are numerous and help young people make their career plans based on the best available information.

Replacement needs—about 28 million in the 1970s—will be the most significant source of job openings in each of the major occupational areas—white-collar, blue-collar, service, and farm. The need to replace workers who leave the labor force—primarily due to death and/or retirement—will account for three in every five job openings during the period 1968–80; occupational growth will account for two in every five openings.

Replacement needs are likely to exceed the overall in those occupations that (*a*) employ many women, who frequently leave the labor force to assume family responsibilities, and (*b*) have a large proportion of older workers who have relatively few years of working life remaining.

---

[1] This balance results, of course, from the assumptions underlying these projections, which were that the growth in employment would match that of the labor force, leaving only a level of unemployment (at either 3 or 4 percent) roughly similar to that in 1968.

Growth needs—about 20 million—reflect industry changes as well as technological changes during the 1970s that, in turn, will determine in large measure which occupations will grow, which will contract.

Changes In Occupational Groups

Employment requirements to 1980 have been projected for the 9 major occupational groups and for about 250 detailed occupations.

Professional, Technical, and Kindred. Employment growth in these occupations has outdistanced that in all other major occupational groups in recent decades. From less than a million in 1890, the number of these workers has grown to 10.3 million in 1968. And requirements for these occupations will continue to lead other categories between 1968 and 1980, increasing half again in size, which is twice the employment increase among all occupations combined. At 15.5 million in 1980, employment in this occupational group will represent 16.3 percent of total employment, up from 13.6 percent in 1968.

The long term rise in demand for goods and services, resulting from population growth and rising business and personal incomes, will account for much of the need for these highly trained workers (as well as for the increases among other groups of workers). The increasing concentration of the population in metropolitan areas also will create new demands for professional and technical personnel to work on environmental protection, urban renewal, and mass transportation systems. In addition, efforts to develop further the nation's resources and industry and the quest for scientific and technical knowledge will generate new requirements for professional workers.

Managers, Officials, and Proprietors. Employment in this occupational group, rising more slowly than total employment, will reach 9.5 million in 1980, up from 7.8 million in 1968. Its share of total employment will continue at about 10 percent.

Changes in the scale and type of business organization have had divergent effects upon the various segments of this occupational group. In retailing, for example, the establishment of chain stores such as supermarkets and discount houses has eliminated many small businesses, thus reducing the number of self-employed proprietors. In contrast, the number of salaried managers and officials has increased significantly. The net result of these opposing trends will probably be a slower increase in employment in the manager-proprietor group as a whole than in any other major group of white-collar workers.

Demand for salaried managers and officials is expected to grow rapidly with the increasing dependence of both business and government on trained management specialists. Technological development will contribute further to employment growth of these occupations. For example, an increasing number of technical managers is needed to plan research and development programs and to make decisions on the installation and use of automated machinery and automatic data processing systems.

Proprietors are expected to continue to decline as the trend toward larger firms restricts growth of the total number of firms, and as small grocery and general stores and hand laundries continue to disappear. The expansion of quick service grocery stores, self-service laundries and drycleaning shops, and hamburger and frozen custard drive-ins, however, will slow the rate of decline.

Clerical. Employment in clerical jobs is expected to grow considerably faster than total employment, rising to 17.3 million in 1980, up from 12.8 million in 1968. This rate of growth, although rapid, is considerably slower than that experienced from 1960–68.

Clerical workers, the largest single category in white-collar employment, will be affected by the rapid technological developments in the fields of computers, office equipment, and communication devices in the 1970s. For some, the effect of these technological improvements will in time retard the growth of employment; for others, the demand for processing the increased information becoming available through these improvements will accentuate growth in their ranks.

Technological developments will limit employment growth for certain types of clerical workers. To illustrate, the use of electronic computers and bookkeeping machines to process routine and repetitive work is expected to reduce the number of clerks in jobs such as filing, payroll, inventory control, and customer billing. On the other hand, laborsaving innovations will be offset to some extent by growing requirements for clerical personnel to prepare computer inputs.

The rapid growth of industries that employ large clerical staffs, particularly those such as finance, insurance, and real estate, is a major factor in the projected level of clerical demand. Clerical employment will increase its share of total employment from 16.9 percent in 1968 to 18.2 percent in 1980.

Sales. The anticipated expansion of trade should increase the demand for sales personnel—particularly for part-time employees—but changing techniques in merchandising may hold down some of the increase. Employment is expected to rise from 4.6 million in 1968 to 6 million in 1980 and at a slightly faster rate of increase than is expected in total employment. Sales share of total employment will continue a little over 6 percent through the 1970s.

Craftsmen, Foremen, and Kindred Workers. Employment in this highly skilled group of occupations is expected to expand more slowly than total employment, rising from 10 million in 1968 to 12.2 million in 1980. The craft share of total employment will slide downward a little to 12.8 percent by 1980.

Different industries employ different proportions of craftsmen. Manufacturing employs a greater number than any other industry. In construction, however, these skilled workers are a much higher proportion of employees than in any other industry group—one out of every two, compared with one in five in manufacturing and transportation and fewer than one in ten in other industries.

Semiskilled Workers. These occupations employ more workers than any other group. Employment in these occupations increased sharply as industry, aided by technological innovations, shifted to mass production processes. But now that these processes are well established, further and more sophisticated technological advances are apt to slow employment growth in these occupations in the years ahead. Employment is projected to rise from 14 million in 1968 to 15.4 million in 1980, at a rate of increase that will be about half the increase projected for total employment; the semiskilled share of total employment will slide downward from 18.4 percent in 1968 to 16.2 percent in 1980.

Three of every five semiskilled workers in 1968 were employed as factory operatives in manufacturing industries. Large numbers were assemblers or inspectors, and many worked as operators of material moving equipment, such as powered forklift trucks. Among the nonfactory operatives, drivers of trucks, buses, and taxicabs by far made up the largest group.

Employment trends among the individual semiskilled occupations since World War II have reflected different rates of growth in the industries in which the workers were employed as well as the differing impacts of technological innovations on occupations. For example, the rapid decline in employment of spinners and weavers reflected not only the relatively small increase in the demand for textile mill products but also the increased mechanization of spinning and weaving processes. Increases in production and growing motor truck transportation of freight will be major factors in expanding demands for operatives in the 1968–80 period.

Nonfarm Laborers. Employment requirements for these laborers are expected to continue at 3.5 million despite the rapid employment rise anticipated in manufacturing and construction, the primary employers of laborers. The nonfarm labor share of total employment, however, will decline from 4.7 percent to 3.7 percent between 1968 and 1980.

Increases in demand are expected to be offset roughly by rising output per worker resulting from the continuing substitution of mechanical equipment for manual labor. For example, power-driven equipment, such as forklift trucks, derricks, cranes, hoists, and conveyor belts, will take over more and more handling of materials in factories, at freight terminals, and in warehouses. Other power-driven machines will do excavating, ditch digging, and similar work. In addition, integrated systems of processing and handling of materials equipment will be installed in an increasing number of plants.

Service Workers. Major factors underlying increased needs for service workers will be a growing population, expanding business activity, increasing leisure time, and higher levels of disposable personal income. This occupational group, a fast growing one, encompasses a wide variety of jobs and a wide range of skill requirements. It includes such diverse jobs as FBI agents, policemen, beauty operators, and janitors.

Employment requirements will rise from 9.4 million in 1968 to 13.1 million in 1980, at a rate of increase that is more than half again as fast as the rate projected for total employment. Private household employment, the slowest growing service area, will expand from 1.7 million to 2.0 million, an increase of about 15 percent between 1968 and 1980. The fastest growing service area will be health service, rising close to 90 percent, from 800,000 to 1.5 million between 1968 and 1980.

Farm Workers. These workers will decline one third, from 3.5 million in 1968 to 2.6 million in 1980. The share of total employment also will fall, from 4.6 percent to 2.7 percent in the same period.

Continuing earlier trends, decreasing requirements for farm workers will be related to rising productivity on the farms. Improvements in farm technology, better fertilizers, seeds, and feed will permit farmers to increase production with fewer

employees. Improved mechanical harvesters for vegetables and fruits will decrease the need for seasonal or other hired labor. Innovations in livestock and poultry feeding and improved milking systems will allow more efficient handling of a greater volume of productivity. The expected development of automatic packing, inspection, and sorting systems for fruits, vegetables, and other farm products also will reduce employment requirements for farm workers. The continued trend toward larger and more efficient farms will also limit employment.

Farms and farm managers are expected to continue to be most affected by the decline in the number of small farms, and requirements for these workers are expected to continue to decline faster than that for farm laborers and foremen.

Employment in a Durables Economy

Under the assumptions embodied in the durables economy, those occupations that predominate in durable goods industries would show different employment levels. Requirements for engineers, for example, would be 1 percent higher in a durables economy; tool and diemakers, carpenters, and cement finishers would each be about 2.5 percent higher; manufacturing salesmen would be nearly 3.5 percent higher. On the other hand, occupations that predominate in services industries such as government; finance, insurance, and real estate; and trade would show somewhat lower employment levels; securities and insurance salesmen, about 2.5 percent less; and waitresses, about 2 percent less.

PROJECTED SHAPE OF THE LABOR FORCE

The labor force is affected by changing labor force participation rates by age groups. Past trends provide clues for predicting how these rates may change. Some past trends suggest that the increase in college enrollments will tend to reduce the labor force activity of the college-age groups as a whole, even though many students continue to work part time. As has been the case in recent years, an expanding economy is likely to provide an abundance of jobs that will tend to encourage students, other young people, and women to move into the labor force, often for part-time jobs, in larger numbers than during the 1960s. Birth rates, which have been declining, are likely to continue to do so with the result that more women will enter the labor force. Finally, the level and coverage of retirement benefits will allow more workers to leave the labor force at earlier ages.

Labor Force Changes

The labor force is constantly changing. Workers enter and leave all the time. The expansion to 100 million by 1980 means that more workers will be coming into the labor force pool (41 million) than will be leaving (26 million). (See Chart 2.)

Three kinds of workers will increase the supply of labor by 41 million through the 1970s:

1. Thirty-four million new, young workers looking for their first jobs.

2. Nearly 6 million women who either delayed their entry into the labor force or picked up the threads of work again after an absence, most frequently devoted to caring for young children.

3. Over 1 million immigrants who will become part of the U.S. work force.

Three kinds of workers will leave the labor force during the 1970s reducing the total by 26 million: workers who die; workers who retire; and workers who decide not to work any longer, although sometimes only temporarily, for a variety of personal reasons including illness and the need to care for family or because of other responsibilities. (See Table 3.)

The net effect of this inflow and outflow on the age composition of the labor force through the 1970s (1968–80) will be as follows:

The huge increase of teen-agers in the 1960s will taper off. The proportion of the labor force that is composed of teen-agers will actually

TABLE 3   Labor Force Balance Sheet, 1960–70, 1970–80 (number in millions)

1960 Decade (1960–70)

Total labor force, 16 years and over, 1960	72.1
Less withdrawals, 1960 through 1969	20.9
1960 total labor force still in labor force in 1970	51.2
Plus new entrants, 1960 through 1969	26.4
Plus all other entrants, 1960 through 1969*	8.0
Total labor force, 16 years and over, 1970†	85.6

1970 Decade (1970–80)

Total labor force, 16 years and over, 1970†	85.6
Less withdrawals, 1970 through 1979	26.3
1970 total labor force still in labor force in 1980	59.3
Plus new entrants, 1970 through 1979	33.7
Plus all other entrants, 1970 through 1979*	7.7
Total labor force, 16 years and over, 1980	100.7

* Primarily reentrants plus immigrants.
† Estimated.

decline a little—from 8.7 percent to 8.3 percent —as the 1970s advance to 1980, but even so their numbers will continue to rise. In 1960, teen-agers in the labor force numbered about 5.2 million. Their average rate of increase through the 1960s (1960–68) was about 3.9 percent per year, resulting in 7.1 million being in the labor force by 1968; by 1980, there will be 8.3 million. Their annual average rate of increase through the 1970s (1968–80) will drop to 1.3 percent, about one third of the growth rate of the preceding decade.

The rate of increase of 20- to 24-year-olds in the labor force will slow down. Young people, 20 to 24 years old, in the labor force will be increasing in numbers during the 1970s but at a slower rate than during the preceding decade. In contrast with the teen-agers, the proportion these young adults constitute of the total labor force will continue to rise from 13.4 percent (11 million) in 1968, to 14.7 percent (almost 15 million) by 1980—a reflection primarily of the increase in population.

Altogether, young people under the age of 25 will account for a little more than a quarter of total labor force expansion of the 1970s, in contrast with over half (54 percent) of labor force growth from 1960 to 1968.

The number of early career workers, 25 to 34 years old, will increase precipitously. The big labor force news of the 1970s will be the significant increase in the numbers of workers in their late twenties and early thirties—the career development years, from 16.5 million in 1968 to over 26 million in 1980, an increase of almost 60 percent. One out of every four workers will be in this age group in 1980 in comparison with one

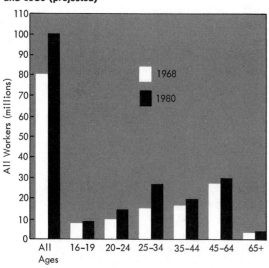

CHART 2   The Shape of the Labor Force, 1968 (actual) and 1980 (projected)

1968
1980

All Workers (millions)

All Ages — 16–19 — 20–24 — 25–34 — 35–44 — 45–64 — 65+

in every five in 1968. For the most part, these workers will have completed their education and training and will be ready to assume full harness in the world of work. The catalyst for the big expansion in young workers is the great upsurge in the fertility rate that occurred following World War II. The annual number of births increased from 2.7 million to 3.8 million between 1946 and 1947 and then moved up to 4.2 million by the late 1950s. Their schooling for the most part completed, these young people born in the early postwar years will provide a large pool of trained, young workers, unprecedented in numbers.

The increasing number of 25- to 34-year-olds in the labor force in the 1970s does not necessarily mean that 800,000 new jobs must be found every year for those moving into this age bracket. A great many of these young workers came into the labor force during the 1960s and found jobs then. During the 1970s, they simply will be moving up the age ladder of the labor force. As they acquire additional training, experience, and maturity in the process of working their way up, they may be able to compensate for the short supply of older workers in the prime career age group where recent labor force expansion has been either slim or nonexistent.

The number of midcareer workers, aged 35 to 44, will show a small increase. Despite growth from 17 million to about 19 million from 1968 to 1980, the supply of these workers in the labor force still will be relatively thin. Their proportion of the total labor force will decline from about 21 percent in 1968 to about 19 percent by 1980. Generally, workers in this age group staff positions of maximum work responsibility and are at the peak of their performance. Their short supply will mean many more midcareer openings will be available for the younger 25- to 34-year-old workers.

A sharp slowdown will occur in the labor force growth rate among older workers, 45 to 64 years of age. These workers, who are normally at the top of their career ladders, will increase in number from 27.5 million in 1968 to just over 29 million in 1980. But the increase will be only one third as great as that between 1960 and 1968. Their proportion of the total labor force will decline sharply from about 33 percent to about 29 percent. This slowdown in the growth rate is related to a sizable decline in population growth in the 45–54-year-old group, reflecting the comparatively small number of people born in the depths of the Great Depression, when birth rates were low, who are moving into this age class.

There will be no significant change for workers beyond the usual retirement age of 65, who will number just over 3 million through the 1970s. They will represent a declining proportion of the work force. The decreased propensity to work after 65 reflects the improvement in retirement benefits that reduces the need for older workers to stay on the job to make ends meet; the greater security that comes with the health protection of medicare and medicaid; and the increased assets that may have resulted from full employment.

Participation Rates

What makes people decide to work? Whatever the incentive for working, 6 in every 10 in the working age group (16 and over) are expected to be either working or seeking work in 1980, about the same as today; in 1890 only 5 in every 10 in the work-age population were workers. The long-run increase in labor force participation reflects primarily the increasing proportion of women who work.

Women in the Labor Force. Women workers —37 million expected in 1980—will continue to represent an increasing proportion of the working population. By 1980, more than 4 in every 10 women (43 percent) will be working, only slightly more than the proportion today (41.1 percent) but double the proportion (2 in 10) in 1890.

Negroes in the Labor Force. The black labor force[2] is expected to total 12 million in 1980, 3 million more than in 1968. Its annual rate of growth, 2.4 percent, exceeds the comparable growth rate for whites, 1.6 percent, by one half. The difference reflects a more rapid increase in the black population of working age than that occurring among whites, particularly among those under 35 years of age.

The pattern of change between 1968 and 1980 for the black work force differs only in degree from that of their white counterparts. Workers under 25 years old will account for a large share of the increase for both blacks and whites but will account for more of the increase among blacks. For both groups, the most spectacular increase will take place in the group 25 to 34 years old, but again, a slightly greater relative increase for blacks. The labor force 35 years old and over will show only a small amount of growth for both blacks and whites.

---

[2] Data refer to all races except white. Nationwide, Negroes make up about 92 percent of races other than white.

The proportion of women who are in the labor force has always been higher for black than for white women, an indication of the greater need for many black women to contribute to family income. The difference between these labor force participation rates has been getting smaller as paid work outside the home has become more common among white women. In 1968, 49 percent of black and 40 percent of white women were workers. By 1980, it is expected that the difference will be reduced further, reflecting an improvement in the economic situation of black men, which, in turn, will mean that black women will be under less pressure to contribute toward the support of their families. Thus, the rate of participation for all black women in 1980 was projected as 47 percent and for white women at 42 percent.

Among black men, small increases are projected in the labor force participation rates from 75.9 percent in 1968 to 77.5 percent in 1980, at the same time that the rate for white males is edging down. These increases reflect the anticipated improvement in black men's employment opportunities, which will tend to minimize irregular work patterns and reduce withdrawals from the labor force that reflect discouragement over job prospects.

Educational Attainment

The nation's labor force will have higher educational qualifications in 1980 than in 1968: the proportion of workers with at least 4 years of high school will be rising among workers at all ages. By 1980, only 1 in 16 adult workers (25 and over)—about 5 million—will have less than 8 years of schooling; and 7 in every 10 adult workers—about 52 million—will have completed at least 4 years of high school. In contrast, over 1 in 10 adult workers in 1968—nearly 7 million—had completed less than 8 years of schooling while 6 in every 10 adult workers—about 37 million—had completed 4 years of high school or more.

Nearly 1 in 6 workers, 25 years and over—about 13 million—will have completed at least 4 years of college in 1980; in 1968, about 8.5 million, or 1 in 7 workers, 25 years and over, had a similar amount of education. The total number of college-educated workers of all ages in the work force would, of course, exceed 13 million, since a significant number of workers under 25—perhaps as many as 2 to 3 million—will have completed 4 years of college in 1980. Moreover, about 9.2 million adult workers—1 in 8—in

1980 will have had some college training but less than 4 years.

The heavy influx to the labor force of relatively well-educated younger workers, which will occur at the same time that many less educated older workers are leaving the labor force, promises a major change in the educational background of the workers in the early age span. By 1980, about 4 out of 5 young adult workers (25 to 34 years old) will be high school graduates or better, and 1 in 5 will have completed 4 years of college or more; by contrast, in the 1968 work force, 3 in 4 workers in this age group were high school graduates and 1 in 6 were college graduates.

SOME IMPLICATIONS OF THE PROJECTIONS

Any set of economic projections carries with it certain implications for the future behavior of all aspects of the economy, including government policy. Three major aspects of the projections warrant further consideration: (1) growth of the economy; (2) demographic changes in the labor force; and (3) higher educational attainment of the labor force.

Growth of the Economy

When the depression years of the 1930s were still within recent memory, optimistic economic projections inevitably raised a question about the ability of the economy to reach the projected levels. The sustained high levels of growth during the 1960s, however, have created confidence that the expected levels indicated for the 1970s may be quite reasonable. The projected GNP level for 1980 will be 65 percent above the level in 1968, a growth rate of 4.3 percent per year. Because of the anticipated higher rate of labor force increase, this is somewhat higher than the potential growth rate of the 1960s. However, the 4.3 percent rate is somewhat lower than the rate actually achieved during the 1960s because advances in the early part of the decade resulted from taking up the slack in the economy.

The projections for certain sectors of the economy raise specific questions:

Expenditures for new or renovated housing, reflecting the needs of new family formation, are expected to about double by 1980. This may make possible attainment of the goal of 26 million housing units for the 1968–78 decade set by Congress in the Housing and Urban Development Act of 1968. However, if this goal is to be fulfilled, major advances will be necessary to assure an adequate supply of trained construction workers, to create sufficient sources of reasonably priced financing, and to put into practice the technological improvements necessary to higher output.

Strong demand for new and renovated housing is evident enough, even today, but the current limited availability of mortgage funds together with a high level of interest rates has caused buyers and builders to hesitate to take on long term commitments. If these conditions continue, the expected surge in residential construction activity may be seriously delayed.

In the decade ahead, special emphasis will undoubtedly be placed on developing new methods of training construction workers, expanding opportunities for minority applicants, and reducing seasonality to make more effective use of skilled craftsmen; and to institute new technology that will permit houses to be built faster and cheaper with the manpower available.

Business investment in plant and equipment is projected to at least maintain the high proportion of GNP attained during the last few years of relatively full employment, thus providing a basis for the continuation of the long-term trend in productivity.

Federal government expenditures for defense purposes will fall as a proportion of total GNP. *Other public expenditures*—state and local and federal nondefense—will rise as a share of the GNP. This implies a possible temporary dislocation of people and jobs in defense industries, particularly if the decline in defense expenditures occurs over a short period of time. Some defense industries may suffer loss of their federal contracts with a companion decline in output; some defense plants will either shut down or curtail their activities; and some regions and localities may experience, at least temporarily, increasing levels of unemployment.

Government programs to meet such dislocation include placement services to workers seeking jobs outside their labor market area and special assistance to enable defense plants hit by cutbacks to diversify production and seek other markets to maintain production levels.

State and local government expenditures between 1968–80 will shift from about half to close to three-fifths of total government expenditures. This shift will occur because of a large increase in state and local expenditures and a relative decline in federal purchases.

While the 1980 projections do not include revenue estimates, it is clear that a major effort will be necessary to obtain the funds to finance this increase in state and local expenditures. Part of this expenditure increase will represent funds channeled from the federal government in the form of grants-in-aid and sharing of federal revenues. At the same time a considerable effort by state and local governments will be necessary to increase their own revenues. A further difficult task will be to develop the programs and the management skills in state and local government to meet the complex problems that they will be facing.

Expenditures for services by both consumers and governments will account for a larger share of the GNP in 1980 than today. It is likely that the trend toward higher manpower requirements to provide these services may contribute to the goal of economic stability since service employment is normally less subject to layoffs at the onset of declines in economic activity.

Productivity, holding steady at 3 percent a year in the private nonfarm sector and remaining at high levels on the farm (5.7 percent a year), will yield an advance in output per man-hour of 3 percent a year for the entire economy through the 1970s. However, as the service sector expands in importance, it may become increasingly difficult to maintain the high level of productivity gains for the economy that have prevailed since World War II. The service industries are unlikely to experience large increases in output per worker because they are less subject to mechanization, and many of them depend for their value upon personal or individual attention. Thus, particular attention will be required to find means of applying cost-saving techniques to the service industries if the nation's productivity is not to fall below the 3-percent level.

Hours of work are expected to decline slightly during the 1970s at a rate of 0.1 percent a year. This relatively small decline reflects in large part the continuing increase in part-time employment and to a lesser degree limited reductions in the scheduled workweek. In addition to this decline, which is based on hours for which payment is received, greater availability of leisure time can be expected as a result of longer paid vacations and an increasing number of paid holidays.

Demographic Changes in the Labor Force

The 100 million labor force of 1980 will exhibit a distinctly different age profile. The rapid growth during the 1960s of teen-agers and persons in their early twenties will inexorably be transferred in the coming decade to those in their late twenties and early thirties. In contrast, the 45–64 age group by 1980 will be barely 5 percent higher than a decade earlier.

For the nation as a whole, the younger work force, averaging 35 years of age, may be a great boon. The large numbers of young workers may provide an abundance of new ideas—the eagerness, imagination, and flexibility of the young may contribute to developing new ways of business organization, production, and marketing.

Differences in the points of view, however, that today seem often to characterize those under and over 30 may, of course, bring some frictions and other problems. Industry's work force may suffer from workers who lack the patience and wisdom that come with age and experience. The differing viewpoints of young and old may bring forth more grievances, more altercations with management.

Likely implications of these changes on specific demographic groups in the population are as follows:

Teen-Agers. The slowdown in their rate of growth in the labor force may improve job opportunities for teen-agers competing in an anticipated expanding economy.

Young Workers. Projected changes may mean keen competition among workers in their twenties for entry-level jobs but better oportunities for advancement to higher levels where the number of competent older workers may be stretched thin.

Experienced Midcareer Workers. The big increase in the number of young trained workers may mean that the mature worker may be pushed hard to hold his own against the young, many of whom will probably be better educated and trained for tomorrow's jobs.

Older Workers. The improved supply of young workers may accelerate pressures on older workers to retire sooner than they might otherwise do. In any case, the trend toward earlier retirement is expected to continue and can be expected to lead to greater emphasis on preretirement planning and the development of community service projects for which retired workers could contribute paid or volunteer part-time work.

Women Workers. The continuing increase in the labor force participation rates of women, particularly young women in their childbearing years, may mean that more day care centers for children must be provided to assure proper protection of the young children of working mothers; more part-time job opportunities must be made available for women whose home responsibilities do not permit full-time employment; some job requirements may need to be adjusted to meet women's physical characteristics.

As an increasing proportion of married women work, the added family income may serve to change patterns of consumption and living styles: More services may be purchased to replace the housewife's home services; more precooked foods may be demanded; more expenditures for leisure time recreational activities may be made.

Negro Workers. The one-third increase expected in the Negro labor force between 1968 and 1980, bringing their total numbers to 12 million workers in 1980, may be accompanied by increased concern for their occupational upgrading during the 1970s. Since upward occupational mobility is conditioned, in part, upon improved job qualifications, the recent steady progress in the educational qualifications of Negroes brings promise of better occupational adjustments to come. The proportion of Negro men between 25 and 29 with 4 years of high school or more rose from 36 percent in 1960 to 60 percent in 1969 while the comparable increase for white males during the same period was from 63 percent to 78 percent. Negro females have made similar but not so striking gains. A major increase in Negroes attending college also took place during the decade.

These higher levels of educational attainment, together with steady progress toward equal employment opportunities, have combined to produce major changes in the occupational progress of employed Negroes. From 1960 to 1969 Negro employment in the professional and technical occupations has more than doubled—from less than 350,000 to nearly 700,000 while white employment in these occupations increased 40 percent from 7 million to 10 million. Similiar improvements have been made in the managerial, clerical, and sales occupations. In the manual occupations, there has been a sharp upgrading of Negro workers with a 70-percent increase in Negro craftsmen compared with a 17-percent increase for whites. At the same time, there has been a drop in Negro nonfarm laborers, private household workers, and farm workers.

Despite these encouraging gains, Negroes are still disproportionately concentrated in occupations, such as nonfarm laborers, that are expected to continue to decline throughout the 1970s or in occupations, such as household workers, which will be increasing only slightly. Moreover, Negro workers in 1969 represented only 6 percent of total employment in professional occupations, 4 percent in sales, and 3 percent in managerial occupations.

The prospects for improved Negro employment in 1980 will depend upon a continuing improvement in education, the relative success of efforts to open employment opportunities that have hitherto remained closed, and the impact of changing occupational patterns. The BLS expects to issue a more detailed study of Negro employment progress and outlook later in the year.

These demographic changes are likely also to affect the country's major job-oriented institutions.

Employers. The large increase in the number of new young workers and women in the labor force will produce pressure for employers to provide improved on-the-job training, more effective supervision, and additional safety education. They will have to expect greater turnover and will have to allow for more part-time workers.

Unions. In a strong economy, their membership swelled by youthful members, unions may lean more toward emphasizing take-home pay rather than job security, seniority, pensions, and other fringe benefits that are usually of greater interest to older workers. Divergent bargaining objectives between young and older workers may lead to intraunion problems.

Schools. The large number of young people entering the labor force directly from high school and vocational school will require improved preparation for obtaining the skills and work attitudes needed for success in the work world. Young workers will need better guidance and counseling as they enter the labor force. Young people who do not complete high school may find it harder to get a job as they compete with their peers who have had more schooling.

Changes in the Labor Market. The projections assume that the 100 million labor force will mesh with the job requirements of the $1.4 trillion economy. This close match between workers and jobs will not just happen. It will require greater flexibility in the labor market through education, realistic training programs geared to shifts in occupational requirements, improved placement services, removal of arbitrary barriers to occupational entry, and the willingness of employers to maintain flexible hiring requirements.

Educational Attainment of the Labor Force

The continuing rise in educational achievement of the labor force has a number of specific implications for the 1980 labor market.

Job Entry Requirements. Faced by a rising supply of more highly educated applicants, some employers may prefer more highly educated job applicants and be reluctant to adjust their educational entry requirements to levels that are consistent with job requirements. Similarly, while job opportunities may open up more readily for disadvantaged workers who improve their educational qualifications, the job outlook for the disadvantaged with limited schooling is likely to remain bleak. These possibilities underscore the importance during the coming decade of encouraging employers to make their educational entry requirements reflect actual job needs rather than simply the availability of a more educated labor supply.

White-Collar Occupations. By 1980, more workers will be in white-collar jobs than in the blue-collar and service groups combined. The impression may grow that white-collar jobs are only for highly educated workers. Jobs within the white-collar group actually have a wide range of educational requirements: Managerial jobs range from the managers of large corporations to managers of hamburger carryout shops; clerical jobs cover executive secretaries and file clerks; and sales occupations include hucksters and peddlers as well as stock brokers.

Since many white-collar jobs do not require even a high school diploma, special means may be needed to keep young people whose education is limited informed of the variety of job openings in this area.

Manual Occupations. The continuing emphasis on higher education poses a threat to the flow of energetic intelligent manpower to the skilled crafts. This emphasis, together with the generally higher esteem in which white-collar occupations are held, may make it difficult to fill blue-collar and service jobs. Whether or not this materializes would seem to depend on the possibility of:

1. A shift in attitudes toward higher education, at least to the extent that youngsters who may not be college material will no longer insist on having a "go" at college nor resist taking useful manual and service employment.

2. Adjustments in labor supply through removal of any remaining racial barriers to job entry and modified immigration policies.

3. Adjustments in pay and working conditions to make such jobs more attractive.

4. Programs to provide greater advancement opportunities for those who enter the manual occupations at the lower level of the job structure.

Highly Educated Manpower. The nation's colleges and universities—principal suppliers of our most highly trained manpower—now are turning out record numbers of graduates and are expected to continue to do so throughout the 1970s. Numbers of persons earning bachelor's degrees will climb by two thirds, and those earning master's and doctor's degrees will double by 1980. Numerically, 13.3 million degrees are expected to be awarded between 1968 and 1980— 10.2 million bachelor's, 2.7 million master's, and 400,000 doctorates.

Using past employment and educational patterns of degree recipients, BLS estimates that between 1968 and 1980 about 9.3 million college-educated persons will enter the civilian labor force after receiving their degrees: 8.4 million at the bachelor's level, 900,000 at the master's, and approximately 18,000 at the doctorate level. Presumably, most persons who will receive degrees during this period and who enter the armed forces will have returned to the civilian labor force by 1980. Therefore, the effect of the conflict in Viet Nam on labor force entry of college graduates was assumed to be limited.

This supply of new graduates will be augmented by another 1.2 million persons with college level training who will come into the labor force between 1968 and 1980. These additions are expected to consist primarily of women who delayed seeking a job but are expected to become available for work in the 1968–80 period, or who were working in earlier years but withdrew from the labor force. Thus, the new supply of college-educated manpower expected to enter the labor force from 1968–80 will total 10.5 million.

The need for workers stems generally from two sources: employment growth in occupations and the need to replace workers who die, retire, or otherwise leave the labor force. But another factor is relevant in considering the need for college educated manpower: rising job entry requirements that make a college degree necessary for jobs once performed by workers with lower educational attainment.

Assessing these three factors—growth, replacement, and rising entry requirements—it is estimated that 10.4 million new college graduates will be needed between 1968 and 1980: (1) 6.1 million to take care of occupational growth and rising entry requirements, and (2) 4.3 million to replace other workers.

Thus, an ample supply of graduates that is roughly in balance with manpower requirements seems in the offing for the 12-year period between 1968 and 1980. The large output of highly educated workers is expected to end many long-time occupational shortages and promises help for other occupations in which shortages may persist because of requirements for highly specialized graduate level training, lack of facilities, or comparatively low salaries. Many professional occupations have suffered from chronic worker shortages for many years, particularly teaching, engineering, physics, oceanography, chemistry, geophysics, and biomedical and health occupations.

An increased supply of graduates offers only the hope that students will elect to enter courses in numbers that match job vacancies by discipline. In an effort to predict how these individual choices will be made, BLS has made projections to 1980 for some of the principal occupations in the professional, technical, and kindred occupational group (see Table 4).

Specific demand-supply assessments indicate potential sharp differences among occupations. Elementary and secondary school teaching is expected to experience the most dramatic change in supply-demand conditions. Long a shortage occupation, teaching is about to undergo a sharp change in prospects: The aggregate supply is expected to significantly exceed demand if recent entry patterns in the occupation continue. The

Table 4   Distribution of College Graduates by Major Occupational Field, 1968 and 1980

	1968			1980		
	Total Employ-ment* (thou-sands)	College Grad-uates† (thou-sands)	Percent Gradu-ates to Total	Total Employ-ment* (thou-sands)	College Gradu-ates† (thou-sands)	Percent Gradu-ates to Total
Occupational Groups						
All occupational groups..................	75,920	9,229	12.3	95,100	15,342	16.1
Professional and technical....................	10,325	6,182	59.9	15,500	10,230	66.0
Managers, officials, and proprietors..........	7,776	1,562	20.0	9,500	2,850	30.0
Sales.......................................	4,647	463	10.1	6,000	780	13.0
Clerical....................................	12,803	583	4.6	17,300	779	4.5
All other...................................	40,369	439	1.1	46,800	703	1.5

* Sixteen years of age and over.
† Data includes persons 18 years of age and over, having 4 years of college or more.

anticipated surplus of applicants trained for elementary and secondary teaching assignments, the biggest single professional opportunity for women, may mean that many college-educated women will have to look to other professions, some long regarded as the principal province of men, such as engineering, law, medicine, dentistry, pharmacy. If employers in these fields accept women readily, this acceptance may help to reduce further some of the discrimination against women in professional schools that has prevailed in the past.

Professional health occupations should continue to experience shortages. The supply of physicians and dentists, for example, is expected to fall short of requirements because of the limited capacity of medical and dental schools currently in operation and scheduled to be in operation by 1980.

Engineers are also expected to continue to be in short supply. If the number of engineering graduates were to keep pace with the expected growth in total college graduates, the new supply would be adequate to meet projected requirements. Recent trends, however, do not suggest this development as bachelor's degrees in engineering continue to become a smaller proportion of total bachelor's degrees awarded.

In scientific fields, shortages of chemists, geologists, and geophysicists seem likely, but surpluses of mathematicians and life scientists may result if students continue to elect these fields in the same proportion as in the past. However, since transfers occur quite frequently among these occupations, part of the supply-demanded imbalances may be remedied by such transfers.

Other areas for which potential shortages are in prospect include counseling, social work, urban planning, and a variety of occupations related to the planning and administration of local governments.

These 1980 projections do have a rosy glow, inspired no doubt by the steady performance of economic growth during the 1960s. But the past decade has, in fact, left the stage to somewhat mixed notices. While economic growth performed beyond expectations, not all aspects of the economy reached the same heights. The current difficulties of meshing the twin objectives of high employment and price stability and solving such social problems as urban congestion, the lack of equal opportunity, rising crime, the disaffection of the young, and environmental pollution are enough to cast doubt on any optimistic view of the future. The challenge to the nation during the 1970s will be to solve these pressing problems before they seriously erode the economy's capacity to realize its growth potential.

4. The Jobless Rate*

Byron E. Calame†

When the government announces the January unemployment rate today, the widely watched economic indicator will be eyed even more closely than usual.

It's generally assumed that the national rate will rise, either now or soon, from the rather low 3.4 percent reported for December. If so, the Nixon Administration may find it increasingly tough to pursue its attack on inflation, thereby running the risk of cooling the economy to the point of a serious recession. And the Federal Reserve Board could feel more inclined to ease credit. If unemployment should continue to mount, the trend would surely haunt Republicans on the campaign trail next fall.

"Probably no other single statistic carries such massive weight in decision-making as the seasonally adjusted unemployment rate," observes Ewan Clague, a Washington statistical consultant and former Commissioner of the Bureau of Labor Statistics.

But even as this little number bulks so large in the nation's economic and political future, questions are swirling around it.

Some critics, including economists and government officials, raise doubts about the accuracy or reliability ·of the figure. They stress its recent gyrations. In September, the seasonally adjusted rate shot up half a percentage point to 4 percent of the civilian labor force—its sharpest jump in nine years. Two months later the rate plunged from 3.9 percent to 3.4 percent—the biggest month-to-month drop in a decade.

---

* Reprinted with permission of *The Wall Street Journal,* Friday, February 6, 1970.

† Byron E. Calame is a staff reporter with *The Wall Street Journal.*

AN INCOMPLETE PICTURE?

Other critics, notably including some liberal Democrats in and out of Congress, assert that the reported rate doesn't present a complete view of the labor-force scene.

"Official unemployment statistics greatly underestimate the seriousness of the problem," insists Sen. Walter Mondale of Minnesota. "They fail to count those who have finally given up through years of frustration and dropped out of the labor market altogether. And they fail to count those who are so poor and so transient that they have never appeared on a census list and can never even be polled by the Labor Department."

Paul Douglas, an economist and former Senate Democrat from Illinois, agrees. He complains that the count of unemployed misses many of the "nonpersons who sleep in the hallways, subways, or motion picture theaters" in the ghetto and have no permanent address. It's believed the 1960 census erred in this fashion.

Other problems with the unemployment rate computation, critics say, center on statistical difficulties in sampling and in compiling the final figure.

A FAULTY MEMORY

Budget Director Robert P. Mayo places part of the blame for the jobless rate's recent gyrations on faulty adjustment for seasonal variations, and most BLS officials concede he's probably right. Weaknesses in the mechanics of gathering the information come to light in talks with economists and statisticians inside and outside the government.

To gather jobless data each month, the BLS sends an army of over 1,100 interviewers to 50,000 carefully picked households across the nation. The interviewers gather information on the labor-force status of about 105,000 adult Americans.

Small errors can be introduced into the rate when a mother with a faulty memory gives an interviewer inaccurate information about the job or job-seeking activity of the teen-age children or when an interviewer poses questions differently from one household to the next. Also, some critics contend that the practice of making changes each month in the makeup of the 50,000-household sample canvassed by its interviewers can cause statistical aberrations in the jobless figure.

But the BLS, which produces the figure, staunchly defends the basic accuracy of the reported employment rate. Officials say scientific methods and the use of a sample that is larger than is statistically necessary make the jobless figure the most comprehensive and carefully compiled in the world. "It tells pretty much what it's supposed to tell," says Harold Goldstein, Assistant BLS Commissioner for Manpower and Employ·ment Statistics.

SAMPLING ERROR

Both he and other BLS officials admit the survey isn't perfect, however. Because of possible sampling error, for example, they can promise only that, in nine out of ten cases, the month-to-month changes in the unemployment rate won't be off by more than 0.12 of a percentage point in either direction. This means the rate usually has to move at least 0.2 of a percentage point before the change can be considered statistically significant. In today's labor force, such a percentage could involve as many as 160,000.

Though the "discouraged jobless" who have quit seeking work are excluded from the unemployment rate by definition, the BLS notes that separate statistics are now being prepared quarterly on this segment of the labor force. The agency concedes that its monthly survey of unemployment may fail to reflect, or "miss," some persons, particularly in low-income areas. But officials contend that many weaknesses in the survey procedures cited by critics cause only relatively minor errors that tend to offset each other or aren't big enough to be statistically significant.

The importance attached to the unemployment statistics by the government is clear: The $4.5 million it spends annually on the household survey is more than it lays out for any other monthly statistical series.

In a separate program dating back to 1915, the BLS also assembles figures on employment. But a way to handle the more complicated chore of finding out who doesn't have a job—but is actively seeking one—wasn't developed until the late 1930s. Officials of the Works Progress Administration, seeking to learn how many Americans might need public-payroll employment, came up with the idea of a random sampling of households. Turned over to the Census Bureau in 1942, the analysis of the Census Bureau figures was a BLS responsibility in 1959 so the results could be announced along with employment data.

"The difficulty of measuring unemployment starts with making up our minds about what we want," says Mr. Goldstein of the BLS. There has long been debate, he notes, on the basic question of what the unemployment figures should represent: a broad economic measure of the unused potential in the labor force, or a more narrow index limited to jobless persons in actual need of work, such as family breadwinners.

Currently an unemployed person is defined as someone over 16 who isn't working but is available to take a job and has made specific efforts to find work within the previous four weeks.

A SUDDEN DROP

This definition, adopted in 1967, made the unemployment category more restrictive than before. It required that a person counted as jobless must have taken "specific" and "overt" steps to find employment within the four-week period rather than have just "looked for work." It also made availability a condition of unemployment, a change that now keeps students seeking summer work out of the jobless category until the end of the school term. The definition immediately lowered total unemployment by 100,000.

The 50,000 households used for the survey are picked at random from among the nation's 61.8 million households, a ratio of about one in 1,220. The process is designed so that every American over 16 who is not in a prison or some other institution has an equal chance of showing up in the sample. The sample's size has a direct bearing on its reliability. Increasing the sample size by 50 percent in 1967 improved reliability by 20 percent, according to the Census Bureau.

The nation's 112 largest metropolitan areas are automatically included in the monthly survey. Then 337 other "primary sampling units" are picked at random from groupings made on the basis of similar population and geographic characteristics. Then within each of the total 449 areas, there's a random selection of "enumeration districts." Within each district, the households to be surveyed are randomly selected, usually by address, from updated lists that were originally drawn up during the 1960 census.

To avoid the resistance that could develop if the same people were burdened with monthly interviews year after year, the Census Bureau "rotates" the households in the sample. One eighth of the 50,000 households are new each month. This new sample "segment" is interviewed for four months, dropped from the sample for eight months, and surveyed again for a final four-month period.

WIDE SWINGS

Though the bulk of the sample remains the same from month to month and gets slightly greater weight in the calculation of the final figures, some statistical experts complain that the introduction of the new segment can cause wide swings in the unemployment figures. Says one expert, "They can run into an Indian reservation, for example; that's happened before." Indeed, Howard Stambler, chief of employment and unemployment analysis for the BLS, concedes that the new segment is one of the first areas automatically checked any time there's a major month-to-month shift in the jobless figures.

But Census Bureau officials contend there's no great problem. "Anytime the new segment includes an Indian reservation in one place, the odds are that a reservation somewhere else is part of the segment being dropped that month," one official maintains.

The 1,100 interviewers swing into action on the Monday following the week in which the twelfth of the month occurs. They have until Saturday to find and question a "responsible person" in each of the 50,000 sample households. In an average month, data are obtained on all but 2,250 households, or about 4.5 percent of the sample, according to Daniel B. Levine, chief of the Census Bureau's demographic survey division.

Typically, the "noninterviews" reflect such situations as a family on vacation or a rural household that can't be reached because of flooded roads. Most disturbing to Mr. Levine is the growing number of people who simply refuse to talk to interviewers (survey participation is voluntary). The average monthly "refusal" rate has more than doubled, to 1.8 percent of the 50,000 households from only 0.8 percent 5 years ago.

"Government workers are the worst about refusing," grumbles one survey staffer.

A visit to the regional Census Bureau office in Philadelphia provides a closer look at how the survey is conducted. Roger A. Barr, regional supervisor for the survey, is responsible for gathering data from about 5,700 households in Pennsylvania, Maryland, the District of Columbia, and parts of New Jersey, Delaware, and Virginia. His 105 part-time interviewers—all but 2 are women—each spend from 35 to 55 hours a month questioning an average of 55 households.

HIGH TURNOVER

Recruiting is one of Mr. Barr's major worries. He says only one of five applicants is qualified for the jobs, which pay from $2.36 to over $3.50 an hour. Nationally, annual turnover is 25 percent and creeping up, especially in urban slums where interviewers fear violence.

Turnover is a "key problem" because the reliability of the survey depends in part on the interviewers' asking the questions in the same way at each household, and experienced interviewers are more likely to be thoroughly familiar with the prescribed procedures.

New interviewers hired by Mr. Barr, like those everywhere, receive the equivalent of six days' training before they are sent out alone. As a check, Mr. Barr and his assistants reinterview a 5 percent subsample of the households in the region each month. Where the discrepancies with the original data exceed certain limits, the interviewer is called in for special training. Nationwide, only one interviewer has been caught making up answers in the past four years, according to Mr. Levine.

Because replies to the household survey questions are confidential, outside observers are barred from sitting in on the interviews. But chats with veteran interviewers shed some light on the process.

The interviewers say they're often relentless in pursuit of their quarry. One reason: Pay raises depend in part on a low "noninterview" rate. Mrs. Adele Herring, who has worked on the survey for four years, recently coaxed one Philadelphia family going on vacation into giving her the phone number of their Fort Lauderdale resort so she could quiz them while they were out of the city. (The government pays the phone bill.)

DRUNK HOUSEWIFE

Another interviewer reports she recently managed to wring enough information out of a "very drunk" housewife to complete a questionnaire. "Of course, I couldn't go through it in the normal way," she says. "It was a little rough; I was shaking."

The rising rate of refusals is a major headache. Mrs. Rose Abrams, a Cherry Hill, N.J., housewife who has been an interviewer for 12 years, finds refusals are particularly frequent each year at tax time. "They hate the government and they take it out on you," she complains. Some interviewees become violent: One angry householder recently grabbed the questionnaire out of an interviewer's hand and ripped it up.

Careful attention to such small matters as dress helps avoid refusals. An interviewer who's often assigned to households in a low-income area of Philadelphia says she makes a point of dressing simply. "You have to sell yourself," she explains. "They couldn't care less that you represent the U.S. Government."

Once the interviewer gets inside and exchanges pleasantries, she is supposed to stick with her prepared script—the questionnaire—to insure maximum uniformity of responses. The interviewer usually deals with the woman of the house. She first questions the woman about her own status and then questions her separately about each of the other persons over 16 in the household. The questions about the husband's status go something like this:

"What was Mr. Jones doing most of last week —working, keeping house, going to school or something else?" If Mr. Jones was working, the interview is wrapped up after three more questions about how many hours he worked. But if he wasn't working and doesn't claim to be too ill to work, the next question serves as a double-check on his wife's memory:

"Did Mr. Jones work at all last week, not counting work around the house?" If the reply is negative, the next question probes the possibility that he was sick or laid off:

"Did Mr. Jones have a job or business from which he was temporarily absent or on layoff last week?" A negative answer produces the first check on his job-seeking activity:

"Has he been looking for work during the past four weeks?" A "no" answers means he won't be counted as part of the labor force. A "yes" points him toward the unemployed category.

PULLING TEETH

But the answer often isn't a definite "yes" or "no," laments Mr. Herring. "They're likely to say something like, 'Not really.' So you have to ask, 'What do you mean by that?' Eventually you get the answer, but it's often like pulling teeth."

If the answer for Mr. Jones turns out to be "yes," the stage is set for the critical question about "overt" job-seeking activity: "What has Mr. Jones been doing in the last four weeks to find work?"

The interviewer's instructions direct her not to offer any suggestions until the person has had a chance to volunteer information. If nothing is volunteered, the interviewer can run down a list of possibilities, including checking with an employment agency, an employer, or friends and relatives about finding work or answering help-wanted ads.

But not all interviewers stop there. "You have to probe a little," says one. "Are they actually doing something to look for work? Or are they just thinking about it? You have to be keen to pick up any contradictions. If it sounds fishy, I always probe a little."

There's some question about how accurately informed the person being interviewed is about the job-seeking activity of others in the home. One of the "inherent disadvantages" of the household survey, a 1962 presidential panel cautioned, is that responses to questions are "influenced by faulty memory." Indeed, Mrs. Herring suspects that many mothers, especially in low-income areas, really don't know what their teen-age children might be doing to look for a job.

But fortunately, says Mr. Goldstein of the BLS, "there is a law of large numbers that watches over statisticians." He refers to the statistical theory that the errors resulting from the practices of different interviewers and from faulty replies tend to cancel out in large enough samples.

NEW QUESTIONS

Partly in response to concern about the "discouraged jobless," the BLS added a final series of questions to the survey in 1967. The idea was to find out how many persons, not counted in the labor force because they have stopped taking specific steps to find a job, really want work. The latest statistics show that 548,000 persons who were not in the labor force during the fourth quarter of 1969 did want a job but had stopped hunting because they thought they couldn't get employment.

With the information from the household sample fed into Census Bureau computers here, Mr. Levine and his colleagues "inflate" the raw data on the approximately 105,000 people covered by the survey into numbers that will equal the whole noninstitutionalized civilian population over 16. After adjusting to account for the households that weren't interviewed, the computers apply statistical ratios to bring the survey data into agreement with independent estimates of the current noninstitutionalized population over 16 and its distribution by age, race, sex, and residence.

But adjusting the survey results to agree with the independent population estimates—which are based on updated 1960 census figures—creates another problem. Since the 1960 census apparently missed an estimated 5.7 million persons, some studies have suggested that this adjustment could contribute to an unemployment undercount of up to 132,000. BLS officials contend, however, that it's almost impossible to take corrective action because there are only rough estimates of the undercount.

Perhaps the most suspect part of the compilation is the seasonal adjustment performed by the BLS each month. When the jobless rate was gyrating last fall, Budget Director Mayo griped that "we haven't got a surefire way of measuring seasonal adjustment yet."

Indeed, a suspicious seasonal regularity seems to be developing: The jobless rate has climbed each September and dropped each November for the past three years. Mr. Stambler of the BLS attributes part of the difficulty to the short period of time that's elapsed since the 1967 changes in the survey procedures. And Geoffrey Moore, BLS Commissioner, says the bureau is "taking a close look" at its seasonal adjustment methods.

5. Discouraged Workers and Changes in Unemployment*

Paul O. Flaim†

Until a couple of decades ago, the many millions of working-age persons outside the labor force were of limited concern to labor economists and policymakers, either as a potential source of manpower or as a possible threat to the stability of the job market. It was then the general assumption that the nation's labor supply consisted only of persons actually working or actively seeking work. The notion that many persons outside the labor force might have wanted work but were not seeking it because they believed that their search would be fruitless was not widely entertained.

This popular concept of the labor supply was probably relevant in the 1930s, when the ranks of the unemployed contained an apparently inexhaustible reservoir of manpower. It had to be gradually abandoned, however, as evidence accumulated during the post-World War II period showed that millions of persons entered and left the labor force each year, not only because of personal reasons but also in apparent response to changing labor market conditions.

Recognizing these facts, the President's Committee to Appraise Employment and Unemployment Statistics (more familiarly known as the Gordon Committee) stated in 1962 that "the relatively .simple dichotomy between those in and out of the labor force . . . [no longer provides] . . . a satisfactory measure of the labor supply." The Committee went on to recommend that special efforts be made, through the Current Population Survey (CPS), to collect detailed data

on persons not in the labor force, particularly on the so-called "discouraged workers" or "hidden unemployed"—those persons who want work but are not looking for a job because of a belief that their search would be in vain. In so doing, it should be noted, the Committee also recommended that these persons *not* be included in the unemployment count.

In 1964–66, following the recommendation of the Gordon Committee, the Bureau of Labor Statistics began to experiment with a special set of survey questions designed to elicit detailed information on the reasons persons outside the labor force did not participate in the job market. In January 1967, these questions were incorporated into the regular CPS questionnaire. The data which they have yielded have been published quarterly since late 1969 in a special set of tables in the monthly BLS periodical, *Employment and Earnings.*

The earlier analyses of these findings were, by necessity, limited to cross-sectional examinations done in snapshot fashion. Obviously, no time-series analysis could have been undertaken until a number of years had elapsed. Moreover, the first three years of data were collected in a period of very low unemployment, so that one could hardly draw any conclusion about their cyclical sensitivity.

Since the data have now been accumulated for 6 years—the last three years being a period in which vast cyclical changes took place in the nation's economy—it is possible to determine, at least tentatively, to what extent workers will refrain from entering the job market or may be induced to leave it because of rising unemployment. Two variables are of particular interest for this purpose: (1) the number of "discouraged workers," and (2) the number of workers leaving

* From U.S. Department of Labor, *Monthly Labor Review,* Vol. 96, No. 3, March 1973, pp. 8–14.

† Paul O. Flaim is an economist in the Division of Employment and Unemployment Analysis, Bureau of Labor Statistics. This article is based on a paper presented at the August 1972 meeting of the American Statistical Association in Montreal, Canada.

the labor force because of "slack work," who may or may not wind up as "discouraged workers" under current definitions.

IDENTIFYING THOSE DISCOURAGED

Determining the extent of discouragement over job prospects is a very difficult task. It involves the measurement of what are essentially subjective phenomena, specifically one's desire for work and one's perception of his or her chances of obtaining a job. The pinning down of these "states of mind" is rendered particularly uncertain by the fact that the housewife is typically the only person interviewed in each CPS household, and she must answer for all members of the household.

Even if interviewed individually, however, some persons may still not always admit their "real" reason for leaving the labor force. It is possible, for example, that some, although having been unable to find a job, may attribute their nonparticipation status to ill health or other "socially acceptable reasons" rather than admit that they have failed in the job market. Conversely, there may be some who indicate that they want a job and who then explain their failure to look for one in terms of unavailability, even though their desire for work is actually of very limited intensity. Given the subjective and elusive nature of "discouragement," the extent of its possible overstatement or understatement cannot be measured.

In order to identify the discouraged workers, the CPS interviewer asks first if the persons not in the labor force "want a regular job now, either full time or part time." If the answer is yes, or even a tentative yes, there is a follow-up question as to the reasons they are not looking for work. In order to be classified as discouraged, a person's principal reasons for not looking for work must fall into one of the following five categories:

1. Believes no work available in line of work or area.
2. Had tried but could not find work.
3. Lacks necessary schooling, training, skills, or experience.
4. Employers think too young or too old.
5. Other personal handicap in finding a job.

It may be argued that this screening process, particularly the requirement that a person must first be reported as wanting a job in order to be questioned about possible discouragement, yields a rather restrictive definition of hidden unemployment. What about those persons, one might ask,

who, upon losing their job, may decide to return to school and who would then not want a job "now"? Should they not also be regarded as discouraged workers? To answer this, it should be noted that if the discouraged workers' data are to be useful as a measure of underutilization of manpower for policy purposes, they should hardly include persons who do not want a job, especially when their current activity may actually prevent them from taking a job.

It is also important to note that separate data are collected and published, from the same survey, on the reasons for leaving the last job for those persons who have recently left the labor force. As will be discussed later, these "flow" data are an important adjunct to the figures on discouraged workers in terms of understanding the dynamics of the labor force under changing economic conditions.

HOW MANY DISCOURAGED WORKERS?

The first examinations of the data on persons not in the labor force, based on 1967–68 findings, showed that less than one-tenth of these persons professed any desire to be holding a job.[1] Among these, only about 700,000 were classified as discouraged—that is, as not looking for work because of a belief that they could not find a job. As shown in Table 1, the other nonparticipants reported as wanting a job turned out either to be in school, in poor physical condition, or prevented from seeking work by household responsibilities. The ranks of the 700,000 discouraged workers, furthermore, were found to contain relatively few men of prime working age—less than 200,000. The great majority of discouraged consisted, instead, of teenagers, housewives, and elderly persons. These findings seemed to run counter to the contentions that there were virtually millions of discouraged workers and that they included large numbers of men.[2]

---

[1] See Robert L. Stein, "Reasons for Nonparticipation in Labor Force," *Monthly Labor Review*, July 1967, pp. 22–27, and Paul O. Flaim, "Persons Not in the Labor Force: Who They Are and Why They Don't Work," *Monthly Labor Review*, July 1969, pp. 3–14.

[2] These contentions were based largely on econometrically derived estimates of hidden unemployment published in various journals during the mid-1960s. Among the first to construct such estimates were Alfred Tella and Thomas Dernburg and Kenneth Strand. See A. Tella, "The Relation of Labor Force to Employment," *Industrial and Labor Relations Review*, April 1964, pp. 454–69, and T. Dernburg and K. Strand, "Cyclical Variation in Labor Force Participation," *Review of Economics and Statistics*, November 1964. Many other economists, using a variety of econometric techniques, have since undertaken similar research. Essentially, they have

TABLE 1   Distribution of Persons Not in the Labor Force, by Reason, 1967–72 (numbers in thousands)

Labor Force Status	1967	1968	1969	1970	1971	1972
Civilian noninstitutional population.................	129,873	132,026	134,335	136,995	139,775	143,325
In civilian labor force............................	77,347	78,737	80,734	82,715	84,113	86,542
Not in the labor force...........................	52,484	53,289	53,596	54,275	55,662	56,783
Do not want job now, total........................	47,787	48,810	49,137	50,396	51,259	52,321
Current activity: In school.......................	5,641	5,892	5,958	6,051	6,373	6,301
Ill, disabled.....................	3,741	3,684	3,826	3,869	4,077	4,313
Homemaker....................	31,239	31,667	31,384	32,162	32,203	32,384
Retired, old.....................	5,313	5,540	5,795	5,918	6,160	6,691
Other.........................	1,853	2,027	2,174	2,396	2,446	2,632
Want a job now, total.............................	4,698	4,477	4,459	3,877	4,404	4,461
Reason not looking: School attendance...........	1,104	1,115	1,126	1,075	1,242	1,200
Ill health, disability..........	768	656	627	489	555	632
Home responsibilities........	1,325	1,263	1,257	926	1,020	1,098
Think cannot get job........	732	667	574	638	774	765
All other reasons...........	769	777	875	749	813	766

Note: Because of separate computation, the figures on the civilian labor force and on persons not in the labor force may not in all cases add up precisely to the civilian noninstitutional population.

However, the data being analyzed in the late 1960s had been collected in a period of unusually low unemployment, when the jobless rate held below 4 percent. Not until 1970, when unemployment rose, could the relationship between changes in the unemployment rate and in the number of discouraged workers be discerned.

That the rise in unemployment in 1970 produced at least a temporary slackening in labor force participation is now a historical fact. The slackening was most evident in the first half of 1971, when the labor force hardly grew at all. The question is the extent to which this slackening in participation can be attributed to discouragement over job prospects caused by the rise in unemployment.

There is, indeed, a positive relationship between the unemployment rate and the number of discouraged workers. Both series trended down-

attempted to measure the elasticity of labor force participation rates, especially for women and youth, in response to the intensity of the demand for labor as reflected by the unemployment rate, the wage rate, and other variables. Optimal participation rates, those consistent with conditions of "full employment," were then applied to the population to obtain a "full employment labor force." To the extent that the actual labor force, as measured through the Current Population Survey, fails to match this theoretical labor force, they ascribe the gap to the discouraged workers phenomenon or hidden unemployment.

For an analytical discussion of the early econometric estimates of "hidden unemployment" or "discouraged workers," see Jacob Mincer, "Labor Force Participation and Unemployment: A Review of Recent Evidence" in R. A. Gordon and M. S. Gordon, eds., *Prosperity and Unemployment* (New York, Wiley, 1966), pp. 73–112. For a comparison of the more recent econometric estimates with the survey data presented in this article, see the discussions by Joseph Gastwirth and Jacob Mincer elsewhere in this issue.

ward, though in differing degrees, during the 1967–69 period; both rose substantially during 1970; both showed little distinct movement during 1971; and both moved downward during 1972. In terms of the actual number of persons involved, however, it should be noted that the 1969–71 increase in the number of discouraged workers was relatively small when compared with the rise in the number of jobless persons. While the number of unemployed rose by 2.2 million between 1969 and 1971 (on an annual average basis), the number of discouraged workers increased by only 200,000.

Despite the positive relationship between unemployment and discouragement, the two series did not correlate very highly with each other. The coefficient of correlation between these two variables, derived on the basis of seasonally adjusted monthly data for the 1967–71 period,[3] was only 0.53. Nor was the coefficient raised when the relationship between the two series was tested on the basis of data disaggregated by age, sex, and race.

Since it may be reasonably assumed that changes in the number of discouraged workers lag behind the changes in the unemployment rate, some experimentation with lags was also conducted. By lagging the discouraged workers' series by three and also by six months behind the unemployment rate, the coefficients of correlation were raised somewhat—to 0.61 in both cases—

[3] Although the not-in-the-labor-force data are published only on a quarterly basis, they are being tabulated monthly. They have also been seasonally adjusted experimentally, although not yet regularly published in this form.

but were still far from indicating a very close relationship between the two variables.

"CYCLICAL" VERSUS "STRUCTURAL" DISCOURAGEMENT

A closer examination of the disaggregated data on discouraged workers for the 1967–71 period revealed a significant change in composition in terms of the specific reason cited by these persons for their belief that they could not obtain a job. Specifically, there was an increase in the proportion of workers whose discouragement appears to have been directly related to the changing conditions of the job market. Conversely, there was a decline in both the number and proportion of persons attributing their discouragement to personal situations or deficiencies.

Table 2 groups discouraged workers into these two broad categories. The first included the workers reported as believing that there were no jobs in their line of work or area and those who had tried unsuccessfully to find a job before giving up the search. The second category includes those workers reported as thinking they could not get a job due to their very young or advanced age, those who saw their lack of education or training as the major obstacle, and those who cited other personal handicaps, such as language difficulties.

It would appear, given the different nature of the reasons for discouragement, that the first category of discouraged workers should be much more cyclically sensitive than the second. Discouragement among the second category appears to be more of a "structural" nature and thus not necessarily related to the tightness, or looseness, of the job market. The data in Table 2 confirm this·hypothesis. As shown, all of the 200,000 increase in the number of discouraged workers between 1969 and 1971 took place among those blaming their situation on job-market weaknesses.

Correlation analysis also lent support to this hypothesis. Whereas, as noted above, the total number discouraged workers did not correlate highly with the overall unemployment rate, yielding a coefficient of only 0.53, the number of workers discouraged because of job market reasons yielded a much higher correlation coefficient —0.79—when regressed against the unemployment rate.

On the other hand, when the number of persons whose discouragement seemed to hinge on personal factors was regressed against the unemployment rate, the result was a negative coefficient of correlation (−0.47). There is no ready explanation for this negative relationship, but some possibilities may be raised. For example, the passage of legislation designed to reduce job discrimination because of age may have accounted for a downward trend in the number of elderly workers who thought that they could not get a job due to their advanced age. It may also be hypothesized that when the unemployment rate rises, some workers who had previously been attributing their discouragement to personal reasons may then attribute their situation to the deteriorating job market.

It is clear, nevertheless, that if we limit our analysis to the group of discouraged workers who link their situation to the conditions of the job market, we find that their number did increase and decrease in line with the underlying move-

TABLE 2   Composition of Discouraged Workers, 1967–72 (numbers in thousands)

Reason	1967	1968	1969	1970	1971	1972
Total...	732	667	574	638	774	765
Job-market factors..................................	383	371	311	437	537	540
Had looked but could not find job..................	168	161	161	244	300	300
Thinks no job available............................	215	210	150	193	237	240
Personal factors....................................	349	297	263	201	236	226
Employers think too young or too old..............	216	171	139	105	112	111
Lacks education, skills, training....................	84	74	78	60	85	78
Other personal handicap..........................	49	52	46	36	39	37
Percent distribution..........................	100.0	100.0	100.0	100.0	100.0	100.0
Job market factors..................................	52.3	55.5	54.2	68.5	69.5	70.6
Had looked but could not find job..................	23.0	24.1	28.0	38.2	38.8	39.2
Thinks no job available............................	29.4	31.4	26.1	30.3	30.7	31.4
Personal factors....................................	47.7	44.5	45.8	31.5	30.5	29.5
Employers think too young or too old..............	29.5	25.6	24.2	16.5	14.5	14.5
Lacks education, skills, training....................	11.5	11.1	13.6	9.4	11.0	10.2
Other personal handicap..........................	6.7	7.8	8.0	5.6	5.0	4.8

Note: Because of rounding, sums of individual items may not equal totals.

ment of the unemployment rate during the 1967–71 period.

UNEXPECTED DISCONTINUITY

One of the findings from the six years of experience in obtaining statistics on labor force nonparticipants is that it apparently makes quite a bit of difference whether the questions about current desire for work and future jobseeking plans are asked in the first month in which they are visited by the CPS interviewer or in subsequent months.

Since a person's reasons for nonparticipation in the labor force are not likely to change from one month to another, this information is asked in only one of the four consecutive monthly interviews conducted in households falling in the CPS sample. From 1967 through 1969, the questions were asked in the month in which a given household first entered the CPS sample and then again 1 year later, when the same household reentered the sample for the second and final 4-month stint after an 8-month hiatus. In January 1970, the questions were switched from the first and fifth month-in-sample to the fourth and eighth. In effect, instead of being asked when a household enters or reenters the sample, they are now being asked only when the household leaves the sample.[4]

This switch turned out to have a noticeable effect on the data on persons not in the labor force. Following the switch, proportionately fewer persons, particularly among the housewives, were reported as either wanting a job at present or as planning to look for work in the near future. Evidently, having become increasingly more at ease with the interviewer with each passing month, a respondent is less likely to exaggerate his (or her) attachment to the labor force in the fourth monthly interview than in the first one.

As far as the data on discouraged workers are concerned, the switch appears to have caused a small drop in the number and proportion of persons attributing their discouragement to personal

reasons (a factor which no doubt contributed to the negative relationship between this variable and the unemployment rate). Although this discontinuity did not have a great effect on the overall numbers, it is a good illustration of the difficulties which arise in the measurement of what are essentially attitudes on the part of workers or potential workers.

PROFILE, 1972

As was the case during the first years for which data on discouraged workers are available, the proportion of men of prime working age among this group is still relatively small. Of the 765,000 persons classified as discouraged workers in 1972, only about 70,000, or less than one-tenth, were men 25 to 59 years of age.

Blacks are even more overrepresented among the discouraged workers than they are among the unemployed. They made up only one-ninth of all the persons of working age outside the labor force but one-fourth of the discouraged workers in 1972. (Blacks also make up one-ninth of the civilian labor force and account for about one-fifth of the unemployed.)

In terms of previous work history, nearly two-fifths of the discouraged workers had been out of the job market less than one year when interviewed. Only 14 percent had never worked before. These findings, however, differ by age and sex.

Evidently, most discouraged workers regard their status as only temporary. Although they do not deem it worthwhile to look for a job at the time of the interview, they are apparently more hopeful in terms of their future prospects. Nearly 80 percent of the total were reported as planning to actively seek work within the next 12 months. It would thus be erroneous to assume that most discouraged workers have permanently given up on the job market.

EXAMINING OUT-FLOWS

While the data on discouraged workers may not fully explain how cyclical changes in the employment situation affect the dynamics of the labor force, other data gathered through the same survey shed additional light on this phenomenon. For example, through the special set of questions asked of the nonparticipants since 1967, it has been possible to group those with recent work experience according to their reasons for leaving their last job—regardless of whether or not they are currently counted as discouraged workers.

[4] The switch was instituted in an attempt to determine whether these added questions were having an effect on the so-called "first-month bias" in the unemployment figures. It had long been evident that the reported incidence of joblessness in households entering or reentering the CPS sample was higher than in households which had been in the sample for two consecutive months or more. This "first-month bias" became even larger around 1967, and it was hypothesized that the increase might have been related to the introduction of the not-in-the-labor-force questions. The reduction in the reported incidence of unemployment for the first and fifth month-in-sample groups and concomitant rise for the fourth and eighth following the January 1970 switch of the not-in-the-labor-force questions seems to have amply confirmed this hypothesis.

Unlike the questions designed to identify the discouraged workers, those designed to determine when and why a person left his last job deal with facts which are of a more overt, observable nature. As such, these questions should present fewer problems, particularly when the respondents, as is often the case, are persons other than those to whom the questions relate. The "flow" data which these questions produce should thus be subject to less response error than those on the actual number of discouraged workers.

The volume of the gross flows out of the labor force has not changed much in recent years, averaging close to 10 million. This would indicate that the cyclical changes in labor force growth during this period have stemmed primarily from fluctuations in the in-flow of new entrants and reentrants into the job market. There have been, however, some cyclical changes in the composition of the out-flows by reasons for leaving last job. Specifically, there was an increase between 1969 and 1971 in the proportion of persons attributing their exit from the labor force to the fact that their jobs had been terminated, either temporarily or permanently, due to economic reasons. Of the three categories under the "economic" heading, "slack work" appears to have been most cyclically sensitive. The changes in this variable have been closely related to the changes in the unemployment rate.

This relationship was also tested through regression and correlation analysis. The coefficient of correlation between the overall unemployment rate and the number of persons reporting they had left the labor force after having lost their jobs due to slack work was 0.83 on the basis of monthly data for the 1967–71 period. The substitution of data on unemployment due to job loss for the overall measurements of unemployment yielded coefficients of roughly similar magnitude.

SUMMARY AND CONCLUSION

After six years of experience in the collection of data on discouraged workers through the Current Population Survey, it appears that this survey is, indeed, a viable vehicle for such a purpose. Although the definition of "discouragement" used for the purposes of the survey might not be universally agreed upon, the data gathered so far have shed important light both on the discouraged-worker phenomenon and other aspects of labor force dynamics.

While six years of data may not be sufficient to enable us to establish with any certainty the relationship between two variables, the hypothesis that changes in the number of discouraged workers are closely related to changes in the unemployment rate can now be verified at least tentatively. The same can also be said for changes in the number of workers leaving the labor force because of slack work.

To the extent that this is true, it would appear that we should take into account these variables, as well as the data on unemployment and underemployment, when assessing the waste of manpower which accompanies an economic recession. In the most recent slowdown, however, the increase in the number of discouraged workers, as currently defined, was relatively small when compared with the magnitude of the changes in unemployment. That being the case, it would be unreasonable to assume that the return of these workers to the job market as economic conditions improve could be of such magnitude as to act as a major brake against the lowering of the unemployment rate.

6. Moonlighters: Their Motivations and Characteristics*

Vera C. Perrella†

Multiple jobholders—moonlighters—are an important, though small, element in the work force. They have been a fairly steady segment of the employed population during the period between 1956 and 1969, both numerically and as a percent of all employed persons. The number of persons who hold down more than one job has ranged between 3 and 4 million, and the multiple jobholding rate has ranged between 4.5 percent and 5.7 percent. The rate for men has been roughly three times that for women. (See box.)

This article deals with information obtained from the May 1969 supplement to the monthly survey of the labor force about reasons for moonlighting, degree of attachment to moonlighting, personal characteristics of multiple jobholders, and occupations, industries, and hours worked on primary and secondary jobs.[1] A brief discussion of some economic and social aspects of moonlighting is included.

MAJOR RESULTS

Four million workers held two jobs or more in May 1969. These moonlighters constituted 5.2 percent of all employed persons. The number of moonlighters was 370,000 higher than at the time of the last survey in May 1966, and the multiple jobholding rate increased somewhat. For men, the rate rose to 6.9 percent from 6.4 percent; however, the women's rate, 2.3 percent, was not significantly different. (See Table 1.)

The net increase in the number of moonlighters was entirely among workers who were nonfarm wage and salary employees in their primary and secondary jobs. In May 1969 almost 60 percent of the moonlighters were nonfarm wage and salary employees in both their first and second jobs. Close to 25 percent worked in agriculture in at least one of their jobs, most often as wage and salary workers off the farm on the first job and as self-employed farmers on the second (Table 2).

Moonlighting was much more common among men than women. White men had a slightly higher multiple jobholding rate than Negro[2] men, but among women there was no difference in rates by color.

REASONS FOR MULTIPLE JOBHOLDING

It is generally assumed that the overriding reason people take on more than one job is financial necessity. Also, there is some speculation as to whether an appreciable proportion of moonlighters have only casual attachment to their moonlighting jobs. Information on these two

* From U.S. Department of Labor, *Monthly Labor Review*, Vol. 93, No. 8, August 1970, pp. 57–64.

† Vera C. Perrella is an economist in the Division of Labor Force Studies, Bureau of Labor Statistics.

[1] Data in the current report are based primarily on information from supplementary questions to the May 1969 monthly survey of the labor force, conducted for the Bureau of Labor Statistics by the Bureau of the Census through its Current Population Survey. The data relate to the week of May 11–17.

This is the eighth in a series of reports on this subject. The most recent was published in the *Monthly Labor Review*, October 1967, pp. 17–22, and reprinted with additional tabular data and explanatory notes as Special Labor Force Report No. 90.

[2] In this report, data for the grouping "Negro and other races" are used to represent data for Negroes, since Negroes constitute about 92 percent of all persons in the grouping. In addition to Negroes, the grouping includes American Indians, Filipinos, Chinese, and Japanese, among others.

SURVEY DEFINITIONS

For purposes of this survey, multiple jobholders are defined as those employed persons who, during the survey week (1) had jobs as wage or salary workers with two employers or more, (2) were self-employed and also held wage or salary jobs, or (3) worked as unpaid family workers but also had secondary wage or salary jobs. The primary job is the one at which the greatest number of hours were worked. Also included as multiple jobholders are persons who had two jobs during the survey week only because they were changing from one job to another. This group is very small—only 1 percent of all multiple jobholders in May 1969.

Persons employed only in private households (as a maid, laundress, gardener, babysitter, and so on) who worked for two employers or more during the survey week were not counted as multiple jobholders. Working for several employers was considered an inherent characteristic of private household work rather than an indication of multiple jobholding. Also excluded were self-employed persons with additional farms or businesses, and persons with second jobs as unpaid family workers.

TABLE 1   Employed Persons with Two Jobs or More, by Sex, 1956–69

Month and Year	Number (thousands)	Multiple Jobholding Rate*		
		Both Sexes	Men	Women
May 1969.......................... 4,008		5.2	6.9	2.3
May 1966.......................... 3,636		4.9	6.4	2.2
May 1965.......................... 3,756		5.2	6.7	2.3
May 1964.......................... 3,726		5.2	6.9	2.1
May 1963.......................... 3,921		5.7	7.4	2.4
May 1962.......................... 3,342		4.9	6.4	2.0
December 1960†.................... 3,012		4.6	5.9	2.0
December 1959.................... 2,966		4.5	5.8	2.0
July 1958........................ 3,099		4.8	6.0	2.2
July 1957........................ 3,570		5.3	6.6	2.5
July 1956........................ 3,653		5.5	6.9	2.5

* Multiple jobholders as percent of all employed persons.
† Data for Alaska and Hawaii included beginning 1960.

aspects of moonlighting was obtained on a nationwide scale for the first time in May 1969, when persons with 2 jobs or more were asked their main reason for moonlighting, whether they had worked at more than one job in every one of the 4 weeks prior to the survey, and in how many of the 12 months prior to May 1969 they had worked on their secondary jobs.

Although statements about motivation must be interpreted cautiously, information on the reasons why people take on extra jobs has significance. Four out of every ten moonlighters said their main reason for moonlighting was to meet regular household expenses for food, clothing, utilities, and rent. One out of ten said paying off debts was his main reason (Table 3). Another one in ten said he was holding a second job mainly to save for the future. The rest of the

moonlighters gave a wide variety of reasons, such as getting experience in a different occupation, building up a business, liking the work, needing money for extras, and helping out friends or relatives who needed work done.

A greater proportion of the Negro than of the white moonlighters gave meeting regular household expenses as the main reason. Among the white moonlighters, the same proportion of men and women gave meeting regular expenses; among the black, this reason was given by an appreciably higher proportion of the women than of the men. Three-fourths of the Negro women who were moonlighters worked at a second job for this reason.

Men and women 25 years old and over were considerably more likely to give the need to meet regular household expenses as the main reason

TABLE 2   Type of Industry and Class of Worker of Primary and Secondary Jobs, for Persons with Two Jobs or More, May 1969 (numbers in thousands)

Type of Industry and Class of Worker of Primary Job	Total Employed	Persons with Two Jobs or More		Type of Industry and Class of Worker of Secondary Job					
				Agriculture			Nonagricultural Industries		
		Number	Percent of Total Employed	Total	Wage and Salary Workers	Self-Employed Workers	Total	Wage and Salary Workers	Self-Employed Workers
Total............................	77,264	4,008	5.2	723	121	602	3,285	2,698	587
Agriculture.......................	3,893	273	7.0	57	41	16	216	210	6
Wage and salary workers.........	1,284	75	5.8	38	22	16	37	31	6
Self-employed workers...........	1,962	167	8.5	13	13	(*)	154	154	(*)
Unpaid family workers...........	647	31	4.8	6	6	(†)	25	25	(†)
Nonagricultural industries........	73,371	3,735	5.1	666	80	586	3,069	2,488	581
Wage and salary workers.........	67,536	3,568	5.3	661	75	586	2,907	2,326	581
Self-employed workers...........	5,264	162	3.1	5	5	(*)	157	157	(*)
Unpaid family workers...........	571	5	.9	—	—	(†)	5	5ₐ	(†)

Note: Because of rounding, sums of individual items may not equal totals.

* Self-employed persons with a secondary business or farm, but no wage or salary job, were not counted as multiple jobholders.

† Persons whose primary job was as an unpaid family worker were counted as multiple jobholders only if they also held a wage or salary job.

TABLE 3   Main Reason for Working at Two Jobs or More, by Age, Sex, Color, and Marital Status, May 1969

	Total		Main Reason for Working at Two Jobs or More				
Characteristic	Number (thousands)	Percent	Meet Regular Expenses	Pay Off Debts	Save for the Future	Get Experience*	Other†
Both sexes, total............	4,008	100.0	40.0	8.8	13.4	8.0	29.8
White..........................	3,640	100.0	38.2	8.8	13.5	8.2	31.2
Negro and other races...........	368	100.0	58.6	9.3	11.4	5.4	15.3
Men, total...................	3,350	100.0	39.6	9.2	14.2	8.4	28.6
White..........................	3,059	100.0	38.2	9.1	14.2	8.6	29.9
Negro and other races...........	291	100.0	54.8	10.3	13.4	5.9	15.5
16 to 24 years....................	395	100.0	27.1	13.9	15.9	8.1	34.9
25 to 44 years....................	1,824	100.0	41.2	10.3	14.5	9.6	24.5
45 years and over................	1,131	100.0	41.5	5.8	12.9	6.5	32.2
Married, wife present............	2,922	100.0	42.5	8.9	13.6	8.4	26.7
Women, total...................	658	100.0	42.2	7.0	9.3	5.9	35.6
White..........................	581	100.0	38.1	7.2	10.0	6.2	38.4
Negro and other races...........	77	100.0	72.7	5.2	3.9	3.9	14.3
16 to 24 years....................	135	100.0	17.8	11.1	14.1	11.9	45.2
25 to 44 years....................	271	100.0	48.1	7.4	8.1	5.9	30.4
45 years and over................	252	100.0	48.8	4.4	7.9	2.8	36.1
Married, husband present........	309	100.0	44.2	5.8	7.4	6.5	36.1

Because of rounding, sums of individual items may not equal totals.
* Including persons who said their main reason was to get experience in a different occupation or to build up a business.
† Includes such reasons as liking the work done on secondary job, needing money for extras, and helping out friends or relatives. Also included are a small number of persons who changed jobs during the week.

than were younger people. The younger men and women are more often single and less likely to have family responsibilities. Paying off debts, saving for the future, and getting experience were more important among the younger moonlighters, decreasing in importance as age increased. This finding accords with the normal pattern of the various stages of career and family phasing linked to age.

There was generally a direct relationship between earnings and the proportion of multiple jobholders who reported they were holding a second job to meet regular household expenses. For example, among the moonlighting men who had usual wage or salary earnings of less than $100 a week, about one half gave this as the main reason, compared with about one third of the men earning $150 a week or more. The men earning $150 or more were more likely to report saving for the future or to get experience at a new job or business.

FREQUENCY OF MOONLIGHTING

Moonlighters apparently have more than a casual attachment to working at more than one job. In May 1969, 7 out of 10 moonlighters had worked at both their main and extra jobs in each of the 4 weeks preceding the survey, and almost half of all the moonlighters had worked at both jobs in all 12 months in the year preceding May 1969. Another 18 percent had moonlighted in at least 7 to 11 of those months.

There was no significant difference between men and women, nor between whites and Negroes, in the proportions who worked in each of the preceding 4 weeks. With respect to age, there was no difference for women, but the men 25 years old and over, most of whom were married, were more likely than the younger men to have worked in each of the preceding 4 weeks. The moonlighters who had worked at both their primary and secondary jobs in each of the preceding 4 weeks were twice as likely to have moonlighted in all 12 months as those who had not worked in each of the weeks. Moonlighting in each of the 4 weeks prior to the survey was just as common (75 percent) among those who were moonlighting to save for the future or to get experience as it was for those who were doing it to meet regular household expenses or pay off debts. Moonlighting in each of the 4 weeks or in all 12 months was more common among those whose second jobs were in agriculture than those whose second jobs were in nonagricultural industries, and among those who were self-employed than those who were wage or salary workers, or second jobs.

The proportion of moonlighters who worked in all 12 months at their second jobs was not directly related to earnings. Among male moonlighters who were wage or salary workers on their first jobs, 54 percent of those with weekly earnings of $150 or more on their primary jobs moonlighted in each of the preceding 12 months, compared with only 28 percent of those who earned less than $60. This does not appear to agree with the finding that the lower earners were more likely to moonlight to meet regular expenses. Several factors may underlie this seeming contradiction. The low earners are mainly the younger moonlighters who, on the one hand, are more likely to be recent labor force entrants and at the lower skill and experience levels and, on the other hand, less likely to have as many dependents or family responsibilities as men in the middle years. The younger men, therefore, may neither want, nor have available to them, as steady a secondary job as the older ones. In addition, they may not have been in the work force all of the preceding 12 months.

Of course, both the regularity and length of time of moonlighting depend upon availability of the work as well as the propensity of the worker to want, need, or persevere in a second job. Older workers more often have the experience and skills which are in demand than do younger workers. For example, 40 percent of the moonlighters were professional workers, farmers, or managers in their secondary jobs. These are the kinds of jobs which generally require both continuity and regularity of work.

MALE HOUSEHOLD HEADS

The tendency to hold more than one job varies with age, sex, and marital and household-head status. A very small proportion of single persons, most of whom are young, have a second job— fewer than 4 percent among the men.

The relatively high multiple jobholding rates of married men emphasize the importance of economic responsibility for their families as a reason for moonlighting. Among these household heads who were wage and salary workers on their primary jobs, the rate increased as the number of children under 18 years old in the family increased:

Number of Children	Multiple Jobholding Rate*
Total	8.2
No children under 18 years	6.0
1 child under 18 years	7.8
2 children under 18 years	8.9
3 or 4 children under 18 years	10.5
5 children under 18 years	11.3

*Persons with two jobs or more as percent of all employed.

INDUSTRY

Workers whose primary jobs were in state and local government and in the postal service had the highest multiple jobholding rates (11 percent and 10 percent, respectively). As in previous surveys, wage and salary workers in construction and in educational services also had high rates. These industries include workers with both high and low earnings and job security. Self-employed persons in agriculture also had rates much higher than average. The high moonlighting rates may result in part from regular work schedules which leave time free when other work is available. On the other hand, the rate for workers in manufacturing, in which working hours may be harder to rearrange, was below the overall average of 5.2 percent.

The industries in which the largest proportions of the moonlighters found their secondary jobs were service and finance, agriculture, and retail trade—industries which have requirements for part-time workers. About 64 percent of all the moonlighters worked in these three industry groups in their secondary jobs; only about 43 percent of all the moonlighters worked in these industries in their primary jobs.

Most of the moonlighters worked in different industries in their primary and secondary jobs. The service, finance, and real estate group was the only one in which close to half of the moonlighters had both their jobs in the same industry. However, the range of different industries included in this very broad major group is extensive, so that many of the moonlighters may in fact have been in quite different industries in their primary and secondary jobs. Of the other broad industry groups, farming (21 percent) and retail trade (19 percent) were the only ones in which the proportion with both jobs in the same industry was much higher than 10 percent.

Although the multiple jobholding rate for factory workers was about average, they were one fourth of all moonlighters, a proportion which has remained relatively unchanged for the past several years for which data are available. Relatively few factory workers who moonlight hold a second factory job. In May 1969, only 11 percent held two jobs in manufacturing; nearly one fourth were in agriculture, mainly as self-employed farmers; and other large groups worked in retail trade and service and finance or were self-employed in nonfarm industries.

OCCUPATION

Persons who were protective service workers (policemen, security guards, and firemen, for example) and farmers on their primary jobs had the highest multiple jobholding rates (Table 4). Among men, the rate for teachers below the college level (17 percent) was more than double the rate for all men. On the other hand, the rate for men who were managers and proprietors was only 5.3 percent. Many of these workers regularly work long hours on their primary job, and average earnings for their occupational group are far above the average for all workers.

Although most moonlighters work at different occupations in their main and extra jobs, there is relatively more correspondence in occupation than in industry. More than half of all the moonlighters whose main jobs were in the professional, technical, and kindred occupations also worked in that group in their extra jobs. Examples of this type of combination are the accountant who is a salaried worker by day but self-employed in the evening or on weekends and the elementary school teacher who has adult education classes in the evenings. This percentage for the professional group was considerably higher than in any other group.

HOURS

Primary Jobs. Most moonlighters work full-time (35 hours or more a week) on their primary jobs; only about 1 out of every 5 worked part time (less than 35 hours a week) in May 1969. The largest single group—41 percent—worked the 40-hour work week, which has become the full-time norm. The large increases in part-time workers, along with some increase in normal

TABLE 4   Multiple Jobholding Rates, by Occupation and Sex, May 1969*

Occupation Group	Both Sexes	Men	Women
All occupations..	5.2	6.9	2.3
Professional, technical, and kindred workers...................	6.9	9.2	3.1
Engineers..	4.6	4.6	—
Medical and other health workers...........................	5.6	12.0	1.6
Teachers, except college...................................	7.1	16.8	2.8
Other professional, technical, and kindred workers..........	7.6	8.6	4.6
Farmers and farm managers.................................	8.6	8.8	2.6
Managers, officials, and proprietors except farm..............	4.7	5.3	1.3
Clerical and kindred workers................................	3.3	6.6	2.1
Sales workers..	4.7	6.3	2.6
Retail trade..	4.0	6.6	2.4
Other sales workers......................................	5.7	6.0	3.9
Craftsmen, foremen, and kindred workers....................	6.4	6.5	2.0
Carpenters and construction craftsmen.....................	6.6	6.7	—
Mechanics and repairmen.................................	7.2	7.2	(†)
Other craftsmen, foremen, and kindred workers.............	5.8	6.0	1.6
Operatives and kindred workers.............................	5.0	6.7	1.1
Drivers and deliverymen.................................	6.9	6.9	5.6
Other operatives and kindred workers.....................	4.6	6.6	1.0
Private household workers..................................	3.6	—	3.6
Service workers, except private household....................	5.1	8.8	2.5
Protective service workers................................	15.7	16.6	—
Waiters, cooks, and bartenders...........................	2.8	3.8	2.4
Other service workers....................................	4.1	6.6	2.6
Farm laborers and foremen.................................	5.1	5.6	4.3
Laborers, except farm and mine.............................	5.6	5.6	3.7

   * Persons with two jobs or more as percent of total employed in each occupation. Total employed is sum of single jobholders in an occupation and those with two jobs or more whose primary job is in that occupation.
   † Percent not shown where base is less than 75,000.

work weeks shorter than the usual 40-hour norm of recent years, have not resulted in significant increases in the proportions of workers who moonlight, because, when unemployment is not high, most people who work part time do so out of choice and because the shorter work hours have not necessarily been accompanied by commensurate decreases in pay. Moreover, most part-time workers are women who work part time out of choice. While a significant number of women work at more than one job, moonlighting continues more a man's than a woman's activity.

Moonlighters whose main jobs were in agriculture had the largest proportion who worked 49 hours or more; of the self-employed among them, more than half worked that many hours on their main jobs. As with the farm workers, the self-employed moonlighters in nonfarm industries on their main jobs had the largest proportion (35 percent) who worked 49 hours or more on those jobs.

Secondary Jobs. Multiple jobholders worked an average (median) of 13 hours on their secondary jobs during the survey week, a number which has changed little over the years for which comparable data are available. About 25 percent of the workers put in only 1 to 7 hours of extra work and another 30 percent, 8 to 14 hours. Teen-agers averaged fewer hours than adults.

Male multiple jobholders were not only more likely than women to be full-time workers on their main jobs (84 percent compared with 50 percent) but also more likely to have worked longer hours on their second jobs. Their median hours were 14 and 10, respectively. Nearly one half of the men but only one third of the women worked 15 hours or more on their secondary jobs.

The industries in which the largest proportions of moonlighters worked 22 hours or more on their second jobs during the survey week were agriculture, manufacturing, and business and repair services. Among those self-employed in agriculture, almost one third worked 22 hours or more. In nonagricultural industries, manufacturing and business and repair services each had about 30 percent who worked 22 hours or more.

By occupation and hours of second job, moonlighters who were farmers and farm managers, nonfarm managers and officials, nonfarm laborers, and operatives had the largest proportions, working 22 hours or more, with the proportions ranging from about one fourth to one third.

Total Hours. Since most of the moonlighters worked full time on their main jobs, the total number of hours worked a week on both jobs

was relatively high. Half of all the moonlighters totaled more than 55 hours a week, and almost 2 out of 5 worked at least 60 hours a week.

The moonlighters who were self-employed in agriculture on their main jobs put in the greatest total number of hours on both jobs; about 3 out of every 5 worked a total of 60 hours or more during the survey week. Among multiple jobholders who were in nonfarm industries on their primary jobs, only those in state and local government had more than 50 percent working at least 60 hours. On the other hand, only 27 percent of the workers in the service and finance industry worked that many hours on both jobs.

SOCIAL AND ECONOMIC ASPECTS

Despite its relatively rare occurrence—or perhaps because of it, since that which is atypical generally draws attention—moonlighting arouses considerable interest and comment, not all favorable. To some people, moonlighting represents a retrogressive practice which undermines efforts to obtain shorter hours and higher pay. Others contend that shortening the work week will only lead to higher moonlighting rates, or that on-the-job accidents are bound to increase because of fatigue caused by excessive work hours. Still others view moonlighting as a threat to job security or rates of pay, arguing that if employers can hire moonlighters at lower wages than union scale, regular workers are threatened through outright job loss, lower regular pay, or loss of overtime pay. Some employers disapprove of moonlighting because they feel it lessens productivity.

To some, the opportunity to hold more than one job, restricted only by the marketability of one's skills and the availability of one's time, represents a desirable exercise of freedom of choice, even though it is recognized that the circumstances which lead some workers to take that option are unfortunate, as in the case of the individual whose primary job earnings are too low to furnish the basic necessities. As indicated by the reasons moonlighters gave for holding more than one job, motivations for moonlighting vary, albeit financial necessity is the single most often given reason.

While data for support or rebuttal of all these arguments are not available, some important points do emerge from what data there are. For instance, neither the number of moonlighters nor the percentage they constitute of all employed persons shows any clear pattern of movement up or down relative to the unemployment rate.

The probability that persons with more than

one job take work away from the unemployed is small. The secondary jobs in which moonlighters are self-employed (1.2 million in May 1969) would provide few job opportunities to the unemployed whose skills and financial resources would probably preclude their taking over a farm or business, however small. Other factors are the difficulty of matching the location of the jobs and jobseekers and of matching jobs usually held only by men or only by women. Also, such jobs are typically for only a small number of hours, with commensurately low earnings; and many of them may be short term or intermittent, while the unemployed look mainly for full-time permanent jobs. Only 8 percent, or 320,000, of the moonlighters had worked the equivalent of a full-time week on their second jobs in the May 1969 survey, whereas about 80 percent of the 2.1 million unemployed in May were looking for full-time jobs.

The role of moonlighting in agriculture cannot be discounted. The small farmer is disappearing rapidly. For a significant proportion of this diminishing group, moonlighting is the only means of continuing as farmers. Without the opportunity to earn money in another job, many small farm owners would be unable to maintain their farms and their chosen way of life. In May 1969, 600,000 moonlighters were self-employed in agriculture on their secondary jobs. At that time, the total number of persons self-employed in primary jobs in agriculture was 2 million. Thus, the moonlighters self-employed in agriculture on the second job represent an addition of nearly one third to the number of persons self-employed in agriculture. In no other industry are multiple jobholders such a high percentage of the employed. And, of course, some of the 165,000 moonlighters who are self-employed in agriculture on their primary jobs must also be assumed to be among the number for whom moonlighting makes the difference between being able to continue in agriculture and having to give it up.

Similarly, moonlighting offers some persons an avenue to self-employment in nonfarm industries, another group which has declined as a proportion of all employed persons. Working at a wage or salary job for security while trying to build up a business of one's own is a not uncommon practice. Without that security, the attempt might be impossible. In May 1969 over half a million moonlighters were self-employed in nonagricultural industries in their secondary jobs, and another 160,000 were self-employed in nonagricultural industries in their primary jobs.

7. Where Women Work—An Analysis by Industry and Occupation*

Elizabeth Waldman and
Beverly J. McEaddy†

The last three decades have been years of extraordinary economic and social change in the status of women—the tremendous response of married women to labor market demand; an increasingly service-oriented economy, accompanied by an increased need for white-collar workers; changing attitudes toward careers for women outside the home; the trend toward smaller families; the increase in the number of households headed by women; and landmark legislation prohibiting employment discrimination based on sex.

Despite these changes, today's figures on the employment of women in American industry bear a striking resemblance to those of yesterday. In 1970, just as in the three previous census years —1940, 1950, and 1960—the service industry ranked first in the employment of women. Over this 30-year span, about 60 percent of all employees in the service industry were women— some 60 percent of the workers in educational services; around 75 percent in the medical-health industry; and about 75 percent in personal services, including those in hotels and private homes. Within other major industrial categories, such as manufacturing and trade, certain subgroups remain as female-intensive today as they were yesterday. Examples are the manufacture of clothing and general merchandising, where at least 50 percent of all employees are women. (See Table 1.)

The recordbreaking growth achieved by American industry since 1940 was made possible, in part, by the phenomenal increase in the number and proportion of women, especially married

women, who were able and willing to join the work force. From 1940 to 1970, nonagricultural employment of all persons expanded from 32.1 million to 69.1 million, with women nearly half of the increase (18 million). In 1940, women were 31 percent of all workers in nonagricultural industries; by 1970, 40 percent, as their numbers almost tripled to 27.5 million. In 1940, almost half the women in the labor force were single and only 30 percent were married; in 1970, about 20 percent were single and 60 percent were married. Over these three decades, the labor force participation rate of married women rose from 15 to 41 percent and the rate of mothers with children under age 6 from 9 to 30 percent.

The enormous expansion in the labor force participation of women has sometimes been referred to as the response of married women to the tidal wave of paperwork that occurred in the industrial world of the 1950s and 1960s. The population explosion of post-World War II contributed to the need for expanding all types of services—among them, medical, educational, personal, and recreational—thus generating more jobs of the types considered to be traditionally female. Many jobs in the service industry can be described as extensions of what women do as homemakers—teach children and young adults, nurse the sick, prepare food.

Another factor contributing to the concentration of women in the service industries is that part-time employment is more readily available there than in other major industry categories (with the exception of retail trade). In recent years, about one-fourth of all employed women held part-time jobs. Also, many service industries employ full-time workers but operate at other than the standard nine-to-five schedule—for example, hospitals, schools, libraries, and hotels.

* From U.S. Department of Labor, *Monthly Labor Review*, Vol. 97, No. 5, May 1974, pp. 3–13.

† Elizabeth Waldman is an economist and Beverly J. McEaddy a social science research analyst in the Division of Labor Force Studies, Bureau of Labor Statistics.

TABLE 1 Women Employed as Wage and Salary Workers in Nonagricultural Industries, 1940–70
(numbers in thousands)

Industry	1940			1970		
		Women			Women	
	Total Employed	Number	Percent of Total	Total Employed	Number	Percent of Total
Total nonagricultural industries.......	32,058	9,794	31	69,115	27,496	40
Mining...................................	869	12	1	616	50	8
Construction.............................	1,603	33	2	3,976	244	6
Manufacturing...........................	10,317	2,323	23	19,566	5,623	29
Durable goods..........................	5,162	604	12	11,596	2,483	21
Nondurable............................	5,155	1,719	33	7,970	3,140	39
Transportation and public utilities...........	2,911	345	12	5,039	1,106	22
Wholesale and retail trade.................	5,522	1,669	30	13,810	5,871	43
Wholesale.............................	1,009	174	17	2,907	699	24
Retail.................................	4,514	1,495	33	10,903	5,172	47
Finance, insurance, and real estate.........	1,294	435	34	3,610	1,870	52
Services..................................	6,984	4,321	62	18,282	11,436	63
Personal, including private household and hotels...........................	3,268	2,449	75	3,010	2,256	75
Private households.....................	2,196	1,931	88	(*)	(1,124)	(*)
Business and repair.....................	583	64	11	2,006	624	31
Professional service....................	2,796	1,736	62	12,707	8,352	66
Medical and health....................	745	543	73	3,907	3,096	79
Education.............................	1,514	976	64	6,080	3,788	62
Private...............................	(*)	(*)	—	1,550	957	62
Government...........................	(*)	(*)	—	4,530	2,831	62
Legal†.................................	156	85	54	386	178	46
Other services, including recreation and amusement.............................	338	72	21	559	204	36
Public administration‡......................	1,758	350	20	4,216	1,297	31
Postal service..........................	309	36	12	719	144	20
Federal public administration.............	299	104	35	1,528	546	36
State and local..........................	848	203	24	1,824	557	31
State.................................	(*)	—	—	538	202	38
Local.................................	(*)	—	—	1,286	355	28
Industry not elsewhere reported...........	800	305	38	—	—	—

* Data not available.
† 1940 figures include engineers and miscellaneous professionals.
‡ 1940 figures are for government instead of public administration.
Note: Because some industries are not included in this table, subgroups do not always add to total for major industrial division.
Source: *Census of Population, Industrial Characteristics,* 1940 (Vol. 3). 1950 (P-E No. 1D), 1960 (PC(2) 7F), 1970 (PC(2) 7C); (Bureau of the Census).

Shift work or other atypical hours of employment may be more attractive to women who have children.

The following sections discuss in greater detail the trends in women's employment by industry and occupation, and are based on, (a) establishment data from the monthly nationwide sample survey of nonagricultural payrolls; (b) the Current Population Survey (CPS), a monthly nationwide sample survey of households; and (c) the U.S. Decennial Census of Population. The establishment series provides a count of jobs; the CPS and Census provide a count of individuals. Despite these differences, data on the industrial employment of women from one series complements and confirms the trends indicated by the others.[1]

___

[1] *Establishment data* are based on payroll records compiled monthly from mail questionnaires by the Bureau of Labor Statistics in cooperation with state agencies. The payroll surveys provide detailed industry information on wage and salary employees in nonagricultural establishments. The *Current Population Survey* (CPS) is conducted each month for the Bureau of Labor Statistics by the Bureau of the Census. It is based on household interviews obtained from a sample of the population 16 years old and over.

The CPS definition of nonagricultural employment comprises persons in nonagricultural industries who were wage and salary workers (including domestics and other private household workers), self-employed, or unpaid and working 15 hours or more during the survey week in family-operated enterprises. The payroll survey

ESTABLISHMENT DATA

Payroll statistics from establishments in non-agricultural industries provide one of the most detailed, up-to-date appraisals of the employment of women in American industry. These data also permit more precise industry identification than that obtained through the household interviews of either the decennial censuses or the monthly Current Population Surveys. Payroll data were first collected in 1919, but until 1964 information on women was available on a regular basis for only a few selected industries. Today, detailed tables on the employment of women in more than 400 industrial categories are published quarterly by the Bureau of Labor Statistics.[2]

covers only wage and salary employees on the payrolls of nonagricultural establishments.

In the household approach, employed persons holding more than one job are counted only once and are classified according to the job at which they worked the greatest number of hours during the survey week. In the payroll series, persons who worked in more than one establishment during the reporting period are counted each time their names appear on payrolls. For example, workers may be counted more than once if they hold two jobs concurrently or leave one job for another during the same reference period and thus appear on the payrolls of both employers.

The household survey includes among the employed all persons who had jobs but were not at work during the survey week—that is, were not working but had jobs from which they were temporarily absent because of illness, bad weather, vacation, labor-management dispute, or because they were taking time off for various other reasons, even if they were not paid by their employers for the time off. In the payroll series, persons on leave paid for by the company are included, but not those on leave without pay for the entire payroll period.

For a detailed description of these series and differences between them, the following publications are available from the Bureau of Labor Statistics: *Concepts and Methods Used in Manpower Statistics from the Current Population Survey,* Report 313 (Bureau of Labor Statistics, 1967); *Handbook of Methods for Surveys and Studies,* Bulletin 1711 (Bureau of Labor Statistics, 1971), chap. 2; and Gloria P. Green, "Comparing Employment Estimates from Household and Payroll Surveys," *Monthly Labor Review,* December 1969, pp. 9–20, reprinted as BLS Reprint 2651.

The *Decennial Census of Population* is conducted by the Bureau of the Census to obtain a house-to-house enumeration of each person by questionnaire. For an employed person, 1970 census information pertains to one specific job held during the reference week. If employed at two jobs or more, the job at which the person worked the greatest number of hours during the reference week was to be represented. Census reports on specific subjects, such as occupation by industry, are frequently based on representative samples of the total population. The intercensal statistics provided by the *Current Population Survey* are generally designed to be comparable to decennial census statistics. For a detailed description of the 1970 decennial census and comparability with earlier censuses and other data, see *Census of Population: 1970, General, Social and Economic Characteristics, Final Report PC(1)–C1, U.S. Summary* (Bureau of the Census).

[2] Detailed establishment data on women employees were first published in the May 1963 *Employment and*

The following discussion uses establishment data to review recent changes for women in major industry divisions, with an eye on prospective trends, and describes changes in the occupational mix within industries.

From January 1964 to January 1973, the number of women on payrolls in nonagricultural industries expanded from 19.1 to 27.9 million. Married or formerly married women, many responsible for school-age or younger children, accounted for the largest share of the increase in payroll employment of women. Most of the 8.8 million labor force entrants or reentrants found jobs in the four major industry divisions that were the fastest growing:

	Millions of Workers
Services	2.5
Government	2.4
Wholesale and retail trade	1.9
Manufacturing	1.1

In the late 1960s, the *service industry* maintained its position as a principal employer of women, and by 1973 had more female workers (6.8 million) than any other industry. Of the several industries within the service sector that recorded a robust expansion, the most spectacular was health care services. The forces that contributed to this industry's growth—gains in the size of the population, a rising affluence that enabled more persons to afford health care and to demand improved services, and increases in the roles of special programs covering medical and health services, such as medicare and medicaid—are expected to continue and to bring similar rapid employment increases in the near future. It seems likely that this industry, in which eight out of ten employees are women, can continue to be a source of jobs for women.

In January 1973, the *trade industry* was the second largest employer of women (6.3 million), most of whom held jobs in retail stores. Women were only one-fourth (900,000) of the employees in wholesale trade, but nearly half (5.4 million) in retail trade. Within retail trade, women made

Earnings. Since 1967, the data have been published in *Employment and Earnings* once each quarter (February, May, August, and November) as Table B–3, "Women Employees on Nonagricultural Payrolls, by Industry." In addition, annual and monthly data appear in *Employment and Earnings, United States, 1909–72.* Bulletin 1312–9 (Bureau of Labor Statistics, 1973), and the *Handbook of Labor Statistics, 1973,* Bulletin 1790 (Bureau of Labor Statistics, 1974).

up two-thirds of the employees in department stores, clothing and accessory shops, and drugstores, and over half in restaurants and other eating and drinking establishments. New job openings in trade during the rest of the 1970–80 decade are expected to be little more than half what they were in the 1960s, because of the greater use of such laborsavers as computers, automated equipment, self-service stores, and vending machines.[3]

Manufacturing still employs the largest share of the male work force, but since the mid-1960s has dropped to fourth place for women. In part, this reflects the fact that in some nondurable goods industries employing relatively larger proportions of women—textile mill products, apparel and related items, and food and kindred items—increased automation and other improved plant processes have boosted output without any great increase in employment. During the 1970s, the need for additional workers in manufacturing is expected to be largest in such durable goods industries as machinery, rubber and plastic products, and instruments, all currently male-dominated.

In the same way that the phenomenal growth of the service industry in the private sector made jobs available for women, services provided by *government agencies* were responsible for the soaring employment of women on government payrolls, especially at the local and state levels. Nearly half (1.1 million) of the entire 1964–73 increase in women's jobs in government occurred at the local level in one industry—education. Two-thirds of all employees in schools and related educational activities supported by city, county, and other local tax jurisdictions were women. In January 1973, the local and state education industry accounted for nearly 60 percent of the 6.1 million women on government payrolls. Demand for workers in the education field is expected to taper off considerably as a result of the decline in birth rates that began in the late 1950s. In contrast, government health and welfare services, industries in which women are also prominent, are expected to increase at a rapid pace through the remainder of the 1970s.

The industry division encompassing *finance, insurance, and real estate* became predominantly female during the 1960s, and by January 1973 women were 52 percent of the employees (the 1940 and 1950 censuses reported much smaller proportions, 34 and 44 percent, respectively). The

1964–73 expansion in this industry's jobs for women occurred primarily in banking and insurance. These industries and credit agencies are expected to continue to expand through the remainder of this decade, providing new opportunities for women.

OCCUPATION BY INDUSTRY

Women, like men, find jobs in the fastest growing industries. However, no matter what industry women are in, they remain clustered in fewer occupation groups than men.

Service

As pointed out earlier, the service industry employs the largest number of working women and ranks third in the employment of men. In 1970 as in 1940, most women in this industry were employed in the same three occupation groups: professional-technical, services, and clerical-sales. Yet there was a striking redistribution which stemmed from the extraordinary demands for clerical support made by the education and health service industries.

In the 30-year span, the proportion of women in the service industry who perform service jobs increased from 20 to 28 percent. Examples of occupations still dominated by women are food services, practical nurses, and dental assistants.

In professional-technical occupations, 2 million women are teachers in elementary and high school. Women also predominate in registered nursing, social work, libraries, dietetics, physical therapy, and dental hygiene.

The 1940–70 redistribution shifted men into the more prestigious, better paying professional-technical group. In the education industry, about 70 percent of the teachers in colleges and universities are men; about 70 percent of the teachers in elementary and high schools are women. Doctors, lawyers, engineers, and many other professional-technical occupations have remained substantially male-intensive.

Trade

Since 1940, very little occupational change has taken place for women in trade. Nearly nine out of ten women in this industry were in retail trade, where sales, clerical, and service jobs predominated, in that order.

In general merchandising, women held the greatest proportion of sales jobs, as well as such clerical positions as bookkeepers, cashiers, office

---

[3] See *Occupational Outlook Handbook, 1972–73 Edition*, Bulletin 1700 (Bureau of Labor Statistics, 1973).

machine operators, secretaries, and typists. A few more were in managerial and administrative jobs as buyers and sales managers, and a relatively small number were in the operative group as dressmakers and seamstresses. Women working in eating and drinking establishments were mostly waitresses, cooks, and clerical workers.

A smaller proportion of men (seven out of ten) were in retail trade. Changes from 1940 to 1970 in their occupational pattern reflect mainly the relative increase in the need for managers and skilled craft workers (carpenters, electricians, mechanics, and repairers) and a decrease in the need for clerical and sales workers.

Manufacturing

In both 1940 and 1970, approximately nine out of ten women working in the manufacturing industry held semiskilled operative or white-collar clerical jobs. Nearly three-fifths were engaged in the production of nondurable goods. In this sector, most women work in the production end as operatives (for example, assemblers), as checkers, examiners, and inspectors, and as sewers and stitchers. About 11 percent of all professionals in nondurable goods were women.

Government

About 22 percent of women on nonfarm payrolls are government employees, mostly (86 percent) in state and local governments working as teachers, administrators, clerical workers, maintenance workers, librarians, nurses, and counselors.

According to a survey by the U.S. Civil Service Commission[4] of women employed by the federal government in 1970, most worked in nonprofessional administrative, clerical, and office service jobs. Roughly 77 out of 100 (compared with 44 of 100 men) were in grades GS–1 through GS–6 in 1970. Another 20 out of 100 women employees (compared with 32 of 100 men) were in grades GS–7 through GS–11, and only 3 out of 100 women (but 23 out of 100 men) were in the highest paying grades, GS–12 and above.

Women's share of full-time white-collar federal employment by individual grade reveals even more dramatically their concentration in the non-

[4] See *Study of Employment of Women in the Federal Government, 1970*, Pamphlet SM 62–06 (Washington, U.S. Civil Service Commission, Bureau of Manpower Information Systems, 1971), Table B.

professional grade series. Grades in which women predominated, GS–1 to GS–4, are entry-level clerical and support positions in the nonprofessional job series. GS–5 is the entry grade for professional employment. Positions in GS–5, GS–7, GS–9, and GS–11 are primarily professional, technical, or administrative jobs, requiring a baccalaureate or higher degree or equivalent professional, technical, or administrative experience.

Other Industries

Most of the occupations women hold in the finance, insurance, and real estate industry are clerical—about 80 percent. Approximately nine out of ten bank clerks and tellers are women, but very few bank officers are. In the transportation and public utilities industry, about 20 percent of the employees are women; over half of these women work in communications, where nine out of ten are telephone operators. Of women employed in the construction and mining industries, most are in clerical occupations.

OCCUPATIONAL SHIFTS

Overall, the 1940–70 changes in the occupational pattern of women, as well as of men, mirror the shift from the predominantly goods-producing economy prior to World War II to the service-producing economy of the 1970s. For women, the occupational pattern changed from half blue, half white collar to one that is decidedly white collar. Today, over 60 percent of women and 40 percent of men employed in nonagricultural industries are in white-collar work.

In 1940, women working in nonagricultural industries were concentrated in three broad occupational groups. Roughly half held service and blue-collar operative jobs (30 and 21 percent), and a third were in the white-collar clerical-sales group. For those in services, prominent occupations were waitress, hairdresser, cook, and practical nurse. Operatives were mostly engaged in the manufacture of clothing (sewing machine operators). The clerical-sales group were mainly stenographers, typists, secretaries, bookkeepers, cashiers, and retail saleswomen. Of the 14 percent in white-collar professional-technical jobs, two out of four were teachers and one out of four were nurses.

Thirty years later, working women were still highly concentrated in the same three broad occupational groups, but a much larger share were in the clerical-sales field, the professional-technical proportion had edged up, and the service and operative proportions had declined.

Do the changes represent an improvement in the lot of employed women? The shift out of service jobs as domestics and into white-collar jobs is a profound improvement, especially among Negro women. And women now are a larger share of employees in a few of the more prestigious, better paying occupations. In 1940 women were only 1 out of 20 physicians, compared with 1 of 8 today (1973 average). From 1940 to 1973, the proportion of real estate agents and brokers who were women grew from 9 to 36 percent.

In the area of job discrimination by sex, there are a few "breakthroughs" into typically masculine jobs. For example, today 30 percent of all bartenders are women, compared with 2.5 percent in 1940, and about 37 percent of the busdrivers are women, a rarity in 1940 when they were less than 1 percent. However, many of today's female busdrivers may operate school buses part time, part of the year, and for low pay. Thus, what appears to some persons to be an occupational improvement—the movement of women out of their homes with its unpaid housework and into the paid labor force—to others represents no gain.

SELF-EMPLOYED WOMEN

Women have made considerable inroads into the traditionally male-intensive province of self-employment, where their share rose from 17 percent in 1940 to 26 percent in 1973. A total of 1.4 million women were self-employed in nonagricultural industries in 1973, nearly 600,000 more than in 1940. Over this period, the number of self-employed men rose only slightly to 4 million —a minor increase, especially when compared with the doubled employment of men in nonfarm wage and salary work. The shift from small owner-operated businesses to corporate ownership contributed to the lack of increase for men. Increased demands in the more female-intensive service and trade industries drew more women into entrepreneurship

Nearly all of the self-employed women in nonagricultural industries in 1973 were in service and retail trade. In the service industry, over six out of ten were in personal services (operating beauty shops, laundries, dressmaking shops, and child care facilities) and three out of ten in professional services (medical enterprises, such as nursing homes and educational services).

The occupational distribution of self-employed women differs from that of women in wage and salary jobs. Proportionately more of the self-employed were managers or proprietors (24 versus 4 percent) and fewer were in clerical-sales (18 versus 43 percent), where self-employed women are found in such fields as court stenography or real estate sales. Self-employed women are generally older than wage and salary women, in part a reflection of the greater experience and maturity necessary to run their own businesses or careers. Median ages in 1973 were about 46 and 36 years.

EARNINGS

Further evidence that women have not yet penetrated the high-skill, high-paying jobs is found in the payroll data on weekly and hourly earnings in nonagricultural industries. In January 1973, most industries paying average weekly earnings of less than $100 were female-intensive. Several were paying under $90 a week, while the weekly paycheck for all industries average $138.[5] Figures on hourly earnings, which exclude the effect of part-time and overtime work, support conclusions based on weekly earnings.

In 1972, women were 28 percent (or 5.5 million) of the total workers in the manufacturing industry, yet most of these women were concentrated in the lower paid and less-skilled jobs. The average salary for all manufacturing workers was $159 a week in January 1973. For those in manufacturing industries that were female-intensive, the average was much lower—for example, the apparel industry, in which 81 percent of employees were women, paid average weekly salaries of only $93.

The service industry—the most female-intensive of the major industry groups, with 55 percent of its workers women—employed 6.8 million women in January 1973; earnings averaged $111 a week. About 1.6 million women worked in hospitals, where weekly earnings averaged $108. Another 600,000 women worked in hotels and laundries-drycleaners, where average weekly wages were $76 and $87, respectively.

Another low-paying female-intensive industry is retail general merchandise, with an average weekly wage of $82. Although part-time work undoubtedly accounts for some of the low earnings, most jobs in department stores and restaurants are known to be low paying.

---

[5] See *Employment and Earnings*, May 1973, Table B–3, "Women Employees on Nonagricultural Payrolls, by Industry," and *Employment and Earnings*, April 1973, Table C–2, "Gross Hours and Earnings of Production or Nonsupervisory Workers on Private Nonagricultural Payrolls, by Industry."

Male-intensive industries are on the higher rungs of the wage ladder: *Construction*—6 percent female, paying $223 average a week; *transportation and public utilities*—21 percent female, paying an average of $196 a week (switchboard operators averaged $126, line construction employees $228); *manufacturing*—here the list is extremely long. In transportation equipment, 10 percent female, average earnings were $210 a week; in food products, the malt liquor industry employed 7 percent women and the average worker earned $229 a week. Among retail trade industries, the most female intensive were the lowest paying. Yet employees on the payrolls of motor vehicle dealers, only 11 percent of whom were women, were among the highest paid workers in retail trade—$152 a week.

Male-female earnings differentials have always existed, but in recent years with the increase in women's labor force activity these differentials have become the focus of great concern. One form of discrimination was the barring of women from the type of jobs men held, such as skilled workers and executives. A typical example was cited in a standard college-level economics text

. . . in a large electrical-goods plant, job evaluation experts divide all factory work into two parts: women's jobs and men's jobs. The lowest pay of the men begins about where the women's highest pay leaves off; yet both management and the union will admit, off the record, that in many borderline jobs the productivity of the women is greater than that of the men.[6]

Many researchers believe the earnings differential results partially from the role that society has traditionally arrogated to women. In a study on wage differentials by sex, using 1959 and 1960 Census of Population and Housing data, Victor Fuchs suggested that the percentage point difference in male-female wages "can be explained by the different roles assigned to men and women. Role differentiation, which begins in the cradle, affects the choice of occupation, labor force attachment, location of work, postschool investment, hours of work, and other variables that influence earnings."[7] He believes a reduction in this role discrimination would eventually result in a narrowing of the male-female differential in earnings. Professor Fuchs also stated that consumer discrimination (such as the preference of customers in expensive restaurants for waiters rather than waitresses) may be more significant than employer discrimination.

Area wage surveys covering six industry divisions recently published by the Bureau of Labor Statistics indicate that on a nationwide basis, pay levels were consistently higher for men than for women working in the same occupation.[8] In a study of pay differences between men and women in the same job, John Buckley—while neither denying nor confirming that wage discrimination by sex existed—acknowledged that "experience in implementing the Equal Pay Act indicates that some discriminatory practices do exist."[9]

Differences in female-male earnings in the federal government occur in part because women remain clustered in the lowest paid grades.

It is not within the scope of this article to explore in depth the various reasons for male-female differentials in pay, but research has continued in this area.[10] Data presented here takes the differential into account as an important factor in women's industrial characteristics.

EDUCATION

For today's working woman to achieve professional status in the higher paying, traditionally male-intensive occupations in many industries, she must acquire more years of formal higher education. To illustrate, doctors, dentists, airline pilots, metallurgists, architects, and certified public accountants must have more years of schooling than are needed for most occupations. For men, the returns on the investment in education are usually high in terms of money and prestige. Women, even with the required years of schooling, often do not obtain returns equal to men's.

The 1972 amendments to the Equal Pay Act and the Civil Rights Act have outlawed many barriers to employment, among them job quotas by sex and unequal male-female wage scales for the same job. While educational attainment alone is not a cure-all for working women (legislation helps), the statistics on women's education and labor force participation indicate that more years of formal schooling would assist in equalizing women's position with that of men.

[6] Paul R. Samuelson, *Economics* (New York: McGraw-Hill Book Co., 1967), p. 120.

[7] Victor R. Fuchs, "Difference in Hourly Earnings between Men and Women," *Monthly Labor Review,* May 1971, pp. 9–15.

[8] *Area Wage Surveys: Metropolitan Areas, United States and Regional Summaries, 1969–70,* Bulletin 1660–92 (Bureau of Labor Statistics, 1971).

[9] John E. Buckley, "Pay Differences between Men and Women in the Same Job," *Monthly Labor Review,* November 1971, pp. 36–39.

[10] See, for example, Paul O. Flaim and Nicholas I. Peters, "Usual Weekly Earnings of American Workers," *Monthly Labor Review,* March 1972, pp. 28–38. Reprinted as Special Labor Force Report 143.

Annual surveys on educational attainment show that, for both men and women, participation in the labor force is lowest and unemployment rates highest for those who complete the fewest years of school. The March 1973 survey shows:

Years of School Completed	Labor Force Rate	Unemployment Rate
11 years or less.....................	32	8.6
12 years...........................	51	5.3
4 years of college or more..........	61	2.7

Women who have graduated from college earn over twice as much annually as women at the lowest end of the education scale. For women employed year round in full-time jobs, median earnings in 1972 were $8,925 for the college graduates, $5,770 for high school graduates, and $4,305 for those who did not complete elementary school. A similar education-earnings relationship was evident for employed men, but their year-round, full-time earnings were substantially above women's—$14,660, $10,075, and $7,575, respectively, for the corresponding groups.

Earnings in the different educational categories are also a reflection of the differences in the industrial distributions of employment. Of the women in nonagricultural jobs who were college graduates, eight out of ten were in service industries, mostly professional services, in March 1973.[11] Women who were high school graduates, but had no college education, were more widely distributed: (1) one-third in the service industry, largely professional services; (2) one-fourth in trade, largely retail stores; and (3) one-fifth in manufacturing. Among working women at the bottom of the educational scale, mostly older women who had either not completed or never attended elementary school, two-fifths were in manufacturing, largely semiskilled employees.

TOWARD TOMORROW

Today's working women are in the throes of obtaining equal consideration with men in the job market through the legislation that prohibits discrimination in employment. Tomorrow's working women will be affected not only by the measure of success achieved today, but also by economic conditions, changes in lifestyle (for example, smaller families), the mode of enforcement of legislation prohibiting discrimination, provision of child care services for mothers on industry payrolls, and the extent of formal education or technical training of women for traditionally male occupations.

---

[11] See William V. Deutermann, "Educational Attainment of Workers, March 1973," *Monthly Labor Review,* January 1974, pp. 58–62. Reprinted as Special Labor Force Report 161.

part two

Some Aspects of the History of the American Labor Movement

A. Explanations of the Labor Movement

During the past century, serious students of the American labor movement have attempted to explain the "how" and "why" of the development of labor organizations. The classical studies made by the Webbs, Hoxie, Commons, Marx, and others have contributed a great deal toward an explanation of the labor movement. These studies, however, have not been completely satisfactory. John T. Dunlop, in the first article, presents a brief summary of the leading explanations of the labor movement and attempts to test them against some important questions which he poses: How is one to account for the origin or emergence of labor organizations? What explains the pattern of growth and development of labor organizations? What are the ultimate goals of the labor movement? Why do individual workers join labor organizations? Subsequent to his investigation, Dunlop finds that no one of the theories of the labor movement answers all of the questions; indeed, the questions themselves are nowhere explicitly stated. He suggests that the labor movement may be more rewardingly studied by examining four interrelated factors:

(1) technology, (2) market structures and character of competition, (3) wider community institutions, and (4) ideas and beliefs. This method would not constitute a theory but it would greatly implement the development of a theoretical system.

In the second article, Walter Galenson deals with a question which confronts many beginning students in the labor field: Are trade unions in the United States socialist oriented? He explains how the American labor movement has developed as a conservative, capitalist institution with limited objectives—limited to an improvement of wages, hours, and working conditions. American unions have practiced "business unionism" directed toward "bread and butter" issues since the days of Samuel Gompers who, when asked by the socialists about labor's objectives, simply replied that the unions want only better conditions, or "more and more." In the realm of politics the labor movement has usually adhered to the principle of rewarding one's friends and punishing one's enemies, regardless of party lines.

8. The Development of Labor Organization: A Theoretical Framework*

John T. Dunlop†

"The facts do not tell their own story; they must be cross-examined. They must be carefully analyzed, systematized, compared, and interpreted."[1] This conclusion is an indictment of the all too frequent approach to the development of the labor movement,[2] in which "history" and "theory" are separate and non-permeable compartments.

Under the caption of "history of labor" are chronicled what purport to be collections of fact and sequences of fact. Under the heading of "theory of labor organization" are found "explanations" conjured out of inner consciousness with only occasional and convenient reference to the past. The "history" and "theory" of the labor movement can have little meaning in isolation.[3] But it is particularly the failure of theoretical apparatus that accounts for the lack of greater understanding of the development of the labor movement and the paucity of significant research. Indeed, despite all the epoch-making developments in the field of labor organization in the past 15 years, there has been virtually no contribution to the "theory" and

scarcely a reputable narrative of this period exists.[4]

This essay constitutes a reexamination of fashions of thinking in theories of the labor movement. It proceeds from the initial conviction that any theory of the labor movement must first establish its criteria. Just what questions is a theory of labor organization supposed to answer? Only after this task has been explicitly recognized can there be critical discussion of the development of the labor movement.

The body of economic theory attempts to explain the allocation of resources.[5] Business cycle theories present systems of propositions to make intelligible the fluctuations of the economic system. In similar terms, what is the pièce de résistance of a theory of the labor movement? By what standards or tests is it possible to prefer one theory to another? What behavior must such a theory explain to be judged a "closer fit" than another model?

EXPLANATIONS OF THE LABOR MOVEMENT

The literature on theories of the labor movement, carefully analyzed, reveals at least four questions which have been the concern of investigators. As far as can be determined, how-

---

* Reprinted with permission of the publisher from R. A. Lester and J. Shister (eds.), *Insights into Labor Issues,* pp. 163–93. Copyright 1948 by the Macmillan Company.

† Professor of Economics, Harvard University. This essay has benefited from helpful comments by J. A. Schumpeter, A. P. Usher, and Selig Perlman.

[1] Talcott Parsons, *The Structure of Social Action* (New York: McGraw-Hill Book Co., 1937), p. 698.

[2] See E. Wight Bakke, *Mutual Survival, The Goal of Unions and Management* (New Haven: Labor and Management Center, Yale University, 1946), p. 12, for a contrast between a "movement" and a "business."

[3] J. B. Bury, *The Ideas of Progress* (New York: Macmillan Co., 1932). See the Introduction by Charles A. Beard, pp. ix–xl.

[4] Selig Perlman's *Theory of the Labor Movement* (New York: Macmillan Co.) was published in 1928. See Horace B. Davis, "The Theory of Union Growth," *Quarterly Journal of Economics,* Vol. 55 (August 1941), pp. 611–37, and Russel Bauder, "Three Interpretations of the American Labor Movement," *Social Forces,* Vol. 22 (December 1943), pp. 215–24.

[5] Frank H. Knight, *Risk, Uncertainty, and Profit* (London: London School of Economics and Political Science, 1933), Preface to reissue.

ever, nowhere are these questions posed explicitly.

1. How is one to account for the origin or emergence of labor organizations? What conditions are necessary and what circumstances stimulate the precipitation of labor organization? Why have some workers organized and others not?

2. What explains the pattern of growth and development of labor organizations? What factors are responsible for the sequence and form in which organizations have emerged in various countries, industries, crafts, and companies? Since there is great diversity in the patterns of development, any theory of the labor movement must account for these differences.

3. What are the ultimate goals of the labor movement? What is its relationship to the future of capitalism? What is its role in the socialist or communist state?

4. Why do individual workers join labor organizations? What system of social psychology accounts for this behavior of the employee?

Most writings on theories of the labor movement have in effect been concerned with one or several of these questions. They show a tendency to seek a single and usually oversimplified statement of the development of labor organization. But the labor movement is highly complex and many-sided. The "history" does not readily lend itself to any single formula.

The pages immediately following constitute a brief summary of the principal contributions to theories of the labor movement. No attempt will be made to present a detailed appraisal of these views; the summary cannot be an exegesis. The discussion is necessarily sketchy. It may be helpful, however, to have in brief compass a summary of views since none exists. Brevity at times has the virtue of concentrating on and compelling attention to essentials.

1. Frank Tannenbaum[6]

To Tannenbaum "the labor movement is the result and the machine is the major cause."[7] The machine threatens the security of the in-dividual worker and the wage earner reacts in self-defense through a union to attempt to control the machine. The individual worker seeks to harness the machine and to stem the tide of insecurity by which his life is menaced.

He intends little more than this security when joining a union, but ". . . in the process of carrying out the implications of defense against the competitive character of the capitalist system he contributes to the well-being of present-day society—a contribution which represents a by-product of the more immediate and conscious attempt to find security in an insecure world."[8] Tannenbaum sees the labor movement ultimately displacing the capitalistic system by "industrial democracy," "an achievement which is implicit in the growth and development of the organized labor movement."[9]

Tannenbaum provides an answer of sorts to at least three of the four questions posed above; he does not examine the pattern of growth of the labor movement. While not concerned with historical detail, Tannenbaum finds the origin of labor organizations in a reaction to the machine (Question 1). The labor movement creates a new society (Question 3). The individual worker joins the union in self-defense in quest of security (Question 4).

2. Sidney and Beatrice Webb[10]

A trade union is a "continuous association of wage-earners for the purpose of maintaining or improving the conditions of their working lives."[11] Its fundamental objective, according to the Webbs, is "the deliberate regulation of the conditions of employment in such a way as to ward off from the manual-working producers the evil effects of industrial competition."[12] The labor organization utilizes, in the well-known schema of the Webbs, the "methods" of mutual insurance, collective bargaining, and the legal enactment. The labor organization chooses among these "methods" depending on the stage of development of the society. An era of the master system requires the enforcement of common rules against "industrial parasitism"; the existence of trusts

[6] Frank Tannenbaum, *The Labor Movement, Its Conservative Functions and Social Consequences* (New York: G. P. Putnam's Sons, 1921).

[7] Ibid., p. 29. As a statement of the origin of labor organizations, this view is to be contrasted with that of John R. Commons, "Whatever may have been its origin in other countries, the labor movement in America did not spring from factory conditions. It arose as a protest against the merchant-capitalist system." (*A Documentary History of American Industrial Society* [Glendale, Calif.: Arthur H. Clark Co., 1910], Vol. 5, p. 23 [with Helen L. Sumner].)

[8] Ibid., p. 32. These lines are in italics in the original.

[9] Ibid., p. 44.

[10] Sidney and Beatrice Webb, *Industrial Democracy* (New York: Longmans, Green & Co., 1897); and *History of Trade Unionism* (New York: Longmans, Green & Co., 1894). Also see Margaret Cole, *Beatrice Webb* (New York: Harcourt, Brace & Co., 1946), pp. 73–83.

[11] Webb, *History of Trade Unionism* (1920 ed.), p. 1.

[12] *Industrial Democracy* (1914 printing), p. 807.

makes legal enactment the only effective method in many cases. The assumption by government of the responsibility for social risks, such as old age and unemployment, greatly curtails the use of the method of mutual insurance on the part of labor organizations.

In the view of the Webbs, trade unionism is ". . . not merely an incident of the present phase of capitalist industry but has a permanent function to fulfill in the democratic state."[13] The special function of the trade union is in the democratic administration of industry. While consumers acting through cooperatives or entrepreneurs may determine *what* is produced, the democratic society requires a labor organization to provide for the participation of workers in the conditions of sale of their services. In the type of democratic society the Webbs eventually expected (the little profit-taker and the trust superseded by the salaried officer of the cooperative and by government agencies), the unions would more and more assume the character of professional associations.

The Webbs used the term "theory of trade unionism"[14] not to refer to answers to any of the four questions posed in the preceding section but as a statement of the economic consequences of a labor organization, virtually a theory of wages or collective bargaining. The trade union is pictured as having only two "expedients" for the improvement of conditions of employment:[15] the restriction of numbers in the trade and the establishment of uniform minimum standards required of each firm. The Webbs condemned the former monopolist policy. They endorsed the latter application of the Common Rule, for it transfers competition from wages to quality. The device of the Common Rule envisages the gradual improvement in these minimum standards of wages and conditions. It is the duty of the labor organization to strive perpetually to raise the level of its common rules. This process may be carried on by collective bargaining or by the use of legislation.[16] Such is the Webbs' "theory of trade unionism," an economic rationalization for the establishment of minimum standards.

What the Webbs called their "theory of trade unionism" would not ordinarily be called a theory of the development of the labor movement. While the Webbs made fundamental and pioneer contributions to the study of trade union government and the narrative of labor organization history, they formulated no systematic, conceptual answers to the first two questions posed in the previous section (the emergence of labor organization and the patterns of development). As for ultimate goals (Question 3), the Webbs see the labor union as an instrument of the democratization of both the work community and the wider society as a whole.

3. Robert F. Hoxie[17]

Hoxie starts from the proposition that wage earners in similar social and economic environments tend to develop a "common interpretation of the social situation."[18] The union emerges when group sentiments have been crystallized. It appears as a "group interpretation of the social situation in which the workers find themselves, and a remedial program in the form of aims, policies, and methods. . . ."[19] To Hoxie, the union constitutes a common interpretation and set of beliefs concerned with the problems confronting the worker and a generalized program of amelioration. Such a persistent group "viewpoint or interpretation"[20] Hoxie calls a *functional* type of unionism. His name has come to be associated almost exclusively with classification of the functional types he suggests (business unionism, uplift unionism, revolutionary unionism, predatory unionism, and dependent unionism) to the detraction of an understanding of his significant contribution.

The account of the origin of labor organizations which Hoxie gives—a crystallization of group viewpoint and programme of action—leads him to question whether the labor movement has any unity: "Seen from the standpoint of aims, ideals, methods, and theories, there is no normal type to which all union variants approximate, no single labor movement which has progressively adapted itself to progressive change of circumstances, no one set of postulates which can be spoken of as *the* philosophy of unionism. Rather

---

[13] Ibid., p. 823.

[14] Ibid., pp. viii and 795. See note 16.

[15] Ibid., p. 560.

[16] ". . . the whole community of wage-earners . . . may by a persistent and systematic use of the Device of the Common Rule secure an indefinite, though of course not an unlimited, rise in its Standard of Life. And in this universal and elaborate application of the Common Rule, the economist finds a *sound and consistent theory of Trade Unionism,* adapted to the conditions of modern industry. . . ." Ibid., p. 795. (Italics added.)

---

[17] Robert F. Hoxie, *Trade Unionism in the United States* (New York: D. Appleton & Co., 1921). See the introduction by E. H. Downey.

[18] Ibid., p. 58.

[19] Ibid., p. 60.

[20] Ibid., p. 69.

there are competing, relatively stable union types. . . ."[21]

Since the labor movement is nonunitary, Hoxie rejects interpretations that look upon trade unionism as fundamentally an economic manifestation of changing methods of production or market developments.[22] The fact of different functional types compels Hoxie to renounce any explanation in environmental terms alone. The subjective factor emphasized in the concept of functional types is equally important.

Hoxie provides an answer to the problem of the emergence of labor organization (Question 1) in terms of "group psychology." He accounts for the divergent forms of unionism but is comparatively unconcerned with an explanation of historical development. One of the factors affecting the classification of functional types is the program for social action developed by the group. In this sense, Hoxie indicates the different answers that have been posed to the problem of the relation of the labor movement to the future of capitalism (Question 3). But there is no sense of historical development here again, for Hoxie is reticent to generalize to a "labor movement as a whole" from his functional types."[23]

4. Selig Perlman[24]

Perlman finds that in any "modern labor situation" there may be said to be three factors operative: "First, the resistance of capitalism, determined by its own historical development; second, the degree of dominance over the labor movement by the intellectual's 'mentality,' which regularly underestimates capitalism's resistance power and overestimates labor's will to radical change; and third, the degree of maturity of a trade union 'mentality.' "[25] By this last factor Perlman means the extent to which the trade union is conscious of job scarcity. "It is the author's contention that manual groups . . . have had their economic attitudes basically determined by a consciousness of scarcity of opportunity. . . . Starting with this consciousness of scarcity, the 'manualist' groups have been led to practicing solidarity, to an insistence upon an 'ownership' by the group as a whole of the totality of economic opportunity extant, to a 'rationing' by the group of such opportunity among the individuals constituting it, to a control by the group over its members in relation to the conditions which they as individuals are permitted to occupy a portion of that opportunity. . . ."[26]

Perlman suggests that there are three basic economic philosophies, those of the manual laborer just indicated, the businessman, and the intellectual. In the United States a "stabilized" unionism was delayed until the labor movement developed job consciousness, until it came to assert a "collective mastery over job opportunities and employment bargains," until wage earners dissociated themselves from "producers" generally who were imbued with the doctrine of abundance and who organized under the slogan of anti-monopoly. The American Federation of Labor constitutes a shift in the psychology of the labor movement, a recognition of the scarcity of opportunity.[27]

Perlman apparently gives a certain primacy to the role of job consciousness in the labor movement. In fact a labor organization can be regarded as fundamentally a manifestation of "economic attitudes" (see quotation cited below in note 26). Nonetheless, labor history cannot deny a "truly pivotal part" to the intellectual. The character of the labor movement in any particular country must depend on the particular combination of the role of the intellectual, the resistance of capitalism, and the development of job consciousness.

Perlman is seen to treat one way or another all four criteria posed in the previous section. Labor organizations develop from a concern with the scarcity of job opportunities (questions 1 and 4). The pattern of development of organization in a particular country depends upon the particular combination of the three factors operative in any "modern labor situation" (Question 2). The relation of the labor movement to the future of capitalism is peculiarly influenced by the role of the intellectual (Question 3).

---

[21] E. H. Downey, Introduction to *Trade Unionism in the United States*, pp. xxiii–xxiv.

[22] See the discussion under the heading of John R. Commons which follows in the text.

[23] See, however, Hoxie, *Trade Unionism*, note 3, p. 59.

[24] Perlman, *Labor Movement*.

[25] Ibid., p. x.

[26] Ibid., p. 4; also see pp. 237–53. The importance attached to job consciousness is the outcome of one of the few explicit statements on the requirements of a theory of the labor movement. "A theory of the labor movement should include a theory of the psychology of the laboring man" (p. 237).

[27] Perlman disagrees with the Webbs' view that there is a tendency for unionism to give up the principle of restriction of numbers in favor of the device of the Common Rule, Ibid., pp. 295–98. Also see *Labor in the New Deal Decade*, Three Lectures by Selig Perlman . . . at the ILGWU Officers Institute, New York City, 1943–45 (Educational Department, International Ladies' Garment Workers' Union, 1945).

5. John R. Commons[28]

Commons believed that labor history should be understood in terms of the interaction of "economic, industrial, and political conditions with many varieties of individualistic, socialistic, and protectionist philosophies."[29] He treats labor history as a part of its industrial and political history.

Commons' thinking on the origin and emergence of labor organization involved an appraisal of the writings of Marx, Schmoller, and Bucher. He posed the problem of explaining the emergence of the labor movement in terms of the growth of new bargaining classes—the wage earner and the employer. He traced the gradual evolution of the employee-employer relationship from the merchant-capitalist dealings with a journeyman. The growth of the market separates from the merchant-capitalist the functions of the custom merchant, the retail merchant, and the wholesale merchant. The employer remains.[30]

While Commons recognized that the changing modes of production influenced to some extent the emergence of labor organization, he attached primary importance to the market expansion. "The extension of the market took precedence over the mode of production as an explanation of the origin of new class alignments."[31]

The pattern of uneven growth in the American labor movement Commons attributed to the fluctuations in economic conditions. Periods of prosperity produced organization while depressions saw the labor movement subside or change its form to political or social agitation.[32]

The theoretical system of Commons seems to have been concerned only with the emergence and the pattern of development of the labor movement (questions 1 and 2 above).

6. The Marxist View

To Karl Marx, the trade union was first and foremost an "organizing center."[33] It provided the locus for collecting the forces of the working class. Without organization, workers competed with each other for available employment. "The trade union developed originally out of the spontaneous attempts of the workers to do away with this competition, or at least to restrict it for the purpose of obtaining at least such contractual conditions as would raise them above the status of bare slaves."[34]

The labor organization provided for Marx the focal point for the functional organization of the working class toward a change in the structure of society. Just as the medieval municipalities and communities were the center of organization of the bourgeoisie, so the trade union for the proletariat. Thus, in addition to its original tasks, the trade union was to learn to take on additional duties, to become the center for organizing the working class for its political emancipation.[35]

It is imperative to distinguish the role of the trade union under capitalism from that after the successful revolution of the proletariat. Left to themselves, labor organizations would remain within the capitalistic framework. Lenin has put this point succinctly. "The spontaneous labour movement, able by itself to create (and inevitably will create) only trade unionism, and working-class trade-union politics are precisely working-class bourgeois politics."[36]

In terms of the fundamental questions posed above, it is apparent that Marx and Lenin, insofar as they formulated a theory of the labor movement, were concerned with the origin or emergence of labor organizations (Question 1) and their ultimate relationship to capitalistic society (Question 3).

A critical comparison of these views is beyond the scope of this essay. There are important similarities of analysis and emphasis that appear at once and more that would be evident save for differences in language. A rather sharp cleavage emerges, however, between writers such as the Webbs and Commons, who look upon the labor movement primarily as the manifestation of economic developments, and those, such as Perlman and Hoxie, who choose to emphasize the habits of mind of wage earners. Compare the *key concepts* of "common rule" (Webbs) and "expansion of the market" (Commons) on the one

[28] John R. Commons, ed., *A Documentary History of American Industrial Society*, 11 vols. (Glendale, Calif.: Arthur H. Clark Co., 1910–11). In particular see the Introduction, Vol. 5, pp. 19–37, written with Helen L. Sumner. Also John R. Commons and Associates, *History of Labor in the United States*, 2 vols. (New York: Macmillan Co., 1918), in particular Vol. 1, pp. 3–21.

[29] Commons and associates, *History of Labor*, Vol. 1, Introduction, p. 3.

[30] Ibid., p. 106.

[31] Ibid., p. 28.

[32] Commons, ed., *Documentary History*, Vol. 5, p. 19.

[33] A. Lozovsky, *Marx and the Trade Unions* (New York: International Publishers Co., 1935), p. 15.

[34] Ibid., p. 16. (Italics deleted.)

[35] Paul M. Sweezy, *The Theory of Capitalist Development* (New York: Oxford University Press, 1942), pp. 312–13.

[36] V. L. Lenin, *What Is To Be Done?* Reprinted from *The Iskra Period* (New York: International Publishers, 1929), p. 90.

hand with "job consciousness" (Perlman) and "functional type" (Hoxie, a persistent exponent of the group viewpoint or interpretation). The Webbs and Commons built their models of the trade union out of changes in observable economic institutions. Hoxie and Perlman were imbued with the necessity of a "psychology" of the labor movement and hold the notion that the outlook of the worker upon his world and his destiny is the cornerstone of a model of trade union development.

This cleavage represents a fundamental failure in the formulation of "theories of the labor movement." For certainly there are significant interrelations between the outlook of members of a community and the economic institutions. Consider, for instance, the shedding of the "producer class" complex of the American labor movement. Commons explains the development in terms of the final development of the national market while Perlman emphasizes that job consciousness and the belief in scarcity of work opportunities had asserted itself. These developments are clearly not independent.

The sections which follow are intended to present a more generalized and more integrated understanding of the development of the labor movement. The next section provides a scaffolding or generalized theoretical framework for an approach to the labor movement.

THE DETERMINANTS OF LABOR ORGANIZATION

The labor movement, or any similarly complex social organization, may be fruitfully explored by an examination of four interrelated factors: technology; market structures and the character of competition; community institutions of control; and ideas and beliefs.

1. Technology. This term includes not only changes in machinery and in methods of production but concomitant developments in the size and organization of production and distribution units.

2. Market Structures and Character of Competition. The term comprehends the growth of markets, the changes in the focus of financial control as distinguished from the size of production units, the development of buying and selling institutions in both product and factor markets, and the emergence of specialized functions and personnel within these organizations.

3. Wider Community Institutions. This phrase is intended to include among others the role of the press, radio, and other means of communication in the society; the formal educational system for both general and vocational training; the courts, governmental administrative agencies; and political parties and organizations.

4. Ideas and Beliefs. This caption is a short cut for the value judgments and mores that permeate and identify a social system.

Such a comprehensive scaffolding or method of approach does not in itself constitute a theory of the labor movement. It claims only to facilitate the development of such a theoretical system. It compels reflection on the range of mutual influences operative in any society. Such a comprehensive framework of reference assists in asking significant questions; the complex interrelations between the labor movement and any society are sharpened. The labor movement is seen in the context of its "total" environment. The fourfold scheme is a set of preliminary tools through which the labor movement may be reconnoitered and analyzed. The facts of labor history may more readily be cross-examined.

It must be emphasized that these four factors are intended not merely to facilitate the cross-sectional study of the labor movement at any one given time but even more to assist in the analysis of the growth and change of the labor movement over time. The interaction among technological and market factors, community institutions, and ideas and beliefs must be used to account for the development of the labor movement.

Social systems or institutions go through periods of relative stability and through other periods of spectacular and tortuous change. Periods of stability may be regarded as involving a certain equilibrium among these four factors. That is, a given system of technology and markets requires or is compatible with only a limited number of community institutions and value judgments and ideas. The converse is equally true; a given system of ideas and community organization is compatible only with particular types of market and technological arrangements. In these terms, equilibrium in the social system may be said to exist when these four groups of factors are compatible one with another. Equilibrium may involve an unchanging condition or rates of change among the factors which are congruous. Change the technology of a system and there are required alterations in the other three factors, or change the value judgments and ideas of a community and there must be changes in market systems and technology.

The actual course of history does not disclose the isolated reaction to the change in a single factor any more than a series of prices reveals directly the unique effects of shifts in demand or movements along demand schedules. A comprehensive theory of a society should indicate the result of varying one of these factors—the others unchanged—when the system as a whole is in initial equilibrium. The actual course of events consists in continuous and inseparable interaction between the secondary effects of the initial change and new impacts on the social system.

The procedure suggested in this section would analyze the labor movement by indicating the change in each of these four factors over the past and the consequent impact on the emergence and the manner of growth of the labor movement. The labor movement is seen as the product of its total environment. As labor organizations grow they become an independent factor affecting the course of their own destiny.

LONG-RUN TRENDS IN UNION GROWTH

In thinking of the development of the labor movement, it will be helpful to distinguish between long-term trends and variations around these tendencies. The evolution of social institutions does not take place at uniform rates. The process is more like waves eating away at the base of a cliff, which eventually crashes into the sea.[37] The present section will be concerned with the trend aspects of the development of the labor movement, while that which follows will adapt this analysis to the pulsation of growth of labor organization.

No working community is ever completely unorganized. Any group of human beings associated together for any length of time develops a community in which there are recognized standards of conduct and admitted leaders. ". . . in industry and in other human situations the administrator is dealing with well-knit human groups and not with a horde of individuals."[38] A group of workers which continues together will establish standards of a "fair" day's work and acceptable norms of behavior in the views of the working group as a whole. Not everyone, of course, will conform to these standards, but there will be recognized norms. In the same way one worker will soon be recognized as a person whose judgment is sought on personal problems; another will be regarded as having superior skill, whose advice on the technical aspects of the job is highly regarded; still another will be accepted as spokesman in expressing the feelings of the group to the management. At times these functions may be combined in the same person. Whenever human beings live or work together the informal group develops. This fact is true today; it no doubt preceded the first formal labor organization.

Formal trade union organization has on many occasions been precipitated out of this type of informal organization. Some danger to the stability and security of the informal group frequently serves as the immediate occasion for formalizing an organization. The threat may come from the management in the form of a wage reduction or a substitution of women on men's jobs, or the arbitrary discipline of a member of the work community. The threat may have its origin outside the firm, as in the introduction of machinery made necessary by competitive conditions. Very frequently the formal organization may last for a short time, only during the period of greatest immediacy of the danger.

The formal group may be assisted and encouraged by outside organizers. The initiative may be taken by the professional organizer, or he may be called in after an initial step. The congealing of these informal organizations into formal structures follows no uniform pattern. The "intellectual" does not here receive the prominence in the development of the labor movement subscribed to by some writers. There can be little doubt that, in any going institution, "rationalizations" are developed—a task necessarily intellectual in content. Such formal statements often help in extending organization. The processes of rationalization are here treated as an essential step in the growth of the union movement, but the "intellectual" does not have a dominant role.

Wage earners join unions for a great many different reasons. They generally involve various aspects of the relation of the individual workman to his immediate work community and, at times, his relation to the larger locality and national life.[39] The fundamental point, however, is that any analysis of the development of labor organizations must proceed from the recognition that work communities, prior to formal organization,

---

[37] For a discussion of historical change refer to Melvin M. Knight, Introduction to Henri Sée, *The Economic Interpretation of History* (New York: Adelphi Co., 1929), pp. 9–37.

[38] Elton Mayo, *The Social Problems of an Industrial Civilization* (Cambridge: Harvard University Press, 1945), p. 111. Also see F. J. Roethlisberger and William J. Dickson, *Management and the Worker* (Cambridge: Harvard University Press, 1940); F. J. Roethlisberger, *Management and Morale* (Cambridge: Harvard University Press, 1942).

[39] E. Wight Bakke, "Why Workers Join Unions," *Personnel*, Vol. 22, No. 1 (1945).

are not simply random aggregates of individual workmen. Typically, informal coagulations exist. While every labor organization probably has not grown out of nor adopted the leadership of the informal group, it is difficult to conceive of a labor organization which has not been substantially influenced by these basic facts of any work community.

There have been, no doubt, many cases in which the informal organization has been precipitated into dramatic formal action only to lapse quickly and pass away. There have been many such outbursts against arbitrary behavior and substantial grievances. But in some circumstances continuing organization has developed and in others it has lapsed. The discussion which follows suggests, with reference to the American scene, two factors that were necessary to the emergence of organization historically and two that have been decisive in determining the trend of development.

1. How is the student of labor organization to account for the location in the productive process of the emergence of continuing unions? Successful organization has required that workmen occupy a *strategic* position in the technological or market structures. In any *technological* process for producing and distributing goods and services, there are some workers who have greater strategic position than others; that is, these workers are able to shut down, to interrupt, or to divert operations more easily than others. They furnish labor services at decisive points in the productive stream where the withdrawal of services quickly breaks the whole stream. The productive process has its bottlenecks. Frequently these workers are skilled. The term strategic, however, is not identical with skill. It means sheer bargaining power by virtue of location and position in the productive process. Locomotive engineers, loom fixers in the textile industry, molders in the casting industry, and cutters in the garment industry well illustrate the concept. The withdrawal of the services of these relatively few almost immediately compels, for technological reasons, the complete shutting down or diversion of operations of the plant.

Analogously, in the *structure of markets* there are firms, and consequently there are employees, who are in strategic positions to affect the whole stream of production and distribution. Employees are technologically strategic by virtue of their position *within* an individual firm. Workers are in a strategic position, marketwise, by virtue of their position in the structure of markets. In the market framework they can most readily exact a

price. Not only are the teamsters in a position to tie up operations (technological position), but also their employers are in a position to pass on cost increases to their customers (market position). Another illustration would be a craft, such as the bricklayers, where cost increases may be passed on to the small house-builder whose bargaining position is such as to force absorption. The musicians constitute probably an even better example. The technological and market strategic positions are never completely disassociated, although it is helpful to make the conceptual distinction.

Labor organization emerges among employees who have strategic market or technological positions. They have bargaining power. They can make it hurt. These strategic employees may be regarded as "points of infection" or "growth cones," to borrow the latter term from embryology, for the spread of labor organization.

How far will organization spread around the original "point of infection?" In some instances organization is confined to these most strategic workers and a pure craft union may result. In other instances these workers become the nucleus of the organization that encompasses other workers in the same plant. The cell wall of the organization may be pushed coextensively with the plant and an industrial union result. The boundary line may be drawn any place in between and may in fact fluctuate a good deal over time. The analogous point applies to the growth of unions in different types of firms. The boundary line of the union may be stopped from crossing into firms with different product market conditions. The phenomenon of a union organized in commercial building but unable or uninterested in pushing into housing is familiar in construction.

There are barriers to extending the cell wall of organization that arise within the strategic group of workers themselves as well as from the opposition of those outside this nucleus. On occasions, the most strategic group will prefer to remain so purist that developments resulting in differentiation of work among these strategic workers will produce a split in the cell and two organizations result. Expanding the group would dilute the gains of organization for the existing nucleus. Labor organizations in the printing industry in this country have taken this pattern of development. From the original group of strategically positioned printers have split off the pressmen, the photo-engravers, the stereo-typers, the bookbinders, and others, as specialized operations have developed.

Resistance to the expansion of the strategic

group may arise from the fact that those outside the nucleus may have such high rates of turnover as to make organization impossible. Thus the butchers in retail outlets did not originally include part-time employees around these stores. The boundary line of the union may be confined because those outside may feel that they can enjoy any benefits won by the strategic group without the costs of organization. It is a mistake to interpret historically the structure (in the sense of boundary lines) of American trade unionism, primarily in terms of a slavish following of the "principle of craft unionism." This analysis suggests a more general view.

Necessary to the emergence and growth of permanent labor organizations have been workers who are located in strategic positions in the market or technological framework. Organization may be treated as expanding from these centers in different patterns and to varying extents. It may be helpful to illustrate this formal analysis with examples from the early growth of labor organizations. In both the men's and women's clothing industry the first group organized was the cutters.[40] Their key position in the technological operation of the making of garments gave them a dominant position in early organizations in these industries. For a while, organization was concentrated in this group. Later the cutters became the nucleus in the women's garment industry for the International Ladies' Garment Workers' Union.

Consider the development of the coal mining industry. Organization was first significant among the contract miners. As a "petty contractor," the miner owned his own tools, purchased his own powder, and worked without supervision. Starting from these strategic employees in the early coal mining industry as a nucleus, organization among the miners gradually expanded to include in a single organization all employees, including those who worked above ground as well as underground.[41]

In the cotton textile industry, the loom fixer has had a position of technological prominence. The failure to keep the looms in running order would soon force the shutdown of the weaving shed. There are other strategic groups of employees, such as the spinners and the slasher

tenders. In a sense, one finds multiple points of organization in this industry. In some cases the craft-like union resulted and in others the nucleus expanded to include sufficient other groups to be designated as a semi-industrial arrangement.

In the steel industry, the Amalgamated Iron, Tin, and Steel Workers Union was formed out of strategically located groups in various branches of the industry. The boilers and puddlers in the making of iron, and the heaters, rollers, and roughers from the finishing operations, formed the bulk of organization.[42] This nucleus failed to expand and in fact could not maintain its own position until the emergence of the CIO. These illustrations could be multiplied many times: the linemen in the growth of the Brotherhood of Electrical Workers,[43] the jiggermen and kilnmen in the pottery industry,[44] and the blowers, gatherers, flatteners, and cutters in the flat glass industry.[45] A union leader described an organizing drive as follows: ". . . we had all of the polishing department, and those men were the core of our whole organization."[46] Such instances provide flesh and blood to the formal scheme outlined above. The simple notion again is a strategic nucleus, which may expand in different patterns, depending on conditions and ideas within the union and the environment without.

The analysis that has just been outlined must be thought of as applicable to the task of understanding the development of the American labor movement in the context of community institutions which prevailed prior to the Wagner Act. Organization by ballot rather than by the picket line places much less emphasis upon strategic employees in the technological and market scene. Organization may proceed instead from those most susceptible to union appeals for votes. Furthermore, the unit or boundary which a union would select for an election is apt to be quite different from that which it would select to defend on the picket line. It has not been generally

[40] See Joel Seidman, *The Needle Trades* (New York: Farrar and Rinehart, 1942), pp. 81–92; also Elden La Mar, *The Clothing Workers in Philadelphia* (Philadelphia Joint Board, Amalgamated Clothing Workers, 1940), pp. 46–47.

[41] Edward A. Wieck, *The American Miners' Association* (New York: Russel Sage Foundation, 1940), pp. 75–77, 85–86.

[42] J. S. Robinson, *The Amalgamated Association of Iron, Steel and Tin Workers* (Baltimore: Johns Hopkins Press, 1920), pp. 9–21.

[43] Michael A. Mulcaire, *The International Brotherhood of Electrical Workers* (Washington: The Catholic University of America, Studies in the Social Sciences, Vol. 5, 1923).

[44] David A. McCabe, *National Collective Bargaining in the Pottery Industry* (Baltimore: Johns Hopkins Press, 1932), pp. 4–7.

[45] Window Glass Cutters League of America, *A History of Trade Unions in the Window Glass Industry . . .*, reprinted from the *Glass Cutter*, March–September 1943.

[46] "From Conflict to Cooperation," *Applied Anthropology*, Vol. 5 (Fall 1946), p. 9.

recognized that the Wagner Act has had as much effect on the organizing strategy and structure of labor organizations as upon relations with the employer.[47]

The concept of strategic workers cannot be as useful to an understanding of the development of the labor movement today as it is for the explanation of the past. Still it may help to explain stresses and strains within unions and particular wage policies.

2. A second necessary condition in the emergence of organization is the view of the employees that they shall look forward to spending a substantial proportion of their lifetime as workmen. This factor has been gradually developing over the past 100 years and has been influenced by the rate of increase in gainful employment. It is also necessary that a substantial proportion in any given work community look forward to remaining in the same or similar work community. Negatively, organization is difficult, if not impossible, where individuals expect to work themselves out of the status of wage earners, or where they expect to remain wage earners but a short time because of anticipated withdrawals from the labor market, or where the rate of turnover and migration is so rapid and so erratic and random as to preclude stability in organization. In a period or in situations in which individual employees expect to become foremen and then owners of their own business, permanent and stable organization is virtually impossible. One of the problems of organizing women arises from the fact that they expect only a short working life and then plan to retire to the more arduous duties of the household. Migratory labor has been notoriously difficult to form into permanent organizations.[48]

3. Certain types of community institutions stimulate, and others retard, the emergence and growth of labor organizations. ". . . There had developed, in effect a double standard of social morality for labor and capital. . . . The story of the gradual modification of this double standard can be read in the history of labor organization and in the record of social legislation on state and federal governments over the past 50 years."[49] The legal system may actually preclude organization, as would have been the case had the doctrine of the early conspiracy cases been generally applied. This is not to suggest that the passage of a law could have wiped out all organization. Such a legal doctrine, however, acted as an obstruction to the growth of organization. Analogously, a policy of government to encourage organization, such as adopted in the Wagner Act, tends to accelerate the growth of labor unions.

The role of the wider community influence on the emergence and pattern of growth of the labor movement must be more broadly conceived than the legal system.[50] Both the struggle for free public schools and the impact of widespread general and technical education have left their mark on the American labor movement. The labor press has drawn heavily on the conventions of the daily newspaper. The hostility of the ordinary press to labor organizations over much of the past in this country in turn helped to set the tone of the labor press.

The *emergence* of labor organizations has been related in preceding pages to the strategic position of wage earners in a market and technological setting. But the subsequent form of the labor organization will be decisively molded by the environment of these wider community and national institutions. In some contexts the labor organization has developed into an almost exclusively political body; in others political activity is minor. Special local or industry conditions, such as prevail in the field of municipal employment, may lead to substantial political activity even though the dominant pattern in the country may involve little such action.

The relation of the labor movement to the future of capitalism (Question 3) must not be viewed narrowly as an issue of the extent or character of political activity. The growth in modern technology in the setting of the business corporation has gradually yielded a society predominantly made up of wage and salary earners. Wage earners have constituted a minor element in previous communities made up largely of self-employed farmers, serfs, slaves, or peasants. Unique in human history has been the

---

[47] The interpretation of the rise of the CIO as a repudiation of the principle of craft unionism neglects the adaptation in structure to these new conditions. A fruitful research enterprise would study these effects of the Wagner Act on union structure.

[48] Carleton H. Parker, *The Casual Laborer and Other Essays* (New York: Harcourt, Brace, and Howe, 1920). Also see Stuart Jamieson, *Labor Unionism in American Agriculture*, Bulletin 836 (Bureau of Statistics, Washington, 1945).

[49] Samuel Eliot Morrison and Henry Steele Commager, *The Growth of the American Republic*, rev. and enlarged ed. (New York: Oxford University Press, 1937), Vol. 2, p. 153.

[50] See W. Lloyd Warner and J. O. Low, "The Factory in the Community," in *Industry and Society*, William F. Whyte, ed. (New York: McGraw-Hill Book Co., 1946), pp. 21–45.

creation of a society where the vast majority of persons earn a livelihood as wage and salary earners. (Two thirds of the national income is wage and salary payment.) Under these circumstances when wage earners organize into labor organizations, as traced in previous sections, these bodies may be expected to exercise considerable political power in the community. The center of political power ultimately shifts as the character of the groups within the community changes.

If the locus of political power shifts to the degree that the labor organization becomes the dominant political power, there is growing evidence that the function and role of the union changes. The attitude toward the right to strike, compulsory arbitration, and production drives shifts away from the customary patterns under capitalism. This transition cannot but involve serious controversy within the labor movement.

4. Over and above these technological, market, and community influences on the labor movement has been the system of values, the ethos, and the beliefs of the community. Professor Schlesinger has summarized the traditional attributes of the American most noted by foreign observers: "a belief in the universal obligation to work; the urge to move about; a high standard of comfort for the average man; an absence of permanent class barriers; the neglect of abstract thinking and of the aesthetic side of life. . . ."[51] Many of these characteristics are to be traced to the "long apprenticeship to the soil."

It should not be hard to understand why labor organization would be difficult in a day in which men believed that individual advancement was to be achieved solely by work,[52] where leisure was a vice, where economic destiny depended solely upon one's ability to work and save, where poverty could only be the reward for sloth, where the poor deserved their fate, and where the public care of the impoverished was regarded as encouragement of idleness. As Poor Richard says:

Employ thy Time well, if thou meanst to gain Leisure;

And, since thou art not sure of a Minute, throw not away an Hour.

Trouble springs from Idleness, and grievous Toil from needless Ease.

For Age and Want, save while you may,
No Morning Sun lasts a whole day.

I think the best way of doing good to the poor, is, not making them easy *in* poverty but leading or driving them *out* of it.

These admonitions of Benjamin Franklin[53] are hardly the ideal text for the organization of a labor union. This set of ethical standards which has pervaded the ethos of the American community until recently places the economic destiny of a workman in his own hands rather than in a labor union.

The political and economic philosophy of the founding fathers, beyond standards of individual behavior, came to be adapted to the advancing order of corporate business. "This ideology was derived in part from deep-rooted folk ideas, in part from the sanctions of religion, in part from concepts of natural science. But whatever the source, its arguments rested upon the concepts of individualism, equality of opportunity, and the promise of well-being under a profit economy. The conservative defense, crystallized by business leaders and by allied members of the legal, educational, and literary professions, was popularized in sermons, speeches, novels, slogans, and essays. It became part and parcel of American popular thought."[54]

Moreover, the dominant economic thinking on the determination of wage rates (the wage-fund doctrine), by the community, could hardly have been favorable a hundred years ago to the growth of labor organizations. ". . . There is no use in arguing against any one of the four fundamental rules of arithmetic. The question of wages is a question of division. It is complained that the quotient is too small. Well, then, how many ways are there to make a quotient larger? Two ways. Enlarge your dividend, the divisor remaining the same, and the quotient will be larger; lessen your divisor, the dividend remaining the same, and the quotient will be larger."[55] There was no place for

[51] Arthur Meier Schlesinger, "What Then Is the American, This New Man?" reprinted from the *American Historical Review*, Vol. 48 (January 1943), pp. 3–4.

[52] "What qualities of the national character are attributable to this long-persistent agrarian setting? First and foremost is the habit of work." (Ibid., p. 10.)

[53] "The Way to Wealth," Preface to *Poor Richard Improved* (1758).

[54] Merle Curti, *The Growth of American Thought* (New York: Harper & Bros., 1943), p. 656. See pp. 605–56. Also, Vernon Louis Parrington, *Main Currents in American Thought*, Vol. 3, *The Beginning of Critical Realism in America* (New York: Harcourt, Brace & Co., 1927).

[55] A. L. Perry, *Political Economy*, p. 123, quoted in Francis A. Walker, *The Wage Question* (New York: Henry Holt & Co., 1886), p. 143. Compare this with the statement by the Webbs, "Down to within the last 30 years it would have been taken for granted, by every educated man, that Trade Unionism . . . was against Political Economy. . . ." *Industrial Democracy*, p. 603.

a union; it could serve no legitimate function. The intellectual climate of political economy changed and became more conducive to labor organization over the years.

The *trend* of standards of personal morality and social and economic philosophy has moved in directions more congenial to the flowering of unionism. Contrast the entreaties of Poor Richard and Horatio Alger with the admonitions of Sir William Beveridge! Leisure is now a virtue rather than a vice; saving may be a community vice rather than the epitome of individual morality; the economically less fortunate are to be sustained by comprehensive social security rather than to be left to sink or swim. The trade union has a more nourishing ethos.

The dominant ethical judgments pervading the community have been a vital factor influencing the growth of labor organization not only as they affect the individual workman but also as they shape and mold the character of the labor organization itself. The primacy of property rights in the American tradition is partly responsible for the dominance of the concept of exclusive jurisdiction in the American Federation of Labor constitution. Each union "owns" its jurisdiction in the same way that a businessman owns a piece of property. These community values have also decisively determined the attitude of the community toward social insurance. It is no accident that the American Federation of Labor was opposed to a program of compulsory insurance until 1932.[56]

The environment of ideas and beliefs in which the labor organization developed has included the special role of the labor intelligentsia or the intellectual. "Capitalist evolution produces a labor movement which obviously is not the creation of the intellectual group. But it is not surprising that such an opportunity and the intellectual demiurge should find each other. Labor never craved intellectual leadership, but intellectuals invaded labor politics. They had an important contribution to make: They verbalized, supplied theories and slogans for it, . . . made it conscious of itself and in so doing changed its meaning."[57] The formulation of a creed or folklore or rationalization is an important function in the development of the labor movement, just as in any organization. The function needs to be kept in proportion. In the American scene this process seems not to have been the province of a special class nor fashioned through different means in labor organizations than in other groups in the community. The English and continental experience is different in this respect.

This section has sketched some suggestions toward an analytical view of the emergence and development of the labor movement out of its total environment, regarding that environment as the technological processes, the market structure, the community institutions, and the value judgments of the society. The emphasis has been upon the long-term *trend* of development.

SHORT-RUN VARIATIONS IN TRADE UNION MEMBERSHIP

The growth of the labor movement has not been uniform and the four factors which have been used to approach the long-term trends in the labor movement were not all operative at the same rate. This section is concerned with the deviations from trend, in particular, the periods of advance in labor organization.

Even a cursory view of the American labor movement identifies seven major periods of rapid expansion in organization. The following tabulation identifies these periods; it also notes the estimated membership[58] of the organizations at the end of a given period.

Periods[59]	Dates	Membership (thousands)
Awakening	1827–1836	300
Nationalism	1863–1872	300
Great Upheaval	1881–1886	1,000
Mass Advancement	1896–1904	2,000
First World War	1917–1920	5,000
New Deal	1933–1937	8,000
Second World War	1941–1945	14,000

These seven periods can be divided into two distinct types. The dominant characteristics of a period do not preclude some elements of the opposite type. The first group of periods were

---

[56] See George G. Higgins, *Voluntarism in Organized Labor in the United States, 1930–40* (Washington: Catholic University of America Press, 1944).

[57] Joseph A. Schumpeter, *Capitalism, Socialism and Democracy* (New York: Harper & Bros., 1942), pp. 153–54.

[58] In any organization it is not always clear who should be counted as a "member." In the case of a union, depending upon the purpose, the significant figure may be those who have signed membership cards, pay dues regularly, attend meetings, vote for the union in a NLRB election, or support the union by joining a strike.

[59] The titles used in Commons and Associates, *History of Labor*, have been adopted for the first four periods. The membership figures for these periods are from the same source.

years of wartime, with rapid increases in the cost of living and stringency in the labor market. This group includes the periods of Nationalism (1863–72), Mass Advancement (1896–1904), the First World War (1917–20), and the Second World War (1941–45). The rapid expansion in membership is to be explained almost entirely by developments in the labor market: the rapid rise in the cost of living and the shortage of labor supply relative to demand. Under these circumstances a trade union helped to enable wage earners to increase their wages to an extent more closely approximating the rise in prices. The individual worker joined unions to push up his wages; the tightness in the labor market and the general level of profits enabled the union to achieve results. Organization in these instances may be regarded as predominately a market reflex.

Contrasting with these years is the second type of period—to be regarded as one of fundamental unrest. Organization of unions represented a basic dissatisfaction with the performance of the economic system and the society in general. Such were the years of Awakening (1827–36), the Great Upheaval (1881–86), and the New Deal (1933–37). It is these three periods which call for special explanation.

It is well established in the analysis of economic fluctuations that modern capitalism has moved in certain long waves.[60] These long waves or Kondratieff cycles are generally regarded as approximately 50 years in length with 25 years of good times and 25 years of bad times, and are distinguished from the shorter business cycles. Professor Alvin H. Hansen's dating scheme is typical.[61] The long wave represents a fundamental structural period in modern capitalism. The first of these waves has been designated as that of the Industrial Revolution,

Good Times	Bad Times
1787–1815	1815–43
1843–1873	1873–97
1897–1920	1920–40
1940—	

the second the Age or Railroads, and the third the Electrical Period.[62] The fourth may be known as that of the airplane and atomic power.

For the present purposes it is significant to note that each one of the three periods of major upheaval and fundamental unrest came at the bottom of the period of bad times in the long wave. The period of good times in the long wave is associated with a cluster of major innovations. There follows a period of generally declining prices (1815–43, 1873–97, 1920–40), during which the shorter business cycles are severe and intense. The three major periods of upheaval follow severe depressions. It is suggested that after prolonged periods of high unemployment for a substantial number in the work force and after years of downward pressure on wages exerted by price declines, labor organizations emerge which are apt to be particularly critical of the fundamental tenets of the society and the economy.

These three fundamental periods of upsurge in the labor movement must also be related to important developments in community institutions and ideas or value judgments. Thus, the first period was the Age of Jacksonian Democracy, the second the Populist, and the third the New Deal. The labor movement of 1827–36 has been treated as an alignment of "producer classes."[63] The Knights of Labor in the period 1881–86 has been referred to as the last great middle-class uprising. The expansion of the labor movement in the New Deal period was primarily a working class movement. The first period rallied around the slogan of free education, the second used the watchword of shorter hours, the third was characterized by the accent on security.

CONCLUDING REMARKS

The scaffolding may now be removed. In the distinctive pattern of growth of the labor movement in this country, one sees in outline form the way in which technology, market structure, community institutions, and the ethos factors have interacted together to yield the labor movement considered as a whole. Special types of these factors in operation in specific industries and localities account for the divergent types and forms of unionism which have developed within the generalized framework. For example, the migratory character of agricultural work and the lumber industry, together with the absence of stability of community, help to account for the

---

[60] Joseph A. Schumpeter, *Business Cycles: A Theoretical, Historical, and Statistical Analysis of the Capitalist Process* (New York: McGraw-Hill Book Co., 1939).

[61] Alvin H. Hansen, *Fiscal Policy and Business Cycles* (New York: W. W. Norton & Co., 1940), p. 30.

[62] Schumpeter, *Business Cycles*, Vol. 1, pp. 220–448.

[63] At the third meeting of the Working Men's Party in New York it was not the employers who were given five minutes to withdraw but "persons not living by some useful occupation, such as bankers, brokers, rich men, etc." Commons, ed., *Documentary History*, Vol. 5, p. 24.

type of unionism that originally emerged in this sector, illustrated by the IWW. The unions in the field of local or national government employment have become lobbying agencies by virtue of the practical prohibitions to effective collective bargaining. These specialized forms or species are variations from the main pattern of growth and development arising from special types of environments. In the same way, peculiar national characteristics shape the operation of these factors in comparing labor movements in various countries.

The framework of approach to the labor movement presented here is intended to be suggestive for a renewed interest in the writing of the history of the labor movement in general and in particular sectors. The emphasis upon the interrelations and mutual dependence of four groups of factors has served as the basis for this analysis. Not only is the analysis schematic, but it must be recognized that any simplified schemata must abstract from many complexities of behavior. The formal analysis must not leave the impression of the labor organization as primarily rationalistic. Professor Knight has well said that there is need for "some grasp of the infinitely complex, intangible, and downright contradictory character of men's interests, conscious and unconscious, and their interaction with equally intricate mechanical, biological, neural, and mental processes in forming the pattern of behavior. The great vice is oversimplification. . . ."[64]

---

[64] Knight in Introduction to Sée, *Economic Interpretation*, p. xxix.

9. Why the American Labor Movement Is Not Socialist*

Walter Galenson†

A Japanese scholar who had spent a year in the United States studying industrial relations visited me recently on the eve of his return to his country. I asked him about the impressions he had gained, and he replied: "We have often been told in Japan that the American labor movement is not Socialist, but we have always regarded this as capitalist propaganda. After a year of observation, I am finally convinced that your trade unions really support the capitalist system, and do not want to replace it with socialism. But when I tell this to my friends in Japan, they will accuse me of having sold out to the capitalists; no one will believe me."

The Japanese are not the only ones to doubt what is simply a matter of fact to Americans. Europeans are equally puzzled by the American scene. This is quite understandable, however, because the American labor movement and the closely allied movement of Canada are unique in their attitudes toward capitalism. Almost everywhere else, labor is dedicated to some form of collectivism, or at least to a very restricted type of capitalism.

In trying to explain why the American labor movement is different, I will first consider the various efforts that have been made during the past century to steer American labor into more orthodox ideological channels. Against that background, I will then discuss the basic economic, social, and political features of American life which have molded the present system.

* Reprinted from the *American Review*, Vol. 1, No. 2, Winter 1961, pp. 1–19.

† Walter Galenson is Professor of Economics at Cornell University.

ATTEMPTS TO RADICALIZE AMERICAN LABOR

Many radical ideologies of Europe, as well as some that were native to the United States, have been urged upon the American labor movement at various times in its history. There were many who believed that one or another had taken permanent root. Martin Tranmael, the founder of Norwegian socialism, once told me that he came to the United States in 1900 in order to study a successful Socialist movement. Daniel De Leon, a prominent American Socialist of the turn of the century, was regarded by Lenin as an outstanding Marxist theorist and practitioner. European Socialists still make pilgrimages to the California ranch of Jack London, although his own countrymen have long forgotten his political views.

The first American labor movement of any importance was the Knights of Labor, established in 1869 as a secret society but converted a decade later into an open trade union federation. Like many of the early European trade unions, the Knights advocated producers' co-operatives as a means of eliminating the exploitation of labor, and the eventual failure of the co-operatives which it sponsored was a major cause of its decline. However, the Knights of Labor was in no sense a revolutionary organization. It was prepared to work within the framework of capitalism provided that the worst abuses were mitigated through collective bargaining and social legislation. One must keep in mind that in the heyday of the Knights, the American worker already enjoyed the right to vote and free public education. These demands of early European socialism did not have to be won by revolutionary activity.

The American Federation of Labor, formed in 1886, supplanted the Knights of Labor as the most representative organization of American workers, and it has occupied that status right down to the present day. It was challenged from the left on numerous occasions, but always emerged unscathed. The AFL was led for many years by Samuel Gompers, a cigar maker by trade, who helped establish the pragmatic approach to political and economic problems which has been its hallmark. Gompers, an immigrant from England, had been a student of Socialist doctrine and was not altogether unsympathetic to the Socialist point of view, but his experience as a labor leader convinced him that it had little chance of success under American conditions. He eventually became a staunch foe of socialism, and its major antagonist within the trade unions.

In 1892, the Socialist Labor party, which had been established two decades earlier, fell under the control of Daniel De Leon, a university teacher and a Marxist fundamentalist. Despairing of making headway within the AFL, he gathered together the remnants of the Knights of Labor and some Socialist-inclined local unions in New York to form the Socialist Trade and Labor Alliance. The Alliance never achieved any real organizational success, though its career was attended by a great deal of furor.

A more serious threat to the Gompers leadership came from Socialist-oriented groups within the AFL. At the AFL conventions of 1893 and 1894, they tried to secure endorsement of collective ownership of the means of production as well as other Socialist demands. Although they were unable to gain a majority for their program, the Socialists teamed up with some personal enemies of Gompers to defeat him for the AFL presidency in 1894, the only time in his long career that Gompers suffered this fate. The moderate Socialists within the AFL continued their efforts to gain control of the organization, and for several decades they were a force to be reckoned with. In 1902, a resolution that would have committed the AFL "to advise the working people to organize their economic and political power to secure for labor the full equivalent of its toil and the overthrowal of the wage system and the establishment of an industrial co-operative democracy" was defeated only by the narrow margin of 4,897 to 4,171 votes. The Socialists ran their own candidate against Gompers at the 1912 convention and gained about one-third of the total vote, being supported, among others, by the delegates of the United Mine Workers, the Brewery Workers, the Machinists, and the Typographical Union. However, Socialist party opposition to American participation in the First World War greatly reduced Socialist strength within the AFL.

Another in the series of efforts to build a radical labor movement independent of the AFL came with the formation of the Industrial Workers of the World in 1905. At its inception, it embraced most of the existing left wing groups, including Daniel De Leon's Socialist Labor Alliance and the followers of Eugene V. Debs, perhaps the most popular Socialist leader in American history. (Debs was imprisoned in 1918 for his opposition to the war, ran for the Presidency of the United States from prison in 1920, and polled close to a million votes for the Socialist party.) But the dominant elements in the IWW came from the western part of the United States, which was then in the process of transformation from a frontier to a settled industrial area. The Western Federation of Miners, an organization of metal miners representing workers in Idaho, Colorado, and Utah, provided the IWW with leadership.

The preamble to the IWW constitution began categorically: "The working class and the employing class have nothing in common"; on this much, the disparate constituency could agree. But differences of opinion soon developed on many issues, including the desirability of political activity within the framework of the capitalist state. Within a few years, Debs, De Leon, and the Western Federation of Miners all withdrew, leaving the IWW in the hands of an uncompromising, direct action group headed by William D. Haywood and Vincent St. John.

The IWW became the spokesman *par excellence* of the migratory workers who at the time constituted a substantial proportion of the labor force in the West. Working in isolated mining camps, in lumbering operations, on large farms, and on the docks of Pacific Coast ports, these men were homeless and rootless, without families, hounded as "hoboes" and "bums" when they were unable to secure work, which was largely seasonal in character at best. Their ideology was a native American syndicalism; its main ingredients were a rejection of capitalism and all its works, and belief in the efficacy of the strike as a means of securing economic gain, and of the general strike in bringing about the eventual overthrow of capitalism. Collective bargaining and the collective agreement were not for them; they were not in one job long enough to make this a feasible procedure, and it was too slow a means of alleviating the poor condition of labor which they faced. The IWW was never very clear about the nature of the Socialist commonwealth which would take over on the great day when all the nation's workers folded their arms and brought capitalism tumbling down. Its job was to prepare for that day by strikes (revolutionary gymnastics), sabotage, and any other means of weakening capitalism.

The formal structure of the IWW was extremely loose. Combined offices and "flop houses," where penniless members could secure a night's lodging and food, were maintained in a number of cities. Dues payments were sporadic, although the members were intensely loyal to the organization and paid when they could. The IWW led some major strikes of metal and lumber workers during the war and suffered severe repression both by the government and by vigilante action. Hundreds of its leaders were imprisoned, some were lynched by mobs. William D. Haywood fled the country while out on bail awaiting trial, escaped to Russia, and died an unhappy man after having learned that communism had as little use for syndicalism as did capitalism.

While the action of the government undoubtedly hastened the demise of the IWW, its days were numbered in any event by changes in the economic conditions which had led to its creation. The West was settling down; miners, loggers, and longshoremen were acquiring steady employment and families. Their trade unions began to adopt collective bargaining. Nevertheless, the IWW tradition has not entirely disappeared; the Mine, Mill and Smelter Workers' Union, successor to the Western Federation of Miners, and the West Coast Longshoremen's Union are among the few American labor unions still controlled by Communists, while in the organizations of West Coast seamen and lumber workers, one can still detect some trace of IWW psychology.

With the eclipse of the Socialists within the AFL and the IWW outside it, the mantle of opposition fell to the Communist party, which had been formed as a breakaway from the Socialist party soon after the Russian revolution. For some years it followed a policy of "boring from within" the AFL under the guidance of William Z. Foster, an able trade union organizer. However, in 1928 it was directed by the Red International of Labor Unions to establish an independent trade union center, and the outcome was the Trade Union Unity League. While the League was never very large, it served an important function as a training ground for Communist organizers.

But a much more serious challenge to the AFL came from within its own ranks. The AFL had declined steadily in membership and vitality after 1920, and the economic depression that hit the country in 1929 weakened it still further. A group of AFL union leaders blamed the AFL difficulties on too strict adherence to craft union structure and advocated industrial unionism as the only way in which workers in the mass production industries could be organized.

The Committee for Industrial Organization (which later became the Congress of Industrial Organizations) was a revolt of the unskilled and semi-skilled workers against the craftsmen who controlled the AFL. Like the "new unionism" of Great Britain in the 1890s, or the transformation of Scandinavian unionism a decade later, it reflected the aspirations of the less privileged labor groups to a greater voice in determining labor conditions and their resentment against exclusion from the union movement. The men who led the CIO were not radicals: John L. Lewis, head of the coal miners' union, was a lifelong Republican, while Sidney Hillman and David Dubinsky, who were presidents, respectively, of the men's and ladies' garment workers' unions, had some early connection with socialism but had long since lost any sympathy for Marxism. The CIO was not established to remake the social order. Its only goal was to organize the workers in the steel, automobile, electrical equipment, rubber, textile, and other mass production industries.

It is fair to say that the CIO was somewhat to the left politically of the AFL, but it was never under the domination of anti-capitalistic elements. Philip Murray, who succeeded John L. Lewis as president in 1940, was a cautious Scotch ex-coal miner, who had been Lewis' chief lieutenant for many years. Walter Reuther, who became president on the death of Murray, had once been a member of the Socialist party but turned later to staunch support of the Democratic party.

However, the CIO did have an internal Communist problem of no mean dimensions. With the advent of the United Front policy in 1934, the Communist party dissolved the Trade Union Unity League and turned its attention once more to the AFL. The organization of the CIO afforded it a tremendous opportunity, for there was a great need of trained organizers, and the Communists were only too willing to oblige. Working for little pay and performing arduous and often dangerous jobs, well disciplined Communist groups established themselves in leadership positions. At the height of their power, they controlled half a dozen major CIO unions and had powerful factions in a number of others.

From the outbreak of war in Europe in September 1939, to the Nazi attack upon the Soviet Union, the Communist-dominated unions were in the forefront of the struggle against American assistance to the democratic nations, and this brought them into sharp conflict with the CIO leadership. But when Russia entered the war, their policy changed over night, and an internal crisis was averted. After the war, tensions once more arose with the growing coolness between the United States and the Soviet Union. When in 1948, the Communist unions supported former Vice President Henry Wallace on a third party ticket in an effort to defeat the Democratic candidate, Harry S Truman, Philip Murray decided that the Communists would have to go, whatever the cost in CIO strength. A number of Communist unions were expelled from the CIO in 1949 and 1950, and in some cases the CIO set up new unions in an effort to hold the members. Communist power in the labor movement declined precipitously thereafter, and today there are not more than 150,000 workers in the few independent unions under Communist control. Even this does not tell the whole story, for few of the rank and file members are Communists, and many of the leaders have only a tenuous relationship with the Communist party.

By 1955, the issues that had divided the AFL and CIO were gone. The mass production workers were organized into powerful trade unions, and many of the AFL craft unions had expanded their jurisdictions until they were almost indistinguishable from the CIO unions. Both federations supported the Democratic party on the political front. As a result, the AFL-CIO merger was consummated, and this organization remains the only labor federation in the United States at the present time.

Until 1950, there was scarcely a period in which socialism, in one of its many forms, did not play a significant role on the American labor scene. But during the past decade, Communist strength has dwindled into insignificance, and no ideology of the left has arisen to take its place. Nor is there any immediate prospect that one will emerge. Not a single responsible trade union leader advocates an independent labor party, and there are no proponents of government ownership of industry. The trade unions are wedded more firmly than ever to the Democratic party. Prediction of events to come is a hazardous undertaking, but few would quarrel with the observation that the future of American socialism does not seem bright.

THE DETERMINANTS OF AMERICAN LABOR IDEOLOGY

European socialists have been prone to attribute the pragmatism of American labor to the "backwardness" of the American worker. The late Harold Laski predicted that eventually the American working class would throw off the blinders that prevented it from seeing the truth about class conflict and catch up with the British. In the light of what is happening in Britain, these views are not as popular as they once were, but there is still enough economic determinism in the European Left to make the thesis seem tenable.

The fact of the matter is that these visions of the future have as little to do with reality as the utopia of Edward Bellamy or the Gehenna of George Orwell. The American worker had the alternative of taking the paths pointed out to him by persuasive prophets—Daniel De Leon, Morris Hillquit, Eugene V. Debs, William Z. Foster, William D. Haywood, or Norman Thomas, to name a few. Yet in the final analysis, he chose to follow such proponents of business unionism as Samuel Gompers, William Green, and George Meany, who promised only a little more of the goods of this world each year. This result flowed from the conjuncture of certain fundamental conditions in the American environment.

The Standard of Living

It should be observed first that there is no necessary one-to-one relationship between living standards and radicalism. In many countries it is among the better paid workers in the metal trades, on the railroads, in the mines, and on the docks, that foci of discontent exist, while the poorer paid textile, service, and farm laborers are quiescent. Yet there does seem to be a general tendency for economic well being and political conservatism to go hand in hand, as European Socialists are beginning to discover.

International comparison of living standards is a slippery business, even for the present, when we have abundant statistics. For the years when the labor movement was in its formative stages, the task is well nigh impossible. Nevertheless, there can be little doubt of the broad outlines. Even before the onset of the American industrial revolution, which began about the time of the Civil War, both workers and farmers in the United States were substantially better off than those in the wealthiest countries of Europe. "Harriet Martineau, observing a demonstration of journeymen mechanics in New York, could hardly believe her eyes: 'Surely never were such dandy mechanics seen; with sleek coats, glossy hats, gay watch-guards, and doeskin gloves!' Similar observations were not wanting a score of years later; and Richard Cobden, who visited the

United States in 1859 after an interval of 24 years, could conclude, 'The people are far better off to my eye as compared with the Europe of today than they were in 1835 as compared with the old world at that time.' " (Henry Pelling, *American Labor*, Chicago, 1960.)

That these differences persisted during the era of rapid industrialization is evidenced by continuous, heavy migration from Europe to the United States. Despite all the hardships and perils, millions came to America to seek their fortunes, and continued to come until the door was slammed in their faces after the First World War.

Of course, there was poverty in the United States. One has only to read Jack London's *Martin Eden*, Upton Sinclair's *The Jungle*, or any one of the many muckraking books written around the turn of the century, for a glimpse of the human costs of industrialization. Yet H. G. Wells, visiting New York in the early years of the present century, was struck by its prosperity compared with London. "Even in the congested entrances, the filthy back streets of the East Side, I find myself saying as a thing remarkable, 'These people have money to spend.' "

The relatively high American standard of living is not difficult to understand. A vast continent, richly endowed with natural resources, was settled by some of the most energetic and ambitious people of Europe. The productivity of labor, both in the factory and on the farm, was high because of its relative scarcity in relation to capital and land. Unemployment was mainly of a frictional or cyclical character and not the permanent structural unemployment found in many countries. If employment opportunities in an area dried up, the American worker simply moved where jobs were more abundant. He had no ancestral village to tie him down. The phenomenal growth of California in the last two decades attests to continuing high labor mobility. It is as though Western Europe were a single nation and the underemployed peasants of southern Italy could move freely to Great Britain and Sweden.

It has often been remarked that it is inequality, rather than absolute living standards, which gives rise to discontent. Karl Marx once observed: "A house may be large or small; as long as the surrounding houses are equally small it satisfies all social demands for a dwelling. But if a palace arises beside the little house, the little house shrinks into a hut." There has always been, and there still is great inequality of income and wealth in the United States. Whether the degree of inequality is greater or less than in Europe is still a matter of statistical debate. But the political consequences of inequality can be quite different, depending upon the absolute base. A small difference in income may be less tolerable to the worker living on the margin of existence than a large difference to the man who is well off. Statistical comparisons cannot convey anything of the resentments felt, respectively, by a worker who, together with his family, occupies a single room and spends his entire income for inadequate food and clothing, and by a worker with a comfortable house, an adequate diet, and money left over for recreation, when each views a millionaire driving by in his limousine.

The Rate of Economic Growth

The rate of growth of the American economy has been very impressive, even by modern, forced-draught standards. By 1900, American industry was producing four times the volume of goods that had been turned out 30 years earlier. During the next 40 years, when the labor movement reached maturity, there was something more than an additional fourfold increase. Since 1940, the increase in manufacturing output has been about 80 percent.

Precisely how this affected real wages is still a matter of some speculation. The best guess is that from 1870 to 1890, real wages in manufacturing rose about 2 percent a year, on the average. Since 1890, the rate of increase declined somewhat to perhaps 1.6 percent per year. These advances in living standards have been persistent, however. Recent research indicates that apart from the years of the Great Depression, real wages have risen quite steadily throughout the entire industrial era.

One of the greatest sources of tension in the modern world is the disparity between the material aspirations of people in underdeveloped nations and the capabilities of their economies. Economic stagnation is not necessarily inconsistent with political stability until the onset of industrialization creates a large class of people who become dissatisfied with their standard of life, and who are able to develop organizational means of protest. We have not yet established the rate of economic advance necessary to prevent undermining of confidence in a prevailing social order. But it is perfectly clear that for the United States, at least, this rate was achieved. It might be objected that European nations developed, too, but that their workers turned to socialism. I would urge in reply that their rates of growth were probably lower during the critical years in which labor's ideology was taking shape; that progress was not nearly as obvious to the working man; and that there was not the optimistic view of the future that prevailed in America. E. H. Phelps Brown, in *The Growth of British Industrial Relations* (London, 1959) has pointed out that "the industrial development of the 25 years before the First World War brought no conspicuous or concentrated changes in the working life of the British people." This can certainly not be said of the United States, when new industries and new factories were everywhere springing up, and old ones were growing.

Not all American workers shared the fruits of industrial growth. The IWW episode was illustrative of the alienation of a substantial group with poor conditions of labor and low expectations for future improvement. But the great majority maintained their faith in capitalism because within their experience, this system delivered the goods.

The Absence of Class Consciousness

A hundred and twenty-five years ago, Alexis de Tocqueville wrote: "America, then, exhibits in her social state an extraordinary phenomenon. Men are there seen on a greater equality in point of fortune and intellect, or, in other words, more equal in their strength than in any other country of the world, or in any other age of which history has preserved the remembrance." A great deal has happened since then. Fortunes have been made, permanent aristocracies of wealth created. Investigators have concluded that social mobility is now greater in the United States than in the industrial nations of Europe. But the belief in equality persists.

Such ideological equalitarianism has played, and continues to play, an important role in facilitating social mobility in the United States. It enables the person of humble birth to regard upward mobility as attainable for himself, or for his children. It facilitates his acceptance as a social equal if he succeeds in rising economically. It mitigates the emotional distance between persons of different social rank. And it fosters in any existing elite the persuasion (however mistaken this may be) that its eminence is the result of individual effort, and hence temporary. The point to emphasize is, not that these beliefs are often contradicted by the experience of those who hold them, but that this equalitarian ideology has persisted in the face of facts which contradict it. We would suggest that the absence of hereditary aristocracy has done much to foster this persistence. Americans have

rarely been exposed to persons whose conduct displays a belief in an inherited and God-given superiority and also demands that others demonstrate (by deferential behavior) their recognition of this superiority. (Seymour Martin Lipset and Reinhard Bendix, *Social Mobility in Industrial Society*, Berkeley, 1959.)

The ideal of equality carries over strongly into industrial life. The great deference shown to European managers is absent in the American plant. There is in its place a certain camaraderie, reinforced by the fact that if manager and worker should chance to meet outside the factory, they are likely to be indistinguishable in dress and speech. As soon as the British worker opens his mouth, it is clear to which class he belongs. But one can sit around a table with American labor and management personnel and not be at all conscious of any class differences.

It might have been anticipated that the myth of equality would be dissipated by the hard facts of reality. It is neither easy nor usual for an ordinary worker to attain high position in a large corporation. Most American workers have no illusions on this score. Nevertheless, there is no indication that a working class in the European sense is developing. Even the worker solidarity that appeared during the union organizing drives of the 1930s is vanishing under the impact of full employment prosperity.

Differences in national origin, cutting vertically through every stratum of the population, are an important cause of weak class consciousness. Italian, Irish, German, Polish, and French-Canadian workers, to name but a few of the major groups found in the American labor force, are just as likely to feel a community of interest with non-workers of the same nationality as with workers of different nationality.

The racial question, which is easily the most pressing social problem of contemporary America, impinges directly upon class solidarity. Substantial numbers of Japanese, Chinese, and Mexican workers, in addition to millions of Negroes, are faced with discrimination at work as well as in social relationships. While the AFL-CIO is opposed to discrimination in employment, a number of local unions affiliated with it, particularly in the South, unofficially bar non-whites from employment. A Negro Labor Council has recently been formed to advance the particular interests of the 1.25 million Negro workers in the labor movement, and the many who are not yet organized. A separate Negro labor movement, while unlikely, is possible if the drive toward racial equality does not speed up.

National and racial divisions among workers

have had a particularly deleterious effect upon the growth of American socialism. The immigrants who brought Marxism to the United States often remained cut off from the native American, and confined their activities to fellow workers from the "old country." In 1917, 33,000 out of 80,000 Socialist party members belonged to 14 semi-autonomous foreign language federations, each with its own newspapers, benefit societies, etc. This situation has been well summarized in the following words:

> The immigrants played a dual role in the development of American socialism. They were largely responsible for its birth. They were also largely responsible for stunting its growth. They could transplant the theory of socialism but they could not naturalize it. In the formative years, therefore, an unequal and uneasy relationship existed between foreign-born and native Socialists. The former enjoyed the prestige of intellectual superiority but could not effectively spread the gospel. The latter suffered from a sense of theoretical inferiority but were indispensable in presenting the face of the party to the general public. It was not unusual for the top leadership of local Socialist groups to be native-born while a majority of the rank and file were foreign-born. (Theodore Draper, *The Roots of American Communism*, New York, 1957.)

The Socialist party was never able to shake off its foreign flavor. Once the stream of immigrants from Europe was cut off, it lost its main source of recruits. The children of immigrants, anxious to demonstrate their Americanism, turned their backs on socialism. There was lacking the European tradition of handing down a political creed from father to son. Many working class children moved into the ranks of professionals, thus depriving the workers of good leadership material.

A final factor militating against the formation of a cohesive working class in the United States was the character and structure of the AFL. At its formation, the AFL represented a revolt of the skilled trades against the heterogeneous Knights of Labor, which, it was felt, tended to subordinate the interests of the craftsman to those of the general worker. Craft structure continued for many years to be the AFL shibboleth. The theory was developed that because of the fragility of American working class loyalties, only the mutual bond of a common craft could prevent unions from splintering, thus providing an ideological basis for craft selfishness.

The exclusiveness of the crafts was strengthened by the very substantial occupation wage differentials that prevailed. In 1907, the American skilled wage level stood at 205 percent of the unskilled, compared to about 150 percent for Great Britain. Occupational differentials have narrowed everywhere since then, but the tendency toward equalization has been weaker in the United States than in Europe. The American "aristocracy of labor" was less than anxious to embrace industrial unionism when craft structure had paid off so well. There were a few industrial unions in the AFL before the New Deal, notably the United Mine Workers and the International Ladies' Garment Workers, but the locus of power was the skilled building trades unions, relatively stable in membership and possessing substantial financial resources.

Conflict between the skilled and unskilled was by no means confined to the United States. The same divisive tendencies had to be overcome in many other countries. But in most cases, the problem was resolved at an earlier stage in labor development, before ideology had been hardened into a fixed mold. The new unionism of the 1890s preceded the formation of the British Labor party, and it has been said of the period:

> The older (craft) unions had a tradition that you should keep party politics out of labour questions; these new ones were organized by Socialists, and Socialism was their aim . . . there was never any question of the new unions supporting any candidates but independent labour men. . . . This was a natural consequence of their lack of an entrenched position in industry; instead, they sought a statutory minimum wage, and compulsory arbitration. It was also a consequence of their not being able to pay enough to provide social insurance for themselves, as the craftsmen did: they had to win the welfare state instead. (E. H. Phelps Brown.)

German unions evolved toward an industrial form at a relatively early stage in their development, while in Norway and Sweden, the unskilled workers captured the labor movement before the First World War. Had American mass production industries been organized 30 years earlier, the political history of American unionism might have been quite different. But powerful employer opposition and indifference of the crafts held the unskilled in check until the catastrophe of the Great Depression unleashed a flood of organization which carried all obstacles before it.

Political Barriers to Socialism

It is almost a cliché that the tradition of the American two-party system provided an insurmountable obstacle to the establishment of a labor party. But putting the matter this way is merely to beg the question. In Britain, one of the great parties of the 19th century, the Liberals, yielded to a newly organized Labour party. In many other countries, the same process occurred as the labor movement asserted its independence. The right question to ask is this: Why did not the Democratic party in the United States yield its paramountcy to a labor party with the rise of the industrial worker?

Apart from the Socialist party, which never outgrew the sectarian stage, there were several 20th century efforts in the United States to build democratic third parties. The Progressive movement of 1912, in which Theodore Roosevelt split the Republican vote and secured the election of Woodrow Wilson, and the Communist-supported candidacy of Henry Wallace in 1948, which almost succeeded in bringing about the defeat of Truman, were ephemeral efforts which did not have the support of organized labor. The Progressive party of the 1920s was more significant. It rallied beneath its banner a number of Midwestern farmer-labor parties, and received the strong support of the labor movement in Chicago and other major cities. Robert M. La Follette was nominated for the Presidency on the Progressive ticket in 1924, and because the candidates of both the major parties were conservatives, the AFL, for the first and last time in its history, endorsed a third party candidate. La Follette got 5 million votes, but despite this promising start, the Progressive coalition fell apart, and in 1928 there were again only two major Presidential candidates.

What these abortive efforts indicated, however, was that from the point of view of election mechanics, a national political campaign could be mounted in a short time, and third parties could get on the ballot. Since 1924, there have been several efforts to establish labor parties on a local basis, mainly in New York State, where the American Labor party and the Liberal party received the backing of the garment unions. But none of these has moved into the national picture.

Samuel Gompers, who more than any other man made explicit the non-partisanship of American labor, wrote in 1920:

The effect of a separate political labor party can only be disastrous to the wage earners of our country and to the interests of all forward looking people. The votes that would go to a labor party candidate would, in the absence of such candidate, go to the best man in the field. In no case would he be an enemy of labor. There can be no hope of success of labor party candidates. The effect, therefore, of a political labor party will be to defeat our friends and to elect our enemies. Labor can look upon the formation of a political labor party only as an act detrimental to the interests of labor and exactly in line with that which is most ardently desired by those who seek to oppress labor.

This statement makes clear the basic reason for the opposition of the leaders of American unionism to independent labor action: the firm conviction that there would be no success. American labor leaders are certainly not averse to winning political power; they would like to sit in the Cabinet, and John L. Lewis once envisioned himself as a Vice-Presidential candidate running alongside Franklin D. Roosevelt. When Lewis broached the subject to Roosevelt, the latter is reported to have replied: "Which place were you thinking of, John?" But they have been realistic enough to realize that such honors, which many European working class leaders have obtained, were unlikely of attainment via the third party route.

Why was this true? For one thing, industrial workers in the United States, the land *par excellence* of industrialization, have never constituted a majority of the population. In 1950, 46 percent of all those employed were classified as professional, technical, managerial, and clerical workers, while another 15 percent were in categories not prone to unionization: private household workers, service workers, and farm laborers. By 1958, the non-worker group percentage had risen to 48 percent, while industrial workers had shrunk to about 37 percent of the labor force. Thus, even if wage earners were a solid bloc, they would still fall far short of a majority unless they could count on substantial support from white-collar employees, who have shown little inclination to vote labor anywhere. In the past it was the farmers who blocked labor's road to political power. Today it is the growing middle class—white-collar workers, professionals, the self employed—which stands in the way.

Secondly, American workers have never voted in the same automatic fashion as European workers. European Socialist parties first gained working class allegiance by elementary democratic demands for universal suffrage and free public education, which American workers have enjoyed for a century, and which therefore could not be utilized as issues by aspiring labor politicians.

Since 1928, most trade unions have supported the Democratic party on the national level, and have urged their members to vote, in turn, for Alfred E. Smith, Franklin D. Roosevelt, Harry S. Truman, Adlai Stevenson, and John F. Kennedy. But even during the Roosevelt era, when American workers were united as never before behind a man whom they felt had rescued them from economic disaster, a minority of trade union leaders and workers supported the Republican party. Among the prominent Republican laborites have been Hutcheson *père* and *fils*, presidents of the large Carpenters' Union; John L. Lewis; and Dave Beck and James Hoffa of the Teamsters' Union.

Apart from formal union support, a number of cross currents have contributed to the splitting of the labor vote. Many Negro workers, for example, support the Republican party as the party of Abraham Lincoln. Prosperous workers who leave working class urban districts and acquire suburban homes tend to take on the political hues of their middle class neighbors. Religion also enters into the picture on occasion, as in the 1960 Presidential campaign.

The political tactics of American labor have not worked badly. The Democratic party is a loose coalition of various interest groups, rather than the representative of a particular economic sector of the population. It includes some of the most anti-labor elements in the country, from the South; the political machines of the large Northern cities, which at best are neutral on issues of labor interest; and staunch labor supporters from areas in which the trade union movement is strong. By operating within the Democratic party structure, the unions are able to secure for themselves, on a *quid pro quo* basis, much broader influence than they could hope for as minority independents.

This method is not without its dangers. If public opinion turns against the unions, as it did after the 1945–47 strike wave, and the 1958–59 corruption exposures, they are left defenseless, since non-labor politicians cannot be expected to brave the wrath of the electorate in support of an unpopular cause. In normal times, however, the unions are able to achieve constant legislative gains, and in periods of economic crisis, the Democratic party has even been transformed into a powerful instrument for major social reform.

The Triumph of Collective Bargaining

The method of collective bargaining, as opposed to the method of legal enactment, to use the terminology of the Webbs, has proven eminently successful in the United States, contributing in no small measure to a reluctance on the part of workers to rely upon the state. A great many objectives which are essentially social in character have been achieved by private bargaining. One need only cite the proliferation of pension plans, health and welfare schemes, and the guaranteed annual wage.

There is one other area, however, in which American collective bargaining has made inroads to an extent matched in few other countries: that of management prerogatives. Fully as important as wages to the working man in this age of the large, impersonal factory is the assertion of his rights as an individual, on the job as well as off, and a sense of participation in the enterprise to which he devotes so large a part of his life. To this end, almost every country of Western Europe has established labor-management or production committees to promote industrial democracy. On the whole, these committees have not lived up to expectations, but this is another story.

Except briefly during the last war, labor-management committees have been exceedingly rare in the United States. Employers are opposed to them on ideological grounds, and unions are suspicious of them as potential competitors. But the real reason for their failure to take root is that unions have penetrated so deeply into the management of enterprise that they would be redundant if established.

The basic instrument of trade union control is the grievance machinery which is found in virtually every collective agreement. Almost any aspect of work can be raised as a grievance, discussed with management, and finally carried to compulsory arbitration by an impartial outsider. There has grown up a comprehensive body of industrial common law which management disregards only at its peril.

It is now difficult for an American business concern to promote or discharge an employee except on the basis of strict seniority. The speed of the assembly line, the size of the working crew on a machine or process, the work load, are all subject to union challenge. Unions may negotiate with management on the quality of meals to be provided employees; on recreational and sanitary facilities; on protection against injuries; in short, on virtually the entire range of subject matter which is within the purview of European labor-management committees. Normally, they still do not have any right to participate in the formulation of production or financial plans, but they are moving in this direction, and it will probably not be too long before this stronghold of management is invaded. Moreover, American trade unions are far better staffed with lawyers, economists, statisticians, accountants, and journalists than their European counterparts, and are in a much better position to gather business information for themselves.

If the unions were ever tempted by public ownership of industry as a goal, they have only to look at the status of the government employee for confirmation of their belief in private ownership. Federal employees, and many state employees, may not strike under pain of immediate discharge and loss of all accumulated rights. There is no formal, and very little informal mechanism, for collective bargaining in government service. It is little wonder that the most vociferous opponents of public ownership are the unions which represent workers on publicly and privately owned utilities, such as gas and electric plants, for they find it much easier to deal with the private employers. I suspect that if the issue were ever put to a vote, even the employees of the postal system would opt for private ownership of post offices.

THE FUTURE

One need not be rash in making the prediction that traditional socialism has little future in the United States. There are still a few advocates around, but their voices are no longer heard. The Communist party and the various splinter Socialist groups have no influence whatever on political events. The trade unions are committed more firmly than ever to working within the existing two-party system.

Time does not stand still, however, and there is no reason to believe that the present scheme of things is frozen immutably. The American labor movement is moving in directions which are likely to be not displeasing to European Socialists who drop Marxist slogans and face the world with an objective eye. American labor unions are insisting that the federal government assume greater responsibility for the economy, and in particular, that it pursue the goal of a more rapid rate of economic growth. They are demanding governmental assistance to the relatively underdeveloped portions of the country. They oppose high interest rates, and advocate monetary and fiscal policies which will bring about greater equality of income. In general, they favor a greater degree of governmental control over economic affairs.

On the collective bargaining front, American unions will undoubtedly continue to push not only for higher living standards for workers, but also for a greater share in the right to manage. The Automobile Workers have already proposed a kind of bilateral price fixing in the interest of selling more automobiles. The building unions are currently discussing with employers means of speeding technological change in construction. A joint labor-management committee has been created in steel to consider the human relations problems of the industry.

The forces that in the past shaped the unique character of the American labor movement continue unabated, for the most part. Material living standards remain the highest in the world, and they are improving at a fairly rapid rate. Of class consciousness, one can only say that everything is tending to diminish the possibility of developing a closely-knit, cohesive working class. The number of industrial workers is shrinking in relation to other groups, and the unions are fully aware of the fact that even to hold their own, they must somehow attract white-collar employees and professionals. Paradoxically, the only development that may foster manual worker cohesiveness is the tendency of manual wages to rise faster than those of white-collar employees, for the manualists may become concerned about protecting their differentials.

The American labor movement, until the last war, was turned inward, engrossed with domestic problems. The realization has grown that what is happening elsewhere in the world may be at least of equal importance in affecting the welfare of the American worker. Contact with the international labor movement has broadened tremendously. Differences of policy and practice between European and American labor are narrowing as both groups are discovering an urgent common interest in the maintenance of democratic institutions in the newly emerging nations of Africa and Asia.

It is my own observation that there is little left today to divide the moderate Socialist unions of Europe from American business unionism. The former may be puzzled, and even outraged, by some of the internal practices of American unions, while the latter may be repelled by the remnants of an earlier Socialist ideology that still prevails in some of the European movements. But when it comes to practical and economic policies, there are precious few differences remaining. It is high time to recognize that the doctrines of the past have very little to do with the kind of world in which we live today.

B. Highlights in the Development of the Labor Movement

Much of the activity and development of the labor movement has added to the mainstream of American economic history. An inquiry into some of the special aspects of the development of the labor movement provides rich insight into an understanding of the role of trade unions in an industrial society. Original sources have been presented in the following articles in order to encompass the thoughts of the early pioneers in the field of labor history and to provide the reader with a flavor not otherwise obtained.

What was an early labor organization like in terms of its goals and functions? In the first article, Commons discusses the cordwainers (shoemakers) as illustrative of the American craft workers. Investigation of the activities of the cordwainers reveals a great deal concerning industrial evolution and conditions in America during various periods.

The Knights of Labor, organized in 1869, and serving as the forerunner to the formation of the American Federation of Labor, was a powerful labor organization during the 1880s. During the period 1878–86, a struggle existed between the reform unionism of the Knights of Labor and the trade unions. Grob discusses the struggle and indicates the important ideological differences between the two groups.

In the third article, Perlman discusses further the importance of the struggle between the principles of labor organization as explained by Grob. Perlman traces the history of the Great Upheaval and explains how craft unionism emerged as the victor over the "one big union" ideas expounded by the Knights of Labor.

Subsequent to the trend in the labor movement during the 1880s toward craft unionism, an opposing philosophy presented itself in the early 1900s with the development of the IWW (Industrial Workers of the World). Hoxie discusses the goals of "revolutionary unionism" and the IWW in his article. He notes that the IWW challenged the conservative, craft unionism advocates on the grounds that the working class should be organized in one great union to fight employers.

In the concluding article, Taft focuses attention on the growth of organized labor during the New Deal period. He discusses the growth of the AF of L and the CIO under the legislation passed in the 1930s protecting the right of labor to organize and bargain collectively.

10. American Shoemakers, 1648–1895*

John R. Commons

The boot and shoe makers, either as shoe-makers or "cordwainers," have been the earliest and the most strenuous of American industrialists in their economic struggles. A highly skilled and intelligent class of tradesmen, widely scattered, easily menaced by commercial and industrial changes, they have resorted with determination at each new menace to the refuge of protective organizations. Of the 17 trials for conspiracy prior to 1842 the shoemakers occasioned 9. Taking the struggles of this harassed trade, it is possible to trace industrial stages by American documents from the guild to the factory. Organizations whose records give us this picture of industrial evolution under American conditions are the "Company of Shoomakers," Boston, 1648; the "Society of the Master Cordwainers," Philadelphia, 1789; the "Federal Society of Journeymen Cordwainers," Philadelphia, 1794; the "United Beneficial Society of Journeymen Cordwainers," Philadelphia, 1835; the Knights of St. Crispin, 1868; the Boot and Shoe Workers' Union, 1895. Each of these organizations stands for a definite stage in industrial evolution, from the primitive itinerant cobbler to the modern factory; each represents an internal contention over the distribution of wealth provoked by external conditions of marketing or production; each was productive of written documents preserving to us the types of social organization that struggled for adaptation to the evolving economic series.

* From *Labor and Administration* (New York: Macmillan Co., 1913), pp. 210–64. Reprinted by permission of the publishers from *The Quarterly Journal of Economics,* Vol. 24, November 1909. Cambridge, Mass.: Harvard University Press. References are to reprints in "Documentary History of American Industrial Society," edited by Commons, Phillips, Gilmore, Sumner, and Andrews, and published by A. H. Clark Co., Cleveland, O.

1. The "Company of Shoomakers," Boston, 1648

Probably the first American guild was that of the "shoomakers of Boston," and its charter of incorporation, granted by the Colony of the Massachusetts Bay, on October 18, 1648, is the only complete American charter of its kind, of which I have knowledge.[1] The coopers were granted a similar charter on the same date. The act recited that on petition of the "shoomakers" and on account of the complaints of the "damage" which the country sustained "by occasion of bad ware made by some of that trade," they should meet and elect a master, two wardens, four or six associates, a "clarke," a sealer, a searcher, and a beadle, who should govern the trade. The "commission" was to continue in force for three years.

A contemporary reference to this incorporation of shoemakers is that of Edward Johnson, in his "Wonder-Working Providence of Sion's Savior in New England," 1651. Speaking of the material progress of the colony and the rapid division of labor, he says,[2] "All other trades have here fallen into their ranks and places, to their great advantage; especially Coopers and Shoomakers, who had either of them a Corporation granted, inriching themselves by their trades very much."

In the charter of the Boston guild, the main object of the shoemakers was the suppression of inferior workmen, who damaged the country by "occasion of bad ware." The officers were given authority to examine the shoemakers, and to secure from the courts of the colony an order suppressing any one whom they did not approve

---

[1] See Appendix to this reading.

[2] Collections of the Massachusetts Historical Society, Vol. 3, 2d series (Boston, 1826), p. 13.

"to be a sufficient workman." They were also given authority to regulate the work of those who were approved, and thus to "change and reforme" the trade and "all the affayres thereunto belonging." And they were erected into a branch of government with power to annex "reasonable pennalties" and to "levie the same by distresse."

At the same time it is evident that the colonial authorities took pains to protect the inhabitants from abuse of these powers by placing their determination "in cases of difficultie" in the hands of the judges of the county, and by allowing appeals to the county court. The two substantial reservations which the colony withholds from the company are the "inhancinge the prices of shooes, bootes, or wages," and the refusal to make shoes for inhabitants "of their owne leather for the use of themselves and families," if required by the latter.

From these reservations we are able to infer the industrial stage which the industry had reached at the time of incorporation.[3] It was the transition from the stage of the itinerant shoemaker, working up the raw material belonging to his customer in the home of the latter, to the stage of the settled shoemaker, working up his own raw material in his own shop to the order of his customer. The reservation for the protection of inhabitants is suggestive of statutes of the 15th and 16th centuries imposing penalties on guild members who refused to work in the house of their customer.[4] The fact that the colony, while granting power to reform the trade, nevertheless thought it necessary to require the shoemaker to continue that he need not go to the house of the customer, indicates the source of the abuses from which the shoemakers were endeavoring to rid themselves. The itinerant was likely to be poorly trained, and he could escape supervision by his fellow craftsmen. He was dependent on his customer who owned not only the raw material, but also the work-place, the lodging, and the food supplies of the shoemaker, leaving to the latter only the mere hand tools. He worked under the disadvantage of a new work-place for each new order, without the conveniences and equipment necessary for speedy and efficient work. He had to seek the customer, and consequently was at a disadvantage in driving a bargain. This made him, however, a serious menace to the better trained shoemaker, working in his own shop and on his own material, but waiting for the customer to come.

The Boston guild represented the union in one person of the later separated classes of merchant, master, and journeyman. Each of these classes has a different function. The merchant-function controls the kind and quality of the work, and its remuneration comes from ability to drive the bargain with the customer in the process of adjusting price to quality. The master-function, on the other hand, controls the work-place and the tools and equipment, and passes along to the journeyman the orders received from the merchant. Its remuneration comes from management of capital and labor. The journeyman-function, finally, is remunerated according to skill and quality of work, speed of output, and the amount and regularity of employment.[5]

Thus, from the standpoint of each of the functions that later were separated, did this primitive guild in self-interest set itself against the "bad ware" of the preceding itinerant stage. From the merchant standpoint the exclusion of bad ware removed a menace to remunerative prices for good ware. From the master standpoint the exclusion of the itinerant transferred the ownership of the workshop and the medium of wage payments from the consumer to the producer. From the journeyman standpoint, this exclusion of the itinerant eliminated the truck-payment of wages in the form of board and lodging by substituting piece wages for a finished product. And this control of the finished product through all the stages of production gave a double advantage to the craftsman. It transferred to him the unskilled parts of the work hitherto done by the customer's family, thus enabling him at one and the same stroke both to increase the amount of his work and to utilize the bargaining leverage of his skills to get skilled wages for unskilled work.

By this analysis we can see that when the three functions of merchant, master, and journeyman were united in the same person, the merchant-function epitomized the other two. It is the function by which the costs of production are shifted over to the consumer. The master looks to the merchant for his profits on raw material, workshop, tools, and wages, and the journeyman looks to him for the fund that will pay his wages.

Now, there is a prime consideration in the craft-guild stage that enhances the power of the merchant to shift his costs to the consumer. This

---

[3] See Bücher, "Die Entstehung der Volkswirtschaft." Citations are from Wickett's translation, "Industrial Evolution" (New York, 1901). Also Sombart, "Der Moderne Kapitalismus," Vol. 1, pp. 93–94.

[4] Bücher, "Die Entstehung," p. 169.

[5] Table 1, showing industrial stages, classes, and organizations, should be consulted in reading this and the following analysis.

TABLE 1   Industrial Stages, Classes, and Organizations of American Shoemakers

(1) Extent of Market	(2) Kind of Bargain	(3) Capital Ownership — Customer, Merchant, Employer, Laborer	(4) Industrial Classes	(5) Kind of Work	(6) Competitive Menace	(7) Protective Organizations	(8) Case
1. Itinerant	Wages	Customer-Employer; Material; Board and lodging; Journeyman; Hand tools	Farm family; Skilled helper	Skilled supervision	Family workers	None	Itinerant individuals, 1648
2. Personal	Custom order	Merchant-Master-Journeyman; Material; Hand tools; Home shop	Merchant-Master-Journeyman	"Bespoke"	"Bad Ware"	Craft guild	Boston "Company of Shoemakers," 1648
3. Local	Retail	Merchant-Master; Material; Finished stock; Short credits; Sales shop; Store-room; Journeyman; Hand tools; Home shop	Merchant-Master-Journeyman	"Shop"	"Market" work; "Advertisers"; Auctions	Retail Merchants' Association	Philadelphia "Society of the Master Cordwainers," 1789
4. Water-ways	Wholesale order	Merchant-Master; Material; Finished stock; Home shop; Journeyman; Hand tools; Home shop	Merchant-Master-Journeyman	"Order"	"Scabs"; Interstate producers	Journeymen's Society; Masters' Society	Philadelphia "Federal Society of Journeymen Cordwainers," 1794–1806
5. High-ways	Wholesale speculative	Merchant-Capitalist; Material; Finished stock; Bank credits; Warehouse; "Manufactory"; Contractor; Work shop; Journeyman; Hand tools	Merchant-Capitalist; Contractor; Journeyman	Team work	Prison; Sweatshop; "Foreigner"; "Speeding up"	Journeymen's Society; Manufacturers' Association*; Employers' Association	Philadelphia "United Beneficial Society of Journeymen Cordwainers," 1835
6. Rail	Wholesale speculative	Merchant-Jobber; Material; Finished stock; Bank credits; Warehouse; "Manufactory"; Contract Manufacturer; Work shop; Journeyman; Footpower machines	Merchant-Jobber; "Manufacturer"; Journeyman	Team work	"Green hands"; Chinese; Women; Children; Prisoners; Foreigners	Trade Union; Employers' Association	Knights of St. Crispin, 1868–72
7. World	Factory order	Manufacturer; Material; Stock; Credits; Power machinery; Factory; Laborer; None	Manufacturer; Wage-earners	Piece work	Child labor; Long hours; Immigrants; Foreign products	Industrial Union; Employers' Association; Manufacturers' Association*	Boot and Shoe Workers' Union, 1895

* The "Manufacturer's Association" is based on the merchant or price-fixing function.

is the fact that his market is a personal one, and the consumer gives his order before the goods are made. On the other hand, the bargaining power of the merchant is menaced by the incapacity of customers accurately to judge of the quality of goods, as against their capacity clearly to distinguish prices. Therefore, it is enough for the purposes of a protective organization in the custom-order stage of the industry, to direct attention solely to the quality of the product rather than the price or the wage, and to seek only to exclude bad ware and the makers of bad ware. Thus the Boston shoemakers and coopers, though enlisting the colonial courts only in the laudable purpose of redressing "the damag which the country sustaynes by occasion of bad ware," succeeded thereby in "inriching themselves by their trades very much." In this they differed from later organizations, based on the separation of classes, to whom competition appeared as a menace primarily to prices and wages, and only secondarily to quality.

II. The "Society of Master Cordwainers," 1789, and the "Federal Society of Journeymen Cordwainers," 1794, Philadelphia

The separation of classes first appears in the case of the cordwainers of Philadelphia, a century and a half later. Here appeared the first persistent discord that broke the primitive American harmony of capital and labor. So intense were the passions aroused, and so widespread was the popular irritation, that they have left their permanent record in 159 pages of "The Trial of the Boot and Shoemakers of Philadelphia, on an indictment for a combination and conspiracy to raise their wages."[6] Here we have a fairly full record of the first American association of employers and the first trade union. They were the "Society of the Master Cordwainers of the City of Philadelphia," 1789, and the "Federal Society of Journeymen Cordwainers" of the same city, organized in 1794.

Other journeymen may have had organizations prior to that time. Mr. Ethelbert Stewart[7] has, indeed, unearthed records showing that the printers in New York as early as 1776, and in Philadelphia as early as 1786, were organized for the purpose of supporting their demands by means of strikes. But these were temporary organizations, falling apart after a brief strike; whereas the cordwainers of Philadelphia in 1799 con-

ducted a strike and lockout of nine or ten weeks. To them goes the distinction of continuing their organization for at least 12 years, and aggressively driving their demands at the end of that period to the extent that the public took notice and the employers sought refuge behind the arm of the law. And it is to this junction of popular excitement and judicial interposition that we owe the record which exhibits this earliest struggle of capital and labor on American soil.

The indictment charged the journeymen with conspiring not to work except at prices and rates in excess of those "which were then used and accustomed to be paid and allowed to them"; with endeavoring "by threats, menaces and other unlawful means" to prevent others from working at less than these excessive prices; and with adopting "unlawful and arbitrary by-laws, rules and orders" and agreeing not to work for any master who should employ any workman violating such rules, and agreeing "by threats and menaces and other injuries" to prevent any workman from working for such a master.

The conspiracy and strike occurred in November 1805, and the matter came to trial in the Mayor's court in March 1806. The court permitted the witnesses to recite the entire history of this and the preceding strikes, as well as the history of the preceding combinations both of journeymen and employers. Consequently we are able to trace from the year 1789 to the year 1806 the development of the boot and shoe industry in Philadelphia, along with the accompanying separation of the interests of the journeymen from those of the masters.

I do not find any record of a guild organization like that in Boston, but there had been a "charitable society" to which both employers and journeymen belonged, and this was still in existence in 1805.[8] It was the masters who first formed themselves, in April 1789, into a separate organization. Their early constitution was laid before the court, showing the purpose of their organization to be that of "taking into consideration the many inconveniences which they labour under, for want of proper regulations among them, and to provide remedies for the same."[9] They were to "consult together for the general good of the trade, and determine upon the most eligible means to prevent irregularities in the same." They were to hold four general meetings each year, and they had a committee of seven "to meet together as often as they think neces-

[6] Doc. Hist., Vol. 3, pp. 59–248.
[7] *Bulletin of U.S. Bureau of Labor*, No. 61, p. 860.

[8] Dic. Hist., Vol. 3, p. 99.
[9] Ibid., p. 128.

sary." The society terminated in 1790, after the fifth quarterly meeting.

Apparently the masters had at that time just two kinds of "inconveniences": the competition of cheap grades of goods offered for sale at the "public market," and the competition of masters who offered bargain prices by public advertisement. This is shown by their qualifications for membership, "No person shall be elected a member of this society who offers for sale any boots, shoes, etc., in the public market of this city, or advertises the prices of his work, in any of the public papers or handbills, so long as he continues in these practices."

Evidently this society of masters was not organized as an employers' association, for nothing is said of wages or labor. It was organized by the masters merely in their function of retail merchant. The attorneys for the journeymen tried to make out that when the latter organized separately in 1794 they did so in self-defense, as against the masters' association, and they contended that in the masters' constitution were to be found "ample powers" not only to regulate prices, but also "to form a league to reduce the wages of their journeymen."[10] And although they admitted that the association had terminated in 1790, yet they held "it was a Phoenix that rose from its ashes."[11] But it was brought out clearly in evidence that the subsequent resurrections in 1799 and 1805 were provoked by the journeymen's aggressive society and were but temporary organizations. The Phoenix that kept on repeatedly rising was not the one that had disappeared. In 1789 it had been an organization of masters in their function of retail merchant. In its later stages it was an organization of masters in their function of employer. The distinction, fundamental in economics, caused a realignment in *personnel*, as will be shown presently. The early organization regulated prices and followed the vertical cleavage between producer and consumer. The later organization regulated wages and followed the horizontal cleavage between employer and laborer. In the early organization the journeyman's interest was the same as the master's. In the later ones the journeyman's interest was hostile to both consumer and master.

The foregoing considerations, as well as the transition to later stages, will become more apparent if we stop for a moment to examine the economic conditions that determine the forms of

organization. These conditions are found, not so much in the technical "instruments of production," as in the development of raw markets. The economic development of the market proceeded as follows: The cordwainer of the Boston guild made all his boots and shoes to the order of his customer, at his home shop. His market was a custom-order market, composed of his neighbors. His product, in the terminology in 1806, was a "bespoke" product. He was in his own person master, custom-merchant, and journeyman.

Next, some of the master cordwainers begin to stock up with standard sizes and shapes, for sale to sojourners and visitors at their shops. They cater to a wider market, requiring an investment of capital, not only in raw material, but also in finished products and personal credits. They give out the material to journeymen to be made up at their homes and brought back to the shop. In addition to "bespoke work," the journeyman now makes "shop work" and the master becomes retail merchant and employer. This was the stage of the industry in Philadelphia in 1789—the retail-shop stage.

Next, some of the masters seek an outside or foreign market. They carry their samples to distant merchants and take "orders" for goods to be afterwards made and delivered. They now become wholesale merchant-employers, carrying a larger amount of capital invested in material, products, and longer credits, and hiring a larger number of journeymen. In addition to "bespoke" and "shop" work the journeyman now makes "order work" for the same employer. This is the wholesale-order stage of the industry.

This was the stage in Philadelphia in 1806. At that time we find the journeyman engaged on one kind and quality of work, with the same tools and workshops, but with four different destinations for his product. Each destination was a different market, with a different level of competition, leading ultimately, after a struggle, to differences in quality. The terms employed at the time recapitulate the evolution of the industry. "Bespoke work," recalls the primitive custom market of the Boston guild, now differentiated as the market offered by the well-to-do for the highest quality of work at the highest level of competition. "Shop work" indicates the retail market of less particular customers at a wider but lower level of competition and quality. "Order work" indicates a wholesale market made possible by improved means of transportation, but on a lower level of strenuous competition and indifferent quality projected from other

<hr>

[10] Ibid., p. 166.
[11] Ibid., pp. 129, 174.

centres of manufacture. "Market work"—i.e., cheap work sold in the public market—indicates the poorest class of customers, and consequently the lowest level of competition, undermining especially the shop-work level, and to a lesser degree, the order-work level, but scarcely touching the "bespoke" level.

It was the widening of these markets with their lower levels of competition and quality, but without any changes in the instruments of production, that destroyed the primitive identity of master and journeyman cordwainers and split their community of interest into the modern alignment of employers' association and trade union. The struggle occurred, not as a result of changes in tools or methods of production, but directly as a result of changes in markets. It was a struggle on the part of the merchant-employer to require the same *minimum quality* of work for each of the markets, but lower rates of wages on work destined for the wider and lower markets. It was a struggle on the part of the journeymen to require the same *minimum wage* on work destined for each market, but with the option of a higher wage for a higher market. The conflict came over the wage and quality of work destined for the widest, lowest, and newest market. This will appear from the evidence brought out at the trial.

In the Boston guild it does not appear that there were any journeymen. Each "master" was at first a traveller, going to the homes of his customers and doing the skilled part of the journeyman's work. Next he was the all-round journeyman, not only "his own master" but, more important, his own merchant. The harmony of capital and labor was the identity of the human person. The market was direct, the orders were "bespoke."

Even in Philadelphia, in 1789, when the masters had added "shop work" and had separated themselves out as an association of retail merchants, the interests of the journeymen coincided with theirs. The journeymen were even more distressed by "market work" than were the masters. At the "market" there was no provision for holding back goods for a stated price. Everything had to be sold at once and for cash. Goods were not carried in stock. Consequently, the prices paid were exceedingly low. Job Harrison, the "scab," testified that, whereas he was regularly paid 9s. for making a pair of shoes, he could get only 3s. to 3s. 6d. on "market work." If he should quit his job by joining the "turnout" under orders from the society, he would be "driven to market work," at which he could not get half a living.[12] So also declared Andrew Dunlap and James Cummings, members of the society who had resorted to "market work" during the turnout.[13] The journeymen's society, in its contest with the masters, permitted its members to send their product to the public market, or to work for merchants who supplied that market. The society members pieced out their strike benefits and what they could get by "cobbling," with what they could get at "market work."[14] "You were at liberty to make market work, or any other work you could get, except of master workmen?" "Yes," was the answer of Job Harrison.[15] This was evidently a war measure, and not an indication that the journeymen were less hostile than the retail merchant towards the public market.

The two other kinds of work that prevailed in 1789 were "shop" work and "bespoke" work. The prices paid to the journeymen for these two kinds of work were originally the same. If they differed in quality, the difference was paid for at a specific price for extra work, as when Job Harrison got 6d. extra a pair if he would "side line" his shoes with silk.[16] But the payment for extras was the same for shop work as it was for "bespoke" work. The same workman made both, and made them in the same way, with the same tools. One of the grievances of the journeymen was the innovation attempted in 1798 by one of the employers to reduce the price for shop work. "I made some work for Mr. Ryan," said John Hayes, "and he made a similar reduction upon me, because they were to go into the shop, when he used before to give the same price for shop goods as he did for bespoke work."[17] The society demanded similar pay for similar work, whether shop or bespoke. "None are to work under the price," said Keegan, a member of the committee that met the employers: "a good workman may get more."[18]

Thus the journeymen were at one with the masters in their opposition to "market work." For the journeyman it was a menace to his wages on shop work. For the master it was a menace to his business as a retail storekeeper.

It was the third, or "export" stage of the

---

[12] Doc. Hist., Vol. 3, pp. 74, 83.
[13] Ibid., pp. 91, 96.
[14] Ibid., pp. 83, 91, 93, 96.
[15] Ibid., p. 88.
[16] Ibid., p. 94.
[17] Doc. Hist., Vol. 3, p. 121.
[18] Ibid., p. 120.

market, with its wholesale "order" work, that separated the interests of the journeyman from those of the master. Here the retail merchant adds wholesale orders to his business. . . .

On the other hand, employers who were not branching out for export work were willing to pay the wages demanded and unwilling to join the employers' association. Wm. Young had belonged to the masters' association in 1789, when it was only a retail merchants' association, and in 1805 he was still doing only bespoke and shop work. . . .

Likewise, the journeymen who did only bespoke and shop work were not inclined to stand by the union for the increase in prices. Job Harrison said,[19] "If shoes were raised to 9s. I should not be benefitted, for I had that price already, but you know it cannot be given only on customers' work." Afterwards he was asked:

Q. Did I understand you to be satisfied all this time with the wages you had been accustomed to receive from Mr. Bedford, and yet they compelled you to turn out?

A. I had as much as any man, and I could not expect more: but they did not compel me to turn out, any other way than by making a *scab* of me. . . . At length I received a note from Mr. Bedford, informing me that if I did not turn in to work I should hereafter have no more than common wages.[20]

The same was true of inferior workmen who could not command the wages demanded. These were doubtless kept on "order" work, and when the union demanded that the price on that work should be brought up to the same level as shop and bespoke work, they secretly worked "under wages." The union had a committee, "to hunt up cases of the kind," and to demand of employers that such men be discharged.[21]

Thus, as intimated above, the organization of the masters according to their employer-function, as compared with their former organization according to their merchant-function, caused a realignment of *personnel*. Both the employer and the workman on high-class custom-work "scabbed" on their respective class organizations struggling to control wholesale-order work.

The several steps in this alignment of interests will appear in the history of the journeymen's society. The first society of the journeymen was organized in 1792, two years after the master's society had dissolved. This was apparently a secret society. At any rate it did not submit a scale of prices to the employers, and did not call a strike, but merely contented itself with a "solemn" oath taken by each member to the effect, "I will support such and such wages, to the utmost of my power, etc." But a number of the journeymen secretly violated their pledge. "I know a number," testified Samuel Logan, at that time a journeyman, but now a master, "to work under wages they had solemnly promised to support. . . . I therefore requested a repeal of this affirmation, which broke up the society."[22] The society dissolved in 1792, the year of its organization.

This society, however, must have had some effect on the price of shoes, for the price which had originally been 4s. 6d.[23] had been raised to 6s. before 1794.

It was in 1794 that the permanent society was organized, which continued until the time of the prosecution in 1806.[24] It secured in that year, and again in 1796, an increase in the price of shoes, first, to something under $1, then to $1 a pair.[25] These increases, affected, however, only shop and bespoke work, so that after 1796 the "settled price" was 7s. 6d.; but Job Harrison, by making a lighter shoe with silk lining "so as to come nearer to London dress-shoes," was paid 9s. a pair.[26] At the other and lowest extreme, only "five eleven penny bits" were paid for "order work." These prices prevailed until 1806. The bespoke and shop work was said to be sold to customers at $2.75 a pair, but the order work was sold to retailers at $1.80 a pair.[27] Thus it was that for nominally the same quality of shoe the journeymen's society was able almost to double their wages on the custom and retail work, but had brought about an increase of only a few cents on the wholesale-order work. In other words, the employer as retail merchant gave to his employees an advance out of the advanced retail price of his goods, but as a wholesale merchant he was not able to give a similar advance. Naturally the better class of workmen gravitated towards the custom and retail work, and the inferior workmen towards the wholesale work so that what was originally the same quality of work, and nominally remained the same, became eventually different in quality. . . .

Notice now the characteristic features of the

---

[19] Ibid., p. 82.
[20] Ibid., p. 84.
[21] Ibid., p. 92.

[22] Ibid., p. 93.
[23] Ibid., p. 118.
[24] Ibid., pp. 174, 217–18.
[25] Ibid., pp. 72, 93.
[26] Ibid., pp. 74, 86.
[27] Ibid., p. 86.

retail and wholesale-order stages of the industry. The master workman at the retail stage has added a stock of finished goods to his business of custom work. This requires a shop on a business street accessible to the general public, with correspondingly high rents. It involves also a certain amount of capital tied up in short credits and acounts with customers. In his shop he has a stock of raw material, besides finished and partly finished goods. The merchant-function has thus become paramount, and has drawn with it the master-function. The two functions have equipped themselves with capital—merchant's capital in the form of finished stock, retail store, and short credits; employer's capital in the form of raw material undergoing manufacture by workmen under instructions. The journeymen are left with only their hand tools and their home workshop.

Thus the retail market has separated the laborer from the merchant. Labor's outlook now is solely for wages. The merchant's outlook is for quality and prices. But the separation is not antagonism. The employer-function is as yet at a minimum. Profit is not dependent on reducing wages so much as increasing prices. Indeed, the journeymen are able almost to double their wages without a strike, and the merchants pass the increase along to the customers.

But it is different when the merchant reaches out for wholesale orders. Now he adds heavy expenses for solicitation and transportation. He adds a storeroom and a larger stock of goods. He holds the stock a longer time and he gives long and perilous credits. At the same time he meets competitors from other centres of manufacture, and cannot pass along his increased expenses. Consequently the wage-bargain assumes importance, and the employer-function comes to the front. Wages are reduced by the merchant as employer on work destined for the wholesale market. The conflict of capital and labor begins.

Before we can fully appreciate the significance and the economic interpretation of these revolutionizing facts, we shall need to consider the next succeeding stage, that of the merchant-capitalist.

III. The "United Beneficial Society of Journeymen Cordwainers," Philadelphia 1835

The organizations of masters and journeymen of 1805 continued more or less until 1835. Then a new and more revolutionary stage of the industry is ushered in. This time it is the merchant-capitalist, who subdues both the master and the journeyman through his control of the new widespread market of the South and West. We read of his coming in the address "to the Journeymen Cordwainers of the City and County of Philadelphia," issued by the 200 members of the "United Beneficial Society of Journeymen Cordwainers."[28] This organization took the lead in bringing together the several trade societies of Philadelphia into the Trades' Union, and in conducting the first great general 10-hour strike in this country. The reasons for their aggressiveness may be inferred from their "Address." They recite that the wages of $2.75 formerly paid for boots have fallen to $1.12½; that their earnings of $9 to $10 a week have fallen to $4 to $6; that, in order to earn such wages they must work, in many instances, 14 hours a day; and that other skilled tradesmen are earning $8 to $12 dollars a week, often "only working 10 hours a day." This depression, they explain, has occurred since "a few years ago." It began with an "unfortunate" cooperative experiment of the journeymen in "opening shops for the manufacture of cheap goods" for the purpose of winning a strike. It was intensified by the appearance of the merchant-capitalist. We are told that

"The cunning men of the East" have come to our city, and having capital themselves, or joining with those who have had, have embarked in our business, and realized large fortunes, by reducing our wages, making large quantities of work and selling at reduced price, while those who had served their time at the trade, and had an anxious desire to foster and cherish its interests, have had to abandon the business or enter into the system of manufacturing largely [i.e., on a large scale] in order to save themselves from bankruptcy.

Then they explain how this has come about "without any positive reduction of our wages."

The answer is plain and simple—by making cheap work, triple the quantity has to be made to obtain a living; this produces, at dull seasons, a surplus of work in the market; and these *large* manufacturers, taking advantage of the times, have compelled their journeyman to make the work so far superior to the manner in which it was originally made for the wages given, that it is now brought into competition with first-rate work. This again lessens the quantity of first-rate work made, and the journeymen, formerly working for employers who gave them $2.75 for each pair of boots made, are forced to seek employment of the very men who had ruined their business.

The dubious position of the employers also, at this stage of the industry, is shown by the

[28] *Pennsylvanian*, April 4, 1835; Doc. Hist., Vol. 6, pp. 21–27.

action of "a large adjourned meeting of the ladies'-shoe dealers and manufacturers." They unanimously adopted a preamble and resolution presented by a committee appointed at a previous meeting reciting that,

Whereas, the laboring portion of this community have made a general strike for what they consider their just rights, knowing that if they were longer to permit the growing encroachments of capital upon labor, they would soon be unable to make any resistance . . . we feel a desire to aid and encourage them in their effort to obtain an adequate compensation for their labor. . . . Knowing that the pittance hitherto earned by them is entirely insufficient for their support, we do hereby agree to and comply with their demands generally, and pledge ourselves to do all in our power to support and sustain them. . . . Believing also that a trifling advance in the price of shoes would scarcely be felt by general society . . . we will agree to be governed hereafter by a list of prices for our work, which will render our business uniform and permanent.[29]

Nine months later these employers were forced by the exactions of the union and their inability to control the merchant-capitalist to take the other side of the question, organizing as an employers' association and making a determined fight against the union.[30]

At this stage of the industry we have reached the market afforded by highway and canal, as well as ocean and river. The banking system has expanded, enabling the capitalist to convert customers' credit into bank credits and to stock up a surplus of goods in advance of actual orders. The market becomes speculative, and the warehouse of the wholesale-merchant-master takes the place of the store-room of the retail capitalist. The former master becomes the small manufacturer or contractor, selling his product to the wholesale-manufacturer, the merchant-capitalist. The latter has a wide range of option in his purchase of goods, and consequently in his ability to compel masters and journeymen to compete severely against each other. He can have his shoes made in distant localities. The cordwainers relate[31] that

. . . there are many employers of this city who have made off of the labor of journeymen a liberal fortune, and now refuse to accede to the justice of our demands, and in order to evade the same they are preparing materials (in this city) in order to send them into the towns of the Eastern states (where living and labor are cheaper and workmanship not so good) to get the same made into shoes, then to be brought here and sold for Philadelphia manufacture.

The merchant-capitalist can also discover new fields for the manufacture of cheap work, and for the first time we read of the competition of convict labor. The cordwainers publish an advertisement[32] warning their members against a firm who "are now getting work manufactured by convicts in the Eastern Penitentiary at less than one-half what our bill of rates call for. . . ." And one of their resolutions asserts that "shoemaking is found to be the most convenient and most lucrative employment of convicts, consequently almost *one-half* of the convicts in our different penitentiaries are taught shoemaking."[33]

The merchant-capitalist has also the option of all the different methods of manufacture and shop organization. He can employ journeymen at his warehouse as cutters, fitters, and pattern makers; he can employ journeymen at their homes to take out material and bring back finished work; but, more characteristic of his methods, he can employ small contractors, the specialized successors of the master cordwainer, who in turn employ one to a dozen journeymen, and by division of labor and "team work" introduce the sweating system.[34]

Through these different methods of manufacture we are able to see how it is that the merchant-capitalist intensifies and even creates the antagonism of "capital and labor." He does this by forcing the separation of functions and classes a step further than it had been forced in the wholesale-order stage. First, he takes away from the retail merchant his wholesale-order business. He buys and sells in large quantities; he assembles the cheap products of prison labor, distant localities, and sweatshops; he informs himself of markets, and beats down the charges for transportation. Thus he takes the wholesale business and leaves to the merchant the retail trade.

Second, he drives off from the retail merchant his employer-function. The retail merchant can no longer afford to employ journeymen on "shop"

[29] *Pennsylvanian,* June 15, 1835; Doc. Hist., Vol. 6, pp. 27–28.

[30] *Pennsylvanian,* March 28, 1836; Doc. Hist., Vol. 6, pp. 32–35.

[31] *Pennsylvanian,* June 20, 1835; Doc. Hist., Vol. 6, pp. 29–30.

[32] *Pennsylvanian,* Sept. 5, 1835.

[33] *Pennsylvanian,* Oct. 1, 1835.

[34] The term "manufactory," as distinguished from "factory," occurs in the merchant-capitalist stage to indicate the combined warehouse and place of employment where material is prepared to be taken out by journeymen or contractors. It is the "inside shop" of the ready-made clothing trade, the contractor's shops being known as "outside shops." See Commons, "Trade Unionism and Labor Problems," p. 316 (1905), article on "sweating system."

work, because he can purchase more cheaply of the merchant-capitalist. A few years ago, say the cordwainers in their "address," "such an article as boots was then unknown in the Market street shops: The manufacturing of that article being confined exclusively to those, who having served an apprenticeship to the business, knew best its value."[35]

Thus the merchant-capitalist strips the former merchant-master both of his market and his journeymen. The wholesale market he takes to himself; the journeymen he hands over to a specialist in wage-bargaining. This specialist is no longer known as "master,"—he takes the name of "boss,"[36] or employer. He is partly a workman, having come up through the trade, like the master, and continuing to work alongside his men. He is an employer without capital, for he rents his workshop, and the merchant-capitalist owns the raw material and the journeymen own the tools. His profits are not those of the capitalist, neither do they proceed from his ability as a merchant, since the contract-prices he gets are dictated by the merchant-capitalist. His profits come solely out of wages and work. He organizes his workmen in teams, with the work subdivided in order to lessen dependence on skill and to increase speed of output. He plays the less skilled against the more skilled, the speedy against the slow, and reduces wages while enhancing exertion. His profits are "sweated" out of labor, his shop is the "sweat-shop," he the "sweater."

Thus the merchant-capitalist, with his widespread, wholesale-speculative market, completes the separation and specializes the functions of the former homogeneous craftsman. The merchant-function, which was the first to split off from the others, is now itself separated into three parts—custom merchant, retail merchant, wholesale merchant—corresponding to the three levels of market competition. The journeyman-function is now segregated on two levels of competition, the highest level of custom work and the lowest level menaced by prison and sweatshop work. The employer-function, the last to split off, makes its first appearance as a separate factor on the lowest level of market competition. Evidently the wide extension of the market in the hands of the merchant-capitalist is a cataclysm in the position of the journeyman. By a desperate effort of organization he struggles to raise himself back to his original level. His merchant-employers at first sympathize with him and endeavor to pass over to their customers his just demand for a higher wage. But they soon are crushed between the level of prices and the level of wages. From the position of a merchants' association striving to hold up prices, they shift to that of an employers' association endeavoring to keep down wages. The result of these struggles of protective organizations will appear when we analyze more closely the economic forces under which they operate. These forces turn on the nature of the bargain, the period and risk of investment and the level of the competitive menace.

* * * * *

We have already seen the cumulative effect in 1806 and 1835, of these three sets of circumstances in dragging down the entire body of workmen. We now proceed to notice the resistance of protective organizations and their ultimate effect in bringing about a segregation of work and workers on non-competing levels.

This may be seen by following again the movement of wages in Philadelphia from 1789 to 1835, on the different classes of work. Prior to 1792, on common boots, the journeyman's wages were $1.40 a pair on both bespoke and shop work. In the course of 15 years the price advanced to $2.75, and this price was paid for both bespoke and shop work, but a concession of $0.25 was made on wholesale-order work, bringing that price to $2.50. In 1835 the price had fallen to $1.12½ for wholesale work, while retail work had dropped out or had come down to the same price as wholesale work, leaving custom work at a higher figure. In the course of this movement, the better class of workmen restricted themselves as much as possible to custom work, and the quality of this kind of work was improved. On the other hand, the wholesale-order and the wholesale-speculative work tended throughout to fall into the hands of inferior workmen, and this brought about an inferiority in quality. These inferior goods, made by inferior workmen, became more and more a menace to the superior goods and the superior journeymen, both on account of the lower levels of the marginal producers and on account of the smaller demand relatively for the production of superior goods.

Herein was the necessity of protective organi-

[35] *Pennsylvanian*, April 4, 1835; Doc. Hist., Vol. 6, p. 22.

[36] The first use that I have found of the Dutch word "bos," meaning manager of a group of workmen, is in the organ of the New York Trades Union, *The Man*, May 30, 1834; Doc. Hist., Vol. 6, p. 92. It was spelled with one "s," though the obstinacy of the printer of the "Documentary History" finally succeeded in using two in the reprint.

zations. In order that these organizations might succeed, it was just as necessary to set up protection against inferior goods as against low wages. In the guild stage of the industry, when the three functions of journeyman, master, and workman were united in one person, the protection sought was against the "bad ware" made by some of the trade. By "suppressing" those who made bad ware, the customers would be compelled to turn to those who were "sufficient" workmen and made good ware. Since the bargain was a separate one for each article, so that the price could be adjusted to the quality before the work was done, nothing more was needed on the part of the guild members for the purpose of "inriching themselves by their trades very much."

But in the later stages of the industry, the merchant-function, and afterwards the employer-function, were separated from the journeyman-function. It is the special function of the merchant to watch over and guard the quality of the work, because his bargain with the consumer is an adjustment of the price to the quality demanded. The journeyman's function is simply that of making the kind and quality of goods ordered by the merchant. The merchant, in his function as employer, gives these orders to the journeyman, and consequently, when the employer-function is separated from the journeyman-function, the employer, as the representative of the merchant, attends to the quality of the work. In this way the journeyman has lost control over quality and is forced to adapt his quality to his price, instead of demanding a price suited to his quality. So, when he forms his protective organization, his attention is directed mainly to the compensation side of the bargain. In proportion as the quality of his work depends on his rate of pay, he directly controls the quality, but the primary purpose of his organization is to control the rate of pay. This he does, first, by demanding the same minimum rate of pay for all market destinations of the same kind of work. It was this demand that forced the alignment of classes and drove the sympathetic merchant over into the hostile employers' association. The employer could yield if he confined himself to the narrow field of the "bespoke" market, but not if he was menaced by the wider field of the wholesale market. On this account it was possible in the retail-shop stage for the interests of employer and workmen to be harmonious. But the employer could not yield in the merchant-capitalist stage, on that part of the field menaced by prison and sweatshop labor. Consequently, the outcome of the strikes of 1835 was the differentiation

of the market into two noncompeting levels, the higher level of custom and high-grade shop work, controlled more or less by the cordwainers' societies for the next 25 years[37] and the lower level of inferior work controlled by prison and sweatshop competition.[38]

IV. Knights of St. Crispin, 1868

We come now to an entirely different step in the progress of industrial stages. Hitherto, the only change requiring notice has been that produced by the extension of the market and the accompanying credit system. These changes were solely external. The next change is internal. Prior to 1837 there had been scarcely a hundred inventions affecting the tools used by the cordwainer. All of these may be described as "devices" rather than machines. Even as late as 1851 all of the labor in the manufacture of shoes was hand labor. In 1852, the sewing machine was adapted to the making of uppers, but this did not affect the journeyman cordwainer because the sewing of uppers had been the work of women. Even the flood of inventions that came into use during the decade of the 50s were aids to the journeyman rather than substitutes for his skill. Indeed, some of them probably operated to transfer the work of women to men, for they required greater physical strength and endurance in order to develop their full capacity. Whether operated by foot power or merely facilitating the work of his hands, they were essentially shop tools and not factory machines. Such were the tin patterns for cutting, the stripper and sole-cutter, adjustable lasts, levellers, skivers, and the machines for heel making, lasting, and sandpapering. Quite different were the pegging machine, introduced in 1857, and especially the McKay sole-sewing machine, introduced in 1862. These usurped not only the highest skill of the workman, but also his superior physique. The McKay machine did in 1 hour what the journey-

[37] Freedley, E. T., "Philadelphia and Its Manufactories," p. 187, says in 1858: "Making men's wear and making women's wear are distinct branches. . . . The Men's men and Women's men, as the workmen are distinguished, have separate organizations, and neither know nor mingle with each other."

[38] "In addition to these there are a large number whose operations, though in the aggregate important, cannot easily be ascertained. They are known by a term more expressive than euphonious, 'garret bosses' who employ from 1 to 12 men each; and having but little capital, make boots and shoes in their own rooms, and sell them to jobbers and retailers in small quantities at low rates for cash. One retailer, who sells $20,000 worth per annum, buys three-fourths of his stock from these makers." Freedley, p. 188.

man did in 80. These machines were quickly followed by others, either machines newly invented or old ones newly adapted, but all of them belted up to steam. The factory system, aided by the enormous demand of government for its armies, came suddenly forth, though it required another 15 years to reach perfection. It was at the middle of this transition period, 1868 to 1872, that the Knights of St. Crispin appeared and flourished beyond anything theretofore known in the history of American organized labor. Its membership mounted to 40,000 or 50,000 whereas the next largest unions of the time claimed only 10,000 to 12,000. It disappeared as suddenly as it had arisen, a tumultuous, helpless protest against the abuse of machinery. For it was not the machine itself that the Crispins were organized to resist, but the substitution of "green hands" for journeymen in the operation of the machines. There was but one law which they bound themselves by constitutions, rituals, oaths, and secret confederacy to enforce and to support each other in enforcing: refusal to teach "green hands" except by consent of the organization. This at least was the object of the national organization. When local unions once were established, they took into their own hands the cure of other ills, and their strikes and lockouts were as various as the variety of shops and factories in which they were employed. The Knights of St. Crispin were face to face with survivals from all of the preceding stages of industrial evolution, as well as the lusty beginnings of the succeeding stages. They were employed in custom shops, in retail and wholesale-order shops, in the shops of the merchant-capitalist and his contractors, in the factories of the manufacturer-capitalist. A comparison of the objects of their strikes reveals the overlapping of stages. All of their strikes turned directly or indirectly on two issues, resistance to wage reductions and refusal to teach "green hands." The wage strikes took place mainly in the shops of the merchant-capitalist, the "green hand" strikes in the factories.[39] The merchant-capitalist was forced by the competition of the manufacturer, either to become a manufacturer himself (or to purchase from the manufacturer), or to cut the wages of his journeymen and the prices paid to his contractors. Neither the journeyman's devices nor his foot power machines yielded a sufficient

increase of output to offset his wage reductions. His aggravation was the more intense in that the wage reductions occurred only on shop work and not on custom work. The anomaly of different prices for the same grade of work, which had showed itself with the extension of markets, was now still more exaggerated and more often experienced under the competition of factory products. Even prison labor and Chinese labor were not cheap enough to enable the merchant-capitalist to compete with the product of "green hands" and steam power.

The factory succeeded also in producing a quality of work equal or even superior to that produced by the journeyman. Consequently its levelling agencies reached upwards to all but the topmost of the noncompeting levels on which the journeymen had succeeded in placing themselves, and brought them down eventually to its own factory level. The Grand Lodge of the Knights of St. Crispin was the protest of workmen whose skill of work, quality of product, and protective unions had for a generation preceding saved for themselves the higher levels of the merchant-capitalist system against the underwash of prison and sweatshop competition. It was their protest against the new menace of cheap labor and "green hands" utilized by the owners of steam power and machinery. . . . Suffice it to note that in the shoe industry the factory system was established in substantially its present form in the early part of the 80s; that detailed piecework has taken the place of team-work and hand-work; that the last vestige of property-right has left the worker; that the present form of labor organization, the Boot and Shoe Workers' Union, has endeavored, since 1895, to bring together all classes of employees, men and women, in a single industrial union rather than a partial trade union; and that the two classes of protective organizations have asserted their political power for protection against low levels of competition, the merchant-manufacturer against free trade in foreign products, the wage-earner against foreign immigrants, prison labor, child labor, and long hours of labor.

APPENDIX

"Company of Shoomakers," Boston, 1648[40]

Vppon the petition of the shoomakers of Boston, & in consideration of the complaynts which haue bin made of the damag which the

[39] For the detailed study upon which this brief summary of the Knights of St. Crispin is based, I am indebted to Mr. D. D. Lescohier, member of my research group. See Bulletin No. 355 of the University of Wisconsin, Economics and Political Science Series, Vol. 7, No. 1.

[40] "The records of the Colony of the Massachusetts Bay in New England," Vol. 3, p. 132.

country sustaynes by occasion of bad ware made by some of that trade, for redresse hereof, its ordred, & the Court doth hereby graunt libtie & powre vnto Richard Webb, James Euerill, Robt Turner, Edmund Jackson, & the rest of the shoomakers inhabiting & howskeepers in Boston, or the greatest number of them, vppō due notice giuen to the rest, to assemble & meete together in Boston, at such time & times as they shall appoynt, who beinge so assembled, they, or the greater number of them, shall haue powre to chuse a master, & two wardens, with fowre or six associats, a clarke, a sealer, a searcher, & a beadle, with such other officers as they shall find nessessarie; & these officers & ministers, as afforesd, every yeare or oftener, in case of death or departure out of this jurisdiction, or remoueall for default, &c., which officers & ministers shall each of them take an oath sutable to theire places before the Gounor or some of the magists, the same beinge pscribed or allowed by this Court; & the sd shoomakers beinge so assembled as before, or at any other meettinge or assembly to be appoynted from time to time by the master & wardens, or master or wardens with two of the associats, shall haue power to make orders for the well gouerninge of theire company, in the mannaginge of their trade & all the affayres therevnto belonging, & to change & reforme the same as occasion shall require & to anex reasonable pennalties for the breach of the same; provided, that none of theire sd orders, nor any alteration therein, shalbe of force before they shalbe pvsed & allowed of by the Court of that county, or by the Court of Assistants. And for the better executing such orders, the sd master & wardens, or any two of them with 4 or 6 associats, or any three of them, shall haue power to heare & determine all offences agaynst any of theire sd orders, & may inflict the pennalties pscribed as aforesd, & assesse fines to the vallew of forty shillings or vnder for one offence, & the clarke shall giue warrent in writinge to the beadle to leuie the same, who shall haue power

therevppon to leuie the same by distresse, as is vsed in other cases; & all the sd fines & forfeitures shalbe imployd to the benefit of the sd company of shoomakers in generall, & to no other vse. And vppon the complaynt to the sd master & wardens, or theire atturny or advocate, in the County Court, of any pson or psons who shall vse the art or trade of a shoomaker, or any pt thereof, not beinge approused of by the officers of ye sd shoomakers to be a sufficient workman, the sd Court shall haue power to send for such psons, & suppresse them; provided also, that the prioritie of theire graunt shall not giue them precedency of other companies that may be graunted; but that poynt to be determined by this Court when there shalbe occasiō thereof; provided also, that no vnlawfull combination be made at any time by the sd company of shoomakers for inhancinge the prices of shooes, bootes, or wages, whereby either or owne people may suffer; provided also, that in cases of dificultie, the sd officers & associats doe not pceede to determine the cause but by the advice of the judges of that county; provided, that no shoomaker shall refuse to make shooes for any inhabitant, at reasonable rates, of theire owne leather, for the vse of themselues & families, only if they be required therevnto; provided, lastly, that if any pson shall find himselfe greiued by such excessiue fines or other illegal pceedinges of the sd officers, he may complayne thereof at the next Court of that county, who may heare & determine the cause. This commission to continue & be of force for three yeares, & no longer, vnles the Court shall see cause to continue the same.

The same comission, verbatim, with the same libtie & power for the same ends, vpon the like grounds is giuen vnto Thomas Venner, John Millum, Samuel Bidfeild, James Mattocks, Wm. Cutter, Bartholomew Barlow, & the rest of the coops of Boston & Charlestowne, for the pventing abuses in theire trade. To continue only for three years, as the former, mutatis mutandis.

11. The Knights of Labor and the Trade Unions, 1878–1886*

Gerald N. Grob†

The year 1886 was destined to be a crucial one in the history of the American labor movement. The eight-hour crusade, the numerous strikes, the Haymarket bomb, the entrance of workingmen into the political arena at the state and national levels, and the mushroom growth of labor organizations all contributed to the agitation and excitement of the year. Yet the importance of these events was overshadowed by a development that was to have such far-reaching implications that it would determine the future of the labor movement for the succeeding half century. That development was the declaration of war by the trade unions against the reform unionism of the Knights of Labor.

The struggle between the Knights and the other unions represented a class of two fundamentally opposing ideologies. The Knights of Labor, on the one hand, grew out of the reform and humanitarian movements of ante-bellum America, and was the direct descendant, through the National Labor Union, of the labor reform tradition of the Jacksonian era. Banking on the leveling influence of technological change, its leaders sought to organize the entire producing class into a single irresistible coalition that would work toward the abolition of the wage system and the establishment of a new society. "We do not believe," a high official of the Knights remarked, "that the emancipation of labor will come with increased wages and a reduction in the hours of labor; we must go deeper than that, and this matter will not be settled until the wage system is abolished."[1] The leaders of the Knights

therefore emphasized education and cooperation, and they bitterly opposed their constituents' participation in such affairs as the Southwest and stockyards strikes of 1886, as well as the very popular eight-hour movement of that same year.

The reform ideology of the Knights, in turn, had an important impact upon the development of its structure, which followed a heterogeneous rather than a homogeneous pattern. Minimizing the utility of organization along trade lines, the Order emphasized instead the grouping of all workers, regardless of craft, into a single body.[2] Highest priority therefore was given to the mixed local assembly, which included all workers irrespective of their trade or degree of skill. Neither a trade, plant, nor industrial union, the mixed assembly could never be more than a study or debating group. Including many diverse elements (even employers), it could not adapt itself to meet the problems of a specific industry or trade. The mixed assembly might agitate for reform or participate in politics, but it could never become the collective bargaining representative of its members.

Given the predominance of the mixed over the trade local, the structure of the Knights inevitably developed along geographical rather than jurisdictional lines, and the district assembly, which included mixed as well as trade locals,

* From *Journal of Economic History*, Vol. 18, June 1958, pp. 176–92.

† Gerald N. Grob is on the faculty of Clark University.

[1] *The Laster*, Vol. 4 (November 15, 1891), p. 3.

[2] For the antitrade unionism of the national leadership of the Knights see the *Journal of United Labor*, Vol. 1 (June 15, 1880), p. 21 (hereinafter cited as *JUL*), Knights of Labor, *Proceedings of the General Assembly*, 1880, p. 169; 1884, pp. 716–17; 1897, p. 37 (hereinafter cited as K. of L., *GA Proc.*); Terence V. Powderly, *Thirty Years of Labor; 1859 to 1889* (Columbus: Excelsior Publishing House, 1889), pp. 155–56; Powderly Letter Books, Catholic University of America, Washington, D.C.; Powderly to James Rogers, December 19, 1892; Gerald N. Grob, "Terence V. Powderly and the Knights of Labor," *Mid-America*, Vol. 39 (January 1957), pp. 41–42.

became the most characteristic form of organization. The highest governmental body of the Knights—the General Assembly—was not intended as a medium for collective bargaining. Indeed, its very inclusiveness precluded such a possibility.

The trade unions, on the other hand, rejected the broad reform goals of the Knights, emphasizing instead higher wages, shorter hours, and job control. Such objectives were clearly incompatible with an organizational structure such as that developed by the Knights. Eschewing the multitrade local that had been so prevalent during the 1860s and was being perpetuated by the Order, the trade unions began to stress the craft-industrial form of organization both at the local and national levels. A relative scarcity of labor, together with a rapidly expanding economy, had created a favorable environment for the trade unions. Gambling on the hope that the rise of a national market made organization along trade rather than geographical lines more effective, union leaders chose to concentrate upon the task of organizing the workers along trade lines into unions designed for collective bargaining rather than social reform.[3]

Therefore, given the inherent differences in ideology and structure, the conflict between the Knights and the trade unions was, if not inevitable, certainly not an unexpected or surprising development.[4] Undoubtedly the antagonistic personalities of partisans on both sides hastened an open rift.[5] Yet the hostilities between the Knights and the trade unions cannot be explained solely in terms of personalities, for the conflict was not simply a struggle for power between two rivals. It was a clash between two fundamentally different ideologies—with the future of the labor movement at stake.

I

The contest between trade unionists and reformers for control of the labor movement developed on two planes. Commencing first as an internal struggle within the Knights, it eventually expanded and soon involved the national unions. Within the Knights the struggle revolved around the unresolved question as to which form of organization best met working-class necessities. On the surface the issue of mixed versus trade locals was simply a structural problem. In reality, however, the differences between the two forms indicated the existence of a fundamental cleavage in ultimate objectives, for the mixed assembly could be utilized only for reform or political purposes, while the trade assembly was generally a collective bargaining organization.

Although the national leadership of the Knights regarded the mixed assembly as the ideal type of unit, a large proportion of its local assemblies were trade rather than mixed. The first local, composed of garment cutters, was strictly craft, and remained so to the end. Most of the other locals that followed were also trade assemblies.[6] On January 1, 1882, according to the *Journal of United Labor*, there were 27 working districts and over 400 local assemblies. Of the latter, 318 were trade and only 116 were mixed. Thirteen additional districts, not functioning, had 53 trade and 87 mixed locals, attesting to the relative instability of the mixed form of organization. Of the 135 locals attached directly to the General Assembly, 67 were trade and 68 were mixed.[7]

Despite the wide latitude given them to organize trade local assemblies, the trade element within the Knights nevertheless found it difficult to function efficiently. Local trade assemblies, no matter how inclusive in their particular area, were often ineffective when operating in a market that was regional or national rather than local in character. So long as employers could find a ready supply of nonunion labor elsewhere, efforts at collective bargaining by locals would be ineffective. The only solution lay in national organization, and the trade exponents within the Knights pressed for national and regional trade districts that would transcend the limited geographical area normally encompassed by the local or district assembly.

The General Assembly, therefore, meeting in January 1879, authorized the establishment of autonomous national trade districts within the framework of the Knights. But only nine months later the Assembly completely reversed itself by

[3] See Lloyd Ulman, *The Rise of the National Trade Union* (Cambridge: Harvard University Press, 1955), pp. 348–77.

[4] See Carroll D. Wright, "An Historical Sketch of the Knights of Labor," *Quarterly Journal of Economics*, Vol. 1 (January 1887), p. 155; *Cigar Makers' Official Journal*, Vol. 11 (June 1886), p. 6; *The Carpenter*, Vol. 6 (February 1886), p. 4 (April 1886), p. 4.

[5] Norman J. Ware emphasized the importance of conflicting personalities. Ware, *The Labor Movement in the United States, 1860–95* (New York: D. Appleton and Co., 1929), pp. 162–63, et passim.

[6] See Wright, "An Historical Sketch Knights of Labor," p. 146.

[7] Ware, *Labor Movement*, p. 158. The statistics on trade locals in the Knights are unsatisfactory and misleading since many of them admitted workers belonging to different trades.

declaring that trade locals were "contrary to the spirit and genius of the Order," and it returned exclusive jurisdiction over all locals to the district assembly of their area.[8]

In December 1881, however, the Federation of Organized Trades and Labor Unions, predecessor of the American Federation of Labor (AF of L), held its first convention. Of the 107 delegates present, no less than 50 came from the Knights.[9]

The following September the General Assembly heard the secretary of the Knights warn that trade sentiment was growing rapidly. "Many trade unions have also written me," he remarked, "stating that they were seriously meditating the propriety of coming over to us in a body, freely expressing the opinion that their proper place was in our Order."[10] To prevent any mass exodus from the Order to the rival Federation, and also to recruit members from the trade unions, the General Assembly enacted legislation authorizing and encouraging the formation of national and regional trade districts. This move was reaffirmed and even extended at the meetings of the General Assembly in 1884 and 1886.[11]

While permissible, at least in theory, the establishment of trade districts was not a simple matter. The basic philosophy of the Knights militated against organization along craft lines, and the establishment of autonomous trade units within the framework of the Order aroused strong opposition. "I do not favor the establishment of any more National Trade Districts," Terence V. Powderly, head of the Knights from 1879 to 1893, told the General Assembly in 1885, "they are a step backward."[12] Other reform unionists, echoing Powderly's sentiments, charged that trade districts violated the fundamental principles of the Knights.[13] Holding tenaciously to their reform concepts, the leaders of the Knights were insistent in their demands that organization should not proceed along trade lines.

Applicants for trade districts therefore could not always be certain that charters would be granted them, even though they had met all the formal requirements. In some cases charters were granted without any questions. Window Glass Workers' Local Assembly (L.A.) 300 was chartered as a national trade district at a time when such districts were contrary to the laws of the Knights, and the telegraphers were organized nationally in 1882 as District Assembly (D.A.) 45. For a while these two were the only national districts, although before 1886 there were two district assemblies composed of miners, five of shoemakers, three of railroad employees, and one each of printers, plumbers, leather workers, government employees, and streetcar employees. Between 1883 and 1885 the General Assembly went on record as favoring the establishment of trade districts of shoemakers, plate-glass workers, and plumbers.[14] On the other hand, after sanctioning the formation of builders' districts in 1882, it refused the following year to permit these districts to be represented on the General Executive Board.[15] Even while passing legislation authorizing trade districts, the General Assembly refused to allow woodworkers, cigarmakers, and carpenters to organize trade districts. Furthermore, it passed a resolution stating that no charter for a trade district would be granted unless the applicants could demonstrate to the satisfaction of the General Executive Board that the craft could not be effectively organized under the system of mixed or territorial districts.[16] The attitude of the board, however, was often conditioned by the antitrade unionism of its officers. In 1886, for example, it refused to sanction the request of five building trade locals that they be permitted to withdraw from D.A. 66 and organize their own district. At the same time it empowered a New Hampshire local to change from a trade to a mixed assembly.[17]

Trade units, generally speaking, were authorized usually in efforts to attract workers to join the Knights. Thus the International Trunkmakers Union came into the Order as a trade district.[18] Once inside, however, workers found it considera-

[8] K. of L., *GA Proc.*, January 1879, pp. 69–70, 72; September 1879, pp. 98, 129.

[9] Federation of Organized Trades, *Proceedings*, 1881, pp. 7–9 (1905 reprinting).

[10] K. of L., *GA Proc.*, 1882, pp. 296–98. See also the statement of the General Executive Board in ibid., p. 334.

[11] Ibid., pp. 364, 368; pp. 705–7, 776; 1886, pp. 265–66.

[12] Ibid., 1885, p. 25.

[13] See the *JUL*, Vol. 7 (June 25, 1886), p. 2100; *John Swinton's Paper*, September 6, 1885; K. of L., *GA Proc.*, 1884, pp. 716–17.

[14] K. of L., *GA Proc.*, 1883, pp. 438, 443, 502; 1884, p. 787; 1885, pp. 127, 133; *JUL*, Vol. 5 (December 10, 1884), p. 856.

[15] K. of L., *GA Proc.*, 1882, pp. 325, 347; 1883, pp. 445, 498.

[16] Ibid., 1882, pp. 311, 351; 1883, pp. 439–40, 498, 502.

[17] Ibid., 1886, pp. 126–27.

[18] Ibid., 1883, p. 506; 1884, p. 619. This was also the case in the affiliation of the harness workers, *JUL*, Vol. 4 (June 1883), p. 511; (July 1883), pp. 520–21. The Knights also aided the barbers, horse railway men, miners, railway men, and ax makers in attempts to get them to join.

bly more difficult to secure trade charters. After affiliating in 1882, to cite one case, the plumbers later left the Knights when they encountered difficulty in obtaining a charter for a national trade district, and they established the International Association of Journeymen Plumbers, Steam Fitters, and Gas Fitters.[19]

The hostility of the national leadership of the Knights was not the sole obstacle to the formation of trade units. Mixed and territorial districts, which were first in the field and were already established as functioning organizations, were also antagonistic toward trade districts. If the latter were formed, not only would a mixed district suffer a loss of membership to a trade district, but it would also surrender its absolute jurisdiction over a given territorial area, since the autonomous trade district would exercise control over the entire craft in that area.

The General Assembly and the General Executive Board often supported the mixed and territorial districts in disputes with trade districts. Frequently the district's consent was a prerequisite to secession and the establishment of a trade district. This consent was not easily obtained. In 1886 D.A. 30 of Massachusetts turned down an application by four of its locals for permission to withdraw and form a national trade assembly of rubber workers.[20] While the General Assembly supported a district court decision that members of trade locals could not be compelled to join mixed locals, the General Executive Board refused to force trade members of mixed locals to transfer to trade assemblies.[21]

Even after obtaining a charter, trade districts encountered difficulties with the mixed district in their areas. Dual jurisdiction often led to friction, though in theory the system of mixed and trade districts appeared perfectly harmonious and compatible. For example, D.A. 64 of New York City, composed of workers in the printing and publishing business, became embroiled in a rivalry with D.A. 49 (mixed). In 1883 D.A. 64 failed to get exclusive jurisdiction over all workers in the trade. Soon afterward D.A. 49 charged that the printers were accepting locals not of their trade, and that these locals had also withdrawn from D.A. 49 without permission. An investigation by the secretary of the

General Executive Board disclosed that D.A. 64 had been initiating lithographers, typefounders, pressmen, and feeders in order to strengthen itself as a bargaining unit, and that it had not engaged in raiding forays against D.A. 49. Although the Board upheld D.A. 64, the decision did not resolve the rivalry, and the two districts continued their feud.[22]

With the single exception of L.A. 300, trade districts did not enjoy any appreciable measure of success between 1878 and 1885.[23] The far-reaching reform goals of the Knights and its structural inclusiveness left the advocates of trade organization in the position of a perpetual minority. The expansion of the Knights into the more sparsely populated regions of the South and West, moreover, further diminished trade influence, since the mixed assembly was dominant in rural areas. Lacking a majority, the trade members were unable to establish a central strike fund or concentrate on collective bargaining, and they found that their immediate goals were being subordinated to and sacrificed for more utopian objectives.

II

The struggle between trade unionists and reformers within the Knights, however, was completely overshadowed by the rupture of relations in 1886 between the Knights and the national unions. The latter, stronger and more cohesive than the trade districts of the Order, were better able to take the lead in the conflict between reform and trade unionism. Disillusioned with labor reformism, the trade unions acted upon the premise that the traditional programs of the past were no longer suitable to the changing environment, and they led the assault against the Knights of Labor in 1886.

During the early 1880s, however, it was by no means evident that the Knights and the national unions were predestined to clash. The Federation of Organized Trades and Labor Unions permitted district assemblies of the Knights to be represented at its annual conventions,[24] and many trade union leaders also belonged to

[19] New York Bureau of Labor Statistics, *Annual Report*, Vol. 5 (1887), pp. 202–3.

[20] *Quarterly Report of District Assembly No. 30 . . . July . . . 1886* (Boston, 1886), p. 69. For a somewhat similar case see New York Bureau of Labor Statistics, *Annual Report*, Vol. 5 (1887), pp. 202–4.

[21] K. of L., *GA Proc.*, 1885, pp. 102–3, 140; 1886, p. 130.

[22] Ibid., 1883, pp. 467, 508; 1884, p. 617; 1885, pp. 125, 135; 1887, pp. 1,714, 1,757.

[23] Even the successful career of L.A. 300 cannot be attributed to the Knights. It was due primarily to the skilled nature of the trade which permitted the window glass workers to organize thoroughly, restrict output, and regulate apprenticeship requirements. See Pearce Davis, *The Development of the American Glass Industry* (Cambridge: Harvard University Press, 1949), pp. 126–30.

[24] Federation of Organized Trades, *Proceedings*, 1882, pp. 5, 16, 20, 23.

the Order.[25] Local unions and assemblies often cooperated in joint boycotts, and expressions of friendliness by the national unions toward Powderly and other officials of the Knights were not uncommon.[26] The International Typographical Union expressed appreciation in 1882 for the aid given it by the Knights in a number of cities, and then went on to adopt resolutions recommending cooperation with other labor organizations and permitting its members to join any body that would further the interests of the craft in their particular locality.[27] In other words, the national unions regarded the Knights as a valuable economic ally.

In turn, the Knights vehemently denied having any hostile designs upon the trade unions, and in a number of prominent cases before 1885 it acted accordingly.[28] Nevertheless, with its structural inclusiveness and reform ideology, it was perhaps inevitable that the Order, in its efforts to bring all workingmen into a single organization, would undercut trade union organizational efforts. Thus the General Assembly authorized a committee in 1883 to confer with union representatives in the hope of incorporating all the trade unions within the Knights.[29]

In the absence of any national or international union, the absorption of local unions by the Knights in the form of trade assemblies created no friction. Indeed, isolated local unions were eager to affiliate with such a powerful national organization.[30] By 1886, therefore, the Knights claimed nearly 1,100 local assemblies, many of which undoubtedly represented local trade unions having no parent national union.

When, however, the Knights began to organize workingmen in trades already having national organizations, friction was quick to arise. The trouble that followed the Order's expansion into the realm of the trade unions was not simply a jurisdictional rivalry between similar organizations. As discussed above, the Order and the national unions had opposing conceptions of the legitimate functions of the labor movement, which in turn had led to different structural forms. The expansion of the Order's mixed units thus served to undermine the economic functions of the trade unions since the heterogeneous character of the former prevented them from exercising any appreciable degree of economic power. Furthermore, the structural diversity of the Knights caused trouble when its trade assemblies sought to perform tasks that logically fell within the purview of the trade unions.[31] The national unions, moreover, took the position that geographical trade assemblies were inadequate to meet the challenge of a nationalized economy and in fact were little better than mixed district assemblies. In defense, union officials generally refused to consent to a mutual recognition of working cards,[32] and they demanded that the Knights cease interfering in trade affairs.[33]

The Knights, however, did not heed the warnings of the national unions, and its organizers continued their sporadic work in trades having national unions. "Every week," John Swinton reported in 1885, "trades unions are turned into local assemblies, or Assemblies are organized out of trade Unions."[34] As early as 1881 a district leader attempted to capture a typographical union local, and by 1884 there were over 40 local assemblies of printers in the Knights.[35] The overzealous activities of the Order's organizers also led to trouble with the Bricklayers and Masons International Union.[36]

The trade unions continuously charged that

[25] For a partial list of trade union leaders belonging to the Knights see *The Painter*, Vol. 2 (February 1888), p. 3.

[26] See *Iron Molders' Journal*, Vol. 19 (June 30, 1883), p. 9; Vol. 20 (June 30, 1884), p. 10; Vol. 21 (November 30, 1885), p. 14; Amalgamated Association of Iron and Steel Workers, *Proceedings*, 1882, p. 955; *The Craftsman*, Vol. 2 (January 17, 1885), p. 2; (August 15, 1885), p. 2.

[27] International Typographical Union, *Proceedings*, 1882, pp. 43, 58, 62, 78, 83, 87.

[28] See K. of L., *GA Proc.*, 1882, p. 270; 1884, pp. 707, 787; 1885, pp. 73, 138.

[29] Ibid., 1883, pp. 460, 467, 505–6. See also Powderly Letter Books, Powderly to J. P. McDonnell, September 24, 1882.

[30] Ohio Bureau of Labor Statistics, *Annual Report*, Vol. 9 (1885), p. 28; Grace H. Stimson, *Rise of the Labor Movement in Los Angeles* (Berkeley: University of California Press, 1955), p. 45.

[31] Differences over wages, hours, and working conditions frequently ensued between trade assemblies and local and national unions, especially since no formal coordinating bodies existed. For an example of such a disagreement see K. of L., *GA Proc.*, 1884, pp. 703, 764, 768.

[32] Iron Molders International Union, *Proceedings*, 1882, pp. 15, 54–55.

[33] See the *National Labor Tribune*, July 7, 1883, cited in John R. Commons, ed., *History of Labour in the United States*, 4 vols., Vol. 2 (New York: Macmillan Co., 1918–35), p. 353. "With other trade unionists," Gompers recalled, "I joined the Knights of Labor for the purpose of confining that organization to theoretical educational work and to see that the Trade Unions were protected from being undermined or disrupted," Gompers Letter Books, AFL-CIO Building, Washington, D.C., Gompers to N. E. Mathewson, October 10, 1890.

[34] *John Swinton's Paper*, April 12, 1885.

[35] *JUL*, Vol. 2 (September–October 1881), p. 158; *John Swinton's Paper*, March 2, 1884.

[36] Bricklayers and Masons International Union, *Proceedings*, 1884, p. 9; Powderly Papers, Henry O. Cole to Powderly, March 9, April 28, 1883.

the Order had accepted scabs and unfair workers.[37] It is probable that the unions greatly exaggerated this grievance, but there is little doubt that the existence of two labor organizations, each purporting to accomplish different ends, created a disciplinary problem. Intraunion disagreements frequently concluded with one party seceding and joining the Order as a local assembly. Thus the trade unions found that the Knights were attracting dissidents who normally might have remained in the union.[38]

Despite the proselytizing activities of the Knights, there was no general conflict with the other unions before July 1885. At this time the membership of the Order was slightly over 100,000, and examples of clashes with the trade unions were generally the exception rather than the rule. When differences did arise, the trade unions often made conciliatory efforts at peaceful adjustment. Thus the convention of the International Typographical Union agreed in 1884 to its president's suggestion that he confer with Powderly in order to iron out existing grievances, although it refused to sanction a proposed amalgamation with the Order.[39]

In only one major case—that involving the Cigar Makers International Union—did the differences between a national union and the Knights erupt in open hostilities before 1886. Historians, placing much emphasis upon this particular conflict, have credited Adolph Strasser and Samuel Gompers, the leaders of the Cigar Makers, with the dual responsibility of helping to precipitate the internecine war between the national unions and the Knights, and then founding the AF of L as a rival national federation.[40]

While the national unions generally supported the Cigar Makers in its struggle with the Knights,[41] it is improbable that sympathy for the Cigar Makers would have led to a fight with the Order. Undoubtedly Strasser and Gompers exerted great efforts to induce the unions to lend them support. The fact is also incontrovertible that both were determined, forceful, and sometimes ruthless men. Nevertheless, their efforts would have been useless unless a solid basis of discontent had already existed. In other words, for the unions to break with the Knights, there must have been more compelling reasons than simply the activities of two individuals.

III

To understand the conflict that split the labor movement, the rapid growth of the Knights after 1885 must be examined. In the 12 months between July 1885 and June 1886 the Order's membership increased from 100,000 to over 700,000. This growth, at least in part, came about at the expense of the other unions. In many cases workers abandoned their trade unions to join the Knights. The Journeymen Tailors National Union found that many of its locals had transferred to the Knights, resulting in a considerable loss of membership. A vice-president of the Amalgamated Association of Iron and Steel Workers complained in 1886 that some sublodges in his area had been disbanded because of inroads by the Order.[42] Further difficulty was caused by overzealous organizers who made determined efforts to transform trade unions into local assemblies. In February 1886 the secretary of the Journeyman Bakers National Union protested against such activities. "We never knew," responded the secretary-treasurer of the Knights, "that the K. of L. was proscribed from bringing into its fold all branches of honorable toil."[43]

The Knights, in other words, had adopted an organizational policy diametrically different from that of the trade unions. The traditional concept of organization held by the AF of L (the representative of the trade unions) required that federal labor unions (local units including workers of all trades having no separate unions of their own) be splintered into separate homogeneous craft units as soon as there were enough workers in that locality to form such bodies. The aim of such a policy was to develop the collective bargaining potentialities of the various trades. The Knights, on the other hand, sought to reverse this strategy and proceed in the opposite direc-

[37] The Carpenter, Vol. 3 (February 1883), p. 3; International Typographical Union, Proceedings, 1884, p. 12.

[38] For typical examples see The Carpenter, Vol. 3 (October 1883), p. 2; Vol. 6 (March 1886), p. 4; Vol. 3 (February 1888), p. 1; Robert A. Christie, Empire in Wood: A History of the Carpenters' Union (Ithaca: Cornell University Press, 1956), pp. 50–51; John Swinton's Paper, February 1 and 8, 1885; K. of L., GA Proc., 1885, pp. 106, 109, 140.

[39] International Typographical Union, Proceedings, 1884, pp. 12, 65–66, 70, 72, 102.

[40] See especially Ware, Labor Movement, pp. 258–79, 285, et passim, and Commons, History of Labour, Vol. 2, pp. 401–2.

[41] Iron Molders' Journal, Vol. 22 (March 31, 1886), p. 14; The Craftsman, Vol. 3 (August 7, 1886), p. 2.

[42] John B. Lennon, "Journeymen Tailors," American Federationist, Vol. 9 (September 1902), p. 599; Amalgamated Association of Iron and Steel Workers, Proceedings, 1886, p. 1,793.

[43] New Haven Workmen's Advocate, December 10, 1887.

tion, and it encouraged the combining of trade units into mixed assemblies, which at most were reform or political units. Beneath the structural and organizational differences of the two groups, therefore, lay opposing goals.

To what extent did the Knights encroach upon the domain of the trade unions? Peter J. McGuire of the Carpenters claimed that between 150 and 160 trade unions, including the Molders, Boiler-Makers, Bakers, Miners, Typographical, and Granite Cutters, had grievances against the Order.[44] Only in the case of the Bricklayers and Masons International Union, however, is the evidence fairly complete. In response to a survey conducted in the summer of 1886, the union's secretary received 87 replies. Eight locals reported the existence of bricklayers and masons assemblies within their jurisdiction, four claimed the Knights were working for subunion wages, and three asserted the Knights were working longer hours. "But there are a large number of such men scattered throughout the country who belong to mixed assemblies," the secretary reported—and herein lay the union's major grievance.[45] The complaints of the Bricklayers and Masons were echoed by most of the other major national unions.[46]

In general, the national unions were fearful of the Knights for two closely related reasons. The mixed assembly, in the first place, was incompatible with trade union goals. In theory both structural forms could exist side by side, each pursuing its own ends. Thus the mixed assembly could concentrate on reform and politics, while the trade unions could develop their collective bargaining functions. This modus vivendi, however, presupposed that workers could belong simultaneously to both trade unions and mixed assemblies. At a time when the labor movement's primary problem was to organize and stay organized, such an assumption was unwarranted, and trade union leaders recognized the mutual hostility of the mixed assembly and trade union.

In the second place, trade union officials opposed the chartering of trade assemblies within the Knights for the reason that these units had proved incapable of developing collective bargaining and other union institutions. Furthermore, the geographical and regional organization of the Knights meant that there was little hope for the mature evolution of the national trade assembly. Since local trade assemblies were often ineffective when operating in an environment marked by a nationalized economy and the geographical mobility of labor, trade union leaders argued that these units were attempting to perform functions that logically belonged to the national unions and in the long run tended to undermine the standards of membership and employment that the unions had struggled so fiercely to establish.[47]

By the spring of 1886 relations between the trade unions and the Knights had so deteriorated that a collision appeared imminent.[48] Five prominent unionists therefore called for a meeting of union leaders to arrange a settlement of differences, while at the same time Powderly summoned the General Assembly in a special session to consider, among other things, the troubles with the trade unions. The conference of trade union officials then appointed a committee of five to draw up a plan of settlement. Under the moderating influence of McGuire, who played the leading role, the committee drew up a "treaty," which it submitted to the General Executive Board of the Knights on May 25, 1886.[49]

By the terms of this treaty the Knights would refrain from organizing any trade having a national organization and also would revoke the charter of any existing trade assembly having a parent union. In the second place, any workers guilty of ignoring trade union wage scales, scabbing, or any other offense against a union, would be ineligible for membership in the Order. Third, any organizer who tampered with or interfered in the internal affairs of trade unions would have his commission revoked. Finally, local and district assemblies were not to interfere while trade unions engaged in strikes or lockouts, and the Knights would not be permitted to issue any

[44] K. of L., GA Proc., 1886 special session, pp. 50–51.

[45] Bricklayers and Masons International Union, Proceedings, 1887, pp. 70–75.

[46] Iron Molders' Journal, Vol. 22 (February 28, 1886), pp. 10, 14; (April 30, 1886), p. 8; (August 31, 1886), p. 6; Vol. 23 (December 31, 1886), p. 7; The Craftsman, Vol. 3 (May 15, 1886), p. 3; Granite Cutters' Journal, Vol. 10 (April 1886), p. 3; The Carpenter, Vol. 6 (May 1886), p. 2; Cigar Makers' Official Journal, Vol. 11 (April 1886), p. 6; Printers' Circular, Vol. 21 (June 1886), p. 66; International Typographical Union, Proceedings, 1886, pp. 90, 93–94; Iron Molders' International Union, Proceedings, 1886, pp. 16, 25, 31.

[47] See The Craftsman, Vol. 3 (February 6, 1886), p. 2; (March 20, 1886), p. 1; The Carpenter, Vol. 24 (December 1904), p. 5.

[48] John Swinton's Paper, March 21, 1886; Illinois Bureau of Labor Statistics, Biennial Report, Vol. 4 (1886), pp. 160–61.

[49] Bricklayers and Masons International Union, Proceedings, 1887, pp. 63–66; The Carpenter, Vol. 6 (May 1886), p. 2; (June 1886), p. 3; Cigar Makers' Official Journal, Vol. 11 (June 1886), p. 7; K. of L., GA Proc., 1886 special session, pp. 1–2; Powderly Letter Books, Powderly to P. J. McGuire and Adolph Strasser, May 11, 1886.

label or trademark where a national union had already done so.[50]

On the surface it appears surprising that the trade unions, which claimed to represent about 350,000 workers (although their actual membership was about 160,000), would present such a document to an organization having 700,000 members. Yet the treaty was neither a bargaining offer nor a declaration of war.[51] It was rather the logical outcome of the duality that had pervaded the labor movement since the Civil War. Under its terms the labor movement would be divided into two separate and distinct compartments. The Knights of Labor, on the one hand, would continue its efforts to abolish the wage system, reform society, and educate the working class. The national unions, on the other hand, would be left paramount in the economic field, and the Order would no longer be permitted to exercise any control over wages, hours, working conditions, or the process of collective bargaining. In other words, trade unionism and reform unionism had come to a parting of the ways.

In one sense the treaty was an expression of the fear of the skilled workers that they were being subordinated to the interests of the unskilled.[52] Yet the polarization implied in such an interpretation should not be exaggerated, for it cannot be said that the Knights themselves represented the unskilled workers. The Order was not an industrial union, nor did it emphasize collective bargaining. It was rather a heterogeneous mass that subordinated the economic functions of labor organizations to its primary goal of reforming society. The mixed assembly, while including workers of all trades and callings, was in no sense an industrial union, since it was not organized either by industry or factory. Moreover, the trade unions had never excluded the unskilled from the labor movement; they simply maintained that organization along craft lines was historically correct. "In truth," remarked Gompers, "the trade union is nothing more or less

than the organization of wage earners engaged in a given employment, whether skilled or unskilled, for the purpose of attaining the best possible reward, [and] the best attainable conditions for the workers in that trade or calling."[53]

The General Assembly of the Knights, in turn, submitted its own proposals to the union committee. Its terms included protection against unfair workers, a mutual exchange of working cards, and the holding of a joint conference before either organization presented wages and hours demands to employers.[54] Clearly the Assembly's position was in fundamental disagreement with that of the trade unions. The latter had demanded unitary control over the economic field, while the Knights had demanded equal jurisdiction over membership and working standards. Thus neither side evinced willingness to compromise over basic issues.

Although failing to conclude a settlement with the trade unions, the special session of the General Assembly did not close the door to further negotiations. For the time being, therefore, the conflict remained in abeyance. While matters were pending, however, the Knights made a determined effort to end friction by intensifying its campaign to bring the national unions under its control. The national unions, however, recognized that the structure of the Knights was incompatible with trade union objectives, and the policy of the Order was only partially successful. Some of the smaller unions, including the Seamen's Benevolent Union, the Eastern Glass Bottle Blowers' League, and the Western Green Bottle Blowers' Association, joined the Knights.[55] The American Flint Glass Workers Union, on the other hand, refused to go along with the other glassworkers because of an earlier dispute with the Order.[56] In New York City the Knights made a determined but unsuccessful attempt to capture

---

[50] A. F. of L., *Proceedings*, 1886, p. 16 (1905–1906 reprinting).

[51] Cf. Ware, *Labor Movement*, p. 284.

[52] Perlman has interpreted the conflict between the Knights and unions largely as one between skilled and unskilled workers. Commons, *History of Labour*, Vol. 2, 396–97. Undoubtedly the skilled workers feared the Knights. The Knights, however, was not necessarily an organization of unskilled workers, as the large number of trade assemblies would indicate. While the unions jealously guarded their autonomy and independence, the conflict that developed in 1886 was more than simply a struggle between the skilled and unskilled, although this aspect was an important element.

[53] Gompers Letter Books, Gompers to George H. Daggett, January 4, 1896. See also Gompers to Albert C. Stevens, No. 1, 1889; Gompers to Frank D. Hamlin, May 6, 1890; Gompers to Charles W. Nelson, April 29, 1892.

[54] K. of L., *GA Proc.*, 1886 special session, pp. 53, 55, 67.

[55] *JUL*, Vol. 8 (August 20, 1887), p. 2,476; K. of L., *GA Proc.*, 1887, p. 1,334; *John Swinton's Paper*, July 25, 1886; David A. McCabe, *The Standard Rate in American Trade Unions* (Baltimore: The Johns Hopkins Press, 1912), pp. 155–56. The glassworkers probably joined the Order in the hope of emulating the success of L.A. 300.

[56] *Iron Molders' Journal*, Vol. 22 (February 28, 1886), p. 10; *Cigar Makers' Official Journal*, Vol. 11 (August 1886), p. 6; Secretary of Internal Affairs of the Commonwealth of Pennsylvania, *Annual Report*, Vol. 16 (1888), Pt. 3, Section F, pp. 18–19.

the German shoemakers and the Associated Jewelers.[57] Most of the larger and more important unions emphatically rejected the Order's overtures. The members of the Amalgamated Associated of Iron and Steel Workers overwhelmingly defeated a referendum on the subject, while a similar poll conducted by the secretary of the Bricklayers and Masons resulted in the same conclusion. The Iron Molders' convention turned down the merger proposal by a vote of 114 to 27.[58] Furthermore, the Typographical Union, the Carpenters, the Plumbers and Gas Fitters, the coal miners, and the Stationary Engineers all rejected the invitation to join the Knights.[59]

At the regular meeting of the General Assembly in October 1886 further negotiations between the trade unions and the Knights again ended in failure. The action by the Assembly in ordering all workers holding cards in both the Knights and the Cigar Makers International Union to leave the latter under pain of expulsion[60] was interpreted by both sides as constituting a final break and an open declaration of war.[61] The trade union committee therefore issued a call on November 10, 1886, for all unions to send representatives to a convention in Columbus, Ohio, on December 8, to form an "American Federation or Alliance of all National and International Trade Unions." Out of this meeting came the AF of L. Completely dominated by the national unions, the December convention excluded assemblies of the Knights from membership and then proceeded to establish the new organization on a firm foundation.[62]

Thus by the end of 1886 the die had been cast, and the Knights and national unions prepared for war. Why had all negotiations failed? Undoubtedly the intractability of leaders on both sides contributed to the difficulties, but there were also those who had made sincere efforts to head off the impending conflict. The trade unions, furthermore, had encountered jurisdictional rivalries with the Knights, but this has been an endemic problem of the labor movement, and one which has not always had an unhappy ending.

The conflict between the Knights and the trade unions, then, had a much broader significance than the negotiations between them indicated and represented the culmination of decades of historical development. The Knights, growing out of the humanitarian and reform crusades of ante-bellum America, emphasized the abolition of the wage system and the reorganization of society. To achieve this purpose it insisted on the prime importance of the mixed assembly, which would serve as the nucleus of an organization dedicated to reform. The trade unions, on the other hand, accepted their environment and sought to take advantage of the relative scarcity of labor and the rising scale of production. Hence they emphasized the collective bargaining functions of labor organizations, thus tacitly accepting the workers' wage status.

Perhaps grounds for compromise did exist, but neither side was prone to make any concessions. The national unions, by insisting upon strict trade autonomy as a sine qua non of settlement, were in effect demanding that the Knights should virtually abandon any pretense at being a bona fide labor organization. It is true that the unions could have organized as national autonomous trade districts if the Knights had been ready to grant permission. The leaders of the Knights, however, were unwilling to permit their organization to be transformed into what the AF of L ultimately became. Indeed, after 1886 many national trade districts left the Order because of their inability to function within the framework of that body.[63] The national unions, moreover,

[57] *The Carpenter*, Vol. 6 (October 1886), p. 1.

[58] Amalgamated Association of Iron and Steel Workers, *Proceedings*, 1886, pp. 1,807–8, 1,818–19, 1,846; 1887, pp. 1,959–62; Bricklayers and Masons International Union, *Proceedings*, 1887, pp. 71, 76; Iron Molders International Union, *Proceedings*, 1886, pp. 17–20.

[59] *John Swinton's Paper*, June 20, 1886; *The Carpenter*, Vol. 6 (October 1886), p. 1. See also *Locomotive Firemen's Magazine*, Vol. 10 (March 1886), p. 141.

[60] K. of L., *GA Proc.*, 1886, pp. 200, 282.

[61] See Joseph R. Buchanan, *The Story of a Labor Agitator* (New York: The Outlook Co., 1903), p. 314.

[62] Bricklayers and Masons International Union, *Proceedings*, 1887, pp. 79–80; A.F. of L., *Proceedings*, 1886, pp. 13–15. A committee from the Knights was also present at the trade union convention in December 1886 but no agreement was reached. See A.F. of L., *Proceedings*, 1886, pp. 17–18; K. of L., *GA Proc.*, 1887, pp. 1,445–47.

[63] The shoemakers, miners, machinists, garment-workers, carriage and wagonmakers, and potters all seceded from the Knights after 1886 because of their inability to function efficiently within the existing framework of the Order. For evidence on this point see the following: *The Laster*, Vol. 1 (March 15, 1889); *Shoe Workers' Journal*, Vol. 11 (July 1910), p. 11; United Mine Workers of America, *Proceedings*, 1911, Vol. 1, p. 581; *JUL*, Vol. 8 (May 19, 1888), p. 1; *Journal of the International Association of Machinists*, Vol. 7 (July 1895), p. 238; *Garment Workers*, Vol. 3 (September 1896), p. 4; *Carriage and Wagon Workers Journal*, Vol. 2 (January 1, 1901), p. 113; United States Industrial Commission, *Report of the Industrial Commission* (19 vols.: Washington, D.C., 1900–2), Vol. 17, pp. 59, 209; Theodore W. Glocker, *The Government of American Trade Unions* (Baltimore: The Johns Hopkins Press, 1913), p. 54.

were not encouraged by the experiences of trade districts within the Knights before 1886. Finally, there was the simple element of power, and both the trade unions and the Knights, as established organizations, were adamant in their refusal to surrender any part of it.

Between reform and trade unionism, therefore, existed a gulf that the leaders of the 1880s were unable to bridge. By 1886 this chasm had widened to such a degree that cooperation between the two seemed virtually impossible, and war seemed to be the only solution. Reform and trade unionism had at last come to a parting of the ways, and upon the outcome of the ensuing struggle hinged the destiny of the American labor movement.

12. The Victory of Craft Unionism and the Final Failure of Producers' Cooperation*

Selig Perlman

We now come to the most significant aspect of the Great Upheaval: the life and death struggle between two opposed principles of labor organization and between two opposed labor programs. The Upheaval offered the practical test which the labor movement required for an intelligent decision between the rival claims of Knights and trade unionists. The test as well as the conflict turned principally on "structure," that is, on the difference between "craft autonomists" and those who would have labor organized "under one head," or what we would now call the "one big union" advocates.

As the issue of "structure" proved in the crucial 80s, and has remained ever since, the outstanding factional issue in the labor movement, it might be well at this point to pass in brief review the structural developments in labor organization from the beginning and try to correlate them with other important developments.

The early societies of shoemakers and printers were purely local in scope, and the relations between "locals" extended only to feeble attempts to deal with the competition of traveling journeymen. Occasionally, they corresponded on trade matters, notifying each other of their purposes and the nature of their demands, or expressing fraternal greetings—chiefly for the purpose of counteracting advertisements by employers for journeymen or keeping out dishonest members and so-called scabs. This mostly relates to printers. The shoemakers, despite their bitter contests with their employers, did even less. The Philadelphia Mechanics' Trades Association in 1827, which we noted as the first attempted federation of trades in the United States if not in the

world, was organized as a move of sympathy for the carpenters striking for the 10-hour day. During the period of the "wild-cat" prosperity the local federation of trades, under the name of "Trades' Union,"[1] comes to occupy the center of the stage in New York, Philadelphia, Boston, and appeared even as far "West" as Pittsburgh, Cincinnati, and Louisville. The constitution of the New York "Trades' Union" provided, among other things, that each society should pay a monthly per capita of 6¼ cents to be used as a strike fund. Later, when strikes multiplied, the Union limited the right to claim strike aid and appointed a standing committee on mediation. In 1835 it discussed a plan for an employment exchange, or a "call room." The constitution of the Philadelphia Union required that a strike be endorsed by a two-thirds majority before granting aid.

The National Trades' Union, the federation of city trades' unions, 1834–36, was a further development of the same idea. Its first and second conventions went little beyond the theoretical. The latter, however, passed a significant resolution urging the trade societies to observe a uniform wage policy throughout the country and, should the employers combine to resist it, the unions should make "one general strike."

The last convention in 1836 went far beyond preceding conventions in its plans for solidifying the workingmen of the country. First and foremost, a "national fund" was provided for, to be made up of a levy of two cents per month on each of the members of the trades' unions and local societies represented. The policies of the

* From *History of Trade Unionism in the U.S.* (New York: Macmillan Co., 1929), pp. 106–29.

[1] In the 30s the term "union" was reserved for the city federations of trades. What is now designated as a trade union was called trade society. In the 60s the "union" became the "trades' assembly."

National Trades' Union instead of merely advisory were henceforth to be binding. But before the new policies could be tried, as we know, the entire trade union movement was wiped out by the panic.

The city "trades' union" of the 30s accorded with a situation where the effects of the extension of the market were noticeable in the labor market, and little as yet in the commodity market—when the competitive menace to labor was the low paid out-of-town product made under lower labor costs selling in the same market as the products of unionized labor. Under these conditions the local trade society, reenforced by the city federation of trades, sufficed. The "trades' union," moreover, served also as a source of reserve strength.

Twenty years later the whole situation was changed. The 50s were a decade of extensive construction of railways. Before 1850 there was more traffic by water than by rail. After 1860 the relative importance of land and water transportation was reversed. Furthermore, the most important railway building during the ten years preceding 1860 was the construction of East and West trunk lines; and the 60s were marked by the establishment of through lines for freight and the consolidation of connecting lines. The through freight lines greatly hastened freight traffic and by the consolidations through transportation became doubly efficient.

Arteries of traffic had thus extended from the Eastern coast to the Mississippi Valley. Local markets had widened to embrace half a continent. Competitive menaces had become more serious and threatened from a distance. Local unionism no longer sufficed. Consequently, as we saw, in the labor movement of the 60s the national trade union was supreme.

There were four distinct sets of causes which operated during the 60s to bring about nationalization; two grew out of the changes in transportation, already alluded to, and two were largely independent of such changes.

The first and most far-reaching cause, as illustrated by the stove molders, was the competition of the products of different localities side by side in the same market. Stoves manufactured in Albany, New York, were now displayed in St. Louis by the side of stoves made in Detroit. No longer could the molder in Albany be indifferent to the fate of his fellow craftsman in Louisville. With the molders the nationalization of the organization was destined to proceed to its utmost length. In order that union conditions should be maintained even in the best organized

centers, it became necessary to equalize competitive conditions in the various localities. That led to a well-knit national organization to control working conditions, trade rules, and strikes. In other trades, where the competitive area of the product was still restricted to the locality, the paramount nationalizing influence was a more intensive competition for employment between migratory out-of-town journeymen and the locally organized mechanics. This describes the situation in the printing trade, where the bulk of work was newspaper and not book and job printing. Accordingly, the printers did not need to entrust their national officers with anything more than the control of the traveling journeymen, and the result was that the local unions remained practically independent.

The third cause of concerted national action in a trade union was the organization of employers. Where the power of a local union began to be threatened by an employers' association, the next logical step was to combine in a national union.

The fourth cause was the application of machinery and the introduction of division of labor, which split up the established trades and laid industry open to invasion by "green hands." The shoemaking industry, which during the 60s had reached the factory stage, illustrates this in a most striking manner. Few other industries experienced anything like a similar change during this period.

Of course, none of the causes of nationalization here enumerated operated in entire isolation. In some trades one cause, in other trades other causes, had the predominating influence. Consequently, in some trades the national union resembled an agglomeration of loosely allied states, each one reserving the right to engage in independent action and expecting from its allies no more than a benevolent neutrality. In other trades, on the contrary, the national union was supreme in declaring industrial war and in making peace, and even claimed absolute right to formulate the civil laws of the trade for times of industrial peace.

The national trade union was, therefore, a response to obvious and pressing necessity. However slow or imperfect may have been the adjustment of internal organizations to the conditions of the trade, still the groove was defined and consequently the amount of possible floundering largely limited. Not so with the next step, namely the national federation of trades. In the 60s we saw the national trade unions join with other local and miscellaneous labor organizations in the

National Labor Union upon a political platform of eight-hours and greenbackism. In 1873 the same national unions asserted their rejection of "panaceas" and politics by attempting to create in the National Labor Congress a federation of trades of a strictly economic character. The panic and depression nipped that in the bud. When trade unionism revived in 1879 the national trade unions returned to the idea of a national federation of labor, but this time they followed the model of the British Trades Union Congress, the organization which cares for the legislative interests of British labor. This was the Federation of Organized Trades and Labor Unions of the United States and Canada, which was set up in 1881.

It is easy to understand why the unions of the early 80s did not feel the need of a federation on economic lines. The trade unions of today look to the American Federation of Labor for the discharge of important economic functions, therefore it is primarily an economic organization. These functions are the assistance of national trade unions in organizing their trades, the adjustment of disputes between unions claiming the same "jurisdiction," and concerted action in matters of especial importance such as shorter hours, the "open-shop," or boycotts. None of these functions would have been of material importance to the trade unions of the early 80s. Existing in well-defined trades, which were not affected by technical changes, they had no "jurisdictional" disputes; operating at a period of prosperity with full employment and rising wages, they did not realize a necessity for concerted action; the era of the boycotts had not yet begun. As for having a common agency to do the work of organizing, the trade unions of the early 80s had no keen desire to organize any but the skilled workmen; and, since the competition of workmen in small towns had not yet made itself felt, each national trade union strove to organize primarily the workmen of its trade in the larger cities, a function for which its own means were adequate.

The new organization of 1881 was a loose federation of trade and labor unions with a legislative committee at the head, with Samuel Gompers of the cigar makers as a member. The platform was purely legislative and demanded legal incorporation for trade unions, compulsory education for children, the prohibition of child labor under 14, uniform apprentice laws, the enforcement of the national 8-hour law, prison labor reform, abolition of the "truck" and "order" system, mechanics' lien, abolition of conspiracy laws as applied to labor organizations, a national bureau of labor statistics, a protective tariff for American labor, an anti-contact immigrant law, and recommended "all trade and labor organizations to secure proper representation in all lawmaking bodies by means of the ballot, and to use all honorable measures by which this result can be accomplished." Although closely related to the present American Federation of Labor in point of time and personnel of leadership, the Federation of Organized Trades and Labor Unions of the United States and Canada was in reality the precursor of the present state federations of labor, which as specialized parts of the national federation now look after labor legislation.

Two or three years later it became evident that the Federation as a legislative organization proved a failure. Manifestly the trade unions felt no great interest in national legislation. The indifference can be measured by the fact that the annual income of the Federation never exceeded $700 and that, excepting in 1881, none of its conventions represented more than one-fourth of the trade union membership of the country. Under such conditions the legislative influence of the Federation naturally was infinitesimal. The legislative committee carried out the instructions of the 1883 convention and communicated to the national committees of the Republican and Democratic parties the request that they should define their position upon the enforcement of the 8-hour law and other measures. The letters were not even answered. A subcommittee of the legislative committee appeared before the two political conventions, but received no greater attention.

It was not until the majority of the national trade unions came under the menace of becoming forcibly absorbed by the Order of the Knights of Labor that a basis appeared for a vigorous federation.

The Knights of Labor were built on an opposite principle from the national trade unions. Whereas the latter started with independent crafts and then with hesitating hands tried, as we saw, to erect some sort of a common superstructure that should express a higher solidarity of labor, the former was built from the beginning upon a denial of craft lines and upon an absolute unity of all classes of labor under one guiding head. The subdivision was territorial instead of occupational and the government centralized.

The constitution of the Knights of Labor was drawn in 1878 when the Order laid aside the veil of secrecy to which it had clung since its foundation in 1869. The lowest unit of organization was the local assembly of ten or more, at least three fourths of whom had to be wage earners at any trade. Above the local assembly was the "district assembly" and above it the "General Assembly." The district assembly had absolute power over its local assemblies and the General Assembly was given "full and final jurisdiction" as "the highest tribunal" of the Order.[2] Between sessions of the General Assembly the power was vested in a General Executive Board, presided over by a Grand Master Workman.

The Order of the Knights of Labor in practice carried out the idea which is now advocated so fervently by revolutionary unionists, namely the "one big union," since it avowedly aimed to bring into one organization "all productive labor." This idea in organization was aided by the weakness of the trade unions during the long depression of the 70s, which led many to hope for better things from a general pooling of labor strength. But its main appeal rested on a view that machine technique tends to do away with all distinctions of trades by reducing all workers to the level of unskilled machine tenders. To its protagonists therefore the "one big union" stood for an adjustment to the new technique.

First to face the problem of adjustment to the machine technique of the factory system were the shoemakers. They organized in 1867 the Order of the Knights of St. Crispin, mainly for the purpose of suppressing the competitive menace of "green hands," that is, unskilled workers put to work on shoe machines. At its height in 1872, the Crispins numbered about 50,000, perhaps the largest union in the whole world at that time. The coopers began to be menaced by machinery about the middle of the 60s, and about the same time the machinists and blacksmiths, too, saw their trade broken up by the introduction of the principle of standardized parts and quantity production in the making of machinery. From these trades came the national leaders of the Knights of Labor and the strongest advocates of the new principle in labor organization and of the interests of the unskilled workers in general. The conflict between the trade unions and the Knights of Labor turned on the question of the unskilled workers.

The conflict was held in abeyance during the early 80s. The trade unions were by far the strongest organizations in the field and scented no

particular danger when here or there the Knights formed an assembly either contiguous to the sphere of a trade union or even at times encroaching upon it.

With the Great Upheaval, which began in 1884, and the inrushing of hundreds of thousands of semi-skilled and unskilled workers into the Order, a new situation was created. The leaders of the Knights realized that mere numbers were not sufficient to defeat the employers and that control over the skilled, and consequently the more strategic occupations, was required before the unskilled and semi-skilled could expect to march to victory. Hence, parallel to the tremendous growth of the Knights in 1886, there was a constantly growing effort to absorb the existing trade unions for the purpose of making them subservient to the interests of the less skilled elements. It was mainly that which produced the bitter conflict between the Knights and the trade unions during 1886 and 1887. Neither the jealousy aroused by the success of the unions nor the opposite aims of labor solidarity and trade separatism gives an adequate explanation of this conflict. The one, of course, aggravated the situation by introducing a feeling of personal bitterness, and the other furnished an appealing argument to each side. But the struggle was one between groups within the working class, in which the small but more skilled group fought for independence of the larger but weaker group of the unskilled and semi-skilled. The skilled men stood for the right to use their advantage of skill and efficient organization in order to wrest the maximum amount of concessions for themselves. The Knights of Labor endeavored to annex the skilled men in order that the advantage from their exceptional fighting strength might lift up the unskilled and semi-skilled. From the point of view of a struggle between principles, this was indeed a clash between the principle of solidarity of labor and that of trade separatism, but in reality, each of the principles reflected only the special interest of a certain portion of the working class. Just as the trade unions, when they fought for trade autonomy, really refused to consider the unskilled men, so the Knights of Labor overlooked the fact that their scheme would retard the progress of the skilled trades.

The Knights were in nearly every case the aggressors, and it is significant that among the local organizations of the Knights inimical to trade unions, District Assembly 49 of New York, should prove the most relentless. It was this assembly which conducted the longshoremen's and coal miners' strike in New York in 1887 and

[2] The constitution read as follows: "It alone possesses the power and authority to make, amend, or repeal the fundamental and general laws and regulations of the Order; to finally decide all controversies arising in the Order; to issue all charters. . . . It can also tax the members of the Order for its maintenance."

which, as we saw, did not hesitate to tie up the industries of the entire city for the sake of securing the demands of several hundred unskilled workingmen. Though District Assembly 49, New York, came into conflict with not a few of the trade unions in that city, its battle royal was fought with the cigar makers' unions. There were at the time two factions among the cigar makers, one upholding the International Cigar Makers' Union with Adolph Strasser and Samuel Gompers as leaders, the other calling itself the Progressive Union, which was more socialistic in nature and composed of more recent immigrants and less skilled workers. District Assembly 49 of the Knights of Labor took a hand in the struggle to support the Progressive Union and by skillful management brought the situation to the point where the latter had to allow itself to be absorbed into the Knights of Labor.

The events in the cigar making trade in New York brought to a climax the sporadic struggles that had been going on between the Order and the trade unions. The trade unions demanded that the Knights of Labor respect their "jurisdiction" and proposed a "treaty of peace" with such drastic terms that, had they been accepted, the trade unions would have been left in the sole possession of the field. The Order was at first more conciliatory. It would not of course cease to take part in industrial disputes and industrial matters, but it proposed a modus vivendi on a basis of an interchange of "working cards" and common action against employers. At the same time it addressed separately to each national trade union a gentle admonition to think of the unskilled workers as well as of themselves. The address said:

In the use of the wonderful inventions, your organization plays a most important part. Naturally it embraces within its ranks a very large proportion of laborers of a high grade of skill and intelligence. With this skill of hand, guided by intelligent thought, comes the right to demand that excess of compensation be paid to skilled above the unskilled labor. But the unskilled labor must receive attention, or in the hour of difficulty the employer will not hesitate to use it to depress the compensation you now receive. That skilled or unskilled labor may no longer be found unorganized, we ask of you to annex your grand and powerful corps to the main army that we may fight the battle under one flag.

But the trade unions, who had formerly declared that their purpose was "to protect the skilled trades of America from being reduced to beggary," evinced no desire to be pressed into the service of lifting up the unskilled and voted down with practical unanimity the proposal. Thereupon the Order declared open war by commanding all its members who were also members of the cigar makers' union to withdraw from the latter on the penalty of expulsion.

Later events proved that the assumption of the aggressive was the beginning of the undoing of the Order. It was, moreover, an event of first significance in the labor movement since it forced the trade unions to draw closer together and led to the founding in the same year, 1886, of the American Federation of Labor.

Another highly important effect of this conflict was the ascendency in the trade union movement of Samuel Gompers as the foremost leader. Gompers had first achieved prominence in 1881 at the time of the organization of the Federation of Organized Trades and Labor Unions. But not until the situation created by the conflict with the Knights of Labor did he get his first real opportunity, both to demonstrate his inborn capacity for leadership and to train and develop that capacity by overcoming what was perhaps the most serious problem that ever confronted American organized labor.

The new Federation avoided its predecessor's mistake of emphasizing labor legislation above all. Its prime purpose was economic. The legislative interests of labor were for the most part given into the care of subordinate state federations of labor. Consequently, the several state federations, not the American Federation of Labor, correspond in America to the British Trades Union Congress. But in the conventions of the American Federation of Labor the state federations are represented only nominally. The Federation is primarily a federation of national and international (including Canada and Mexico) trade unions.

Each national and international union in the new Federation was acknowledged a sovereignty unto itself, with full powers of discipline over its members and with the power of free action toward the employers without any interference from the Federation; in other words, its full autonomy was confirmed. Like the British Empire, the Federation of Labor was cemented together by ties which were to a much greater extent spiritual than they were material. Nevertheless, the Federation's authority was far from being a shadowy one. If it could not order about the officers of the constituent unions, it could so mobilize the general labor sentiment in the country on behalf of any of its constituent bodies that its goodwill would be sought even by the most powerful ones. The Federation guaranteed to each union a certain jurisdiction, generally coextensive with a craft, and protected it against encroachments by adjoining unions and more especially by rival unions. The guarantee worked absolutely in the case of the latter, for the Federation knew no mercy when a rival union attempted to undermine the strength of an organized union of a craft. The trade unions have learned from experience with the Knights of Labor that their deadliest enemy was, after all, not the employers' association but the enemy from within who introduced confusion in the ranks. They have accordingly developed such a passion for "regularity," such an intense conviction that there must be but one union in a given trade that, on occasions, scheming labor officials have known how to checkmate a justifiable insurgent movement by a skillful play upon this curious hypertrophy of the feeling of solidarity. Not only will a rival union never be admitted into the Federation, but no subordinate body, state or city, may dare to extend any aid or comfort to a rival union.

The Federation exacted but little from the national and international unions in exchange for the guarantee of their jurisdiction: a small annual per capita tax; a willing though a not obligatory support in the special legislative and industrial campaigns it may undertake; an adherence to its decisions on general labor policy; an undertaking to submit to its decision in the case of disputes with other unions, which however need not in every case be fulfilled; and lastly, an unqualified acceptance of the principle of "regularity" relative to labor organization. Obviously, judging from constitutional powers alone, the Federation was but a weak sort of a government. Yet the weakness was not the forced weakness of a government which was willing to start with limited powers hoping to increase its authority as it learned to stand more firmly on its own feet; it was a self-imposed weakness suggested by the lessons of labor history.

By contrast the Order of the Knights of Labor, as seen already, was governed by an all-powerful General Assembly and General Executive Board. At a first glance a highly centralized form of government would appear a promise of assured strength and a guarantee of coherence amongst the several parts of the organization. Perhaps, if America's wage earners were cemented together by as strong a class consciousness as the laboring classes of Europe, such might have been the case.

But America's labor movement lacked the unintended aid which the sister movements in Europe derived from a caste system of society and political oppression. Where the class lines were not tightly drawn, the centrifugal forces in the labor movement were bound to assert themselves. The leaders of the American Federation of Labor, in their struggle against the Knights of Labor, played precisely upon this centrifugal tendency and gained a victory by making an appeal to the natural desire for autonomy and self-determination of any distinctive group. But originally perhaps intended as a mere "strategic" move, this policy succeeded in creating a labor movement which was, on fundamentals, far more coherent than the Knights of Labor even in the heyday of its glory. The officers and leaders of the Federation, knowing that they could not command, set themselves to developing a unified labor will and purpose by means of moral suasion and propaganda. Where a bare order would breed resentment and backbiting, an appeal, which is reinforced by a carefully nurtured universal labor sentiment, will eventually bring about common consent and a willing acquiescence in the policy supported by the majority. So each craft was made a self-determining unit and "craft autonomy" became a sacred shibboleth in the labor movement without interfering with unity on essentials.

The principle of craft autonomy triumphed chiefly because it recognized the existence of a considerable amount of group selfishness. The Knights of Labor held, as was seen, that the strategic or bargaining strength of the skilled craftsman should be used as a lever to raise the status of the semi-skilled and unskilled worker. It consequently grouped them promiscuously in "mixed assemblies" and opposed as long as it could the demand for "national trade assemblies." The craftsman, on the other hand, wished to use his superior bargaining strength for his own purposes and evinced little desire to dissipate it in the service of his humbler fellow worker. To give effect to that, he felt obliged to struggle against becoming entangled with undesirable allies in the semi-skilled and unskilled workers for whom the Order spoke. Needless to say, the individual self-interest of the craft leaders worked hand in hand with the self-interest of the craft as a whole, for had they been annexed by the Order they would have become subject to orders from the General Master Workman or the General Assembly of the Order.

In addition to platonic stirrings for "self-determination" and to narrow group interest, there was a motive for craft autonomy which could pass muster both as strictly social and realistic. The fact was that the autonomous craft union could win strikes where the centralized promiscuous Order merely floundered and suffered defeat after defeat. The craft union had the advantage, on the one hand, of a leadership which was thoroughly familiar with the bit of ground upon which it operated and, on the other hand, of handling a group of people of equal financial endurance and of identical interest. It has already been seen how dreadfully mismanaged were the great Knights of Labor strikes of 1886 and 1887. The ease with which the leaders were able to call out trade after trade on a strike of sympathy proved more a liability than an asset. Often the choice of trades to strike bore no particular relation to their strategic value in the given situation; altogether one gathers the impression that these great strikes were conducted by blundering amateurs who possessed more authority than was good for them or for the cause. It is therefore not to be wondered at if the compact craft unions led by specialists scored successes where the heterogeneous mobs of the Knights of Labor had been doomed from the first. Clearly then the survival of the craft union was a survival of the fittest; and the Federation's attachment to the principle of craft autonomy was, to say the least, a product of an evolutionary past, whatever one may hold with reference to its fitness in our own time.

Whatever reasons moved the trade unions of the skilled to battle with the Order for their separate and autonomous existence were bound sooner or later to induce those craftsmen who were in the Order to seek a similar autonomy. From the very beginning the more skilled and better organized trades in the Knights sought to separate from the mixed "district assemblies" and to create within the framework of the Order "national trade assemblies."[3] However, the national officers, who looked upon such a move as a betrayal of the great principle of the solidarity of all labor, were able to stem the tide excepting in the case of the window glass blowers, who were granted their autonomy in 1880.

The obvious superiority of the trade union form of organization over the mixed organization, as revealed by events in 1886 and 1887, strengthened the separatist tendency. Just as the struggle between the Knights of Labor and the trade unions on the outside had been fundamentally a struggle between the unskilled and the skilled portions of the wage-earning class, so

the aspiration toward the national trade assembly within the Order represented the effort of the more or less skilled men for emancipation from the dominance of the unskilled. But the Order successfully fought off such attempts until after the defeat of the mixed district assemblies, or in other words of the unskilled class, in the struggle with the employers. With the withdrawal of a very large portion of this class, as shown in 1887, the demand for the national trade assembly revived and there soon began a veritable rush to organize by trades. The stampede was strongest in the city of New York where the incompetence of the mixed District Assembly 49 had become patent. At the General Assembly in 1887 at Minneapolis all obstacles were removed from forming national trade assemblies, but this came too late to stem the exodus of the skilled element from the order into the American Federation of Labor.

The victory of craft autonomy over the "one big union" was decisive and complete.

The strike activities of the Knights were confessedly a deviation from "First Principles." Yet the First Principles with their emphasis on producers' cooperation were far from forgotten even when the enthusiasm for strikes was at its highest. Whatever the actual feelings of the membership as a whole, the leaders neglected no opportunity to promote cooperation. T. V. Powderly, the head of the Order since 1878, in his reports to the annual General Assembly or convention, consistently urged that practical steps be taken toward cooperation. In 1881, while the general opinion in the Order was still undecided, the leaders did not scruple to smuggle into the constitution a clause which made cooperation compulsory.

Notwithstanding Powderly's exhortations, the Order was at first slow in taking it up. In 1882 a general cooperative board was elected to work out a plan of action, but it never reported, and a new board was chosen in its place at the Assembly of 1883. In that year, the first practical step was taken in the purchase by the Order of a coal mine at Cannelburg, Indiana, with the idea of selling the coal at reduced prices to the members. Soon thereafter a thorough change of sentiment with regard to the whole matter of cooperation took place, contemporaneously with the industrial depression and unsuccessful strikes. The rank and file, who had hitherto been indifferent, now seized upon the idea with avidity. The enthusiasm ran so high in Lynn, Massachusetts, that it was found necessary to raise the shares of the Knights of Labor Cooperative Shoe

[3] The "local assemblies" generally followed in practice trade lines, but the district assemblies were "mixed."

Company to $100 in order to prevent a large influx of "unsuitable members." In 1885 Powderly complained that "many of our members grow impatient and unreasonable because every avenue of the Order does not lead to cooperation."

The impatience for immediate cooperation, which seized the rank and file in practically every section of the country, caused an important modification in the official doctrine of the Order. Originally it had contemplated centralized control under which it would have taken years before a considerable portion of the membership could realize any benefit. This was now dropped and a decentralized plan was adopted. Local organizations and, more frequently, groups of members with the financial aid of their local organizations now began to establish shops. Most of the enterprises were managed by the stockholders, although, in some cases, the local organization of the Knights of Labor managed the plant.

Most of the cooperative enterprises were conducted on a small scale. Incomplete statistics warrant the conclusion that the average amount invested per establishment was about $10,000. From the data gathered it seems that cooperation reached its highest point in 1886, although it had not completely spent itself by the end of 1887. The total number of ventures probably reached 200. The largest numbers were in mining, cooperage, and shoes. These industries paid the poorest wages and treated their employees most harshly. A small amount of capital was required to organize such establishments.

With the abandonment of centralized cooperation in 1884, the role of the central cooperative board changed correspondingly. The leading member of the board was now John Samuel, one of those to whom cooperation meant nothing short of a religion. The duty of the board was to educate the members of the Order in the principles of cooperation; to aid by information and otherwise prospective and actual cooperators; in brief, to coordinate the cooperative movement within the Order. It issued forms of a constitution and bylaws which, with a few modifications, could be adopted by any locality. It also published articles on the dangers and pitfalls in cooperative ventures, such as granting credit, poor management, etc., as well as numerous articles on specific kinds of cooperation. The Knights of Labor label was granted for the use of cooperative goods, and a persistent agitation was steadily conducted to induce purchasers to give a preference to cooperative products.

As a scheme of industrial regeneration, co-operation never materialized. The few successful shops sooner or later fell into the hands of an "inner group," who "froze out" the others and set up capitalistic partnerships. The great majority went on the rocks even before getting started. The causes of failure were many: hasty action, inexperience, lax shop discipline, internal dissensions, high rates of interest upon the mortgage of the plant, and finally discriminations instigated by competitors. Railways were heavy offenders, by delaying side tracks and, on some pretext or other, refusing to furnish cars or refusing to haul them.

The Union Mining Company of Cannelburg, Indiana, owned and operated by the Order as its sole experiment of the centralized kind of cooperation, met this fate. After expending $20,000 in equipping the mine, purchasing land, laying tracks, cutting and sawing timber on the land, and mining $1,000 worth of coal, they were compelled to lie idle for nine months before the railway company saw fit to connect their switch with the main track. When they were ready to ship their product, it was learned that their coal could be utilized for the manufacture of gas only, and that contracts for supply of such coal were let in July, that is, nine months from the time of connecting the switch with the main track. In addition, the company was informed that it must supply itself with a switch engine to do the switching of the cars from its mine to the main track, at an additional cost of $4,000. When this was accomplished they had to enter the market in competition with a bitter opponent who had been fighting them since the opening of the mine. Having exhausted their funds and not seeing their way clear to securing additional funds for the purchase of a locomotive and to tide over the nine months ere any contracts for coal could be entered into, they sold out to their competitor.

But a cause more fundamental perhaps than all other causes of the failure of cooperation in the United States is to be found in the difficulties of successful entrepreneurship. In the labor movement in the United States there has been a failure, generally speaking, to appreciate the significance of management and the importance which must be imputed to it. Glib talk often commands an undeserved confidence and misleads the wage earner. Thus by 1888, three or four years after it had begun, the cooperative movement had passed the full cycle of life and succumbed. The failure, as said, was hastened by external causes and discrimination. But the experiments had been foredoomed anyway—through the incompatibility of producers' cooperation with trade unionism. The cooperators, in their eagerness to get a market, frequently undersold the private employer expecting to recoup their present losses in future profits. In consequence, the privately employed wage earners had to bear reductions in their wages. A labor movement which endeavors to practice producers' cooperation and trade unionism at the same time is actually driving in opposite directions.

13. The Industrial Workers of the World and Revolutionary Unionism*

R. F. Hoxie

The American public has been frightened by the impressionist school of reporters and magazine writers into vital misconception and tremendous overestimate of the power and significance of the Industrial Workers of the World. This is the one outstanding fact revealed by the eighth annual convention of that organization held in Chicago late in September 1913.

The first significant fact revealed by this convention, and by the whole history of the IWW as well, is that this body, which claims as its mission the organization of the whole working class for the overthrow of capitalism, is pathetically weak in effective membership and has failed utterly in its efforts to attach to itself permanently a considerable body of men representative of any section of American workers.

In spite of eight years of organizing effort and unparalleled advertisement, the official roll of the convention indicated that its present paid-up membership[1] entitled to representation does not much exceed 14,000 men, while the actual constitutional representation on the convention floor was probably less than half that number. Nor was there anything to make it appear that this was regarded by the leaders or members as an exceptional or disappointing showing. The fact is, impossible as it may seem to those who have read the recent outpouring of alarmist literature on the subject, that this number probably comes near to representing the maximum, permanent, dues-paying membership at any time connected with the organization. For notwithstanding extravagant statements made in the past and a present claim of an enrollment approximating 100,000,[2] it is admitted by the highest official of the Industrial Workers that up to the time of the Lawrence strike the membership never reached 10,000, the highest yearly average being but 6,000, and the convention debates indicated clearly that the great bulk of those enrolled during that strike and in the succeeding period of unusual agitation and activity have retained no lasting connection with the organization. It was shown that the effective force of the union at Lawrence is already spent.[3] The representatives of the whole textile industry, indeed, cast but 31 votes in the convention, developing the fact that the total paid-up membership in this line of work probably does not now exceed 1,600,[4] and a communication was received from one of the local unions still remaining at Lawrence complaining of the methods of the organization and threatening adhesion to the American Federation of Labor. At Akron, again, where during the

---

* From *Trade Unionism in the United States* (New York: D. Appleton-Century-Crofts Co., Inc., 1924), pp. 139–74.

[1] November 1913.

[2] The actual membership of the IWW is unknown even to the officials. The records of the general office show an average paid-up membership for the year of 14,310. It is estimated that local and national bodies have an additional dues-paying membership of 25,000 on which no per capita tax has been paid to the general organization, and that there is, besides, a nominal nondues-paying enrollment of from 50,000 to 60,000. The truth seems to be that 100,000 or more men *have had* IWW dues cards in their possession during the past five years. How much of this outlying membership fringe is now bona fide it is impossible to estimate. Some part of it represents members out of work or on strike and therefore temporarily unable to pay dues. Even this portion, however, is organically ineffective and is constantly dropping out. We seem justified, therefore, in taking the actual paid-up membership as the nearest approximation to the permanent effective strength of the organization.

[3] The membership now claimed at Lawrence is 700. After the strike it was said to be 14,000.

[4] By constitutional provision one vote is allowed in the convention for every 50 members or major fraction thereof.

120

rubber strike early this year apparently more than 6,000 were added to the roll, the convention vote cast indicated a present membership of 150 or thereabouts, and statements on the floor revealed the fact that most of those who joined at the time of the strike did not retain official connection with the union long enough to pay the second assessment of dues.[5]

Evidence to the same general effect might be multiplied almost indefinitely. Everywhere the history of the organization has shown this same inability to maintain a stable and growing membership. There are without doubt reasons for this fact apart from the special character and methods of the IWW, but these are beside the point. The point is that by reason of lack of sufficient membership this body is and seems destined to be utterly inadequate to the tasks which it has set itself to accomplish. It aims to educate and organize the working class and claims to have discovered the effective ideals and organic basis to this end, but during eight years of strenuous effort it has succeeded in reaching and holding less than one in 2,000 of the workers of this country alone. Its first great organic tasks, if it is to attain this end, are the displacement of the American Federation of Labor, the railway brotherhoods, and the Socialist party, but it has not been able to organize effectively for these purposes a body of men equal to 1 percent of the membership of the American Federation alone, or to one sixtieth of those who act with the Socialist party; it proposes a united and successful direct industrial assault upon capitalism, but it has not thus far drawn to itself on this basis a permanent enrollment equal in number to the employees of many a single capitalist enterprise. Plainly no further proof is needed that those who are attached to the present order have nothing now to fear from IWW-ism judged from the standpoint of mere numbers and power of appeal to the great body of the working class.

But numerical weakness is not after all the chief handicap of the IWW in its struggle for positive achievement. This convention secondly brought into clearest relief the fact that this feeble body is in a state of organic chaos as the result of apparently irreconcilable internal conflict, and the history of the organization makes it appear that this state of affairs is chronic and inevitable. The conflict, the keynote of IWW history, was waged in the present convention under the guise of centralization versus decentrali-zation. It is at present, objectively, a contest virtually between the East and the West. The so-called decentralizers, mainly westerners, sought in the convention by every conceivable means to cut down the power and authority of the central governing body. This central authority already had been reduced almost to a shadow. As the result of previous phases of the contest the office of general president had been abolished; the executive board had been placed under control of the general referendum which could be initiated at any time and on all subjects by ten local unions in three different industries, while its efficiency had been minimized by inadequate financial support; and the locals had become to all intents and purposes autonomous bodies. But all this has brought no permanent satisfaction to the decentralizing faction. Its ultimate ideal apparently is, and has been from the beginning, not "one big union" but a loosely federated body of completely autonomous units, each free to act in time and in manner as its fancy dictates, subject to no central or constitutional guidance or restraint—in short, a body of local units with purely voluntary relationships governed in time, character, and extent of cooperation by sentiment only.

Actuated by this ideal, the decentralizers conducted in the recent convention a 12-days' assault upon what remained of central power. They attempted to abolish the general executive board; to paralize the general organization by minimizing its financial support; to abolish the convention and provide for legislation by means of the general referendum only; to place the official organizers under the direct control of the rank and file; to reduce the general officers to the position of mere clerks, functioning only as corresponding intermediaries between the local organizations; and by other means to give to each of these local bodies complete autonomy in matters of organization, policy, action, and financial control. It matters little that at this particular convention the centralizing faction, mainly by virtue of superior parliamentary tactics, succeeded in staving off the attacks of its opponents and in saving, at least until the matter goes to referendum, the present form of the organization. The significant facts are that the same factional strive has existed from the moment when the IWW was launched; and that it apparently is bound to exist as long as the organization lasts; that the decentralizing forces, though often defeated formally, have in practice succeeded and seem bound to continue to succeed in working their will inside the organization, with the inevitable result of disintegration and organic chaos. Evidence of

    [5] At the time of the strike the local purchased 11,000 dues stamps from the general office. A membership of 2,000 is claimed at present.

this is everywhere apparent. During the past year 99 locals, ignored and uncared for, went out of existence entirely; in New York the relatively strong local assembly is working at cross-purposes with the central organization and successfully defying its power; in the West, locals are being formed and managed on extra-constitutional lines; throughout this part of the country members are being expelled by one local and straightway admitted by another; so diverse are the local ideals and so uncertain the means of intercommunication that in practice it has been found generally impossible to get ten locals into the requisite harmony to initiate a referendum; sabotage is being openly practiced by the local membership against the organization itself and has recently resulted in the suspension of one of its two official organs, the *Industrial Worker;* in fact, it is freely admitted and apparently is looked upon with satisfaction by the decentralizing faction, that there are at present 57 varieties of Industrial Workers of the World.

The net result is that the IWW, instead of being the grim, brooding power which it is pictured in popular imagination, is a body utterly incapable of strong, efficient, united action and the attainment of results of a permanent character—a body capable of local and spasmodic effort only. True, it has a constitution which provides in a most logical manner for the welding of the workers into a great, effective, organic body. But this constitution is a mere mechanical structure in the interstices of which organic accretions have here and there settled. The little organic bodies are sovereign, each of their members is a sovereign, and to both member and organic unit the constitution is a thing subject to their will. The fact is that the IWW is not an organization but a loosely bound group of uncontrolled fighters. It is a symptom if you will, and in that alone, if anywhere, lies its present social significance. But decentralized as it is to the extent of organic dissipation, atomistic, and rent by bitter factional strife, it has no present power of general persistent or constructive action.

The IWW, however, is not only weak in membership and organic unity; it possesses, further, no financial resources even in a slight degree adequate to advance and maintain its proposed organization of the working class or to carry forward any consistent assault on capitalism; and, moreover, it has shown itself incapable of controlling for its main purposes even the financial resources which it does possess. Advocates of the movement, it is true, minimize the importance of mere money in the kind of warfare

which they propose to conduct. This is supposed to be one of the pregnant ideas of the direct actionists. They do not propose, it is said, like the Socialists, to support a horde of parasitic labor politicians, nor, like the trade unions, to out-wait the capitalist. They will force the capitalists to abdicate by the simple process of making it unprofitable for them to conduct industry. And this can be done practically without funds— where it will suffice—simply by keeping the worker's hands in his pockets—where this will not produce the desired result, by striking on the job. I do not propose in this connection to enter into any discussion of the theory of direct action. All that I wish to do is to point out the fact that much of the present weakness of the IWW is due to financial want and a constitutional inability to control the actual financial resources at hand. Time after time the IWW has been obliged to let slip favorable opportunities for organization and has lost local bodies because it could not furnish the carfare and meal tickets necessary to send the gospel to the workers groping in darkness. Time after time it has seen promising demonstrations collapse and the workers drift away from the point of contest and from its control because it could not finance organizers and supply food and lodging to tide over the period of temporary hardship. The whole experience of the organization has, in fact, proved that, short of a condition of general and desperate distress, progressive and permanent working-class organization requires ready and continuous financial support. And here lies the most vital error in the practical theory and calculations of the IWW. The American workmen as a body are not, and are not likely to be, in a condition of general and desperate distress. It is, therefore, to the unskilled and casual laborers alone that the IWW can bring home its appeal and to these only that it can look for the funds to put through its organizing projects. It is this chronic financial distress that more than anything else has caused the dissipation of its membership after each of its brilliant but spasmodic efforts.

The case is made more hopeless by the inability of the organization to control the little financial power it can command. This lack of financial control is another outcome of the decentralizing mania which grips the membership. The average local has not developed the ability to conserve its own resources. Rather than support the central authority and submit to its financial management, the local suffers its funds to be dissipated by incompetent members or stolen by dishonest officials. Nothing was more striking in the recent convention than the stories of local financial losses. "All down through the line," said one delegate, "we have had experience with secretaries who absconded with funds." "No less than three have done the same thing (in our local)," was the testimony of another. This has happened three times to one local in one year according to a third statement. Indeed, so loose is the local financial control and the general interrelationship of organic units, especially in the western country, that there appears to exist a body of circulating professional agitators who make it their business to go from locality to locality for the sole purpose of getting themselves elected to the treasurer's office and absconding with the funds. The local unions do not seem to be in sufficiently close touch to ferret out the malefactors and check the practice, nor will they heed the warnings of the general office. Indeed, in some locals the feeling seems to prevail that the local secretary is entitled to what he can make away with. Such are the financial conditions in the organization which claims to have the only means of opposing to the capitalist class a solid and effective organization of the workers, and asserts that it is training the workers for the task of reorganizing and managing the industries of the country.

From what has already been said it might readily be inferred that the IWW would be incapable of successful general assault on the present social and industrial organization or of any effective reconstructive effort, even though it should succeed in greatly enlarging its membership, reconciling its factions, and overcoming its financial difficulties. Such a conclusion in fact seems amply warranted. It rests on a threefold basis of fact: First, the membership of the IWW is and is bound to be of such a character that united, sustained, constructive action is practically impossible for it without a consistent body of ideals and a relatively permanent leadership of the highest organizing and directive quality.

As already intimated, the IWW must depend for the bulk of its membership on the least capable, least developed, lowest trained, and poorest paid of American workmen. To these may be added an element made up of irresponsible atomists who are so constituted that to them all authority is an ever-present challenge. No American workman of constructive mind will permanently affiliate himself with a revolutionary industrial organization which abhors half-measures and political action so long as he can see ahead the hope of immediate betterment through the gradual development and enforcement of an im-

proved system of working rules and conditions. This does not mean that the IWW is composed of the so-called bum element, as is so often asserted. Far from it. But it does mean that it is the desperate elements of the working class, the men who have not developed and cannot develop, under the existing system, organic discipline, and constructive ability, to whom the IWW appeals—in the East the "Hunkies" and underpaid mill hands, for the most part unassimilated Europeans; in the West the "blanket stiffs," the "timber wolves," "the dock wallopers," and the padrone-recruited construction gangs; and everywhere the man who because of temperament or oppression has become a self-directing enemy of whatever stands for authority or things as they are. One had but to observe the recent convention to recognize these types and these characteristics as predominant even in this picked assembly. Undernourishment and underdevelopment were prominent physical characteristics of the group. The broad-headed, square-jawed, forceful, and constructive type, so marked in trade-union assemblies, was conspicuous by its absence. By many of those present organic strength and action were evidently regarded as correlatives of oppression. To some these ideas seemed so foreign that the general character of the organization appeared to be unknown to them. The rule of the majority, except in so far as it applied to the local group, was repudiated many times during the course of the debates. Add to all this the presence in the assembly of members of secret committees whose actions are beyond even the knowledge and control of the local groups—and we have a fair conception of the difficulty here presented of united and controlled action. Obviously only a body of leaders strong in intelligence and personality, bound to a consistent body of ideals, harmonious in action, and long in the saddle, could hope to weld such elements into an effective, organic whole.

But, secondly, the IWW has failed to develop and sustain such a stable body of leaders and shows no capacity to do so. Of the original group of men who organized and outlined the policies of this new venture in unionism, only one was seated in the convention and only one or two besides are prominently connected with the organization at present. Moyer, Debs, Mother Jones, Pinkerton, and others, signers of the original manifesto, effective leaders of the past, many of them yet effective leaders in other labor organizations, have all disappeared from the councils of the IWW—nagged out, kicked out, or driven out by despair or disgust. This result has been in part the inevitable outcome of the hatred of authority which expresses itself in the decentralizing movement. Partly, as will be shown later, it is the outcome of an incongruity and shifting of ideals within the organization; but, to no small extent, it is the product of a strong force of romantic idealism which, strange as it may seem, exists in the minds and hearts of the downtrodden constituency of the IWW. In spite of the fact that these men will have none of the regularly constituted authority when it makes for strength, they are hero-worshipers and are easily led for the moment by the "heroes of labor." These heroes are the momentary leaders of strikes and of battles with the police and militia, those especially who have gone on trial and suffered imprisonment for violence or the disturbance of the public peace. They are, in general, men who themselves have not involuntarily suffered at the hands of society but have provoked its vengeance. They are largely well nourished, quick, and intelligent, but, with exceptions, they are men who have deliberately discarded all constructive ideals, deliberately thrown off social restraint, and, in the spirit of the medieval knight or the revolutionist of the well-to-do classes in Russia, have constituted themselves the personal avengers of the wrongs of the working class. Such men grip the imagination of the rank and file and make of what would otherwise be an ultra-democratic organization, relatively unfitted for constructive effort, a positively destructive force in spirit and action. They are the inventors of new forms of sabotage, the guerrilla leaders, the members of "secret committees," the *provocateurs* in the free-speech fights; the men who create the sentiment that the only existing standard of right is might, that opposition to authority is a virtue, that imprisonment is an honor. It is these labor heroes, rising from time to time before the admiring vision of the undisciplined membership of the IWW, who have displaced the men already in power and, to a large extent, have made impossible the development of a stable body of leaders capable of welding the membership by patient effort into an organic whole.

Underneath all this, however, making consistent action and therefore permanent development impossible for the IWW, there exists and has existed, thirdly, a fundamental conflict of ideals. Much has been made of the sabotage and other modes of direct action current among the members of the IWW. Because of the prevalence of these methods, the conclusion has been accepted uncritically that IWW-ism is another name for syndicalism. This, however, is but a half-truth and even as such it needs qualification. The truth is that the IWW is a compound entity whose elements are not entirely harmonious. It was launched in 1905 as a protest against craft unionism and the conservative attitude and policies of the American Federation of Labor. It was originally composed prevailingly of a body of men socialistically inclined who believed that betterment of the condition of the workers as a whole and permanently could be attained only by organizing all of them by industries into one big union with the ultimate object of the overthrow of the capitalist system. In order to attain this end they outlined an organization which should bring the skilled and unskilled workers into one structural body with highly centralized authority so that the whole power of the organization—especially its financial power—could be quickly concentrated at any one point where contest existed between the employers and the workmen, and which should cooperate with the Socialist party on the political field. The slogans of the organization were: "Labor produces all wealth"; "might makes right"; "an injury to one an injury to all"; "no contracts and no compromise"; "industrial organizations"; "one big union"; "workers of the world, unite." The IWW showed at this time no essential characteristics of what has since become familiar as revolutionary syndicalism.

No sooner, however, had the organization been launched than a conflict of ideals appeared. The first year saw a fatal blow struck at the idea of one big union with strong, centralized authority —in a disruption which resulted in the abolition of the office of general president of the organization. In 1908 a second split occurred which banished the Socialist element from power. Political action was stricken from the preamble to the constitution and direct action as a revolutionary slogan arose alongside the notion of one big, centralized, industrial union. From this time forward the internal history of the IWW has been a history of the conflict of these two ideals—the one, industrial unionism, standing for permanent organization of the workers and immediate benefits, requiring a strong central authority well financed; the other, revolutionary syndicalism, standing for uncontrolled agitation, and guerilla warfare, whose adherents chafe against central authority and its financial support.

Out of this conflict of ideals the contest between centralization and decentralization arose. The decentralizers, mainly westerners, imbued with the revolutionary ideal because they were for the most part casual workers with no big industries to organize, whose main recourse was to stir up trouble, argued that since this was the purpose of the organization all central authority was to be reckoned as irksome restraint. The local membership could best judge when the time had come to act. A central treasury was not needed since one or a few individuals acting on their own responsibility could wreck machinery, destroy materials, and precipitate a contest with political authority. Therefore they raised the banner of decentralization and direct revolution. Thus was syndicalism born and nourished in the IWW. But it was mainly an instinctive syndicalism, a blind, destructive force, lacking in general the vision and well-rounded doctrine of the European syndicalists. Even yet it is safe to say that few among the rank and file who call themselves syndicalists could state the theory of the European movement. Meanwhile in the East the relatively permanent character of the unskilled workers, and the necessity of wrenching from great industrial organizations immediate and permanent gains, still emphasized the need of regularity, authority, and permanent power—in short, industrial unionism in its original connotation. Hence syndicalism and industrial unionism have remained as conflicting ideals within the organization, preventing the development of that leadership which alone can give to the IWW consistent action, permanent growth, and effective power. So long as the conflict holds, the organization must remain weak, spasmodic in action, and destructive in results.

But it is doubtful if the final triumph of either of these ideals would suffice to make of the IWW a real power in this country. In this connection two points need emphasis: First, in so far as the IWW aspires to represent syndicalism pure and simple the conditions are not here for its growth. Syndicalism as it has developed in this country is a doctrine of despair. However much its proponents may attempt to stress its ultimate ideal—the rebuilding of industrial society—it is essentially a destructive philosophy. As stated above, it will not be adopted, except temporarily and under special stress, by any body of workmen who see hope ahead in gradual betterment through constructive industrial and political action. Such a body is the organizing element of the American working class as evidenced by the 2.5 million trade unionists, and the growth of the Socialist party since it has taken an opportunist position.

Secondly, in so far as the IWW aspires to represent the movement toward industrial unionism, the field of action is already occupied. The American Federation of Labor through its local councils, its central organizations, its system federations, its departments, and its amalgamated craft unions, is creating the machinery for the practical expression of the industrial union ideal as rapidly as the circumstances of the worker's life and needs allow of its development. The process is perhaps slow but it is sure and effective. It is proceeding by the trial-and-error method which alone has proved adequate to the permanent advancement of the interests of the workers. And when it is considered further that within the American Federation one industrial union alone outnumbers in membership the whole effective force of the IWW in the proportion of 20 to 1, the prospect that the latter will be able to oust its rival from the field becomes too small for consideration.

The fact is that the IWW faces a perpetual dilemma. The bulk of the American workmen want more here and now for themselves and their immediate associates and care little for the remote future or the revolutionary ideal. These will have none of the IWW. The others have not and, under the existing conditions, cannot develop the capacity for sustained organic effort. Whichever way the organization turns, then, it seems doomed to failure.

Viewing the situation in any reasonable light, therefore, we find it difficult to escape the conclusion that the Industrial Workers of the World as a positive social factor is more an object of pathetic interest than of fear. It has succeeded in impressing itself upon the popular imagination as a mysterious, incalculable force likely to appear and work destruction at any time and place. It has terrified the public because its small body of irresponsible and foot-loose agitators scent trouble from afar and flock to the point where social rupture seems to be for the moment imminent. They are like Morgan's raiders. By rapidity of movement and sheer audacity they have created the impression of a great organized force. But in reality they are incapable of anything but spasmodic and disconnected action. As a means for calling attention to the fact that machinery is breaking down the distinction between skilled and unskilled labor and is thus rendering craft organization ineffective; as an instrument for rousing the public to a consciousness of the suffering and needs of the unskilled and transient workers and of the existence here of a compelling social problem; as a spur to the activity of the more conservative and exclusive labor organizations, the IWW may have a useful social function. As a directly effective social force, however, it has no considerable significance.

The conclusion, so far as it concerns the problem of syndicalism in the United States, would seem to be obvious. But I am well aware that those who feel a vital, constitutional need for visualizing and magnifying such a problem will not abandon their beliefs merely on this showing of evidence. They will doubtless point to the undeniable growth of industrial unionism within the American Federation of Labor and to the many sporadic outbreaks of violent and predatory action with which the history of our labor movement has been checkered, as indicating the development of syndicalism in spirit and action within the American labor movement quite apart from any formal organization or teaching—a great ground swell, they will say, carrying the whole movement onward toward the syndicalist bourne. But let us see whether these are really syndicalistic manifestations. I doubt it, and for these two reasons:

First, I venture to affirm that there is no more necessary connection between industrial unionism and syndicalism than between capitalism and monarchy. Industrial unionism on the face of it is merely an attempt to parallel capitalist organization. It is perfectly compatible with collective bargaining and with what we might call business unionism, as is illustrated by the case of the United Mine Workers. It is the ideal type of unionism advocated by the socialists. On the other hand, it may grow up along with nonsocialist political action, as in the American Federation of Labor, where a strong tendency toward industrial organization has gone hand in hand with a robust development of legislative and political activity. Evidently, then, it indicates a hopeless confusion of ideas to identify syndicalism with industrial unionism, and it is a misuse of reason to predicate the one as necessarily the result of the other.

How then about union violence and predation? Do they show any necessary affinity between unionism and syndicalism? In order to answer this question correctly let us look for a moment at the most usual occasion for deliberate violence and predation on the part of old-line unionists. It is a fact that almost any body of union men, whatever their principles and ordinary methods, and for that matter almost any body of workers, will tend to resort to violence and perhaps predation if they are face to face with systematic and long-continued aggression, or are brought up against a blank wall of resistance to demands for the absolute essentials of a safe and decent existence, *provided there is no relief in sight through law or public opinion.* But the same is true of any body of men with red blood in their veins or of women, for that matter. Shall we

then dissipate our concept of syndicalism by making it cover the actions of the Boston Tea Party, the Ku-Klux Klan, the Mexican revolutionists and the militant suffragettes? Surely we must not confuse spasmodic outbreaks against specific oppression with direct action as the corollary of a fixed and general aversion to peaceful opportunist effort and political action. Only, then, when union violence and predation have been the outgrowth of a permanent aversion of this kind, or when such aversion has grown up with the violence and has become a fixed creed of a union can we rightfully speak of them as syndicalistic in character.

But shall we nowhere find this permanent attitude outside of the Industrial Workers of the World? The American Railway Union was not adverse to political action; the Western Federation of Miners has again joined forces with the American Federation of Labor; the Bridge and Structural Iron Workers show no signs apparently of going over to the syndicalist camp.

Must we not then conclude that, in drawing the Industrial Workers of the World into the picture in its proper character and proportion, we have pretty thoroughly disposed of syndicalism as a serious American problem?

So far so good; but have we any assurance that we shall not soon have to face a serious syndicalist problem in America? To satisfy ourselves on this point we should have to discuss our third question, namely: What are the causes of syndicalism, and what are the prospects of its future development? I shall not attempt to discuss this question fully, but shall be content to make one or two suggestive statements indicating why syndicalism has not developed and is not likely to develop on American soil, and the conditions which would be necessary for its development here.

Successful trade unionism as it exists in America today is not a made-to-order affair; it is not imitative of anything to be found abroad, nor is it the objectification of any general social theory. It is a means, slowly forged by experience, of meeting the immediate needs and of solving the immediate problems of the American workers. It has been developed by the trial-and-error method; it is experimental, opportunistic, and pragmatic. And, if you will look back over the last century and a quarter you will find that this is the only kind of labor organization that has survived and worked in this country. Even socialism, before it could make any successful appeal to American workmen, had to cut loose from the ultrarevolutionists, thrust its theories into the background, and develop a program for meeting immediate needs and problems.

The immediate reason for all this lies in the character of the organizing element of American workmen. The great mass of organized American workmen are not conscious revolutionists, but optimistic opportunists. They want more here and now. Their attention is fixed on meeting immediate needs and solving immediate problems. They see hope ahead in a gradual improvement of existing conditions. They have little capacity for or patience with speculative theorizing. They are unwilling to leave the path which has been marked out by experience with its slow but sure advance, to plunge into theoretically assumed shortcuts charted only by the imagination. This is the general attitude of that portion of the American working class which has alone proved itself capable of sustained organic effort.

This attitude is the outcome partly of the racial character of American workmen, and partly of American economic and social conditions. The hard-headed, tradition-bound, empirical element predominates in our labor movement just as it does in our business affairs, in law and politics, and in our social ideals and affairs generally, and this characteristic, perhaps racial, has been re-enforced by the fact that the economic and social conditions have for generations been such that the workers *could* see hope ahead in gradual betterment through constructive industrial and political action. The labor movement thus given character has assimilated and Americanized foreign accretions, just as in general we have assimilated and Americanized the immigrant, socially and politically.

It is true in the one case as in the other that assimilation and transmutation have not been complete, but if our labor history has proved anything, as indicated especially by the career of the Industrial Workers of the World, it is that those elements which have not been assimilated are incapable of consistent and effective organic union and action, and that the spasmodic organic efforts of such a body as the Industrial Workers of the World fail to check the growth and do not essentially modify the ideals and methods of the American and Americanized labor movement.

On account of all this there is no syndicalist problem of consequence in this country. We shall have none of consequence, I believe, unless and until the great organic American labor movement finds its way barred to empirical advance. It is now feeling its way toward the organizing of the unskilled and will doubtless organize them as fast as the psychology of the situation will permit;

it is advancing experimentally toward the industrial form of organization, as anyone must concede who is at all familiar with the organic history and the declarations of the American Federation of Labor; it is at the same time forging ahead on the line of political action as fast as tradition will safely allow; it is gradually overcoming the employers' claims of autocratic rights and establishing the principles and working rules of industrial democracy. Whenever it comes face to face with a blank wall of resistance in law and administration, whenever it encounters trusts and employers' associations bent upon its extermination, it is apt to adopt secret, violent, and predatory methods. But when the temporary occasion is past it quickly returns to its ordinary ideals and tactics. And if I read the character and spirit of the American labor movement aright, it would take a deal of useless battering against an impenetrable wall of legal and industrial resistance to create in the American labor movement the general psychology compatible with a real and robust development of syndicalism.

The Industrial Workers of the World is one aspect of revolutionary unionism. To understand it, therefore, we must have some understanding of the larger thing of which it is a part. In the popular conception of things revolutionary unionism is generally distinguished by violence and sabotage. The tendency, however, to make violence the hall-mark of revolutionary unionism is a great mistake. The bulk of revolutionary unionists embraces the most peaceful citizens we have, and on principle. Most violence in labor troubles is committed by conservative unionists or by the unorganized.[6] In Chicago, violence has become inseparably associated in the public mind with organizations in the building trades. "Slugging" raids and shooting affairs have come to be taken as a matter of course and excite little interest. A few years ago these union tactics attained their highest development under the leadership of "Skinny" Madden, then in control of the central building trades organization. But Madden and his men were not looking to any overthrow of existing conditions. His were the methods of predatory hold-up unionism. Nor was the recent dynamiting campaign of the Bridge and Structural Iron Workers the product of revolutionary unionism. Here, rather, was a case of a conservative union fighting with its back to the wall against a campaign of annihilation by an employers' combination. In the last ditch, it turned,

---

[6] That is to say, the violence which is due to the labor unions.

not to revolution, but to guerilla warfare and *guerilla* unionism. And this also to a large degree characterizes the recent violent acts of the miners in Colorado. In short, violence in labor troubles is a unique characteristic of no kind of unionism but is a general and apparently inevitable incident of the rise of the working class to consciousness and power in capitalistic society.

Secondly, revolutionary unionism is not to be marked off from other kinds of unionism by its employment of sabotage as an offensive and defensive weapon. It is true that sabotage is a weapon whose use is highly characteristic of revolutionary unionism, but the notion that its use is confined to revolutionary unionists fades out the moment its true character and varied forms are known.[7] It is moreover distinctly repudiated by many revolutionary unionists, is not confined to revolutionary unions, and it might be added, is not confined to the workers alone.[8] It is clear then that revolutionary unionism cannot, by this practice, be marked off and made a definite and clearly recognizable thing.

What, then, is revolutionary unionism, and how are we to distinguish and recognize it? Revolutionary unionism is in essence a spiritual something, a group viewpoint, a theory and interpretation of society and social relationships held by groups of militant wageworkers and an attempt to realize this theory and interpretation by means of a program of action. A distinct organization committed to this program and viewpoint is a thing always striven for, but is not an essential feature nor at present a general characteristic of revolutionary unionism in the United States. That is to say, while there are distinct revolutionary organizations in this country, such as the Industrial Workers of the World and lately the Syndicalist League, most revolutionary unionists are found within conservative trade unions, with no separate organic expression of their own. To distinguish revolutionary unionism, therefore, and to get an accurate understanding of the matter in hand we must distinguish its varieties before going further. The first, *socialistic* unionism, is represented organically by the Detroit Industrial Workers of the World and by a small number of national unions in the American Federation of Labor. The larger number of socialist unionists, however, have no separate union organization. They are to be found in the supposedly conservative business and uplift unions of the American Federation of Labor and the Railway Brotherhoods. The mine workers, the painters, the bakers, for example, are largely socialist unionists. The second variety of revolutionary unionism found in this country is *anarchistic,* or more accurately, *quasi anarchistic.* It is best represented by the Chicago Industrial Workers of the World. But, again, there are quasi anarchistic unionists scattered through the conservative and socialistic unions.

Revolutionary unionism, in both its forms, starts with the assumption that society is divided into two warring classes, between which there are no common interests and no possibility of compromise. The workers produce all wealth; the employers systematically rob them. The workers cannot secure and enjoy what they produce until they rule society.[9] In this fight, the revolutionary unionists refuse to recognize the validity of the standards of right and justice, the laws and the rules of the game current in society. There is no such thing as society as a whole. Established notions of right, established rights, and the institutions in their support are the devices of the employing class designed to keep labor down and exploit the workers. Therefore, the workers are not bound by these things. For the workers—just as well as for the employers—whatever is for their interests as a class, whatever furthers their

[7] Sabotage is an elusive phenomenon and is difficult of accurate definition. Briefly described it is called "striking on the job." J. A. Estey, in his "Revolutionary Unionism," does well when he says: "In Syndicalist practice it [sabotage] is a comprehensive term, covering every process by which the laborer, while remaining at work, tries to damage the interests of his employer, whether by simple malingering, or by bad quality of work, or by doing actual damage to tools and machinery" (p. 96). This definition puts admirably the essential, underlying characteristics of sabotage, but in practice it ranges even beyond such limits. There are almost an indefinite number of ways of "putting the boots to the employer" which have come properly to be included under the general designation, and some of them have been employed by conservative unionists time out of mind. *Ca' Canny* or soldiering is one of them, which was a practice long before revolutionary unionism was known to the mass of the workers. In essence it is practiced by every union that sets a limitation on output. Living strictly up to impossible safety rules enacted by the employers for their own protection is another method. Wasting materials, turning out goods of inferior quality or damaging them in the process, misdirecting shipments, telling the truth about the quality of products, changing price cards, sanding the bearings, salting the soup and the sheets, "throwing the monkey wrench into the machinery"—all are methods of practicing sabotage that have become familiar.

[8] As the unionists point out, essentially the same thing is practiced by employers and dealers who adulterate goods, make shoddy goods, conceal defects of products, and sell goods for what they are not.

[9] See Constitution, Industrial Workers of the World, Preamble §§ 1, 2; also Industrial Unionism vs. Anarchy and Reform, p. 4, Detroit Industrial Workers of the World. But see also Declaration of Principles of Bakery and Confectionery Workers, a compound craft union in the American Federation of Labor.

ends, is *right*. In short, in the last analysis, there is no standard of right and rights but might. This doctrine is held without reserve by quasi anarchistic unionists. It justifies to them violence, destruction of property, and even killing. It would be unfair, however, to say this of the socialistic unionists. While they declare that actual rights are based on might, they refuse to admit that might *ought* to make right and, therefore, stop short of justifying violence and killing.

It is the primary aim of all revolutionary unionists to overthrow the existing institutional order; to do away with individual ownership of the means of production and the profit system; to put social and industrial control into the hands of the workers. To accomplish this, they propose to unite the workers not by crafts, as is the case generally of conservative unionism, but by industries, and, finally, into one great working class organization so that in a fight workers cannot be used against workers, but the whole power of the class can be brought to bear against the employers at any point. But beyond this, the socialist unionists and the quasi anarchistic unionists differ vitally and widely. They differ as to ultimate aims, as to program, and as to methods.

The socialist unionists look forward to a state of society which, except for common ownership and control of industry and strong centralized government in the hands of the working class, does not differ essentially from our own. They would in general attain this end by peaceful means, both industrial and political. Industrially, they would organize the workers into larger and larger units, and by the usual trade union methods secure for them better conditions and a greater and greater voice and place in the control and management of industry. Politically, they would unite the same workers into a great party designed to educate them and others in civil affairs, to push for legislation in the social and industrial interests of the workers, and ultimately to secure control of the legislative, administrative, and judicial powers of the government. Ultimately, the industrial employer would be eliminated by the working class state.

The quasi anarchistic unionists have a different ultimate aim. They look forward to the *complete* abolition of the state and of existing governmental machinery. They visualize not a political but an industrial society where the *unions* would be the government. All political action is abhorrent to them, partly because the state is outside their scheme of things and political action is a recognition of a compromise with it, but largely because they believe that experience has proved

it to be not only useless as a working-class weapon but positively harmful to working-class interests. They have noted that political associations and political gains make the workers soft, conservative, and nonrevolutionary. Revolution degenerates into mere reform, and political preferment makes traitors of working-class leaders. The middle-class tendencies of the Socialist parties in Germany, France, and the United States, and the action of such men as Briand and John Burns have brought them to this view. Direct action, therefore, has become their slogan, that is, the making and enforcing of demands upon the enemy directly by the workers, through demonstrations, strikes, sabotage, and violence. At this point, however, the quasi anarchistic revolutionary unionists themselves split into two camps, centralizers and decentralizers.

The centralizers believe that the actual building up of the industrial organization will train and educate the workers in the conduct, not only of industry, but of all social affairs, so that when the organization has become universalized it can perform all the necessary functions of social control now exercised by the state in its legislative, executive, and judicial capacities. This universal organization of the workers will then displace the state, government, and politics in the present sense; private ownership, privilege, and exploitation will be forever abolished. The one big union will have become the state, the government, the supreme organic and functional expression of society; its rules and decisions will be the law.

The decentralizers look forward to what they call a free industrial society. Each local group of workers is to be a law to itself. They are to organize as they please. The present industrial and social arrangements are to be overthrown simply by making it unprofitable for the employing class to own and operate industries. Future society is to consist of independent groups of workers freely exchanging their products. The proper proportions of investment and production, the ratio of exchange of goods, etc., will automatically be determined, just as they are under competitive industry, only then the competition will be between groups of workers, instead of between individuals. Universal knowledge and a superior morality, which will spring up as soon as capitalist society is abolished, will take the place of our present complicated system of social control and do away with the necessity of government in the present sense.

Beyond this, the characteristic theories, policies, and methods of the two varieties of quasi anarchistic unionists, in general, agree. The central purpose of all their efforts, as we have seen, is the overthrow of the capitalist system, and the establishment of working-class social control. But this cannot be accomplished by a gradual process of immediate gains in the form of better wages, shorter hours, better working conditions, etc. The end is retarded rather than advanced by such immediate concessions and advantages because these tend to make the workers conservative, satisfied with the present system, and those who gain most become selfish and detached in interest from the whole working class. The main immediate object of all their efforts is not material results, but agitation, education, a rousing of the workers and employers to mutual hatred and bitterness. Hence they count everything in the way of a fight, whether won or lost, as a gain. To them, no strike can be lost, since the very failure, in the common way of looking at it, is the surest way to secure the psychological results they are after. Therefore, they are always alert to take every opportunity for fighting, whatever the odds against them. Their motto is anything to stir up trouble between the workers and the ruling class. A contest with the police over free speech or with the church is as good an opportunity as a strike. And they count all things as good that may irritate the employers or authorities to action against them. Trouble is what they thrive on.

The revolution, then, must be the work of the unskilled—the true proletariat. They must be roused and united and educated—the whole object of the agitation is this. But is this possible when we consider the character and conditions of these unskilled workers? The great mass of them are untrained, unintelligent, cowed, subservient, satisfied with things as they are because they know nothing better. Get them together and there is no unanimity of ideas; poll them and the sodden majority would overwhelmingly outvote the alert, revolutionary minority. How, then, can the unskilled proletariat create the revolution? The quasi anarchistic unionists answer with what is perhaps their most distinctive and pregnant idea, *the theory of the militant minority.* They are no levelers; they do not propose to poll the proletariat; they do not really believe in democracy. Throughout the history of the world, they will tell you, everything has been achieved, every advance has been pushed through, by the intelligent minority. Every revolution has thus been accomplished. The mass of men in all grades of society are unintelligent, but they are imitators. Given a sufficiently intelligent and active minority which understands this and does not allow itself to be swamped by democratic ideals and arrangements, and the mass can be roused to action and be made to work its will. The quasi anarchistic unionists are the intelligent minority of the workers. The proletariat is their instrument. Their task is to tune it up to the revolutionary pitch and use it as a revolutionary force. But how? Obviously the way is to stimulate a constant and ever-growing fight between the proletariat and their enemies. This can be done partly by general agitation, but the fight must be conducted also on the industrial field. And how best conduct this industrial fight?

Here the quasi anarchistic unionists are moved partly by theory and partly by the necessities of the situation. On the basis of theory alone, the thing is not to work primarily for material gains. Such gains, we have seen, put the instrument out of tune, relax the strings. Hence the old-fashioned strike is not appropriate. And, beyond this, necessity makes it an impossible weapon. The old-fashioned strike is essentially a trial of financial strength between the employers and the workers. Its success also requires sustained cooperative effort on the part of the mass. But the proletariat has no financial strength and cannot be held to its task for long periods. The ordinary strike then is out of the question as a revolutionary weapon. If it succeeds it weakens the revolutionary spirit of the workers; if it fails it strengthens the employers. A weapon, then, must be devised which shall keep alive the revolutionary spirit, be inexpensive to the workers, require no sustained cooperation, and weaken the employers. Here, finally, we reach the raison d'être of the great industrial weapons of the quasi anarchistic unionists—the intermittent strike and sabotage. They keep the workers and employers constantly embroiled in a way to arouse mutual bitterness and hatred. They are inexpensive to the workers; the intermittent strike does not demand continuous cooperation over long periods, while sabotage need not require cooperation at all; it can be carried on by the individual alone. They hit the employer at his most vulnerable point by making it unprofitable for him to operate. Hence the great industrial slogan is "Strike on the job." But all these methods we have mentioned are not the ultimate means of the quasi anarchistic unionists. They are but the *means to the means* for the final end. Agitation of all sorts, the intermittent strike, sabotage, and violence[10] have

---

[10] But note that this is said only of the quasi anarchistic, revolutionary unionists. The socialistic revolutionary unionists, who are by far the majority in this country, altogether repudiate violence, sabotage, etc.

the primary purpose of developing solidarity among the proletariat which will make possible ultimately the general strike that shall finally overthrow capitalism and of educating the workers to a capacity for the conduct of social affairs.

There is no way of arriving at even a moderately accurate estimate of the strength of revolutionary unionism in America. As has been seen, most socialist unionists are scattered through nonrevolutionary organizations. This is true to a lesser extent of quasi anarchistic unionists. Unions keep no records of character of membership. They would not give it out if they did, and the records would not be worth anything if given out. The national officers of the Socialist Party refuse to estimate. In the 1912 convention of the American Federation of Labor, the Socialist candidate for president polled 5,073 out of a total of 17,047 votes cast. Estimating the American Federation of Labor membership at 2 million, the socialistic membership, if this vote were indicative, would number 846,000, or 42 percent.

But a vote of unions one way or another is no indication of the strength of internal factions. The Socialist Party vote is somewhere near 30 percent as large as the estimated number of trade unionists, but it is to a considerable extent a nonunionist vote. The best we can say is that socialist unionists are a fairly large and apparently growing minority. The quasi anarchistic unionists are probably mostly in separate organizations, but no accurate figures can be obtained of these. The Industrial Workers of the World claim to have issued cards to something over 200,000 since its establishment. The Syndicalist League is only a handful, if it exists. It is possible that all revolutionary unionists combined in this country number perhaps one third of the organized workers, or in the neighborhood of 800,000. Lacking statistics of its growth, the only way we can discuss the prospects of revolutionary unionism is in the terms of its causes and the character of its adherents.

In attempting to account for revolutionary unionism, stress has ordinarily been laid almost entirely on industrial conditions and forces. It has been pointed out that, with the development of modern industry under the stimulus of machinery and the machine process, the relationships between employers and workers are becoming remote and impersonal, and each class is coming to be subjected to a different environment and is thus developing different sets of ideals and interests. To those who accept this theory, class conflict and the growth of class conflict alike are inevitable. Revolutionary unionism is one aspect of this conflict based on industrial conditions. It is bound to exist and bound to develop rapidly in this country now that our free land is exhausted, and that in other respects the opportunities for escape from the working class are being cut off. There is a strong element of truth in this explanation and prediction, especially as applied to socialistic unionism. On the other hand, economic conditions alone cannot account for revolutionary unionism. This is evidenced by the fact that in the same trades and industries, and notably in the same unions, we find both conservative business and revolutionary unionists. I am inclined to think that revolutionary unionism, especially as regards the quasi anarchistic variety, is largely a matter of individual and racial temperament.

To judge of the outlook for revolutionary unionism in this country, we must consider both our temperamental and environmental situation and tendencies. A large proportion of our organized workers are probably temperamentally conservative and would never become revolutionary unionists no matter what the industrial development. A growing portion of the workers—largely as the result of our recent immigration—are temperamentally radical. In so far as they become unionists at all they are bound to be revolutionaries. Between these extremes are the floaters, the negative mass, perhaps the largest proportion of the workers. They will be swayed by their associates and by industrial and political conditions. As skilled workers they are likely to be conservative; as unskilled, revolutionary. In times of prosperity they will become satisfied and temperate; in times of stress, radical. Political disability and casual work, such as the migratory worker suffers, will draw them into the revolutionary camp. Reforms—workmen's compensation, health and safety legislation, old-age pensions—will tend to make them supporters of the existing system. Militant action by employers' associations and trusts, and unfavorable legislative action and court decisions will make militants of them. Speaking, then, of revolutionary unionism as a whole, and not of syndicalism or the Industrial Workers of the World, we shall see more rather than less of it. It is bound to develop with unregulated immigration and the lack of a comprehensive and thoroughgoing program of reform. It is one of the big problems of our time.

14. Organized Labor and the New Deal*

Philip Taft†

The American labor movement has a long and multicolored history reaching back to the days of the founding fathers. But not until almost the close of the 19th century did it attain a definite form and character. Then, with the triumph of the American Federation of Labor over the huge, sprawling Knights of Labor, it turned away from political and reform movements and settled down to the business of getting better employment and working conditions for its members—mostly skilled craftsmen.

Its achievements were considerable. Notable systems of collective bargaining had their start in the years around 1900, some of them earlier. But they were limited to a small number of industries—the building and printing trades, the railroads, coal mining, and a few others. And this remained true up to the First World War, when trade-union membership spurted and many hitherto open-shop areas temporarily yielded recognition. It was true also of the 1920s, a decade whose first three years saw over half the wartime gains swept away and whose last seven prosperous years were a period of almost complete union stagnation.

Still centering nearly all their efforts on improving the material position of the skilled crafts, and handicapped by political and economic developments, the labor unions showed no signs of ability or desire to reach more than a small fraction of American workers. There was no indication that the millions of unorganized employees in the mass production industries, the clerical and service trades, or agriculture would ever be organized. And when depression hit the country, even the old union strongholds received what seemed a mortal blow. Membership fell off, and the disintegration and lack of vitality so evident in the 20s became much more pronounced. With little apparent hope for a successful comeback, the labor movement retreated before the gathering economic storm.

1. GOVERNMENT ENCOURAGEMENT OF LABOR ORGANIZATION

Not until the spring of 1933, when a new administration took over in Washington, did organized labor come out of its slough of despond. Then, for the first time in the nation's history, unionism and the right to bargain collectively came under strong government protection and encouragement.

Yet this new policy was not so much an innovation as a revival and extension of previously enunciated principles. During the First World War, the War Labor Board upheld collective bargaining and forbade interference with it. That stand was not entirely abandoned even in the 20s, despite organized labor setbacks. On the contrary, what was once a wartime regulatory policy was written into a federal statute and survived the test of the courts.

This was the Railway Labor Act of 1926, which had the blessing of both carriers and rail labor organizations—the first law ever passed by Congress to specify in so many words the right to organize without interference and coercion.[1] It applied to only one, though important,

* From *Organized Labor and the New Deal* (New York: 20th Century Fund, 1942), pp. 3–30.

† Professor Emeritus, Brown University.

[1] Section 2 of the law provided that: "Representatives, for the purposes of this Act, shall be designated

group of organized labor, and even the power of Congress to do this was challenged. But the Supreme Court of the United States upheld that power in the case of *Texas & New Orleans Railroad Co.* v. *Brotherhood of Railway & Steamship Clerks.*[2]

Less than two years after this decision came the Norris–La Guardia Anti-Injunction Act which stated the same principles and, in effect, encouraged their application in wider fields.[3] But however encouraging, this legislation was limited. It remained for the National Industrial Recovery Act of 1933 to affirm in explicit terms in the famous Section 7(a), labor's right in Code industries to organize without employer interference and to bargain collectively.[4]

Effect of Early New Deal Legislation

Although Section 7(a) and the act of which it was a part were not destined to live more than two years, it served as a catapult for rapid organization of labor. Workers flocked into old unions and set up new ones. From June to October 1933 the American Federation of Labor chartered 584 directly affiliated federal unions with 300,000 members—more than in any other comparable period in the Federation's existence.[5] At the same time, national and international unions affiliated with the AF of L chartered 2,953 locals. Although its convention report showed an average of 2,126,796 members for 1933, the Federation estimated its membership in October of that year at 3,926,796.[6] Total trade union membership is estimated to have risen from an

average of 3,144,300 during 1932[7] to 4,200,000 by the beginning of 1935.[8]

Even more significant than new charters or increased membership was the wide geographical and industrial spread of union activity. In many mass production industries there were marked gains. In rubber tire manufacturing in 1934 there were 75 local unions, almost all of them organized since the enactment of the NRA. In June 1933 no AF of L unions existed in the automobile industry; a little over a year later 106 federal locals were active. Between July 1933 and July 1934 locals in the aluminum industry rose from 1 to 20, and in lumbering, from 4 to 130 in 21 states and Canada.[9]

Although designed to protect the code worker's right of self-organization, Section 7(a) did not prevent company unions. The fact is that it placed a premium upon their establishment. As efforts were made to thwart attempts at independent organization, a race began between outside and company unions. Hundreds of employee representation plans were introduced, and company-union coverage increased from an estimated 1,263,194 employees in 1932[10] to about 2,500,000 in the beginning of 1935,[11] or almost 60 percent of the total trade-union membership—an all-time high.[12]

Replies to a Bureau of Labor Statistics questionnaire from 14,725 firms employing 1,935,673 workers showed 30.2 percent in April 1935 employed in establishments dealing with some or all workers through trade unions, 19.9 percent in establishments dealing through company unions,

---

by the respective parties in such manner as may be provided in their corporate organization or unincorporated association, by other means of collective action, without interference, influence, or coercion exercised by either party over the self-organization or designation of representatives by the other." 44 Stat. L. 578, Pt. 2.

[2] 281 U.S. 548 (1930).

[3] Section 2.

[4] For a discussion of Section 7(a), see Paul Brissenden, "Genesis and Import of the Collective Bargaining Provisions of the Recovery Act," *Economic Essays in Honor of Wesley Clair Mitchell* (New York: Columbia University Press, 1935), pp. 27–62.

[5] *Report of the Proceedings of the Fifty-Third Annual Convention of the American Federation of Labor . . . 1933,* p. 78.

[6] *United Mine Workers Journal,* October 15, 1933, p. 9.

AF of L total membership in October 1933 3,926,796
Reported as paying the per capita tax 2,526,796
Exempt from dues 100,000
In new federal unions 300,000
In new international local unions 500,000
Recruits in old international unions 450,000
Recruits in old federal locals 50,000

[7] Leo Wolman, *Ebb and Flow in Trade Unionism,* National Bureau of Economic Research (New York, 1936), p. 16. (In 1933 the average declined to 2,973,000.) Canadian membership of approximately 150,000 at the close of 1932 and 140,000 at the close of 1933 should be subtracted. See the Department of Labour of Canada, *Twenty-Second Annual Report on Labor Organization in Canada, 1934,* p. 80; and *Twenty-Third Annual Report, 1934,* p. 140.

[8] *Labor and the Government* (New York: Twentieth Century Fund, 1935), pp. 21–24. This figure does not include Canadian membership.

[9] AF of L, *Proceedings, 1934,* pp. 43–55.

[10] National Industrial Conference Board, *Collective Bargaining through Employee Representation* (New York, 1933), p. 16.

[11] Twentieth Century Fund, *Labor and the Government,* p. 79.

[12] This comparison is subject to criticism, for the trade-union and company-union figures are not closely comparable. In connection with company union figures, it will be noted that the word "coverage" is used. The figures are for employees in the plants with company unions. Prior to 1937, only a small proportion of the company unions were associations with memberships and dues; the great majority were merely plans for the election of representatives.

7.4 percent in establishments with both company and trade unions, and 42.5 percent in establishments without any recognized labor organization. Company unions were widespread in iron and steel, chemical, and transportation equipment industries and in "miscellaneous manufactures." And while trade-union strength was concentrated in plants employing less than 2,500, the company union was prevalent among firms employing 2,500 or more. Over 60 percent of the company unions had been organized between 1933 and 1935.[13]

NRA Administrative Machinery

Organized labor's vigorous drive and employers' counteroffensives sharply increased labor disputes in the summer of 1933[14] and threatened the hoped-for industrial revival. The National Recovery Administration lacked machinery to handle these disputes until August 5, when President Roosevelt established the National Labor Board, with Senator Wagner as impartial chairman and three representatives each from labor and industry. This body heard complaints, undertook strike settlements, and held plant elections to determine collective bargaining representatives. A large proportion of the cases filed with it grew out of contests between trade and company unions or were charges of discrimination against employees engaging in union activity.

Similar duties were undertaken by its successor, the first National Labor Relations Board, which came into being in July 1934, by the National Mediation Board for the railroads, and by special boards handling labor disputes in such industries as automobiles, textiles, steel, and coal.[15] Although many elections conducted by these government labor boards were held by consent, their authority in other cases was contested in the courts. Frequently the results of elections held without employer consent were ignored, as were some board decisions in non-election cases. With such uneven accomplishments the boards' effectiveness diminished rather than increased. Generally speaking, all these bodies were ineffective in getting industry to accept their interpretations of Section 7(a), and

their usefulness steadily declined until May 1935, when the NRA was declared unconstitutional.[16]

The National Labor Relations Act

To meet this situation—to salvage principles laid down by the National Labor Board and the first National Labor Relations Board, and to provide for enforcement of decisions—the Wagner bill was introduced early in 1935. After amendment, it passed in the following July, not many weeks after the NRA died. Not, however, until the Supreme Court upheld its constitutionality and gave it broad coverage in April 1937[17] did the National Labor Relations Act become a powerful instrument for the widespread extension of collective bargaining. Employers were required to meet with the accredited representatives of a majority of their employees and to make an honest effort to reach agreements on issues raised; though actual agreement was not required, collective bargaining became compulsory when requested by an appropriate labor organization. . . .

The Split in the Labor Movement

The forward surge in union membership is one outstanding act of the New Deal years. It was offset, in part at least, by the split in the labor movement arising in 1935 out of general dissatisfaction and dissent within the American Federation of Labor over the issue of industrial organization.

Although the AF of L sent organizers to many areas, it did not take full advantage of the opportunities presented by the receptive attitude of mass production workers. Its 1933 convention authorized a conference of national and international unions to devise methods of organizing the unorganized. Meeting in January 1934, the conference affirmed that:

The paramount issue is not what particular form of organization shall be allowed in this emergency and this unusual situation. The demand of the government is to promote organization in whatever form or method is best designed to rally the wage earners to the cause of Organized Labor, bearing in mind that in the pursuit of organization the present structure, rights, and interests of affiliated National and International Unions must be followed, observed, and safeguarded.[18]

---

[13] "Characteristics of Company Unions, 1935," *Bulletin No. 634*, U.S. Bureau of Labor Statistics, 1938, pp. 37–38, 48, 51.

[14] Florence Peterson, "Strikes in the United States," *Bulletin No. 651*, U.S. Bureau of Labor Statistics, 1938, p. 45.

[15] For a detailed history of the labor boards under the NRA, see Lewis L. Lorwin and Arthur Wubnig, *Labor Relations Boards* (Washington, D.C.: Brookings Institution, 1935).

[16] *A.L.A. Schechter Poultry Corp., et al.* v. *United States*, 295 U.S. 490 (1935).

[17] *Associated Press* v. *NLRB*, 301 U.S. 103; *NLRB* v. *Jones & Laughlin Steel Corp.*, 301 U.S. 1; *NLRB* v. *Fruehauf Trailer Co.*, 301 U.S. 49; *NLRB* v. *Friedman-Harry Marks Clothing Co.*, 301 U.S. 58; and *Washington, Virginia & Maryland Coach Co.* v. *NLRB*, 301 U.S. 142.

[18] AF of L, *Proceedings, 1934*, p. 41.

This resolution posed the Federation's dilemma —to organize the wage earners into the most suitable type of organization without encroaching upon the jurisdictions staked out by its international affiliates in the past. The Federation's inability to solve this problem was the chief cause of the split in the ranks of labor. The AF of L 1934 convention tried to conciliate the divergent groups with a compromise resolution, but a careful reading of the resolution shows that each side could interpret it to suit its own interests. While authorizing industrial charters in a number of mass production industries, it reiterated the Federation's "duty to formulate policies which will fully protect the jurisdictional rights of all trade unions organized upon craft lines. . . ."[19]

Even though they had few members in mass production industries, craft and semindustrial unions were unwilling to give up their jurisdictional rights. Another obstacle was the AF of L's slowness to provide the organizational and financial support needed for the campaigns in these sectors. As a central body of autonomous unions, the Federation was never intended to assume general responsibility for labor's organizing efforts. It had neither the equipment nor the personnel for such tasks, and the leaders of the internationals were reluctant to risk thousands of dollars of defense funds in attempts to organize groups that had been indifferent to organized labor's appeal.

By the summer of 1935 little doubt remained that union gains of 1933 and 1934 were fast being destroyed, partly because vigorous organization along industrial lines was not being pressed and partly because the NRA guarantee of the right to organize failed to be as effective as anticipated. But despite these clear warnings, a resolution to organize the mass production workers into industrial unions was voted down at the 1935 convention, 18,024 to 10,993, after sharp and bitter debate.[20]

Rise of the CIO

Less than a month later, officers of eight unions[21] representing 940,000 members met in Washington and formed the Committee for Industrial Organization to promote unionization of the unorganized workers in the mass production industries and elsewhere. The Committee's announced functions were "educational and advisory"; ostensibly it would organize within the framework of the AF of L. But shortly after its formation it was ordered to disband. Rejecting this demand, the CIO taunted the Federation for failing to organize the steel industry and offered to raise $500,000 for a campaign by its own organizers. The AF of L Executive Council spurned this offer, then suspended all but two of the original CIO unions[22] and four others which had later affiliated with it. With the insurgent unions unrepresented, the 1936 convention overwhelmingly upheld the Council's action.[23]

The labor movement was thus divided into two rival groups, although not until two years later did the Committee for Industrial Organization change its name to Congress of Industrial Organizations and become an independent federation. Despite the defection of the Hatters in 1936 and the Ladies' Garment Workers in 1938, the CIO has continued to prosper; it weathered a serious business slump which hit hardest those industries where its strength was concentrated.

Time and conflict widened AF of L–CIO differences and encouraged mutual recriminations and raiding of jurisdictions. The CIOs initial position was that "it is not the purpose to take from any national or international union any part of their present membership, or any part of their potential membership employed in certain types and plants of industry [i.e., where craft distinctions are important]."[24] But it later invaded building construction and other industries. The AF of L reciprocated. The differences became more difficult of solution owing to the evolution of the CIO into an independent institution performing functions paralleling those of the AF of L. Moreover, pride and fear of loss of prestige or political influence handicapped all efforts to bring the two organizations together.

Organizational Gains, 1937–41

This very dissension was partly responsible for the extraordinary organizational efforts and ex-

[19] Ibid., pp. 586–87.

[20] Ibid., 1935, pp. 521–75.

[21] Amalgamated Clothing Workers; United Hatters, Cap and Millinery Workers; International Ladies' Garment Workers; Mine, Mill and Smelter Workers; United Mine Workers; Oil Field, Gas Well and Refinery Workers; United Textile Workers; International Typographical Union.

[22] The International Typographical Union and the United Hatters, Cap and Millinery Workers were not suspended because their affiliation with the CIO was in doubt.

[23] AF of L, Proceedings, 1936, pp. 416–17; Committee for Industrial Organization, "Industrial Unions Mean Unity," Washington, pamphlet (no date), pp. 5–8.

[24] Committee for Industrial Organization, "Industrial Unionism," Washington, pamphlet (no date), p. 13. The quotation is from a speech by President Howard of the Typographical Union at the 1935 AF of L convention.

penditures after 1936. Beginning in the rubber tire and automobile industries, CIO unions won collective bargaining rights by organized pressure or peaceful persuasion on a wide industrial front —in steel, electrical manufacturing, shipbuilding, and textiles, among others. It was a cyclonic campaign. In March 1934, a high official of the General Motors Corporation asserted that his company would neither recognize unionism nor agree in advance to an election of bargaining representatives.[25] Three years later both General Motors and Chrysler signed agreements with the CIO automobile union. Perhaps even more important was the peaceful acceptance of collective bargaining by the United States Steel Corporation. Many other basic and fabricating firms in the steel industry followed, and finally, in 1941, "little steel's" resistance collapsed. Earlier in the same year, another antiunion stronghold surrendered when Ford signed a very favorable contract with the CIO.

CIO victories prodded AF of L leadership into more rigorous action. Many international unions increased their organizational staffs and not infrequently extended their jurisdictions. Indeed, many unions that had formerly shied away from the semiskilled and unskilled welcomed them with open arms. Moreover, the Federation decided to take the leadership in campaigns in the unorganized industries. In May 1937 a conference of international and national unions voted to assess themselves one cent per member a month to support an organization campaign.[26] The organizing staff was enlarged, and a division with a director in charge was created to supervise its activities.[27] Organizational expenditures by the Federation increased from $338,576 (a sum larger than usual) in 1935 to $1,174,015 for the 12 months ending on August 31, 1938; in 1940–41, $1,039,759 was spent.[28] In spite of losses from the expulsion of CIO affiliates, the AF of L enlarged its membership.

The Old Unions

Since 1933 only a few national or international unions have decreased in size. The Wood Carvers, The Metal Engravers, the Sleeping Car Con-

ductors, the Rural Letter Carriers, the Plasterers, and the Stonecutters have all lost; so have a few others.[29] Most unions of this group, however, play minor roles in both the labor movement and the national economy. The overwhelming majority of trade unions have increased in size and influence. While some gains were only moderate after 1933—usually because organization was already fairly inclusive—an impressive number had tremendous growth.

Membership in such old and strongly intrenched organizations as the Brotherhood of Railway Carmen, the Photo Engravers', and Pressmen's unions increased rather slowly—from 10 to 30 percent from 1933 to 1941. The same was true of the International Typographical Union, the Sheet Metal Workers' Union, and the National Federation of Post Office Clerks. But unions in coal mining, clothing, baking, and other industries grew by leaps and bounds. Between 1933 and 1941 the United Mine Workers' membership rose from 300,000 to 600,000, the Amalgamated Clothing Workers from 125,000 to 275,000, and the Brotherhood of Electrical Workers from 94,000 to 201,000. The Machinists more than tripled—from 65,000 to 222,000. The Bakery Workers, with some 84,000 members in 1941, showed about a fivefold increase, and the Teamsters, with over 400,000, almost a sixfold increase. At the same time membership of the Meat Cutters and Butcher Workmen jumped nearly eightfold—from 11,000 to 85,000—and that of the Hotel and Restaurant Employees, over ninefold—from 23,000 to 214,000.

The growth of these old unions reflects not only more complex coverage of traditional jurisdictions but also, in many cases, inclusion of related trades and industries or of unskilled and semiskilled workers. Almost half the 1940 members of the Amalgamated Clothing Workers were journeymen tailors, and shirt, neckwear, laundry, and cleaning and dyeing workers. Before the New Deal, members of the Brotherhood of Electrical Workers were largely in the railroad and construction industries, but after 1933, powerhouses and electrical manufacturing plants were organized, which accounted for 105,000 of the union's 203,000 members in November 1939.[30] The Machinists set out to organize the aircraft industry, among others, on an industrial basis, and the Bakery Workers after 1936 sought bargaining rights in mechanical bakeries. These

[25] Lorwin and Wubnig, *Labor Relations Boards,* p. 355.

[26] AF of L, *Proceedings, 1937,* pp. 110–11. This assessment was abolished at the 1940 New Orleans convention and the per capita tax increased from one cent to two cents a month. Ibid., 1940, pp. 444–46.

[27] Ibid., 1937, p. 80.

[28] Ibid., 1935, p. 26; 1938, p. 65; *Report of the Executive Council, 1941,* p. 3.

[29] AF of L, *Report of the Executive Council, Annual Convention, 1941,* pp. 10–11.

[30] Information submitted by the organization.

are only a few examples of the greater inclusiveness of long-established unions.

The Rise of New Unions

Even more striking than the gains of the old unions has been the appearance of new ones in hitherto unorganized, or practically unorganized, trades and industries. Hundreds of thousands of workers have been drawn into strong industrial unions in such mass production industries as iron and steel, autos, and electrical and radio manufacturing. The Steel Workers Organizing Committee claimed in 1941 roughly 600,000 members; the United Automobile, Aircraft and Agricultural Implement Workers 600,000; and the United Electrical, Radio and Machine Workers, around 300,000. Additional thousands of union members were in the rubber, aluminum, and flat glass industries. Other fields of economic activity, such as office and professional work, agriculture and canning, and editorial and commercial work on newspapers, have also been reached by the organized labor movement.

2. THE COLLECTIVE BARGAINING SITUATION

Although not all union members have achieved collective bargaining rights, the number of unorganized employees whose employment and working conditions are directly determined by collective agreements is probably large enough to make union control coequal with union membership.[31] Collective labor agreements, therefore, cover roughly 11 million, or more than a quarter of the nearly 40 million wage and salary workers actually employed. . . .

Importance of Collective Bargaining in Various Industries

In 1940 only two giant American industries were almost 100 percent covered by union agreements—the railroad, with about 1 million employees, and coal mining, with 0.5 million. But about three fourths of the 500,000 auto workers were under contract; so were over three fifths of the 500,000 steel workers[32] and the 400,000 in electrical manufacturing, together with well over half of the nearly 2 million in construction. The

addition of such industries as rubber, private shipbuilding, men's and women's clothing, and meat packing, each employing over 100,000 and from half to almost 100 percent covered by labor agreements, makes clear the vital role that collective bargaining plays in the United States.

Plus these, collective agreements embraced from 50 to over 90 percent of the workers in other, less important industries—glass, brewing, hosiery, and flour milling and cereal manufacturing. Moreover, in a number of otherwise poorly or only moderately well-organized industries, strong craft unions determined the employment and working conditions of certain occupational groups. The International Brotherhood of Blacksmiths, Drop Forgers and Helpers claimed that early in 1940 its agreements covered 100 percent of the craftsmen within its jurisdiction employed by small hardware and tool manufacturers. In the textile industry, the International Spinners Union bargained for all of the spinners of textile yarns; and agreements of the Metal Polishers, Buffers, Platers, and Helpers International Union applied to some 60 percent of the eligible workers in the chrome furniture industry. The Association of Machinists and the Brotherhood of Electrical Workers had contracts covering maintenance and repair workers in textiles, food products, paper and pulp, and chemicals, and the Pattern Makers' League of North America bargained for skilled pattern makers in the aircraft and other industries.

Collective bargaining has advanced on most fronts. Formerly limited to the building, printing, and needle trades, the railroads and coal mining and a relatively small number of other industries, it is now found in nearly every branch of the American economy. Before 1933 it was in the main confined to urban centers, except in the case of coal mining and the railroads; it appears now in middle-sized and small manufacturing communities as well. No longer limited geographically or industrially, collective bargaining is fast becoming the most important single device for determining wages, hours, and working conditions in the United States. Transportation, mining, construction, and manufacturing are more and more coming under its sway.

Yet in spite of this rapid progress since 1933, nearly three quarters of American wage and salary workers are not members of trade unions or covered by collective agreements. Collective bargaining has made little headway among the 6.5 million wholesale and retail trade employees, the more than 4 million in the financial and service trades, the 4 million government em-

---

[31] See text for reference to the decline in relative importance of closed-shop agreements.

[32] About 200,000 union members were in steel processing and fabricating concerns, not classified as part of the iron and steel industry.

ployees, or the 3 million agricultural workers. In addition, hundreds of thousands in textiles, in chemicals, and in other important industries are without union agreements.

The Bargaining Unit

The rise of industrial unionism, already referred to, was partly, if not largely, responsible for the extension of collective bargaining. Today industrial or semi-industrial unions provide the dominant organizational and bargaining patterns.

A second development of recent years has been a tendency for agreements to cover a wider geographical area. The most common agreement is still local, negotiated with single employers or local associations of employers and tending to set standards for the local market. But regional and national agreements are increasing. They are found, for example, in stoves, hosiery, coal, shipping, paper and plup, clothing, glass containers, and pottery. Such agreements usually result in standardization of labor conditions over wider areas—often an important contribution to the stability of collective bargaining. In the face of large wage differences, the standards in any one firm or plant may be subject to severe pressure, and the union's position jeopardized. During the last decade such pressure was intensified; unions were forced to give greater attention to the relationship between wage rates in different plants; and, except in such cases as the building trades and cleaning and dyeing, where the market is local, they have increasingly sought industry-wide agreements or industry-wide uniformity of agreements to make less difficult the problem of enforcement.

Of course enforcement of uniform piece or hourly rates also involves difficulties, since technical and organizational conditions vary from plant to plant. Weak firms may be unable to continue in business unless the uniform rate is set at an extremely low level. Confronted by such a problem, unions may have to make concessions to less efficient establishments, as in the hosiery industry.

However, reduction of inequalities in labor standards promises to continue as a very important trade-union objective. It has been a factor in the tendency toward multiple-plant or company-wide agreements in such branches of industry as motor vehicle production, dominated by a few large concerns. Multiple-unit agreements which equalize labor costs remove reasons for diverting work from one plant to another; they reduce the time allotted to bargaining, leaving national officers free for other activities; and they increase union prestige and so aid organizational effort.

More recently the exigencies of national defense have also encouraged wider agreement coverage. For example, to prevent "labor pirating" and to stabilize industrial relations in shipbuilding, defense officials promoted the negotiation of regional contracts for each of the three coasts.

Union Status

The status of the union varies considerably from industry to industry (and within industries), depending, in the main, upon the age of the organization and the length of time collective bargaining has been in effect. Most unions seek a closed, union, or preferential shop,[33] but newly organized ones usually have difficulty in winning any one of these from employers traditionally opposed to unionism. Ten years ago most agreements provided for the closed shop. In recent years there have been more exceptions than at any time since the 1880s; unions were willing to take what they could get in order to secure a foothold in areas previously closed to them. For example, many agreements signed in the 1930s with new industrial unions in the mass production industries stated that the union was to bargain for its members only. However, as collective bargaining gained more general acceptance and as unions won National Labor Relations Board elections, these "membership" agreements were generally replaced by contracts designating the union as exclusive representative of all employees, except certain groups such as supervisors and salaried employees. Agreements of this type are prevalent in the rubber and auto industries.

A number of employers have yielded to union demands for greater security. Often this step was taken as a result of employer recognition that a financially secure union can be a more responsible bargaining agent. Sometimes the motive was removal of friction between organized and unorganized workers in a plant; sometimes both employer and union have wanted protection against a rival union. And so an increasing minority of "exclusive bargaining" contracts is being replaced by some form of the closed or

---

[33] Under the closed shop only union members can be hired and workers must remain union members to retain employment. Under the union shop nonmembers can be hired, but to retain employment must become union members after a certain period. The preferential shop gives union members preference in hiring or lay-off, or both.

preferential shop. However, except for the rail-roads, where it is illegal, the closed shop is most prevalent in industries where labor organization and collective bargaining have been long accepted—building construction, printing, and the needle trades, among others.

The closed shop was an important issue in disputes certified to the National Defense Mediation Board, established early in 1941. This body of union, employer, and public representatives was given investigatory and mediatory powers to deal with the problem of strikes in defense industries. The Board never formally announced any general policy on the closed shop but attempted to decide each case on its merits. It recommended adoption of the closed shop in one case and in a number of others suggested a union membership maintenance clause, under which all present or future union members must remain in good standing as a condition of continued employment, though no employee has to join the union. But in the captive mines dispute in the fall of 1941, the Board rejected the United Mine Workers' demand for a union shop. This led to the resignation of all CIO members and destroyed the Board's usefulness. With America's formal entrance into the war, steps were taken to reorganize the machinery for dealing with industrial disputes. In January 1942 the Defense Mediation Board was replaced by the National War Labor Board, to which were given greater powers than those of its predecessor.

Collective Bargaining Machinery

The machinery for negotiating an agreement is usually comparatively simple—formal conferences on a local, regional, or national basis between union representatives and employers or their representatives, sometimes with provision for arbitration when the two sides cannot agree.[34] Such machinery does not, of course, guarantee peaceful settlement of the issues involved. Strikes and lockouts may often be the ultimate deciding factor, their frequency and extent varying with such things as the business cycle and employer resistance to unionism and collective bargaining.

As industrial activity in the United States picked up because of defense spending, strikes naturally increased. In the first seven months of 1941 they numbered almost twice those in the corresponding period of the preceding relatively inactive year; the number of man days lost was more than five times as great. When 1941 is com-pared with the five-year period 1935–39, how-ever, the contrast is not so marked. From January through July 1941, there were some 2,500 strikes involving 1.3 million workers, and 15.8 million man days were lost; the figures for the corresponding period in 1935–39 were 1,800, 0.7 million, and 10.9 million, respectively.[35] Main causes of 1941's strikes were union efforts to get greater recognition, a more secure status, and wage increases.[36]

Administration of Agreements. More complex than the procedure for negotiating an agreement is the machinery for administering it—for peacefully settling disputes over its interpretation and application. The procedure followed varies, of course, among industries, but there are certain similarities. First, an attempt must be made to settle a dispute by the worker involved, or his union representative, and the foreman. Then there is a system of appeals to higher union and management officials. In industries where collective bargaining has been long established, such as coal, printing, hosiery, and the needle trades, final appeal is often to a standing body composed of an equal number of representatives from each side, plus an impartial third person, or to a permanent impartial chairman alone. Arbitration is less frequent in newly organized industries. Practically every agreement makes it mandatory that the established procedures, rather than strikes or lockouts, be used to settle disputes arising during its life.

Obviously here, too, the machinery alone, no matter how well conceived, is not enough to insure successful relations. More depends on the attitudes, experience, and judgment of the persons involved, and consequently on the length of time collective bargaining has been in effect. The process of training union and management officials in handling grievances is a slow one. Wholehearted acceptance of collective bargaining and mutually satisfactory delimitation of its scope come slowly. For these reasons violations of agreements may be rather frequent in newly organized industries. But as collective bargaining becomes more firmly established, little trouble is usually encountered in securing observance, the established machinery is relied on to secure adjustment, and it in turn tends to function more

---

[34] See the special studies for detailed descriptions.

[35] U.S. Bureau of Labor Statistics figures, as published in *The New York Times,* August 27, 1941.

[36] Until the captive mines dispute, the National Defense Mediation Board's efforts to minimize strikes in defense industries had a good deal of success. There were few cases where strikes were called after a dispute was certified to it, and few failures to abide by its recommendations.

smoothly and expeditiously. More disputes are settled close to the source of trouble, thus preventing delays and the accumulation of discontent.

The Terms of Employment

The extent to which the terms and conditions of employment are directly determined by collective bargaining varies. In the newly organized mass production industries, management, jealous of its prerogatives, has frequently opposed joint determination of individual wage rates, for example. It prefers to set the rates itself, with opportunity for union protest through the grievance machinery. On the other hand, many unions have independently developed and enforced their own rules. Thus the scope of collective bargaining may be wide or narrow. Here an attempt is made to indicate very briefly some of the more important developments of the last decade in the terms and conditions of employment as they have been affected by the rapid spread of trade unionism and collective bargaining.

Wages. Wage increases in the middle 30s were considerable. And to a large extent trade unions were responsible, as they were for the maintenance of rates in the 1937–38 recession. According to one estimate,[37] hourly earnings of industrial wage earners were 11 percent higher in 1938 than in 1928 and 1929; at the same time real hourly earnings were 30 percent above the 1928–29 level. More recently, as the defense boom got under way, union pressure has again resulted in substantial increases—in steel, autos, coal, aircraft, and shipbuilding, among others—though these have been at least partially offset by the rise in the cost of living.

The increase in wage rates is one result of the greater strength and inclusiveness of unionism and collective bargaining. Another is the reduction in the differences between wage rates for similar jobs,[38] to which earlier reference was made. At the same time has come a narrowing of the spread between the rates for different jobs—in part a result of the rapid growth of industrial unionism and of agreements covering all or a large proportion of the workers in a plant. Hitherto skilled wages in the United States had been much higher—when compared with

unskilled and semi-skilled wages—than in countries like England and Australia. Relative scarcity of skilled labor plus concentration of union organization in this group largely accounted for such a situation. In recent years, with an increasing number of agreements written on an industrial basis, the tendency has been to reduce the difference between skilled and unskilled wages by establishing high minimum rates and granting larger relative increases in the lower brackets. Introduction of minimum wage legislation has also contributed to this trend.

Seniority and Work Sharing. An outstanding development of the depression was greater union interest in the problem of layoffs. To provide a measure of job security for the individual and to protect him from discrimination, an increasing proportion of collective agreements provide that layoffs, rehirings, and promotions shall be based on seniority. This development has been a controversial matter and a prominent issue in labor disputes during the New Deal years. Union men maintain that seniority is the most equitable criterion on which to base layoffs, rehirings, and promotions. But management has been opposed to its use, unless "other things," such as "ability," are equal, claiming that otherwise efficiency would be reduced by removing incentive for self-improvement and by increasing the age of the work force. However, in layoffs and rehirings, seniority is apparently becoming less of a bone of contention. As its administration improved, management has often come to regard the system with toleration, or even approval.

Unions have not always been happy about the way seniority systems have worked out. There are problems of administration in mass production industries. Conflicts frequently arise within the union when seniority is applied on a divisional or plant-wide basis, those laid off protesting strenuously. Even when it is applied only on a departmental basis it is, of course, a source of dissatisfaction and protest on the part of the younger men against whom it discriminates.

To meet objections to sole reliance on seniority, work sharing has been widely practiced. In highly seasonal industries, such as the needle trades and boots and shoes, equal division of work during slack seasons—not layoffs based on seniority—is usually the rule. In a large number of other cases, work sharing is combined with seniority: Sometimes short-service employees are dropped before work is divided; sometimes work is equally shared until average hours fall to a certain level, and thereafter layoffs are made on a seniority basis; sometimes these two methods

[37] Spurgeon Bell, *Productivity, Wages, and National Income* (Washington, D.C.: Brookings Institution, 1940), p. 16.

[38] Of course, in some cases, these differentials have been increased as a result of only partial organization of an industry.

are combined. Such arrangements are rather common in steel and rubber agreements and in electrical and radio manufacturing.[39]

The share-the-work movement was probably more important in its effect than reductions secured by unions in full-time working hours. These reductions were, of course, considerable— in a large majority of collective agreements, the standard work week is 40 hours, spread over five days; in many it is less than 40. But in general during the 30s, actual hours worked were less than the standard number. Part of the reduction was merely an inevitable accompaniment of the depression. Part, however, was due to work sharing instituted by the trade unions.

Variations in Collective Bargaining

Collective bargaining does not have a uniform pattern. The geographical coverage of the agreement, its scope, the status of the union, machinery for adjusting disputes, and ways of meeting fluctuations in employment are only some of its aspects which vary among industries. Others are policies with regard to technological change and methods of wage payment. Some unions with a high degree of control have promoted unusually restrictive policies and practices; others have undertaken extensive programs for the rehabilitation of a part, or even the whole, of an industry.

---

[39] For an analysis of methods of controlling layoffs in unionized industries, see Sumner H. Slichter, *Union Policies and Industrial Management* (Washington, D.C.: Brookings Institution, 1941), chap. 4.

part three

The Structure and Government of Unions
A. Union Structure and Government

The governments of American unions, like those of nations, run the gamut from democracy to dictatorship. Since union government and structure have important repercussions both on union policies and on the economy as a whole, a knowledge of union structure and government is an essential background to a study of the economics of labor.

The first article by Dunlop offers a general introduction to the study of the structure and government of trade unions. Dunlop addresses himself to two questions: In what respect have long-established characteristics in the American labor movement been continued? and, What have been the principal changes in labor organizations, in managements, and in their interactions in our collective bargaining system? He also places in perspective the changes in the American industrial relations system which have occurred since the 1920s.

Subsequent to Dunlop's discussion, two articles are presented that provide additional data on the unions' structure, functions, and membership. Material drawn from the *Directory of* *National and International Labor Unions in the United States* gives an excellent picture of the membership status of American trade unions as well as a guide to organizing and bargaining activities in the recent past. Virginia A. Bergquist's article discusses women as trade union members and as union officers, and reports on their current status.

William Leiserson analyzes the national union as the locus of power in the labor movement. Following Leiserson's discussion, John Hutchinson explains how the AFL-CIO, as a federation, and particularly George Meany, has both supported and controlled the principle of national union autonomy. Under the guidance of Samuel Gompers, the AFL was built on the idea that national unions should be responsible for their own activities, but events occurring in the 1950s led George Meany to take direct action toward restraining the "wayward" activities of some national bodies. Hutchinson presents interesting case studies on corruption in various national unions, and he evaluates the role Meany and the AFL-CIO have played in these matters.

15. Structural Changes in the American Labor Movement and Industrial Relations System*

John T. Dunlop†

The AFL-CIO merger is a good vantage point from which to survey major developments of the past generation in the American labor movement and in our collective bargaining system.[1] In what respects have long established characteristics been continued, and what new tendencies have arisen since the 1920s? What have been the principal changes in labor organizations, in managements, and in their interactions in our collective bargaining system?

1. UNION STRUCTURE AND GOVERNMENT

Changes in union structure and government have in the past provided an outward indicator of the inward pressures created by changes in environments:[2] in product and labor markets and in the larger community. Issues of internal government have been focal points of debate and conflict within the labor movement reflecting these shifting external pressures.

The traditional AFL structure, given decisive form by the conflict with the Knights of Labor, was based upon two principles in the relations of the national unions and the federation: exclusive jurisdiction and autonomy. In introducing the majority report of the Resolutions Committee in the 1935 Convention, John Frey stated these principles as follows:

This contract [between the Federation and an international union] called for loyalty to the purposes of the American Federation of Labor. In return the National and International Unions were guaranteed two specific things: first, jurisdiction over all workmen doing the work of the specific craft or occupation covered by the organization; secondly, guaranteeing to the National or International Unions complete autonomy over all its internal affairs.[3]

While these principles have been said to be basic to the merged Federation,[4] there has been a substantial transformation in their meaning and application. Union government has been more drastically reconstructed in the 20 years 1935–55 than in any other period since the AFL first took form.

Developments affecting union structure and government will be examined under four headings: (1) the policy toward competition within the labor movement, the reappraisal of the exclusive jurisdiction doctrine; (2) the occupational scope of the form of organization, the craft-industrial range of questions; (3) the relations between the confederation level or trade union center (AFL and CIO) and the constituent national unions, the reappraisal of the autonomy doctrine; and (4) the relations within the national unions among the national office, the

* From Industrial Relations Research Association, *Annual Proceedings* 1956, pp. 12–31.

† Secretary of Labor.

[1] Sumner H. Slichter, "The American System of Industrial Relations," *Arbitration Today, Proceedings of the Eighth Annual Meeting, National Academy of Arbitrators,* Boston, Massachusetts, January 27 and 28, 1955 (BNA Inc., Washington, D.C., 1955), p. 168. For a discussion of the meaning of "collective bargaining systems," see unpublished paper "Systems of Management-Employee Relations and Economic Development," 12th annual conference on Industrial Relations Research, University of Minnesota, May 25–26, 1956.

[2] Lloyd Ulman, *The Rise of the National Union* (Cambridge, Mass.: Harvard University Press, 1955), p. 569.

[3] *Report of the Proceedings of the Fifty-fifth Annual Convention of the American Federation of Labor, 1935,* p. 522. See, Article II, Section 3 and Article IX, Section 11 of the 1935 constitution for the constitutional statement of these principles. Also see, Sumner H. Slichter, *The Challenge of Industrial Relations* (Ithaca: Cornell University Press, 1947), pp. 8–14.

[4] Arthur J. Goldberg, *AFL-CIO Labor United* (New York: McGraw-Hill Book Co., Inc., 1956), pp. 142–45.

subordinate local and regional bodies and the membership.

1. Exclusive Jurisdiction

The doctrine of exclusive jurisdiction provided that each affiliated national union should have a clear and specified job territory and boundary ordinarily defined in terms of work operations, crafts, trades, occupations, or industrial grouping of jobs, and occasionally defined in terms of geography.[5] Jurisdiction was exclusive in the sense that no two national unions were to have jurisdiction over the same work operations. In this way conflict and competition within the labor movement was supposed to be constrained; each national union was to keep within its jurisdiction and not poach or trespass on the jurisdiction of another union.

Under the logic of exclusive jurisdiction, the AFL by establishing jurisdictional lines also determined the union the individual employee should join. The worker with a job had no direct influence nor expressed any preference in the selection of a particular union. The employer likewise was to deal with the union with exclusive jurisdiction. The government had no role in matching unions and workers or unions and employers. The assignment of jurisdiction and the regulation of competition was supposed to be the exclusive concern of the American Federation of Labor.

The system of exclusive jurisdiction required procedures and machinery to make decisions and to enforce them. The Executive Council and the convention was the machinery of last resort. The ultimate use of expulsion of a national union, particularly if a large union, was shown by experience to be both a poor method of enforcement and seldom to contribute to the settlement of the dispute over jurisdiction. The ideological and moral force of legitimacy[6] was of some, although limited, effectiveness in securing compliance with decisions of the Federation on jurisdiction. The system of exclusive jurisdiction never developed a satisfactory method for making jurisdictional decisions or agreements nor for enforcing them. Although the constitutional doctrine provided for exclusive jurisdiction and

thereby for an elimination of competition, in actual practice the degree of competition in the American labor movement was very high.

In the years before World War I the AFL made many jurisdictional decisions. Final action was taken less frequently in the 20s and early 30s. The Committee on Adjustment tended to refer problems to the Executive Council or to recommend further meetings between the contending unions. Between the split in the 30s and merger in the 50s only a relatively few decisions were made although not from a lack of problems or fighting issues. The will to make final decisions, the machinery to enforce decisions, and the consequences of non-agreement or expulsion all led to a gradual abandonment of decision making and to greater resort to presures for agreement, postponement, and ad-hoc solutions to particular situations. Internally, the system of exclusive jurisdiction had seriously declined in its vitality before it was challenged from outside.[7]

The system of exclusive jurisdiction was largely displaced by a combination of two developments in the mid-30s; the government determination of the election district under the Wagner Act (continued under the Taft-Hartley law) and the rise of the CIO. The Wagner Act without a split in the labor movement probably would have resulted only in minor or gradual variations in the system of exclusive jurisdiction,[8] a split in the labor movement without government determination of election districts probably would have provided no effective challenge to the principle of exclusive jurisdiction although in many sectors possession and control over jurisdiction would have changed. Matthew Woll in the 1935 Atlantic City debate stated clearly the implications of the Wagner Act:

Bear in mind that we now have legislation on our books which does not make us the sole factor in determining the form and character of organization that shall hereafter prevail in the labor movement.

With all of this we are merely playing into the hands of those who would delegate the power of self-organization of wage earners, not into the hands of the councils of the American Federation of Labor or

---

[5] Jurisdiction was defined in charters, certificates of affiliation, decisions of the AFL conventions or Executive Council, formal agreements, exchanges of letters, and informal understandings between the unions, or the decisions of specialized tribunals.

[6] Walter Galenson, "The Unionization of the American Steel Industry," *International Review of Social History*, 1956, p. 15.

[7] There is need for a definitive study of the "decisional process" and substantive actions of the Federation on jurisdiction from the 1880s to the 1930s. See Lewis L. Lorwin, *The American Federation of Labor* (Washington, D.C.: The Brookings Institution, 1933), pp. 340–41, note 3.

[8] Compare developments in the railroad industry where the National Mediation Board determines the appropriate craft or class and certifies the exclusive bargaining representative. See *Determinations of Craft or Class of the National Mediation Board, July 1, 1934– June 30, 1948* (Washington, D.C.: Government Printing Office, 1948).

its Executive Council . . . but to delegate it to governmental bodies.[9]

The rapid expansion of the labor movement in the spurts of the mid-30s and the war, with a good deal of grass roots growth, the AFL-CIO split and government determination of election districts, were factors contributing to a widespread blurring of jurisdictional lines. The jurisdiction of a national union depended upon elections won and contracts signed rather than upon charter rights or claims. While there was always a significant difference between jurisdiction claimed and jurisdiction exercised, in the period of the 30s and 40s the ideal of traditional jurisdiction in most sectors of the labor movement became largely nonoperational.

In the post-war period the costs and disadvantages of competition, unrestricted from within the labor movement, came increasingly to the fore as the rate of growth of membership tapered off and few new sectors were penetrated. Raiding increased with craft severance and the isolation of the communist dominated unions.[10] Rivalry was expensive and frequently led to the mere transfer of members or to reorganizing the organized. The Taft-Hartley law permitted decertifications so that contesting unions could both lose to a non-union vote.[11] In the period after the war a tendency developed within the labor movement to limit in certain directions the extent of competition and rivalry among unions.

At least six types of agreements among contesting unions are to be observed. Particular agreements, of course, extend beyond the scope of a single pure type and may be illustrative of several types.

a. Agreements to negotiate jointly with employers or to coordinate strike action where both unions are significantly represented in plants of a company or association.

b. No-raiding agreements to restrict competition for workers already certified or covered by agreements or to restrict competition for runaway plants.

c. Agreements for joint organizing campaigns with an interim or permanent division of new members[12] or a specific division of plants and agreements to regulate the conduct of competitive organizing campaigns or to establish Marquis of Queensberry rules.

d. Agreements defining jurisdiction between the organizations and settling disputes over exclusive jurisdiction. Among unions in the Building and Construction Trades Department approximately 25 agreements of this type have been signed since 1948.

e. Agreements merging national unions may also be mentioned, although a merger makes internal to the combined union problems which were formerly between organizations. Mergers arise for a variety of reasons other than to solve problems of rivalry and conflicting jurisdiction, such as to secure financial support for a weaker organization and for economies of organizational and administrative arrangements. A number of mergers have been made without formal signed agreements.

f. Agreements creating machinery providing for final and binding decisions by arbitrators in disputes over (*b, c,* or *d*): raiding of workers already organized by parties to the agreement, the organization of workers unorganized or organized by unions not parties to the agreement, or work jurisdiction disputes. There are four such agreements currently in effect:[13] that creating the National Joint Board in the construction industry established in 1948 concerned with work jurisdiction alone; the CIO agreement governing organizational disputes established in 1951 concerned with both raiding and new organizing disputes; the AFL internal disputes plan established in 1954 with raiding, new organizing, and work jurisdiction disputes; and the no-raiding agreement between the AFL and CIO established in 1953–54 concerned solely with problems of raiding.[14]

The accompanying table lists approximately 50 agreements made between national unions

[9] *Report of the Proceedings of the Fifty-Fifth Annual Convention of the American Federation of Labor, 1935,* pp. 529–30.

[10] See Joseph Krislov, "The Extent and Trends of Raiding among American Unions," *Quarterly Journal of Economics,* February 1955, pp. 145–52; "Raiding among the 'Legitimate' Unions," *Industrial and Labor Relations Review,* October 1954, pp. 19–29.

[11] See statement of President George Meany, *Proceedings of Conference of International Representatives A.F.L. to Consider Tentative Draft American Federation of Labor Internal Disputes Plan, Chicago, Illinois,* May 14, 1954, pp. 9–10.

[12] See Marten S. Estey, "The Strategic Alliance as a Factor in Union Growth," *Industrial and Labor Relations Review,* October 1955, pp. 41–53.

[13] See *Arbitration Today, Proceedings of the Eighth Annual Meeting, National Academy of Arbitrators,* Boston, Massachusetts, January 27 and 28, 1955 (BNA Inc., Washington, D.C., 1955), pp. 149–66; Arthur J. Goldberg, *AFL-CIO,* pp. 271–82, 291–302 for the text of three agreements; David L. Cole, "Jurisdictional Issues and the Promise of Merger," *Industrial and Labor Relations Review,* April 1956, pp. 391–405.

[14] One of the significant developments of the period since World War II has been the general willingness (as the lesser of evils) to allow jurisdictional issues to be referred to outsiders for decisions.

since 1948 classified according to the types just noted.

This is an age of bilateral agreements; at no time in the history of the labor movement have so many agreements between national unions been made.[15] The central system of exclusive jurisdiction had become largely inoperative, and a central system under the merged Federation has not been established. In the absence of final decisions within the labor movement, the practical insistence on solutions to problems has tended to stimulate agreements. Moreover, the law provided penalties for jurisdictional strife and appeared to give management unlimited rights to assign work and a limited right to re-quest elections. The unions could do no less between themselves than they and the law of the land expected of employers, to bargain for an agreement. While a system of bilateral agreements is not logically consistent with the doctrine of exclusive jurisdiction since decisions are not made by a single central body, agreements may prove a practicable substitute by keeping competition within limits, by preventing further departures from established jurisdictional lines and by yielding the equivalent to exclusive jurisdiction in many cases.

The AFL-CIO merger, and the writing of a new constitution,[16] provided an opportunity for a fresh and systematic review of the doctrine of exclusive jurisdiction. But there was no extensive constitutional debate in convention as there had been in 1935, except in the corridors, bars, and in a few journals.[17] An analysis of the new constitution indicates that the older constitutional doctrine of unqualified exclusive jurisdiction was substantially modified, if not abandoned.

a) All jurisdictional claims against national unions in the merged federation alleging past trespass of jurisdiction were in effect denied. No matter how meritorious a claim based on previous exclusive jurisdiction, possession was to prevail and to provide constitutional protection in the future. The jurisdiction actually exercised by each affiliate at the time of merger was to be preserved intact.[18] Historical jurisdiction is replaced by "established collective bargaining relationship." This constitutional principle apparently applies not only between former affiliates of the AFL and CIO but also between unions within each group. Voluntary agreements and mergers may ultimately eliminate extreme instances of overlapping jurisdiction.

b) A new term "organizing jurisdiction" was introduced[19] to provide that with respect to an unorganized group or to one represented by a union outside the merged Federation, a union was free to assert its historical jurisdiction. But once a group is organized and certified or a collective bargaining relationship established, it would appear that traditional jurisdiction is again lost to the actual possessor. While "organizing jurisdiction" could have significance if the AFL-CIO were to assign rights and priorities in unorganized sectors and in organizing campaigns, at the present time "organizing jurisdiction" has little significance as a standard for settling disputes over organizing or providing an indication of legitimacy.

c) Jurisdictional rights may be asserted when consideration is given by the merged federation to adding a new affiliate which would be in conflict with the jurisdiction of an existing affiliate.[20] Charters are not to be issued in conflict with the jurisdiction of an affiliate. Jurisdiction apparently has most significance in the new constitution when it is asserted against a prospective national union rather than against one of the charter members of the new Federation.

The principle of exclusive jurisdiction, the constitutional principle used to regulate competition within the labor movement from the 1880s, was weakened from within before the mid-30s by an unwillingness to make decisions and a lack of enforcement machinery. The government determination of election units and the split in the labor movement combined to render the doctrine largely inoperative. Some vestiges remain in the new concept of "organizing

---

[15] Agreements among unions have been made from the earliest days; thus, the Knights of Labor and the Federations discussed a "treaty."

[16] AFL-CIO, *Constitution of the AFL-CIO and Other Official Documents Relating to the Achievement of Labor Unity,* January 1956.

[17] For critical discussion see Martin P. Durkin, "Toward a Lasting Merger" and "What Price Merger?" *United Association of Journeymen and Apprentices of the Plumbing and Pipe Fitting Industry Journal,* October and November, 1955; "ITU Seeks Merger Constitution Changes," *Labor's Daily,* July 7, 1955, pp. 7–10; "What Price Bigness," *Pattern Makers' Journal,* January–February 1955, pp. 1–2; "Merger," July–August, 1955, pp. 1–2; "ITU Autonomy Is Fundamental Matter," *The Typographical Journal,* January 1956, pp. 18–21.

[18] Article III, Section 4: "The integrity of each such affiliate of this Federation shall be maintained and preserved. Each such affiliate shall respect the established collective bargaining relationship of every other affiliate and no affiliate shall raid the established collective bargaining relationship of any other affiliate."

[19] Article III, Section 3: "Each such affiliate shall retain and enjoy the same organizing jurisdiction in this Federation which it had enjoyed by reason of its prior affiliation. . . ." Also see Article II, para. 8.

[20] Article II, Section 7.

jurisdiction," in the rights against new affiliates and in the rights of unions parties to the AFL internal disputes plan to assert evidences of traditional jurisdictional rights.[21] The new constitutional principles relied upon to regulate competition within the labor movement are the principle of the "integrity of affiliates" and "established collective bargaining relationships" and the stated hope for the voluntary extension of the voluntary no-raiding and internal disputes plans.

In practice the principle of exclusive jurisdiction is inoperative except in the building and construction industry, where the provision for government determination of bargaining units by elections is impractical and inoperative, and to some degree in sectors such as the railroad and printing industries which were highly organized and where elections have not radically affected the pattern of jurisdiction except as between pairs of contending unions on some properties or in some plants.

The "established bargaining relationship" has become the standard of legitimacy both within the law of the labor movement and the land. Unlike the state of affairs under the principle of exclusive jurisdiction, there is effective machinery in the government to make decisions concerning bargaining representatives and to enforce them. In a sense, the merged Federation largely abandoned its previous standard for regulating competition and accepted that of the law of the land, availing itself thereby of effective decisional and enforcement machinery as a last resort. Voluntary machinery, with use of an impartial no-raiding umpire, in this legal framework can operate more rapidly and appear to keep the regulation of competition relatively within the labor movement. In the sector of the labor movement where exclusive jurisdiction is still applicable, in the building trades, new decisional machinery was established and the enforcement machinery of the government materially assists the voluntary machinery.

The labor movement is as reluctant as ever to yield the determination of inter-union competition to the preference of workers, to employers, or to the government. The bilateral agreements between national unions and the setting up of no-raiding and internal disputes plans are designed to bring these decisions in large measure back within the scope of the labor movement.

The relation between union growth and inter-union competition is complex. While some degree

and types of inter-union competition probably have inhibited growth, there is also merit in the view that "competition, not unity, is responsible for the gains made by workers over the past 20 years."[22] The significant problem for the future is the forms and degrees of competition to be permitted within the Federation as a matter of public policy and union government.

2. The Craft-Industrial Problem

The occupational scope of the form of union organization dominant in the AFL was a trade, craft, or group of related crafts. Organization seems to have started with strategically placed groups of workers[23] and to have grown outward from these centers. In some relatively specialized cases, starting from these key workers, organization spread to form industrial unions as in the case of the isolated mining communities,[24] the brewing industry with the strong socialist traditions of its immigrant work force, and the garment industry where craft and immigrant origins were preserved as an industrial union, grew under the need for market control. The dominant form of trade organization traditionally characterized union structure in the major organized industries: railroad, buildings, printing, and shipbuilding.

The practical needs for survival, and unhappy experience with extreme forms of industrial unionism, confirmed the dominant pattern of organizational form save in special cases. A rationalization or philosophy of the trades or craft form of organization slowly emerged which achieved the status of received doctrine. This doctrine and policy was the center of all attacks from rival labor organizations: on the left for industrial unionism[25] and on the right for company unionism.

The traditional policies were displaced in the direction of a somewhat larger occupational

[22] "What Price Bigness," *Pattern Makers' Journal*, January–February 1955, p. 1.

[23] John T. Dunlop, "The Development of Labor Organization: A Theoretical Framework," in article 8 in this volume.

[24] *Report of Proceedings of the Twenty-First Annual Convention of the American Federation of Labor, 1901*, p. 240.

[25] "But the basic measure for the concentration of the forces of organized labor is the amalgamation of the six score craft unions into a few industrial unions." William Z. Foster, *Misleaders of Labor* (Trade Union Educational League, 1927), p. 321; Anthony Bimba, *History of the American Working Class* (New York: International Publishers, 1927), p. 227. See, however, Louis Adamic, *Dynamite, The Story of Class Violence in America* (New York: The Viking Press, 1931), pp. 194–95.

[21] Article V of the plan sets forth the standards to be considered by the umpire.

grouping—in the industrial union direction—by the events of the mid-30s. The decisive factors were two: (*a*) The government determination of the scope of the "bargaining unit" under Section 9 of the Wagner Act, and (*b*) the competition within the labor movement. The size of unit which can be organized and defended against employer opposition and worker apathy is much larger with government determination of election districts, certification depending on a majority vote, government enforcement on employers of the obligation to bargain for the unit as a whole, and government protection against rival unions save at specified periods. It is a quite different task to organize and to defend a unit on the picket line, with few limitations to employer opposition and rival unions, than to organize through quasi-political methods and to persuade an electorate to place an "x" on a ballot. The type of union, and the relation of union organization to member, is also likely to be different from the product of the older picket-line or nonelection organizing.

While the range of organizational forms in the labor movement has not been altered, the occupational scope of most national unions has been substantially increased. There are some few exceptions on the extreme narrow side such as the Patternmakers, Lathers, and Horseshoers. The industrial union, instead of being an exception to "organization on trade lines" warranted by special circumstances, such as the isolation of the coal mining industry (Scranton Declaration), is now recognized to be on a parity with the "trade union." In the language of the constitution of the merged Federation, ". . . giving recognition to the principle that both craft and industrial unions are appropriate, equal and necessary as methods of union organization."[26]

The issue of craft versus industrial unionism was for many years an issue of ideology within the labor movement. Since the events of the 30s, the occupational scope of organization has become largely a question of tactics and strategy in the particular organizing or bargaining context and a practical problem of internal union administration.[27] It is now evident that there are problems confronting unions with either wide or narrow groupings of occupations. Neither organizational form is without difficulties which at times make the other appear attractive both to the union officers and to groups of members.

A narrow grouping of occupations may require coordination in bargaining with other labor organizations and may, for practical purposes, abdicate the initiative and independent decision making in collective bargaining since tails do not ordinarily wag dogs. Technological change and shifting tastes and demand may threaten a narrow grouping. A union with a limited occupational scope and a small membership may not achieve many of the economies of scale in union organization. On the other hand, a wide grouping of occupations may have difficulty holding together. A number of industrial unions have had skilled-trades trouble,[28] and they have experimented with a variety of devices to give special recognition to their problems within a larger group: a skilled trades department, special wage increases, and apprenticeship programs. The larger scope of occupations also presents difficulties in bargaining, in finding internal agreement on an acceptable collective bargaining contract, where there may be differences over the extent of wage differentials and where high seniority employees may have different views than low service workers on pensions and supplementary unemployment compensation. The policies of organizations are affected by the relative number of workers in unskilled, semiskilled and skilled occupations under an agreement.

The developments within the labor movement on the occupational scope of the union—the craft-industrial problem—have been in the direction of further diversity. A number of intermediate forms have arisen to compromise the extremes of the craft-industrial clash. Among the more prominent are the following:

a. The council of occupationally narrow unions has had some limited sucess as a bargaining representative in atomic energy installations, in sectors of shipbuilding, munitions plants, the hotel industry, and in isolated establishments.[29] The council idea was advocated by John Fry who sought to introduce this form of organiza-

---

[26] Article II, Section 2.

[27] Industrial unions have, for example, sought to carve out craft groups from a unit organized on an industrial basis by traditional craft unions. See, for example, the decision of October 22, 1956 of the AFL-CIO umpire David L. Cole, involving the Oil, Chemical and Atomic Workers International Union and various unions affiliated with the Metal Trades Department. Traditional craft unions have petitioned for wide or narrow election districts depending almost solely on their chances of success.

[28] "Dissidence in the Auto Field," *Business Week*, March 10, 1956, p. 150; "To Prevent Revolt, UAW Takes New Tack," *Business Week*, December 22, 1956, pp. 84–87.

[29] See *Proceedings to the Forty-Sixth Annual Convention of the Metal Trades Department of the American Federation of Labor*, November 28, 1955, pp. 12–19, 25–30.

tion in the Western mining industry as an alternative to pure industrial unionism. Councils had long been established in the building and printing industries, but they were ordinarily used as a device to coordinate activities rather than serve as a collective bargaining instrument. Their development on a wide basis as a bargaining agent was an innovation of the split in the labor movement.

b. Some unions with a narrow occupational scope, to protect a central core, and in anticipation of conflict with other unions, simply extended the occupations within the union and covered by agreements to include the whole plant. The Moulders and Glass Bottle Blowers are illustrative. The problems and tensions of adaptation then took place inside the unions. At times new locals were formed and at other times the new groups were included in the same locals. The leadership of the narrower groups frequently continued for a period, and many still continue, making for gradual adaptation to the largest scope of organization.

c. One of the most striking developments of the period is the way in which unions which were predominantly craft in the 30s have expanded to include industrial groups and various intermediate forms while continuing craft organizations in some sectors. The Machinists and Electricians, strong AFL leaders against the CIO in the 30s, are perhaps the clearest illustrations, although much the same developments have taken place in all but a few craft unions.[30] The craft unions of the 30s have become both craft and industrial in varying proportions. Union structure has been most pliable. As a consequence new problems of internal government have arisen for these unions: the dues structure, union death benefits and health features, and the distribution of union offices. As a general rule the craft groups still control these groups, but they have developed quite flexible policies toward the non-craft groups who enjoy considerable autonomy. Special departments, conferences, and councils have frequently been established within the framework and supervision of the national union with specialized personnel. In some cases a limited number of executive board places have been assigned to give these groups representation in the top councils of the union.

The craft-industrial issue is no longer a question of ideology but rather a matter of organizing and bargaining tactics and internal union govern-

ment. There have been such widespread modifications in the scope of the occupations in the craft unions of the 30s that there no longer exists among national unions a craft-industrial issue. The adaptations in structure of the national unions have created new and difficult questions of internal government. The craft-industrial issue has been turned inward to take almost a different form in each national union.

3. The Doctrine of Autonomy

The principle of autonomy, its origins in the struggle in the 1880s between the Knights of Labor and the national unions affiliated with the Federation, is reaffirmed in the constitution of the AFL-CIO. A stated purpose is ". . . to protect the autonomy of each affiliated national and international union."[31] There has been no change in the statement of the constitutional principle, except that procedures have been established to implement the constitutional purpose that unions shall be free of corrupt influences and totalitarian agencies. The Executive Council is empowered to conduct an investigation, to give directions to an affiliated national union on these matters, and on a two-thirds vote to suspend the affiliate.[32]

While these new constitutional provisions do limit the principle of autonomy, at least in the form it had previously been expressed,[33] the change does not significantly alter the basic fact of the dominance of the national union in the American labor movement, relative to the influence and authority of the confederation or trade union center.[34]

These new provisions reflect an increased sensitivity to public opinion and a new status in the community. A labor movement with one third of the non-agricultural work force enrolled, in this respect, may be expected to be more responsive to public opinion than a union movement with only 5 or 10 percent of the work force.

The way in which these new constitutional principles are in fact applied will be a better measure of the extent to which the principle of autonomy has undergone change. The principle of autonomy historically did not preclude con-

---

[30] See the affiliations of the building trades and metal trades unions to the industrial union department of the AFL-CIO.

[31] Article II, Paragraph 11.

[32] Article VIII, Section 7.

[33] Report of the Proceedings of the Sixtieth Annual Convention of the American Federation of Labor, 1940, pp. 504–6.

[34] See J. E. Barnett, "The Dominance of the National Union in American Labor Organization," Quarterly Journal of Economics, May 1913, pp. 455–81.

Agreements among National Unions, 1948–56* (classified by type)

Organizations	Date	Joint Action in Collective Bargaining or Dealing with Employers (a)	No Raiding (b)	Joint Organizing Campaigns; Standards for Competitive Organizing (c)	Work Jurisdiction (d)	Merger or Transfer of Members (e)
Laborers/Electricians	July 13, 1948	—	—	—	X	—
Laborers/Plumbers	May 24, 1949	—	—	—	X	—
UAW/Machinists	Sept. 9, 1949,	X	—	—	—	—
Carpenters/Laborers	June 2, 1953	—	X	X	—	—
Carpenters/Asbestos Workers	Oct. 3, 1949	—	—	—	X	X
Boilermakers/Blacksmiths	July 21, 1950	—	—	—	X	X
Boilermakers/Plumbers	April 15, 1951	—	—	—	—	—
Iron Workers/Sheetmetal Workers	July 9, 1951	—	—	—	X	—
Machinists/Teamsters	Feb. 6, 1952	—	—	—	X	—
	Feb. 4, 1953					
Iron Workers/Elevator Constructors	Sept. 13, 1955	—	X	X	X	—
Iron Workers/Carpenters	May 26, 1953	—	—	—	X	—
Machinists/Rubber Workers	June 3, 1953	X	X	X	—	—
Packinghouse/Meat Cutters	June 15, 1953	X	X	X	—	—
Machinists/Rubber Workers	June 23, 1953	—	X	X	—	—
Boilermakers/Iron Workers	Aug. 10, 1953	X	—	—	X	—
Insurance Agents/Insurance Workers	Sept. 23, 1953	X	—	X	—	—
Machinists/Pressmen	Dec. 13, 1953	—	—	X	X	—
Laborers/Engineers	Dec. 16, 1953	—	—	—	X	—
Boilermakers/Plumbers	Dec. 18, 1953	—	—	—	X	—
Bricklayers/Asbestos Workers	Dec. 29, 1953	—	—	—	X	—
Laborers/Engineers	Jan. 28, 1954	—	—	—	X	—
Laborers/Engineers	Feb. 3, 1954	—	—	X	X	—
Teamsters/Upholsterers	Feb. 17, 1954	—	—	—	X	—
Machinists/Plumbers	Feb. 17, 1954	—	—	X	X	—
Carpenters/Laborers	April 29, 1954	—	—	—	X	—

Unions	Date					
Laborers/Engineers	Sept. 17, 1954	—	—	x	—	—
Carpenters/Machinists	Sept. 18, 1954	—	x	—	x	—
Teamsters/Meat Cutters	Sept. 24, 1954	—	x	—	x	—
Musicians/Variety Artists	May 29, 1950	(withdraw legal action)	—	—	—	—
	Nov. 15, 1954		—	x	—	—
Meat Cutters/Fur Workers	Dec. 28, 1954	—	x	—	x	x
Teamsters/Bakery Workers	Feb. 5, 1955	—	—	—	—	x
Oil Workers/Gas, Coke, Chemical	Feb. 25, 1955	—	—	—	—	—
Cement, Lime and Gypsum/Stone and Allied Workers	March 19, 1955	—	x	x	—	x
Iron Workers/Machinists	March 22, 1955	—	x	—	x	—
Iron Workers/Electricians	May 5, 1955	x	—	—	x	—
Five Printing Trades Unions (amendments to the 1911 agreement)	June 29, 1955	(union label)	—	—	—	—
Retail Clerks/Meat Cutters	Dec. 12, 1955	x	—	x	x	—
Electricians/Carpenters	Feb. 1, 1956	—	—	—	x	—
Lathers/Sheetmetal Workers	April 26, 1956	—	—	—	x	—
Oil, Chemical and Atomic/Chemical Workers	May 11, 1956	—	—	x	x	—
Furniture Workers/Upholsterers	May 24, 1956	—	—	x	x	—
Meat Cutters/Packinghouse	June 6, 1956,	—	—	—	—	—
	Sept. 10, 1956	—	—	—	—	—
State, County and Municipal/Civic Employees	June 30, 1956	—	—	—	—	—
Barbers/Barber and Beauty Culturists	July 1, 1956	—	—	—	—	x
Machinists/Metal Engravers	July 24, 1956	—	—	—	—	x
Sheetmetal Workers/Plumbers	Aug. 31, 1956	x	x	x	x	—
Machinists/Boilermakers	Sept. 1, 1956	x	x	x	x	—
Teamsters/Flight Engineers	Oct. 12, 1956	—	—	x	x	x
Painters/Asbestos Workers	Nov. 1, 1956	—	—	—	—	—
Painters/Plasterers	Nov. 29, 1956	—	—	—	—	—

* The list contains those agreements between national unions which have come to the writer's attention. He would welcome copies of agreements not here reported. For a partial listing (18), see Bureau of National Affairs, "Jurisdictional Dispute Settlement Agreements," Vol. LRX pp. 346 a–e.

Only formally signed agreements have been included in the list; informal understandings or clarifications of old agreements have not been listed. Agreements formally repudiated also have been excluded. The classification by type is the writer's judgment and does not constitute a formal interpretation. In addition to these agreements are the four creating general plans for settling various types of disputes noted in paragraph (f) in the text. There are some formal procedural agreements limited to settling disputes between two unions not listed above, such as Iron Workers/Plumbers, October, 8, 1953, and Painters/Plumbers, August 5, 1954, amended February 2, 1956.

siderable influence upon smaller unions and even directions on occasions from the Executive Council or President on matters that might be regarded as autonomous in the case of a larger or more influential union.[35] The meaning of autonomy under the new constitution will be significantly tested when the powers of Article VIII, Section 7 on corruption and communism are applied not against an international union or its officers but rather sought to be applied through an international to some local union or local officer.

4. The Internal Government of National Unions

While the last generation has seen few basic changes in the autonomy of the national unions relative to the confederation, there have been significant developments in the relations between the national union and both the constituent local and regional bodies and the membership.

a. Intermediate bodies between the national union office and the local union have come to play an increasing role in the life of the national union and in the negotiation or administration of collective bargaining agreements. It may be a regional office as in the Steelworkers and Hod Carriers, a district council as in the Carpenters, a market or regional office as in the Ladies' Garment Workers, a conference as in the Teamsters and Glaziers, or a less formal grouping of locals in a number of states or a product branch of the industry under an international representative. These bodies have gained responsibility and new functions both as compared to the local unions and the national office.[36] There is a variety of reasons for this development including the growing size of unions with larger administrative duties and the organization of firms in specialized product markets. The growing ease of transportation and the expansion of metropolitan centers also played a role in the consolidation of many locals.

While policy making is kept typically in the national office, these regional and product or market groups are significant agencies of administration and typically also points of political control within the hierarchy of the international union. It is thus politically easier to control ten local unions in an area (count on their votes in a convention) through a district council or regional office than to maintain control within each separate local union. While most international unions exercise considerable control over local unions directly through international representatives and the telephone, there is some tendency for administration to be decentralized to these intermediate bodies.

b. There is a growing specialization of union staff, a greater use of technicians and experts, and a growing professionalism in the conduct of union affairs and collective bargaining. The growth in union size with resulting administrative problems, the growth of personnel and specialized staffs in management, the passage of legislation affecting collective bargaining, peace time and war time governmental agencies, the growth of arbitration and the increased complexity of some collective bargaining issues such as pension plans have all been factors operating in this direction.

c) The relationship of the membership to the local and national unions has also undergone significant changes.[37] In part, this arises from the way in which members are recruited. Members organized by a vote in a government-conducted election or by the application of the union security provisions of an agreement, whose dues are checked off by the employer to the union, can hardly be expected to hold the same attachments to the union that arose when men were organized on the picket line. Long-term contracts operate in the same direction to create new attitudes toward the union. In part, the labor force itself is changing, affecting the nature of its attachment to the union: a higher proportion of women and older workers, a higher level of education, a change of residence frequently to the suburbs, a higher proportion of home ownership, a considerable level of installment debt, the habits of television affect the union's communication with its members, and a rising proportion of skilled and technical occupations. Then, too, the continuing high levels of employment, the absence of serious unemployment affects the attitudes of the union member. Finally, mention should be made of the change in policies of many managements, as exemplified in employee rela-

---

[35] See Herbert R. Northrup, "The Tobacco Workers International Union," *Quarterly Journal of Economics*, August 1942, p. 621.

[36] See G. D. H. Cole, *What Is Wrong with the Trade Unions?* Fabian Tract 301, September 1956, p. 7.

[37] Much contemporary discussion fails to draw a distinction between long-term or secular trends and the changes in relationship within the early years of the life of any national union. The changes in many unions formed in the late 30s or in the war period are no more than the passing of an initial stage. For perspective, see Robert F. Hoxie, *Trade Unionism in the United States* (New York: D. Appleton and Co., 1921), chap. 7, "The Leaders and the Rank and File."

tions and plant and community communications programs.

These factors have not been enumerated to suggest that union members are necessarily less loyal or less willing to strike. Rather they suggest that workers may be joining unions (except at the frontiers of union growth) more normally and naturally and that the attachment is less an emotional and personal experience and more another affiliation in a pluralistic society.

II. THE AMERICAN INDUSTRIAL RELATIONS SYSTEM

Any industrial relations system reflects the environment in which it arises and the characteristics of the management and labor organizations which interact. Systematic analysis of industrial relations systems requires the isolation of a limited number of characteristics of a system and a statement of the interrelations between the features of the environment and the labor and management organizations on one hand and the observed characteristics of the industrial relations system on the other.

While the present paper is no place for extensive analysis of the American industrial relations system, the changes in that system since the 20s need to be placed in perspective. The principal features of the American industrial relations system which existed prior to the 1930s may be analyzed in the following terms:

Features of the Total Environment

1. High ratio of natural resources to labor.
2. Large geographical environment with diverse regions.
3. Wide market area for products and labor.
4. Economic instability.
5. Industrialization did not have to transform a settled social system.

Workers and Labor Organizations

1. Individualistic workers.
2. Economic unionism.
3. Dominance of national union and career union leaders.
4. Local unions have large function and no rivals from works councils or labor parties.
5. Competitive unionism restrained by exclusive jurisdiction.

Management

1. Competitive and aggressive management.
2. Few strong employers associations.
3. Anti-union in the main.

4. Little staff organization for labor matters; foreman and line without assistance or general policy.
5. Drawn from no single class.

Features of the Industrial Relations System

1. High wage rates.
2. Wide differentials for skill.
3. Small sector organized (10 percent of nonagricultural work force).
4. Local bargaining predominates.
5. Large number of strikes and considerable violence.
6. Periods of union growth were sporadic.

In the period since the 1920s there has been a number of changes in the total environment in which the industrial relations system operates. The most prominent of these changes, in their effect upon the system, are the following:

1. The cessation of immigration was to have a significant effect upon the homogeneity of the work force, to accelerate the withdrawal of labor from agricultural regions and to raise unskilled and semi-skilled wages relative to compensation for skilled work.

2. The prolonged depression of the 30s and then the high employment levels of the war and decade after were to shape attitudes in the community, and among workers and managements, toward union organization. They were to set the stage for a vast expansion in collective bargaining. In two spurts, in the mid-30s and in the war, union membership was to rise from 10 percent to one third of the non-agricultural work force. "For economic and political power—reinforced by moral power—has brought about a complete change during our lifetime in the social and economic structure of the nation."[38]

3. The government policies represented by the Wagner Act and the War Labor Board were to have significant effects on the industrial relations system. The Wagner Act established the policies of: (a) an exclusive bargaining representative, in line with the public tradition of majority rule and the tradition of exclusive jurisdiction in the labor movement, and (b) government determination of the election district. The war followed soon upon the birth of many new bargaining relationships; four years of preoccupation with a common wartime effort under maintenance of membership and other policies determined by governmental agencies

[38] Sylvia and Benjamin Selekman, *Power and Morality in a Business Society* (New York: McGraw-Hill Book Co., Inc., 1956), p. 7.

were to assist in firmly establishing collective bargaining beyond serious possibility of disruption and for long enough to permit changes in basic attitudes among many parties. The war produced transformations in attitudes and policies which otherwise might have taken many years; its long run effects must be rated very high.

4. The expansion in collective bargaining and the implications of the Wagner Act were to lead, particularly in a post-war context, to some degree of public regulation of union organization and collective bargaining in the Taft-Hartley law.

These changes in the environment of the parties created important changes within management organizations and labor unions. In large managements particularly, there was a great expansion in staff concerned with employees and collective bargaining. Policies involving employees were centralized and, in varying degree, also their administration.[39] Except for a minority and for unorganized companies, large managements had shed much of their open anti-unionism. Opposition was more subtle. Human relations policies and techniques were widely adopted. On the union side, large organizations were to require more modern methods of administration, and larger labor organizations had to learn the hard way, as business before it, to be more sensitive to public opinion. The labor movement had shed almost all ideological elements which contested any of the basic institutions of the society.[40]

These transformations in the environment, and in management and labor organizations since the 1920s, were not to change the main features of the industrial relations system that was received from the past. Some significant modifications and refinements, however, are to be noted:

1. The labor movement is much less a minority movement. The present plateau of membership, as a percentage of the non-agricultural work force, appears stable, and substantial growth depends on a major break through to new sectors or areas which does not appear imminent.

2. Collective bargaining has become a settled and orderly process except at the frontiers of growth. Management has retained the major features of its discretion and policy making unimpaired, and it enjoys a high prestige by and large among workers, the unions, and the community. While strikes continue above the level of poorer and smaller countries or those with more centralized industrial relations systems, the extent of violence in labor disputes has very significantly declined in the United States.

3. Arbitration of grievances has become the final step of grievance procedures. The wide extent of private arbitration and the resort to private neutrals has become a unique feature of the American industrial relations system.

4. The compensation system has become more complex with fringe benefits (pensions, health and welfare programs, supplementary unemployment compensation), job evaluation plans, incentive plans, and production bonus arrangements in which the unions play a significant administrative role. These developments reflect a less ideological position and the growth of the administrative functions under collective bargaining.

5. The extent of occupational wage differentials has been substantially reduced when expressed in percentage terms.

6. The government through the NLRB (and the NMB) has come to play a large role in setting the details of the framework of collective bargaining, when comparison is made with systems of industrial relations abroad.

The American industrial relations system in the past generation has adapted to the evolving features of the total environment in which industrial relations take place, to its historical path and to the changes within union and management organizations. It is the task of industrial relations research to document and to analyze this interaction.

[39] See Charles A. Myers and John G. Turnbull, "Line and Staff in Industrial Relations," *Harvard Business Review,* July–August 1956, pp. 113–24.

[40] See, in contrast, the prediction and analysis of Werner Sombart, *Socialism and the Social Movement,* Translated by M. Epstein (New York: E. P. Dutton and Co., 1909), pp. 276–78.

16. The Unions: Structure, Functions, and Membership*

U.S. Department of Labor

PART 1. STRUCTURE OF THE LABOR MOVEMENT

The AFL–CIO

The constitution of the American Federation of Labor and Congress of Industrial Organizations, adopted at its founding convention in 1955, established an organizational structure closely resembling that of the former AFL, but more authority over affiliates was vested in the new Federation. The chief members of the Federation continued to be the national and international unions, the trades departments, the state and local bodies, and the directly affiliated local unions. (See Chart 1.)

The supreme governing body of the AFL-CIO is the biennial convention. Each union is entitled to convention representation according to the membership on which the per capita tax ($0.10 a month) has been paid.

Between conventions, the executive officers, assisted by the Executive Council and the General Board, direct the affairs of the AFL-CIO. In brief, the functions of the two top officers and of the two governing bodies are as follows:

Executive Officers. The president, as chief executive officer, has authority to interpret the constitution between meetings of the Executive Council. He also directs the staff of the Federation. The secretary-treasurer is responsible for all financial matters.

Executive Council. The Executive Council, consisting of 33 vice-presidents and the 2 executive officers, is the governing body between conventions. It must meet at least three times each

* Reprinted from U.S. Department of Labor, *Directory of National Unions and Employee Associations,* 1973.

year, on call of the president. Among the duties of the council are proposing and evaluating legislation of interest to the labor movement and keeping the Federation free from corrupt or communist influences. To achieve the latter, the council has the right to investigate any affiliate accused of wrongdoing and, at the completion of the investigation, make recommendations or give directions to the affiliate involved.

Furthermore, by a two-thirds vote, the Executive Council may suspend a union found guilty on charges of corruption or subversion. The council also is given the right to (1) conduct hearings on charges that a council member is guilty of malfeasance or maladministration, and report to the convention recommending the appropriate action; (2) remove from office or refuse to seat, by two-thirds vote, any executive officer or council member found to be a member or follower of a subversive organization; (3) assist unions in organizing activities and charter new national and international unions not in jurisdictional conflict with existing ones; and (4) hear appeals in jurisdiction disputes.

General Board. This body consists of all 35 members of the Executive Council and a principal officer of each affiliated international and national union and department. The General Board acts on matters referred to it by the executive officers or the Executive Council. It meets upon call of the president. Unlike members of the Executive Council, General Board members vote as representatives of their unions; voting strength is based on per capita payments to the Federation.

Standing Committees and Staff. The constitution authorizes the president to appoint standing committees to carry on legislative, political, educational, and other activities. These commit-

CHART 1   Structure of the AFL-CIO

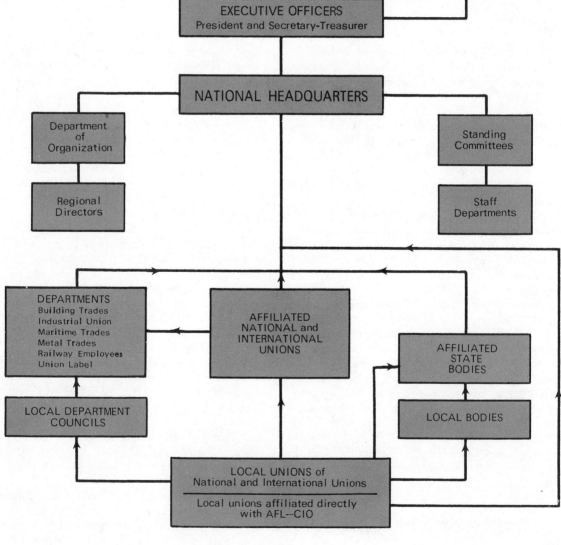

tes operate under the direction of the president and are subject to the authority of the Executive Council and the convention. Fifteen standing committees are operating at present. Staff departments are established as needed.

Department of Organization and Field Services. Meeting just prior to the opening of the 1973 general convention, the AFL-CIOs Executive Council revised the role and function of the Department of Organization, integrating the regional offices of the former department with all AFL-CIO operations and programs. Reflecting this expanded role, the name of the department was changed to the "Department of Organization and Field Services." The director of the department is appointed by the president, subject to the approval of the Executive Council. The department has its own staff and other resources necessary to carry out its activities.

Trade and Industrial Departments. The AFL-CIO constitution provides for six trade and industrial departments. An Industrial Union Department was added to the five departments which were carried over from the AFL. A department made up of unions in the food and beverage industry, chartered in 1961, was disbanded at the 1965 convention. Affiliation with departments is open to "all appropriate affiliated national and international unions." Affiliates are obligated to pay a department per capita tax which is determined by the number of members coming within their jurisdiction.

State and Central Bodies. Under the AFL-CIO constitution, the Executive Council is authorized to establish central bodies on a city, state, or other regional basis, composed of locals of national unions, organizing committees, and directly affiliated local unions. In 1973, there were approximately 735 local central bodies in existence.

Organizing Committees. The Executive Council has the authority to issue charters to groups not eligible for membership in national unions and combine directly affiliated local unions into organizing committees. These committees have the same status as national unions except that they are under the direct control of the Federation. In 1973 only one organizing committee was still in existence—the School Administrators & Supervisors Organizing Committee. The United Farm Workers of America, formerly an organizing committee, became a full-fledged AFL-CIO union in 1972.

Directly Affiliated Local Unions. At the time of the Federation's formation, local trade and federal labor unions (AFL) and local industrial unions (CIO) had a combined membership of 181,000. These local unions, having received charters from both federations, became directly affiliated local unions of the AFL-CIO and in 1973 claimed 55,000 members. Under the constitution of the merged Federation, the Executive Council of the AFL-CIO has responsibility for issuing charters and controls the affairs of these locals. The council also is under obligation, at the request of the locals, to combine them into national unions, organizing committees, or national councils where appropriate.

Jurisdictional Problems. Former AFL and CIO affiliates joined the Federation as fully autonomous unions and retained the same jurisdictional rights they held before the merger. These principles are expressed as follows in Article III, Section 4 of the constitution: "The integrity of each . . . affiliate of this Federation shall be maintained and preserved." The concepts of autonomy and jurisdictional rights find further support in Article III, Section 7, which gives the Executive Council the right to issue charters to new organizations only if their jurisdiction does not conflict with that of present affiliates because "each affiliated national and international union is entitled to have its autonomy, integrity, and jurisdiction protected and preserved." On the problem of craft versus industrial form of organization, the issue primarily responsible for the 1935 split, the new constitution recognizes that "both craft and industrial unions are appropriate, equal, and necessary as methods of trade union organization . . ." (Art. VIII, Sec. 9). The constitution acknowledges the existence of overlapping jurisdictions which might lead to conflict within the Federation. Affiliates are urged to eliminate such problems "through the process of voluntary agreement or voluntary merger in consultation with the appropriate officials of the Federation" (Art. III, Sec. 10).

New and enlarged machinery to replace the procedures previously provided for under the No-Raiding Agreement (Art. III, Sec. 4) was adopted at the 1961 convention and incorporated in a new section of the constitution, Article XXI, Settlement of Internal Disputes, effective as of January 1, 1962. Under the terms of this article, affiliates are required to respect both the established collective bargaining and the work relationships of every other affiliate. In a dispute, the case first goes to a mediator chosen from a panel of mediators "composed of persons from within the labor movement" (Sec. 8). Should the mediator not be able to settle the dispute within 14 days, it is then referred to an impartial umpire selected from a panel "composed of prominent and respected persons . . ." (Sec. 9), for a decision which is to go into effect 5 days after it has been handed down, unless an appeal has been filed. An appeal case is first referred to a subcommittee of the Executive Council which can either dismiss it or submit it to the full Executive Council for a final decision. A variety of sanctions are provided against noncomplying unions, including loss of the right to invoke the disputes settlement machinery and possible suspension. The Federation is further authorized to publicize the fact that a union has refused to comply with a decision and it can extend "every appropriate assistance and aid" (Sec. 15) to an aggrieved union.

A panel of impartial umpires and a panel of officers of international unions handle the mediation of internal disputes. All members of the Federation's Executive Council serve on the subcommittees which screen appeals and hear complaints of noncompliance.

According to the Executive Council's report to the AFL-CIO convention in 1973, a total of 1,401 cases had been filed under the Internal Disputes Plan since its inception in 1962 through the first seven months of 1973. Nearly 57 percent (796) of the complaints were settled by mediation; 562 were decided by the impartial umpires. In addition, the umpires issued fact-finding reports in 16 cases. Only 19 decisions were rejected by unions found in noncompliance with a decision, and in these cases sanctions were imposed by the Executive Council.

Councils

The Government Employees Council was formed in 1945 as a planning organization through which leaders of unions having members in government service could prepare programs for legislative and administrative action. This council is composed of 30 AFL-CIO organizations.

The Council of AFL-CIO Unions for Professional Employees was organized in Washington, D.C., in March 1967. Its goals include cooperation among members of scientific, professional, and cultural unions, encouragement of all professionals to become union members, participation in legislative activities of interest to professionals, and promotion of greater public interest in scientific, educational, and cultural activities. The council is composed of 17 organizations.

Railway Labor Executives' Association

The Railway Labor Executives' Association is composed of the chief executives of 15 labor organizations, all but one of which is affiliated with the AFL-CIO. Nine of these organizations have virtually all of their membership in the railroad industry, and the remaining six are principally established in other industries. RLEA is not a federation of unions; rather it functions as a policymaking body on legislative and other matters of mutual interest to railroad workers.

Congress of Railway Unions

The Congress of Railway Unions was formed during December 1969, after five unions withdrew from the Railway Labor Executives' Association over a dispute involving proposed compulsory retirement and pension benefit legislation. The six unions composing the organization are AFL-CIO affiliates. The Congress acts as a policymaking body on legislation and other matters of interest to railroad workers.

Other Federations

Two organizations act as a federation or have some of the characteristics of a federation, such as the issuance of charters to, and the maintenance of, a formal affiliation among autonomous labor organizations. The Assembly of Governmental Employees (AGE), founded in 1952 as the National Conference of Independent Public Employee Organizations, is made up of affiliated organizations in 40 States and Puerto Rico. The AGE is primarily concerned with the establishment and maintenance of the merit principle, although its affiliates have considerable autonomy on specific policy issues, including work stoppages. The second organization is the National Federation of Independent Unions (NFIU). Unions affiliated with the NFIU which had negotiated agreements covering different employers in more than one state are included among the unaffiliated, or independent, unions discussed below.

Unaffiliated or Independent Unions

A total of 64 national or international unions not affiliated with the AFL-CIO were known to the Bureau in 1972. All of the unaffiliated unions, other than those organizing government employees, reported agreements covering different employers in more than one state.[1] The combined membership of these unions for 1972 was estimated at 4.4 million. They included long-established and well-known organizations such as the Brotherhood of Locomotive Engineers and the United Mine Workers of America. Approximately four-fifths of the membership in unaffiliated national and international unions in 1972 was in unions once affiliated with the AFL-CIO and the former CIO, including expelled unions such as the International Brotherhood of Teamsters, the United Electrical Workers (UE), the Longshoremen's and Warehousemen's Union, and the Distributive Workers, as well as the Automobile Workers.

Unaffiliated local unions are generally confined to a single establishment, employer, or locality, and therefore do not meet the Bureau's definition of national unions. A 1967 Bureau survey showed about 475,000 members in 884 unaffiliated local unions. According to the Bureau's findings, these local independent unions represented approximately 2.3 percent of the total 1972 union membership in the United States.

Professional and State Employee Associations

Thirty-seven professional and state employee associations were known to be engaged in collective bargaining activities and responded to the Bureau's questionnaire. Thirty-five associations, with 2.2 million members, are included in the membership series.

PART II. DEVELOPMENTS IN ORGANIZED LABOR, 1971–73

A bitter jurisdictional dispute between the Farm Workers (AFL-CIO) and the Teamsters (Ind.) for the right to represent agricultural workers in California highlighted labor affairs during the period from 1971 to 1973. A significant number of new union presidents also assumed office during the period, including Mr. Arnold Miller, who was elected president of the United Mine Workers of America (Ind.) in a court-ordered election conducted by the U.S. Department of Labor. Several labor organizations

[1] The requirement pertaining to collective bargaining agreements was waived for organizations of government workers. Since the issuance of Executive Orders 10988 and 11491, the Bureau has attempted to include those federal government unions holding exclusive bargaining rights. Organizations representing postal employees have been included. Some unaffiliated unions, interstate in scope, may have been omitted because adequate information as to their existence or scope was not available.

formed alliances to better achieve common goals, while new measures were instituted by the AFL-CIO to improve its organizing capabilities, in recognition of organized labor's declining share of the nation's work force.

Farm Workers versus Teamsters

A bitter and, at times, violent dispute between the AFL-CIOs United Farm Workers of America and the independent International Brotherhood of Teamsters, Chauffeurs, Warehousemen and Helpers of America over the right to represent California grape and lettuce field workers emerged in 1973. Despite the mediatory efforts of AFL-CIO President George Meany, a peaceful settlement did not appear at hand by the end of 1973. In fact, at the close of the year, the Farm Workers pledged to intensify its nationwide boycott of Teamster-picked lettuce and grapes.

Trouble in the lettuce fields erupted in mid-January when the Teamsters and 170 growers renegotiated the final two years of a number of 5-year agreements originally signed in 1970. The new contracts, which covered 30,000 field workers, undercut attempts by the Farm Workers to organize the pickers and to force the lettuce growers to sign labor agreements. Less than a month before, the California Supreme Court ruled that the growers had, in 1970, signed contracts with the Teamsters without assessing the support the Teamsters held among field workers. As a result, the court decided that no jurisdictional dispute existed between the unions, and the Farm Workers were free to organize. Under California law, a jurisdictional dispute bars one union from competing with another in organizing workers. An injunction forbidding picketing and striking by the Farm Workers was also lifted by the court. Following the renegotiation of the Teamster agreements, the Farm Workers announced plans to conduct a nationwide boycott of Teamster-picked lettuce, similar to their boycott of grapes in the mid-1960s.

The struggle intensified during the summer when the California grape growers in the Coachella Valley, San Joaquin Valley, and the Delano area signed agreements with the Teamsters rather than renegotiate expired contracts with the Farm Workers. Failure to reach new contract terms with the Delano growers was particularly significant for the Farm Workers, not only because the Delano growers were the largest employers of agricultural labor in the State, but also because the efforts to organize the growers began there in 1965, and it was there that the first contract was signed in 1970. Since farm workers are not covered by the National Labor Relations Act, no representation election for the field workers was required before the contracts were awarded to the Teamsters. Mr. Cesar Chavez, President of the Farm Workers, insisted that a majority of the field workers covered by the Teamsters agreements were, in fact, supporters of his union.

Although negotiations with individual employers differed on specific points, several issues, including the use of hiring halls versus the labor contractor, labor camp conditions, and the use of pesticides in the fields, were of paramount importance and, according to UFW officials, were responsible for the impasse which developed in each bargaining situation. The growers, on the other hand, attributed the breakdown in negotiations to one particular issue—the insistence by the UFW that all labor be obtained through union hiring halls. As expressed by a spokesman for the Delano Growers Negotiating Committee, "The UFW demanded to have absolute control over who was going to work in the grape fields, refusing to agree that growers would be allowed to employ their regular seniority work force because many of these workers had shown a preference for the Teamsters Union." Contending that hiring halls lead to intimidation and coercion of workers, the Teamsters permitted hiring from all sources, including labor contractors.

Strikes were called by the Farm Workers against all growers who would not renegotiate their agreements. Picketing in the San Joaquin Valley, however, was curtailed following the shooting and killing of two Farm Worker members and the arrest of hundreds of pickets. A nationwide boycott of California grapes, initiated by the Farm Workers following the loss of the agreements to the Teamsters, was intensified as the union changed its tactics.

Monetary support for the striking farm workers was given by the AFL-CIO. At the spring session of the Federation's Executive Council, the AFL-CIO voted to donate $1.6 million, assessing each member of a federation union $0.12 to raise the funds.

AFL-CIO President George Meany sought personally to end the dispute, meeting with Teamsters President Frank E. Fitzsimmons in hopes of reaching an accord. On August 21, the end of the jurisdictional conflict seemed at hand when Mr. Fitzsimmons repudiated the 30 contracts signed with the Delano growers. In late September, Mr. Meany announced that an "agreement in principle" had been reached, under which the Teamsters would have abandoned its contracts with the grape growers immediately and would relinquish its lettuce contracts when they expired. The Teamsters would retain jurisdiction over food workers in packinghouses, canneries, and warehouses. The accord, however, proved shortlived. On November 7, President Fitzsimmons denied that an agreement with the head of the AFL-CIO had ever existed and announced that the Teamsters would honor their "moral and legal" obligations to the growers.

Nine days later Meany stated that the Teamsters had repudiated the agreement he and Fitzsimmons had reached "after long, formal negotiations." Meany also released the text of the agreement and a "chronology of events that led to it." At the present date, the issues remain unresolved and the conflict continues.[2]

1972 United Mine Workers of America Election

In one of the most significant legal decisions affecting organized labor in recent years, U.S. District Court Judge William Bryant ruled on May 1, 1972 that the 1969 United Mine Workers election was invalid. Judge Bryant, of the Washington, D.C., Court, upheld charges brought by the U.S. Department of Labor that the 1969 contest between the incumbent W. A. (Tony) Boyle and the late Joseph A. (Jock) Yablonski was marked by massive violations of union election laws. (As reported extensively in the press, Mr. Yablonski, his wife, and daughter were slain three weeks after the 1969 election, the victims of a complex murder conspiracy.)

Included in the list of violations were the union's illegal and prejudicial use of its newspaper to promote Mr. Boyle's candidacy; the use of UMW funds to finance Mr. Boyle's campaign; and the inability of Yablonski's observers to monitor voting at the polls because of interference by UMW officials. On June 16, a new election was ordered by Judge Bryant. The Department of Labor was directed by the Court to closely monitor the election, and strict procedures were established to govern the union's activities prior to the voting. Representatives of the Department of Labor were assigned to union offices with "specific authority to disapprove any financial transaction." Tight restrictions were placed on the activities of the union and its officials. In addition, the union was enjoined from repeating

[2] California has passed legislation permitting farm workers to hold union elections effective September 1975. This should assist in resolving the conflict. [Editor's Note]

the violations which impeded the first election.

The 49-year-old Mr. Arnold Miller, a victim of black-lung disease, was chosen in May 1972 to replace Yablonski as the candidate of the Miners for Democracy, the mine worker group opposed to President Boyle. Mr. Miller, while stressing he would put an end to the corruption and dishonesty which he charged pervaded the Boyle administration, also called for basic improvements in health and safety laws, pensions, and economic benefits. Mr. Boyle's platform was also geared towards increasing mine worker benefits.

Approximately two-thirds of the eligible UMW members participated in the election, which was accomplished without incident during the first week of December. On December 16, the Department of Labor announced that Mr. Miller had defeated the incumbent, receiving 70,353 of the 126,707 votes cast.

Upon certification of his election, Mr. Miller announced that major changes would be made in the administration of the union. He promised to cut the salaries of all Mine Workers' officials and staff members by 20 percent, move union headquarters from Washington, D.C., to a mining area, and explore the union's possible return to the AFL-CIO. He also dismissed 20 of the 24 members of the Mine Workers Executive Board, charging they had been illegally appointed by Boyle. Fourteen "interim" appointments were made, while six of the seats were left vacant to be filled by district elections.

Tony Boyle did not leave the public view with his defeat for reelection. On September 6, 1973, the Federal Bureau of Investigation arrested Mr. Boyle in connection with the Yablonski slaying. Boyle was arrested under a federal grand jury indictment which charged him with conspiracy in violating the civil rights of Mr. Yablonski by ordering his death. Simultaneously, the State of Pennsylvania filed murder charges against Boyle, citing him for the initiation and instigation of the assassination plan. Mr. Boyle was hospitalized, the victim of an apparent suicide attempt, only days before a Pennsylvania grand jury was scheduled to hear the charges against him. Mr. Boyle was tried by the State of Pennsylvania early in April 1974 and was found guilty of the charges.

Turnover of Union Presidents

The relatively high turnover among union presidents reported previously declined somewhat during the current survey period Thirty-six unions, 16 of which were affiliated with the AFL-CIO, reported that an individual who had not previously held the office of president was elected to that position in the 2-year period since 1971. Thus, there were leadership changes in 20 percent of the national unions compared to 28 percent during the last survey period.

From secondary sources, the Bureau has identified the reasons for 33 of these changes. (See Table 1.) Due to the Bureau's reliance on the labor and public press for this information, these reports should be viewed with caution; they do provide, however, some basis for determining the general reasons for change.

Historically, turnover has been most frequent among smaller unions, often those made up of government employees. This trend continued in the 1971–73 period: 16 of the 36 unions which experienced changes in their presidencies had fewer than 10,000 members, while 25 had fewer than 100,000. More than one-third of the changes in union presidencies occurred in unions that represent government employees.

Six unions with memberships exceeding 100,000—the Carpenters, the Clothing Workers, the American Federation of Government Employees, the Hotel and Restaurant Employees, the Mine Workers (Ind.), and the Textile Workers— changed their presidencies between 1971 and 1973.

Retirement or resignation for various reasons, including ill health, accounted for a turnover of 19 presidents. Mr. Joseph W. DePaola, president of the 50,000-member Barber's union, resigned in 1971 after a federal grand jury indictment on charges of accepting kickbacks for loans from the union's pension fund. Mr. DePaola was replaced as president by Richard A. Plumb, the former eighth vice-president.

Joseph Curran, the first and only head of the National Maritime Union for 36 years, retired in 1973 and was replaced by Secretary-Treasurer Shannon J. Wall. At the time of his retirement, Mr. Curran's longevity in office had exceeded that of nearly all other union presidents. (Harry

TABLE 1   Reported Reasons for Change of Union Presidents, 1971–73

Reason	Number of Presidents
Total	36
Retirement	8
Resignation or failure to seek reelection	11
Death	4
Election defeat	6
Limitation on number of terms	4
Reason unknown	3

Bridges, president of the International Longshoremen's and Warehousemen's Union (Ind.), and Sal B. Hoffman, head of the Upholsterers' International Union of North America (AFL-CIO) were both elected chief officials in 1937 and still remain in office.) Mr. Curran was most widely noted as a staunch foe of communism, and in 1948 headed a slate that ousted communist elements from posts in the maritime union.

An important transition occurred in the leadership of some of the major clothing and textile unions, when four longtime incumbents left office. William Pollock, 72, president of the Textile Workers Union of America since 1956, decided not to seek reelection in 1972 and was succeeded by Sol Stetin, the union's secretary-treasurer. Jacob S. Potofsky, president of the Amalgamated Clothing Workers since 1946, retired and was replaced by Murray Finley, one of 23 vice presidents. Throughout his tenure in office, Mr. Potofsky had been active in the civil rights movement and in the establishment and operation of union-sponsored cooperative housing and health care centers. Francis Schaufenbil, former secretary-treasurer of the United Textile Workers of America, succeeded George Baldanzi as president of the 52,000-member union. Mr. Baldanzi died in April 1972. In an additional change, Albert Buglione resigned from the presidency of the Textile Foremen's Guild and was replaced by William Carafello.

Four presidents died during their terms of office. These individuals headed the Asbestos Workers, Leather Goods, Machine Printers, and the United Textile Workers.

Election defeats were responsible for the replacement of six incumbents. The most publicized contest involved the United Mine Workers' (Ind.) W. A. (Tony) Boyle, president since 1964. As mentioned earlier, Boyle was defeated by Arnold Miller in an election conducted by the Department of Labor in December 1972.

In another contested election supervised by the Labor Department, the international officers of the Bricklayers, Masons and Plasterers were reelected by delegates to a special convention. The union's 1972 convention was reconvened after the Labor Department found defects in the procedures used to elect local union delegates to the earlier convention. Thomas F. Murphy was reelected president, along with the slate that had won the previous election.

Turnover also resulted from the policy of some labor organizations of limiting the number of terms national officers may serve. Four small independent unions, all with membership in the

federal government, have constitutional provisions of this nature. Three of the organizations, the Quarantine Inspectors (Ind.), the Trademark Society (Ind.), and the Aeronautical Controllers Association (Ind.), limit national officers to two terms. The constitution of the Federal Veterinarians (Ind.) requires the election of new national officers each year.

Alliances of Public Employee Organizations

NEA-SCME-IAFF Coalition. In March 1973, the Coalition of American Public Employees (CAPE), a lobby and political action group comprising the National Education Association (NEA), the American Federation of State, County and Municipal Employees (SCME), and the International Association of Fire Fighters (IAFF), announced plans to implement a legislative and legal program designed to effect major changes in current public sector bargaining statutes. Towards this end, three major goals were adopted by the coalition's executive board: (1) seek congressional legislation which would set national standards governing collective bargaining for public employees; (2) seek the repeal of the Hatch Act; and (3) bring to an end the current policy of taxing public employees' retirement withholdings. In addition to the establishment of these legislative goals, the executive board authorized a separate fund of $75,000 to hire a full-time director and staff to implement them. (Ralph Flynn, a former official of the NEA, was subsequently named executive director.) Twenty state and local CAPE units were also formed to work for the advancement of public policy favorable to government employees in their respective regions. A fourth public sector organization, the National Treasury Employees Union, joined the coalition in August 1973. The Fire Fighters, however, withdrew from CAPE one year after its formation.

AFT-NCUEA Coalition. While CAPE invited other organizations to join, the American Federation of Teachers (AFT) declined to do so because it felt that such a step might frustrate its eventual goal of merger with the NEA. Furthermore, leaders of the AFT characterized CAPE as a "false substitute for true unity." In an apparent contradiction, however, the AFT has formed a National Coalition for Teacher Unity (NCTU) with the National Council of Urban Education Association (NCUEA), which represents about 400,000 members of the NEA's large city locals. Many problems have beset the coalition, including the censure of the NCUEA president by the group's executive board for entering into an unauthorized alliance with the AFT.

Mergers under Consideration

After years of resisting merger proposals by the AFT, the NEA at its June 1973 annual convention invited the American Federation of Teachers to participate in merger talks without preconditions. The leaders of both organizations had hoped that the September 1973 talks would mark the end of years of antagonism between their groups. Both sides recognized, however, that their fundamental differences, primarily the NEAs historical aversion to affiliation with the AFL-CIO, must be resolved prior to the culmination of the merger on a national level.[3] Locals of the NEA and AFT previously had merged in New York State, Los Angeles, New Orleans, and Miami.

At the December 1973 session of the AFTs executive council, severe criticism of President David Selden's handling of the merger talks with the NEA surfaced, resulting in the passage of a resolution calling for his immediate resignation. Most of the council members claimed that Mr. Selden had made "proposals to the NEA that the union's merger-negotiating committee had not authorized." It was asserted that the "unauthorized proposals" might jeopardize the future of the merger. Should Mr. Selden resign, First Vice President Albert Shanker, head of the United Federation of Teachers in New York City and generally regarded as the dominant figure in the union, would most likely be named as interim president until the next scheduled election in the summer of 1974.

Merger negotiations between the two organizations collapsed during late February 1974 after only four meetings. According to Dr. Helen Wise, president of the NEA, the AFT leadership refused to compromise on its basic demand that any merged group be affiliated with the AFL-CIO. This charge was challenged by President Selden who claimed that compromise solutions were offered to the NEA, including the right of individual association members to reject AFL-CIO membership after the merged union joined the Federation. Observers predict that the nation's school systems will now be subject to a bitter interunion organizing battle as competition for new members is heightened.

Consolidation of all printing union members into one union, an avowed goal of several labor leaders in this industry, moved several major steps towards fruition since 1971. In addition to the mergers which created the Graphics Arts International Union (GAIU-AFL-CIO) and the International Printing and Graphic Communications Union (IPGCU-AFL-CIO) in 1972, exploratory merger talks have been opened between the International Typographical Union and the IPGCU and the Newspaper Guild and the GAIU. Confronted with common problems—the emergence of a new technology, a decline in employment, and an expansion in the use of nonunion workers—union leaders have concluded that craft representation may be obsolete and merger the only solution.

AFL–CIO Reaffirms Commitment to Organizing

Labor's long-term commitment to organizing was reasserted recently through measures taken by the AFL-CIOs tenth convention, held in October 1973 at Bal Harbour, Florida. A five-part program on organizing was adopted by the convention, primary impetus being directed towards the passage of legislation removing so-called state right-to-work laws from the scope of the Labor Management Relations (Taft-Hartley) Act. AFL-CIO state and local central bodies were to assume a greater responsibility in organizing and to assist in educating the public on the aims and acomplishments of the labor movement. Improvements in organizing techniques through more extensive training for staff members were also suggested.

In addition, the AFL-CIO's Executive Council, meeting just prior to the opening of the general convention, directed that the Federation's organizing arm be completely revamped. Recognizing that effective organization could not take place "in a political, legislative, and climatic vacuum," the Council broadened the role and function of the regional directors and field staff who previously were engaged principally in organizational activities. The regional offices were to be made "an integral part of the full-range of AFL-CIO operations and programs." The Executive Council maintained that it was essential "to develop a structure that is fully responsive to objectives uppermost, at any given time, in the labor movement's order of priorities." To more efficiently participate in advancing labor's goals, the restructured staff was to develop a close

---

[3] For a comprehensive discussion of the obstacles confronting a merger, see Edward F. Hanley, "National Education Association Again Focuses on Merger Issues," *Monthly Labor Review*, September 1973, and Carl A. Batlin, "American Federation of Teachers Endorses Merger Talks," *Monthly Labor Review*, October 1973.

liaison with the Federation's departments which rely on strong field support, particularly the Committee on Political Education (COPE), and the committees on legislation, community services, and urban affairs. As a means of creating greater flexibility, the 16 regions were to be consolidated into 8.

Mr. Alan Kistler, assistant to the director of the former Department of Organization, was selected to direct the new department. As a result of its "broader mission," the Department of Organization was renamed the Department of Organization and Field Services. Mr. Kistler's initial responsibility will be to develop working relationships between the regional directors and all AFL-CIO field personnel.

Employee Associations

Professional and public employee organizations that engage in collective bargaining and related activities have experienced a period of sustained growth in recent years and have emerged as a major factor in public sector labor relations. In many cases, these groups have had to meet the challenges of labor unions for the right to represent public employees. Recognizing the significant impact associations have had in public sector negotiations, the Bureau has continued its efforts, since 1971, to identify all employee associations which negotiate agreements or represent employees in related activities. In the interest of continuity the Bureau will maintain separate membership statistics on organizations traditionally identified as unions.

Employee associations have been represented on the national level since 1952 by the Assembly of Governmental Employees (AGE), the largest organization of nonteaching public employees in the nation. The assembly is comprised of 32 state employee associations and 12 other affiliated groups with approximately 700,000 members. Since each affiliate retains complete autonomy in local matters, the national headquarters' staff and officials in Washington, D.C., function primarily as a lobby, proposing legislation to improve the rights and benefits of state and local government employees.

PART III. UNION MEMBERSHIP

Total Union Association Membership

Membership in the nation's 177 labor unions and 35 professional and State associations reached 23,059,000 in 1972. Reports from 166

national unions, supplemented by Bureau estimates for 11, yielded a total of 20,838,000 union members in the year, including members outside the United States. The addition of 55,000 members in local unions directly affiliated with the AFL-CIO raises the total to 20,894,000, the figure consistent with the Bureau's historical series for total union membership. Membership of 35 professional and state associations was 2,221,339 in 1972. Not included in these totals, however, are approximately 475,000 members of single-firm or local unaffiliated unions in the United States and an estimated 235,000 members in municipal public employee associations.

By affiliation, 1972 union membership figures were distributed as follows: AFL-CIO, approximately 16,507,000; unaffiliated national and international unions, about 4,386,000. For 1971, a year also covered by this survey, AFL-CIO affiliates claimed approximately 16,183,000 members and unaffiliated unions about 4,399,000, yielding a total of about 20,582,000. With the inclusion of association members in the count, the 1972 total equaled 23,115,000; 1971 total was 22,697,000. (See Table 2.)

Comparable membership statistics for 1970 were as follows: AFL-CIO, 15,978,000, and unaffiliated, 4,774,000. The membership of 23 state and professional associations in 1970 totaled 1,868,000.

Over the 2-year span, membership in unions affiliated with the AFL-CIO increased by well over 500,000; in contrast, unaffiliated unions experienced a loss of nearly 400,000 members. Most of the shift was due to the merger of District 50

TABLE 2   Reported and Estimated Membership of National Unions and Employee Associations, 1971 and 1972

Organization and Source of Data	1971	1972
Total unions and associations...................	22,697,000	23,115,000
Unions......................	20,582,000	20,894,000
AFL-CIO affiliates............	16,183,000	16,507,000
Membership reports*......	15,563,000	16,011,000
Per capita data†.........	558,000	441,000
Locals directly affiliated....	62,000	55,000
Unaffiliated unions.........	4,399,000	4,386,000
Membership reports‡......	3,859,000	4,321,000
Membership estimates§...	540,000	65,000
Employee associations (state and professional)‖.....	2,115,000	2,221,000

* 105 unions in 1971; 107 in 1972.
† 10 unions in 1971; 6 in 1972.
‡ 53 unions in 1971; 59 in 1972.
§ 11 unions in 1972; 5 in 1972.
‖ 35 unions in 1971 and 1972.

(Ind.) with the AFL-CIOs Steelworkers. In the aggregate, unions gained 142,000 members between 1970 and 1972, the smallest increase in both absolute and relative terms since the 1960–62 period, when union rolls actually declined. Unions and associations increased their combined membership by nearly 500,000, with associations accounting for about 70 percent of the total gain.

Membership in the United States. The figures previously cited, which cover membership in 1971 and 1972 of national unions and employee associations with headquarters in the United States and of directly affiliated AFL-CIO local unions, include members outside the United States. As noted, these membership data exclude the approximately 475,000 members of unaffiliated unions which confine their activities to a single employer or to a single locality. The Bureau used this estimate for single-firm and local unaffiliated unions to compute the 1972 total membership in the United States. Table 3 contrasts membership in the United States with membership of all national unions and employee associations headquartered in the country.

Table 3 may not include specific classifications of workers with a direct attachment to the labor movement in 1972. Past reports received by the Bureau indicate that many unions include only their dues-paying members in their membership totals, and exclude all those who are, in whole or in part, dues-exempt (unemployed workers, strikers, retirees, those in the armed forces, etc.). Largely because of recordkeeping problems at national headquarters, accurate figures on the number so excluded are difficult to obtain. Esti-

mates furnished by unions able to respond to an inquiry of this type in the past yielded totals as high as 930,000. Information obtained from the 1971 questionnaire indicated that retirees were included in the membership count of 30 unions. In addition to these unions, which reported 291,-000 retirees in their membership, 11 unions reported that they included retirees but were unable to provide figures. This item was not included in the 1973 questionnaire.

Membership Outside the United States. Unions and associations reported 1,585,000 members outside the United States in 1972, an increase of about 7 percent over the number reported in 1970. One hundred and thirteen of the 177 national unions claimed 1,579,000 members in areas outside the United States, an increase of 109,000 over 1970. Only 6,000 association members were employed abroad. Union membership outside the United States grew at a faster rate than membership within. Thus, in 1972, 7.6 percent of the membership in all unions was located outside the United States, compared with 7.1 percent of membership in 1970. Canadian membership increased by approximately 87,000, Puerto Rican by 14,000, and membership in other areas by 10,000; membership in the Canal Zone declined by 1,000.

The significant membership gain experienced in Canada was made by unions representing workers in both manufacturing and nonmanufacturing industries, particularly primary metals and service. At the same time a number of unions reported minor losses. In addition, Canadian members of the Communications Workers withdrew from the national organization at its

TABLE 3 Derivation of Union and Association Membership in the United States, 1972

Membership Item	Number	
Membership claimed by all national unions with headquarters in the United States.	20,838,000	—
Subtract: Members outside the United States.	1,579,000	—
National union membership in the United States.	—	19,259,000
Add: Membership of locals directly affiliated with AFL-CIO.	55,000	—
Add: Membership of single-firm and local unaffiliated unions.	475,000	530,000
Total union membership in the United States.	—	19,789,000
Add: Membership of professional and state employee associations.	2,221,000	—
Subtract: Members outside the United States.	6,000	—
Add: Membership of municipal employee associations*.	235,000	—
Total association membership in the United States.	—	2,450,000
Total union and association membership in the United States.	—	22,239,000

* See Municipal Public Employee Associations, Bulletin 1702 (Bureau of Labor Statistics, 1971). Membership adjusted to account for duplication.

April 1972 convention but continued their affiliation with the Canadian Labor Congress. Although the Canadian membership of most of the 113 U.S. unions remained relatively unchanged, 18 unions reported gains of 1,000 members or more each since 1970 and 11 reported losses.

In Puerto Rico, large membership increases by the Distributive Workers (Ind.) and the Longshoremen more than offset losses by several unions, including the Teachers and State, County, and Municipal Employees.

Union Membership Trends and Changes

Union membership quadrupled in the period following the enactment of the Wagner Act (1935) and the end of World War II. In the second half of the 1940s membership remained fairly constant; the early 1950s, in contrast, saw many new entrants to union rolls. After peaking in 1956 at 17.5 million (excluding Canadian), membership began a downward trend that was not reversed until the mid-1960s. As indicated by Chart 2, union membership (exclusive of Canadian) has increased each year but one since 1964, reaching its highest point in 1972 with 19.4 million members. (See Table 4). Growth

in the future will depend to a great extent on how successfully unions organize in the expanding sectors of the economy and compete with employee associations for the right to represent public sector workers.

The small absolute increase in union membership in 1972, when coupled with a sharp rise in the labor force, resulted in a decline in the proportion of organized workers. This decline, to 21.8 percent, continued the long-term downward movement in this measure.

As a proportion of employees in nonagricultural establishments, the sector where most members are found, the downward trend has also continued, falling to new lows of 27.2 percent in 1971 and 26.7 percent in 1972. Since 1970 the number of employees in nonagricultural establishments increased 3 percent, while union membership grew by only 0.3 percent.

In contrast to the 1968–70 period, when the number of unions gaining members exceeded those which lost, more unions experienced declines (74) than increases (62) in the 1970–72 period. Sixteen of the unions for which comparable information was available reported virtually no change in membership. A significantly greater proportion of unions experienced losses

TABLE 4 National Union and Employee Association Membership as a Proportion of Labor Force and Nonagricultural Employment, 1958–72 (numbers in thousands)*

Year	Membership Excluding Canada	Total Labor Force		Employees in Nonagricultural Establishments	
		Number	Percent Members	Number	Percent Members
Unions and associations					
1968	20,721	82,272	25.2	67,915	30.5
1969	20,776	84,240	24.7	70,284	29.6
1970	21,248	85,903	24.7	70,593	30.1
1971	21,327	86,929	24.5	70,645	30.2
1972	21,657	88,991	24.3	72,764	29.8
Unions					
1958	17,029	70,275	24.2	51,363	33.2
1959	17,117	70,921	24.1	53,313	32.1
1960	17,049	72,142	23.6	54,234	31.4
1961	16,303	73,031	22.3	54,042	30.2
1962	16,586	73,442	22.6	55,596	29.8
1963	16,524	74,571	22.2	56,702	29.1
1964	16,841	75,830	22.2	58,331	28.9
1965	17,299	77,178	22.4	60,815	28.4
1966	17,940	78,893	22.7	63,955	28.1
1967	18,367	80,793	22.7	65,857	27.9
1968	18,916	82,272	23.0	67,915	27.9
1969	19,036	84,240	22.6	70,284	27.1
1970	19,381	85,903	22.6	70,593	27.5
1971	19,211	86,929	22.1	70,645	27.2
1972	19,435	88,991	21.8	72,764	26.7

* Membership includes total reported membership excluding Canadian. Also included are members of directly affiliated local unions. Members of single-firm unions are excluded.

CHART 2   Membership of National Unions, 1930–72*

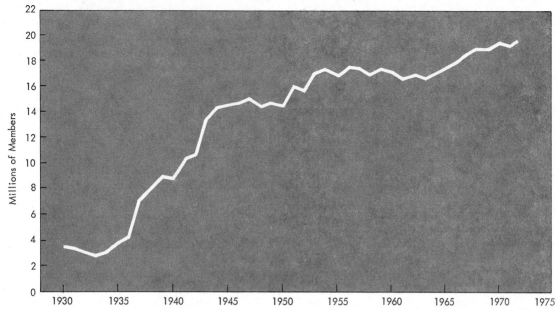

* Excludes Canadian membership but includes members in other areas outside the United States. Members of AFL-CIO directly affiliated local unions are also included. For the years 1948–52, midpoints of membership estimates, which were expressed as ranges, were used.

(39) than gains (26) of 10 percent or more of total membership between 1970 and 1972. Most of the 11 unions which grew by 20 percent or more were smaller unions, with membership not exceeding 50,000 each.

Most of the changes which occurred in the 1971–72 period were minor. Reports from 103 of 159 unions, 65 percent, showed membership changes of less than 5 percent. Nearly twice as many unions lost (17) as gained (19) 10 percent or more of their membership.

Between 1951 and 1972, only 18 of 113 unions for which reports were available showed membership changes of less than 10 percent. Almost 4 of every 10 unions increased their membership by more than 20 percent; 3 of 10, on the other hand, reported declines of greater than 20 percent. Unions experiencing substantial increases over the 21 years were those with a significant proportion of their membership in government, service, trade, and transportation (airline and trucking). Indicative of the shifts that have occurred within the economy over the past two decades, unions with members in railroads, textiles, shoes, and furniture industries experienced substantial declines in membership.

It is extremely difficult to assess the many factors that contribute to a union's gain or loss of membership. Increases in individual unions may be attributed to the merger of organizations,

successful organizing campaigns, and increased employment in plants covered by union shop agreements. Changing employment patterns, such as a shift from blue-collar to white-collar occupations, can cause a loss in membership.

Of the 57 unions which claimed 100,000 members or more during the 1960–72 period, the largest gains were made by unions that organize in predominantly white-collar or service-oriented industries: government, service, and trade. The Teamsters (Ind.), representing workers in a wide array of industries, but particularly in trucking, showed the largest absolute gain over the period (371,000). Several unions have consistently reported growth over the 12-year period. Among these are: the Electrical Workers (IBEW); Operating Engineers; Retail Clerks; Service Employees; State, County and Municipal Employees; Teachers; Letter Carriers; and the Communications Workers. Reflecting the effects of its merger with District 50 (Ind.), the Steelworkers showed the largest 2-year gain—200,000.

Size Distribution

As has been noted previously, union membership is concentrated in a relatively small number of unions. This trend continued into 1972. Fifteen unions, less than 10 percent of the total, represented 11.7 million union members, or 56 percent of all those on union rolls during the year. Ten of these unions, each with membership exceeding 500,000, claimed 9.4 million members, or 45 percent of the total. In 1970, the 8 unions in this size class accounted for 40 percent of all union members. At the opposite end of the distribution, 86 unions, nearly one-half of the total, had membership of less than 25,000 each in 1972, and represented only 3 percent of all members.

The membership of employee associations was also highly concentrated. Over one-half of association membership was located in one organization, the National Education Association (NEA); 24 associations, nearly 70 percent, had fewer than 25,000 members on their rolls. It should be noted, however, that most of the associations represent employees of a particular state and thus are subject to a built-in limitation on their size. Unions which organize workers in more than one state do not face such restrictions.

Table 5 lists the 48 unions which reported 100,000 members or more. The number of associations in this size class increased by one from 1970. Although the number of unions in this class

did not vary from 1970, several changes did occur in the composition of the listing. Two unions which were included in the 1970 list reported that their membership had fallen under 100,000: the Chemical Workers (AFL-CIO) and the Federation of Federal Employees (Ind.). In addition, District 50 (Ind.) joined the Steelworkers and thus no longer qualifies for listing. As a result of mergers, two new unions appear for the first time: the Paperworkers (AFL-CIO) and Graphic Arts (AFL-CIO). Both the Pulp, Sulphite and Paper Mill Workers (AFL-CIO) and the Papermakers and Paperworkers (AFL-CIO) had over 100,000 members prior to their merger creating the United Paperworkers of America. The Woodworkers (AFL-CIO), Railway Carmen (AFL-CIO), and Government Employees (NAGE) (Ind.) increased their membership sufficiently since 1970 to be added to the 1972 list.

Based on information supplied by individual unions, the most significant change in the size ranking of the top 11 since 1970 was the displacement of the Auto Workers (Ind.) from second place, a position it had held for over a decade. While the Auto Workers experienced a

TABLE 5   National Unions and Employee Associations Reporting 100,000 Members or More, 1972*

Organization	Members (thousands)	Organization	Members (thousands)
Unions		Unions (continued)	
Teamsters (Ind.)	1,855	Retail, wholesale	198
Steelworkers	1,400	Rubber	183
Automobile workers (Ind.)	1,394	Iron workers	176
Electrical (IBEW)	957	Textile workers	174
Carpenters	820	Oil, chemical	172
Machinists	758	Electrical (UE) (Ind.)	165
Retail clerks	633	Fire fighters	160
Laborers	600	Sheet metal	153
Meat cutters	529	Transport workers	150
State, county	529	Bricklayers	149
Service employees	484	Bakery	146
Hotel	458	Maintenance of way	142
Communications workers	443	Boilermakers	132
Ladies' garment	428	Transit union	130
Operating engineers	402	Printing pressmen	115
Paperworkers	389	Typographical	115
Clothing workers	365	Graphic arts	106
Musicians	315	Woodworkers	106
Government (AFGE)	293	Railway carmen	104
Electrical (IUE)	290	Government (NAGE) (Ind.)	100
Teachers	249		
Transportation union	248	Associations	
Postal workers	239		
Railway clerks	238	Education association	1,166
Plumbers†	228	Civil service (NYS)	202
Letter carriers	220	Nurses association	157
Mine workers (Ind.)	213	Police	125
Painters	208	California	103

* Based on union and association reports to the Bureau with membership rounded to the nearest thousand. All unions not identified as (Ind.) are affiliated with the AFL-CIO.
    † 1973 AFL-CIO per capita.

decline in membership between 1970 and 1972, the Steelworkers recorded a significant gain, principally as a result of its merger with District 50. After losing more than 10 percent of its membership since 1970, the Machinists (AFL-CIO) dropped from fifth to sixth place. Both State, County and Municipal Employees (AFL-CIO) and the Service Employees (AFL-CIO) moved ahead of the Hotel and Restaurant Employees, which slipped from 10th to 12th place.

As a consequence of strong and successful organizing efforts among government employees, unions which organize exclusively in the public sector have shown the largest increases in membership. Between 1962 and 1972, for example, Government Employees (AFGE) (AFL-CIO) and Teachers (AFL-CIO) have more than doubled their membership. In 1972, Government Employees ranked 19th in size; in 1962, the union was 43d. The Teachers, which did not appear on the 1962 listing, ranks 21st in 1972. State, County, and Municipal Employees with 220,000 members was ranked 21st in the list a decade ago; in 1972, the union reported 529,000 members and is now the 10th largest union in the country.

Industrial Distribution of Membership

Changing employment patterns within the U.S. economy over the past decade have had an impact on the industrial composition of union membership.[4] Employment in the manufacturing sector, where unions have traditionally been strongest, has remained relatively stable since 1962, while employment in service-producing industries, including government, has increased by 41 percent. Thus, it is not entirely coincidental that unions have made their most sizable gains in the government and nonmanufacturing sectors. In fact, since 1956, only the government sector has consistently gained both in total number and as a percentage of total membership. Union membership in the manufacturing sector, while slightly higher than the 1956 level, has declined significantly as a proportion of the total organized work force.

Between 1956, when the Bureau first requested information by industry, and 1968, membership was available only in broad industry classes. Data for 2-digit Standard Industrial Classification (SIC) industry groups have been available only since 1968.

Since 1970, unions which organize primarily

---

[4] Data by industry include members outside the United States, retired workers, and others.

in the manufacturing sector have lost approximately 250,000 members. The most substantial loss was registered in the fabricated metal products industry (247,000), due primarily to a shift in the industrial composition of the Steelworkers, which reported 227,000 fewer members in this industry group in 1972 than in 1970. Ten other industry groups experienced declines; none, however, approached the loss registered in fabricated metal products. This decline in union representation resulted in part from membership losses experienced by the Machinists and Automobile Workers (Ind.), which represent workers in a wide variety of manufacturing industries.

Union membership in nonmanufacturing increased by 260,000 between 1970 and 1972, due principally to the higher demand for and employment in services. Gains of 362,000 in services and 176,000 in contract construction more than offset losses of 265,000 in wholesale and retail trade and 83,000 in transportation.

Unions and associations represented 4.5 million workers employed in government, an increase of 11 percent over 1970. Professional and public employee associations accounted for about 68 percent of the overall gain, but most of this was due to the inclusion of 13 additional associations in the survey. All of the 142,000-member increase by unions was registered at the state and local government levels. Much of this gain was attributable to the State, County and Municipal Employees which increased its rolls by 85,000 since 1970 and the Teachers (AFT) which gained 43,000 members. In 1972 the Bureau, for the first time, requested separate information on the extent of organization at the state and local government levels. Previously, this membership had been grouped. Since nearly three-fifths of all government workers are employed at the local level, it is not surprising that most organized government workers (51 percent) are employed in this sector. Association members outnumbered those in unions at the state and local levels, but were of secondary importance within the federal government.

One-half of the 23.1 million organized workers were employed in four industry classifications: government, 4.5 million; construction, 2.8 million; transportation, 2.4 million; and services, 1.8 million. Union and association membership exceeded 1 million in three additional industries: wholesale and retail trade, electrical machinery, and transportation equipment .

Between 1970 and 1972, AFL-CIO membership increased in both the manufacturing and nonmanufacturing sectors, although the increase in manufacturing (1 percent) was less than that in nonmanufacturing (4 percent). The increase in each sector was in part attributable to the merger of District 50 (Ind.) with the Steelworkers and the readmission of the International Chemical Workers to the Federation. Nearly 300,000 union members were added to AFL-CIO rolls as a consequence of these actions. Thus, the predominance of unaffiliated membership over AFL-CIO affiliates in several industries, including chemicals and allied products and scientific instruments, which existed in 1970, was reversed. Unaffiliated membership in 1972 ranked ahead of the AFL-CIO in the mining, transportation equipment, and agriculture and fishing industries.

The Bureau has long been aware of the lack of data on the extent of union organization by industry. Industry membership as reported by unions or estimated by the Bureau includes members in areas outside the United States, and in many cases, members not currently in the labor force, and therefore cannot be applied to industry employment totals with precision. Also, union membership totals are not necessarily identical with collective bargaining coverage. By making rough adjustments for these factors, the Bureau has ranked in broad percentage categories 35 industries and industrial divisions by the degree of union organization as follows:

75 Percent and Over

1. Transportation
2. Contract construction
3. Ordnance
4. Paper
5. Electrical machinery
6. Transportation equipment

50 Percent to Less than 75 Percent

7. Primary metals
8. Food and kindred products
9. Mining
10. Apparel
11. Tobacco manufactures
12. Petroleum
13. Manufacturing
14. Fabricated metals
15. Telephone and telegraph
16. Stone, clay, and glass products
17. Federal government
18. Rubber

25 Percent to Less than 50 Percent

19. Printing, publishing
20. Leather
21. Furniture
22. Electric, gas utilities

23. Machinery
24. Chemicals
25. Lumber

Less than 25 Percent

26. Nonmanufacturing
27. Textile mill products
28. Government
29. Instruments
30. Service
31. Local government
32. State government
33. Trade
34. Agriculture and fishing
35. Finance

Some shifts occurred in the ranking of industries by degree of organization since 1970. To some extent this was a result of changes in estimates prepared by reporting officials, rather than an actual modification in membership composition. The decline in the extent of organization within the fabricated metal products industry, which fell from the 75 percent and over classification to the 50–75 percent category, was attributable to the reported redistribution of Steelworker membership, the largest union in the industry. Downward moves were also experienced by the printing and publishing industry, chemicals, furniture, and nonmanufacturing. As in 1970, it was estimated that approximately three-fifths of all production employees in manufacturing were organized, compared with one-quarter in nonmanufacturing and one-fifth in government. With the addition of association membership, the extent of organization in government was estimated at one-third; for both state and local government, the rate was about three workers out of ten.

The growth and effectiveness of the labor movement depend heavily on how successfully unions are able to expand their representation of employees. At this time, a large proportion of the major establishments in heavily organized industries are operating under contracts with unions. While further organizing may significantly increase the number of employers under contract, current employment trends indicate that the proportion of the work force that is organized will be affected only slightly. Furthermore, additions to union rolls may be somewhat offset by representation and employment losses.

In recent years, advances have been achieved in several of the less highly organized industries, particularly in nonmanufacturing. However, due to the large number of employees in some of these industries, the percentage of penetration is still low. In some of the traditionally unorganized industries, many of the deterrents to unionization remain.

As a basic dictum of growth, many unions organize in different industries. Thus, union membership exhibits a remarkable degree of industry dispersion. With the exclusion of those unions which represent only government employees, 106 unions, or 60 percent of the total number of unions, have 80 percent or more of their membership in a single industry. The highest degree of industry dispersion was clearly found in manufacturing. For example, in the transportation equipment industry, only one of 15 unions, representing just 2 percent of union membership in the industry, reported that 80 to 100 percent of its members were in the industry. The remaining members (1,011,000) were distributed among 14 unions, 8 of which reported having less than 20 percent of their membership in that industry. Twenty-one of the 23 unions in the chemicals industry and 14 of the 15 in scientific instruments reported less than 20 percent of their members in the industry.

17. Women's Participation in Labor Organizations*

Virginia A. Bergquist†

While the growth of labor unions has slackened in the past few years, a considerable spurt has appeared in the number of women members. From 1968 through 1972, a 500,000 increase in women union members in the United States equaled the overall gain in union enrollment, an especially significant gain since women make up only one-fifth of union membership. This increasing enrollment by women in labor organizations has not been reflected in the higher elective and appointive positions held by women at national levels, according to the forthcoming *Directory of National Unions and Employee Associations, 1973.*[1]

In the last 20 years women have become increasingly important in the civilian labor force and in most labor unions. However, labor force gains by women have far outpaced their membership in unions. In 1972, only 12.6 percent of working women were active union members compared with over 15 percent in 1952. (See Table 1.) This decline paralleled the general percentage decline in all unionized workers, from 24 percent in 1952 to 22 percent 20 years later.

More women have recently joined the work force in response to the diminishing stigma against women working, increasing cost of living, higher general wage levels, increasing education levels among women, and improved technology, which allows women in the home more spare time.[2] Women made up almost 40 percent of the civilian labor force in 1972, compared with 31 percent 20 years earlier. In labor unions, women's proportion of total membership rose from 18.1 percent in 1952 to 21.7 percent in 1972.

OCCUPATION AND INDUSTRY

The type of industry in which women are most frequently employed may partially explain the small proportion of women in unions. Unions have organized less than 25 percent of the workers in five of the nine industries in which women constitute more than 40 percent of total employment: textiles, finance, service, and state and local governments. In none of the industries with over 40 percent women were as many as 75 percent of the workers unionized.

According to the *Manpower Report of the President, March 1973,* "virtually all increases in female employment between 1960 and 1971 were in either the white-collar or service sectors, continuing the patterns established between 1947 and 1960."[3] Thus, the types of occupations women have entered most frequently in the last 10 years have been among the traditionally less organized. In 1972, over 60 percent of all women workers were in white-collar jobs. Only 40 percent of all men were employed in those occupations.

However, the rate at which women have been joining unions was more rapid from 1962 to 1972 than during the previous ten years. Some 37 percent more women were members of unions in the United States in 1972 than in 1962, compared with a 6-percent growth during the preceding 10 years.

While only 13 unions had 50,000 women or

* From U.S. Department of Labor, *Monthly Labor Review*, Vol. 97, No. 10, October 1974, pp. 3–9.

† Virginia A. Bergquist is an economist formerly in the Division of Industrial Relations, Bureau of Labor Statistics.

[1] *Directory of National Unions and Employee Associations, 1973,* Bulletin 1813 (Bureau of Labor Statistics, 1974).

[2] *Manpower Report of the President, March 1973,* U.S. Department of Labor, pp. 64–65.

[3] *Manpower Report,* p. 65.

Year	Civilian Labor Force		Membership		Women as a Percent of Total Civilian Labor Force	Women Membership as a Percent of—	
						All Women in Labor Force	Total Union Membership in the United States
	Total	Women	Total	Women			
Unions and Associations*							
1970.......................	82.7	31.5	21.1	5.0	38.1	16.0	23.9
1972.......................	86.5	33.3	21.5	5.3	38.5	16.0	24.9
Unions							
1952.......................	62.1	19.3	16.0	2.9	31.0	15.1	18.1
1954.......................	63.6	19.7	16.7	2.8	30.9	14.1	16.6
1956.......................	66.6	21.5	17.2	3.2	32.2	14.9	18.5
1958.......................	67.6	22.1	16.8	3.1	32.7	13.8	18.2
1960.......................	69.6	23.2	16.9	3.1	33.4	13.3	18.3
1962.......................	70.6	24.0	16.4	3.1	34.0	12.8	18.6
1964.......................	73.1	25.4	16.7	3.2	34.8	12.5	19.1
1966.......................	75.8	27.3	17.8	3.4	36.0	12.6	19.3
1968.......................	78.7	29.2	18.8	3.7	37.1	12.5	19.5
1970.......................	82.7	31.5	19.2	4.0	38.1	12.6	20.7
1972.......................	86.5	33.3	19.3	4.2	38.5	12.6	21.7
Change—Unions							
1952–72							
Number..................	24.4	14.0	3.3	1.3			
Percent..................	39.3	72.7	20.4	44.1			
1952–62							
Number..................	8.5	4.7	.4	.2			
Percent..................	13.6	24.6	2.8	5.6			
1962–72							
Number..................	15.9	9.3	2.8	1.1			
Percent..................	22.6	38.6	17.1	36.5			

* Associations were first surveyed in 1970. That survey covered 23 associations while the 1972 study covered 35. The number of unions covered in 1952 was 215; in 1962, 181; in 1970, 185; and in 1972, 177.

more in their ranks in 1952 and 17 in 1962, this number rose to 24 in 1972 (Table 2), about 14 percent of all unions. The concerted organizing campaigns carried on by AFL-CIO unions during the 1960s was partly responsible for this growth. The Retail Clerks, with 125,000 women in 1952 and 317,000 in 1972, and the Electrical Workers, 150,000 women in 1952 and 287,000 20 years later, showed particularly marked increases. Unionization drives during the late 1960s among all levels of government employees, 43 percent of whom are women, also organized significant numbers of women. In 1952, three public employee unions (Teachers; Government Employees; and State, County and Municipal Employees) had a combined membership of 60,000 women. These same three groups accounted for over 420,000 women unionists in 1972. In addition, the New York Civil Service Association and the National Education Association together reported over 800,000 women in 1972.

The number of large unions with at least 50 percent women has remained virtually unchanged since 1952. These include the Clothing Workers, Communications Workers, Ladies' Garment Workers, Retail Clerks, and Teachers. The Office Employees, for which there was no 1952 membership estimate, also reported that in 1972 over half of its members were women. Estimates for the National Education Association and the Nurses Association, also first surveyed in 1970, showed that women constituted more than three-fifths of their membership in 1972.

Most (13 of 18) unions in which women were less than half of the membership in 1972 but which had more than 50,000 women on their rolls reported an increase in the proportion of women over the 20-year period. The Postal Workers,

TABLE 2 Women in Unions and Associations with 50,000 Women Members or More, 1952 and 1972 (numbers in thousands)

Union	1952		1972	
	Number of Women Members	Percent of Total Membership	Number of Women Members	Percent of Total Membership
Total, all unions	3,000	17.9	4,524	21.7
Total, selected unions	1,862	21.0	3,674	28.9
Total, all unions and associations	—	—	5,736	24.9
Total, selected unions and associations	—	—	4,646	32.6
AFL-CIO				
Bakery Workers*	60.2	35.0	51.0	35.0
Clothing Workers	261.8	68.0	273.8	75.0
Communications Workers	(†)	(†)	230.5	52.0
Electrical Workers (IUE)	(†)	(†)	116.0	40.0
Electrical Workers (IBEW)	150.0	30.0	287.0	30.0
Government Employees (AFGE)	(†)	(†)	(†)	(†)
Hotel and Restaurant Employees	(†)	(†)	(†)	(†)
Ladies' Garment Workers	292.5	75.0	342.4	80.0
Machinists	(†)	(†)	106.1	14.0
Meat Cutters‡	59.3	18.1	92.5	17.5
Office Employees	(†)	(†)	52.8	64.0
Paperworkers§	35.7	13.6	(†)	(†)
Postal Workers‖	(†)	(†)	107.4	45.0
Railway Clerks	36.0	12.0	(†)	(†)
Retail Clerks	125.0	50.0	316.6	50.0
Retail, Wholesale, and Department Store Union	14.6	15.1	79.1	40.0
Rubber Workers	(†)	(†)	(†)	(†)
Service Employees	55.5	30.0	145.2	30.0
State, County, and Municipal Employees	(†)	(†)	195.7	37.0
Steelworkers	80.0	7.3	175.0	12.5
Teachers	37.5	75.0	129.2	52.0
Textile Workers Union of America	(†)	(†)	69.6	40.0
Unaffiliated				
Auto Workers#	118.4	10.0	195.1	14.0
Teamsters	(†)	(†)	(†)	(†)
Employee Associations				
Civil Service (NYS)	(†)	(†)	(†)	(†)
Education Association	(†)	(†)	736.7	63.2
Nurses Association	(†)	(†)	(†)	(†)

* Includes the Bakery and Confectionery Workers' International Union of America (Ind.) and the American Bakery and Confectionery Workers' International Union (AFL-CIO).
† Figure not reported to the Bureau or not available.
‡ Includes Packinghouse Workers (AFL-CIO) in 1952 and 1962.
§ Includes Papermakers (AFL), Paperworkers (CIO) and Pulp, Sulphite Workers (AFL) in 1952; the Papermakers and Paperworkers (AFL-CIO) and Pulp, Sulphite Workers (AFL-CIO) in 1962 and 1970; and the United Paperworkers (AFL-CIO) in 1972.
‖ Includes the National Postal Union (Ind.), Postal Clerks (AFL-CIO), Special Delivery Messengers (AFL-CIO), General Services Maintenance Employees (AFL-CIO), Motor Vehicle Employees (AFL-CIO), and Postal Workers Union (AFL-CIO). On July 1, 1971, these five unions merged to form the American Postal Workers Union (AFL-CIO).
Affiliated with the CIO in 1952 and with the AFL-CIO in 1962.
Note: Unlike Table 1, figures include members in areas outside the United States, primarily in Canada.

Railway Clerks, Retail, Wholesale and Department Store Union, State, County and Municipal Employees, and Teamsters showed especially marked increases.

CONCENTRATION AND EARNINGS

Since 1952, more than one-fifth of all unions have reported that there were no women in their ranks. These included unions in predominantly "male" industries such as construction, maritime, coal mining, and air transportation (pilots). Four fewer unions reported that they had no women members in 1972 than in 1952. In percentage terms, however, the proportion of all unions that have no women actually increased from 1952 due to the shrinking number of unions resulting from mergers and dissolutions.

In the same 20-year period, the proportion of unions with some women but less than 10 percent declined from 39 to 30 percent. As in 1952, only 14 percent of all trade unions had more women

TABLE 3   Selected Union and Association Offices Held by Women, 1952, 1962, 1970, 1972*

Position	Unions				Associations†	
	1952	1962	1970	1972	1970	1972
Total positions held by women...........	31	28	37	37	31	44
Total women............................	30	24	34	33	30	41
Elective Offices						
President.............................	2	0	1	2	2	6
Secretary-treasurer....................	9	7	10	13	18	17
Appointive Positions						
Director of organizing activities........	(‡)	1	1	0	0	2
Research director......................	10	3	7	3	0	3
Research and education director.......	1	3	0	0	0	0
Education director.....................	2	2	2	3	0	0
Director of social insurance............	(‡)	5	7	6	0	1
Editor................................	6	6	4	3	5	5
Legal activities........................	(‡)	1	1	1	0	1
Legislative activities...................	(‡)	(‡)	2	3	0	0
Public relations activities..............	(‡)	(‡)	2	3	1	1
Other................................	1	0	0	0	5	8

* In 1952, 215 unions were surveyed; in 1962, 181; in 1970, 185; and in 1972, 177. In 1970, 23 associations were surveyed; in 1972, 35.
† Associations were first surveyed in 1970.
‡ Not surveyed.
§ Appointive positions surveyed for unions and associations varied somewhat. Appointive positions included in the category "other" for associations are executive director, collective bargaining director, and government relations director. In 1952, the union position included in the category "other" is executive secretary.

than male members in 1972. These 25 unions represented 37 percent of all women trade unionists in 1972, slightly less than ten years earlier.

A number of Bureau of Labor Statistics and Census Bureau studies have shown that union women and men employed year round on a full-time basis earn more than nonunion employees. A 1970 Bureau of Labor Statistics study found that for blue-collar workers, nonunion women averaged $4,297, [which is] $647 less than their union counterparts.[4] White-collar workers (both men and women) showed a similar differential—nonunion workers earned an average of $8,532 a year and union workers earned $8,858.

PROBLEMS OF PARTICIPATION

Regardless of the financial benefit, women have faced numerous obstacles to participation in labor unions. A study by the New York State School of Industrial and Labor Relations of Cornell University grouped barriers to women's participation in labor unions into three categories: (1) personal-cultural—including extensive home responsibilities and a lack of personal self-confidence; (2) job related—including discrimination by employers against union employees; and (3)

union related—including unfamiliarity with union procedures and a need for encouragement to participate.[5]

The 7.6 million women who were part-time employees in 1972 probably felt less incentive to participate in the union movement due to their frequent entry into and exit from the labor market, as well as the traditionally low level of unionization in the two industries in which over 64 percent of all voluntarily part-time employees work—wholesale and retail trade, and finance and service.

WOMEN OFFICIALS

Women have remained rare at the governing and high appointive levels of almost all of the 177 unions in the United States. Despite the progress women have achieved in the past 20 years in union membership, the number of women in the highest national union offices (both elective and appointive) increased only slightly. (See Table 3.) As in 1952, women held the highest elected office, the national presidency, in two unions in 1972—the Stewards and Stewardesses Division of the Air Line Pilots and the Veterinarians. Women were more common in the

---

[4] *Selected Earnings and Demographic Characterstics of Union Members, 1970,* Report 417 (Bureau of Labor Statistics, 1972).

[5] Barbara Wertheimer and Anne Nelson, "The American Woman at Work," *Personnel Management,* March 1974, p. 22.

office of secretary-treasurer, but seldom in unions with more than 50,000 members.

As shown in Table 3, women were infrequently appointed to head a department at the national level. Women were most commonly research directors (10) and editors (6) in 1952; they were most frequently appointed editors or heads of social insurance departments in 1962, 1970, and 1972. Fewer women in all four years were named to head other major departments, most frequently education and research and education.

Statistical data concerning women in leadership roles below the national union level were not collected in the union directory survey because an estimated 71,000 locals would have had to be surveyed. However, fragmentary information from studies done by several unions, such as the Bakery Workers, the Auto Workers, and the Packinghouse Workers, indicates that women more frequently held leadership roles at local than at national levels.

Women accounted for approximately 7 percent of the members of elected governing boards of unions and employee associations.[6] These boards, generally consisting of the union president, secretary, treasurer, and vice presidents or other comparable elected officials, serve as the decision-making body for unions between conventions. Among their duties are the allocation of funds, interpretation of the laws of the union, and application of the constitution to its workings. Of 4,800 positions on the governing boards of both the unions and associations, only 350 were reported held by women,[7] although a number of the organizations failed to provide complete information on this subject.

Women were better represented at the higher appointive and elective levels of the 35 professional and state employee associations. The high proportion of women (60 percent) in the associations explains their comparative prominence in association governance. The 737,000 women in the National Education Association—63 percent of total NEA membership—accounted for the largest proportion of all association women.

Only 13 of 35 associations had no women officers or officials, compared with 149 of the 177 trade unions. The Connecticut, Illinois, Maine,

Massachusetts, North Carolina, Vermont, and Washington State Associations had two women officers. Two organizations understandably had a larger than usual number of women officers—5 officers of 6 in the Licensed Practical Nurses Association and 8 of 11 in the Nurses Association. Six associations were headed by women in 1972 —Alaska State Employees, Classified School Employees, National Education Association, Licensed Practical Nurses, American Nurses, and Washington State Employee Association. Association presidents and secretary-treasurers made up more than half of the 44 elective and appointive positions surveyed which were held by association women in 1972.

The number of women holding appointive positions in associations increased markedly from 1970 to 1972, the only two years for which data are available. Compared with 1970, when a total of only 11 women occupied 3 top appointive categories (editor, public relations activities, and other), some 21 women held 7 top appointive positions in associations in 1972. This increase is partly the consequence of the 12 additional associations (to a total of 35) which fell within the scope of the 1972 survey.

Women were similarly better represented on the governing boards of associations than on those of unions. Only 4 of 35 associations reporting stated that women were not represented on their boards. Nine associations included more than five women as board members. Of the 187 selected national officers and appointed officials reported by the 24 unions with at least 50,000 women members, 6 were women. The Clothing Workers, Electrical Workers, Ladies' Garment Workers, and Railway Clerks all reported one woman official; the Textile Workers Union had two. Of the 556 members of executive boards in these unions, 18 were women.

This low level of women representation was evident throughout the entire labor movement. In the remaining 153 unions with less than 50,000 women in 1972, 27 women were reported as elected officers or appointed officials at the national level. In more of these unions did women constitute as much as 50 percent of the total number of officers and appointed officials. Only five unions had two women officers or officials and none had more than two.

The AFL-CIO has established organizations at the state level made up of locals of affiliated national unions. Functioning as lobbyists and coordinators for AFL-CIO programs, the state labor councils are headed by an elected governing

---

[6] The number of women on governing boards may reflect double counting, since officers are members of unions' executive boards.

[7] In addition, 26 women are members of the governing boards of the Stewardesses Division and the Air Line Pilots. These 26 are not included in the total.

board and several officers. Of the 173 officers and officials elected by these organizations in 1972, 8 were women.

AID TO UNION WOMEN

In June 1963 the Equal Pay Act went into effect, erasing wage discrepancies between employees based on sex. A year later, Title VII of the Civil Rights Act invalidated all laws which were supposedly protective of women but which in practice often provided a legal foundation for discrimination between the sexes. The Equal Rights Amendment, now awaiting ratification by three-fourths of the states, would invalidate all state and federal laws making any distinction between the sexes. Labor organizations such as the AFL-CIO (reversing its previous opposition to the ERA), Auto Workers, Teamsters, Steelworkers, Communications Workers, and Electrical Workers (IUE) have endorsed the Equal Rights Amendment.

A Bureau of Labor Statistics study of 1,300 labor agreements in effect on July 1, 1972, and covering at least 1,000 workers noted the prevalence of several contract clauses particularly significant for women.[8] Slightly less than two-thirds of the 1,300 agreements, covering more than three-fourths of these workers, prohibited discrimination due to sex. Contract clauses insuring equal pay for equal work were included in 145 of the contracts and maternity leaves in 503 agreements (39 percent).

Since March of 1970 when the Wisconsin State Federation hosted the first AFL-CIO women's conference, other state organizations, including Illinois, Arkansas, California, and Iowa, have held such meetings.[9] International unions, such as the Auto Workers, Communications Workers, Electrical Workers (IUE), Teachers (AFT),

and the Newspaper Guild, have also held conferences directed at women's needs and problems.[10]

The Coalition of Labor Union Women (CLUW), convening in Chicago in March 1974 with 3,200 CLUW delegates coming from over 58 labor unions, resolved to work within the labor movement. The trade union women (nonunion women are ineligible to join) defined several goals: (1) to encourage the 30 million nonunion working women to take advantage of the tangible economic benefits of unionists by joining unions; (2) to increase women's participation within unions; (3) to seek "affirmative action" on the part of unions against employers' discriminatory practices; and (4) to press for legislative action which would further women's interests, such as child care assistance and passage of the Equal Rights Amendment. CLUW's first official convention is planned for early or mid-1975.

POTENTIAL GROWTH IN GOVERNMENT

Employment at all levels of government exceeded 13 million in 1972. At the state and local government levels, employment more than doubled over the last two decades—from 4.2 million in 1952 to over 10.6 million in 1972. Though historically poorly organized, all levels of government are now feeling the impact of concerted organizing drives by unions and associations, such as the State, County and Municipal Employees, Teachers, National Education Association, and Government Employees. Less than 25 percent of all government personnel are now estimated to be union members (not including associations). With women constituting 43 percent of the 13.7 million government workers in 1972, the number and proportion of organized women will probably grow along with government unions and associations.

[8] *Characteristics of Agreements Covering 1,000 Workers or More, July 1, 1972,* Bulletin 1784 (Bureau of Labor Statistics, 1973).

[9] "Women Workers, Gaining Powers, Seeking More," *U.S. News and World Report,* Nov. 13, 1972, pp. 104–7.

[10] Edna E. Raphael, "Working Women and Their Membership in Labor Unions," *Monthly Labor Review,* May 1974, pp. 27–33.

18. The National Union: Basic Governmental Unit*

William M. Leiserson

Ask a union man to what organization he belongs, and he may answer: AFL, CIO, or he may name an organization like the Machinists, Autoworkers, Teamsters, Carpenters, Steelworkers, Railway Carmen. Again he may say he belongs to Local 3 or 600 or some other numbered local union or lodge. These typical responses may reflect pride in being associated with an organization that is powerful and well known, or loyalty to a subdivision of a union which looks after the member's interests in dealing with the management of the shop in which he works. They do not ordinarily indicate his status as a citizen, so to speak, under the union government which is the source of his rights, privileges, and immunities as an organized worker, and whose laws he is bound to obey.

There are no individual members of the AFL-CIO. Only unions are members of this labor confederation, as only nations are members of the United Nations. In the manner of any alliance of nations, the confederations deal with and act through the governments of the member unions. Unlike our own federal government, they do not have direct authority over the subjects or the citizens of the various union governments. They may not tax individual union members, adopt laws or working rules for them, try them for offenses, discipline or expel them. These are prerogatives of the separate member unions. With certain exceptions comparable to the territories and possessions of the United States, each affiliated union is a national organization, self-governing like a sovereign state.

A union worker is normally a member of one

of these national unions. Its government is the highest authority over him in American organized labor. He ordinarily holds this membership in a subdivision of the national union for the locality or plant in which he works, but when he moves to another place he must transfer to another such local union. As the constitution of the Ladies' Garment Workers Union puts it: "The membership of the ILGWU shall consist of individual workers organized in local unions in the manner provided in this constitution."

A new member is usually initiated in a local where he pledges allegiance to the constitution and laws of the national union, sometimes without mentioning the local constitution, which must conform to the national and be approved by a national officer. Applicants are ordinarily prohibited from applying or being admitted to membership in any local other than the one designated for this place of work. Many unions also provide for holding membership directly in the national organization, and for initiation by national officers. The qualifications for membership are prescribed by the national constitution, and the obligation the member takes when initiated is essentially to the union as a national organization. Typical is the statement he must repeat and sign to become a member of the International Brotherhood of Electrical Workers: "I . . . do sincerely promise and agree to conform to and abide by the Constitution and laws of the IBEW and its Local Unions. I will faithfully further, by every means in my power, the purposes for which the IBEW is instituted."

Thus the basic unit of union government is the national union, and not the local as is often supposed. It commonly calls itself "international" because it has members and branches in Canada and sometimes in other North American coun-

---

* From William M. Leiserson, *American Trade Union Democracy* (New York: Columbia University Press, 1959), pp. 85–101.

tries. Some of the older unions, in the fashion of fraternal organizations, name their national or international union the Grand Lodge to distinguish it from subordinate government units. We shall continue to refer to them as national unions since their membership outside the United States is a small fraction of the total.[1]

All sovereign powers are in these national unions. Their governments are supreme over all members, local unions, and other subordinate governing bodies. The AFL-CIO derives its powers from them. They decide to form, join or not join, any such association of unions. Some belong to the "National Independent Union Council" or the "Confederated Unions of America," which are small and relatively unknown. Many remain independent.

In terms of citizenship a union member is a citizen under the government of his national or international union. The location of his work determines the branch or local to which he must belong, just as a citizen of one of our states must vote in the locality where he resides. But he does not have dual citizenship as an American is a citizen of one of the 48 states as well as of the United States. He is a citizen of his union only, not of the confederation of labor with which it may be affiliated.

Local unions are mere subdivisions of the national organizations whose constitutions provide for their government as a state does for its counties, cities, towns, and villages. The amount of home rule they enjoy is determined by the national, and they are bound by the laws of their national governments. They are authorized to adopt local constitutions and by-laws and the national constitution usually prescribes the form of local government. National laws provide for the suspension, merging, and abolition of local unions. Local officers may be removed by the national executives who may appoint administrators to manage their affairs, sometimes without the consent of the local members.

The national union has other subordinate governmental units—district and regional councils, joint boards, trade or craft councils, and often also state councils. These are delegate bodies composed of representatives from local unions, and their powers and duties are defined by the national constitution. Some of them are given extensive supervisory powers over the locals. They are subject to the authority of na-

tional union officials, and the locals are usually required to join such councils.

Historically national unions were built by local trade unions joining to form a national organization to govern their particular trades, related occupations, or industries. But once they joined they became subject to the laws of the new national governments they created. The local unions did not merely delegate certain limited powers and reserve others to themselves, although sometimes they insisted on and were granted a certain amount of home rule. There are examples, also, of two or more national unions forming a single organization with each retaining autonomous rights over its own trade. But usually the national union has a centralized government ruling all members and all subordinate organizations.

As every political state has some definite territory, so every national union has what it calls its jurisdiction—the kind of work and workers it claims the exclusive right to organize and govern. The feeling of inviolability of its jurisdiction is not less strong in a union than is the sacredness of its territory to a national state. Woodruff Randolph, President of the International Typographical Union, expressed it this way: "The ITU is a craft union exercising jurisdiction over all composing room work. Our jobs are dependent on that work. The life of our trade is dependent upon that jurisdiction. Whatever weakens or destroys our jurisdiction destroys our union."

Industrial unions feel much the same way about the industries they stake out as their domains. Some unions, like the Pacific Coast Marine Firemen's Association, are sectional, and do not claim jurisdiction outside the areas in which they operate. Nor do the international unions which extend beyond the boundaries of the United States vigorously pursue exclusive jurisdictional claims in the foreign countries.

Although few unions succeed in enrolling within their ranks all workers in their asserted jurisdiction even in the home country, they nevertheless are intolerant of any trespassing of their exclusive domains; and one union will often demand that workers organized by another in what it considers its territory shall be turned over to it. Thus, like nations, unions have their boundary disputes and irredentist movements which at times break out in interunion wars—jurisdictional strikes, picketing, and boycotts, not infrequently accompanied by violence. Like nations also, national unions form or join alliances to deal with such problems of conflicting interests as well as common defense against employers, and pro-

---

[1] In 1949 less than 5 percent of the members of American unions were located in Canada, but a majority of Canadian organized workers are included in this membership.

motion of common interests. The AFL and the CIO (and now the AFL-CIO) are merely the most comprehensive of these. The railroad unions have a Railway Labor Executives Association, and there are other alliances, comparable to the Benelux combination and the North Atlantic Alliance.

Being alliances or leagues rather than supergovernments, the AFL and CIO had as little success in preventing conflicts among the national unions or settling them peacefully as the League of Nations did among the national states, or as the United Nations has thus far been able to achieve. Perhaps in the American world of labor, an overall government of organized workers will be needed to assure peace among the national unions as many think world government is the answer to wars among the nations. For the present, however, relinquishment of any of its sovereignty is as abhorrent to a national union as it is to a national state.

Industrial unionism has reduced jurisdictional disputes among the organizations—CIO unions were not as plagued with them as the AFL unions—but it has not abolished them. On the other hand the existence of two competing confederations created new conflicts of jurisdiction between the unions affiliated with one against those of the other, and the independent United Mine Workers through its so-called District 50 extended its jurisdictional claims over workers in many industries. Failure of organized labor to develop its own governmental machinery for settling interunion controversies makes it most likely that the U.S. government will supply this lack. A beginning has been made in the Taft-Hartley Act of 1947, which authorized the National Labor Relations Board to decide such controversies.

In dealing with the problems of organizing nonunion workers and establishing new national unions, the leagues or confederations have been more successful because national unions have been more willing to delegate to them adequate powers for these purposes, at least in recent years. Both the AFL and the CIO were authorized to organize local unions, known respectively as "federal labor unions" and "local industrial unions," and to charter and govern them in the same manner that a national union does with its own locals. The merged AFL-CIO has similar powers. Until the members of such local unions are assigned to affiliated national organizations which claim jurisdiction over them, or until the locals can be combined to form a new national union, the federation in effect acts like a national union in relation to them. The workers in such

locals may perhaps be considered exceptions to the rule that there are no individual members in the AFL-CIO.

Prior to the organization of the CIO, the jurisdictional claims of the craft unions made it almost impossible for the AFL to organize the mass production industries. Joint committees of a score or more craft unions were established to do the organizing, and each wanted the skilled mechanics that came within its jurisdiction rather than the establishment of a new industrial union. After 1934 when the AFL convention adopted a resolution authorizing the organization of industrial unions in specific mass production industries, it was less hampered in this respect. The merged Federation may still labor under difficulties, because a union is not ordinarily admitted to membership if any organization that is a member objects. Thus jurisdictional claims of the crafts may still prevent an industrial union from affiliating with the Federation on equal terms with the other organizations; but the objections are more easily overcome, and adjustments are usually made permitting the craft unions to retain jurisdiction over workers in the industry who are covered by their agreements with employers.

In establishing new national unions, the old AFL joined existing federal labor unions of the same craft or industry under a national council which governs them under its supervision until they are considered ready for self-government and affiliation as autonomous national unions. The CIO likewise was empowered to combine its local industrial unions into national unions, but it more generally reversed the process by creating national organizing committees for particular industries which functioned like national unions from the beginning. They carried on active organizing campaigns and set up their own locals. A national organizing committee remained a subordinate organization until in the judgment of the CIO, it was ready for self-government, when it was admitted as an autonomous member union equal in status with the other affiliated national organizations.

Thus the local unions attached directly to the AFL and the CIO were governed like the dependencies of the United States such as Guam and Puerto Rico, while the national councils and organizing committees are similar to territorial governments of Alaska or Hawaii. The affiliated national unions, however, did not occupy the subordinate position of the states in the federal government of the United States. They had all the sovereign powers that wholly independent unions have which are not affiliated with any confederations. But it is significant that in practice the CIO exercised a measure of authority over its affiliated national unions that the AFL organizations ordinarily would not permit. Whether this was due to so many of them having grown out of organizing committees which the CIO created or whether this is the beginning of a trend toward a federal union government superior to those of the national unions, only the future can tell.[2]

Establishment of national unions as the supreme governmental units of organized labor was a slow development. A full century had elapsed from the time when trade unions first appeared before these independent labor states emerged as survivors in the struggle of different forms of government with which workers experimented as they strove to meet new conditions and new problems.

In labor circles today, independence and equality of the government of each separate union is accepted as normal and permanent regardless of whether the workers are organized by trades, crafts, industries, or any combinations or divisions of these. When the CIO was formed to promote industrial unionism, it did not question the desirability of national government of the unions which the craft organizations of the AFL had worked out. Sixty years earlier, when the AFL was battling with the Knights of Labor the main issues between them did involve differences as to how unions should be governed. The Knights attempted to set up a centralized government over all American labor with the national unions subordinated to it.

The earliest unions had town meeting governments subject to no higher authority, except as all unions then and now have been subject to the general public law. They were local unions, but self-formed and autonomous. Each union, or trade society as it was known, was governed by the meeting of its members. Its officers had few duties and little power. When anything was to be done the meeting appointed a committee for the purpose. The members governed directly, not through representatives. Internally, these first trade unions were popular democracies.

The beginnings of representative government came when the separate trade organizations in a city leagued together in a joint movement against employers. Then each society elected delegates to a local assembly which became known as a "trades' union." This union of trades, however,

did not combine the memberships under a single government. Each society continued to rule its own affairs, and retained authority over its members. The trades' union could act only through the separate organizations, and it got its funds from them, not from individual members.

Through the trades' union, the organizations helped each other in strikes and dealt with problems common to all the trades. Representing all organized labor in the city, it concerned itself largely with promoting legislation in behalf of the wage earners, and from the first, political action rather than trade union activity became its sphere. Direct bargaining with employers and regulation of employment by working rules were matters that each trade society handled for itself. Union laws were local laws; today a local union gets permission from its national organization to adopt local laws.

As these local delegate bodies spread through the country, they in turn set up a national representative body on the same model. The first of these was established in 1834 when at a convention of delegates from city trades' unions the National Trades' Union was formed. The local trade organizations were only indirectly represented in this. It was an association of city associations of unions. Reflecting the general disillusionment with the workingmen's parties with which the city unions became identified during the last year of the previous decade, it adopted a resolution that "no party, political, or religious questions shall be agitated or acted upon in the Union." But it did not condemn lobbying for legislation in the interest of working people, and concerned itself a good deal with agitation and pressure for such legislation.

Prior to this time several attempts had been made to combine local societies of the same trade in different cities under a national government of the trade, but no such national trade organizations succeeded in establishing themselves. Thus a pattern of union government was set quite different from that which prevails today. The basic governmental unit was an autonomous local craft organization which alone had authority to make rules binding on the individual members, to tax and judge them, to bargain and make agreements with employers for them. Beyond this there was no higher authority over the memberships. The meeting of this organization was the final judge as to whether it would go along with any action taken by a city trades' union or the National Trades' Union.

This pattern prevailed down to the last quarter of the 19th century. During the long depression

---

[2] In general, the merger of the AFL and CIO has not changed these structural relationships between the national unions and the Federation.

that followed the Panic of 1837, what labor organizations there were took the form of mutual benefit societies, producers and consumers' co-operatives, and political and social reform associations, although their memberships were by no means confined to wage workers. Delegates from such organizations met several times in national industrial congresses, but these concerned themselves with politics and social reform.

When trade-unionism revived in the 1850s and 1860s, it followed the pattern set in the earlier years. Again a multitude of local trade organizations sprang up, and these joined in forming city representative bodies which they called "trade assemblies." The term "trade union" had become the customary name for the local trade societies. In 1864 an attempt was made to set up an "international industrial assembly" modeled on the former National Trades' Union, but the effort went to naught. In the 30 years that had elapsed, a new method of governing unions nationally had developed which departed from the old pattern.

While the local unions still found the city trade assemblies useful for common local purposes, a national association of such city assemblies no longer met the needs of some of the trades. As national markets developed, more and more of the local unions found that a wider governing unit than a local community was needed for effective union regulation of wages and working conditions. Competition of employers of the same trade in distant cities threatened the standards of the local union, and when the members struck to maintain or better conditions, they often found their work transferred to an employer in another city. This led unions of the same trade in different cities to give up some of their autonomy and combine under the government of a single national union of their trade, of which they eventually became subordinate local divisions.

In the 1850s a few such nationally governed unions had established themselves, but the following decade saw a rapid growth of national trade unions. Some well-known existing national unions date from this period.[3] The main body of organized labor, however, still followed the old pattern. Rising living costs during the Civil War brought new crops of local unions, and these

formed or joined city trade assemblies. This movement culminated in the organization of the National Labor Union in 1866 which also was an assembly of unions on the model of the old National Trades' Union.

Although the nationally governed craft organizations participated in its formation, its delegates represented mainly city trade assemblies and local unions. It also accepted delegates from various kinds of social reform organizations.[4] Despite its title, it was not a higher organ of authority among labor unions and was not concerned with integrating local unions in wider governmental units. It was a political rather than a labor organization. Its main objective when first established was the 8-hour workday, to be secured by legislation rather than by union bargaining or strikes, and it soon turned itself into a "national labor and reform party."[5]

The national trade unions began to withdraw earlier, dissatisfied with the concentration on politics. Thereafter they twice attempted to set up a "national labor congress" that would confine itself to trade union problems, but without success. Nevertheless the nationally governed unions won the day. Most of them survived the Panic of 1873 and the depression that followed, while other workers' organizations went to pieces. With the upturn of business in the late 70s, country-wide organizations by crafts or trades spread and gained strength, and by the end of the century, the pattern of nationally governed union organizations had become dominant.

But this was not achieved without a bitter

---

[3] International Typographical Union (1850), International Molders Union (1859), Brotherhood of Locomotive Engineers (1863), National Union of Cigar Makers (1864), Order of Railway Conductors (1868). Four of the building trade unions, Carpenters, Bricklayers, Painters and Plasterers were organized in 1865.

[4] Susan Anthony appeared as a representative of the women suffragists, and an attempt was made to exclude her, but after a debate she was seated.

[5] At the 1871 convention of the Typographical Union the following report was received: "The undersigned, delegates from your body in the Labor Congress held in Cincinnati, August 1870, report that we attended said Labor Congress from the opening to the close of the session and failed to discover anything in the proceedings, with the exception of the report of the committee on obnoxious laws, that would entitle the congress to representation from a purely trade organization. The congress was made up of delegates, with few exceptions, who openly avowed the object to be the formation of a political party. Played-out politicians, lobbyists, woman-suffragans, preachers without flocks, representatives of associations in which politics are made a qualification for membership, and declaimers on the outrages perpetrated on poor Lo, formed the major part of the congress. The session was one of continuous confusion, in which personalities abounded, and charges and countercharges were made of attempts to run it in the interest of both the old political parties. The only thing accomplished was the formation of the Labor Reform party and the adoption of a platform announcing its principles." John Collins, Harry P. Temple, delegates (George A. Tracy, History of the Typographical Union [Indianapolis: International Typographical Union, 1913], p. 256).

struggle for survival lasting almost two decades with another type of union organization and government which sought to unify all labor organizations under a single supreme authority. The Noble Order of the Knights of Labor met in open convention for the first time in 1878. It had been formed as a secret society with vague idealistic aims by a group of tailors in Philadelphia led by Uriah Stephens. At the convention it adopted a constitution designed to embrace "all toilers" in one organization governed by a centralized authority at the top. It aimed at establishing an empire of labor including not only wage workers, but "all the producing classes." The central government would have direct authority over individual members however they might be distributed among subordinate organizations. Its motto, "An injury to one is an injury to all," expressed its ideal.

At the top was a national assembly composed of elected representatives in which was lodged all powers—"constitutional, legislative, judicial, and executive." "It alone possesses the power and authority to make, amend, or repeal the fundamental laws and regulations to the Order; to finally decide all controversies arising in the Order; to issue all charters (to subordinate organizations). . . . It can also tax the members of the Order for its maintenance." Between sessions of the assembly a national executive board exercised its powers, presided over by a Grand Master Workman. Beneath the national assembly were district assemblies, and at the bottom local assemblies which any ten or more workers could form upon receipt of a charter from the national executive board.

The jurisdiction of the Order covered all work and workers excepting only lawyers, bankers, stockbrokers, professional gamblers, and saloon keepers. Its governmental subdivisions were based on geographical units rather than on craft or industry. Although three-fourths of the members of local assemblies were required to be wage earners, these did not have to be of the same trade or occupation, or even related employments. The membership of the locals could be mixed or of the same trade depending on the kind of "toilers" that wanted to join them. A majority were mixed, but many local trade unions joined in a body, became local assemblies, and continued to function as they had before joining.

As the Knights of Labor grew in numbers and prestige after it shed its secrecy, it also absorbed some existing national trade unions and it organized some new ones. For these it made a place under its all-inclusive government by establishing them as trade districts or trade assemblies on a par with its territorial district assemblies. At one time it had as many as 22 national trade assemblies. The national governments of these unions were thus made subordinate divisions of the Order, subject to its general laws and to the authority of its executive board.

Although the Knights rose to great power for a brief period, the plan never did work out in practice. Many of the subordinate assemblies went pretty much their own way, disregarding the central authority. Diverse interests among the heterogeneous membership—farmers, tradesmen, professional people, wage workers, and political reformers—caused constant conflict within the organization and led to early disintegration.

For some years, however, it looked as if the centralized empire of labor about which the Knights dreamed would become a reality. Between 1880 and 1886 the membership of the Knights of Labor increased from 28,000 to more than 700,000. It absorbed many national unions and established them as subordinate trade districts, while numerous locals of the craft unions went over to it en masse. Even the most prominent leaders of the national unions, men like Samuel Gompers of the Cigar Makers and P. J. McGuire of the Carpenters, who sponsored and led the American Federation of Labor, had been members of the Knights of Labor. At the same time, it was attracting every variety of reformist group to its ranks.

But even while it was having its spectacular growth and success, the trade unions feared they were being submerged in the conglomerate organization and fought to establish their autonomy while the various reform groups struggled to have their pet programs adopted as the official platform of the Order. The most important opposition came from the national unions, however. In 1881 they launched the Federation of Trades and Labor Unions as a rival to the Knights of Labor to promote the cause of self-governing national craft or trade organizations. The drift of skilled as well as unskilled workers to the all-inclusive organization was too strong, however, and by 1885 this alliance of unions was little more than a name.

Then the trade unions started a movement for the 8-hour day to be secured directly from employers by bargaining or strikes which the Knights of Labor condemned, though it was not averse to legislation to secure the same end. This movement made great headway the following year, and the national unions profited by their sponsorship, while the Knights began to lose members. The same year a committee of trade unionists issued a call for a convention to form an "American federation or alliance of all national and international trade unions," to which representatives from 25 organizations responded. "Moved by a common feeling of the menace of the Knights, these delegates agreed to form themselves into an American Federation of Labor for mutual aid and assistance."[6]

This absorbed the defunct Federation of Trades, and under its leadership the national unions succeeded in establishing their supremacy. By this time the Knights of Labor had already passed the crest of its power; and further weakened by struggles with socialist and anarchist groups among its members, it disintegrated as rapidly as it had grown. By the end of the next decade nationally ruled trade organizations were firmly established as the dominant form of union government.

In the early years of the present century, the national unions perfected their internal government and administration, established adequate revenue systems, developed methods of making joint agreements with groups of employers, and extended their working rules into national laws. To safeguard the stability of the organizations and the collective relations with employers established by the agreements, they gave national officers more control over locals and disciplining of members, required national authorization or approval of strikes, and established strike benefit funds as a means of enforcing the controls.

This process had begun earlier. The Molders' Union pioneered in the 1860s in developing techniques for integrating local unions into the national union governments, and the Cigar Makers some years later carried its methods further. In fighting the Knights of Labor the national unions found it necessary to restrict autonomy of their locals and to exercise more direct control over their members. Building on this experience, most unions lodged more and more power in their national governments and officers, with little in the way of checks on their authority.

Later, the adoption by many unions of the referendum and recall of officers marked a reversion to popular government, and this was reflected also in restrictions on the appointive power of union executives. More recent years have witnessed a resumption of growth of appointive and other powers of union officials, and development of new agencies and techniques for mass organi-

zation from the top down, with less reliance on self-organization of the workers. New administrative departments have sprouted—for research, labor education, political activity, and community service, as the unions began to make their strength felt in national, state, and local community affairs.

While the national unions were strengthening their internal governments, the American Federation of Labor was developing organs for interunion cooperation among them all along the line on local, state, regional, and national levels, and on an industry basis where different craft unions operated within the same industry.

For these purposes it made use of the old machinery of trade or labor assemblies, but it established these representative bodies as subordinate governmental divisions of the Federation. In every city where there were local branches of national unions affiliated with the AFL, it issued a charter to a city central body which was variously known as Central Labor Union, Trades and Labor Assembly, or City Federation of Labor and was composed of delegates from the locals within the city or urban area. Similarly, state federations of labor were formed and chartered to include representatives from the subordinate organizations of the affiliated national unions located within their boundaries.

But for common action along industrial lines, the interunion agencies were established at the national level by creating "departments subordinate to the American Federation of Labor" at the headquarters in Washington. The national unions in the building industry were joined in the Building and Construction Trades Department, railway unions in the Railway Employees Department, metal workers' organizations in the Metal Trades Department. Affiliated with these were local, regional, and state trade councils. There was also formed the Union Label Trades Department composed of organizations which have labels or similar devices to advertise the insignia among consumers and otherwise promote the use of goods made by union labor.

The CIO paralleled the AFL with local, district, and state interunion organizations known as industrial councils, but because it rarely had more than one national union for each industry, it did not need and made no provision for departments like those of the AFL.

Despite the establishment of these interunion agencies as subordinate divisions of the AFL and the CIO, the national unions did not lose, and under the merged AFL-CIO have not lost, control over their locals and other branches that were

---

[6] Lewis L. Lorwin, *The American Federation of Labor* (Washington, D.C.: Brookings Institution, 1933), p. 22.

joined in the various councils. Although the Federation insists that locals of affiliated national organizations must join city and state federations or industrial councils, some refuse to join, or having joined they not infrequently withdraw. The national unions decide for themselves whether they will or will not participate in such interunion organizations. Moreover they may enter into cooperative arrangements with other unions which are not affiliated with the confederations to which they belong. In the railroad industry, for example, the Railway Labor Executives Association includes officers of independent unions and AFL-CIO unions.

Thus, though the AFL-CIO has the main responsibility for interunion relations, participation in these subordinate agencies remains essentially voluntary, and each national union reserves its autonomous or sovereign rights.

This devotion of each union to its independent governing authority is a constant source of criticism in and outside of organized labor. The jealousies and jurisdictional conflicts which it engenders are apparent contradictions of the ideal of labor unity. But the struggle between the Knights of Labor and the national unions led by the AFL taught the lesson that one big union embracing all workers is not the way to real unity. The Knights, despite their solidified government, were more torn by dissension in their ranks than are the self-governing national unions in the AFL-CIO. Workers learned that the basis of labor organization must be their specific interests in their jobs, wages, and working conditions, not the general interests that all wage earners have in common and together with other disadvantaged groups.

Nevertheless the vision of all workers joined in a single organization has remained a strong motivating force in American labor movements. In 1905 the IWW (Industrial Workers of the World) revived the idea of a centralized empire of labor. It assumed leadership of many strikes, conducted them in a spectacular manner, and won much publicity, creating the impression of a powerful organization which its meager membership belied. Being made up mainly of unskilled, seasonal, and migratory workers, and opposed to making contracts with employers, its organizations proved ephemeral. It disintegrated during World War I. After that war another movement for "One Big Union" received a good deal of publicity, but nothing came of it. More recently there has been the successful effort in 1955 to unite the AFL and the CIO in a single confederation. Even before the merger, the AFL, CIO, and independent Railroad Brotherhoods formed the United Labor Political Committee for the purpose of planning and pursuing common action in national election campaigns, in lobbying, and in dealing with government departments and agencies. In all these developments, the autonomy or sovereignty of each national labor union has been acknowledged, but the tendencies in these unifying movements toward subjecting the autonomous national unions to the rule of an overall government of labor organizations are not to be underestimated.

19. George Meany and the Wayward*

John Hutchinson†

"We have made it clear that union autonomy can not be used as a cloak for corruption."[1] Thus spoke AFL-CIO President George Meany in 1956.

The statement represented a revolution in trade-union government. From his assumption of the presidency of the American Federation of Labor in 1952, but particularly as president of the merged AFL-CIO from 1955, Meany was the chief architect of a doctrine which—in contrast to one of the most powerful traditions of the American labor movement—affirmed that the parent Federation had jurisdiction over the morals of its affiliated unions.

The autonomy of affiliated unions was a bedrock principle of the AFL. Founded in 1886, the Federation was a completely voluntary organization, a gathering of sovereign bodies for limited ends. It was in fact a confederation, a creature of delegated and meager authority, concerned more with consensus than with conformity. "The Federation," said AFL founder and president Samuel Gompers, ". . . has no power to enforce

its judgement."[2] Suspension and expulsion were the only sanctions, something less than mortal for the great majority of AFL unions, and almost never used. From time to time the AFL did take action against erring affiliates, but discipline seemed to be a function of size. Gompers and his successor, William Green, respected the sensitivities of the larger affiliates, seldom assayed more than circumspect advice, and always paid homage to autonomy.

In 1931 the AFL Executive Council heard that International Vice-President Theodore Brandle of the Iron Workers had accepted a bribe from New Jersey employers. Green twice asked Iron Workers' President P. J. Morrin to act to protect the good name of the union. Brandle was eventually expelled, but hardly in haste. Meanwhile Green was careful to state that the Executive Council made "no charges. It has no authority to make charges. . . . You have the power to deal with this case."[3]

In 1932 Green discussed with President John Possehl of the Operating Engineers the various charges of misbehavior levelled against International Vice-President Joseph Fay. Although Fay was convicted in the courts, Possehl told Green that there was no corruption in his organization. Apparently no further action was taken by either the union or the Federation.

The repeal of Prohibition in 1933 moved the American underworld—already entrenched in many local unions for bootlegging purposes—to

* Copyright © 1971 by The Regents of the University of California. Reprinted from the *California Management Review*, Vol. 14, by permission of the Regents.

The meticulous documentation supplied with the manuscript of this article was abridged perforce. Specific sources not now footnoted are either from AFL-CIO files or from Convention Proceedings. Background information from well-known sources—including the well-indexed hearings of the Douglas Subcommittee and the McClellan Committee of the United States Senate—is not footnoted. For the full account and complete documentation, see John Hutchinson, *The Imperfect Union: A History of Corruption in American Trade Unions* (New York: E. P. Dutton, 1970).

† John Hutchinson is Professor of Industrial Relations, Graduate School of Business Administration, UCLA.

[1] *AFL-CIO News*, September 1, 1956.

[2] Samuel Gompers, *The American Labor Movement*, Washington: American Federation of Labor 1914(?), pp. 7–9.

[3] See Philip Taft, *The A.F. of L. From the Death of Gompers to the Merger* (New York: Harper and Brothers, 1957), p. 423.

infiltrate the higher levels of trade unionism in search of substitute revenues. At four conventions during the 1930s the AFL warned against racketeering influence, but punishment was absent.

In 1940 President George Brown of the International Association of Theatrical and Stage Employees, together with his Capone-appointed assistant Willie Bioff, was under indictment and was soon to go to jail for extortion, but he nevertheless was reelected to the AFL Executive Council. President George Scalise of the Building Service Employees International Union was already in prison for embezzlement of union funds, but no comment was made in convention about that. The International Ladies Garment Workers Union, itself long embroiled in a battle against racketeers, proposed to the 1940 AFL convention that the Federation be given summary power to order the dismissal of any union representative who used his official position for private gain, and that all union constitutions be amended to provide for adequate discipline against the corrupt. The convention rejected the first proposal and adopted only an advisory version of the second. Fay of the Operating Engineers physically assaulted ILGWU President David Dubinsky later in the convention. Someone asked Green if the convention would take note of the incident. "Oh, no," Green evidently said, "that's just personal. It has nothing to do with us."

The tradition of tolerance prevailed until Green's death in 1952. Meany succeeded him. A new constitutional system was soon in the making.

LONGSHOREMEN

Meany was the prime mover in the unprecedented expulsion in 1953 of a powerful affiliate, the International Longshoremen's Association, on grounds of corruption. The Executive Council said,

The founders of the American Federation of Labor saw to it that there was no police power given to the central organization. . . . However, no one should make the mistake by concluding that the American Federation of Labor will sit by and allow *abuse of automomy* on the part of any of its affiliates to bring injury to the entire movement. The exercise of automomy . . . presupposes the maintenance of minimum standards of trade union decency.

There was an order. "The Executive Council," Meany wrote to the ILA, "will expect a report from you . . . on or before April 30, 1953."

The 1953 AFL convention expelled the ILA by an almost unanimous vote. The Federation chartered the International Brotherhood of Long-

shoremen and appointed five trustees for the new organization—Meany, President Dave Beck of the Teamsters, Secretary-Treasurer Paul Hall of the Atlantic and Gulf District of the Seafarers, President Albert J. Hayes of the Machinists, and President William C. Doherty of the Letter Carriers. Only Hall and Beck became involved to any extent, the Seafarers assuming almost all of the organizational burden.

The IBL lost two representation elections to the ILA. On the approach of a third election in 1956, International Vice-President James R. Hoffa of the Teamsters announced his readiness to lend the ILA up to $400,000 for organizing purposes.

Meany objected in a letter to Beck:

As you know, the [ILA] was expelled from the American Federation of Labor. . . . You supported this. . . . To what extent the [proposed loan] . . . might make the Teamsters International Brotherhood an ally with the corrupt influence that still seems to dominate the Longshoremen's Union is a matter of concern. . . . I would request you to advise me as early as possible as to the full details . . . whether such financial assistance has received your approval . . . if the view expressed by Mr. Hoffa . . . actually express your views and the views of the International Brotherhood of Teamsters.

The loan, together with a proposed organizing agreement between the Teamsters and the ILA, was dropped.

Meanwhile Beck had an idea. He wrote to President Harry Bates of the Bricklayers, who was also a member of the AFL Executive Council and one of Meany's closest associates,

I have worked very hard to try to find a solution to the waterfront problem. . . . There is no permanent solution . . . except that the Executive Council vest in the Teamsters International Union jurisdiction over this classification of employment. . . . We will guarantee 100 percent clean-cut international wage, hour, and condition procedure for every union affiliated with us under this jurisdiction. . . . We cannot continue to have our working relations continually jeopardized by the present procedure. . . . The IBL is but a paper organization, completely devoid of financial or physical resources. . . . We would be ready to assimilate it, to play fair in every respect. . . . I will be deeply appreciative of your personal support in this direction.

Bates was apparently unresponsive. Beck made his plea to the Executive Council in May 1955. Meany replied that there was nothing to indicate that the Teamsters could handle the waterfront problem. He accused the Teamster leadership in New York City of being "openly hostile" to the AFL on the waterfront, despite the fact that

Beck had assured the Federation that the international union could "take care" of its New York affiliates. Further, the Teamsters were reported still to have an organizing alliance with the ILA. "If the Teamsters should get into an organizational campaign against the International Brotherhood of Longshoremen, AFL, what are the Teamsters going to do about that?" Jurisdiction was refused, but damage had been done. Many New York longshoremen were now convinced that Beck's interest in them was essentially proprietary. In 1956 the IBL lost its third and last fight against the ILA.

After the merger of the AFL and CIO in 1955 the ILA had continued its supplications for reaffiliation. In September 1956, ILA President William V. Bradley met with Meany. The encounter was unfruitful. Meany announced that he would not "even bother" to refer the ILA's request to the AFL-CIO Executive Council. "It would be insulting to their intelligence," he said. "It is my opinion that the ILA officials have done nothing to rectify the conditions for which they were expelled. . . . The matter is closed.[4]

There was another irritation. Meany called for united labor support of the IBL in its 1956 contest, describing the ILA as "a disgrace to the good name of organized labor." However, on the eve of the election, President Joseph Curran of the National Maritime Union—a major influence in East Coast maritime unionism and a rival of the Seafarers—announced that he would support the ILA and suggested that Meany do the same. Meany was not amused. He wrote to Curran:

I note with interest your statement that you stand for honest, responsible, constructive trade unionism. . . . I note that you are aware of the shortcomings of the independent ILA and that your union has a prime interest in seeing that these faults and shortcomings are corrected forthwith. . . . Did this interest just become manifest to you on October 15, 1956? . . . Just what have you done in this regard either in your capacity as president of the NMU, or as a member of the Executive Council of the AFL-CIO, or as a member for the past ten months of the AFL-CIO Ethical Practices Committee? I am unaware of any effort on your part. . . . You wrote to me and transmitted the contents of your letter to the newspapers of New York City in the early evening of October 15 FOR ONE PURPOSE—AND ONLY ONE PURPOSE—TO ASSIST THE OLD ILA GANG TO RETAIN THEIR CONTROL OVER LONGSHOREMEN IN THE NEW YORK AREA. . . . Under these circumstances, I have serious doubts as to any effective contribution you could make as a member of the Ethical Practices Committee. . . .

[4] See *New York Times*, September 10 and 26, 1956.

The AFL-CIO now gradually withdrew from the waterfront, and the IBL declined. Early in 1959 the ILA, hardly a paragon but a much-improved organization, applied again for affiliation. "The situation," Meany told the 1959 AFL-CIO convention, "did change. . . . The average take-home pay . . . went from $52 to $102.50 in 1957 due to the elimination of this so-called casual labor that was representing the outside racketeer. . . . Bookkeeping is now the order of the day. They now have officers for their union. . . . We did some good when we kicked them out and we are now ready to take them back." An AFL-CIO committee recommended that affiliation be permitted, provided that the ILA reach an approved agreement with the IBL, submit to any orders from Meany, provide any reports required by the AFL-CIO, allow Meany to attend any meeting of the ILA Executive Council, and accept the right of the AFL-CIO to impose on the union any discipline it thought appropriate. The ILA agreed and affiliated—incidentally putting an end to rumors that it might join the Teamsters—and later, with Federation approval, absorbed the IBL. "It is encouraging," Meany said, "because now we have developed an element inside the ILA that is as much interested in fighting corruption and fighting for decent unionism as we were when we put them out in 1953."

TEXTILE WORKERS

"To make a long story short," Secretary-Treasurer Lloyd Klenert of the AFL United Textile Workers of America wrote to AFL Secretary-Treasurer Meany in 1952, "we have just about reached the end of our rope. This week no salaries will be paid starting from [UTWA President Anthony] Valente and myself all the way down the line. . . ."

The UTWA was trying to wean a dissident group away from the CIO Textile Workers Union of America. Expenses for this and other activities were allegedly heavy, and Klenert asked Meany for a loan. "I was somewhat surprised at this," Meany said later, "because the campaign had been going for only six or seven weeks. . . ." He asked Klenert for a financial report, then condemned it as "phoney." Now there were rumors that Valente and Klenert had used union funds to buy private houses and other personal goods for themselves. Meany told the two officers that they could appear before the AFL Executive Council in support of their loan application, with the understanding that they would be questioned about their financial report. They refused to attend. "They now felt," Meany said, "that the question of financial assistance to the United Textile Workers was of no importance compared to the question of their integrity."

Valente and Klenert later met with Meany, conceding that their report was "a complete fabrication," but defending their duplicity as a necessary means of concealing the UTWA's assets from its CIO rival. Meany told them he thought their purpose was to deceive the AFL. Meany reported to the AFL Executive Council: "We built this organization by the expenditure of thousands and thousands of dollars. . . . For a number of years . . . the American Federation of Labor paid the salaries and expenses of the organizing staff of the United Textile Workers, including the salaries of Valente and Klenert. . . . I felt that the American Federation of Labor should take immediate action to protect the 90,000 members of the United Textile Workers." Green appointed a committee consisting of Meany, Doherty, and President Dan Tracy of the International Brotherhood of Electrical Workers. The committee met in New York with the Executive Board of the UTWA.

Valente: Before we start, we thought you wanted an opportunity to address our Council, and we have no objection to that. . . . However, I don't think we should have the record kept. . . . We are not on trial; we are not going to have cross-examination. I think this is a family matter.
Meany: Weil, this [stenographer] is taking record for the American Federation of Labor.
Valente: Well, our counsel objects to it.
Meany: Your counsel objects to it?
Valente: Yes.
Meany: Well, so far as I am concerned, that is the end of the meeting.

The hearing proceeded with the stenographer at work. The discussion covered the complex financial transactions of Valente and Klenert in buying real estate and personal goods, in listing unusual organizing expenses, and other matters. Members of the UTWA Board admitted they knew the report was fraudulent, but repeated the argument that its purpose was legitimate. The union's counsel argued that Valente and Klenert were acting to protect the union.

Meany: All I can say is you are going to have a great opportunity from now on to protect . . . because God knows it will need protection. O.K. Let's go.

Meany reported the exchange to the Executive Council. The Council referred the matter back to the UTWA Executive Board, which

cleared Valente and Klenert. Apparently the AFL took no further action.[5]

The McClellan Committee of the U.S. Senate conducted an investigation of the UTWA in 1957, after which the AFL-CIO Committee on Ethical Practices held its own inquiry. The latter committee concluded that the real purpose of the 1952 financial report was to conceal the attempted use of union funds to buy two houses and other personal possessions, and that "but for Mr. Meany's intervention in 1952 the Union might well have sustained a loss from that transaction. . . ."

Meany told the 1957 AFL-CIO convention that

The record on this union . . . would make fantastic reading. . . . We asked this [UTWA] committee . . . if Klenert had now resigned. They said, "Oh, yes, he is out." . . . "Have there been any financial arrangements made with him?" . . . They said, "Oh, yes, we are paying him $100 week." "For how long?" it was asked. "Oh, for 20 years. . . ." They made a simple arrangement when he resigned to pay him $100 a week as a reward for stealing the union's money to the extent of well over a quarter of a million dollars. . . . That action was rescinded. We got the resignation of the president. . . ."

The AFL-CIO placed the UTWA under a monitorship. Peter McGavin, Meany's personal assistant, administered the affairs of the union while it undertook the reforms required by Meany. Valente, Klenert, and UTWA Counsel Joseph Jacobs—not labor attorney Joseph Jacobs of Chicago—were barred permanently from office. The union elected new officers by secret ballot, adopted the AFL-CIO Codes of Ethical Practices, agreed to submit periodic reports to the AFL-CIO Executive Council, and later instituted further reforms—including the prohibition of personal loans to officers, the tightening of financial procedures, and the bonding of officers. In time McGavin reported to Meany his satisfaction with the progress of the UTWA. The Executive Council dissolved the monitorship in February 1960.

JEWELRY WORKERS

In 1952 a committee of the AFL Executive Council—composed of Meany, Dubinsky, and President William McFetridge of the BSEIU—investigated the affairs of the International Jewelry Workers Union. The committee reported to

[5] *Report,* Meeting of a Sub-Committee of the Executive Council of the American Federation of Labor and the Executive Board of the United Textile Workers of America, September 24, 1952, n.p. (AFL-CIO files). All the above chronology and citations subsequent to the Klenert-Meany letter are taken from this report.

the 1952 AFL convention that the IJWU had agreed to revoke a charter issued outside of its normal jurisdiction. Under pressure from the committee, the union also suspended the officers of New York Local 222 after the arrest of Business Agent George ("Muscles") Futterman for the alleged intimidation of a prime witness in the case of the murder of ILGWU Organizer William Lurye.

Matters lay dormant until 1957. In that year an AFL-CIO group in New York—the Committee to End Exploitation of Puerto Rican and Other Minority Workers—reported to Meany a number of malpractices in the IJWU, including family nepotism in the union's welfare fund and the complete absence of effective representation of the members. The IJWU ostensibly undertook a number of reforms, but the Minority Workers' Committee told Meany that no progress had been made. Meany asked the Committee on Ethical Practices to investigate. That committee reported that the union "had become thoroughly demoralized . . . on the verge of moral and financial bankruptcy . . . rapidly disintegrating." It found numerous violations of the AFL-CIO Codes of Ethical Practices, including kickbacks, the stealing of elections, the molestation of intra-union opponents, the padding of expense accounts, and in one case the prodigious use of entertainment allowances. There was a protest on that. "I can assure the Committee," IJWU Secretary-Treasurer Hyman Powell testified, "that I did not see *My Fair Lady* 23 separate times."

Meany was unsatisfied. "Under the circumstances," he wrote to Powell and IJWU President Joseph Morris, "I have no other course of action except to direct you to end these practices forthwith and to take whatever steps are necessary, including the expulsion of all officers who refuse to abide by the Code of Ethics . . . and to end exploitation of any of the workers in any of your shops in your jurisdiction." Meany met with the IJWU Executive Board, which asked the Federation to assume full powers over the union. Morris and Powell, who had resigned from elective office to become employees of the union, now lost their jobs. Other reforms were undertaken. The Executive Council raised the IJWU's probation before the union's 1962 convention.

LAUNDRY WORKERS

"It is the sincere desire and firm intention of the Laundry Workers International Union," LWIU President Sam J. Byers wrote to Meany in 1955, "to take such action with respect to its welfare fund as it may find to be necessary, appropriate, and legally proper. . . . I request the assistance of the American Federation of Labor." A Senate subcommittee under the chairmanship of Senator Paul Douglas of Illinois had just reported unfavorably on the operation of the LWIU's welfare fund.

Meany promised his help and sent Nelson Cruikshank—director of the AFL Department of Social Security—to LWIU headquarters. Cruikshank recommended various measures to end conflict-of-interest activities by LWIU officials, to replace several welfare-fund trustees, and to improve the insurance available to the beneficiaries of the fund. Meany, urging prompt action by the union, wrote to Byers.

I am sure you recognize that to take the position that no action by any union is called for until action is instituted by the Department of Justice or by a state, and finally determined by the courts, would be tantamount to an abdication of the responsibility of a trade union to protect the interests of its members. It is a firm and cherished principle of the American Federation of Labor that our unions are capable of exercising their own discipline . . . [but] any failure to measure up to this responsibility . . . would put in jeopardy the freedom from control of the internal affairs of all unions."

Byers referred the matter to the welfare fund trustees.

In 1956 Meany ordered an AFL-CIO staff report on the LWIU. The report stated that some reforms had been undertaken by the trustees, but that LWIU Secretary-Treasurer Eugene ("Jimmy") James—who had been accused by the Douglas Subcommittee of diverting, in cooperation with broker Louis Saperstein, some $900,000 from the welfare fund—was still in office. The Committee on Ethical Practices found a wide range of abuses still in practice, but no impetus for effective reform within the union. Byers retired and was succeeded by Ralph T. Fagan of James's Local 46 in Chicago. "Fagan is clean, honest, and has integrity," James announced. "I know him well. He is my employee." James also retired, but allegedly dominated the union from behind the scenes.

The AFL-CIO Executive Council suspended the LWIU in June 1957. The union's counsel, Herbert S. Thatcher, argued in a letter to Meany that the LWIU was now essentially in compliance with the standards of the Federation. Meany countered with a last offer, proposing that within 90 days the union hold a special convention presided over by an AFL-CIO official, require all incumbent officers to submit themselves for re-election, read the Committee on Ethical Practices' report to the delegates and print it in the proceedings, and start court action against James.

The LWIU rejected Meany's proposals, offering only to hold a special convention with Meany attending as an observer, and appealed to the 1957 AFL-CIO convention. "Our rank and file," Fagan told the delegates, "has shown complete satisfaction with the results reached at our convention. . . . We have not received a single letter, nor even a postcard, from any member of our International criticizing our action in this regard."

Meany's experience had been different. An LWIU laundress had written,

Dear Mr. Meany. I would like to know *Why* our laundry only starts with 65 cents an hour. . . . Every year you get a nickel raise till the amount comes to a *Dollar*. That is a union Ha Ha Ha. . . . No contract on wall or Labor law hung up in shop so that we can see what we should know. . . . When we have our meetings some of the girls have to say some things to the other girls and they are told to shut there mouth and to sit down or do not attend any more meetings or be fined 5 dollars. . . . We work like horses and I mean horses. . . . Our Boss said that our Union is nothing and is not worth the paper it is wrote on. . . . They make you pay the full month dues when you are sick and that is 2.50 a month. The books say 35 cents a month and they wrote the contract that way. . . . Well all I have to say is I do hope you will help us out and get us a good Union in. . . . Send some one down to help us PLEASE PLEASE.

"He looks like a very reasonable person," Meany said of Fagan to the delegates, "His remarks make me wonder why it is he could not accept our proposal . . . [but] there is every reason to believe that up until this present moment the same forces that controlled this Union may still be in control. . . . Has Mr. Fagan any further comment?"

Fagan was silent. The convention expelled the LWIU and chartered a new union, The AFL-CIO Laundry and Dry Cleaning International Union. The LWIU affiliated with the Teamsters.

DISTILLERY WORKERS

In 1954 the Douglas Subcommittee reported adversely on the AFL Distillery Workers. A New York grand jury then indicted Secretary-Treasurer Sol Cilento on charges of bribery and conspiracy in connection with the union's welfare fund. Cilento's co-defendants were former BSEIU president George Scalise, and Anthony ("Little Augie Pisano") Carfano—once a bootlegger with the Capone organization. Louis Saperstein, the welfare-fund broker already sentenced to five years in jail for embezzling money from the LWIU welfare fund, turned state's evidence. He was forced, he said, to turn over 50 percent of his commissions—some $540,000 altogether—to the three defendants, Cilento allegedly receiving more than $100,000. The defendants were acquitted on a technicality.

The union was evidently uncooperative with the authorities, an AFL-CIO staff group said, in this and another indictment against Cilento for grand larceny, its attitude having had "the obvious effect of shielding Cilento from effective prosecution." President Joseph O'Neill had preferred charges against Cilento, and the union's General Executive Board had suspended him from his offices as secretary-treasurer and as trustee of the welfare fund. Cilento then resigned, but retained his position as executive vice-president of Local 2. "So far as is known," the staff group said, "neither the international union nor the local union has made any effort to remove him from this key local union position." In June 1956 the Committee on Ethical Practices conducted its own investigation of the union, and the AFL-CIO Executive Council directed the Distillery Workers to "show cause" why they should not be suspended from the federation.

"I desire to assure the [Executive Council] and you personally," O'Neill wired to Meany, "that upon evidence that the Distillery Workers International Union has not conformed in any respect to the principles and policies of the AFL-CIO Constitution I will take immediate and necessary action." The union held a special convention, ostensibly to reform, but Meany was unsatisfied and appointed McGavin as monitor over the union. McGavin arranged a second convention which, according to the *New York Times,* was "a near-riot of cursing and name-calling." McGavin, in the chair, ordered a secret ballot for new officers, whereupon irate delegates stormed the platform, shouting "Hitlerism" and other expletives. McGavin adjourned the convention and left, followed by a number of delegates. The remainder, representing about two-thirds of the union's membership, re-elected O'Neill and replaced Cilento with George Oneto. "The undemocratic tactics employed by Brother McGavin," O'Neill wrote to Meany, "naturally provoked the delegates into a demonstration. . . .

Indeed, admirable restraint was exercised by the delegates. . . ."

Conversations were held, and the Distillery Workers agreed to hold another convention chaired by an AFL-CIO representative and to conduct elections by secret ballot. "Under these circumstances," Meany reported to the 1957 AFL-CIO convention, "the Executive Council decided to go along with this Union to see if they straightened themselves out."

The union instituted various reforms, but absolution was delayed. "It appears," McClellan Committee chief counsel Robert F. Kennedy wrote to Meany in 1959, "that some of the matters we have uncovered in the course of our investigation of the [Distillery Workers] are as serious as those uncovered in the Textile Workers." The McClellan Committee made charges of nepotism, careless bookkeeping, and munificent salaries and expenses for union officers. An AFL-CIO auditing committee appointed by Meany seemed to confirm the charges. Meany asked the union for an explanation, informing the 1959 AFL-CIO convention that "the President's office is investigating certain conditions in the union."

The new president of the Distillery Workers, Mortimer Brandenburg, wrote to Meany. He said the charges of the McClellan Committee came in "poor grace" when the Congress so often authorized millions of dollars in expenses for the President of the United States for which no accounting was required. There was also the matter of status at the bargaining table. "The officials of the employers who negotiate with the officials of these local unions," Brandenburg said, "also receive compensation in high surtax brackets and, needless to say, the interests of the locals are not disserved by having union officials on a comparable prestige and remuneration level." There was a patriotic by-product. "The Federal Internal Revenue," Brandenburg continued, "has been a principal beneficiary of the salary situation. For example, Dr. [Max] Drexler [of New York Local 2] paid over $25,000 in Federal taxes on his 1958 compensation . . . Mr. Brandenburg more than $67,000 [in the last five years]." Finally, inflation was a leveller. "If the officers' compensation is computed on the basis of an inflated forty-five cent dollar after taxes," Brandenburg concluded, "the notion of excessiveness is rapidly dissipated."

The monitorship continued, but the union evidently complied rapidly with whatever directives were given. "I do want to . . . record," McGavin wrote to Brandenburg later in the year, "my satisfaction with the substantial progress being made by your International Union. . . . The Distillery Workers' Union has irrevocably committed itself in practice to the AFL-CIO Codes." There was a further period of probation, then the AFL-CIO Executive Council dissolved the monitorship in January 1961, restoring the union to full standing in the federation.

AUTOMOBILE WORKERS

John DioGuardi, a New York hoodlum more popularly known as Johnny Dio, became active in the affairs of the AFL United Automobile Workers in the early 1950s. Meany, hearing rumors, asked UAW-AFL President Lester Washburn for an explanation.

"First of all," Washburn replied, "I believe I should explain the extent to which we have been involved with the two individuals Paul Dorfman and Sam Berger." Dorfman was the head of AFL Federal Local 20647, a waste materials handlers' union in Chicago. He was, according to the McClellan Committee, an intimate of various leaders of the Chicago underworld, and was in fact later removed from office by the AFL-CIO for malpractice. Berger was the business manager of ILGWU Local 102 in New York—later resigning under pressure from the union—and a partner with Dio in a flower shop. Dorfman and Berger had persuaded the UAW-AFL to grant them a charter for UAW-AFL Local 102, also in New York. Dio was not among the original charter applicants, nor a member of the union, nor had he worked in the industries in which Local 102 was given jurisdiction, but he was appointed business manager of the local. "The situation," Washburn explained to Meany, "required that competent leadership be established for this local."

"While living in New York," a member of Local 102 wrote to Meany, "I was employed in a plant where the union is the AFL Auto Workers. . . . The union is run by an ex-convict, John Dio, and his henchmen. I tried to protest a contract sell-out at a meeting and was called at home by these thugs and told if I loved my children to shut up. . . . I'm no hero, so I did." Meanwhile Dio had been convicted of income tax evasion, and accused of various misdeeds by the New York Anti-Crime Committee and District Attorney Frank Hogan.

Meany threatened action against the union, which then disbanded Local 102. Washburn expelled Dio from office and membership and withdrew the charters of six local unions allegedly dominated by Dio. The UAW-AFL's Executive Board reinstated Dio and restored the charters of three of the locals. Washburn resigned in protest and was succeeded by Earl Heaton. The Executive Board took note of Dio's record. Although he had been arrested in the past for vagrancy, coercion, extortion, and an unregistered liquor still, and had been in jail for extortion, the Board concluded that "by all New York standards our operations are clean." The Board judged Dio innocent of any improper activities connected with the union, but he resigned, later going to jail on the income tax charge.

"Dear Mr. Meany," wrote a member of UAW-AFL Local 286 in Chicago, "I hope you will act on this story. . . . A local hoodlum, Angelo Inciso, runs this union. . . . I was told to keep my mouth shut or I would be thrown down the steps. . . . I do not sign my name as such action might bring swift reprisal on my family. . . . Hope you can clean up this menace to all American unionism." Inciso had been convicted for theft, grand larceny, shoplifting, and violation of the federal liquor laws, and had been in jail twice. In 1956 the Douglas Subcommittee condemned him for misuse of union funds. The UAW-AFL Executive Board revoked the charter of Local 286 in February 1956, but then rescinded its action on advice of counsel and allowed Inciso to disaffiliate his local, taking with him one-fifth of the dues income of the international union.

The Committee on Ethical Practices investigated the union, which had changed its name to the Allied Industrial Workers of America, and condemned its tolerance of Dio and Inciso. The AIW accepted a monitorship, expelled four New York locals, adopted the Codes of Ethical Practices, and instituted other reforms. However, AIW Secretary-Treasurer Anthony Doria—who had been charged with condoning the loose financial controls which permitted Inciso's mishandling of union funds—demanded that he be allowed to resign with severance pay of $150,000 and a car. The Executive Board agreed, then reversed itself, voting to give Doria only $5,000 and a car. Heaton reported to McGavin that Doria had resigned, but did not mention the financial arrangement; then he evidently signed an agreement with Doria—without informing the Executive Board—to pay him $80,000 over a period of two years. McGavin heard of the agreement and reported it to Meany. Heaton said afterwards that he did not think McGavin would be interested in the matter.

Meany summoned Heaton and the entire Executive Board to a meeting. The Board cancelled the agreement with Doria. The AIW then held a special convention in August 1957 at which Carl W. Griepentrog succeeded Heaton as president. The convention set new limits to the power of the international president, introduced annual audits for local unions, and voted to move the union's headquarters from Beverly Hills in California back to the Midwest. It also commended Meany and the AFL-CIO Executive Council "for their forthright action and leadership in fighting this small cancerous element of corruption which foisted itself on the labor movement."

"I note with satisfaction," Meany wrote to Griepentrog, "the progress that your international union has made." The Executive Council ended the AIW's probationary status in October 1957. The AIW, the Council reported, was the only union disciplined by the Federation up to that point to have accepted in full the Council's recommendations on reform. The monitorship stayed in force a short period, McGavin continuing to advise the officers of the union. It was ended in May 1958 since the AIW, according to Meany, "had done an outstanding job in rebuilding the international union."

BAKERY AND CONFECTIONERY WORKERS

President James G. Cross and other officers of the Bakery and Confectionery Workers International Union were accused by the McClellan Committee of financial and other malpractices. The Committee on Ethical Practices condemned them as well, and the Executive Council ordered the Bakers to correct the abuses revealed and to expel the officers responsible. The Bakers' Executive Board refused to comply, but when Meany announced the suspension of the union it asked for a meeting with him. Meany agreed, "with the understanding that this [Bakers'] committee will not include in its membership the President of your organization." The meeting was abortive. Cross—who had been accused of dictatorial rule, the use of violence against internal opponents, excessive expenditures, and conflict-of-interest activities in collusion with bakery industry employers—appealed the suspension to the 1957 AFL-CIO convention, claiming he was being made a scapegoat.

Meany said,

I find myself listening to Brother Cross in the position of wondering whether the Appeals Committee [of the convention] should not have taken more summary action. . . . There is every evidence right at this minute that there is no intention to comply.

. . . This [Cross] is a remarkable guy. But I have seen both sides of him, and I can tell you frankly that this union is in a bad way if he continues to run its affairs, whether he runs them from one of his two homes in Palm Beach or whether he runs them from his other mansion, or whether he runs them in conjunction with the Employers' Association. . . . This is a workers' organization. . . . Let's keep it that way.

The convention expelled the Bakers and chartered a new union, the American Bakery and Confectionery Workers International Union. The two organizations reunited in 1970 with the approval of the AFL-CIO.

TEAMSTERS

"I have nothing to fear," President Dave Beck of the Teamsters said after his appearance before the McClellan Committee. "My record is an open book. I make this fight for others, not for myself."[6] Beck, threatening to "blow the lid right off the Senate" when he testified, instead invoked the Fifth Amendment more than 200 times. Meany declared that any union official who refused to testify about his handling of union funds had no right to hold office. Beck, accused among other things of stealing hundreds of thousands of dollars from the Teamsters, took his case to the AFL-CIO Executive Council, saying he would not remove any union official for exercising his constitutional rights. "I know all the things you're not going to do," Meany said. "What I want to know is what you are going to do to clean things up." The Council suspended Beck from its membership and ordered an investigation of the Teamsters. Beck protested, arguing that his suspension was improper, depriving the Teamsters of rightful representation.

Meany wrote to Beck,

I wish to point out that membership of the Executive Council is a personal matter. Members of the Council do not sit on the Council as representatives of any particular union but are required to act in the interests of the general membership of the entire trade union movement. The action of the Council in suspending you as a member was based on your personal actions and not on any actions of the Teamsters Brotherhood as such. . . . I will, however, convey your request [for a meeting] to the Executive Council.

---

[6] *New York Times*, March 29, 1957.

The Council heard out Beck's claim that his suspension was invalid, expelled him, and appointed Teamster Secretary John F. English in his place.

The condemnations by the McClellan Committee and the Committee on Ethical Practices led to formal action against the Teamsters at the 1957 AFL-CIO convention. Meany wound up the debate. He noted that the Teamsters' constitution provided for the discipline or expulsion of any member convicted of a crime, or who engaged in racketeering, or who brought dishonor on the union. "The Teamsters," he said, "have made no move . . . to live up to their own Constitution in regard to these crimes against the trade union movement. . . . Their [1957] convention took up this matter not at all. . . . They read the Ethical Practices Report in an atmosphere of hilarity. They had a nice time doing it. . . . They didn't do anything, they didn't investigate anything." Meany had agreed several times through an intermediary to meet with newly elected Teamster President James R. Hoffa, but evidently on each occasion Hoffa had cancelled the appointment. "I have the door open," Meany said. "It was open until 11 o'clock last night; it will be open after you have finished voting. . . . But you have got to give these members a chance. . . . When you vote for the [Appeals] committee's report you are voting to free the Teamsters from the dictatorship of these men." The convention expelled the Teamsters.

THE DOCTRINE OF CONDITIONAL AUTONOMY

The government of trade union federations in the United States has been characterized overwhelmingly by persuasion rather than by authority. Prior to the expulsion of the ILA from the AFL, there had in fact been only two examples of major punitive action taken by a federation: the expulsion of John L. Lewis's Committee for Industrial Organization from the AFL in 1936, and the expulsion of the Communist-influenced unions from the CIO in 1949. There were special circumstances involved. The AFL's action against the CIO was redundant; the Committee was already a de facto separate and independent organization, and its chairman cared not at all about the calumny of the AFL. The CIO's own disbarment of the far left, on the other hand, was to some extent an act of political necessity, since—because of prevailing congressional and public opinion—failure to take some such action could easily have led to most unwelcome legislative reprisal.

Much the same could be said about the AFL-CIO's expulsions of the Teamsters and Bakers and Laundry Workers. The charges of corruption against one union or another were serious, highly visible, and occasionally magnified by both the Congress and the press beyond proper proportions. But they were made, and widely and strongly believed. Retribution was a clear and present danger. The expulsions were unprecedented only in their price, since no organization occupies so central a place in the economics of American trade unionism as the Teamsters.

What was quite new was the promulgation and application of the doctrine of conditional autonomy, the assertion of the right of the parent federation to prescribe and control the constitutional and administrative practices of an affiliate as a condition of its association. It was a step without a precursor. The reversal of tradition could hardly have been more complete.

The monitorships were the instruments of conditional autonomy. Gompers and Green often spoke of standards, and were usually ready to make known to erring affiliates the displeasure or misgivings of the AFL; but there was never any question of the right to internal control. Lewis dominated the affairs of the CIO from 1935 to 1940. He led at the bargaining tables of other unions and often influenced their ways, but even as leader he was essentially a guest. Unlike Meany's his presidency was never custodial.

Nor can the reversal of tradition under Meany be explained wholly as a matter of political necessity. There were fears of legislative reprisal in the event of inaction, but the AFL-CIO could easily have resorted to less stringent methods with some hope of escape. The merger of the AFL and the CIO created a much-expanded aggregation of unions which, by diminishing the relative power of individual large unions, made them easier to criticize; but autonomy was still a cherished idea. The record lends much substance to the proposition that the steps taken by the AFL-CIO against the corrupt were in great measure due to the convictions and capability of its president. There is simply no evidence that Gompers, Green, CIO President Philip Murray, or his successor Walter Reuther ever exercised such sustained *authority* on any issue as did Meany. Again only Lewis bears comparison, but by 1940 even he was threatening resignation over

challenge to his leadership, particularly on the matter of peace negotiations with the AFL.

THE IMPACT OF MEANY

Meany seems never to have encountered divisions within either the AFL or the AFL-CIO sufficient to cause him to change direction or to threaten resignation. It is at least part of the folklore of the Federation that he had his way on virtually every issue of importance. On corruption he observed most of the proprieties, but his influence was manifest. Albert J. Hayes, former president of the Machinists and chairman of the Committee on Ethical Practices, wrote:

> Because of Meany's concern over corruption, this matter was discussed . . . by the Executive Council. As a result the Ethical Practices Committee was established. President Meany appointed the members of the Committee. . . . Although he did not interfere with the work of the Committee, nor attempt to impose his views, he did favor the adoption of ethical standards and insisted upon a full investigation of all charges and allegations. . . . He vigorously supported the Committee's reports and recommendations. . . . Largely because of President Meany's vigorous support the AFL-CIO convention took action.[7]

The quality of Meany's general stewardship of the AFL and AFL-CIO remains to be assessed. In the meantime it is certain that on the matter of corruption his role was both assertive and innovative in constitutional theory and practice, greatly a matter of personal conviction, and without effective opposition.

How should he be judged? It could be argued that discipline was incomplete; but it could hardly have been pushed much further without endangering the life of the Federation, even on the debatable assumption that it would have been justified by the evidence. What Meany did might be regarded as an act of expediency to ward off the Congress, but few American union leaders have such a public record of repeated and explicit opposition to corruption. Meany also risked displeasure, not only of those whom he berated or punished, but of those among the innocent who suspected his assumption of authority lest some day he might use it against them on other grounds. He could have chosen an easier, more palliative way. But he did not; and it is at least arguable that, in acting as brusquely and firmly as he did, he not only saved the

---

[7] Letter to the author, December 3, 1968.

American labor movement from legislation even more unwelcome than the Landrum-Griffin reform act of 1959, but was instrumental in the proclamation of a body of trade union standards surely as specific, demanding, and admirable as any. It was a service hardly open to reproach, one of great prescriptive value to the institution of trade unionism, one in which the affiliates of the AFL-CIO might well feel glad to have shared.

Arthur J. Goldberg, former counsel of the CIO and an architect of both the AFL-CIO merger and the Codes of Ethical Practices, had a comment on the matter. He told the 1961 AFL-CIO convention,

Law or no law, the trade union movement has an old and eternal obligation to exercise vigilance against those who would corrupt it and use it for their personal gain. . . . I think it was the finest hour of the trade union movement in America when you took the action that you did.

B. The Administration of Union Affairs

In a previous article, Leiserson indicates that the locus of power in the American labor movement is in the national union. Does this mean that the national union leader is able to act without restraint and run the organization as a one-man show? Bok and Dunlop, in discussing how union policy is made, dispel any notion that the union leader is all-powerful. They find that "union behavior is the product of four broad influences that are constantly interacting upon one another: the desires of the members, the nature and abilities of the leadership, the capacities and opinion of subordinates, and the pressures of the environment."

The problem of democracy in labor unions is discussed by Kerr who examines the question of the union's impact on the worker's freedom with emphasis on six aspects of the problem: local union autonomy, a new faith for the union movement, secret elections of officers, independent judicial processes, permissive rules on union entry and on movement within industry, and narrow limits to union functions. He proposes that legislation may be drawn up in some of these areas to insure individual freedom and democracy within the union.

In the concluding article, Galenson and Prickett debate the issue of Communism and trade union democracy.

20. How Trade Union Policy Is Made*

Derek C. Bok and John T. Dunlop†

At present, most commentators seem to assume that the future of the labor movement rests mainly in the hands of its leaders. This point of view is reflected in the constant criticism of labor leaders, and it is buttressed by a mass of opinion data to the effect that unions are run pretty much as the top officials see fit. Yet one must beware of such opinions, for each of the groups that most influence the public view of organized labor has its special reasons for misconceiving the role of the union leader and exaggerating his influence.

The businessman, for example, is accustomed to organizations where the leader enjoys considerable power (though not so much as the outsider tends to suppose). As a result, many executives assume instinctively that the union leader enjoys comparable authority; they overlook the fact that union officials must win office by election. Businessmen may also exaggerate the role of the union leader as a result of their natural tendency to assume a "harmony of interests" between themselves and their employees. This assumption has suffused the literature of business for decades and stems, once again, from understandable motives. Few managements wish to harbor the thought that they are pursuing their own interests at the expense of their employees. It would be most disagreeable to concede that wages are kept unfairly low or that the quest for efficiency has led to harsh supervision or uncomfortable working conditions. As a result, when employees organize or protest or strike, many employers assume that

harmonious relations within their plants have been disrupted by some opportunistic union leader who has succeeded in leading the workers astray. This reaction, once again, is not a simple matter of tactics; it springs naturally from a network of beliefs that help many executives to justify their behavior as businessmen and human beings.

Intellectuals also have their reasons for ascribing great influence to the union leader. As Bertrand Russell has pointed out, the liberal critic has traditionally been sentimental toward the underdog. He has been unable to champion the cause of the poor and the disadvantaged without idealizing them as well. As a result—until recently, at any rate—these critics could seldom bring themselves to blame union shortcomings on the members; instead, they concluded that the leaders must somehow be responsible.

Other forces also helped to reinforce this bias. After the rush of organizing in the 30s, union members seemed to have become representative of the entire working class. Under these circumstances, it would have been most awkward to fault the members for labor's failure to press for social reform. How could the liberal justify his programs if the beneficiaries themselves were indifferent to them? Unless the rank and file were on his side, how could he urge the unions to reform and still keep true to his democratic principles? Above all, how could he harbor any optimism at all if the entire working class had to be persuaded to support his programs? With all these difficulties, it was far easier to assume that unions were made up of willing members who were held back by the stubbornness and selfishness of powerful leaders. These beliefs could begin to weaken only when union members were no longer seen as representative of the lower classes and unions were no longer the only organized

* From U.S. Department of Labor, *Monthly Labor Review*, Vol. 93, No. 2, February 1970, pp. 17–20. Permission granted by Simon & Schuster, Inc. This article is drawn from *Labor and the American Community*, published by Simon & Schuster in 1970.

† Derek C. Bok is President of Harvard University. John T. Dunlop is Secretary of Labor.

force for social reform. Thus, it is no accident that intellectuals did not acknowledge the lack of liberal, reformist sentiments among the members until the 1960s, when students, black militants, and other groups had already begun to offer organized support for fundamental social reforms. (Characteristically enough, now that the pendulum has begun to swing, it has swung very far indeed in the minds of many critics. Union members are now viewed not only as apathetic and undisposed to social reform; they are erroneously perceived as a highly conservative force in the society.)

Because of these tendencies to exaggerate the influence of the labor leader, one must take pains to construct a more realistic picture of how union policy is actually made. Otherwise, society will often misdirect its energies by flailing away at union officials for actions that are not really within their power to change. In the process, deeper forces may be overlooked, forces that actually determine union behavior and must ultimately be changed if the conduct of unions is to change.

In the end, union behavior is the product of four broad influences that are constantly interacting upon one another: the desires of the members, the nature and abilities of the leadership, the capacities and opinions of subordinates, and the pressures of the environment. In the brief space remaining, it is possible only to distill these influences into a more succinct, more general statement.

WHAT THE MEMBERS WANT

Starting first with the rank and file, a mass of data suggests that the members are primarily interested in their union as an agent for negotiating with the employer and administering the collective bargaining agreement. Where these functions are involved, the members exert influences through many different channels to impose certain restraints upon their leaders. Sometimes the demands of the members are very high, even impossibly so; sometimes they can be modified by the leaders through education and persuasion. Once formed, however, these demands can be ignored only at the risk of decertification, election defeat, refusals to ratify contracts, wildcat strikes, or other forms of withholding cooperation.

The members expect little and ordinarily demand even less in other areas of union activity, such as organizing, political action, or community service. Their main interest is simply that these programs not require too large an expenditure of dues or demand too much time and attention from union officials. To enforce this interest, members exert pressure either by refusing dues increases and special levies to pay for the programs or by withholding their cooperation or participation, which is often essential if the programs are to succeed.

Throughout the entire range of union programs, the members tend to impose closer restraints upon local leaders than upon national officials, especially if the local organizations are small. At the national level, it is much more difficult to marshal an effective protest or to oust the incumbent officials, since opposition must be mounted in many widely scattered groups of members. But in the national as well as in the local union, the influence of the member expresses itself more insistently and through many more channels than most observers have been prepared to concede. On the whole, moreover, the influence has been much less salutary than critics of unions like to acknowledge. A candid appraisal compels the conclusion that the rank and file has contributed to most of the widely condemned union shortcomings: racial discrimination, excessive wage demands, featherbedding, and—in many instances—irresponsible strikes. Corruption, of course, is one form of union misbehavior that cannot be attributed significantly to the membership. Critics may often respond to the above-mentioned arguments by asserting that autocratic unions can also indulge in featherbedding, racial discrimination, etc. This is undoubtedly correct, but one reason may be that democratic elections are only one way by which the views of the members are impressed upon the leader; there are other highly effective conduits for transmitting membership demands and values, even in seemingly autocratic unions.

INFLUENCE OF SUBORDINATES

The union leader is also limited by his subordinates. In many cases, of course, the subordinate is simply a vehicle for pressures arising from the membership. Thus, local officials will resist advice or commands which, if carried out, would threaten defeat at the next local election. But subordinates can limit their superiors in ways quite independent of any rank-and-file sentiments. Local leaders may develop personal ambitions that can be furthered by resisting the international. Staff personnel may have views and priorities that conflict with those of the union leaders they serve. Local officials or staff can simply lack the ability to carry out orders effectively. In theory, of course, the higher official may have formal authority to order his subordinates about. In practice, however, the situation is not so simple. The leader must normally obtain genuine cooperation and even enthusiasm from his subordinates, and this cannot often be achieved if the leader does not accommodate himself, to some extent at least, to the abilities and desires of those whom he commands.

EFFECT OF ENVIRONMENT

The environment presses in upon the union from many directions: through the policies of employers; the market pressures affecting the firm, the industry, and the entire economy; the attitudes of the public; and the provisions of the law. With all its endless variety, the environment affects the union in three essential ways.

To begin with, the environment acts upon the members and shapes their outlook, their expectations, and their preferences. For example, the openness of the society and the lack of class divisions have had much to do with the unwillingness of union members to support a labor party. The educational system and the gradual evolution of community values have produced large changes in the attitudes of union members toward the Negro. The restless disaffection of the young pervades the unions as it does so many other institutions. Advertising and the widespread emphasis on material success inflate the demands that members make in collective negotiations. As a general rule, influences of this sort play their most vital role in helping to determine union goals.

The environment also affects the methods unions can use to achieve their goals and the degree of success that they will achieve. Thus, the creation of vast conglomerate firms has impelled many different unions to join in "coalition bargaining" to increase their bargaining power. In turn, the effectiveness of this strategy will be conditioned by the financial health and competitive position of the firm and its separate units, as well as by conditions in the economy as a whole. In similar fashion, labor's success in organizing mass-production industries in the 30s (after repeated failures in the past) was greatly helped by such factors as the impact of the Depression, the personnel policies of the firms involved, and the newly enacted federal law to protect union organization. Conversely, the inability of many of the same labor officials to organize the South ten years later was due to another set of social and community pressures that hampered the organizer

and dulled the incentive of employees to join a union.

The environment affects the union movement in still another way by helping to shape the quality of labor leadership. The political traditions and the laws of this country insure that union leaders will be chosen by the members. This policy in turn implies that the leaders will be chosen from the ranks and will be generally representative of the membership. At the same time, the educational system, the programs of scholarships and student aid, the emphasis on social mobility, and the willingness to recognize talent whenever it appears, all create opportunities through which promising individuals can escape the shop floor and the assembly line from which tomorrow's labor leaders must be drawn. The low prestige that society accords to union leaders also helps to insure that many employees will take advantage of these opportunities instead of seeking a union post. In this way, environmental forces diminish the pool of talent available for union office.

THE LIMITS OF LEADERSHIP

What freedom of action remains to the union leader caught between the pressures of the environment and the demands of the rank and file? To begin with, he can experiment and innovate, at least on a modest scale. He may not always be able to launch new programs costing large sums nor will he be quick to experiment at the risk of failing to meet the critical demands imposed by his members. Moreover, his innovations will eventually have to win acceptance by the rank and file in order to survive and flourish. Nevertheless, the activities and achievements of the union will ultimately reflect the capacity of its officials to offer up new goals, new programs, and new benefits for the members to consider.

Union leaders can also do something to alter the opinions of the members and affect their attitudes toward the goals and policies of the organization. On specific trade-union issues—to accept or reject the contract; to strike or not to strike—the leader may have great influence, especially if he is popular and without vocal opposition. On more general matters of value, social attitude, and political choice, his opportunities for exerting influence may be sufficient to deserve attention, but they are not large. Where these issues are concerned, it is normally too difficult to reach the members, too hard to engage their attention seriously, too arduous to overcome all the competing messages reaching them through other media and other sources.

Finally, and perhaps most important, the leader can have the imagination to conceive of new strategies and new opportunities in the environment to help the union make fresh progress toward its goals. This capacity is partly a matter of knowing the environment well, but it is ultimately dependent on the intuition, the judgment, and the imagination of the leader. It is this type of influence and power that John L. Lewis demonstrated so tellingly in perceiving that the time was ripe for massive organizing in the 30s.

It is very hard to guess how much an able, imaginative leader could accomplish to make progress toward union goals. Nevertheless, it is safe to say that the process of selecting union officials—while admirably suited for certain purposes—is not likely to produce an unusual number of leaders with exceptional vision or imagination. Indeed, one would frankly expect less talent of this sort in unions than in most other major institutions. In addition, many of the forces that press upon the labor leader are strong indeed and leave him with much less freedom of action than many critics seem to recognize. For example, those who exhort the unions to exercise wage restraint, eliminate featherbedding, or refrain from strikes seem greatly to underestimate the pressures from the members. Although most union leaders have a degree of influence over the policies of their organizations, few would stay in office very long if they slighted their members' concern for safeguards against the loss of work or ignored their desire to seek pay raises—and go on strike if need be—to keep pace with wage and price increases they see occurring all around them.

One can readily sympathize with the visions of other critics who deplore the failure of union leaders to seize opportunities to turn their talents to new fields: organizing the poor, mobilizing the members to fight for consumer protection, and taking the lead in searching for a more meaningful life for workers caught between their television set and the tedium of a semiskilled, repetitive job. In one sense, unions seem naturally suited to such tasks in view of their experience in organizing mass movements, their large memberships, and their commitment to high social purposes. Yet, critics invariably overlook the enormous difficulties involved; the members' lack of interest in undertaking ventures outside the traditional union domain, their unwillingness to see their dues expended for such purposes, the shortages of talented leadership in labor's ranks, and the pressures on existing leaders, whose time and energy are already stretched thin attending to conventional union tasks. In the face of such limitations, even a leader as gifted and energetic as Walter Reuther has been unable to make noteworthy progress in organizing the poor, expanding union membership, altering Detroit politics, or expanding the skilled job opportunities for Negro members. By underestimating these problems, liberal critics have succeeded—after two decades of biting prose—in accomplishing virtually nothing except to antagonize the union leadership.

THE CRITIC'S ROLE

This sketch of union behavior has clear implications for the critic's role in assessing social institutions. In reality, union members, leaders, subordinates, and environmental forces interact in such an intimate way that it is treacherous to single out one set of actors in the drama and heap responsibility upon them. Union behavior must be seen as the product of a complex, interrelated process. In order to be effective and fair, the critic must seek to identify the various centers of initiative throughout this process and suggest the actions that can be taken by each of these groups to make it easier for unions to progress toward desirable goals.

21. Unions and Union Leaders of Their Own Choosing*

Clark Kerr†

A quarter of a century ago in the United States the great issue in industrial relations was "unions of their own choosing." The country was in the depth of a profound depression, and a great ferment was in process. A new orientation of the American economy was in the making—an orientation toward full employment, government-sponsored security for workers and farmers, government regulation of business practices, and the creation of workers' organizations to balance the power of employers in the industrial labor markets of the nation. The American economy, previously largely monistic in the management-labor area, in a few short years became pluralistic. Ranged alongside the power of the private employer was now the power of the state and the power of the union.

As it turned out, this new balance of power made less difference than once supposed, for the employers generally adapted quite well to the new situation and found they could prosper within it; but there was a new environment, largely set by government, and within this new environment the employer faced the union as well as the individual employee.

A quarter of a century later—today—unions are well established and secure in most major industries of the nation. Their members number 18 million. They can close down even the giants of American industry—General Motors and United States Steel. They negotiate 100,000 contracts covering the working rules that guide and govern important aspects of the life of industrial men in nearly every trade and every industry and nearly every town. Income, leisure, job security, retirement, pace of work, job opportunities, discipline

—are all affected by union participation in the rule-making process. And union influence extends outside the industrial government of the nation into its political processes, too. Unions affect the selection and the election of candidates. They are intimately woven into much of our economic and political life.

This quarter century has been a most eventful and crucial period in American economic history. It has seen the great change in the power structure of our economy—from monism to pluralism. It has seen new wealth, new security, new satisfaction for nearly all the people. It has seen the creation of a "modern capitalism" which can stand as a vital alternative in the great ideological, economic, scientific, and military contest that enthralls and engulfs the world—an alternative that has amply produced both goods and freedom. These developments in the United States have resulted in an acceptance of the surrounding society by its members which can hardly be matched in our earlier history or elsewhere in the world at any time in history. It is a society with consensus.

This consensus and the great achievements of the recent period should not obscure the fact that our society is still changing. Industrialization is new to the United States and to the world. The final form of the industrial society cannot yet be clearly seen. In particular, the ultimate adjustments between institutional power and individual choice within the state, the private economic organization, and the economic process (such as the labor market) are not yet settled and, of course, may never be in any final way. Many large and open—and even more small and silent—battles will be waged in the process of adjustment. Nor should this consensus and these achievements obscure the fact that all is not for the best even in "the best of all possible worlds." There are no

* From Center for the Study of Democratic Institutions of the Fund for the Republic (1958).

† Professor, University of California.

really dramatic internal crusades today either in existence or needed; but there are some reforms which are both needed and in the making. This discussion relates to one of them.

NEEDS FOR LABOR SELF-SCRUTINY

American government has been under critical scrutiny almost since the founding of the nation. American industry was subjected to an intensive national review, particularly in the 1930s. It had become big and powerful and sometimes corrupt. The great depression was laid at its doorstep, since it was the most prominent doorstep around at the time. American unions are today undergoing similar scrutiny. They, in turn, have become big and powerful and sometimes corrupt.

Now it is said by some that only the unions can scrutinize themselves—that it is not the proper business of anybody else. They are private, voluntary associations. The corporations said this once also and they were scrutinized; and the unions will be too. Unions are private associations but their actions are clothed with the public interest, for they affect the levels of wages and prices, the access of individuals to jobs, the volume and continuity of production, and many other important aspects of society. Also, they are seldom really voluntary. Even in the absence of the closed or union shop, social pressure often assures membership.

At the same time, along with external efforts, the unions should scrutinize themselves, and the more effectively they undertake this scrutiny (and they are doing surprisingly well) the less need there is for external scrutiny and external reform. Our pluralistic system has three main organized elements: state, corporation, and union. It is essential that each element function effectively and consequently that each element be subject to both internal and external criticism.

Several issues involving labor are abroad in the land. Three of them are inherently simple issues confined to specific segments of the labor movement and, beyond that, issues which run also into American life generally. These are corruption, collusion, and violence.

Corruption exists, and it is bad; but right and wrong are quite evident and hardly open to debate. Few unions are involved, and other institutions in society have known and do know it also. Some remedies, including proper accounting procedures, are relatively easy to identify although not always so easy to apply effectively.

Collusion also exists, and it also is bad; but again the nature of virtue is not hard to define, although the line where it ends may be hard to draw in particular cases. (Virtue and this problem of the drawing of lines have met before on other stages.) Relatively few unions are affected and then nearly always jointly with their employers; and collusion, too, accompanies human nature almost throughout the span of social relationships.

Violence also is to be condemned. It has decreased greatly as a union tactic, however, and is subject to control by the many devices civilized man has created to insure law and order.

These are issues, and they will be for a long time; they deserve attention, but they are peripheral to the main contemporary controversy.

CENTRAL ISSUE: UNIONS AND WORKER FREEDOM

The great issue is the impact of the union on the freedom of the worker. This issue is not simple; it is most complex. It is an issue which runs through all or nearly all of the union movement and is central to its very existence. While not unknown as an issue in the spheres of government and the corporation, it is less intensely manifested there at the present time. Our nation has had a long and most successful experience in creating a democratic framework for our government and protecting the liberties of individual citizens. Our corporations are not expected to be run on a democratic basis. They are founded on the model of the individual entrepreneur making his own decisions; seldom do corporations have either a captive labor force or captive consumers, and when they have captive consumers they are usually subject to state control.

The unions are different. They have not had, like our government, a long and successful experience in developing a system of checks and balances, in limiting their sphere of endeavor, in defining and protecting the internal rights of their members. Unlike the corporation, they are founded on the assumption of internal democracy. They are associations of individuals, not collections of capital funds. Moreover, increasingly they have a captive membership. It is usually not possible just to withdraw in protest without penalty, if the member does not like the organization, its leaders, or its policy. We have here most frequently a more or less compulsory organization with substantial impact on the lives of its members.

American unions do make a major overall contribution to a democratic industrial society, and this is the first and also the most important observation to be made about their impact on worker freedom. They usually create a two-party legislative system governing the life of the work place. In their absence, the rules would be set exclusively by the employer. Through the unions, the workers can have a direct impact on the nature of the rules under which they work. Without a union they can also have an impact, by their choice of employers, but this is much less direct. Also, unions usually insist on a grievance mechanism and this brings a judicial process into industrial life which is more impartial than when the employer sits as both prosecutor and judge. Beyond that, they create a new power center which can, if it wishes, stand against the power centers of the state and the corporation, and these latter power centers have gained in their absolute strength in recent years. A rough balance between private and public power centers is the essence of a pluralistic society, and a pluralistic society is the only firm foundation for democracy in an economy based on industrial production.

Thus the unions have generally brought a better legislative and judicial process into industrial life and a better balance among the power groups of society. They have done this without the feared consequences that gave rise to such apprehensions in times just past. It was feared that industrial conflict would tear society apart. In fact, industrial peace is now the commonplace; and, except for the few unions still under Communist domination, American unions most certainly contribute to the social stability and security of our whole system. It was feared that unions would hamper productive efficiency and stifle progress. Undoubtedly many union rules do retard production, but there is no evidence that the overall effect has been anything but relatively minor; and some new methods have been better received because of union consultation than they otherwise would have been in the light of the inherent conservatism of the work place. It was feared that unions might distort inter-industry wage structures and also that their actions would assure wild inflation. In fact, it is one of the wonders of the economic world that unions have had so little effect on wage structures. Their impact on price levels, while open to dispute, has certainly been no more than moderate. Exaggerated fears of costly social conflict, strangled production, and rampant inflation due to unions have proved largely without substance.

But a fear does remain that unions may take too much freedom from the worker; and this fear may not prove so groundless. If they do, they will not be the only institutions in our mass society which have conduced toward conformity. Big unions, big corporations, big government, and small individuals seem to be the order of the day.

Unions almost of necessity reduce the freedom of the worker in some respects. If freedom is defined as the absence of external restraint, then unions reduce freedom, for they restrain the worker in many ways. They help to establish formal wage structures, seniority rosters, work schedules, pace of output, and the pattern of occupational opportunities, all of which limit his freedom of choice. They decide when he shall strike and not strike. They are—and this is one of the essentials to an understanding of unionism—disciplinary agents within society. They add to the total network of discipline already surrounding the workers through the practices and rules of the employer. They too insist upon order and obedience—inherent in their very existence. Two bosses now grow where only one grew before.[1]

Some loss of freedom, however, is inevitable in an effective industrial system. It will occur, more or less, whether the system is run by the employers alone, by the state alone, or even by the unions alone. Industrial society requires many rules and reasonable conformity to these rules. There must be a wage structure, a work schedule, and so forth, no matter who operates the system. This loss of freedom is one of the prices paid by man for the many benefits in income and leisure that can flow from industrial society. The challenge is that this price not be any higher than necessary.

The issue lies in the "more or less." The loss of freedom of the industrial worker will be substantial, as compared with the self-employed farmer or craftsman, but it may be less rather than more; and unions can make it both less or more.

UNION DEMOCRACY: DIFFICULTIES, DETRIMENTS, AND VIRTUES

Before turning to how the reduction of freedom may be less rather than more, three introductory observations will be made.

1. Democracy in unions is inherently difficult to achieve. A union is variously expected to be at one and the same time, as Muste[2] so well pointed

---

[1] This is not to suggest that it is not often and perhaps almost universally better to have two bosses than one, for the union boss may help liberate the worker from the unilateral rule of the employer boss; but the worker is still subject to a web of rules, and this web tends to be more thickly woven as a result of the presence of the union.

[2] A. J. Muste, "Factional Fights in Trade Unions," in *American Labor Dynamics* (New York: Harcourt Brace, 1928).

out long ago, an army, a business, and a town meeting. Unions have usually ended up by being a business, serving the members but sometimes with little more influence over the conduct of the business by the members than stockholders have over a corporation. They have sometimes ended up as an army and have justified it, as Lloyd Fisher once remarked, just as the Communists have tried to justify their "people's democracy," by reference to "capitalist encirclement." They have almost never ended up as a town meeting. The pull is most insistently toward being a "business."

2. A good deal more democracy exists in unions than these comments and most external observations would indicate. The national unions are the most visible entities, and they are usually the least subject to democratic pressures. But at the local level, in many unions, there are contested elections, substantial turnover of officers, and face-to-face relations between members and leaders, and there is the least entrenched bureaucracy. Particularly at the shop level, between shop stewards and workers, is there a responsive relationship. To the workers, the local level is usually the most important. That is where he lives and where his grievances are handled.

3. It is sometimes argued that unions need not or even should not be democratic. Different reasons are given for this conclusion. One line of argument is that unions have become largely functionless organizations, and nobody really cares whether they are democratic or not. The state guarantees full employment and social security, and the employer has been seduced by human relations. Consequently, the worker has a job—often paid above the contract rate—a pension, and also a friend, perhaps even a psychiatrist; and there is nothing for the union to do. Or, it is sometimes said, unions have become quasi-governmental bureaus. They help set minimum wages and schedules of hours and process grievances, as government bureaus sometimes do both here and abroad. Their work is largely routine and best handled in good bureaucratic fashion; and so again why worry about democracy? Occasionally, it is also noted that unions function best if they are removed from the pressures of democratic life. They must respond to many pressures, not those of the membership alone but also the needs of the industry, the welfare of society, the concerns of other unions. They should take a longer view of events than the current membership is likely to take, for they are organizations with a continuing life. They will be more widely responsible to society and more businesslike in their operations

if they are not subject to the uncertainties of active democratic participation. It is concluded that democracy causes internal and external strife and irresponsibility.

Each of these reasons has some point to it. Unions perform less of a function than two decades ago; their work has become more routine with pattern-following and grievance precedents; and internal democracy can cause external trouble, particularly for employers.

But the case for democracy can still be persuasive. If democracy is a superior form of government, as most of us would insist, it should be preferred in practice wherever it is possible. Also, the workers can have a more effective voice in industry if they have an effective voice in their unions; and they are more likely to be satisfied with society if they have a sense of participation. Additionally, if the unions lose responsiveness to worker interests, an opportunity is created for other organized elements more politically motivated to move in to represent these interests, as has happened in certain European countries.

ONE-PARTY GOVERNMENT—THE UNION CASE

The overwhelming majority of all the organizations of man throughout history have been ruled by one-party governments. Most of the time in most parts of the world all organizations have been under one-party rule. In certain parts of the world at certain times in history there have been a few two-party (or multi-party) organizations; but one-party rule is the standard and well nigh universal case. The trade union is no exception. The International Typographical Union in the United States is the single deviant specimen on a national level.

Even in the democratic United States the corporation, the political party, the fraternal order, the religious denomination, the farm organization, the welfare group, the student government are all one-party organizations. Only in the public area, where it is by all odds the most essential, do we have two-party government.

The neglect of the one-party model of government, in the light of its great significance, is most astounding. The rare instances of two-party and multi-party government have attracted most of the study. Certain it is that two-party government, as Lipset[3] has so persuasively argued, does have much to recommend it. It provides criticism of

---

[3] S. M. Lipset, M. Trow, and J. Coleman, *Union Democracy* (Glencoe, Ill.: Free Press, 1956).

the existing government, makes ready an alternative government if the members want it, reduces apathy, and does much else of value. But most men all of the time—and all men some of the time—function in one-party social organizations, as do union members.

Why are unions one-party governments? The answers are several. Partly, it is the requirement of unity in the face of external conflict. Partly, it is the control exercised by the leaders over the mechanism of the organization. But the root of the problem is much deeper. It goes beyond the fear of the enemy and the desire of the leaders. It is that there are no continuing conflicts except over ideology, and ideological conflicts tend to split unions rather than to create two-party systems within them. Witness the separate unions in several European countries and the split-off of Communist unions in the United States. Ideology aside, issues over wage increases, the handling of grievances, and so forth may lead to factions and leadership rivalry but not to two-party systems on a continuing basis.

So unions are one-party governments. Does this mean that they are inevitably "undemocratic?" If only two-party systems are really democratic, then the answer is obviously in the affirmative. But if organizations where the supreme power is retained by the members and which are reasonably responsive[4] to membership desires may be called "democratic," even in the absence of a two-party system, then unions may be and many are "democratic."

---

[4] There are those, of course, who would argue that the proper test of an organization is not the degree of responsiveness to the needs of those involved but rather the degree to which the persons involved actually and directly participate in the decision-making process. For them, only town meeting democracy is fully satisfactory; and, given the nature of industrial society, their test can be met by very few consequential organizations. It should be noted that "responsiveness" is not only a different test from "participation" but is also different from the test of "performance." "Performance," in the sense of "bringing home the bacon," may be quite exceptional without, at the same time, having any or at least much connection with "responsiveness." "Performance" refers to results; "responsiveness" to the processes which connect leadership behavior with membership desires. Performance, however, will usually be superior in the long run where responsiveness exists; and this is one of the basic tenets of democratic thought. And perhaps it should also be noted that active participation, where it is possible, is often an effective means of assuring responsiveness but is by no means a guarantee of such responsiveness—in fact, it can serve as a technique of control. The view taken here is that performance alone is not enough and that participation, as through a two-party system, is more than can be expected under the circumstances and consequently, that the appropriate test is responsiveness. Responsiveness rests on a minimum degree of participation and will yield, usually, a reasonable measure of performance.

HISTORICAL PRESSURES ON UNION GOVERNMENT

There are dangers in any one-party government,[5] but the one-party government may serve its members well. It is most likely to do so in the long run, however, if it is under the proper pressure. Traditionally, this pressure on trade union government in the United States has come from four sources; all of them, unfortunately, now largely of historical importance only. In the passing of these four sources of pressure lies much of our current problem.

1. When union membership was more voluntary, leaders had to be responsive to the workers to find and retain members, and this was an effective check on authority. As noted earlier, union membership is now—one way or another—often compulsory, the law notwithstanding; and it is likely to become more so. Union security—with all its other advantages—and leadership responsiveness tend to move in somewhat opposite directions. The voluntary sale and the forced sale lead to different behavior in any walk of life. This is not to support voluntary membership through the compulsion of the state, for it seems neither possible in many situations nor, on balance, wise.

2. When dual unionism, now largely a relic of the past, was an active force, it had somewhat the same impact as voluntary membership. Not individuals but groups of people could and did shift allegiance, and this acted as a check and balance. The idea of one union in one jurisdiction, however, is so firmly bedded in American union philosophy that dual unionism can exist only sporadically and temporarily.

3. The more or less permanent faction, stopping short of a second party but hovering in the wings ready to rush out on any inappropriate occasion, was a check on the leadership in many unions. The old-line Socialists served this function for many, many years, but the New Deal and time brought their demise. The Catholic faction continues in a few unions but usually only in those under left-wing control; otherwise there is little basis for a Catholic faction. There are few permanent factions today and fewer still in prospect.

4. The employer, particularly the recalcitrant employer, has historically been a check and balance on the union leadership. We have here two organizations—the company and the union—appealing to the same constituency. If they are in

---

[5] This is true particularly if there is no judicial protection against the use of arbitrary power, as is often the case. Due process can be as important as democratic assent to the leadership.

conflict, each will criticize the other and may even stand ready to attempt to destroy the other. But the day of fighting the unions is largely past, at least under conditions of full employment. The separation of interests between the leaders of the two organizations is decaying. Industrial peace pays. Consequently, company pressure on most unions has been greatly reduced or has even totally disappeared.

NEW ELEMENTS IN
UNION DEMOCRACY

With union membership increasingly compulsory, dual unionism declining, the permanent faction disappearing, and company opposition more rare, is there any hope for "democracy" or leadership responsiveness to membership interests in trade unions? There still is, for there are substitutes for these historical pressures. Six such possibilities will be suggested, with particular emphasis on the sixth.

1. Membership Interest. Union memberships are traditionally apathetic except in some crisis; and very little can be done about it. Compulsory strike votes proved a farce in World War II, and most bargaining issues cannot properly be put to membership vote. But some experiments might be undertaken with polling of membership opinion and with advisory referenda, and even the use of television as a means for leaders to reach members (since members seldom will come to meetings) might be profitable.

2. "Professional" Leaders. Much is written currently about management as a profession. Perhaps union leaders might also become professional in the sense that they might be specifically trained for their jobs and might develop an "ethic" to guide their conduct—an ethic which sets boundaries to their behavior.[6]

3. A New Faith for the Union Movement. In unions where the last vestiges of active democracy disappeared long ago, certain leaders today still serve their members well because of their adherence to the "old faith" of the union movement. But the "old faith" attracts few new adherents. It was a fighting faith growing out of evil conditions for the workers and union-busting by the employers. The conditions which gave rise to it no longer exist in the United States. They do continue to a degree even today in England and Germany, and there the "old faith" still sets standards for union

leaders. The social reformer holds himself and is held by his environment to a higher code of conduct than the business leader of the business union who quickly takes on the coloration of the industry with which he deals. If its ethics are high, his will be also; if they are low, so are his. The business union is a segment of the business.

What might this new faith be? It cannot be either "more, more, more, and now" or a vision of class conflict. It might be, as suggested later, the development of the unions as a liberating force in industrial society; and there might be a consequent integration of the union leader more into the intellectual and less into the business community.

4. Local Autonomy. Local unions, by their inherent nature, clearly can provide more opportunities than can national unions for democratic participation by the members. Consequently, the more autonomy there is at the local level, the greater the democratic life on the union movement is likely to be. The big drop in democratic participation comes in the move from the one plant to the multi-plant local or the district union. In the one plant, rival leaders can become known and be effective, issues can be discussed on a face-to-face basis, and democracy can be effective.[7] The multi-plant unit serves the interests of the entrenched leadership in a most emphatic way. The one-plant local with real authority is the most democratic entity in the trade union movement. Considerable constitutional reform in most unions would be prerequisite to effective single-plant locals. Among other things, the institution of the "receivership" by regional and national officials would need to be curtailed.

5. Union Decertification. It is certainly desirable to continue some mechanism through which members can exercise an option in favor of another or no union at all. Such an option will rarely be employed, but it should be available. If it is available and is used occasionally, it can act as a minor check and balance on union leadership.

6. Discharge through Rebellion. The two-party system within unions, as we have seen, is an historical oddity. The regularly contested election is a rarity. Yet union officials do get changed other than as a result of death or retirement. Union officials are, in effect, "hired" by the membership for the duration of their good behavior as tested imprecisely by the membership. The trouble comes when they need to be "fired." The mechanism then is a contested election in which the old

---

[6] They might, like city managers, for example, be specifically trained for their jobs and responsible to an elected governing board.

[7] In several European countries it is the local works council, with substantial powers, which arouses worker interest and participation.

leader is voted out of office. For such a contested election to take place two prerequisites are necessary: It must be possible for a faction to form and for its members to be reasonably free from retaliation through the operation of an impartial judicial process; and there must be secret elections at appropriate intervals. Other actors must be allowed to stand in the wings and be permitted to move on stage when the audience calls them. The dissatisfied individual and the antagonistic faction must be given an opportunity.

The term "competitive discharge" might be used in the sense that the leader is subject to constant evaluation by the members and is also subject to discharge through the process of electing a competitor who is free to appear when the conditions warrant.[8] In the two-party system, the question is as to the better person; in the "competitive discharge" case, it is whether the incumbent should be fired or not.[9] Deposed union leaders usually feel—and they are correct in their feeling—that they have been fired, not that they have been defeated. Among other things, they almost never seek election again, once having been discharged. They are like the old bull in the buffalo herd brought to his knees by the young challenger.

If trade union democracy is defined as a system of government where the supreme power is largely retained by the members and can be exercised by them in an emergency at any and all levels, then the effective right of competitive discharge, by itself, is a sufficient basis for trade union democracy. The essential feature of a trade union constitution is whether it guarantees this right of competitive discharge. This is the most we can reasonably expect, and it is also probably enough.

THE NEW INDUSTRIAL FREEDOM?

The central issue presented earlier was the impact of unionism on worker freedom. This issue goes beyond the internal relationship of leader to member which we have just been discussing, to the rules the union makes or helps to make affecting the life of the worker as worker and to the span of activity of the union.

Industrial society, as we have noted, requires a great web of rules to bind people together and to secure their cooperative performance within an extraordinarily complex and interrelated productive mechanism. And the burden of these rules on the individual can vary quite substantially. It can be comparatively heavy or comparatively light.

For it to be comparatively light, two principles are basic. First, the rules should provide the maximum power of individual choice consistent with efficient production; the greatest possible provision to move freely within limits set by the imperatives of industrial society itself.

Second, each institution should be narrowly oriented toward its primary function, whether production of goods, representation of economic interest, or salvation of souls. The individual will have greater freedom if the span of control of each institution with which he is associated is relatively narrow. The institution which encompasses the totality of the life of the individual can subject him to its power and control in a way no limited-function institution can.

The power to do as one pleases, which is the essence of freedom, rests on rules with broad limits and institutions with narrow limits. One of the great and continuing—and even eternal—challenges of industrial society is how to structure it to maximize not only the wealth of the world but also the freedom of man.

These general principles apply also to unions. The rules they make or join in making can channel a great deal of the occupational life of an individual. To begin with, all unions should be open unions—open to everyone without discrimination except on the grounds of ability to perform the work. In addition, the rules governing a man's working life should give him maximum freedom of choice inside the union. Illustrations from three important areas will indicate the possibilities.

1. Seniority rights are important in almost all areas of human relationships. They are the basis for settling many problems; but they can be a prison too. Some unions allow the transfer of

---

[8] In one major Icelandic union, for example, this principle is explicitly recognized rather than being camouflaged. The incumbent officers are automatically re-elected at each "contract reopening period" (if the stated election time may be so designated) unless a certain number of members petition for an opposition slate on the ballot, in which event a contested election is conducted. More common practice in the United States is to go through the formality of an election each time, but usually there is opposition only if the incumbent is in an unfavorable position.

[9] Such question is most likely to be raised in an urgent fashion at the time of a "crisis" (a strike, an attack by a rival union, an unsuccessful wage negotiation, the disclosure of misuse of funds, etc.). Such crises hold within themselves the possibilities of constructive democratic action, if a minimum of democratic machinery is available; otherwise an open revolt, usually taking the form of the organization of a rival union, is the only alternative and a very difficult one. Unfortunately, under the "competitive discharge" system an ineffective leader can retain his position much longer (i.e., until a crisis creates the condition for his downfall) than he could under the competitive election system. The machinery which is used to handle the "competitive discharge" can, of course, also be employed to handle the problem of replacement after the death of a leader.

seniority rights from one place of employment to another, or permit some percentage of positions, in one case every fourth position, to be filled outside of local seniority lists. Such arrangements increase the mobility opportunities of workers.

2. Private pension plans often have no vesting provisions, and this tends to tie the worker for life to a single place of employment. His status becomes not unlike that of the serf on the manor tied to his lord, who in our case may be plural—the company and the union. Reasonable vesting rights aid the mobility and thus the freedom of workers.

3. Hours of work must be scheduled, but these schedules can provide for local option by individual groups of workers instead of a uniform national schedule. (A local group may prefer one holiday to another or longer vacations and as a consequence longer hours per week.)

They can provide some part-time jobs for the aged or for women or for men who want a second job. Developing an appropriate balance between the time spent on earning income and time spent on leisure is an important aspect of welfare in any society, and it can best be done on an individual basis. The opportunities for experiment in this area are great.

A union, like many another institution, often seeks to extend its sphere of activity unit it covers more and more of the life of its members, not only as workers but also as consumers and citizens. If the limited-function corporation and the limited-function state and the limited-function church are desirable, so also is the limited-function union. Union paternalism (housing projects, vacation resorts, recreation facilities) has little more to recommend it than employer paternalism. Union political activity, while inevitable and often desirable, should not infringe on the rights of the member as citizen.[10] He should not be required to support, financially or otherwise, a political party or candidate not of his own choice. The union should find its primary function in relating to the worker as worker, not also as consumer and as citizen.

Trade unions have historically been fighting organizations. They have emphasized unity within their own circles and the "standard rate" in the labor market. But now they are established, secure, and accepted. Full employment in the econ-

omy and grievance machinery in the plant give the individual worker a status largely unknown 25 years ago. The union attitude of limited class warfare directed at the surrounding society and of discipline directed at the individual member no longer is required by the new situation.

Might the unions turn their attention from the old slogans and the old dogmas, to undertake a new orientation toward their role in industrial society? This new role might well be that of a liberating force in industrial society, of a force helping to structure industrialization to meet the desires of the single individual as well as the organized group. This would be an historic mission and a mission which employers might well join for they too have pressed for conformity and against individuality among the workers.

THE WORKER, THE UNION, AND THE STATE

The title of this paper suggests that national policy might move from the "unions of their own choosing" of the 1930s to "union leaders of their own choosing" and even, to a degree, to "union rules of their own choosing." But how is this to be accomplished? Action by the unions themselves would be most desirable, and there has been a surprising amount of it during the past year. Experience here and abroad, however, suggests it will not be sufficient and that behind the good intentions of most union leaders will need to stand the power of the law, as in the case of corporations in the past.

This is a troublesome issue. The pluralist will defend the private association from the control of the state. The individual, however, also needs defense against the control of the private government of the trade union, and ultimately this can be guaranteed only by the state. If the state is to interfere in the internal life of trade unions—and it does so quite significantly already—then it is important that this interference be wisely conceived, for the power to control is the power to destroy. Unions should in no way be destroyed as independent power centers. Clyde Summers has recently suggested[11] four guide lines for such interference, and each one seems worthy of consideration: It should be minimal; it should be segregated from laws on other matters; it should encourage responsible self-regulation by the unions; and it should be enforceable.

---

[10] The traditional union political activities in the United States, lobbying in regard to legislation affecting unions and workers as workers and distributing informational data on the records of candidates in the same areas, do not interfere with the rights of the union member as a citizen. Compulsory political levies and political strikes do interfere with these rights and also with the proper functioning of a democratic society.

[11] "Legislating Union Democracy," paper presented to annual meeting of the Industrial Relations Research Association, September 1957 (to be published in the *Proceedings*).

In this discussion of the impact of unions on the freedom of workers, six aspects of the problem were particularly emphasized: local union autonomy, a new faith for the union movement, secret elections of officers, independent judicial processes, permissive rules on entry to the union and on movement within industry, and narrow limits to union functions.

Four of these areas may lend themselves properly to legislation:

1. In Australia,[12] union members can, under certain circumstances, ask the state for the conduct of secret elections of officers.

2. Again in Australia and to an increasing extent in the United States, union members can appeal to the courts for protection against retaliation for internal political dissent. In this connection the private external review boards of the Upholsterer's Union and the United Automobile Workers are a most interesting device, paralleling private arbitration of grievances against companies.[13]

3. Protection from discrimination in getting

---

[12] See L. S. Merrifield, "Regulation of Union Elections in Australia," *Industrial and Labor Relations Review*, January 1957.

[13] The encouragement of such private judicial processes better fits a pluralistic society with its independent power centers than the institution of a public labor court approach, as in Germany.

into a union, as well as in getting a job, is already provided in some states. Such provisions call for the open union instead of the open shop.

4. Prohibition of compulsory political contributions is now provided in both the United States and Great Britain.

Adequate legislation in these four areas would assure a reasonable degree of democracy and of individual freedom. Beyond what the law might require, many unions have provided and may provide considerably more democratic life and individual liberty. The Ethical Practices Committee of the AFL-CIO has made a substantial contribution in these directions.

The trade unions, as noted at the start, are going through a period of crisis. This crisis originates as much from self-examination by labor leaders as from the more obvious external criticisms. Out of this crisis may well come more representative government within unions and more rights for the individual worker. Since they are an important element in our pluralistic society, the effective functioning of the trade unions is contributive to the national welfare. As an element of a democratic society, they should be responsive to their members. As an element of a society founded on the significance of the individual, they should contribute to his freedom. "More, more, more, and now" is no longer enough.

22. Communism and Trade Unionism: An Exchange*

A. ANTI-COMMUNISM AND LABOR HISTORY

James R. Prickett†

Many labor economists, historians, and political scientists who have written about Communists in the labor movement have made two assumptions. First, they have assumed that Communists were unique among workers, union officials, and labor organizers in that they were not interested in building strong unions which could win better working conditions and higher wages for themselves and other workers. It has even been argued that "once taken over by the Communists, a trade union ceases to be a trade union, for all that it may retain the charter and outward appearance of a trade union."[1] Second, they have assumed that whatever influence individual Communists or the Communist movement attained in the labor movement must have been due to deception and manipulation. These two assumptions have led to the conclusion that the expulsion of Communists from the Congress of Industrial Organizations (CIO) returned the CIO to the path of genuine trade unionism and that the anti-Communist victories in various CIO affiliates restored democratic unionism to a grateful membership.

Actually, the unions led or influenced by Communists were, if anything, more democratic than the strongly anti-Communist unions. Particularly striking, as the discussion of the National Maritime Union later in this article reveals, was the frequent decline in union democracy when an anti-Communist administration defeated a pro-Communist

one. Anti-Communist scholars—and this is the major point of this paper—have been so constrained by their basic anti-Communist framework that they have been unable to concede, much less explain, this decline in union democracy. In this note, I would like to explore several selected issues dealing with the treatment of Communists in the labor history literature.

Doublethink

Perhaps the key element of the anti-Communist framework is the pervasive and curious vocabulary in which commonplace activities engaged in by all political individuals, Communist and non-Communist alike, are described in quite different terms. For example, non-Communists win union elections, but Communists "capture" a union. Non-Communists join unions; Communists "infiltrate" or "invade" them.[2] A non-Communist states his or her position; a Communist "peddles the straight party line."[3] Non-Communists influence

* Reprinted with permission from *Industrial Relations,* Vol. 13, No. 3, October 1974, pp. 219–43.

† Doctoral candidate in History, University of California, Los Angeles.

[1] Max M. Kampelman, *The Communist Party vs. the CIO: A Study in Power Politics* (New York: Praeger, 1957), p. 249.

[2] Most readers will be familiar with this sort of rhetoric, but one example will be given for those who are not. On three pages of Taft's essay on "Radicalism in American Labor," the word "capture" appears five times. In the same essay, Taft indicates that Communists can invade organizations to which they already belong: "The Communists operating through the Trade Union Educational League planned to invade all unions, but the affiliation of their adherents determined which unions were to feel the brunt of the pressure." Philip Taft, *The Structure and Government of Labor Unions* (Cambridge: Harvard University Press, 1954), pp. 5, 8–9, 10–11.

[3] David Shannon wrote that "the well known radio news commentator Johannes Steel . . . was invited to speak at IWO conventions, where he peddled the straight party line." Shannon would never say that anyone peddled the Democratic Party line or the liberal line; this rhetoric is reserved for those branded as Communists. David A. Shannon, *The Decline of American Communism: A History of the Communist Party of the United States since 1945* (New York: Harcourt-Brace, 1959), pp. 115–16.

or lead groups; Communists dominate them.[4] A non-Communist political party passes resolutions or makes decisions, but a Communist party invariably issues "directives."[5] One sentence, taken virtually at random from an anti-Communist essay, employs several of these themes: "In 1935, according to a variety of witnesses, the party dispatched an agent named Jeff Kibre to organize the infiltration of the talent and technical unions."[6] The key phrase of the sentence is, of course, "the party dispatched," which conveys the image of the Communist Party as a huge machine in which human beings are processed, but each phrase conveys a distinct anti-Communist image.[7]

When Communists perform good, constructive, trade union work, it is simply assumed that this work is little more than a camouflage for other, less admirable, purposes. As Jensen has argued:

They [the Communists] often pushed grievances energetically to foster the belief that collective bargaining and the workers' interests were their chief . . . objectives. The militant emphasis upon collective bargaining was a camouflage for gaining freedom to pursue other objectives as it suited them. A penetrating look reveals that control of the organization . . .

was their primary goal. . . . Policy formation was, of course, not enough. The union had to be built. What better way to achieve control than to build local unions and hand-pick and control the local officers?[8]

There is, of course, no way to empirically test Jensen's argument, since the actual behavior of Communists is seen as nothing but camouflage hiding their real (and assumed) objectives. In Jensen's view, a Communist organizer who spent several years organizing workers in a basic industry, risking, as many did, physical assault and even death, could be shown to have been uninterested in organizing workers if he so much as made a single speech at a union meeting in support of any one of the positions of the Communist Party.

Criticisms of Communists

When stated explicitly, many criticisms of the Communists appear ludicrous or vicious, or both. The preoccupation of southern racists with possible interracial sex in the Communist movement is well known. Less well known, perhaps, is the fascination the topic holds for northern social scientists. Using a somewhat subtler style, Glazer explored a favorite theme of southern conservatives: "In the party, Negro members were treated with more than equality, and white female party members went out of their way to demonstrate how serious Communists were in eliminating all social barriers between the two races."[9] Communists are pictured as moral monsters who are never quite so happy as when reading about the lynching of a black man. As Record put it, "What more welcome event could occur for such [Communist] propagandists than a lynching in Georgia, legal or otherwise?"[10] A rather common assumption appears to be that it is perfectly all right to destroy a movement or an organization in order to rid it of Communists:

Today this union [the International Ladies Garment Workers' Union] is safe from Communist dis-

[4] In one paragraph, Taft uses the phrase "Communist domination" four times. Taft, Structure and Government, p. 14. Incidentally, the phrase "Communist domination" appears 12 times in the essay, while the term "Communist-led" never appears.

[5] Jack Barbash, The Practice of Unionism (New York: Harper and Brothers, 1956), p. 324.

[6] John Hutchinson, "Trade Unionism and the Communists: American and International Experiences," in William Peterson, ed., The Realities of World Communism (Englewood Cliffs, N.J.: Prentice-Hall, 1963), p. 171.

[7] This sentence deserves a close examination:
"In 1935." This phrase appears reasonably straightforward, although it has, as we shall see, some anti-Communist overtones.
"according to a variety of witnesses." The term "witnesses" is chosen rather than "sources" to convey the image of a criminal court proceeding. Note also that the witnesses are not identified.
"the Party dispatched." As noted above, this portrays the Party as a vast machine in which individual people are mere parts to be processed and dispatched. It implies, of course, that the man being "dispatched" had no part in the decision.
"an agent named Jeff Kibre." If Kibre had belonged to any other political group, he would be called an organizer rather than an agent. Actually, Kibre had been in Hollywood since the late 20s. Moreover, he did not plan to bring Communists into the unions but to win those already in the unions to aspects of the Communist program.
"to organize the infiltration of the talent and technical unions." The key word here is infiltration: a Communist, no matter where he or she comes from, is always an infiltrator. Kibre had been in Hollywood since the late 20s. Moreover, he did not plan to bring Communists into the unions but to win those already in the unions to aspects of the Communist program.
This brings us back to "in 1935." Since Kibre had been in Hollywood prior to 1935, the phrase "in 1935" coupled with "the Party dispatched" is also anti-Communist.

[8] Vernon H. Jensen, Nonferrous Metals Industry Unionism, 1932–1954: A Study of Leadership Controversy (Ithaca: New York State School of Industrial and Labor Relations, 1954), pp. 296–97.

[9] Nathan Glazer, The Social Basis of American Communism (New York: Harcourt, Brace and World, 1961), p. 171. Glazer continued in the next sentence: "The slightest hesitation in social relations with Negro party members, and indeed, some felt, in sexual relations, made a member suspect, and might lead to denunciation." The notion (no documentation is given, incidentally) that the Communist Party forced white women to sleep with black men (or any woman with any man) is sexist as well as racist and anti-Communist.

[10] Wilson Record, The Negro and the Communist Party (New York: Atheneum, 1951, 1971), p. 259.

ruption. The issue was fought through to a finish, mostly because its outstanding leaders had had a long experience in appraising and dealing with factional feuds and were quick to recognize the menacing proportions of Bolshevism. . . . *And though after the struggle the International was almost gone, what was left of it was healthy and progressive.*[11]

That the [Communist] party was willing, even during this united front period . . . to infiltrate and even destroy [Negro organizations] was evidenced in the Workers' Councils of the NUL [National Urban League]. Lester Granger later described what happened: "That [Workers' Council] was an ideal organization for the Communists to capture. They grabbed one in New York City, *we had to kill it off. They grabbed another in Pennsylvania, and we had to kill that off.*"[12]

Stolberg and Record are describing, with considerable approval, the destruction of organizations by anti-Communists simply because the Communists have attained positions of leadership in those organizations. Similarly, Jensen, quoted above, described with considerable disapproval the building of a union by the Communists. The sincerity of these scholars is not at issue. There is little doubt that Record believes that black workers in New York were better off without any workers' council than they would be with one led by the Communists, or that Stolberg believes that a weak union of 30,000 members with anti-Communist leadership is preferable to a stronger union of 90,000 workers in which the Communists share leadership.[13] But sincerity is no substitute for judgment. If anti-Communists are unable to be critical of an anti-Communist purge which loses or forces out two-thirds of a union's membership, they are probably unable to be critical of any anti-Communist drive. A closer look at the treatment of the controversies over communism in CIO unions reveals a number of serious distortions growing out of the uncritical support given to anti-Communist unionists.

Walter Reuther and Joseph Curran

In their influential study, *The UAW and Walter Reuther,* Howe and Widick argue that Reuther's victory in the UAW can be traced to the rise of a democratic, rank-and-file movement

"against the evils of Stalinism."[14] To minimize Reuther's consistent support of measures designed to curtail the political rights of Communists within the UAW, Howe and Widick fabricate an incident in which the Communists were more undemocratic than Reuther:

The Stalinists tried to counter Reuther's resolution by introducing a motion to bar Socialists as well as Communists from UAW office, but this silly maneuver failed. Actually, their motion was a stupid blunder. . . . By countering the possible anti-democratic implications of Reuther's proposal with an even less democratic motion, they simply proved that Reuther's characterization of them had been accurate.[15]

The anti-Socialist, anti-Communist resolution to which Howe and Widick refer was actually prepared by a group of unionists opposed to both the Communists and the Socialists, and the Communists spoke against both resolutions at the UAW convention.[16]

Since Reuther was possibly the most liberal and attractive of the anti-Communists within the CIO, it is not hard to understand the support given him by anti-Communist scholars. More difficult to understand is the consistent support of liberal anti-Communists for Joseph Curran's anti-Communist campaign in the National Maritime Union (NMU). A number of studies have painted Curran's victory in the NMU as a victory for rank-and-file democracy which "returned" the union to the membership after it had been "captured" by the Communists.[17] In fact, Curran was more committed to union democracy during his pro-Communist years than he was when he became an anti-Communist union leader. During his cam-

---

[14] Irving Howe and B. J. Widick, *The UAW and Walter Reuther* (New York: Random House, 1949), passim; see also Irving Howe and Lewis Coser, *The American Communist Party: A Critical History* (New York: Praeger, 1962), pp. 458–59.

[15] Howe and Widick, *The UAW,* p. 80.

[16] For a Communist speech against both resolutions, see International Union, United Automobile, Aircraft, and Agricultural Implement Workers of America, *Proceedings of the Sixth Convention* (1941), pp. 702–3; for the speeches of those in favor of the anti-Socialist amendment, see ibid., pp. 692, 700, 703–4, 706.

[17] For studies maintaining this position, see Joseph Goldberg, *The Maritime Story: A Study in Labor-Management Relations* (Cambridge: Harvard University Press, 1960); Jack Barbash, *The Practice of Unionism* (New York: Harper and Brothers, 1956), pp. 361–63; Taft, *Structure and Government,* pp. 198–205; Howe and Coser, *American Communist Party,* pp. 378–79, 459–62; Murray Kempton, *Part of Our Time: Some Ruins and Monuments of the Thirties* (New York: Simon and Schuster, 1955), pp. 86–104; Philip Selznick, *The Organizational Weapon: A Study of Bolshevik Strategy and Tactics* (Glencoe, Ill.: Free Press, 1960), pp. 184–96.

---

[11] Benjamin Stolberg, *Tailor's Progress: The Story of a Famous Union and the Men Who Made It* (Garden City: Doubleday, Doran and Company, 1944), pp. 108–9.

[12] Record, *The Negro,* pp. 147–48.

[13] For membership figures, see *American Labor Year Book* (New York: Labor Research Department, Rand School of Social Science, 1929), p. 115.

paign against the Communists, Curran assured NMU members that he could continue to respect the rights of all union members. In his weekly column in the union newspaper, Curran wrote, "it is not the intention nor the objective of the rank and file committee [the Curran caucus] to eliminate from the Union members because of . . . political belief, although the Communists in the Union attempt to confuse you, the membership, into believing those things."[18] Again and again, Curran insisted, "I am against, and will always be against, any type of repression, discrimination, or any brand of witchhunt."[19]

Only after incomplete election returns indicated that Curran's caucus would win a sweeping victory did he introduce the idea of expulsion: "The [Communist] party officials know that they are on their way . . . out of the Union because of their crimes against the membership."[20] Since NMU workers strongly opposed political expulsions, Curran promised that no one would be tried simply for being a member of the Communist Party. "Only those who violated the constitution" or had committed "crimes against the membership" were to be subjected to expulsion.[21] Yet a complete list of the charges against expelled members reveals that Communism was clearly the key factor. Here are a few sample charges:

Making false statements against the Port of Houston, the Trial Committee, and the membership; bringing the Union into ill repute through his misconduct; belonging to a radical organization that is dedicated not only to overthrow the constitutional rights of this Union, but also the democracy in which we believe.

Distributing subversive literature for the sole and deliberate purpose of creating disruption in the Union hall.

Anti-Union activity; being aboard ship without being cleared through the Union hall, for the purpose of distributing leaflets put out by members of the Communist Party to be used for confusing and disrupting the membership.[22]

Ostensibly nonpolitical charges had political overtones. One seaman was charged with missing a ship and causing it to sail short-handed. The usual penalty for that offense was a $35 fine, but since this was "the same Boehm who was a mem-

ber of the Communist Party," the committee recommended expulsion from the union.[23] By the 1949 NMU convention, an estimated 500 seamen had been expelled from the Union,[24] and several times that number were expelled in the years following the convention. A recent article in *The Nation* described the fate of the latest opposition leader in the NMU, James M. Morrissey:

His program asks for a return of the NMU to democracy through rank and file control, and his openly declared strategy during the summer was that the opposition should organize for the NMU 14th National Convention, then two months away.

On September 14, two weeks before the convention, Morrissey was attacked by three large men with lead pipes who beat him and broke his skull. He had just left NMU National Headquarters, the Joseph Curran building in New York.[25]

Armed with information about the actual aftermath of Curran's victory, one can reread the anti-Communist accounts profitably. The first observation is that nowhere in any of the accounts is there any specific information about undemocratic activity on the part of the Communists. In fact, it rapidly becomes clear that the Communists were consistent democrats. One anti-Communist has suggested that "seldom has so meticulous an adherence to the outer forms of democracy so thoroughly violated its spirit and intent."[26] When Curran was part of a Communist-dominated union leadership, his opponents were able to publish anti-Curran and anti-Communist letters in the *Pilot* (the union newspaper). Opponents of the union leadership and of the Communist Party were not subject to expulsions. The crimes of which the Communists have been accused are fairly trivial: knowing parliamentary procedure, staying "all night" at union meetings, and serving on convention committees.[27] The second observation is that the indifference of anti-Communists to Curran's later tactics contrasts sharply with their indignant response to the Communists.

Socialists versus Communists

Discussions of the conflict between the Socialist leadership and the rank-and-file oppositions in

[18] NMU *Pilot* (New York), January 9, 1948.

[19] Quoted in M. A. Verick, "Rebel Voices in the NMU," *New Politics*, 5 (Summer 1966), 33.

[20] NMU *Pilot*, July 16, 1948.

[21] Ibid., July 30, 1948.

[22] National Maritime Union of America, *Proceedings of the Seventh Convention* (1949), pp. 529, 535, 560. These are complete lists of the charges leveled against three NMU members, not excerpts from the charges.

[23] Ibid., p. 528.

[24] Ibid., pp. 349, 364.

[25] Dorian J. Fliegel, "Curran's NMU: Headquarters vs. the Men at Sea," *The Nation*, 205 (January 30, 1967), p. 144.

[26] Howe and Coser, *American Communist Party*, p. 383.

[27] Curran's charges are quoted in Kampelman, *Communist Party*, pp. 83–84.

which Communists were prominent all obscure (but cannot really hide) the majorities which those oppositions won and the methods used to prevent them from coming to power. For example, all students of the International Ladies Garment Workers' Union (ILGWU) know that, as Schneider noted, "the anti-administration forces, though outvoted in the [1925 ILGWU] convention, actually represented a majority of the members of the International."[28] Yet Schneider is the only one to state this clearly. Laslett simply said that the administration retained the presidency in a "relatively close contest," and Howe and Coser noted that the administration defeated the left by the "unimpressive margin of 158 to 110."[29] Epstein came closer to the truth when he wrote that "the left delegates . . . from the majority of the important locals" were outvoted "largely by delegates from small locals—many of them in semiexistence—garnered throughout the country."[30] Nor are historians at all critical of the consequences of the administration's victory. The loss of two-thirds of the union's membership is seen as a reasonable price to pay to defeat the Communists.

Throughout the discussion of the controversy, it is simply assumed that the Socialist leaders of the garment unions were high-minded democrats and that their Communist opponents were unprincipled totalitarians. Contemporaries knew better. Explaining his reluctance to run for alderman in New York, Norman Thomas pointed out that "the political campaign next fall cannot be separated from internal labor controversy" inside the garment unions. As Thomas saw it, there were two major problems. First, most workers in New York supported the Communist-led oppositions rather than the Socialist trade union leaderships. He indicated that "it is not occasional Communist hecklers that I mind but the general feeling of the district." Second, Thomas could not support the Socialist leaders uncritically. He thought that many of them were "associated with strong armed methods of labor organization which are absolutely fatal in the long run to the Socialist idealism

to which we must appeal to defeat Tammany Hall." Thomas made these criticisms privately since any "public criticisms would tend to play into the hands of the lefts."[31]

The attitudes of the Socialist Party in the 20s, as Thomas described them, were remarkably similar to the attitudes of liberal labor historians in the 50s. Thomas complained that the "one issue on which a great many of our comrades tend to arouse themselves, the one thing that brings into their eyes the old light of battle, is their hatred of Communism." The *Jewish Daily Forward* and "a considerable element in the party" would support "any crook, any incompetent in power in the ILGWU or the Furriers who shouted right wing slogans."[32] Not all the leaders in the garment unions supported by the Socialists were gangsters or incompetents, by any means. But Socialists did consciously ally with gangsters to defeat the Communists.

Conclusions

None of the above discussion is meant to suggest that the Communists were above criticism or that they did not make some extremely questionable alliances themselves. What it does suggest is that our notion of the factional struggles inside CIO unions is highly distorted. These distortions flow from a notion which I think must be discarded; namely, that Communists are somehow external to the working class movement. The current weakness of Communism in the American working class should not obscure the fact that the Communist movement was the major expression of working class radicalism for the second quarter of the 20th century. As even their bitterest enemies within the movement would concede, many Communists dedicated (and sometimes lost) their lives working to build the CIO unions in basic industry. The assumption has been that these men and women were nothing more than extensions of *Daily Worker* editorials or, in the more dramatic phrase, agents of a foreign power. In fact, they were among the most active working class militants during a period of intense and militant working class struggle. While there is no need to canonize them, there is a need to take them seriously as workers, as organizers, and as Communists.

[28] David M. Schneider, *The Workers' (Communist) Party and the American Trade Unions* (Baltimore: Johns Hopkins, 1928), p. 95.

[29] John H. M. Laslett, *Labor and the Left: A Study of Socialist and Radical Influences in the American Labor Movement, 1881–1924* (New York: Basic Books, 1970), p. 129; Howe and Coser, *American Communist Party*, p. 248.

[30] Melech Epstein, *Jewish Labor in U.S.A., 1914–1952: An Industrial, Political, and Cultural History of the Jewish Labor Movement* (New York: Trade Union Sponsoring Committee, 1953), p. 142.

[31] Norman Thomas to Morris Hillquit, June 14, 1927, Morris Hillquit Papers (microform edition), State Historical Society of Wisconsin, 1969.

[32] Thomas to Hillquit, December 21, 1926.

B. COMMUNISTS AND TRADE UNION DEMOCRACY

Walter Galenson[†]

Mr. Prickett's revisionist view of the role of the Communist Party in the American labor movement might have been interesting if he had marshalled some solid evidence with which to refute the conclusions of the writers he takes to task. Unfortunately, there is little in his article except sweeping and unsubstantiated charges of bias. Moreover, he has failed to focus on the central problem: the limited functions of trade unions in a democratic capitalist society and the difficulty of accommodating Communist leaders who do not accept such limitations but rather seek to use the unions for the purpose of achieving a proletarian dictatorship along Soviet lines. This is the essence of the problem, not the forms of procedure on which Prickett concentrates.

While it would be unseemly for me to defend all the writers against whom Prickett inveighs, and unwise because there is considerable unevenness in the quality of their work, a few examples may serve to illustrate how Prickett fails to observe the normal canons of scholarly discourse.

1. The assertion that there is "no way to empirically test Jensen's argument," advanced in *Nonferrous Metals Industry Unionism* . . . , simply ignores 300 pages that went into the conclusion quoted by Prickett. Jensen analyzed the history of Mine Mill; he explained the nature of the internal controversy, what the various factions were doing, and their motives. He certainly does not deny "that many of the devices and tactics which the Communists employed have been used also by nonideological factions in the labor movement in their ruthless efforts to gain control in their respective organizations."[1] But he demonstrates conclusively that the main purpose of the Communists was not to further collective bargaining but rather to gain control of labor organizations in key industries which they could and did use for political purposes in the interests of the Soviet Union.

Jensen wrote in a similar vein about the struggles in the Woodworkers' Union. It is just not enough simply to assert that the work of a meticulous scholar is biased. To sustain his thesis, Prickett must demonstrate that Jensen went wrong either factually or analytically, and this he has failed to do.

2. The technique of guilt by association is—if Prickett will forgive me—an old Communist trick. The full quotation from Glazer's work, from which he excerpts, is as follows:

The Communists used more characteristic and more effective tactics. They showed themselves as the one element in American life that demanded the goal that even Negro political organizations hesitated to put forward: the complete merging of Negro and white in a common society. There was no hesitation, no equivocation in the demanding of such a merger. In the party, Negro members were treated with more than equality, and white female party members went out of their way to demonstrate how serious Communists were in eliminating all social barriers between the two races. The slightest hesitation in social relations with Negro party members, and indeed, some felt, in sexual relations, made a member suspect and might lead to denunciation. Social relations between Negroes and whites in the Communist Party were far more effective in permitting the party to reach Negroes than any higher policy hammered out by Moscow.[2]

The issue is not whether interracial sex was a favorite theme of southern conservatives or anyone else. It is, rather, whether Glazer's statement is true or false, but Prickett fails to enlighten us on this point.

3. Reference to the civil war in the ILGWU in the 20s is another example of Prickett's hit-and-run tactics. "Not all the leaders in the garment unions supported by the Socialists were gangsters or incompetents, by any means. But Socialists did consciously ally with gangsters to defeat the Communists," we are told. How many of the leaders were gangsters? Who were they? This sweeping generalization, unsupported by evidence, is based entirely on an unpublished letter from Norman Thomas to Morris Hillquit that is neither factual nor specific. However, Epstein, whom Prickett cites approvingly on another point, described the assistance given to the Communists by Arnold Rothstein, who "controlled most of the gangs in New York, the traffic in gambling, narcotics, and bootlegging." There is no evidence that this support was either solicited or welcomed, but Rothstein did provide it, perhaps because he hoped in this way to gain a foothold in the garment industry.[3]

[†] Professor of Economics, New York State School of Industrial and Labor Relations, Cornell University.

[1] Vernon H. Jensen, *Nonferrous Metals Industry Unionism, 1932–1954* (Ithaca: New York State School of Industrial and Labor Relations, 1954), p. 295.

[2] Nathan Glazer, *The Social Basis of American Communism* (New York: Harcourt, Brace and World, 1961), pp. 170–71.

[3] Melech Epstein, *Jewish Labor in U.S.A., 1914–1952* (New York: Trade Union Sponsoring Committee, 1953), pp. 149–51.

Prickett ascribes to labor historians the view that "the loss of two-thirds of the union membership was not an unreasonable price to pay to defeat the Communists." What he fails to say is that the virtual bankruptcy of the ILGWU in 1926 was due to a disastrous 28-week strike called by the Communist-led Joint Board that cost the union $3.5 million. Nor does he tell us that a few years after Communist influence had been eliminated from the ILGWU, it was "within reach of fully recuperating its losses."[4] The Great Depression temporarily stopped the Union, but by 1936 it had rebuilt both its membership and fortunes so that it was able to play an important role in founding the CIO.

4. The debate at the 1941 United Automobile Workers' convention to which Prickett refers was an interesting one. The interpretation of the Communist position that he gives is by no means self-evident, but the Howe and Widick position is certainly not proven. It is incumbent upon them, as it is on Prickett, to sustain their statements with facts.

One might observe, however, that the Communist speech cited by Prickett contained the following attack on Walter Reuther that tells us a good deal about Communist tactics:

The Royal Family [Reuthers] that sponsored this resolution has in its ranks a man that would sooner face cameras than bullets. Let me make this point clear. I say that our union has got the right to ask for deferment [from the draft] for our key men. If industry has this right our union has this right. But this man was not deferred because of that. He was deferred because he told the government of the United States that his wife was depending on him. He hid behind the skirts of his wife, and every man in this hall knows that.[5]

This *ad hominem* attack, which Reuther fully refuted, is difficult to reconcile with the consistent democracy that Prickett finds in the record of American communism.

5. The quotation from Wilson Record does not describe Communists as moral monsters. It is a fact that the Communists were always prepared to gear their propaganda (or should I say "publicity"?) to outrages against blacks or any other groups. Sometimes their intervention was not to the advantage of the victims, as the famous Scottsboro case suggests.[6]

Trade Union Democracy

Let us turn now to the basic problem with Prickett's paper. His major point is that "unions led or influenced by Communists were, if anything, more democratic than the strongly anti-Communist unions." His principal evidence consists of some brief remarks on the National Maritime Union before and after the Communists were expelled.

The difficulty with this approach lies in the use of the term "democracy" as it applies to American trade unions.[7] This is an exceedingly complex problem and cannot be handled quite as simply as Prickett does. If a necessary condition for a trade union to qualify as democratic is that it have a permanent, legitimate opposition to the administration, as in political life, only the International Typographical Union would be on the list. Other tests can be applied: the frequency of opposition slates in national and local elections,[8] the extent of rank-and-file participation in union affairs, the use of the referendum for ratification of agreements, and others.[9]

One could hardly interpret Goldberg's study of the NMU as a paean of praise for its democratic proclivities either before or after Curran broke with the Communists. And it would be unrealistic to deny that by almost any standard, many American trade unions have been dominated by autocratic or corrupt leaders for shorter or longer periods. John L. Lewis, one of the most formidable figures in American labor history, ran the United Mine Workers of America as a personal fiefdom during his long tenure as president. By keeping many union districts in permanent receivership, he was able to hand pick a substantial majority of convention delegates. He was scrupulous in maintaining the outward forms of democracy; oppositionists were permitted to speak at conventions and then voted down. But these were never serious opponents; the men who could really have challenged him were simply expelled from the union.

In spite of his autocratic leadership and not-

---

[4] Ibid., p. 156.

[5] United Automobile Workers of America, *Proceedings of the Sixth Convention* (1941), p. 702.

[6] See Wilson Record, *The Negro and the Communist Party* (New York: Atheneum, 1951), pp. 86–90.

[7] See, in particular, William M. Leiserson, *American Trade Union Democracy* (New York: Columbia University Press, 1959); S. M. Lipset, Martin Trow, and James Coleman, *Union Democracy* (Glencoe, Ill.: Free Press, 1956); and Derek C. Bok and John T. Dunlop, *Labor and the American Community* (New York: Simon and Schuster, 1970).

[8] See Philip Taft, *The Structure and Government of Labor Unions* (Cambridge: Harvard University Press, 1954).

[9] For an attempt to apply some of these criteria to European trade unions, see Walter Galenson, *Trade Union Democracy in Western Europe* (Berkeley: University of California Press, 1961).

withstanding the fact that the UMW Constitution barred Communists from membership, the Communists found Lewis to their liking as long as they thought they could use him. The Communist organ *New Masses* declared in 1937: "In a series of remarkable speeches . . . he demonstrated that the leadership of the progressive trade union movement was his right of ability and program."[10] After Lewis had spoken at a meeting of a Communist-front organization, Earl Browder, the general-secretary of the Communist Party, declared: "Lewis emerged with this speech not merely as the greatest American trade union leader, not only as one of the most potent representatives of American democracy, but as a leader of world democracy."[11] Needless to say, Lewis forfeited his world leadership when he stubbornly remained an isolationist after the German attack on the Soviet Union in 1941.

It is sometimes argued that trade unions, as limited-purpose organizations, should not be expected to conform fully with the requirements of political democracy. The argument is that they are established by workers to advance parochial economic interests, and that if they do a good collective bargaining job, the form of government is irrelevant. Those who disagree with this point to the malpractices unearthed by the McClellan Committee as a possible consequence of oligarchy unchecked. But both sides would agree that a necessary, if not sufficient, condition for a claim to union democracy is the acceptance by the organization and its leadership of political democracy in the broader sense and their basic devotion to the rule of law in a pluralistic society. Unions controlled by totalitarians of the Left or the Right, by authoritarian governments, or by racketeers, clearly do not meet this condition.

It has been maintained that trade unions controlled by Communists are democratic if the term is used, say, in the sense of the "democratic centralism" that characterizes trade union government in the Soviet Union. However, American Communists have never professed their devotion to American democratic government. When the interests of the United States came into conflict with those of the Soviet Union, they could justify their support of the latter by arguing that the future well being of American workers, whether they knew it or not, was linked inextricably with that of the Communist motherland. The defense of Soviet communism against internal and external enemies certainly came before the improvement of wages and working conditions for the American working man and woman and, it goes without saying, before the defense of capitalist democracy in the United States.

Some Examples

Let us consider a few examples of Communist trade union behavior by way of illustration. From the outbreak of World War II in 1939 until June 1941, when the Soviet Union was invaded, the Communist-dominated trade unions mounted campaigns against any form of U.S. intervention in the war, even against aid to the embattled British when they were facing the Nazi war machine alone. The Maritime Federation of the Pacific adopted the following resolution in June 1940:

Resolved, that this 6th Annual Convention of the Maritime Federation of the Pacific calls upon the American people to fight each and every action, large and small, subtle and significant, which ignores our stated policy of absolute neutrality in the present conflict, whether by selling munitions to one side or the other, or attempting to drum up public sympathy for either side; and that the organizations represented at this conference continue to cooperate on issues of common interest tending to spread the message to all the world that The Yanks Are Not Coming.[12]

This slogan was echoed by the entire Communist labor press. But more serious were strikes called against plants engaged in defense production. One of the most notorious was that at the North American Aviation Company in Los Angeles in 1941. The demand of the local Auto Workers' Union for a wage increase was before the National Defense Mediation Board, and Richard Frankensteen, the UAW vice-president in charge of the aviation division, had pledged to the Board that in return for a retroactivity commitment, no strike would be called until three days after the Board had completed its findings. The Communist-dominated local struck the plant nonetheless. Its charter was revoked by the national union, provisional officers installed, and the plant reopened with the help of troops sent in by President Roosevelt. The majority of a UAW special committee established to investigate the strike had this to say about it:

The interference of the Communists into the strike gave basis to the charge of Frankensteen that

[10] Quoted in Max M. Kampelman, *The Communist Party vs. the CIO* (New York: Praeger, 1957), p. 16.

[11] Ibid., p. 16.

[12] Maritime Federation of the Pacific, *Proceedings of the Sixth Annual Convention*, June 3–8, 1940, p. 185.

the wildcat strike was engineered by Communists, inside and outside the union, who were interested in carrying out the policy they were then fostering in trade unions. They were interested in demonstrating their effectiveness in obstructing national defense. Communist leaflets were distributed on picket lines. The leaflets distributed by the strike committee were written by a well-known Communist writer and signed by one of the union strike leaders. The same individual was active in planning strike strategy and organizing the picket lines.[13]

That Great Britain might be conquered by the Nazis was apparently a matter of no concern to American workers. But as soon as Russia was attacked, the war became a people's war in which their vital interests were at stake, even though the United States was still not involved. Joseph Curran, head of the National Maritime Union, had condemned the Lend Lease Act as fascist legislation, but in June 1941, the NMU declared in a policy statement:

We recognize the present struggle of Great Britain and the Soviet Union against the forces of Fascism to be sincere and requiring the full support of liberty-loving people throughout the world.[14]

The Communists placed themselves at the forefront of the production drive. They supported an unconditional no-strike pledge for the duration of the war, a policy about which many non-Communist trade unionists had serious reservations. Labor leaders who called strikes were branded as traitors. Earl Browder charged that John L. Lewis, who mounted the most spectacular wartime strikes, was part of a conspiracy to put him in charge of the United States as Nazi gauleiter.[15]

With the end of the war and the divergence of American and Soviet policies, the Communist unions came down on the Soviet side and soon effectively isolated themselves from the rest of the labor movement. The Marshall Plan was attacked by Communist union leaders, who claimed that "huge sums of the Marshall Plan are being given to these Nazis to rebuild the German cartels and trusts in heavy industry."[16] They joined together with the Communist Party in a political campaign designed to defeat President Truman in 1948, despite the fact that he had vetoed the Taft-Hartley Act and was one of the most pro-

labor presidents in American history. These activities prompted the following observation by Philip Murray, President of the CIO, with which all of the Communist unions were then affiliated:

I have asked all these so-called apostles of democracy to stand somewhere, sometime upon the floor of a national convention of the CIO and to criticize the Cominform, or criticize Russia's policy of expansionism, to criticize any of the policies of Russia, and these hypocrites run from me. They dare not stand upon their dirty feet and give any expression of opposition to anything the Soviets are doing. They are inbred with a feeling of hatred against democratic institutions and democratic countries. They lend assistance to every satellite of Communist dictated Russia. . . . Their allegiances are pledged to a foreign government.[17]

Over almost a century, the leaders of the mainstream of American labor, Samuel Gompers, William Green, and George Meany, have spoken out repeatedly against oppression and for the rights of individuals. It would help his case if Prickett could supply us with even one example of protest by an incumbent American Communist trade union leader against the Stalin regime, which tortured and killed millions of people, including workers. The democracy they advocated was the democracy of the concentration camp.

Prickett's claim that "the Communist movement was the major expression of working class radicalism for the second quarter of the 20th century" is a parody of history. The American Communist Party never achieved even minimal success at the polls, although it put up candidates in many elections. Its first attempt at independent union action was in 1928, when the Red International of Labor Unions in Moscow directed its constituent bodies to abandon the previous policy of boring from within the existing labor movements. The Trade Union Unity League (TUUL) was created in the United States. It chartered a number of affiliates, most of which never got beyond the paper stage, and, at its height, the TUUL claimed 125,000 members, and even this was an exaggeration. With the switch to the United Front in 1935, the TUUL was dissolved; some of its leaders joined the CIO drives of 1937–40 and managed to gain positions of influence in new unions. They were on the way to exclusion in 1939–41 because of their support of the Hitler-Stalin pact but were saved temporarily by the invasion of the Soviet Union. After the war, they hung on for a few years in an increasingly hostile environment. A combination of palace revolutions

---

[13] United Automobile Workers of America, *Proceedings of the 1941 Convention*, p. 243.

[14] Quoted in Kampelman, *The Communist Party*, p. 20.

[15] Joel Seidman, *American Labor from Defense of Reconversion* (Chicago: University of Chicago Press, 1953), p. 144.

[16] Cited in Philip Taft, *Organized Labor in American History* (New York: Harper and Row, 1964), p. 626.

[17] Quoted in Taft, *Organized Labor in American History*, p. 628.

led by top leaders who deserted them (Joe Curran, Mike Quill, Morris Muster), and expulsions from the CIO marked the end of any Communist influence in the American labor movement. Certainly, there have been organizations which represented the more radical aspirations of American workers—the Knights of Labor, the Industrial Workers of the World, the CIO—but communism was an alien philosophy that never flourished on American soil.

Conclusions

A lawyer would define a conspiracy as an agreement by two or more persons to commit a crime, fraud, or other wrongful act. If racketeers are engaged in an attempt to establish or capture a labor organization, they are clearly involved in a conspiracy. Communists in the American labor movement were committing a fraud: although professing that their purpose was to engage in collective bargaining to improve wages and working conditions of union members, they were actually attempting to establish bases of political power that could be and were used at the behest of the Soviet Union in times of crisis. It is, therefore, quite appropriate to use such conspiratorial terms as "infiltrate" and "dominate" to describe their activities. There is no "heavy burden" on labor historians to prove these charges; the evidence they have already gathered is overwhelming. The burden of proof is rather upon the modern revisionists, like Prickett; they must eschew vague, inaccurate accusations and get down to the difficult job of gathering facts and marshalling them into convincing arguments. This they have not done, and until they do, few will take them seriously.

C. REPLY TO PROFESSOR GALENSON

Perhaps the most interesting passage in Professor Galenson's comment is his curious argument that it is impossible for a Communist-led union to be democratic since "a necessary, if not sufficient, condition for a claim to union democracy is the acceptance . . . of political democracy in the broader sense and . . . devotion to the rule of law in a pluralistic society." This is a splendid example of the sort of anti-Communist reasoning I find objectionable. No matter how democratically a Communist leader might behave, to Galenson he could never be truly democratic because he does not accept liberal, pluralist theory. The absurdity of the argument becomes apparent when one applies it to the IWW whose leaders had

nothing but contempt for "the rule of law in a pluralistic society." Was the IWW undemocratic?

The way one determines whether Communists were democratic or undemocratic leaders is by examining the way they exercised leadership, not by asking, as Galenson does, whether or not they criticized the Soviet Union. Galenson objects to this approach and takes me to task for concentrating on what he calls "forms of procedure." What he calls "forms of procedure" I would call "basic democratic rights." I agree that it is difficult to formulate a precise definition of union democracy (the two-party system is not my definition either inside or outside of the labor movement), but it seems clear to me that a union in which members are denied access to the union press, beaten for expressing opposition to the leadership, and expelled for political affiliations is less democratic than one in which members can criticize the leadership in the union press, can speak and organize against that leadership, and can belong to any political group without losing membership rights. Similarly, a union in which members vote on contract settlements is more democratic than one in which they do not. By any criteria involving actual practice, the unions expelled from the CIO were, if anything, more democratic than those which remained.

Galenson claims that I have "failed to focus on the central problem: the limited functions of trade unions in a democratic capitalist society and the difficulty of accommodating Communist leaders who do not accept such limitations but rather seek to use the unions for the purpose of achieving a proletarian dictatorship along Soviet lines." Is he serious? Communists never worked for the dictatorship of the proletariat in the CIO, and as a number of recent historians have suggested, Communists were probably far too willing to accept the limitations of orthodox trade unionism.[1]

Let me also say something about Galenson's efforts to show that "Prickett fails to observe the normal canons of scholarly discourse." Here my numbering follows his.

[1] See, for example, Stanley Aronowitz, *False Promises: The Shaping of American Working Class Consciousness* (New York: McGraw-Hill, 1973), pp. 214–63; Norman Markowitz, *The Rise and Fall of the People's Century: Henry A. Wallace and American Liberalism, 1941–1948* (New York: Free Press, 1973), pp. 204–12; Ronald Radosh, "The Corporate Ideology of American Labor Leaders from Gompers to Hillman," *Studies on the Left,* 6 (November–December 1966), 85–86; Staughton Lynd, "The Possibility of Radicalism in the Early 1930s: The Case of Steel, *Radical America,* 6 (November–December 1972), 37–64; James Weinstein, "The Left, Old and New," *Socialist Revolution,* 10 (July–August 1972), 30–33; Jeremy Brecher, *Strike* (San Francisco: Straight Arrow Books, 1972), pp. 204, 257, 317.

1. We obviously disagree on whether Jensen has demonstrated—conclusively or otherwise—that Communists were interested in control of the union rather than collective bargaining. My point was that Jensen's argument was based upon his *assumption of hidden Communist motives,* and he was, therefore, incapable of unbiased empirical investigation.

2. The point here is not whether interracial sex occurred but whether the Party denounced white women for not sleeping with black men. Glazer's snide speculations are racist, sexist, and, above all, false. By the way, is Galenson suggesting in his opening sentence—itself a rather nice example of guilt by association—that I am a Communist? If not, the sentence is pointless; if so, it is false and libelous.

3. Galenson makes no attempt to deny the existence of a Socialist-gangster alliance against the Communists; he merely wants me to be more precise about its extent. For that, he and others may refer to my dissertation.[2]

4. Galenson ducks the issue raised in my criticism of Howe and Widick and then introduces a new one by quoting a nasty Communist attack on Reuther which proves only that some Communists sometimes used *ad hominem* arguments against their bitter enemies. This should surprise no one.

5. Galenson also sidesteps the issue raised by Record's statement. The point is not whether Communists "geared their propaganda to" (a more accurate phrase would be "fought against") outrages against blacks but whether they were pleased when those outrages occurred. Record claimed that Communists found nothing so pleasing, no event more welcome, than a lynching. Would Galenson agree? Incidentally, recent scholarship indicates that Record and Galenson are wrong about the Scottsboro case.[3]

---

[2] James R. Prickett, "Communists and the Communist Issue in the American Labor Movement, 1920–1950" (unpublished doctoral dissertation, University of California at Los Angeles, 1974). The dissertation should be available from University Microfilm by the end of 1974. It offers a far different view of the Communist role in the American Labor movement than the popular indictment summarized by Galenson.

[3] Although critical of the Communists, one author has recently indicated that the International Labor Defense did not exploit the case for financial gain and that it saved the lives of the defendants. See Dan T. Carter, *Scottsboro: A Tragedy of the American South* (Baton Rouge: Louisiana State University Press, 1969), pp. 170–73. It should be remembered that the NAACP was reluctant to defend the boys at first because rapists gave the race a bad name and that an NAACP leader described the boys' parents as "the densest and dumbest animals it has yet been my privilege to meet." What would have occurred without the Communists is suggested by a second case: "The International Labor Defense offered to come to the aid of Peterson, but on

In his conclusion, Galenson repeats Jensen's thesis that Communists only pretended to be interested in improving wages and working conditions. It is possible to believe this only if one considers the men and women who worked in the plants and belonged to the Party as abstractions rather than people. Does he really believe that Wyndham Mortimer, for instance, who spent 40 years as an industrial worker, including nearly two decades in an automobile plant before the UAW was formed, was uninterested in ending the speedup and winning higher wages for auto workers? As even some former leaders of the anti-Communist crusade in the unions have realized, this highly ideological and abstract model collapses when the actual behavior of Communists is examined. For example, Father Charles Owen Rice, a leading figure in the anti-Communist grouping in the United Electrical Radio and Machine Workers (UE), noted that "so far as the day-to-day conduct of the union was concerned, communism . . . didn't have a bad effect." Rice's interview included this important exchange:

> Interviewer: The charges against the UE members who are supposedly communists were always based on the support of the foreign policy line. . . .
> Rice: Sure, we couldn't find any—I mean we'd look and look we couldn't—we examined it with a fine tooth comb to try to find things wrong with them other than that. The indictment was very weak.[4]

In spite of Professor Galenson's efforts, the indictment remains very weak.

D. REJOINDER TO MR. PRICKETT

Let me make a few specific points before responding to Mr. Prickett's general strictures:

1. I have no knowledge whatever of Prickett's politics; I never heard of him prior to the request that I reply to his original article. In my parenthetical aside, I was merely suggesting that my statement was meant to be objective rather than pejorative. The statement is not pointless; the

---

the advice of white interracial leaders in Birmingham, he stuck with his court-appointed attorney. The second time, the jury deliberated only 20 minutes before returning with a guilty verdict. Peterson was sentenced to die in the electric chair." He did not even fit the physical description of the rapist, so he later received life imprisonment rather than death. Ibid., pp. 90, 132–34.

[4] Charles Owen Rice, Oral History Interview, Pennsylvania Historical Collections, Pennsylvania State University (1967–68), p. 13. For a discussion of Rice's activities, see his papers at Pennsylvania State (perhaps the best collection on anti-Communism in the CIO) and Michael Harrington, "Catholics in the Labor Movement," *Labor History,* 1 (Fall 1960), 231–63.

technique of argument cited is a standard communist method, though of course anyone can use it.

2. Glazer's analysis impresses me as neither snide, racist, sexist, nor false; I believe that it is valid. For me to defend the factual basis of Glazer's statement would be an act of supererogation. I would just like to make the observation that for a man who is so sensitive about the possibility of implied libel, Prickett is both careless and arrogant in his characterization of the work of an eminent scholar.

3. It looks as though we will all have to be patient until Prickett's doctoral dissertation becomes available for the final and conclusive proof of Socialist iniquity in the 1926 ILGWU imbroglio. Let us hope that his evidence is stronger than what he set forth in his original article. (For anyone who cannot wait, there is already a substantial body of literature available which casts considerable doubt on Prickett's assertion).

4. Although personally I was not surprised by the Communist attack on Walter Reuther, it is nice to have Prickett's firm statement that Communists could be nasty at times.

5. Let me quote the "Record statement" a bit more fully than Prickett does:

Whether or not world-wide propaganda campaigns such as the Communists have conducted around court cases involving Negro Americans have any appreciable influence on the trials themselves is difficult to determine. Actually, legal justice is a secondary consideration for the Party. One thing is certain; the treatment accorded American Negroes in the courts, particularly in the South, is one of the most important bases for the anti-United States propaganda campaign waged by the U.S.S.R. among colored peoples all over the world. What more welcome event could occur for such propagandists than a lynching in Georgia legal or otherwise.[1]

Taken in context, there is nothing about Communists being "pleased"; that is Prickett's term. That lynchings were welcome grist for the Soviet propaganda mill does not strike me as an unreasonable observation. But beyond that, does Prickett really believe that Stalin's minions would have had the slightest concern for a few American blacks when they were engaged in the brutal murder of hundreds of thousands of their own people? "Moral monsters" would be an apt term for them at that.

6. As for Scottsboro and the sincerity of the American Communist Party on the race question,

here is what Roy Wilkins had to say years after the event:

We remember the Scottsboro case and our experience then with the [Communist] International Labor Defense. . . . We remember that in the Scottsboro case the NAACP was subjected to the most unprincipled villification. We remember the campaign of slander in the *Daily Worker*. . . . We of the NAACP remember that during the war when Negro Americans were fighting for jobs on the home front and fighting for decent treatment in the armed services we could get no help from organizations of the extreme left. . . . As soon as Russia was attacked by Germany they dropped the Negro question. During the war years the disciples of the extreme left sounded very much like the worst of the Negro hating Southerners.[2]

7. Was the IWW a democratic organization? This is an extremely complicated question, as I learned many years ago from my dissertation supervisor.[3] But at least one thing is clear: while they rejected capitalism, they were equally opposed to authoritarian socialism. "The rule of law in an atomistic society" is perhaps not a bad description of their inchoate philosophy.

8. Prickett asserts that "the two-party system is not my definition [of democracy] either inside or outside of the labor movement." We agree on the unions, but I would be curious to know whether he would agree that the existence of more than one party is a necessary, if not sufficient, condition for the existence of political democracy. If not, the source of some of our differences is clear.

Prickett's contention that the Communist-dominated unions expelled by the CIO were democratic simply flies in the face of the evidence.[4] In the case of the Mine, Mill, and Smelter Workers' Union, for example, the CIO found that its policies "were determined in secret meetings with high officials of the Communist Party prior to their submission to the union's governing body and to the membership."[5] There were similar findings for the rest of the expelled unions, as well as for those, like the ILWU, that chose to disaffiliate voluntarily.

We are asked to believe, on the other hand, that some substantial number of the 80 percent of the CIO members in the United Auto Workers,

---

[1] Wilson Record, *The Negro and the Communist Party* (New York: Atheneum, 1951), p. 259.

[2] Quoted in ibid., pp. 260–61.

[3] Paul F. Brissenden, *The IWW* (New York: Columbia University Press, 1919).

[4] The reader is referred to the voluminous transcripts of the hearings conducted by CIO investigating tribunals prior to the expulsions.

[5] Max M. Kampelman, *The Communist Party vs. the CIO* (New York: Praeger, 1957), p. 177.

the Steelworkers, the Rubber Workers, the Amalgamated Clothing Workers, the Textile Workers, the Oil Workers, and 23 other unions were "denied access to the union press, beaten for expressing opposition to the leadership, and expelled for political affiliations." Has Prickett ever attended any union conventions or read union newspapers? As I have already indicated, it would be silly to maintain that all non-Communist unions have always been paragons of democratic virtue. But there is simply no doubt that in general, the unions that remained in the CIO were far more responsive to the views of their members than the expelled unions and never sacrificed their economic interests at the behest of an alien power.

Prickett cites the case of Wyndham Mortimer as a typical example of a Communist activist whose major concern was improving the lot of working people, not politics.[6] In fact, Mortimer never deviated from the Party line regardless of its impact on his constituents. His leadership role in the highly political North American Aviation strike attests to this. How typical a rank-and-file American worker he was is suggested by the fact that to him, President Roosevelt was just a millionaire concerned with saving capitalism, and by his conviction that the executive council of the AFL-CIO "believes in and advocates a system by which private capital has monopolized the earth and robbed the common people." Writing in 1965, he was willing to concede that Stalin had his shortcomings, "but by no stretch of the imagination could he be regarded as an enemy of the auto workers of America, or of the working people generally."[7] What Prickett does not seem to understand is that while many American Communist activists may have been sincere, hard working, and fully committed to the welfare of their constituents, they were always prepared to make what they could rationalize as "temporary" sacrifices in behalf of the higher good, which by definition was furtherance of the interests of the Soviet Union, as interpreted by the Comintern.

They might build up a union at great personal risk only to collapse it unhesitatingly if the line changed from "dual unionism" to "boring from within." This was their fatal flaw.

Prickett appears to believe that Communists, in their union activities, acted like good business unionists, and to view them as concerned with such goals as the dictatorship of the proletariat is to set up a "highly ideological and abstract model." But Wyndham Mortimer makes it perfectly clear in his autobiography that he viewed his CIO activities as part of the class struggle.[8] Arthur Goldberg, who was probably the best informed person in the CIO on Communist activities within the organization, pointed out that "if the Communist attaches any importance to collective bargaining he sees it only as a temporary way station on the road to upheaval and the ultimate Communist dictatorship."[9] A Communist union official could be a very tough bargainer one year and sign a sweetheart agreement the next; it all depended on the higher strategy.

I can understand the impulses that have led to current romanticism about the Molly Maguires, the Knights of Labor, and the IWW. But I find it incomprehensible that anyone, with the advantage of hindsight, should attribute a positive role in the development of the American labor movement to as vicious and corrupt a movement as Stalinism—and make no mistake, American Communists of the 30s and 40s were ardent sycophants of the Soviet dictator. It is almost like arguing that Adolf Hitler was a benefactor of the German working class because he reduced the rate of unemployment from 42 percent in 1932 to 3.2 percent by 1938. Hubert Humphrey once observed that the "Communist infiltration of the CIO was a direct threat to the survival of all our country's democratic institutions."[10] Senator Humphrey may have overstated the power of the Communists, but he was on the right track.

Walter Galenson

---

[6] I have never seen any proof that Mortimer was actually a Communist Party member, although there is no doubt about his alignment with the Communist faction in the UAW.

[7] Wyndham Mortimer, *Organize* (Boston: Beacon Press, 1971), pp. 151, 187.

[8] Ibid., p. 219.

[9] Arthur Goldberg, *AFL-CIO United* (New York: McGraw-Hill, 1964), p. 7.

[10] Introduction to Kampelman, *The Communist Party*, pp. vii–viii.

part four

Collective Bargaining

A. The Development and Structure of Collective Bargaining

Collective bargaining has become an institutionalized and legally protected mechanism for determining wages, hours, and working conditions in the United States since the passage of the Wagner Act in 1935. Essentially a two-party process involving labor unions and management, collective bargaining has an interesting origin, and its development has experienced interesting structural changes.

In the first article, Vernon Jensen presents an historical perspective on collective bargaining. Jensen's major theme is "that collective bargaining has always been basically a moderate, businesslike process." John Dunlop discusses the major characteristics and framework of the collective bargaining system in the 1970s, and Herbert Northrup reflects on bargaining structure change through union mergers, management instigated restructuring, government pressures, and international developments.

George Hildebrand's article considers some of the "recent shifts in the balance of bargaining power between unions and managements in the United States." He explores the concepts of coalition bargaining, selective strikes on the railroads, and inflation and relative bargaining power.

In the last article, the president of the Steelworkers' union, I. W. Abel, explains a new experiment in bargaining in the steel industry. This new procedure, known as the Experimental Negotiating Agreement—ENA—is looked upon by Abel as a real breakthrough in collective bargaining in that it promises to eliminate strikes in a basic industry.

23. Notes on the Beginnings of Collective Bargaining*

Vernon H. Jensen†

The origin of an institution often throws light upon its subsequent role, notwithstanding that institutions often change in their purposes and functions as they develop, mature, and become accommodated to other institutions. Despite its importance in American industrial life, too little is known about the early history of collective bargaining. Its pedigree still needs tracing thoroughly, if we are to understand more fully the institutional role of collective bargaining in a capitalistic society.

The judgment that collective bargaining is anticapitalistic and its opposite, that it is basic to capitalism, both appear in the literature. Both assertions, contradictory as they appear, seem to have relevance within certain frames of reference. However, if collective bargaining was at first antagonistic to some of the institutional arrangements of our society—and many times it emerged and established itself only through conflict—this does not necessarily mean that as an institution it is not at present compatible with other institutions of a capitalistic society. While struggling to live it may have been asserting only its rightful place among the various institutional arrangements of a more fully developed capitalistic society. As a matter of fact, there are very close parallels in the development of "freedom of capital" and the development of "freedom of labor," and it can be argued that "free labor" is as necessary as "free capital" to a capitalistic or enterprise society.

The true nature and function of collective bargaining have been overshadowed by the turbulence frequently associated with its establishment. The thesis of this article is that collective bargaining has always been basically a moderate, businesslike process. That this was its true character from the beginning is clearly revealed if one looks at the institution apart from the conflicts over recognition which fill the pages of the early history of unionism.

BRITISH ORIGINS

The term collective bargaining is younger than the practice. To Sidney and Beatrice Webb is given the credit for the term and for establishing it in the literature just before the turn of the century. What is not often known or remembered is that before the term collective bargaining came into use, the term arbitration had a more general meaning than it carries today. Prior to the turn of the century the term arbitration was often used in a generic sense and encompassed among other things practices we would nowadays refer to as collective bargaining.[1] Also, the term conciliation was sometimes used to describe the phenomenon later called collective bargaining, but it, too, was used loosely.

Some of the most interesting early developments of collective bargaining took place in England. One development, which had a later parallel in the United States, was the espousal by British labor of arbitration under govern-

* Reprinted with permission from *Industrial and Labor Relations Review,* Vol. 9, No. 2, January 1956, pp. 225–34. Copyright © 1956 by Cornell University. All rights reserved.

† Vernon H. Jensen is a professor in the New York State School of Industrial and Labor Relations, Cornell University.

[1] Sidney and Beatrice Webb, *Industrial Democracy* (London: Longmans, Green and Co., 1920 ed.), pp. 223–24; Edwin E. Witte, *Historical Survey of Labor Arbitration* (Philadelphia: University of Pennsylvania Press for the Labor Relations Council of the Wharton School of Finance, 1952), p. 4.

mental auspices. That British labor used the term "arbitration" and looked to the government to help establish the practice they had in mind, need not surprise students of collective bargaining. This espousal of arbitration under governmental auspices was designed to secure recognition and a voice in determining the conditions of their working lives which, under the existing legal restraints, organized workers were relatively powerless to secure alone. In England this agitation by labor for governmentally sponsored arbitration disappeared with the enactment of the Trade Union Acts of 1871–75. With the new status achieved under these laws to pursue freely their self-help objectives, British unions quickly turned away from the search for governmental support and sought to develop private bargaining relations with employers.

Sidney and Beatrice Webb clearly perceived this. In speaking of arbitration and "why the Trade Unionists from 1850 to 1876 so persistently strove" for it, they stated that it was because "the majority of employers asserted their right to deal individually with each one of their 'hands'" and "habitually refused even to meet the men's representatives in discussion, and sought to suppress Collective Bargaining altogether by the use of ambiguous statutes and obsolete law." Because the trade unions knew that it was an immense gain for them to get their fundamental principle of a "Common Rule adopted," they had sought it by advocating arbitration under governmental auspices. It was noted carefully that "Arbitration was accordingly opposed by the more clear-sighted of the opponents of Trade Unionism."

The Webbs then quoted significantly from the book *Trade Unionism* by James Stirling: "'Our main objection,' said one of the leading critics, 'both to arbitration and conciliation, as palliatives of Unionism, is that they sanction, may necessitate, the continuance of the system of combination, as opposed to that of individual competition.'" The same spokesman explained why acceptance of arbitration was impossible. "'In so doing we lend the authority of public recognition to the pestilent principle of combination, and sanction the substitution of an artificial mechanism for that natural organism [the unobstructed, competitive market] which Providence has provided for the harmonious regulation of industrial interests.'"[2]

The point to be noted is that employers were opposed to dealing with their employees collectively, while their organized workers—unable to use economic pressures effectively—had sought a form of recognition through governmentally sponsored arbitration. They hoped that such sponsorship would give them some voice in determining the conditions of their employment.

Even before the Trade Union Acts of 1871–75, some interesting developments in collective bargaining had taken place in England. It is significant that employers as well as unionists took some initiative in the matter. One of the most noteworthy developments is associated with the name of A. J. Mundella, an employer in the hosiery trade, who has been hailed as "the father of conciliation"[3] (what we now call collective bargaining).

Mundella's work has been succinctly described in his own words by Henry Crompton, an early exponent of conciliation and chairman for many years of the board of arbitration and conciliation of the lace trade in England. (The Webbs said the latter's writings were "the classic work upon the whole subject.")[4] It was in 1860, after three prolonged strikes at Nottingham, that the manufacturers in the hosiery trade met to consider what they should do in their defense. They shrank from the proposition of a lockout. As Crompton put it, in part quoting Mundella:

Wisely and nobly they resolved to try a better alternative . . . a handbill was issued inviting a conference between masters and men. "Three of us," says Mr. Mundella, "met a dozen leaders of the trades unions. We . . . told them the present plan was a bad one, that they took every advantage of us when he had a demand, and we took every advantage of them when the trade was bad, and it was a system mutually predatory. Well, the men were very suspicious at first; indeed, it is impossible to describe . . . how suspiciously we looked at each other. Some of the manufacturers also deprecated our proceedings, and said that we were degrading them. However, we had some ideas of our own, and we went on with them, and we sketched out what we called 'a board of arbitration and conciliation.'"

Crompton continued:

They agreed to refer all questions in dispute to the board . . . composed of an equal number of

[3] See Henry Crompton, *Industrial Conciliation* (London: P. S. King and Co., 1876), pp. 20, 33; Lanford I. F. R. Price, *Industrial Peace* (London: Macmillan and Co., 1887), p. xvi; Lujo Brentano, *The Relations of Labor to the Law Today* (New York: G. P. Putnam's Sons, 1891), pp. 139–40.

[4] Sidney and Beatrice Webb, *History of Trade Unionism* (New York: Longmans, Green and Co., 1920), pp. 323; *Industrial Democracy*, p. 223.

[2] Sidney and Beatrice Webb, *Industrial Democracy*, pp. 223–25.

manufacturers and workmen. . . . The proceedings of the board are very informal, not like a court, but the masters and men sit around a table. . . . The proceedings are without ceremony, and the matter is settled by what the men call a "long jaw" discussion and explanation of views. . . . They agree by coming to the best arrangement possible under the circumstances. . . . The "long jaw," ending in agreement, may take a longer time, but it is the true practical way out of the difficulty.[5]

It is significant that the Webbs recognized that much of what is called arbitration or conciliation in the earlier writings on the subject amounts to nothing more than organized Collective Bargaining.

They further stated:

The Nottingham hosiery board, established in 1860, often described as a model of arbitration was, in effect, nothing more than machinery for Collective Bargaining, no outsider being present, the casting vote being given up, and the decisions being arrived at by what the men called "a long jaw."

Also, to make the point clear, they quote Mundella's observation:

It is well to define what we mean by arbitration. The sense in which we use the word is that of an arrangement for open and friendly bargaining . . . in which masters and men meet together and talk over their common affairs openly and freely.[6]

This procedure of friendly bargaining fitted the British temperament and was so appealing in contrast to the formality, and possible governmental compulsion, of arbitration that it rapidly became the practice throughout industry.

EARLY AMERICAN CONCEPTS

The basic kinship, both in law and custom, created certain parallels with English experience in the development of the collective bargaining concept in the United States. As in England, the rise of labor unions in the United States was met with mixed reactions, and the development of peaceful labor and management relations was not easily achieved. Many experiments, often sporadic, and many ideas about the proper relationships of employers and workers fall into the history of such developments.

In the late 1870s and early 1880s, American labor entered a more vigorous organizing phase. Many employers at this time feared organized labor and thought labor unions had no legitimate place in our society. At the same time labor, confronted with an unfriendly legal system and with meager resources, knew full well the hazards of using economic pressures to gain recognition. Parallel to the earlier situation in England, American labor advocated arbitration, whereas employers opposed it.

In 1885 two significant investigations of labor unrest were made in the United States, one by the Commissioner of Labor Statistics of the State of New York and the other by the Committee on Education and Labor of the United States Senate. The New York Commissioner conducted a three-month investigation during which hearings were held in several of the major communities of the state. Hundreds of workers and many employers were interviewed and, among other things, were asked for their opinions on remedies for industrial unrest. Specifically, they were requested to give their views regarding the place of strikes and lockouts in labor-management relations and the usefulness of the device of "arbitration."[7]

In reporting to the state legislature following this investigation, the Commissioner said,

As long as there is no other way of settling trade disputes save by strikes, there will be cause for apprehension, if not a real danger. There are many who see . . . cause for alarm . . . a few who advocate repressive measures, because they imagine they see in the prevailing discontent the spread of socialistic influences . . . But there is another way of settling labor disputes, and a peaceful way, too. The workingmen want it, and many employers indorse their opinion regarding it. That way is by arbitration.

Yet he hastened to add that

the first obstacle in the way of the successful introduction of arbitration is the hostile attitude or contemptuous indifference of employers to the wants and needs of their employees.

Also, the lack of practical knowledge of the remedy because of the dearth of experimentation, he thought, would involve the passage of "some time" before laws could be secured which would provide for "boards of arbitration." Meanwhile, he said, "the initial steps to reach arbitration

<hr />

[5] Crompton, *Industrial Conciliation*, pp. 35–37. That the term "long jaw" might not be misunderstood, for it does not imply a set or firm jaw, or stubbornness, it should be mentioned that "to jaw" was a colloquialism in England meaning to argue. As the phrase sometimes was put, "What are you 'jawing' about?" Hence, it was roughly synonymous with bargaining in its argumentative sense.

[6] Sidney and Beatrice Webb, *Industrial Democracy*, pp. 223–24.

[7] *Third Annual Report of the Bureau of Statistics of Labor of the State of New York, 1885*, pp. 11–12, 195–476. The term arbitration was being used in a very broad sense, as will be seen shortly.

must be taken by the trade unions themselves, as the capitalist seems half satisfied with the present system."[8]

With the Commissioner, as with others at the time, the term "arbitration" was used very broadly, for the term "collective bargaining" had not yet come into use. The Commissioner noted quite correctly that a good deal of the agitation for a system of "arbitration" came from the labor organizations. This, of course, was not unnatural where they were seeking more status and greater acceptance. Unionists generally did not relish use of the strike weapon. American experience in this respect, with a slight time lag, paralleled the British. The clamor for "arbitration," a joint meeting of workers and employers, was also due to the belief that it was a "fair thing."

ARBITRATION AS A FORM OF UNION RECOGNITION

Evidence that many unions formally espoused arbitration, by which they meant a conciliatory rather than a belligerent approach to securing their demands, is easily found in the records. One of the aims of the Knights of Labor, in the period of its ascendancy during the mid-80s, was stated in its Declaration of Principles as follows:

To persuade all employers to agree to arbitrate all differences which may arise between them and their employes, in order that the bonds of sympathy between them may be strengthened, and that strikes may be rendered unnecessary.

The constitution of the International Typographical Union contained similar language:

Recognizing strikes as detrimental to the best interests of the craft, it (the ITU) directs subordinate unions not to strike until every possible effort has been made to settle the difficulty by arbitration.

This was not an uncommon union position, but it is well to keep in mind the loose use of the term arbitration.

The real interest on the part of labor spokesmen in the development of arbitration at this time—apart from a basic desire to avoid the consequences of strike action—was the desire to achieve union recognition. An examination of the objectives and language of men who were active in workers' organizations makes this quite clear. Recognition is what the unions needed and were after. In the early meetings where the founda-

tions were laid for the formation of the American Federation of Labor, the questions of arbitration and incorporation of unions were discussed most favorably. The reasons for favorable consideration were two, as revealed in the remarks of Adolph Strasser, who argued that they would give protection to unions, but what was more important, would also

give our organization more stability, and in that manner we shall be able to avoid strikes by perhaps settling with our employers, when otherwise we should be unable to do so, because when our employers know that *we are to be legally recognized* [recognized before the law] that will exercise such moral force upon them that *they cannot avoid recognizing us themselves.*[9]

The important emphasis was upon achievement of recognition of unionism—the prerequisite of agreement making. Similarly, the words of W. H. Foster of the Cincinnati Trade and Labor Assembly, who also favored incorporation of unions, reveal the prevailing interest in governmentally sponsored arbitration as a device with which to achieve such recognition. He wanted a national law to "legalize arbitration," but in his own words, he wanted it for the reason that

when a question of dispute [should arise] between the employers and employed instead of having it as now, when the one often refuses to even acknowledge or discuss the question with the other, if they were required to submit the question to *arbitration,* or to *meet on the same level* before an impartial tribunal, there is no doubt but what the result would be more in our favor than it is now, when very often public opinion cannot hear our cause.[10]

It seems clear that such representatives as Strasser and Foster sought compulsory dealing with unions, not compulsory arbitration in the sense that a third party would make an award to settle a difference. Unions were seeking status which they did not have and which was too costly and uncertain of achievement through strike action. As for the arbitration they were suggesting, the parties were to be free to accept proposals for settlement—provided, however, "that *once they do agree* the agreement shall remain in force for a fixed period."[11]

---

[8] Ibid., pp. 365–67.

[9] Senate Committee on Education and Labor, *Report upon the Relations between Capital and Labor,* 1885, I, p. 461 (italics supplied).

[10] Ibid., p. 404 (italics supplied). It is to be noted that the phrase "or to meet on the same level" undoubtedly involves the use of the word "or" as a connective of alternate expressions rather than in the conjunctive sense of joining two separate things.

[11] Ibid., p. 404 (italics supplied).

BROAD USE OF "ARBITRATION"

Samuel Gompers, when testifying at the New York State hearings in 1885 about the desirability of arbitration instead of strikes, also revealed the broad usage of the term arbitration. He was asked if his organization had made any efforts to establish a board of arbitration. He replied affirmatively, but then added, "This I speak of is hardly arbitration—it is conciliation; the committee endeavors to conciliate the matter, meet the employer, if possible, half way. . . ." He went on to say that the recent Cincinnati convention of his international union had adopted a law, then being voted upon by the membership, obligating every local union "to endeavor to arbitrate" with the employer before a strike could be authorized.[12]

Gompers certainly did not intend that matters pertaining to working conditions should be turned over to third parties for decision. Rather, the intent was to secure recognition from the employer and, if possible, to bargain with him over the terms of employment prior to taking strike action. In any event, the Cigarmakers' Union was also seeking internal control against hasty, ill-conceived strike action and was voting on the issue of requiring efforts to bargain with employers before strikes could be called. A common procedure in these days was to call a strike to enforce demands,[13] but the results were often disastrous to the unions. From this they desired to escape.

An example of the loose use of the word arbitration and the obvious lack of a term for collective bargaining is found in the testimony of Adolph Strasser, who appeared at the same hearing. His testimony also confirms the interpretation made above of Gompers' remarks. When asked, "What steps are taken before a strike is declared?" Strasser answered, "We as a rule, have a committee on arbitration [obviously what we nowadays would call a bargaining committee] to meet with the employer, and inquire into the matter and try to bring about a settlement." Furthermore, when asked if they had tried to establish "a board of arbitration," he replied, "We have; we have really practically enforced it; we always elect committees; it has always been advocated." Yet he added, interestingly, "we have not yet inaugurated the system of arbitra-

tion which is prevailing in England that of selecting an umpire in case both parties cannot agree."[14] It is obvious that the term arbitration was used broadly enough, if not more or less synonymously, to include bargaining as well as intervention of third parties.

It is of interest too, in this same connection, that the establishment in New York City, by various crafts in the building trades and their employers, of joint committees of a permanent sort were contemporaneously described as "arbitration committees." No third parties were involved, although sometimes several local unions were represented by the same committee, as when H. Oscar Cole was the chairman of the committee representing five bricklayers' unions. Their work was described as a "sort of friendly conference."[15]

Another piece of interesting evidence of the broad usage given to the term arbitration, in the absence of the term collective bargaining, is found in the report of the New York Commissioner of Statistics of Labor in 1885. He explained, "there are several forms of so-called arbitration in practices in the state at the present time." Among the types, he listed the following: "the appointment of a committee to see the employer to protest against a reduction or to urge an increase . . ."; "grievance committees to whom such matters are referred"; "others have what are called shop committees, who are also termed arbitration committees." He even included a process in union government as constituting a form of arbitration, for he said,

A form of arbitration which has prevailed in the City of New York during the past few years, [which] has seemingly met the approval of a large number of organizations . . . consists in referring the trouble which arises in a subordinate union to a central body in which a large number of trades and callings are represented. This possesses the merit of being impartial as far as the special abuse is concerned, and as the committee appointed by this central body has, as a rule, met committees of manufacturers, it would seem that it is as near perfection as an experiment of this kind can reach. . . .

Continuing, he said, "But the most general form is to refer the matter to the executive committee of the trade . . . their government gives them a sort of power as boards of arbitration."[16]

Although arbitration was often synonymous

[12] *Third Annual Report of the Bureau of Statistics of Labor of the State of New York, 1885,* p. 450.

[13] Neil W. Chamberlain, *Collective Bargaining* (New York: McGraw-Hill, 1951), p. 5, passim. This practice had been common in England earlier; see Crompton, *Industrial Conciliation,* p. 6.

[14] *Third Annual Report of the Bureau of Statistics of Labor of the State of New York,* 1885, p. 451.

[15] Ibid., p. 441.

[16] Ibid., pp. 368–69.

with collective bargaining, the term was also used in its narrower modern meaning of adjudication by private persons appointed by mutual agreement of the parties involved to decide matters in the dispute. Even so, the practice of this type of arbitration was very limited.

In discussing the settlement of strikes, for example, the report of the New York Bureau of Statistics of Labor in 1887 observed that 1,162 disputes were settled by conciliation. Then it was explained,

> The term "conciliation" is used as the proper one and in place of the more generally used, but, nevertheless, improper expression, arbitration. The two are entirely different in meaning, although the latter is almost universally applied to any settlement made between employer and employe. Practically, two interested parties to a controversy cannot arbitrate their differences without calling in a third and disinterested party. Where two aggrieved parties settle a difference between themselves, it is done, and can only be done, by concessions on the part of one or both. In other words, one or both conciliated the other.[17]

EARLY BARGAINING PRACTICES

Although a name had not yet been found for union-management negotiation, the practice of collective bargaining was already evident by the middle of the 19th century. It hardly needs to be emphasized that the development of collective relationships between management and labor in the United States had been spotty and discontinuous up to this time. Nevertheless, a few noteworthy antecedents of modern collective bargaining can be found in the fragmentary records of joint employer and worker relations. Some significant cases of collective bargaining occurred in the half century prior to the Civil War.[18] During and after the war, as unions became active once again, there were more cases of joint relationships, even if the development must be characterized as slight. Collective action without organization, however, cannot be continuous, and unions experienced great difficulty before this time in staying organized for any purpose. Of necessity, organized labor had concerned itself either with unilateral establishment and maintenance of standard rates, or with political or reform programs. Its approach was always pragmatic, whether centering in the advocacy of reform legislation, welfare programs, or economic force.

One of the earliest significant examples on record in the United States of what might be called collective bargaining occurred in 1850. In that year, the printers and their employers in New York City met jointly to set rates of pay, but the practice was not long-lived; within a couple of years they reverted to unilateral actions.[19]

In the printing industry we also find one of the early advocates of collective bargaining. Horace Greeley, as president of the New York printers' local union in 1853 and later as an employer, spoke lucidly of the desirability of joint negotiations. He did not like the customary "directed scale" of wages, which the union was promulgating unilaterally, but advocated scales drawn after joint participation of workers and employers. The prevailing custom of the organized printers—true also of other organized workers at the time—was to promulgate their scales unilaterally, relying upon economic strength to make the scales effective. This practice was based partly upon the fact that employers were unwilling to meet with them. The unionists usually had no other recourse than unilateral action supported by economic power. Greeley argued against the practice in principle and urged the workers to change their policy. Later, as an employer, Greeley consistently advocated the same approach. On one occasion, while still a unionist, he said,

> . . . the journeymen made a mistake in proceeding of themselves to fix a new and advanced scale of prices and then asking the employers to accede to it. They ought to have asked the employers to unite with them in revising the scale and adapting it to the existing state of things.[20]

An example of conciliation, or collective bargaining, which occurred at the end of the Civil War in the Pittsburgh iron trade may be men-

[17] Fourth Annual Report of the Bureau of Statistics of Labor of the State of New York, 1887, p. 707.

[18] John R. Commons and Associates, History of Labour in the United States, Vol. 1 (New York: The Macmillan Co., 1921), pp. 121–22, 601–4; Chamberlain, Industrial Conciliation, pp. 1–22.

[19] George A. Stevens, New York Typographical Union No. 6—A Study of a Modern Trade Union and Its Predecessors (Albany: J. B. Lyon Co., 1913), p. 253; Commons and Associates, History of Labor, Vol. 1, pp. 121–22, date the first attempt at negotiations in 1799 when the Philadelphia Cordwainers were locked out for refusing to accept a decrease in wages but shortly sued for peace and waited upon the employers with an offer of a compromise which was accepted after negotiation.

[20] Stevens, New York Typographical, pp. 252–53; Chamberlain quotes this statement by Greeley, which appeared originally in the New York Daily Tribune as an editorial, and says of it, "perhaps the first concisely ordered statement in this country" of collective bargaining. Chamberlain, Industrial Conciliation, p. 26.

tioned because it involved negotiation with an employers' association.[21] The United Sons of Vulcan was organized in 1858, secretly, for the men feared discharge. With the outbreak of the Civil War and a more favorable labor market, union activities were brought into the open. By 1863 the power of the organization began to be felt and the union was recognized. A general conference of representative workers and employers reached an agreement, dated February 13, 1865. It has been described as "probably the first important attempt at conciliation in this country."[22] After some alteration, following the first year's experience, the agreement remained in force for seven years. Conciliation in this sense also developed in the anthracite region of Pennsylvania as early as 1870.[23]

Another example of early joint relations which occurred in the shoe industry at Lynn, Massachusetts, has sometimes been cited as an early example of arbitration.[24] Although the parties themselves referred to their procedure as a joint board of arbitration, it is another example of the loose use of the term arbitration. A reading of the account of the joint dealings of the employers and organized workers reveals very clearly that the program was so akin to collective bargaining as we know it, that one should not now describe it as an example of arbitration. The arrangement, at first, consisted of a committee of five from the union, a local of the Knights of St. Crispin, and five from the employers, set up "to meet . . . and talk over matters in an amicable manner; so that, if possible, some agreement might be reached which would be mutually satisfactory."[25] In 1870 the two committees worked out an

agreement, and the men "were jubilant, and considered they had gained a point *in being recognized by* employers as a body *to be negotiated with on equal terms.*"[26] This arrangement was destroyed by employers in the economic crisis of 1873 but was revived, in part, in 1875 "with considerable countenance and aid . . . from some of the manufacturers" with a larger "board of arbitration [as it was called] . . . composed of 11 members, each from a different branch of labor." This time no employer committee or board was established, but even so, many disputes were settled informally, "amicably and without much trouble." Obviously this "board of arbitration" was simply a union committee empowered to deal with employers after investigation of complaints to "endeavor to effect a settlement . . . before giving their consent to a strike" by meeting "a committee appointed by the employer." There was no appeal to an outside party, only to "the lodge" of the union.[27]

CONCLUDING OBSERVATIONS

Events like those that have been described, not the spectacular conflicts over recognition which fill the pages of the early history of unionism, give us the clearest insights into the real nature of the institution of collective bargaining. A moderate, conservative process is its true picture. One may avidly read the story of early labor and management warfare and may reflect with admiration upon the great courage and fortitude with which unionists sought to establish the right to bargain collectively, yet have only a partial understanding of the practice that has become a marked feature of our industrial society. The true nature of the institution of collective bargaining is better portrayed— although less spectacularly—in those situations where relationships were being worked out on a man-to-man basis. Conflict was the manifestation of lack of acceptance or of frustration, whereas the humble structural and procedural developments were the promise and the hope of the future. The latter were basic, the former transitory.

The fundamental character of early collective bargaining was clearly seen by a contemporary who, as much as anyone in his day, had studied the problem of industrial unrest. J. D. Weeks wrote with knowing insight:

While there has been little or no conciliation in this country, such as exists in the trades in England,

[21] State of Pennsylvania, Department of Internal Affairs, Bureau of Industrial Statistics, *Annual Report of the Secretary, 1878–79,* Part 3; Cf., Joseph D. Weeks, *Report to the Governor of Pennsylvania on the Practical Operation of Arbitration and Conciliation in the Settlement of Differences between Employers and Employees in England* (Harrisburg: Lane S. Hart, 1879), pp. 109–119; Commons and Associates, *History of Labor,* Vol. 2, p. 80.

[22] Weeks, *Report to the Governor,* pp. 111; In Commons and Associates, *History of Labour,* Vol. 2, p. 80, it is stated, "it deserves attention . . . for it offers the first instance of a trade union entering into a trade agreement with an employers' association."

[23] Carroll D. Wright, *Industrial Conciliation and Arbitration* (Boston: Rand, Abery, 1881), pp. 121–32. This report prepared under the jurisdiction of the Massachusetts Bureau of Statistics of Labor is mostly the work of Joseph D. Weeks.

[24] *Eighth Annual Report of the Bureau of Statistics of Labor,* Massachusetts Department of Labor and Industries, 1877, p. 19; Cf. Chamberlain, *Industrial Conciliation,* p. 32.

[25] *Eighth Annual Report of the Bureau of Labor Statistics,* Massachusetts, 1877, p. 27.

[26] Ibid., pp. 27, 30 (italics supplied).

[27] Ibid., pp. 41–43.

that is, systematic through the medium of permanent committees organized for the purpose of conciliation, there are certain forms that have a history. . . . Unfortunately for the advance of mutual confidence and sympathy between the two parties to labor contests . . . examples of conciliation, for the most part, never come to the knowledge of the world. They are worked out in the quiet of the countinghouse and office, where employer and employed meet as equals, and as man should meet man, and then and there in all kindliness and good feeling settle their differences before they become disputes.[28]

These brief notes and reflections on the beginnings of collective bargaining reveal it as a process conceived in the best heritage of our democratic traditions. It is founded, not in radicalism or necessarily in militance, but in the desire to be conciliatory, fair, and businesslike. Institutionally, collective bargaining, apart from any need to establish itself or to fight for survival as a process, is completely compatible with the other institutions of a capitalistic or enterprise society.

---

[28] Wright, *Industrial Conciliation*, p. 108. One should not minimize, however, the importance of power in the practical working of collective bargaining. Without the right to strike, collective bargaining could not function. It is a phenomenon based on power; but the rational use of power of which the parties are aware while the public often is not. The deadline and the possibility of the use of power to effect a shutdown are instruments of agreement making. The point to be made is that collective bargaining, although an instrument for peace, is not a guarantee of peace. Its value lies in the fact that it generally produces peace and preserves the essence of democracy and enterprise. No other method will do as much. There is no other satisfactory, realistic alternative; not by legislation, not by arbitration—although it has its proper place—but only by collective bargaining can we preserve the values of democracy and enterprise.

24. Structure of Collective Bargaining*

John T. Dunlop†

DISTINCTIVE FEATURES OF U.S. COLLECTIVE BARGAINING

Collective bargaining is carried on within a framework of law, custom, and institutional structure that varies considerably from one country to another. The framework of bargaining in the United States has certain characteristics that sharply distinguish it from that of most other industrial democracies.

Perhaps the most significant characteristic of the American collective-bargaining system is that it is highly decentralized. There are approximately 150,000 separate union-management agreements now in force in the United States. A majority of union members work under contracts negotiated by their union with a single employer or for a single plant. Only 40 percent of employees covered by collective agreements involve multi-employer negotiations, and the great bulk of these negotiations are confined to single metropolitan areas.

In the United States, unlike most countries in Western Europe, one union serves as the sole representative for all the employees in a plant or other appropriate bargaining unit. This practice conforms to the American political custom of electing single representatives by majority vote. It can also be traced back to the tradition of conflict among the autonomous international unions.

* From Gerald S. Somers (ed.), *The Next Twenty-Five Years of Industrial Relations*, Industrial Relations Research Association, © 1973, pp. 10–18. Adapted and exerpted from Derek C. Bok and John T. Dunlop, *Labor and the American Community* (New York: Simon and Schuster, 1970), chaps. 7 and 8. A final section reports briefly on the application of the analysis to recent problems of the construction industry.

† John T. Dunlop was Professor of Economics at Harvard University when this article was written; he is currently Secretary of Labor.

To restrain such conflict, the American Federation of Labor—as far back as the 1880s—developed the concept of exclusive jurisdiction. Under this principle, only one union was authorized to represent employees in a particular occupation, a group of jobs, or, occasionally, an industry. Employers generally accepted exclusivity since it stabilized labor relations by diminishing disputes among competing unions. It was natural, therefore, for the principle to be embodied in public policy when the government began to develop detailed regulation over collective bargaining. Thus, during World War I and under the Railway Labor Act of 1926, a system of elections was adopted to enable groups of employees to select a single representative by majority vote. The same procedures were subsequently carried forward on a broader scale in the National Labor Relations Act of 1935 and its subsequent amendments.

Under almost any system, collective bargaining leaves room for a degree of individual negotiation over certain terms and conditions of employment. Even in the United States, the law explicitly provides that an employee can discuss individual grievances with representatives of management. And in a few fields—for example, the performing arts—agreements typically leave employees free to bargain individually for salaries above the minimum. For the most part, however, collective agreements in the United States specify the actual wages and terms of employment which in fact govern the workers in the bargaining unit, and individual employees do not negotiate different terms on their own behalf.

The absence of any authority in law to extend a collective-bargaining contract to others who have not accepted the agreement is rooted in the structure of the American industrial-relations systems. It is comparatively easy to extend a contract containing a few minimum terms and conditions, particularly when the contract has been negotiated by an association representing a large and representative group of firms. In the United States, however, where rival unions may coexist in a single industry, where contract terms set actual rather than minimum requirements, and where provisions are highly complex and often vary from one firm to another, it would be very difficult to find a single set of terms that would be suitable for all firms in the industry.

In another respect, the structure of bargaining in this country has caused the law to play a more ambitious role in collective negotiations than it does abroad. Although we rely less heavily on legislation to fix the substantive terms of employment, there is much more regulation in the United States over the tactics and procedures of bargaining. Thus, law in the United States defines the subjects that must be bargained about. It requires the parties to "bargain in good faith" and clothes this obligation with detailed rules proscribing stalling tactics, withholding of relevant information, and other forms of behavior that are considered unfair. The net result is a complex of regulations that greatly exceeds anything to be found in other industrialized countries.

THE PARTIES AND THE STRUCTURE OF BARGAINING

These special characteristics help to define the framework of the American system of collective bargaining. Within these contours, several types of negotiation go on. The most familiar aspect of bargaining involves the discussions between the parties over the terms and conditions of employment for the workers involved. But a vital part of the bargaining process has to do with determining the structure and the procedures through which these discussions will take place.

One question of structure has to do with the level at which different issues should be resolved. This problem is particularly significant in any negotiation that affects more than one place of work. In a situation of this kind, the parties must decide which issues should be agreed upon at the negotiating table and incorporated into a master agreement and which should be left for labor and management representatives to settle at the company, plant, or departmental level. Agreements made at these subsidiary levels are called local supplements. Sometimes the interdependence between the two settlements creates prob-

lems. Is one settlement contingent upon the other, and is a failure to conclude one a basis for a strike or lockout in all units? Which settlement will be made first?

These questions are often difficult to resolve. In a multiplant company, for instance, such matters as the amount of time allowed for wash-up before the end of a shift or the allocation of parking facilities might be best handled at the plant level. But it is also clear that policies or precedents on these matters at one plant may influence decisions elsewhere. Considerations of bargaining power and market competition may also influence the level at which particular issues are treated. As technological and market changes take place, it may be necessary to alter these arrangements and provide for more centralization on some issues, as with the introduction of containers in the East Coast longshore industry, and greater decentralization in other instances, such as the determination of the number of trainmen in a crew on the railroads. Since conditions vary widely from one plant or industry to another, there is little uniformity among collective-bargaining relationships in the pattern of centralization and decentralization in negotiations.

A second problem in arranging negotiation procedures concerns the range of jobs, territory, and employees to be governed by the ensuing agreement. Several illustrations may be helpful. The basic steel companies took major strikes in 1946 in part to achieve separate negotiations for their fabricating facilities from their basic steel operations. As a result, separate agreements with different expiration dates and different wage scales now are negotiated at different times, reflecting the different competitive conditions that affect these two types of operations. In view of differing market conditions for the different products involved, the major rubber companies have on occasion insisted on differential wage increases for tire plants and those plants making rubber shoes and other rubber products. Conversely, 26 cooperating international unions sustained an 8-month strike in the copper negotiations of 1967–68 in an effort to obtain collective-bargaining agreements with the same expiration dates and identical wage increases for all employees of a company.

A third set of structural problems has to do with the relations among different craft unions bargaining with a common employer. In recent years, the newspaper printing industry, the West Coast shipbuilding industry, and the construction industry have suffered many strikes growing out of disagreements over the wage pattern or sequence of settlements among a group of inter-related crafts agreements. For example, the 114-day New York newspaper strike of 1962–63 was fought by Bertram Powers, president of Local 6 of the International Typographical Union, largely to change a system of bargaining which had existed since the early 1950s. Under the prior agreement, wage settlements had been made with the Newspaper Guild and then extended to other newspaper unions. As a result of the strike, contract expiration dates were negotiated which removed the five-week lead the Guild has pre-viously held and thus eliminated its ability to impose an industrywide pattern on the other unions before they ever got to the bargaining table. Thus, the strike enabled Powers to put an end to a follow-the-leader pattern that had deprived his union of any real power to negotiate its own wage agreements.

Serious questions may arise also in deciding which subjects should be encompassed within the scope of collective bargaining. The subjects that are dealt with vary widely, reflecting in each contract the problems of the relevant workplace and industry. Some maritime agreements specify the quality of meals and even the number of bars of soap, towels, and sheets that management is to furnish to the crew. Such provisions are natural subjects for negotiation, since they are vital to men at sea, but they would make no sense in a normal manufacturing agreement. In some contracts in the ladies' garment industry, com-panies agree to be efficient and to allow a union industrial engineer to make studies of company performance. These provisions would be regarded as ludicrous in the automobile industry. Detailed procedures respecting control over hiring are central to collective bargaining in industries with casual employment, where employees shift con-tinually from one employer to another, as in construction and stevedoring; but in factory and office employment, new hiring typically is left to the discretion of management. In this fashion, the topics raised in collective bargaining tend to reflect the problems of the particular workplace and industry.

The law also plays a part in deciding the subjects for negotiation, since the National Labor Relations Act (Section 9a) requires the parties to bargain in good faith over "rates of pay, wages, hours of employment, or other conditions of employment." Pursuant to this Act, the National Labor Relations Board and the courts have de-cided which subjects are mandatory topics for collective bargaining and which are optional. In some instances, particular subjects or bargaining proposals have been held to be improper or illegal and hence nonnegotiable, such as a union's insistence on a closed shop or an employer's demand that the union bargain through a par-ticular form of negotiating committee or take a secret ballot prior to calling a strike. On the whole, however, the Board and the courts have steadily broadened the scope of mandatory bar-gaining to include Christmas bonuses, pensions, information on plant shutdowns, subcontracting, provisions for checkoff of union dues, and many other topics.

The provisions of the National Labor Rela-tions Act would appear to make legal rulings decisive as to the scope of bargaining. And on a few issues, such as pension plans, litigation undoubtedly played a significant role. In the main, however, although the law may help to define the outer limits of bargaining, the actual scope of negotiations is largely decided by the parties themselves.

DISPUTE SETTLEMENTS AND THE STRUCTURE OF BARGAINING

In disputes over the terms of an agreement, there are three elements that may shape the procedures, beyond ordinary mediation, to be used for settling differences.[1] The first involves the *substantive terms* in dispute—wages, pen-sions, technological displacement, crew size, in-centive systems, job evaluation, promotion cri-teria, and the like. Some subjects are more com-plex than others; some issues treat all employees equally, while the essence of others is that they involve differential treatment among groups of employees. Some questions are easily compro-mised; other arise from differences of principle or involve matters that virtually affect the institu-tional security and well-being of one or both of the parties.

The second critical feature of a dispute has to do with the *relations between the particular labor and management organizations.* The character of the negotiation may differ enormously between the first contract and, say, the fifteenth to be negotiated by the parties. One or both parties may be afflicted with intense internal leadership rivalry; expectations among constituents may be very high with respect to the results of negotia-tions, thereby complicating agreement-making

---

[1] While no scheme is ideal for all purposes, practi-tioners will readily recognize the types of disputes which follow. These do not, of course, constitute an exhaustive list. In fact, disputes seldom occur in the pure forms here cited, since actual cases typically involve mixtures.

and ratification; the preceding contract period may have been most difficult to administer, with the consequence of a large backlog of unresolved grievances that shape attitudes in the negotiations.

A third feature, present in some disputes, is the determination of one side to change the *structure of bargaining*. Such disputes involve a change in the design of collective bargaining negotiations themselves—the scope of employees to be covered by the agreement, the timing of expiration dates of various agrements, the selection of a leader among a group of unions—as much as disagreement over wages, hours, and working conditions. Two subtypes are especially significant: (*a*) disputes involving relationships of two or more unions, typically craft unions, bargaining with the same management or an association of employers, and (*b*) controversies over the range of plants or companies or employees to be included, formally or informally, within the scope of the negotiations. In cases of rivalry among unions, managements are often seeking to expand the scope of bargaining with a group of craft unions. In coalition bargaining it is typically the union which seeks to expand the effective coverage of the agreement and enlarge the scope of possible future strikes.

Disputes arising from attempts to change the structure of bargaining no doubt involve the most difficult negotiations, with the most serious and longest work stoppages. A list of the disputes and stoppages that have attracted the greatest public attention in the private sector in recent years would include the following cases where the structure of bargaining was a major issue.

Stoppage	Years	Time
New York City newspapers	1962–63	114 days
East coast longshore industry	1964–65	60 days
Cleveland construction industry	1965	39 days
Maritime industry, East and Gulf coasts	1965	78 days
Pacific Shipbuilding Association, electricians	1966	5 months
New York plumbers	1966–67	6 months
Railroad shop crafts	1967	1 day
San Diego shipbuilding	1967–68	4 months
Copper industry	1967–68	8 months
East Coast longshore industry	1968–69	2 months

Disputes over bargaining structure often lead to prolonged work stoppages and substantial money settlements without ultimately resolving the underlying structural issue. Since adjustments in bargaining structure are not readily negotiated, higher money settlements are simply a rough compromise to postpone the ultimate day of reckoning. As a result, disputes over bargaining structure can persist over many years, with an accommodation in bargaining arrangements being made bit by bit through negotiations that are often characterized by prolonged stoppages.

RECENT APPLICATIONS OF THE ANALYSIS TO CONSTRUCTION

The collective bargaining structure in construction was, in my view, a major contributing factor to the high level of work stoppages over the terms of agreements and to the rapid rate of inflation of wage rates and benefits in the late 1960s and early 1970s.[2] The level of effective demand or the degree of monopoly power of labor organizations or their control over hiring, often alleged to be the operative factors, do not provide a very convincing explanation nor do they provide much of a reason why such results had not taken place earlier in periods of strong demand. Moreover, they do not provide much of an understanding of the accelerating inflationary process as it spread throughout large segments of the industry and diffused geographically in the period prior to the imposition of wage controls in this industry alone on March 29, 1971. By early 1971 first year settlements were running 16–18 percent a year and one out of three expiring agreements resulted in a work stoppage.

The collective bargaining structure in many regions of the country, particularly in the East,[3] and in many branches of the industry had become increasingly obsolete as contractors and workers had increased the range of their movement with the highway system, as the pension, health and welfare, and other benefit funds were less appropriate to a single locality, and as union contractors in various branches of the industry confronted quite different forms of competition. In many areas the role of the strike or lockout ceased to be a means to encourage conventional collective bargaining as many contractors and workers continued to work in nearby areas and

[2] For a discussion see Daniel Quinn Mills, *Industrial Relations and Manpower in Construction* (Cambridge: The M.I.T. Press, 1972), chap. 3.

[3] For a careful study see the report of the Construction Industry Collective Bargaining Commission on the geographical bargaining structure of New York State, 1970.

as national agreements tended in many cases to undermine local negotiations.

The Construction Industry Stabilization Committee from the outset sought to encourage reforms in the structure of collective bargaining in the industry as a long run contribution to stabilization "in furtherance of effective collective bargaining in the industry," to use the language of the executive order. The tripartite Committee, working through the national union and association leaders, developed the following program to improve the structure of collective bargaining:

a. Each branch of the industry should develop a bi-partite national craft board to play an active role in the settlement of local disputes over terms of agreements.

b. The geographical scope of agreements was reviewed by the national organizations, and in many cases agreements were consolidated with appropriate adjustments in the local union and contractor organizations for collectivetive bargaining purposes. Special attention was directed to the need for several wage zones in many enlarged agreements in order not to adversely affect union contractors in rural regions.

c. Separate and lower wage schedules were developed by many crafts for some branches of the industry, such as residential construction.

d. The geographical scope of funded benefits were reviewed to reduce in many cases the administrative costs of benefits in small locals and contractor groups.

e. The work rules in agreements should be reviewed both to secure greater uniformity and to encourage productivity.

f. The Committee itself has been concerned with the timing of the expiration of agreements among related crafts in a locality.

While not all crafts and employer organizations have been equally interested in promoting a structure of collective bargaining which is less prone to strife and to inflation, the operations of the Committee and the craft boards have made a significant contribution in these directions. Indeed, these larger and longer run objectives of national leaders of both sides have made it possible to achieve the shorter run purposes of stabilization and significant retardation in the rate of inflation.

25. Reflections on Bargaining Structure Change*

Herbert R. Northrup†

INTRODUCTION

The structure of collective bargaining in the United States is a fascinating polyglot of craft, industrial, local, regional, national, and miscellaneous arrangements that derive from history, accident, ambition, relative power, governmental interference, and a host of other factors. Certainly it is not possible to describe this system in a brief paper. Hence these remarks will be confined to the potential for change in a few key areas.

The cornerstones of the mixed American system are the principles of exclusive representation and majority rule, which make changes in the structure, for the most part, dependent upon the consent of the parties. Hence changes in structure are not easy to obtain, however well or indifferently they serve the parties or the public interest. A structural change upsets both the existing power balance and the political status quo. If, for example, bargaining is altered from a local to a regional basis, it is likely that the economic advantage of one party over the other is lessened while, at the same time, the importance and/or political stature of the local union officials and plant personnel and line officials suffer a decline. It is readily apparent that changes of this nature are not universally welcome.

Nevertheless, change does occur and is occurring, and for a variety of reasons. In this paper, I shall focus on four instruments of change: (1) union mergers; (2) management instigated restructuring; (3) governmental pressures; and (4) international developments. Of

course, there are many other factors involved, and even for the subjects covered, space constraints permit only the highlights to be noted.

UNION MERGERS AND BARGAINING STRUCTURE IMPACT

As Professor John T. Dunlop has pointed out, union organization in the United States is under considerable stress, not for ideological reasons as the intellectual left and other romanticizers would have us believe, but for the mundane facts of financial realities.[1] Three-fourths of American unions have a membership of 100,000 or less. With scattered membership, with, like universities and other nonprofit bodies, costs rising in an inflationary period much faster than income, and with membership disinclined readily to increase dues, many of these smaller unions do not have the finances to serve their memberships adequately. Recently, for example, the International Chemical Workers Union required the injection of a one dollar per month dues increase merely to survive. Consequently, we have seen quite a few union mergers, and more are likely to develop.

On the other hand, a few large unions, particularly the Teamsters and the Steelworkers, see the plight of smaller unions as an opportunity. Both have become conglomerate unions. Devoid of ideological hangups, they merge smaller organizations in a manner analogous to their industry counterparts, providing for guaranteed employment and pensions for the officers and

* From Gerald S. Somers (ed.), *Proceedings of the Twenty-Sixth Annual Winter Meeting*, Industrial Relations Research Association, December 1973, pp. 137–44.

† Herbert R. Northrup is Professor of Industry and Director of the Industrial Research Unit, the Wharton School, University of Pennsylvania.

[1] John T. Dunlop, "Future Trends in Industrial Relations in the United States," address before 3d World Congress, International Industrial Relations Association, London, 1973, mimeo.

staff of the merged union at rates higher than the small impecunious unions could possibly pay, thus securing support for the merger action. Then like the conglomerate corporation which assures the world that "no changes in personnel or staff are contemplated," the conglomerate union removes the frequently less-than-expert newly acquired staff from positions where their bumbling could be hurtful or where their possible disloyalty could be upsetting, and sets out to reorganize bargaining structure in the industry.

The United Steelworkers' experience in non-ferrous mining and its entry into chemicals are cases in point. In the former case, it merged the Mine, Mill and Smelter Workers in 1967 and attempted immediately to put bargaining on a company-wide, if not industry-wide basis. Apparently, its optimism that this could be accomplished out of hand was based on the USW experience in steel, aluminum, and can, and the former MMS bureaucracy's belief that all it required was unity and the USW's resources. Fearful that such a structure would doom their converting businesses, the Big Four nonferrous mining concerns refused to yield. After a nine-month strike, settlement was finally achieved on the basis of a compromise, but new structure worked out by an extra-legal board headed by the late George W. Taylor. This structure maintained the separation of primary and secondary processing and manufacturing operations.[2]

Now the Steelworkers has become the largest union in the chemical industry by absorbing District 50. This industry has featured a low degree of unionization, weak unions, and plant bargaining units. All this the Steelworkers is determined to change. It has set out to unionize DuPont, the industry's giant. A majority of DuPont's plants are unorganized; the second largest group bargains with local independents; and about five plants are unionized by the International Chemical Workers Union. The Steelworkers' organizing drive had yielded one victory in a small facility and a defeat in a larger one by the end of 1973. Meanwhile, it is wooing the independents to merge them and actively attempting to organize other plants.

Elsewhere in the industry, the Steelworkers have induced Allied Chemical to agree to regional bargaining in New York state and, with a union coalition, have succeeded in gaining limited company-wide bargaining at Union Carbide on pensions and insurance.[3] For the Steelworkers to accomplish its mission, it needs not only to increase the degree of unionization in the chemical industry, but to effectuate further expansion of bargaining units. Single plant units allow companies to transfer production and to withstand strikes, especially since chemical production processes permit maintenance of a high degree of production at single facilities by supervisory and salaried personnel during strikes. Needless to note, success of the Steelworkers' organizing and restructuring plans in the chemical industry would result in a fundamental shift of bargaining power there and a further enhancement of union power generally.

MANAGEMENT INSTIGATED RESTRUCTURING

In terms of relative bargaining power, the construction industry is at the other end of the spectrum from chemicals. Union power is so overwhelming that the unions have only to watch the clock tick the employer into submission. As a result of excesses resulting from the abuse of this raw power, not only contractors, but also users and even government have moved to redress the balance. Yet it is the dismal science, economics, in the guise of nonunion competition, that is in fact having the greatest impact in this regard.

Historically construction bargaining has been largely on a local basis, and although multicraft bargaining has always occurred, there have been in most jurisdictions, several key crafts that bargain on an individual basis. Management representation has been split up into a plethora of associations, many of which seem more interested in the survival of their bureaucracies than in containing union power. In case a strike occurred, strikers could drive a few miles and work during the strike. Contractors, many of whom are small and financially weak, had no such easy method to sustain themselves. Moreover, each contractor was subject to strikes by several crafts, any one of which could shut him down.

To make matters worse, the industry has a number of national contractors with national agreements. These contractors traditionally kept working in a locality during a strike against local firms. When that occurred, strikers did not even have to travel to keep working. Meanwhile, contractors, national or local, who experienced a

[2] For a detailed account of these events, see William N Chernish, *Coalition Bargaining*. Industrial Research Unit Study No. 45 (Philadelphia: University of Pennsylvania Press, 1969), chap. 9.

[3] Union Carbide previously had fought hard to avoid coalition bargaining. See Chernish, *Coalition Bargaining*, chap. 7.

strike would receive unremitting pressure from manufacturing companies and other users to end the strike "regardless of the cost." And just in case the construction unions might suffer from the consequences of having everything going their way, the federal government has been there to bolster their power through the Department of Labor's propensity to define the Davis-Bacon prevailing rate as the union rate whenever doubt existed, and/or by the National Labor Relations Board and the courts interpreting the restrictions on secondary boycott to mere shadows of their purported substance.[4]

The results of such imbalance have led to a special stabilization program, a rethinking by the users and national contractors of their roles, and attempts by industry, government, and users to alter bargaining strategy, tactics, and structure. In the Dallas–Ft. Worth areas of Texas, for example, local associated general contractor and specialty contractor associations have assigned bargaining rights to a broad regional group, countered union whipsawing, and effectuated a much better bargaining balance. Similar restructuring of the bargaining units have had like results elsewhere. These results have achieved some success, at least in part, because of a number of key developments:

1. Users formed the construction Round Table, now a part of the Business Round Table, in order to support, instead of pressure, contractors, and have done just that.

2. Partially as a result of the Round Table's efforts, national contractors are now contributing to local negotiations and not working if a local stoppage occurs.

3. The construction stabilization program has apparently aided in slowing wage increases, thus in effect bolstering contractors.

All these developments might have been in vain, however, if the union construction wage inflation and continued productivity decline, had not induced an increasing number of users and contractors to see an alternative and contractors to take advantage of that alternative which is, of course, nonunion construction. In a study now underway at the Wharton School's Industrial Research Unit, we have found a surge of nonunion construction throughout the country in areas and types of work that just a few years ago were

monopolized by union construction. This expansion of the nonunion sector, widely acknowledged by unions and contractors, has created a number of union responses, including contract concessions, violence, and especially pertinent here, a willingness to agree to bargain on a different structural basis, as for example, the Dallas–Ft. Worth example just noted.

At this point, I should like to add a caveat against the trend to wider bargaining units. I can well understand the reasoning, and I agree that some widening might be necessary to avoid whipsawing in construction. Experience generally, however, indicates that in the long run, wide bargaining units may enhance already inflated union power, not modify it.

Indeed, those who see larger bargaining units as a panacea for bargaining weakness might well pause and study experience before they act. Certainly there is little in the history of national collective bargaining in the railroad, bituminous coal, flat glass, or steel industries that would automatically cry out for emulation, and overrated regional bargaining structures, such as those in the West Coast paper industry, have been reappraised on the basis of later developments. The larger the unit and the farther away from the employee that the decisions are made concerning wages, hours, and working conditions, the less are the problems of employee concern likely to be addressed, or the needs of local union officials likely to be considered. If an attempt is made to localize some of the bargaining to avoid ignoring workplace problems, as in practice is likely to be necessary, then the potential of separate national and local strikes exists. For the building contractor, being liable for only two strikes is a great advance, but in the less underdeveloped areas of work, this is a retrogression. Moreover, local strikes become more difficult over time because employers who settle economic matters at the national or regional level have little or nothing to give locally. Hence, they are unable or unwilling to make concessions to please employees or to provide political salve for local union business agents—at least until forced to by recurring local strikes.

Perhaps a better way of coping with the construction crisis is to permit economic forces to make their pressure felt. Ideally, this would involve repeal or modification of the Davis–Bacon Act so that where unions are not strong, union rates would not be artificially inflicted on the tax paying public. It would also include repeal or modification of the Norris–La Guardia Act so that union tactics, such as harassment picketing,

[4] A forthcoming Industrial Research Unit study will examine Davis-Bacon policy in detail. On secondary boycotts, see Ralph M. Dereshinsky, *The NLRB and Secondary Boycotts*. Labor Relations and Public Policy Series, Report No. 4 (Philadelphia: Industrial Research Unit, The Wharton School, University of Pennsylvania, 1972).

secondary boycotts, and organizational strikes can be dealt with. (The latter is, of course, what Congress thought it was doing with the 1958 Landrum–Griffin amendments to the Taft–Hartley Act, but the National Labor Relations Board and the courts have essentially rewritten these provisions.) And finally, it would involve enforcement of laws against violence, destruction, and personal injury—or treatment of such actions in a labor dispute no different than they are handled in other cases. Unfortunately, I must conclude that since these fundamental reforms are not on the horizon, construction employers must do what is possible—and today that means widening the bargaining unit and considering either going nonunion or forming a "double-breasted" nonunion subsidiary.

GOVERNMENT PRESSURES

Within our essentially mixed private-government collective bargaining system, government pressures on the structure of bargaining will continue to be significant. Only a few can be noted here. Bargaining unit determination by the NLRB has always been a strong shaper of bargaining structure, and will surely continue to be.[5] If, as it appears, the stabilization period drags on, changes in structure are likely to occur under the aegis of Dr. Dunlop, whose interest in the subject is obvious. In late 1973, for example, the cement and the supermarket industries were key targets for restructuring pressure from the Cost of Living Council. In both, the industry has performed very poorly in bargaining, and unions have demonstrated little restraint.

Although the direction of restructuring emphasis by the Cost of Living Council is not fully clear at this writing, it does appear that it is toward wider bargaining units at least in so far as cement is concerned. My caveats about this trend have already been made. I do believe that such industries as cement and supermarkets should take a good hard look at mutual aid a la the airlines, if they are to withstand union pressures. The supermarket industry is beset, like construction, with nonunion competition, and its unionized sector desperately needs some social engineering to remain viable. Its plight is similar to that of the construction contractor, and more than restructuring of the bargaining system is required for relief.[6]

For more than 20 years it has been very clear that the power of the Retail Clerks and, to a lesser extent, Meat Cutters in the supermarket industry, rested almost entirely on the boycott power of the Teamsters.[7] Reducing the efficiency of that boycott power, as I have proposed, would do much to bring collective bargaining in the supermarket industry closer to the public interest. Absent this basic reform, the inexorable forces of economics should result in a continued expansion of the regional and local supermarkets. They use separately owned cooperative or wholesaler warehouses, trucks, and in most cases, unionization. They are able therefore to utilize manpower more efficiently. Even if they pay equivalent wage rates to the union ones, like their nonunion construction counterparts, they then have significantly lower manpower costs. Sooner or later, this competition must affect the supermarket unions, although they have yet to face up to the clear results of their power.

INTERNATIONAL DEVELOPMENTS

Today there is much publicity and discussion concerning the potential of multinational collective bargaining. Much of this is self-appreciating bombast by a few officials of International Trade Secretariats, particularly the Secretary-General of the International Federation of Chemical and General Workers Unions (ICF), Charles Levinson. He has claimed credit for a host of successful confrontations with multinational companies. These claims have now all been investigated—Saint Gobain, AKZO, Michelin, Dunlop-Pirelli, and a host of others—in a recently completed article by a colleague and myself.[8] In all cases, the claimed results have been falsified, or exaggerated, or both, but accepted as fact by business journals and/or scholars too inefficient or lazy to delve behind cleverly written press releases.

Nevertheless, there are significant develop-

[5] For an analysis of the NLRB in this regard, see John E. Abodeely, *The NLRB and the Appropriate Bargaining Unit,* Labor Relations and Public Policy Series, Report No. 3 (Philadelphia: Industrial Research Unit, The Wharton School, University of Pennsylvania, 1971); especially chap. 4, "Unit Modification."

[6] Some discussion of similarity between construction and supermarkets is found in Herbert R. Northrup et al., *Restrictive Labor Practices in the Supermarket Industry.* Industrial Research Unit Study No. 44 (Philadelphia: University of Pennsylvania Press, 1967).

[7] See Marten Estey, "The Strategic Alliance as a Factor in Union Growth," *Industrial and Labor Relations Review,* Vol. 9 (October 1955), pp. 41–53.

[8] Herbert R. Northrup and Richard L. Rowan, "Multinational Collective Bargaining Activity: The Factual Record in Chemicals, Glass, Rubber Tires, and Petroleum," *Columbia Journal of World Business* (March and June 1974).

ments which could lead to multinational bargaining in the European Economic Community. These developments involve not the traditional trade secretariats but regional groups under the aegis of the European Confederation of Trade Unions, and particularly its affiliate, the European Metal Workers Federation. The latter, which has no official ties to the International Metalworkers Federation (IMF), has conducted several multinational union discussions with Philips and Fokker-VFW and with the European shipbuilding industry. That these discussions could lead to new bargaining structures that could involve American multinational concerns, and eventually American unions, seems clear. Although it is easy to overlook problems, difficulties, and national institutions which stand in the way of fruition of union aims, we do anticipate some multinational bargaining structures in Europe within this decade.

CONCLUDING REMARKS

In this paper, I have confined my attention to the private sector. Just a glance at the public sector indicates that all the mistakes ever made relating to bargaining structure in the private sector are being made in the public one, plus a few new ones. Moreover, whereas economic realities do assert themselves in the private sector, however hesitantly, they are blocked by political considerations in the public one. The imbalance of power there is so monstrous as to raise very serious questions whether collective bargaining among public employees is a viable method of determining employee wages, hours, and working conditions, and the current bargaining structure, with its fragmented units and special groups, adds to the problem. The viability of local and state government, as well as the need to gain effective control of the national government, all require that we thoroughly rethink and reanalyze what was done when the private collective bargaining model was applied to the public sector.

At the same time, it would seem to behoove all of us to examine critically where we are headed in the structure of bargaining in the private sector. Is not the whole question of structure grounded in the concept of relative power? If that is so, is the thinking of the 1930s, so strong in the views of the NLRB and Department of Labor bureaucracies, not lacking in the public interest for the social setting of the 1970s? If the answer remains affirmative, should we not question much of the law and administration which underpins union and management power in order to determine whether it is in the public interest? Obviously I believe so, and I invite particularly the younger scholars to rethink this question most seriously.

26. Bargaining Structure and Relative Power*

George H. Hildebrand†

In what follows, I propose to consider three recent shifts in the balance of bargaining power between unions and managements in the United States. One involves an effort by certain unions to enlarge the scope of negotiations by forming coalitions of separate bargaining units. The second concerns the substitution of "selective" for industry-wide strikes by one of the leading unions in the railroad industry. The third involves the impacts of seven years of inflation upon union demands and management resistance.

I. COALITION BARGAINING

Probably the most dramatic attempt to alter the balance of bargaining power in recent years has been the movement for coalition bargaining mounted by the Industrial Union Department of the AFL-CIO during the period 1962–68. The campaign extended over a broad range of industries, among them petroleum refining, nonferrous metals, chemicals, metal products, electrical equipment, and food processing. Several very prominent firms have been involved.

In each instance, the initial target situation was one in which a multi-plant concern had been conducting separate negotiations with several different locals, frequently affiliated with more than one international union. As I have pointed out elsewhere,

The initial object of a coalition is to enlarge the scope of bargaining beyond the limits of each of the existing units—*without, however, technically re-placing either the units themselves or the unions recognized to be their respective bargaining agents.*[1]

Put a little differently, the goal of a coalition is to bring about unilaterally an enlargement of the scope of negotiations and of decision-making to embrace a fragmented group of bargaining units that hitherto had negotiated separately; and to accomplish this while leaving these separate units technically intact.

Typically, coalitions have emerged in the following contexts. In the first, the employer has several competing plants, each with a different local belonging to the same national union, and with a separate agreement for the particular plant. This was a situation confronted by an early coalition directed against bargaining in Standard Oil of Ohio. Where it occurs, the employer has the advantage of being able to substitute among alternative sources of supply, which enables him to take local strikes more effectively, and to bargain successfully to recognize differences in wages and other conditions according to locality, to the disadvantage of the locals and their parent organization, as they see the matter.

The second situation is a variant of the first: Here there is more than one parent international. Each suffers from incomplete jurisdiction, rivalry with the other organizations, inability to mount companywide strikes, and the risk of being undercut because it cannot effectively "take wages out of competition." This roughly describes the situation confronting the coalition in General Electric and Westinghouse. Only a carefully coordinated common strategy among the unions can overcome

* From Richard L. Rowan (ed.), *Collective Bargaining: Survival in the '70s?*, © University of Pennsylvania, 1972, pp. 10–23.

† George H. Hildebrand is Maxwell M. Upson Professor of Economics and Industrial Relations, Cornell University.

[1] George H. Hildebrand, "Cloudy Future for Coalition Bargaining," *Harvard Business Review*, Vol. 46 (November–December 1968), pp. 114–28. My colleague, Professor Frederic Freilicher, has been most helpful in discussions of coalition bargaining and selective striking.

these inherent weaknesses of fragmented bargaining.

In the third situation, the basic problem for the unions is the vertical integration of the company—in the case of copper, from mine to concentrator to smelter to refinery to fabricating plant. At any one stage, the problem is as in our first case: substitute plants under the control of the same employer, with local bargaining. But with vertical integration combined with separate bargaining, the employer is better able to take strikes at any link in the chain. If the mines and smelters are closed, he can buy metal for his fabricating plants in the open market, avoiding a complete shutdown of operations. If the finishing plants are struck instead, the mines can continue to produce either for stock or for sale in the open market. In basic steel, the technical circumstances are quite similar, but because the industry has been organized by a single large union that bargains companywide, there is no problem of strike effectiveness devolving from the fact of vertical integration. By contrast, in nonferrous there is such a problem from the union point of view. Its solution requires a coalition of monumentally complex character, as in fact was put together by the United Steelworkers back in 1967 after this organization had absorbed the former Mine-Mill Union.

Finally, there is the case of the conglomerate producing company, for example, Union Carbide. Within given lines of production, some plants in such a concern will be substitutes for one another. But the very existence of a broad array of products will bring about diversity in technology and in occupational requirements. Add fractional bargaining to this mixture and the result will be a complex bargaining system in which the employer is likely to have the initiative. No local union is likely to be strong; indeed, no national union is either. Thus the incentive for concerted action will be present and acutely felt, though putting together a combination will be unusually difficult.

Over the past five years ample opportunity became available to test the strategy and tactics of coalitions in the courts and before the NLRB. Although I lack space to develop them fully, the following now seem to be relatively settled points of law.

First, as the Board found in the *Phelps Dodge* case,[2] it is "nonmandatory" that negotiations be conducted on a basis broader than the established bargaining unit. To insist, as the Respondents did in that case, that the employer bargain companywide and therefore beyond the scope of the established units, and to strike in behalf of this demand, were violations of Section 8(b)(3) of the Act.

Second, the parties have a duty to execute local settlements once reached, even if other units remain without agreements.[3] In short, it is violative of the Act for a party to a system of local agreements to follow an all-or-nothing strategy as regards a return to work in any one unit in which settlement separately has been achieved. This, of course, denies to the coalition a central element in the typical strategy of such combinations.

Third, an employer is within his rights to try to preserve a system of local bargaining, provided he observes his own obligations under the law. Thus, he can insist that the bargaining be confined to the scope of the established unit whose agreement is before the parties for renegotiation. But he cannot refuse to undertake such negotiations simply because the union's bargaining team may include persons belonging to other unions or from "outside" of the unit as such.[4] And if the employer can also show that he has bargained to an impasse on mandatory items, he may lock out the particular plant as part of his strategy for countering a coalition.

Finally, in view of the foregoing it seems clear that the Board will continue to emphasize the scope of existing bargaining units except where the parties themselves agree to change that scope. This was not so clear in 1968, when the Board decided over the employer's opposition in the *Libbey-Owens-Ford* case that separate self-determination elections could be directed over the question of whether the locals involved should now be represented by an established multi-plant unit for other locations of the same company.[5] The company successfully contested the majority view in Federal District Court, but the Board obtained a reversal in the Court of Appeals, and the Supreme Court denied certiorari. The elections were then held, but there-

[2] AFL-CIO Joint Negotiating Committee for *Phelps Dodge* v. *Phelps Dodge Corp.*, 184 N.L.R.B. No. 106, 74 L.R.R.M. 1705 (1970). See also the Report of the Trial Examiner in *Kennecott Copper Corp.* v. *United Steelworkers of America*, 176 N.L.R.B. No. 13, 71 L.R.R.M. 1188 (1969).

[3] *Standard Oil Co. of Ohio*, 137 N.L.R.B. 68 (1962).

[4] *American Radiator & Standard Sanitary Corp.*, 155 N.L.R.B. 69 (1965).

[5] *Libbey-Owens-Ford Glass Co.* v. *United Glass and Ceramic Workers of North America*, 169 N.L.R.B. 2 (1968). See also *Libbey-Owens-Ford Co.* v. *McCulloch*, 67 L.R.R.M. 2712 (1968); and *McCulloch* v. *Libbey-Owens-Ford Glass Co.*, 68 L.R.R.M. 2447 (1968).

after the company refused to bargain with the enlarged unit in order to test the majority view of the Board's powers in disputed cases involving changes in the scope of a unit.

During the pendency of a complaint on this aspect of the matter, Mr. Edward B. Miller became Chairman of the NLRB. By his joining the earlier minority members, a new majority emerged that found that the Board should not have made the earlier "clarification" of the original certification, nor have conducted the ensuing elections. In the Chairman's own words, "the principle which the Board so boldly announced in 1968 has proved to have extremely limited utility."[6] However, he was careful to distinguish his majority colleagues' position—that statutory authority was lacking for the Board's original order—from his own—that the authority was available to merge units but was inappropriately used in this instance, where the parties' relationships had been long established.

As matters now stand, the record of the various coalitions is a spotty one. It has not proved possible to compel the enlargement of the scope of a negotiating unit where the employer is opposed to the move. This is not to say that the employers have not had to pay a high economic price, both to withstand long strikes and to obtain ultimately separate settlements of those disputes. Rather it is to say that as things have turned out, the law now leans heavily against the more obvious forms of coalition strategy. In the legal sense, then, the balance of bargaining power is not likely to shift in the near term.

But to those who would seek such a shift de facto, a subtler strategy still remains open: This is to try gradually to narrow down the spread between the expiration dates in the separate agreements. Eventually a companywide strike then would become feasible, whereupon the negotiations can be made interdependent even though they remain legally separate. In this way uniformity in settlement terms at the end of a dispute can be approached although the integrity of the separate units is left free from direct attack.

Thus the apparent failure of several coalitions should not be taken to mean that negotiating scope ultimately cannot be enlarged because unit scope has successfully been preserved. In turn, this means that it is still possible legally to shift the center of negotiating gravity from the plant to the entire company. And where this difficult exercise can be successfully executed, a shift in the locus of union power also seems a likely next step. The national office would gain relative to the locals. Parallel national unions would acquire incentive to merge. And where a dominant national organization has provided successful leadership to a coalition involving weaker nationals as well, its prestige, influence, and ability to expand are all likely to grow. By the same token, all of these tendencies together would diminish the bargaining power of those multi-plant companies that now have fractional local systems. These concerns would lose the ability to resist strikes by substituting one plant for another, and therewith the means for preserving major inter-plant differences in their local agreements.

The logical extension of the concept of coalition bargaining is from all company plants within the United States and Canada to those owned by the same firm overseas. Although nothing lasting so far has emerged from this interesting conception, the possibility has been discussed in recent years for automobiles, chemicals, textiles, and radio-tv sets. Superficially, it seems plausible to argue that if wage uniformity is "fair" for all automobile workers in the United States, it is equally so for those throughout the world. The more interesting question is whether the automobile workers in the plants abroad would actually want wage parity with their brethren in the United States. Would they press equalitarianism to this extreme?

I doubt it. Competitive economic analysis tells us that the principal reason for international differences in wages is differences in the economic productivity of labor. If, then, an international coalition were to be proposed, the first item on the agenda would be wage standards. If the U.S. level were proposed, the more astute foreign bargainers would quickly point out that this would serve as a protectionist device for the United States, by equalizing wages but not unit labor costs throughout the industry—with attendant sizable loss of jobs abroad. But anything less than international wage uniformity for the industry would require the acceptance of the "competition of cheap foreign labor"—hardly an attractive goal for an American union. And so I conclude that a proposed international coalition would founder at once on the shoals of wage policy. If it could survive this passage, its course toward effective strike control for all competing plants anywhere in the world still would be perilously difficult to carry out. In turn this is indeed fortunate for industrial workers in the

---

[6] *Libbey-Owens-Ford Glass Co.* v. *United Glass and Ceramic Workers of North America*, 189 N.L.R.B. No. 139, 76 L.R.R.M. 1806 (1971).

developing countries in particular, for otherwise their jobs would be at forfeit.

II. SELECTIVE STRIKES ON THE RAILROADS

The unspoken and unexamined premise of the foregoing discussion is that a coalition of separate bargaining units to enlarge the scope of negotiations will increase the relative bargaining power of the union, to the disadvantage of the employer. Otherwise why would the coalition be undertaken?

But at this point we encounter a paradox: If the premise is correct, how are we to interpret the recently judicially recognized right of the United Transportation Union to strike selectively against any of some 170 railroad carriers who are joined together for multi-employer bargaining? Presumably the UTU switched to the tactic of striking selectively because it believed that this would increase its power to attain its objectives. Collaterally, by fighting these strikes vigorously in the courts, the carriers must have reasoned that the tactic would weaken their own position. Yet the tactic itself calls for substituting selective strikes for a mass stoppage of the whole industry —in short, partial disintegration of a coalition, at least so far as strikes are concerned. By contrast, the ability to mount a companywide strike is the central tactical argument for a coalition itself.

Fortunately, there is a way out of this dilemma. On the railroads, a selective strike already involves an entire company rather than a subdivision thereof. Within the struck carrier, there is no counterpart to the substitute plants of the multi-plant manufacturer. In consequence, the UTU is already in a position to impose companywide strikes upon as many carriers as it chooses, to the same effect as that arduously sought by an industrial coalition in pursuit of simultaneous expiration dates for its separate contracts. Accordingly, the carrier's normal revenues can be completely cut off. If it stands out for any length of time, its losses can be enormous, and it will also run the risk of a permanent loss of some customers.

Thus the proper comparison is not between an industrial coalition against a single multi-plant employer and selective striking of separate railroad companies. Rather it lies between a coalition against all companies in a given industry and one directed against a single employer alone. Perhaps, then, to paraphrase Karl Marx, to the multi-plant industrial employers the rail-road case presents "the image of their own future," just as England was supposed to do for the other less developed industrial countries of the 19th century. With dialectical inevitability the movement of bargaining history may well be from the plant locus of negotiations to the entire company, and finally from the entire company to the entire industry. And once the goal of multi-employer bargaining is attained, then divide-and-conquer tactics—that is, selective striking—become the next order of business. And if industry-wide bargaining of this type becomes widespread, then we would have a change of quantity becoming a change of quality, again in Marxian dialectical fashion. Can the system of organizational laissez-faire that we call free collective bargaining survive this kind of evolution? I defer this question until later. Meanwhile I want to refer briefly to the judicial reasoning by which selective railroad strikes were upheld.

Between 1969 and 1971, a manning dispute existed between the carriers and four railroad unions. The issue involved "national handling" in that it embraced the regional associations that bargain jointly for some 170 carriers. National handling, as Herbert R. Northrup has pointed out in an outstanding recent paper, is a requirement sought successfully by the railroads themselves in the 30s to overcome their vulnerability to whipsawing tactics under the earlier more decentralized bargaining systems.[7] In the case at hand, three of the unions settled, but the UTU held out. After bargaining had gone to an impasse and the procedures of the Railway Labor Act had been exhausted, the union began a series of strikes against selected properties. The carriers responded by seeking injunctions. In the *Delaware and Hudson* case they were successful, but met reversal in the Court of Appeals. In *Burlington Northern,* the lower court denied their request.[8]

Both cases rest on the same line of reasoning. First, the courts held, where a dispute begins under national handling, both parties remain obligated to keep negotiations at that level, and to settle on a multi-carrier basis. On the precedent in *Atlantic Coast Line,* both "practical appropriateness" and "historical experience" so dictate.[9]

Second, so long as the union seeks only to

[7] Herbert R. Northrup, "The Railway Labor Act: A Critical Reappraisal," *Industrial and Labor Relations Review,* Vol. 25 (October 1971), p. 9.

[8] *Delaware & Hudson Railway* v. *United Transportation Union,* 76 LRRM 2898 (1971); *United Transp. Union* v. *Burlington Northern, Inc.* 76 LRRM 2838 (1971.

[9] *Brotherhood of Railroad Trainmen* v. *Atlantic Coast Line Railroad Co.,* 66 LRRM 2115 (1967).

bring pressure to bear upon the whole carrier group on behalf of a joint settlement, and not to coerce the individual struck properties into making separate settlements, it is legally free to employ its basic right to strike in a selective manner. Essentially this is a matter of good faith. It cannot be decided beforehand, as the lower court attempted to do in *Delaware and Hudson*. Therefore an anticipatory injunction was inappropriate. Furthermore, the Appellate Court chose to believe the UTU President, Charles Luna, when he declared that his purpose in striking selectively was only to bring pressure to bear toward a national settlement, and not to extract separate agreements for the struck properties.

Third, the carriers are not without weapons in their own defense. They can impose their own work rules unilaterally, and they can resort to a nationwide lockout if they wish.

By these findings, the Appellate Court rejected the contentions of the carriers: that they are extremely vulnerable to whipsawing because they are weak financially and because they cannot produce for inventory; that the unions respect each other's picket lines and can easily close the roads down; that the railroad strikers can draw unemployment compensation paid for entirely by the company; and that the majority cannot reasonably be expected to yield to a pattern achieved on one property alone, under conditions of extreme inequality lying against the employer.

There can be little doubt that these rulings strengthen the position of the unions against the carriers. To combat whipsawing, the latter must risk a total shutdown at costs they can no longer easily absorb. They also risk ensuing congressional intervention, with politically dictated settlements that, if the Railroad Signalmen's case is typical, are likely to increase their burdens even further.[10] I also share Northrup's view that in addition to representing the most complete form of government control of collective bargaining now present in the country, the Railway Labor Act discourages voluntary settlements, rewards intransigent behavior, and perpetuates obsolete rules and work practices.[11] If this is typical of

full-scale government intervention, then its extension indeed bodes ill for the survival of collective bargaining itself.

Yet, at the same time, I have to say that as these selective strikes eventually worked out, they yielded an almost unheard-of novelty in the dismal record of the railroad industry: a dispute that was allowed to run its full course without government intervention to bail out the intransigent party, but instead with a voluntarily negotiated settlement that includes some built-in provisions for resolving surviving issues. Compared with experience since 1941 under the Emergency Board procedures and subsequent interventions, this consummation is indeed as welcome as it was unexpected.

III. INFLATION AND RELATIVE BARGAINING POWER

We have arrived now at the point where we ought to stand back and take stock before looking further into the question of changes in relative bargaining power in the economy. First, I contend that the right way to view the coalition movement is as an attempt to introduce the bargaining systems of basic steel and automobiles to a group of large companies that by chance rather than design emerged three decades or so ago with localized and fragmented rather than centralized and consolidated bargaining arrangements. The number of these concerns and their relative importance for aggregate production and manpower are not large. But if their systems eventually can be centralized, this will contribute significantly to the problems now confronting our general policy of relatively unhampered collective bargaining. Under that policy, some strong national unions have already emerged. If the efforts of coalition succeed, these organizations will grow even stronger. With this increase in strength, their political influence will also expand.

This leads me to my second point. The wave of inflation that set in early in 1965 has already seriously tilted the balance of bargaining power against management and toward the unions. In general impact, it has released the considerable potential of collective bargaining as an independent source of inflation of its own. It is in this context that the New Economic Policy of August 15 should be interpreted.

NEP is an incomes policy for the United States. In fact it is the second one attempted in peace time, the first having been introduced in 1962 and killed by the airline strike settlements

---

[10] The Signalmen were offered and rejected a pattern accepted by other unions, and instead went on a brief strike in May 1971. Congress intervened statutorily to end the strike; in doing so, it imposed a 13.5 percent retroactive wage increase upon the carriers, while doing nothing whatever about proposed legislation to improve the handling of emergency disputes. Thus the union gained a 13.5 percent increase as a reward for its irresponsible act. (Northrup, as cited, p. 14.)

[11] Ibid., pp. 29–31.

of 1966.[12] Both versions involve guidelines. Both include prices along with wages. Both are attempts to restrain the use of market power by sellers, in particular the power of unions to raise wage costs through collective bargaining. And, finally, neither version contemplates any direct attack upon the sources of this market power. Rather, both of them aim only at restraint in the exercise of that power.

The only way that one can rationalize the 90-day wage-price freeze together with the subsequent creation of the Pay Board and Price Commission is to assume that the country now suffers from sellers' inflation, in particular, wage-push by the trade unions. In turn this implies a shift in relative bargaining power that for now at least cannot be adequately controlled by the indirect method of fiscal and monetary restraint alone.

General inflation contributes to excessive increases in wages through collective bargaining because it reduces the costs of larger demands to the unions at the same time that it lowers the costs of larger settlements to the employers. On the union side, the threat of ensuing layoffs is lowered; it is easier for men to quit and to get another job quickly; and rank-and-file militancy is increased by a rising cost-of-living and, initially at least, higher profits. To management, it is more costly to take a strike and an excessive quit rate than it is to settle largely on the union's terms and then to recoup through higher prices without fear of reduced sales. In this way inflationary expectations develop for both sides, finding recurrent expression in ever larger wage settlements and price scales. Once started, the process becomes extremely difficult to check by the indirect method of fiscal and monetary restraint, not because the method will not work but because political considerations forbid its exercise to the possibly drastic degree required. Before August 15, 1971, this approach was in fact working slowly in the right direction. However, the fatal combination of some continuing inflation with relatively high continuing unemployment was more than the community seemed prepared to accept for much longer. In short, the old policy had lost popular support.

The current inflation had its inception in the beginning of 1965, when plenty of slack existed in the economy, both in plant capacity and in manpower. As both the money supply and public spending were rapidly expanded, the wage and price levels entered their sustained rise and inflationary expectations began to be built up. By this time the economy was undergoing an inflation based upon excess demand. As we can expect with excess demand, profits were strongly inflated as well. But by 1970 the period of excess demand had been passed, and excess resources had reappeared. At the same time, corporate profits had been declining sharply since 1968. Although fiscal and monetary restraint were now the order of the day, general price inflation continued, interest rates soared, and the cost of wage settlements continued to rise. Thus we entered the period of "stagflation," that is, an inflation without excess demand in which there exists a substantial margin of unused resources and little or no growth in real output. The situation is rather like that of 1957–60. It has also been experienced recurrently in Great Britain ever since World War II.

At this point, the question of relative bargaining power comes up once more and some observations are in order. Cost-push inflation is primarily wage-push inflation. Its cause cannot be product-market monopoly because final price mark-ups have not been widening as this notion requires. Quite the contrary. Mark-ups must have been shrinking, because profits have been falling for over three years although output has been slowly rising. Thus we have to look specifically at wage costs as the source of the trouble.

What has been happening is that increases in the costs of compensation in 1970 alone, for example, were averaging 7 percent in the private sector; output per manhour (labor productivity) was advancing on average by only 1.0 percent; and unit labor costs accordingly were edging upward by about 6.0 percent. In short, these higher costs were slowly contracting. Finally, for the collective bargaining sector in 1970 the mean annual rates of increase for union wage settlements were running at over 10 percent throughout all industry, at between 15 and 21 percent in construction, and at over 8 percent in manufacturing. That is why the present situation can be attributed to wage-push inflation.

Now the mechanism by which the union sector of the economy serves as the pace-setter for wage-push inflation over the system is complex and cannot be examined here.[13] At the same time, it must be emphasized that this peculiar

---

[12] The previous policy carried no sanctions other than "moral suasion."

[13] See George H. Hildebrand, "Structural Unemployment and Cost-Push Inflation in the United States," in George Horwich, ed., *Monetary Process and Policy: A Symposium* (Homewood, Ill.: Richard D. Irwin, 1967), pp. 15–29.

kind of inflation cannot emerge without an initiating impulse from excessive expansion of money. Nor can it continue indefinitely without renewed monetary expansion. Money, in short, remains the root of the inflation problem. Here again the mechanism is complex and cannot be considered. For present purposes, all that need be said is that inflations begin with the mismanagement of money by governments. Let the process persist and the inflationary expectations will become general. If, now, monetary restraint is introduced to check the inflation, it will take considerable time to become effective—all the more so if the inflation has been running for several years, as this one has. Meanwhile, during this lag before monetary slack is taken up, the accumulated force of wage-push begins asserting itself with increasing vengeance, prolonging the general rise of prices well after money restraint has taken over. This is the situation in which the NEP system of direct control has been introduced.

Just as the freeze can have brief effectiveness for dampening inflationary expectations, the control apparatus of Phase II can contribute to the same end for a short period. But the success of the Pay Board, for which we all hope, will depend upon that Board's ability to influence specific settlements. For, as Gottfried Haberler has pointed out, it is these individual settlements and not the wage level as a whole that are the controllable policy variable. Furthermore, the Board's success will also depend upon the continuing support of fiscal and monetary restraint. Without such restraint, we would find ourselves in a period of suppressed inflation, which is the worst of all economic worlds.[14]

Whatever one's view of the effectiveness of peacetime direct controls with sanctions, their introduction is a symptom of a loss of faith in the ability of relatively unregulated labor and commodity markets to produce wages and prices compatible with non-inflationary full employment. Thus the central question of the hour is: Will these controls ultimately disappear, or will they be extended and made permanent? To this I have no answer, only a closing comment.

The theme of this paper is changes in relative bargaining power and their significance for the survival of collective bargaining in the 1970s.[15] Collective bargaining has emerged as an institution over the years as part of what Clark Kerr once called the "system of liberal pluralism," or what Theodore Lowi more recently has termed "interest-group liberalism."[16]

However described, pluralism views modern society as a collection of independent groups—in our case, unions and employing companies—no one of which is dominant and all of which function under a government of limited powers. For the labor market, the basic premise is organizational laissez-faire. That is, the state sets the rules of the game. The parties are then left free to make their own private bargains. Above all, the key underlying assumption is that this bargaining struggle will produce a socially and politically acceptable economic equilibrium, compatible with sustained growth and non-inflationary full employment.

It is this system of self-equilibrating countervailing power that is now threatened by the several tendencies we have been considering. Are we about to enter an age of what we may call the socialism of interest-groups, or will we return eventually to the economy of private bargains in due course? That is the central economic issue for today.

---

[14] Gottfried Haberler, *Incomes Policies and Inflation: An Analysis of Basic Principles* (Washington: American Enterprise Institute, 1971), p. 24.

[15] Unions and managements as such of course can survive without collective bargaining in a new environment of direct government controls, where political influence and bargaining would take over.

[16] Clark Kerr, "Industrial Relations and the Liberal Pluralists," *Proceedings of Seventh Annual Meeting of Industrial Relations Research Association* (1954), pp. 2–17; Theodore Lowi, *The End of Liberalism: Ideology, Policy, and the Crisis of Public Authority* (New York: W. W. Norton, 1969).

27. Steel: Experiment in Bargaining*

I. W. Abel†

The Steelworkers and the ten basic steel companies have agreed to an unprecedented experiment in collective bargaining. This new approach did not come about with any suddenness. When I appeared before the Collective Bargaining Forum in New York City in 1969, I talked about our efforts to find a better way to resolve our differences through collective bargaining. I reviewed at that time the discussions that had been underway then between the union and representatives of the basic steel industry for utilizing voluntary arbitration as a means of resolving contractual disputes. We mutually agreed, at that time, that we had to solve the twin problems of stockpiling and imports but could not agree then on all the elements that would make a voluntary arbitration arrangement work in collective bargaining.

What did finally emerge in the Spring of 1973, thus, is part of an evolutionary process that had its beginning in the late 1960s. Development of this new approach involved much study and a great deal of discussion and old-fashioned bargaining. But because of the attitude of both sides, because of the spirit of cooperation, and because both sides recognized the importance of what we were seeking to accomplish, we were able to agree on a brand new approach for settling our bargaining differences.

The new bargaining procedure is officially known as the Experimental Negotiating Agreement—ENA for short. We are excited about it. We regard it as a historic breakthrough on the collective bargaining front. It's called an experimental agreement because we are going to test the usefulness of this approach in our bargaining talks in 1974 when the present 3-year agreement expires. Both sides are committed to the procedure only for the 1974 negotiations. If it works to the satisfaction of both sides—and we hope it does—we will continue to utilize it. If it proves unsuccessful, then it's back to the drawing board. But I am personally convinced it will work.

This is what the new negotiating plan does: it provides certain guaranteed preliminary benefits for our members in the basic steel industry; it protects certain existing employe benefits and rights; it allows the parties to negotiate freely in almost all economic and fringe benefit areas; it safeguards certain management rights; it eliminates the possibility of a nationwide strike or lockout in the steel industry; and it provides for voluntary arbitration of any unresolved bargaining issues.

This new approach is something that the founder and first president of our union envisioned about 33 years ago. At that time, Phil Murray co-authored a book on the evolution of relations between management and unions called *Organized Labor and Production*.

As both sides become more nearly equal in bargaining power, he predicted, they will "either wage war to gain the spoils of production restriction and scarcity prices, or they will together devise improved production practices that increase social income."

Phil Murray was writing primarily about the development of more mature labor-management relations. Yet his words clearly apply to what we have evolved in the form of a new bargaining procedure in steel. What he tried to tell us in

† I. W. ABEL, an AFL-CIO vice president, is president of the Steelworkers and of the AFL-CIO Industrial Union Department.

* Reprinted from The American Federationist, AFL-CIO, Washington, D.C., Vol. 80, No. 7, July 1973, pp. 1–6.

1940 was that both sides could either wage war or work together when confronted with problems of common concern.

There's no doubt that we've done our share of waging war with the basic steel industry over the years. Those of us still around have the scars to prove it. Sometimes the fighting amounted to little skirmishes, but at other times the future of the union and the industry was on the line. But after our shoot-outs and bargaining hassles, down through the years, conditions began to change, and problems of mutual concern began to emerge.

In the late 1950s, foreign steel producers started to make inroads on the U.S. domestic market. The 116-day strike in 1959—the last one, incidentally—provided foreign steel makers an initial opportunity to acquire and cultivate American customers. That was when our problems started to build up each time we went to the bargaining table. During our negotiating periods, the market was being glutted with more and more imported steel while the industry kept stepping up production to satisfy the stockpiling which steel customers were undertaking as a hedge against a possible strike.

The stockpiling had its impact not only on our bargaining and on our successes at the bargaining table, but it also had a tremendous impact on the ups and downs of production and employment.

This resulted in a "feast and famine" or "boom-bust" treadmill for our members in the basic steel industry. Most steelworkers enjoyed steady work and many worked overtime just prior to the negotiating periods and during the negotiating period. But then came the peaceful settlements, the working off of stockpiles, partial plant shutdowns, and prolonged layoffs.

Shortly after I assumed office as president of the Steelworkers in October 1965, I appointed a special committee to study the union's collective bargaining procedures and to explore methods of improving them.

The 1965 basic steel agreement contained a provision that required union and company representatives to study issues not resolved by the 1965 negotiations and "other possible topics of mutual interest."

The union's international officers and general counsel and a four-man group representing the steel companies began informal discussions on possible steps that could be taken in the 1968 negotiations.

From the beginning of such informal discussions, however, there was a clear understanding that such discussions involved no commitment by either party. It was also clearly understood that any matter that might be viewed favorably by the spokesmen of the parties would not be binding until there had been full examination and approval by appropriate ratifying groups.

These discussions brought forth a highly tentative approach to bargaining for study by both sides in 1967. The suggested procedure outlined a concept of arbitrating any issues which could not be resolved by bargaining in the 1968 negotiations.

The procedure was studied thoroughly by the executive board of our union. After a full exploration of the proposal, the board said it believed that while the new concept was worthy of serious consideration, there were certain safeguards and guarantees that should be part of any new bargaining procedure before it could be taken to the union's policy-making councils.

"In short," the board noted in a public statement December 2, 1967, "it was essential that the interests of our members be fully protected; that there be reasonable assurances that we can obtain essential improvements without jeopardizing our existing benefits and protections; that the procedure will promote, not hamper, effective collective bargaining; and that we share with the industry in the economic benefits inherent in any new bargaining procedure."

It was clear to us in 1967 that the industry was not prepared to agree to those safeguards, guarantees, and inducements that were necessary for the development of a completely sound approach. However, the board, in its statement, pledged to continue the search for new and better methods of bargaining. What is needed, the board said, is an approach to bargaining that is not only free of any potential disputes but one that also offers our membership genuine hope of achieving results equal to those obtainable when the traditional freedom to strike prevails.

The search for the new way continued but it was not found in time for the 1971 negotiations when the "boom-bust" cycle became worse. And in 1971, for the first time in the history of this country, we witnessed the steel industry laying off workers and shutting down mills and plants one full month in advance of the expiration date of our contracts and the possible commencement of a strike. Following the peaceful settlement in 1971, many production units were shut down and complete plants were closed. Some of our members went jobless for more than seven months because of stockpiling that year. Steel imports in 1971 set an all-time record—18.3 million tons.

Since 1 million tons of imported steel represents the export of 6,000 full-time job opportunities in the steel industry, the 18.3 million tons of steel imported in 1971 represented the export of at least 108,000 full-time job opportunities. The stockpiling and related problems following the 1971 negotiations also cost the 10 largest steelmakers an estimated $80 million. These harsh economic after-effects of the 1971 negotiations spurred both sides on with renewed vigor in the search for a new bargaining approach.

This time our efforts succeeded, and the result was the Experimental Negotiating Agreement that assures labor peace in the steel industry at least until 1977. The plan was approved overwhelmingly by the union's 600-member Basic Steel Industry Conference on March 29, 1973, and was signed a few days later by officials of the ten major steel firms. In a joint union-industry statement following installation of the new procedure, we made this comment:

Both parties feel sure that the action taken today will assure the nation and steel customers a constant supply of steel and an end to the "boom-bust" cycles associated with past labor contract negotiations . . . The new agreement not only provides for additional wages and benefits for employes, but will also provide an opportunity for the companies to increase production through stability of operations and enhance the steel industry's competitive position.

The new agreement applies only to the ten companies that bargain together as the Coordinating Committee Steel Companies. This includes Allegheny Ludlum, Armco, Bethlehem, Inland, Jones & Laughlin, National, Republic, U.S. Steel, Wheeling-Pittsburgh and Youngstown Steel & Tube.

Here are the major elements of our experimental negotiating agreement:

Our members employed by the ten companies —some 350,000 workers—will be guaranteed wage increases of at least 3 percent each year of the 3-year agreement, due on August 1 of each of the years 1974, 1975, and 1976. I want to emphasize that these are guaranteed minimums that do not prevent us from seeking greater pay increases in the negotiations. The wage increases of 3 percent in each of the three years of the agreement will also be included in the incentive calculation wage scales.

Also, each of our members having employe status as of August 1, 1974, will receive a one-time bonus of $150. The companies agreed to pay this amount in recognition of the production savings they anticipate from avoiding the effects of stockpiling. This one item will mean a payout by the ten companies to our members in excess of $50 million.

The Experimental Negotiating Agreement assures that the cost-of-living clause we won in 1971 will continue to operate through 1977. There will be no "floor" and no "ceiling" on the amount of cost-of-living adjustments that can become payable during the life of the new agreement.

Also, there are certain fundamental safeguards in our existing collective bargaining agreements that each side wants to protect and preserve. These pertain to local working conditions—or past practices; the union shop and checkoff provisions; the no-strike and no-lockout provisions; and the management rights provisions.

Under the new procedure there will be one bargaining procedure to resolve national issues and another to resolve local issues. On the national level, both sides will start talks no later than February 1, 1974. If an agreement is not reached by April 15, either party can submit its unresolved bargaining issues to an Impartial Arbitration Panel which will have authority to render a final and binding decision on such issues. This arbitration panel will be made up of one union representative, one representative of the companies, and three impartial arbitrators selected by both sides. At least two of these three arbitrators to be chosen by both sides will be persons thoroughly familiar with collective bargaining agreements in the steel industry. This panel will hear any disputes during the month of May 1974 and must render its decisions no later than July 10, 1974. The balance of July will be available for implementation of the panel's award. The renewal date for the basic steel agreement is August 1 of next year.

On local issues, for the first time in the union's history, we have established a separate right to strike over such issues. At the same time, the companies will have the right to decide upon a lockout on local issues at the plant level. We believe—and so does the industry—that if such local plant strikes or lockouts do materialize, there will be little likelihood of any significant disruption of domestic steel production.

These, then, are the basic ingredients of the new bargaining formula that both sides sincerely believe will prove to be the answer to the problems that have plagued our previous negotiations.

Support among our basic steel members for the new procedure has not been unanimous. It has been overwhelming, but not unanimous. Some of the opposition is based on a sincere concern over third-party influence and impact on our negotiations. And some is based on an unwarranted fear that the union will be powerless to negotiate effectively without a big club.

A review of early union experience and an examination of our bargaining disputes with the steel industry will show that our collective bargaining historically has been subjected to third-party influence and impact. As far back as 1937, in the days of the Steel Workers Organizing Committee, the forerunner of the United Steelworkers of America, Inland Steel and the Steel Workers Organizing Committee reached agreement in the office of the governor of Indiana after the company recognized the committee as the workers' collective bargaining agent.

During the years of World War II, steelworkers received a number of beneficial awards from the National War Labor Board, including wage increases, union security, improved vacations, and rate adjustments.

In 1949, after negotiations based on recommendations of a presidential fact-finding board, we won a trail-blazing, non-contributory pension plan with a minimum payment of $100 a month, plus social security, for employes with 25 years service; and also hospital and surgical care benefits.

In 1959, the date of our last strike in basic steel, intervention by third parties in that rather bitter 116-day strike was credited with convincing the industry to soften its hard-headed position and settle with the union. The third parties at that time were the then Vice President, Richard M. Nixon, and the Secretary of Labor, James P. Mitchell.

In 1965, when our negotiations were completely deadlocked, President Lyndon B. Johnson invited—if that is the correct word—both sides to Washington. And just to make sure we came, he sent his own plane to get us there. He then put both sides under virtual house arrest in the Executive Office Building next to the White House, saw that meals were not too appetizing or nourishing, and engaged in some arm twisting as only he could do. As a result, we wound up with an excellent settlement, including the first general pay increase in many years, and with major benefit gains on pensions and in other areas.

And in 1968 we got hung up over incentive pay coverage and finally turned the matter over to a voluntary arbitration panel for final and binding disposition. The end result, in 1969, was a decision directing the major steel companies to provide incentive pay opportunities to at least 85 percent of their total production and maintenance workforce and to at least 65 percent at each plant. The decision extended incentive pay coverage to an additional total of almost 50,000 steelworkers employed by the 11 largest steel firms.

So, we have had a history of third-party influence on our negotiations, although only twice have we applied voluntary arbitration in resolving collective bargaining issues—the incentive pay coverage issue of 1968 and now the Experimental Negotiating Agreement. Our decision to use voluntary arbitration in negotiations adds a new, refreshing element to third-party intervention: Both sides agreed voluntarily to the procedure in 1968 and 1973 without having someone impose it upon them.

When we officially established the new bargaining procedure I stated that we were confident this experiment can work.

I am optimistic for a number of reasons. First, the industry and the union have agreed to try this experimental approach on a one-time basis. The parties know that if the experiment fails, there may never be another chance to establish a long period of industrial peace in the industry. We realize that failure this time could lead to a long, disastrous strike three years later. I believe that these realities will be uppermost in the minds of both company and union negotiators as they meet next year. And it will put on all of us a degree of pressure that we may never have felt before—if the parties sincerely seek a long-range, stabilized labor-management relationship, and I think we do.

Also, it is only natural for both sides to prefer a settlement shaped by themselves, and not by a third party. The parties themselves know the problems best, and they also know what solutions will work best. A third party dictating the terms of a settlement might not be aware of technical problems that may, unwittingly, stem from an imposed settlement.

The need to formulate contract conditions that are workable and acceptable to both sides will serve as additional pressure to resolve issues independent of the arbitration machinery that has been established. In fact, I predict that chances are reasonably good that an entire agreement on national issues could be negotiated without submitting anything to the Arbitration Panel. This, certainly, will be the objective of the union.

Another positive factor in the 1974 negotiations is the fact that local unions will have the right to strike over local issues, which have always been a festering sore in our negotiations and which often produced demoralizing reactions from our members—even when we negotiated good national economic terms. Since local unions, in 1974, will for the first time have the right to strike over local issues, we expect speedier resolution of major issues and more effective bargaining on the local issues. Faced with the genuine possibility of a strike locally—however limited—the companies will have reason to bargain out such issues promptly in negotiations. This should help produce a more satisfactory settlement. The right to strike over local issues is an essential ingredient of the experimental procedure and the plan could not succeed without it.

The preliminary "sacred cow" concessions are also a vital part of the new procedure that will help ensure its success. The initial wage increases of 3 percent in each year of the 3-year contract, the $150 bonus, and retention of the union security, cost-of-living, and local working conditions clauses demonstrate to our members that the companies are acting in good faith. They also demonstrate to our members that the companies really want a settlement based on equity and are willing to back up that desire with a down payment—so to speak—even before contract negotiations begin. This will help put at ease any fears that management is out to weaken or undermine the union, or that the industry is seeking a cheap, cut-rate settlement. It creates the type of climate for bargaining that will lead to success. The preliminary concessions are, of course, another integral part of the experimental agreement and no approach to strikeless bargaining could have taken place without them.

There is an additional factor motivating both sides to reach a prompt, peaceful, and trouble-free settlement: the import threat. The experimental procedure was designed to mitigate crisis bargaining and reduce steel imports that always thrive during steel negotiations. Since the union and the industry acknowledged the import threat by agreeing to the new procedure, it is only logical that both sides will want to protect themselves further against steel imports by making the new bargaining approach work.

One additional point along this line: An experiment of this type could never have come about without a long, and often painful, collective bargaining relationship to set the stage for it.

The union underwent many critical strikes in the steel industry in its early years as the industry resisted bargaining progress every step of the way. In fact, the entire relationship nearly went up in smoke during the long 1959 strike. But that lengthy and bitter dispute brought both sides to their senses and paved the way for a healthy new dimension in steel bargaining that promises to be mutually beneficial and which may last a very long time.

We believe this unprecedented experiment will prove there is a better way for labor and management to negotiate contracts. The new procedure will not only relieve both sides of the pressures of a potential shutdown, but will also offer us a genuine opportunity to achieve results equal to those obtainable when the threat of a strike exists.

We have carefully preserved the nature and role of our bargaining relationship. What we have done is to extend and refine the tools of collective bargaining to solve a special and highly vexing problem afflicting our industry. Fourteen years of uninterrupted industrial peace in the steel industry have gradually established the maturity and respect for each other that justified this sort of an advanced step in our collective bargaining relationship.

We believe it will vindicate our faith in the free collective bargaining process. Both sides are determined to make this a successful endeavor so that those we represent can continue to enjoy substantial economic progress and the nation can be assured of continued stability in this most essential industry.

B. Strikes and Compulsory Arbitration in the Private Sector

Over the years one of the most interesting questions in the field of collective bargaining has been that which pertains to the usefulness of the strike in bringing about a meeting of minds. It has been argued by some that work stoppages should not be permitted, particularly in those cases where a significant part of the public would be affected. In order to prevent a strike and eliminate the inconveniences that accrue therefrom, compulsory arbitration has been proposed in various places.

The two articles in this section express interesting points of view in regard to the strike and compulsory arbitration. Thomas Kennedy argues that the right to strike is a fundamental factor in a free collective bargaining system. In his judgment, the price of the strike is not too severe when compared to the costs of compulsory settlements in labor-management disputes.

In the second article, Orme W. Phelps offers some "defense" of compulsory arbitration. He argues that "we have compulsory arbitration of labor-management controversies with us now. It is in large-scale operation in the United States today." Phelps concludes that a system of compulsory arbitration may have positive attributes and that it should not be discarded without further consideration.

28. Freedom to Strike Is in the Public Interest*

Thomas Kennedy†

FOREWORD

As public frustration grows over strikes, more voices are being raised in favor of some form of compulsory settlement of labor-management disputes. Freedom to strike comes at a price. But when this price is compared with the costs of compulsory settlements, it does not look nearly so high; free collective bargaining is vital to our private enterprise system. The author reaches these conclusions after first examining the reasons for increasing strike activity, the nature of collective bargaining, and the current trends in automation and conglomerate corporations which affect strike power.

Activities on the labor front have confirmed earlier forecasts to the effect that 1970 would be a difficult year. There have been numerous strikes and threats of strikes—and there are more to come.

The year opened with 147,000 General Electric workers already engaged in a stoppage which was to last for more than three months. The GE strike was followed by these events:

1. The threat of a nationwide rail strike or lockout, which ended only after Congress legislated a compulsory settlement.

2. The first major strike of federal employees, when postal workers in New York City and other metropolitan areas refused to work until the government agreed to bargain with their representatives.

3. A second work stoppage of federal employees, when a number of the air traffic controllers suddenly became "sick."

4. The refusal of members of the Teamsters Union in a number of the major cities to drive their trucks, in order to protest the terms of a new agreement negotiated by their national leaders.

5. The threat of a strike of the New York City newspapers.

The indications are that 1970 will continue to be a year of heavy activity on the strike front. Major contracts are open or will be open before the end of the year in a variety of major industries, including railroads (more than 500,000 workers not covered in the April 1970 settlement), over-the-road trucking, rubber, automobiles, farm equipment, New York City taxicabs, and New York City newspapers. It may well be that, when the year has ended, the record will show that the percent of working time lost as a result of strikes will have been the greatest since 1959 (the year of the 116-day steel strike), although it is not likely to approach the postwar record of 1946, when the percent of lost time was four times greater than it was in 1969.

IMPELLING FACTORS

Why are so many strikes being waged or threatened? There are at least eight major reasons. Let us review them briefly, limiting ourselves to a few highlights for each.

1. Numerous Negotiations

Labor contract terminations tend to peak at 3-year intervals in the United States. Thus 1967 was a big year for terminations, 1968 was a

* Reprinted with permission from *Harvard Business Review*, Vol. 48, No. 4, July–August 1970, pp. 45–57. © 1970 by the President and Fellows of Harvard College; all rights reserved.

† Thomas Kennedy is Professor of Business Administration at the Harvard Business School and formerly Director of Industrial and Public Relations at Atlas Chemical Company.

smaller one, and 1969 was still smaller. But in 1970 we are back again to a big year; contracts covering about 5 million workers have been or will be subject to renegotiation or reopening, in contrast to contracts covering only about 2.7 million workers in 1969.

Considering the great difference in the number of employees affected by contract terminations, it does not follow that labor relations are worse in 1970 simply because the time lost in strikes may have increased over 1969. Even if the batting average on settlements in 1970 should remain the same as in 1969, by the time this year is finished we can expect to have had almost twice as much strike activity.

2. Great Expectations

The peak in terminations in 1970 comes at a time when the demands and expectations of workers are very high. These high aspirations are due to a number of factors, one of the more basic of which is the continuing high rate of inflation.

Although some workers whose contracts terminate in 1970 have had their real hourly wages protected against the erosion of price increases by cost-of-living escalator clauses, this has not been true of the great majority of workers. The Bureau of Labor Statistics estimates that only 2.6 million workers are covered by cost-of-living escalator clauses; and of these employees, 1.8 million are covered by clauses which have ceilings on the amount of cost-of-living increase that is permitted. To illustrate the significance of this fact:

The 1967–70 contract in the automobile industry provided for no cost-of-living increase during the first year and limited the increases in the next two years to a maximum of $0.08 per hour per year. As a result, auto workers have been receiving considerably less in terms of real wages than they had anticipated. In September 1967, when the prior automobile contract terminated, the Consumer Price Index stood at 117.1, compared with 133.2 in March 1970, indicating a 14-percent rise during that period. By September 1970, when the current contract terminates, we may anticipate that the total cost-of-living increase during the contract period will be at least 16 percent.

The average hourly rate for unskilled workers at Ford, prior to the 1967 contract, was $3.30. The 1967 contract added $0.20, plus two 3-percent increases, bringing the total to $3.71. At the end of the contract in September 1970, unskilled workers would have had to receive an additional 16 percent, or $0.59 per hour, in order for their real wages to equal what they would have earned had there been no increase in the cost of living. Instead, they will have received only $0.16, leaving a deficit of $0.43. For Ford skilled workers, the deficit will be about $0.60.

Moreover, the decrease in real wages per hour has been accompanied in many industries by a decrease in the number of hours worked per week, especially the premium-wage overtime hours. From January 1969 to January 1970, gross average weekly hours in manufacturing decreased only from 40.6 to 40.2, but during the same period overtime hours decreased by almost 20 percent.

Finally, workers whose last general wage increase occurred in 1967 have watched workers whose contracts terminated in 1968 or 1969 receive increasingly higher settlements than those made in 1967. The 1967 median package increase of wages and benefits, when averaged out over the full term of the contract, was only 5.5 percent, compared with 6.6 percent for 1968 and 8.2 percent for 1969. Living under contract rates negotiated in 1967 has been especially painful for skilled craftsmen, who have seen their counterparts in the building trades receive an average increase of 12.9 percent in 1969.

3. Inability to Pay

Unfortunately, the peak in worker expectancy has come at a time when managements feel less able and willing to grant sizable wage and benefit increases. As the various economic indexes show, the trend of the economy has been downward. First-quarter profits in 1970 fell 9 percent from the first quarter of 1969, for all industries, and 39 percent in autos and equipment. As a result, managements' bargaining posture has hardened.

When the economy was booming and labor cost increases could be passed on to customers, the "message from above" to the company's men at the bargaining table was "get a reasonable settlement if possible, but in any event avoid a strike." Now the message is more likely to be the reverse: "Avoid a strike if possible, but in any event insist on a reasonable settlement."

4. Other Income Sources

The ability of a union to wage a long strike depends in part on the alternative sources of income which are available to the striking members.

The major sources of this type are welfare payments, union strike benefits, unemployment compensation, and employment elsewhere.

In cases where the union can arrange for only a small fraction of its membership to be on strike at any one time, it may be able to afford sizable strike benefits. This is the case with the International Typographical Union. If it strikes the New York City newspapers again in 1970, its members will receive union strike benefits which will be close to their regular pay. In the steel, coal, aluminum, and automobile industries, however, and in many others as well, the unions have such a large percentage of their membership on strike at any one time that strike benefits can amount to only a very small percentage of the employees' regular pay. For example:

The UAW had a strike fund of $67 million for the 1967 strike. When one realizes, however, that a strike at General Motors involves 390,000 members, the fund does not appear to be so large. In 1967, the strike benefits per week paid by the UAW were only $20 for a single employee, $25 for a married employee, and $30 for an employee with a family. It was calculated that the fund would last only seven weeks if a strike had been called at GM.

Welfare payments are in many cases more important than union strike benefits. The old management cliche, "starve them out," is no longer applicable in many communities. Instead, when strikers' resources reach the level where they cannot meet certain minimum needs, welfare funds are made available to them. In the 1969–70 General Electric strike, it was reported that 2,500 of the 12,000 strikers in the Lynn, Massachusetts, area received welfare payments of between $65 and $110 per week in addition to $20 per week of union strike benefits. It was reported also that it was very easy to get on the welfare roll in Lynn: "A family only had to have less than $1,000 in savings to qualify."[1]

In New York and Rhode Island, after a waiting period of six weeks in addition to the regular one week, striking employees are eligible for state unemployment compensation payments. As a result, the pressure on employees to settle, when a strike has lasted more than seven weeks, is greatly diminished.

During a period of relatively full employment, if a strike occurs in a community where there are other plants not on strike, some of the strikers may find temporary jobs. This, too, reduces their willingness to come to terms. During one recent strike it was reported that the vast majority of the strikers who were not on welfare found full-time or part-time jobs or else had wives who worked. Appeals for temporary bus drivers and for men to deliver telephone books went unfilled as many strikers took their choice of jobs.[2]

5. Revolt of Rank and File

Even when management and union representatives at the bargaining table are able to reach an agreement, a strike may occur because the rank and file in the union refuse to ratify the settlement and insist on a better package. In 1969, the number of such incidents reached an all-time high, and this trend has continued into 1970.

Unfortunately, management has sometimes been willing to sweeten its offer following a negative vote. Such action makes acceptance of future contracts on the first vote highly unlikely. One group of union employees now has as its motto, "First vote *no*, then *go*." Moreover, such action is very contagious. After all, employees say to themselves, if another group of workers gets more by voting down a contract, why not try it ourselves? Refusals to ratify cause strikes because the vote frequently occurs too close to the contract termination date to allow bargaining officials time to negotiate a change in the agreement. Moreover, if the package finally agreed to by the employees represents a major gain, it not only undermines the influence of the reasonable union leadership, but also causes management in future negotiations to hold back its final offer until after the first vote by the employees. As a result, negotiations become more difficult and strikes more likely.

6. Vetoes by Skilled Workers

Closely related to the revolts of the rank and file as a factor in recent strike activity have been the revolts of the skilled workers. Believing that settlements by the big industrial unions have favored the unskilled majority, the skilled minority has threatened to secede unless it is given more control over the nature of the bargains. For example:

In the automobile industry, a large group of the skilled workers appealed to the National Labor Relations Board to establish it as a separate bargaining unit. The NLRB turned down the

---

[1] David Gumpert, "Striking the Modern Painless Way," *The Wall Street Journal*, February 5, 1970.

[2] Ibid.

Types of Strikes

The kind of strike described in this article as essential to the free collective bargaining system—the strike over contract terms—is only one of several types. Categorized according to the purposes which they are intended to serve, there are at least four others: the political strike, the organizational strike, the jurisdictional strike, and the grievance strike.

Fortunately, the political strike has never been significant in modern labor relations in the United States. The organizational, jurisdictional, and grievance strikes, on the other hand, were once very important. However, as time has passed, successful alternatives to each of these have been developed and used. Today the total number of man-hours per year lost as a result of these three types of strikes has become quite small. The contract strike alone now accounts for the great part of strike activity in this country.

With this background in mind, let us look at the distinguishing features of each type of strike.

1. A *political* strike, as the name implies, is one which is called in the hope of influencing government action. In France and Italy, where the unions tend to be affiliates of political parties, such strikes are common.

2. An *organizational* strike is used to force an employer to accept the union as the representative of his employees. Prior to 1935, a strike was the only means a union had to force a stubborn employer to bargain with it. Organizational strikes occurred frequently and were among our most violent industrial conflicts. However, the NLRA provided a peaceful alternative method for securing recognition through an election procedure. By 1967, organizational strikes accounted for less than 1 percent of the number of workers involved in strikes and only slightly above 1 percent of the man-days lost because of strikes.

3. A *jurisdictional* strike occurs when two or more unions each claim that certain work should be done by their members. Some years ago such strikes were frequent in the building trades. For example, the carpenters, the electricians, and the sheet-metal workers might disagree with respect to whose members should do certain tasks involved in the installation of indirect lighting in a ceiling. If the management assigned the work to one of them, the other two would picket the building site and stop the construction. Since they were the victims of interunion disputes over which they had no control, both management and the public reacted strongly against this type of strike action. Consequently, Section 10(k) of the Taft-Hartley Act in 1947 accorded the NLRB the power to decide such disputes. Later the unions established their own settlement procedures, and these included arbitration.

As a result, jurisdictional strikes are no longer a very significant part of the overall strike picture. In 1967 they accounted for only 2.5 percent of the number of workers involved in strikes and less than 2 percent of the man-days lost because of strikes.

4. A *grievance* strike occurs when the employees stop production because of disagreement with management's handling of some day-to-day problem in the shop, such as promotion or discipline. In the early days of unions in this country, such strikes were frequent. Both unions and management came to realize, however, that the right to use the strike power every day could be very detrimental to both of them. As a result, the parties developed the labor contract, which is simply a kind of peace treaty.

It is estimated that there are approximately 300,000 labor contracts in effect in the United States, and that 94 percent of them provide there shall be no strikes or lockouts during the term of the contract; instead, grievances shall be subject to final and binding arbitration by an impartial person selected by the parties. Because not all contracts require arbitration, we still have some grievance strikes, especially in the construction, trucking, and coal-mining industries.

Some contracts provide for arbitration of most issues that arise under the terms of the contract but do permit strikes on certain issues. For example, the automobile contracts permit strikes over work standards, although most other disputes are subject to binding arbitration. Moreover, sometimes employees engage in wildcat stoppages over grievances in violation of the no-strike and arbitration clauses of their contracts. Hence we still have some grievance strikes. However, throughout most of the unionized section of industry, the system for handling day-to-day disputes through use of the contract grievance procedure, which culminates in arbitration, works remarkably well. As a result, grievance strikes form only a small part of the total strike picture.

5. A *contract* strike occurs when the employees stop work because the union and the company are unable to reach an agreement regarding the terms of a new labor contract. While most labor agreements provide for arbitration of disputes which arise during their life, as indicated earlier, it is very unusual for the parties to agree to the arbitration of new contract terms. When the contract terminates, either side is free to use its economic power in the form of the strike or the lockout. In 1967, the majority of U.S. strikes were of this variety, and they accounted for more than 90 percent of the man-days lost as a result of all strikes.

appeal, but at the union's convention in 1966 the constitution was changed to provide that all labor agreements henceforth be ratified not only by the majority of all the employees covered, but also by a majority of the skilled employees.

The right of the skilled group to veto a contract settlement makes it harder for negotiators to develop a package which satisfies everyone.

7. The Generation Gap

There is a generation gap today not only between young people and their parents but also between young workers and old workers. This gap is reflected in what workers want their union to insist on at the bargaining table. The young (the group which includes most of the minority workers) want money now plus more income security in case of layoffs; their seniors want better medical care and improved pensions. (The UAW demand will be a $500-per-month pension after 30 years of service regardless of age.) In a year in which economic conditions require a limited total package, it will be difficult to satisfy both types of demands.

8. Unrest in Public Sector

Public employee unions are the fastest-growing labor organizations in the country. Despite the fact that strikes against government agencies (whether federal, state, or local) are illegal, stoppages in the public sector have been occurring with increasing frequency during the past several years. In many cases these stoppages have been highly successful in securing for the workers sizable wage and benefit increases, and except in a few instances, penalties have not been invoked. Of special significance in this respect has been the recent postal employees' strike.

Strikes by federal employees probably will continue to be prohibited *de jure*, but since the postal strike, everyone understands that *de facto* strikes can occur and succeed without the penalties being enforced.

In the long run, strikes in the public sector will probably decrease as the parties become more skilled and government workers achieve pay parity with private industry employees. But for the next several years a sizable increase of strike activity in this sector can be anticipated.

BARGAINING IN REVIEW

The public has become irritated and frustrated by the strikes and threats of strikes which have caused inconvenience and hardship. It is disturbed by the increases in prices and taxes which have followed many of the settlements. Of particular concern have been the strikes by the postal employees and the air traffic controllers. Until this year, the public has assumed that the federal employment sector, with its vital services, was immune to work stoppage.

Strong pressure may develop for legislation to outlaw strikes in the private sector as well as in the public sector and to replace collective bargaining with some method whereby wages, hours, and other conditions of employment are determined by compulsory arbitration, labor courts, or government boards. This is an appropriate time, therefore, for a careful review of the free collective bargaining system which we have in the private sector, an essential element of which is the freedom to strike.

How the System Works

While it has always been illegal in this country for public employees to strike,[3] in the private sector of the economy strikes have not been illegal except during wartime. The National Labor Relations Act of 1935 (NLRA) requires a private employer and the union that has been certified as the bargaining agent for a group of the employer's workers to bargain in good faith with respect to "wages, hours, and other conditions of employment." Before a contract terminates, the employer and the union must make an honest attempt to reach agreement. However, no union and no company is forced by the government to continue to work under conditions to which it will not agree. Instead, when the labor agreement terminates and an impasse is reached, either party is free to use its economic power in the form of the strike or the lockout to try to force the other party to terms which it considers more reasonable. We refer to this system as *free collective bargaining*.

Under the Taft-Hartley amendments to the NLRA, one exception was made to the free collective bargaining system. If the President is of the opinion that a strike or lockout will create a national emergency, he may seek a court injunction which will prohibit the strike for a period of 80 days, during which the parties must continue to operate under the terms of their old contract. At the end of the 80-day cooling-off period, however, the injunction is removed, and the parties are again free to use the strike or the

---

[3] See Executive Order 10988 (1962) and Executive Order 11491 (1969), which provide for collective bargaining for federal employees. In the states, strikes by public employees are prohibited by statute or by common law.

lockout. The President then reports the matter to Congress, which can take whatever legislative action it deems necessary.

Collective bargaining in the railroad and airline industries is not covered by the NLRA. Instead, they operate under the Railway Labor Act (RLA). The RLA also provides for free collective bargaining. The railroad and airline unions are free to strike if they cannot reach a satisfactory agreement, and likewise, the carriers are free to lock out their employees. However, the RLA does provide an extensive mediation procedure which the parties must pursue before they are legally free to use their economic power.

On three occasions in recent years, strikes have occurred or have appeared imminent on the railroads, and in each case Congress has ordered a compulsory settlement. Aside from these cases, the free collective bargaining system has been maintained during peacetime in the private sector of the economy.

Where the Strike Comes In

The possibility of a strike and the costs which strike action will place on the union, the employees, and the company are inducements to the parties to bargain effectively. To illustrate:

When I used to bargain for a company, there were times when I had made an offer of, say, $0.08; but knowing that the union would indeed strike if I held at that point, I was willing to move up a little more rather than assume the costs of a strike for the company. Likewise, without the threat of the strike, the union might have held at, say, $0.12; but knowing that I would indeed take a strike if it held at that level, the union was willing to move down rather than face the costs of a strike for it and its membership. Thus the threat of a strike forced both of us to move from an offer and a demand which we would have preferred to a point where agreement was reached.

The threat of the strike was not always successful in forcing us to reach agreement. On a few occasions both parties felt that the other side was so adamant that we had to take a strike. Then the cost of the strike itself began to put pressure on both of us to settle. The loss of production and sales was translated into a loss of profits for the company. Some of our customers who had to turn to our competitors for delivery might be lost for good. The longer the strike lasted, the greater the pressure within the company to reach a settlement and get back into production.

On the union side, the pressure to settle built up in the same way. The early days of the strike were accepted by the employees with a carnival attitude, but after several paydays without checks, the cost of the strike action to them and their families caused them to put pressure on the union to seek a settlement. Eventually, the pressures forced a retreat from one or both of the previous positions, and with the help of a mediator a settlement was reached.

It is the threat of the strike and, if that is not successful, it is the strike itself which creates the kind of pressures necessary at times to force the parties to reach agreement under our free collective bargaining system. Without the right to strike, our system would not be so effective in bringing about settlements.

IMPACT OF AUTOMATION

In the late 1940s, the United States experienced a series of strikes and threats of strikes in the privately owned utility field which caused great public fear and anxiety. There was good reason for this reaction. A strike by utility employees in those days could paralyze an entire community. Pittsburgh learned this when the employees of the Duquesne Light Company engaged in a stoppage. A blackout of the street lights resulted in a high rate of burglary and other crimes. Hospitals and other institutions, as well as private homes, were without light, heat, and power.

Today, however, the public does not exhibit the same anxiety regarding strikes in public utilities—and for good cause. Strikes in this area no longer result in discontinuance of service. The reason is automation.

True, the early effect of automation is to expand the strike power of a union by increasing the overhead or fixed costs of a company in comparison wtih labor costs. But the situation changes over time. Thus:

If a company is engaged in manufacturing panama hats by hand and the employees strike, practically all of the company's costs go out the door with the strikers. As a result, the strike power of the union is not very great. However, if the company decides to mechanize, then as it invests more and more money in hat-making equipment, a smaller and smaller part of its costs go out the door with the strikers. Thus the strike power of the union becomes greater and greater as automation proceeds. This is illustrated in Exhibit 1, where the trend line represents strike power at various stages of automation.

EXHIBIT 1   Strike Power Increases during Early Stages of Automation

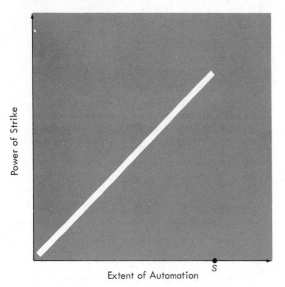

Extent of Automation

The apex of the union's strike power is reached at Point S, where the automation has been very extensive but not quite enough to enable the nonunion management employees to operate the plant. Once that point is passed, however, and Point M is reached (see Exhibit 2), the strike power diminishes quickly. Unable to stop production and sale of the product, the employees and their union have lost the power to cause the company to suffer heavy losses by withdrawing their services. Management personnel are now able to operate the plant.

EXHIBIT 2   When Automation Is Advanced, Strike Power Drops

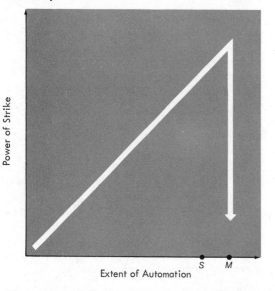

Extent of Automation

Reduced Strike Power

Automation has already reached Point M in the electric power, telephone, gas, and oil refining industries, and in some chemical industries. Let us look at some examples:

1. In 1963, when the Utility Workers Union of America struck Boston Edison Company for two weeks, the company was able to report that "management, supervisory and other nonunion employees operated essential services without inconvenience to customers."

2. When the installers, repairmen, building maintenance, and construction personnel of the New England Telephone and Telegraph Company struck from April to September in 1968, the company was able to report that "during the strike supervisory people and employees not involved in the strike maintained excellent service."

3. In 1969, when its 1,000 unionized employees struck for a period of 11 weeks, the Boston Gas Company was able to report that "gas service was maintained by nonunion employees during the strike."

4. Similar results have been reported following strikes in oil refineries and chemical plants. In 1962, when the Oil, Chemical, and Atomic Workers Union struck the Shell Oil Company's refinery in Houston, Texas, for 353 days, the company, by using supervisory, technical, and clerical employees, was able to operate at more than 100 percent of rated capacity, processing 140,000 barrels per day although the rated capacity was only 130,00 barrels per day.[4]

Although the development of automation in utilities, oil, and chemicals has led the public to lose interest in eliminating free collective bargaining in those areas, the effect on the unions may be quite the opposite. Having lost the power to bring pressure on the companies by means of a strike, the unions may view with favor a move away from collective bargaining to some kind of compulsory settlement. They may prefer to have a neutral arbitrator or a government board rather than have management dictate the terms of employment. For the first time in our history we may see a sizable segment of labor move to support compulsory arbitration of new contract terms.

HOW COSTLY ARE STRIKES?

Despite the fact that peaceful alternatives have replaced most organizational, jurisdictional, and grievance strikes, and despite the fact that strikes in utilities, oil refineries, and some chemi-

---

[4] *The Wall Street Journal*, August 5, 1963, p. 3.

cal plants no longer create crises, strikes over new contract terms still do occur, and these can be quite costly to companies, employees, unions, suppliers, customers, and the general public. Also, of course, when the strike involves a critical material or service, the effect on the economy as a whole may be disastrous if the stoppage continues beyond a certain point.

Thus, while the strike performs a valuable function in our free collective bargaining system, it is legitimate to question whether the costs are too great in relation to the benefits. Might some alternative to the strike, such as compulsory arbitration, serve the interests of the parties and the public better? To answer this question, let us begin by examining the costs of strikes. We can next compare these with the costs of alternative procedures.

Because of the publicity which strikes get, it is easy for their extent and their impact on the economy to be overestimated. When one reads in the headlines that 147,000 GE employees have been on strike for over three months, one is likely to be greatly impressed. But when one realizes that the GE strikers represent only 0.2 percent of the 71 million nonagricultural employees in the country, one sees it in a different light (although for the company, its dealers, and its employees, the strike is still very significant).

It is estimated that there are approximately 300,000 labor agreements in the United States.[5] On the average, about 120,000 of these agreements terminate each year. Thus, across the country during an average year, 120,000 management bargaining teams sit across the table from 120,000 union bargaining teams and try to work out agreements on new contract terms. The issues which they deal with are wages, benefits, hours, and other important working conditions. These are matters which are extremely vital to the companies, the unions, and the employees. Despite the difficulties of these issues, the parties are successful in 96 percent or more of the negotiations. Only 4 percent or less of the negotiations result in strikes, and in most cases these strikes are short-lived. The problem is that a peaceful settlement is seldom front-page news, whereas a strike may be good for a number of headlines.

The Bureau of Labor Statistics estimates that the amount of working time in the total economy which was lost directly as a result of strikes in 1969 was only 0.23 percent. Moreover, the gen-

[5] This figure and the ones immediately following are from a forthcoming book by William Simkin, former Director of the Federal Mediation and Conciliation Service.

EXHIBIT 3   Working Time Lost in Strikes, as a Percent of Working Time in Total Economy

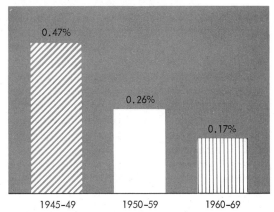

Source: Data in Table 140, "Work Stoppages in the U.S., 1881–1967," in *Handbook of Labor Statistics 1969* (Washington D.C.: Bureau of Labor Statistics, 1970), pp. 352–53, plus data for 1968 and 1969 reported currently by the Bureau of Labor Statistics.

eral trend has been down. As illustrated in Exhibit 3, from 1945 to 1949 the average time lost per year was 0.47 percent, compared with 0.26 percent from 1950 to 1959, and only 0.17 percent from 1960 to 1969. We have been losing far more time in coffee breaks than in strikes!

Industrywide Bargaining

The effect of a strike on the economy depends, among other things, on the nature of the product or service and the structure of the bargaining. In the steel industry, where the product is essential to many other industries and where the bargaining is practically industrywide, one might expect that a strike of any sizable duration would have drastic effects on the overall economy. Such studies as are available, however, indicate that such is *not* the case.

Following the 116-day steel strike in 1959, E. Robert Livernash of the Harvard Business School made an extensive study for the Department of Labor of the impact of that and earlier steel work stoppages on the economy. Livernash concluded that:

The actual adverse effects of steel strikes on the economy have not been of serious magnitude. A major reason why steel strikes have had so little measurable impact is that when a strike approaches a critical state, pressure upon parties to settle becomes substantially irresistible. . . . It is significant that the public interest has not been seriously harmed by strikes in steel or by steel collective bargaining agreements, despite common public opinion to the contrary.[6]

In January 1970 the Department of Labor published an extensive study of the effect on the economy of the 1963, 1965, and 1969 longshore strikes.[7] The study concluded that, although the companies and workers involved suffered losses, as did some workers and owners in collateral industries, "the strike had no visible impact on the economy as a whole." Many companies, according to the report, prepared for the strikes by stepping up their business before the stoppages and catching up again afterwards. "There appears to be no evidence," the report stated, "of a permanent loss of export markets because of the strikes." In talking to newsmen when he released the longshore strikes study, Secretary of Labor George P. Shultz stated that "despite warnings of catastrophic economic effects during some major strikes such results are kind of difficult to find afterwards."[8]

Bargaining in Conglomerates

Unions tend to be organized along industry lines. Accordingly, a particular union may find it difficult to bring heavy economic pressure on a conglomerate, since it can close down only a small part of the corporation's total business. To illustrate with one case I know of:

A union had been able to conduct several successful strikes against one company during a period of a number of years. The union was of the opinion that it had established a strong bargaining position. However, a few years ago the company was bought out by a conglomerate that owned companies in a dozen other industries. Some of the other companies were unionized, but none of them had the same union as the first company. As a result, the union's strike power greatly decreased because the conglomerate as a whole could continue to operate at a profit, albeit a somewhat smaller one, during the period of a work stoppage.

In order to meet the threat of the conglomerate, unions are taking two actions—they are supporting legislation which opposes conglomeration, and they are developing coalition bargaining. Coalition bargaining is a technique whereby a number of unions that have contracts with the

same conglomerate cooperate for bargaining with it.[9] The NLRB and the courts have ruled that coalition bargaining is permissible, and union leaders involved in the GE strike of 1969–70 have expressed the opinion that the new approach is a viable procedure which proivdes them with much more economic power when dealing with a conglomerate.

Whether the growth of conglomerates and coalition bargaining will result in more or fewer strikes remains to be seen. When such strikes do occur, they are likely to be on a grander scale. Yet they are not so likely to create national emergencies as are strikes which involve industry-wide bargaining, such as those in the steel and coal industries.

HIGH PRICE OF COMPULSION

It has often been proposed that strikes in the private sector be made illegal. The managements of the railroads and the maritime industry openly advocate compulsory arbitration as a desirable alternative to free collective bargaining. There is reason to believe, as indicated earlier, that unions in industries where automation has reduced the strike power will also move to that position. Suppliers and customers hurt by a strike are likely to mutter, "It should be outlawed."

Unfortunately, it is not a matter of eliminating strikes by devices which have no costs. The various compulsory settlement methods also are expensive, and it may be that managements, unions, and the public would find such costs more onerous than the costs of strikes. We should be fully aware of these costs before abandoning the present free collective bargaining system in the private sector.

Specter of More Failures

As stated earlier, the costliness of a strike to management and labor is in itself a strong incentive for them to reach agreement. What happens if that incentive is removed? There is reason to believe that the number of failures to reach agreement would increase greatly. This was our experience during World War II, when the strike was replaced with compulsory settlement by a government agency. It was also our experience in the late 1940s, when a number of

[6] Collective Bargaining in the Basic Steel Industry (Washington, D.C.: U.S. Department of Labor, January 1961), p. 18.

[7] Impact of Longshore Strikes on the National Economy (Washington, D.C.: 1970).

[8] The New York Times, January 11, 1970.

[9] For a detailed analysis of coalition bargaining, see George H. Hildebrand, "Cloudy Future for Coalition Bargaining," Harvard Business Review, (November–December 1968), p. 114, and Article 27 herein.

states replaced free collective bargaining in public utilities with compulsory arbitration.

There are two reasons that the companies and unions find it more difficult to reach agreement when the possibility of the strike has been removed:

1. The parties are not under so much pressure to work out a contract because, while the compulsory settlement may be less desirable than the contract that could have been negotiated, it does not carry a threat of immediate loss of production and wages.

2. If the compulsory settlement authority—whether it be a government board, a court, or an arbitrator—has the right to decide on what it thinks is a fair settlement, then the company and the union may well hesitate to make a move toward a settlement, fearing that the other party will hold at its old position and that the board, court, or arbitrator will split the difference. If, for example, the company is offering a $0.10-per-hour increase, and the union is asking for $0.16 per hour, why should the company move to $0.12 when there can be no strike anyhow and when the authority might then decide between $0.12 and $0.16 instead of between $0.10 and $0.16? For like reasons, the union hesitates to move down from $0.16 to $0.14. Thus, compulsory settlement interferes with the process of voluntary settlement.

In order to avoid the effect just described, the Nixon Administration now proposes that when strikes are threatened in the transportation industries, the President be permitted to order arbitration proceedings in which the arbitrator is required to decide only which of the two final offers of the parties is the more reasonable. It is believed that this method would remove one of the undesirable effects of the usual type of arbitration—that is, the hesitancy of the parties to improve their offers for fear that the arbitrator will split the difference. However, the new proposal has the disadvantage of forcing the arbitrator to choose between two proposals, both of which may seem unfair to him.

While the type of arbitration now proposed by the Administration would probably be less harmful than ordinary compulsory arbitration in terms of hampering efforts to reach a voluntary settlement, it would still have some such effect, for management and labor would not be prodded by fears of strike costs. I believe it is erroneous to expect that the number of disputes which would go to an arbitrator would be the same as the number of strikes which would occur without compulsory settlement. The removal of the strong incentive

to settle would result in a great many more failures to reach agreement voluntarily. It would therefore be necessary to establish a sizable government bureaucracy to handle the increased volume of unsettled contract disputes.

More Federal Intervention

The size of the bureaucracy could be lessened by using private arbitrators (with the parties given an opportunity to choose the men they like) instead of a labor board or a labor court. However, the government would have to become involved when the parties were unable to agree on an arbitrator. Moreover, while the Federal Mediation and Conciliation Service has been free from political bias in placing arbitrators' names on its lists for selection by the parties in grievance arbitrations, there can be no guarantee that politics would not play a role in the selection process if the stakes were high enough—as they would be in the compulsory arbitration of new contract terms in the steel, coal, automobile, and other major industries.

If a board or labor court were used to settle disputes, it would have the possible advantage of being able to establish continuing policies. Nevertheless, appointment of at least some of the members would be made by the Administration. (A board could be tripartite, in which case some members would be appointed by labor and some by management.) One of the costs of compulsory settlement, therefore, would be to move management-labor disputes—to some degree at least—from the economic to the political arena.

Will Force Really Work?

Under the free collective bargaining system, the government has no problem of enforcement. For instance, while both the company and the employees suffered serious losses during the 14-week GE strike, once it was over both the management and the workers returned to their jobs voluntarily. This illustrates an important advantage of the present system which is often overlooked—that no use of force by the government is required. Moreover, since the agreement is one which the parties themselves have negotiated, the day-to-day operations under it are likely to be more cooperative. The company representatives sell it to management, and the union representatives sell it to the employees. Since the contract is the negotiators' own handiwork, they make a real effort to get it to work —a greater effort, I believe, than they would make if the agreement were the work of some authority appointed by the government.

This country's experience with legislation that has prohibited strikes on the part of public employees indicates that such legislation does not automatically put an end to the strikes. The Condon-Wadlin Act, which prohibited strikes by state and local government employees in New York State from 1947 to 1967, was violated often, but on only a few occasions were its penalties actually enforced. Since 1967 the Taylor Act, which also prohibits strikes by public employees in New York State, has been subject to numerous violations. Likewise, the illegality of strikes by federal employees has not prevented them from leaving the job.

What would happen, under compulsory settlement, if workers in the coal, steel, automobile, trucking, or some other major industry decided that they did not wish to accept the terms prescribed by the arbitrator or labor court and refused to work? How does a democratic government force 100,000 coal miners, 400,000 steel workers, 700,000 automobile workers, or 450,000 truckers to perform their tasks effectively when they elect not to do so? Perhaps it can be done —but I suggest that this is a question which it is well not to have to answer. It is unwise to run the risk of placing government in a position where the government may reveal its impotence unless it is absolutely necessary to do so.

Threat to Capitalism

Finally, if government becomes involved in the determination of labor contract terms in order to avoid strikes, it may not be able to stop there. With our democratic political structure it would be impossible, I believe, to prevent compulsory settlement of wages for union members from leading to compulsory determination of *all* wages; that, in turn, would lead to government decisions concerning salaries, professional fees, and finally, prices and profits.

So long as free collective bargaining is permitted, it forms an outer perimeter of defense against government regulation in other areas. If it falls, the possibility of more regulation in the other areas becomes much greater. It is worth noting that George Meany, the president of the AFL-CIO, stated several months ago that he would not be opposed to wage controls if similar controls were placed on salaries, prices, and profits. Meany's view of these relationships is one that many people might share.

In Exhibit 4 I have tried to portray the notion just described by showing how government inroads in one area make other areas more vulnerable. In some industries, such as the utilities, the railroads, and the maritime industry, which are already heavily controlled, the threat of inroads may not be an important argument for free collective bargaining, but in the major part of our private economy it is very significant. Businessmen who believe in the effectiveness and desirability of private enterprise should recognize that free collective bargaining constitutes the outer defense of the entire system. In terms of what they consider of most value in our economic system, the ultimate costs of compulsory settlement would be very high indeed.

CONCLUSION

In 1970 we are in a period of heavy strike activity which is likely to continue for some time.

EXHIBIT 4   Compulsory Arbitration Threatens the Private Enterprise System

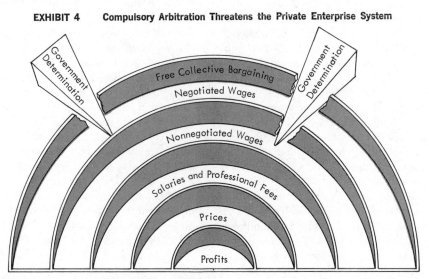

As the public becomes more and more irritated and frustrated by the inconveniences and hardships these strikes cause and by the increases in prices and taxes which follow the settlements, political pressure will probably develop, as it has on similar occasions in the past, to replace free collective bargaining with some method of compulsory settlement. How do the costs of the right to strike compare with the costs of the alternative, compulsory settlement? Taking strike costs first, my analysis indicates that:

1. It is easy to overemphasize the costs of strikes.

2. Much progress has already been made in replacing organizational strikes, jurisdictional strikes, and grievance strikes with peaceful alternatives.

3. Strikes—even the big industrywide ones—have a minimal effect on the economy.

4. Some strikes, such as those in public utilities, which once were very critical, are no longer so because of automation.

5. The number of man-days lost because of strikes is a very small part of the total (only 0.23 percent in 1969), and the trend has been definitely downward.

On the other hand, my analysis indicates that compulsory settlement involves major costs like these:

1. The elimination from collective bargaining of the strongest incentive to reach agreement which management and labor now have.

2. A great increase in the number of failures to reach agreement.

3. The development of a large government bureaucracy to adjudicate the larger number of unsettled disputes.

4. An increase in political aspects of collective bargaining.

5. The difficulty of enforcement of compulsory orders, with the attendant danger of divulging the impotence of government.

6. The likely development of other wage, salary, price, and profit controls by government.

I conclude that the right to strike is preferable to a compulsory settlement system. It does not follow that the government should never move to protect the public against strikes which create serious hardships, but it does folow that any move to prohibit the use of the strike in the private sector should be made cautiously and only to the extent which is clearly required. Any broad prohibition of strike freedom would prove to be very costly in itself and also lead to major government controls over other parts of the economy. Free collective bargaining, which includes the right to strike and the right to lock out, constitutes the outer defense of the private enterprise system.

29. Compulsory Arbitration: Some Perspectives*

Orme W. Phelps†

Over the years, the case against compulsory arbitration of labor disputes has been argued with such skill and conviction that the brief for the defense seems to have been lost. Quite apart from the merits, this is a curious development in a community where the compulsory arbitration of other types of dispute is considered an ornament of a free society. If a neighbor commits a trespass or a business associate fails to honor his contract, he is hailed before a magistrate and the matter is compulsorily arbitrated rather than settled by force of arms. Even in the difficult and delicate area of domestic relations, questions of child custody and separate maintenance may be brought to compulsory arbitration at the option of an aggrieved party. Our whole system of jurisprudence relies on the idea that anyone with a grievance is able to compel an antagonist to meet him peaceably at a public hearing where, after argument, a binding third-party settlement is handed down. No one apologizes for this; more often than not the courts are referred to as protectors of our liberties, defenders of freedom. The unanimity with which it has been held that labor disputes must be exempted from this process is remarkable in itself.

In the case against compulsory arbitration there are distinguished prosecutors galore, and the catalog of inevitable disasters runs the gamut from simple bad decisions to dislocation of the economic foundations of free enterprise. The division is not liberal/conservative, nor labor/management—there is no division. All the principal authorities are in agreement. Says Senator Wayne Morse of Oregon, an arbitrator of long experience and high repute:

> However, Mr. President, if you go into arbitration—and there are some who want to go into compulsory arbitration—you are taking away from the parties, management and labor, some very precious freedoms. You are substituting a third party and asking that third party, in effect, to tell them how they are going to run their business and under what conditions they are going to work. This is a dangerous situation. It is a situation that attacks, in my judgment, some basic foundations of economic freedom in this Republic.[1]

Whereupon, Senator Morse yields to Senator Goldwater:

> It is not often that the senior Senator from Oregon and the junior Senator from Arizona find themselves in agreement, but on this particular subject, compulsory arbitration, I am in complete agreement. . . . I agree with the Senator from Oregon that if this is forced upon the American people, it can mean price control, wage control, quality control, and even place of employment control.[2]

The senators were not making news. They were merely seconding the opinions of Secretary of Labor Wirtz,[3] former Secretary of Labor Mitchell,[4] the AFL-CIO: "Compulsory arbitration means loss of freedom,"[5] the National Association of Manufacturers: "Arbitration through compulsion of law violates the American concept of free-

* From *Industrial and Labor Relations Review,* Vol. 18, No. 1, October 1964, pp. 81–91.

† The author is senior professor of economics, Claremont (California) Men's College. His article was first developed while he was a Brookings research professor, 1962–63.—Editor.

[1] *Congressional Record,* February 20, 1963, p. 2,492.

[2] Ibid.

[3] Address before the National Academy of Arbitrators, Chicago, Illinois, February 1, 1963.

[4] "Mitchell Opposes Compulsory Arbitration," Address to the Safety Awards Dinner of the Brotherhood of Locomotive Firemen and Enginemen, January 13, 1959.

[5] "Labor's Position on Compulsory Arbitration," n.d.

dom under which the government is the servant rather than the master of the people,"[6] and scores of other commentators, including such an experienced observer of labor-management relations as the *New York Times'* labor editor, A. H. Raskin.[7]

FORMS OF THIRD-PARTY INTERVENTION

A careful reading of the indictments, however, produces a disquieting sense of unreality. No one alludes in any detail to the institution being rejected. The implication is that compulsory arbitration is an easily recognizable thing, with a size, shape, mass, and specific gravity varying but little from case to case or situation to situation. This of course is inaccurate. There are many varieties of the species. For example, arbitration may be compulsory in every case, as was true of wage settlements under the Wage Stabilization Board during the Korean War, but it does not have to be so. It may also be at the option of either party or of a public authority (President, Governor); it may be restricted to certain industries or types of disputes (as is now the case in the National Labor Relations Act); the compulsion may be absolute or partial—that is, recommendatory; the arbitrators may be *ad hoc*, permanent, tripartite, or public member only; they may be selected by the parties or appointed by public or private authority;[8] there may be statutory guidelines or not; the issues to be put to arbitration may be inclusive or selective; review and appeal procedures may be made available; and so on. Finally, arbitration may be combined with delay (cooling off) or mediation or both. Any combination is possible, and what is useful in one case may be quite unlike the appropriate instrument in another.

A second very interesting conclusion to be drawn from recent critiques is the assumption that compulsory arbitration is an evil so far largely avoided in this best-of-all-possible labor markets. One can read extensively in the critical literature without finding reference to any existing system of compulsory dispute settlement other than passing references to national emergency strike procedures under the Taft-Hartley Act or perhaps emergency boards on the railroads. This assumption is quite misleading. There is currently a very large volume of labor disputes in the United States in which third-party settlement may be

compelled at the option of one or both of the principals to the dispute. They are not commonly designated as "compulsory arbitration," but the vagaries of terminology should not be allowed to obscure this basic fact.

LABOR DISPUTES

In numerical terms the three principal categories of labor disputes are: (1) grievances, (2) contract disputes, and (3) disputes over organization. Two of these classes (the first and third) are already practically eliminated, either by legislation or by contract, as a basis for strikes or lockouts, with adjudicated third-party settlement substituted instead. Strikes over organization are now a rarity, the disputes being taken either to the National Labor Relations Board or to state labor relations boards. The overwhelming majority of grievances are also subject to compulsory settlement (often—perhaps usually—as a *quid pro quo* for a no-strike commitment) as a result of clauses written into labor agreements by the parties, and with at least one large system—the National Railroad Adjustment Board—created by law. Only the second category, contract disputes, is still generally subject to "direct action," and this area of freedom of choice has been nibbled away by boards of inquiry under the Taft-Hartley Act and by the provision for emergency boards in the Railway Labor Act. In total volume of dispute settlement, probably as many issues go to compulsory arbitration in the United States each year as are settled by the parties on their own.[9]

We have compulsory arbitration of labor-management controversies with us now. It is in large-scale operation in the United States today. Labor disputes are settled regularly and in large numbers by compulsory submission to third-party decision making. They have been ever since 1935, when the Wagner Act was passed, with a notable increase in volume since World War II, when grievances began going to arbitration in quantity as a result of National War Labor Board awards adding arbitration clauses to union contracts.

THE NLRB

The volume of such settlements is impressive, in both its formal and informal aspects.[10] Between

---

[6] *Industry Believes*, April 1962, n. 34.

[7] "Labor's Crisis of Public Confidence," *Saturday Review*, March 30, 1963, pp. 21–25, 52.

[8] The American Arbitration Association, for example.

[9] If all grievance settlements at all steps are included, the compulsory total will be many times that of the voluntary one. Statistically, this is not too far out of line. Once a grievance is formally docketed, in 90 percent of the cases it is on the way to settlement, by compulsion if necessary.

[10] See below, p. 337, for data on informal settlements.

1948 and 1962 the National Labor Relations Board alone disposed of 298,614 cases, of which 109,689 were charges of unfair labor practice, 134,964 raised questions of representation, 53,416 were union shop authorization elections (during the years 1948–52), and 545 involved union shop de-authorization petitions.[11] These disputes arose in all 50 states, the District of Columbia, Puerto Rico, and the Virgin Islands, in literally thousands of communities from one end of the country to the other. The employers and unions involved numbered in the tens of thousands. In the 5 years 1958 through 1962, the NLRB averaged just under 21,000 case dispositions per year, divided as follows: approximately 11,200 unfair labor practice charges, 9,700 representation elections, and 60 union shop de-authorization proceedings.

The decisions and awards of the National Labor Relations Board are classic examples of compulsory arbitration. They involve authoritatively binding third-party decisions over issues which may be brought to the tribunal at the option of either party, and from which the responding party may not abstain or abstains at his peril. The NLRB is a labor court of limited jurisdiction. It handles specific types of dispute: mainly those arising out of organizational contests or involving jurisdictional boundaries.[12] Unlike the National War Labor Board in World War II or the Wage Stabilization Board during the Korean War, the NLRB does not have plenary jurisdiction. Instead, the parties may resolve their differences without going to the Board, if they so wish and are able to do so. Nobody knows, of course, how many conflicts are settled in this manner, but the number is unquestionably large.

GRIEVANCES

The largest class of disputes currently settled by compulsory methods involves grievances. Here the compulsion arises from contract clauses agreed to by the parties which require the submission of unresolved disagreements over interpretation or administration of the contract to an impartial third party for final and binding settlement. The practice is now almost universal, and

the number of disputes so settled each year unquestionably runs to the tens of thousands, but there are as yet no data from which to arrive at any fair estimate of the actual total. Guesses have ranged from 10,000 to 100,000 per annum. No legislative framework is involved, except in the case of the National Railroad Adjustment Board, an agency created by amendment of the Railway Labor Act of 1934 to dispose of grievances which the carriers and railway unions could not settle among themselves. In 25 years of operation, 1935 through 1959, the NRAB rendered decisions in 47,097 disputes, or something less than 2,000 per year.[13] Grievance arbitration blankets the country, involving the services of hundreds of arbitrators, many of them full-time. The contractual undertaking to submit unresolved issues to arbitration is voluntary but, once incorporated in an agreement, is compulsory and legally enforcible, as leading Supreme Court decisions have held.[14]

CONTRACT ISSUES AND THE NATIONAL INTEREST

There is still a third group of labor disputes presently being settled on a quasi-compulsory basis. These are: (1) contract issues arising on the railroads, which, under the terms of the Railway Labor Act, may be referred to a Presidential emergency board if they fail to yield to mediation; and (2) disputes which are found by the President to "imperil the national health or safety" under Title II of the Taft-Hartley Act. Both are subject to mediation, cooling-off, and fact-finding by special *ad hoc* boards appointed by the President. In neither, however, is the compulsion final; lawful strikes may be called or renewed at the end of the cooling-off period. In addition, on the railroads, the parties frequently agree to arbitrate contract issues. Technically, it is voluntary, not compulsory, arbitration. Nevertheless, the parties' willingness to arbitrate must be judged in the light of the National Mediation Board's authority to intervene and to request the appointment of a Presidential emergency board if mediation fails.

The volume of semicompulsory adjudication from these sources is not overwhelming, but it is

[11] *Annual Reports of the National Labor Relations Board,* 1948 through 1962. In the process, the Board applied for 1,525 injunctions (under Sections 10(1) and 10(j) of the act), was either petitioner or respondent in 1,572 cases before the Circuit Courts of Appeal, and tried 83 cases before the Supreme Court of the United States.

[12] Plus a miscellaneous category which includes work assignments, secondary boycotts, "hot goods" boycotts, featherbedding, and other prohibited grounds for work stoppages.

[13] *Annual Report of the National Mediation Board,* 1959, p. 85.

[14] *Textile Workers Union of America* v. *Lincoln Mills of Alabama,* 353 U.S. 448 (1957). *United Steelworkers* v. *Warrior and Gulf Navigation Company,* 363 U.S. 574 (1960); *United Steelworkers* v. *American Manufacturing Company,* 363 U.S. 564 (1960); *United Steelworkers* v. *Enterprise Wheel & Car Company,* 363 U.S. 593 (1960).

significant, and has been going on consistently for a number of years with some measure of success. For example, there were 22 Taft-Hartley boards of inquiry appointed during the 15-year period, 1948–62, as follows:

President Truman, 10 boards in 5 years: 7 in 1948; 1 in 1949; 1 in 1951; 1 in 1952;

President Eisenhower, 7 boards in 8 years: 1 in 1953; 2 in 1954; 1 in 1956; 1 in 1957; 2 in 1959;

President Kennedy, 5 boards in 2 years: 1 in 1961; 4 in 1962.

The key step in the national emergency strike procedure is the 80-day injunction. In only 5 of the 22 cases did strikes occur after the end of the injunction period. Four of these were longshore disputes, three of which were on the East Coast.[15]

On the railroads during the same 15-year period, there were 109 emergency boards created by Executive Order of the President, or an average of 7 a year. There were also 187 agreements to arbitrate, an average of 13 a year. Total settlements by emergency board and arbitration were 296, or approximately 20 per year. During the 15 years, there were 13 strikes following the final reports of emergency boards. Seven of these were concentrated in two years: 4 in 1948 and 3 in 1959.[16]

What all this adds up to—the National Labor Relations Board and National Mediation Board experience (along with that of state labor relations boards in New York, Wisconsin, and elsewhere) and grievance arbitration—is very extensive familiarity on the part both of labor and of management in dealing with compulsory procedures for settling disputes. It is a rare union or company that has not been through a quasi-judicial hearing of one sort or another (and frequently of several kinds), thus learning the methods, procedures, and standards used by trial examiners and arbitrators. These include the proper manner of developing and presenting a case: the introduction, examination, and cross-examination of witnesses; the use of exhibits; techniques of argument; the types, varieties, and relative value of different kinds of evidence; and certainly not least, the self-discipline called for by the acceptance of adverse decisions. Hearings

may be very complicated and lengthy affairs, with legal counsel on both sides a full transcript of proceedings being taken by a court reporter, voluminous briefs, and so on. Whether aided by counsel or not, both company and union are customarily represented by their own official personnel.

UTILITY OF COMPULSORY ARBITRATION

In evaluating the utility of compulsory arbitration in contract disputes, this already extensive training of the parties in the quasi-judicial process must not be disregarded. It is unlikely that compulsory arbitration will be employed except in the settlement of disputes of some importance. In such cases, it can also safely be assumed that both union and management officials will be experienced—or at least have the assistance of experienced counsel—in all phases of adjudication. There are few substitutes for adjudication in laying bare the heart of a controversy. Given informed parties, able counsel, and a competent judge, the adversary process is a powerful instrument to get at the truth of things. For fact-finding and decision making in controversial affairs, it is virtually unsurpassed: not by research, nor by bargaining, persuasion, intuition, or revelation. In some of the recent and more prolonged contract disputes in this country, it is conceivable that illumination of the issues would have been a major contribution to acceptable settlement.

Would the adoption of a policy of compulsory arbitration of contract disputes be the equivalent of a death sentence for collective bargaining in the areas to which the policy applied? One argument on the affirmative side is based on the dope habit analogy. As stated by Secretary of Labor Wirtz, "a statutory requirement that labor disputes be submitted to arbitration has a narcotic effect on private bargainers . . . they [will] turn to it as an easy—and habit forming—release from the obligation of hard, responsible bargaining."[17] Although stated as a fact, this is merely an opinion. To begin with, the Secretary's statement, like that of other critics, is based on a narrowly restricted definition of "compulsory." Of course, legislation might require that *all* disputes go to compulsory arbitration, but it does not have to and probably would not.[18] Compulsory arbitra-

[15] Federal Mediation and Conciliation Service, *Synopsis of Presidential Board of Inquiry Created under National Emergency Provisions of the Labor Management Relations Act, 1947.* Revised January 1963.

[16] *Annual Reports of the National Mediation Board,* 1948 through 1962.

[17] Address before the National Academy of Arbitration, p. 10.

[18] This statement of the issue is a carryover from the wartime experience (NWLB in World War II and WSB in the Korean War) when submission was compulsory in all cases.

tion can also be at the option of either party or of the responsible public authority. Then, with work stoppages prohibited, bargaining would be under threat of recourse to arbitration. Would effective bargaining thenceforth cease?[19]

The experience of the National Labor Relations Board may be instructive, in this connection. In the fiscal year 1961, the Board disposed of 12,116 unfair labor practice cases. However, it closed 10,082, or 82 percent of the total, even before the issuance of a formal complaint. It "adjusted" 1,651, dismissed 3,539, and 4,892 were withdrawn. That is, the disputes were settled, without recourse to litigation. In labor-management terms, they were mediated: misunderstandings were cleared up, practices changed, parties appeased, differences reconciled. The National Labor Relations Act makes no provision for mediation, yet over four fifths of the unfair labor practice cases coming to the Board are regularly disposed of in this manner. Nor is this all. To return to fiscal 1961, some 955 more cases were closed after issuance of the complaint but before the opening of the hearing, to wit: 497 adjusted, 4 in compliance with stipulated decision, 380 upon compliance with consent decree, 51 withdrawn, and 23 dismissed. One hundred forty-seven more were closed out after the hearing opened but before the trial examiner had made his report: 43 adjusted, 2 by stipulated decision, 85 by consent decree, 15 withdrawn, and 2 more dismissed. Thus, in the final analysis, only 932 (8 percent) of 12,116 cases actually went to a formal decision or award.[20]

The issues before the NLRB are not, of course, those facing the parties in contract bargaining, but neither are they completely unrelated. The parties are the same and the issues involved similarly crucial: rights of representation, and freedom to organize effectively and to bargain collectively. The very high percentage of informal settlements at least leaves open the question whether, under threat of recourse to arbitration, the parties might not be able to bargain out a reasonable proportion of their contract demands. Thus far, the only widespread experience of compulsory arbitration of contract issues in this country has been in wartime. In spite of the fact that the statutes were rigid, the coverage comprehensive, and submission compulsory, the results were surprisingly good. Nevertheless, war-

time is not a good environment for "hard, responsible" bargaining of any sort, and it may be doubted that conclusions drawn from such periods are applicable to more normal times.

ACCEPTABILITY

One of the strongest arguments against compulsory arbitration in the eyes of many is the question of acceptability. Will labor and management accept from third parties decisions affecting their vital interests: wages, hours, job security, on the one hand, and on the other, the impact on costs, prices, operating procedures, and competitive positions? Of course, no one can say in advance and certainly not for every situation that might arise. There are, however, some points to consider.

In the first place, compulsory arbitration of contract disputes should not and need not be resorted to in the absence of very strong and widespread opinion that a work stoppage in a given case is clearly contrary to the public interest. A blanket imposition of compulsory dispute settlement in peacetime is unthinkable for the foreseeable future. The decision to require arbitration could well be left to a responsible public authority, such as the President. There would, in all probability, be wide publicity attending all the steps antecedent to submission to arbitration. It is surely not unreasonable to believe that this would both influence the attitudes of the parties and encourage self-discipline in the face of adverse decisions. It should also be remembered that the level of acceptance in previous cases has been very high: before the NLRB and NMB, in Taft-Hartley national emergency situations, in grievance arbitration, and during wartime before the NWLB and WSB. In a society where compulsory arbitration before the courts is so widely practiced and due process of law has such prestige, there are strong pressures for the acceptance of decisions arrived at by judicial processes.[21]

In the long run, acceptability might well be affected by considerations of equity. It is at least arguable that the judicial process is as well designed to produce an equitable (fair, reasonable) decision as either bargaining or force. Equity does not necessarily correspond to the power positions of the parties, nor is it sure to be reached through the strategies of bargaining which include, along with the interplay of per-

[19] If it did, then the impassioned assertions of both management and labor representatives that compulsory arbitration is not for them will have a slightly hollow ring.

[20] *Annual Report of the National Labor Relations Board, 1961,* pp. 226–27.

[21] It can also be argued as a matter of psychology that adverse decisions are usually more acceptable from duly constituted third parties than from adversaries.

sonalities, misstatements of fact, bluffs, and threats as manipulated by experienced dialecticians.[22] Although equity undoubtedly has a subjective element and is fundamentally not quantifiable, it is also a function of the evidence as related to issues. Though not a mathematical process, it is a rational one, and the weight of the evidence usually gets the decision. How the conclusions of the judges are arrived at can be examined in thousands of published decisions and awards of the National Labor Relations Board, in *Labor Arbitration Reports*,[23] *Labor Arbitration Awards*,[24] and elsewhere. It may be that equity is of no importance or of only minor importance in the negotiation of labor agreements, but such a hypothesis is not self-evident. In these days of tighter and tighter integration of industrial processes into a high-speed, interlocking economy, fair and reasonable settlements arrived at through judicial processes may be preferable, in some sensitive areas, to work stoppages pushed to the limit by ambitious leaders or stubborn negotiators.

ARBITRATION OF "INTERESTS"

It has been said and will be said again that compulsory arbitration of the terms of a labor agreement is a very different thing from compulsory arbitration of what that agreement means, which is grievance arbitration. The former is a matter of the "interests" of the parties, the latter a question of "rights" already established by contract. Permitting compulsory arbitration of contract terms means, in the words of Senator Morse "substituting a third party . . . to tell [management and labor] how they are going to run their business, and under what conditions they are going to work." Or, as Senator Goldwater has extended the argument, "it can mean price control, wage control, quality control, and even place of employment control." There is some truth to what Senator Morse says, but it is not the whole truth nor does it clearly distinguish the arbitration of interests (terms of the agreement) from the arbitration of rights (grievances); the issue is just not that black and white. There is also some truth in Senator Goldwater's more extreme specifics, but very little and the probability still less. Compulsory arbitration *could*

mean all these things, but it does not have to and there is no likelihood at all that it will.

Nevertheless, the issue of "interests" should be faced. Contract negotiation is a different thing from either disputes over organization or grievance bargaining. To use a governmental analogy, it is more of a "legislative" act, whereas arbitration is a judicial process. In grievance arbitration, the arbitrator has the contract to use as a guide; in organizational disputes, the NLRB has the terms of the act. But in contract negotiation, the interests of the parties have no theoretical limits, and numerous imaginative innovations have shown that management and labor can get together in a variety of unexpected patterns. What, then, would be the limits or the clues to guide the arbitrator to a proper settlement?

PRIVATE DECISION MAKING

The first answer is, of course, that it is always to be preferred if the parties can work out a settlement between themselves. The primary argument is the desirability of reserving the largest possible area in the economy for private decision making, especially those decisions affecting the way businesses are run and the conditions under which employees work; a secondary, though still major reason is acceptability, which is almost always enhanced if the decision is bargained out. Assuming, however, that an arbitration tribunal is faced with a set of contract issues, there are still several factors which will assist in reaching a decision. They are: (1) the terms of submission, (2) the composition of the tribunal, (3) the existing agreement, (4) the proposals of the parties, and (5) the classic criteria which have been used by bargainers and third parties over the years to test the logical strength of bargaining demands.

No arbitration—contract or grievance—has to be thrown wide open to unlimited adjustment, either in range of issues or scale of decision. Such a proceeding would be practically unheard of—and quite unsettling for both the parties and the arbitrator. The customary procedure is to specify carefully and limit the issues to be passed upon and the range within which the decision is to fall. An example is the railroad arbitration of 1963, in which the issues placed before the board were two: the elimination of unneeded firemen, and the crew size dispute. The remaining issues were remanded to the parties for further bargaining. A frequent form that such adjudication takes is the negotiation of all issues but one, perhaps

[22] See "The New York City Newspaper Strike: A Step-by-Step Account," A. H. Raskin, *New York Times,* April 1, 1963, for some detailed illustrations of the bargaining process.

[23] Washington, D.C.: Bureau of National Affairs.

[24] Chicago, Ill.: Commerce Clearing House, Inc.

wages, and submission of that single unsettled item to the arbitrator for final determination. The neutral arbitrator or arbitrators will often be helped in making this determination by the arguments of his (their) colleagues on the board representing management and the union. In other words, the proper and customary form of a contract arbitration tribunal is tripartite. Since the labor and industry members know the issues and the arguments, they can at a minimum help the neutral member to avoid serious error.

The existing agreement and the proposals of the parties also form a pattern which may not automatically point the way to a solution but which will certainly set some practical limits to the range of decision making. These may be and often are supplemented by transcripts of earlier negotiations, review of contract development through the years, and tests of conformity to related agreements in the same or other industries. These are the standard criteria for supporting, denying, and compromising the demands of the parties. By far the most important of them are interfirm and interindustry comparisons.[25] They are fully set forth in Irving Bernstein's *The Arbitration of Wages*,[26] in which the author also reaches the conclusion that the results of arbitration in the cases he studied did not differ appreciably from what might have been expected had the parties bargained out the issues themselves.[27]

It is also arguable that the distinction between the effect of grievance decisions and contract negotiation is not quite as sharp and clear as the classification "rights/interests" sounds. There are many company managers and quite a few union officials who will testify that through arbitration of grievances the former have been told "how they are going to run their business," at least in part, and the latter have discovered under what conditions their members are going to work. Subcontracting is an example of the former;[28] and there are thousands of cases involving wages, hours of work, discipline, authority of shop stewards, and so forth, in which union members have been told by arbitrators the conditions under which they are required to work.

The decisions and awards of the NLRB are

equally difficult to fit into a dichotomy. Although the freedom to organize and bargain collectively is a right guaranteed by law, it took a very long time and a large number of decisions and appeals to find out what some of the terms meant.[29] The Board's decisions have dealt with some of the most basic issues in labor-management relations. Would it have been better, over the 15 years 1948–62, for the parties to fight out the more than a quarter of a million highly volatile and inflammatory issues brought before the agency, or was it better to have them compulsorily arbitrated by a staff of specialists trained in labor-management relations?

The negotiation of the terms of an agreement is not as sensitive an issue as the right to organize. It is generally conceded to be a more sensitive issue than the settlement of a grievance. Both unfair labor practice charges and grievance issues are now subject eventually to compulsory settlement by third parties if the union and management are unable to reconcile their differences. There are few critics of either system generally, although there are often criticisms of details of the procedures. The key question is: Will the same system or some modification of it necessarily fail if applied selectively, by issue or industry or *ad hoc*, to disputes over the negotiation of contracts?

The unfortunate fact is that current tendencies in both bargaining and industrial technology raise expectations of more disputes inviting public intervention, not fewer. Industry continues to automate, and both unions and management keep broadening the area of bargaining to industry-wide or community-wide negotiations. The union bargaining under threat or fact of automation faces that most difficult of economic issues, the contracting market. Not all unions faced by mechanization are so placed as to bargain out a deal for their members (as the ILWU did on the West Coast), and the losses may be more than the union as a political organization can afford to take without a battle. The industry-wide or community-wide shutdown has both the intent and effect of denying a certain type of goods or service to all potential customers. Where the loss of such goods or services has an immediate impact on public convenience, intervention to restore service is already recognized as a political necessity for public officials.

[25] See Arthur M. Ross, *Trade Union Wage Policy* (Berkeley: University of California Press, 1948).

[26] Berkeley and Los Angeles: University of California Press, 1954.

[27] Ibid., pp. 112–13.

[28] See D. Crawford, "The Arbitration of Disputes over Subcontracting," in Jean T. McKelvey, ed., *Challenges to Arbitration* (Washington, D.C.: Bureau of National Affairs, Inc., 1960), pp. 51–77.

[29] The problem continues. See, for example, the Trial Examiner's Intermediate Report on "Boulwarism" as a permissible form of collective bargaining, in "General Electric Company and International Union of Electrical, Radio and Machine Workers, AFL-CIO, Case Nos. 2-CA-7581–1, 7581–2, 7581–4, 7864 (Post 10-CA-4682)."

Whether or not a given work stoppage may be more inimical to the public interest than denial of the right to strike or to lock out is to the interests of the parties is a question of public policy. The answer may be "never," as is implied in position statements of both the National Association of Manufacturers and the AFL-CIO, previously cited,[30] but the facts of industrial life cast doubt on this simple conclusion. The railroad example of 1963,[31] the public reaction to shutdowns of recent years in steel, airlines, shipping, newspapers, and missile production, as well as statements by responsible public officials, lead to different projections. As Secretary Wirtz has said: "A decision has been made, and that decision is that if collective bargaining can't produce peaceable settlements of these controversies, the public will."[32]

PEACEABLE ALTERNATIVES

What are the "peaceable" alternatives? They are mediation, delay (cooling-off), fiat (government seizure), bargaining, and arbitration. The first two have proved ineffective in the major disputes of recent years; they should be retained, of course, but not relied upon. Government seizure rarely settles anything, although it does permit an imposed settlement, by administrative decree. Bargaining without the possibility of recourse to strike or lockout may prove to be a mirage, but then again it may not. There is more than one form of threat. It remains to be seen whether bargaining under threat of recourse to arbitration will be ineffective. If it proves so, if the availability of arbitration turns out to mean the certainty of arbitration, then the solution is to limit its availability—by size or type of dispute, by industry, by administrative decision, or by some other criterion. This should be no insuperable obstacle to a Congress that has enacted the Railway Labor Act, the Wagner Act, the Taft-Hartley Act, the Labor Reform Act, among others.[33]

The sensible final resort for disputes which are judged to be outside the range of direct action is resolution by a properly constituted board of arbitration after full hearings, argument, and all the guarantees of due process now widely employed and well understood by both management and labor. There is no lack of qualified people to hear and resolve such disputes. Men with broad experience in labor relations, as negotiators and arbitrators, can be found at all levels of government, from the Supreme Court and the Cabinet on down through senators, congressmen, agency heads, governors, mayors, deans, professors, and presidents of universities, and scores of private arbitrators practicing throughout the country. All have had the confidence of both labor and management to the extent of being called in to settle significant disputes concerning the interpretation and administration of agreements; many have also served as mediators and on public boards of all kinds. A tripartite board of arbitration, with the public members selected by the parties from a national panel, might not arrive at precisely the same conclusions as the parties themselves, but it would be unlikely to commit any major errors and might well come to both an equitable and an acceptable solution.

The essential argument here is that the judicial process has not yet been proved inappropriate to labor-management disputes. If the point is reached where certain classes or individual cases of work stoppage are judged to carry too high a social cost to be tolerated, experimentation with some type of compulsory arbitration is a logical extension of past experience. The employer-employee relationship is a dispute-breeding relationship. The best method of adjustment is bargaining between union and management. If that does not work, two alternatives are left: fiat or argument. Settlement by decree raises far more difficult questions than resolution by due process. If the method to be used is argument, then compulsory arbitration appears to be the best answer yet devised. It is at least worth examining in the light of the evidence of past experience and without prejudgment based on sweeping generalizations or haphazard analogies.

---

[30] See above, pp. 378–79.

[31] Special arbitration board, No. 282, established by joint resolution of Congress, P.L. 88–108, approved August 28, 1963. See *Monthly Labor Review*, January 1964, pp. 36–43, 70–71, for summary.

[32] Address before the National Academy of Arbitrators.

[33] As a reasonable first step, a clause might be added to the emergency board of the Railway Labor Act and to

---

the national emergency dispute procedure of the Taft-Hartley Act giving to the President the power, at his option, of requiring arbitration at the close of the cooling-off period.

C. Issues in Jurisprudence

Under a system of collective bargaining, employees, through their union, participate with management in establishing the rules and regulations that govern the employment relationship. Issues in industrial jurisprudence growing out of this relationship become important to both the union and management. What does the union security issue involve? What is a grievance procedure? What is the function of an arbitrator? These are some of the questions dealt with by the contributors to this section.

Union security has had an interesting development in the United States. Closed shop was given a legal status in the Wagner Act in 1935; it was made illegal in Taft-Hartley in 1947; and in the Landrum-Griffin Act in 1959, it was declared legal once again in a modified sense for the building and construction industry. On the other hand, the union shop was protected under the Wagner Act as amended by Taft-Hartley, except in those cases where a state establishes the right of an employee to work without belonging to a union under a right-to-work law.

Daniel Pollitt discusses the historical and legal background of union security. In the second article, James Kuhn explores the issue of right-to-work laws and their impact on union membership.

Today, about 90 percent of all labor-management agreements contain grievance procedures with a final step of arbitration. In making a comparison with the Australian system, DeVyver explains how grievance systems were developed in the United States. This is followed by Aaron's article, which also contains some international comparisons in evaluating some of the issues pertaining to the grievance and arbitration process.

30. Union Security in America*

Daniel H. Pollitt†

Union security in America was until recent years chiefly embodied in the "closed shop" agreement. Closing the shop to all employes other than those who belong to a union is as old as America.

As early as 1674, a New York colonial court ordered brewers and bakers to hire only union members, as "formerly was accustomed." Prior to the Civil War, the cordwainers (shoemakers), the carpenters, the cigar makers, the tailors, the glass blowers, the hatters, the mule skinners, the carpet weavers, the stone cutters, the potters, and the longshoremen had all formed unions with provisions similar to that found in the 1842 constitution of the Baltimore Typographical Society: "Every person working at the business will be required to make application to join the Society within one month from the time of his commencing work at any office in the city."

Requiring all employes to be union members at the time of their initial employment is but one of the forms of "union security" provisions developed in American industry. There is also the union shop agreement, permitting the employer to hire union or non-union employes as he sees fit, but requiring all new employes to join the union within 30 days or some other period following his employment. There is the union shop with preferential hiring agreement, whereby the empoyer agrees to give preference to union members when he hires but is permitted to hire non-union employes when union members are not available. There is the maintenance of membership agreement, requiring all members of the union at the

time a contract is signed to maintain their membership during the period of the agreement. There is the agency shop agreement, whereby employes are not required to join the union but are required to pay to the union an amount of money—usually equivalent to union dues—for performing functions as their agent in collective bargaining activities.

American unions and their members insist on some form of union security arrangement for many reasons. First and foremost is the need for self-protection against the anti-union employer. The historic technique, still utilized in some areas and industries today, for destroying a union is to discharge the more active and popular union members and to replace them with more "docile," or anti-union employes. The closed shop form of union security was a practical method for depriving the anti-union employer of this weapon; it benefits him not to discharge a "militant" if the union can fill the vacancy with a member equally steadfast.

A second major reason for the union security arrangements is that without them there may be no union at all. This is true in the construction, maritime, tourist resort, entertainment, and other industries where jobs are of brief duration and marked by rapid turnover. The union agreement must be made before employment begins or not at all. In the building trades industry, for example, it is a sheer impossiblity to choose a union, select a spokesman, and negotiate a collective bargaining agreement before the job is completed and the employes scatter to new employment. The realities of this situation were recognized by Congress in the 1959 Landrum-Griffin amendments to the National Labor Relations Act, which authorize the pre-hire contract between the union and employer governing the working conditions to

* Reprinted from *The American Federationist*, AFL-CIO, Washington, D.C., Vol. 80, No. 10, October 1973, pp. 16–22.

† *Daniel H. Pollitt is a professor of law at the University of North Carolina.*

prevail when the job subsequently begins. Such prehire contracts may (the employer and union willing) contain provisions requiring employes to join the union within seven days after employment; requiring the employer to notify the union of employment opportunities; and requiring the employer to give preference in employment opportunities based upon length of service with the employer, within the industry, or in the particular geographical area.

A third major reason for union security agreements is the resentment of the American workers against the "free rider." Union organization and recognition often comes hard and, once attained, is costly to maintain. But the results are worth the price. Numerous studies demonstrate that the wages paid in union establishments exceed the wages paid in non-union plants and that union plants far surpass non-union plants in pension, health, vacation, and other fringe benefits.

More importantly, only in union plants can the worker protest his grievances with outside assistance through regularized channels. And his seniority system gives him protection from "personalized" selection in the event of a layoff or when he seeks to improve himself by bidding on a better job. The union member who pays and supports these benefits with his dues naturally resents the worker who wants to ride on the union train without cost. Thus when given the vote under a since-repealed section of the 1947 Taft-Hartley amendments (requiring a majority vote of the employes before a union shop contract could be negotiated), 96 percent of approximately 2 million workers balloted by the NLRB voted in favor of authorizing their union negotiators to seek a union shop.

In short, the pressure for the union shop and against the free rider comes from the rank-and-file union members at the shop level. Rank-and-file employes are not the only persons who see advantages in a union security agreement. Surveys by business-oriented organizations demonstrate that experienced employers favor a union security agreement. Why? Because employe morale, loyalty, and productivity increase when the employer signs a union shop agreement.

Over 30 years ago, the National Industrial Conference Board, a research agency wholly supported by employers, ran a survey which came up with some of the reasons why experienced employers favor the union shop:

"the elimination of friction and strife within the working force . . .

"gives employes greater feeling of responsibility and interest in their jobs because they feel they have something to say about their conditions of work . . .

"more responsible unions. It does not have to struggle to hold its membership by repeatedly demonstrating its ability to obtain new advantages. . . ."

With the strength of a union security agreement behind it, a union can make constructive concessions helpful to management, even though these concessions may be detrimental to the short-run interests of some union members. Without this security, unions must press for demands desired by the member even when the result may be to the overall detriment of management and worker alike.

An academic expert in the field once observed: "An assured status for the union is not a guarantee of successful union-employer relations but it is a prerequisite, and the closed shop or its equivalent is the only way of assuring the status of the union." Congress was cognizant of these considerations for union security arrangements when it approved them in the original National Labor Relations Act in 1935.

In the 1935 Wagner Act, Congress expressly authorized an employer to sign a closed shop contract with a bona fide union, but not with a company union. This congressional authorization for the closed shop was sustained by the Supreme Court in a 1949 decision involving some employes represented by the CIO who were unhappy with a limited wage increase negotiated by the union and went on an unauthorized strike. Thereafter, the wildcatters began to organize a rival union and sought affiliation with the AFL. The union expelled 17 of them from membership, and they consequently were discharged by the employer under the closed shop agreement.

The National Labor Relations Board filed unfair labor practice charges against the company on the theory that the discharges interfered with and restrained the right of the employes to shift their union allegiance from the CIO to the AFL. Even under these facts, the Supreme Court rejected the Labor Board's argument and upheld the closed shop agreement. The court noted that a union "has the natural right of self-preservation, and may with propriety expel members who show their disloyalty by joining a rival organization."

It then wrote:

One of the oldest techniques in the art of collective bargaining is the closed shop. It protects the integrity of the union and provides stability to labor relations.

To achieve stability of labor relations was the primary objective of Congress in enacting the National Labor Relations Act. Congress knew that a closed shop would interfere with freedom of employes to organize in another union. . . . Nevertheless, with full realization that there was a limitation in the section which authorizes the closed shop agreement upon the freedom to join any union of one's choice. Congress inserted the proviso. . . .

The Supreme Court continued to uphold and sustain the various forms of union security agreements authorized by Congress or by state law. In 1956, dissenting railway employes argued that the "union shop" agreement authorized by the Railway Labor Act violated their rights under the First and Fifth Amendments. The court upheld the requirement that all employes join and pay union dues as a condition of continued employment, with the comment that there is no more infringement of First Amendment rights under the union shop agreement "than there would be in the case of a lawyer who by state law is required to be a member of an integrated bar." Again in 1963, the Supreme Court sustained the validity of an agency shop agreement authorized under the Indiana right-to-work law as a mandatory matter for collective bargaining.

In 1947 Congress determined that the pendulum had swung too far toward the union security side, and amended the Wagner Act in this area as well as others. These 1947 Taft-Hartley amendments did a number of things:

First, the closed shop, requiring all employes to be union members at time of original hire, was outlawed.

Second, all union security agreements requiring the employer to give preference to union members in employment opportunities were outlawed.

Third, employers and unions representing a majority of the employes were permitted (but not required) to negotiate for a union shop, requiring union membership after 30 days of employment, but only after a majority first voted to authorize their union negotiators to enter into such negotiations.

Fourth, the workers retained the right at any time by majority vote—triggered by a petition of 30 percent of the employes—to "de-authorize" the union shop agreement.

Fifth, if the company and union sign an agreement requiring union membership after the initial grace period of 30 days, the union cannot compel the employer to discharge an employe for any reason other than failure of · the employe "to tender the periodic dues and the initiation fees uniformly required as a condition of acquiring or retaining union membership."

In other words, the employe cannot be discharged under the Taft-Hartley union shop as long as he pays his fair share even if, as a local union leader, he "sells out" in an unsuccessful attempt to replace his own union with an outside rival. Nor can the union cause the discharge of the employe who refuses to join the union, refuses to do picket duty, or continues to work when his union is on strike. All of these rulings were tested in court cases between 1951 and 1953. Nor can a union, under Taft-Hartley, impose a fine on a union member who votes for a strike but then resigns from the union and crosses the picket line. That decision came in a 1972 Textile Workers case in which the court ruled that when Congress enacted the Taft-Hartley "union security" amendments, it intended to prevent the utilization of these agreements for "any purpose other than to compel payment of union dues and fees."

"Congress recognized the validity of unions' concern about 'free riders,' that is, employes who receive the benefits of union representation but are unwilling to contribute their share of financial support to such union, and gave unions the power to contract to meet that problem while withholding from unions the power to cause the discharge of employes for any other reason," the court said in a 1954 decision.

Any union security requirement as a condition of employment "is whittled down to its financial core," as it was expressed in a 1963 case involving General Motors.

Consequently, in a current case involving the Television and Radio Artists, the right-to-work forces are entirely erroneous when they allege that plaintiffs William F. Buckley Jr., Fulton Lewis, and M. Stanton Evans must join and remain union members "in good standing" as a condition of continuing their broadcasts. As long as the three dissidents contribute their share of financial support, the union is specifically barred from seeking their discharge, no matter how anti-union their conduct is otherwise.

Sixth, if and when the employer and union agree that all employes must pay the union dues as a condition of continued employment, other sections of the Taft-Hartley amendments require that the NLRB make sure that the union fees and dues are not "excessive or discriminatory." The levels or amounts of union dues are voted by the union membership and are generally quite low. Monthly union dues vary in amount, but usually represent the wages received in two hours of work.

Seventh, the Taft-Hartley amendments also provided that the limited union shop agreement authorized in one section of the act could be outlawed in any state which enacted a right-to-work law. That's the famous section 14(b) through which some 19 states in the South, northern Great Plains, and southern Rocky Mountain areas have enacted right-to-work statutes.

In most of those states, an employe can enjoy all the benefits of a union bargaining contract without paying a cent. Thus, when a union in Texas attempted to impose even a nominal charge of $15 upon non-member employes who utilized the union-financed grievance and arbitration machinery, the union was told by the NLRB that it could not impose a fee upon non-union members, and that the union must provide its services free of charge to the employes who refused to join or support the union.

It has long been illegal for a union, voted in by a majority of the employes, to sign a contract which gives benefits to "members only." One of the last tests establishing that came in 1954. A union representing a majority of the employes cannot in any way discriminate against non-members, but instead must represent all the employes without charge, without discrimination, and in good faith, even when the non-member who gets this union protection refuses to give the union any quid pro quo.

The short of the matter is that the "union shop" agreement permitted by Taft-Hartley is a far cry from the original "closed shop" agreements traditional in the American labor movement.

The employer cannot agree to give perference to union members when he hires new employes. Once hired, employes can be required after 30 days of initial employment to meet union obligations to pay dues and initiation fees but cannot be discharged if they refrain or refuse to become union members in "good standing." The employes under a "union shop" agreement can refuse to attend meetings and can refuse to support strikes voted by a majority of the membership without fear of discharge. They can even engage in a "wildcat" strike in breach of a "no-strike" contract, without fear of union punishment, although their strike may well subject the union to an employer suit for damages. At regular intervals, a majority of the employes can vote out, or "deauthorize," the union shop agreement in secret

ballot elections conducted by the NLRB. In like vein, if a majority of the voters in any state are so minded, they can enact a right-to-work law and prohibit even this limited form of union security agreement. The employes can be required to pay or tender union dues (after the 30-day grace period), but the dues cannot be either "excessive" or "discriminatory."

In sum, the Taft-Hartley law permits employes and unions to sign agreements requiring all employes who enjoy union benefits to pay their fair share of the costs; and thereby permits the elimination of the strife and conflict caused by the "free rider." It does no more. Thus, the Taft-Hartley "union shop" agreement does not deprive the individual workers of their freedoms at the job site—despite the extravagant claims of what are now known as "right-to-work" organizations.

The right-to-work movement had its genesis at the turn of the century, when recovery from the 1893–96 depression caused trade union membership to increase rapidly—membership in the AFL rose from 265,000 in 1897 to more than 1.6 million in 1904. This tremendous multiplication in union membership won attention from employers, and they retaliated in 1903 with an "open shop" drive.

The term was coined by the National Association of Manufacturers at its 1903 convention. It was intended to convey the impression that the shop or factory was "open" to all workers, union or non-union; whereas by contrast, the "closed shop" was closed to all but union members. The "open shop" drive was spearheaded by the NAM, the National Trades Federation, the National Erector's Association, and a number of "citizens' alliances" at the local level. The local "citizens' alliances" were organized nationally through the Citizens' Industrial Association of America, whose first head was also the head of the NAM.

In reality, the "open shop" was closed to union members. The featured speaker at the 1905 NAM convention warned the delegates to "discharge union men promptly," for "it is the common practice of union men in an open shop to harass the upright and capable workman who may not choose to join a union."

The National Erector's Association restricted its membership to "such firms as pledge themselves to the open shop" principle; and this was defined by the association as meaning "not only no dealings with the union but no employment of union members."

Pursuant to this "open shop" principle, Bethlehem Steel and other companies refused to sell their products to contractors who employed union men.

This tactic has continued over the years. The late UAW president, Walter Reuther, was once discharged from the Murray Body Company because it sold most of its products to Ford, and Ford insisted upon clearing everyone employed by Murray. Reuther's experience was a continuation of company blacklisting, the most common practice whereby employers unite to prevent the spread of unionism. Blacklisting has claimed plenty of victims. In his labor history, *Toil and Trouble,* Thomas R. Brooks tells the story of the blacklisting of Thomas Lewis, the father of John L. Lewis, after he took part in a coal strike called by the Knights of Labor. The Lewis family experiences through 15 years of moving repeatedly from job to job and discharge to discharge was to have a lasting impression on young John L. Lewis.

Recently, an Operating Engineers organizer told a House committee how his union had lost an NLRB election (despite the fact that over two-thirds of the eligible voters had signed union cards) after the employer had announced that if the workers voted for a union, he would no longer be able to sell his products to the Springs Cotton Mills, J. P. Stevens & Co., or to the Burlington Industries—the major textile concerns in the area, all of which refused to purchase supplies from "union" firms.

When the idea was started early in the century, the National Metal Trades Association established an "employment bureau" and issued "certificates of recommendation" to employes. To win a "certificate of recommendation," it was necessary to work "not less than 60 days during strike conditions" in shops of the members of the association. Not surprisingly, the "open shop" drive was successful. In two years, from 1904 to 1906, the AFL lost over 114,000 members.

During World War I, the AFL membership doubled—from 2 million in 1914 to 4 million in 1920. Again, the American employer decided to do something about it and did so under what was called the "American Plan." The supporters of the plan purported to recognize the right of voluntary unionism but were dead set against the "un-American" closed shop.

It was in these "American Plan" days that Finley Peter Dunne had his characters Mr. Dooley and Mr. Hennessy discuss the American Plan in the famous, oft-quoted dialogue:

"What's all this that's in the papers about the open shop," asked Mr. Hennessy.

"Why, don't you know?" asked Mr. Dooley. "Really, I'm surprised at yer ignorance, Hennessy. What is th' open shop? Sur, 'tis where they kape the doors open to accommodate the constant stream av min coming in t' take jobs cheaper than the min what has the jobs. Tis like this, Hennessy: Suppose wan av these freeborn citizens is working in an open shop for the princely wages av won large iron dollar a day av tin hours. Along comes anither son-av-a-gun and he sez t' the boss, Oi think Oi could handle the job nicely f'r ninety cints. Sure, sez the boss, and the wan dollar man get the merry jinglin can and goes out into the crool world t' exercise his inalienable rights as a freeborn American citizen an' scab on some other poor devil. An' so it goes on, Hennessy. An' who gets the benefit? True, it saves the boss money, but he don't care no more f'r money thin he does for his right eye. It's all principle wid him. He hates to see men robbed av their indepindense. They must have their indipindense, regardless av anything else."

"But," said Hennessy, "these open shop men you mention say they are for the unions if properly conducted."

"Sure," said Mr. Dooley, "if properly conducted and how would they have them conducted: no strikes, no dues, no contracts, no scales—hardly any wages, and damned few members."

The scheme of the American Plan was the same as the earlier "open shop" drive. The work was carried on by proliferating employer associations. By late 1920, New York had over 50 organizations dedicated to propagandizing the open shop, Illinois had 46, Michigan 23, and Connecticut 18. In January 1921, some 22 state organizations met in Chicago to draw the assorted local bodies together under the so-called American Plan.

The plan was a smashing success. The National Metal Trade Association was a leader in the "plan," and membership in the Machinists dropped from 330,000 in 1920 to 78,000 in 1924. This decrease in union membership was typical. Wartime union gains in the meat packing and shipping industries were completely wiped out. The Mine Workers had over 500,000 members in 1920; by the end of the decade there were half that many. Total union membership approximated over 5 million in 1920 and was down to 3.6 million in 1923.

Many years later, after World War II, union membership was again on the increase and anti-union employers once more utilized the techniques of the past—this time under the slogan "right to work." As the struggle shifted to the state legislatures, Florida became the first right-to-work state.

The story begins in 1939 when the Associated Industries, a Florida state organization of manufacturers, businessmen, and industrialists sponsored a number of bills in the state legislature designed to weaken unions. Nothing came of this effort, but when the legislative session next met in 1941, the association narrowed its efforts to support a bill which would make the "closed shop" illegal on all projects financed by public funds. This too failed. After the legislature adjourned, Attorney General Tom Watson (assisted by an attorney connected with the Associated Industries) filed a suit against the Tampa Shipbuilding Corporation alleging that the closed shop agreement between the corporation and various unions violated the "public policy" of Florida. This too failed.

In 1943, the Associated Industries decided upon a constitutional amendment as a device for enacting their proposals. A right-to-work proposal was put on the ballot as an amendment to the state constitution, and it passed.

Supporting the proposal were the following organizations: Florida Citrus Canners Cooperative; Florida Citrus Exchange; R. D. Keene, Inc.; Winter Haven Citrus Growers Association; Waverly Growers Cooperative; Campbell Cattle Company; Princess Growers, Inc.; United Growers and Shippers Association; Florida Citrus Producers Trade Association; and the United Growers and Packers—all working with the Florida Farm Bureau. It was no coincidence that the CIO was then engaged in a drive to organize the citrus industry. Also active in support of the right-to-work drive were the Greater Miami Restaurant Association and the Florida State Hotel Association, representing employers who were then untouched by unionism but feared its arrival.

The proposal was resisted in the populous industrialized counties but enacted with the votes from what the Miami Citizen termed the "backward, low-wage sections of the state, where lumber and turpentine interests rule workers like barons of old."

The current right-to-work movement is merely the latest phase in the long-standing opposition of employer groups to union security and unions

themselves. It is the direct descendant of the "Open Shop" and "American Plan" drives of earlier years. It is not known who coined the current name for this historic anti-union movement. As early as 1935 the Automobile Manufacturers Association opposed the enactment of the Wagner Act with the statement that "men have an inalienable right to work," free from coercion by unions. In 1939, the National Association of Manufacturers referred to "the right to work," and in 1936, there was something called the "right-to-work union," but little is known of its activities.

In any event, the formation of the present National Right to Work Committee was announced in 1955 by E. S. Dillard, president of the Old Dominion Box Co. of Charlotte, N.C., and Fred A. Hartley Jr., the former congressman and co-sponsor of the Taft-Hartley Act. By then, some 17 states had enacted right-to-work laws. The other "founders" include P. M. French, president of an apparel manufacturing concern in Nashville, Tenn.; Robert A. Englander, president of the Dacam Corp. of Lynchburg, Va.; Nathan Thorington, President of a Richmond construction company; and two workers: S. D. (Duke) Cadwallader, a former railroad conductor on the B&O, and William Harrison, a former clerk with the Louisville and Nashville. Harrison served as the executive secretary until 1959, when he was succeeded by Reed Larson.

In 1968, the committee created the "legal defense and education" foundation with a nearly identical board of directors. The two organizations work in tandem: the committee in the area of publicity and lobbying, the foundation in the area of litigation. The common purpose is to discredit and weaken the strength of unions with employers whose workers they have organized or might seek to organize in the future. Since creation of the legal foundation, the group has put considerable effort into litigation aimed at undermining unions.

Much of the litigation sponsored by right-to-work forces boils down to an attack upon union political activity. But it is axiomatic that what a union wins at the bargaining table may be lost in the legislative halls. At least since Samuel Gompers and the AFL embarked upon a political program "to reward our friends and punish our enemies," trade unions were in the front lines in the struggle for such social objectives as the public school system, the 10-hour day, minimum wages, equal pay for women, fair employment opportunities, safe and hygienic working conditions, and so on. Few labor organizations today confine their activities simply to "business unionism."

The 1947 Taft-Hartley amendments made it unlawful for a union to make any "contributions or expenditures" in connection with political campaigns for federal office. CIO President Philip Murray promptly challenged the law by publishing a front page editorial in the CIO News explaining why he would support a particular candidate for Congress. Extra copies were sent to Baltimore where the election campaign was in progress. Ultimately, the Supreme Court held that Congress had not intended to prevent this union-financed, "in house" type of political communication; otherwise "the gravest doubt would arise in our minds as to its constitutionality." Four of the nine Supreme Court justices went even further and held that the statute was "patently invalid" under the First Amendment protection of speech, press, and assembly.

Writing for the four concurring judges, Justice Wiley Rutledge said:

The expression of block sentiment is and always has been an integral part of our democratic electoral and legislative processes. They could hardly go on without it. . . . To say that labor unions as such have nothing of value to contribute to that process and no vital or legitimate interest in it is to ignore the obvious facts of political and economic life and of their increasing interrelationship in modern society. . . . That ostrich-like conception, if enforced by law, would deny those values both to unions and thus to that extent to their members, as also to the voting public in general.

Thereafter, the United Auto Workers ran afoul of the statute when it sponsored (out of union funds) a continuing Sunday evening television program in which invited participants discussed topical issues of the day. During the fall of 1956, the participants on the UAW program discussed the issues involved in the pending federal elections. With the elections over, the union was indicted for "having used union dues to sponsor commercial television broadcasts designed to influence the electorate to select certain candidates for Congress."

On appeal by the government from dismissal of the indictment, the Supreme Court commented that the lawsuit "raises issues not less than basic to a democratic society" and rather than decide the issues on what the majority of the court believed to be an inadequate record, sent the case back for the factual elucidation of the issues at trial. When this information was presented, the jury acquitted the UAW. Three of the Supreme Court justices did not see the need to send the case back to the lower court for a trial. They believed that, no matter what the evidence might disclose:

"Making a speech endorsing a candidate for office does not, however, deserve to be identified with antisocial conduct. . . . Nor can the fact that it costs money to make a speech—whether it be hiring a hall or purchasing time on the air —make the speech any the less an exercise of First Amendment rights."

Subsequently, Congress has amended the "political expenditure" clause of the Taft-Hartley law, to make it doubly clear that nothing in the federal law was intended to prevent or preclude a union from using its funds (1) to communicate with its members and their families "on any subject"; (2) to support nonpartisan registration and get-out-the-vote drives aimed at members and their families; or (3) to establish, administer, and solicit contributions to a separate fund to be utilized for political purposes. In a 1972 decision, the Supreme Court sustained the right of a local union under these provisions to solicit voluntary contributions from its members and then to utilize such funds in connection with a federal election. Consistent with that decision, a federal circuit court recently affirmed rulings against union political contributions from "involuntary" funds "actually or effectively required for employment or union membership."

These decisions seem eminently fair. Unions operate by majority vote in the political field as well as in all other areas of activity. In politics, as in the other areas, the majority of union members "has an interest in stating its views without being silenced by the dissenters," as it was expressed in 1961 and 1963 cases. In these two cases, railway employes in Georgia (the *Street* case) and North Carolina (the *Allen* case) alleged that they were required to pay union dues under a "union shop" agreement and that a portion of their dues was used to support "political candidates and causes which they opposed." They asked the courts to enjoin the enforcement of the union shop agreement (the *Street* case), or to relieve them from the obligation to pay union dues (the *Allen* case), and the state courts granted most of this relief. The Supreme Court held that this went too far, that such injunctions "would work a restraint on the expression of political ideas (by the majority) which might be offensive to the First Amendment." The Supreme Court did hold, however, that the protesting union dues-payers were entitled, upon request, to a rebate of that portion of their dues which was spent on political activities to which they were opposed.

But the right-to-work forces, not content with minority protection, continue to seek to block majority political action. Many of the cases sponsored by the National Right to Work Legal Defense and Education Foundation are an attempt to relitigate the law clearly settled by numerous previous cases. For instance, in one current case involving the UAW, the plaintiffs alleged (just as the plaintiffs in Street and Allen had alleged at a much earlier date) that as employes at the McDonnell Douglas Corporation, they are required to pay fees to the union pursuant to an agency shop agreement between their employer and the union, and that the union uses a portion of their "compulsory agency fees in the support of political and economic doctrines, ideologies, and legislative programs to which they are opposed." They asked the court to relieve them of their obligation to pay any dues—just as had been asked by plaintiffs in Allen. Recently, a circuit court refused this request, ruling that the UAW authorizes a dissenting dues-payer to recover, upon request, a pro rata rebate of that portion of his dues spent for political and ideological causes to which he objects. The court concluded that this union remedy negates the unfair representation claim made by the political dissenters.

The Machinists, like the Auto Workers, has adopted an internal procedure authorizing minority political protestors to recover that portion of their dues which is used for political objectives. Also, on July 12, 1973, the State, County, and Municipal Employes adopted "a system for permitting the rebate of that portion of union dues and service fees used for partisan political and ideological purposes to those who object to such uses."

Thus, it appears from all the cases that Congress and the courts have created a workable balance: The minority union member or the agency shop member cannot handcuff the majority of the union if it wishes to engage in political activities; on the other hand, neither can the majority compel dissenters to contribute to support those political candidates and causes they oppose when their disapproval and objection is duly noted.

The federal labor laws are carefully balanced to protect dissenters without destruction of the rights of the majority. The dissenter who works under a union security contract must pay his "fair share" of the costs of administering the bread-and-butter economic issues which arise under the union agreement. He need pay nothing to support the political activities favored by the majority within the union. This arrangement protects the First Amendment freedoms of both the majority and the minority. Much of the litigation financed by the right-to-work forces seeks to upset this balance. That effort is hardly surprising, because these forces are a conduit of funds for employers using the "right-to-work" slogans to advance their anti-union cause.

31. Right-to-Work Laws—Symbols or Substance?*

James W. Kuhn†

The major protagonists in the long-continuing debate over right-to-work laws have taken ironic positions. Autocratic managers of business bureaucracies unabashedly proclaim their devotion to individual freedom—in unions, of course—and denounce the union shop. Elected leaders of democratically organized unions, on the other hand, stridently demand the right to force union membership upon unwilling workers.

Managers who espouse right-to-work laws may be genuinely concerned with workers' freedom, but one cannot fail to note that their concern takes a particularly convenient form, an attack upon a uniquely American union device. To be able to champion so high a good as individual freedom in a way which denies unions an additional provision for security must be gratifying.

If gratifying to managers, it is embarrassing to many sympathetic students of labor. The coercion implicit in forced membership and the appeal of a unionism that requires dues as a condition of employment weigh uneasily upon

many who wish to defend individual freedom and also to promote union security. A recent study by Frederic Meyers does nothing to quiet our unease and probably increases it. He concludes in his report to the Fund for the Republic, *"Right to Work" in Practice* (1959), that right-to-work laws do not weaken unions, at least not in Texas and probably not elsewhere either. He believes that "'right-to-work' proposals are of much less importance than either side to the controversy has been willing to admit. The issue is a symbolic one. What is at stake is the political power and public support of management and unionism."[1] He could find only minimal effects upon growth and bargaining power of Texas unions after 11 years of a right-to-work law.

If right-to-work laws are important to unions only as symbols of political power and public support, many an observer may find it difficult to look with great favor or enthusiasm upon dragooning reluctant or unwilling workers into unions. To allow unions to enjoy the union shop just to demonstrate their public support or to expunge right-to-work laws from the statute books as evidence of unions' political power, while undoubtedly of significant value to union leaders and of real loss to managers, is not apt to be a particularly persuasive argument for infringing individual rights. Unless unionists can more cogently justify coercive membership as being necessary and vital to the continued strength and well-being of unions, they may well lose a large measure of support for the union shop.

One may wonder if hard-headed, practical union leaders and businessmen would agree with Meyers and on the basis of his findings admit

* From *Industrial and Labor Relations Review*, Vol. 14, No. 4 (July 1961), pp. 587–94.

† Associate Professor, Graduate School of Business, Columbia University.

Editor's note: In recent years, some students of industrial relations have concluded that the substantive issues in the continuing controversy over "right-to-work" legislation are much less important than the symbolic ones. Labor and management groups, according to this view, are basically engaged in a struggle to win public support for their respective objectives, but the laws have had little effect on the balance of economic power in the labor market. The author of this discussion contests this view. His analysis of union success in voluntary recruitment of members and of the effects of a loss of union security on union membership and revenues leads him to conclude that basic practical considerations may be at stake in the right-to-work issue. Tentatively at least, he urges, the verdict on the right-to-work laws should be withheld until there has been more research on their actual effects on union strength and collective bargaining.

[1] Meyers, p. 45.

that "union shop" and "right to work" are important political symbols but matters of only minimal substance in the life and activities of unions. Would businessmen have supported and campaigned for right-to-work laws as they did in the 1958 state elections if they had thought that right to work was merely a political symbol with no practical effect upon union bargaining strength? Would labor leaders have worked as hard as they did to defeat the right-to-work proposals if they had not believed them a substantial threat to union growth and membership? The Teamsters alone spent $800,000. In California, unions spent about $1.5 million to defeat right-to-work proposals and probably raised $500,000 for the same purpose in Ohio. The Chamber of Commerce estimated that labor unions spent more than $10 million to defeat right-to-work proposals in 1958 and that proponents had spent about $2 million.[2]

VOLUNTARY RECRUITMENT AND THE UNION-SHOP POLLS

Political symbols are often important to men, and for them men may sacrifice much, possibly even life. Whether the cash contributions of business-like Teamster leaders to defeat right-to-work proposals and of business-minded General Electric officers to enact the proposals, for example, were intended to secure merely political satisfaction is doubtful. The director of industrial relations of a large firm active in the 1958 campaign told the writer that he did not intend to give in to the demands for a union shop in his plants because "We don't want that money from non-members going into the union treasury." He was convinced that bargaining with unions would be much easier if fewer firms in the industry had granted union shops or if right to work were generally in effect.

Union leaders can very well have the same conviction—that the more widespread right-to-work laws, the more advantageous will be management's bargaining position. Their experience with American workers gives them good reason to believe that a union shop is not only a convenience, but that it is also a substantial prop to effective, stable collective bargaining. Right-to-work laws strike at unions' main resource, dues. If all workers within a bargaining unit always sought membership and willingly paid their dues, right-to-work laws could have little significance for collective bargaining. American workers have not been noted, however, for their whole-hearted devotion to, and voluntary support of, unions. Even craft workers, who have appeared to be devoted union members—so devoted they would sell their tools to pay union dues if need be—were responding to the inescapable fact of their union's control of employment opportunities.

American workers have often displayed little or no initiative in taking out union membership. If they could avoid signing up they did, taking out a union card and paying dues only when constantly dunned by shop stewards. In the absence of union or closed shops, unions have always been able to increase their membership by signing up workers whom they already represented and for whom they bargained. For example, in 1941 the United Auto Workers enrolled only three quarters of the workers it represented.[3] As late as March 1948, the United Auto Workers was able to recruit among the workers then in the bargaining unit over 25,000 new members in General Motors, a firm that had been organized for over a decade. The new members amounted to about 10 percent of all the represented workers in company plants. Two years later when the union secured a modified union shop from General Motors, a check-off from Chrysler, and union shops from a number of other plants, union officials estimated that approximately 50,000 new members would be added to union rolls, an increase of over 5 percent in the international's total membership.[4]

The Taft-Hartley provision for free and secret union-shop votes a few years ago gave union leaders an opportunity to find out how strong worker support was for the union shop. Although the votes were generally favorable, they were hardly overwhelming demonstrations of support. They must have strengthened the belief among union leaders that compulsory membership is a valuable and substantial aid in the shop and at the bargaining table. As reported by the unions, workers voted impressively for the union shop. Union newspapers and labor spokesmen proudly and loudly touted the results of the NLRB-conducted, union-shop elections. They pointed out that 97 percent of the 46,146 elections held between 1947 and 1951 favored the union shop and that 91 percent of *those voting* cast their ballots for the union shop.

The elections did demonstrate that a majority of organized workers liked the union shop—or at least unions. A close observer of many of these

[2] *New York Times,* November 14, 1958, 1:4, and December 9, 1958, 19:5.

[3] *Report of the President,* United Automobile Workers, August 4, 1951, p. 3.

[4] *United Auto Worker,* August 1950, p. 9.

elections, Sanford Cohen, reported that many workers thought they were voting on the more basic issue of unionism itself,[5] but the size of the majorities was not as impressive as unionists would have us believe. While the majorities were large enough to get the union shop, they were certainly not large enough to make the union shop unnecessary. Enough workers voted "no" or did not bother to vote at all, so that only an unperceptive union leader could have viewed the election results as signs of an irresistible enthusiasm for unionism.

Though only about 7 percent of the 6,545,001 eligible workers voted against the union shop between August 1947 and October 1951, 15 percent did not choose to vote, with the result that the majority of eligible workers favoring the union shop was no more than 77 percent. A noticeably smaller portion of eligible workers among large, mass-production plants supported the union shop than did workers in small plants. In 1948, about 83 percent of eligible workers, mostly in small craft shops, voted for the union shop, 5 percent against, with 12 percent not voting. By 1951, when the number of elections held in plants of over 1,000 workers had greatly increased since 1948, only 72 percent of the eligible workers voted for union shops, 10 percent against, with 18 percent not voting. In the larger plants, the vote again doubled and the proportion of those not voting increased by half.[6]

The results of the vote in the following firms suggests that several large unions found the union shop a useful and even necessary device for recruiting many workers whose voluntary and eager support may have been lacking. In General Motors plants in early 1950, the United Auto Workers won support for a union shop from about 75 percent of those eligible to vote, was rebuffed by 9½ percent, and could not get about 13½ percent to the polls.[7] In late 1950, the United Steel Workers mounted an intense campaign in 162 steel plants to get out the vote and to produce an "overwhelming demonstration" that steel workers really wanted a union shop. While the final outcome must have been gratifying, since the union shop won in 153 plants and lost in only 9, the size of the vote must have been a bit disappointing to union leaders in view of

TABLE 1   Percent of Eligible Workers Voting "No" or Not Voting in NLRB-Conducted Union-Shop Elections*

	Voted "No"	Did Not Vote	Total
Total NLRB elections, 1947–51	7.6	15.2	22.8
Small plants, 1948–49	5.1	12.0	17.1
Large plants, 1950–51	12.1	18.6	30.7
General Motors	7.0	13.3	20.3
Briggs	4.1	c.13.7	c.17.0
Ford	1.2	7.5	8.7
162 steel plants	14.2	19.6	33.8
Boeing Aircraft	11.6	24.2	35.8
Curtis-Wright	8.7	5.6	14.3
Local 131, UAW	7.1	7.8	14.9
Local 644, UAW	9.5	4.1	13.6

* Data calculated from election figures in: *17th Annual Report*, NLRB, 1952, p. 302; *Monthly Labor Review*, August, 1953, p. 837; *Business Week*, March 3, 1951, pp. 125–26, October 8, 1955, pp. 127–28; and union newspapers between 1947 and 1951.

their ardent campaign. Two thirds of the eligible workers voted for the union shop, a surprisingly large 14 percent voted against it, and 20 percent did not vote.[8] Still later, in early 1951, the Machinists asked for a union-shop election at Boeing in Seattle. Slightly less than two thirds, 64 percent, of the eligible workers voted yes, 12 percent voted no, and nearly one fourth cast no ballot. Table 1 shows the votes in these and a few other plants.

In some plants the vote gave evidence that outright opposition might decline where workers had had some experience with the union shop. After more than six and one half years under union shop, from late 1941 to July 1948, only 1.2 percent of Ford workers voted against the union shop and 7½ percent did not vote. In one of the biggest majorities in union-shop elections in any auto plant, 90 percent of the eligible Ford workers voted for the union shop.[9]

Experience under the modified union shop, which allowed workers to "escape" union membership after a year, also showed that once workers were forced to join the union, their opposition to dues paying declined. A union leader

[5] Sanford Cohen, "Union Shop Polls: A Solution to the Right-to-Work Issue," *Industrial and Labor Relations Review*, Vol. 12, No. 2 (January 1959), p. 254.

[6] *Seventeenth Annual Report*, National Labor Relations Board, 1952, p. 306.

[7] The other 2 percent of the eligible voters are accounted for by voided and challenged ballots.

[8] *Business Week*, March 3, 1951, pp. 125–26.

[9] No earlier union-shop election is available for comparison, but the vote on the Ford representational election may give some hint of the change in worker opposition to the union and its proposals. In the 1941 vote, 2½ percent of eligible workers had voted for "no union" and 11 percent had not voted. (*Report of the President*, UAW, 1941, p. 3.) While the difference between the 1948 and 1941 "yes" vote is only about 5 percentage points, the important changes are that the relative size of the "no" vote declined by over half and the proportion of those not voting declined by nearly a third.

would note, however, that such opposition did not disappear. In 1952, Jones and Laughlin reported that 6 percent of its new employees were "escapees"; another large steel firm reported that about 4 percent of its new employees chose to escape union membership; and Allegheny-Ludlum said that it had only a few escapees. *Fortune* magazine estimated that of 150,000 new steel workers, about 5 percent dropped out of the union under the 1952 steel agreement. Another 4 to 5 percent of the new workers would not have joined initially if they had not been required to do so, but they did not feel strongly enough one way or the other to leave the union.[10]

Auto workers at General Motors showed little interest in "escaping" from union membership under a provision of the 1950 agreement that allowed new members to drop out after one year of employment. Between 1950 and 1955, the company hired 600,000 new employees, but only 600 elected to drop out at the end of their year. By June 1955, when General Motors agreed to the full union shop, 16,000 workers, less than 5 percent of the total eligible were not union members. At Chrysler, too, only several hundred out of 110,000 employees (excluding 30,000 union-shop workers at Briggs) were not members when the company, and the union signed a union-shop agreement in 1955.[11]

EFFECTS ON UNION INCOME AND EFFICIENCY

As he contemplated the results of the union-shop elections and the number of escapees under the modified union-shop plans, a union leader would not necessarily be at all reassured that support for his union was so general that loss of the union shop under a right-to-work law would not be a substantial blow to the union. On the average, somewhere between 5 and 12 percent of all eligible workers had definitely opposed union shops and might be presumed to oppose joining a union and paying dues. Contemplating the proportion of opponents and the 12 to 19 percent who did not bother to vote, he might well wonder what it would take to get these workers to support the union and how willingly they would pay dues without a union shop. The non-voters had not responded to the active, publicized campaigns to vote for the union shop—and the union; would it take that much continued union effort, or more, to get the apathetic workers, at least, to

pay their dues? A union leader might prudently assume that loss of the union shop would allow a fair number of non-voters to evade or neglect dues payment. The Ford vote and the small proportion of escapees indicate that some of those who had not voted earlier or who had voted "no" might pay their dues now, after having lived under a union shop for some time, of course.

Once the union shop was prohibited, however, unions could not rely upon it to educate new workers to the responsibility of paying dues; from among new hires union leaders could expect some "uneducated" rejection of voluntary membership so that within a few years the proportion of non-members would probably rise above the escapee percentage. If unions were then to maintain their membership they would have to maintain added educational programs, extra shop services, and shop canvassing. The loss of the union shop would thus necessitate a diversion of union resources from present activities under the best of circumstances; and it would bring in no more income, though it could bring in less. There is no guarantee that diverting expenditures and efforts and offering new services would hold members. Added programs and extra services *might* offset membership losses and even strengthen unions internally as well; an outside observer might wonder if a union would not be strengthened by some cuts in staff and by eliminating unimaginative, unrewarding programs. Union leaders, however, are not apt to be impressed with such an argument for which there is no proof, but they will not underestimate the cost to the union of continued, aggressive dues collection among the workers, not overestimate the possible gains of such work.

The evidence clearly suggests that loss of the union shop to unions now enjoying it would, in itself, bring about a drop in membership. The union shop has brought in an average of one new member for every six voluntary members. Under the modified union shop in steel and autos during the early 50s, as noted above, around 5 percent of the workers dropped or stayed out when they could. Were there no period of forced membership, as in most of these steel and auto plants, to initiate workers into the union, the percentage would no doubt be higher. Meyers' study of unions under the right-to-work law supports such a conclusion. A larger proportion of Texas workers do not belong to the unions that represent them than do workers in steel and autos who first had to join the union. In Jefferson County, Texas' most highly organized industrial area, 9 percent of represented workers did not

[10] *Fortune*, December 1952, p. 90.
[11] *Business Week*, October 8, 1955, pp. 127–28.

belong to a union and in Dallas County, where labor is weak, 21 percent of represented workers did not belong to unions.[12]

These fragmentary data on escapees in steel and autos, and on Texas workers, considered along with the proportion of workers who did not vote or who voted "no" in the union-shop elections, provide a reasonable basis for union leaders to guess that unions now enjoying the security of the union shop could lose perhaps as low as 6 to 8 percent to as high as 10 to 15 percent of their present members if right-to-work laws were widely enacted. Whether union leaders—or businessmen—would agree that a loss in union membership of from 6 percent to 15 percent is minimal is doubtful. Unionists might very well consider such a suggestion gratuitous, for the exclusive representation of all workers, whether members or not, imposes upon unions overhead expenditures that are relatively insensitive to changes in membership and that magnify revenue losses.

If membership and dues income should fall off as the result of a right-to-work law, unions would still have to provide the full services of representing and protecting all workers that they now furnish. Negotiations, grievance processing, arbitration, and administration costs would continue at about the same level as under the union shop. If unions increased their services to hold wavering and doubtful members and to attract uninterested new workers, costs would go up while, at best; income would no more than remain the same. Meyers suggests that grievance activity may rise when there is no union shop, though his data are too sketchy to suggest by how much or to indicate clearly whether union leaders became more responsive to worker needs or workers became more irresponsible.

In any case, the burden of decline in any union income would fall disproportionally upon the less immediate and crucial, though none-the-less vital, programs such as research, white-collar organizing, publicity, education, shop-steward training, voters' registration, and perhaps even strike funds. Since these programs in total account for no more than half to a quarter of a union budget, a 6 to 15 percent decline in dues can be magnified easily into a major and substantial cut in any one or several programs.

The United Auto Workers' experience in 1958 provides some indication of union response to a decline in income of the size possible under right-to-work laws. Per capita tax income fell off from 1957 by about 12 percent as laid-off and permanently displaced workers discontinued their dues payments. Loss of these workers to the union tended to reduce representational demands, of course, in a way that member loss under right-to-work laws would not, yet the union dropped 188 staff members, sharply curtailed TV and radio programs, and cut back *Solidarity*, the weekly newspaper, to a monthly. Also, officers and board and staff members took two voluntary pay cuts— 10 percent for 18 weeks in 1958 and 5 percent for 16 weeks in 1959. To strengthen the United Auto Workers' general financial condition and to build up a diminishing strike fund, Walter Reuther sought approval of a 67 percent increase in dues for 1959.

The general effects of right-to-work proposals, if enacted, might not be nearly as serious as the cutbacks experienced by the United Auto Workers in 1958; there may not be in fact as large a loss in membership and income as our highly speculative calculations suggest. Yet, union leaders could well find the calculations persuasive enough to convince *them* that right-to-work laws would inflict something more than a minimal or symbolic political loss upon their organization.

NEED FOR FURTHER RESEARCH

A loss of income and membership is not welcome by unionists at any time, but today even a small additional loss can have a serious impact upon union strength. Desmond Walker, secretary-treasurer of the United Rubber Workers, told his members last year, "Through automation we're losing membership in the big locals. But we're organizing more plants, and these locals need more men to service them. Our operating expenses keep going up, but our income remains the same."[13] Smaller plants require a higher expenditure of organizing time and money per worker than did the large, mass-production plants organized in the 30s. Automation not only brings smaller plants, but also more white-collar workers who are rapidly supplanting and displacing the core of union members, the production workers. Unions will need a more persuasive and sophisticated, and thus probably a more expensive, approach to organize white-collar men. Any loss of income that bears heavily upon union publicity, education, and organizing activities can have serious consequences.

What the actual effect of right-to-work laws upon union strength and bargaining is in a single

---

[12] Meyers, p. 30.

[13] *United Rubber Worker*, September 1959, p. 11.

state, or would be if made general throughout the nation, we do not know. After considering union experience under right to work in Texas, Meyers asserts that the law had a minimal direct effect upon union growth for two reasons. First, unions and employers in the traditional areas of the closed shop have ignored the law, and second, workers can secure a union shop only after union organization and recognition. As proof, he points out that organization of the unorganized in Texas has proceeded at a remarkably rapid rate since 1947.[14] The difficulties are that he has no unambiguous standard by which to judge the growth rate and, further, that he has no way of demonstrating whether the growth rate would have been less or more rapid if there had been no right-to-work law. After passage of the law, the rate at which unions organized in large manufacturing establishments declined, but whether the right-to-work law contributed to the decline is impossible to tell from Meyers' data.[15]

Whatever the effect of right to work may be on union growth and bargaining in a single state, one must be cautious in inferring that a right-to-work law generally applied would have the same effect. To do so is to fall into the fallacy of com-

[14] *"Right to Work" in Practice*, p. 4, and "The Growth of Collective Bargaining in Texas—A Newly Industrialized Area," *Annual Proceedings*, IRRA, 1954, pp. 286–97.

[15] The rate of organization of small establishments remained steady, but whether the rate was the same as it would have been without a right-to-work law is impossible to say without some appropriate standard to use in comparison.

position. If Texas unions suffered any loss of membership and revenue because of the right-to-work restriction, it well might not be noticeable since the parent international unions, soundly and securely organized in the great industrial states, have contributed a large share of the organizing effort and have provided the bulk of bargaining strength in top negotiations. Were right-to-work laws generally applied, however, any resulting loss of income would affect all locals within a union. None would have any outside resources to draw upon, and the impairment of present union programs and activities would become plainly and immediately apparent.

The difficulty in speculating about the possible effects of right-to-work laws applied to unions generally, as was attempted in this article, is quite as great as that faced by Meyers in estimating probable union growth and bargaining in Texas if the state had had no right-to-work law. The difficulties should warn us that conclusions based so unsteadily had better be tentative and that more than one ought to be explored. The speculations here do no more than suggest that the effects of right-to-work laws are complex and call for much more careful research than was done here or elsewhere. Until someone carries out that research, others may wish to join me in passing a Scotch verdict of "not proven" upon the effect of right-to-work laws: We believe they have a decided and substantial effect upon union strength and bargaining, but we cannot prove it.

32. Grievance Systems in American Industry*

Frank Traver de Vyver†

Formalized procedures for handling plant-level disputes between management and labour have become a regular part of the American industrial relations systems. In fact, during the past 30 years, the institution has developed rapidly and, with arbitration as the final step, has lead to many variations in union-management relationships. A grievance procedure is a formal arrangement under which decisions by one level of management may be appealed through channels to higher levels of management. Under nearly all American collective bargaining contracts a third party, *viz.* an arbitrator, is called in if the claimant is not satisfied with top management's decision. In the English engineering industry there may be an appeal from decisions of one firm to regional associations and then to the York Conference, which is attended by representatives of the national association and of the national unions. The system in the United States, however, is generally limited to plant or company. Formalization of such appeals systems seems to be an American institution. It certainly is rarely found in Australia.

Prior to the passage of the Wagner Act in 1937, trade unions in America were legally accepted, but their right to exist was unprotected. Management could and some did do everything possible to keep out unions. Labour spies employed by some of the best firms reported to the companies the names of union leaders and of new members who were then immediately discharged. Union leaders were sometimes bribed, and as the records show, company policy and

strike breakers were available to break up strikes or any other demonstrations. Those were the days of the "open-door policy." With a nostalgic view of the era of the small owner-operated factory, corporation presidents announced that no worker needed a union to speak for him. "The president's door is always open" read the signs posted throughout the multi-storied plant. Theoretically any worker dissatisfied with his foreman's decision could drift into the president's office for a man-to-man discussion of his problem. Strangely enough there were and are examples in American industry where this open-door policy has worked. In general, however, although the door may have been open, the hurdles in the way of getting there were insurmountable. Much as he might like the friendly approach, the modern corporation executive has far too much to do at the macro level to spend much time with the detailed problems of the worker-foreman relationship on the factory floor. Even if the worker could obtain his foreman's permission to leave his job he would have to see several secretaries on his perilous journey to the president's office where the door might be open but the president himself might be off to New York to negotiate with bankers or potential customers.

The passage of the Wagner Act did protect the workers' rights to organize and bargain collectively through representatives of their own choosing and forbade management's interference with those rights. With this right protected rather than simply allowed, collective bargaining became the way of industrial life for many additional millions of American workers. The motor companies, the steel companies, the rubber industry, the aluminum industry, and the textile industry, to mention a few, which previously had operated free from union interference, soon

* Reprinted from the *Australian Quarterly*, June 1965, pp. 34–43.

† Vice Provost and Professor of Economics, Duke University. Fulbright Lecturer, University of Western Australia.

were widely organized on a company or plant basis. The myth of the open-door policy gave way to a search for some method to satisfy the worker and his representative when, from the worker's standpoint, a foreman made an incorrect decision.

The method generally used is the step grievance procedure. Labour contracts all have a clause which describes what is to happen if a worker is dissatisfied. A typical opening statement might read as follows: "Complaints, grievances, or disputes arising out of the operation and interpretation of this agreement involving wages (other than general wage increase or decrease proposals as provided for in Article VI), hours, or other conditions of employment shall be presented within 15 days of the time that the aggrieved party has knowledge of the grievance and shall be handled and settled in the following manner." A more simple opening statement from another contract defines a grievance "as a violation of the terms of this agreement or any type of supervisory conduct which unjustly denies to any employee his job or any benefit arising out of his job and notice of which has been given in writing within six calendar weeks after its occurrence."

The steps for handling the grievance depend to a large extent upon the organizational structure of the company and to a lesser extent upon the union's structure. Typically, however, the parties agree that efforts will be made to settle the differences at the lowest level of management before the difference actually becomes a formal grievance. For example, one agreement reads, "Should any difference arise between the employee covered by this agreement and a representative of the Company, the employee and/or the Job Steward shall discuss such difference informally with the immediate supervisor for the purpose of settling differences in the simplest and most direct manner in order to avoid grievances."

If the decision at the informal step is unsatisfactory, the difference becomes a grievance and more formal procedures are prescribed. The first formal step would ordinarily involve the foreman or his assistant, the aggrieved worker, and the representative of the union, who at this first stage is usually the elected shop steward. Often the grievance has to be written down but, that requirement may come at a later step. At any rate the foreman is expected to give a reasonably prompt answer and a time limit for receipt of the answer is provided.

If the worker or the union representative is not satisfied with the foreman's answer either he or the union may appeal to the foreman's immediate boss, likely the superintendent. At this step the superintendent listens to the facts and the union's arguments. Again with a specified time limit the superintendent is required to reply to the union in writing and may be expected to give reasons for his decision.

Unless the superintendent has overruled his foreman or has persuaded the union that the foreman's actions were in accordance with the terms of the contract, the union will probably appeal to the next higher step, perhaps the manager of a particular plant of the corporation. By this stage the original grievant and his shop steward are likely to be left out at the discussion. The manager meets with a union official, a business agent perhaps, and often with a general shop committee which is an elected group of workers from various departments. Minutes would ordinarily be kept at this stage of the procedures, and probably more than one grievance would be heard at these regularly scheduled meetings of union and employer representatives. Without the original disputants present the manager and the union agent theoretically can debate with less heat and more light. Presumably the manager makes a further investigation of the facts and within a prescribed time limit must give his answer to the complaint.

The manager may overrule the superintendent or the union's business agent may drop the case if he thinks the worker and the shop steward were wrong. If the union is not satisfied, however, the next appeal is to executive management. At this point the president of the corporation or his deputy discuss all unresolved cases with a representative of the national union. Completely removed as they are from the pressures of the active participants, these men are expected to have a broad view of industrial relations and be able to reach logical conclusions. Sometimes they may be willing to swop, with the union giving in on some cases and the company on others.

Well over 90 percent of the grievance procedures found in American collective bargaining contracts provide for arbitration before a mutually agreed upon outsider, if the union remains unsatisfied with the executive management's decision. Ordinarily, therefore, the final step in a grievance procedure describes the details involved in getting the dispute to the arbitrator and provides that both parties agree to abide by the arbitrator's decision.

Before discussing the advantages and disadvantages of such formal procedures some mention should be made of the clear distinction between grievance settlement and the negotiation of a contract, and of the subject matter and purpose of grievances in American style collective bargaining.

The reason grievances are carefully defined in the introductory sections of a contract's grievance clause is because in the United States a sharp distinction is made between disputes arising during the negotiation of an agreement or contract and those arising over interpretation of the terms of the agreement or over management's decisions on matters included in the contract. During what might be called the more naive days of bargaining when neither management nor unions had learned the pitfalls of loose wording, grievances' were not defined. The first General Motors agreement, for example, signed in 1937, merely indicated that "any employee having a grievance in connection with his work, or any group of employees having a joint grievance in connection with their work, should first take up the matter with the foreman of the department."

It soon became evident, however, that workers could and did grieve about unusual matters. Perhaps a group of them did not like a foreman. Under a wide-open grievance clause such a dislike could be appealed to arbitration, a possibility which management viewed with alarm. Such items might, of course, be kept from the grievance system by a strong management rights clause now a part of most contracts. More difficult to handle were the large number of *bona fide* disputes which arose about matters not included in the basic agreement, omitted either because of neglect or as the result of bargaining. Suppose, for example, the contract contained no mention about the assignment of overtime work but some worker felt he was not getting his share of that work. He certainly would have a complaint and in his mind a grievance. Without clear definitions of the meaning of the term "grievance" such a complaint could come through the grievance procedure and even to arbitration. In such event the arbitrator would be deciding an interest or contract dispute, the type of arbitration which neither American management nor labour wants. This same event might have become a rights dispute if the parties had previously agreed that overtime should be shared equally and the individual worker felt he had not had his proper share. In other words it is one thing to agree that overtime be shared and argue whether a particular person had shared properly; it is an entirely different matter to have an outside arbitrator decide that in his

opinion overtime should be shared no matter what the parties had agreed to. From such experiences with grievance decisions actually changing the contract, management and labour have learned to define carefully the meaning of the term grievance and generally to limit the coverage to those disputes arising out of the terms of the contract or from an action taken by management under the contract.

An examination of the subject matter of grievances is also important in understanding the American system. Matters which in Australia are usually not even considered comprise an important part of the usual American collective bargaining contract. For example, except for long service leave a leave of absence is almost unknown in Australian industry. If a person wishes to be off the job for an extended period, he gives notice and leaves employment. In the United States, on the other hand, elaborate procedures are often provided for application and approval of requests for leaves. Since the details are involved, differences over interpretation may easily arise. When, for instance, is a worker absent without leave if his 30-day leave expires on Monday and he is on a third shift which starts at 12:30 Sunday night?

Examples like this could be multiplied. Fundamentally, however, the concept of job ownership and the absence of any enforcement agency for collective bargaining contracts are the two major factors which increase the possibilities for differences over individual rights.

The ordinary American collective bargaining contract provides sufficient checks so that once a worker has spent a probationary period on a job, except under strong provocation, that job remains his until he retires or decides to give it up. Under such a system a discharge is almost bound to create a grievance. Likewise any type of discipline which may build up a record leading to eventual discharge will be likely to be the subject of a grievance. In my own experience I have listened to and then arbitrated grievances over an oral warning. Again arising from the ownership of the job, grievances are filed because of job assignments, transfers, lay-offs either because of redundancy or as discipline, leaves of absence, and absenteeism.

Related to the job ownership concept is the concept that seniority is all pervasive. Contracts usually have an entire section devoted to seniority rules; that is, how seniority is determined, how it is lost, and the rights which it carries. One contract reads, "Seniority is defined as the length of an employee's service with Company, uninterrupted by quitting or discharge, and the purpose of which is to provide a declared policy of right of preference measured by such length of service. The rules governing the application of above policy are mutually agreed to as follows, and shall apply to all employees covered by this agreement." Furthermore, seniority is mentioned throughout the contract. Jobs are to be assigned according to seniority if the senior person is qualified or can qualify. Redundancy lay-offs must be according to seniority; recalls to jobs have to follow the seniority list, and even overtime may be assigned according to seniority. Certain union officials may even be given super-seniority during their incumbencies. In the necessary daily decisions on seniority rights the chances for misunderstanding are numerous. If, for example, a senior worker is to be assigned to a job provided he is qualified, neither the worker nor the union is likely to accept management's decision that a man with less seniority is really more qualified. And when a lay-off is scheduled there is even less chance of convincing the older worker that his qualifications are not adequate for the jobs which are being retained. Unions have even been known to increase the number of shop stewards when a redundancy lay-off was imminent so that super-seniority provided for shop stewards would allow the faithful to be kept on the job. Needless to say that action brought numerous grievances from senior members not among the elite.

The second reason for large numbers of grievances is because the machinery is in reality the enforcement machinery for the contract. If an Australian award, for example, requires extra pay when a plant permanently closes, this is a matter of law and the enforcement up to the Court. In the United States, on the other hand, if an employee felt he was entitled to severance pay and did not get it, his procedure would be to file a grievance. Or, if an Australian employee felt he was not receiving the award rate or the skill margin, he could appeal to the Court. An American worker would file a grievance. Only after the grievance procedures had been exhausted will American courts ordinarily step in to enforce an arbitrator's decision.

There are no available statistics to measure the causes of grievances but one study of 1,728 grievances which did go to arbitration gives some indication of the possible reasons for grievances. Of the 1,728 cases, 456 involved discipline and discharge, grievances, in other words, arising from the job ownership concept. An additional 301 cases involved seniority disputes, disputes closely related to the job ownership idea. The remaining 971 cases were mostly concerned with issues involving enforcement of the agreement, with 223 of those items having to do with job evaluation issues, matters which in Australia would be found in the margins sections of the award.

Although American grievance procedures have been used successfully to handle hundreds of rights disputes, there are certainly defects which must be recognized.

In the first place the long appeals system is based upon a theory which in practice may be untenable. In theory the further the parties are removed from the heat around the spot where the grievance originated, the more likely they can use pure reason to settle the issue. In practice both management and union officials find it difficult to overrule decisions made by those in lower echelons. Such a feeling is understandable. A union president who kept overruling a shop steward after he had been upheld by other persons in the union hierarchy would surely lose the loyalty of the members and might even be replaced. And a corporation president or his deputy who overruled a decision successively upheld by two or three in the management group would surely destroy morale if he did it very often. The point is even stronger when the superintendent is asked to overrule a foreman or the local business manager of a union to overrule a shop steward. There will be times when a grievance is so obviously without merit or so patently a management error that the business manager of the union or the superintendent will change the earlier decision. By and large, however, the steps of the grievance procedure offer time for lines to be drawn. By the time the executive management and the national officer of the union hear the case, facts and argument disclose a right side and the other man's side. Arbitration becomes the only way out. No statistics are available on the plant settlement of grievances, but my own experience would indicate that once a grievance had been put in writing it almost always reached executive management and probably went on to arbitration.

Another difficulty with a grievance system is that the immediate supervisor, knowing that there may be an appeal from his decision, may be tempted to take action without considering all of the ramifications of that action. Although he would probably resent being overruled, the foreman nevertheless may make snap judgments because he knows that his decision may be modified. In other words the grievance system with arbitration as the final step may be a way of "passing the buck." Knowing the possible results of unfair disciplinary actions or departures from award provisions, an Australian foreman must give careful consideration to any action involving members of the work force. My observation has been that too many American foremen may act precipitously, aware that an error can always be corrected.

In the third place a grievance procedure may take considerable time. Although the typical contract provides time limits, the carrying of a complaint through arbitration may take nearly a year. The worker has, let us say, 15 days to file, the foreman has from 3 to 5 days to make his decision. Appeal must be within two weeks and then the superintendent may have another two weeks to give his answer. After another two weeks for appeal the manager is likely to have two to four weeks for his investigation and reply. Executive management hears cases only once a month so there is the possibility of another 30 to 45 days wait before management's final decision is given. After that the parties must agree upon an arbitrator, agree with him on a date when all can be present, then wait about 30 more days for the arbitrator's decision. I recently arbitrated a two-year-old grievance and it was not my delay. The company and the union lawyers had busy schedules as did the national representative of the union. By the time I heard the case, the worker who had started it by claiming he should have had overtime instead of the man who did work had withdrawn any claim for compensation, and the argument evolved about matters of principle. Both management and labour seek prompt settlement of complaints as the proper way to attain good personnel relations. There is doubt whether a formal grievance procedure meets this requirement.

Finally, what started as a way to get a prompt hearing from top management, instead of the haphazard "open-door" policy, has developed into a mechanical set of successive hearings sometimes with more interest given to who wins than to what is right. The proper papers must be filed at the proper times; the proper schedule for meetings must be adopted; only the proper persons may attend the meetings; and records must be kept not only of decisions but of what participants actually said. Such a system must be confusing to the worker who was disciplined for tardiness although he was late because his car broke down or to the foreman who was using his best judgment as a manager when he reprimanded an employee for poor workmanship. An American slang expression expresses the situation accurately. A grievance system seems to "make a production" out of some very minor differences between management and labour. An example of the legalism that has become part of the system was a case decided by one of America's more famous arbitrators. During a strike which had created considerable violence several employees had been arrested and convicted for assault. At the conclusion of the strike the company agreed to return everyone to work except those who had been convicted. The union arbitrated the case. The arbitrator reversed the company's decision not because it was incorrect (which it might have been) but rather because a provision in the agreement had not been fulfilled. It read "In the case of discharge or imposition of a disciplinary penalty upon an employee, the penalty will be imposed in the presence of a shop steward." Since the discharge took place while all shop stewards were on the picket line it was impossible to follow the provision. Therefore said the arbitrator, the discharged workers must be returned to work, and they were. This type of legalistic approach to a grievance procedure is surely one of the drawbacks of the system.

Yet grievance systems are a viable part of American collective bargaining. Because of their existence with the final step being arbitration, the incidence of strikes over disputes subject to the grievance procedure is extremely low. A no-strike clause is part of most American collective bargaining contracts. The grievance procedure does supply the escape valve which used to be the strike or other direct action.

33. Contemporary Issues in the Grievance and Arbitration Process: A Current Evaluation*

Benjamin Aaron†

INTRODUCTION

The grievance and arbitration process, as developed in the United States, can fairly be characterized as an immensely successful social invention. To be sure, the process is not encompassed within a single structure: It is better described as a fundamental theme in our system of industrial relations that appears in numerous variations based on pragmatic considerations. It is also true that grievance and arbitration procedures, of whatever kind, have never lacked able and outspoken critics, who have attacked them for being too formal or too informal, too legalistic or too freewheeling, too expensive, too pretentious, and so forth. Most of these strictures, however, have generally inspired the collective bargaining parties, their representatives, and arbitrators to engage in greater self-examination and to attempt to correct obvious abuses. Thus, private voluntary grievance and arbitration procedures have, for the most part, escaped the arid formalism and stultification of, say, the statutory procedures of the Railway Labor Act.

To a degree as yet uncertain, however, the integrity of the grievance and arbitration process has been undermined by its own success. In a series of now-familiar decisions construing the somewhat Delphic declarations of Congress in Section 301 of the Taft-Hartley Act,[1] the U.S.

Supreme Court has exalted arbitral decisions beyond the reach, in most instances, of judicial review. Similarly, the National Labor Relations Board, although not going quite so far, has adopted the policy of deferring to arbitration awards involving conduct allegedly consisting of both an unfair labor practice and a violation of contract, if certain specified conditions have been met.[2] Moreover, the question whether the Board will, in such cases, refuse to entertain the unfair labor practice charge if the grievance and arbitration procedure is available to adjudicate the dispute, is still open.[3] As a consequence, the process has been attacked by some as a system of private decision-making that vitally affects the rights of third parties and is yet above the law of the land.

Nor is that all. During a somewhat longer period than that encompassing the developments just referred to, the courts have gradually built up a sizeable corpus of doctrine in respect of the collective agreement. The basis of the doctrine is that the principals to that agreement are the employer and the union, and that the union, in its capacity of exclusive bargaining representative, "owns" the grievances challenging the interpretation or application of the agreement, or at the very least, is virtually in complete charge of their processing.[4] Of course, the union owes equally to all employees in the bargaining unit,

* Reprinted by permission from *Collective Bargaining Today* (Proceedings of the Collective Bargaining Forum —1971) copyright © 1972 by The Bureau of National Affairs, Inc., Washington, D.C., 20037.

† Professor of Law and Director, Institute of Industrial Relations. University of California, Los Angeles, Calif.

[1] *United Steelworkers* v. *American Mfg. Co.*, 363 U.S. 564, 46 LRRM 2414 (1960); *United Steelworkers* v. *Warrior & Gulf Navigation Co.*, 363 U.S. 574, 46 LRRM 2416 (1960); *United Steelworkers* v. *Enterprise Wheel & Car Corp.*, 363 U.S. 593, 46 LRRM 2423 (1960); *Textile Workers* v. *Lincoln Mills of Alabama*, 353 U.S. 448, LRRM 2113 (1957).

[2] See *Spielberg Mfg. Co.*, 112 NLRB 1080, 36 LRRM 1152 (1955), discussed in text at note 27, *infra*.

[3] The leading NLRB decision on this point is *Adams Dairy*, 147 NLRB 1410, 56 LRRM 1321 (1964), discussed in text at note 23, *infra*. But see *Joseph Schlitz Brewing Co.*, 175 NLRB No. 23, 70 LRRM 1472 (1968). The courts have so far taken a view contrary to that of the Board. *Square D. Co.* v. *NLRB*, 332 F.2d 360, 56 LRRM 2147 (9th Cir. 1964): *Sinclair Refining Co.* v. *NLRB*, 306 F.2d 569, 50 LRRM 2830 (5th Cir. 1962).

[4] See Cox, "Rights under a Labor Agreement," 69 *Harvard Law Review* 601 (1956).

whether union members or not, a duty of fair representation;[5] but the courts will grant it "a wide range of reasonableness . . . in serving the unit it represents"[6]—wide enough, in fact, to legitimize by its concurrence some employer actions against individual employees which, if taken unilaterally and opposed by the union, might well be condemned by the NLRB or the courts.[7]

The final link in this constricting circle around individual employee rights was forged by further refinements in the doctrine of exhaustion of remedies. It now seems settled that if the grievance and arbitration procedure is available to an aggrieved employee, he is without standing to bring an action for contract violation under Section 301 of the Taft-Hartley Act unless and until he has exhausted that procedure.[8] Furthermore, there are at least four Justices on the present Supreme Court who believe that the grievant should not be permitted to sue his employer for breach of contract unless he can first establish that the union violated its duty to represent him fairly.[9] To many observers, there seems to be operating here a kind of "Catch 22" insofar as the individual employee is concerned.

A number of issues arise from the developments I have described. Time does not permit a thorough discussion of any one of them, but I shall attempt at least a superficial exploration of three: (1) judicial review of labor arbitration awards; (2) deference by administrative agencies and courts to arbitral decisions involving alleged violations of both the collective agreement and an applicable statute; and (3) rights of an employee under an agreement when the grievant's position is manifestly at odds with that of his bargaining representative.

JUDICIAL REVIEW OF LABOR ARBITRATION AWARDS

Although, of the three I have chosen to explore in this paper this issue has generated perhaps the most emotion, it gives me the least

trouble. The reason is that I have not found it difficult to distinguish the somewhat overblown and sententious rhetoric of the Supreme Court's opinion in the *Warrior & Gulf* case[10] from the more modest but similar conclusions of other, more knowledgeable observers. One does not have to agree with Mr. Justice Douglas' unqualified assertions that the labor arbitrator "performs functions which are not normal to the courts," or that the "ablest judge cannot be expected to bring the same experience and competence to bear upon the determination of a grievance, because he cannot be similarly informed,"[11] in order to defend the thesis that most arbitrators are better qualified than most judges to handle the types of grievances commonly submitted to arbitration. By the same token, one need not accept Judge Paul Hays' even more extravagant claims that only a "handful" of arbitrators possess "the knowledge, training, skill, and character to make them good judges and therefore [sic] good arbitrators," and that the remainder, who decide "literally thousands of cases every year," are "wholly unfitted for their jobs,"[12] in order to concede that arbitrators occasionally render decisions that insult our intelligence or outrage our sense of fairness.

It is entirely fitting that we should be concerned about this latter type of case, which although it is not nearly so common as Judge Hays asserts, occurs too frequently to be dismissed on de minimis grounds. Unfortunately, the proposals of how to deal with the problem are either demonstrably unfeasible or would open the door to a return to the bad old days of *Cutler-Hammer*,[13] when judges simply substituted their own notions of what ought to be done for those of the parties or of the arbitrator. In the former category, I would place the suggestion made by the late Harry Shulman in 1955,[14] and more recently revived by Judge Hays[15] and Professor Harry Wellington,[16] that the courts should refuse

[5] *Syres* v. *Oil Workers*, 223 F.2d 739, 36 LRRM 2290 (5th Cir. 1955), rev'd and remanded per curiam, 350 U.S. 892, 37 LRRM 2068 (1955); *Steele* v. *Louisville & N.R.R.*, 323 U.S. 192, 15 LRRM 708 (1944).

[6] *Ford Motor Co.* v. *Huffman*, 345 U.S. 330, 338, 31 LRRM 2548 (1953).

[7] E.g., *Hildreth* v. *Union News*, 315 F.2d 548, 52 LRRM 2827 (6th Cir.), cert. denied, 375 U.S. 826, 54 LRRM 2312 (1963).

[8] *Republic Steel Corp.* v. *Maddox*, 379 U.S. 650, 58 LRRM 2193 (1965).

[9] *Vaca* v. *Sipes*, 386 U.S. 171, 64 LRRM 2369 (1967). The four Justices are White, Douglas, Brennan, and Stewart.

[10] 363 U.S. 574, 46 LRRM 2416 (1960).

[11] Id. at 581–82.

[12] Hays, *Labor Arbitration: A Dissenting View* (New Haven: Yale University Press, 1966), 112.

[13] *Int'l Ass'n of Machinists* v. *Cutler-Hammer, Inc.*, 271 App. Div. 917, 67 N.Y.S.2d 317, 19 LRRM 2232, aff'd 297 N.Y. 519, 74 NE2d 464, 20 LRRM 2445 (1947). This case held, "If the meaning of the provisions of the contract sought to be arbitrated is beyond dispute [in the view of the court] there cannot be anything to arbitrate and the contract cannot be said to provide for arbitration." 271 App. Div. at 918, 67 N.Y.S.2d at 318.

[14] Shulman, "Reason, Contract and Law in Labor Relations," 68 *Harvard Law Review* 999, 1024 (1955).

[15] Hays, supra note 12, at 116.

[16] Wellington, *Labor and the Legal Process* (New Haven: Yale University Press, 1968), 123–24.

to entertain actions to compel arbitration or to enforce arbitral awards. The trouble is that Dean Shulman's suggestions were rejected by the Supreme Court in *Lincoln Mills* and its numerous progeny. Adoption of his position after almost two decades of experience in the development of the opposite thesis would be much more than a "strategic retreat";[17] it would, in fact, require a major restructuring of collective bargaining in this country. I see not the slightest possibility that the proponents of such a drastic reversal of policy, themselves a small minority, could persuade Congress to take this step.

In the category of proposals that would recreate old problems in the effort to solve new ones, I would include another of Professor Wellington's suggestions, as well as one offered by Professor Bernard Meltzer. Wellington favors "serious judicial review of whether the parties agreed to arbitrate a particular dispute in a post-arbitration proceeding."[18] This would be accomplished, apparently, not by allowing the court to hold a hearing de novo, but by requiring the arbitrator "to write a reasoned and unambiguous opinion," and a determination by the court whether the arbitrator's award was "reasonable in the light of the language of the collective agreement, projected against its industrial background and revealed in the opinion of the arbitrator."[19] In a similar vein, Meltzer suggests that courts be required to enforce an award unless it clearly lacks a "rational basis in the agreement read in the light of the common law of the plant where appropriate."[20]

Of the two proposals, Meltzer's is much to be preferred. Wellington's is apparently limited to review of arbitrability issues, and would not cover those cases in which the arbitrator's judgment, rather than his jurisdiction, is challenged. Moreover, the mind boggles at the prospect of establishing standards for determining what constitutes a "reasoned and unambiguous opinion." Meltzer's proposal, however, suffers from the fatal defect of excessive flexibility. The phrases "rational basis in the agreement" and "where appropriate" would provide more than enough leeway for judges so inclined to substitute their conclusions for those of the arbitrator selected by the parties.

My own view is that we would be better off trying to improve the present system rather than trying to change it in a revolutionary way. I suspect that both the relative and the absolute numbers of arbitration awards that most persons would concede to be outrageous or indefensible are extremely small. Moreover, the effects of such awards are seldom, if ever, catastrophic and can often be remedied by subsequent changes in the collective agreement. Incompetent arbitrators, unlike incompetent federal judges, can be, and frequently are, fired. In sum, I believe the present doctrine limiting judicial review both on questions of arbitrability and on challenges going to the merits of arbitration awards should be preserved, despite its imperfections.

DEFERENCE BY ADMINISTRATIVE AGENCIES AND COURTS TO ARBITRAL DECISIONS

The archetypical case under this heading is one in which it is alleged that the same conduct violates both a collective agreement and an applicable statute. The questions I should like to discuss are first, whether the grievant must exhaust his rights under the collective agreement before filing either a charge with an administrative agency or an action in court; and second, whether the grievant, if he elects to proceed with arbitration and loses, may then take his complaint to an administrative agency or initiate a law suit. The statutes most commonly involved are the National Labor Relations Act, the Taft-Hartley Act, and Title VII of the Civil Rights Act of 1964.[21]

As previously indicated, an employee who alleges that his employer's treatment of him has violated both the collective agreement and the NLRA must exhaust the grievance and arbitration procedure before suing under Section 301 of the Taft-Hartley Act for breach of contract.[22] But suppose the employee decides to file an unfair labor charge with the NLRB instead of pursuing his remedy under the grievance and arbitration procedure under the collective agreement: Assuming probable cause, should the Board issue a complaint?

---

[17] Id. at 124.

[18] Id. at 122.

[19] Id.

[20] Meltzer, "Ruminations about Ideology, Laws, and Labor Arbitration, in *The Arbitrator, the NLRB, and the Courts, Proceedings of the 20th Annual Meeting, National Academy of Arbitrators,* ed. Dallas L. Jones (Washington: BNA Books, 1967), 1, 13.

[21] Exhaustion of arbitration procedures is not required as a condition precedent to a suit by a seaman for recovery of unpaid wages accruing from services rendered in foreign commerce. U. S. Bulk Carriers, Inc. v. Arguelles, 91 Sup. Ct. 409, 76 LRRM 2161 (1971). And see *Thompson* v. *Iowa Beef Packers, Inc.,* 19 WH Cases 1060, 1066 (Ia. 1971) (state court suit for wages allegedly due under Fair Labor Standards Act on account of employees' "on call" status during lunch period not barred by their failure to seek contract arbitration).

[22] *Republic Steel Corp.* v. *Maddox,* 379 U.S. 650, 58 LRRM 2193 (1965), supra note 8.

Apparently, the Board still adheres to the policy that it will not defer to arbitration procedures unless (1) the case turns on the interpretation of a specific contract provision; (2) the disputed issue is unquestionalby encompassed by the contract arbitration procedure; and (3) it is reasonably probable the arbitrator's decision will not only dispose of the grievance but will also settle the unfair labor practice controversy in a manner that will effectuate the policies of the Act.[23] Member Gerald Brown has espoused the view, however, that "it is inconsistent with the statutory policy favoring arbitration for the Board to resolve disputes which, while cast as unfair labor practices, essentially involve a dispute with respect to the interpretation or application of the . . . agreement."[24] Accordingly, he favors a policy that whenever it appears that the parties have by practice, bargaining history, or contract waived their statutory rights, bargained them away, or bargained to agreement in respect of the subject matter of the dispute, the Board should "leave to the arbitrator the question of the nature of their bargain and the respective rights and obligations of each party."[25]

Of course, as the Supreme Court has said, the Board's authority is "superior" to arbitration and "may be invoked at any time."[26] This is all the more reason, it seems to me, why the Board should require charging parties to exhaust available arbitration procedures in cases of the type described by Member Brown before seeking relief under the NLRA. By so doing, the Board can reduce its own caseload while also encouraging the private settlement of labor disputes.

Now, let us suppose that our hypothetical grievant takes his dispute to arbitration, loses, and then files an unfair labor practice charge with the Board: Should he be entitled to a "second bite"? The three standards applied by the Board in such cases are well known: it will not defer to the arbitrator's award unless (1) the arbitration procedures have been fair and regular; (2) all parties have agreed to be bound by the arbitrator's award; and (3) the award must not be repugnant to the provisions and policies of the Act.[27] The third criterion obviously contains a good deal of flexibility; and perhaps

flexibility is needed, particularly in the so-called "pretext cases" in which an employee discharged allegedly for good cause claims that the real reason was the employer's anti-union bias. In such situations the Board has refused to defer to the arbitration award unless it appears that the arbitrator knew of and dealt with the allegation of an unfair labor practice.[28] At least one circuit court of appeals has ruled, however, that the Board must enforce the arbitrator's award in this type of case unless it "affirmatively finds an improper reason" for the discharge.[29]

The *Spielberg* standards, with the *Raytheon* gloss, represent, in my view, a sensible balance between the encouragement of private settlement and the protection of rights guaranteed by the NLRA. But is this a proper model for cases arising under Title VII of the Civil Rights Act? Suppose an employee claiming discrimination because of race, religion, or sex files a grievance under a collective agreement that expressly prohibits such discrimination. If the arbitrator denies the grievance, should the courts defer to the arbitrator's judgment?

The arguments, pro and con, are presented in two recent cases. In *Dewey* v. *Reynolds Metals Co.*[30] the plaintiff claimed adverse discrimination because of religious beliefs in violation of the collective agreement. The grievance was carried to arbitration but was denied by the arbitrator. Plaintiff then brought suit in federal district court under Title VII and prevailed. The court of appeals reversed by a divided vote, holding that the district court lacked jurisdiction of the cause. The majority pointed out that if the arbitration award had been in plaintiff's favor, it would have been "final, binding, and conclusive" on the employer. Therefore, it reasoned, allowing plaintiff to relitigate the issue in the courts after losing in arbitration "could sound the death knell to arbitration of labor disputes," because "[e]mployers would not be inclined to agree to arbitration clauses . . . if they provide . . . that the awards are binding on them but not on their employees."[31]

In *Hutchings* v. *United States Industries, Inc.*[32] the facts were similar except that the alleged discrimination was based on race. The federal

---

[23] *Adams Dairy,* 147 NLRB 1410, 56 LRRM 1321 (1964), supra note 3.

[24] Id. at 1423.

[25] Id.

[26] *Carey* v. *Westinghouse Electric Corp.,* 375 U.S. 261, 272, 55 LRRM 2042 (1964).

[27] *Spielberg Mfg. Co.,* 122 NLRB 1080, 36 LRRM 1152 (1955), supra note 2.

[28] *Monsanto Chemical Co.,* 130 NLRB 1097, 47 LRRM 1451 (1961).

[29] *Raytheon Co.* v. *NLRB,* 326 F.2d 471, 55 LRRM 2101 (1st Cir. 1964).

[30] *Dewey* v. *Reynolds Metals Co.,* 429 F.2d 324, 2 FEP Cases 687 (6th Cir. 1970), aff'd by equality divided Court, 402 U.S. 689, 3 FEP Cases 508 (1971).

[31] 429 F.2d at 332.

[32] 428 F.2d 303, 2 FEP Cases 725 (5th Cir. 1970).

district court granted the employer's motion for summary judgment, basing its decision in part on the ground that plaintiff had made a binding election of remedies by first taking his grievance to arbitration. The court of appeals reversed. Its opinion stressed the different functions performed by the federal district courts and by arbitrators in Title VII cases. The trial judge, it said,

[b]ears a special responsibility in the public interest to resolve the employment dispute, for once the judicial machinery has been set in train, the proceeding takes on a public character in which remedies are devised to vindicate the policies of the Act, not merely to afford private relief to the employee.[33]

The arbitrator's role, the court continued,

[i]s to carry out the aims of the agreement that he has been commissioned to interpret and apply. . . . The arbitrator, in bringing his informed judgment to bear on the problem submitted to him, may consider himself constrained to apply the contract and not give the types of remedies available under Title VII, even though the contract may contain an anti-discrimination provision. . . .

In view of the dissimilarities between the . . . grievance-arbitration process and the judicial process under Title VII, it would be fallacious to assume that an employee [who seeks a remedy under both] . . . is attempting to enforce a single right in two forums. . . . [T]he arbitrator's determination under the contract has no effect upon the court's *power* to adjudicate a violation of Title VII rights.[34]

The court concluded that "[i]f the doctrine of election of remedies is applicable at all to Title VII cases, it applies only to the extent that the plaintiff is not entitled to duplicate relief in the private and public forums which would result in an unjust enrichment or windfall to him."[35]

The Supreme Court has granted certiorari in the *Dewey* case, so we can expect that the conflict between the Fifth and Sixth Circuits will eventually be resolved. Meanwhile, I should like to suggest two additional reasons why I think the decision in the *Hutchings* case should be sustained. First, there is some reason to doubt that the average arbitrator has any unique qualifications that would justify his being allowed to make unreviewable decisions on the merits of cases involving employment discrimination based on race, color, religion, sex, or national origin. Indeed, arbitrators, being human, are likely to have the same conscious or unconscious prejudices in these matters as those found in the population at large. This is especially true in sex discrimination cases; most arbitartors are men, and recent research discloses that some of them have upheld employment discrimination against women because of their sex on the flimsiest of grounds.[36]

Second, the likelihood of conflict between the grievant and his bargaining representative and of collusion between the employer and the union is much greater in cases of alleged race and sex discrimination than in those involving alleged discrimination for union activity. We cannot ignore the continued existence in some companies and in some unions of open or covert discrimination against racial minorities and women; nor should it surprise us that some members of those disadvantaged groups may put less trust in the contract grievance and arbitration procedure than in the remedies against discrimination provided under Title VII.

I do not mean to suggest that cases of this type should never be submitted to arbitration; indeed, if the matter in dispute is plainly covered by a valid provision in the collective agreement, arbitration may be the best procedure by which to resolve the question. Nevertheless, I would not require exhaustion of contract remedies as a condition precedent to initiating a Title VII proceeding. Conciliation in the early stages by the state or federal equal employment opportunity agencies may serve the same purpose as the contract grievance procedures. And if conciliation proves unsuccessful, there is no guarantee that an arbitrator will be more or as well qualified as a federal court judge to resolve the dispute. In fact, the opposite must be assumed if the issue involves the legality of the contract provision rather than its application or interpretation.

For these reasons, I would not in race and discrimination cases impose the same strict limitations upon judicial review that are invoked in actions under Section 301 of the Taft-Hartley Act to set aside arbitration awards. A more appropriate analogue, I submit, is the one set forth in Section 10(e) of the NLRA, which declares that the standard of review applicable to courts of appeals in NLRB decisions shall be that "the findings of the Board with respect to questions of fact if supported by substantial evidence on the record considered as a whole shall be conclusive."

RIGHTS OF INDIVIDUAL EMPLOYEES

The most serious structural weakness in the American grievance and arbitration process is, in

---

[33] Id. at 311.

[34] Id. at 312–13 (italics in original).

[35] Id. at 314.

[36] See McKelvey, "Sex and the Single Arbitrator," 24 *Industrial and Labor Relations Review* 335 (1971).

my opinion, its seeming inability to provide adequate protection to the bargaining unit member who is at odds with the designated bargaining representative. This charge is easier made than proven, but I base it on some 25 years of experience as an arbitrator and student of labor law and industrial relations. The kinds of cases that come to mind are the exception rather than the rule, but they occur frequently enough to cause me deep concern.[37] A few examples will indicate the general scope of the problem, but there are many variations on these basic themes.

1. A union routinely takes to arbitration every grievance involving discipline or discharge, regardless of merit. Then one day the employer fires X, a constant critic of the incumbent union officers and of the company management. Both parties say, "good riddance"; X files a grievance, but the union decides that it lacks merit and refuses to process it.

2. The union appeals X's grievance to arbitration, but presents it in such an inadequate way that the arbitrator quickly understands that the union wants to lose.

3. The parties have a bipartite arbitration board; only if the board deadlocks is a neutral called in. Y is arguing a position opposed by the bargaining representative. The bipartite arbitration board reaches a decision against Y without calling in a neutral.

It goes without saying that in many of these cases the grievant deserves to lose. In others, however, his claim may be meritorious. The point is that the nature of the process encourages the principals to the collective agreement to further their mutual institutional interests even if this sometimes results in unfair treatment to individual employees. Of course, the employee has the theoretical remedy of a law suit or unfair labor practice charge against the union for breach of its duty of fair representation; but as I indicated earlier, the odds in such cases are overwhelmingly in the union's favor.

Unfortunately, most of the suggested means of providing greater protection of individual rights under the collective agreement also present serious risks to the collective bargaining relationship between the employer and the union. For example, to permit an aggrieved employee to carry any case he wishes to arbitration over the union's objection is neither practicable nor desirable. The union has valid institutional interests

of its own to protect, and these would be seriously endangered if every dissatisfied employee were guaranteed the right to compel arbitration of a grievance based on an interpretation of the collective agreement rejected by the union and the employer. Similarly, it would be equally inappropriate either to require the union to assume the costs of these arbitrations or to insist that the grievant pay. The former approach would quickly bankrupt many local unions; the latter might make it impossible for many employees to pursue their legal remedies. In any case, a majority of the Supreme Court in *Vaca* v. *Sipes* expressly rejected the theory that every employee should have the right to take his grievance to arbitration.[38] It reasoned, correctly in my view, that adoption of this principle would substantially undermine the collective bargaining relation between union and employer; for it would destroy the employer's confidence in the union's authority, return the individual grievant "to the vagaries of independent and unsystematic negotiation,"[39] and very likely overburden the arbitration process to the point of rendering it inoperable.

Several academic writers have argued that the individual employee has rights under the collective agreement which cannot be compromised or ignored by the principals without his consent. If I read Professor Summers correctly, he would permit the individual employee to file an action against his employer for breach of contract, under Section 301 of the Taft-Hartley Act, if his union refused to process the grievance to arbitration. Presumably, the union, as an interested party, could intervene.[40] Professor Blumrosen would limit the individual employee's independent right to proceed against the wishes of his union to discharge and seniority cases involving "critical job interests." These, he argues, should be heard on their merits in some impartial forum, where "the employee should be allowed to prove that his claim is meritorious" and the union should "be required to demonstrate why it rejected his claim."[41]

But if it is unwise to permit employees to insist that their grievances be arbitrated when

[37] I have dealt with this problem at greater length in my article, "The Union's Duty of Fair Representation under the Railway Labor and National Labor Relations Acts," 34 *Journal Air Law & Commerce,* 167 (1968).

[38] The leading case supporting the theory is *Donnelly* v. *United Fruit Co.,* 40 N.J. 61, 190 A.2d 825, 53 LRRM 2271 (1963).

[39] 386 U.S. at 191.

[40] Summers, "Individual Rights in Collective Agreements and Arbitration," 37 *New York University Law Review* 362 (1962).

[41] Blumrosen, "The Worker and Three Phases of Unionism: Administrative and Judicial Control of the Worker-Union Relationship, 61 *Michigan Law Review* 1435, 1485 (1963).

the union is unwilling to do so, it seems no less so to allow them to proceed in court. A decision in either forum in the employee's favor might seriously undermine the structure of rules and mutual understandings established by the employer and the union and might also adversely affect the rights of the great majority of employees in the bargaining unit.

In only one situation does it seem to me that the employee can safely be permitted to sue his employer for breach of contract under Section 301 without first proving, as he is now required to do, that the union has violated its duty to represent him fairly. That is the case in which an employee claims he has been discharged in violation of the collective agreement and in which he expressly waives any right to reinstatement and asks only for damages. I would favor allowing such suits upon a showing that the union, for whatever reason, has refused to exhaust the grievance and arbitration procedure in the employee's behalf. Although there is always the possibility that the court, in upholding the employee's claim, might construe the agreement in such a way as to undermine important understandings between the employer and the union, the risk seems to be minimal, and the consequences correctable.

In other types of cases I think individual employee rights will probably have to be protected through new and more informal mechanisms. The United Auto Workers Public Review Board is one example of such a mechanism, but it is clearly not feasible for many unions. I have elsewhere suggested the possibility of employing a number of ombudsmen, appointed by and answerable to an agency of the federal government, to aid in preventing serious violations of the rights of individual employees within the framework of a government-sanctioned collective bargaining relationship.[42] Neither that nor any other arrangement can be made to work, however, unless the parties to the collective agreement—the employer and the union—recognize the need to insure that in pursuing their commendable objective of mutual accommodation, they do not ignore the legitimate complaints of individual employees, no matter how annoying and inconvenient these may be.

CONCLUSION

One way of assessing the effectiveness of the grievance and arbitration process in this country is to compare it with procedures for settling disputes over rights in other countries. For the past five years I have, together with five European colleagues, been engaged in a comparative study of these procedures in Britain, France, West Germany, Italy, Sweden, and the United States.[43] Precise comparisons are, of course, impossible, but I believe that a few generalizations are valid.

It is true that the average cost of taking disputes over rights to the labor courts in France, Germany, and Sweden, and to the courts in Italy, is far less than the average cost of arbitration in the United States. In Britain, which is the only one of the six countries that draws no distinction between disputes over rights (what we would call "grievances") and disputes over interests (what we would call new contract terms), every complaint becomes a matter for negotiation rather than adjudication; so it is difficult, if not impossible, to estimate the costs involved.[44]

Excessive delay is perhaps the most frequently criticized aspect of the American grievance and arbitration procedure. In this respect the record of the labor courts in France, Germany, and Sweden is much better than ours, even if time consumed by appeals to higher tribunals, which are permitted in France and Germany,[45] is included. In Italy, however, where disputes over rights are heard by the regular courts, delays are a serious problem.[46]

I have stressed the disadvantages of the American grievance and arbitration process for the individual worker, who cannot maintain control of his own grievance. Yet countervailing advantages become apparent when we compare his status with that of the Italian worker; the latter, rather than his union, "owns" the grievance.

---

[43] Publications resulting from this collaboration include: Aaron, ed., *Labor Courts and Grievance Settlement in Western Europe* (Berkeley: University of California Press, 1971); Wedderburn & Davis, *Employment Grievances and Disputes Procedures in Britain* (Berkeley: University of California Press, 1969); Aaron, ed., *Dispute Settlement Procedures in Five Western European Countries* (Institute of Industrial Relations, University of California Printing Department, 1969); Aaron, "Labor Courts: Western European Models and Their Significance for the United States, *U.C.L.A.L. Rev.* 847 (1969), and *A Comparative Study on Industrial Action in All Six Countries,* now in press.

[44] See Wedderburn & Davies, supra note 43. The situation in Britain could change drastically, however, if the present Government's Industrial Relations Bill, which seeks, inter alia, to amend the law relating to employers and workers and their respective organizations, and to establish a National Industrial Relations Court, is adopted.

[45] Aaron, supra note 43, at 866–872.

[46] Guigni, "The Settlement of Labor Disputes in Italy," in *Labor Courts and Grievance Settlement in Western Europe,* supra note 43.

---

[42] Aaron, supra note 37, at 207.

Judicial decisions by the Italian courts frequently undermine the entire collective agreement.[47]

Another area of comparison, in which the American organized worker appears to have a distinct advantage, is reinstatement of workers dismissed without just cause. This remedy is virtually unknown in France and Italy, is available only on limited grounds in Sweden, exists but is rarely resorted to in Germany, and is obtainable only through "job action" in Britain. Moreover, organized American workers seem to have far greater job security against employer retaliation than do those in France, Germany, and Italy, who typically wait until their individual contracts of employment have expired before bringing suits for redress of grievances. These delays often susbtantially limit or prevent the possibility of adequate remedies.[48]

It cannot be emphasized too often, however, that each country's system of dispute settlement is part of an entire economic and social system. Comparisons between countries that focus on only one part of the total system are thus inevitably misleading and of no real value. To give but one example, the American organized worker appears to do as well or better under our grievance and arbitration system than do his foreign counterparts under the labor court systems of France, Germany, and Sweden, the civil court system of Italy, and the private, loosely structured system in Britain. But the great mass of unorganized workers in the United States have considerably less statutory protections and guarantees than do those in the other countries.

In the last analysis, therefore, we must evaluate our grievance and arbitration process in terms of the extent to which it has realized its full potential within our own unique economic and social system. Despite its shortcomings, I think it must be rated an outstanding success. That judgment is not, of course, uniformly true of each of the thousands of grievance and arbitration procedures we have in this country; but I am prepared to defend the generalization that this system of "industrial jurisprudence," considered as a whole, represents one of the greatest achievements of our society.

[47] Id.

[48] Aaron, "Introduction" to *Labor Courts and Grievance Settlement in Western Europe,* supra note 43.

D. Collective Bargaining in the Public Sector

The determination of working conditions through collective bargaining is a growing activity among employees in the public sector. There has been much discussion pertaining to the adaptability of private sector bargaining and industrial relations techniques to the public sector, the right to strike by public employees, and the development of public policy applicable to public employee labor relations.

Wellington and Winter distinguish between the public and private sector in terms of the labor-management environment. This provides an excellent framework for studying the article by Burton and Krider, which analyzes the role and consequences of strikes in the public sector. A third article in this section explains the approach taken by various state legislatures in regard to public sector strikes.

In a concluding article, Fogel and Lewin explore wage determination in the public sector. The authors explain the wage differences found between public and private sector employees in blue-collar, white-collar, and managerial and professional occupations.

34. The Limits of Collective Bargaining in Public Employment*

Harry H. Wellington and Ralph K. Winter†

Writing in the March 1969 issue of the *Michigan Law Review,* Mr. Theodore Kheel, the distinguished mediator and arbitrator, placed the weight of his considerable authority behind what is fast becoming the conventional wisdom. In the public sector, as in the private, Mr. Kheel argues, "the most effective technique to produce acceptable terms to resolve disputes is voluntary agreement of the parties, and the best system we have for producing agreements between groups is collective bargaining—even though it involves conflict and the possibility of a work disruption."[1] Clearly for Kheel, as for others, the insistence upon a full extension of collective bargaining—including strikes—to public employment stems from a deep commitment to that way of ordering labor-management affairs in private employment. While such a commitment may not be necessary, a minimal acceptance of collective bargaining is a condition precedent to the Kheel view. Those skeptical of the value of collective bargaining in private employment will hardly press its extension. But even if one accepts collective bargaining in the private sector [. . .] the claims that support it there do not, in any self-evident way, make the case for its full transplant. The public sector is *not* the private, and its labor problems *are* different, very different indeed.

THE CLAIM FOR COLLECTIVE BARGAINING IN THE PRIVATE SECTOR

Four claims are made for private-sector collective bargaining. First, it is said to be a way to achieve industrial peace. The point was put as early as 1902 by the federal Industrial Commission:

> The chief advantage which comes from the practice of periodically determining the conditions of labor by collective bargaining directly between employers and employees is that thereby each side obtains a better understanding of the actual state of the industry, of the conditions which confront the other side, and of the motives which influence it. Most strikes and lockouts would not occur if each party understood exactly the position of the other.[2]

Second, collective bargaining is a way of achieving industrial democracy, that is, participation by workers in their own governance. It is the industrial counterpart of the contemporary demand for community participation.[3]

Third, unions that bargain collectively with employers represent workers in the political arena as well. And political representation through interest groups is one of the most important types of political representation that the individual can have. Government at all levels acts in large part in response to the demands made upon it by the groups to which its citizens belong.[4]

Fourth, and most important, as a result of a belief in the unequal bargaining power of employers and employees, collective bargaining is claimed to be a needed substitute for individual

* Reprinted from *The Unions and the Cities,* © The Brookings Institution, 1971, pp. 7–32.

† Members of the Brookings' associated staff in Economic Studies and professors at the Yale Law School.

[1] "Strikes and Public Employment," 67 *Michigan Law Review* 931, 942 (1969).

[2] *Final Report of the Industrial Commission* (Government Printing Office, 1902), p. 844.

[3] See, for example, testimony of Louis D. Brandeis before the Commission on Industrial Relations, January 23, 1915, in *Industrial Relations,* Final Report and Testimony Submitted to Congress by the Commission on Industrial Relations, S. Doc. 415, 64 Cong. 1 sess. (1916), 8, 7657–81.

[4] See generally H. Wellington, *Labor and the Legal Process* (Yale University Press, 1968), pp. 215–38.

bargaining.[5] Monopsony—a buyer's monopoly,[6] in this case a buyer of labor—is alleged to exist in many situations and to create unfair contracts of labor as a result of individual bargaining. While this, in turn, may not mean that workers as a class and over time get significantly less than they should—because monopsony is surely not a general condition but is alleged to exist only in a number of particular circumstances[7]—it may mean that the terms and conditions of employment for an individual or group of workers at a given period of time and in given circumstances may be unfair. What tends to insure fairness in the aggregate and over the long run is the discipline of the market.[8] But monopsony, if it exists, can work substantial injustice to individuals. Governmental support of collective bargaining represents the nation's response to a belief that such injustice occurs. Fairness between employee and employer in wages, hours, and terms and conditions of employment is thought more likely to be ensured where private ordering takes the collective form.[9]

There are, however, generally recognized social costs resulting from this resort to collectivism.[10] In the private sector these costs are primarily economic, and the question is, given the benefits of collective bargaining as an institution, what is the nature of the economic costs? Economists who have turned their attention to this question are legion, and disagreement among them monumental.[11] The principal concerns are of two intertwined sorts. One is summarized by Professor Albert Rees of Princeton:

If the union is viewed solely in terms of its effect on the economy, it must in my opinion be considered an obstacle to the optimum performance of our economic system. It alters the wage structure in a way that impedes the growth of employment in sectors of the economy where productivity and income are naturally high and that leaves too much labor in low-income sectors of the economy like southern agriculture and the least skilled service trades. It benefits most those workers who would in any case be relatively well off, and while some of this gain may be at the expense of the owners of capital, most of it must be at the expense of consumers and the lower-paid workers. Unions interfere blatantly with the use of the most productive techniques in some industries, and this effect is probably not offset by the stimulus to higher productivity furnished by some other unions.[12]

The other concern is stated in the 1967 Report of the Council of Economic Advisers:

Vigorous competition is essential to price stability in a high employment economy. But competitive forces do not and cannot operate with equal strength in every sector of the economy. In industries where the number of competitors is limited, business firms

---

[5] See, for example, *Final Report of the Industrial Commission*, p. 800:
It is quite generally recognized that the growth of great aggregations of capital under the control of single groups of men, which is so prominent a feature of the economic development of recent years, necessitates a corresponding aggregation of workingmen into unions, which may be able also to act as units. It is readily perceived that the position of the single workman, face to face with one of our great modern combinations, such as the United States Steel Corporation, is a position of very great weakness. The workman has one thing to sell—his labor. He has perhaps devoted years to the acquirement of a skill which gives his labor power a relatively high value, so long as he is able to put it to use in combination with certain materials and machinery. A single legal person has, to a very great extent, the control of such machinery, and in particular of such materials. Under such conditions there is little competition for the workman's labor. Control of the means of production gives power to dictate to the workingman upon what terms he shall make use of them.

[6] The use of the term monopsony is not intended to suggest a labor market with a single employer. Rather, we mean any market condition in which the terms and conditions of employment are generally below those that would exist under perfect competition.

[7] There is by no means agreement that monopsony is a significant factor. For a theoretical discussion, see F. Machlup, *The Political Economy of Monopoly: Business, Labor and Government Policies* (Johns Hopkins Press, 1952), pp. 333–79; for an empirical study, see R. Bunting, *Employer Concentration in Local Labor Markets* (University of North Carolina Press, 1962).

[8] See L. Reynolds, *Labor Economics and Labor Relations* (3d ed. Prentice-Hall, 1961), pp. 18–19. To the extent that monopsonistic conditions exist at any particular time one would expect them to be transitory. For even if we assume a high degree of labor immobility, a low wage level in a labor market will attract outside employers. Over time, therefore, the benefits of monopsony seem to carry with them the seeds of its destruction. But the time may seem very long in the life of any individual worker.

[9] See *Labor Management Relations Act*, § 1, 29 U.S.C. § 151 (1964).

[10] The monopsony justification views collective bargaining as a system of countervailing power—that is, the collective power of the workers countervails the bargaining power of employers. See J. Galbraith, *American Capitalism: The Concept of Countervailing Power* (Houghton Mifflin, 1952), pp. 121 ff. Even if the entire line of argument up to this point is accepted, collective bargaining nevertheless seems a crude device for meeting the monopsony problem, since there is no particular reason to think that collective bargaining will be instituted where there is monopsony (or that it is more likely to be instituted there). In some circumstances collective bargaining may even raise wages above a "competitive" level. On the other hand, the collective bargaining approach is no cruder than the law's general response to perceived unfairness in the application of the freedom of contract doctrine. See Wellington, *Labor and the Legal Process*, pp. 26–38.

[11] Compare, e.g., H. Simons, "Some Reflections on Syndicalism," *Journal of Political Economy* 1–25 (1944), with R. Lester, "Reflections on the Labor Monopoly Issue," 55 *Journal of Political Economy* 513 (1947).

[12] A. Rees, *The Economics of Trade Unions* (University of Chicago Press, 1962), pp. 194–95. Also see H. Johnson and P. Mieszkowski, "The Effects of Unionization on the Distribution of Income: A General Equilibrium Approach," 84 *Quarterly Journal of Economics* 539 (1970).

have a substantial measure of discretion in setting prices. In many sectors of the labor market, unions and managements together have a substantial measure of discretion in setting wages. The responsible exercise of discretionary power over wages and prices can help to maintain general stability. Its irresponsible use can make full employment and price stability incompatible.[13]

And the claim is that this "discretionary power" too often is exercised "irresponsibly."[14]

Disagreement among economists extends to the quantity as well as to the fact of economic malfunctioning that properly is attributable to collective bargaining.[15] But there is no disagreement that at some point the market disciplines or delimits union power. As we shall see in more detail below, union power is frequently constrained by the fact that consumers react to a relative increase in the price of a product by purchasing less of it. As a result any significant real financial benefit, beyond that justified by an increase in productivity, that accrues to workers through collective bargaining may well cause significant unemployment among union members. Because of this employment-benefit relationship, the economic costs imposed by collective bargaining as it presently exists in the private sector seem inherently limited.[16]

---

[13] Economic Report of the President together with the Annual Report of the Council of Economic Advisers, January 1967, p. 119.

[14] Ibid., pp. 119–34. See generally J. Sheahan, The Wage-Price Guideposts (Brookings Institution, 1967).

[15] See H. Lewis, Unionism and Relative Wages in the United States: An Empirical Inquiry (University of Chicago Press, 1963), and earlier studies discussed therein.

[16] See generally J. Dunlop, Wage Determination under Trade Unions (Macmillan, 1944), pp. 28–44; M. Friedman, "Some Comments on the Significance of Labor Unions for Economic Policy," in D. Wright (ed.), The Impact of the Union, p. 204 (Harcourt, 1951); Rees, The Economics of the Trade Unions, pp. 50–60.

In A. Ross, Trade Union Wage Policy (University of California, 1948), the argument is made that the employment effect of a wage bargain is not taken into account by either employers or unions (pp. 76–93). One reason given in support of this conclusion is the difficulty of knowing what effect a particular wage bargain will have on employment. But the forecasting difficulty interferes in any pricing decision, whether it is raising the price of automobiles or of labor, and it certainly does not render the effect of an increase on the volume purchased an irrelevant consideration. Uncertainty as to the impact of a wage decision on employment does not allow union leaders to be indifferent to the fact that there is an impact. If it did, they would all demand rates of $100 per hour.

Ross's second argument is that there is only a loose connection between wage rates and the volume of employment. It is not clear what he means by this assertion. It may be a rephrasing of the uncertainty argument. Presumably he is not asserting that the demand curve for labor is absolutely vertical; although proof of that phenomenon would entitle him to the professional immortality promised by Professor Stigler (see G. Stigler, The Theory of Price [3d ed., Macmillan, 1966] p. 24), the un-

THE CLAIMS FOR COLLECTIVE BARGAINING IN THE PUBLIC SECTOR

In the area of public employment the claims upon public policy made by the need for industrial peace, industrial democracy, and effective political representation point toward collective bargaining. This is to say that three of the four arguments that support bargaining in the private sector—to some extent, at least—press for similar arrangements in the public sector.

Government is a growth industry, particularly state and municipal government. While federal employment between 1963 and 1970 increased from 2.5 million to 2.9 million, state and local employment rose from 7.2 to 10.1 million,[17] and the increase continues apace. With size comes bureaucracy, and with bureaucracy comes the sense of isolation of the individual worker. His manhood, like that of his industrial counterpart, seems threatened. Lengthening chains of command necessarily depersonalize the employment relationship and contribute to a sense of powerlessness on the part of the worker. If he is to share in the governance of his employment relationship as he does in the private sector, it must be through the device of representation, which means unionization.[18] Accordingly, just as the increase in the size of economic units in private industry fostered unionism, so the enlarging of governmental bureaucracy has encouraged public employees to look to collective action for a sense of control over their employment destiny. The number of government employees, moreover, makes it plain that those employees are members of an interest group that can organize for political representation as well as for job participation.[19]

The pressures thus generated by size and bureaucracy lead inescapably to disruption—to labor unrest—unless these pressures are recognized and unless existing decision-making procedures are accommodated to them. Peace in government employment too, the argument runs, can best be

---

supported assertion hardly merits serious consideration. But if the curve is not vertical, then there is a "close connection" since the volume of employment is by hypothesis affected at every point on a declining curve. Probably he means simply that the curve is relatively inelastic, but that conclusion is neither self-evident, supported by his text, nor a proposition generally accepted on the basis of established studies.

[17] U.S. Bureau of the Census, Public Employment in 1970 (1971), Table 1, and Bureau of the Census, State Distribution of Public Employment in 1963 (1964), Table 1.

[18] See Final Report of the Industrial Commission, p. 805; C. Summers, "American Legislation for Union Democracy," 25 Mod. L. Rev. 273, 275 (1962).

[19] For the "early" history, see S. Spero, Government as Employer (Remsen, 1948).

established by making union recognition and collective bargaining accepted public policy.[20]

Much less clearly analogous to the private model, however, is the unequal bargaining power argument. In the private sector that argument really has two aspects. The first, just adumbrated, is affirmative in nature. Monopsony is believed sometimes to result in unfair individual contracts of employment. The unfairness may be reflected in wages, which are less than they would be if the market were more nearly perfect, or in working arrangements that may lodge arbitrary power in a foreman, that is, power to hire, fire, promote, assign, or discipline without respect to substantive or procedural rules. A persistent assertion, generating much heat, relates to the arbitrary exercise of managerial power in individual cases. This assertion goes far to explain the insistence of unions on the establishment in the labor contract of rules, with an accompanying adjudicatory procedure, to govern industrial life.[21]

Judgments about the fairness of the financial terms of the public employee's individual contract of employment are even harder to make than for private sector workers. The case for the existence of private employer monopsony, disputed as it is, asserts only that some private sector employers in some circumstances have too much bargaining power. In the public sector, the case to be proved is that the governmental employer ever has such power. But even if this case could be proved, market norms are at best attenuated guides to questions of fairness. In employment as in all other areas, governmental decisions are properly political decisions, and economic considerations are but one criterion among many. Questions of fairness do not centrally relate to how much imperfection one sees in the market, but more to how much imperfection one sees in the political process. "Low" pay for teachers may be merely a decision—right or wrong, resulting from the pressure of special interests or from a desire to promote the general welfare—to exchange a reduction in the quality or quantity of teachers for higher welfare payments, a domed stadium, and so on. And the ability to make informed judgments about such political decisions is limited because of the understandable but unfortunate fact that the science of politics has failed to supply either as elegant or as reliable a theoretical model as has its sister discipline.

Nevertheless, employment benefits in the public sector may have improved relatively more slowly than in the private sector during the last three decades. An economy with a persistent inflationary bias probably works to the disadvantage of those who must rely on legislation for wage adjustments.[22] Moreover, while public employment was once attractive for the greater job security and retirement benefits it provided, quite similar protection is now available in many areas of the private sector.[23] On the other hand, to the extent that civil service, or merit, systems exist in public employment and these laws are obeyed, the arbitrary exercise of managerial power is substantially reduced. Where it is reduced, a labor policy that relies on individual employment contracts must seem less unacceptable.

The second, or negative, aspect of the unequal bargaining power argument relates to the social costs of collective bargaining. As has been seen, the social costs of collective bargaining in the private sector are principally economic and seem inherently limited by market forces. In the public sector, however, the costs seem economic only in a very narrow sense and are on the whole political. It further seems that, to the extent union power is delimited by market or other forces in the public sector, these constraints do not come into play nearly as quickly as in the private. An understanding of why this is so requires further comparison between collective bargaining in the two sectors.

THE PRIVATE SECTOR MODEL

Although the private sector is, of course, extraordinarily diverse, the paradigm is an industry that produces a product that is not particularly essential to those who buy it and for which dissimilar products can be substituted. Within the market or markets for this product, most—but not all—of the producers must bargain with a union representing their employees, and this union is generally the same throughout the industry. A price rise of this product relative to others will result in a decrease in the number of units of the product sold. This in turn will result in a cutback in employment. And an in-

[20] See, for example, *Governor's Committee on Public Employee Relations, Final Report* (State of New York, 1966), pp. 9–14.

[21] See N. Chamberlain, *The Union Challenge to Management Control* (Harper, 1948), p. 94.

[22] This is surely one reason that might explain the widely assumed fact that public employees have fallen behind their private sector counterparts. See J. Stieber, "Collective Bargaining in the Public Sector," in L. Ulman (ed.), *Challenges to Collective Bargaining* (Prentice-Hall, 1967), pp. 65, 69.

[23] See G. Taylor, "Public Employment: Strikes or Procedures?" 20 *Industrial and Labor Relations Review* 617, 623–25 (1967).

crease in price would be dictated by an increase in labor cost relative to output, at least in most situations.[24] Thus, the union is faced with some sort of rough trade-off between, on the one hand, larger benefits for some employees and unemployment for others, and on the other hand, smaller benefits and more employment. Because unions are political organizations, with a legal duty to represent all employees fairly,[25] and with a treasury that comes from per capita dues, there is pressure on the union to avoid the road that leads to unemployment.[26]

This picture of the restraints that the market imposes on collective bargaining settlements undergoes change as the variables change. On the one hand, to the extent that there are nonunion firms within a product market, the impact of union pressure will be diminished by the ability of consumers to purchase identical products from nonunion and, presumably, less expensive sources. On the other hand, to the extent that union organization of competitors within the product market is complete, there will be no such restraint and the principal barriers to union bargaining goals will be the ability of a number of consumers to react to a price change by turning to dissimilar but nevertheless substitutable products.

Two additional variables must be noted. First, where the demand for an industry's product is rather insensitive to price—that is, relatively inelastic—and where all the firms in a product market are organized, the union need fear less the employment-benefit trade-off, for the employer is less concerned about raising prices in response to increased costs. By hypothesis, a price rise affects unit sales of such an employer only minimally. Second, in an expanding industry, wage settlements that exceed increases in productivity may not reduce union employment. They will reduce expansion, hence the employment effect will be experienced only by workers who do not belong to the union. This means that in the short run the politics of the employment-benefit trade-off do not restrain the union in its bargaining demands.

In both of these cases, however, there are at least two restraints on the union. One is the employer's increased incentive to substitute machines for labor, a factor present in the paradigm and all other cases as well. The other restraint stems from the fact that large sections of the nation are unorganized and highly resistant to unionization.[27] Accordingly, capital will seek nonunion labor, and in this way the market will discipline the organized sector.

The employer, in the paradigm and in all variations of it, is motivated primarily by the necessity to maximize profits (and this is so no matter how political a corporation may seem to be). He therefore is not inclined (absent an increase in demand for his product) to raise prices and thereby suffer a loss in profits, and he is organized to transmit and represent the market pressures described above. Generally he will resist, and resist hard, union demands that exceed increases in productivity, for if he accepts such demands he may be forced to raise prices. Should he be unsuccessful in his resistance too often, and should it or the bargain cost him too much, he can be expected to put his money and energy elsewhere.[28]

What all this means is that the social costs imposed by collective bargaining are economic costs; that usually they are limited by powerful market restraints; and that these restraints are visible to anyone who is able to see the forest for the trees.[29]

THE PUBLIC SECTOR MODEL: MONETARY ISSUES

The paradigm in the public sector is a municipality with an elected city council and an elected mayor who bargains (through others) with unions representing the employees of the city. He bargains also, of course, with other permanent and ad hoc interest groups making claims upon government (business groups, save-the-park committees, neighborhood groups, and so forth). In-

---

[24] The cost increase may, of course, take some time to work through and appear as a price increase. See Rees, *The Economics of Trade Unions*, pp. 107–9. In some oligopolistic situations the firm may be able to raise prices after a wage increase without suffering a significant decrease in sales.

[25] *Steele* v. *Louisville & Nashville Railroad Co.,* 323 U.S. 192 (1944).

[26] The pressure is sometimes resisted. Indeed, the United Mine Workers has chosen more benefits for less employment. See generally M. Baratz, *The Union and the Coal Industry* (Yale University Press, 1955).

[27] See H. Cohany, "Trends and Changes in Union Membership," 89 *Monthly Lab. Rev.* 510–13 (1966); I. Bernstein, "The Growth of American Unions, 1945–1960," 2 *Labor History* 131–57 (1961).

[28] And the law would protect him in this. Indeed, it would protect him if he were moved by an antiunion animus as well as by valid economic considerations. See *Textile Workers Union of America* v. *Darlington Manufacturing Co.,* 380 U.S. 263 (1965).

Of course, where fixed costs are large relative to variable costs, it may be difficult for an employer to extricate himself.

[29] This does not mean that collective bargaining in the private sector is free of social costs. It means only that the costs are necessarily limited by the discipline of the market.

deed, the decisions that are made may be thought of roughly as a result of interactions and accommodations among these interest groups, as influenced by perceptions about the attitudes of the electorate and by the goals and programs of the mayor and his city council.[30]

Decisions that cost the city money are generally paid for from taxes and, less often, by borrowing. Not only are there many types of taxes but also there are several layers of government that may make tax revenue available to the city; federal and state as well as local funds may be employed for some purposes. Formal allocation of money for particular uses is made through the city's budget, which may have within it considerable room for adjustments.[31] Thus, a union will bargain hard for as large a share of the budget as it thinks it possibly can obtain, and even try to force a tax increase if it deems that possible.

In the public sector, too, the market operates. In the long run, the supply of labor is a function of the price paid for labor by the public employer relative to what workers earn elsewhere.[32] This is some assurance that public employees in the aggregate—with or without collective bargaining—are not paid too little. The case for employer monopsony, moreover, may be much weaker in the public sector than it is in the private. First, to the extent that most public employees work in urban areas, as they probably do, there may often be a number of substitutable and competing private and public employers in the labor market. When that is the case, there can be little monopsony power.[33] Second, even if public employers occasionally have monopsony power, governmental policy is determined only in part by economic criteria, and there is no assurance, as there is in the private sector where

the profit motive prevails, that the power will be exploited.

As noted, market-imposed unemployment is an important restraint on unions in the private sector. In the public sector, the trade-off between benefits and employment seems much less important. Government does not generally sell a product the demand for which is closely related to price. There usually are not close substitutes for the products and services provided by government and the demand for them is relatively inelastic. Such market conditions are favorable to unions in the private sector because they permit the acquisition of benefits without the penalty of unemployment, subject to the restraint of non-union competitors, actual or potential. But no such restraint limits the demands of public employee unions. Because much government activity is, and must be, a monopoly, product competition, nonunion or otherwise, does not exert a downward pressure on prices and wages. Nor will the existence of a pool of labor ready to work for a wage below union scale attract new capital and create a new, and competitively less expensive, governmental enterprise.

The fear of unemployment, however, can serve as something of a restraining force in two situations. First, if the cost of labor increases, the city may reduce the quality of the service it furnishes by reducing employment. For example, if teachers' salaries are increased, it may decrease the number of teachers and increase class size. However, the ability of city government to accomplish such a change is limited not only by union pressure but also by the pressure of other affected interested groups in the community.[34] Political considerations, therefore, may cause either no reduction in employment or services, or a reduction in an area other than that in which the union members work. Both the political power exerted by the beneficiaries of the services, who are also voters, and the power of the public employee union as a labor organization then combine to create great pressure on political leaders either to seek new funds or to reduce municipal services of another kind. Second, if labor costs increase, the city, like a private employer, may seek to replace labor with machines. The absence of a profit motive, and a political concern for unemployment, however, may be deterrents in addition to the deterrent of union resistance. The

[30] See generally R. Dahl, *Who Governs? Democracy and Power in an American City* (Yale University Press, 1961). On interest group theory generally, see D. Truman, *The Government Process: Political Interests and Public Opinion* (3d printing; Alfred A. Knopf, 1955).

[31] See, for example, W. Sayre and H. Kaufman, *Governing New York City: Politics in the Metropolis* (Russell Sage, 1960), pp. 366–72.

[32] See M. Moskow, *Teachers and Unions* (University of Pennsylvania, Wharton School of Finance and Commerce, Industrial Research Unit, 1966), pp. 79–86.

[33] This is based on the reasonable but not unchallengeable assumption that the number of significant employers in a labor market is related to the existence of monopsony. See R. Bunting, *Employer Concentration in Local Labor Markets,* pp. 3–14. The greater the number of such employers in a labor market, the greater the departure from the classic case of the monopsony of a single employer. The number of employers would clearly seem to affect their ability to make and enforce a collusive wage agreement.

[34] Organized parent groups, for example. Compare the unsuccessful attempt of the New York City Board of Education to reduce the employment of substitute teachers in the public schools in March 1971. *New York Times,* March 11, 1971, p. 1.

public employer that decides it must limit employment because of unit labor costs will likely find that the politically easiest decision is to restrict new hirings rather than to lay off current employees.

Where pensions are concerned, moreover, major concessions may be politically tempting since there is no immediate impact on the taxpayer or the city budget. Whereas actuarial soundness would be insisted on by a profit-seeking entity like a firm, it may be a secondary concern to politicians whose conduct is determined by relatively short-run considerations. The impact of failing to adhere to actuarial principles will frequently fall upon a different mayor and a different city council. In those circumstances, concessions that condemn a city to future impoverishment may not seem intolerable.

Even if a close relationship between increased economic benefits and unemployment does not exist as a significant deterrent to unions in the public sector, might not the argument be made that in some sense the taxpayer is the public sector's functional equivalent of the consumer? If taxes become too high the taxpayer can move to another community. While it is generally much easier for a consumer to substitute products than for a taxpayer to substitute communities, is it not fair to say that, at the point at which a tax increase will cause so many taxpayers to move that it will produce less total revenue, the market disciplines or restrains union and public employer in the same way and for the same reasons that the market disciplines parties in the private sector? Moreover, does not the analogy to the private sector suggest that it is legitimate in an economic sense for unions to push government to the point of substitutability?

Several factors suggest that the answer to this latter question is at best indeterminate, and that the question of legitimacy must be judged not by economic but by political criteria.

In the first place, there is no theoretical reason —economic or political—to suppose that it is desirable for a governmental entity to liquidate its taxing power, to tax up to the point where another tax increase will produce less revenue because of the number of people it drives to different communities. In the private area, profit maximization is a complex concept, but its approximation generally is both a legal requirement and socially useful as a means of allocating resources.[35] The liquidation of taxing power seems neither imperative nor useful.

Second, consider the complexity of the tax structure and the way in which different kinds of taxes (property, sales, income) fall differently upon a given population. Consider, moreover, that the taxing authority of a particular governmental entity may be limited (a municipality may not have the power to impose an income tax). What is necessarily involved, then, is principally the redistribution of income by government rather than resource allocation,[36] and questions of income redistribution surely are essentially political questions.[37]

For his part, the mayor in our paradigm will be disciplined not by a desire to maximize profits but by a desire—in some cases at least—to do a good job (to implement his programs), and in virtually all cases by a wish either to be reelected or to move to a better elective office. What he gives to the union must be taken from some other interest group or from taxpayers. His is the job of coordinating these competing claims while remaining politically viable. And that coordination will be governed by the relative power of the competing interest groups. Coordination, moreover, is not limited to issues involving the level of taxes and the way in which tax moneys are spent. Nonfinancial issues also require coordination, and here too the outcome turns upon the relative power of interest groups. And relative power is affected importantly by the scope of collective bargaining.

THE PUBLIC SECTOR MODEL: NONMONETARY ISSUES

In the private sector, unions have pushed to expand the scope of bargaining in response to the desires of their members for a variety of new benefits (pension rights, supplementary unemployment payments, merit increases). These benefits generally impose a monetary cost on the employer. And because employers are restrained by the market, an expanded bargaining agenda means that, if a union negotiates an agreement over more subjects, it generally trades off more of less for less of more.

---

[35] See generally R. Dorfman, *Prices and Markets* (Prentice-Hall, 1967).

[36] In the private sector what is involved is principally resource allocation rather than income redistribution. Income redistribution occurs to the extent that unions are able to increase wages at the expense of profits, but the extent to which this actually happens would seem to be limited. It also occurs if unions, by limiting employment in the union sector through maintenance of wages above a competitive level, increase the supply of labor in the nonunion sector and thereby depress wages there.

[37] In the private sector the political question was answered when the National Labor Relations Act was passed: The benefits of collective bargaining (with the strike) outweigh the social costs.

From the consumer's point of view this in turn means that the price of the product he purchases is not significantly related to the scope of bargaining. And since unions rarely bargain about the nature of the product produced,[38] the consumer can be relatively indifferent as to how many or how few subjects are covered in any collective agreement.[39] Nor need the consumer be concerned about union demands that would not impose a financial cost on the employer, for example, the design of a grievance procedure. While such demands are not subject to the same kind of trade-off as are financial demands, they are unlikely, if granted, to have any impact on the consumer. Their effect is on the quality of life of the parties to the agreement.

In the public sector the cluster of problems that surround the scope of bargaining are much more troublesome than they are in the private sector. The problems have several dimensions.

First, the trade-off between subjects of bargaining in the public sector is less of a protection to the consumer (public) than it is in the private. Where political leaders view the costs of union demands as essentially budgetary, a trade-off can occur. Thus, a demand for higher teacher salaries and a demand for reduced class size may be treated as part of one package. But where a demand, although it has a budgetary effect, is viewed as involving essentially political costs, trade-offs are more difficult. Our paradigmatic mayor, for example, may be under great pressure to make a large monetary settlement with a teachers' union whether or not it is joined to demands for special training programs for disadvantaged children. Interest groups tend to exert pressure against union demands only when they are directly affected. Otherwise, they are apt to join that large constituency (the general public) that wants to avoid labor trouble. Trade-offs can occur only when several demands are resisted by roughly the same groups. Thus, pure budgetary demands can be traded off when they are opposed by taxpayers. But when the identity of the resisting group changes with each demand, political leaders may find it expedient to strike a balance on each issue individually, rather than as part of a total package, by measuring the political power of each interest group involved against the political power of the constituency pressing for labor peace. To put it another way, as important as financial factors are to a mayor, political factors may be even more important. The market allows the businessman no such discretionary choice.

Where a union demand—such as increasing the disciplinary power of teachers—does not have budgetary consequences, some trade-offs may occur. Granting the demand will impose a political cost on the mayor because it may anger another interest group. But because the resisting group may change with each issue, each issue is apt to be treated individually and not as a part of a total package. And this may not protect the public. Differing from the private sector, non-monetary demands of public sector unions do have effects that go beyond the parties to the agreement. All of us have a stake in how school children are disciplined. Expansion of the subjects of bargaining in the public sector, therefore, may increase the total quantum of union power in the political process.

Second, public employees do not generally produce a product. They perform a service. The way in which a service is performed may become a subject of bargaining. As a result, the nature of that service may be changed. Some of these services—police protection, teaching, health care—involve questions that are politically, socially, or ideologically sensitive. In part this is because government is involved, and alternatives to governmentally provided services are relatively dear. In part, government is involved because of society's need for it. This suggests that decisions affecting the nature of a governmentally provided service are much more likely to be challenged and are more urgent than generally is the case with services that are offered privately.

Third, some of the services government provides are performed by professionals—teachers, social workers, and so forth—who are keenly interested in the underlying philosophy that informs their work. To them, theirs is not merely a job to be done for a salary. They may be educators or other "change agents" of society. And this

[38] The fact that American unions and management are generally economically oriented is a source of great freedom to us all. If either the unions or management decided to make decisions about the nature of services provided or products manufactured on the basis of their own ideological convictions, we would all, as consumers, be less free. Although unions may misallocate resources, consumers are still generally able to satisfy strong desires for particular products by paying more for them and sacrificing less valued items. This is because unions and management generally make no attempt to adjust to anything but economic considerations. Were it otherwise, and the unions—or management—insisted that no products of a certain kind be manufactured, consumers would have much less choice.

[39] The major qualification to these generalizations is that sometimes unions can generate more support from the membership for certain demands than for others (more for the size of the work crew, less for wage increases). Just how extensive this phenomenon is, and how it balances out over time, is difficult to say; however, it would not seem to be of great importance in the overall picture.

may mean that these employees are concerned with more than incrementally altering a governmental service or its method of delivery. They may be advocates of bold departures that will radically transform the service itself.

The issue is not a threshold one of whether professional public employees should participate in decisions about the nature of the services they provide. Any properly run governmental agency should be interested in, and heavily reliant upon, the judgment of its professional staff. The issue rather is the method of that participation.

Conclusions about this issue as well as the larger issue of a full transplant of collective bargaining to the public sector may be facilitated by addressing some aspects of the governmental decision-making process—particularly at the municipal level—and the impact of collective bargaining on that process.

PUBLIC EMPLOYEE UNIONS AND THE POLITICAL PROCESS

Although the market does not discipline the union in the public sector to the extent that it does in the private, the municipal employment paradigm, nevertheless, would seem to be consistent with what Robert A. Dahl has called the "'normal' American political process," which is "one in which there is a high probability that an active and legitimate group in the population can make itself heard effectively at some crucial stage in the process of decision," for the union may be seen as little more than an "active and legitimate group in the population."[40] With elections in the background to perform, as Mr. Dahl notes, "the critical role . . . in maximizing political equality and popular sovereignty,"[41] all seems well, at least theoretically, with collective bargaining and public employment.

But there is trouble even in the house of theory if collective bargaining in the public sector means what it does in the private. The trouble is that if unions are able to withhold labor—to strike—as well as to employ the usual methods of political pressure, they may possess a disproportionate share of effective power in the process of decision. Collective bargaining would then be so effective a pressure as to skew the results of the "'normal' American political process."

One should straightway make plain that the strike issue is not simply the importance of public services as contrasted with services or products produced in the private sector. This is only part of the issue, and in the past the partial truth has beclouded analysis.[42] The services performed by a private transit authority are neither less nor more important to the public than those that would be performed if the transit authority were owned by a municipality. A railroad or a dock strike may be more damaging to a community than "job action" by police. This is not to say that governmental services are not important. They are, both because the demand for them is inelastic and because their disruption may seriously injure a city's economy and occasionally impair the physical welfare of its citizens. Nevertheless, the importance of governmental services is only a necessary part of, rather than a complete answer to, the question: Why be more concerned about strikes in public employment than in private?

The answer to the question is simply that, because strikes in public employment disrupt important services, a large part of a mayor's political constituency will, in many cases, press for a quick end to the strike with little concern for the cost of settlement. This is particularly so where the cost of settlement is borne by a different and larger political constituency, the citizens of the state or nation. Since interest groups other than public employees, with conflicting claims on municipal government, do not, as a general proposition, have anything approaching the effectiveness of the strike—or at least cannot maintain that relative degree of power over the long run —they may be put at a significant competitive disadvantage in the political process.

The private sector strike is designed to exert economic pressure on the employer by depriving him of revenues. The public employee strike is fundamentally different: Its sole purpose is to exert political pressure on municipal officials. They are deprived, not of revenues but of the political support of those who are inconvenienced by a disruption of municipal services. But precisely because the private strike is an economic weapon, it is disciplined by the market and the benefit/unemployment trade-off that imposes. And because the public employee strike is a political weapon, it is subject only to the restraints imposed by the political process and they are on the whole less limiting and less disciplinary than those of the market. If this is the case, it must be said that the political process will be radically altered by wholesale importation of the strike weapon. And because of the deceptive simplicity of the analogy to collective bargaining in the

---

[40] R. Dahl, *A Preface to Democratic Theory* (University of Chicago Press, 1956), p. 145.

[41] Ibid., pp. 124–25.

[42] See, for example, Spero, *Government as Employer*, pp. 1–15.

private sector, the alteration may take place without anyone realizing what has happened.

Nor is it an answer that, in some municipalities, interest groups other than unions now have a disproportionate share of political power. This is inescapably true, and we do not condone that situation. Indeed, we would be among the first to advocate reform. However, reform cannot be accomplished by giving another interest group disproportionate power, for the losers would be the weakest groups in the community. In most municipalities, the weakest groups are composed of citizens who many believe are most in need of more power.

Therefore, while the purpose and effect of strikes by public employees may seem in the beginning designed merely to establish collective bargaining or to "catch up" with wages and fringe benefits in the private sector, in the long run strikes may become too effective a means for redistributing income; so effective, indeed, that one might see them as an institutionalized means of obtaining and maintaining a subsidy for union members.[43]

As is often the case when one generalizes, this picture may be considered overdrawn. In order to refine analysis, it will be helpful to distinguish between strikes that occur over monetary issues and strikes involving nonmonetary issues. The generalized picture sketched above is mainly concerned with the former. Because there is usually no substitute for governmental services, the citizen-consumer faced with a strike of teachers, or garbage men, or social workers is likely to be seriously inconvenienced. This in turn places enormous pressure on the mayor, who is apt to find it difficult to look to the long-run balance sheet of the municipality. Most citizens are directly affected by a strike of sanitation workers. Few, however, can decipher a municipal budget or trace the relationship between today's labor settlement and next year's increase in the mill rate. Thus, in the typical case the impact of a settlement is less visible—or can more often be concealed—than the impact of a disruption of services. Moreover, the cost of settlement may fall upon a constituency much larger—the whole state or nation—than that represented by the mayor. And revenue sharing schemes that involve unrestricted funds may further lessen public resistance to generous settlements. It follows that the mayor usually will look to the electorate that is clamoring for a settlement, and in these circumstances the union's fear of a long strike, a

major check on its power in the private sector, is not a consideration.[44] In the face of all of these factors other interest groups with priorities different from the union's are apt to be much less successful in their pursuit of scarce tax dollars than is the union with power to withhold services.[45]

With respect to strikes over some nonmonetary issues—decentralization of the governance of schools might be an example—the intensity of concern on the part of well-organized interest groups opposed to the union's position would support the mayor in his resistance to union demands. But even here, if the union rank and file back their leadership, pressures for settlement from the general public, which may be largely indifferent as to the underlying issue, might in time become irresistible.[46]

The strike and its threat, moreover, exacerbate the problems associated with the scope of bargaining in public employment. This seems clear if one attends in slightly more detail to techniques of municipal decision making.

Few students of our cities would object to Herbert Kaufman's observation that:

Decisions of the municipal government emanate from no single source, but from many centers; conflicts and clashes are referred to no single authority, but are settled at many levels and at many points in the system: no single group can guarantee the success of any proposal it supports, the defeat of every idea it objects to. Not even the central governmental organs of the city—the Mayor, the Board of Estimate, the Council—individually or in combination, even approach mastery in this sense.

Each separate decision center consists of a cluster

---

[43] Strikes in some areas of the private sector may have this effect, too. See below, p. 320.

[44] Contrast the situation in the private sector: ". . . management cannot normally win the short strike. Management can only win the long strike. Also management frequently tends, in fact, to win the long strike. As a strike lengthens, it commonly bears more heavily on the union and the employees than on management. Strike relief is no substitute for a job. Even regular strike benefits, which few unions can afford, and which usually exhaust the union treasury quite rapidly (with some exceptions), are no substitute for a job." E. Livernash, "The Relation of Power to the Structure and Process of Collective Bargaining," 6 *Journal of Law & Economics* 10, 15 (October 1963).

[45] A vivid example was provided by an experience in New Jersey. After a 12-hour strike by Newark firefighters on July 11, 1969, state urban aid funds, originally authorized for helping the poor, were diverted to salary increases for firemen and police. See *New York Times,* August 7, 1969, p. 25. Moreover, government decision makers other than the mayor (for example, the governor) may have interests different from those of the mayor, interests that manifest themselves in pressures for settlement.

[46] Consider also the effect of such strikes on the fabric of society. See, for example, M. Mayer, *The Teachers Strike: New York, 1968* (Harper and Row, 1969).

of interested contestants, with a "core group" in the middle, invested by the rules with the formal authority to legitimize decisions (that is to promulgate them in binding form) and a constellation of related "satellite groups" seeking to influence the authoritative issuances of the core group.[47]

Nor would many disagree with Nelson W. Polsby when, in discussing community decision making that is concerned with an alternative to a "current state of affairs," he argues that the alternative "must be politically palatable and relatively easy to accomplish; otherwise great amounts of influence have to be brought to bear with great skill and efficiency in order to secure its adoption."[48]

It seems probable that such potential subjects of bargaining as school decentralization and a civilian police review board are, where they do not exist, alternatives to the "current state of affairs," which are not "politically palatable and relatively easy to accomplish." If a teachers' union or a police union were to bargain with the municipal employer over these questions, and were able to use the strike to insist that the proposals not be adopted, how much "skill and efficiency" on the part of the proposals' advocates would be necessary to effect a change? And, to put the shoe on the other foot, if a teachers' union were to insist through collective bargaining (with the strike or its threat) upon major changes in school curriculum, would not that union have to be considerably less skillful and efficient in the normal political process than other advocates of community change? The point is that with respect to some subjects, collective bargaining may be too powerful a lever on municipal decision making, too effective a technique for changing or preventing the change of one small but important part of the "current state of affairs."

Unfortunately, in this area the problem is not merely the strike threat and the strike. In a system where impasse procedures involving third parties are established in order to reduce work stoppages—and this is common in those states that have passed public employment bargaining statutes—third party intervention must be partly responsive to union demands. If the scope of bargaining is open-ended, the neutral party, to be effective, will have to work out accommodations that inevitably advance some of the union's claims some of the time. And the neutral, with his eyes fixed on achieving a settlement, can hardly be concerned with balancing all the items

on the community agenda or reflecting the interests of all relevant groups.

THE THEORY SUMMARIZED

Collective bargaining in public employment, then, seems distinguishable from that in the private sector. To begin with, it imposes on society more than a potential misallocation of resources through restrictions on economic output, the principal cost imposed by private sector unions. Collective bargaining by public employees and the political process cannot be separated. The costs of such bargaining, therefore, cannot be fully measured without taking into account the impact on the allocation of political power in the typical municipality. If one assumes, as here, that municipal political processes should be structured to ensure "a high probability that an active and legitimate group in the population can make itself heard effectively at some crucial stage in the process of decision,"[49] then the issue is how powerful unions will be in the typical municipal political process if a full transplant of collective bargaining is carried out.

The conclusion is that such a transplant would, in many cases, institutionalize the power of public employee unions in a way that would leave competing groups in the political process at a permanent and substantial disadvantage. There are three reasons for this, and each is related to the type of services typically performed by public employees.

First, some of these services are such that any prolonged disruption would entail an actual danger to health and safety.

Second, the demand for numerous governmental services is relatively inelastic, that is, relatively insensitive to changes in price. Indeed, the lack of close substitutes is typical of many governmental endeavors.[50] And, since at least the time of Marshall's *Principles of Economics,* the elasticity of demand for the final service or product has been considered a major determinant of union power.[51] Because the demand for labor is derived from the demand for the product, inelasticity on the product side tends to reduce the employment-benefit trade-off unions face. This is as much the case in the private as in the

---

[47] "Metropolitan Leadership," quoted in N. Polsby, *Community Power and Political Theory* (Yale University Press, 1963), pp. 127–28.

[48] Polsby, ibid., p. 135.

[49] Dahl, *Preface to Democratic Theory,* p. 145.

[50] Sometimes this is so because of the nature of the endeavor—national defense, for example—and sometimes because the existence of the governmental operation necessarily inhibits entry by private entities, as in the case of elementry education.

[51] A. Marshall, *Principles of Economics* (8th ed.; Macmillan, 1920), pp. 383–86.

public sector. But in the private sector, product inelasticity is not typical. Moreover, there is the further restraint on union power created by the real possibility of nonunion entrants into the product market. In the public sector, inelasticity of demand seems more the rule than the exception, and nonunion rivals are not generally a serious problem.

Consider education. A strike by teachers may never create an immediate danger to public health and welfare. Nevertheless, because the demand for education is relatively inelastic, teachers rarely need fear unemployment as a result of union-induced wage increases, and the threat of an important nonunion rival (competitive private schools) is not to be taken seriously so long as potential consumers of private education must pay taxes to support the public school system.

The final reason for fearing a full transplant is the extent to which the disruption of a government service inconveniences municipal voters. A teachers' strike may not endanger public health or welfare. It may, however, seriously inconvenience parents and other citizens who, as voters, have the power to punish one of the parties—and always the same party, the political leadership—to the dispute. How can anyone any longer doubt the vulnerability of a municipal employer to this sort of pressure? Was it simply a matter of indifference to Mayor Lindsay in September 1969 whether another teachers' strike occurred on the eve of a municipal election? Did the size and the speed of the settlement with the United Federation of Teachers (UFT) suggest nothing about one first-rate politician's estimate of his vulnerability? And are the chickens now coming home to roost because of extravagant concessions on pensions for employees of New York City the result only of mistaken actuarial calculations? Or do they reflect the irrelevance of long-run considerations to politicians vulnerable to the strike and compelled to think in terms of short-run political impact?

Those who disagree on this latter point rely principally on their conviction that anticipation of increased taxes as the result of a large labor settlement will countervail the felt inconvenience of a strike, and that municipalities are not, therefore, overly vulnerable to strikes by public employees. The argument made here, however— that governmental budgets in large cities are so complex that generally the effect of any particular labor settlement on the typical municipal budget is a matter of very low visibility—seems adequately convincing. Concern over possible taxes will not, as a general proposition, significantly deter voters who are inconvenienced by a strike from compelling political leaders to settle quickly. Moreover, municipalities are often subsidized by other political entities—the nation or state—and the cost of a strike settlement may not be borne by those demanding an end to the strike.

All this may seem to suggest that it is the strike weapon—whether the issue be monetary or nonmonetary—that cannot be transplanted to the public sector. This is an oversimplification, however. It is the combination of the strike and the typical municipal political process including the usual methods for raising revenue. One solution, of course, might well be a ban on strikes, if it could be made effective. But that is not the sole alternative, for there may be ways in which municipal political structures can be changed so as to make cities less vulnerable to strikes and to reduce the potential power of public employee unions to tolerable levels. . . .

All this may also seem to suggest a sharper distinction between the public and private sectors than actually exists. The discussion here has dealt with models, one for private collective bargaining, the other for public. Each model is located at the core of its sector. But the difference in the impact of collective bargaining in the two sectors should be seen as a continuum. Thus, for example, it may be that market restraints do not sufficiently discipline strike settlements in some regulated industries or in industries that rely mainly on government contracts. Indeed, collective bargaining in such industries has been under steady and insistent attack.

In the public sector, it may be that in any given municipality—but particularly a small one —at any given time, taxpayer resistance or the determination of municipal government, or both, will substantially offset union power even under existing political structures. These plainly are exceptions, however. They do not invalidate the public-private distinction as an analytical tool, for that distinction rests on the very real differences that exist in the vast bulk of situations, situations exemplified by these models. On the other hand, in part because of a recognition that there are exceptions that in particular cases make the models invalid, we shall argue that the law regulating municipal bargaining must be flexible and tailored to the real needs of a particular municipality. The flexibility issue will be addressed directly, and in some detail, after consideration of the contemporary setting in which public bargaining is now developing.

35. The Role and Consequences of Strikes by Public Employees*

John F. Burton, Jr. and Charles Krider†

> *Reason is the life of the law.*
> Sir Edward Coke

> *The life of the law has not been logic: It has been experience.*
> Oliver Wendell Holmes

The vexing problem of strikes by public employees has generated a number of assertions based largely on logical analysis. One common theme is that strikes fulfill a useful function in the private sector but are inappropriate in the public sector because they distort the political decision-making process. Another is that strikes in nonessential government services should not be permitted because it is administratively infeasible to distinguish among the various government services on the basis of their essentiality. The present article attempts to evaluate these assertions in terms of labor relations experience at the local level of government.

The assertions concerning strikes by public employees which we shall discuss have been drawn mainly from *The Taylor Report,* a report on public employee labor relations submitted to the Governor of New York State,[1] and "The Limits of Collective Bargaining in Public Employment," a recent article by Harry Wellington and Ralph Winter.[2] Most of the evidence used to evaluate these assertions has been gathered in connection with the Brookings Institution *Study of Unionism and Collective Bargaining in the Public Sector.*[3] Statistical information on all local public employee strikes which have occurred between 1965 and 1968 has been provided by the Bureau of Labor Statistics.[4] Because education is outside the scope of our portion of the Brookings study, the data used in this article primarily relate to strikes by groups other than teachers.

* Reprinted by permission of The Yale Law Journal Company and Fred B. Rothman & Company from *The Yale Law Journal,* Vol. 79, pp. 148–440. This paper was prepared as part of a Study of Unionism and Collective Bargaining in the Public Sector which is being conducted by the Brookings Institution with financial support from the Ford Foundation. The views are the authors', and are not presented as those of the officers, trustees, or staff members of the Brookings Institution or of the Ford Foundation.

Helpful comments on an earlier draft of this paper were received from Paul F. Gerhart, Robert B. McKersie, Arnold R. Weber, and Harry H. Wellington.

† John F. Burton, Jr., is Associate Professor of Industrial Relations and Public Policy, Graduate School of Business, University of Chicago. Charles Krider is a graduate student, University of Chicago; and Research Assistant, Brookings Institution.

[1] Governor's Committee on Public Employee Relations, Final Report (State of New York 1966) [hereinafter cited as *Taylor Committee Report*]. The committee chairman was George W. Taylor.

[2] Wellington and Winter, "The Limits of Collective Bargaining in Public Employment," 78 *Yale L.J.* 1107 (1969) [hereinafter cited as Wellington and Winter].

[3] Some 50 cities, counties, and special districts were visited during 1968–69, and numerous interviews were conducted. Specific references to these interviews are not included because of our guaranty of anonymity to those we interviewed.

[4] We would like to express our appreciation to the Bureau of Labor Statistics for making this unpublished data available to us.

I. THE ROLE OF STRIKES IN THE PRIVATE SECTOR

Wellington and Winter have catalogued four claims which are made to justify collective bargaining in the private sector.[5] First, collective bargaining is a way to achieve industrial peace. Second, it is a way of achieving industrial democracy. Third, unions that bargain collectively with employers also represent workers in the political arena. Fourth, and in their view the most important reason, collective bargaining compensates for the unequal bargaining power which is believed to result from individual bargaining. Wellington and Winter recognize that the gains to employees from collective bargaining, such as protection from monopsony power, are to be balanced against the social costs resulting from the resort to collectivism, such as distortion of the wage structure. While noting that considerable disagreement exists among economists concerning the extent of the benefits and costs, they stress the fact that costs are limited by economic constraints. Unions can displace their members from jobs by ignoring the discipline of the market. These four justifications for private sector collective bargaining are presumably relevant to some degree whether or not strikes are permitted. Nonetheless, one can conceptualize two models of collective bargaining—the Strike Model, which would normally treat strikes as legal, and the No-Strike Model, which would make all strikes illegal—and evaluate whether, in terms of the above justifications, society benefits from permitting strikes.

Most scholars of industrial relations accept the view that the right to strike is desirable in the private sector. Chamberlain and Kuhn assert, "[T]he possibility or ultimate threat of strikes is a necessary condition for collective bargaining."[6] The distinguished scholars who comprised the Taylor Committee asserted similarly, "[T]he right to strike remains an integral part of the collective bargaining processes in the private enterprise sector and this will unquestionably continue to be the case."[7] One reason for this endorsement of the strike is that its availability is often essential to the union in its bid for recognition by the employer.[8] In addition, once the bargaining relationship is established, the possibility that work may be interrupted forces the parties to bargain seriously.[9] The possibility of a strike thus increases the likelihood that the parties will reach an agreement without third-party intervention. More important, the ability to strike increases the bargaining power of employees and their union so that, unlike the No-Strike Model, the employer cannot dominate the employer-employee relationship.

Use of the Strike Model instead of the No-Strike Model appears to enhance all but the third of the four claims for private sector collective bargaining offered by Wellington and Winter.[10] While they do not provide a claim by claim analysis of the consequences of permitting strikes, their endorsement of strikes in the private sector must indicate that they believe the Strike Model preferable to the No-Strike Model.

II. THE ROLE OF STRIKES IN THE PUBLIC SECTOR

What are the virtues of collective bargaining in the public sector, and what are the consequences of permitting strikes by public employees?

The advocates of one view presumably assume that the four reasons offered by Wellington and Winter to justify collective bargaining in the private sector have equal relevance in the public sector. They also assert that strikes play the same role in the public and private sectors, and that our private sector strike policy should be replicated in the public sector. Strikes would not be banned *ab initio* in any function but could

[5] Wellington and Winter, supra note 2, at 1112–13.

[6] N. Chamberlain and J. Kuhn, *Collective Bargaining* 391 (2d ed. 1965).

[7] *Taylor Committee Report,* supra note 1, at 15.

[8] Private sector unions subject to the Labor Management Relations Act (Taft-Hartley Act), 29 U.S.C. §§ 141–97 (1947), have little need for recognition strikes because the right of self-organization is protected by statute.

[9] "Since a strike hurts management by stopping production and workers by cutting off their wages, neither party is apt to reject terms proposed by the other without serious consideration. . . . Without such a threat they may continue to disagree indefinitely and never bargain seriously, each simply refusing to give ground in an effort to reach a settlement acceptable to both." Chamberlain and Kuhn, supra note 6, at 391.

[10] The first reason offered—it is a way to achieve industrial peace—appears to be inconsistent with the notion of permitting strikes as a method of increasing the employees' bargaining power. One possible resolution of this apparent contradiction is that the enhanced bargaining power of the employees will enable them to work out mutually satisfactory terms with their employer without having to resort to the strike, while workers with limited bargaining power will often engage in strikes as an expression of their futility. This explanation is not totally compelling, however, and one may therefore have to justify collective bargaining among parties with equal power on grounds other than the diminution of strikes. The favorable consequences of the last three claims offered by Wellington and Winter for private sector collective bargaining presumably offset any possible increase in strikes.

be dealt with *ex post facto* by injunction if an emergency occurred.

This approach has been argued by Theodore W. Kheel, a noted labor arbitrator. He asserts that it is now "evident that collective bargaining is the best way of composing differences between workers and their employers in a democratic society. . . ." The only alternatives to collective bargaining are two: "either the employer makes the final determination or it is made by a third party, an arbitrator." While collective bargaining is the superior type of industrial relations, "collective bargaining cannot exist if employees may not withdraw their services or employers discontinue them."

[However, this does not mean] that the right to strike is sacrosanct. On the contrary, it is a right like all other rights that must be weighed against the larger public interest, and it must be subordinated where necessary to the superior right of the public to protection against injury to health or safety. . . .

These principles, in my judgment, apply to the private sector as well as to the public sector. Moreover, their application cannot be determined in advance.[11]

Instead, Kheel believes, a procedure should be developed which would halt a strike only after it could be demonstrated that the public health and safety were endangered.

Proponents of the opposing view of public sector strikes argue that such strikes are invariably inappropriate. The Taylor Committee concluded that in the public services, "the strike cannot be a part of the negotiating process."[12] And Wellington and Winter clearly believe that overall the four claims for collective bargaining are valid in the public sector only if strikes are illegal. Their primary concern is the fourth reason offered for collective bargaining—collective activity is needed as a substitute for individual activity because individuals are weak.[13] This reason is always troublesome because increased bargaining power involves costs as well as benefits. They do not endorse the Strike Model in the public sector because the costs which result from increasing employee bargaining power by permitting strikes are higher and the benefits are

less in the public sector than in the private sector.

The benefits of collective action are less in the public sector for several reasons. The problem of employer monopsony is not as consequential, not only because employer monopsony is less likely to occur, but also because existing monopsony power is less likely to be utilized. In addition, the low pay given to certain groups in the public sector, such as teachers, may reflect society's view about the best uses of its resources, while low pay in the private sector for a particular occupation presumably reflects a misallocation of resources.

The costs of substituting collective for individual bargaining are also likely to be higher in the public sector. According to Wellington and Winter, the market restraints on trade union activity are weak, reflecting the inelastic demand for public services, a lack of substitutes for these services, and the fact that many public services are essential. Second, strikes in the public sector lead to public pressure on officials which compels quick settlements. Further, there are no other pressure groups competing for public resources which have weapons comparable to the strike, and, thus, unions have a more advantageous arsenal of weapons. The net result of the lack of market restraints, the pressure on public officials to settle strikes quickly, and the absence of comparable weaponry by other pressure groups is that strikes in the public sector impose high costs by distorting the normal political process.

Because the cost-benefit ratio which results from the substitution of collective action, including strikes, for individual action is so high in the public sector, Wellington and Winter argue that public employee strikes should be illegal. Their argument is based on their notion of sovereignty. This is not the traditional doctrine of sovereignty, which they specifically reject,[14] but a new version of sovereignty which asserts that the government has the right, through its laws, "to ensure the survival of the 'normal' American political process."[15] This rationale for sovereignty, fully articulated in Wellington and Winter and implicit in the Taylor Report analysis, deserves a careful scrutiny in terms of empirical evidence.

III. CONSEQUENCES OF STRIKES IN THE PUBLIC SECTOR

The best procedure for evaluating public sector strikes would be to investigate the respective

---

[11] All quotations are from Kheel, "Resolving Deadlocks without Banning Strikes," 92 *Monthly Lab. Rev.* 62–63 (July 1969).

[12] *Taylor Committee Report,* supra note 1, at 16.

[13] "In the area of public employment the claims upon public policy made by the need for industrial peace, industrial democracy, and effective political representation point toward collective bargaining." Wellington and Winter, supra note 2, at 1,115. "Much less clearly analogous to the private model, however, is the unequal bargaining power argument." Id. at 1,116.

[14] *See* id. at 1,125–26.

[15] Id.

impacts of the Strike Model and the No-Strike Model on each of the claims made for collective bargaining. Such an analysis should consider the economic, political, and social effects produced. An inquiry into these effects is particularly important since several authors who have implicily endorsed the Strike Model in the private sector have done so more on the basis of noneconomic reasons than economic reasons.[16] Nonetheless, the attack on the Strike Model in the *public* sector has been based largely on the evaluation of the fourth claim for collective bargaining, that relating to unequal bargaining power. We will attempt to meet this attack by confining our discussion to the economic consequences of collective bargaining with and without strikes.

Even an examination confined to economic consequences is difficult. The most desirable economic data, which would measure the impact of unions on wages and other benefits, is unavailable. A major examination of the relative wage impact of public sector unions is now being conducted by Paul Hartman,[17] but pending the outcome of his study we have to base our evaluation on less direct evidence. Our approach will be to review carefully the various steps in the analytical model developed by Wellington and Winter by which they arrive at the notion of sovereignty. If we find that the evidence available on public sector strikes contradicts this model, we shall conclude that the differential assessment they provide for public and private strikes is unwarranted.

A. Benefits of Collective Bargaining

Wellington and Winter believe the benefits of collective action, including strikes, are less in the public sector than in the private sector since (1) the problem of employer monopsony is less serious, and (2) any use of monopsony power in the public sector which results in certain groups, such as teachers, receiving low pay may reflect, not a misallocation of resources, but rather a political determination of the desired use of resources.

Wellington and Winter assert that employer monopsony is less likely to exist or be used in the public than in the private sector.[18] But as they

concede,[19] referring to Bunting, monopsony is not widespread in the private sector and, except in a few instances, cannot be used as a rationale for trade unions. They provide no evidence that monopsony is less prevalent in the public than in the private sector. Moreover, other labor market inefficiencies, common to the public and private sectors, are probably more important than monopsony in providing an economic justification for unions. For example, the deficiencies of labor market information are to some extent overcome by union activities,[20] and there is no reason to assume that this benefit differs between the public and private sectors.

Assuming there is monopsony power, Wellington and Winter believe that collective bargaining in the private sector can eliminate unfair wages "which are less than they would be if the market were more nearly perfect."[21] They assert, however, that low pay for an occupation in the public sector may reflect a political judgment which ought not to be countered by pressures resulting from a strike. To say, however, that the pay for an occupation would be higher if the employees had the right to strike than if they did not is not independent proof that strikes are inappropriate. The same criticism could be made of any activity by a public employee group which affects its pay. An independent rationale must be provided to explain why some means which are effective in raising wages (strikes) are inappropriate while other means which are also effective (lobbying) are appropriate. Whether the Wellington and Winter discussion of the politically based decision-making model for the public sector provides this rationale will be discussed in more detail subsequently.

B. Costs of Collective Bargaining

Wellington and Winter's discussion of the cost of substituting collective for individual bargaining in the public sector includes a chain of causation which runs from (1) an allegation that

[16] A. Rees, *The Economics of Trade Unions* 194–97 (1962).

[17] Paul Hartman of the University of Illinois is examining the impact of public sector unions on wages as part of the Brookings Institution's *Study of Unionism and Collective Bargaining in the Public Sector.*

[18] Wellington and Winter, supra note 2, at 1,120.

[19] Id. at 1,113.

[20] "Under purely competitive conditions, it is assumed that perfect knowledge of existing wage rates in other firms, regions, and occupations, and mobility of both labor and capital would tend to eradicate unnecessary wage differentials (i.e., differentials which did not truly reflect the marginal productivity of labor). Both knowledge and mobility, however, are very imperfect in the real market. The existence of trade unions to a large extent compensates for the lack of knowledge and represents a force tending toward wage standardization for similar work." A. Cartter and F. Marshall, *Labor Economics: Wages, Employment, and Trade Unionism* 324–25 (1967).

[21] Wellington and Winter, supra note 2, at 1,116.

market restraints are weak in the public sector, largely because the services are essential; to (2) an assertion that the public puts pressure on civic officials to arrive at a quick settlement; to (3) a statement that other pressure groups have no weapons comparable to a strike; to (4) a conclusion that the strike thus imposes a high cost since the political process is distorted.

Let us discuss these steps in order:

(1) *Market Restraints:* A key argument in the case for the inappropriateness of public sector strikes is that economic constraints are not present to any meaningful degree in the public sector.[22] This argument is not entirely convincing. First, wages lost due to strikes are as important to public employees as they are to employees in the private sector. Second, the public's concern over increasing tax rates may prevent the decision-making process from being dominated by political instead of economic considerations. The development of multilateral bargaining in the public sector is an example of how the concern over taxes may result in a close substitute for market constraints.[23] In San Francisco, for example, the Chamber of Commerce has participated in negotiations between the city and public employee unions and has had some success in limiting the economic gains of the unions. A third and related economic constraint arises for such services as water, sewage, and, in some instances, sanitation, where explicit prices are charged. Even if representatives of groups other than employees and the employer do not enter the bargaining process, both union and local government are aware of the economic implications of bargaining which leads to higher prices which are clearly visible to the public. A fourth economic constraint on employees exists in those services where subcontracting to the private sector is a realistic alternative.[24] Warren, Michigan, resolved a bargaining impasse with an American Federation of State, County and Municipal Employees (AFSCME) local by subcontracting its entire sanitation service; Santa Monica, California, ended a strike of city employees by threatening to subcontract its sanitation operations. If the subcontracting option is preserved, wages in the public sector need not exceed the rate at which subcontracting becomes a realistic alternative.

An aspect of the lack-of-market-restraints argument is that public services are essential. Even at the analytical level, Wellington and Winter's case for essentiality is not convincing. They argue:

> The Services performed by a private transit authority are neither less nor more essential to the public than those that would be performed if the transit authority were owned by a municipality. A railroad or a dock strike may be much more damaging to a community than "job action" by teachers. This is not to say that government services are not essential. They are both because they may seriously injure a city's economy and occasionally the physical welfare of its citizens.[25]

This is a troublesome passage. It ends with the implicit conclusion that all government services are essential. This conclusion is important in Wellington and Winter's analysis because it is a step in their demonstration that strikes are inappropriate in all governmental services. But the beginning of the passage, with its example of "job action" by teachers, suggests that essentially is not an *inherent* characteristic of government services but depends on the specific service being evaluated. Furthermore the transit authority example suggests that many services are interchangeable between the public and private sectors. The view that various government services are not of equal essentiality and that there is considerable overlap between the kinds of services provided in the public and private sectors is reinforced by our field work and strike data from the Bureau of Labor Statistics. Examples include:

1. Where sanitation services are provided by a municipality, such as Cleveland, sanitationmen are prohibited from striking. Yet, sanitationmen in Philadelphia, Portland, and San Francisco are presumably free to strike since they are employed by private contractors rather than by the cities.

2. There were 25 local government strikes by the Teamsters in 1965–68, most involving truck drivers and all presumably illegal. Yet the Teamsters' strike involving fuel oil truck drivers in

---

[22] "It further seems to us that, to the extent union power is delimited by market or other forces in the public sector, these constraints do not come into play nearly as quickly as in the private." Wellington and Winter, supra note 2, at 1,117.

[23] McLennan and Moskow, "Multilateral Bargaining in the Public Sector," 21 *Ind. Rel. Res. Assn. Proceedings* 31 (1968).

[24] The subcontracting option is realistic in functions such as sanitation and street or highway repairs, and some white collar occupations. Several other functions, including hospitals and education, may be transferred entirely to the private sector. The ultimate response by government is to terminate the service, at least temporarily. In late 1968, Youngstown, Ohio, closed its schools for five weeks due to a taxpayer's revolt. 281 *Gov. Lab. Rel. Rep.* B 6 (1969). In late 1969, 10 Ohio school districts ran out of money and were closed down. *Wall Street Journal*, December 19, 1969, at 1, col. 1.

[25] Wellington and Winter, supra note 2, at 1,123.

New York City last winter was legal even though the interruption of fuel oil service was believed to have caused the death of several people.[26]

(2) *Public Pressure:* The second argument in the Wellington and Winter analysis is that public pressure on city officials forces them to make quick settlements. The validity of this argument depends on whether the service is essential. Using as a criterion whether the service is essential in the short run, we believe a priori that services can be divided into three categories: (1) essential services—police and fire—where strikes immediately endanger public health and safety; (2) intermediate services—sanitation, hospitals, transit, water, and sewage—where strikes of a few days might be tolerated; (3) nonessential services— streets, parks, education, housing, welfare and general administration—where strikes of indefinite duration could be tolerated.[27] These categories are not exact since essentiality depends on the size of the city. Sanitation strikes will be critical in large cities such as New York but will not cause much inconvenience in smaller cities where there are meaningful alternatives to governmental operation of sanitation services.

Statistics on the duration of strikes which occurred in the public sector between 1965 and 1968 provide evidence not only that public services are of unequal essentiality, but also that the a priori categories which we have used have some validity. As can be seen from Table 1, strikes in the essential services (police and fire) had an average duration of 4.7 days, while both the intermediate and the nonessential services had an average duration of approximately 10.5

days. It is true that the duration of strikes in the intermediate and nonessential services is only half the average duration of strikes in the private sector during these years.[28] However, this comparison is somewhat misleading since all of the public sector strikes were illegal, and many were ended by injunction, while presumably a vast majority of the private sector strikes did not suffer from these constraints. It would appear that with the exception of police and fire protection, public officials are, to some degree, able to accept long strikes. The ability of governments to so choose indicates that political pressures generated by strikes are not so strong as to undesirably distort the entire decision-making process of government. City officials in Kalamazoo, Michigan, were able to accept a 48-day strike by sanitationmen and laborers; Sacramento County, California, survived an 87-day strike by welfare workers. A 3-month strike of hospital workers has occurred in Cuyahoga County (Cleveland), Ohio.

(3) *The Strike as a Unique Weapon:* The third objection to the strike is that it provides workers with a weapon unavailable to the employing agency or to other pressure groups. Thus, unions have a superior arsenal. The Taylor Committee Report opposes strikes for this reason, among others, arguing that "there can scarcely be a countervailing lockout."[29] Conceptually, we see no reason why lockouts are less feasible in the public than in the private sector. Legally, public sector lockouts are now forbidden but so are strikes; presumably both could be legalized. Actually, public sector lockouts have occurred. The Social Service Employees Union (SSEU) of New York City sponsored a "work-in" in 1967 during which all of the caseworkers went to their office but refused to work. Instead, union-sponsored lectures were given by representatives of organizations such as CORE, and symposia were held on the problems of welfare workers and clients. The work-in lasted for one week, after which the City locked out the caseworkers.

A similar assertion is made by Wellington and Winter, who claim that no pressure group other than unions has a weapon comparable to the strike. But this argument raises a number of questions. Is the distinctive characteristic of an inappropriate method of influencing decisions by public officials that it is economic as opposed to political? If this is so, then presumably the threat

TABLE 1   Duration of Strikes by Essentiality of Function*

	Average Duration in Days	Standard Deviation in Days†
Essential.	4.7	7.9
Intermediate.	10.3	18.5
Nonessential.	10.6	20.1
Education.	7.2	8.9

* Based on data collected by the Bureau of Labor Statistics on strikes during 1965–68 involving employees of local government.

† Standard deviation is a measure of dispersion around the average or the mean.

---

[26] *New York Times,* December 26, 1968, at 1, col. 1, and December 27, 1968, at 1, col. 5.

[27] We consider education a nonessential service. However, because our portion of the Brookings Institution study excludes education, our analysis in this article will also largely exclude education.

[28] U.S. Bureau of Labor Statistics, Dep't of Labor, Bulletin no. 1611, *Analysis of Work Stoppages 1967,* at 4 (1969).

[29] *Taylor Committee Report,* supra note 1, at 15.

of the New York Stock Exchange to move to New Jersey unless New York City taxes on stock transfers were lowered and similar devices should be outlawed along with the strike.

(4) *Distortion of the Political Process.* The ultimate concern of both the Taylor Committee and Wellington and Winter is that "a strike of government employees . . . introduces an alien force in the legislative process."[30] It is "alien" because, in the words of the Taylor Committee Report:

Careful thought about the matter shows conclusively, we believe, that while the right to strike normally performs a useful function in the private enterprise sector (where relative economic power is the final determinant in the making of private agreements), it is not compatible with the orderly functioning of our democratic form of representative government (in which relative political power is the final determinant).[31]

The essence of this analysis appears to be that certain means used to influence the decision-making process in the public sector—those which are political—are legitimate, while others—those which are economic—are not. For several reasons, we believe that such distinctions among means are tenuous.

First, any scheme which differentiates economic power from political power faces a perplexing definitional task. The *International Encyclopedia of the Social Sciences* defines the political process as "the activities of people in various groups as they struggle for—and use— power to achieve personal and group purposes."[32] And what is power?

Power in use invariably involves a mixture of many different forms—sometimes mutually reinforcing—of persuasion and pressure. . . .

Persuasion takes place when A influences B to adopt a course of action without A's promising or threatening any reward or punishment. It may take the form of example, expectation, proposals, information, education, or propaganda. . . .

Pressure is applied by A upon B whenever A tries to make a course of action more desirable by promising or threatening contingent rewards or punishments. It may take the form of force, commands, manipulation, or bargaining. . . .

Physical force is a blunt instrument. . . . Besides, more flexible and reliable modes of pressure are available. Rewards, in the form of monetary payments, new positions, higher status, support, favorable votes, cooperation, approval, or the withdrawl of any anticipated punishment, may be bestowed or promised.

Punishment, in the form of fines, firing, reduction in status, unfavorable votes, noncooperation, rejection, disapproval, or withdrawal of any anticipated reward, may be given or threatened. . . .

Bargaining is a still more fluid—and far more persuasive—form of using pressure. In bargaining, all sides exercise power upon each other through reciprocal promises or threats. . . . Indeed, force, command, and manipulation tend to become enveloped in the broader and more subtle processes of bargaining.[33]

We have quoted at length from this discussion of the political process because we believe it illustrates the futility of attempting to distinguish between economic and political power. The former concept would seem to be encompassed by the latter. The degree of overlap is problematical since there can be economic aspects to many forms of persuasion and pressure. It may be possible to provide an operational distinction between economic power and political power, but we do not believe that those who would rely on this distinction have fulfilled their task.[34]

Second, even assuming it is possible to operationally distinguish economic power and political power, a rationale for utilizing the distinction must be provided. Such a rationale would have to distinguish between the categories either on the basis of characteristics inherent in them as a means of action or on the basis of the ends to which the means are directed. Surely an analysis of ends does not provide a meaningful distinction. The objectives of groups using economic pressure are of the same character as those of groups using political pressure—both seek to influence executive and legislative determinations such as the allocation of funds and the tax rate. If it is impossible effectively to distinguish economic from political pressure groups in terms of their ends, and it is desirable to free the political process from the influence of all pressure groups, then effective lobbying and petitioning should be as illegal as strikes.

If the normative distinction between economic and political power is based, not on the ends desired, but on the nature of the means, our

[30] Id.

[31] Id. at 18–19.

[32] 12 *Int'l Encyc. Social Sciences* 265 (1968).

[33] Id. at 269–70.

[34] It is interesting to note that some who would differentiate between economic and political considerations apparently view public sector strikes as *political* activity. Stieber, "Collective Bargaining in the Public Sector," in *Challenges to Collective Bargaining* 83 (L. Ulman ed. 1967): "The basic question is whether the strike, which in the United States has been viewed primarily as an economic weapon, is equally appropriate when used as a political weapon." If Stieber's characterization of public sector strikes is correct, then presumably the rationale of the *Taylor Committee Report* should make these strikes legal.

skepticism remains undiminished. Are all forms of political pressure legitimate? Then consider the range of political activity observed in the public sector. Is lobbying by public sector unions to be approved? Presumably it is. What then of participation in partisan political activity? On city time? Should we question the use of campaign contributions or kickbacks from public employees to public officials as a means of influencing public sector decisions? These questions suggest that political pressures, as opposed to economic pressures, cannot *as a class* be considered more desirable.

Our antagonism toward a distinction based on means does not rest solely on a condemnation of political pressures which violate statutory provisions. We believe that perfectly legal forms of political pressure have no automatic superiority over economic pressure. In this regard, the evidence from our field work is particularly enlightening. First, we have found that the availability of political power varies among groups of employees within a given city. Most public administrators have respect for groups which can deliver votes at strategic times. Because of their links to private sector unions, craft unions are invariably in a better position to play this political role than a union confined to the public sector, such as AFSCME. In Chicago, Cleveland, and San Francisco, the public sector craft unions are closely allied with the building trades council and play a key role in labor relations with the city. Prior to the passage of state collective bargaining laws such unions also played the key role in Detroit and New York City. In the No-Strike Model, craft unions clearly have the comparative advantage because of their superior political power.

Second, the range of issues pursued by unions relying on political power tends to be narrow. The unions which prosper by eschewing economic power and exercising political power are often found in cities, such as Chicago, with a flourishing patronage system. These unions gain much of their political power by cooperating with the political administration. This source of political power would vanish if the unions were assiduously to pursue a goal of providing job security for their members since this goal would undermine the patronage system. In Rochester, for example, a union made no effort to protect one of its members who was fired for political reasons. For the union to have opposed the city administration at that time on an issue of job security would substantially have reduced the union's influence on other issues. In Chicago,

where public sector strikes are rare (except for education) but political considerations are not, the unions have made little effort to establish a grievance procedure to protect their members from arbitrary treatment.

Third, a labor relations system built on political power tends to be unstable since some groups of employees, often a substantial number, are invariably left out of the system. They receive no representation either through patronage or through the union. In Memphis, the craft unions had for many years enjoyed a "working relationship" with the city which assured the payment of the rates that prevailed in the private sector and some control over jobs. The sanitation laborers, however, were not part of the system and were able to obtain effective representation only after a violent confrontation with the city in 1968. Having been denied representation through the political process, they had no choice but to accept a subordinate position in the city or to initiate a strike to change the system. Racial barriers were an important factor in the isolation of the Memphis sanitation laborers. Similar distinctions in racial balance among functions and occupations appear in most of the cities we visited.

Conclusions in Regards to Strikes and the Political Process

Wellington and Winter and the Taylor Committee reject the use of the Strike Model in the public sector. They have endorsed the No-Strike Model in order "to ensure the survival of the 'normal' American political process."[35] Our field work suggests that unions which have actually helped their members either have made the strike threat a viable weapon despite its illegality or have intertwined themselves closely with their nominal employer through patronage-political support arrangements. If this assessment is correct, choice of the No-Strike Model is likely to lead to patterns of decision making which will subvert, if not the "normal" American political process, at least the political process which the Taylor Committee and Wellington and Winter meant to embrace. We would not argue that the misuse of political power will be eliminated by legalizing the strike; on balance, however, we believe that, in regard to most governmental functions, the Strike Model has more virtues than the No-Strike Model. Whether strikes are an appropriate weapon for all groups or public employees is our next topic.

[35] Wellington and Winter, supra note 2, at 1,125–26.

IV. DIFFERENTIATION AMONG PUBLIC SECTOR FUNCTIONS

The most important union for local government employees, The American Federation of State, County and Municipal Employees (AFSCME), issued a policy statement in 1966 claiming the right of public employees to strike:

AFSCME insists upon the right of public employees . . . to strike. To forestall this right is to handicap free collective bargaining process [sic]. Wherever legal barriers to the exercise of this right exist, it shall be our policy to seek the removal of such barriers. Where one party at the bargaining table possesses all the power and authority, the bargaining becomes no more than formalized petitioning.[36]

Significantly, AFSCME specifically excluded police and other law enforcement officers from this right. Any local of police officers that engages in a strike or other concerted refusal to perform duties will have its charter revoked.

Can a distinction among functions, such as is envisioned by AFSCME, be justified? In view of the high costs associated with the suppression of strikes, could each stoppage be dealt with, as Theodore Kheel suggests, only when and if it becomes an emergency?

Despite arguments to the contrary, we feel that strikes in some essential services, such as fire and police, would immediately endanger the public health and safety and should be presumed illegal. We have no evidence from our field work to support our fears that any disruption of essential services will quickly result in an emergency. But the events which occurred on September 9, 1919, during a strike by Boston policemen provide strong proof; those which occurred on October 7, 1969, following a strike by Montreal policemen would appear to make the argument conclusive. Contemporary accounts amply describe the holocausts:

Boston, 1919

About me milled a crowd of aimless men and women, just seeing what they could see. . . . There was an air of expectancy without knowing what was expected.

There came the sound of two hard substances in sharp impact, followed a second later by a louder one and the thrilling crash of falling splintering glass. A plate show-window had been shattered. Instantly the window and its immediate vicinity were filled with struggling men, a mass of action, from which emerged from time to time bearers of shirts, neckties, collars, hats. In a few seconds the window was bare. Some with loot vanished; others lingered.

Lootless ones were attacking the next window. Nothing happened. That is, the fear of arrest abated after the first shock of the lawless acts. I saw men exchanging new shirts each with the other, to get their sizes . . . good-looking men, mature in years, bearing all the earmarks of a lifetime of sane observance of property rights.[37]

Montreal, 1969

"You've never seen the city like this," said the owner of a big women's clothing store surveying his premises, strewn with dummies from which the clothing had been torn. "It's like the war." [38]

A taxi driver carrying a passenger up Sherbrooke Street in Montreal today blamed the police for "not knowing the effect their absence would have on people." He continued: "I don't mean hoodlums and habitual lawbreakers, I mean just plain people committed offenses they would not dream of trying if there was a policeman standing on the corner. I saw cars driven through red lights. Drivers shot up the wrong side of the street because they realized no one would catch them." [39]

In the case of strikes by essential employees, such as policemen, the deterioration of public order occurs almost immediately. During the first few hours of the police walkout in Montreal, robberies occurred at eight banks, one finance company, two groceries, a jewelry store, and a private bank.[40] In the case of the Boston police strike of 1919, outbreaks began within four hours after the strike had commenced. Such consequences require that strikes by police and other essential services be outlawed in advance. There is simply no time to seek an injunction.

Even if a distinction in the right to strike can be made among government functions on the basis of essentiality, is such a distinction possible to implement? The Taylor Committee based their argument against prohibiting strikes in essential functions but allowing them elsewhere on this difficulty:

We come to this conclusion [to prohibit all strikes] after a full consideration of the views . . . that public employees in non-essential government services, at least, should have the same right to strike as has been accorded to employees in private industry. We realize, moreover, that the work performed in both

---

[36] International Executive Board AFSCME, *Policy Statement on Public Employee Unions: Rights and Responsibilities* 2 (July 26, 1966).

[37] C. Wood, "Reds and Lost Wages" 9–10 (1930), as quoted in D. Ziskind, *One Thousand Strikes of Government Employees* 45 (1940).

[38] *New York Times,* October 9, 1969, at 3, col. 1.

[39] *New York Times,* October 10, 1969, at 2, col. 6.

[40] *New York Times,* October 8, 1969, at 3, col. 1.

TABLE 2   Partial Operation by Essentiality of Function (noneducation)*

	Essential		Intermediate		Nonessential		Total†	
	Number	Percentage	Number	Percentage	Number	Percentage	Number	Percentage
Total number of strikes..........	37	100.0	221	100.0	43	100.0	301	100.0
Partial operation.......	34	91.9	175	79.2	33	76.7	242	80.4
Supervisors..........	(28)	(75.7)	(154)	(69.7)	(29)	(67.4)	(211)	(70.1)
Nonstrikers..........	(27)	(73.0)	(137)	(62.0)	(28)	(65.1)	(192)	(63.8)
Replacements.......	(3)	(9.1)	(34)	(15.4)	(4)	(9.3)	(41)	(13.6)
Volunteers...........	(5)	(13.5)	(16)	(7.2)	—	—	(21)	(7.0)
No partial operation..........	3	8.1	46	20.8	10	23.3	59	19.6

* Based on data collected by the Bureau of Labor Statistics on strikes during 1965–68 involving employees of local governments.
† Twenty-eight strikes in such miscellaneous functions as libraries, museums, and electric or gas utilities were not classified. There was partial operation in 18 (64.3 percent) of these strikes.
‡ The sub-totals for partial operation do not add to 100 percent because more than one may have been used in each strike.

sectors is sometimes comparable or identical. Why, then, should an interruption of non-essential governmental services be prohibited?

To begin with, a differentiation between essential and non-essential governmental services would be the subject of such intense and never ending controversy as to be administratively impossible.[41]

Despite the conclusion of the Taylor Committee it appears that in practice a distinction is emerging between strikes in essential services and strikes in other services. Employee organizations and public officials do in fact treat some strikes as critical, while other strikes cause no undue concern.

Our analysis of the Bureau of Labor Statistics strike data pertaining to the last four years suggests that it is possible to devise an operational definition of essential service. First, as we have indicated above, strike duration was considerably shorter in the essential services than in the intermediate or nonessential services [see Table 1]. These data suggest that, except in police and fire services, public officials have some discretion in choosing to accept long strikes. Second, the statistics reveal that managers have been able to distinguish between essential and nonessential services in their use of counter sanctions. In strikes involving essential services, injunctions were sought more frequently and employees, because of their short run indispensability, were fired less frequently. Injunctions were granted in 35 percent of the essential strikes, and in 25 percent of the intermediate, but only in 19 percent of the nonessential strikes. Third, partial operation was attempted more frequently in essential services [see Table 2]. By using non-

[41] *Taylor Committee Report*, supra note 1, at 18.

strikers, supervisors, replacements or volunteers, local governments were able to continue partial operation during 92 percent of the essential strikes, but in only 80 percent of the intermediate, and 77 percent of the nonessential strikes. Such data suggest that it may be administratively feasible to differentiate among public services so as to permit some, but not all, public employees to strike. Indeed, public administrators already seem to be making such distinctions.

The idea that distinctions among functions are appropriate is also beginning to emerge among legislators. The first state to move in this direction has been Vermont, which apparently restricts municipal employee strikes only if they endanger the health, safety, or welfare of the public.[42] Unfortunately—at least from the viewpoint of researchers—there has been no experience under the statute. Montana prohibits strikes in private or public hospitals only if there is another strike in effect in a hospital within a radius of 150 miles.[43] Study commissions in other states have accepted the distinction between essential and nonessential services. In 1968, the Governor's Commission in Pennsylvania recommended a limited right to strike for all public employees except police and firemen.[44] In 1969, the Labor Law Committee of the Ohio State Bar Association recommended repeal of the Ferguson Act, which prohibits strikes by public employees.[45] They proposed a Public Employment Relations

[42] *Ver. Stat. Ann.* tit. 21, § 1704 (Supp. 1969).

[43] *Rev. Codes of Montana* tit. 41, § 2209 (Supp. 1969).

[44] The Governor's Commission to Revise the Public Employee Laws of Pennsylvania, Report and Recommendations, in 251 *Gov. Emp. Rel. Rep.* E-1 (1968).

[45] *Ohio Rev. Code* §§ 4117.01–4117.05 (1964).

Act which would permit strikes by recognized employee organizations in nonessential occupations following mandatory use of fact-finding procedures.[46] The proposed statute states:

[I]n the event a public employer and a certified labor organization are unable to reach an agreement within 45 days following the date of the receipt of the recommendation of the fact-finding board, the public employees in the bargaining unit . . . and/or the labor organization shall not thereafter be prohibited from engaging in any strike until such time as the labor organization and the public employer reach agreement on a collective bargaining agreement.[47]

V. IMPLICATIONS FOR PUBLIC POLICY

We have expressed our views on the market restraints that exist in the public sector, the extent of the public pressure on public officials to reach quick settlements, the likely methods by which decisions would be made in the No-Strike Model, and the desirability and feasibility of differentiating among government services on the basis of essentiality. In this light, what public policy seems appropriate for strikes at the local government level?

In general, we believe that strikes in the public sector should be legalized for the same reasons they are legal in the private sector. For some public sector services, however—namely, police and fire protection—the probability that a strike will result in immediate danger to public health and safety is so substantial that strikes are almost invariably inappropriate. In these essential functions, the strike should be presumed illegal; the state should not be burdened with the requirement of seeking an injunction. We would, however, permit employees in a service considered essential to strike if they could demonstrate to a court that a disruption of service would not endanger the public. Likewise, we would permit the government to obtain an injunction against a strike in a service presumed nonessential if a nontrivial danger to the public could be shown.[48]

The decision to permit some, but not all, public employee strikes cannot, of course, take place in vaccus publicum jus. Mediation, fact finding, or advisory arbitration may be appropriate for those functions where strikes are permitted. Where strikes are illegal because of the essential nature of the service, it may be necessary to institute compulsory arbitration.[49] The choice of a proper role for third parties in the public sector is difficult, and we do not wish to leave the impression that we are unaware of the problem. In our portion of the Brookings Institution study, we will examine the experience which many cities have had in the use of neutral third parties. Our initial reaction is that such experience does not undermine the feasibility of a public policy which would permit some, but not all, public employees the right to strike, and include that decision in a comprehensive public policy for collective bargaining.

While we have indicated our support for the right of public employees to strike, we do not mean to suggest that all strikes are desirable. In particular, strikes which are necessary solely because the employer refuses to establish a bargaining relationship seem anachronous. The right of employees to deal with their employer through a representative of their choosing should be reflected in our public policy. The obligation on employers to recognize and to bargain with properly certified unions has eliminated many strikes in the private sector. The evidence in Table 3 suggests that, in the public sector, strikes on such issues can be sharply reduced. In those states in which local governments are required to recognize and to bargain with unions representing a majority of their employees, strikes to establish the bargaining relationship have been virtually eliminated. States with permissive laws, which require minimal recognition of unions and which require only that employers "meet and confer," as opposed to "bargain," with these unions, have perhaps aggravated the strike problem.

Similarly, our general endorsement of public sector strikes does not mean that we are unconcerned about the circumstances under which

---

[46] 42 Ohio Bar 563 (1969).

[47] Id. at 576.

[48] The Labor Management Relations Act (Taft-Hartley Act) is a statute which presumes strikes are legal unless an emergency is involved. 29 U.S.C. §§ 176–180 (1969). The President may delay or suspend an actual or threatened strike which if permitted to occur or continue will constitute a threat to the national health or safety. The emergency procedures have been invoked 29 times since 1947. This experience should provide some guidance in formulating an operational version of our policy which would permit strikes in nonessential functions unless a nontrivial danger to the public could be shown. We real-

ize that it may be more difficult to formulate an operational version of our policy for essential functions. We are not aware of any experience with a statute which permits the presumption of illegality for strikes to be rebutted under appropriate circumstances.

[49] Michigan has recently enacted a statute applicable to public police and fire departments which imposes penalties on striking employees and establishes a binding arbitration procedure for negotiating disputes. Arbitration is available upon the request of either party in the dispute. Mich. Comp. Laws §§ 423.232–.247 (1948).

TABLE 3   Local Government Strikes by Public Policy and Issue*

	Noneducation Strikes		Education Strikes	
	Number	Duration in Days	Number	Duration in Days
Mandatory law				
Strikes to establish bargaining relationship†	1	10.0	5	3.4
Other strikes	56	6.7	104	8.7
Permissive law				
Strikes to establish bargaining relationship	20	19.6	2	7.0
Other strikes	34	10.4	16	6.5
No law				
Strikes to establish bargaining relationship	68	21.6	29	5.9
Other strikes	150	5.8	93	6.2

* Based on data collected by the Bureau of Labor Statistics on strikes during 1965–68 involving employees of local governments.

† Includes strikes where union was demanding recognition as well as strikes where union was demanding bona fide collective bargaining.

such strikes take place. Public policy has an important role to play in shaping the structure and, hence, influencing the outcome of collective bargaining.[50] An example is the inclusion or exclusion of supervisors in the bargaining unit. As indicated in Table 2, supervisors are often used during strikes to provide partial operation. Presumably, this enhances the ability of local governments to resist union demands. Some states, such as Wisconsin,[51] have wisely stipulated that supervisors are to be excluded from bargaining units, while other states, such as New York, have not. A supervisor who belongs to a striking union is likely to be of limited usefulness to management in attempting to counteract the strike. Another way in which a state's public policy could enhance local government's ability to resist strikes would be to enact a statute prohibiting employers from signing away their right to subcontract. The absolute right to subcontract operations would thereby be preserved. While it is unlikely that some services, such as police and fire protection, will ever be placed under private management, other services can be subcontracted if union demands raise the cost of a public

service to a level at which private service becomes competitive. Excluding the education sector, subcontracting was threatened by management in 16 local government strikes and implemented in 5 between 1965 and 1968.

VI. CONCLUSIONS

This article has offered a policy to deal with public sector strikes. It has also examined several propositions concerning public sector strikes which have been based largely on logical analysis. The assertions that strikes by public employees inevitably distort the decision-making process in the public sector and that differential treatment of public employees in their right to strike would be infeasible have been found to be wanting when evaluated in the light of our actual experience with public sector strikes. This evaluation suggests that logic alone is an inadequate basis for public policy in this area. Yet we would not want to suggest that a literal interpretation of Holmes' view on the relative merits of logic and experience is appropriate. If we were forced to choose a mentor in any debate concerning the proper bases for law, we endorse Cardozo:

My analysis of the judicial process comes then to this, and little more: logic, and history, and custom, and utility, and the accepted standards of right conduct, are the forces which singly or in combination shape the progress of the law.

[50] For a discussion of collective bargaining structure, see Weber, "Stability and Change in the Structure of Collective Bargaining," in *Challenges to Collective Bargaining* 13 (L. Ulman ed. 1967).

[51] *Wis. Stat. Ann.* § 111.81(12) (Supp. 1969), relates to state employees.

36. Public Sector Strikes—Legislative and Court Treatment*

Jerome T. Barrett and Ira B. Lobel†

Historically, public policy toward public sector work stoppages was typified by Franklin D. Roosevelt's feeling that they were "unthinkable" and Calvin Coolidge's thought that they were a form of "anarchy." That attitude persisted into the 1960s, despite the number of public sector collective bargaining relationships which had been established and the occurrence of some work stoppages. In the mid-1960s, it would be accurate to say that public policy in all states clearly prohibited work stoppages of public employees by statute, court decision, or attorney's general opinion.

The federal government's policy toward work stoppages by its employees has been spelled out in section 19(b)(4) of Executive Order 11491, which makes it an unfair labor practice for a public employee labor organization to "call" or engage in a strike, work stoppage, or slowdown, to picket an agency in a labor-management dispute, or to condone any such activity by failing to take affirmative action to stop it. Just as explicit is 5 U.S.C. section 7311(3) which provides, "An individual may not . . . hold a position in the Government of the United States . . . if he . . . participates in a strike . . . against the Government of the United States. . . ."

Some federal courts have enjoined U.S. employees from striking, and in *Postal Clerks* v. *Blount*,[1] a federal district court rejected the union's argument that an absolute prohibition of strikes by such employees was a denial of their First Amendment rights and equal protection of the law. These rights could not be denied, simply because they do not exist, the court said.

With a few highly publicized exceptions in the last several years, the absolute ban on work stoppages by federal employees has been respected by employee organizations. The same condition certainly does not prevail in state and local governments today. In 1960, 36 public sector strikes resulted in 58,400 man-days lost, compared with 412 work stoppages in 1970 involving a man-day loss of 2,023,000.[2]

Because of the growing unwillingness of public employees to continue the tradition of respecting the public policy prohibiting work stoppages, some state legislatures and courts have begun to adjust public policy regarding such stoppages. This article summarizes these changing attitudes.

LEGISLATIVE ACTIONS

Most of the states have established public policy through legislation which prohibits work stoppages. In 1967, the Vermont legislature became the first to give public employees a limited right to engage in a legal strike. Since that action, Montana, Pennsylvania, Hawaii, Alaska, Minnesota, and Oregon have enacted legislation allowing a limited opportunity for legal strikes by certain types of public employees.

The Vermont enactment of 1967 gave all municipal employees, except teachers, the right to strike so long as there was no danger to health, safety, or welfare. Not even policemen or firemen were denied this right. A 1973 amendment to the law established three conditions for a legal

* From U.S. Department of Labor, *Monthly Labor Review*, Vol. 97, No. 9, September 1974, pp. 19–22.

† Jerome T. Barrett is Director of the Office of Technical Services, Federal Mediation and Conciliation Service. Ira B. Lobel is a labor relations specialist in the Office of Technical Services.

[1] 325 F. Supp. 879 (D.-D.C. 1971)—See *Monthly Labor Review*, July 1971, pp. 60–61; aff. 404 U.S. 802 (1971).

[2] See *Work Stoppages, 1958–68*, Report 348 (Bureau of Labor Statistics, 1970); and BLS Report 1727, 1972.

strike: 30 days must elapse after the delivery of a factfinding report to the parties; the dispute must not be one subject to final and binding arbitration or must not have been ruled upon by an arbitrator; and the strike must not endanger the public health, safety, or welfare.[3] In 1969, the state's legislature extended the right to strike to teachers, provided the stoppage does not present a clear and present danger to a "sound program of school education." The law instructs courts considering a strike injunction to enjoin only those specific acts expressly found to impose a clear and present danger.[4] That same year, the Montana legislature passed a law giving nurses in public and private health care facilities a limited right to strike when two conditions are met: The union has given the employer a 30-day written notice of its intention to strike, and no other work stoppage is in effect in another health care facility within a 150-mile radius.[5]

The two most highly publicized laws allowing public employee work stoppages were passed in 1970 in Hawaii and Pennsylvania. The Hawaii law, covering all public employees, provides a limited right to strike when these conditions are met: There must be no danger to the public health or safety; the employees involved must be in a unit certified by the Public Employment Relations Board; the unit must not be one where arbitration is required to resolve interest disputes; the parties must have exhausted in good faith mediation and factfinding efforts to resolve the dispute; if an unfair labor practice exists, the parties must have exhausted all proceedings under the statute; 60 days must have elapsed since the factfinding report was made public; and the union must file a 10-day written notice of its intent to engage in a work stoppage.[6] The statute authorizes the Hawaii Public Employment Relations Board to decide whether these prerequisites have been met. The Board is also authorized to set requirements to avoid or remove imminent or present dangers found in a situation which may lead to a work stoppage.

The Pennsylvania statute covers all public employees except policemen, firemen, prison and mental hospital guards, and court employees.[7]

The statute establishes two principal requirements which must be met if the work stoppage is to be legal: The parties must have exhausted all mediation and factfinding requirements, and the stoppage must not endanger public health, safety, or welfare.[8] The law also provides that an unfair labor practice does not constitute a defense for an otherwise illegal strike, and that strikers may not be paid for the period of their strike.

The Alaska statute, passed in 1972, allows strikes but makes them contingent on the essentiality of the employee's functions. Employees are divided into three groups.[9] The first group, which includes police and fire protection employees, guards in prisons and other correctional institutions, and hospital employees, are absolutely prohibited from engaging in a work stoppage. Bargaining impasses for these employees must be submitted to arbitration. For the second group of employees, which includes employees of public utilities and those engaged in sanitation, snow removal, and public school teaching, a work stoppage is legal if it does not threaten health, safety, or welfare, the parties have utilized mediation, and a majority vote of the employees has supported the stoppage. In applying the law, the court must consider "total equities"—the effect of the strike and the extent to which the parties met statutory obligations—and, if it enjoins such a strike, it must direct arbitration of the issues in dispute.

All other employees may engage in work stoppages, provided a secret ballot election has been conducted. The statute refers to this category as "those services in which work stoppages may be sustained for extended periods without serious effect on the public."

In 1973, the legislatures of Minnesota and Oregon passed laws which dealt with the right to strike. The Minnesota statute, covering all public employees, does not legalize strikes but provides that the failure of a public employer to utilize arbitration in an interest dispute with "nonessential" employees may result in the court's refusal to enjoin their strike if it does not create a clear and present danger to the public health or safety. An employer's refusal to use arbitration may either be a refusal to request arbitration or a failure to comply with an arbitration award. In either case, the union representing nonessential

[3] Vermont Municipal Labor Relations Act, U.S.A., Title 21, Chap. 20, L. 1973, Act III, eff. 7/1/73, Sec. 1730.

[4] Labor Relations for Teachers, U.S.A., Title 16, Ch. 57, L. 1969, No. 127, Sec. 2010.

[5] Revised Codes of Montana, Secs. 41–2201–2209, L. 1969.

[6] Hawaii Revised Statutes, Ch. 89, Laws of 1970, Ch. 171.

[7] Police and Firemen are covered by Penn. Stat. Annot., Title 43, L. 1968, No. 111, which provides for final and binding arbitration of disputes. Ch. 19, No. 195 (footnote 9) prohibits strikes for guards and court employees.

[8] Pennsylvania Stat. Annot., Ch. 19, L. 1970, No. 195, Sec. 1101.1103.

[9] Alaska Statutes, Title 23, Ch. 40, L. 1972, Ch. 94.

employees may use the employer's refusal as a defense against enjoinment of a strike.[10]

The new Oregon law allows strikes by all employees in the state except policemen, firemen, and guards at the correctional and mental institutions. Impasses for the employees denied the right to strike are resolved through binding arbitration.[11] For all other employees, the statute provides certain criteria which must be met before a strike would be legal: a 30-day period must elapse after the factfinder's report has been made public; a 10-day strike notice must be given by the union stating the reasons for the strike; and there must be an absence of a threat of a clear and present danger to public health, safety, or welfare. An unfair labor practice does not constitute a defense against an otherwise illegal work stoppage. If a work stoppage is enjoined by the court, arbitration of the dispute is required to begin within 10 days.

In addition to the above states with statutes clearly allowing strikes in certain situations, there are several states whose laws may be interpreted as granting its employees a limited right to strike. Massachusetts, for example, prohibits strikes by public employees, but its Labor Relations Commission has the authority to determine "whether a strike occurs." It may institute appropriate proceedings in court when a violation of the strike prohibition takes place. It seems clear that the initiative for enforcement of the strike ban rests with the Commission, not the courts, and that the Commission has discretion in seeking injunctions against an illegal strike.[12]

Montana's new statute,[13] covering all employees other than nurses and teachers, makes no mention of strikes. However, the rights section of that statute, in a language similar to that found in the Taft-Hartley Act, gives employees the right to engage in concerted activity. A state district court has recently interpreted the act as granting employees the right to strike.[14] In Idaho, the statute for firefighters provides that "upon consummation and during the term of the written contract or agreement, no firefighters shall strike. . . ."[15] It is not certain what the right of firefighters are after the agreement has expired.

JUDICIAL ACTION

Despite this legislative progress in the matter of strikes, it is clear that public employee work stoppages are prohibited in the vast majority of states. Typically, the courts in those states are asked to enjoin the work stoppage and impose the penalties where the statute provides for penalties. Of course, it is interesting to note that one of the major reasons for the enactment of the New York State Taylor Law in 1967[16] was that the severe strike penalties of the Condon-Wadlin Act had proved both unenforceable and unworkable. At least one state, South Dakota, has recently decreased strike penalties, while the laws of several others, such as Massachusetts and Wisconsin, simply do not mention strike penalties.

Several court decisions in recent years have indicated that, in the future, the availability of injunctive relief during a public employee work stoppage may be reduced.[17]

One possible approach of state courts to this question is to apply antiinjunction statutes to public employees. These laws, which are similar to the federal Norris-LaGuardia Act, are found in 26 states. In 1973, an appellate court of Illinois, in *City of Pana* v. *Crowe*,[18] held that the state's antiinjunction statute prohibited the issuance of an injunction against a strike of municipal workers despite an allegation of interference with the operation of the city's water, sewer, street, and police departments. The court found that the concern for public health, safety, and welfare was insufficient to override the mandate of the antiinjunction statute. Although the case was overturned by the Illinois Supreme Court in May 1974, this interpretation may be applied in other states.

Another approach was used by the Supreme Court of Michigan in *Holland School District* v. *Holland Education Association*.[19] The court found that the state's Hutchison Act, which prohibits public employee strikes, was constitutional, but the mere illegality of the stoppage could not compel a court of equity to issue an injunction in "every instance." The criterion for the court to enjoin a strike is "a showing of violence, irreparable injury, or breach of peace." The court also reasoned that public employer, to obtain an injunction, would have to enter the court

[10] Minnesota Statutes, Secs. 179.61–179.76, L. 1971, Ch. 33.

[11] Oregon Revised Statutes, Secs. 243.711–243.795 as last amended, L. 1973, Ch. 536, Sec. 17–18.

[12] Massachusetts Statutes, L. 1973, Ch. 1078, Secs. 2–2–B, 4–8, Sec. 9–A.

[13] Montana Stat., L. 1973, Ch. 441.

[14] 561 *Government Employee Relations Report*, July 1, 1974, B–2.

[15] Idaho Code, Sec. 44–1801–1811, L. 1970, Ch. 138.

[16] New York State Civil Service Law, Secs. 200–214, L. 1967, Ch. 392.

[17] See *Peoria* v. *Benedict*, 47 Ill. 2d 166 (1970).

[18] 519 *Government Employee Relations Reports B–4*, 1973.

[19] 151 NW 2d 206, 1966.

with "clean hands," i.e., having bargained in good faith, free of having committed unfair labor practices, having exhausted impasse procedures, and not being viewed as having unduly provoked the strike. The result is that in Michigan, in spite of a clear statutory prohibition against strikes, the actual practice differs little from those of the states which grant a limited right to strike.

In 1973, the Supreme Court of Rhode Island[20] became the first state court to apply the principles enunciated in the *Holland* case. The court reasoned that while the statutory ban on public employee strikes was valid and constitutional, "every time there is a concerted work stoppage by employees, it should not be subject to an automatic restraining order." Relying on the reasoning in *Holland,* the court embraced the irreparable harm standard and held, "we must concede that the mere failure of a public school system to begin its school year on the appointed day cannot be classified as a catastrophic event. We are also aware that there has been no public furor when schools are closed for inclement weather, or on the day a presidential candidate comes to town, or when the basketball team wins a championship."

The New Hampshire Supreme Court[21] recently used a similar rationale in denying an injunction against an illegal strike of teachers in the absence of a showing of irreparable harm. The Court noted that the parties had not exhausted the possibilities of finding compromise in the collective bargaining process.

Generally, the proper course to follow is to obey the injunction while testing its validity through an appeal. For when employees disregard an injunction which later proves to be invalid, they nevertheless are usually found to be guilty of contempt of court.

In California, the rule is different. Generally, the violation of an order in excess of the jurisdiction of the issuing court cannot justify a judgment of contempt. In the work stoppage of the Sacramento County welfare workers, the California

Supreme Court applied[22] the general California rule after it found the injunction to have been overboard, and therefore, the lower court did not need to determine whether or not the strike was legal. As a result of this case, unions in California defy injunctions and then try to prove that the injunctive order was too vague and uncertain, or prescribed more than was necessary. The consequence has been a diminished use of injunctions to restrain California's public employees from striking and a reduction in the effectiveness of those that are issued.

In several other states, it is clear that there has been a reluctance to apply vigorously the letter of the law in imposing penalties. For example, in a strike involving the Troy firefighters, the New York Public Employment Relations Board refused to enforce the strike penalties since the city's lack of good faith in bargaining precipitated the strike.[23]

Thus, in the last five years, a number of states have become receptive to the concept of legalized public employee strikes, as indicated by their legislative actions or the decisions of their courts. Whether legislatures will continue to move toward eliminating prohibitions against work stoppages, and whether the courts will continue to limit injunctions of strikes, is anyone's guess. However, one recent decision created doubt about the effectiveness of legislative liberalization on the strike question. In the *Ross* v. *Sullivan* case,[24] involving the 1973 Philadelphia teachers' strike, the court found that the increased threat of gang warfare, the additional cost of beefing-up police patrols, and the threat to continued state funding of education were, in fact, a sufficient threat to health, safety, and welfare of the public to justify the injunction against that strike despite the presence of the legal right to strike. The decision has caused concern as to whether a legislative thrust toward relaxing the strike prohibition will really make any difference.

---

[20] *Westerly* v. *Teachers Association, 491 Government Employee Relations Report E-1, 1973.*

[21] *550 Government Employee Relations Report B-19,* April 15, 1974.

[22] 436 P. 24273, C8 Cal. 2d 137, 1968.

[23] *City of Troy* v. *Uniformed Firefighters Association,* 2 NYS Public Employment Relations Board 3077 (1969).

[24] *493 Government Employee Relations Report F-1,* 1973.

37. Wage Determination in the Public Sector*

Walter Fogel and David Lewin†

There is a growing body of evidence that government employment is attractive in terms of both wages and job security. A recent U.S. Bureau of Labor Statistics survey found that clerical, data processing, and manual workers employed by municipalities in 11 large urban areas were substantially better paid than their counterparts in private industry.[1] In most cases, federal employees in the same cities were also paid more than comparable private sector workers. Fringe benefits in the public sector are also as good or better than those in the private sector, according to a national survey of U.S. municipalities.[2] Furthermore, job hiring and tenure practices provide considerable security to public workers: In 1971, 57 percent of nonfarm private employees worked a full year, whereas in the public sector, the proportion was 77 percent.[3] Attractive wages and salaries, steady demand for public services, and tenure practices all combine to produce low rates of employee turnover—19 percent in state and local government and 22 percent in the federal service in 1970, compared to 58 percent in private manufacturing.[4]

Because these rather surprising findings conflict with popular notions about government pay, it is appropriate to examine the process of wage determination in the public sector and the outcomes of this process for different occupational groups in government employment. Governmental wages and salaries affect the respective government budget and, therefore, the citizens' tax burden; they influence the relative attractiveness of employment in the public and private sectors; and they are an important factor in the continuing debate over the size and role of government in American society.

THE PREVAILING WAGE PRINCIPLE

Almost all levels and agencies of government in this country, at the city level or higher, are

* Reprinted with permission from *Industrial and Labor Relations Review*, Vol. 27, No. 3 (April 1974), pp. 410–31. Copyright © 1974 by Cornell University. All rights reserved.

† Walter Fogel is Professor of Industrial Relations in the Graduate School of Management at the University of California, Los Angeles. David Lewin is Assistant Professor of Business at Columbia University. The authors appreciate the comments they received on this paper from John H. Keith, Jr., Paul J. McNulty, and Daniel J. B. Mitchell.

[1] Stephen H. Perloff, "Comparing Municipal Salaries with Industry and Federal Pay," *Monthly Labor Review*, Vol. 94, No. 10 (October 1971), pp. 46–50.

[2] Edward H. Friend, *First National Survey of Employee Benefits for Full-Time Personnel of U.S. Municipalities* (Washington, D.C.: Labor Management Relations Service, October 1972). As an example, municipal workers in New York City receive four weeks' paid vacation after just one year of service. In New York's private industries, less than one fourth of plant and one third of office workers are eligible for four weeks' vacation, *even after 15 years' service*. See U.S. Department of Labor, Bureau of Labor Statistics, *Wages and Benefits of Local Government Workers in the New York Area*, Regional Reports, No. 26 (Washington, D.C.: G.P.O., 1971), pp. 40–42.

[3] *Manpower Report of the President—March 1973* (Washington, D.C.: G.P.O., 1972), Table B-16, p. 185. Also see Bennett Harrison, "Public Employment and the Theory of the Dual Economy," in Harold L. Sheppard, Bennett Harrison, and William J. Spring, eds., *The Political Economy of Public Service Employment* (Lexington, Mass.: D.C. Heath and Co., 1972), pp. 66–67.

[4] Jacob J. Rutstein, "Survey of Current Personnel Systems in State and Local Governments," *Good Government*, Vol. 87 (Spring 1971), p. 6; and U.S. Civil Service Commission, Bureau of Manpower Information Systems, *Federal Civilian Manpower Statistics* (Washington, D.C., May 1971), Table 6, p. 14. See also Robert E. Hall, "Turnover in the Labor Force," *Brookings Papers on Economic Activity*, No. 3 (Washington, D.C.: The Brookings Institution, 1972), p. 715. The data cited in the text are separation rates.

required to pay wages comparable to those received by private employees performing similar work. This rule is commonly called the "prevailing wage" principle. For example, the Federal Salary Reform Act of 1962 requires that "federal pay rates be comparable with private enterprise pay rates for the same levels of work." The city of Los Angeles, one of the largest local government employers in the United States, is required by its charter to "provide a salary or wage at least equal to the prevailing salary or wage for the same quality of service rendered to private employers."[5]

These prevailing wage requirements are sensible in terms of both equity and efficiency. The output of government does not pass through the marketplace where its relative worth can be assessed by customers. In the absence of a product market discipline imposed on pay practices (a discipline which, incidentally, is not present in all parts of the private sector), what could be more fair than to pay government employees what their private industry counterparts are getting? Furthermore, to attract employees of at least average quality to the government, the pay offered must be comparable to that available in the private sector. For the government to pay more than the private sector, however, would be unnecessary and would waste government revenues. Therefore, the prevailing wage rule is efficient as well as equitable.

On the surface, the procedure seems quite simple and "fair" for all concerned. As one examines the application of this rule closely, however, things appear less simple and certainly not "fair" for everyone. Aside from the administrative problems of applying the prevailing wage rule to an occupational structure that may include hundreds or even thousands of job classifications, this rule is dependent on the existence of smoothly functioning private labor markets. If these markets all operated like the textbook model of perfect competition, the prevailing wage rule would always provide efficient and equitable wages—and, in fact, such laws would probably not be needed at all. Private markets, however, are influenced by noncompetitive forces and also contain jobs that differ widely with respect to their nonwage attractiveness. The latter phenomenon produces a range of wage rates, rather than a single rate; the noncompetitive forces often produce a wage

(or range of wages) above or below that which would prevail in a truly competitive market.

The existence of a range of wages for most occupations presents difficult administrative problems for government wage-fixing authorities. What rules should be applied to the range in order to come up with a prevailing wage? Should the average of the entire range be used, or the first quartile, or the mean, or the median? The decision could be made simpler by precisely defining the labor markets in which the government employer must compete for a work force. Rarely is this done, however. Instead, it will be shown that the more common practice is to seek wage information over the geographical area included within the governmental jurisdiction and then only from medium- and large-sized employers. Although this practice holds down the cost of wage surveys—surveying small firms or firms outside of the local market is costly relative to the information obtained—it also imparts an upward bias to prevailing wage determinations, since only the "core" economy is surveyed. The "periphery" economy, which pays low wages, is excluded.[6]

OTHER PROBLEMS

The existence of a private sector market that pays wages that are either above or below the competitive wage presents a more difficult policy problem for governmental wage setters. Suppose that a private sector wage is depressed because the market is monopsonistic or, more likely, because discrimination or other factors that impede mobility confine some workers to a small part of the total labor market. In such cases, is it appropriate for government to pay a wage that has resulted from the market power of the employer or from employee inability to compete? We will show that many government wage-setting authorities apparently think not, and in these cases they will often establish rates above those prevailing in such private markets.

This assumption is the basis for some of the support currently voiced for public employment programs. Advocates of these programs assume that governments will provide low-skilled workers with better compensation than they now receive in private "secondary" markets and hope that the

[5] Charter of the City of Los Angeles, Section 425. Also see *Pay Policies for Public Personnel: A Report of the Municipal and County Government Section of Town Hall* (Los Angeles, 1961), p. 15.

[6] These concepts underlie developing theories of labor market behavior. See Harrison, "Public Employment and the Theory of the Duel Economy," especially pp. 45–55; and Barry Bluestone, "The Tripartite Economy: Labor Markets and the Working Poor," *Poverty and Human Resources*, Vol. 6 (July–August 1970), pp. 15–35.

scope of public employment efforts will be large enough to raise wages and improve working conditions in the "secondary" markets.[7] The latter objective is almost certain to be frustrated, however, since labor supply to most "secondary" markets is highly elastic at prevailing wages over the range relevant to feasible public employment programs.

On the other hand, suppose that a union, professional association, or licensing agency has achieved a wage above that which would otherwise prevail. For example, Lewis has estimated that, on average, American unions have a 7 to 15 percent impact on the wages of those for whom they bargain,[8] and, because of their ability to influence labor supply, some unions, especially craft unions, have an even larger impact on wages. Should governments match wage rates that have been achieved through the exercise of private market power and, in effect, support and expand such power? For reasons to be stated later, we assume that, in their wage-setting actions, governments will indeed tend to match private market rates that have been raised through market power, even in instances in which lower rates would clearly attract an adequate supply of labor.

Another potential bias in government wage-setting practices occurs because of the narrow view of employment compensation contained in most prevailing wage statutes. Any reasonably sophisticated view of the labor market recognizes that the wage is merely the most variable part of employment compensation, the part that firms most easily adjust to offset other aspects of compensation (fringe benefits, working conditions, location, etc.) that are discernibly advantageous or disadvantageous. A private firm can experiment with its wage rates, relative to those of other firms, in order to discover the rates that, along with other characteristics of the firm, will attract an adequate work force. In contrast, government employers required to pay prevailing wages almost always interpret that requirement as precluding any attempt to take into account the attractiveness of nonwage aspects of government employment. As previously noted, one such nonwage aspect—job security—appears to be very attractive in government compared to the private sector. Failure to consider this difference in job

security on the part of government wage setters would seem, *a priori*, to produce public wage rates that are higher than necessary to attract a work force.

Finally, for some public sector jobs (e.g., policemen, firemen, social workers), there is either no private market or, because of government's dominant employment position in these occupations, wage rates in the private market that does exist are pegged to the public sector rather than the reverse. Government employers probably overestimate the number of occupations of this type, but some do exist. How should the pay for such jobs be established?

To summarize, four aspects of labor markets create serious policy problems whenever public employers attempt to translate prevailing wage statutes into wage rates for their employees: the wide range of wages paid for most private sector jobs; the existence of wage rates established through the exercise of market power; the multifaceted nature of employment compensation; and the absence of a private market for some government occupations.[9] Because of these factors, much discretion must be exercised by public authorities in implementing prevailing wage statutes and fixing public sector wages. It will be argued here that this discretion in decision making, plus the political processes involved in wage setting, produce upwardly biased wage rates for most government jobs.

THE POLITICS OF WAGE SETTING

Recently, several analysts have summarized the shortcomings of traditional wage theory in explaining public sector wage determination.[10] Major weaknesses include the absence of a motive for profit maximization in government and

---

[7] See Sheppard, Harrison, and Spring, *The Political Economy of Public Service Employment*, pp. 13–82.

[8] H. Gregg Lewis, *Unionism and Relative Wages in the United States* (Chicago: University of Chicago Press, 1963), p. 193.

[9] We have purposely avoided some additional, largely administrative problems of governmental wage determination, e.g., deciding which public jobs should be directly compared with their private sector counterparts. These problems are reviewed in David Lewin, "The Prevailing Wage Principle and Public Wage Decisions," *Public Personnel Management*, Vol. 3 (November–December 1974), forthcoming.

[10] Robert J. Carlsson and James W. Robinson, "Toward a Public Employment Wage Theory," *Industrial and Labor Relations Review*, Vol. 22, No. 2 (January 1969) pp. 243–48; Donald Gerwin, "Compensation Decisions in Public Organizations," *Industrial Relations*, Vol. 9, No. 2 (February 1969), pp. 175–84; Robert J. Carlsson and James W. Robinson, "Criticism and Comment: Compensation Decisions in Public Organizations," *Industrial Relations*, Vol. 9, No. 1 (October 1969), pp. 111–13; and James A. Craft, "Toward a Public Employee Wage Theory: Comment," *Industrial and Labor Relations Review*, Vol. 23, No. 1 (October 1969), pp. 89–95.

the related lack of a conventional demand curve for labor. Public employers' demand curves are inferred indirectly through "voter expressed demands for government services and directly through political bargaining between governments and employee groups," rather than through a marginal revenue product curve.[11] Thus, construction of a relevant public sector wage model apparently requires more explicit consideration of the motivations of public managers and public workers, as well as the political processes through which these motivations are filtered.

In his seminal work on democratic theory, Anthony Downs notes that "the main goal of every party (defined as a team of individuals) is the winning of elections. . . . Thus, all its actions are aimed at maximizing votes."[12] In pursuit of that goal, parties view the electorate as a number of interest groups, and they seek to determine and respond to the relative importance of such groups.

Thus, in their wage-setting decisions, political bodies are sensitive to two constituencies. First, there are the government employees directly affected by public wage decisions. In general, the larger the group whose wages will be affected by a legislative decision, the more responsive elected decision makers will be to the preferences of this group. The second constituency is the general public. The public is, of course, interested in keeping down its tax burden, but beyond this general constraint, it is usually uninformed and not especially interested in the specifics of government wage setting.

In order to influence government policy-making in any area of decision, a citizen must be continuously well-informed about events therein. . . . The expense of such awareness is so great that no citizen can afford to bear it in every policy area. . . . If he is going to exercise any influence at all, he must limit his awareness to areas where intervention pays off most and costs least.[13]

Consequently,

many voters do not bother to discover their true views before voting, and most citizens are not well enough informed to influence directly the formulation of those policies that affect them.[14]

These considerations suggest that lawmakers are relatively more responsive to the first group—

those directly affected by wage decisions—than to the second. Government employees will watch lawmakers' reactions to their proposed wage increases, and these reactions, especially negative reactions, can be the major determinants of employee voting behavior in subsequent elections. The general public, however, will probably not recall the lawmakers' votes on government wage questions and, furthermore, will be concerned with a variety of other issues in its voting decisions. In general, then, the combination of the direct interest of government employees in their wages and the diffusion of issues (including public sector pay issues) among the general constituency create the potential for an upward bias in public sector wage rates. Obviously, the potential bias increases with the size of the government sector in question.

Particular circumstances, of course, can operate to restrain this bias or even reverse it. At times, the public strongly oposes (further) tax increases; at these times, lawmakers are quite cautious in their wage decisions. Indeed, in these instances, lawmakers may be able to profit from negative decisions on the wages of some kinds of public employees, either because the group in question is in public disfavor or because it lacks political clout. College and university faculties are good illustrations of this phenomenon. Policemen may currently illustrate the opposite phenomenon, i.e., a situation in which lawmakers gain from making positive wage decisions for a group riding the crest of public favor.

An organization of public employees will attempt to exploit this political condition. First, it will try to bring about solidarity among employees who are to be directly affected by wage decisions. Second, it will attempt to convey the force of this solidarity to the appropriate political body. Finally, it may attempt to gain broad support for its wage objectives by appealing directly to the public. At least part of the relative increase in public sector wage rates over the last 10 to 15 years is due to the effectiveness with which some public employee organizations have carried out these activities.[15]

---

[11] Mark V. Pauley, "Discussion Comments: Manpower Shortages in Local Government Employment," *American Economic Review*, Vol. 59, No. 2 (May 1969), p. 565.

[12] Anthony Downs, *An Economic Theory of Democracy* (New York: Harper and Row, 1957), p. 35.

[13] Ibid., p. 258.

[14] Ibid., p. 259.

[15] The other major influence over this period has been the growth in the number of public employees, as this number (votes) has been brought to bear on the wage-setting process.

Some authors casually assign a large wage impact to public employee unions. Cf. Harry H. Wellington and Ralph K. Winter, Jr., *The Unions and the Cities* (Washington, D.C.: The Brookings Institution, 1971), especially pp. 7–32. Yet, as Lewin suggests, the extent to which governmental wage increases are due to unionization as distinct from the increasing politicization of public wage-setting processes is not clear. See David Lewin, "Public Employ-

In summary, because of the nature of the political process involved, there is a tendency for lawmakers and other elected officials to support the wage perferences of government employees. Indeed, "the position of public employees as voters and opinion-makers who partially determine whether or not the employer retains his job" has been cited as the major factor underlying motivational differences between public employers and private, profit-maximizing employers.[16] The tendency toward "high" public wages varies with the size of the group in question, its public "image," and its cohesiveness. Finally, this tendency has been increasing as government services have expanded and as employee organizations continue to develop in the public sector.

MAJOR PATTERNS

In the balance of this paper, we shall present evidence showing that wage determination in the public sector tends to be characterized by the following practices:

1. Government employers deal with the range of private sector wages for any given occupation, in part, by excluding small firms from their wage surveys. This has the effect of giving an upward bias to the results of such surveys.

2. The public sector pays rates that are higher than existing private rates for jobs for which the private sector wage is relatively low because of monopsony or highly elastic supplies of unskilled laborers who are relatively immobile.

3. The public sector pays wages that are at least equal to those that exist in private markets where wage levels have been increased by supply-side institutional power.

4. Public agencies do not take into account favorable nonwage aspects of public sector employment or unfavorable aspects of private sector employment that have affected the private market wage.

5. Administrative procedures used to fix wages for "unique" public sector jobs bias the results upward.

These practices result from the effect of the political process underlying public sector wage setting on the discretionary areas inherent in the prevailing wage concept as it is applied to imperfect labor markets. The general result of these practices is that public sector wages tend to exceed those of the private sector for all occupations except high level managers and professionals. These relationships flow directly from the politicization of public sector wage determination. There are many more votes in the low-skill and middle-skill occupations than in managerial-professional jobs. Furthermore, public employees in the latter jobs tend to be more visible to a public that is skeptical, at best, of the contributions of "highly paid" government employees.

THE EVIDENCE

Government employers deal with the range of private sector wages for any given occupation, in part, by excluding small firms from their wage surveys. The Bureau of Labor Statistics (BLS) annually conducts wage surveys of (*a*) office clerical, (*b*) professional and technical, (*c*) maintenance and power plant, and (*d*) custodial and material movement occupations in more than 90 major metropolitan areas of the United States. In reporting the results of these surveys, BLS states explicitly that "establishments having fewer than a prescribed number of workers are omitted because they tend to furnish insufficient employment in the occupations to warrant inclusion."[17] Therefore, to be included in the survey in most areas, an establishment must employ at least 50 workers in manufacturing; transportation, communication, and other public utilities; wholesale trade; retail trade; finance, insurance, and real estate; or services. In 12 of the largest areas, the minimum establishment size is 100 workers in manufacturing; transportation, communication and other public utilities; and retail trade.[18] Because wages vary directly with firm size,[19]

ment Relations: Confronting the Issues," *Industrial Relations*, Vol. 12, No. 3 (October 1973), pp. 309–21.

[16] Bernard Lentz, "A Democratic Theory of Economics: Wage and Salary Determination in Municipal Employment" (Ph.D. dissertation, Yale University, in progress). Stanley notes further that "employees in the public sector exert influence not only as employees, as do private workers, but also as pressure groups and voting citizens." See David Stanley, *Managing Local Government under Union Pressure* (Washington, D.C.: The Brookings Institution, 1972), p. 20.

[17] See, for example, U.S. Department of Labor, Bureau of Labor Statistics, *Area Wage Survey, The Los Angeles–Long Beach and Anaheim–Santa Ana–Garden Grove, California, Metropolitan Area, March 1972*, Bulletin No. 1725–76 (Washington, D.C.: G.P.O., 1972), p. 1.

[18] U.S. Department of Labor, Bureau of Labor Statistics, *Wage Differences among Metropolitan Areas, 1970–71* (Washington, D.C., July 1972), p. 1. Major exclusions from BLS wage surveys are construction, the extractive industries, and government.

[19] See Richard A. Lester, "Pay Differentials by Size of Establishment," *Industrial Relations*, Vol. 7, No. 1 (October 1967), pp. 57–67.

these procedures have the effect of biasing survey results upward. Public wages set on the basis of survey rates will be similarly biased.

Since 1959, the BLS has also conducted the *National Survey of Professional, Administrative, Technical and Clerical Pay* (PATC), the results of which are used in the determination of wages for white-collar (i.e., "general schedule") civil service workers as well as employees in the postal field service and those covered by a few other statutory pay systems. Minimum establishment size requirements in this survey range from 100 employees in most industry divisions to 250 employees in manufacturing and retail trade. As in the area wage surveys, exclusion of relatively small, low-wage establishments results in upwardly biased wages in the PATC survey.

State and local government employers, especially those with large labor forces, sometimes undertake their own wage surveys. For example, in Los Angeles, four local public jurisdictions jointly conduct an annual survey of wages and salaries in Los Angeles County. To be included in this survey, an establishment regardless of its industry classification must employ more than 250 persons. Industry coverage parallels that of the BLS survey.

The exclusion of small establishments from public wage surveys produces both a direct and indirect upward bias in the survey results. The direct bias occurs, of course, because of the positive relationship that exists between size of firm and wage levels. The indirect bias occurs from the overrepresentation of high-wage industries and underrepresentation of low-wage industries produced by the exclusion of small establishments. For example, wholesale and retail trade accounted for only 9 percent of surveyed employment in Los Angeles County in 1970, when actually 26 percent of all workers in that county were employed in those industries. On the other hand, employment in the manufacturing and utilities-transportation sectors is overrepresented in this survey.[20]

The magnitude of the bias produced by the exclusion of small firms from wage surveys is probably large. Approximately 60 percent of all nonfarm private sector employees work in establishments employing fewer than 250 employees.[21]

Such workers are likely to be paid 15 to 20 percent less than employees of establishments with 1,000 or more employees.[22]

LOW-WAGE JOBS

The public sector pays more than existing private rates for jobs for which the private sector wage is relatively low because of monopsony or highly elastic supplies of unskilled laborers who are relatively immobile. Rather than ferret out the existence of monopsony and labor supply characteristics of private labor markets, we will present evidence on the simpler proposition that, *for most low-wage occupations, government pays more than the private sector.*

Table 1 shows that there is proportionately more low-wage employment in the private sector of the American economy than in the governmental sector. For example, among full-time, year-round, privately employed workers, about 12 percent earned less than $4,000 and 42 percent earned less than $7,000 in 1971, when the comparable proportions in the public sector were only 6 and 30 percent. Note that the proportion of low-wage employment is particularly small in the federal government, in which the median annual salary was $11,809 in 1971.[23] The relative advantage of the public sector would be increased by inclusion of private self-employed workers in the comparisons and, of course, by inclusion of part-time and part-year workers.

These public-private differences in earnings distributions could reflect differences in occupational composition rather than rates of compensation. Table 2 therefore, presents salary comparisons for low-wage occupations common to municipal, federal, and private employment in 11 large cities, including 5 of the 6 U.S. cities with populations over 1 million. In nine of these cities, municipal governments consistently paid higher salaries than private employers in 1970. Only in New Orleans and Kansas City did private-sector pay exceed municipal pay for the occupations listed. The size of the municipal-private differential is often substantial. Of the 56 observations in Table 2, 27 show a municipal wage advantage of 10 percent or more and 19 show a

---

[20] David Lewin, "Wage Determination in Local Government Employment" (Ph.D. dissertation, University of California, Los Angeles, 1971), pp. 77–110. The Los Angeles survey does not weight its sample results to reflect the actual industry composition of the county.

[21] U.S. Bureau of the Census, *County Business Patterns: 1970* (Washington, D.C.: G.P.O., 1971), p. 29.

[22] Lester, "Pay Differentials by Size of Establishment," p. 59.

[23] U.S. Civil Service Commission, Bureau of Manpower Information Systems, *Pay Structure of the Federal Civil Service, June 30, 1971* (Washington, D.C., 1971). Table 2, p. 18. The data are for domestically employed general schedule employees.

TABLE 1   Earnings Distribution for Full-Time, Year-Round Wage and Salary Workers in the United States, by Sex and Employment Sector for 1971 (in percentages)

Employment Sector and Sex	Earning Below				
	$3,000	$4,000	$5,000	$6,000	$7,000
Private sector					
Male....................................	3.4	6.5	11.3	18.2	26.3
Female..................................	11.4	25.7	45.0	64.3	77.9
Average................................	5.8	12.3	21.5	32.1	41.8
Public sector					
State and local government					
Male....................................	1.5	3.6	7.2	12.5	19.8
Female..................................	4.4	10.8	20.3	32.3	45.8
Average................................	2.6	6.4	12.4	20.3	30.1
Federal government					
(both sexes)...........................	0	1.6	2.7	6.6	16.2

Source: U.S. Bureau of the Census, "Money Income in 1971 of Families and Persons in the U.S.," *Current Population Reports,* Series P-60, No. 85 (Washington, D.C.: G.P.O., 1972), Tables 52 and 58, pp. 135–38; and U.S. Civil Commission, *Pay Structure of the Federal Civil Service* (Washington, D.C.: G.P.O., June 30, 1971), Tables 11–14, pp. 29–32.

municipal advantage of at least 20 percent.[24] It should be remembered, as well, that the private sector wages that are used to make the comparisons in Table 2 contain some upward bias, since they do not encompass the rates paid by small establishments.

The superiority of municipal over private pay in major American cities is further accentuated when hours of work are considered. In Los Angeles, Houston, Kansas City, and Atlanta, municipal white-collar employees worked a "standard" 40-hour week in 1970, but in Philadelphia, the work week for these employees was 37.5 hours; in Chicago, Boston, New Orleans, and Buffalo, 35 hours; in Newark, 30 hours; and in New York City, municipal employees worked a 35-hour week for nine months and a 30-hour week during the remainder of the year.[25] Although these differences in work schedules partially reflect differences in area practices generally, the municipal work week is typically shorter than the work week in private employment. For example, in New York City in 1970, "96 percent of the white-collar workers in local government worked 35 hours or less per week as compared with 58 percent of private office workers."[26] Thus, pay differentials between municipal

and private employment are even greater when considered on an hourly rather than monthly basis.

The pattern of relatively high government pay for low-skill occupations may be even more pronounced in suburban areas than in central cities. This very tentative conclusion emerges from analysis of recently published data, presented in Table 3, on the salaries of local government workers in the New York City area. For the individual occupations shown in that table, average salaries in the two types of suburban governments ranged from 18 percent above to 6 percent below those in New York City. In only two cases, however, did suburban pay fall below central city pay in the New York area. Pay differentials between New York counties and the City exceeded 10 percent in four occupations; differentials between suburban municipalities and New York City exceeded 10 percent in five occupations. It is possible, of course, that this differential is "neutralized" by similar differentials in private industry salaries between the suburbs and the central city.

Relatively high minimum wages in government employment are sometimes explicitly mandated by legislative statute. In 1970, for example, the salary ordinance governing the largest local government employer in Southern California, the county of Los Angeles, required that, "notwithstanding any other provisions of this ordinance, the minimum salary for all positions . . . shall be $417 per month . . . or $2.40 per

[24] As a proportion of private pay, municipal salaries for the entire group of 16 office clerical positions surveyed by the BLS were as follows: New York—101; Chicago—108; Los Angeles—118; Philadelphia—133; Boston—109; New Orleans—93; Kansas City—97; Atlanta—108; Buffalo—122; and Newark—106. Perloff, "Comparing Municipal Salaries with Industry and Federal Pay," Table 2, p. 49.

[25] Ibid., Table 1, pp. 47–48.

[26] U.S. Department of Labor, Bureau of Labor Statistics, Middle Atlantic Regional Office, *Wages and Benefits*

of Local Government Workers in the New York Area, Regional Report No. 26 (Washington, D.C.: G.P.O., December 1971), p. 53.

TABLE 2   A Comparison of Monthly Salaries in Municipal Government and Private Industry in 7 Low-Wage Occupations and 11 Cities for 1970 (private industry salary = 100)

Occupation	Equivalent Federal Salary (GS) Grade	New York	Chicago	Los Angeles	Phila-delphia	Houston	Newark	Boston	New Orleans	Kansas City	Atlanta	Buffalo
Messenger..............	1	114	98	107	136	123	125	107	86	—	—	—
Keypunch operator—B..........	2	102	101	120	114	111	120	103	91	95	104	115
Switchboard operator—B........	2	105	112	134	—	142	107	—	105	—	119	135
Typist—B................	2	102	105	123	142	—	107	102	89	101	102	122
Tabulator machine, operator—C........	2	109	107	—	140	—	—	—	—	—	—	—
Tabulator machine, operator—B........	3	—	103	—	131	—	—	114	83	—	112	—
Janitors, porters, and cleaners..........	—	98	137	122	131	124	109	127	88	95	100	111

Source: Stephen H. Perloff, "Comparing Municipal Salaries with Industry and Federal Pay," *Monthly Labor Review*, Vol. 94, No. 10 (October 1971), Tables 1–3, pp. 47–50.

Occupation	New York City Municipal Government Earnings (dollars)	New York Area Earnings as a Percentage of New York City	
		Counties	Suburban Cities and Towns
Typist—B..	102.50	102	100
Messenger.......................................	103.00	102	112
Keypunch operator—B...........................	106.00	108	116
General stenographer............................	107.50	102	107
Accounting clerk—B..............................	108.00	116	113
Transcribing machine operator—B...............	111.00	101	94
Janitors, porters, cleaners.......................	111.20	112	113
Bookkeeping machine operator—B...............	113.50	118	100
Switchboard operator—B.........................	114.00	97	106
Senior stenographer.............................	125.00	113	111

* Includes New York City municipal government and the governments of five counties and 53 cities and towns located in the New York standard metropolitan statistical area.
    Source: U.S. Department of Labor, Bureau of Labor Statistics, *Wages and Benefits of Local Government Workers in the New York Area,* Regional Reports, Number 26, December 1971 (Washington, D.C.: G.P.O., 1972), Tables 2, 4, and 6; and pp. 16, 21, and 25.

hour, as the case may be."[27] Similarly, the city of Los Angeles required that

the salary rate of any person . . . employed in any class, the salary schedule of which is fixed at Schedule 23 or lower, and who is receiving salary at a lower rate than the third step of the schedule for such class . . . shall be increased to the third step of the schedule prescribed for his class of position.[28]

The city's statute resulted in a minimum wage of $2.54 per hour in 1969. Minimum wages in the county and city of Los Angeles were thus 50 percent and 59 percent higher, respectively, than the minimum hourly wage of $1.60 then mandated for private employment under the Fair Labor Standards Act. These ordinances account for at least some of the public-private differentials that exist in the Los Angeles area, as shown in Table 2 and also, using different sources and data, in Table 4.

There is at least one important occupation, however, in which government wage levels have often accurately mirrored monopsony (low-wage) conditions in the private market. This is the case of hospital nurses as described by Devine.[29]

Private labor markets for hospital nurses are frequently characterized by monopsony, with the local hospital association serving as the cartelizing agency. Devine's survey of hospital associations in major metropolitan areas found each one maintaining in the mid-1960s a "wage stabilization" program for nurses. These collusive agreements were predicated on the view that it is "undesirable for council members to enter into a competitive race among themselves to see which can offer the most favorable conditions of employment."[30]

Although local government hospitals are typically not enrolled in the hospital associations, their wage policies (and rates) do reflect institutional wage determinations in the private sector. Municipal hospitals have continually incurred shortages of nurses (vacancy rates have sometimes exceeded 20 percent in recent years; this is about three times larger than the average overall vacancy rate in local government employment).[31] In the late 1960s, for example, the county of Los Angeles experienced a 27 percent vacancy rate in its hospital nursing positions,

---

[27] County of Los Angeles, *Salary Ordinance of Los Angeles County,* Ordinance No. 6222, as amended to July 1, 1969, p. 30

[28] City of Los Angeles, *Salary Standardization Ordinance,* Ordinance No. 89, 100, revised to September 20, 1966, amended to July 1, 1969, p. 25.

[29] Eugene J. Devine, *Analysis of Manpower Shortages in Local Government* (New York: Praeger, 1970), pp. 49–62. For econometric support of the monopsony thesis,

see R. W. Hurd, "Equilibrium Vacancies in a Labor-Market Dominated by Non-Profit Firms: The 'Shortage' of Nurses," *Review of Economics and Statistics,* Vol. 50 (May 1973), pp. 234–40.

[30] Devine, *Analysis of Manpower Shortages in Local Government,* p. 56.

[31] During 1970, vacancy rates of 6.6 and 6.7 percent were reported for counties and cities respectively. See Rutstein, "Survey of Current Personnel Systems in State and Local Governments," p. 6.

TABLE 4 Average Monthly Salaries in Low-Skill Occupations in the Private and Public Sectors for the County and City of Los Angeles, Fiscal Year 1969–70

| | Median Monthly Salary (dollars) | | | Differences between Public and Private Sectors (percentages) | |
| | Private Sector | Public Sector | | | |
Occupation		County	City	County	City
Laundry worker.............................. 287		428	—	49.1	—
Institutional food service worker............... 358		447	—	24.9	—
Hospital attendant........................... 385		453	—	17.7	—
Clerk.. 385		428	464	11.1	20.5
Clerk typist................................... 418		447	489	6.9	17.0
Custodian.................................... 447		489	491	9.4	9.8
Gardener.................................... 495		—	591	—	19.4
Transcriber typist............................. 480		518	—	7.9	—
Bookkeeping machine operator................ 475		489	516	2.9	8.6
Telephone operator........................... 474		489	505	3.1	6.5
Vocational nurse.............................. 494		577	—	16.8	—

Sources: Derived from City of Los Angeles et al., *Wage and Salary Survey in Los Angeles County*, March 1, 1969 (Los Angeles: City of Los Angeles, Printing Division, 1969); County of Los Angeles, *Salary Ordinance of Los Angeles County*, Ordinance Number 6222, as amended to July 1, 1969; and City of Los Angeles, City Administrative Officer, *Salary Recommendations* (processed, April 1969).

and vacancy rates for nurses in New York City municipal hospitals were about 60 percent![32] Salaries for nurses in each of these cities were based on rates set by the respective local hospital associations. Not surprisingly, both of these cities invested heavily in recruitment activities, frequently extending their search for nurses nationwide. The federal government, on the other hand, experienced less severe shortages of nurses than local governments (and some private hospitals), apparently because, under administrative provisions of the Federal Salary Reform Act of 1962, federal hospitals raised their nurses' salaries well above those offered by other hospitals.

In recent years, the loosening of cartel arrangements among private hospitals, along with a more aggressive collective bargaining stance among nurses' unions, have contributed to a substantial improvement in the relative wage position of hospital nurses, including those employed by government.

CRAFT WAGES

The public sector pays wages at least equal to those that exist in private markets where wage levels have been increased by supply-side institutional power. Among American unions, market power is perhaps most strongly exercised by construction unions. Moreover, governmental pay policies have broadened the wage impact of

construction unions in the private sector and have extended it to public employment.

For example, at the federal level, the Davis-Bacon Act requires private contractors engaged in construction work valued at $2,000 or more and paid for by federal funds to compensate employees on the basis of prevailing wages. Secretaries of Labor have generally considered the union rate to be the prevailing rate even in nonunion areas. Consequently, "unions need only secure a wage increase in a few locations where their control of the labor supply is firm . . . and under the law the government extends the wage gain far and wide."[33] It is little wonder that this act has been labeled a "superminimum wage law."[34]

At the state and local level, especially in very large cities, this approach has been carried one step further: Through explicit policy or administrative practice, government craft employees are often paid construction industry rates and frequently only the union rates within construction. In these cases, public employers ignore the lower wages paid by nonconstruction employers for the same jobs. This practice undoubtedly accounts, at least in part, for the relatively high salaries for public craft workers in 5 of the 11 major cities for which data are presented in Table 5.

[33] James W. Kuhn, "The Riddle of Inflation: A New Answer," *The Public Interest*, Vol. 27 (Spring 1972), p. 73.

[34] Gordon F. Bloom and Herbert R. Northrup, *Economics of Labor Relations*, 7th ed. (Homewood, Ill.: Richard D. Irwin, Inc., 1973), p. 493.

[32] Devine, *Analysis of Manpower Shortages in Local Government*, pp. 51 and 57.

TABLE 5   Municipal Salaries as a Proportion of Private Industry Pay in Selected Crafts, 1970* (private industry salary = 100)

Occupation	New York	Chicago	Los Angeles	Phila-delphia	Houston	Boston	New Orleans	Kansas City	Atlanta	Buffalo	Newark
Carpenter, maintenance	162	125	118	106	91	91	76	80	98	88	141
Electrician, maintenance	162	148	121	107	113	—	87	87	91	82	141
Helper, maintenance trades	—	—	—	113	—	99	—	—	—	83	171
Painters, maintenance	136	108	107	114	95	101	75	81	100	93	139
Plumbers, maintenance	160	111	121	113	—	—	—	—	—	—	144

* Comparisons are of monthly salaries.
Source: Stephen H. Perloff, "Comparing Municipal Salaries with Industry and Federal Pay," *Monthly Labor Review*, Vol. 94, No. 10 (October 1971), p. 49.

Public employers are not unaware of the substantial public-private differentials for craft workers. In Los Angeles, for example, local government employers annually obtain data on craft wages in all sectors of the private market. Yet, when setting wages for municipal craft workers, these employers discard all market rates obtained through their survey and adopt, instead, construction industry-negotiated wage levels. This occurs despite important differences (to be discussed later) in the characteristics of craft employment between the public and private sectors. Consequently, an analysis of the 1969 local agency survey (not the BLS data reported in Table 5) showed that Los Angeles government agencies paid craft workers salaries that were between 10 and 46 percent higher than those paid by private employers, and those differences would have been even larger if small (low-wage) employers had been included in the government's wage survey.[35]

NONWAGE FACTORS

Public agencies do not take into account favorable nonwage aspects of public sector employment or unfavorable aspects of private sector employment that have affected the private market wage. As previously noted, government employment generally offers more favorable fringe benefits, employment stability, and job security than private employment. Yet government employers fail to take this into account when establishing their own wage rates.

In addition to the evidence previously cited of the favorable nonwage aspects of much government employment,[36] it is useful to examine comparative turnover data in more detail. Among 33 federal agencies reporting separation data, only 3—Interior, Agriculture, and the Tennessee Valley Authority—experienced rates higher than those experienced by manufacturing industries in 1972, and the layoff rate alone was 75 percent lower in the federal service than in manufactur-

ing.[37] Although state governments experienced about the same separation rate as the federal sector (22 percent) in 1970, county and city governments experienced rates only three quarters and two thirds as large, respectively, as the federal government.[38] These rates are especially significant in light of the fact that local governments employ more than two and one-half times as many workers as state governments in the United States.

The failure of public employers to consider the nonwage aspects of employment is most generally shown by the methods commonly used to implement the prevailing wage rule. When they are undertaken, governmental wage surveys generally solicit only wage and salary information. Recently, the Department of Labor expanded some (but not all) of its area wage surveys to include selected fringe benefits, such as work scheduling, paid vacations and holidays, and health and welfare plans.[39] Most state and local public employers, however, have not similarly intensified their survey efforts, and the government has not yet sought unemployment or turnover data from private employers as part of its wage-setting process. Thus, public employers focus too narrowly on wages to the exclusion of other factors determining comparative net advantage in the labor market.

Inconsistent treatment of nonwage differences in employment is shown by pay determination procedures for public craft occupations. On the one hand, the higher public fringe benefits are often recognized by setting public wages for these jobs at the level of unionized industry rates minus some percentage reduction for the superior fringe benefits paid by the public jurisdiction. On the other hand, use of the negotiated construction rates ignores the fact that most public sector craft employees are more fully employed and apparently perform much more nonconstruction work (for which private sector wages are lower) than private sector construction workers. These procedures help to bring about heavy civil

---

[35] Derived from Lewin, "Wage Determination in Local Government," pp. 187–90.

Because construction unions have recently shown increased willingness to exercise market power, the differences between public and private sector craft wages are probably even larger than suggested here. By 1972, the hourly earnings of construction workers were about 60 percent more than those of manufacturing workers; in 1947, the differential was little more than 25 percent. See *Manpower Report of the President—March, 1973* (Washington, D.C., 1972). Table C-3 pp. 190–91.

[36] See the first paragraph of this article and the sources cited in footnotes 2, 3, and 4.

[37] Derived from U.S. Civil Service Commission, Bureau of Manpower Information Systems, *Federal Civilian Manpower Statistics* (Washington, D.C., March 1973), Tables 7 and 8, pp. 17–18.

[38] Rutstein, "Survey of Current Personnel Systems in State and Local Governments," p. 6. In this survey, counties reported a separation rate of 16.6 percent, cities 14.5 percent.

[39] See U.S. Department of Labor, Bureau of Labor Statistics, Area Wage Survey, *The Newark and Jersey City, New Jersey, Metropolitan Areas, January 1972,* Bulletin 1925–52 (Washington, D.C., 1972), pp. 28–35.

service filing and waiting lists for most craft occupations in many cities.[40]

UNIQUE JOBS

Administrative procedures used to fix wages for "unique" public sector jobs bias the results upward. Various methods are used to set pay for jobs unique to the public sector.[41] Although these procedures do not uniformly result in upwardly biased wage rates, on balance, they have probably escalated rates beyond efficient levels.[42]

Because private market wage data are unavailable for jobs exclusive to government, public administrators often set pay for these positions on the basis of interagency or intergovernmental comparisons. For example, in Los Angeles, the Department of Water and Power, a city agency with independent salary-setting authority, has historically been a high-wage employer, compensating some uniquely public occupations at rates more than 20 percent above those of other departments. Because of this, city agencies in similar positions face continual upward pressures on wages, even in cases in which substantial civil service eligibility and waiting lists are maintained.

The county of Los Angeles determines pay for social work, probation, property appraisal, sanitation, and inspection positions by comparing its rates with those of the ten other largest counties in California and then making any pay adjustments required to maintain at least a third-place ranking among these governments.[43] Because the county is the principal employer of public service personnel in southern California, its wage decisions set the pattern for other governmental bodies in the area. To the extent that the other large California counties (and local governments) make similar pay comparisons, this practice creates the potential for circular wage escalation in positions exclusive to the public sector.

A procedure that establishes wage rates for many "unique" public employees is the "parity" arrangement. Wage parity between policemen and firemen is especially widespread: This arrangement was adhered to by more than 60 percent of all American municipalities in 1969. Because of dissimilarities between the labor markets for policemen and firemen, the parity rule probably results in the underpayment of policemen and certainly the overpayment of firemen, judged by market criteria.[44]

Shortages of policemen and excess supplies of firemen are well known and widespread. In Los Angeles, the police vacancy rate in 1970 was about twice that for all other occupations, a situation that mirrors the national pattern. New York City, which has the country's largest police and fire departments, reports substantial queues for fire positions and, like Los Angeles, administers entrance examinations for the fire service only once every two to three years. In contrast, New York has experienced shortages in the police ranks and has counteracted this by investing heavily in the recruitment of police applicants and offering police entrance examinations several times each year.[45] The attractiveness of a fireman's job, compared to a policeman's at the same salary, is further reflected in a recent study that found that among a cohort of 1,915 men appointed to the New York City Police Department in 1957, 38 percent of those who left over the next 11 years obtained jobs with the city's fire department![46] No firemen transferred to the city's police force during the same period.

In some cities, sanitation workers are treated as a component (with police and firemen) of the uniformed services. Where this occurs, there exists pressure for a more expanded form of wage parity—tripartite parity. Although sanitationmen have not yet achieved outright parity with police, and are generally paid about one quarter less than police, the differential in 1970 was only about 15 percent in the largest cities (those with populations of more than 1 million) and about

---

[40] Lewin, "Wage Determination in Local Government," pp. 165 and 196–98; and Devine, *Analysis of Manpower Shortages in Local Government,* Tables 5 and 6, pp. 42–43.

[41] Some jobs commonly regarded as unique to government, such as teaching and protective service positions, are also found in private markets. In this section, we discuss occupations for which government is an exclusive or dominant employer.

[42] "The method of salary setting for . . . classes peculiar to the public service . . . may have raised the cost of government without a demonstrated need to increase these salaries as high as they have gone." See Louis J. Kroeger et al., *Pricing Jobs Unique to Government* (Chicago: Public Personnel Association, n.d.), p. 5.

[43] Lewin, "Wage Determination in Local Government Employment," pp. 260–75.

[44] For further analysis of this issue, see David Lewin, "Wage Parity and the Supply of Police and Firemen," *Industrial Relations,* Vol. 12, No. 1 (February 1973), pp. 77–85.

[45] David Lewin and John H. Keith, Jr., "Managerial Responses to Perceived Labor Shortages: The Case of Police," processed (New York: Columbia University, 1974).

[46] Bernard Cohen and Jan M. Chaiken, *Police Background Characteristics and Performance* (New York: The New York City Rand Institute, August 1972), p. 45.

13 percent in Northeastern cities.[47] In New York, sanitationmen now earn 90 percent of police base pay, up from 60 percent in 1940, and the differential is even smaller when interdepartmental variation in overtime scheduling is considered. Because of this wage level, New York City experiences substantial queuing for positions in the sanitation service.

It has been suggested that pay for uniquely public jobs should be based on private sector wages for "occupations . . . to which individuals of comparable training and interests might be attracted."[48] Thus, in some cities, police and fire salaries are based on rates paid to skilled trades occupations in the local labor market, on the assumption that the two occupational groups attract persons of similar characteristics.[49] Aside from its dependence on a market sector that is strongly influenced by union power, this is not an unreasonable procedure, provided that its results are periodically checked against job turnover and vacancy experience.

A widely practiced procedure for dealing with exclusively public jobs is to establish their wage *levels* at a point in time by some system of internal job evaluation or salary comparisons and to base subsequent wage *increases* on the average rate of wage change occurring in the local private labor market. This is a generally commendable technique and is practically the only means of setting wages for some public jobs. All job evaluation systems, however, incorporate a large element of subjectivity and, consequently, are subject to the politicization process described earlier.

Two important occupations almost exclusive to the governmental sector—teachers and social workers—appear not to conform to our generalization about the upward bias in wage determination for unique jobs. Until recently, wage levels for these occupations were not high enough to equate supply with demand.[50] If the salaries of teachers and social workers had been based on salaries paid in alternative occupations, such as

the salaries of college graduates with business administration degrees, the result would have been considerably higher wages for these public occupations. So far as is known, however, this inferential method was never employed for teachers and social workers. One possible explanation for the teacher—social worker experience is that most employees in those occupations are women, and public wage fixing for them may have reflected general discrimination against women.

THE TOTAL WAGE STRUCTURE

Public sector wages tend to exceed those of the private sector for all occupations except high-level managers and professionals. Evidence demonstrating a tendency for public wages to exceed private levels for low-skilled and craft occupations has already been presented. There is ample information showing the reverse relationship for high-level occupations.

The National Manpower Council noted in 1964 that

government employers have been handicapped by the salaries they offer . . . scientific, professional, and managerial and executive personnel. . . . The discrepancy between public and private compensation for these categories of personnel . . . are larger on the upper rungs of the salary ladder.[51]

Table 6 presents federal government–private industry salary comparisons for the ten lowest and ten highest ranking positions included in the most recent *National Survey of Professional, Administrative, Technical and Clerical Pay*. These data show that in 1972, for jobs with GS1 through GS3 classifications, the federal government paid between 1 percent less and 13 percent more than private industry, whereas for jobs with GS13 through GS15 grades, federal salaries ranged between 1 percent above and 19 percent below private salaries. In the same year, the highest pay schedule in government, that for the federal executive branch, contained salaries ranging from $36,000 to $60,000—well below the $144,000 median salary then paid to the chief executive officers of America's 774 highest paying corporations.[52] Although progress has been made, the conclusion reached ten years ago by the Advisory

[47] See Urban Data Service, Stanley M. Wolfson, *Salary Trends for Police Patrolmen, Firefighters and Refuse Collectors* (Washington, D.C.: International City Management Association), Vol. 4, No. 10 (October 1972), pp. 5–6. These data are for cities with populations in excess of 100,000.

[48] Kroeger et al., *Pricing Jobs Unique to Government*, p. 4.

[49] See the Jacobs Company, *Report on Police and Fire Classification and Pay Studies*, City of Los Angeles (Chicago: The Jacobs Company, 1970), p. 31.

[50] Devine, *Analysis of Manpower Shortages in Local Government*, pp. 39–44 and 103–20.

[51] National Manpower Council, *Government and Manpower* (New York: Columbia University Press, 1964), pp. 34–35.

[52] Derived from "Who Gets the Most Pay," *Forbes*, May 15, 1972, pp. 205–36. The cited federal salaries exclude those of the President and Vice President.

TABLE 6 Relationship of Federal Salaries to Private Industry Salaries for Selected Occupations, 1972

Occupation and Job Grade	Average Annual Salary for Private Industry (dollars)	Annual Federal Salaries as a Percentage of Private Industry Salaries
File clerk I (GS 1).....................................	4,602	109
File clerk II (GS 2)....................................	5,027	113
Messenger (GS 1).....................................	5,087	99
Typist I (GS 2)..	5,229	109
Keypunch operator I (GS 2)...........................	5,756	99
Accounting clerk I (GS 3).............................	5,870	109
Typist II (GS 3).......................................	6,093	105
General stenographer (GS 3)..........................	6,181	104
File clerk III (GS 3)..................................	6,214	103
Draftsmen–Tracer (GS 3)..............................	6,288	102
Engineer VI (GS 13)...................................	21,402	96
Attorney IV (GS 13)...................................	23,443	88
Engineer VII (GS 14)..................................	24,367	99
Director of personnel IV (GS 14)......................	24,738	98
Chemist VII (GS 14)...................................	25,888	93
Chief accountant IV (GS 14)..........................	26,521	91
Attorney V (GS 14)...................................	27,528	88
Engineer VIII (GS 15).................................	27,885	101
Chemist VIII (GS 15)..................................	30,827	91
Attorney VI (GS 15)...................................	34,828	81

Source: Derived from U.S. Department of Labor, Bureau of Labor Statistics, *National Survey of Professional, Administrative, Technical and Clerical Pay, March, 1972,* Bulletin 1764 (Washington, D.C.: G.P.O., 1973), Appendix D, pp. 68–69.

Panel on Federal Salary Systems still holds: "Federal agencies . . . lag far behind private employers in the monetary rewards they can offer executive and managerial . . . personnel even though they have duties and responsibilities equal to or greater than any to be found in private enterprise."[53]

Similar relationships between public and private occupational pay exist in state and local government. An analysis of wage data for 100 governmental job classifications in Los Angeles produced public-private wage ratios ranging between 153.3 for the lowest ranked position (Laundry Worker) to 76.5 for top-ranking executive jobs (Health Officer, M.D., and County Counsel). Moreover, 8 of the 12 lowest ranked positions in these governments had ratios exceeding 100 percent, whereas all 16 highest ranked occupations had ratios below 90 percent.[54] The low salaries of city managers and chief executive officers in major cities, as displayed in Table 7, provide additional support, when compared to the average salary of $144,000 of top executives in industry, of the fact that the occupational pay

[53] National Manpower Council, *Government and Manpower,* pp. 159–61.

[54] David Lewin, "Aspects of Wage Determination in Local Government Employment," *Public Administration Review,* Vol. 34 (March–April 1974), forthcoming.

TABLE 7 Average Salaries for Chief Administrative Officers or City Managers of Selected Major U.S. Cities, 1971 (in dollars)

City	Mean Salary
Atlanta....................................	$29,068
Boston....................................	27,500
Chicago...................................	31,000
Dallas....................................	40,452
Los Angeles..............................	42,888
New York.................................	45,000
Philadelphia..............................	34,000
Phoenix..................................	37,500
Seattle...................................	25,188
Washington, D.C..........................	36,000

Source: International City Management Association, *The Municipal Yearbook—1971* (Washington, D.C., 1972), p. 244.

structure is more compressed in the public sector than in private industry.

Some observers believe, however, that the U.S. Bureau of Labor Statistics exaggerates the content of federal jobs when it conducts wage surveys of "comparable" private sector jobs. This charge has never been publicly documented, to the best of our knowledge, but it is clear that if such a bias in public-private job comparisons does exist, then a public-over-private wage differential extends farther up the occupational hierarchy than is shown by the available wage data. Unless the bias is greater for high- than low-level jobs, however, the finding of a more compressed wage structure for the public sector is still valid.

CONCLUSION

The available data indicate that public-private pay relationships in the United States can be explained, at least in part, by a combination of two factors: the discretion that public employers must exercise in implementing the prevailing wage rule adopted by most cities and larger government units and the nature of the political forces that affect governmental wage decisions. The result is an occupational pay structure that is more "equalitarian" in the public sector than that in private industry, in the sense that public employers tend to pay more than private employers for low-skill and craft jobs and to pay less for top executive jobs.[55]

It is not appropriate for us to render a judgment about the equity of the public sector wage structure. The collective judgment of the American people may be that government wage structures should be more egalitarian than those existing in private industry. This is doubtful, however, since the relevant political pressures work toward producing that kind of public wage structure, without benefit of any implicit or explicit public judgment about the equity question.

We can, however, draw a conclusion about the market efficiency of the public sector wage structure, and that conclusion is negative. Government employers frequently pay more than necessary to attract a work force at the low- and middle-skill ranges and generally pay less than necessary to attract employees of average quality at the upper managerial and professional levels. It is doubtful that high worker productivity offsets the high public wages, although research on this question is needed.[56]

Given the great increase in the number of college graduates expected during this decade, the public wage structure may well be a precursor of a general restructuring of wage relationships in society as the wages of highly educated workers suffer a relative decline. Such restructuring, however, is far from certain,[57] and until it occurs, there is need for a dialogue on whether the equity benefits of the public sector wage structure are worth their costs in efficiency.

Finally, Ehrenberg has recently presented evidence confirming a widely held view that employment elasticities in state and local government are very low. Thus, "market forces do not appear to be sufficiently strong to limit the size of real wage increases which state and local government employees may seek in the future."[58] Consequently, he suggests, and we agree, that careful attention should be given to the evolving structure of collective bargaining in the public sector.

---

[55] Obviously, we do not purport to explain all elements of public wage structures. For example, we suspect that in some regions and in relatively nonurban areas, public sector wages are comparatively low. If, indeed, this is correct, our hunch would be that the political forces described in this article, particularly public worker organization, have not developed very far in these areas.

[56] A strong believer in the efficiency of markets might argue that high government wages attract highly qualified workers but that productivity is unaffected because government agencies are unable or unwilling to identify and hire these workers or are unable to use them efficiently when they are employed.

[57] See Lester Thurow, "Education and Economic Equality," The Public Interest, Vol. 28 (Summer 1972), pp. 66–81.

[58] Ronald G. Ehrenberg, "The Demand for State and Local Government Employees," American Economic Review, Vol. 53, No. 3 (June 1973), p. 378.

part five

Economics and Labor Relations
A. Labor Markets, Wage Theory, and Hours

Wage theory and labor market structure are fundamental aspects of the economics of labor relations.

In the first article, Gallaway discusses the significance of the labor market in terms of its relationship to unemployment, economic growth, inflation, poverty, and the Negro. He concludes that "a good many of the . . . economic problems of today have a labor market dimension, and consequently, the way in which labor markets react to these problems has some significance for the formulation of public policy with respect to such issues."

In the second article, Pierson is concerned with the lack of an acceptable framework within which wage-setting can be studied. He provides a review of competitive, noncompetitive, general equilibrium, and income theory as it relates to wage theory.

Elbing, Gadon, and Gordon discuss the flexible working hours system that has been used in Europe, and they forecast that it may become acceptable to U.S. companies. The authors present a favorable view pertaining to flexible hours, whereas in the article by Hedges considerable doubt is cast on its adoption where "the data show that the 5-day workweek still dominates the work schedules of U.S. wage and salary workers."

38. The Significance of the Labor Market*

Lowell E. Gallaway†

In the past 15 years the American economy has experienced almost the full gamut of possible labor market conditions. Commencing with the Korean war episode and its accompanying inflationary pressures we have moved through a period in which there has been, first, a steady secular drift upwards in unemployment rates in the economy; second, a concerted use of fiscal policy to "beat down" unemployment; and finally, the reemergence of inflationary pressures as the result of the combination of the use of fiscal policy and the increasing commitment of military power in Viet Nam. Thus, we have in a sense gone full cycle from what is popularly called "high" full employment during the Korean war to less than full employment during the late 50s and early 60s and then back to "low" full employment in 1965 with every prospect of a return to "high" full employment conditions in the very near future.

Not surprisingly, this great variation in labor market conditions over the past 15 years has been accompanied by a considerable amount of controversy with respect to the desirability of one policy measure vis-à-vis another. As cases in point one need merely recall the "growthmanship" issue of some six years past, or the more recent argument with respect to whether the upward drift in unemployment rates from 1957 to 1963 was caused by "structural" change or "a deficiency of aggregate demand," or the present concern of policy makers, viz., how to limit inflationary pressure while maintaining satisfactory levels of growth and unemployment.

As if this assortment of policy problems with labor market overtones were not sufficient, the immediate past has seen the addition of questions such as the relationship between economic opportunity and the presence of poverty and the broad issue of the Negro's position in the labor market. These latter problems of course reflect the recent emphasis on facilitating the elimination of poverty in the economy as well as the society's concern with providing equality of economic opportunity to its citizens regardless of their race.

1. THE LABOR MARKET AND UNEMPLOYMENT

To this point it has simply been asserted that problems such as the level of economic growth, unemployment, inflation, poverty, and the economic status of the Negro have significant roots in the way in which labor markets in our economy function. In some cases this is self-evident. For example, the matter of the level of the unemployment rate is rather obviously related to the manner in which labor markets perform the task of bringing jobless workers in contact with available jobs. In its simplest form this merely involves the question of whether the labor market is able to equate the quantity demanded of labor with the quantity supplied. If these two magnitudes are not equal, the result is unemployment. Such a view of the labor market is a gross oversimplification in that it compresses the great diversity of American labor markets into a single generalization. Rather than there being one broad market for labor there are a great many smaller markets which interact with one another to produce an exceedingly complex set of labor supply and demand relationships.[1]

---

* This essay is part of an unpublished manuscript prepared by the author. It is used by permission.

† Professor of economics, Ohio University.

[1] There is a great variety of evidence relating to the diversity of American labor markets, evidence which has sometimes been interpreted as indicating that the gen-

For example, if unemployment develops in one region or one industry, the unemployed workers in that market may seek employment elsewhere, and an adjustment process is set in motion. If that process functions smoothly, unemployment will be gradually eliminated through unemployed workers in one sector finding jobs in other areas. Whether all the unemployment disappears as the result of movement of this sort depends upon not only the efficiency of the adjustment process but the degree of flexibility of wage rates throughout the economy. If wages are relatively inflexible, job opportunities may not be available in sufficient quantities in other sectors to absorb the initial unemployment.[2] Of course, implicit in the assumption of an original amount of unemployment in a particular market is at least temporary wage inflexibility in that sector. Otherwise, the adjustment to unemployment could presumably be made within the sector itself through downward movements of wage levels.[3]

Moving to the level of multiple labor markets alters things only slightly. Regardless of whether the labor market is viewed as a simple or complex arrangement the overall level of unemployment is integrally related to the effectiveness of the labor market adjustment process. The linkage may take one of two forms. First, in the case of a general decline in aggregate demand in the economy, such as that which accompanies a downturn of the business cycle, the responsiveness of labor markets in general to the presence of unemployed workers has an influence on the general level and duration of unemployment. If these markets respond to unemployment by exhibiting flexible money wages,[4] some or all of the impact of the decline in aggregate demand may be absorbed. However, if in general money wage rates are inflexible downward, little of the unemployment generated by the downturn of the business cycle will be eliminated. Thus, the effectiveness of labor markets in adjusting to the presence of unemployment has a significant effect on the severity of cyclical unemployment.

In addition to its impact on the level of cyclical unemployment the nature of the labor market adjustment process also has an effect upon the amount of unemployment which is observed during periods of what we choose to call full employment. At any point in time displacement of workers is occurring due to dynamic changes in the economy. Shifts in consumer demand and technological innovations introduce random shocks which generate unemployment which puts pressure upon labor market adjustment mechanisms. To the extent that such unemployment is absorbed rapidly by labor markets in other sectors of the economy the level of unemployment associated with full employment is reduced. In effect, the ability of labor markets to react to such changes determines in fact what may be thought of as a normal minimal level of unemployment in the economy. This is commonly thought to lie in the range of from 3 to 4 percent for the United States, a part of which, perhaps 2 percentage points, can be viewed as minimal "frictional" unemployment where frictional unemployment may be thought of as unemployment resulting from the lapse of time required for workers to change jobs in the economy under "true" full employment condi-

eralizations of conventional economic theory may be of limited usefulness in dealing with labor market phenomena. One of the earlier suggestions along this line may be found in J. E. Cairnes, *Some Leading Principles of Political Economy, Newly Expounded* (London, 1874), in which the concept of noncompeting groups in the labor force is developed. For a latter-day treatment of this matter see Clark Kerr, "The Balkanization of Labor Markets," in *Labor Mobility and Economic Opportunity* (New York and Cambridge, 1954), pp. 92–110.

[2] It has been argued by J. M. Keynes in *The General Theory of Employment, Interest, and Money* (New York, 1936), that flexible money wages rates may not be sufficient to produce labor market equilibrium in the aggregate. The crux of this argument is the matter of interdependencies between wage rates, aggregate demand, price levels, and costs. For a treatment of this subject in the literature see Martin Bronfenbrenner, "A Contribution to the Aggregate Theory of Wages," *Journal of Political Economy*, December 1956, pp. 459–69 and "Aggregative Wage Theory and Money Illusion: Reply," ibid., October 1957, pp. 445–47; P. E. Junk, "A Macroeconomic Theory of Wages: Comment," *American Economic Review*, September 1957, pp. 679–82; K. W. Rothschild, "Aggregative Wage Theory and Money Illusion," *Journal of Political Economy*, October 1957, pp. 442–45, and "Aggregative Wage Theory and Money Illusion: Rejoinder," ibid., pp. 447–48; and Sidney Weintraub, "A Macroeconomic Approach to the Theory of Wages," *American Economic Review*, December 1956, pp. 835–56, and "A Macroeconomic Theory of Wages: Reply," ibid., September 1957, pp. 682–85. My own view on this matter is that the Keynesian contentions are valid logically under certain assumptions but that the assumptions are not likely to be realized.

[3] When discussing a single sector of the overall market for labor the aggregation problems indicated in the previous footnote can be disregarded with relative safety as long as the sector in question is small relative to the entire market for labor. When this is the case the effect of the interdependencies which create aggregation problems is in large part "washed out."

[4] The question of how much and how rapidly the impact of declining aggregate demand will be absorbed by flexible money wage rates depends on the impact of the various interdependencies referred to in footnote 2. In short, it depends upon the validity of Keynes', *General Theory of Employment*, basic argument that flexible money wage rates may not be sufficient to produce an aggregate labor market equilibrium.

tions.[5] The remainder represents the contribution made to normal unemployment by the inability of labor market mechanisms to shift workers between jobs in the time required in a true full employment situation. Of course, the matter of what constitutes the normal length of time for job changing under full employment is a question of judgment.[6]

II. THE LABOR MARKET AND ECONOMIC GROWTH

It follows quite naturally and rather obviously that if the labor market mechanism has a significant impact on the overall level of human resource use, i.e., on the unemployment rate, it also has an effect on the process of economic growth in an exchange economy, for one of the major determinants of levels of economic activity is the extent to which an economy's human or labor resources are used. The effect of the functioning of the labor market on economic growth can take one or both of two forms. First, it may alter the growth rate of an economy by means of a "once-and-for-all" or "one-shot" type change. An example of this would be some alteration in the circumstances of the labor market sufficient to produce a permanent shift in the level of human resource use. Such a shift might have the effect of reducing the labor force participation rate in the economy or it might alter the intensity or degree of labor force participation of those still active in the labor market. Both of these are exemplified by the reaction of workers to the availability of retirement benefits of either a public or private character. The provision of such benefits operates through the labor market both to shift older workers out of the labor force and to reduce the amount of labor force participation among those older workers who remain in the labor force.[7] Such shifts have the effect of deterring economic

growth during the period in which they occur. However, if they represent merely a transition from one set of retirement institutions to another, once the transition is completed the negative impact of the labor force changes on economic growth will no longer be felt although the economy will be operating at a lower level of measured real output than previously.[8] Thus, an alteration of labor market conditions of this type merely shifts the economy from one growth path to another without necessarily affecting its growth rate other than during the period in which the shift occurs.[9]

By contrast, there are aspects of the manner in which labor markets function which have a direct bearing on the size of the long-term growth rate of an economy. For one thing, the ability of an economy to grow is dependent on its capacity to adjust to the technological changes which are vital to increasing productivity and output. One aspect of this ability is the ease with which workers who are displaced as the result of an altered technology are absorbed elsewhere in the economy. If such absorption takes place relatively rapidly, unemployment among displaced workers is minimized, and more important, the society's willingness to accept and incorporate technological change is in all probability enhanced. Historically, there has been substantial opposition among workers to the introduction of labor-saving machinery.[10]

---

[5] In a paper entitled "Long Term Unemployment, the Structural Hypothesis, and Public Policy," *American Economic Review,* December 1964, pp. 985–1001, N. J. Simler estimates that if long-term unemployment (15 weeks or longer) were eliminated, the residual amount of unemployment would be about 2 percent. In a crude sense, this may be thought of as "frictional" unemployment although I would regard it as a maximum estimate.

[6] In the previous footnote I have implied that a normal length of time for job changing under "true" full employment is less than 15 weeks. If such a definition is accepted, the Simler estimate of 2 percent unemployment with zero long-term (15 weeks or greater) unemployment measures frictional unemployment.

[7] For a discussion of various aspects of the labor market response of the aged to retirement benefits see my *The Retirement Decision: An Exploratory Essay,* Research Report No. 9, Social Security Administration, Washington, 1965.

[8] Such a transition does not imply a lower level of social welfare even though measured output may have declined because of it. What has happened is that increased leisure has been substituted for goods and services which are priced by the market mechanism. However, leisure is not priced in this fashion and, according to our income accounting conventions, consequently, is not included in measured national output.

[9] It is possible for shifts of this sort to have a permanent effect on the economy's growth rate if it results in changes in the quality of the labor force. For example, if the general level of adaptability of the labor force to economic change is altered due to shifts in the composition of the labor force that result from the types of movements discussed here, the result may be a permanently changed growth rate for the economy.

[10] It would require a lengthy tome to chronicle all the examples of such opposition. One of the most famous, though, is the Luddite riots in England in 1830. However, this is not the first of such happenings. The following citation is illustrative:

"Popular or state opposition was easily aroused against any invention that threatened to injure some strong vested interest, or to reduce the demand for labor and thus cause more people to need poor relief. At various times mobs destroyed sawmills, ribbon looms, and knitting frames. Guilds condemned equipment or methods that gave one member an advantage over his fellows. The city of Danzig forbade the use of a loom which wove several strands of ribbon, and suffocated its inventor (1586). Charles I of England ordered the destruction of a needle making machine

Admittedly, such efforts have not been able to permanently forestall the introduction of new techniques with their accompanying contribution to increasing economic growth. However, it is not clear that the rate of technological progress has not been slowed at certain times by efforts to protect workers from the rigors of the ensuing adjustment process. In fact, there are indications that this very thing may be occurring to some extent in the contemporary United States. Increasing emphasis in collective bargaining negotiations on smoothing the technologically displaced worker's transition to other employment at the expense of the introducer of the new technology has the effect of increasing the cost of such changes to the producer. In a market economy this results in a slowing of the rate of adoption of technology due to the reduced level of profitability produced by the higher cost of introduction. Consequently, if the pressure for such cost increasing arrangements is reduced by the presence of a smoothly functioning labor market mechanism, economic growth is encouraged and facilitated.

In addition to its impact on private devices for dealing with the problem of workers who have been displaced by technological change, the effectiveness of labor market processes in producing necessary adjustments may also significantly influence public policy with respect to the introduction of technological change. For example, labor markets that produce a relatively inefficient adaptation to advancing technology may engender public policies such as those adopted in France where significant restrictions are placed upon the rights of employers to displace workers from their existing employment.[11] Not all public policy measures dealing with problems of displaced workers have to take the form of restricting their movement out of or between jobs but public figures seem to have an unfortunate predilection in that direction.[12] Consequently, an ineffective labor market adjustment mechanism is more likely than not to produce public policies which aim at limiting worker movement rather than encouraging it. And, if this does happen, the impact is apt to be a diminution in the rate of economic growth for the system.

III. THE LABOR MARKET AND INFLATION

The discussion of the relationship between the nature of labor market mechanisms and the problems of unemployment and economic growth suggest that these two phenomena are quite clearly interrelated. Unemployment levels affect economic growth, and the manner in which growth is generated influences unemployment levels. And, of course, both are greatly affected by the manner in which labor markets function to produce the adjustments required by both growth and the presence of unemployment. This pattern of interrelationship is repeated when the connection between the labor market and the phenomenon of price inflation is considered.

Price stability, or its inverse—price inflation—has been a constant source of concern in the United States over the past quarter century. Commencing with World War II there have been few periods in which the fear of substantial upward movements in the price structure was not present. And, in those instances where such fear did not manifest itself, unsatisfactorily high levels of unemployment were generally present. This suggests the existence of a basic conflict between the policy objectives of full employment

---

(1623) and banned the casting of brass buckles (1632) on the ground that six casters would endanger the livelihood of six hundred guildsmen who were making buckles in the old way." (Herbert Heaton, *Economic History of Europe*, rev. ed. [New York, 1948], p. 481.)

In more recent times the so-called featherbedding controversies are reminiscent of this type of opposition.

[11] The following citations from *International Trade Union Seminar on Active Manpower Policy, Supplement to the Final Report*, Organization for Economic Co-operation and Development, 1963, are illustrative of the types of control which government instrumentalities may exercise in France:

(1) "By law the public authorities enjoy the most extensive privileges on the labour market, since their authorization is required before any recruitments or dismissals in industry or commerce can take place" (p. 13).

(2) "In the matter of collective dismissals . . . authorization is given only if it can be proved that the dismissals are justifiable, either because of a real reduction in activity or in the development of new production methods, or because of the company's obligation to cut down overhead expenses" (p. 13).

In addition, approval is required of the Labour Inspector before overtime work can be undertaken and the courts have ruled in some cases that "workers whose dismissal has been brought about through the inefficient management of the enterprise could also suffer 'direct and special prejudice of sufficient gravity' to demand legal redress" (p. 14).

No matter how loosely administered such an environment can hardly be conducive to the implementation of new technology.

[12] In general, public officials seem to be reluctant to encourage individuals to migrate from the areas which they govern. I first encountered this phenomenon when writing a doctoral dissertation on the subject of the economic problems of depressed industrial areas. For a summary of my conclusions at that time see "Proposals for Federal Aid to Depressed Industrial Areas: A Critique," *Industrial and Labor Relations Review*, April 1961, pp. 365–66.

FIGURE 1

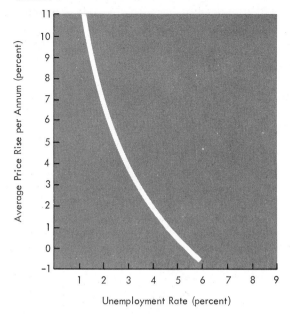

and price stability in our economy. The empirical evidence on this count rather clearly indicates that this is the case. For example, a comparison of unemployment rates and increases in the price level for individual years can be summarized in the form of what has come to be called a Phillips' curve.[13] The Phillips' curve is a conceptual device for expressing the "trade-off" between the unemployment rate and the rate of price inflation that exists in an economy and takes the general shape shown in Figure 1. That particular delineation of a Phillips' curve is taken from a 1960 paper by Paul Samuelson and Robert Solow and roughly approximates the relationship between the unemployment rate and the rate of price inflation for the American economy in the post-World War II world.[14] Of particular interest is the negative slope of the Phillips' curve of Figure 1, for this negative slope reflects the basic conflict between the policy objectives of full employment and price stability. In effect, the relationship shown in Figure 1 says that it is only possible to obtain lower unemployment rates at the expense of greater price inflation or price stability at the expense of higher unemployment rates.

Thus, it depicts what is sometimes a painful choice for a society that on occasion seems to have a rather low tolerance for price inflation. The choice shown here is made all the more painful by the fact that price stability may also be incompatible with high real growth rates for the economy as a whole. It is rather obvious that the conflict between full employment and price stability must be carried over at least in part to the relationship between the growth rate and price stability. But the conflict extends even beyond this rather straightforward linkage, for it is quite clear that a rapidly growing economy is more likely to put greater demands on its resources and thus generate the increases in prices that we call price inflation.

The dilemma presented by the conflict between the various policy alternatives that face the economy has part of its roots in the operation of the economy's labor markets, for there are some clear relationships between the way in which these markets function and levels of economic growth and unemployment. Interpreted in the context of the Phillips' curve discussion, a more efficient labor market mechanism implies a more favorable relationship between the rate of unemployment and the rate of price inflation. This follows from the fact that at a given level of aggregate demand a more efficient labor market will produce a lower level of unemployment and, presumably, a higher level of output and a lower price level. Consequently, the particular workings of the labor market have a substantial impact upon the position of the Phillips' curve for the American economy and the set of policy alternatives which are available to the society. The more efficient the labor market, the less painful the choice that has to be made between full employment, economic growth, and price stability.

IV. POVERTY AND THE LABOR MARKET

After observing a slackening in the rate at which poverty was being eliminated in the United States in the past several years a number of people have argued that there is some fundamental shortcoming in the economy as it now stands which seriously limits the ability of individuals with extremely low levels of income to move to a nonpoverty level of income.[15] As usually defined this means an inability to obtain a level of money income in excess of $3,000 per

---

[13] The concept of the Phillips' curve arises out of the work of A. W. Phillips, "The Relation between Unemployment and the Rate of Change in Money Wage Rates in the United Kingdom, 1862–1957," *Economica*, November 1958, pp. 283–99.

[14] P. A. Samuelson and R. M. Solow, "The Analytics of Anti-Inflationary Policy," *American Economic Review*, May 1960, pp. 177–94.

[15] See, for example, Michael Harrington, *The Other America* (Baltimore, 1963), and J. K. Galbraith, *The Affluent Society* (Boston, 1958), chap. 22

year, but this definition is somewhat flexible.[16]

Those who are dissatisfied with the performance of the contemporary American economy in eliminating poverty usually argue that certain groups in the society are relatively isolated from its normal market processes and, consequently, do not share fully in the largesse generated by the system. Implicit in this position are some very clear attitudes with respect to how labor markets in the United States function, for a very substantial source of the economic isolation that is claimed for some portions of the population must lie in a lack of full contact with those labor markets. In fact, some argue rather specifically that for many this isolation from the economy's labor markets is so complete that normal measures to stimulate economic activity, such as monetary-fiscal policy, will prove quite ineffective in eliminating their poverty.[17]

Specific reasons for the relative isolation of certain groups from the mainstream of American economic life vary, but, in general, they seem to focus on a lack of marketable skills among these groups, either because of those skills being rendered obsolete by the process of technological change or because the skills were never acquired to begin with due to lack of educational opportunity and the like. Examples of the first type would be individuals with marginal labor force skills who are displaced by the introduction of labor-saving machinery and find themselves unable to locate another job over a protracted period of time. Obviously, this case is almost identical to that treated in the discussion of the significance of the labor market for the level of growth in the economy. However, when the displacement from employment becomes protracted, true isolation from the labor market process can develop. To begin, after a substantial lapse of time without work an individual may become "discouraged" and simply stop looking for work, i.e., he may withdraw from the labor force.[18] Further, as he is divorced from work activity for longer and longer periods of time the possibility of erosion of his already meager labor force skills cannot be ignored.[19] Thus, a sequence of progressive isolation from the labor market may develop in situations such as this.

The process by which individuals may be progressively isolated from the labor market is somewhat similar for those who have never acquired skills of any particular significance. People in this category are more likely to undergo protracted periods of unemployment which in turn may lead to labor force withdrawal, erosion of what little skill they may have had, and finally, a settling into a permanent life of poverty. The possibility of large numbers of individuals slowly slipping into an economic way of life that leaves them without meaningful access to the economy's labor markets and, consequently, relatively untouched by the normal processes of growth that characterize this economic system is not a pleasant one. However, it is certainly not clear that this type of isolation from the labor market mechanism occurs in quantitatively significant numbers. For one thing, the concept of skill is a variable thing. With low levels of aggregate demand in the economy and low levels of employment employers can afford to be quite selective in their hiring practices. For example, with an abundance of workers (a "loose" labor market) it may be feasible to insist on a credential, such as a high school diploma, before employing someone in a relatively unskilled job.[20] On the other hand, if the economy is operating with high levels of aggregate demand and a tight labor market, employers begin to find that such credentials are not necessary to carry out that particular job, and in

[16] A more sophisticated set of definitions of poverty which take into consideration varying family size have been developed by the Social Security Administration. See Mollie Orshansky, "Counting the Poor: Another Look at the Poverty Profile," *Social Security Bulletin*, January 1965.

[17] An exploration of this thesis on an aggregative level may be found in my "Foundations of the War on Poverty," *American Economic Review*, March 1965, pp. 122–31. On a much more disaggregated level see W. H. Locke-Anderson, "Trickling Down: The Relationship between Economic Growth and the Extent of Poverty among American Families," *Quarterly Journal of Economics*, November 1964, pp. 511–24 and my "The Aged and the Extent of Poverty in the United States," *Southern Economic Journal*, October 1966.

[18] A good deal of recent research on the "discouragement" effect has been reported. See W. G. Bowen and T. A. Finegan, "Labor Force Participation and Unemployment," in A. M. Ross, ed., *Employment Policy and the Labor Market* (Berkeley, 1965), pp. 115–61; T. F. Dernberg and K. T. Strand, "Hidden Unemployment 1953–62: A Quantitative Analysis by Age and Sex," *American Economic Review*, March 1966, pp. 71–95; K. T. Strand and T. F. Dernberg, "Cyclical Variation in Civilian Labor Force Participation," *Review of Economics and Statistics*, November 1964, pp. 378–91; A. Tella, "The Relation of Labor Force to Employment," *Industrial and Labor Relations Review*, April 1964, pp. 454–69 and "Labor Force Sensitivity to Employment by Age and Sex," *Industrial Relations*, February 1965, pp. 69–83.

[19] Simler, *"Long Term Unemployment,"* develops a full theory of long-term unemployment which incorporates the phenomenon of skill erosion explicitly.

[20] Such policies by business enterprises are not arbitrary and capricious. Given a choice between workers with specific credentials and workers with none, on balance, it is probably safer to employ those with the credentials.

general, there is an upgrading of skills as the labor market tightens. Such upgrading does reach down into the lower levels of the skill hierarchy but whether it reaches far enough to break down the isolation of many individuals from the labor market can only be answered in an empirical fashion. Regardless of the nature of that answer it is clear that the manner in which labor markets function is an important aspect of the poverty problem.

V. THE LABOR MARKET AND THE NEGRO

The recent civil rights revolution has projected the economic status of the Negro into the forefront of discussions of contemporary American life. Such discussions have been quite varied, ranging from esoteric treatments of the theory of economic discrimination[21] all the way to the most naive form of casual empiricism. However, irrespective of the quality of the discourse, it has been characterized by an emphasis on the Negro's labor market position relative to that of whites. A number of statistical measures suggest a basic weakness in that position.[22] Unemployment rates among Negroes are larger than those of whites by approximately a multiple of two.[23] Further, income levels of Negroes are only slightly more than half those of whites and actually showed a relative decline over the decade of the 1950s, although there are signs of improvement in more recent years.[24]

The apparent weakness of the Negro in the labor market can be explained in a variety of ways: (1) discrimination against the Negro due to his race, (2) lack of educational opportunity for Negroes which operates to deprive them of necessary labor market skills, (3) the differential impact of variations in levels of economic activity upon the economic position of Negroes and whites, or (4) factors associated with the Negro culture in the United States which make it difficult for him to participate fully in the American economic system.[25] The impact of this complex of factors in producing such a markedly lower economic status for the American Negro makes a great contribution towards generating many of the tensions and difficulties that have marked the racial scene in recent years. That these factors exert their impact through the labor market mechanism almost goes without saying. Discrimination against Negroes in employment opportunities because of employer attitudes regarding the desirability of hiring them,[26] inability of Negroes to compete effectively for jobs either due to prior educational discrimination or the problems arising out of the existence of a Negro sub-culture in the United States, and the differential impact of cyclical swings in economic activity are all labor market manifestations of basic characteristics of the contemporary American society.

In many respects the remarks concerning the relationship between poverty and the labor market are applicable to the economic problems of Negroes. Discrimination, lack of education, and the like operate to make many Negroes "margi-

[21] See Gary Becker, *The Economics of Discrimination* (Chicago, 1957), and Anne O. Krueger, "The Economics of Discrimination," *The Journal of Political Economy,* October 1963, pp. 481–86.

[22] An excellent analysis of the causes and significance of the economic status of the Negro in contemporary America may be found in James Tobin, "On Improving the Economic Status of the Negro," *Daedalus, Journal of the American Academy of Arts and Sciences,* Fall 1965, pp. 878–98.

[23] United States Department of Labor, *Manpower Report to the President,* March 1966, Table A-11.

[24] For discussions of the behavior of relative incomes of Negroes, see Alan B. Batchelder, "Decline in the Relative Income of Negro Men," *Quarterly Journal of Economics,* November 1964, pp. 511–24; Becker, *Economics of Discrimination;* Rashi Fein, "Relative Income of Negro Men: Some Recent Data," *Quarterly Journal of Economics,* May 1966, p. 336; and Elton Rayack, "Discrimination and the Occupational Progress of Negroes," *Review of Economics and Statistics,* May 1961, pp. 209–14. Becker and Rayack find that during the relatively prosperous 1940s Negro relative income improved. However, Batchelder shows that in the 1950s, with a somewhat more sluggish economy, the relative income of Negro males declined. Recent evidence presented by Fein indicates that the prosperity of the 60s has re-established the trends observed by Becker and Rayack.

[25] In an as yet unpublished paper entitled "Theory and Cost of Racial Discrimination," Donald W. Katzner estimates that the total cost of economic discrimination in 1959 was 4.36 percent of national income. He divides the cost into two categories: (1) that accruing from a failure to provide equal educational opportunities for Negroes (1.23 percent of national income) and (2) that arising out of a non-optimal utilization of existing skills of Negroes (3.13 percent of national income). His concept of non-optimal utilization of skills is really a residual cost which includes everything but the educational factor. In another unpublished paper I have estimated that "race" and education are about equally important in explaining poverty levels of income among Negroes, *The Negro and Poverty,* unpublished, 1966. My race factor corresponds to Katzner's non-optimal utilization of Negro skills. H. J. Gilman discusses Negro unemployment levels in his "The White/Non-White Unemployment Differential," in *Human Resources in the Urban Economy* (Resources for the Future, Inc., Baltimore, 1963), pp. 75–113 and "Economic Discrimination and Unemployment," *American Economic Review,* December 1965, pp. 1077–96. A treatment of the impact of variations in general levels of economic activity may be found in Locke-Anderson, *"Trickling Down."*

[26] It should be kept in mind that employer prejudices in hiring may be derived from either the prejudices of other workers against working with Negroes or consumer prejudices against being served by Negroes.

nal" participants in the labor market. And, with marginal participation in the labor market go the possibilities of progressive isolation from the mainstream of economic life and poverty levels of income. Consequently, it is no surprise to find that, relatively, Negroes account for about two and one-half times as much poverty as whites.[27] While one cannot say exactly what the contribution of this relative lack of success of the Negro in the labor market is toward generating the current racial unrest in the United States, it is fairly clear that it is a significant factor. Certainly, elimination of the differential results of Negro and white labor market participation would be helpful in easing the bitterness that presently characterizes interracial relations.

---

[27] For specific data on Negro income levels in the post–World War II period, see U.S. Bureau of the Census, *Trends in the Income of Families and Persons in the United States, 1947–60*, Technical Paper No. 8, Washington, 1963.

VI. CONCLUDING REMARKS

With almost monotonous regularity the importance and significance of labor market mechanisms in the American economy have been reiterated. This is not to say that labor markets are the mechanism with the greatest influence on contemporary economic life. However, some poetic license must be granted the researcher whose primary interest is labor markets if he seemingly exaggerates the importance of his subject. But, even discounting the previous discussion to take account of such exaggeration it seems clear that labor market mechanisms are a significant factor in today's economy. At least, it does seem that a good many of the very pressing economic problems of this day and age have a labor market dimension and, consequently, the way in which labor markets react to these problems has some significance for the formulation of public policy with respect to such issues. . . .

39. An Evaluation of Wage Theory*

Frank C. Pierson†

In contrast to developments in the field of wage-setting techniques, little progress has been made of late in our understanding of wage-setting fundamentals. Today employers and labor representatives can draw on an impressive fund of knowledge concerning such matters as how to run a community wage survey, establish a job-evaluation plan, or install an incentive system, but on broader issues of principle, wage analysis commands surprisingly little esteem—probably less now than it did 50 or 100 years ago.

The dangers attending this state of affairs need no elaboration. The wage question is too important, its ramifications too numerous, to be dealt with by piecemeal or opportunistic means. The fact that wage decisions often have to be made under rapidly changing conditions, with consequences which can be only dimly foreseen, helps explain but does not justify this lack of an acceptable conceptual framework.

DEDUCTIVE VERSUS INDUCTIVE ANALYSIS

One factor contributing to the muddled state of wage economics is the gap which has come to exist between deductive and inductive wage analysis. An axiom of all scientific endeavor is that these two methods of inquiry should closely parallel one another, each enriching and forwarding the other. The study of wage phenomena,

however, is marked by no such mutuality. Theorists frequently appear to be dealing with one subject, empiricists with another, the work of each suffering as a result.

There are a number of reasons for the unhealthy cleavage which has developed between these two approaches to the field. As in other areas, the training and temperament of the investigator are bound to be reflected in the way he looks at his subject. More important, the nature of the subject itself makes this sharp dichotomy quite understandable. The "price" for labor in a given market at a given time or over a given period is notoriously hard to pin down, and any number of pitfalls exist to trap the investigator. For some, this suggests that little is to be gained by inductive studies and that deductive analysis is the only route left open. For others, these difficulties are taken as further evidence that the essence of the subject lies in its variety and detail, underscoring the need for intensive inductive investigations.

The major reason for the sharp division in this field, however, grows out of a difference in viewpoint or vision. Fundamentally, interest in deductive work has centered on how the buying and selling of labor's services fits into the workings of the economy as a whole. The assumptions made about how employers and workers, either individually or collectively, approach their dealings with one another are the same as those made about purchases and sales in all other spheres of economic life. The conception of the entire system, as it were, comes first, and each of the individual parts, including the determination of wages, is fitted into the general framework wherever or however the logic of the system dictates. Thus, at the outset of his analysis of wages, Alfred Marshall stated:

* From George W. Taylor and Frank C. Pierson (eds.), *New Concepts in Wage Determination*, pp. 3–31. Copyright 1957. McGraw-Hill Book Company, Inc. Used by permission. Abridged by the editors.

† Professor of economics, Swarthmore College.

Author's Note: In addition to my colleagues in the economics department at Swarthmore College, I wish to express my thanks to George H. Hildebrand and Sidney Weintraub for their many helpful suggestions. Any errors of commission or omission are the author's sole responsibility.

The nominal value of everything, whether it be a particular kind of labour or capital or anything else, rests, like the keystone of an arch, balanced in equilibrium between the contending pressures of its two opposing sides; the forces of demand press on the one side, and those of supply the other.[1]

J. B. Clark put the matter in these words:

Looking at the transactions between employers and employed, can we see in them anything that causes wages to fluctuate about a standard which is more or less akin to the natural prices of goods? We shall at once find that there is a similarity between what the classical economists distinguished as the market price of goods and the market rate of wages. . . . We shall find that it [the wage rate] is fixed in a way akin to that in which the immediate selling prices of goods are determined. Later we shall find that, in both cases, the market rates fluctuate about permanent standards.[2]

It need hardly be pointed out that an analysis of wages along these lines must proceed at a high level of abstraction. Differences tend to drop from view; details about how wage rates behave in individual firms, industries, or regions are likely to be swallowed up in broad averages, long-term trends, or vague references to differences in efficiency and in the net advantages of the terms of employment. Thus, out of the myriad forces and changes continuously at work in the wage field, deductive analysis singles out only the barest number deemed to be of controlling importance. The *method* is deliberately designed to remove many elements of the real world, but the *results* are said to reveal underlying forces which shape wage relations.[3]

The parallelism between this view and the attitude of many employers toward wage questions is striking. For management, labor is but one of a number of essential elements in the production-selling process. The nature of the market for the firm's product and the nature of the firm's relation to its principal customers on the one hand and to its principal rivals on the other largely dictate the amount of labor and other productive elements which can be employed. As to the terms on which labor is hired, employers tend to think of labor's price as being set "by the market" in much the same way as the price of raw materials,

of equipment, or of any other factor of production. Phrases like "meeting our competitors' wage" and "paying what the market demands" are not mere euphemisms; they are part of the cost-price calculus which employers use to appraise every transaction and contract into which they enter. . . .

The parallelism between the deductive approach to wages and the attitude of employers is hardly accidental. The individual employer stands at the center of the economic theorist's world, and the greater part of the latter's work consists of translating into precise (some might say unintelligible) language, the principles which underlie business management's actions and decisions. Similarly, in emphasizing the influence of broad, impersonal market forces on wages as well as on all other transactions, the theorist and the businessman are inclined to stress the futility or danger of any efforts to deflect these forces through government or trade union means. By no means all theorists, nor all businessmen for that matter, have subscribed to this view. Two of the greatest economists who wrote in the classical tradition, Marshall and Pigou, were far from doctrinaire on the question, but the tone of their writings, as with most of the better known theorists, was hostile to direct government-union efforts to raise wages.

Marshall's temperate viewpoint on the issue is indicated in the following passage:

The power of unions to raise general wages by direct means is never great; it is never sufficient to contend successfully with the general economic forces of the age, when their drift is against a rise of wages. But yet it is sufficient materially to benefit the worker, when it is so directed as to cooperate with and to strengthen those general agencies, which are tending to improve his position morally and economically.[4]

A. C. Pigou, in his *The Economics of Welfare*, takes essentially the same position as Marshall; nonetheless, he deals at considerable length with cases in which wages are "unfair" and in which interference to raise pay levels is justified and desirable.[5]

[1] Alfred Marshall, *Principles of Economics*, 8th ed. (New York: St. Martin's, 1920), p. 526.

[2] *The Distribution of Wealth* (New York: Macmillan, 1902), pp. 81–82.

[3] J. R. Hicks, *The Theory of Wages* (New York: St. Martin's, 1932), pp. 4–5. Deductive or theoretical analysis can be thought of merely as a tool of inquiry or as a set of generalizations about actual behavior; the term is used in the latter sense here.

[4] *Elements of Economics of Industry* (New York: St. Martin's, 1892), p. 408.

[5] A. C. Pigou, *The Economics of Welfare*, 4th ed. (New York: St. Martin's, 1932), chaps. 14–17. For an uncompromising attack on such interferences, written by a contemporary theorist, see W. H. Hutt, *The Theory of Collective Bargaining* (Glencoe, Ill.: Free Press, 1954); this book was originally published in 1930. A more recent and much more balanced treatment is contained in K. W. Rothschild, *The Theory of Wages* (New York: Macmillan, 1954). The ideas of earlier classical economists on wages

By contrast, the work of empiricists reflects a rather deep-seated skepticism about the notion that dealings between employers and workers are subject to the same principles or "laws" as are transactions in other spheres. While a certain surface similarity may be said to exist, empiricists tend to regard this notion as a source of much mischief. In their view, the essence of wage relationships is to be found in the details of individual firm, industry, or regional experience. While simplifying assumptions have to be made in order to keep the analysis manageable, it is felt they should be kept as close as possible to the particular class of cases under investigation. Broad propositions about wages and how they are related to the economic system as a whole are not stressed. To writers of this school, "it seems questionable in fact whether there can be one all-embracing theory of wages, which will sufficiently satisfy our sense of reality, and stand the test of historical experience."[6]

In a number of respects, . . . the viewpoint of empiricists toward wages is in accord with the general approach of trade union spokesmen. Both underscore the variability of wage relationships and the essential difference between labor and commodity markets. Both emphasize the latitude which employers frequently enjoy in adapting themselves to wage changes and the new dimensions which are added to wage setting when competing firms bargain as a single group. Both tend to distrust any analysis which reduces dealings in the labor field to a single rule of behavior, especially when such reasoning is applied to worker-union decisions to offer or withhold labor. Since empiricists stress the scope which the parties often enjoy in deciding wage questions, it is hardly surprising that their approach has proved congenial to trade unionists.[7]

The limitations of these two methods of inquiry when pursued independently of one another are obvious. The weakness of deductive analysis in the wage field is that its findings are impossible to prove or disprove by appeal to the facts. The marginal-productivity theory of wages, for example, was arrived at almost wholly by deductive means many years ago; yet to this day it lacks any solid factual underpinnings, since it embodies concepts which defy empirical verifi-

cation.[8] In this connection one cannot help being struck by the rigor with which writers of a theoretical bent analyze wage relationships deductively in contrast to the extremely casual, unscientific methods they employ in checking their findings against the facts.[9]

The besetting weakness of inductive work, on the other hand, is its inability to link its conclusions together in some kind of unified whole. Indeed, the results of this work to date have been too limited, too pluralistic, and too loosely related to one another to justify being characterized as a body of principles at all. It would appear that if theorists have been too daring in drawing broad implications from their materials, empiricists have been too timid. Thus whatever preeminence equilibrium-wage theory still enjoys seems largely attributable to the fact that no alternative system of thought has been developed to replace it.

The need, then, is for fashioning concepts which will facilitate both deductive and inductive work—concepts which will prove general enough to provide a framework for more intensive analysis, yet flexible enough to allow for major differences in observed behavior. This, in turn, appears to call for a careful review of the wage field at a level of inquiry considerably nearer to day-to-day experience than the more traditional deductive analysis makes possible. . . .

CONTEMPORARY THEORETICAL ISSUES

In canvassing the possibilities for bringing deductive and inductive wage analysis more closely together, consideration must first be given to the general role which a theory of wages can be expected to play. The answer turns on what are the most pressing questions currently being asked about wages, since these are the issues on which theory is expected to throw light. . . . Our initial task, then, is to determine what questions in this field call for intensive examination at the present time.

To help in the task of finding answers to these central questions, wage theory need not include many of the details of observed behavior; in fact, the essence of theory is that it simplifies, i.e., abstracts from reality so that the essential can be distinguished from the nonessential. On the other hand, the theory need not be so abstract as to exclude all differences of detail either. The nature of the field or the present extent of knowl-

and unions are briefly summarized in Lionel Robbins, *The Theory of Economic Policy* (New York: St. Martin's, 1952), pp. 103–10.

[6] J. W. F. Rowe, *Wages in Practice and Theory* (London: Routledge, 1928), p. 192.

[7] Two noteworthy examples of this school are Sidney and Beatrice Webb, *Industrial Democracy* (London: Longmans, 1914), Part III, and Rowe, *Wages in Practice.*

[8] See Machlup, "Marginal Analysis and Empirical Research," *American Economic Review,* Vol. 36 (September 1946), pp. 519–54.

[9] See Hicks, *Theory of Wages,* pp. 61, 76.

edge about it may mean that a less generalized and perhaps less precise theory might well be more useful. . . .

The wage field seems to be in this in-between position. Understanding of the subject is still in a rather primitive state. The field is broken up into a number of quite different and isolated parts. At this stage, the most that can be expected is a theory that reduces the bewildering variety of cases to a manageable number of broad categories and provides a general framework for studying the relationships between them. If there are ultimate principles which can be said to underlie these relationships, their formulation can wait until this interim kind of theorizing is more advanced.

Issues of Primary Interest: Three Questions

Speaking broadly, the wage issues commanding most interest today center around questions of wage-rate *levels* and wage-rate *structures*, i.e., questions concerning the level of wage rates in the plant or firm, industry, region, or nation, and the spread of wage rates around these different levels.[10] Interest in each of these four areas, in turn, can be said to fall under three broad headings: (1) how choices in the determination of wages mesh with related choices or activities of worker and employer organizations; (2) why different kinds of wage relationships assume particular forms or patterns; and (3) what effects follow from changes in wage relationships.

These three parts of the subject are closely linked. An understanding of how wage-determination choices are related to a broad complex of employer-union-worker activities is essential to an understanding of why various wage patterns emerge and what their major effects appear to be; similarly, it is impossible to go very far in analyzing the determinants of wage levels and structures without considering how wage-setting choices are related to other aspects of employee-employer behavior or what repercussions follow from wage changes. In each instance, attention is focused on the particular factors deemed to be critical, but in reality these three parts of the subject are merely different aspects of a single whole.

A decision about wage rates in a given situation has to be reconciled with a variety of other, often rather remote, considerations. Such matters

as when wage rates should be changed and by how much, how they should be distributed among different employees, and what firms should be covered affect a wide range of personal and organizational interests. Disputes between employers and unions over wages are often part and parcel of conflicts over such diversified questions as union recognition, the closed shop, or the relative standing of rival union leaders. What is deemed a "good" wage settlement by one party or the other may depend on such considerations as what improvements in labor efficiency now become possible, what wage gains have been secured by other workers in nearby plants, or whether lower wage competitors will be brought into line. A somewhat "higher-than-average" wage increase can work to the advantage of a particular company or employer group if it fits in with special recruiting requirements, enhances the firm's reputation as a good employer, or is a logical counterpart of a broad program for improving industrial relations. Similarly, a somewhat "lower-than-average" wage increase can work to the advantage of a particular group of workers or union if it means avoiding a prolonged strike, winning certain safeguards over discharges, or improving job prospects for certain skills. The fact that such terms as "average increase" and employer or worker "advantage" are difficult to define is itself an indication of the variety of objectives that a given wage change is likely to reflect.

Implicit in the foregoing is the view that the parties to wage settlements typically confront a rather wide range of choices and that the final outcome in a given case depends on how much weight they elect to give to a number of varying and perhaps conflicting considerations. Do these circumstances apply to less important wage adjustments as well as to the so-called pace-setting or key wage bargains? With certain modifications, the answer appears to be in the affirmative. If attention is focused solely on a few strategic rates, many pace-following settlements appear to be wholly mechanical in nature; this is especially likely to be true in highly inflationary periods, such as existed in the years immediately following World War II. If account is taken, however, of changes in the whole structure of a firm's rates, in such important "nonrate" elements in labor costs as shift premiums, pension contributions, etc., and in the way a company's wage structure is administered in terms of overtime premiums, promotions, and job-duty assignments, the parties typically exercise a considerable element of choice even in pace-following situations. Indeed, the

---

[10] Unless otherwise indicated, the discussion refers to straight-time hourly rates (or earnings in the case of pieceworkers) plus the value of so-called fringe benefits in cents per hour.

very fact that there is some type of a pattern settlement to which it has been decided particular firms should adhere is itself evidence of conscious design and deliberate choice.

Thus, a major task of wage theory is to help explain what alternatives confront parties to wage settlements and what considerations enter into making one choice or combination of choices rather than another. In this connection, there is a temptation to speculate about the "ultimate" objectives of employers, unions, and workers, but it is difficult to believe that anything very solid can be developed in this direction. Rather than try to pierce the inner recesses of the human or "collective" mind it would probably be more rewarding to find out what kinds of choices have been made in actual practice.

Closely related to these matters is the broad question of the determinants of wage relationships. As in the analysis of how choices are reconciled in the wage field, highly simplified theorizing is likely to prove of little help. At the outset, it is important to make clear what kind of wage-rate relationship is under consideration—whether wages are being studied on a plant, industry, regional, or national level—since the controlling influences in each case are likely to differ. Attention must be given to the nature of wage-decisionmaking bodies—their size, degree of centralization, internal and external rivalries, etc. —to get an understanding of different traditions and customary attitudes that have developed in individual firms or industries; what is considered a "fair wage," for example, cannot be understood without probing into the different employer-worker groups' attitudes on such matters. . . .

Thus, in some contexts, the standards and mores of a particular locality or region can have an important bearing on wage-rate relationships. In others, the chief controlling influence may be a gradual or sudden change in technology, in sources of labor supply, in the firm's competitive standing or in the general sales-and-profits prospect of the industry.

The task of theory is to help reduce this bewildering array of influences to some kind of order without allowing the crucial elements in the wage-setting process to be lost from sight. Indeed, the test to apply is whether a given theory, in simplifying wage relationships, helps bring out the most significant features of the wage-setting process. It is easy enough, on the one hand, to catalogue all the conceivable factors that impinge on different wage-rate levels and structures or, on the other, to set up a model from which almost all the complexities of the subject have been removed. The more difficult and important job is to develop generalizations that show how these determinants of wage-rate levels and structures are interrelated and what significance should be attached to each in different classes of cases.

Analysis of the effects following wage-rate adjustments at the plant, industry, regional, or national level is subject to much the same type of difficulty. Mention has already been made of the fact that the parties can materially alter the effects of a given wage change simply by the way wage systems are administered. One of the most elusive but important aspects of the matter is the effect of a wage change on the productiveness of workers and on the managerial efficiency of employers.[11] A hardly less complex issue is the relation between wage-rate changes and shifts in labor *supply* between firms, industries, or regions, and the impact of wage changes on employer *demand* for different labor skills or for machine substitutes.

These matters call, in turn, for analysis of a wide range of subjects—the impact of wage changes on costs, prices, profits, and even employer-consumer expectations—the study of any one of which is beset with many difficulties and pitfalls. Beneath these issues lie such important but imponderable questions as the effect of wage changes on the growth or strength of unions, the development of employer bargaining associations, the competitive product positions of different firms and industries, and the level and distribution of new capital expenditures, savings, and national income.

These issues pose a dilemma even more baffling than that encountered in the analysis of choices and determinants: If in the interest of clarity a narrow framework is used, many important elements of the subject will doubtless be excluded; if in the interest of realism a broad framework is used, anything like definite conclusions will be put completely out of reach. Again, there seems to be no other recourse than to pick one's way between these two extremes, using theoretical constructs or hypotheses which are neither unduly simplifying nor hopelessly complicating. As before, the most fruitful approach would appear to be to formulate and test generalizations about the effects of wage changes in terms of a number of classes of cases. . . .

To a considerable degree, the results derived from analyzing wage relationships in terms of

[11] See Sumner H. Slichter, *The Challenge of Industrial Relations* (Ithaca, N.Y.: Cornell University Press, 1947), chap. 2.

choices, determinants, and effects depend on what concept of time is used. The results will differ, of course, depending on whether a very short or a very long period is assumed, since adjustments can be made under the latter circumstances that are ruled out under the former. In any given period, however, the investigator has to ask himself the more basic question: whether the different sources of change are to be studied singly, the remaining changes being held constant, or whether attention is to be centered on the interrelationships between changes occurring in given situations. In short, the investigator must choose between a predominantly static and a predominantly dynamic kind of analysis. Under static analysis, the adjustments which follow a given change yield a precise result; under dynamic analysis, a variety of results become possible. Under static analysis, a given wage adjustment is viewed as occurring within a system of unchanging relationships in which a delicate balancing of counter-acting forces is continuously being realized; under dynamic analysis, the system of relationships within which wage adjustments occur is itself changing, the outcome being very possibly a cumulative, rather than a self-correcting, change. . . .

POSTULATES OF EQUILIBRIUM
WAGE THEORY

Wage theory consists of two quite different branches: partial- and general-equilibrium analysis. Theorists customarily use partial analysis to explain the wage levels of individual firms or industries, and until recently, they have used the same framework to analyze the national wage level and labor's share in the national income. Today, the approach to wages in this latter area has been greatly altered by Keynesian general-equilibrium analysis, although many economists still use the traditional approach in explaining labor's income share.[12] Moreover, the fact that there is a basic similarity between these two ways of analyzing wage issues should not be overlooked. Both use essentially the same method of investigation; both proceed on the same underlying assumptions about individual economic behavior; and while the results of the two approaches *may* be interpreted as mutually contradictory, logical necessity does not require it.

As in other aspects of economics, the foundations of partial- and general-equilibrium wage

[12] The term "general equilibrium" as used here refers to the Keynesian theory of national-income determination, not to the general-equilibrium system of pre-Keynesian economists like Leon Walras.

analysis consist of three main elements: the concept of maximization, the method of static analysis, and the conditions of equilibrium. As to the first, the notion that buyers and sellers of labor's services seek to maximize some magnitude (profits, real income, net satisfactions, etc.) is considered essential, since in the absence of some such assumption there would be no rational basis for expecting one wage rate to prevail rather than some other. The maximizing calculations are assumed to relate to the price paid for labor; that is, it is assumed that the changes which buyers and sellers are constantly making to achieve maximum gains result from, and are reflected in, changes in the wage rate for the labor in question. It is assumed that a wage increase, for example, will lead employers to recalculate how much labor should be hired in order to maximize profits, while workers will be led to recalculate how much labor or labor effort should be expended in order to maximize the net benefits from their work. This same highly simplified view of employer-worker motivations has been carried over into general-equilibrium analysis, although in the latter, attention is focused on aggregate, not individual-firm, equilibrium conditions.

The second characteristic of theoretical work in the wage field is the use of static or stationary analysis. According to this method, certain severely limiting conditions are set up which are assumed to remain unchanged for the period under examination, while the effects of altering one variable in the system are traced through various paths of adjustment. Later, the limiting conditions may be relaxed in order to bring the analysis closer to reality. Thus, in order to isolate the effects of a change in wage rates on a particular group of firms, the assumption is made in partial-equilibrium analysis that all other conditions affecting the firms' revenues and costs, such as consumers' tastes, the level and distribution of national income, the techniques of production, and the number of competitors in both the product and labor market, remain the same. If the period of time under study is very short, it is postulated that the amount of capital invested cannot be changed and that there will be no opportunity for firms to enter or leave the industry. If a longer period is involved, shifts in the so-called fixed factors can be allowed for. The essential feature of this method of inquiry is that the various limiting conditions are relaxed one at a time so that the effect of each change can be made clear as the analysis is brought closer to reality.

In general-equilibrium analysis this same procedure is followed, although the relationships which explain the national income level and the national wage level are, of course, not the same as those involved in the theory of the firm. According to so-called Keynesian theory, the determinants of national income can be reduced to a few simple relationships, and if certain assumptions are made about the nature of the supply of labor and of other factors of production, these same determinants also control the nation's real-wage level. As before, the analysis consists of changing one of the determinants, the others being assumed to remain the same, and tracing the effects through different channels. If, as in dynamic analysis, the other determinants are not assumed to remain unchanged, the effects of altering a given variable become less predictable and the results less precise.

The third element in the approach which theorists have taken to wage determination, the notion of equilibrium, is a logical counterpart of the two points just discussed. If the market for a given type of labor is assumed to be subject to a specified set of conditions and all buyers and sellers are assumed to be seeking to maximize some definable magnitude, then a change in any one of the specified conditions will call forth certain adjustments until maximum gains of all parties are once again realized. This holds true for analysis of national income levels as well as of individual firms or industries. The channels through which the equilibrating forces move are different, but the notion that the system is essentially self-balancing or self-correcting underlies both approaches. On the other hand, dynamic treatments stress the possibility that the adjustments may, at least within certain limits, assume a cumulative character.

Weaknesses of
Stationary-Equilibrium Analysis

A number of questions, as noted below, can be asked about the appropriateness of an analysis of wage relationships based on these three elements. The single point emphasized here is that stationary-equilibrium analysis puts wage issues into a frame of reference which can be considered as either highly restricting or extremely broad; especially is this true of partial-, as opposed to general-, equilibrium formulations.

Consider for example, the notion of maximizing behavior on which the entire structure of partial-equilibrium theory rests. If this notion is given specific content, as when it is said that

employers seek to maximize profits, other hardly less important objectives are lost from view. If it is broadened to allow, say, for differences in the net satisfactions or aspirations of different workers or worker groups, the notion can be said to explain everything—and at the same time nothing. Or take the concept of stationary equilibrium as a way of getting at the major forces shaping wage relationships. An essential aspect of the subject is that these forces, either as determinants or effects, do not refer to the same point of time but are continually changing and interacting with one another over periods of time. Thus, some part of any one decision made by buyers and sellers of labor depends on decisions made in prior periods under conditions probably quite different from those now in existence; another part depends on expectations of future conditions regarding prices, costs, output, employment, and the like.[13] Stationary-equilibrium analysis, as such, precludes attention to these all-important facets of market behavior, and any observations which theorists may make about these matters must rest on grounds which lie wholly outside their system of thought.

This rather harsh judgment is somewhat modified, but not fundamentally changed, when the principles of stationary-equilibrium wage theory are examined more directly and in somewhat greater detail. These principles can be grouped under three headings: competitive, noncompetitive, and general-equilibrium theory. Attention is now turned to an evaluation of theoretical work in these three areas.

COMPETITIVE THEORY

The three postulates of stationary-equilibrium theory just discussed, when combined with the assumption that labor is bought and sold under conditions of pure competition, form the core of traditional wage theory.[14] This view of the major forces controlling wage relationships, commonly referred to as the marginal-productivity theory, envisages a world of many individual buyers and sellers, so many that no one of them can affect the prevailing wage; a world in which all buyers and sellers are seeking to maximize their satisfactions (i.e., their "returns" over "costs") and in which the effects on total costs and returns

[13] Joseph A. Schumpeter, *History of Economic Analysis* (New York: Oxford, 1954), p. 963.

[14] The importance of the competitive assumption for the general body of economic theory is indicated by Hicks, when he states that abandonment of the competitive hypothesis threatens "wreckage . . . of the greater part of general equilibrium theory." J. R. Hicks, *Value and Capital*, 2d ed. (New York: St. Martin's, 1939), p. 84.

resulting from small (marginal) changes in the amounts of labor offered or demanded can be determined; a world in which the units of labor in question are perfectly homogeneous and the workers supplying this labor are perfectly mobile; finally, and most importantly, a world of stationary equilibrium in which all other conditions—including the prices of products, technological conditions, and the flow of money purchasing power through the economic system—remain unchanged.

Under these conditions the only wage rate that will satisfy the conditions of equilibrium is the one at which each buyer and seller is receiving a money return for an added unit of product which just covers the amount of expenditures or sacrifice incurred in producing such additional output. Various demand and supply configurations can be assumed, notably those associated with different time dimensions, different ratios of variable to fixed costs, and different technological data, but the essential element in all cases is that added output (and thus added input) will eventually entail more cost or sacrifice than is gained in the way of added revenue or benefit. If every buyer and seller has reached a position where the addition of another unit of output will entail more in the way of cost than in revenue, there will be no incentive for anyone to move or change his scale of operations, and a condition of equilibrium will have been achieved.[15]

Bearing of Competitive Theory on Three Main Questions

How does this view of wages answer the three main questions with which contemporary wage theory is concerned—how choices among alternative wage policies are made, what determinants shape wage relationships, and what effects follow from wage changes? The answer in each case is essentially the same—any change in conditions on either the supply side or the demand side of the market for labor will touch off a series of adjustments which will automatically bring about a new equilibrium position. The competitive theory of wages says nothing about policy choices among alternatives, because in a perfectly competitive market, buyers and sellers

must either sell on the same terms as rivals or be excluded altogether. The theory does not explain in any detail what the determinants of wages are—only that the sole basis for every increase or decrease in wages is a change in labor's marginal product and that whenever such a change occurs, the buyers and sellers of labor automatically adjust themselves to the new situation.

Nor does the theory throw much light on the manifold effects that are likely to follow from wage changes beyond the proposition that individual employers and employees must meet the "terms of sale" prevailing in the market or suffer displacement. Wages under competitive conditions are extremely, if not perfectly, flexible and the amounts of labor demanded by employers and offered by workers under these conditions are extremely, if not perfectly, responsive, or elastic, with reference to such changes. Accordingly, a rise in the relative wage level of a particular firm, industry, or region will cause the quantities of labor being bought and sold to change until equilibrium is regained.[16] In short, the competitive hypothesis is about the simplest, most straightforward view of wage determination imaginable, with all the advantages and disadvantages associated with highly abstract formulations of this type.

When viewed against the complex and shifting network of relationships involved in the wage-determination process, discussed above, competitive theory seems completely out of touch with the world of actuality.[17] Except in a very loose or general sense, this hypothesis affords a poor basis for explaining wage relationships; when combined with the other assumptions of partial-equilibrium analysis, it provides too limited a framework for analyzing the issues which command greatest interest in the wage field today.

✺   ✺   ✺   ✺   ✺

NONCOMPETITIVE THEORY

In view of the limitations which mark theorizing about wages on the assumption of pure com-

[15] If allowance is made for effects of general wage increases on either the efficiency or supply of labor, more than one equilibrium position is possible, but this involves going outside the assumptions of stationary analysis. Economic theorists have long given attention to such effects, but the discussion of such matters has been inconclusive; see, for example, J. R. Hicks, *The Theory of Wages* (New York: St. Martin's 1932), chap. 5, and Rothschild, *The Theory of Wages*, pp. 29–31, 38–48.

[16] Strictly speaking, the purely competitive hypothesis assumes that the individual firm is able to expand its labor force by any desired amount without raising wages because its size is small relative to the total number of buyers. An entire industry could hardly be assumed to do so without attracting labor from other uses, which in turn would entail raising the industry's relative wage level; thus, the industry's supply curve of labor is generally assumed to be upward sloping.

[17] See, for example, Richard A. Lester, *Hiring Practices and Labor Competition* (Princeton, N.J.: Princeton University Press, 1954), especially chaps. 4–6.

petition, it is not surprising that economists have long given attention to formulations based on the noncompetitive hypothesis. The simplest construct, pure monopoly, stands at the other extreme from pure competition, and it has the advantages as well as the disadvantages of any polar case. In a pure selling monopoly, a single organization controls all the supply, and buyers (in this case, employers) have no alternative sources or substitutes to draw on; in a pure buying monopoly, or monopsony, there is only one buyer, and sellers have no opportunity to sell their services elsewhere.[18] In either case, the wage is set at whatever level the party enjoying the monopoly advantage decides will yield him the best possible results. The theory should not be interpreted as meaning that the monopolist can adjust the wage to any degree without suffering adverse effects but only that within a given range he suffers no adverse effects from rival sellers or buyers offering more attractive conditions of sale. Moreover, within this range he need have no concern about possible rivals invading his private domain in the future; in fact, he can count on receiving a supernormal level of returns indefinitely.

It need hardly be pointed out that this conception of wage setting is quite as far removed from the real world as that of pure competition, a complete monopoly in which there is only one buyer or seller of labor being rarely, if ever, found in practice. Few types of labor are sold to only one employer or even to one closely knit employer group. Few unions have been able to cut off employers from *all* sources of substitute labor or methods of production for any considerable length of time. There may be some instances in which local skilled-worker groups have achieved this measure of power for rather long periods, but there is no evidence to suggest that employers in such situations are incapable of forming their own "countermonopoly" bargaining organizations.

More importantly, both monopoly and competitive theory use essentially the same narrow frame of reference based on the same highly restrictive postulates of partial-equilibrium analysis. The notions that an employer monopoly seeks to maximize some definite magnitude, such as short-run or long-run profits, that regardless of its size it can act as a monopolist and still keep within the *ceteris paribus* bounds of partial-equilibrium analysis, and that any disturbance

pushing a monopolist away from its equilibrium position sets in motion forces tending to restore this position again—these notions are hard to vest with much meaning. When conditions permit the employer a considerable range of discretion in choosing between various wage policies, hiring practices, and the like, differences between choices, not their common elements, become the center of interest.

As for its applicability to trade union activities, monopoly theory can easily become downright misleading. Without the anchor of maximum profits, what becomes of the theory? If union wage rates move together throughout an industry or group of industries, what is left of the *ceteris paribus* assumption? In what sense can it be said that the wage for a particular class of union labor is in equilibrium but for another class it is not? It would seem that the concepts of monopoly theory, which of course were originally designed to explain a certain type of commodity market, throw very little light on the major aspects of wage-setting behavior.

Main Contribution of Monopoly Theory

The principal contribution of monopoly theory to the wage field is the general direction it has given to the study of the subject. The essential characteristic of monopoly is absence of competition, in the sense that a seller or buyer is insulated against compelling or exacting pressures from rivals. This is also a common characteristic of labor markets. In describing the determinants and consequences of wage changes, labor economists repeatedly stress the numerous barriers to the operation of competitive adjustments in this area, both on the side of employees and employers. If workers are attached to a particular firm, area, or industry in such a way that a decrease in their wage will have little or no effect on the amount of labor supplied, the employers can act as monopsonists and can lower rates without losing workers. If the employers, on the other hand, continue to hire the same amount of labor even when wages go up, a union representing all the workers involved can act like a monopolist and raise wages without losing job opportunities. The fact that they do not always do so or that conditions in the real world are not so clear-cut as the foregoing suggests should not be allowed to obscure the substantial element of truth which monopoly theory contains.

If the theory is modified to include different degrees of monopolistic or noncompetitive control, the concept becomes somewhat blurred, but

---

[18] If the employer's monopoly is in the sale of products rather than in the purchase of labor, the effects on labor's wage and employment result from restrictive practices followed in the product market.

its essence remains. Thus some of the most important advances in wage theory in recent years have been built around formulations of this type. That wage rates are typically rigid rather than flexible, that wage rates in different markets frequently move together, that wage-rate differences persist indefinitely among workers doing the same work at the same level of efficiency in the same industry or area—these are facts which can hardly be reconciled with the competitive hypothesis but which the noncompetitive hypothesis can readily explain.

Bilateral Monopoly View of Wage Theory

One type of noncompetitive market deserving special mention is bilateral monopoly. Roughly speaking, this type of monopoly obtains whenever a union can raise the wage level of a firm or industry within a certain range without causing any adverse effects on the demand for labor and whenever employers can reduce the wage level without any adverse effects on the supply of labor. More precisely, the upper limit is the point at which the wage (and amount of labor employed) would be set if all the monopoly advantage were on the side of the union, and similarly, the lower limit is the wage that would be set if all the monopoly advantage were on the side of the employer. In a bilateral monopoly situation, the wage and amount of labor hired would usually fall somewhere between these upper and lower limits. Note, however, that above the "no-reaction" range, there is virtually no labor demanded at all and that below it, hardly any supplied. If the top and bottom limits are very close to one another, the parties have little latitude for bargaining, but in many situations this is not the case and the resulting wage will depend on such vague considerations as the type of leaders involved, public pressures to reach agreement, and relative bargaining strengths. Each party can be said to enjoy a certain advantage by reason of its monopoly position, but each likewise suffers a certain disadvantage by reason of the other's monopoly power.[19]

This view of wage determination deserves serious consideration for at least three reasons:

1. Experience in many bargaining situations indicates that relative to wages for comparable work elsewhere, there is a considerable range within which wage levels can be adjusted up and down without any observable effects on employment, methods of production, amounts of labor supplied, etc., but that outside this range further adjustments cause serious repercussions.

2. By directing attention to the limits within which wage adjustments can be made, this view highlights one of the most critical elements in wage determination. Objective circumstances such as the cost levels of competing producers, the availability and substitutability of other factors of production, consumer resistance to higher prices, and actual and prospective profit margins may mean that there is a fairly well-defined ceiling to possible wage increases. If there are other job opportunities to which the workers can readily turn, conditions of labor supply may even mean that there is something like a specific floor below which wage levels cannot fall. But in either case, estimates by the parties of what the other will probably do, what their own constituents will insist upon, and how their customers, suppliers, and rivals may react will also affect judgments as to how far a change in wages can be allowed to go.

3. In explaining when a particular wage or wage change falls within a given range, this view leaves room for a wide variety of influences which lie outside the usual frame of reference of equilibrium analysis. As noted earlier, objectives and strategies in wage determination can vary from industry to industry and from period to period, so even at the loss of a certain precision and clarity, theory must allow for this diversity of behavior. The major weakness of the competitive hypothesis, it will be recalled, is the extremely simple framework it employs for analyzing wage relationships. Formulations built around the notion of bilateral monopoly, on the other hand, set the stage for a more meaningful kind of analysis.

Most of the work in the latter direction has been kept within the severe limitations of partial-equilibrium theory and cannot be said to have added significantly to our understanding of wage principles.[20] Some noteworthy attempts have been made, however, to go beyond the usual bounds of theory and in some cases they have already yielded important insights. One such, which has received a great deal of attention, introduces

[19] For a formal treatment of these issues, see William Fellner, *Competition among the Few* (New York: Knopf, 1949), chap. 10. Lloyd Reynolds has used much the same approach in analyzing the wage level of the individual firm; see his chapter in Richard A. Lester and Joseph Shister (eds.), *Insights into Labor Issues* (New York: Macmillan, 1948), chap. 11.

[20] The most ambitious attempt to apply competitive and monopoly theory to wage issues is contained in Joan Robinson, *The Economics of Imperfect Competition* (New York: St. Martin's, 1936), Book VII; perhaps the most important contribution of this book to wage theory is its treatment of monopsony and minimum-wage problems.

"political" as well as "economic" influences into the explanation of wage relationships. . . .[21]

GENERAL-EQUILIBRIUM THEORY

To the 19th-century economist, the wage question was largely one of analyzing the real share of the nation's product going to labor. In one sense, this entailed a quite different approach to the study of wages from that involved in partial-equilibrium analysis, since it meant that labor was treated as a single homogeneous factor, differences among workers in particular areas, industries, and skill categories being disregarded. Attention was focused on the nation's total output rather than on outputs of individual firms or industries and on the real income position of the laboring class as a whole over long periods of time.[22]

In a more fundamental sense, however, the approach in both partial- and general-equilibrium analysis was the same. National demand for labor was simply viewed as the sum of the offers made by all the firms in the country; national labor supply as the sum of the offers of all the workers at different wage levels—all expressed in real terms. If the real-wage level was reduced, other things being equal, more labor would be hired. The intersection of the two schedules gave both the national wage level and the total volume of employment, the product of wage times employment giving labor's total income for the period in question. The same reasoning was followed to explain the price and income paid to the other factors of production, of which the most important was payment for the use of capital.

This view of the relationships governing real wages in the country considered as a single market is wholly analogous to the approach taken by classical economists to the study of wages in individual submarkets or industries. The concepts that individual buyers and sellers are maximizing a definable magnitude, such as net profits, that certain conditions such as consumer tastes and the state of technology remain unchanged, and that a variation on the side of either demand or supply will set in motion certain equilibrating adjustments—these concepts underlie the reasoning in both cases. As in partial-equilibrium analysis, the system as a whole is viewed as tending toward a position in which labor everywhere is employed in such a way that value of added output equals added cost. Employers and workers in the aggregate behave just as they do in individual markets—the same analysis governing their choices among alternatives, the determinants of wages—the effects following wage changes holds true for both.

Pure Competition or Pure Monopoly?

In line with this view, one of the crucial questions is whether the buying and selling of labor are done typically under conditions approaching pure competition or pure monopoly. If the former, the real-wage level and the total amount of labor employed can be said to be the result of countless transactions entered into by individuals, no one of whom can affect the wage prevailing in a given market. Every employer will continue to hire additional workers at the prevailing wage until the value of any one worker's contribution to the firm's output falls below the added or marginal cost involved in hiring him. Accordingly, workers everywhere will receive a wage equal to the value of their marginal products. Moreover, involuntary unemployment will be no more than a limited or transitory phenomenon, since wages will automatically fall until all those seeking work find jobs. Just as in any one submarket, labor and capital will continue to shift throughout the country until net returns derived from utilizing small increments of each factor are made everywhere the same.

If labor is bought and sold typically under conditions approaching pure monopoly, however, the real-wage level does not adjust itself automatically in such a way as to bring about full employment, nor is labor allocated everywhere in such a way that workers receive wages equal to the value of their marginal physical products.[23] If employers generally possess a monopoly advantage in their dealings with employees, both the national wage level and the level of employment will tend to be less for a given number of workers than would be the case under pure competition, since employers will find it to their interest to restrict employment below what it would otherwise be. If the monopoly advantage, through unionism, lies on the workers' side, the real-wage level for those who remain employed will tend to be higher than under purely competitive con-

---

[21] Arthur M. Ross, *Trade Union Wage Policy* (Berkeley, Calif.: University of California Press, 1948).

[22] Sidney Weintraub has suggested to me that classical theory was only concerned with the absolute real share going to labor, not its relative share.

[23] Wages should still equal marginal-revenue products, however—the difference being that, under monopoly, changes in outputs of individual firms affect product prices, while under monopsony, changes in amount of labor hired by individual firms affect wages.

ditions; on the other hand, employment of labor generally will tend to be less since the labor organizations will find it to their advantage to restrict the amounts of labor offered in order to keep the wage for employed workers above the level it would otherwise be. It follows that neither full employment nor optimum allocation of labor will be realized if the buying and selling of labor are carried on under noncompetitive conditions.

Extended evaluation of this approach to the study of the national wage level, and of labor's share in the national product, is unnecessary, since it is subject to many of the same criticisms already noted in connection with partial-equilibrium analysis. The notion of an average wage level for all labor throughout the economy is so all-inclusive as to be devoid of much meaning. The competitive hypothesis makes it possible to speak of a normal or equilibrium wage level in some highly abstract sense, but if the noncompetitive hypothesis is used (and realism seems to require it), the notion of equilibrium becomes considerably less precise. The principal value of this formulation is realized when it is applied to labor's long-term real-wage position in different industries, regions, or countries. Clearly, the relatively high real-wage level in a country like the United States is tied, in a general way, to the value of labor's marginal product in this country. Moreover, broadly speaking, the shares of the national income going to labor and capital in a particular region or country reflect the relative abundance or scarcity of these two factors of production.[24]

Perhaps the main lesson to be learned from classical wage theory is that, at any given moment of time, a rise in the money-wage level is unlikely to entail a rise in the real-wage level, and if it does, the increase in the money- and real-wage level is even less likely to entail an increase in labor's total real income. Over a period of time, however, classical doctrine teaches us that the entire marginal-product schedule of labor may shift upward as mechanical methods of production or other improvements in efficiency are introduced on a widening scale; under these conditions, a rise in the real-wage level, in labor's total real income, and, conceivably, in labor's share in total output becomes possible. When stated in these broad terms, which are almost in the category of homely truths, few economists would take exception to the classical formulation, and in this sense it still appears to afford the best frame of reference for getting at long-term influences bearing on the nation's real-wage level.

MODERN INCOME THEORY

In modern income theory, in contrast to the classical system, the question of the level of aggregate demand comes to the forefront of attention. According to this view, even a country with a well-trained work force, an elaborate money and credit structure, a large stock of capital equipment, and a highly competitive business system may suffer from a low real-wage level and considerable unemployment. This anomalous result (the paradox of poverty in the midst of plenty) follows from the fact that there is no assurance that the principal spending propensities in the private sector—the propensity to consume, the propensity to lend, and the propensity to borrow (or invest)—will yield a total volume of expenditure which will fully utilize the country's physical and human resources. If these propensities—or, more strictly, the relationships among them—are such as to discourage spending, it follows that aggregate output, employment, and income will settle at a point well below the full-employment potential and that the real-wage, as well as the money-wage, bill will be reduced. If, on the other hand, the spending propensities are favorable, all the advantages flowing from a full utilization of the nation's resources will be realized, and the real-wage bill will be correspondingly greater.[25] Once full employment is attained, moreover, the important considerations become the same as those stressed by the classicists in explaining long-run changes in real wages. . . .

While modern income theory has put analysis of the national wage level in a wholly new light,

---

[24] The fact that labor's *relative* share in the national income has apparently remained stable for a long period of time has intrigued many economists, but a satisfactory explanation has yet to be developed. Starting from the assumption of imperfect competition, Kalecki makes the interesting suggestion that the stability in labor's share in England and the United States between 1880 and 1935 can be attributed to a decline in raw material prices which just about offset an increase in the degree of monopoly among business firms; the latter part of the proposition is extremely dubious. See Michael Kalecki, *Essays in the Theory of Economic Fluctuations* (New York: Rinehart, 1939), chap. 1.

[25] A concise statement of wage theory as it relates to modern income analysis is contained in James Tobin's essay in Seymour H. Harris (ed.), *The New Economics* (New York: Knopf, 1947), chap. 40. Reference is made to the wage bill rather than the wage level in order to avoid making any assumption as to whether production is occurring under conditions of decreasing returns.

it suffers from certain limitations or weaknesses which deserve mention.[26]

1. The theory is couched in broad aggregative terms. The consumption function, the marginal efficiency of capital, and the liquidity-preference schedule (to use Keynesian jargon) embody relationships of a most general character, and in applying these concepts it is easy to overlook important differences among consuming and investing groups. The analysis has been especially criticized for losing sight of the importance of cost-price relationships, differences in supply elasticities among industries, and variations in the sales-profit positions of different firms—considerations which are handled with considerable facility in partial-equilibrium analysis. This criticism seems justified, although it is more applicable to the way in which modern income theory has sometimes been applied than to the validity of the theory itself.

2. Income theory, strictly speaking, deals only in static, short-run relationships. In this respect, the theory is subject to the same weaknesses as the earlier formulations based on partial-equilibrium analysis; in fact, by concentrating on short-run conditions, one could argue, it is even more open to censure on this score. For many economists it is hard to attach much meaning to the notion that if a change occurs in one of the key determinants of national income, a series of adjustments will follow which will restore the balance of the system again. On the other hand, if the determinants are assumed to vary over time and if the relationships between the different spending categories are treated as cumulative within limits rather than self-limiting, the analysis is greatly complicated. Once again, theory seems to be faced with almost a Hobson's choice: to be either simple and meaningless or extremely complex and relevant.

3. Income theory has not yet successfully bridged the gap between money values and real values. As long as the analysis is confined to one basis or the other, this problem does not arise, but when the two sets of values are combined within a single system of relationships, serious difficulties occur. This was clearly evident in the comments already made concerning the determinants of the national wage level, when the leap was made from money terms to real terms.

4. As the foregoing suggests, the theory has been no more successful than any of its predecessors in dealing with the supply of labor. In order to close the system, some kind of supply curve of labor has to be introduced, but lacking a better means for handling the matter, a supply curve of labor has simply been assumed. In other words, the forces determining the national wage level are treated as lying largely outside the system of income relationships. A first order of business for those working in the wage field is to try to fill this void.[27]

In the perspective of subsequent developments, the greatest contribution of modern income analysis has come primarily as a by-product, for while the theory is essentially static in conception, it has given an enormous impetus to the study of dynamic relationships. The analysis of wages has as yet received little benefit from this new development in economics, but it can be confidently predicted that it will do so in the future.

CONCLUSIONS

In this brief review of wage theory, emphasis has been put on those features of deductive analysis which have added most to our understanding of contemporary wage issues. Broadly speaking, partial- and general-equilibrium theory have been found to provide an unsatisfactory framework for analyzing wage relationships in terms of choices, determinants, and effects—the three questions of major interest today. On the other hand, the direction in which recent work in these two areas has been moving shows considerable promise. In the area of partial-equilibrium analysis, theorists are putting less emphasis on the rather simple, almost mechanical view of wage determination based on the hypothesis of pure competition and developed in its most elaborate form in the theory of marginal productivity. Increasing attention is being given to formulations based on the noncompetitive hypothesis, such as bilateral monopoly, and on the interplay between competitive and noncompetitive influences. Thus, while contemporary theorists (quite properly, it seems) still use the competitive or marginal-productivity hypothesis to explain wage movements of a broad, long-term nature, they

[26] These issues, particularly the second and third, are discussed in Lawrence R. Klein's essay in Kenneth K. Kurihara (ed.), *Post Keynesian Economics* (New Brunswick, N.J.: Rutgers University Press, 1954), chap. 11.

[27] Concerning this element in his empirical model of the Keynesian system, Klein writes: "A labor supply equation is not explicitly reproduced. At this stage, the model assumes the labor force to be an exogenous variable, but obviously this approximation eventually will have to be dropped." See Lawrence R. Klein's essay in Kurihara, *Post Keynesian Economics*, p. 317.

tend to approach the study of structural wage differences and short-term wage movements in terms of the noncompetitive hypothesis.

This accords with the view that influences other than the compulsions of competitive markets play a large role in shaping wage relationships. An understanding of these other influences calls particularly for an analysis of salient aspects of industrial relations: how managements and unions approach their wage bargains, how the prospect of nonagreement affects their dealings, how various intra- and interplant wage structures emerge, and the like. . . .

Our critique of general-equilibrium theory has yielded somewhat similar findings. Except for explanations of long-term movements, modern theorists no longer use the marginal-productivity framework in analyzing the general wage level. The controlling forces emphasized today are those associated with modern income analysis. This analysis, however, yields rather fuzzy results; it is impossible to speak with much definiteness about the relationships between changes in the general wage level and the other elements of national income determination. Again, the way is open for further work which will help fill the gap that modern theory has exposed.

The principal conclusion to which this critique has come is that in both branches of deductive analysis, theorists are now saying that wage determination cannot be reduced to a single rule of behavior, that in so far as economic influences as such are concerned, there is an element of uncertainty or even indeterminateness in wage setting, which earlier economists were inclined to minimize. This accords with the main line of development in empirical work, suggesting that it is in this direction that deductive and inductive wage analysis may yet be able to reach common ground.

40. Flexible Working Hours: It's about Time*

Alvar O. Elbing, Herman Gadon, and John R. M. Gordon†

The changing workweek is no longer just an idea—it is a reality, and one that appears to be here to stay. On both sides of the Atlantic, management, workers, and unions are actively engaged in discussing and trying out new organizations of working time that represent permanent shifts away from the classic 5-day, 9 to 5, 40-hour week.

Though changes have occurred in both Europe and North America, the forms they have taken until now have been quite different. In Europe, companies have usually adopted some form of a flexible working-hours plan. Started in West Germany in 1967, the idea was picked up in Austria and Switzerland, and then in Scandinavia. From there it spread southward to France, Benelux, Italy, Spain, and to the United Kingdom. Today in West Germany alone, over 3,000 companies use some form of flexible hours; this directly involves over 1 million employees.

In North America, on the other hand, the shorter workweek (4 10-hour days or 3 12-hour days, for example) has been tried almost exclusively. According to the April 30, 1973 *Wall Street Journal*, some 3,000 U.S. companies have adopted the 4-day week, compared to an estimated 40 in 1970. The article also mentioned, however, that after introduction to the 4-day week, there is frequent disenchantment and a decline in enthusiasm for it. Experience has revealed unforeseen problems that have reduced

its appeal and limited its extension; the 4-day week does not deal with the central issue of autonomous distribution of one's own time.

In Europe, by contrast, enthusiasm for flexible working hours continues and appears to be on the increase. The concept of flexible working hours bypasses the length of the workweek and allows individuals to settle their own work- and leisure-time allocations, within limitations. Perhaps this is the reason why the concept of flexible working hours is at last catching on and gaining acceptance in North America.

At a conference in New York City in March 1973 on the Changing Work Ethic (sponsored by the Urban Research Corporation of Chicago), the view was often expressed among participants that the current trend toward flexible hours would virtually halt consideration of the shorter workweek as the primary alternative to the 5-day week. Similar views were expressed by U.S. managers of MNCs [multinational corporations] who have had experience in Europe with flexible working hours and who were aware of American experimentation with the shorter workweek. If the U.S. experience parallels Europe's, flexible working hours should sweep the country during the next few years. Just what do U.S. companies have to look forward to?

THE CHANGING WORKWEEK

The flexible-hours system is just one of several ways to organize working time. In general, one can speak about fixed, staggered, flexible, or variable working hours. This hierarchy represents an increasing level of flexibility in working-hour arrangements between employees and employers: Fixed and staggered hours do not change once established; flexible and variable hours can change from day to day. In the latter cases, a

* Reprinted with permission from the *Harvard Business Review*, Vol. 52, No. 1, January–February 1974, pp. 18–33. Copyright © by the President and Fellows of Harvard College.

† Mr. Elbing and Mr. Gordon are both professors of business administration at IMEDE Management Development Institute in Lausanne, Switzerland. Mr. Gadon was in residence at IMEDE during 1971–73, and is now professor of management at the Whittemore School of Business and Economics, University of New Hampshire.

system of record keeping is necessary so that the number of hours worked can be balanced over some time period, usually a week or a month.

In general, the 4-day workweek used in North America fits into the first category of fixed hours. Once the normal workday is established, the employee has no mobility within the set hours.

The concept of staggered hours does allow a certain degree of flexibility for the company. Under that system separate groups of employees arrive at different times, resulting in overlapping schedules, but all must still work a predetermined number of hours during their workday.

The system known as flexible working hours introduces flexibility for the employee. He has the right to determine the number of hours he will work in any particular day, outside the core times when all employees must be present.

Finally, the most flexible of working arrangements involves variable working hours. In contrast to flexible hours, the variable-hours system does not specify a core time. Under the variable-hours system, the employee may work whenever he wishes. He may take time off without specific permission, as long as his function is covered in his absence.

The most advanced example of this method that we have observed is in the German time-recording meter assembly plant of the Hengstler Gleitzeit ("gliding time") Company, a subsidiary of Hengstler Company. Not only can the 100 employees schedule their own workdays, but they also all have keys to the plant; they can let themselves in at any hour and turn on the assembly line. In order to do this, the employees learned how to fill in at all positions on the line. Now the two plant supervisors spend their time on systems design rather than on personnel problems. Willi Haller, managing director of Hengstler Gleitzeit, is delighted with the results, which have produced a fourfold increase in output over three years.

Although some companies in Europe are clearly pleased with the variable-hours system, the flexible working-hours concept is more widely accepted. The many instances of its acceptance in Europe and elsewhere seem to forecast a similar experience for North America.

Experience Abroad

In Europe flexible hours began less from a philosophical conviction about employee participation than from practical organization needs produced by the external environment. The first experiment with flexible hours occurred in Germany as a result of traffic congestion.

At the Ottobrunn research and development plant of Messerschmitt-Bölkow-Blohm, a German aerospace company, employees were finding that it took a little longer every day to get to work on time. While encouraging automobile transportation, an extension of the autobahn led commuter traffic close to the plant but not directly to it. During rush hours the local routes from the autobahn to the plant were totally inadequate to absorb the traffic, and the community could not be motivated to improve them. It looked as if there were no solution to the congestion problem until the employees themselves leveled out the traffic by distributing their arrivals over a lengthier time period.

Thus in 1967 the flexible working-hours system was established at Ottobrunn, and unexpected side benefits surfaced. As it was now legitimate to arrive late for work, or rather at an hour of one's choosing, there was a remarkable drop in sick-leave calls. The experiment worked so well, in fact, that it was extended to the entire facility. By 1969 an estimated ten companies in Germany had adopted the system.

At first, managements were apprehensive. The flexible-hours system might reduce traffic problems, but would it not also reduce efficiency? Some feared that management would lose control of output, be unable to plan production, or lose contact with employees. Others worried that the system would increase operating costs. Experience, however, has proved otherwise. According to a survey carried out in 1973 by the Deutsche Gesellschaft für Personalführung (German Personnel Management Association), to which 30 companies replied, 24 reported improvement in working atmosphere; 25, reduction of paid absences; 23, self-adjustment of work time to work load; 15, reduction of overtime; 17, increased individual productivity; 19, improved recruitment success; and 6, reduced personnel turnover.

The German Industrial Institute (DII) predicts that 50 percent, or 6 million, of the white collar workers in Germany will be on flexible hours by 1975. It is anticipated that this trend will be followed in most European countries.

The rest of German-speaking Europe has been quick to follow the German experience, and in Sweden, Denmark, Norway, and Finland the flexible working-hours concept is gaining in popularity. In Great Britain 80 companies and 500,000 civil servants are on some form of the system; in Italy, France, and Spain it is spreading. Perhaps the most surprising use of the system to date is not in Europe but in Japan, where it was first introduced in 1971. Because, it was argued, the system violated Japanese working traditions, quick failure was forecast. On the contrary (and much to the delight of the Japanese Ministry of Trade), the system is still employed and working well. In the crowded cities and paternalistic companies that characterize Japan, the value of flexible working hours is high.

North America Next

The experience with flexible hours outside Europe has not totally excluded North America. In Canada, the Excelsior Life Insurance Company of Toronto, Taylor Instruments, and Canadian Liquid Air Ltd. all use the system. A recent decision by the Canadian Treasury Board may be a dramatic turning point. After considerable analysis and experimentation, the board both approved flexible hours and denied the short workweek. The results of this decision for the balance of Canadian civil service, as well as for Canadian industry, should be very interesting.

Although until recently the Canadian experience was ahead of that of the United States, the situation is rapidly changing. The Flextime Corporation, a New York-based subsidiary of the Hengstler Gleitzeit Company, recently reported a 100 percent increase in orders for its flexible-hours systems equipment. In September 1973, Bernhard Keppler, president of Flextime, disclosed that in May 1973, when his company began operations in North America, only 12 companies in the United States had installed Flextime equipment. But since that time, he has received orders from 12 other companies to introduce flexible working hours by the end of November 1973. These 24 firms—primarily banks, insurance companies, and government offices, but also including a few engineering firms, a meter manufacturer, a library, and a technical institute—collectively employ 5,000 people.

The popular press (*Wall Street Journal,* July 7, 1973; *Newsweek,* September 10, 1973) indicates that the idea is spreading and gaining favor with U.S. domestic companies as well as with foreign subsidiaries in the United States. Considerable coverage has been given to Hewlett-Packard, Scott Paper, Occidental Insurance, Samsonite, Sun Oil, and the Industrial National Bank of Providence, Rhode Island, as well as to Nestlé in White Plains, New York, and Lufthansa German Airlines.

While the flexible-time concept is spreading in the United States, there is considerable variation in the systems adopted. Hewlett-Packard, for instance, requires employees to work a given number of hours every day, though they can decide each day when between the hours of 6:30 and 8:30 A.M. they will come to work; starting time automatically determines quitting time. The U.S. headquarters of Nestlé Alimentana Company asks each employee the week before to decide what hours he will work during the following week. At the Industrial National Bank in Providence, the employee balances his time each week and decides for himself how many hours in addition to core times he will work each day, as well as when he will work them.

What Is Meant by Flexible Working Hours?

The system of flexible working hours is a way of arranging work time that gives employees some freedom in choosing the hours they will work each day. A typical example is the system recently adopted by a Swiss company, using the following regulations for 300 administrative employees. They can report for work in the morning any time between the hours of 7:00 and 9:00, but they must be there between 9:00 and 11:30. Lunch can be taken between 11:30 and 1:00 as long as at least 30 minutes are used as required by law. All employees are required to be at work during the afternoon core hours of 1:00 to 4:00 P.M. It is possible to leave work any time between 4:00 and 6:00. Total hours (plus or minus ten) must balance monthly against the work-time requirement.

An employee may work as little as 5½ hours or as much as 10½ hours (excluding ½ hour for lunch) in any one day; as little as 27½ hours or as much as 52½ hours in any one week. The only stipulation is that he must be present every day during the core times of 9:00 to 11:30 and 1:00 to 4:00. If the usual monthly work requirement is 168 hours, and the employee works more than 178 hours in the month, he still carries over only 10 hours as a credit balance. He is also allowed to carry over a debit balance of 10 hours, which means that in a given month he may work as little as 158 hours (assuming no credit balance on which to trade) or 148 hours (if he has carried forward a 10-hour credit balance from the previous month).

Theoretically, each employee could maintain a debit balance of 10 hours carried over from month to month. The companies from which we have information, however, report a *credit* balance averaging 3½ hours per employee.

In general, time credit has been applied only to working days and has not been added to vacation time, but this is another option.

As the experience with flexible working hours in the United States increases, it will be important to examine closely the usefulness of the system in the North American work environment. As yet no form of the system is perfect. Implementation sets enormous challenges for organizations, and before adopting the system, U.S. managers need to be convinced of its worth for their own companies.

WHERE IT WILL WORK, AND WHY

When discussing flexible working hours, most executives inevitably say, "That's all very well, but is it appropriate for my organization?" This question is usually followed by a series of reasons to explain why the cited examples of flexible working hours are limited to special cases, or why the individual concerned considers his own potential application a unique case.

The historic origins of flexible working hours indicate that it is an appropriate system in a research and development setting, like that at Ottobrunn. Further, the system can easily accommodate relatively professional employees who work on an independent basis rather than in interdependent teams. More probing usually reveals that many clerical activities could also be handled quite well under flexible working hours.

The system has been successfully installed and used in a number of production operations, all the way from heavy industrial manufacturing of hydroelectric equipment to assembly lines in the watch industry. Even job-shop applications do not seem beyond the realm of feasibility when one considers that most job shop operations already involve a significant amount of in-process inventory that tends to buffer individual operations from one another. The additional discrepancies caused by flexible working hours from work center to work center would, therefore, probably have only limited impact on the total amount of in-process inventory required to maintain a smoothly operating shop.

On the other hand, when flexible working hours are used in an assembly line operation, the line may have to be redesigned to include larger amounts of in-process inventory so that there is some element of independence among workers. In instances where this has been done, the increase in inventory has been recognized but has not been a deterrent.

It has not yet been determined whether there is a net added cost of carrying the additional inventory; a precise cost/benefit analysis will be necessary to settle this question. (In most of the European assembly-line operations that we observed, the workers generally carried over a credit balance per employee averaging 3½ hours a month. Since this represents labor for which payment has not been made, it is in the company's favor and is an offset against extra inventory carried as a buffer between work stations.)

Also, few basic demands for output or service occur in a uniform and regular manner. Most work demands are variable. Because of management's inability to predict the pattern of this variability, and because of its preoccupation with uniform work loads, it has attempted to create an illusion that work demands themselves are uniform. It may be to everybody's advantage to permit variable scheduling for variable work loads; in fact, when the work is truly uniform and repetitive, some attempt to make it variable may be more productive in the long run.

One further example of the application of flexible working hours, in an apparently low-feasibility production situation, is its use in shops that are operating on two shifts. Brown Boveri in Switzerland has successfully implemented flexible working hours on a two-shift installation; the comings and goings of operators manning the same piece of equipment are coordinated by the two workers themselves.

We have encountered most concern about the limits of flexible working hours from managements contemplating application to three-shift operations, where it is difficult for employees among whom there are interdependencies to arrange simultaneous communications. This does not appear, however, to present formidable problems of coordination. We have found that in more than 80 German EDP centers operating on three shifts, the system is working well.

Many managers also feel that the size of the organization is a determining factor in the applicability of flexible working hours. The concept of a rather loose system of attendance for a large organization creates an image that is not comforting to most supervisors. Most people also seem to feel that flexible working hours would not be a successful system in a service organization, where close interdependencies among individuals working in groups, or interaction between individuals and clients, is essential. Specific examples show, however, that this is not necessarily the case:

1. A German department store with over 100 salesclerks and a supervisory staff of three has all employees coming and going as they wish. The ability to make commissions on sales ensures that there is coverage during peak hours, and informal

agreements between the clerks guarantee coverage during the slower early morning and late afternoon hours.

2. A German insurance company was worried about the personal service which customers expected and which they might miss if employees were not available outside of core-time periods. The company solution was to print the core times on its letterhead. The employees themselves dealt with the problem another way. There had always been times when agents were unavailable, and client coverage by other agents at those times had been unsatisfactory.

With the introduction of flexible working hours and a potential decrease in contact hours between the client and his agent, all the agents assumed responsibility for each other's clients. Customer service and satisfaction actually increased. The client felt that someone was looking after him when his own agent was away, and the agent was better informed when he returned to work.

Certainly there are potential problems with both external and internal communications. The difficulties are not hard to overcome, however, since members of the organization adjust rather quickly to the new arrangements. First, in most instances, they have approved of flexible working hours and therefore have a stake in making the system work. Second, there are clear benefits to individuals in retaining the system and, therefore, in coping with difficulties it generates. Third, experience reveals that wasted time decreases—Parkinson's law seems to be an operational one.

For instance, we have often found that there are fewer meetings, and they take less time. Apparently, we tailor our work to the time available to do it. We have yet to come across an instance in which the reduced contact hours have resulted in decreased efficiency, although some executives remember complaining at first that it felt inconvenient not to have people available when needed, either on an individual basis or for meetings. On the other hand, it is commonly reported that people use the time they have before and after core hours to concentrate on correspondence, projects, clearing backlogs, and so forth, without fear of interruption. Also, in most cases where the system has been adopted, the absentee level has dropped so that there have actually been more people on the job than before.

The key to success in the above examples appears to be that the employees have an opportunity to take some responsibility for their own performance and to coordinate their personal time with their work time. In fact, these factors have been present in all the applications of flexible working hours that have succeeded. In one of the German EDP centers mentioned earlier, management left the prime responsibility of function performance to the person whose job it was. It was up to him to arrange his time with others on whom he depended or who depended on him. In the company that could not afford large stocks of in-process inventory, the employees on successive operations took the responsibility of making reciprocal agreements between themselves, a plan that ensured the operators of sufficient materials for uninterrupted production.

Flexible working hours may not be universally applicable, but where the system does work, success must be attributed to trust, mutual confidence, and a shared commitment that grows out of a problem-solving effort on behalf of both management and employees.

INTRODUCING THE SYSTEM

To succeed, the flexible working-hours system requires that members of an organization have mutual trust and confidence. In particular, management must believe that employees will not abuse the trust placed in them. Unlike other benefits, which are "given" to employees and are passively accepted, flexible working hours require active response: Employees must live up to expectations of their performance. Also, employees must believe that management does, in fact, trust them.

No matter who introduces the idea, support of the concept by other involved groups is necessary sooner or later. Though motives may vary, the differences are not likely to be critical as long as interested parties are given an honest opportunity to participate early enough in the consideration process.

In one of the few instances in Europe where the flexible working-hours system was rejected by employees, a well-meaning management asked a personnel committee to approve a plan without first providing employees with the opportunity to understand it, ask for more information, or influence features of the plan that were important to them. After a referendum administered by the committee, the employees turned down the company's proposal. On reflection, some company executives felt that the employees reacted to what appeared to them to be the relative arrogance of management rather than to their own doubts about the actual value of the plan.

This case dramatically illustrates the importance of the process of introduction. In no instance where arrangements have been made to treat employee views seriously have we heard of a rejection of a proposed application of flexible working hours. In the present case, top management had not resolved its own mixed feelings about giving up control over the workday schedule. This ambivalence was sensed as a lack of trust by the personnel committee and was ultimately passed on to the employees. In an environment that reflected doubts and suspicion rather than confidence in their integrity, the employees reacted negatively to management's proposals.

If a flexible working-hours system is to be successfully introduced, top management must be unequivocally enthusiastic. And the decision is a policy matter that must be decided at the highest level to ensure the support of line managers. Once its own commitment to the plan has been made, top management must make sure its immediate subordinates share its commitment.

First-Line Supervisors

In the operation of the system first-line supervisors play a key role; it is they who represent to subordinates the operational meaning of policies announced by higher levels of management. If they do not put the intent of policy declarations into practice, the result will be failure. Time and again we have seen that first-line supervisors have been extremely sensitive to the introduction of flexible working hours. In fact, they must face what is probably the hardest job of adjustment.

Perceiving pressure from top management as a demand to "control" subordinates, supervisors often take refuge in one of the oldest organization myths—presence equals performance. When all else fails, they can take comfort from insisting on attendance and punctuality. Under flexible working hours, first-line supervisors are deprived of recourse to this time-honored tool and are asked instead to trust their subordinates before they acquire the reassuring experience that the subordinates will honor that trust.

Three types of initial supervisory reactions to flexible hours have been observed. In some cases, the supervisors fear something will happen when they are not present, so they increase their own working hours. In other cases, supervisors try to learn each other's jobs, so they can rely on colleagues during flexible-time periods. Most often, however, supervisors learn the benefits of having employees organize their own work and are then free to concentrate on long-range planning.

Others Down the Line

In some organizations other special groups need to be identified and their reactions anticipated. We have seen professional staffs, already operating on a flexible-hours basis, who resented extension of the privilege to the rest of the organization because it removed a distinction through which the professional employees saw themselves as having higher status.

There are some personnel who cannot easily adapt their activities to a flexible working-hours arrangement, for example, linear assembly-line operators on three shifts. Groups that are excluded, or who see themselves as losing something when others gain, need explanations in advance. Where management had the courage not only to inform these people of the difficulties, but to entrust them with the elimination of problems that seemed insurmountable, employees sometimes rewarded management with ingenious solutions to which they were committed.

Where employees are represented by a union, it too will have to be taken into consideration. In some cases in Europe, union officials have opposed introduction of flexible working hours only to be pressured into active support by members themselves. In Sweden, a national union refused the request of a local union to negotiate a flexible-hours plan with management. It changed its position, however, after the local threatened to buy television time to expose the resistance of the national union. In another instance, in Germany, this turnabout was reflected by changing the demand for payment of a premium for personnel working *with* flexible working hours to a demand for a premium for workers *not* receiving the "benefit" of such arrangements.

By and large, unions in Europe have supported flexible working hours and deliberately shied away from quibbling about sharing gains in productivity. Apparently, union leaders have not wanted to jeopardize a development that seems so clearly in the best interest of workers. In the United States, the UAW has expressed interest in flexible working hours through its participation as a panel member in the April 4, 1973, conference on the subject that was sponsored by the American Management Association.

TURNING IT ON

Once the decision has been made to introduce flexible working hours, it is necessary to define the operational features of the system. Decisions must be made about the length of the accounting period, core times, carry-over allowed from one accounting period to the next, payment for overtime, and so on. In some instances, joint committees of management and employees have worked well to provide these operational guidelines. Some of these decisions involve legal issues. In the United States, for instance, companies are currently installing the system within the limits of a weekly accounting period, or even within a day, because of overtime pay problems connected with the Fair Labor Standards and Walsh-Healey acts.

Sometime during the design of the proposed system the question of recording the work time must be decided. There are at least five different methods now in use. The most simple are self-recording systems maintained by the individual employee. In one, he keeps his own record and balances it himself; in another, he signs in and out at some central point, but the balance is kept by someone else. A third system uses the classic time clock, which mechanically checks and records the employee's punctuality.

A fourth system uses a special time-recording meter which, unlike the time clock, is merely an accounting machine that provides the employee with a correct tally but does not store or use the information. Finally, some organizations use a centralized computer. Nestlé headquarters in Vevey, Switzerland, uses one with visual displays located in easily accessible places throughout the office building; employees can record and check their time at their convenience.

While each device can be adapted to the demands of the system, the special-purpose time-recording equipment seems to entail the least difficulties while offering overall advantages of simple administration and continuous, easy access to information at a low cost.

After the general guidelines of the system have been defined, all interested parties must be informed. Following a general announcement, a series of meetings with employees is usually necessary to answer any questions and deal with unexpected problems.

To administer the system properly, the first-line supervisor must become completely familiar with all its operational details. Experience indicates that the best-prepared supervisor is the one who helps design the system before it is installed. In developing the details of a system it is desirable to have as much interaction as possible between the first-line supervisor and his superior. Sometimes the development work and training of first-line supervisors is done by staff men from the accounting or personnel departments. While these specialists should be available, direct involvement of the first-line supervisor's boss signifies management support and commitment to the new system. And involvement of the first-line supervisor gives him an opportunity to identify and cope with the real or fancied problems he believes the new system will create for him. In these ways, each system can be tailored to the organization's needs.

In general, organizations interested in considering a change in working-hour patterns experiment with it in some part of the organization where reliable observation of the results is possible. The experiment usually runs for several months, after which there is an objective evaluation of the system.

At this point, an interesting phenomenon has been observed: The organization cannot go back. Experimenting with flexible hours is like stepping on a moving sidewalk—the organization just keeps going. In thousands of cases observed in Europe, the vast majority rapidly expanded the system throughout the organization regardless of the evaluation. Some organizations expanded even before the completion of the trial period.

CONCLUSIONS

The flexible working-hours system is not a panacea for traffic congestion, overloaded facilities, or the malaise that accompanies boring and repetitive work. But experience in Europe has shown us that when it is installed in the presence of an appropriate managerial environment, productivity improves, morale rises, turnover drops, absenteeism decreases, and overtime declines.

For the employee, being able to arrive and depart when he chooses has significant advantages for travel and personal circumstances. If both husband and wife work, flexible working hours make it possible for them to arrange their schedules so that one of them can, for instance, be at home when the children get out of school.

For the community, flexible working hours can lead to a more uniform use of recreational and support facilities. With spread-out work peaks, it is possible to ensure better utilization of golf courses, power and fuel supplies, traffic routes, and even of human patience.

And finally, for organizations themselves, a flexible working-hours system can not only increase productivity by opening up new scheduling opportunities but also provide a new measure of self-respect for employees at every level.

41. How Many Days Make a Workweek?*

Janice Neipert Hedges†

The number of days worked per week has been little discussed in the research on worktime. Weekly hours have been tracked since 1870, but no systematic record exists of the transition that began in the 1920s from workweeks of 6 or 5½ days to 5 days. Not until recently have data been available to detect whether a further reduction in workdays may be underway.

Interest in the configuration of weekly hours has mounted in the past few years as new types of work schedules have drawn attention to the fact that full-time weeks are being worked in 3 to 7 days. In addition, there has been a growing awareness of the implications of the allocation of the week between workdays and "free days."

Discussions of 4-day workweeks often range, for example, over the potential effects on the health and activities of workers and their families, and on their demands for goods and services. Within firms, their effects on absence, tardiness, injuries, plant and equipment utilization, and energy and other costs are at issue. At the national level, their potential impact on commuter traffic, productivity, employment, and energy have been of greatest interest.

This article reports on the first national survey of the number of days usually worked by wage and salary employees who typically work full time, that is, 35 hours or more a week.[1] The major

source of data was a special question ("How many days a week does . . . usually work at this job?") on the May 1973 and May 1974 supplements to the Current Population Survey (CPS), a national sample survey of 47,000 households which is conducted by the Bureau of the Census for the Bureau of Labor Statistics.

The data refer to usual days worked (whether scheduled or not) on their sole or primary job by wage and salary workers, except farm and household workers.

They cover "shorter workweeks" of 3, 4, or 4½ days, "standard workweeks" of 5 days, and "extended workweeks" of 5½, 6, or 7 days.[2] All of the 3- and 4-day weeks and about half of the 4½-day weeks (those of 38 hours or more) involve workdays in excess of 8 hours. The data refer to the hours of workers as distinct from the hours of the establishment. Workers on a 4½-day week, for example, may be employed in an establishment that operates 5 days or more a week.

OVERALL PATTERNS

The CPS data show that the 5-day workweek still dominates the work schedules of U.S. wage

* From U.S. Department of Labor, *Monthly Labor Review*, Vol. 98, No. 4, April 1975, pp. 29–36.

† Janice Neipert Hedges is an economist in the Division of Labor Force Studies, Bureau of Labor Statistics.

[1] Beginning with 1972, the Bureau's Area Wage Survey program has compiled national and area data on days worked per week in metropolitan areas. Data for these surveys are obtained from employers and relate to work schedules for the majority of workers in each establishment. See *Area Wage Surveys: Metropolitan Areas, United States and Regional Summaries, 1971–72*, Bulletin 1725–96 (Bureau of Labor Statistics, 1974) and individual area bulletins.

[2] In those cases where the respondent either was unable to answer the question on the number of days usually worked or asked how the data should be computed, the interviewer was instructed to count as 1 full day each day during which a person worked his regular hours or more, and as a half day each day during which a person worked more than 2 hours less than his regular hours. The 7-day category includes 6½-day weeks. Data on daily hours were calculated from the data collected on usual days and usual weekly hours. In deriving daily hours, it was assumed that each whole day reported by an individual was of equal length, and that a "half-day" was literally half of a whole day.

and salary workers. Workweeks longer than 5 days are still much more prevalent than workweeks shorter than 5 days.

The average number of days in a workweek in May 1974 ranged from 5.8 for schedules of 51 hours or more a week to 5.0 for schedules of 35–39 hours. Five-day workweeks predominated among employees who worked from 35 to 45 hours and, as expected, were most widespread among those who worked 40 hours. Above that level, they yielded progressively to schedules of 5½ days or more. Interestingly, below 40 hours, schedules of 4½ days or less and 5½ days or more both increased. (See Table 1.) Even among employees who worked 35–39 hours, however, almost 9 out of 10 worked 5-day weeks.

Arrangements of weekly hours are affected by collective bargaining agreements and by laws. Many agreements, for example, tend to limit daily hours and/or the number of workdays through premium pay provisions. Some directly stipulate the number of scheduled workdays.[3] Among the laws that encourage a limit on daily hours (by requiring premium pay after 8 hours a day) are the Contract Work Hours and Safety Standards Act and the Walsh-Healey Public Contracts Act, which apply to most workers in firms holding government contracts.[4] The Federal Pay Act, which applies to most federal employees, has a similar provision.[5] The amended Fair Labor Standards Act,[6] which requires that employees in interstate commerce and in public administration be paid overtime after 40 hours of work a week, sometimes combines with other legal and collective bargaining provisions concerning daily overtime to encourage a 5-day workweek.[7]

The force of the various influences for 5-day weeks and 8-hour days is suggested by the fact that in May 1974, about 38.3 million wage and salary workers regularly worked a 5-day week of 8-hour days. An additional 10.5 million worked a 5-day week (but not 8-hour days) and over 2 million worked 8-hour days (but not 5-day weeks).

The CPS data also indicate a tendency for

---

3 *Characteristics of Agreements Covering 1,000 Workers or More, July 1, 1973,* Bulletin 1822 (Bureau of Labor Statistics, 1974).

4 Public Law 87–581, August 13, 1962 and Public Law 74–846, June 30, 1936.

5 United States Code, title 5, chapter 61.

6 Public Law 93–259, April 18, 1974.

7 Five 4-day workweeks are legislated for many employees by the Monday Holiday Law, which reschedules a number of national holidays (Washington's Birthday, Memorial Day, Labor Day, Columbus Day, and Veteran's Day) to provide 3-day weekends. See Public Law 90–363, June 28, 1968.

TABLE 1   Number and Percent Distribution of Nonfarm Wage and Salary Workers Who Usually Work Full Time, by Usual Number of Days and Hours per Week, May 1974

Hours per Week	Total Reporting*	Fewer than 5 Days	5 Days	More than 5 Days
		Number in thousands		
35 or more....	59,187	1,096	48,807	9,283
35 to 39.......	5,090	334	4,430	326
40..........	39,868	466	38,263	1,140
41 to 45.......	4,178	72	2,721	1,386
46 to 50.......	5,749	87	2,436	3,226
51 or more....	4,301	137	958	3,206
		Percent distribution		
35 or more....	100.0	1.9	82.5	15.7
35 to 39.......	100.0	6.6	87.0	6.4
40..........	100.0	1.2	96.0	2.9
41 to 45.......	100.0	1.7	65.1	33.2
46 to 50.......	100.0	1.5	42.4	56.1
51 or more....	100.0	3.2	22.3	74.5

Note: Data apply to nonfarm wage and salary workers, excluding private household workers. Because of rounding, sums of individual items may not equal totals.
* Total reporting for 1974 in Tables 1 and 2 differ since fewer workers report hours per week than days worked.

---

workweeks to consist only of full days.[8] Although 4½- and 5½-day schedules fall nearer the standard 5-day week than 4- or 6-day schedules, about half as many work the former as the latter. In all, only 5 percent of all wage and salary workers usually work 4½- or 5½-day weeks.

CURRENT DEVELOPMENTS

In May 1974, several years after the 4-day week was heralded as a revolution in working time, about 650,000 full-time wage and salary employees usually worked such a schedule.[9] An additional 190,000 regularly worked full time 3 days a week. When employees on 4½-day weeks (who may have been on such schedules for some time) were included, 1.1 million workers or 2 percent of all full-time wage and salary workers, regularly were working less than 5 full days a week.

Wage and salary workers who regularly put in 5½, 6, or even 7 days a week were far more numerous. Totaling over 9 milion employees, they accounted for 16 percent of all full-time workers.

---

8 The data also seem to indicate a preference for whole hours per day. Although average days tend to decrease as hours shorten, more workers work 5-day weeks in weekly hours categories that are evenly divisible by 5 (35, 40, 45, and 50) than in categories that are 1 to 4 hours higher.

9 Riva Poor, ed., *4 Days, 40 Hours,* (Cambridge, Mass.: Bursk and Poor Publishing, 1970).

TABLE 2   Number and Percent Distribution of Nonfarm Wage and Salary Workers Who Usually Work Full Time by Usual Number of Days Worked and Industry Group, May 1974 (numbers in thousands)

Industry Group	Number Reporting	Percent Distribution		
		Fewer than 5 Days	5 Days	More than 5 Days
Total...................................	59,442	1.9	82.2	15.9
Goods producing*...........................	23,471	1.3	85.4	13.3
Mining.......................................	562	.6	70.9	28.5
Construction...............................	4,059	2.3	87.0	10.7
Manufacturing.............................	18,641	1.1	85.8	13.1
Service producing...........................	35,971	2.2	80.2	17.6
Transportation............................	4,725	2.0	84.8	13.2
Trade.......................................	9,817	1.6	66.9	31.6
Finance.....................................	3,505	1.9	84.5	13.6
Professional...............................	10,820	1.6	88.7	9.7
Other.......................................	3,033	3.2	69.2	27.5
Public administration.....................	4,070	5.2	88.9	5.8
Federal and state........................	2,800	.6	94.9	4.5
Local.......................................	1,270	15.5	75.8	8.7

Note: Data apply to nonfarm wage and salary workers excluding private household workers. Because of rounding, sums of individual items may not equal totals.
* Total includes nonfarm workers in the agricultural industry.

The 5-day week remained clearly the standard or, as its detractors term it, the "mold."[10] Almost 49 million full-time wage and salary workers, or four-fifths of the total, usually worked 5 days a week in 1974. Recent developments suggest, however, that significant changes in the configuration of hours and days worked might be anticipated.

Work schedules are being used by management, for example, as strategies for problem solving. Scheduling by objectives led in the early 1970s to flexitime and variable schedules as well as compressed 4- and 3-day schedules.[11] The common objective is to improve the functioning of the firm, although the specific target varies. Sometimes it is adjusting the flow of man-hours to peak workloads, or increasing the utilization of plant and equipment, or improving customer service. In others it is improving recruitment, lowering absence rates, reducing turnover, or raising morale.

The interest of workers in larger blocks of leisure and their problems with inconvenient schedules and excessive hours also can be ex-

pected to influence work schedules.[12] An agreement signed by Chrysler Corp. and the United Automobile Workers (UAW) in September 1973 may herald significant changes in days worked when economic conditions improve. The agreement, which set a pattern in the automobile industry, permits workers to turn down assignments on Saturdays under certain conditions and, if attendance requirements are met, on any Sunday.

WORKERS ON SHORTER WORKWEEKS

Workers on shorter weeks in May 1974 differed from those on 5-day weeks in their industry and occupational distribution and in certain demographic characteristics. Local public administration, for example, accounted for 2 percent of all full-time workers, but 18 percent of those on shorter workweeks. About 16 percent of all full-time workers in this industry worked less than 5 days a week in May 1974. (See Table 2.)

By occupation, service employees had the highest proportion, 7 percent, on workweeks of less than 5 days. (See Table 3.) This occupation, which includes protective and health service personnel and workers in food and personal

[10] See, for example, Linda G. Sprague, "Breaking the 5-Day Mold: Scheduling Issues," in Riva Poor, ed., 4 Days, 40 Hours, pp. 71–78.

[11] Flexitime refers to a work schedule that gives employees some limited options in the time that they arrive and depart but does not change total hours over a given time period. Variable hours permit employees to work whenever they wish. Again, total hours are not usually affected, although the term is used occasionally to refer to an arrangement in which the only control is getting the work done.

[12] See Juanita Kreps, "Lifetime Trade-offs between Work and Play," *Proceedings of the 21st Annual Winter Meeting of the Industrial Relations Research Association, 1968*, pp. 307–16 and Robert P. Quinn, Thomas W. Mangione, Martha S. Baldi de Mandilovitch, "Evaluating Working Conditions in America," *Monthly Labor Review*, November 1973, p. 36.

TABLE 3 Number and Percent Distribution of Nonfarm Wage and Salary Workers Who Usually Work Full Time, by Usual Number of Days Worked and Occupation, May 1974 (numbers in thousands)

Occupation	Number Reporting	Percent Distribution		
		Fewer than 5 Days	5 Days	More than 5 Days
Total..................................	59,442	1.9	82.2	15.9
White-collar..................................	29,766	1.2	83.0	15.8
Professional, technical, and kindred workers..................................	9,466	1.2	87.2	11.6
Managers and administrators, except farm......................................	6,487	.9	68.3	30.8
Sales workers...............................	3,024	1.5	69.9	28.6
Clerical and kindred workers.................	10,789	1.2	91.9	6.9
Blue-collar..................................	24,214	1.6	82.8	15.6
Craftsmen...................................	9,504	1.6	82.0	16.4
Operatives, except transport.................	9,104	1.3	85.4	13.4
Transport equipment operatives.............	2,539	3.2	74.1	22.7
Laborers, except farm.......................	3,066	1.5	84.9	13.5
Service workers, except private household.....	5,462	6.6	75.7	17.7

Note: Data apply to nonfarm wage and salary workers excluding private household workers. Because of rounding, sums of individual items may not equal totals.

service, accounted for less than 10 percent of all full-time employees but one-third of those on shorter weeks.

Employees who worked less than 5 days a week were several years younger on the average than other workers. (See Table 4.) The age difference may be due to employers feelings that young workers will be less fatigued by workdays that stretch to 10 or more hours, or possibly to the special appeal of long weekends to younger workers.

Three-day workers were disproportionately higher among men (80 percent), while the 4½-day group had the highest proportion of women (50 percent). The sex distribution of 4-day workers resembled that of 5-day workers, about two-thirds men.

Although the proportion of college graduates is smaller among those who work less than 5 days than for other workers, the proportion who completed from 1 to 3 years of college is about the same. Hourly earnings for those who usually worked less than 5 days a week in May 1974 averaged about $3.80, or nine-tenths as much as for those who worked 5-day weeks.

THE 4-DAY WEEK

The 4-day week discussed in the United States in the early 1970s was not the 4-day 32-hour week that labor officials refer to from time to time as their long-term goal. It was a "shorter

workweek" in days only; in most cases, a 40-hour week was compressed into 4 days.

The 4-day week raised many issues. Was an additional day off a good exchange for 10-hour workdays? Would a 3-day block of free time be used for recreation and leisure—or for working a second job? Would more days off reduce unscheduled absences from work?[13] And would the adoption of 4-day, 40-hour schedules lead to a 32-hour week?

The merits of 8-hour days versus 3-day weekends have been argued from several perspectives, including fatigue and family life. Most labor officials oppose 4-day workweeks that increase daily worktime beyond 8 hours, but the survey revealed that union members were as likely as nonunion members to be working such schedules. The survey did not provide information on the effect of the 4-day weeks on fatigue or family life, but confirmed that the family question was indeed relevant, inasmuch as three-fourths of the men and three-fifths of the women on these schedules were married (spouse present), about the same proportion as for the work force as a whole. Four-day workers are, however, only about 10 per-

---

[13] Unscheduled absence is defined as absence that results from (1) illness or injury, or (2) miscellaneous personal reasons. It excludes absence due to vacations, holidays, strikes, or weather. For further details, see Janice Neipert Hedges, "Absence from Work—A Look at Some National Data," *Monthly Labor Review*, July 1973, pp. 24–30.

TABLE 4   Selected Data on Nonfarm Wage and Salary Workers Who Usually Work Full Time, by Usual Number of Days Worked, May 1974 (numbers in thousands)

Selected Data	Number Reporting			Percent Distribution		
	Fewer than 5 Days	5 Days	More than 5 Days	Fewer than 5 Days	5 Days	More than 5 Days
Sex						
Both sexes......................	1,108	48,891	9,443	100.0	100.0	100.0
Men................................	728	30,450	7,725	65.7	62.3	81.8
Women...........................	380	18,441	1,718	34.3	37.7	18.2
Age						
Total, 16 years and over..........	1,108	48,891	9,443	100.0	100.0	100.0
Under 35 years......................	573	22,476	4,344	51.7	46.0	46.0
16 to 24 years......................	236	9,405	1,867	21.3	19.2	19.8
25 to 34 years......................	336	13,071	2,477	30.4	26.7	26.2
35 years and over...................	536	26,415	5,099	48.3	54.0	54.0
35 to 54 years......................	412	19,778	3,789	37.1	40.4	40.1
55 years and over..................	124	6,638	1,311	11.2	13.5	13.9
Median age........................	34	37	37	—	—	—
Education						
Total.............................	1,108	48,891	9,443	100.0	100.0	100.0
Less than 4 years high school......	296	12,469	2,649	26.7	25.6	28.1
Elementary: 8 years or less............	143	5,305	1,114	12.9	10.9	11.8
High school: 1 to 3 years..............	153	7,164	1,535	13.8	14.7	16.3
High school: 4 years.................	510	20,265	3,734	46.0	41.4	39.5
College: 1 to 3 years..................	180	7,537	1,506	16.2	15.4	16.0
4 years or more.....................	123	8,621	1,554	11.1	17.6	16.5
Median years completed..............	12.5	12.6	12.6	—	—	—
Hourly earnings						
Total.............................	954	40,584	7,688	100.0	100.0	100.0
Less than $2..........................	73	1,392	793	7.7	3.4	10.3
$2 to $2.99............................	243	8,451	1,915	25.5	20.8	24.9
$3 to $3.99............................	203	9,305	1,616	21.3	22.9	21.0
$4 to $4.99............................	143	6,812	1,226	15.0	16.8	15.9
$5 to $6.99............................	192	9,584	1,447	20.1	23.6	18.8
$7 or more............................	99	5,040	692	10.4	12.4	9.0
Median hourly earnings................	$3.79	$4.17	$3.70	—	—	—
Weekly earnings						
Total.............................	957	40,608	7,779	100.0	100.0	100.0
Less than $100........................	199	5,409	1,070	20.8	13.3	13.8
$100 to $149..........................	209	10,605	1,609	21.8	26.1	20.7
$150 to $199..........................	201	9,320	1,479	21.0	23.0	19.0
$200 or more..........................	348	15,274	3,621	36.4	37.6	46.5
$200 to $399..........................	319	13,686	3,027	33.3	33.7	38.9
$400 or more.........................	29	1,588	594	3.0	3.9	7.6
Median weekly earnings..............	$168	$173	$191	—	—	—

Note: Data apply to nonfarm wage and salary workers, excluding private household workers. Because of rounding, sums of individual items may not equal totals.

cent of all those who usually work 10-hour days.

Whether a schedule that provides 3 days off a week would lead employees to take a second job was a leading issue. The concern was twofold: the effect of dual jobholding on the health and productivity of dual jobholders and on unemployment.

In the past, multiple jobholding[14] has not been considered a major factor in unemployment. The proportion of wage and salary workers who hold more than one job has been relatively low, about 5 percent for the past decade. Moreover, relatively few multiple jobholders are in competition with unemployed jobseekers, either because they are self-employed, or in different occupations or geographic areas than the unemployed.

[14] Multiple jobholders are defined by the Bureau of Labor Statistics as those employed persons who, during the survey week (1) had jobs as wage or salary workers with two employers or more, (2) were self-employed and also held wage or salary jobs, or (3) worked as unpaid family workers and also held secondary wage or salary jobs. For further information, see Allyson Grossman, "Multiple Jobholding in May 1974," *Monthly Labor Review*, February 1975, pp. 60–64.

The survey indicated that in May 1974 workers on 4-day weeks were roughly twice as likely as all full-time workers to hold a second job (8.6 and 4.7 percent, respectively). Workers on shorter weeks included a disproportionate number of protective service workers, who normally have a high rate of dual jobholding, but standardizing the occupational structure of 4-day workers indicated that their higher dual jobholding rate was not due simply to occupational composition.

Absence rates were widely expected to decline with the adoption of 4-day weeks. The reasoning was that workers would find 3 free days sufficient to take care of all personal obligations and, in addition, would be more reluctant to take off a 10-hour day than an 8-hour day, because of the additional cost in leave or earnings. Many managers, in fact, have reported a decline in absence;[15] others have observed that absence returned to normal levels after the novelty of the 4-day week wore off.[16]

The survey data show that 4-day workers were about as likely as 5-day workers to be absent. While groups of workers with above-average absence rates may be overrepresented on such schedules, the data do not indicate that 4-day weeks are effective in reducing absence from work.

Finally, would a 4-day, 40-hour week be the opening wedge for a substantial reduction in weekly hours? It concerned management that it would be, although labor officials were more inclined to see such a schedule as an obstacle to achieving a 4-day, 32-hour week.[17]

The surveys provide benchmark data for determining over time whether 4-day weeks lead to a reduction in working hours. The proportion of 4-day workers who worked less than 40 hours a week increased slightly between May 1973 and May 1974, in contrast to a small decrease in the proportion of 5-day employees who worked less than 40 hours.

The Department of Labor decided in 1972 that sufficient evidence had not been presented on which the Department could base a recommendation for a statutory change to permit employers subject to the daily overtime standards of the Walsh-Healey Public Contracts Act or the Contract Work Hours and Safety Standards Act to adopt 4-day weeks involving more than 8 hours work a day without paying overtime.[18]

These developments, together with the discontinuance of some 4-day schedules and the introduction from Europe of a different type of new workweek—flexitime[19]—apparently resulted in a slower growth of 4-day weeks from 1973 to 1974 than from 1970 to 1973.[20] The actual experience contrasted with the widespread expectation that their growth would accelerate as the 1970s progressed.[21]

GROWTH OF 5-DAY WEEK

The long-run future of 4-day weeks, however, should not be gauged by current growth. The 5-day week, which now seems so firmly entrenched, went through a developmental period in the 1920s that in some ways resembles the present situation in 4-day weeks. This is not to imply, however, that the course of the 4-day week will replicate that of the 5-day week, or that the 4-day week will necessarily become the "standard."

Many of the early 5-day weeks rearranged rather than reduced hours. That is, weekly hours were maintained but workdays were lengthened in order to provide a 2-day weekend, precisely as most 4-day schedules now lengthen workdays to provide a 3-day weekend. Many 5-day schedules were introduced on a temporary, trial basis, or as a summer schedule, as many 4-day weeks been. And sometimes they were discontinued.[22]

The 5-day week grew selectively from 1920[23] to 1926, first and principally in the manufacture of men's clothing[24] then gradually in foundries and machine shops, laundries, and the building

[15] Kenneth E. Wheeler, Richard Gurman, Dale Tarnowieski, The Four-Day Week, An American Management Association Report (New York: American Management Association, Inc., 1972).

[16] See The Altered Work Week: A Symposium Held in November 1973 (Ottawa: The Conference Board in Canada, 1974).

[17] "Can the Four-Day Week Work?" Dun's Review, July 1971, pp. 40–45.

[18] Federal Register, March 15, 1972, p. 5,416.

[19] See Janice Neipert Hedges, "New patterns for working time," Monthly Labor Review, February 1973, pp. 3–8.

[20] This assumes that 4-day workers numbered less than 10,000 in 1970. See Riva Poor, ed., 4 Days, 40 Hours, p. 14.

[21] See, for example, Wheeler and others, The Four-Day Week, p. 6.

[22] Arthur James Todd, Industry and Society (New York: Henry Holt and Co., 1933), p. 252.

[23] The first published report of a 5-day week apparently appeared in Factory, August 15, 1920. The Monthly Labor Review of December 1920 (p. 80), referred to this article which noted that the adoption of the 5-day week resulted in a saving of power, reduced absenteeism, a new source of labor (women), and "more balanced production."

[24] "Prevalence of the 5-Day Week in American Industry," Monthly Labor Review, December 1926, pp. 1–17.

trades. The first major advance came in 1926, with its adoption in the Ford industries and in the New York City building trades.[25] In 1929, the National Industrial Conference Board concluded: "The evidence does . . . remove the 5-day week from the status of a radical and impractical administrative experiment and places it among the plans which, however revolutionary they may appear to some, have demonstrated both practicability and usefulness under certain circumstances."[26] Soon after, the depression "forced . . . attention to the shortening of working time as a means of passing the jobs around. . . ."[27] By mid-1932, although the debate was still going on, a Bureau of Labor Statistics survey of 38,000 establishments in 77 industries showed that one-fourth had permanently adopted the 5-day week for all or part of their employees.

Among the major differences in the early development of 5-day and 4-day workweeks are those of objectives. In most cases, for example, the major goal of the 4-day week has been to improve the functioning of the firm, with productivity figuring importantly. In the 1920s, in contrast, a need to balance production and consumption was sometimes a major objective. Henry Ford expressed this view in saying: "It is the influence of leisure on consumption that makes the short day and the short week so necessary. . . . People who consume the bulk of goods are the people who make them."[28]

Differences in objectives account for an important difference in implementation. Many firms who have adopted a 4-day week for their employees have used multiple shifts of workers on the shorter weeks to extend the days and hours of the firm, whereas a 5-day week for employees generally meant a 5-day week for the firm. This might suggest that adoption of a 4-day week is a less radical step for employers than was the adoption of a 5-day week.

The performance of 4-day weeks in solving the initial set of problems to which they had been applied seems only moderately successful. Other problems against which they might be tested include shortages and rising costs of energy, and unemployment. As yet, however, there has been no movement to shorten the number of days worked in order to effect savings in energy, either at the firm or through a reduction in commuter trips. Nor is there extensive discussion, despite increasing concern about unemployment, of a 4-day week as a work-sharing device.

EXTENDED WORKWEEKS

Over 9 million wage and salary workers in May 1974, 16 percent of the total, usually worked more than 5 days a week. The largest group, 5.8 million, worked 6 days a week, followed by those who worked 5½ and 7 days.

Many workers on long workweeks in May 1974 worked long days as well. About two-fifths of those who usually worked 5½ days or more put in 9 hours or more daily. The proportion who worked these long days was more than three times the proportion of 5-day employees who worked 9 hours or more a day.

Weeks of 5½ days or more were about twice as prevalent in 1974 among unorganized workers as among the organized (18 and 10 percent, respectively). This held true for both men and women. But among those who worked 41 hours or more, union members were almost as likely as nonunion workers to work 5½ days or more.

By occupation, managers were heavily overrepresented on all of the extended workweeks. Two other white-collar groups were overrepresented on some extended workweeks: notably sales workers on 5½- and 6-day weeks, and professional workers on 7-day weeks.

Long weeks were less common among blue-collar workers, with the exception of truck drivers and delivery and route workers. Service workers, however, were overrepresented on 6- and 7-day weeks. Both service and transportation equipment workers also were overrepresented on workweeks of less than 5 days.

Service-producing industries tended to have disproportionate numbers of workers on long weeks. In trade, the proportion on 5½- and 6-day weeks was about double what might have been expected on the basis of trade's proportion of all workers. The transportation industry and the professional service industry (which includes the hospital and health industries) were overrepresented in 7-day weeks.

The proportion of workers on each of the longer workweeks who were men was higher than among 5-day workers. For both men and women, the distribution by marital status among those on extended weeks was similar to that of workers on 5-day weeks. However, men who usually worked 5½ days were more likely to be married (spouse present) than men who worked 5 days. Women on 6-day weeks were more likely

[25] "The 5-Day Week in the Ford Plants," *World's Work*, October 1926.

[26] Todd, *Industry and Society*, p. 255.

[27] Ibid., p. 253.

[28] "The 5-Day Week in the Ford Plants," *World's Work*.

to be separated, divorced, or widowed than those on 5-day weeks.

Median hourly earnings for workers in 1974 declined as the workweek lengthened. In comparison with average hourly earnings of $4.17 for 5-day workers, those who usually worked 5½ days earned $3.87 an hour and those who worked 6 or 7 days a week earned a little over $3.60 hourly. Workers on extended weeks included high-paid as well as low-paid workers, but the latter were overrepresented. About one-tenth of all workers who usually worked 5½ days or more earned less than $2 an hour, three times the proportion for 5-day workers. Median weekly earnings, however, were higher for those on extended schedules than for those on 5-day schedules. Apparently, many employees compensated for low hourly rates by working long weeks.

B. Wage Policy

In an effort to moderate inflationary trends in the economy, the federal government has experimented, using varying degrees of vigor, with wage and price guidelines. The articles in this section deal with various aspects of wage policy.

Milton Derber presents an historical perspective of the wage stabilization program in the period from World War II to the early days of Phase II under the Nixon administration. Daniel Mitchell elaborates more fully on Phase II and Phase III of the wage stabilization program and analyzes what he considers to be the future of U.S. wage controls. In the concluding article, Quinn Mills reviews the wage stabilization experience in the construction industry which, given its "economic and institutional peculiarities . . . requires, and has received, special treatment in periods of economic stabilization by direct controls."

42. Wage Stabilization: Then and Now (The Wage Stabilization Program in Historical Perspective)*

Milton Derber†

Since 1940, the U.S. government has found it expedient to adopt wage-price stabilization programs on five occasions—during World War II (1942–45), in the postwar reconversion period (1945–46), during the Korean War (1951–52), during the Kennedy-Johnson administration (1962–66), and currently in the Nixon regime (1971–   ). In this brief paper, I propose to compare the Nixon stabilization program with the first three of the prior programs. I omit the guidepost policy of the 60s because it was largely voluntaristic (apart from a few cases of government arm-twisting), it focused on only a small array of major collective bargaining and public units, and it was adopted under circumstances that contained no serious inflationary tendencies.

In making the comparisons, I shall examine the four programs on a topical basis rather than treating each as an entity: (1) origins; (2) organizational or structural characteristics in relation to assigned functions; (3) major substantive wage control policies; and (4) political and economic results.[1]

ORIGINS

The Nixon program was adopted by an ideologically reluctant administration that had refused for a year to utilize the comprehensive powers provided in the Economic Stabilization Act of 1970, except in the special case of the construction industry. A combination of political and economic factors appears to explain the unexpected wage-price freeze of August 15. The political calculation seemed to be based on a concern that the recovery from the anomalous condition of rising prices and a 6 percent unemployment rate would not occur rapidly enough to safeguard the administration's position in the 1972 presidential and congressional elections. The economic calculus seemed to be geared to the rapidly deteriorating condition of American foreign trade and mounting pressures on the dollar. Perhaps the most striking feature of this sudden turn to a comprehensive direct incomes policy was that it was unrelated to any of the traditional demand-pull forces of the marketplace. Cost-push inflation was in evidence in some sectors of the economy (for example, in the largely nonunion health services and in centers of union power like metal products, railroads, and construction) but to many economists it appeared to have peaked.

World War II Experience

In contrast to the 1971 circumstances of de-escalation, the forces leading to the World War II and Korean War stabilization programs were part of a mounting involvement in new wars.[2] Both cases reflected classical demand-pull inflation, although in very different degrees and forms. When the European War broke out in September 1939, the United States was still

* From the *Labor Law Journal*, Vol. 23, No. 8, August 1972, pp. 453–62.

† Milton Derber is Professor of Labor and Industrial Relations, University of Illinois.

[1] Because of limitations of space and time, important issues regarding internal administrative machinery and enforcement procedures are not discussed.

[2] The chief source is the three-volume *Termination Report of the National War Labor Board* (Washington: Government Printing Office, undated). An important interpretive work is W. Ellison Chalmers, Milton Derber, and William H. McPherson, editors, *Problems and Policies of Dispute Settlement and Wage Stabilization During World War II* (Washington: U.S. Department of Labor, Bulletin No. 1009, 1950).

deeply enmeshed in economic depression. As the defense program expanded, and the unused capital and labor resources were redirected to the needs of the largest war in American history, it was clear that severe price inflation was inevitable without comprehensive economic controls. Thus, the nation moved gradually from no controls to selective price controls to general price controls—wage controls lagged. None were introduced during the defense period nor even under the Price Control Act of January 31, 1942, the directive to government agencies merely was "to work toward a stabilization of prices, fair and equitable wages, and cost of production." The Executive Order establishing the National War Labor Board on January 12, 1942 made no reference to wage stabilization. The Board, of course, became concerned with wage policy in the settlement of labor disputes and played a major role in the fashioning of wartime wage controls through its case decisions. Nevertheless, when President Roosevelt issued his comprehensive seven-point stabilization program of April 27, 1942, the Board was still confined to controlling wages of firms whose labor disputes came before it. "Voluntary" wage increases by employers or by employer-union agreement were uncontrolled and threatened to undermine the Board's work. The passage of the Stabilization Act of October 2, 1942, at the request of the President, gave the NWLB responsibility for voluntary as well as dispute cases, and the control program became truly comprehensive. The control movement reached its peak with the hold-the-line Executive Order of April 8, 1943.

Korean War Experience

The Korean experience developed somewhat differently because of the limited scope of the war.[3] When the nation entered the conflict in June of 1950, there was great uncertainty as to the nature of the involvement. The Truman administration referred to it as a "police action," but many were fearful that a third world war might develop. With World War II fresh in the minds of most adults, scare-buying by both consumers and business combined with rapid stock-

piling by the military led to an inflationary trend despite the fact that the country was just coming out of the recession of 1948–49 and the unemployment rate in early 1950 was nearly 6 percent. Between June 1950 and January 1951, the Consumer Price Index rose about 6.6 percent and the Wholesale Price Index about 15 percent.

Mindful of the then current public antipathy to economic controls, the administration was hesitant about adopting them. Despite the passage of the Defense Production Act of September 1950 with its authorization of comprehensive controls and the appointment of a Wage Stabilization Board within the Economic Stabilization Agency, general controls over prices and wages were not imposed until January 25, 1951. Part of the delay was due to the reluctance of experienced labor relations experts to become involved and to political infighting in regard to the administrative structure. The Chinese military involvement in November 1950 heightened concern about the war, and made economic control action urgent.

Postwar Reconversion—1946

The economic stabilization program of 1946, in contrast, was an effort to facilitate a smooth economic transition from war to peace after World War II.[4] President Truman had hoped that his postwar, industry-labor conference would reach an agreement on reconversion labor policies, but he was to be disappointed. The country was weary of the wartime controls, and the members of the National War Labor Board, particularly union and management representatives, were anxious to return to their respective organizations and to free collective bargaining. On October 16, 1945, the Board announced that its termination would take place on January 1. While recognizing that the arbitration machinery of the Board could not be carried over into peacetime, the administration was concerned to continue some of the Board's wage-stabilization functions. The unions were pressing for substantial wage increases to maintain the wartime level of earnings that were threatened by a reduction of weekly hours from 48 or more to the

[3] A detailed account of Korean wage stabilization development is to be found in Bruno Stein, *Labor Participation in Stabilization Agencies: The Korean War as a Case Study* (New York: New York University Ph.D. thesis, 1959). Other valuable sources are the symposium entitled *"Wage Policies of the WSB"* in *Industrial and Labor Relations Review*, Vol. 17, No. 2, January 1954; and the fourth and fifth annual *Conference on Labor* sponsored by New York University (New York City: Matthew Bender, 1951 and 1952).

[4] An official account is United States Department of Labor, *The National Wage Stabilization Board, January 1, 1946–February 24, 1947* (Washington: U.S. Government Printing Office, undated). Perceptive analyses of contemporary thinking are found in John T. Dunlop, "The Decontrol of Wages and Prices," in Colston E. Warne, editor, *Labor in Postwar America* (Brooklyn: Remsen Press, 1949) and in Joel Seidman, *American Labor from Defense to Reconversion* (Chicago: University of Chicago Press, 1953) chap. 12.

peacetime standard of 40; there was a vast, pent-up demand for houses, autos, and domestic goods; and economists feared either a repetition of the post-World War I experience of rapid demand-pull inflation followed by severe depression or immediate serious unemployment upon the demobilization of millions of men from the armed forces. The tensions were revealed in the greatest outburst of major strikes in American history, including General Motors, basic steel, and petroleum refining. The new National Wage Stabilization Board had the unenviable responsibility of ruling upon wage increases which "might be used as a basis for increasing prices or rent ceilings or which might result in higher costs to the government."[5]

STRUCTURE

Phase I—Phase II and NWLB

When the current stabilization program was established, two perennial questions of structure were raised. One was whether controls should be determined and administered by a single agency responsible for both prices and wages or by multiple agencies. The other was whether the administrators of the wage program should be a tripartite body (representing labor, management, and the general public) or a wholly public unit. The answers were different for Phase 1 and Phase 2. The initial 90-day "freeze" program was governed by a Cost of Living Council, comprised of the Secretaries of five Cabinet departments and other top administration officials. There was logic to such a council, because it was expected by the administration that the "freeze" would be temporary and firmly adhered to.

The Phase 2 structure was envisaged in very different functional terms—flexible and pragmatic policy-making, reliance on the administrative cooperation of the major interest groups, and of indefinite duration. Thus, while the Cost of Living Council was retained as general policy coordinator and overseer, the main administrative responsibility was given to a 7 public-member Price Commission and a 15-member, tripartite Pay Board, with equal representation from organized labor, business, and the public. When four of the five labor members resigned in March, the tripartite structure was preserved symbolically by retaining one business and one union member with the five public members.

The Phase 2 structure was in line with the three preceding wage stabilization programs. The National War Labor Board consisted of 12 members, 4 each representing organized labor, employers, and the public. As noted above, the NWLB started out as a dispute settlement agency and acquired wage stabilization responsibilities later. It had no role in price determination—that was the responsibility of the Office of Price Administration, headed by a single director. The coordinating and overall policy-making role was filled by a Director of Economic Stabilization, who was responsible to the President.

1946 WSB and Korean WSB

The Wage Stabilization Board of 1946–47 had essentially the same structure as the War Labor Board although it was smaller (six members equally divided among public, labor, and industry) and had a considerably reduced staff in Washington and in its regional boards and industry commissions. The chief difference was that the WSB had, with a few limited exceptions, no dispute settlement function. In this respect it was similar to the current Pay Board.

The Korean Wage Stabilization Board was also tripartite in structure, originally with 9 members, later with 18 equally divided among labor, management, and the public. Price controls were administered by an Office of Price Stabilization. The Administrator of Economic Stabilization served as top policy-maker and coordinator.

For a considerable period of time, the relation between the Board and the Administrator over policy-making was a source of discord and confusion.[6] The first Administrator regarded the Board as merely an advisory body, even as to specific cases and the selection of key personnel.[7] The unwillingness of Board members to accept such a role contributed to his resignation.[8] His successor was willing to delegate substantial policy-making as well as administrative authority to the Board. Despite these concessions, the Board functioned for less than a month before the labor members walked out on February 15, 1951 in a controversy over General Wage Regulation Six (that was concerned with the idea of a cost-of-living "catch-up" adjustment) and other

[6] See Bruno Stein, cited at footnote 3, and Morris A. Horowitz, "Administrative Problems of the Wage Stabilization Board," *Industrial and Labor Relations Review*, Vol. 7, No. 3, April 1954, pp. 391–92.

[7] Horowitz, cited at footnote 6, at p. 391.

[8] The desire of the Price Stabilization head for autonomy was an equally important factor in the resignation.

[5] *The National Wage Stabilization Board,* cited at footnote 4, at p. 7.

policies. The Board continued to function without labor representatives until May when it was reconstituted on a tripartite basis.

Board structure was also affected by the issue of whether the Board should have responsibility for the settlement of labor disputes. The initial Executive Order did not provide for a dispute settlement role, but when labor returned to the Board in May 1951, it was authorized to make recommendations on disputes seriously threatening the defense effort. This function was later narrowed to apply only to wage issues and finally eliminated entirely after a 53-day steel strike that severely damaged the stabilization effort.[9] From the outset, management spokesmen strongly objected to Board intervention in the collective bargaining process which they judged favorable to labor, and the management representatives (as well as the public chairman) withdrew from the Board in November 1952 after the President reversed the Board in a national coal case.

WAGE POLICIES

Phase II

The announced objective of the Nixon administration for Phase II was to reduce the rate of inflation to between 2 and 3 percent by the end of 1972. This entailed limiting pay increases to an average of between 5 and 6 percent, on the assumption that the workers would continue to share in the nation's long-run productivity gains of about 3 percent per annum and that prices would rise in the same proportion as labor costs. Exceptions to correct for inequities were intended to be quite limited. Some were mandated by Congress when it extended, with several significant amendments, the Economic Stabilization Act in December of 1971. The congressional amendments were a response to labor pressures against what labor regarded as restrictive policies adopted by a public-employer majority on the Pay Board. Particularly important were the directives to the Board to approve retroactive payments under agreements reached before the August 15 freeze date and deferred increases in such agreements provided that they were not "unreasonably inconsistent" with stabilization standards relating to the prevention of "gross inequities."

Little Steel

The heart of the War Labor Board's policy was the Little Steel formula, adopted in a dispute case on July 16, 1942 prior to the passage of the Stabilization Act of October 1942. The intent of this formula was to sever the tie between general wage increases and future cost-of-living rises by allowing general increases only up to the point that would cover the 15 percent rise in the Consumer Price Index between May 1942 and the base date of January 1941. The idea of a wage freeze was explicitly rejected. The Board was authorized to approve increases if necessary to "correct maladjustments or inequalities, to eliminate substandards of living, to correct gross inequities, or to aid in the effective prosecution of the war."

For a time the "inequalities" and "inequities" exceptions were given liberal interpretation, particularly after Little Steel adjustments were exhausted, but as rising labor costs continued to press against price ceilings, tensions between the wage and price programs mounted. On April 8, 1943, the administration issued a very tight, "hold-the-line" order (Executive Order 9328) although strong Board protests, including threats of a labor walkout, resulted in a partial relaxation the following month. Thereafter the Board responded to the inflationary pressure by carefully opening small escape hatches through its interplant wage-bracket system, fringe adjustments, and internal wage rationalization.

EXECUTIVE ORDERS 9599, 9651, 9697

The aim of the administration at the end of World War II was to eliminate controls as rapidly as possible consistent with price stability. Thus, Executive Order 9599 of August 18, 1945 continued comprehensive price controls but, except for construction and, to a lesser degree, basic steel, employers were free to institute wage increases of any size without government approval as long as such increases did not serve as the basis for price increases or increases in charges on government contracts. On October 30, Executive Order 9651 permitted price adjustments to take into account unapproved wage increases after they had been in effect for six months.[10] The standards for approval of wage increases as a basis for immediate price increases differed little, however, from the wartime standards. This policy proved untenable in the face of the great labor

---

[9] The steel crisis is analyzed in detail by Harold L. Enarson in Irving Bernsten et al., editors, *Emergency Disputes and National Policy* (New York: Harper, 1955) chap. 3.

[10] See H. M. Douty, Department of Labor Bulletin No. 1009, pp. 146–47.

disputes in the fall of 1945 and the winter of 1945–46. The wage settlements that were essential to labor (on the order of 17.5 percent) required price increases in industry's view that were incompatible with the price ceilings. Voluntary wage increases without immediate price adjustments by profitable firms created serious inequity issues for related, less profitable firms and industries.

In an effort to save the stabilization program, Executive Order 9697 was issued on February 14, 1946 with considerably liberalized wage-price standards. The Wage Stabilization Board was directed to approve any wage increase that was consistent with industry or local labor market area increases put into effect between August 18, 1945 and February 14, 1946. In the absence of such patterns, the Board was authorized to approve similar increases to eliminate gross inequities, to correct substandards of living, or to correct disparities between wage increases and the increase in living costs between January 1941 and September 1945. Since the major disputes involved the centers of union strength and the most profitable industrial firms, the patterns of the settlements were relatively high. The stabilization constraints therefore had little significance, and by June 1946, the program was practically dead, although formal dissolution did not occur until November 9.

Regulations 6, 8, 10—Korean WSB

The Korean War wage stabilization policy was one of steady relaxation from a base that was in itself far more liberal than World War II policy. The wage regulations adopted shortly after the freeze order of January 25, 1951 embodied two main principles—cost-of-living "catch-up," and tandem or interplant inequity adjustments. Regulation 6 paralleled the Little Steel formula by permitting general wage increases up to a level of 10 percent above January 1950 (this figure was actually 1.9 percentage points above the rise in the Consumer Price Index between the base date and January 1951). Regulation 8 permitted wage increases on the basis of cost-of-living escalation clauses in contracts or plans in effect prior to January 25, 1951—a reflection of the importance of the 1948 UAW–General Motors escalator agreement. Regulation 10 permitted increases of wage followers to keep pace with their historical pattern setters. In addition, the WSB adopted an interplant, inequity adjustment policy (based on a weighted average of comparable rates) which was more liberal than the wage bracket system of the War Labor Board (first significant cluster or 10 percent below the weighted average).

These policies were relaxed significantly in the next six months under labor and management pressures. Regulation 8 was amended on August 23, 1951 to permit the adoption of new escalator plans as well as wage increases corresponding to cost of living increases, thus establishing the opposite of the WLB approach. The interplant, inequity policy was further loosened by the conduct of periodic wage surveys embodying approved wage adjustments. Beyond these changes, on June 6, 1951 the Board authorized UAW-GM, productivity, "annual improvement" adjustments based on collective agreements negotiated before January 25, a policy that was widely extended, not only by similar agreements but even more by the application of the tandem and interplant inequity principles. Finally, the Board gave a considerable boost to fringe adjustments that did not exceed "prevailing industry or area practice as to amount or type." Health, welfare, and pension plans were given special consideration and were finally largely excluded from the limitations on wage increases.

RESULTS

Nixon Stabilization

As of this writing (mid-April 1972), it is not feasible to attempt a conclusive assessment of the Nixon economic stabilization program. Phase I must be accounted an impressive success on both political and economic grounds. It snapped, at least temporarily, what appeared to be a strong inflationary mood throughout the nation and enjoyed widespread public support—even among groups like school teachers who were disadvantaged by the timing of the freeze. It checked the rise in living costs.

Phase II was not expected to maintain this pace. Administration spokesmen warned, correctly, that a temporary bulge in wages and prices was to be expected as an outgrowth of the freeze. The CPI returned to the pre-August rate of increase between mid-November and mid-February. Average, straight-time hourly earnings in manufacturing, adjusted for inter-industry shifts, rose 2.9 percent over the three months. The worrisome problem was whether the "temporary bulge" was not extending too far and whether the wage and price controls were either too loose or were being flouted.

World War II Stabilization

The earlier programs can be assessed with more confidence. The stabilization record during World War II is generally regarded as a success.[11] Between January 1941 and October 1942, before comprehensive controls were imposed, estimated basic wage rates went up 15 percent and unadjusted, straight-time hourly earnings in manufacturing rose 26.4 percent. During the control period, October 1942–July 1945, when inflationary pressures were much stronger, the comparable figures were 8 and 15.5 percent.[12] The Consumer Price Index, adjusted for the disappearance of low-cost items and quality deterioration factors, increased about 20 percent in the pre-control period and about 13 percent in the control period.[13]

Postwar Stabilization

The postwar stabilization program, however, proved incapable of maintaining the wartime record. The Wage Stabilization Board was set up too late and with too limited powers (especially with reference to disputes) to have an effective impact on the swarm of major disputes in late 1945 and 1946. As a result, the program never took hold and it ended, for all practical purposes within less than a year, in total disarray. Between August 1945 and October 1946, urban manufacturing wage rates rose 18 percent and straight-time hourly earnings 13 percent while the adjusted Consumer Price Index went up 14 percent.[14]

Korean Stabilization

The Korean stabilization record was more comparable to that of World War II, without its aftermath. Both the 6.6 percent consumer price rise and the 15 percent wholesale price rise between June 1950 and January 1951 prior to stabilization were attributable almost entirely to demand forces. Average hourly earnings in manufacturing, excluding overtime, rose 6.6 per cent. By the spring of 1951, fears of a third world war had largely dissipated, and the market psychol-

ogy was more "normal" reflecting mainly the high levels of output and employment. The unemployment rate fluctuated between 2.5 and 3.0 percent throughout the last 9 months of 1951 and averaged 2.7 percent in 1952 and 2.4 in 1953. During the stabilization period between January 1951 and January 1953, average hourly earnings for factory workers rose 11.5 percent, but the Wholesale Price Index for commodities other than farm products and foods actually declined by about 3 percent and the Consumer Price Index rose only about 5 percent despite a much more liberal price policy than in World War II. Clearly, inflation was not a problem during the control period or immediately thereafter, the wage gains being mainly absorbed by higher productivity.

CONCLUSIONS

1. The reluctance with which each administration introduced wage-price controls is indicative of the important political dimension of an incomes policy in this country. Without widespread public support, such programs are not likely to be introduced, let alone successfully implemented. This may complicate proper timing from an economics viewpoint. Both the post-World War II and the Korean programs appear to have been delayed too long, the former with disastrous consequences. It may be argued that the World War II program should have been initiated full-blown immediately after Pearl Harbor and that the Nixon program should have started earlier on a more gradual basis.

2. All four programs adopted the same structural principles, that is, separate wage and price agencies under the coordination of a general stabilization unit; and a tripartite wage board. Persuasive arguments have been made for both of these principles. They both raise problems, however, that may justify different approaches in future control efforts. One is the interrelatedness between wage and price decisions. Separate agencies have a tendency to formulate their policies independently and on grounds that are often incompatible or at least difficult to match. A single wage-price board might integrate policies more effectively than a general economic coordinator reacting to pressures from rival and largely autonomous agencies. The difficulty with tripartism is that important interests are often neglected while some special interests are disproportionately represented.

The role of the wage board in labor disputes is another topic of concern. Except for the War

---

[11] For a dissenting view, see Jules Backman, "The Economic Environment of Collective Bargaining," *Fourth Annual Conference on Labor,* New York University (New York: Matthew Bender, 1951), pp. 193–95.

[12] See *Termination Report of the National War Labor Board,* Vol. 1, p. 549.

[13] Cited at footnote 12, at p. 550.

[14] *Report of The National Wage Stabilization Board,* p. 298.

Labor Board, which started as a disputes settlement agency and acquired wage stabilization responsibilities afterwards, the boards have had only an indirect relationship to collective bargaining disputes. The 1946 Wage Stabilization Board was virtually destroyed by the great conflicts of its time; the 1952 steel strike undermined the integrity of the Korean Board; and the longshore dispute was the springboard for labor's withdrawal from the Nixon Board. Because such conflicts often involve package deals, Board action on only the wage and fringe items may distort the total effect of a settlement. There is no simple answer to this dilemma. Whatever policy is adopted will require adjustments in the collective bargaining process.

3. Two central issues on basic wage policy have emerged from the four stabilization programs. One is the appropriate tie between wages and living costs; the other is the scope for inequity adjustments. The War Labor Board rejected the cost of living tie, the 1946 Wage Stabilization Board ignored it, the Korean Board encouraged it, and the Nixon Board assumed it within specified limits. If, as a result of the total economic stabilization program, the cost of living can be restrained to acceptable limits, then recognition of the connection between wages and living costs serves a psychologically potent role.

If, however, the inflationary pressures are not quickly brought under control, the tie merely fuels an inflationary spiral.

Inequity adjustments are the other side of the coin. Human imagination being what it is, the possible range of such adjustments is almost unlimited. A liberal cost of living policy may necessitate a tight inequity policy. A tight general wage increase standard may require inequity adjustments as a useful escape valve. Obviously, the appropriate balance depends on the inflationary pressures at work at a particular time. The War Labor Board was obliged to tighten a relatively liberal inequity approach in 1943 because the cost pressures were becoming too strong, while the Korean Board found it possible to be increasingly liberal on both cost of living and inequity. The Nixon Board has adopted a rather liberal general increase policy and has tried to play down the inequity issue.

4. Can wage stabilization be a useful (if partial) tool in the fight against inflation? The answer in the wartime years 1942–45 and, to a lesser degree, in 1951–52 would appear to be in the affirmative; the answer in postwar 1946 was negative but that was at least partly due to miscalculations of the trend and delays in introducing the program. For 1971–72, the answer lies in the months immediately ahead.

43. The Future of American Wage Controls*

Daniel J. B. Mitchell†

The American economy is still in the midst of an experiment with wage/price controls— incomes policy, as the Europeans call them. To date, the experience with the overall experiment suggests that there is still much to learn about the use of controls. The price inflation problem, particularly with food during Phase III, obscured observation of the wage side of the program. Wages did not "take off" during Phase III, despite the foreboding of many industrial relations experts. Naturally, there was little official bragging about wage restraint in the face of rapid price inflation. But the episode does suggest that our ability to control wages is more advanced than our ability to control prices.

Whatever the final outcome of the current experiment with controls, there will be other episodes of incomes policy in the future. The same forces that led to the adoption of controls in 1971 will recur in the United States, just as they have in other countries. Both political parties are willing to dabble in controls. The program that began in 1971 was authorized by what was essentially a Democratic bill, the Economic Stabilization Act of 1970. This bill was intended to be as much an embarrassment to a Republican administration as it was an invitation to an incomes policy. But the bluff was called by that same administration. The degree of lip service paid to the free market may vary between the parties, but ultimately no politician wants to be considered "pro-inflation."

THE THEORY BEHIND CONTROLS

Any rationale for an anti-inflation device must be based on a theory of inflation. One theory, which may be termed the "self-starting" approach, explains general price increases as the by-product of a struggle over the income distribution between interest groups. Sometimes the journalist's version of the "wage/price spiral" seems to fit into this category. Unions push up wages in an attempt to raise the real incomes of their members. But to the extent these increases are not offset by rising productivity, firms raise prices to restore their profit margins. This, in turn, leads to another wage round, and the spiral continues. The story has no beginning and no end and seems to relegate monetary and fiscal policy which most American economists regard as important to no role at all in the inflation process. A somewhat more sophisticated version of the theory recognizes monetary and fiscal policy, but it assumes that political pressures will permit them to play only a passive role.

The self-starting view of inflation is more popular in Europe than it is in the United States. Indeed, the European phrase "incomes policy" demonstrates the relative stress on the income distribution in contrast to the American phrase "wage/price controls." The European version of the interest-group struggle sometimes takes on a Marxist flavor. Inflation is seen as the unfortunate result of a struggle between labor and capital over a share of the national product. The French, in particular, seem to favor this view, probably as a result of the strained industrial relations system in France.[1]

* Copyright © 1974 by The Regents of the University of California. Reprinted from *California Management Review,* Vol. 17, No. 1, pp. 48–57, by permission of the Regents.

† Daniel J. B. Mitchell is Associate Professor at the Graduate School of Management, UCLA. During Phase II, he was Chief Economist at the U.S. Pay Board.

[1] See Daniel J. B. Mitchell, "Incomes Policy and the Labor Market in France," *Industrial and Labor Relations Review,* Vol. 25 (April 1972), pp. 315–35.

A theory of inflation based on a struggle over the distribution of income suggests that the only feasible approach is a permanent problem of reconciling conflicting demands. A number of European countries have established formal mechanisms whereby interest group representatives are brought together in an attempt to hammer out a consensus. It is thought that forcing the groups to consider the limits to the real income available for distribution will bring forth a set of mutually consistent income claims.

Most American economists have not accepted the European-style "self-starting" theories, although Galbraith is perhaps an exception.[2] Instead, those American economists who see a role for incomes policy follow some sort of "self-perpetuation" theory. Inflation in this view does not arise because of some structural conflict in the economy; but once it is started by a monetary/fiscal excess, inflation either perpetuates itself or slows down gradually. The self-starting and the self-perpetuation theories are not mutually exclusive. If the slowing-down process is believed to take a long time, then except for the initial spark, the two viewpoints are similar. But if slowing down is a relatively short process, the policy prescription is different. Incomes policy may be needed to hasten the process, but the policy should be temporary. And if the adjustment is very fast, then no justification for incomes policy exists.

The self-perpetuation theory generally revolves around the notion of inflationary expectations.[3] In this view, once inflation has been present for a period of time, it is believed that it will continue. Wage and price decisions are formulated accordingly, thus helping to realize the expected inflation. Monetary and fiscal policy break the cycle by creating an environment hostile to inflationary behavior, but the adjustment process is painful. Essentially, the economy must be pushed into a recession severe enough so that wage and price decision-makers are not capable of acting in accordance with their expectations. After a time, the forced slowdown of inflation contributes to a new pattern of expectations— only moderate price rises are anticipated. The rate of inflation is permanently reduced unless jarred again by a monetary/fiscal push. Incomes policy fits into this framework by shortening the needed slowdown or even permitting moderate expansion.

It is clear that the controls that were established in 1971 fell into the self-perpetuation framework. Advertised as a temporary remedy, the controls were to be administered by temporary agencies staffed by employees with such civil service descriptions as "temporary, emergency, indefinite," and the bureaucracy created was to be kept small.[4] When Phase II ended, it was rumored that one of the reasons that the Pay Board and Price Commission were not retained to administer the Phase III controls was to prevent these bodies from becoming "entrenched."

Without considering questions of economic validity, it is easier for an administration originally opposed to controls to accept them as a temporary measure. But once controls are established, the administrative mechanisms for operating them will be similar, whether the program is viewed as permanent or transitory. The main difference lies only in the amount of resources devoted to administration. Thus, it is quite possible that at some future date the United States will find itself with permanent controls founded on a temporary rationale.

WHAT NEEDS TO BE CONTROLLED?

Wages versus Prices

If controls are imposed, should they cover both wages and prices? Since the main object is to control inflation (that is, prices) a simple view would suggest price controls by themselves would be sufficient. It might be argued that with price controls, wages will take care of themselves. Employers would resist large wage demands strongly if they could not pass along the added labor costs.

There are problems with a price-only approach. First, it is based on stiffening employer resistance without attempting to reduce union wage demands. It is therefore a formula for increased strike activity. Second, almost by definition, a price-only system of controls would mean little unless it were based on absolute price ceilings rather than on historical markups over costs. If the system were to be based on markups, there would be a complete labor-cost pass-through, and the incentive for employer resistance would be eliminated. An attempt to squeeze traditional markups would not be very effective without

---

[2] John Kenneth Galbraith, *The New Industrial State* (Boston: Houghton Mifflin, 1967), pp. 247–61.

[3] An elaboration of this approach may be found in Daniel J. B. Mitchell, "A Simplified Approach to Incomes Policy," *Industrial and Labor Relations Review*, Vol. 22 (July 1969), pp. 512–27.

[4] See *Economic Report of the President* (Washington: Government Printing Office, 1972), pp. 22.

cost controls. The average pre-tax markup on sales (7½ percent in manufacturing in 1972) is too small to provide much room for squeezing. Hence, a price-only system would soon require detailed government price-fixing.

Absolute ceilings on prices are not readily adjusted for changes in supply conditions (costs), nor are they responsive to demand pressures. Aside from the shortages on the produce market that such ceilings can cause, they can also distort the labor market. Industries with high rates of productivity growth could afford large wage increases without suffering large increases in unit labor costs, but those with low rates of productivity increase would be forced to offer stiff resistance to such demands. These unequal incentives for employer resistance would disrupt traditional patterns in the inter-industry wage structure and stimulate industrial strife in industries with slow productivity growth. Moreover, distortions in the wage structure would eventually create a wage bubble after controls were relaxed. Industries whose wage levels had been relatively depressed would be pressed to catch up with the other sectors.

If a price-only system is undesirable, the remaining choices are either a wage-only system or a combined wage and price system. The political problems of implementing a wage-only system are insurmountable. In all countries where incomes policy is under consideration, organized labor always demands that all forms of incomes be covered, not just wages. (For example, the AFL-CIO has repeatedly stated this position. Lloyd Ulman and Robert Flanagan suggest that the existence of price controls helps unions "sell wage restraints to their members.")[5] As a result, the systems adopted always have both price and wage aspects. The question, however, is whether the price side is largely redundant and adopted only to make controls acceptable.

This question is invariably avoided by governments in public statements. But price controls in mixed wage/price systems are usually markup controls. Given restraints on increasing markups, the prime determinants of controlled price movements, at least in the short run, will be wage movements, productivity developments, and the prices of exempted items. A controls system will affect only wage movements directly. Thus, the unspoken premise of the controllers is that wage controls are the heart of incomes policy.

The American Phase II system bears witness

to this premise. As originally formulated, the Pay Board's wage target was set at 5.5 percent, a figure formulated by adding a long-term productivity trend of about 3 percent per annum to the 2 to 3 percent price target. The Price Commission essentially was to operate a markup system. When the Pay Board seemed to falter in its first wage case by approving a 16.8 percent increase for coal miners, the Price Commission announced it would hold firms to a 5.5 percent labor cost increase for pricing purposes. In effect, the Commission was ready to push for wage restraint by increasing employer resistance to wage demands if the Pay Board could not confront those demands directly. But the Price Commission and Pay Board definitions of what the 5.5 percent meant were different, part of the difference stemming from the alternate reporting units used by the two agencies. The Pay Board used the wage decision-making unit for reporting (this could be smaller or larger than a single firm) while Price Commission reporting requirements were based on the firm. Although reduced price inflation was the main target, wage restraint was to be the chief route to obtain it.

Economists have a simple model of the firm which appears in all elementary microeconomic textbooks. Based on demand conditions and production technology, the firm prices its output according to the principle of profit maximization. Users of this model point out that even if the firm is a pure monopoly, it chooses some optimum price, *not a rate of price increase*. Thus, opponents of controls argue, there is no reason to suppose that non-competitive market conditions cause inflation.[6] Obviously, it is possible to produce counter models in which some inflationary consequences follow from non-competitive markets. But the simple model prevails in the minds of most economists.

On the wage side, the picture is different, particularly where collective bargaining is concerned. There is no neat model of wage determination under collective bargaining. Most industrial relations specialists reject the view expressed in the economic literature that a union is analogous to a profit-maximizing firm.[7] Moreover, on the surface, there is some plausibility of wage push models. After all, unions are in the business of

[5] Lloyd Ulman and Robert J. Flanagan, *Wage Restraint: A Study of Incomes Policies in Western Europe* (Berkeley: University of California Press, 1971), p. 244.

[6] See Milton Friedman, "What Price Guideposts" in George P. Shultz and Robert Z. Aliber, *Guidelines: Informal Controls and the Market Place* (Chicago: University of Chicago Press, 1966), p. 21.

[7] See Daniel J. B. Mitchell, "Union Wage Policies: The Ross-Dunlop Debate Reopened," *Industrial Relations*, Vol. 11 (February 1972), pp. 46–61.

obtaining increases in wages. And there is always the classic quote of Samuel Gompers, first president of the AFL, that the goal of the union movement was simply "more."

The view is superficial, however. In 1960, the median union wage increase in manufacturing was 3.2 percent; in 1971, it was 10.1 percent. Yet the degree of unionization was about the same in the two years. Thus, there must be something more behind inflation than simply wage push. Indeed, union spokesmen hasten to point out that prices moved first in the inflation that began in the mid-1960s.

It is necessary to be cautious in citing union wage data as evidence of wage push. Major collective bargaining contracts typically averaged close to three years in duration prior to controls. Such relatively long-term agreements are formulated to reflect expectations of future price increases. Unexpected inflation can lead to a wage lag, followed by a period of catching up. Thus, base developments in a given year reflect prior conditions as well as the immediate state of the labor market.

Figure 1 illustrates this tendency during 1972. The private sector has been divided into industries that had a less-than-median average hourly earnings increase in 1972 (Sector A—ordnance; food; tobacco; apparel; lumber; furniture; printing and publishing; rubber; leather; electrical equipment; miscellaneous manufactures; wholesale and retail trade; finance, insurance, and real estate; and services) and those that had above-median increases (Sector B—textiles; paper; chemicals; petroleum; stone and glass; primary metals; fabricated metals; machinery; transportation equipment; professional instruments; mining and quarrying; construction; transportation; telephone and telegraph; and utilities).[8] Sector B is characterized by features that suggest bargaining power. It is more heavily unionized (almost 60 percent versus less than 20 percent in A), pays higher average wages, and tends to have larger wage determination units. Some might cite these characteristics as the reason for the more rapid wage growth in B compared with A. Yet, in the latter part of the 1960s, it was A that experienced the faster rate of wage increase. The year 1972 (largely Phase II) was a period of catching up, aided by the economic upturn; Sector B was regaining the ground it had lost relative to Sector A in earlier years. Wage controls in effect then

[8] Data on the characteristics of the two sectors were drawn from *Employment and Earnings, Directory of National Unions and Employee Associations*, 1971, and Pay Board computer records.

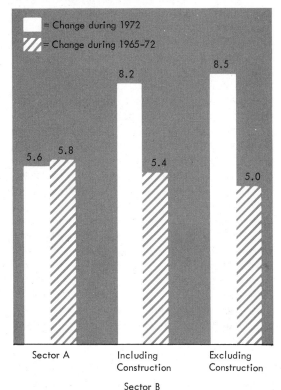

FIGURE 1   Increase in Average Hourly Earnings at Annual Rates (percent)

☐ = Change during 1972
▨ = Change during 1965–72

Sector A — 5.6, 5.8
Sector B — Including Construction: 8.2, 5.4; Excluding Construction: 8.5, 5.0

Source: Calculated from Bureau of Labor Statistics data.

were expected to prevent an overshooting of the catching-up process, but not to suppress it.

In short, the unspoken emphasis of a controls program will always tend to be on the wage side. This is not because all inflation is the result of wage push, or even because there is substantial evidence that wage-push inflation is a continuing problem. It is simply because despite the substantial research that has developed in the postwar period, wage determination is still something of a mystery. To some degree, the wage emphasis is a measure of our ignorance. Wage determination does not always respond to monetary/fiscal policies as we would like for reasons that are not always apparent. Wage control then appears as an attractive mechanism to help the adjustment, but it will always be accompanied by some sort of price control mechanism.

Union versus Non-Union

Within the labor force, there is also the question of who should be covered by a wage-control program. The earlier discussion emphasized the collective bargaining aspect of wage determination. If there is anything to wage push, it is hard to imagine it as emanating from the private nonunion sector. Presumably, private non-union employers raise wages for two basic reasons: Either they find that wage increases are necessary for recruitment and controlling turnover, or they wish to stay abreast of the union sector in order to discourage organization. This suggests that control of private non-union units is largely redundant. Indeed, the Phase II data from the Pay Board suggest such is the case. Table 1 shows that average requests and approvals received at, and granted by, the Pay Board in the larger cases involved 1,000 or more workers. The table shows that most of the cutbacks were centered in new union cases. (New cases were those negotiated during Phase II; old cases were negotiated prior to Phase II.) The non-union sector came in low and went out low, generally with a rubber-stamp approval from the board. And an examination of Pay Board rollbacks reveals that most of those cases came from the union sector.

Of course, there is a certain amount of illusion built into Table 1. Non-union employers were most apt to go along with the program and keep their initial requests down. But despite this element of illusion, it does not appear that Phase II would have been a period of a non-union wage upsurge, even if that sector had been exempt from controls. The limitations on the union sector, combined with the relatively loose labor market of Phase II, would have been an effective restraint. Even during Phase III, as the labor market tightened, there was no non-union upsurge, although the Phase III reporting requirements made the non-union sector largely "invisible" to the Cost of Living Council.

The public sector is still heavily non-union—a little over one-quarter of state and local employees belong to unions or associations. But its wage determination mechanism differs from that of the private non-union sector. Govern-ments do not make profits, and their internal processes are too complicated to be susceptible to any simple economic model. Too many intangible political factors are involved.

State and local government employment has been expanding. It has become more important in the overall labor force than it was two decades ago when government was exempted from the Korean wage controls. From 1952 to 1972, state and local employment grew 154 percent compared with 27 percent for the rest of the employed civilian labor force. Moreover, the government sector is particularly visible. As might be expected, during Phase II, the Internal Revenue Service received relatively few complaints about wages from the public. Most complaints were about prices and rents; only 3 percent involved wages, and many of these wage complaints stemmed from publicized increases granted to public officials.[9] Under future wage control programs, therefore, the state and local sectors should not expect exemption.

For the private non-union sector, a blanket exemption based solely on lack of organization is not politically feasible, but it is possible to tailor a program so that the non-union sector is not the center of controls. For example, during Phase II, units with less than 1,000 workers (Category III) did not have to report to the wage authorities unless they wished to exceed the standards, and there was an exemption for most employers with fewer than 60 employees. Since non-union units tend to be smaller than union units, the impact of the reduced reporting requirements and exemption fell most heavily on non-union workers. Special exemptions for low-paid workers, as mandated by Congress in 1971 and 1973, also have their impact mainly on the non-union sector. For example, the average straight-time wage for all non-supervisory employees in manufacturing during 1972 was $3.65. Although exact figures are not available, the average for union workers in that sector was something over $4.[10]

Administrative Considerations

In a program with generalized reporting requirements, such as Phase II, workload considerations can be critical. During Phase II, the Pay Board handled over 16,000 cases. The In-

TABLE 1   Pay Board Requests and Approvals: Categories I and II

Type of Case	Average Request (percent)	Average Approval (percent)
All cases	5.6	5.4
Union cases	6.2	5.9
New	7.6	6.9
Old	5.7	5.6
Non-union cases	5.0	4.9

Source: Pay Board computer records as of March 2, 1973.

[9] Data obtained from Cost of Living Council, Bi-Weekly Summary, January 1–12, 1973.

[10] Data from Current Wage Developments (June 1973), p. 48.

ternal Revenue Service, which handled Category III, processed 15,683 exception requests through January 12, 1973. Clearly, the more types of units that are exempted in such a program, the less will be the caseload.

The small employer exemption was the most critical during Phase II. It removed roughly one-fourth of the employed labor force from the program, with a resultant benefit to the wage authorities and to the small employers who were relieved of the burden of a regulatory program. Congress mandated a "working-poor" exemption in 1971, without defining who the working poor were. After a court test, the definition became a straight-time wage of $2.75 or less. Roughly, a third of the private non-supervisory labor force fell under the working-poor exemption. Because of overlaps, the combined exemptions probably covered about half of the total labor force. But the working-poor exemption was not a workload saver. In many units there were both exempt workers and non-exempt workers, and so the usual reporting requirements continued. An exemption based on wage rates of *individuals* does not lift the administrative burden of a program based on *units*. In fact, the Pay Board was forced to adopt complex regulations to remedy the conflicting concepts.

Phase III wage controls, in contrast, concentrated mainly on the pattern-setting super-large union contracts. The process was generally not a quasi-judicial review after a contract had been reached, but informal pressure before and during negotiations. Such a system does not create a workload problem. During Phase III, staff time on wages was spent largely in finishing up old Phase II business and on processing cases gener-ated by the few sectors still under Phase II-type controls. Under a system of informal pressure on lead settlements, the meaning of small-employer and working-poor exemptions is largely symbolic.

WHAT HAPPENED DURING CONTROLS?

Wages

There is no doubt that wage growth slowed during Phase II. Table 2 illustrates this tendency with a variety of indexes. The hourly earnings index for private, non-farm, non-supervisory workers was rising at an annual rate of 7.4 percent prior to Phase I. During Phase II, after a post-freeze bulge when deferred increases scheduled during the freeze were allowed to take effect, the index rose at a 6.1 percent annual rate. Compensation per man-hour, which covers fringes and compensation of supervisors, shows a similar movement.

The degree to which this slowdown can be attributed to the program is unclear. Evidence from econometric wage equations is, and will remain, inconclusive. The area where the effect is apparent is on the collective bargaining settlements. First-year settlements during 1971 averaged 11.6 percent, mainly prior to Phase I; in 1972, the first-year average dropped to 7.3 percent. Construction settlements controlled by the Construction Industry Stabilization Committee, fell from 17.6 percent in 1970 to 12.6 percent in 1971 and 6.9 percent in 1972. In the non-construction sector, settlements dropped to 7.4 percent. Pay Board records indicate that under Bureau of Labor Statistics definitions, the 7.4 percent average approval represented about

TABLE 2   Wage Adjustments during Phase II Compared with Earlier Pre-Control Adjustment (percent change at annual rates)

	Before		After
Hourly earnings index*.........................	1970-II to 1971-II 7.4%		Dec. 1971–Jan. 1973 6.1%
Compensation per man-hour†...................	1970-II to 1971-II 7.5%		1972-I to 1972-IV 6.1%
Major collective bargaining settlements‡	*1970*	*1971*	*1972*
First-year wage adjustments.....................	11.9	11.6	7.3
Excluding construction........................	10.9	11.6	7.4
Life-of-contract wage adjustments..............	8.9	8.1	6.4
Excluding construction........................	7.9	7.9	6.5

* Adjusted for overtime in manufacturing and interindustry shift.
† Private non-farm sector.
‡ Situations involving 1,000 or more workers.
Source: Bureau of Labor Statistics.

an 8.3 percent average request. That is, for major settlements, rollbacks reduced the average increase by 0.9 percent. The 8.3 percent is a lower-limit estimate of the average settlement that would have occurred in the absence of controls, since requests to the Pay Board contained a degree of self-moderation in response to the program.

It is not surprising that the new union settlements would be most affected by controls; such settlements were most likely to conflict with Pay Board standards. Union workers got more than non-union workers during Phase II due to the pressures of catching up. But they were cut back more too. Future wage control programs will produce similar results. Controls will concentrate their attention on new union settlements, even if they are nominally comprehensive. New union settlements in any given year cover only a small portion of the entire work force. As a result, the impact of controls on aggregate wage measures for the total economy tends to be small initially. But the effects on collective bargaining settlements will be far more noticeable. As time passes, if the controls are continued, more and more workers will be involved in settlements scrutinized by the wage authorities, and the influence of controls will spread.

Response to Loopholes

How rapidly will wage decision-makers seek out "loopholes" in a wage control program? Phase II indicates that the answer is "not very fast." A number of features of the Pay Board's regulations might be regarded as loopholes that could have been used to obtain more than the basic 5.5 percent. For example, the board in its tripartite state permitted cost-of-living escalators to be "time-weighted." Under time weighting, a 3 percent increase half-way through the year counts as 1.5 percent. It would have been to the advantage of union negotiators to make an escalator adjustment just prior to the end of their first control year, raising wages with only a small charge against the allowable 5.5 percent for that year. And it would have raised the base wage against which the following year's 5.5 percent would have been computed. Yet despite this incentive, escalators seemed to decline in popularity, probably because expectations of high inflation had lessened. During 1971, 54.5 percent of workers under major non-construction union settlements were covered by escalators. In 1972, the proportion fell to 25.8 percent.

"Qualified" fringe benefits were another avenue for obtaining more than the basic 5.5 percent. Originally, the Pay Board covered all benefits, wages, and fringes under its 5.5 percent guideline. But Congress, after intense lobbying by the insurance industry, amended the Economic Stabilization Act to provide preferential treatment for qualified fringe benefits. These benefits consisted of most pensions, health and welfare plans, and thrift schemes.

In response to the congressional mandate, the Pay Board adopted a basic guideline, with liberal exceptions, of 0.7 percent for qualified benefits. The additional amount raised the overall compensation standard from 5.5 percent to 6.2 percent. But despite the incentive to install or contribute to fringe benefits, 1972 was not a year of fringe upsurge. Total private employer contributions to pension and welfare funds rose faster than wage payments (11.5 percent versus 9.3 percent) according to the Commerce Department. This trend has been in evidence for some time, but the two rates were much closer than in the past. In the major union settlements, 52.1 percent of the workers covered received pension benefits in 1972, down from 70.6 percent in 1971. For health and welfare benefits, the percentages were 62.5 percent and 77.9 percent, respectively. Again, there was no evidence of a surge to take advantage of the incentive created by Phase II rules.

Another area where avoidance of the intent of the regulations was possible was productivity-incentive plans. The "Percy Amendment" to the Economic Stabilization Act required exemption of productivity-based earnings from such programs. Productivity-incentive plans are normally intended to stimulate worker output. But in order to implement the amendment, the Pay Board had to issue a complicated set of rules outlining the appropriate nature of a legitimate plan. In fact, the Board had no means to ensure that such rules were being followed. It would have been possible to use productivity plans, ranging from simple piece rates to Scanlon-type programs, to evade the program. In July 1972, about 46 percent of the workers under major non-construction union agreements were paid on an incentive basis. No hard evidence is available as to whether this evasion in fact occurred, but informal reports from the field suggest that it did not happen.

The fact that Phase II was known to be a short-term program, combined with the relatively loose labor market that existed, limited the incentive to seek out potential loopholes in the Pay Board's regulations. Thus, the Phase II experience has provided an important lesson. The formulators of a realistic wage program need not concern themselves with closing all possible avenues of escape, so long as they intend to operate a short-duration transitionary system of controls. This assumes, of course, that the basic guidelines are in realistic accord with labor-market conditions.

Distortions and Side Effects

Any wage/price control program carries the risk of creating economic distortions, particularly shortages. These situations arise when the program restricts wages or prices to levels at which suppliers do not meet the total demand. During Phase II, there were some developments of this type on the price side, notably in the lumber industry. Phase III controls were associated with a beef shortage, a gasoline shortage, and a paper shortage. But distortions of this type on the labor side were absent.

Pay Board staff members searched for evidence of occupational shortages in late 1972, and were unable to find any.[11] The quit-rate in manufacturing during that year was about what econometric equations would have predicted. Turnover was not artificially stimulated by controls. While the Board's rules did provide an exception for labor-shortage situations, its evidence requirements were so strict that the exception was seldom used. A loose labor market and a realistic guideline were the main reasons for the lack of economic distortion on the wage side.

Aside from economic distortions, a wage control system has the potential for damaging the industrial relations system. For example, there was some fear that controls would erode collective bargaining. It was thought that employers might accept any union demand, thereby avoiding the costs of a strike, hoping that the Pay Board would eventually pare back the contract to a reasonable level. Some instances of this strategy did occur during Phase II, notably in the retail food industry, but the problem never seemed widespread. Perhaps employers were not sure that their contracts would be cut back, or it may simply be that habits of normal bargaining are slow to change.

The presence of controls did disturb average contract durations. An important feature of American industrial relations has been the ability to negotiate multi-year contracts that provide periods of labor peace and stability. Hence, the disturbance is a matter of some concern. The pattern was especially evident in the union construction sector where controls were imposed in the spring of 1971. During the preceding year, 1970, only 7 percent of construction contracts were negotiated for one year's duration, according to a survey of the Bureau of National Affairs.[12] In 1971, the proportion rose to 63 percent. It reached 81 percent in 1972. The pattern was less severe, but still noticeable, in the non-construction sector. Six percent of contracts negotiated in that sector were of one year's duration in 1971. The figure increased to 15 percent in 1972. In some cases, the nominal contract duration was left intact, but early wage re-opener clauses were included in the contract.

The shortening of contract life apparently was a reaction to the anticipated short-term nature of Phase II. No one could be certain how long the controls would last, nor what would follow them. This uncertainty created an incentive to keep options open by permitting renegotiation after a shorter period of time than usual. It may be expected that future wage controls, if advertised as temporary, will produce a similar effect. Whether the announcement of a "permanent" system of controls would have such a result is unknown.

Controls during earlier wartime programs sometimes fostered unionization, or at least union security. In some cases, union security devices were offered in exchange for wage and strike restraint. However, during Phase II the Pay Board did not involve itself in the negotiations process. Thus, a "distortion" of the propensity to unionize probably should not have been expected. Still, there were some who felt that the existence of a wage guideline might *discourage* unionization. Workers might have thought that they would not get more than 5.5 percent even if they unionized, and so might have resisted organization. On the other hand, it could have been argued that the fact that unions seemed to get more during Phase II might have stimulated the desire to organize.

Although many hypotheses could be advanced, the evidence is that the wage program had no significant effect on unionization. Unions won 53 percent of representation elections conducted by the National Labor Relations Board during Phase II, compared to 53 percent in 1971 and 55 percent in 1970 and 1969.[13] This was not

---

[11] The results of the search were reported in Pay Board staff paper number OCE-103.

[12] Bureau of National Affairs, Inc., *Collective Bargaining Negotiations and Contracts* (Washington: BNA, 1973), pp. 18:935–18:938.

[13] Data on representation elections appear in *Annual Reports* of the National Labor Relations Board. Monthly

much different from the preceding decade. Elections involving the Teamsters—the "insiders" at the Pay Board after the other four labor members walked out—also show no break from past results. Thus, wage controls need not change the balance between the union and non-union sectors.

The number of strikes in 1972 was less than in the immediately preceding years, although not much different from 1971; but the number of workers involved and man-hours lost declined substantially. A total of 3.3 million workers participated annually in strikes in 1970. Of course, in 1972, the number of workers involved in major contract expirations was lower than in previous years. Major expirations and re-openers covered 2.8 million workers in 1972, down from 4.8 million in 1971. This factor would tend to limit worker involvement in strikes, but there are other influences on strike activity. The drop in worker involvement, and therefore the severity of strikes, appears to be larger than can be accounted for by the combined influence of changes in expirations and cyclical factors. It is noteworthy that during Phase II there were practically no strikes aimed specifically at the wage program. Of course, had the program continued to shorten contract durations, there would have been larger and larger numbers of workers with expirations in future years. This increase might have led to increased strike activity. But the experience under Phase II indicates that short-term controls programs need not lead to heightened labor strife.

CONCLUSIONS

It is probable that the United States, and other Western countries will be using incomes policy from time to time in the future. The unhappy experience on the price side during Phase III should not prevent learning whatever lessons can be gathered from the experience with the controls inaugurated in 1971. Phase III, in retrospect, appears to have been founded on two misapprehensions. On the wage side, it was feared that the Pay Board could not handle the upcoming big contracts of 1973: rubber, trucking, electrical equipment, and autos. Although tripartism was useful to the Board in the early days, the lack of it after the walkout was less of a problem than the administration seemed to think. On the price side, the Cost of Living Council believed that the Price Commission was mismanaged and that its rules were ineffective. Although there were serious management problems at the Commission, these did not necessarily mean that it was having no restraining effect on inflation. The sudden move to Phase III released the pressure on the industrial front at the same time the (uncontrolled) food price situation was known to be worsening. These two price problems brought on political pressures which forced a second freeze and created product-market distortions. It is hoped that more gradualism and less ideology will characterize future American programs.

It may also be hoped that the political problems which incomes policy entail will be lessened in the future by a more cooperative Congress. The American system of government ensures that Congress will have an influence on incomes policy, whether its views are sought or not. During Phase II, Congress changed the nature of the wage program through a variety of amendments. And it was fear that the Congress would act unilaterally which forced the adoption of the second freeze during Phase III. Had Congress been more actively involved in the planning prior to the announcement of the various phases, some of the difficulties that arose could have been avoided.

Phase III did provide one useful lesson. The change in the price control format did provoke a reaction, but the wage side remained quiet, despite the switch from mandatory Pay Board controls to "self-administration" and backroom cajoling. Price-setters are quicker to react to changes in the institutional framework than wage-setters. Paradoxically, although economists tend to concentrate on the wage aspects of incomes policy, the price side is the more complicated to regulate.

summaries are available from the NLRB. The win rate for Phase II was calculated for the period December 1971–December 1972.

44. Wage Stabilization in the Construction Industry: An Historical Perspective*

D. Quinn Mills†

The military construction program of the United States began in earnest in the spring and summer of 1941. In June 1941, the Office of Production Management authorized negotiations leading to a labor stabilization agreement for construction. There was issued on July 22, 1941, a "Memorandum of Stabilization Agreement between Certain Government Agencies Engaged in Defense Construction and the Building and Construction Trades Department of the AFL." The Agreement provided for uniform overtime rates and uniform shift pay on all national defense projects. It also provided a no-strike pledge from the unions and for settlement of grievances and disputes by conciliation and arbitration. In return for these concessions, the government accorded the building trades unions "unprecedented recognition . . . that they represented the workers of the construction industry."[1] By this agreement, a no-strike pledge was established in construction five months prior to that in industry generally.

In the spring of 1942, the government initiated discussions with the building trades regarding a wage stabilization agreement. On May 22, 1942, such an agreement was executed. The Secretary of Labor then issued an order establishing the Wage Adjustment Board to administer wage control in construction. The WAB was formally liquidated on February 14, 1947. During the existence of the National War Labor Board and the National Wage Stabilization Board, the WAB

administered general stabilization policies in the construction industry. Thus, wage controls came to construction by agreement five months prior to being imposed on industry in general, and were retained by agreement for more than a year following the effective abolition of wage and price controls.

On September 8, 1950, President Truman signed the Defense Production Act of 1950, and on the following day issued an Executive Order establishing the Wage Stabilization Board. On November 28, 1950, the WSB held its first meeting; and on January 25, 1951, a general wage-price freeze was announced. Shortly after the imposition of the freeze, construction industry leaders sought a meeting with the Board regarding wage stabilization in their industry. At its first meeting on May 8, 1951, the reconstituted Board discussed a request for a separate construction board. Finally, on May 31, 1951, General Wage Regulation 12 of the WSB established the Construction Industry Stabilization Commission, including employer, labor, and public representation. Because of employer objections, no reference was made in Regulation 12 to a dispute settlement function for the Commission, and during its existence only two dispute cases were formally referred to the Commission by the WSB. In 1953, both the WSB and the Construction Industry Stabilization Commission were abolished by President Eisenhower.

On March 29, 1971, following several months of discussion among government, labor, and employer representatives, President Nixon invoked the Economic Stabilization Act of 1970 to establish the Construction Industry Stabilization Committee (by Executive Order 11588). The Committee was given jurisdiction over collective bargaining agreements in the contract construc-

---

* From the *Labor Law Journal,* Vol. 23, No. 8, August 1972, pp. 462–68.

† D. Quinn Mills is on the faculty of Harvard University.

[1] John T. Dunlop and Arthur Hill, *The Wage Adjustment Board: Wartime Stabilization in the Building and Construction Industry* (Cambridge, Mass.: Harvard University Press, 1950), pp. 18–20.

tion industry. The Committee was tripartite in composition, including representatives of labor, contractors' associations, and the public. All newly negotiated collective bargaining agreements in construction required the approval of the Committee before they could be placed into effect. Four and one-half months later, the President imposed a general wage-price freeze which included construction. In mid-October an Executive Order established a tripartite Pay Board to administer wage controls generally. The Construction Industry Stabilization Committee (CISC) was explicitly continued by the new Order, but the criteria for wage adjustments included in the March 29 Order were removed, in order that the general wage policy adopted by the Pay Board should also apply to construction. On January 29, 1971, the Pay Board and the CISC jointly announced agreement on the authority of the CISC to administer wage stabilization policy in construction and the general criteria which the Committee should apply in 1972. A most important aspect of the agreement extended authority to the CISC to review all deferred increases in existing collective bargaining agreements and to prohibit their being placed into effect if inconsistent with stabilization policies in the industry.

THE ECONOMIC ENVIRONMENT OF CONTROLS

Economic Conditions in Construction Prior to and during Controls

The economic environment of a program of wage controls is a major determinant of the form which the program must take and of the results which can be expected from it. The economic environment of the wage stabilization program as a whole in 1971–72 was very different from previous periods, and this situation was especially marked in construction.

The context of the first part of the stabilization program in World War II was one of rapidly expanding over-all construction demand, very rapid adjustment to a very different composition of demand, and tightening labor markets. In 1943, however, the war-time construction boom was over and demand pressures fell off substantially until the end of the war. However, 1946 was a year of great expansion in construction, particularly in housing. In summary, the period 1940–47 was characterized by rapid fluctuations in the total volume of construction, and equally rapid variations in its composition. A more unsettled

period in construction demand is hard to imagine.

The Korean period was far more moderate with regard to fluctuations of demand. Industry volume had been steadily expanding after World War II and continued to do so during the Korean War. The composition of expenditures shifted toward military and industrial work, but to a far lesser degree than in the mid-1940s. Unemployment rates fell during the war, but not as precipitously as during World War II.

Perhaps the most important characteristics of both war-time periods as contrasted to 1971 was the experience of years of relative stability prior to the sudden expansion of demand and the imposition of controls. This description is less true of the Korean years than of World War II; but even in the case of Korea, 1949 and 1950 had been years of generally loose labor markets. However, when controls were imposed on construction in 1971, the industry had been through the longest boom in its history (1964–69). Further, and more importantly, the inflationary pressures of 1968–69 had been unconstrained by controls, and collective bargaining had resulted in a badly distorted wage structure. In construction, wage rates are established in separate negotiations with each trade in each geographic area. The uneven pattern of the timing of negotiations (most trades in the late 1960s negotiated on a three-year basis) was such as to allow those trades negotiating in 1969 and 1970 to introduce great distortions into the wage structure. In some areas laborers were receiving, in 1970–71, higher wage rates (including fringes) than certain of the skilled trades. In other areas, wage differentials among the skilled trades no longer bore any resemblance to the traditional structure of rates. There existed, therefore, in 1971 as the bargaining season opened in the spring, a situation of great instability in the wage structure in construction—a circumstance very much unlike that confronting stabilization authorities in previous periods.

The Wage Stabilization Record

During much of World War II and Korea, the wage stabilization program in construction was a holding action against the pressure on wages created by rising construction volume and falling unemployment. The program in World War II was largely successful in restraining the rate of increase in wage rates, though earnings expanded rapidly. "Union wage-rate scales in construction increased less than in manufacturing generally during the defense period prior to the imposition of wage controls and in the subsequent period of direct wage controls when . . . measured in percentage terms."[2] This assessment for the World War II period[3] was based on special studies of wage-rate changes and urban wage rates developed by the BLS during World War II and cannot be replicated for the Korean period. However, indications from average hourly earnings data are that the rate of wage increases in construction was approximately equal to that in manufacturing and followed the same year-to-year pattern during stabilization.

Judgments as to the results of wage stabilization activities during the current period are necessarily tentative. There is distinct seasonality to the collective bargaining process in construction, with most negotiations taking place between April 1 and September 30 so that it is possible to evaluate the performance of the Stabilization Committee during 1971 (the change of policy which accompanied the freeze on August 15 affected only the final six weeks of this period). During the second and third quarters of 1970, average first-year increases in negotiated settlements in construction covering 1,000 or more workers were at the annual rate of 17.1 and 21.3 percent, respectively. The first quarter of 1971, prior to controls, showed an average increase of 15.7 percent (the highest first quarter increase in recent years). With the advent of the stabilization program in construction on March 29, 1971, second and third quarter increases in construction, on the average, were at the annual rate of 12.0 and 11.4 percent, respectively. As compared to the experience of manufacturing, this retardation in the rate of increase in construction settlements is quite marked. Manufacturing increases continued to accelerate through 1971 until, in the third quarter of the year, the average rate of increase in new manufacturing settlements[4] exceeded that in construction for the first time since the 1960s.

DISPUTE SETTLEMENT

Dispute settlement in wartime was directed at maintaining production as well as effectuating the stabilization program. In the 1970s, dispute settlement was a critical element in maintaining the integrity of the wage control program. During World War II, the unions gave a no-strike pledge, and the activities of the Review Board (under the July 22, 1941 agreement) and its successor, the Wage Adjustment Board, included the settlement of disputes. However, because the distinction between a voluntary wage adjustment request and a dispute case was less sharp in construction than in industry generally, there were only a limited number of formally certified dispute cases.[5] In the context of the no-strike pledge, dispute settlement was a less significant factor in the stabilization program than in the 1970s. Conversely, during the Korean period, there was no no-strike pledge and also there was no official delegation of authority to the Construction Industry Stabilization Commission in dispute cases. Nonetheless, the Commission was inevitably involved in some dispute situations.

During 1971, dispute settlement was a major function of the stabilization machinery. Records of the Federal Mediation and Conciliation Service indicated that, in 1970, more than 500 work stoppages had occurred, involving one of every three negotiations in construction. In many localities strikes by one trade after another occurred, keeping the industry in turmoil throughout the work season. Unable to secure a no-strike pledge for 1971, the government did seek and obtain agreement from the national unions and employer associations to establish procedures to assist in the settlement of disputes at the local level. The Executive Order of March 29 therefore provided for "craft disputes boards" to be created in each trade at the national level, bipartite in composition, for the purpose of advising and assisting local parties in the negotiations process. The Committee, working in concert with the craft boards, was able to significantly reduce the incidence of work stoppages. In 1971, one third the number of strikes occurred in construction as in 1970, and the working time lost due to work stoppages over economic issues was cut by 60 percent.[6]

WAGE STABILIZATION—CONSTRUCTION VERSUS INDUSTRY GENERALLY

The question of the establishment of industry-specific commissions in a wage stabilization program has always been a contentious one. Whatever the merits of the issue in general, it has proven necessary, in each of the three periods

---

[2] Cited at footnote 1, at p. 120.

[3] Dunlop and Hill further note a comparison of wage differentials among trades and regions as a result of stabilization activities, cited at footnote 1, at p. 123.

[4] The third quarter, 1971 manufacturing estimate was largely due to settlements in steel and at Western Electric.

[5] Cited at footnote 1.

[6] Unpublished data of the Federal Mediation and Conciliation Service.

with which we are concerned, to establish a special board for construction. In large part this was to provide criteria for wage adjustments appropriate to the peculiar circumstances of construction but equivalent on balance to those in industry generally. Yet, during World War II and Korea, the existence of the special construction industry boards raised difficult problems of coordination with regional bodies of the general machinery.[7] In the current context, at least to this date, there have been no such problems because the Pay Board has not created regional bodies.

The peculiar arrangements of construction are reflected not only in administrative matters but also in policy application. On January 28, 1972, the Pay Board and the CISC announced a set of "Substantive Policies" to be applied by CISC in 1972. The document stated that "specific policies of the Pay Board with respect to matters such as tandem relationships, deferred increases, merit increases, incentives, and the like may not be directly applicable in all instances to construction and will need supplementation. . . . CISC policies should be applied so as to conform as closely as the special conditions of the construction industry permit to those of the Pay Board." In addition, the Pay Board-CISC agreement provides that, in construction, "no agreement is automatically entitled to the 'general pay standard' . . . of the Pay Board."[8] Further, procedures for reporting or pre-notification of increases and for the handling of deferred increases (those provided for in agreements negotiated before the stabilization program) are very different in construction than in industry generally. There is, for example, an interesting parallel from World War II in the relationship of the Wage Adjustment Board to the National War Labor Board with respect to the application of NWLB policies by the WAB in construction. General Order No. 13 of the NWLB (adopted October 13, 1943) says as follows:

Section F.2. Sound and Tested Rates
The provisions of the May 12 supplement to Executive Order No. 9328 with respect to "brackets of sound and tested going rates" are inapplicable to the Building Construction Industry.

[7] See Clark Kerr, "The Distribution of Authority and Its Relation to Policy," in W. E. Chalmers, M. Derber and W. H. McPherson, editors, *Problems and Policies of Dispute Settlement and Wage Stabilization during World War II*, BLS, Bulletin No. 1009, 1950, pp. 291–321.

[8] See text, published in Bureau of National Affairs, *Daily Labor Report*, No. 20 (January 28, 1972), pp. AA1–AA4.

Section F.3. Little Steel
The Little Steel formula . . . shall be applied by the Wage Adjustment Board in the following manner:

a. No employee or groups of employees is entitled automatically to a Little Steel adjustment.

b. Generally, employees enjoying relatively high rates of pay should receive a smaller percentage adjustment than those receiving lower rates of pay"[9]

In the current situation, as before, the day-to-day operations of the construction industry machinery is qutie different from that of the all-industry board. Because of the multitude of separate bargaining units in the industry, the overlapping of geographic coverage among units of different trades, and the complex interrelationships among trades and areas, the construction boards have operated as expert panels, examining in detail virtually all adjustments submitted to them. There has been far less delegation of authority to staff or subordinate bodies than has, of necessity, characterized the general industry board. In construction, policy has been made on a case-by-case basis on the record of particular situations. During 1971, for example, the CISC, meeting weekly, and its subcommittees composed *only* of members of the Committee (no substitutes), examined in detail more than 1,700 new collective bargaining agreements.

CONCLUSIONS

Two general conclusions may be drawn from this brief review of wage stabilization experience in construction. First, there are economic and institutional peculiarities of the industry which require, and have received, special treatment in periods of economic stabilization by direct controls. Inflationary pressures in construction both prior to World War II and in the late 1960s were so acute as to result in the inposition of controls on the industry in advance of those on the economy generally. Further, in the application of stabilization policy, special boards were established for construction in all three periods, and special policies were applied in construction. Problems sometimes arose in the administration of stabilization policy because special treatment was feared by some to be a special license for construction to ignore general stabilization regulations, and because the existence of a construction board created certain problems of coordination with the general machinery of stabilization. Yet there can be little doubt that the special arrangements created for construction con-

[9] Cited at footnote 1.

stituted an element of strength in stabilization policy generally. Those familiar with construction on all sides (labor, management, and the public) have been in agreement that the application to the industry of policies developed for industry generally could only result in chaos.

Second, in both World War II and the current period, wage stabilization programs for construction have had important long-range objectives that have not characterized stabilization efforts in the rest of the economy. During World War II, the administration of the no-strike pledge involved the settlement of jurisdictional disputes as well as disputes over wages and conditions of work. "The experience in industry-wide responsibility represented by the WAB . . . was to provide (personal) associations which were to seek more effective settlement of wage contract disputes and machinery for the problem of jurisdictional work stoppages in the postwar era."[10] The

CISC in the current period has viewed a major aspect of its work to be the development of institutional arrangements which will operate to improve collective bargaining in the industry in the future. The most important such arrangements are the craft boards established at the national level in each trade by employers and the unions (as specifically provided by the Executive Order establishing the CISC). The craft boards have been charged by the Secretary of Labor with concern for dispute settlement, local bargaining structure, and working rules in the industry.[11] Stabilization authorities cannot, of course, assure the continued existence and effectiveness of the craft boards after the stabilization machinery is abolished, but they may attempt to establish as firm a foundation for the future of the boards as possible.

---

[10] Cited at footnote 1, at p. vii. The National Joint Board for the Settlement of Jurisdictional Disputes was established in 1948 with John T. Dunlop as its first Impartial Chairman.

[11] Speech by Secretary of Labor James Hodgson to the craft boards, Washington, D.C., January 13, 1972.

C. The Negro and Employment

The Negro's job position has been a precarious one throughout most of our economic history. The unemployment rate for blacks has always been about twice the rate for whites in the United States, and when employed, blacks have been concentrated in the most menial jobs. Two articles are presented in this section that deal with Negro employment problems.

James Tobin discusses the general economic status of Negroes and stresses the importance of a healthy economy and tight labor market for an improvement in the position of Negroes. Andrew Brimmer analyzes recent changes in the pattern of black employment in both the private and public sectors, and he assesses the job opportunities for blacks in the years ahead to 1985.

45. On Improving the Economic Status of the Negro*

I start from the presumption that integration of Negroes into the American society and economy can be accomplished within existing political and economic institutions. I understand the impatience of those who think otherwise, but I see nothing incompatible between our peculiar mixture of private enterprise and government, on the one hand, and the liberation and integration of the Negro, on the other. Indeed the present position of the Negro is an aberration from the principles of our society, rather than a requirement of its functioning. Therefore, my suggestions are directed to the aim of mobilizing existing powers of government to bring Negroes into full participation in the main stream of American economic life.

The economic plight of individuals, Negroes and whites alike, can always be attributed to specific handicaps and circumstances: discrimination, immobility, lack of education and experience, ill health, weak motivation, poor neighborhood, large family size, burdensome family responsibilities. Such diagnoses suggest a host of specific remedies, some in the domain of civil rights, others in the war on poverty. Important as these remedies are, there is a danger that the diagnoses are myopic. They explain why certain individuals rather than others suffer from the economic maladies of the time. They do not explain why the overall incidence of the maladies varies dramatically from time to time—for example, why personal attributes which seemed to doom a man to unemployment in 1932 or even in 1954 or 1961 did not so handicap him in 1944 or 1951 or 1956.

Public health measures to improve the environ-ment are often more productive in conquering disease than a succession of individual treatments. Malaria was conquered by oiling and draining swamps, not by quinine. The analogy holds for economic maladies. Unless the global incidence of these misfortunes can be diminished, every individual problem successfully solved will be replaced by a similar problem somewhere else. That is why an economist is led to emphasize the importance of the overall economic climate.

Over the decades, general economic progress has been the major factor in the gradual conquest of poverty. Recently some observers, J. K. Galbraith and Michael Harrington most eloquently, have contended that this process no longer operates. The economy may prosper and labor may become steadily more productive as in the past, but "the other America" will be stranded. Prosperity and progress have already eliminated almost all the easy cases of poverty, leaving a hard core beyond the reach of national economic trends. There may be something to the "backwash" thesis as far as whites are concerned.[1] But it definitely does not apply to Negroes. Too many of them are poor. It cannot be true that half of a race of 20 million human beings are victims of specific disabilities which insulate them from the national economic climate. It can-

[1] As Locke Anderson shows, one would expect advances in median income to run into diminishing returns in reducing the number of people below some fixed poverty-level income. W. H. Locke Anderson, "Trickling Down: The Relationship between Economic Growth and the Extent of Poverty Among American Families," *Quarterly Journal of Economics*, Vol. 78 (November 1964), pp. 511–24. However, for the economy as a whole, estimates by Lowell Gallaway suggest that advances in median income still result in a substantial reduction in the fraction of the population below poverty-level incomes. "The Foundation of the War on Poverty," *American Economic Review*, Vol. 55 (March 1965), pp. 122–31.

* From *Daedalus*, The Journal of the American Academy of Arts and Sciences, Fall 1965, pp. 878–98.

† Sterling professor of economics, Yale University.

not be true, and it is not. Locke Anderson has shown that the pace of Negro economic progress is peculiarly sensitive to general economic growth. He estimates that if nationwide per capita personal income is stationary, nonwhite median family income falls by 0.5 percent per year, while if national per capita income grows 5 percent, nonwhite income grows nearly 7.5 percent.[2]

National prosperity and economic growth are still powerful engines for improving the economic status of Negroes. They are not doing enough, and they are not doing it fast enough. There is ample room for a focused attack on the specific sources of Negro poverty. But a favorable overall economic climate is a necessary condition for the global success—as distinguished from success in individual cases—of specific efforts to remedy the handicaps associated with Negro poverty.

THE IMPORTANCE OF A TIGHT LABOR MARKET

But isn't the present overall economic climate favorable? Isn't the economy enjoying an upswing of unprecedented length, setting new records almost every month in production, employment, profits, and income? Yes, but expansion and new records should be routine in an economy with growing population, capital equipment, and productivity. The fact is that the economy has not operated with reasonably full utilization of its manpower and plant capacity since 1957. Even now, after four and one-half years of uninterrupted expansion, the economy has not regained the ground lost in the recessions of 1958 and 1960. The current expansion has whittled away at unemployment, reducing it from 6.5 to 7 percent to 4.5 to 5 percent. It has diminished idle plant capacity correspondingly. The rest of the gains since 1960 in employment, production, and income have just offset the normal growth of population, capacity, and productivity.

The magnitude of America's poverty problem already reflects the failure of the economy in the second postwar decade to match its performance in the first.[3] Had the 1947–56 rate of growth of median family income been maintained since 1957, and had unemployment been steadily limited to 4 percent, it is estimated that the fraction of the population with poverty incomes in

1963 would have been 16.6 percent instead of 18.5 percent.[4] The educational qualifications of the labor force have continued to improve. The principle of racial equality, in employment as in other activities, has gained ground both in law and in the national conscience. If, despite all this, dropouts, inequalities in educational attainment, and discrimination in employment seem more serious today rather than less, the reason is that the overall economic climate has not been favorable after all.

The most important dimension of the overall economic climate is the tightness of the labor market. In a tight labor market unemployment is low and short in duration, and job vacancies are plentiful. People who stand at the end of the hiring line and the top of the layoff list have the most to gain from a tight labor market. It is not surprising that the position of Negroes relative to that of whites improves in a tight labor market and declines in a slack market. Unemployment itself is only one way in which a slack labor market hurts Negroes and other disadvantaged groups, and the gains from reduction in unemployment are by no means confined to the employment of persons counted as unemployed.[5] A tight labor market means not just jobs, but better jobs, longer hours, higher wages. Because of the heavy demands for labor durnig the second world war and its economic aftermath, Negroes made dramatic relative gains between 1940 and 1950. Unfortunately this momentum has not been maintained, and the blame falls largely on the weakness of the labor markets since 1957.[6]

---

[2] Anderson, "Trickling Down," Table 4, p. 522.

[3] This point, and others made in this section, have been eloquently argued by Harry G. Johnson, "Unemployment and Poverty," unpublished paper presented at West Virginia University Conference on Poverty amidst Affluence, May 5, 1965.

[4] Gallaway, "War on Poverty." Gallaway used the definitions of poverty originally suggested by the Council of Economic Advisers in its 1964 Economic Report, that is: incomes below $3,000 a year for families and below $1,500 a year for single individuals. The Social Security Administration has refined these measures to take better account of family size and of income in kind available to farmers. Mollie Orshansky, "Counting the Poor: Another Look at the Poverty Profile," Social Security Bulletin, Vol. 28 (January 1965), pp. 3–29. These refinements change the composition of the "poor" but affect very little their total number; it is doubtful they would alter Gallaway's results.

[5] Gallaway, "War on Poverty," shows that postwar experience suggests that, other things equal, every point by which unemployment is diminished lowers the national incidence of poverty by 0.5 percent of itself. And this does not include the effects of the accompanying increase in median family income, which would be of the order of 3 percent and reduce the poverty fraction another 1.8 percent.

[6] For lack of comparable nationwide income data, the only way to gauge the progress of Negroes relative to whites over long periods of time is to compare their distributions among occupations. A measure of the occupational position of a group can be constructed from decennial Census data by weighting the proportions of the group in each occupation by the average income of the

The shortage of jobs has hit Negro men particularly hard and thus has contributed mightily to the ordeal of the Negro family, which is in turn the cumulative source of so many other social disorders.[7] The unemployment rate of Negro men is more sensitive than that of Negro women to the national rate. Since 1949 Negro women have gained in median income relative to white women, but Negro men have lost ground to white males.[8] In a society which stresses breadwinning as the expected role of the mature male and occupational achievement as his proper goal, failure to find and to keep work is devastating to the man's self-respect and family status. Matriarchy is in any case a strong tradition in Negro society, and the man's role is

further downgraded when the family must and can depend on the woman for its livelihood. It is very important to increase the proportion of Negro children who grow up in stable families with two parents. Without a strong labor market it will be extremely difficult to do so.

Unemployment

It is well known that Negro unemployment rates are multiples of the general unemployment rate. This fact reflects both the lesser skills, seniority, and experience of Negroes and employers' discrimination against Negroes. These conditions are a deplorable reflection on American society, but as long as they exist Negroes suffer much more than others from a general increase in unemployment and gain much more from a general reduction. A rule of thumb is that changes in the nonwhite unemployment rate are twice those in the white rate. The rule works both ways. Nonwhite unemployment went from 4.1 percent in 1953, a tight labor market year, to 12.5 percent in 1961, while the white rate rose from 2.3 percent to 6 percent. Since then, the Negro rate has declined by 2.4 percent, the white rate by 1.2.

Even the Negro teenage unemployment rate shows some sensitivity to general economic conditions. Recession increased it from 15 percent in 1955–56 to 25 percent in 1958. It decreased to 22 percent in 1960 but rose to 28 percent in 1963; since then it has declined somewhat. Teenage unemployment is abnormally high now, relative to that of other age groups, because the wage of postwar babies is coming into the labor market. Most of them, especially the Negroes, are crowding the end of the hiring line. But their prospects for getting jobs are no less dependent on general labor market conditions.

---

occupation. The ratio of this measure for Negroes to the same measure for whites is an index of the relative occupational position of Negroes. Such calculations were originally made by Gary Becker, *The Economics of Discrimination* (Chicago, 1957). They have recently been refined and brought up to date by Dale Hiestand, *Economic Growth and Employment Opportunities for Minorities* (New York, 1964), p. 53. Hiestand's results are as follows:
Occupational position of Negroes relative to whites:

	1910	1920	1930	1940	1950	1960
Male	78.0	78.1	78.2	77.5	81.4	82.1
Female	78.0	71.3	74.8	76.8	81.6	84.3

The figures show that Negro men lost ground in the Great Depression, that they gained sharply in the 1940s, and that their progress almost ceased in the 1950s. Negro women show a rising secular trend since the 1920s, but their gains too were greater in the tight labor markets of the 1940s than in the 1930s or 1950s.

Several cautions should be borne in mind in interpreting these figures: (1) Much of the relative occupational progress of Negroes is due to massive migration from agriculture to occupations of much higher average income. When the overall relative index nevertheless does not move, as in the 1950s, the position of Negroes in the non-agricultural occupations has declined. (2) Since the figures include unemployed as well as employed persons and Negroes are more sensitive to unemployment, the occupational index understates their progress when unemployment declined (1940–50) and overstates it when unemployment rose (1930–40 and 1950–60). (3) Within any Census occupational category, Negroes earn less than whites. So the absolute level of the index overstates the Negro's relative position. Moreover, this overstatement is probably greater in Census years of relatively slack labor markets, like 1940 and 1960, than in other years.

The finding that labor market conditions arrested the progress of Negro men is confirmed by income and unemployment data analyzed by Alan B. Batchelder, "Decline in the Relative Income of Negro Men," *Quarterly Journal of Economics*, Vol. 78 (November 1964), pp. 525–48.

[7] Differences between Negro men and women with respect to unemployment and income progress are reported and analyzed by Alan Batchelder, *op. cit.*

[8] Differences between Negro men and women with respect to unemployment and income progress are reported and analyzed by Alan Batchelder, "Income of Negro Men."

Part-Time Work

Persons who are involuntarily forced to work part time instead of full time are not counted as unemployed, but their number goes up and down with the unemployment rate. Just as Negroes bear a disproportionate share of unemployment, they bear more than their share of involuntary part-time unemployment.[9] A tight labor market will not only employ more Negroes; it will also give more of those who are employed

---

[9] Figures are given, for example, in the articles by Rashi Fein in *Daedalus* (Fall 1965) and by Daniel Patrick Moynihan in *Daedalus* (Fall 1965).

full-time job. In both respects, it will reduce disparities between whites and Negroes.

Labor-Force Participation

In a tight market, of which a low unemployment rate is a barometer, the labor force itself is larger. Job opportunities draw into the labor force individuals who, simply because the prospects were dim, did not previously regard themselves as seeking work and were therefore not enumerated as unemployed. For the economy as a whole, it appears that an expansion of job opportunities enough to reduce unemployment by one worker will bring another worker into the labor force.

This phenomenon is important for many Negro families. Statistically, their poverty now appears to be due more often to the lack of a breadwinner in the labor force than to unemployment.[10] But in a tight labor market many members of these families, including families now on public assistance, would be drawn into employment. Labor-force participation rates are roughly 2 percent lower for nonwhite men than for white men, and the disparity increases in years of slack labor markets.[11] The story is different for women. Negro women have always been in the labor force to a much greater extent than white women. A real improvement in the economic status of Negro men and in the stability of Negro families would probably lead to a reduction in labor-force participation by Negro women. But for teenagers, participation rates for Negroes are not so high as for whites; and for women 20 to 24 they are about the same. These relatively low rates are undoubtedly due less to voluntary choice than to the same lack of job opportunities that produces phenomenally high unemployments for young Negro women.

Duration of Unemployment

In a tight labor market, such unemployment as does exist is likely to be of short duration. Short-term unemployment is less damaging to the economic welfare of the unemployed. More will have earned and fewer will have exhausted private and public unemployment benefits. In 1953 when the overall unemployment rate was 2.9 percent, only 4 percent of the unemployed were out of work for longer than 26 weeks and only 11 percent for longer than 15 weeks. In contrast, the unemployment rate in 1961 was 6.7 percent; and of the unemployed in that year, 17 percent were out of work for longer than 26 weeks and 32 percent for longer than 15 weeks. Between the first quarter of 1964 and the first quarter of 1965, overall unemployment fell 11 percent, while unemployment extending beyond half a year was lowered by 22 percent.

As Rashi Fein points out [*Daedalus* (Fall 1965)] . . . one more dimension of society's inequity to the Negro is that an unemployed Negro is more likely to stay unemployed than an unemployed white. But his figures also show that Negroes share in the reduction of long-term unemployment accompanying economic expansion.

Migration from Agriculture

A tight labor market draws the surplus rural population to higher paying non-agricultural jobs. Southern Negroes are a large part of this surplus rural population. Migration is the only hope for improving their lot, or their children's. In spite of the vast migration of past decades, there are still about 775,000 Negroes, 11 percent of the Negro labor force of the country, who depend on the land for their living and that of their families.[12] Almost a half million live in the South, and almost all of them are poor.

Migration from agriculture and from the South is the Negroes' historic path toward economic improvement and equality. It is a smooth path for Negroes and for the urban communities to which they move only if there is a strong demand for labor in towns and cities North and South. In the 1940s the number of Negro farmers and farm laborers in the nation fell by 450,000 and 1.5 million Negroes (net) left the South. This was the great decade of Negro economic advance. In the 1950s the same occupational and geographical migration continued undiminished. The movement to higher income occupations and locations should have raised the relative economic status of Negroes. But in the 1950s Negroes were moving into increasingly weak job markets. Too often disguised unemployment in the countryside was simply transformed into enumerated unemployment, and rural poverty into urban poverty.[13]

---

[10] In 34 percent of poor Negro families, the head is not in the labor force; in 6 percent, the head is unemployed. These figures relate to the Social Security Administration's "economy-level" poverty index. Mollie Orshansky, "Counting the Poor."

[11] See *Manpower Report of the President*, March 1964, Table A-3, p. 197.

[12] Hiestand, *Economic Growth*, Table 1, pp. 7–9.

[13] Batchelder, "Income of Negro Men," shows that the incomes of Negro men declined relative to those of white men in every region of the country. For the country

Quality of Jobs

In a slack labor market, employers can pick and choose, both in recruiting and in promoting. They exaggerate the skill, education, and experience requirements of their jobs. They use diplomas or color or personal histories as convenient screening devices. In a tight market, they are forced to be realistic, to tailor job specifications to the available supply, and to give on-the-job training. They recruit and train applicants whom they would otherwise screen out, and they upgrade employees whom they would in slack times consign to low-wage, low-skill, and part-time jobs.

Wartime and other experience shows that job requirements are adjustable and that men and women are trainable. It is only in slack times that people worry about a mismatch between supposedly rigid occupational requirements and supposedly unchangeable qualifications of the labor force. As already noted, the relative status of Negroes improves in a tight labor market not only in respect to unemployment, but also in respect to wages and occupations.

Cyclical Fluctuation

Sustaining a high demand for labor is important. The in-and-out status of the Negro in the business cycle damages his long-term position because periodic unemployment robs him of experience and seniority.

Restrictive Practices

A slack labor market probably accentuates the discriminatory and protectionist proclivities of certain crafts and unions. When jobs are scarce, opening the door to Negroes is a real threat. Of course prosperity will not automatically dissolve the barriers, but it will make it more difficult to oppose efforts to do so.

I conclude that the single most important step the nation could take to improve the economic position of the Negro is to operate the economy steadily at a low rate of unemployment. We cannot expect to restore the labor market conditions of World War II, and we do not need to. In the years 1951–53, unemployment was roughly 3 percent, teenage unemployment around 7 percent, Negro unemployment about 4.5 percent, long-term unemployment negligible. In the years

---

as a whole, nevertheless, the median income of Negro men stayed close to half that of white men. The reason is that migration from the South, where the Negro-white income ratio is particularly low, just offset the declines in the regional ratios.

1955–57, general unemployment was roughly 4 percent, and the other measures correspondingly higher. Four percent is the official target of the Kennedy-Johnson administration. It has not been achieved since 1957. Reaching and maintaining 4 percent would be a tremendous improvement over the performance of the last eight years. But we should not stop there; the society and the Negro can benefit immensely from tightening the labor market still further, to 3.5 or 3 percent unemployment. The administration itself has never defined 4 percent as anything other than an "interim" target.

WHY DON'T WE HAVE A TIGHT LABOR MARKET?

We know how to operate the economy so that there is a tight labor market. By fiscal and monetary measures the federal government can control aggregate spending in the economy. The government could choose to control it so that unemployment *averaged* 3.5 or 3 percent instead of remaining over 4.5 percent except at occasional business cycle peaks. Moreover, recent experience here and abroad shows that we can probably narrow the amplitude of fluctuations around whatever average we select as a target.

Some observers have cynically concluded that a society like ours can achieve full employment only in wartime. But aside from conscription into the armed services, government action creates jobs in wartime by exactly the same mechanism as in peacetime—the government spends more money and stimulates private firms and citizens to spend more too. It is the *amount* of spending, not its purpose, that does the trick. Public or private spending to go to the moon, build schools, or conquer poverty can be just as effective in reducing unemployment as spending to build airplanes and submarines—if there is enough of it. There may be more political constraints and ideological inhibitions in peacetime, but the same techniques of economic policy are available if we want badly enough to use them. The two main reasons we do not take this relatively simple way out are two obsessive fears, inflation and balance of payments deficits.

Running the economy with a tight labor market would mean a somewhat faster upward creep in the prive level. The disadvantages of this are, in my view, exaggerated and are scarcely commensurable with the real economic and social gains of higher output and employment. Moreover, there are ways of protecting "widows and orphans" against erosion in the purchasing power of their savings. But fear of inflation is strong both in the U.S. financial establishment and in the public at large. The vast comfortable white middle class who are never touched by unemployment prefer to safeguard the purchasing power of their life insurance and pension rights than to expand opportunities for the disadvantaged and unemployed.

The fear of inflation would operate anyway, but it is accentuated by U.S. difficulties with its international balance of payments. These difficulties have seriously constrained and hampered U.S. fiscal and monetary policy in recent years. Any rise in prices might enlarge the deficit. An aggressively expansionary monetary policy, lowering interest rates, might push money out of the country.

In the final analysis what we fear is that we might not be able to defend the parity of the dollar with gold, that is, to sell gold at $35 an ounce to any government that wants to buy. So great is the gold mystique that this objective has come to occupy a niche in the hierarchy of U.S. goals second only to the military defense of the country, and not always to that. It is not fanciful to link the plight of Negro teenagers in Harlem to the monetary whims of General de Gaulle. But it is only our own attachment to "the dollar" as an abstraction which makes us cringe before the European appetite for gold.

This topic is too charged with technical complexities, real and imagined, and with confused emotions to be discussed adequately here. I will confine myself to three points. First, the United States is the last country in the world which needs to hold back its own economy to balance its international accounts. To let the tail wag the dog is not in the interests of the rest of the world, so much of which depends on us for trade and capital, any more than in our own.

Second, forces are at work to restore balance to American international accounts—the increased competitiveness of our exports and the income from the large investments our firms and citizens have made overseas since the war. Meanwhile we can finance deficits by gold reserves and lins of credit at the International Monetary Fund and at foreign central banks. Ultimately we have one foolproof line of defense—letting the dollar depreciate relative to foreign currencies. The world would not end. The sun would rise the next day. American products would be more competitive in world markets. Neither God nor the Constitution fixed the gold value of the dollar. The United States would not be the first country to let its currency depreciate. Nor would it be the first time for the United States—not until we stopped "saving" the dollar and the gold standard in 1933 did our recovery from the Great Depression begin.

Third, those who oppose taking such risks argue that the dollar today occupies a unique position as international money, that the world as a whole has an interest, which we cannot ignore, in the stability of the gold value of the dollar. If so, we can reasonably ask the rest of the world, especially our European friends, to share the burdens which guaranteeing this stability imposes upon us.

This has been an excursion into general economic policy. But the connection between gold and the plight of the Negro is no less real for being subtle. We are paying much too high a social price for avoiding creeping inflation and for protecting our gold stock and "the dollar." But it will not be easy to alter these national priorities. The interests of the unemployed, the poor, and the Negroes are under-represented in the comfortable consensus which supports and confines the current policy.

Another approach, which can be pursued simultaneously, is to diminish the conflicts among these competing objectives, in particular to reduce the degree of inflation associated with low levels of unemployment. This can be done in two ways. One way is to improve the mobility of labor and other resources to occupations, locations, and industries where bottlenecks would otherwise lead to wage and price increases. This is where many specific programs, such as the training and retraining of manpower and policies to improve the technical functioning of labor markets, come into their own.

A second task is to break down the barriers to competition which now restrict the entry of labor and enterprise into certain occupations and industries. These lead to wage- and price-increasing bottlenecks even when resources are not really short. Many barriers are created by public policy itself, in response to the vested interests concerned. Many reflect concentration of economic power in unions and in industry. These barriers represent another way in which the advantaged and the employed purchase their standards of living and their security at the expense of unprivileged minorities.

In the best of circumstances, structural reforms of these kinds will be slow and gradual. They will encounter determined economic and political resistance from special interests which are powerful in Congress and state legislatures. Moreover, Congressmen and legislators represent places rather than people and are likely to oppose, not facilitate, the increased geographical mobility which is required. It is no accident that our manpower programs do not include relocation allowances.

INCREASING THE EARNING CAPACITY OF NEGROES

Given the proper overall economic climate, in particular a steadily tight labor market, the Negro's economic condition can be expected to improve, indeed to improve dramatically. But not fast enough. Not as fast as his aspirations or as the aspirations he has taught the rest of us to have for him. What else can be done? This question is being answered in detail by experts elsewhere [see *Daedalus* (Fall 1965)]. I shall confine myself to a few comments and suggestions that occur to a general economist.

Even in a tight labor market, the Negro's relative status will suffer both from current discrimination and from his lower earning capacity, the result of inferior acquired skill. In a real sense both factors reflect discrimination, since the Negro's handicaps in earning capacity are the residue of decades of discrimination in education and employment. Nevertheless for both analysis and policy it is useful to distinguish the two.

Discrimination means that the Negro is denied access to certain markets where he might sell his labor and to certain markets where he might purchase goods and services. Elementary application of "supply and demand" makes it clear that these restrictions are bound to result in his selling his labor for less and buying his livelihood for more than if these barriers did not exist. If Negro women can be clerks only in certain stores, those storekeepers will not need to pay them so much as they pay whites. If Negroes can live only in certain houses, the prices and rents they have to pay will be high for the quality of accommodation provided.

Successful elimination of discrimination is not only important in itself but will also have substantial economic benefits. Since residential segregation is the key to so much else and so difficult to eliminate by legal fiat alone, the power of the purse should be unstintingly used. I see no reason that the expenditure of funds for this purpose should be confined to new construction. Why not establish private or semi-public revolving funds to purchase, for resale or rental on a desegregated basis, strategically located existing structures as they become available?

The effects of past discrimination will take much longer to eradicate. The sins against the fathers are visited on the children. They are deprived of the intellectual and social capital which in our society is supposed to be transmitted in the family and the home. We have only begun to realize how difficult it is to make up for this deprivation by formal schooling, even when we try. And we have only begun to try, after accepting all too long the notion that schools should acquiesce in, even reinforce, inequalities in home backgrounds rather than overcome them.

Upgrading the earning capacity of Negroes will be difficult, but the economic effects are easy to analyze. Economists have long held that the way to reduce disparities in earned incomes is to eliminate disparities in earning capacities. If college-trained people earn more money than those who left school after eight years, the remedy is to send a larger proportion of young people to college. If machine operators earn more than ditchdiggers, the remedy is to give more people the capacity and opportunity to be machine operators. These changes in relative supplies reduce the disparity both by competing down the pay in the favored line of work and by raising the pay in the less remunerative line. When there are only a few people left in the population whose capacities are confined to garbage-collecting, it will be a high-paid calling. The same is true of domestic service and all kinds of menial work.

This classical economic strategy will be hampered if discrimination, union barriers, and the like stand in the way. It will not help to increase the supply of Negro plumbers if the local unions and contractors will not let them join. But experience also shows that barriers give way more easily when the pressures of unsatisfied demand and supply pile up.

It should therefore be the task of educational and manpower policy to engineer over the next two decades a massive change in the relative supplies of people of different educational and professional attainments and degrees of skill and training. It must be a more rapid change than has occurred in the past two decades, because that has not been fast enough to alter income differentials. We should try particularly to increase supplies in those fields where salaries and wages are already high and rising. In this process we should be very skeptical of self-serving arguments and calculations—that an increase in supply in this or that profession would be bound to reduce quality, or that there are some mechanical relations of "need" to population or to Gross National Product that cannot be exceeded.

Such a policy would be appropriate to the "war on poverty" even if there were no racial problem. Indeed, our objective is to raise the earning capacities of low-income whites as well as of Negroes. But Negroes have the most to gain, and even those who because of age or irreversible environmental handicaps must inevitably be left behind will benefit by reduction in the number of whites and other Negroes who are competing with them.

ASSURING LIVING STANDARDS
IN THE ABSENCE OF
EARNING CAPACITY

The reduction of inequality in earning capacity is the fundamental solution, and in a sense anything else is stopgap. Some stopgaps are useless and even counterproductive. People who lack the capacity to earn a decent living need to be helped, but they will not be helped by minimum wage laws, trade union wage pressures, or other devices which seek to compel employers to pay them more than their work is worth. The more likely outcome of such regulations is that the intended beneficiaries are not employed at all.

A far better approach is to supplement earnings from the public fisc. But assistance can and should be given in a way that does not force the recipients out of the labor force or give them incentive to withdraw. Our present system of welfare payments does just that, causing needless waste and demoralization. This application of the means test is bad economics as well as bad sociology. It is almost as if our present programs of public assistance had been consciously contrived to perpetuate the conditions they are supposed to alleviate.

These programs apply a strict means test. The amount of assistance is an estimate of minimal needs, less the resources of the family from earnings. The purpose of the means test seems innocuous enough. It is to avoid wasting taxpayers' money on people who do not really need help. But another way to describe the means test is to note that it taxes earnings at a rate of 100 percent. A person on public assistance cannot add to his family's standard of living by working. Of course, the means test provides a certain incentive to work in order to get off public assistance altogether. But in many cases, especially where there is only one adult to provide for and take care of several children, the adult simply does not have enough time and earning opportunities to get by without financial help. He, or more likely she, is essentially forced to be both

idle and on a dole. The means test also involves limitations on property holdings which deprive anyone who is or expects to be on public assistance of incentive to save.

In a society which prizes incentives for work and thrift, these are surprising regulations. They deny the country useful productive services, but that economic loss is minor in the present context. They deprive individuals and families both of work experience which could teach them skills, habits, and self-discipline of future value and of the self-respect and satisfaction which comes from improving their own lot by their own efforts.

Public assistance encourages the disintegration of the family, the key to so many of the economic and social problems of the American Negro. The main assistance program, Aid for Dependent Children, is not available if there is an able-bodied employed male in the house. In most states it is not available if there is an able-bodied man in the house, even if he is not working. All too often it is necessary for the father to leave his children so that they can eat. It is bad enough to provide incentives for idleness but even worse to legislate incentives for desertion.[14]

The bureaucratic surveillance and guidance to which recipients of public assistance are subject undermine both their self-respect and their capacity to manage their own affairs. In the administration of assistance there is much concern to detect "cheating" against the means tests and to ensure approved prudent use of the public's money. Case loads are frequently too great and administrative regulations too confining to permit the talents of social workers to treat the roots rather than the symptoms of the social maladies of their clients. The time of the clients is considered a free good, and much of it must be spent in seeking or awaiting the attention of the officials on whom their livelihood depends.

The defects of present categorical assistance programs could be, in my opinion, greatly reduced by adopting a system of basic income allowances, integrated with and administered in conjunction with the federal income tax. In a sense the proposal is to make the income tax

---

[14] The official Advisory Council on Public Assistance recommended in 1960 that children be aided even if there are two parents or relatives *in loco parentis* in their household, but Congress has ignored this proposal. *Public Assistance: A Report of the Findings and Recommendations of the Advisory Council on Public Assistance,* Department of Health, Education and Welfare, January 1960. The Advisory Council also wrestled somewhat inconclusively with the problem of the means test and suggested that states be allowed to experiment with dropping or modifying it for five years. This suggestion too has been ignored.

symmetrical. At present the federal government takes a share of family income in excess of a certain amount (for example, a married couple with three children pays no tax unless their income exceeds $3,700). The proposal is that the Treasury pay any family who falls below a certain income a fraction of the shortfall. The idea has sometimes been called a negative income tax.

The payment would be a matter of right, like an income tax refund. Individuals expecting to be entitled to payments from the government during the year could receive them in periodic installments by making a declaration of expected income and expected tax withholdings. But there would be a final settlement between the individual and the government based on a "tax" return after the year was over, just as there is now for taxpayers on April 15.

A family with no other income at all would receive a basic allowance scaled to the number of persons in the family. For a concrete example, take the basic allowance to be $400 per year per person. It might be desirable and equitable, however, to reduce the additional basic allowance for children after, say, the fourth. Once sufficient effort is being made to disseminate birth control knowledge and technique, the scale of allowances by family size certainly should provide some disincentive to the creation of large families.

A family's allowance would be reduced by a certain fraction of every dollar of other income it received. For a concrete example, take this fraction to be one third. This means that the family has considerable incentive to earn income, because its total income including allowances will be increased by two thirds of whatever it earns. In contrast, the means test connected with present public assistance is a 100 percent "tax" on earnings. With a one-third "tax" a family will be on the receiving end of the allowance and income tax system until its regular income equals three times its basic allowance.[15]

Families above this "break-even" point would be taxpayers. But the less well-off among them would pay less taxes than they do now. The first dollars of income in excess of this break-even point would be taxed at the same rate as below this point, one third in the example. At some income level, the tax liability so computed would be the same as the tax under the present income

tax law. From that point up, the present law would take over; taxpayers with incomes above this point would not be affected by the plan.

The best way to summarize the proposal is to give a concrete graphical illustration. On the horizontal axis of Figure 1 is measured family income from wages and salaries, interest, dividends, rents, and so forth—"adjusted gross income" for the Internal Revenue Service. On the vertical axis is measured the corresponding "disposable income," that is, income after federal taxes and allowances. If the family neither paid taxes nor received allowance, disposable income would be equal to family income; in the diagram this equality would be shown by the 45° line from the origin. Disposable income above this 45° line means the family receives allowances; disposable income below this line means the family pays taxes. The broken line OAB describes the present income tax law for a married couple with three children, allowing the standard deductions. The line CD is the revision which the proposed allowance system would make for incomes below $7,963. For incomes above $7,963, the old tax schedule applies.

Beneficiaries under Federal Old Age Survivors and Disability Insurance would not be eligible for the new allowances. Congress should make sure that minimum benefits under OASDI are at least as high as the allowances. Some government payments, especially those for categorical public assistance, would eventually be replaced by basic allowances. Others, like unemployment insurance and veterans' pensions, are intended to be rights

15 Adjusting the size of a government benefit to the amount of other income is not without precedent. Recipients of Old Age Survivors and Disability Insurance benefits under the age of 72 lose one dollar of benefits and only one dollar for every two dollars of earned income above $1,200 but below $1,700 a year.

FIGURE 1   Illustration of Proposed Income Allowance Plan (married couple with three children)

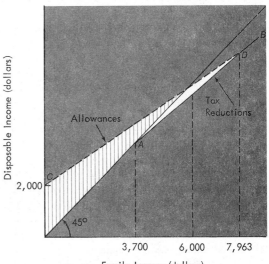

earned by past services regardless of current need. It would therefore be wrong to withhold allowances from the beneficiaries of these payments, but it would be reasonable to count them as income in determining the size of allowances, even though they are not subject to tax.

Although the numbers used above are illustrative, they are indicative of what is needed for an effective program. It would be expensive for the federal budget, involving an expenditure of perhaps $15 billion a year. Partially offsetting this budgetary cost are the savings in public assistance, on which governments now spend $5.6 billion a year, of which $3.2 billion are federal funds. In addition, savings are possible in a host of other income maintenance programs, notably in agriculture.

The program is expensive, but it need not be introduced all at once. The size of allowances can be gradually increased as room in the budget becomes available. This is likely to happen fairly rapidly. First of all, there is room right now. The budget, and the budget deficit, can and should be larger in order to create a tight labor market. Second, the normal growth of the economy increases federal revenues from existing tax rates by some $6 to $7 billion a year. This is a drag on the economy, threatening stagnation and rising unemployment unless it is matched by a similar rise in federal spending or avoided by cutting taxes. With defense spending stable or declining, there is room both for increases in civilian spending, as in the war on poverty, and for further tax cuts. Indeed, periodic tax reduction is official administration policy, and President Johnson agrees that the next turn belongs to low-income families. Gradually building an allowance system into the federal income tax would be the best way to lower the net yield of the tax—fairer and more far-reaching than further cuts in tax rates.

I referred to programs which make up for lack of earning capacity as stopgaps, but that is not entirely fair. Poverty itself saps earning capacity. The welfare way of life, on the edge of subsistence, does not provide motivation or useful work experience either to parents or to children. A better system, one which enables people to retain their self-respect and initiative, would in itself help to break the vicious circle.

The proposed allowance system is of course not the only thing which needs to be done. Without attempting to be exhaustive, I shall mention three other measures for the assistance of families without adequate earning capacity.

It hardly needs emphasizing that the large size of Negro families or non-families is one of the principal causes of Negro poverty. There are too many mouths to feed per breadwinner, and frequently the care of children keeps the mother, the only possible breadwinner, at home. A program of day care and pre-school education for children five and under could meet several objectives at once—enriching the experience of the children and freeing the mother for training or for work.

The quality of the medical care of Negroes is a disgrace in itself and contributes to their other economic handicaps.[16] Even so the financing of the care of "the medically indigent" is inadequate and chaotic. Sooner or later we will extend the principle of Medicare to citizens under 65. Why not sooner?

As mentioned above, much Negro poverty in the South reflects the inability of Negroes to make a livelihood in agriculture. As far as the traditional cash crop, cotton, is concerned, mechanization and the competition of larger scale units in the Southwest are undermining the plantation and share cropping system of the Southeast. The Negro subsistence farmer has too little land, equipment, and know-how to make a decent income. Current government agricultural programs, expensive as they are to the taxpayer, do very little to help the sharecropper or subsistence farmer. Our whole agricultural policy needs to be recast, to give income support to people rather than price support to crops and to take people off the land rather than to take land out of cultivation. The effects on the social system of the South may be revolutionary, but they can only be salutary. Obviously there will be a tremendous burden on educational and training facilities to fit people for urban and industrial life. And I must emphasize again that substantial migration from agriculture is only possible, without disaster in the cities, in a booming economy with a tight labor market.

CONCLUSION

By far the most powerful factor determining the economic status of Negroes is the overall state of the U.S. economy. A vigorously expanding economy with a steadily tight labor market will rapidly raise the position of the Negro, both absolutely and relatively. Favored by such a climate, the host of specific measures to eliminate discrimination, improve education and training,

[16] See the statistics summarized by Rashi Fein in *Daedalus* (Fall 1965).

provide housing, and strengthen the family can yield substantial additional results. In a less beneficent economic climate, where jobs are short rather than men, the wars against racial inequality and poverty will be uphill battles, and some highly touted weapons may turn out to be dangerously futile.

The forces of the marketplace, the incentives of private self-interest, the pressures of supply and demand—these can be powerful allies or stubborn opponents. Properly harnessed, they quietly and impersonally accomplish objectives which may elude detailed legislation and administration. To harness them to the cause of the American Negro is entirely possible. It requires simply that the federal government dedicate its fiscal and monetary policies more wholeheartedly and singlemindedly to achieving and maintaining genuinely full employment. The obstacles are not technical or economic. One obstacle is a general lack of understanding that unemployment and related evils are remediable by national fiscal and monetary measures. The other is the high priority now given to competing financial objectives.

In this area, as in others, the administration has disarmed its conservative opposition by meeting it halfway, and no influential political voices challenge the tacit compromise from the "Left." Negro rights movements have so far taken no interest in national fiscal and monetary policy. No doubt gold, the federal budget, and the actions of the Federal Reserve System seem remote from the day-to-day firing line of the movements. Direct local actions to redress specific grievances and to battle visible enemies are absorbing and dramatic. They have concrete observable results. But the use of national political influence on behalf of the goals of the Employment Act of 1946 is equally important. It would fill a political vacuum, and its potential long-run pay-off is very high.

The goal of racial equality suggests that the federal government should provide more stimulus to the economy. Fortunately, it also suggests constructive ways to give the stimulus. We can kill two birds with one stone. The economy needs additional spending in general; the wars on poverty and racial inequality need additional spending of particular kinds. The needed spending falls into two categories: government programs to diminish economic inequalities by building up the earning capacities of the poor and their children, and humane public assistance to citizens who temporarily or permanently lack the capacity to earn a decent living for themselves and their families. In both categories the nation, its conscience aroused by the plight of the Negro, has the chance to make reforms which will benefit the whole society.

46. Widening Horizons: Prospects for Black Employment*

Andrew F. Brimmer†

I spend a fair amount of time on college campuses, and whenever I can I try to get an appreciation for the expectations of black students regarding their careers. I am frequently told by many of them that they "want to help the black community" rather than engage in a "middle class race for economic security."

I undertook an analysis of recent changes in the pattern of black employment. This was done against the backdrop of the efforts to reduce racial discrimination in employment led by the Equal Employment Opportunity Commission created by Title VII of the Civil Rights Act of 1964. I have also reviewed the job progress made by blacks employed by the federal, state, and local governments. Finally, an effort was made to assess job opportunities for blacks out to 1985. The main conclusions of this analysis can be summarized as follows.

To a considerable extent, employment advances made by blacks during the 1960s were partly the result of the long period of economic expansion culminating in 1969. However, these gains were also partly a reflection of the rising educational level and the acquisition of skills within the black community.

Moreover, legislation adopted in 1964 aimed at fostering equal opportunity in employment

also played a role. The evidence reported by companies subject to the law indicates that they are opening jobs to blacks at a rate much faster than is true for all employers in the country as a whole. However, it appears that the expansion is much slower in the upper reaches of the occupational job categories than at the lower end. Thus, the task of occupational upgrading remains considerable.

The extent of occupational integration varies greatly among different regions of the country. But in the last seven years, the greatest gains in white-collar employment have been made in the South—although the absolute shortfall in that region remains the largest.

Blacks have made relatively more job progress in public service than they have in the private sector. But, with employment opportunities likely to expand more slowly in the federal government in the years ahead, blacks would do well to look more to the private sector for future careers.

Among the promising opportunities available to blacks, careers in protection are especially worthy of examination. Given the persistence of high crime rates in the black community (and blacks are the principal victims), there will be a strong demand for sympathetic police officials with better-than-average educations.

LONG-TERM TRENDS IN BLACK EMPLOYMENT

During the decade of the 1960s, blacks made substantial economic progress. This was evident in terms of the number and range of jobs held by them. In general, blacks expanded their share of white-collar jobs while their share of lower-paying service jobs shrank somewhat. The proportion of blue-collar occupations held by blacks rose

* From the *Labor Law Journal,* Vol. 25, No. 6, June 1974, pp. 323–35. Dr. Brimmer wishes to thank Mr. John Austin and Mrs. Ruth Robinson of the Board's staff for assistance in the preparation of the article; also Chairman John H. Powell, Jr., of the Equal Employment Opportunity Commission for authorizing the special tabulations of reports to the Commission on which much of the analysis is based. The views expressed here are Dr. Brimmer's own and should not be attributed to anyone else.

† Andrew F. Brimmer was a Member of the Board of Governors of the Federal Reserve System when this article was written; he is presently a Professor at the Harvard Graduate School of Business.

moderately. Blacks left agriculture (both as farmers and as farm laborers) at a much faster rate than American workers at large.

Within these broad trends, a number of important specific developments were occurring. For example, among white-collar workers, the largest relative gains were made by those engaged in professional and technical occupations. In 1960, 4.7 percent of all black workers (versus 11.4 percent for all workers) were in this category. By 1970, the fraction for blacks had climbed to 9.1 percent and that for all workers to 14.2 percent. Over the decade, blacks' share of these jobs at the top of the occupational scale expanded from 4.4 percent to 6.9 percent. However, the greatest growth occurred in technical fields (especially in fields requiring only moderate skills) rather than in those professions demanding long years of college education or advanced training.

Another sub-trend worthy of note is the relatively modest advances made by blacks as managers, officials, and proprietors. This category includes the self-employed as well as public and private salaried officials and administrators. In 1960, blacks held 2.5 percent of the managerial jobs, and their share had climbed to only 3.6 percent in 1970. Within the economy at large, the number of self-employed businessmen continued to decline over the decade. When the figures are adjusted for this trend, it is evident that the number of salaried managers expanded appreciably. Blacks shared in this expansion—but to a much smaller degree than was true in the case of professional and technical workers.

The steady progress made by blacks during the 1960s was seriously interrupted by the recession of 1970. In fact, between blacks as a group and whites as a group, blacks suffered all of the recession-induced decline in jobs—while whites made further job gains. From the fourth quarter of 1969 through the fourth quarter of 1970, total employment decreased by 66 thousand. This was the net result of a drop of 174 thousand in the number of jobs held by blacks which was partly offset by an increase of 108 thousand jobs held by whites. During the sluggish recovery of 1971, job gains by blacks lagged considerably, and unemployment in the black community continued to rise.

Only last year did the rate of job improvement among blacks resume the pace recorded during the 1960s. For the most part, the basic trends noted earlier are still evident. The proportion of white-collar jobs held by blacks had risen further. The relative advances by professional and tech-

nical workers were again striking. But the gains by those in the managerial group were also noticeable.

To a considerable extent, employment advances made by blacks during the 1960s were partly the result of the long period of economic expansion culminating in 1969. However, these gains were also partly a reflection of the rising educational level and the acquisition of skills within the black community. Moreover, legislation adopted in 1964 aimed at fostering equal opportunity in employment also played a role.

THE CAMPAIGN FOR EQUAL EMPLOYMENT OPPORTUNITY

Title VII of the Civil Rights Act of 1964 created the Equal Employment Opportunity Commission (EEOC), and the Commission began operations on July 2, 1965. However, it was preceded by a generation of essentially voluntary action at both the federal and state and local levels. It was against this background that EEOC came into being. Actually, EEOC was not part of the legislation proposed by President John F. Kennedy in mid-1963 which became the Civil Rights Act of 1964. He thought that the inclusion of such a controversial provision would further decrease the already unpromising prospect of the bill's passage. Instead, he thought it best to expand further—through executive action—the existing efforts to check job discrimination. As the bill moved through the legislative process, the fair employment provision was added at congressional initiative. Lyndon Johnson—who had by then succeeded to the presidency—threw his strong support behind the entire measure.

Nevertheless, EEOC started life with a number of handicaps. In the first place, its start-up was delayed for a full year after the bill was signed. Its coverage was severely limited—being restricted for the most part to private companies in interstate commerce with 25 or more employees. Its actions had to depend on the filing of complaints by individual workers. This was an extension of the voluntary approach followed at the federal level during World War II—and despite evidence accumulated in the intervening years under state fair employment programs which demonstrated that the complaint mechanism had not been particularly successful. For the first seven years of its life, the Commission had no enforcement powers of its own. The Attorney General could bring suit when a "pattern or practice" of discrimination was discovered by EEOC. But, for the most part, the

Commission was left to rely on education and persuasion—along with the provision of technical assistance—in its efforts to end discrimination in employment.

After nearly eight years of effort, the EEOC's authority was strengthened by the 1972 amendments to the Act. The most important of these gave the Commission enforcement powers of its own. Once the new authority was implemented in March, 1973, EEOC could initiate civil actions in federal courts to enforce the provisions barring job discrimination and to remedy instances of their violation. Coverage of the statute was extended to employees of state and local governments and their instrumentalities, employees of educational institutions, and firms or labor organizations with 15 or more workers or members. Additional protection was also provided federal government employees.

Armed with this new authority and an enlarged budget, EEOC in the last two years has accelerated its drive against employment discrimination—concentrating on sex and language bias as well as on racial barriers. It achieved a landmark settlement of its suit against AT&T in January 1973, which will result in cash payments (mainly to blacks and white women) in excess of $50 million in compensation for past discrimination and as bonuses for transferring to better-paying jobs. The Commission has also worked out agreements in the trucking and steel industries which will yield greatly improved job opportunities for blacks in the years ahead.

MIXED PATTERN OF JOB EXPANSION

Given the efforts of EEOC to broaden job opportunities for blacks and other minorities (and more recently for women), one can naturally ask just what has been the impact of the campaign. Unfortunately, no direct answer can be given. But the indirect evidence does suggest that the Commission's activities are having generally favorable results. Employers, trade unions, and others covered by the statute are required to report the racial and sexual composition of their work forces to the Commission at least once each year. So far EEOC has required annual reports from those with 100 or more employees. On the basis of these reports, one can get a fairly good idea of the changing composition of jobs held by blacks compared to others.

Several conclusions stand out. Black employment in EEOC-reporting firms rose much faster than employment in the economy as a whole. For instance, blacks accounted for 21 percent of the growth in jobs in EEOC-reporting firms versus 15 percent in the total. However, within the white-collar category, only clerical workers and sales workers recorded relatively larger gains on EEOC-reported payrolls (34 percent versus 22 percent and 10 percent versus 8 percent, respectively). In the case of professional and technical workers, EEOC figures show blacks getting 10 percent of the increase in jobs versus 14 percent for black professionals and technicians in the economy at large. The lag was especially noticeable among managers and officials. In the country as a whole, blacks accounted for 14 percent of the expansion; their share in EEOC reporters was only 7 percent. In contrast, blacks got a much larger share of the new craft and service jobs in EEOC-reporting firms—e.g., 26 percent of craft jobs versus 12 percent for all firms and 31 percent of service jobs versus 10 percent for all employers combined. The relative gains were about the same in the case of operatives (56 percent). In the case of laborers, blacks in EEOC firms accounted for a smaller proportion of the rise in employment—18 percent versus 45 percent.

On the basis of these figures, I conclude that the companies reporting under the EEOC requirements are opening jobs to blacks at a rate much faster than is true for all employers in the country as a whole. At the same time, however, it appears that the expansion is much slower in the upper reaches of the occupational scale than it is among job categories at the lower end. Thus, the task of occupational upgrading for blacks remains considerable.

The EEOC data also enable one to get a feeling for the extent to which blacks have *not* made headway in gaining employment in specific types of firms. In response to my request, the Commission prepared special tabulations showing the number of firms which have black employees and those which do not. The number of total employees and the number of blacks on the payroll of each group of firms are also shown. The tabulations for 1973 covered 50 industry groups and 145,877 firms—which had 31,838,867 employees. Of the latter, 3,448,535 (or 10.8 percent) were black. Of the total number of firms, 106,624 (or 73.1 percent) had 28,502,748 employees. In these companies, 3,448,535 blacks were employed, representing 12.1 percent of the total. The remaining 39,253 firms (26.9 percent of the total) had 3,336,119 employees—10.5 percent of the total. None of these was black. In 1966, the data are based on the experience of 117,600 establishments and total employment of 25,571,000—

of whom 2,097,000 (or 8.2 percent) were black.

Among the 22 industry groups identified in the table, securities' and commodities' brokers in 1973 had the largest proportion of firms (53 percent) with no black employees. Jobs in these firms represented 18 percent of total industry employment. Eating and drinking places with no black workers accounted for 32 percent of the firms—but for 23 percent of the jobs—in that industry. The insurance industry also had a sizable proportion of firms with no black workers on their payroll—e.g., 34 percent of insurance carriers and 38 percent of agents and brokers. On the other hand, the percentage of firms without black employees in 1973 was substantially smaller in all but a few industry groups than was the case in 1966. In the latter year, almost half (47 percent) of the EEOC reporters had no black workers. Among credit agencies, insurance firms, and securities' and commodities' brokers, the proportion in that year was in the neighborhood of three-quarters of the reporters.

So, from these data, a general conclusion emerges: While blacks are making considerable headway in finding new job opportunities, there remain many doors on which they must still knock. A substantial number of these are to be found in the banking and finance industry.

GEOGRAPHICAL PATTERN OF BLACK EMPLOYMENT

In tracing trends in black employment, I also wanted to know the extent to which significant differences are observable in various geographical areas of the country. Perhaps the most striking change (between 1966 and 1973) is the sharp expansion in white-collar jobs held by black workers in the South. These relative gains were largest in the technical, sales, and clerical categories. However, noticeable improvement also occurred among professional workers and managerial personnel. In the Northeast and Midwest, blacks also made significant gains in white-collar employment, but the strides were proportionately less dramatic than those observed in the South.

An even more graphic picture of geographic differences in blacks' employment status emerges when the proportion of jobs held by blacks in each occupational category is viewed on the basis of data relating to metropolitan areas. The situation is put in even sharper focus when blacks' representation in a given occupation in a given standard metropolitan statistical area (SMSA) is related to blacks' proportion of total employment in the area. For this purpose, an "Index of Occupational Integration" was calculated. The index was derived as follows: (1) blacks' share (percentage) of total employment and their share of employment in each occupational group in each metropolitan area was calculated; (2) next, blacks' share (percentage) in each occupation group was divided by their share (percentage) of total employment. The result is the "Index of Occupational Integration." An index number of 100 indicates equality; an index number less than 100 indicates an occupational deficit, and an index number greater than 100 indicates a surplus or overrepresentation of blacks in a particular occupation. Indexes were calculated for the United States as a whole and for each of the 13 SMSAs (see Table 1).

Several conclusions stand out in these data. In the country at large, blacks have a white-collar job deficit of 48 percent. But the biggest deficit (75 percent) is evident in the managerial category—followed by professionals (70 percent), sales workers (53 percent), and technical workers (31 percent). The closest blacks come toward occupational equality is in the clerical category (where the deficit is 21 percent). In contrast, blacks are heavily overrepresented in blue-collar jobs—except in the case of craft workers (where there is a deficit of 40 percent). In the case of operatives, the index was 143, and it was 192 for laborers. Among service workers, it was 229.

The degree of occupational integration enjoyed by blacks in individual SMSAs in broad job categories in 1973 was as shown in Table 2.

Several comments can be made with respect to this array. In general, the cities in the South and Southwest are the farthest behind in the integration of blacks in white-collar jobs. On the other hand, only a handful of cities in the North and West are doing appreciably better than the national average. The deficit in black employment in jobs is enormous all over the country. Likewise, every area recorded a surplus of blacks in blue-collar occupations—except in the case of craft workers, where all areas reported deficits. Here also, the lesson is clear: Blacks all over the country still have a long way to go before they achieve occupational equality in the better-paying jobs. Much of the current deficit undoubtedly reflects the legacy of racial discrimination and exclusion suffered by blacks in the past. The effects are observable not only in the large deficit in white-collar jobs but also in the skilled crafts—where trade union practices have frequently kept blacks out of those fields. On the other hand, lack of skills has prevented blacks

TABLE 1   Index of Occupational Integration in Major Metropolitan Areas, 1973*

Metropolitan Area	White-Collar Workers						Blue-Collar Workers				Service Workers
	Total	Professional	Technical	Managers and Officials	Sales	Clerical	Total	Craftsmen	Operatives	Laborers	
United States........	52	30	69	25	47	79	129	60	143	192	229
New York City........	77	40	106	31	50	117	118	70	130	173	224
Baltimore........	45	24	68	22	40	65	136	58	152	230	241
Philadelphia........	53	26	85	25	43	80	130	68	139	222	260
Washington, D.C........	61	30	76	33	59	92	148	73	178	238	213
Detroit........	47	20	56	24	41	77	139	43	180	147	202
Chicago........	52	23	60	23	40	83	144	70	160	196	199
St. Louis........	56	77	92	22	44	65	114	49	130	187	268
Atlanta........	45	26	51	20	41	67	148	53	153	293	270
New Orleans........	37	11	44	18	48	50	140	70	148	258	241
Dallas........	37	11	55	16	36	57	158	70	179	237	335
Houston........	45	24	73	17	51	63	141	62	178	256	267
Los Angeles........	65	33	87	31	58	99	128	79	158	162	233
San Francisco........	69	31	100	29	60	102	129	65	145	215	249

* The index is calculated as follows: (1) Blacks' share (percentage) of total employment and of employment in each occupation group in each metropolitan area is calculated. (2) Blacks' share (percentage) in each occupation group is divided by their share (percentage) of total employment. An index number of 100 indicates equality. An index number of less than 100 indicates an occupational deficit, and an index number greater than 100 indicates an over-representation in a particular occupation.

Source: Calculated from Table 6.

TABLE 2

Total White-Collar	Deficit (percent)	Professional	Deficit (percent)
1. Dallas	63	1. Dallas	89
2. New Orleans	63	2. New Orleans	80
3. Atlanta	55	3. Detroit	80
4. Baltimore	55	4. Chicago	77
5. Houston	55	5. Houston	76
6. Detroit	53	6. Baltimore	76
7. Chicago	48	7. Atlanta	76
8. Philadelphia	47	8. Philadelphia	74
9. St. Louis	44	9. Wash., D.C.	70
10. Wash., D.C.	39	10. S.F.–Oakland	69
11. Los Angeles	35	11. Los Angeles	67
12. S.F.–Oakland	31	12. New York	60
13. New York	23	13. St. Louis	23

Total Blue-Collar	Surplus (percent)	Craft Workers	Deficit (percent)
1. Dallas	58	1. Detroit	57
2. Wash., D.C.	48	2. St. Louis	51
3. Atlanta	48	3. Atlanta	47
4. Chicago	44	4. Baltimore	42
5. Houston	41	5. Houston	38
6. New Orleans	40	6. S.F.–Oakland	35
7. Detroit	39	7. Philadelphia	32
8. Baltimore	36	8. Chicago	30
9. Philadelphia	30	9. New York	30
10. S.F.–Oakland	29	10. New Orleans	30
11. Los Angeles	28	11. Dallas	30
12. New York	18	12. Wash., D.C.	27
13. St. Louis	14	13. Los Angeles	21

from taking advantage of many opportunities which have emerged—especially in recent years. The task of remedying this deficit in skills should be high up on the agenda of the black community in the years ahead.

EMPLOYMENT OPPORTUNITIES IN THE PUBLIC SECTOR

While I have dwelt on the employment status of blacks in private industry, we must not overlook the still unsatisfactory situation in public service. Historically, a larger proportion of employed blacks (especially of those in professional positions) has been on the public payroll than has been true for the population as a whole. For example, while blacks represented about 10 percent of total employment in nonfarm occupations in private industry in 1973, they accounted for nearly 16 percent of all civilian employees in the federal government. Moreover, while federal employment absorbed 3 percent of the total civilian labor force, about 4.8 percent of the blacks in civilian jobs were on the federal payroll.

Behind these overall statistics is an even heavier reliance by blacks on the public sector for a disproportionate share of the better jobs they hold. The extent of this reliance was fully documented in the 1960 and 1970 Census of Population. In 1960, employment in public administration at the federal, state, and local level accounted for about 4.9 percent of total employment. The percentage of blacks so employed was roughly the same, 5 percent. However, while just 6 percent of all professional and technical workers were employed by public agencies, 7.3 percent of black workers in the same occupations were employed by such agencies. By 1970, public administration represented 5.5 percent of total employment, but the proportion for blacks had risen to 6.6 percent.

The much greater reliance of blacks on the public sector for better-paying white-collar jobs is particularly noticeable. For instance, in 1960 about 1 in 8 of all salaried managers (both black and the total) worked for public institutions; by 1970, the ratio had declined to under 10 percent for the total—but it had risen to 16 percent for blacks. Nearly one-fifth of the black engineers worked for government bodies in 1960 and 1970 compared with only 8 percent for all engineers. For accountants, the ratios were roughly one-third for blacks and only 13 percent for all accountants in both years. Some 18 percent of black lawyers were employed by public agencies in 1960, compared with only 12 percent of all lawyers. By 1970, the proportion of all lawyers employed in public administration had risen to 18 percent, but for blacks the figure was 26 percent.

Clerical workers provide the most striking example of all. In 1960, about two-fifths of all black women employed as secretaries, stenographers, and other classes of clerical workers were on the public payroll. Only 14 percent of the white women employed as clerical workers were on the public payroll. Moreover, while black women represented less than 4 percent of all women with such jobs, they accounted for 10 percent of those employed in the public sector. By 1970, these proportions had changed very little. Black women still constituted only 3.6 percent of all clerical workers—but 10 percent of those in public administration. And 30 percent of all black female clerical workers were on the public payroll.

Although the details obviously have changed since 1970, the broad conclusions probably still hold. While private industry has greatly accelerated its hiring of blacks in recent years, so has the public sector. For example, in 1963, blacks constituted 13 percent of total employment in the federal government; by 1973, the ratio had risen to almost 16 percent of the work force. In the 10-year period, the number of blacks employed by the federal government rose from 302 thousand to 395 thousand, a gain of 93 thousand —representing 41 percent of the increase in total federal civilian employment.

However, while great strides have been made in the employment of minority groups in the federal government, the vast majority of blacks is still concentrated in the low- and middle-grade jobs. Again, of the 395 thousand blacks employed by the federal government in 1973, two-fifths (162 thousand) were in the regular civil service grades, and three-fifths were in the postal field service or held blue-collar (wage board) jobs. Moreover, in regular civil service categories, blacks are heavily concentrated in the low- to middle-salary grades.

The employment status of blacks in state and local governments appears to be generally less favorable than it is in the federal government. The extent to which this is the case cannot be determined because of a lack of comprehensive information. However, a survey conducted in 1967 by the U.S. Civil Rights Commission casts considerable light on the situation.

The Commission collected information on government employment in seven major metropolitan areas—representing 628 governmental units. The areas were San Francisco-Oakland, Baton Rouge, Detroit, Philadelphia, Memphis, Houston, and Atlanta. In all, nearly 250,000 jobs were involved. About one-fourth of these jobs were held by blacks.

Of the black workers in state and local governments, more than half were on the payrolls of central city governments. In four of these areas (San Francisco, Philadelphia, Detroit, and Memphis), the percentage of total city jobs held by blacks was equal to—or exceeded—their proportion of the population. In both Baton Rouge and Oakland, the city employment rate for blacks was roughly one-half of their representation in the population.

The data from the survey also show that blacks are heavily concentrated in the low-skill, low-pay occupations in all of the central cities listed. In fact, in each of the cities (except San Francisco and Oakland), blacks held 70 percent or more of all laborer jobs. In three of the cities (Philadelphia, Detroit, and Memphis), they made up about one-third of all service workers. In only two cities—Philadelphia and Detroit—did the number of blacks in white-collar positions come near to reflecting their proportion of the population.

On the basis of these results of the survey, one must share the Commission's conclusion: State and local governments have fallen far short of meeting their obligation to assure equal employment opportunity to all of their citizens. Consequently, the quest for job equality must still be pressed at city halls and in state capitals —as well as in the federal government.

On the other hand, I am personally convinced that blacks would do well to look more to the private sector—and less to public payrolls—for expanded job opportunities in the years ahead. This is especially true of the federal government —where the expansion of employment is likely to be quite sluggish.

OUTLOOK FOR BLACK EMPLOYMENT: SELECTED OCCUPATIONS

Over the next decade, job prospects for blacks will be especially good—if they have marketable skills and can take advantage of the unfolding opportunities. According to projections published by the Bureau of Labor Statistics, the civilian labor force is expected to expand as follows (Table 3).

Thus, by 1985, more than 13 million black workers will be holding jobs or seeking work.

TABLE 3

Category	Actual		Projected	
	1973	1975	1980	1985
Total civilian labor force (millions).....	88.7	90.1	98.0	104.4
Black labor force (millions).....	10.2	10.5	11.9	13.2
Percent of total..	11.5	11.6	12.1	12.6

Between 1973 and 1985, the black labor force will expand substantially faster than the civilian labor force as a whole. As a consequence, their share of the total will rise from 11.5 percent to 12.6 percent. Moreover, the demand for skills over the next decade will strengthen considerably, and workers with few skills—whites as well as blacks—will find the competition for jobs especially keen.

Aside from trying to get an appreciation for the general outlook for black employment in the years ahead, I have attempted to assess the prospects in those fields which may be of particular interest to the black community. For this purpose, a combination of data was used. Blacks' share of employment in selected occupations was obtained from the 1970 Census of Population. An assessment of employment prospects in particular occupations was derived from the Bureau of Labor Statistics' *Occupational Outlook Handbook*, 1974–75 edition. The specific occupations were grouped under ten headings—beginning with those which appear central to the solution of some of the most pressing problems facing the black community (health, education, social services, urban improvement, and protection) and fanning out into fields more related to the economy as a whole.

In drawing up this array, however, I must stress the fact that I am not suggesting that blacks who pursue occupations in categories . . . [placed in parentheses above] . . . should work only—or even primarily—in the black community. Rather, I am suggesting that young blacks who place special emphasis on service to the black community may well find it rewarding to consider those lines of career development. Although the annual incomes one might expect in those fields may not be as high as in some other areas of specialization, many young people may still find them attractive.

. . . Job opportunities in the health field are likely to be very good out to 1985. With the spread of prepaid medical care, the demand for health personnel is likely to be quite strong. So while the supply of workers with such skills will also grow appreciably, the number of job openings may expand even faster. In contrast, the demand for school teachers is expected to be quite weak. The supply of college graduates going into education is expected to slacken somewhat, but a sizable surplus of teachers is expected to prevail for some time. The field of social services (including both recreation and social workers) is expected to offer good job prospects. This is a field into which blacks have gone in considerable numbers in the past, and undoubtedly many will continue to find it attractive.

I would especially urge young blacks to consider opportunities in the area of urban improvement and protection. The need to rebuild or rehabilitate urban facilities will give rise to strong demands for architects, urban planners, and other professionals with similar skills. But even more strongly, I would urge young blacks to examine the prospects for careers involved with protection. The persistent high crime rates in the black community (in which blacks are the principal victims) clearly call for an increased number of blacks interested in fighting crime and improving the security of the community. So far, the representation of blacks in most city police departments is proportionately quite small. In most state police forces, the situation is much worse.

Among the other occupations . . . [mentioned] . . . I would call attention particularly to those associated with electronic computers and banking and finance. Undoubtedly, the computer will continue to transform the techniques for controlling the production and distribution of goods in the economy. Moreover, further inroads will be made in the handling of financial and other service transactions—including the provision of medical care. Blacks have already established a toehold in computer-related occupations, and considerable scope will exist for broadening these. The demand for workers in the banking and financial field will also remain strong. Here, too, blacks can expect to find better-than-average career opportunities. Many of these will be at the officer—rather than clerical—level; they will also involve lending as well as community relations functions.

In the final analysis, however, the extent to which blacks can take advantage of the widening opportunities on the horizon will depend as much on them as on the continuing efforts by government and business to eradicate the legacy of racial discrimination and deprivation which still restricts blacks' chances for economic development.

part six

Multinational Industrial Relations
International Labor Developments

While some work in comparative labor systems has been done by American academicians (for example, Windmuller, Kassalow, Sturmthal, Dunlop, Meyers), the field of multinational industrial relations has been relatively unexplored. Perhaps this can be explained by the fact that until the late 1960s there was little interest on the part of international trade union bodies (such as the International Metalworkers' Federation, International Chemical and General Workers' Federation, and the International Union of Food and Allied Workers) in multinational collective bargaining. The scene has changed rapidly in the past decade, and it now behooves us to become aware of the pressures toward developments such as multinational bargaining and the expansion of concepts involving worker participation, such as codetermination.

In the first article, Everett Kassalow presents an analysis of the West European industrial relations systems and the changes that have been occurring in recent years. This presentation is followed by two articles on codetermination. Hartmann discusses the major features of codetermination as they were set forth in the German Co-determination Law of 1951 and as experienced in the iron, coal, and steel industries. He concludes that the concept has functioned

very well and that it probably will be utilized on a broader scale in the future. A second article by McIsaac and Henzler, however, finds that the American multinational firms will be faced with considerable problems if they must operate under an expanded codetermination formula. If the German model becomes the pattern for worker participation in other European countries, Americans operating abroad (as well as others) will be challenged to do some creative planning in the industrial relations sphere.

The last article in this section presents an analysis of efforts made to effectuate multinational bargaining in the metals and electrical industries. This article is one of six prepared by Rowan and Northrup in a research project on multinational industrial relations. The authors conclude that it appears to be very difficult to develop multinational bargaining in the metals industry, but in recent years the International Metalworkers' Federation (a Geneva-based International Trade Secretariat) has shown a strong interest in accomplishing such an objective. Other trade secretariats covering industries such as rubber, chemicals, oil, glass, and food have shown similar interests as those expressed by the IMF, and the future is uncertain in regard to transnational or multinational bargaining.

47. Conflict and Cooperation in Europe's Industrial Relations*

Everett M. Kassalow†

The 1969–71 outbreak of serious strikes in several continental West European countries can be seen, in retrospect, as a clear signal of tension and change in the industrial relations systems of that part of the world.[1] By the mid-1950s and early 1960s, European industrial systems, with the exception of France and Italy (chronic exceptions, anyway!), seemed to have reached a very stable equilibrium. National union-management agreements (generally by industry, sometimes by industry within broad regions) had become firmly established. These were complemented by legislation regulating weekly hours of work, overtime rates, and the number of paid holidays and annual vacations for the entire work force. Extensive legislated social insurance programs covered the health and retirement fields so fully as to make American-style collective negotiation of these fringe benefits largely unnecessary.[2]

In the past six or seven years, however, major eruptions and changes have occurred in these industrial relations systems. The 1969–71 strikes were an indicator of growing discontent with existing union-management machinery at the enterprise and shop-floor levels. Even as discontent seemed to grow at these levels, however, major economic gains continued to be registered nationally, and some of these broke paths into new social and economic areas where union influence was previously absent (and sometimes hardly imaginable). This note briefly explores some of these changes in a few West European countries.

WEST EUROPEAN INDUSTRIAL RELATIONS SYSTEMS

To understand what has been happening, it is useful to briefly review the economic and political forces which have conditioned West European industrial relations systems. West European countries have generally experienced over two decades of unprecedented sustained economic growth, accompanied by very low unemployment rates, especially if measured against U.S. standards).[3] This period of economic growth has also been accompanied nearly everywhere in Western Europe by substantial trade union membership advances. With France and Italy somewhat excepted, the rates of unionization in Western Europe are now significantly beyond those in the United States (see Table 1).

These union movements have used their grow-

* From *Industrial Relations*, Vol. 13, No. 2, May 1974, pp. 156–63.

† Professor of Economics, University of Wisconsin, Madison.

[1] I have excluded Great Britain from consideration. Special economic circumstances—notably a low rate of economic growth and chronic balance-of-payments difficulties, as well as some different union-management traditions and practices—justify this exclusion. Space has also precluded my treating the growing pressures for workers' participation on company boards of directors as well as the so-called autonomous work group experiments aimed at meeting worker dissatisfaction in routine jobs by widening the areas of workers' control at the job level.

[2] While a substantial number of European countries have supplementary pension plans, in most countries (except France) these plans are not as entwined in union-management relations as they are in the United States.

[3] Italy is something of an exception so far as unemployment levels are concerned, but in some respects Italy has barely emerged from a state of lesser economic development compared to almost all other West European countries. This paper was completed before the onset of the energy crisis, with its possible impact on the future of employment and unemployment in Western Europe.

TABLE 1 Total Union Membership as a Percentage of All Nonagricultural Wage and Salary Employment in the United States and Western Europe

	Approximate Trade Union Membership (millions)	Approximate Percentage of Unionization (percent)
France	2.4	23
United States	21.2	30
Italy	4.0	33
Germany	8.3	38
Netherlands	1.6	41
Ireland	.7	43
Great Britain	11.0	48
Denmark	1.1	58
Austria	1.6	65
Norway	.7	65
Belgium	2.2	71
Sweden	2.6	80

Note: Data are for 1971, but in a few instances for 1970 and 1972. In the U.S. case, we have included employee associations which the U.S. Bureau of Labor Statistics includes in its directory of unions. Sources vary from the unions themselves to different government agencies. The definition of union membership is somewhat different from country to country, and this can affect membership figures (especially in France and Italy).

ing strength to negotiate important gains at the national level. In these efforts, they have often been assisted by large, well established labor parties in government (or in the wings as plausible alternatives to incumbent governments).

The more prosperous (compared to pre-World War II and the immediate postwar years) and more unionized work force has also been a better educated one. The number of compulsory school years has been extended in virtually all countries, higher education has been opened to the wider population, and the generally greater affluence of most families has made it possible for working-class children to remain in school for longer periods of time than was the case in the prewar period. Western Europe's better educated labor force is also one whose aspirations may be rising. It is a labor force with little memory of any great depression and consequently likely to be more assertive and less wedded to or dependent upon particular employers or plants.

The steady state of full employment accounts for the vast influx of workers from the Mediterranean area. Almost everywhere in Western Europe, thousands of Turkish, Yugoslav, Spanish, Algerian, and Italian workers are to be found, especially in low-level labor jobs in construction, services, and factories. Quiescent for a long period of time, this immigrant labor bloc has become a less predictable, sometimes disruptive element in much of European industrial relations.

Finally, while more difficult to assess, in several countries the New Left socialist and student groups (produced to some degree by the growing affluence of Western Europe as well as the demands for greater "quality of life") have surfaced from time to time as one of the new forces at work in European labor circles.

Stronger union movements, more deeply institutionalized in their countries' economic and political structures, along with a more confident, less deferential work force have combined to produce significant changes at both the local and national levels of the various industrial relations systems.

PLANT AND JOB LEVEL CHANGE

The 1969–71 strike wave offers some clues regarding changes at the shop level.[4] In almost every instance, these strikes did *not* originate within the regular national union machinery; that is, they were usually wildcat or unofficial strikes. A common cause was dissatisfaction with some aspects of the established systems for negotiating collective agreements and settling local problems. At the same time, despite the new militance they suggested, the strikes appeared to be largely free of the older socialist-revolutionary ideology (with the possible exception of those in Italy).[5]

Sweden

In the case of the Kiruna coal mines in Sweden, all parties mentioned neglect of local working conditions by the central miners union and management negotiators who held their meetings at remote locations. Significant, also, in the Kiruna case was a protest by the miners against the so-called solidaristic wage policy long practiced by the Swedish Federation of Trade Unions (LO).[6] Miners had seen the differentials

---

[4] The single best resource on these strikes is the colloquium edited by Guy Spitaels, which contains a number of country reports (some in French). See *Crisis in the Industrial Relations in Europe: Diversity and Unity, Possible Responses* (Bruges: DeTempel, Tempelhof, 1972).

[5] The French strikes of May 1968 were, to a still not quite clear extent, also more ideological in character than those elsewhere. I have already noted that Italy and France frequently deviate from general West European patterns.

[6] Without going into elaborate discussion, the LO's wage solidarity policy has aimed at reducing unjustifiable differentials (e.g., those not based on skill differences) between industries, sexes, etc. For a recent discussion of the solidarity wage policy, see Rudolf Meidner and Berndt Uhman, *Fifteen Years of Wage Policy* (Stockholm:

between their own wages and those of workers in other industries narrowed by almost 20 percent between 1958 and 1970. The workers sensed that their particular enterprises were earning profits far above the average, which contributed to their discontent with the overall average wage increase being centrally negotiated by the LO with the employers' association in Stockholm.

The presence of substantial numbers of foreign workers (especially Finns) in the mines was also cited as a cause of difficulty. These foreign workers accumulated special problems on the job and in the community, but cultural and linguistic barriers often made the regular labor-management machinery for solving such problems inaccessible to them. Finally, the media, notably Swedish government-operated television, seemed to have played up the strike and protracted it, as did left-wing intellectuals and student groups.[7] (It was contended that the TV editors responsible were left, anti-establishment, anti-LO, etc., and that they had colored their treatment of the Kiruna rebels accordingly.)

Germany

The wildcat strikes in the German metal industry in the fall of 1969 seem to have been aimed primarily at earlier negotiated regional wage bargains. These agreements, which were signed during a period of economic recession in 1969, provided only modest wage increases and yet were to run for 18 months, a somewhat longer than usual period. The quick return of prosperity and a high level of business profits and rising prices touched off discontent in many local situations.[8]

While the strikes had real economic roots, they appear to have been widened and strengthened by the example of the highly publicized student strikes and demonstrations occurring during this same period, even though the more conservative union workers apparently did not cooperate in any direct manner with the leftist students. Again, some sense of dissatisfaction with

remotely negotiated agreements was a factor, especially in large prosperous firms.

Belgium

In the Belgium coal mine wildcat strikes of 1970, the economic decline of the mines themselves was cited as a major causal factor. A feeling of economic insecurity was especially widespread in the Limbourg region. The weakness of union communications lines down to the work level clearly played a role in deepening the workers' insecurity and dissatisfaction. Conflict between the workers' committees at the job level on the one hand, and the official union hierarchies on the other, surfaced during the conflict.

A serious strike at the Michelin plant seems also to have been caused by a lack of communication between the workers and the union hierarchy. At Michelin, however, the presence of large numbers of foreign workers with special problems not being met by regular union and management machinery was an aggravating factor, accompanied by student and media agitation.

The head of the Belgian Federation of Labor (FGTB) concluded from this 1970 strike experience that the existing system of national collective bargaining agreements was not sufficiently flexible to deal with the growing problems at the enterprise level. The national agreements themselves, he said, must be made more "open" and subject to modification under changed circumstances.[9]

What seems to stand out in all of these strike situations, as well as others in Western Europe, is some loss of control on the part of national trade union leaders. A new sense of economic and social power on the part of workers at the enterprise level from time to time touches off strikes or other action, unsanctioned by the union headquarters, to redress grievances or achieve new gains at the local level. But in almost no case can one find serious persistent hostility on the part of workers toward the structure of their national unions. The workers seem to accept them for certain important tasks but increasingly look beyond them to solve problems at the local level.[10] Presently, it does not seem likely that na-

---

Swedish Trade Union Confederation, 1972). In an as yet unpublished paper, Meidner claims a considerable degree of success for this wage policy over nearly two decades.

[7] See the interesting report of the Kiruna and related strikes by R. Tersmeden, in Spitaels, *Crisis in the Industrial Relations.*

[8] Another wave of strikes in 1973, especially in several large German automobile plants, seemed to have similar causes, especially as regards higher prices; but immigrant worker discontent was also a contributing cause of strikes in some German plants in 1973.

[9] G. Debunne in Spitaels, *Crisis in the Industrial Relations.* Worker protest at the local level in Belgium in recent months has increasingly come in the form of taking over the premises to demonstrate opposition to threatening management plans. See "Sit-In, the Belgian Experience," in International Confederation of Free Trade Unions, *Free Labour World,* December 1972.

[10] Mention should be made of the fact that beginning in the late 50s many major French and German enterprises paid wages above the minima prescribed by national industrial collective agreements as they sought to

tional union leaders will be able to gain much control over these local processes and increasing worker power.

ADVANCES AT THE NATIONAL LEVEL

Although hindered by unofficial action at the local level, national trade union power has nevertheless accounted for notable advances in most West European countries. National trade unions have played an ever-widening role, for example, in industrial and manpower planning, especially in Dutch, French, and Belgian economic and social policy councils, as well as in the manpower boards in Sweden and other countries. In addition, there have been cooperative government-union-management efforts to reach national consensus on wage price policies in a number of countries.

At the national collective bargaining level, important settlements have been negotiated. Some of these are so significant that they seem, at times, to transform the national bargaining process into a kind of social-legislative machinery. France provides a number of useful instances where this has occurred. In recent years, as a result of union-management agreements (with government also assisting), the hourly or blue-collar worker has had his status equalized with that of salaried employees in many basic respects. No longer, for example, will French factory workers be paid on an hourly basis, as they are gradually being converted to monthly salary status (equalization of many benefits is also occurring). Following a national joint statement approving this change, made by the major labor federations and the employers' association in 1970, unions and management at the national level of different industries have worked out the details of the transformation in their industry-wide collective agreements. Since these changes have implications for social insurance programs, government has been, to a degree, a partner in these negotiations.[11]

The collective bargaining process has been employed, usually at the industry level, to make a somewhat similar though more limited (in terms of numbers of industries) transformation of workers to salaried status in Germany and Switzerland. Similar steps are being taken in Belgium as a result of a union-management agreement on a national inter-industry basis.

In France, union-management controlled vocational training and retraining programs have been established. Under these plans, workers can receive as much as a year's training, with weekly cash benefits that equal or approach their regular wages.[12]

Important new protections against layoffs have been negotiated by unions and management in the metal and chemical industries in Germany. Under these agreements, no worker 50 (or 55) years or older, with at least 10 years' service, can be dismissed as a result of technological change, while those 40 (or 45) years or older with 10 to 15 years' seniority are to receive many months of prior notice and up to approximately one year's gross pay as severance compensation.[13]

The practice of concluding union-management agreements at the highest levels and of setting inter-industry wages, working, and social conditions has probably been developed most fully in Belgium. In 1960, the major union federations and the employers' association signed an agreement for joint "social programming," operating through a National Labor Council. Agreements growing out of this arrangement, as Blanpain puts it, are "tending to make the National Labor Council a kind of social parliament enacting general rules that apply to the whole private sector of the economy."[14] In 1971, for example, the three Belgium labor federations signed an agreement with the employers' association on an inter-industry basis, providing for important modifications of the social security laws of the country. The agreement made it contingent upon the parties to persuade the government to make the necessary legal changes in pensions and benefits. If government action did not occur (unlikely in the political context of Belgium), the parties would reopen their own agreement. In this same

---

attract and hold a better than average work force. Sometimes this action was taken after consultation with local workers' or union committees, but often it was made unilaterally. In the major enterprises, at least, the workers now seem to have learned the possibilities for local initiative in demanding special advantages at the shop level.

[11] See the interesting article by Yves Delamotte, "Recent Collective Bargaining Trends in France," *International Labour Review*, April 1971, esp. 365–66 on the salary status conversion agreements.

[12] Ibid., pp. 362–63.

[13] A description of these and some other recent innovating developments in European collective bargaining can be found in Charles Levinson's paper in *New Perspectives in Collective Bargaining*, paper prepared for a Regional Trade Union Seminar, November 4–7, 1969 (Paris: OECD, 1971). Also see E. M. Kassalow, *New Directions in European Unionism* (Madison: University of Wisconsin, Industrial Relations Research Institute, Reprint No. 165, 1971).

[14] Roger Blanpain, "Recent Collective Bargaining Trends in Belgium," *International Labour Review*, July-August 1971, pp. 116–18.

general agreement, again on an inter-industry basis, management agreed to periodically release trade unionists for several weeks of management-paid training for safety and grievance committee work. A fourth week of vacation was agreed upon for all eligible workers, as well as maternity benefits for women.[15]

I noted above that despite their manifest discontent with some local wage and working conditions and the machinery for handling these difficulties, West European workers still seem quite loyal to their national unions and federations.

[15] "National Agreement Covering All Trades and Occupations, 1971–72," ICFTU, *Social and Economic Bulletin*, September–October 1971. The same machinery in 1970 produced the collective agreement for a guaranteed monthly wage for all workers on an inter-industry basis. Often a breakthrough in a particular area (e.g., an increase in vacation pay) may be accomplished by the national unions bargaining in one sector of the Belgian economy (the metal unions are conspicuous in this regard). This new gain can later be generalized for workers in other industries through an "inter-professional" national agreement.

The foregoing major national advances are an indication of this loyalty.

CONCLUSIONS

Changes at both the local and national levels are likely to continue for some time. Recent outbreaks in major auto plants in France and Germany, triggered in part by a "revolt" of foreign workers (e.g., largely North Africans in the French Renault plant and Turks in the Ford Cologne case), attest to the continued volatility of the plant level labor situation.[16] Significant socioeconomic progress via national negotiations is also evident. This combination of change at the local and national levels will provide a continuously interesting, creative period in European industrial relations.

[16] In the German case, the late summer 1973 strikes were extended to a number of metal working plants. As in the 1969 case (see above), national union officers seemed to have underestimated the impact of a sharply rising cost of living on a collective agreement which had been signed some months earlier.

48. Co-Determination Today and Tomorrow*

Heinz Hartmann†

The term "co-determination" is an awkward, almost forbidding one. There are some, like Professor Lyon-Caen, who think that the German word *Mitbestimmung* is entirely untranslatable.[1] There are advantages, however, in using the term co-determination. For one thing, it calls attention to the fact that this is in some respects a peculiarly German product. Secondly, the word "determination" reminds us that we are dealing with decision-making, joint decision-making, rather than information or consultation. This helps to make the discussion more to the point. Finally, there is the terminological affinity of co-determination to self-determination; and this affinity helps to uncover the idealistic element in co-determination.

In dealing with the merits and prospects of co-determination it may be wise to state again the major objectives and attributes of co-determination. I shall do this briefly since the formal features of co-determination are reasonably well known.[2] Next, we need to look at its record. Has it been a success or failure? That is the evaluative side of the topic. Finally, we must look into proposed changes in co-determination as a social institution. What are its chances of survival and growth? This is of some interest, too, outside West Germany, since there is a new and general

concern with participation in most highly industrialized countries. There are also more specific reasons, such as the efforts of the European Commission to harmonize company laws in the member states and to create a statute for the European firm—efforts which in large measure are based on the co-determination model.[3]

This article will be mainly concerned with discussing the central principles of co-determination as set out in the Co-Determination Law of 1951 and as practised in the iron, coal, and steel industries. The law provides for the introduction of a labour director in the executive committee, and for a parity agreement in the supervisory board: half its members to be representatives of owners and shareholders, half representatives of company employees—plus a neutral chairman. The law of 1951 formalized and generalized a pattern of employee representation which had been demanded by German unions in the iron and steel industries immediately after the second world war and which was agreed to in 1947 by the British Military Government, an extension of the then Labour Government of Britain.[4]

Outside the iron, coal, and steel industries industrial relations are subject to a lesser kind of co-determination which in a large part revolves around the works councils. Co-determination here also extends into the supervisory board, but employees occupy no more than one-third of the seats. No provision is made for a labour director. Legislation on this watered-down version of co-determination was passed in 1952. Although this occurred only a year after Parliament passed the

---

* From *British Journal of Industrial Relations*, Vol. 13, No. 1, March 1975, pp. 54–64.

† Professor of Sociology, Münster University, Federal Republic of Germany.

[1] Gérard Lyon-Caen, *Beitrag zu den Möglichkeiten der Vertretung der Interessen der Arbeitnehmer in der Europäischen Aktiengesellschaft*, Kollektive Studien, Reihe Wettbewerb-Rechtsangleichung Nr. 10, Brussels 1970, p. 9.

[2] For a recent statement in English, see A. Szakats, "Workers' Participation in Management: The German Experience," *The Journal of Industrial Relations*, Vol. 16 (March 1974), pp. 29–44.

---

[3] *Proposal for a Council Regulation Embodying a Statute for European Companies*, Brussels, Commission of the European Communities, 1970.

[4] For a recent reminiscence from a British participant, see W. Harris-Burland, "Worker Codetermination" (letter to *The Times*), *The Times*, 4 March, 1974.

1951 law, this one year proved crucial. As Clark Kerr brilliantly explained in his early analysis of the redistribution of power in postwar Germany, the interim period of 1951 to 1952 was used by the conservative Christian Democrats to entrench themselves firmly in defensive positions against the forces of organized labour.[5]

When the trade unions pressed for a German co-determination law, their motives had much to do with what they had been through in the Nazi era; trade unions were dissolved very soon after Hitler came to power, and they wanted to make certain that German industrialists would never again finance an extremist party. This option for political control—by way of co-determination—no longer applies but there has been much concern instead with control in the areas of personnel and general management. There is little interest in "participation"—in the literal sense where running the firm might be considered a venture at the joint risk of management and labour. Labour concentrates on maintaining a system of pressure groups. That labour has given way on the issue of conflict and control implies no more than consent to the institutionalization of conflict, that is, to agreement on the provision of rules to regulate conflict. This means that even with co-determination German unions are fully prepared to use strikes as an additional instrument of collective coercion. Co-determination has kept down the instances of open conflict; the shutdown of many mines in the Ruhr could hardly been effected without strikes if labour directors had not been in office to protect the interests of dismissed employees. But the elimination of strikes could hardly be called an overt motive for co-determination.

As one would expect, the interest in control is most pronounced among the trade unions, while employees as individuals (in their relationship with management) are often satisfied with co-operation. It is important at this point to emphasize that German trade unions are organized at the local or district level, not at the level of the firm; there is no formal trade union representation in the firm. Trade unions do make their influence felt, of course, in each of the three major instruments of co-determination: the works council, the office of labour director, the supervisory board. Most of the council members are organized and so are very nearly all council chairmen. The labour director is almost always appointed by the supervisory board from a trade union slate. Finally, in the coal and steel industries three of the five employee representatives in the supervisory board are recommended by the trade unions; they are elected by a meeting of shareholders, but the meeting can only vote on trade union nominations. So there is considerable opportunity for the trade unions to intervene even though unions formally stay outside the firm.

It is precisely this leverage of organized labour which has caused some observers to challenge the value of co-determination; they talk of "remote control" of company affairs by the trade unions. Others have expressed a fear that controversies over conflicting interests will delay decision-making, or that labour directors will break down from split loyalties—and so on. What is the record of co-determination? Has it been a success or has it failed significantly on many points? In trying to evaluate co-determination, it is possible, for the most part, to rely on the Report of the Biedenkopf-Commission, a government appointed group of experts.[6] The Commission was established in 1967. The appointment was made by a government which at the time consisted of Christian and Social Democrats, so that political bias in the Commission was in all probability evenly distributed. The findings were published in 1970, roughly two decades after co-determination was put into effect. The basic results of the hearings, interviews, and survey by the Commission were that co-determination as an institution was accepted by all and worked reasonably well. This is not to say that the Report did not refer to partial failure and some weaknesses. But in general this commission of experts gave co-determination a reasonably clean bill of health. Moreover, the Commission devoted some thought to the possibilities of adding new features to the existing co-determination machinery and extending the system to industries outside the coal, iron, and steel industries.

On balance, the Commission was apparently more impressed with the pacifying effects which co-determination had on organized labour than by the sense of participation which it imparted to individual employees. And it was further impressed by the fact that co-determination, while satisfying the trade unions, did not seem to interfere with the economic and technical efficiency of the firm. A critical test of adverse effect on company efficiency was the question of whether the parity composition of the supervisory board would lead to stalemates in decision-making. To

[5] Clark Kerr, "The Trade Union Movement and the Redistribution of Power in Postwar Germany," *The Quarterly Journal of Economics*, Vol. 48 (November 1954), pp. 535–64.

[6] *Deutscher Bundestag, 6. Wahlperiode, Drucksache VI/334*, Bonn, 1970.

begin with, adverse effects on this score should not be seen as fatal to the firm. For, contrary to what is often assumed in discussions about the system of two-tier boards, the supervisory board in Germany has not been a strong instrument of control, although it was intended to be. In fact management, or members of the executive committee, occupy a stronger position (in terms of organized influence) than do members of the supervisory board. Nevertheless it is important to note that the Commission found next to no evidence of stalemate in decision-making on the supervisory boards. It is interesting, however, to look at some of the reasons for this. The Commission found that the issues reaching the supervisory board for decision had not only been screened to some extent by the executive committee, but in addition executive committees had taken pains in many cases to clear these issues with the works councils—so that, as far as company employees were concerned, most of the controversy on any given issue had been ironed out before the supervisory board came to vote on it. This is not the same as a situation where labour would have its say early in the process of decision-making and therefore appear passive in the final voting, for two sets of labour representatives are involved: employee representatives on the works council, who are more likely to follow a company-centered policy, and employee representatives on the supervisory board, the majority of whom are more likely to follow a union-centered policy. The Commission goes so far as to indicate that there is a kind of collusion between the executive committee and the works council against the supervisory board and that this policy tends to pre-empt the powers of the supervisory board—which are not overly impressive to begin with.

In considering the labour director the Commission clearly indicates that labour directors have divided loyalties. It is hard to see how this division of loyalties—to other members of the committee, on the one hand, and to employees and trade unions on the other—could be avoided. A number of studies had established this very fact before the Commission drew attention to the problem. The Commission does, however, point to exceptions. Significantly the Report in these exceptional cases refers to instances of "integration" of the labour director into the executive committee. Exemption from split loyalty obviously is to be had only by siding with one of the two parties.

Findings on the so-called economic committee are even more negative. Under co-determination arrangements the economic committee is to run as a joint committee of labour and management to provide information on the economic situation of the firm. These committees have failed in most companies. They were made redundant by the exchange of information on other levels, especially in cases where employee representatives shared in decision-making and did not have to wait for management to volunteer specific items of information.

There are a number of weaknesses in co-determination which the Commission did not take up explicitly but which to my mind should not go unmentioned. In particular I am thinking of those which relate to worker satisfaction with co-determination. A number of empirical studies have shown that the problem of growing alienation between representatives and their constituency is as much of a liability to co-determination as it is to other representative systems. This problem, which was especially evident during the years of general labour unrest in western Europe —1968 to 1971—is a familiar one. Roberto Michels, in his study of trade unions, dealt with this phenomenon more than 60 years ago when he formulated his "iron law of oligarchy." Elected representatives are likely to acquire such superiority of information and know-how (when compared to the competence of the rank and file) that it becomes difficult to revoke their mandate and unseat them. In the 50s Richard Lester took up this subject again, in his book *As Unions Mature*.[7] The same process can be observed in the co-determination system. This is especially true on the level of the works council, where we find that members stay in office for years and years and that dissidents hardly ever have a chance of getting in. This phenomenon, of course, is a barrier to direct involvement of the employees in their participation scheme.

Here may be the key, perhaps, to the apparent contradictions in employee statements on their satisfaction with co-determination. As long as the question is geared to co-determination as a scheme, to its general desirability in West German society, the answers are unequivocally positive. There can be no doubt that the institution as such is endorsed not only by the trade unions but also by individual employees. But when people are questioned on the degree of personal satisfaction and asked, "How well are you personally satisfied with co-determination? Did you get out of co-determination what you wanted person-

[7] Richard A. Lester, *As Unions Mature: An Analysis of the Evolution of American Unionism* (Princeton, N.J.: Princeton University Press, 1958).

ally?" there is a noticeable lack of satisfaction.[8]

This comparative dissatisfaction may stem from the impersonality, the relative anonymity of the system. Co-determination is centered very much at the top level of the company. It is not embedded in parallel institutions at the higher national level or the lower level of the shop floor. Some will say that "it operates in a void." Clearly this is not so. But there is a definite detachment from other levels. To illustrate this point: Workers on the shop floor rarely know the employee representatives personally at the board level.[9] And it can hardly be said that this is due to individual negligence or to the fact that employees do not keep themselves informed when they should. It is known from social psychologists that perceptual awareness in general tends to be limited in terms of social space.

The record is clear. On the whole, co-determination is functioning well enough in spite of several flaws. But what are its propensities for growth? Will we see more of it? The answer is a definite yes, if the present government in the Federal Republic is to have its way. Early last year the coalition partners, Social Democrats and Free Democrats, concluded an agreement on the expansion of co-determination and this agreement will become law later this year.

At first sight the draft seems to be a compromise between the two versions of co-determination now in operation in West Germany, that is, the more advanced version extant in the coal and steel industries which provides "full parity" on the supervisory board and a "labour director" on the executive committee, and the less advanced version which provides "one-third-parity." The current draft primarily applies to the supervisory board; it limits the proportion of trade union representatives on the board while upholding the concept of full parity. Depending on company size, supervisory boards are to be staffed by 12, 16, or 20 members. In the small and medium companies trade unions would be represented by two officers only while in larger boards they would fill three of the ten seats allotted to labour.

Board membership for labour representatives would be dependent on the votes of an electoral college which itself is elected by employees in the company. Seats in the electoral college are distributed among three categories of employees: manual workers, white collar employees, and executive level employees (*Leitende Angestellte*),

according to their relative share in the total workforce of the firm. There are special provisions, however, to safeguard the representation of minorities. Nominations for the electoral college may be made by one-tenth of the members of each category or, at any rate, by at least 100 employees of the respective category. The same number of votes (or one-fifth of the vote in each category) will suffice for the endorsement of candidates for the supervisory board, except that the representatives of the trade unions are to be elected by the shareholders' assembly.

Since previous surveys did not exactly attest to the value of neutral chairmen in the supervisory boards of the coal and steel industry,[10] the present government decided to drop this feature from future co-determination legislation. This, in turn, necessitated elaborate precautions for the election of board chairmen in case the two parties involved could not agree on any one candidate. Present provisions are that in case of deadlock, each party is to elect its own candidate; these two candidates will then take turns at occupying the positions of chairman and vice-chairman, respectively.

Finally, provisions have been made for the election of top management, i.e., members of the executive committee. A regular procedure has been laid down for their election by the supervisory board on the basis of a two-thirds majority. "Fail safe" arrangements in this case are even more elaborate than in the staffing of supervisory boards; assorted mechanisms are to cover all contingencies in the election of top managers. In the last resort, the shareholders' assembly will be asked to settle controversial candidacies.

The government proposal is being discussed in Parliament at the time of writing, and its sponsors themselves have admitted that it needs improvement: It suffers from unnecessary formalism and is very unwieldy. Criticism by the opposition has either tended also to be formalist, or in contrast has been strongly oriented towards principles. A further disadvantage is that important substantive distinctions of the current proposal vis-à-vis earlier stages in the evolution of co-determination have been neglected. These distinctions will be analysed later, after a brief review of actual objections by the adversaries of the draft.

As indicated above, the election procedure for the supervisory board and its chairman seem excessively complicated and of little use in situations in which there is need for promptness and clarity in decision-making. The institution of a

---

[8] For an early summary see Erich Potthoff, Otto Blume, Helmut Duvernell, *Zwischenbilanz der Mitbestimmung*, J. C. B. Mohr (Paul Siebeck), 1962, p. 321.

[9] Ibid., pp. 311, 313 et passim.

[10] *Deutscher Bundestag . . . ,* p. 40.

neutral chairman in the past may not have added much to the functional achievements of the supervisory board. But it has found new support in view of problems arising when two parties in conflict must agree on someone who, in spite of his partisanship, will be entrusted with the office of chairman. Besides, there is criticism of the two-stage election procedure for ordinary members; the institution of an electoral college to many appears expendable in favour of direct elections.

Secondly, the provisions of top management have aroused little enthusiasm. Because this may well be an area riddled with antagonism, the government has devised four different solutions which must be tried in turn in case of conflict and successive failure; it is only after these elaborate efforts of bipartisan problem-solving that the shareholders' assembly may advance its presumably unilateral decision.

Thirdly, there is the contentious issue of the *Leitende Angestellte*, managerial employees at the middle and upper ranks in the hierarchy. This group aims at independent representation of its collective interests. It sees itself as a third force in the enterprise and has taken steps to organize on its own. The government, however, prefers to treat managerial employees like other employees of varying functions and status. The present draft will offer some assurance that *Leitende Angestellte* may elect representatives from their own group, but they will serve on the labour bench in the board. There are fears they may be voted down by other labour representatives when they speak up on behalf of their own group.

While much of the debate has consisted of haggling over legal safeguards for minorities and other such technicalities, a second criticism has been basic to a degree of wholesale rejection. Statements to this effect were made both by trade unions and employers. Some trade unions claimed that nothing but the full application of the most advanced forms of co-determination will promote the cause of worker participation, and some employers fear the breakdown of the entire economy if co-determination is extended to industries outside coal and steel even in a modified version.

More plausible than either of these arguments is the claim that the government draft threatens the bargaining autonomy (*Tarifautonomie*) of trade unions and employers' federations. Under German law the settlement of wages and working conditions by contract is left to the free interaction of unions and employers' associations. Labour influence on the staffing of the executive

committee is feared by some as likely to subvert the ranks of employers. If a top manager should feel dependent on the approval of labour representatives in the supervisory board, he might favour labour interests while officially serving on the bargaining committee of his own association. Critics are prone to point to experience in the coal and steel industries where managers appointed to the executive committee from a trade union slate (labour directors) have become members of the industry's employers' association and participate in bargaining on the employers' side (*Uber-Paritat*). The bargaining process in coal and steel indeed differs from the interaction common in other industries under the bargaining autonomy of the two major parties.

All in all, however, the real problems of the new draft seem to be intermediate to such basic issues and to the technicalities of voting or other procedures. Little effort has been made so far, for example, to examine the implications of this intended law in the evolution of co-determination. If it is a new step, how does this draft compare to earlier and to future objectives in worker participation? It is not sufficient to interpret this law as a mere effort of quantitative extension, i.e., of spreading co-determination into areas so far untouched. The draft law implies substantive change along three major axes: First, the present draft calls for joint legitimation of managerial power; secondly, it brings up the question of participation on the job; finally, it promotes the concept of management by mandate.

Observers should realize that in recent debates co-determination has been defended and promoted as conducive to the "democratic legitimation of power." This slogan introduces a new note into the plea for co-determination. If co-determination was at first pressed in the interest of "control over capital" and, in later years, has become a means for introducing a new party to decision-making, the current drive is for consent in the use of power, for consensus on the acceptability of managerial direction. During the early years, managerial discretion was taken for granted. The major objective was to limit the exercise of power: to prevent its political abuse, as in the support of extremist parties, and to curb autocratic leadership inside the firm. In the next stage the quest was for pluralism: The special interests of labour, alongside the motives and values of management, were to find recognition in decision-making. Now, the cry is for consent.

As yet this escalation of demands is hardly backed by systematic reasoning. There is no explicit controversy concerning alternative bases of power. Consensus is required mostly on persons and procedures; the discussion rarely involves challenges to positions and ideology. But there is a new insistence on agreement, a stubborn plea for bipartisan action, a telling reluctance to abandon the pressure for consensus and yield to a managerial agency like the shareholders' assembly or to mediation. Clearly, the ultimate aspiration is for agreement not only in decision-making but on the very bases of decision-making powers. Labour is coming forward to vote on the acceptability of superiority or subordination in the industrial hierarchy.

This is not a tug-of-war between company and trade union officers, for another feature of the present stage is the involvement of the rank and file. Co-determination has long been a high-level affair. As surveys have shown, employees rarely master the mechanics of the procedure and often do not even know who are the officials concerned. This trend would only be encouraged by the new institution of an electoral college to vote on membership in the supervisory board. In reaction to the growing anonymity of the officers concerned, critics of the draft have been very much in favour of the "common employee" voting directly on his cause and his representatives. Co-determination is to be made the immediate concern of each and every one among the employees.

This may seem to be a surprising ambition on the part of the opposition, ordinarily a rather conservative grouping. Upon closer inspection part of the critical drive proves to be directed against the trade unions. The opposition claims that anonymity is greatest when the electoral college votes on candidates put forward by the trade unions which, under German law, are organized outside the individual firms. Indeed, German trade unions have been loath to carry co-determination to the rank and file. Recent suggestions for worker participation on the floor by some labour ideologists have met with little enthusiasm among trade union officers. Now the opposition has picked up this flag. We may have some doubts at this stage, of course, on whether the sponsors of direct involvement would, if given the opportunity, really be willing to follow up the initiative and invest employees with more of a say on matters concerning them. In fact, the opposition may soon wonder whether its concept of "direct voting" may not become a ticket for a ride on the tiger called plebiscite.

In fact current proposals for the staffing of top management do imply a relationship of dependency on group-centered voting. If government plans materialize, labour representatives on the board may vote only in favour of an executive considered to be reliable from their own political point of view. A logical outgrowth of this could be management by mandate as it is practised in the Yugoslav model.

These implications are directly linked to some of the idealistic elements in co-determination. If we want to assess the future of co-determination, clearly we must take into account its ultimate objectives. By and large, the idealistic aims of this institution seem to be well served by current developments, and this positive relationship augurs well for its future growth. The argument is that whatever the origins of the scheme (and they appear to be accidental and pragmatic rather than fundamental), co-determination today promises to give concrete fulfilment to several Utopian desires among what used to be called the labour movement. This linkage with Utopia provides sufficient traction for co-determination to subsist and grow for some time to come—especially if we recognize that these desires are shared widely in society at large.

Take the issue of parity. What is behind the issue is the desire for inside control of business on a par with the owner and his trustee management. There always was a strong tendency among the Catholic Labour Movement to press for the equality of labour and capital. For reasons of their own the non-Catholic part of labour was interested in the same objective. But, until recently, everybody felt this to be a very remote, inaccessible objective. As indicated, however, things are changing rapidly. If the government succeeds in its current policy, we are about to witness the partial fulfilment of what was—and to some extent, still is—a Utopian goal.

Since we are well on the way towards this part of the objective, two other objectives ought also to be discussed. One is the objective of democratization, the other the desire of self-determination in industry. Obviously, co-determination has so far resulted in the implementation of some lesser features of democratization. One of the most quoted examples is the mining industries which were formerly notorious for their authoritarian patterns of leadership: Co-determination has significantly reduced this former source of friction and strife. But what of the more ambitious goals of democratization?

If by democratization is meant that groups with some sense of collective identity should find some organized representation of their own, then this Utopian idea is being implemented gradually; following blue- and white-collar labour, managerial employees are now setting up independent bodies of representation in the enterprise. The prospective law will also award them 1 seat in 20 on the supervisory board. In practice this latter concession will mean little or nothing, but independent councils do mean something. The first such council (analogous to the works councils) was established in 1971, and in the meantime a very large number of them has sprung up.[11] Within three years they have wrought significant changes in German industrial relations: They have advanced the democratic stature of industrial relations in one important respect. It is developments like these, sudden, inspired, successful, which should make it necessary to consider the probabilities of still higher degrees of democratization.

But what of the last of the Utopian ideas which we proposed to take up, self-determination? Is it at all meaningful to link this idea to co-determination? As pointed out at the beginning of this article, the concept of co-determination relates, terminologically, to self-determination. And it was none other than Otto Brenner, the late president of the Metal Workers' Union and one of the most eager, powerful and considerate champions of co-determination in Germany, who tied the two concepts together in terms of substance when he said, repeatedly: "Co-determination to us is a stepping stone towards self-determination." Admittedly, this is the one Utopia which is least imminent. We have only just begun to discuss the pros and cons of autonomous groups on the company floor; we are still at a loss for a practical mix of independence and interdependence for individual employees. It certainly looks as if we have a long way to go towards realizing this objective.

But movements towards the incorporation of values into ongoing social concerns are still widespread, and co-determination continues to be one of the notions most widely shared and applied. It is difficult to overestimate its importance in many different fields, especially of course in industrial relations. Its influence on employees compares with that of the Protestant ethic on early entrepreneurs and industrialists. Just as this ethic held sway over the minds of what is today called top management, co-determination now (and for some time to come) will be of prime value to employees as an end-in-view of their working lives.

[11] Heinz Hartmann, "Managerial Employees—New Participants in Industrial Relations," *British Journal of Industrial Relations*, Vol. 12 (July 1974), pp. 274–75.

You can't lay off 5,000 employees at once,

49. Codetermination: A Hidden Noose for MNCs*

George S. McIsaac and Herbert Henzler†

For most large U.S. companies, any prospect of worker representation on their boards of directors —to say nothing of actual top-management power-sharing with labor union representatives —has always seemed incomprehensibly remote. If it couldn't quite be dismissed as impossible, at least it never came high on any rational top manager's list of things to lie awake worrying about. "Codetermination"—a German problem— was no concern of his.

Suddenly, all this is changing. Codetermination with teeth, until now confined to the German iron and steel industry, is highly likely to be extended to all major German enterprises, including scores of subsidiaries of U.S. and other foreign-based multinationals. In short, barring a political miracle, many U.S. companies may soon become the involuntary subjects of a painful and hazardous learning experience. The details of the experience, and the lessons that can be drawn from it, are important for two reasons: First, they may well constitute a foretaste of a trend toward labor partnership in management affairs that is not confined to Germany; second, they represent a critical test of the relationship between the MNC [multinational corporations] and a sovereign host nation.

Within Germany, of course, it is not only the daughters of U.S.-based multinationals whose way of doing business is suddenly threatened. Faced with the prospect of increased worker involvement in the most critical corporate decisions, German industrial managers are exhibiting reactions ranging from dismay to outrage.

* Reprinted with permission from the Winter 1974 issue of the *Columbia Journal of World Business*. Copyright © 1974 by the Trustees of Columbia University in the City of New York.

† George S. McIsaac is director of McKinsey and Co., Washington, D.C. Herbert Henzler is a McKinsey principal in Germany.

To Dr. Mathias Seefelder, the new head of the managing board at BASF, the chief executive of any big German company needs the same kind of reflexes as an aircraft pilot in a thunderstorm. The proposed codetermination (*Mitbestimmung*) law, by giving labor equal Board of Directors representation with capital, would make impossible the quick reactions required to maneuver through corporate up- and down-drafts. And Dr. Martin Schleyer of Mercedes Benz, head of the German employers' association, sums up the new law as "nothing less than cold expropriation." Yet neither man is optimistic about the chance of avoiding it. The current plans of Germany's ruling coalition call for a vote before May 1975, and the prospects are that a new law establishing extensive rights of codetermination will readily pass the Bundestag.

Privately, Germany's seasoned and extraordinarily skillful top executives are preparing to live with the additional burdens imposed by the new law—and they are far from despairing of their ability to do so. After all, the German iron and steel industry has survived rather handsomely for more than 20 years with nearly 50–50 labor participation on the Board of Directors (*Aufsichtsrat*). Indeed, Heinz Oskar Vetter, Chairman of the DGB (Deutsche Gewerkschafts-Bund, Germany's all-powerful trade union federation) claims that labor participation has benefited the industry by keeping managers constantly on their toes. Nobody would suggest that Herr Vetter is unbiased, but off the record, many German steel executives would grant this point.

In contrast to the anguished reactions of German managers, little was heard until recently from the MNC's with major asset commitments in Germany. Then, in mid-October, the American Chamber of Commerce in Germany lodged a protest with the Federal Chancellor, Helmut

449

Schmidt, and the heads of the party groups in the Bonn parliament, as well as with the U.S. State Department. The Chamber of Commerce document, based on a specially commissioned legal brief, flatly denies that the new law can legitimately be applied to existing foreign-owned companies. Its author, Wilhelm Wengler, a noted professor of law at Berlin's University, argues that the provisions of *Mitbestimmung* violate the German-American trade treaty of 1954, which spelled out the "residual rights" of American companies operating in the Federal Republic after the country had obtained sovereignty.

This action has stung German labor and government leaders into a counter-barrage of public protests against what is seen as U.S. business meddling in internal German affairs. Heinz Oskar Vetter led off with a ringing declaration, "We are no banana republic!" And indeed hardly anyone expects the Bonn government to grant all U.S. subsidiaries extra-territorial status, exempting them from the requirements of domestic law.

The anxieties of the multinationals, then, are probably well-founded. Under the new law, which is highly likely to go into effect in 1975, it will almost certainly be plausible for work-force representatives on the *Aufsichtsrat* to block decisions on major investments or divestments, the repatriation of dividends, the appointment or replacement of key managers, and other critical matters.

For foreign-based companies, of course, these decision areas are especially vulnerable to possible interference on nationalistic grounds. German labor, like labor all over the world, has always tended to give very high priority to national self-interest, and it takes no great amount of imagination to detect a strain of economic nationalism in the current German mood. Depending on the aggressiveness of labor representation on the *Aufsichtsrat*, it could be but a short step from the decisions mentioned above to such delicate matters for multinationals as transfer pricing and financing policy. This could be the hidden noose of *Mitbestimmung*.

In the balance of this article we will describe how the major U.S.-based multinationals have been operating in Germany, how their operations will be affected, and how MNC management can prepare for the changes.

THE OLD BALL GAME

With few exceptions, the German "daughters" of American industrial companies are legally or-ganized either as limited-liability, nonpublicly held companies (the GmbH form) or as publicly held stock corporations (AGs). In all AGs and GmbHs with more than 500 employees, a Board of Directors (*Aufsichtsrat*) is legally responsible for supervision of the Board of Managers (*Vorstand*), which actually operates the enterprise. Under current law, two-thirds of the *Aufsichtsrat* are elected by the shareholders and one-third by labor—except in the mining and iron and steel industries (covering some twoscore totally German-owned companies) where the Board positions are shared equally by labor and owners' representatives, with one neutral member elected by both sides.

In U.S. subsidiaries, German nationals are often conspicuously present on the *Aufsichsrat*. Almost invariably, however, they comprise less than 50 percent of the Board, and in any case they are typically responsive to headquarters' wishes. In effect, then, the *Aufsichtsrat* is dominated by the representatives of the majority (frequently the sole) shareholder. Whenever a test of support for a managerial decision occurs, it merely rubber-stamps whatever headquarters has decided or approved. In more than one instance, minority shareholders have been bought out by the parent to preclude any possibility of labor members and minority shareholders getting together to block majority decisions.

Since *Vorstand* members (including the resident manager or *Vorstand-vorsitzer* of an MNC) are prohibited by law from sitting on the *Aufsichtsrat*, it is futile for the resident manager, whether American or German, to protest a headquarters decision except through traditional line channels. And, of course, too much opposition to headquarters, just like poor performance, means replacement—an easy matter with a rubber-stamp *Aufsichtsrat*. Confronted with an unwelcome directive, therefore, the resident manager generally swallows hard and holds his peace, unless he is prepared to argue up the line to headquarters. Given this situation, U.S. multinationals have had no reason to temper their accustomed management style where their German subsidiaries are concerned. Typically, the daughter organization is run as just another operating division, which happens to be located in Germany. And that is very different indeed from the way most indigenous German companies are run.

Most sizable German companies carefully follow established patterns of collective responsibility at the top management (*Vorstand*) level. Compared with the typical American or British management, they are more concerned with the views of their workers and more sympathetic in practice to workers' efforts to assert their rights. Frequently this approach has cost little more than management time, and the history of relative labor peace in Germany indicates that this time has, in many cases, been well invested.

In comparison, U.S. labor-management relations at home tend to be marked by tough bargaining confrontations and highly formalized grievance procedures, with strong "you-we" connotations. Perhaps inevitably, the same spirit shows up in the subsidiaries of U.S. multinationals in Germany.

Unlike the German *Vorstand-vorsitzender,* the chief executive of the American multinational is just that—not a *primus inter pares.* He has full responsibility for running the company and cannot share his accountability with his top management colleagues on the *Vorstand.* In the U.S. multinational, moreover, superior-subordinate lines are typically more clearly drawn, and limits of delegation more precisely established. Decisions and orders flow easily down the line, and performance or non-performance is readily discernible. Finally, the U.S. MNC style is definitely less tolerant of dissent than German companies, which have traditionally placed a major premium on managers' skills in negotiation and persuasion vis-a-vis fellow executives, immediate subordinates, and the work force.

To date, even with partial *Mitbestimmung,* there has been little pressure on the U.S. multinational to change. But if even German executives, accustomed as they are to dissent and conciliation, are anguished by the prospect of 50–50 *Mitbestimmung,* picture the approaching trauma for the U.S. subsidiary whose management style is tilted towards confrontation. Almost certainly, when the new-style *Mitbestimmung* comes into effect, broad conflicts will result in costly, even dangerous delays in key decisions. And German labor is quite evidently in no mood to duck such confrontations.

THE NEW BALL GAME

The new law now moving through the Bundestag hearing process will not change the fundamental decision power of the Board of Directors. As always, certain matters are prescribed by law as requiring the *Aufsichtsrat's* attention. Beyond this, the *Aufsichtsrat* also has the power to specify what matters are reserved for its own decision.

In U.S. subsidiaries, little use has been made of this flexibility: A rubber-stamp *Aufsichtsrat* has no reason to push very hard to expand its traditional scope. With the new-style *Mitbestimmung,* this picture will drastically change. In the words of Heinz Oskar Vetter, "The *Aufsichtsrat* member has a responsibility for long-term job security; he should therefore make full use of the rights implicit in the *Aktiengesetze* (stock corporation laws) to influence key management decisions." Given the opportunity of new-style *Mitbestimmung,* there is no reason for labor members not to follow that advice.

The key to the effect of *Mitbestimmung* on the top-level decision processes of a company, then, lies primarily in the composition of the *Aufsichtsrat.* The new law, as currently proposed, will call for 50 percent work force representation making for a powerful new interest group (see Exhibit 1). In the case of a foreign-based multinational, it is clear that the priorities governing the behavior of the interest group will be: first, employment and income security (in a sense identical with the well-being of the division); second, the well-being of the national community; and third and last, the well-being of the total enterprise.

This hierarchy of interests is nothing more or less than can be expected from any working man —or, for that matter, from most managers of any nationality. Yet its implications can be disturbing. As just one example, consider the occasional disagreements between a German-located *Vorstand* and multinational headquarters on how to deploy cash flowing into the German operations. Given a choice of expanding these operations, or paying or loaning the cash back to headquarters by one means or another, managers seem to prefer the former course two-thirds of the time. Headquarters, however, can find higher-return uses for the cash outside Germany two-thirds of the time. To be sure, these seeds of conflict between headquarters and overseas subsidiaries are nothing new. What is new is the prospect that with *Mitbestimmung,* a subsidiary manager who is at odds with headquarters may find allies within the labor faction of the *Aufsichtsrat.*

Faction-building, indeed, is the major risk. In theory, German managers could get together with worker representatives on the Board of Directors to effectively block, for the short-term benefit of the national division, decisions taken by headquarters in the interest of the total corporation. And since the *Aufsichtsrat* determines

EXHIBIT 1   Makeup and Role of Aufsichtsrat under Mitbestimmung (as currently proposed)

MEMBERSHIP: Half indirectly elected by a
workers electoral committee.....................half elected by shareholders

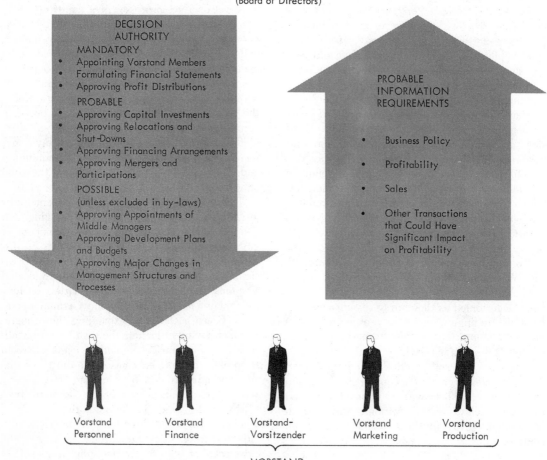

Supervisory
Employee

Nonemployee-
Trade Union
Representatives

Blue- & White-
Collar Employees

Shareholder Directors

AUFSICHTSRAT
(Board of Directors)

DECISION
AUTHORITY
MANDATORY
• Appointing Vorstand Members
• Formulating Financial Statements
• Approving Profit Distributions
PROBABLE
• Approving Capital Investments
• Approving Relocations and
  Shut-Downs
• Approving Financing Arrangements
• Approving Mergers and
  Participations
POSSIBLE
(unless excluded in by-laws)
• Approving Appointments of
  Middle Managers
• Approving Development Plans
  and Budgets
• Approving Major Changes in
  Management Structures and
  Processes

PROBABLE
INFORMATION
REQUIREMENTS

• Business Policy

• Profitability

• Sales

• Other Transactions
  that Could Have
  Significant Impact
  on Profitability

Vorstand
Personnel

Vorstand
Finance

Vorstand-
Vorsitzender

Vorstand
Marketing

Vorstand
Production

VORSTAND
(Managing Board)

management appointments and sets salaries, it is easy to see that—given some disposition to horse-trading on the part of local management—the parent multinational could lose its most effective check-rein on unruly executives, namely the power to fire.

As a taste of what could transpire, some major German concerns with overseas stakes have already found out what growing labor influence can mean. The chief executive of Volkswagen, Rudolf Leiding, was seriously interested in building an assembly plant in the United States. Indeed, he has been quoted as saying a U.S. plant is "a must to keep VW alive." Dissenting *Vorstand* members were supported by labor representatives on the *Aufsichtsrat* in blocking Leiding since German labor can't help being concerned about the loss of jobs to the United States. Leiding exited from Volkswagen in December 1974, and the issue of building the U.S. plant seems to be evaporating.

Since the German subsidiaries of U.S. companies repatriate more cash to the United States than German-owned overseas companies bring home, the noose of *Mitbestimmung* could lie tighter still about their necks. True, the law provides that a stalemate in the *Aufsichtsrat* can be resolved by the verdict of an extraordinary shareholders' meeting. But since it usually takes more than two months to call such a meeting, the remedy may be too cumbersome to be useful.

Not all the implications of the new law, however, are negative. Where internal management processes are concerned, some of its effects could be beneficial. For example, planning and information systems will have to be better. The labor members of the *Auftsichtsrat* will take their jobs seriously. They will expect managements to produce detailed plans and analyses or performance to support their major decisions. As a result, in most companies, standards of staff work, analysis, and presentation are almost certain to improve. Since the Board of Directors will command greater respect from managers, processes will be designed to provide routine documentation for management decisions and actions. Seat-of-the-pants management will become less prevalent. Managers, in short, will direct more of their attention to keeping the *Aufsichtsrat* "on board" so that it can keep the enterprise moving.

By implication, then, collective bargaining— formerly confined to wage rates, fringes, and work conditions—will move to the board room. It will cover a far more significant range of decisions, from key management appointments to budget allocations.

Portents of these developments are already at hand. Vetter has said: "The *Aufsichtsrat* must ensure that the company and the worker suffer as little as possible from the ups and downs of business cycles. Thus, it will have to be involved in all fields that may have an impact on the labor side." This is not an extremist viewpoint. Throughout Germany, unions are becoming more aggressive. At the same time, their concerns are broadening from getting their share of the economic pie to winning an equal voice in decisions affecting the future health of the company, in which labor feels it has just as big a stake as do the shareholders. Since over 90 percent of the majority party in the German Bundestag are union members, this concept is likely to prevail.

Nor, for that matter, is it confined to Germany alone. Similar movements are afoot elsewhere on the Continent. With the political winds blowing in Europe as they are today, the big multinationals should be thinking hard about how they can best accommodate these forces. Legal defenses, however carefully constructed, are vulnerable to both interpretation and political reversals. The companies that adjust most adroitly are going to suffer considerably less pain over the next two decades than their less flexible competitors.

PREPARING A NEW POSTURE

Successful adjustment to *Mitbestimmung*, however, is not a matter of passively accepting the realities of power-sharing. Rather, it will call for positive, constructive efforts by top managements to secure a far better information base, acquire new habits of precision, relearn some important human relations lessons, and perhaps develop some new political sensitivities. Elements that might be involved in such an effort include:

1. Gathering comprehensive information on the scope and functioning of codetermination. By studying the *Mitbestimmung* application model within the company, analyzing the codetermination experience of the coal and iron and steel industries, and exchanging information with comparable companies, the daughter *Vorstand,* together with corporate headquarters, can determine precisely how the new law will affect the company. Preparation for D-day also requires a realistic documentation of imminent management problems, including an analysis of labor representatives' goals and tactics, a list of issues subject to labor decision in the foreseeable future, and a review of past management decisions that would have been controversial under codetermination. Ideally, this documentation might take the form of a top-management handbook.

2. Analyzing and updating the company's by-laws and articles. More often than not, companies' by-laws and articles are outdated, vaguely worded, ambiguously designed, and far from specific about the respective responsibilities of *Vorstand* and *Aufsichtsrat*. Since neither corporation law nor the proposed codetermination law spells out the tasks of the two tiers in sufficient detail, the foreign-based headquarters, together with their German *Vorstand,* should work out by-laws that carefully fill the gap. In addition, a clear definition of responsibilities and authority within the reporting lines of the company is needed to convince a critical *Aufsichtsrat* that everybody in the company knows what his responsibilities are.

3. *Installing long-range plans for management succession and for personnel management.* Ad hoc hiring and firing of top-management personnel, in which U.S. headquarters of German subsidiaries have been known to indulge, will become difficult if not impossible under co-determination; instead, long-range management succession programs will become a must. German companies like BASF, Deutsche Bank, and Daimler-Benz have traditionally placed heavy emphasis on such long-range plans. As a result, the existing *Vorstand* often proposes the appointment of new *Vorstand* members (mostly from within the company), and the *Aufsichtsrat* usually agrees to these proposals.

Special needs in the field of personnel planning are for fair and readily understandable compensation systems, formal career and training plans and performance evaluations keyed both to local industry practice and to the corporate requirements of the MNC.

4. *Winning works council support.* Despite severe and well-publicized problems at such companies as Opel and Ford, many German subsidiaries of U.S. companies have enjoyed good relations with their works councils in the past. Many works council members (and labor board representatives from within the company) feel a stronger commitment to their company than to their unions. In the words of Germany's present Labor Minister, excoal miner and union leader Walter Arendt, "They aren't puppets in the hands of union officials." But works councils, too, are undergoing a generation change. Top management will be well advised to keep on good terms with them, since they can definitely temper the more aggressive spirit of outside union experts on the Board. The action of Daimler-Benz in sponsoring a one-week seminar for works council members to inform them of their rights and duties when the new shop constitution law came into effect exemplifies the sort of move that can only improve management's standing with the work force.

5. *Reviewing corporate policies, objectives, and strategies.* Far-reaching strategic decisions are typically handed down to German subsidiaries by their foreign headquarters like edicts

from Mount Olympus. Strategic decisions like IBM headquarters' divestment of a sizable property they had bought in Hanover to create 3,000 jobs will be a lot harder to execute in the future. Labor representatives on the *Aufsichtsrat* will want to weigh corporate policy decisions in the context of a well-thought-out long-term corporate strategy. Even today, long-range planning in many companies leaves far too much to be desired.

6. *Overhauling existing planning and control systems for management decisions.* Many companies generate great volumes of accounting data without providing the *Vorstand* or the *Aufsichtsrat* with adequate appropriate information for direction and control of the business. Here the experience of the German iron and steel companies is instructive. Typically, the labor members of the *Aufsichtsrat* have insisted on their legal right to be fully briefed by the *Vorstand*—and the more fully the *Vorstand* has informed the labor side about its intentions, the less interference it has encountered.

7. *Introducing a more cooperative management style.* A cooperative, collegial management style, both at the *Vorstand* level and in relations between *Vorstand* and lower management levels, will be a primary goal of the labor side on the board. This will be a slow and painful process for the U.S.-based headquarters and the present members of the *Vorstand*. But even a little more communication and a tacit acknowledgement of common interests will be an improvement on the style practiced in the past.

These, in our view, are the most important and generally applicable elements of a thoughtful corporate response to the coming change. Obviously, particular company circumstances may call for different courses of action. In preparing their own corporate programs, however, company headquarters executives and *Vorstand* members alike should bear in mind that an active—even aggressive—but not confrontation-oriented management posture will best serve their interests in the long run. Unlike their British or U.S. counterparts, the German unions have a remarkable record of entrepreneurial understanding and capability, thanks largely to the ample training they have received through *Aufsichtsrat* representation in large union owned enterprises like the Bank for Gemeinwirtschaft and Neueheimat. It is worth remembering that 25 years ago, German iron and steel industry executives visualized management lock-outs and other doomsday usurpations of authority when parity board representation was introduced. Even with that event, however, they managed to run their enterprises efficiently and to turn out higher profits than comparable private and nationalized companies in other countries.

In a very broad sense, Germany today is something of a "learning laboratory" for international managers. In the words of Walter Arendt: "German codetermination has been designed for the work force in German, but sooner or later it is bound to become the pattern for other modern European countries." When and if that should happen, U.S. companies with subsidiaries in Germany need not be caught unprepared.

50. Multinational Bargaining in Metals and Electrical Industries: Approaches and Prospects*

Richard L. Rowan and Herbert R. Northrup†

INTRODUCTION

The prospects for multinational collective bargaining have been widely discussed, and much has been made of the activities of various international labour bodies which have been directed toward achieving meetings between multinational companies and various coalitions representing unions in different countries.[1] The purpose of this article is to analyse reports of what has occurred in this regard in several metals industries—automobiles, farm machinery and construction equip-

* From the *Journal of Industrial Relations* (Australia), Vol. 17, No. 1, March 1975, pp. 1–29.

† Richard L. Rowan and Herbert R. Northrup are both professors of Industry and Co-Directors of the Industrial Research Unit, the Wharton School, University of Pennsylvania.

The authors would like to thank the numerous companies, unions and government officials in the United States and abroad for assistance in fact-gathering. The study, part of a larger work in the field, has been financed by the Labor Relations Council and the Research Advisory Group of the Wharton School.

[1] See, e.g., W. P. Hogan, "Multinational Firms, Labour Migration and Trade Flows," *The Journal of Industrial Relations*, Vol. 14 (September 1972), pp. 225–37; George Polites, "Multinational Corporations: The Employees' View," ibid., Vol. 15 (March 1973), pp. 64–74; I. A. Litvak and C. J. Maule, "The Union Response to International Corporations," and Karl F. Treckel, "The World Auto Councils and Collective Bargaining," in *Industrial Relations*, Vol. 11 (February 1972), pp. 62–79; Charles Levinson, *International Trade Unionism* (London: George Allen & Unwin Ltd, 1972); Duane Kujawa, *International Labor Relations Management in the Automotive Industry: A Comparative Study of Chrysler, Ford, and General Motors* (N.Y.: Praeger, 1971); Herbert R. Northrup and Richard L. Rowan, "Multinational Bargaining Activity: The Factual Record in Chemicals, Glass, and Rubber Tires," *Columbia Journal of World Business*, Vol. 9 (Spring 1974), pp. 112–24, and (Summer 1974), pp. 46–63; and Herbert R. Northrup and Richard L. Rowan, "Multinational Bargaining in Food and Allied Industries: Approaches and Prospects," *Wharton Quarterly*, Vol. 7 (Spring 1974), pp. 32–40.

ment, aerospace, and shipbuilding—and in the electrical machinery and electronics industries. The labour organizations involved are the International Metalworkers' Federation (IMF)—the largest and one of the oldest "international trade secretariats"[2] based in Geneva, Switzerland—and a relatively new organization, with which the IMF is often confused but with which it has no formal ties—the European Metalworkers' Federation in the Community (EMF), a Brussels-based European regional group. After a brief background on IMF policy development, we shall review its activities in the bargaining field and then turn to those of EMF, which has approached more closely the goal of leading a coalition of unions from various countries into bargaining sessions with multinational companies.

THE IMF ORGANIZATION FOR MULTINATIONAL BARGAINING

Despite the fact that it dates back to 1894 and was officially organized in 1904, the IMF did not move toward multinational bargaining approaches until the post-World War II years. Prior thereto, it was a socialist-oriented organization devoted to the exchange of information among European unions. As late as 1959, a history of IMF, written under U.S. Department of Labor auspices, devoted only two paragraphs to co-

[2] For succinct explanations of the organization of the world trade union movement and the role of the international trade secretariats, see the works of John P. Windmuller, particularly *Labor Internationals*, Bulletin 61 (Ithaca: N.Y. State School of Industrial and Labor Relations, Cornell University, 1969), and *International Trade Union Organizations: Structural, Functions, and Limitations*, Reprint No. 235, ibid., n.d.

cordinated bargaining potential across national boundaries.[3]

In 1949, however, the direction of IMF had commenced shifting. By then American unions were playing a key role in IMF for the first time. Under the leadership of Konrad Ilg, who in that year was both Secretary-General of IMF and head of the Swiss Metal and Watchmakers' Union, and backed energetically by the late Walter Reuther, then the newly elected President of the U.S. United Automobile Workers' Union, the IMF was restructured into industry departments. From its inception until his death in 1970, Reuther headed the Automotive Department, which, like those for steel, shipbuilding, and engineering, was organized in 1950. A department covering electrical industry employees was established in 1967.

The Automotive Department and the Auto Councils

The IMF Automotive Department has been influenced heavily by the United Automobile Workers since its formation in terms of both leadership and financial support. Personnel attached to the Automotive Department were originally led by Daniel Benedict, a former General Electric Company employee, who worked first as a UAW-IMF representative in South America, then, after serving as executive of the Automotive Department, became Assistant General Secretary of the IMF. The recent election of Herman Rebhan, formerly co-ordinator of the IMF World Auto Councils in Geneva and director of the UAW's International Affairs Department, as General Secretary of the IMF will probably strengthen the UAW's influence in the Automotive Department.

In 1962 the UAW established a Free World Labor Defense Fund which has been used in part to support IMF activities. The fund was created by a constitutional provision and financed by earnings on the investment of strike funds during 1962–64. By the end of 1964 a total of $4,346,221.49 had accumulated in the fund and the UAW International Executive Board decided to suspend further additions since income from

strike funds exceeded the Free World Labor budget. Disbursements continued to be made from the fund and a deficit was finally created in 1970 coinciding with a depleted UAW treasury following a long strike in the U.S. automobile industry. Deficit spending occurred from 1970 until the end of 1973. The financial report for the year ended December 31, 1973, shows a beginning deficit of $1,521,308.19 in the Defense Fund, financed by a transfer from the General Funds in the amount of $1,948,345.98. Disbursements for 1973 were at the lowest point since 1963 at $409,780.25. Confusion over the financing and disbursing of the fund led to its abolishment at the 1974 UAW Convention. Future disbursements for international affairs will be made through the General Funds.[4]

From the beginning Reuther urged the Automotive Department to organize itself for multinational bargaining by setting up separate subgroups for each major automotive concern, and thereby increasing communication and co-operation among unions dealing with a common employer. Thus, at the 1953 Paris meeting, he submitted a memorandum proposing "subcouncils to facilitate the exchange of ideas" that could "lay the basis for international coordination of collective bargaining with international companies."[5] This proposal was adopted, but acted upon very slowly. Studies were made, largely through UAW efforts, of labour conditions in Ford and General Motors plants throughout the world. European unions, however, appeared considerably less interested in multinational bargaining than did the UAW—perhaps fearful that it was a device to reduce the foreign threat to American car makers by raising their standards to American levels and thus equalizing American and European wage costs. At the 1957 IMF Automotive Department Conference, the UAW succeeded in getting a number of foreign unions to send representatives to the United States, partly at its expense, to be present during the 1958 American collective bargaining negotiations and to inspect U.S. practices and conditions in the automotive industry.[6] It was not, however, until the mid-1960s that the automotive councils were formally organized and began to operate as Reuther might have envisioned 15 years earlier.

---

[3] U.S. Department of Labor, Office of International Labor Affairs, *The International Metalworkers' Federation* (Washington: Government Printing Office, 1959), p. 64. See also Everett M. Kassalow, "The International Metalworkers' Federation and the World Automotive Industry: The Early Years, Another View of the Forest," paper presented at the International Industrial Relations Research Association 3d World Congress, London, September 3–7, 1973; and Treckel, *loc cit.*

[4] Financial data contained in reports of the UAW, *Labor Solidarity*, for years stated. See report of Emil Mazey in UAW, *Labor Solidarity*, July–August 1974, pp. 5 and 7, and financial report, p. 9.

[5] Kassalow, *International Metalworkers'*, p. 8.

[6] U.S. Department of Labor, *The International Metalworkers*, p. 17.

THE WORLD AUTO COUNCILS IN ACTION

At the 1964 Automotive Department meeting in Frankfurt, the IMF finally gave its formal commitment for the creation of world auto councils. Two years later at a meeting in Detroit, permanent councils were established for Ford, General Motors, and Chrysler. Since then six others have been organized: Volkswagen-Daimler Benz and British Leyland (1966), Renault-Peugeot (1971), and Toyota and Nissan (1973). A Fiat-Citroen Council was formed in 1971 and became the Fiat Council in 1973 when the two companies dissolved their partnership agreement.

Reuther made it clear at the 1966 Detroit meeting that the purpose of the auto councils was to further international union co-operation which would eventually lead to multinational collective bargaining:

When a GM worker discusses a problem at a bargaining table in Brazil or in Great Britain, in Canada, in Australia, in Germany, or in any other part of the world, he ought to know precisely what GM is doing about that kind of problem in every other part of the world. He should not be talking about vacation pay as though he were the only one dealing with that problem; he ought to know precisely what everybody else is doing about that demand. What is true about vacation pay is true about every other basic collective bargaining demand whether it concerns pensions, holidays, wage rates, production standards, etc., because only as we can bring our collective effort to bear upon these practical collective bargaining problems can we really begin to give meaning and purpose to the slogans of international trade union solidarity.[7]

Prior to the meeting, the UAW research department, with IMF and other union co-operation, had prepared detailed analyses of the leading automobile corporations' production, profits, plant locations, and union contract provisions. These company booklets have served as guides for automotive bargaining throughout the world. Company officials interviewed attest to their significance, pointing out that especially for unions in underdeveloped countries these booklets have led to increased aspirations and greater sophistication in demands and bargaining, and that evidence of a "Detroit psychology" and UAW and/or IMF advice is generally present, particularly in South American countries' negotiations, but also at those in various Asian countries as well.[8]

Publicity and Australian Intervention

At the 1966 Detroit meeting, Reuther forged another tactic that has been utilized not only by IMF groups but also by other secretariats: amplification of the significance of meetings with company officials in order to give the impression that multinational bargaining is close at hand. Arrangements were made for the delegates to tour facilities and to meet with the top labour relations personnel at Ford and General Motors. According to an IMF acount:

Although these were not collective bargaining sessions as such, delegates took the opportunity to make known a number of the stronger grievances, particularly those arising from the anti-union attitudes, unfair practices and reluctance to bargain on the part of company officials in various countries.[9]

The companies' version is that they agreed to the meetings most reluctantly, and only on the clear understanding that there would be no collective bargaining discussions. When the delegates began discussing issues at various foreign plants, the U.S. industrial relations personnel referred them to their respective home plants.[10] The net effect of the 1966 conclave was a propaganda coup for the IMF Auto Councils and a basic wariness on the part of General Motors and Ford to meet with international union groups.

Even before the 1966 meeting, the UAW evidenced its international concern by sending officials to Australia to support the case of the union representing employees of General Motors' Australian affiliate, General Motors-Holden's Pty Ltd. The Australian union demanded "a prosperity loading of $6 p.w. for some 17,000 employees of the company" is a case before Australia's Commonwealth Arbitration Court.[11] The Court denied the union position:

The union case had some unfortunate aspects: It followed the American precedent, especially observable in the vehicle industry, of "picking off" either the most vulnerable or the most prosperous employer in the field, obtaining a contract from that employer, and then following this up by claims for a similar contract with other employers in the same field. The origin of the dispute was a claim, backed by strike action, against GM-H two years ago, and this was reinforced by calling in aid the evidence of the regional director of the United Automobile Workers

---

[7] The IMF, Automotive Department, *World Company Councils: Auto Workers' Answer to World Company Power*, Geneva, 1967, p. 7.

[8] Interviews with major American automobile company officials, 1972–74.

[9] The IMF, Automotive Department, *World Company Councils*, p. 28.

[10] Interviews with company officials, and company transcript of meetings in authors' possession.

[11] The decision was handed down, September 12, 1966, and is found in 1966 A.I.L.R. Rep. 323.

Union most directly concerned with that union's relations with General Motors Corporation in the U.S., Mr. E. S. Patterson. Mr. Patterson's evidence was obviously meant to be the lynch-pin of the union's case, but it was bypassed by the Commission on the ground that the internal affairs of General Motors, whether in Australia or the U.S., were no concern of the Commission: Its main concern was with the principle of uniformity between employees doing the same class of work, the principle of comparative wage justice.[12]

General Motors corporate officials did not participate directly in the case, although they undoubtedly supplied information to their Holden affiliate from the wings. Their concern was that any appearance before the Commonwealth Commission would lend credence to the UAW claim that strings were pulled from Detroit and that if the Commission should have considered the total corporation profit picture not just its Australian operation in making its award, as the UAW and the Australian Vehicle Builders desired, a big step toward multinational bargaining would have occurred.[13]

Further Studies, Objectives, and Problems

Since the 1966 conclave, the IMF Automotive Department and the world auto councils have met on a regular basis. The Turin Conference in 1968 emphasized the need for regional coordination and the UAW commitment to raise standards in Latin American plants, and the general IMF support for harmonization of plants in the European Economic Community and Britain. Detailed data on production, bargaining, labour conditions, and collective bargaining agreement provisions were distributed to unions in the industry and, as noted, have influenced union demands and bargaining ever since.

At the 1971 London Conference, chaired by Leonard Woodcock, who succeeded to the presidency of the UAW upon Mr. Reuther's death, the delegates emphasized the need for common expiration dates of contracts, "so that the full weight of the totality of the firms' organized workers can be brought to bear upon each corporation, under conditions when all unions involved are free of contractual restrictions."[14]

This call for common contract termination dates for all unions within a multinational auto manufacturing company has been one of the auto councils' most fundamental and necessary goals. It is obvious, however, that multinational auto firms have been reluctant to permit this type of co-ordinated action and that they will undoubtedly continue to resist this IMF objective. Moreover, the different national bargaining systems make its realization difficult. Thus in Germany, national bargaining in the metals industries encompasses the automobile industry; in Britain, a variety of disparate unions are involved; in Australia, procedures under the arbitration laws must be considered; and in several countries, the systems of bargaining involve not only national or multiplant arrangements, but also local ones, with local unions, workers' councils, or stewards' committees. A sorting out of these arrangements to achieve common bargaining arrangements would be difficult even if the major automobile concerns were inclined to co-operate.

The problems on the union side are further illustrated by the dissimilarity in priorities among the objectives of the various auto council subgroups within the IMF Automotive Department which were enunciated at the 1971 conference. The General Motors council, for instance, listed hours of work and security of employment as their primary concerns, while the Ford council was more concerned with pension systems and health benefits. The Renault-Peugeot council, on the other hand, was more interested in safety control and rest periods. This lack of uniformity was evident in every council except Chrysler whose first priority was commensurate with that of General Motors, all of which serves to demonstrate further the immense problems involved in seeking a multinational agreement.

Strike Support and Company Meetings

The 1971 London Conference was held during the eighth week of a 9-week strike by 15 unions against Ford in England. Leonard Woodcock, President of the UAW, joined pickets outside the Ford Dagenham stamping and body plant for a brief appearance. On the last day of the conference, a declaration of solidarity with the strikers was issued.[15]

Ford management in Britain was not able to detect any immediate effects of the IMF con-

---

[12] See "Legislation and Decisions," *The Journal of Industrial Relations*, Vol. 8 (November 1966), pp. 301–2.

[13] These views are ascribed to General Motors by the authors after discussion with GM personnel.

[14] IMF, "Declaration of London IMF World Auto Company Councils, 23–25 March 1971," *Reports of the Secretariat and National Affiliates 1968–71, 22d International Metalworkers' Congress*, p. 137.

[15] IMF, "Declaration of Solidarity for the Strike of British Ford Workers," March 25, 1971.

ference or the declaration on the strike.[16] The parties reached a settlement at the end of the week following the IMF conference.

At a Ford World Auto Council meeting in Geneva on June 14, 1972, 16 union representatives from England, Germany, Belgium, Netherlands, France, and Ireland concluded that they would propose a meeting with the management of Ford of Europe to discuss items such as short and medium term investment, production plans of Ford Motor Company in Europe, differences in working conditions and fringe benefits, and the feasibility of common expiration dates for collective bargaining contracts in European Ford operations. Representatives were urged to do everything possible to bring the dates of regional and plant contracts in line with one another.[17]

IMF Secretary-General Ivar Noren then wrote a letter to the President of Ford of Europe requesting a meeting between management of Ford's European automotive operations, the IMF, and trade union representatives.[18] Ford of Europe declined the request, emphasizing the efforts that Ford national companies make to assure effective collective bargaining and consultative relationships at the national company level, and expressing the belief that such meetings would hinder and confuse local and national company relationships.[19]

In December 1972, several months after Ford of Europe declined to meet with the IMF, the UAW requested a meeting with representatives of the UAW, IMF, and trade unions in Belgium, Britain, and Germany that represent Ford's employees, to discuss production planning as it affects jobs and working conditions in Ford's European plants. Management at Ford's world headquarters in Dearborn, Michigan, refused this request, stating that it would not have ongoing meetings with the IMF. It was agreed, however, that Ford's management in Dearborn would meet with representatives from the IMF secretariat for the purpose of affording IMF officials an opportunity to present their reasons for believing that Ford's interest would be served by following a different course than the one they had announced.

The meeting was held on February 9, 1973, at Ford world headquarters in Dearborn. Representatives at this meeting included the IMF General Secretary, Assistant General Secretary, and the Co-ordinator of the World Automotive Councils; the UAW representatives included its President, the chief Ford union negotiator, and a representative from the UAW International Department; Ford's representatives included the Vice-President—Labor Relations, the Director of the Labor Affairs Office, and the liaison manager in overseas industrial relations.

The Dearborn meeting was brief with most of the time spent by the IMF in an attempt to explore Ford's intentions in regard to investments abroad. No commitment was made by Ford to hold such further meetings.[20] Subsequent to this meeting, Ford of Europe was approached in May 1974 by the trade union side of the British "Ford" National Joint Negotiating Committee on behalf of the IMF to discuss the company's European investment strategy and, in particular, the anticipated effects of building a new plant in Spain. Ford's British management responded to the request maintaining the view that the matter could be discussed by British union/company representatives in the joint negotiating committee. The chairman of Ford of Europe has agreed to meet informally with local union and company managers in preparation for a proffered meeting by Ford of Britain's managing director with the National Joint Negotiating Committee. As of November 8, 1974, these meetings have not been arranged, but the IMF World Council meeting in London on November 4–5, 1974, apparently encouraged the British union officials to accept Ford of Britain's proposal.

Burton Bendiner, co-ordinator of the IMF World Auto Councils, announced at the IMF congress in Stockholm in July 1974 that "In Europe trade unionists will meet the director of Ford European subsidiaries. . . . The discussion at Ford's will concentrate on investments by this multinational in dictatorships."[21] An IMF Ford Auto Council meeting has been scheduled for November 4 and 5, 1974, in London, and the IMF states in its September 1974 *News* that "High on the agenda will be a discussion of the Company's increased investment in a new plant now under construction in Spain, where the repressive government is making collective bargaining difficult. There is a possibility of an informal meeting with Ford of Europe management to

[16] Interviews, London, England, and Dearborn, Michigan, USA, 1972–73.

[17] *IMF News,* No. 24, June 1972, p. 2.

[18] IMF, *Press Release from the IMF Auto Councils,* Circular No. 37, June 1972; see also *The Times* (London), June 15 and 16, 1972.

[19] Company interviews; and Robert Copp, "The Labor Affairs Function in a Multinational Firm," *Labor Law Journal,* Vol. 24 (August 1974), especially pp. 457–58. Mr. Copp is Ford's liaison manager in international industrial relations.

[20] Copp, "Labor Affairs Function."

[21] *IMF News,* No. 23, July 1974, p. 4.

discuss long term production policies of the company in Europe, as these affect members' jobs and income security."[22]

In addition to calling for a meeting with Ford, Bendiner announced that "This year a work session of the Fiat World Auto Council will be followed by an interview with Fiat Director General Giovanni Agnelli. The discussion with Agnelli will cover the overall production plans in the worldwide plants of Fiat as they affect the jobs of members of our affiliates and working conditions in these plants."[23] On September 11, 1974, the IMF postponed the Fiat World Auto Council meeting scheduled to be held in Rome on November 18–20, 1974, because of "internal problems in Italy at present and at the suggestion of the Italian affiliate." Also IMF stressed the importance of "the complicated Italian labour situation involving the unity of the metal unions, including our affiliates and the Communist metal-workers."[24] Fiat claims that as of September 13, 1974, they had not received any official request for a talk with the IMF.[25]

Negotiation Visitations— World Agricultural Implement Council

In view of the interest of the world automobile councils in developing multinational contacts with managements, it might have been expected that in the 1973 contract negotiations the UAW would have some foreign visitors present. Apparently this did not occur, although during the General Motors negotiations an Australian unionist was in Detroit. He allegedly participated in UAW caucuses, but did not appear at the actual negotiations.

At the 1973 key farm equipment and construction machinery negotiations, in which the UAW is also the union representative, an international flavour was added on a purely *pro forma* basis. The UAW addressed separate letters to John Deere, International Harvester, and Caterpillar Tractor, advising each company that they had invited foreign unionists as visitors for the opening session, and requesting that they be given a plant tour. For Caterpillar, those present included representatives from the Belgian Metal-workers' Union, the French General Federation

of Metalworkers, the National Officer for the Metal Industry of the British Municipal Workers' Union, and the IMF Co-ordinator of the World Auto Councils; and for Harvester and Deere, representatives from Force Ouvrière, France, IG Metall, Germany, and the Amalgamated Union of Engineering Workers, Britain.

In each case, the visitors remained only the first day, or half-day, were given a plant tour, and departed. In no case did they participate in negotiations, but they had an opportunity to address the union's negotiating committees in advance of bargaining. Their presence would seem to indicate a greater IMF and/or UAW multi-national interest in these large concerns and their industries. Certainly IMF gave that impression in its expansive press release, which also noted the existence of a World Agricultural Implement Council that had met in Brussels in 1972.[26]

PROSPECTS FOR AUTOMOBILE MULTINATIONAL BARGAINING

As of this writing, the IMF and its constituent bodies in the automotive industry have moved toward multinational co-ordination of bargaining only by exchanging information and increasing somewhat the commonality of some demands put forward in separate local or national bargaining negotiations. Even here, demands maintain an overwhelming national flavour. Attempts to develop common contract termination dates, to influence national wage policy, or to engage in meaningful discussions with companies on a multinational basis, have been largely unsuccessful.

Unlike the public relations activities of some international trade secretariats, the IMF's World Auto Council co-ordinator, Burton Bendiner, has been "against romanticising accomplishments especially towards 'international collective bargaining.'"[27] In an article analyzing the problems of effectuating multinational bargaining in the automobile industry, Bendiner states that "The work of the World Auto Councils has occasionally given rise to press reports that international collective bargaining is just around the corner or that global union contracts, covering all of General Motors, Ford, Fiat, or Volkswagen plants in a single country, are imminent. That is a naive

[22] *IMF News*, No. 28, September 1974, p. 1.

[23] *IMF News*, No. 23, July 1974, p. 4.

[24] Memo to affiliated organizations, IMF, September 11, 1974, and correspondence with IMF, January 13, 1975.

[25] Letters to one of the authors from Fiat, September 13, 1974.

[26] Information from companies involved; and "A 'First' Scored in Agricultural Implement Company Negotiations as Union Participant Observers Attend Caterpillar Negotiations from Overseas Plants," release from IMF World Auto Councils, Circular No. 47, July 13, 1973.

[27] Letter to one of the authors from Burton Bendiner, August 8, 1974.

and somewhat hasty conclusion."[28] Bendiner insists that "our main route at present involves greater coordinated action and cooperation among unions in resolving problems of labor organization vis-a-vis the multinational automotive companies."[29]

Management Policy

Nevertheless, one should not write off the potential for multinational bargaining. Several automobile companies have rationalized their operations so that the assembly of vehicles in one country is dependent on parts manufactured in another. This has been especially true in small countries, or in areas such as the underdeveloped countries where demand is insufficient to support a totally integrated operation. Elimination of tariff barriers has caused the major American companies to integrate their U.S. and Canadian operations; the expanding European Economic Community is encouraging the same process; and world competition for markets in Asia, Africa, and Latin America is seeing companies locate central regional parts facilities and national assembly plants in order to compete at the lowest costs.[30]

If this regional and world rationalization process continues, it could cause major automobile companies to rethink their opposition to multinational bargaining as means of avoiding a series of strikes which, under such a production arrangement, would shut down a whole region's operations. Conceivably, it might seem preferable to management to risk one major interruption through multinational bargaining rather than several such production stoppages resulting from a number of national strikes. This is, of course, an argument advanced by IMF and the adherents of multinational bargaining, such as those in the European Economic Community staff organization.[31]

There are, however, serious arguments against such a change in managerial philosophy. One has already been noted: The varied and complex national bargaining arrangements make it difficult to conceive how a multinational arrangement could be put together other than by creating a tri-level structure. This would involve multinational discussions, followed by national ones, and in turn by local arrangements. The companies' belief that this would add a complicating factor which would expand the potential scope of stoppages without compensating relief therefrom seems difficult to refute.

The experience under the bargaining system in America appears to add credence to the argument against widening of bargaining coverage. General Motors, Ford, and Chrysler each bargain on a national basis for overall economic and policy issues; then they bargain with local unions on a multitude of local issues involving plant rules, seniority, etc. Initially, national settlements meant a virtual guarantee against local stoppages. More and more, however, regardless of national settlements, strikes have occurred over local issues, sometimes with far-reaching effects on total company production, as local union officials attempt to gain for their members what is important locally, insignificant nationally, but costly, or potentially so, to the corporations.

It is not far-fetched to envision multinational bargaining followed by a few years of labour peace and then a gradual breakdown, as local and national interests, tired of having their desires and aspirations "swept under the rug" by multinational negotiators who see only the large view, institute an increasing number of strikes to satisfy their constituents. It is this vision, combined with a fear of flexibility loss and bargaining power decline, which causes management in the automobile industry to examine cautiously the IMF's enticements down the multinational bargaining road.

Cracks in Union Solidarity

The UAW has traditionally been the most internationally minded union in America; as noted, it provided the intellectual and financial basis for establishing IMF multinational bargaining policy and the organization to implement this policy in the automobile and in related industries. Until 1974, the UAW had not supported the protectionist policy which in recent years has been advocated by the AFL-CIO and many of its constituent unions. The UAW even opposed the AFL-CIO sponsored Burke-Hartke Bill, which

<hr>

[28] Burton Bendiner, "Unions' Expanding International Coordination," *Harvard Business Review*, March–April 1974, pp. 12–14, 16.

[29] Ibid.

[30] For a vivid description of the Asian struggle for markets and the impact on multinational integration, see Louis Kraar, "Detroit Finds New Routes across the Pacific," *Fortune*, Vol. 88 (October 1973), pp. 164–7, 208, 210.

[31] See, e.g., the article by Jack Peel, Director—Industrial Relations, EEC-Commission, "Industrial Relations: The Bridge or the Barrier," *Industrial Relations—Europe Newsletter*, Vol. 1 (July 1973) supplement, in which he states: "The next priority is to forge the machinery for achieving collective agreements on a European scale between workers and employers in the same industries throughout the nine countries."

would impose numerous restrictions on foreign investment by American corporations, as well as curtail imports. Nevertheless, the UAW responded to the early 1974 layoffs in the American automobile industry by having a bill introduced into Congress that would place limiting quotas on small car imports, which comprise the bulk of all imports. Such a bill would seriously affect Volkswagen and the Japanese car makers. The bill did not receive serious consideration in the 1974 congressional session, but could be revised as a result of the worsening automobile sales slump.[32]

German automobile unionists have responded to the current depressed automobile sales picture with at least as much nationalistic fervour. Union representatives on the Volkswagen supervisory board have strongly opposed the management's plan to establish a plant in the United States and have been supported by government representatives on the board who are aligned with the unions politically. (Volkswagen is 16 percent owned by the German Federal Government, 20 percent by the State of Lower Saxony, both of which have Social Democratic Governments.) The German unions make no secret that their opposition is based on a fear of loss of jobs to the United States.

These obvious departures from international solidarity apparently have not as yet weakened automotive unity among unions of the three largest automotive producing companies. Leonard Woodstock visited Germany in July 1974 and supported the German union position. In an interview, Woodcock said the "temporary crisis" in the automobile industry has made the "primary" responsibility of German auto makers its own people. Woodcock had earlier favoured a move to the United States by VW.[33]

Herman Rebhan, then director of the UAW International Department, visited Japan in March 1974, apparently to urge the Japanese to restrict exports to the United States, without known results. In the 1974 IMF Congress, the American, German, and Japanese automobile unions supplied most of the votes to elect Rebhan General

Secretary and Eugen Loderer of IG Metall, Germany, President. Rebhan defeated Daniel Benedict, another American. Benedict had fallen from UAW favour but was supported by a majority of labour organizations, 39 for Benedict and 30 for Rebhan. The large automotive unions and their allies, however, had sufficient votes to win handily.

THE IMF AND THE ELECTRICAL INDUSTRY

The pattern of IMF organization in the automobile industry has been copied in electrical machinery and electronics. An Electrical-Electronics Department was established in 1967, headed by Paul Jennings, President of the U.S. International Union of Electrical, Radio and Machine Workers (IUE), an AFL-CIO affiliate. Within that framework, world councils have been organized to bring together unions representing employees of particular companies, as was done for automobile unionists. Most active of these councils have been those representing unions in General Electric and Honeywell Inc. plants. In addition, an IMF-led group has met with Brown Boveri.

General Electric Company

The General Electric council held its first International Union Conference in Bogota, Colombia, April 18–19, 1969, a second one in London in 1971, and a third in New York City in March 1973. The 1969 and 1973 meetings were timed to antedate opening of triennial negotiations between General Electric, the largest U.S. and world electrical machinery company, and a coalition of unions of which IUE has the largest membership in GE Messrs. Jennings and Benedict have repeatedly stressed that their aim is to include unions from other countries within this coalition.[34] They have succeeded in doing so to the extent of having foreign unionists attend a few negotiating meetings as non-participating visitors.

Over the objections of General Electric and other companies, National Labor Relations Board rulings, sustained in the courts,[35] permit unions certified to represent a particular bargaining unit to include representatives of other unions or other

---

[32] See "The UAW Wants a Lid on Small-Car Imports," *Business Week*, April 6, 1974, pp. 20–1. The bill H.R. 13920 was introduced in Congress on April 4, 1974. See *Daily Labor Report*, No. 66, April 4, 1974, p. A-10, for story and text. Also, see "Labor Unrest and Strikes, Once Rare, Become More Frequent as Workers Push Demands" and "VW Talks with Other Firms of Sharing Equity Stake in Possible U.S. Auto Plant," *The Wall Street Journal*, March 6 and October 2, 1974, respectively; also "VW Beetle Begins Final Bows," *The New York Times*, June 6, 1974.

[33] "Woodcock Warns VW Not to Build in U.S.," *International Herald Tribune*, July 13–14, 1974, p. 9.

[34] See, e.g., "Bargaining Tables that Circle Earth," *IUE News*, February 4, 1971, p. 7.

[35] *General Electric Co.*, 173 NLRB 253 (1968): enforced *General Electric v. NLRB*, 412 F.2d 512 (2d Cir., 1969).

bargaining units on their bargaining committees provided the fiction is maintained that these outside representatives are representing the unit then bargaining. General Electric deals with two unions on a multiplant, national basis: the IUE, and the United Electrical, Radio and Machine Workers (UE), from which the IUE seceded in 1949 when the UE's communist domination caused its expulsion from the CIO. In addition, GE deals with numerous other unions on a local basis. To form a united coalition front, representatives of the unions which have bargaining rights on a local basis have sat in on the national IUE negotiations since 1966.[36]

In 1969, Daniel Benedict also sat in on a few of the GE-IUE negotiating sessions. He did not attempt to participate in any discussions.[37] In 1972, a meeting of the General Electric World Council was held, as noted, just prior to the commencement of IUE-GE negotiations. The IUE asked if the world council group could attend the initial negotiating session. Since IUE could have brought them in any case *as IUE representatives*, and General Electric could not then legally object provided the outside unionists conformed to the court interpretation in their conduct, as discussed below, the company gave its assent.

Foreign unionists attending the opening of General Electric negotiations on March 22, 1973, included those from West Germany, South Africa, Mexico, Colombia, Venezuela, and Argentina, besides Benedict. In addition, German and Mexican union representatives attended the UE negotiations that day. Both IUE and UE groups had their pictures taken with the company negotiators. No substantive discussions occurred on the first negotiating day for the 1972 contract; the international contingent made no speeches nor otherwise participated in the negotiations and did not appear again at negotiations.

Prior to the 1972 negotiations, Jennings told *The Wall Street Journal* that the forthcoming appearance of the IMF council members from abroad was " 'a very important symbol' to re-

mind GE of the backing that the negotiators have."[38] Certainly, it was symbolic only. General Electric is not strong in Europe, and the IMF council is largely a Central and South American group. It is difficult to believe that employees in those countries would give up income to support their much better compensated brothers in the north. What has been important to unionists there is the technical and financial support from U.S. unions and the IMF which, as in the case of the automobile unions, has resulted in greater bargaining sophistication in dealing with General Electric within their countries. The only overt foreign support for the IUE cause in relation to General Electric, exclusive of Benedict's and the foreign union representatives' "symbolic" presence, occurred during the 1969–70 strike when the IMF "made a small token contribution in Swiss francs to the IUE strike fund . . . [and] the Japanese electrical workers council contributed $5,000; the presentation took place at a picket line in Newark, N.J."[39] Although one author termed the Japanese action as "perhaps more significant"[40] than that of the IMF, realistically, both appear symbolic at most.

If, however, the IMF, or any other group, would attempt to alter the bargaining structure with General Electric by insisting that GE bargain about matters pertaining to plants not included within the IUE bargaining unit (or any other legally defined bargaining unit for which those bargaining were the duly certified agent), such an attempt would be contrary to the court order which has compelled General Electric to admit outsiders chosen by the IUE to the bargaining sessions. For the law, as interpreted by the courts, requires that the outsiders maintain the legal fiction that they are IUE representatives and that they bargain only for matters pertaining to the IUE bargaining unit. If, at an IUE-GE bargaining session, union representatives persisted in attempting to bargain about, for example, labour conditions in the General Electric plants in Colombia, the company could not only refuse to discuss the matter, but would be able to bring a refusal to bargain in good faith charge against the American union involved.[41]

The General Electric operations in Colombia

[36] For the background on this coalition movement, and on General Electric employee relations, see William N. Chernish, *Coalition Bargaining*, Industrial Research Unit Study No. 45 (Philadelphia: University of Pennsylvania Press, 1969), esp. chap. 6; and Herbert R. Northrup, *Boulwarism* (Ann Arbor: Bureau of Industrial Relations, University of Michigan, 1964).

[37] In the *IUE News*, February 4, 1971, it was stated that Benedict ". . . sat in on several GE negotiations sessions. . . ." In July 1971, the *IUE News* reported that Benedict "participated in the 1969–70 GE and W[estinghouse] coordinated bargaining in the U.S. . . ." The first statement is accurate.

[38] Bryon E. Calame, "Import Curbs Could Hurt U.S. Labor's Ties to Unions Abroad, AFL-CIO Officials Say," *The Wall Street Journal*, February 27, 1973, p. 4.

[39] Richard L. Barovick, "Labor Reacts to Multinationalism," *Columbia Journal of World Business*, Vol. 5 (July–August 1970), p. 42.

[40] Ibid.

[41] This charge would be brought pursuant to Section 8(b)(3) of the Taft-Hartley Act.

are a favourite source of IMF publicity relating to the company because a former plant manager there permitted an international union committee and Benedict to tour the facility. The unionists claimed to have found conditions below those elsewhere. In an interview with the *New York Times,* Benedict claimed that IUE "confronted" GE repeatedly during the 1969–70 negotiations with alleged GE malpractices in Colombia and it was "too embarrassing" for GE, so that the practices ceased.[42] The reporter did not contact the company, whose negotiators told the authors that Colombia or Bogota were not mentioned in the negotiations; that one day a claim was made of poor treatment of workers outside of the United States, to which the reply was made that the company negotiators were familiar with U.S. but not foreign laws; and that no other like reference could be found in the negotiation minutes. The company denied the allegations reported in the *New York Times.*[43]

The IUE and IMF personnel have claimed several other international actions, none of which we have been able to confirm. For example, it has been alleged that during a 1965 strike at GE's Rome, Georgia, plant, IMF pressure prevented GE from sending "struck work" overseas.[44] The company denies that any such interference occurred or was a factor in the strike. An IMF regional paper merely stated that Jennings sent a cable asking the IMF for support and that the "IMF" asked Brother Jennings to assure the strikers of its decided support."[45]

During a 1971 strike at a GE plant in Ireland, John Shambo, a Schenectady, New York, IUE official, who also heads the IUE General Electric Conference Board, visited the strikers after attending a Zurich union meeting. According to Jennings, this resulted in GE not only recognizing the Irish union, "but also other unions in other parts of the world who saw this fight as their own."[46] In fact, the Irish Transport and General Workers' Union put up a picket line at GE's Shannon, Ireland, plant after it had agreed to a representation election and was rejected by the employees as a representative by a 3-to-1 majority. Despite acts of violence, the picket line failed

to deter employees from working. After some months, the issue was settled through mediation by the Irish Minister for Labour with the company agreeing to meet with the union officials a few times per year to discuss plant conditions generally. The union was not recognized as a bargaining agent.[47]

Claims such as those made in reference to the Irish situation and unsupported statements in various sources, such as "The IUE . . . has intervened frequently with U.S. embassies on behalf of Latin American unions negotiating with General Electric,"[48] cloud the fact that multinational bargaining is nowhere near at hand at General Electric. The fact that GE is not a major operator in the European Economic Community and that its plants in South America continue to avoid the union attempts to achieve common expiration dates, all indicate that it may be many years before such bargaining is approached, whatever symbolic acts occur in the ensuing few years. Moreover, the active support of the Burke-Hartke Bill, and of other protective tariff or quota legislation by the IUE,[49] raises serious questions about the solidarity of unions involved in the GE or other IMF Electrical Department councils.

Honeywell Inc.

The IMF has designated Honeywell as a prime target for its first worldwide collective bargaining agreement.[50] It has a very active Honeywell World Council which, however, has been unable to obtain a meeting with Honeywell management. It has had regular meetings since 1971 attended by representatives from France, Germany, Italy, Netherlands, United Kingdom, and the United States.[51] After the initial meeting in March 1971 in Geneva, Switzerland, an IMF representative journeyed to Minneapolis, site of Honeywell's headquarters, to advance the idea of a meeting

---

[42] Clyde H. Farnsworth, "Big Business Spurs Labor toward a World Role," the *New York Times,* December 26, 1972.

[43] Company interviews, January 25, 1973.

[44] *IUE News,* September 29, 1966, p. 12.

[45] *Metal,* April–May–June 1965. This is the organ of the IMF Regional Office for Latin America and the Caribbean, published in Mexico City.

[46] Speech before the World Conference of General Electric—Bogota, Colombia, April 18, 1969, p. 6.

[47] Based upon documents and interviews in 1969, 1973, and 1974.

[48] Barovick, "Labor Reacts," p. 43. This article, by the Washington editor of *Business Abroad* and *International Reports,* repeats many exaggerated and unsupported claims of union successes with multinational companies.

[49] See, e.g., Calame, "Import Curbs"; and articles in the *IUE News,* which have taken a very strong protectionist line for several years.

[50] See Monty Meth, "World Unions Pick Their Target," *Daily Mail* (London), April 15, 1971; and Ian McGregor, "Multinational Companies Will Be under Spotlight at Metalworkers Congress," *The Times* (London), October 25, 1971.

[51] See, e.g., *IMF News,* No. 33, September 1972, p. 4; and No. 34, September 1973, p. 2.

with Honeywell, but the company declined to meet with him.[52]

In 1973, *The Wall Street Journal* carried a story indicating that Honeywell would deal with the IMF coalition, purportedly based on an interview with its Honeywell Bull subsidiary in Paris:

It'll take three to five years for them to really get together. But there are distinct signs that it's coming, says a spokesman for Honeywell Bull. . . .

One distinct sign pointing toward the future is that Honeywell, which has so far dealt strictly with national unions on labor questions, now says it is prepared in principle to talk with unions on an international basis.[53]

Honeywell emphatically denies this report, and attempted without success to have *The Wall Street Journal* publish this statement issued the next day:

Honeywell today denied a report published in *The Wall Street Journal* on April 23 that it agreed in principle to talk with unions on a multinational basis. The Company's policy continues to be to deal with a union only in regard to the bargaining unit which that particular union is certified to represent.[54]

Honeywell did have one brush with the IMF during a strike in its French Bull subsidiary in late 1972 and early 1973. Like many walkouts in France and Italy, this strike was not a complete one. About 50 percent of the workforce would report one day, 30 percent another day, etc. *The Wall Street Journal* reported the union version of what happened in the same article in which it incorrectly stated Honeywell's bargaining policy. Its story maintained that Honeywell sought to import workers during the strike from other European countries, but that none came because they were advised not to by IMF affiliates.[55]

In actual fact, Honeywell did import workers from Cologne, West Germany, but sent them home after about ten days following a threat by IG Metall, their German union, that "something would be organized" if they remained in Paris.[56] Soon thereafter, the strike was settled when

agreement was reached between Honeywell Bull and the Communist Confédération Général du Travail (CGT) which left the IMF affiliate and Honeywell World Council member, the now deconfessionalized Christian union, Confédération Française Démocratique du Travail (CFDT), a much smaller union, little to do but to accept the results.[57]

In the United States, Honeywell operates a sizable number of plants non-union and bargains individually with various unions in others on a strictly local basis. At its largest plant in Minneapolis, the bargaining agent is the Teamsters' Union, which is not affiliated with IMF and has not joined other U.S. unions that are attempting to alter Honeywell's bargaining policies.

In January 1974, however, the President of the Teamsters of Minneapolis Joint Council 32 wrote the President of Honeywell requesting again that Honeywell agree to a meeting with representatives of the IMF. The request further noted that it was being transmitted at the suggestion of the Secretary-Treasurer of the International Brotherhood of Teamsters who had recently been designated a vice-president of another international trade secretariat, the International Federation of Chemical and General Workers Union (ICF). Honeywell declined again, citing its fundamental philosophy of placing primary labour relations philosophy at the local level.[58]

In France and Italy, IMF affiliated unions are minority ones. The dominant French union, as noted, both nationally and at Bull plants there, is affiliated with the Communist CGT. In Italy, two unions affiliated with the Confederazione Italiana Sindicato Lavoratori (CISL) and the Unione Italiana del Lavoro (UIL) are members of the IMF-Honeywell council. Both are much smaller in Italy and in Honeywell plants than the Confederazione Generale Italiana del Lavoro (CGIL), the Communist union. All three are now working together under Communist leadership. Thus in the three key countries where Honeywell operates—the U.S., France, and Italy —the affiliates of the IMF-Honeywell World Council are in a minority representation position. Obviously, this weakens the council's potential to achieve multinational bargaining.

---

[52] Letter to one of authors from Honeywell executive, January 25, 1972.

[53] Neil Ulman, "Talk of the Globe. Multinational Firms Face a Growing Power: Multinational Unions," *The Wall Street Journal*, April 23, 1973, p. 1.

[54] Supplied to one of the authors by Charles E. Brown, Vice-President, Honeywell Inc., by letter dated April 24, 1973.

[55] Ulman, "Talk of the Globe."

[56] Interview, Paris, August 1973.

[57] *IMF News*, No. 6, February 1973, p. 2. The claim of IMF that the "most militant" of the CFDT stayed out and won additional demands is denied by the company, and does not seem realistic in view of CFDT's small size and relative weakness.

[58] Interviews, company personnel, January and March, 1974.

Other U.S. Electrical Companies

Although Westinghouse Electric Corporation, the second largest American concern in this industry, is more broadly based in Europe than is General Electric, it has not been the target of any significant multinational union activity. In 1969, during the period when Daniel Benedict sat in on a few General Electric negotiations, he visited Pittsburgh, the headquarters of Westinghouse, while negotiations were in progress but did not sit in on the negotiations.[59] In 1972, no international unionists attended Westinghouse negotiations, nor, as far as we are able to determine, visited Pittsburgh while they were in progress.

Texas Instruments, which operates non-union in the United States, is another company that the IMF, and particularly Benedict, has claimed has been forced to act because of IMF pressures. In a *New York Times* interview, it was reported that:

Some 1,400 Curaçao [sic] women integrated circuit workers wanted to organize a union in the new Texas Instruments plant; the company was opposed and the women struck last September. Workers at the company's plants in West Germany, Italy, and the Netherlands supported them by refusing production transfers and after two weeks the company gave in to the women.[60]

The company maintains that there was no stoppage at Curaçao. When some supervisors imported from South America tried to take over an existing union, the company shut down for vacation, sent the supervisors home, and has since negotiated amicably with the union. The only union pressure in Europe was an exchange of "solidarity" telegrams between leaders in Curaçao and Europe with no impact or publicity in Europe.[61]

IMF joined with another international trade secretariat, the International Union of Food, Drink and Allied Workers' Associations (IUF), to sponsor "a working party" meeting for unions dealing with the International Telephone and Telegraph Company (ITT). Twenty delegates from nine countries met in Geneva on July 6, 1972, to launch an ITT council and to hear reports on such matters as company structure and finances. Emphasis in the resolutions passed by the delegates was on the exchange of information and opposition to work transfer from one country to another.[62] Apparently nothing since has developed. ITT has a firm policy of local bargaining and would oppose multinational union approaches.

Brown Boveri

Effective January 1, 1970, Brown Boveri, the large Swiss-based heavy electrical machinery concern, announced a general management reorganization in part centralizing managerial control over some operations that were formerly highly decentralized. Later in 1970, IMF's Daniel Benedict telephoned the company headquarters in Baden, Switzerland, requesting to pay a "visite de politesse" in order to become acquainted with the new organization of the company. The company agreed to the meeting without ascertaining what the proposed agenda might be or who would represent IMF. Company management discovered only a few days before September 4, 1970, the day of the meeting, that Benedict and Karl Casserini, IMF economist, would be accompanied by members of union and workers' committees from the various European countries in which Brown Boveri has operating facilities, and that the IMF agenda covered basic employee relations and investment policies of the company.[63] A previous informal meeting between IMF officials and Brown Boveri representatives had included no national unions or plant work representatives.[64]

Besides Messrs. Benedict and Casserini, the IMF delegation included one union and one Brown Boveri plant worker committee representative each from Germany, Norway, and Austria, the secretaries of the Swiss Metal and Watchmakers' Unions plus one worker committeeman from the Baden plant, one representative each from the French CFDT and the Force Ouvrière, and one each from the Italian CISL and the UILM. The IMF proposed agenda included the following:

International policy of the Brown Boveri Group and its repercussions on the management and labour organization of its member companies.

---

[59] According to the *IUE News* ("Bargaining Talks that Circle Earth," February 4, 1971, p. 7), "In last year's GE and Westinghouse negotiations, Dan Benedict . . . sat in on several GE negotiating sessions . . . and was in Pittsburgh during some of the *W* talks."

[60] Farnsworth, "Big Business."

[61] Telephone interview, January 23, 1973.

[62] *IMF News*, No. 27, July 1972, p. 2; IUF, *Documents of the Secretariat, 17th Congress, Item 5: Report on Activities—8 Multinational Companies*, 1973, p. V-8/18.

[63] This section is based on communications and interviews with company and IMF personnel.

[64] See *IMF News*, No. 33, 1969; No. 30, September 1970.

Basic mission and major tasks of the newly created Group Staff, Management Development.

Business prospects and possible implications on employment as a result of the new organization.

Personnel policy and social security plans in different Brown Boveri factories.

Personnel and social problems connected with mergers and acquisitions in which Brown Boveri might be involved.

Efforts to put everyone on salary.

Possibilities of future negotiations on specific problems aiming at a better information of IMF on BBC's business policy and its consequences on the labour side; possibilities of continuous consultations.

The meeting was relatively short and most of the topics were discussed only in a general way. Both parties attest to the friendly atmosphere which prevailed at the meeting, but no additional meetings have been held or scheduled. The reason, as in the case of Philips (discussed later), is apparently the different objectives of the parties.

In its press release concerning the meeting, IMF stated that there was "agreement to meet yearly and when important problems arose, to renew contacts."[65] Brown Boveri management, however, states that:

No promises were made, especially there was no agreement on future negotiations or regular consultations. . . . A subsequent press release by the IMF created some disturbances not only in Brown Boveri subsidiaries but also in other business circles, because the announcement made believe that our top management had agreed to institutionalize meetings and talks at the level of the IMF.[66]

Perhaps the key to this disagreement lies more in the different objectives of the parties than in what occurred. The IMF makes no secret of the fact that it regards such meetings as an initial step toward multiplant bargaining. The company, however, is dubious of the efficacy of meetings with this objective. Our impression is that the company is particularly concerned at inferences that it is engaged in a collective bargaining relationship with IMF and that decisions concerning plant employee relations have resulted from the September 1970 meeting. It claims to have taken no such action and believes that claims made otherwise have been "harmful."

As an example of such claims, the company notes that between April 1970 and April 1971 it put all Swiss blue collar employees on salary

with all rights of salaried workers. In addition, hours have been made variable with considerable employee choice. The company told the authors that "The relevant management decision was the result of an intensive study which lasted several years and had absolutely nothing to do with IMF's visit."[67] The changes were, of course, discussed with union representatives at the national level.

IMF did not take direct credit for this change, but, in the *IMF News*, reported that it was done "in the framework of negotiations between plant representatives of the Swiss Metal and Watchmakers' Union and the Brown Boveri Company. . . ."[68] Charles Levinson, Secretary-General of the ICF, also attributed these innovations to "recent negotiations" between the Swiss unions and the company.[69] The inference in these reports that it was not the company initiative apparently makes Brown Boveri management wary of future meetings. Such meetings are, of course, desired by IMF, not only as a step toward multinational bargaining but also because with Brown Boveri headquartered in a non-European Economic Community country, the IMF is exerting coordinating leadership rather than, as in the case of Philips and Fokker-VFW, the European Metalworkers' Federation in the Community. The latter, of course, is affiliated with the European Trade Union Confederation and maintains only "fraternal relationships" with IMF, as discussed in a later section of this article.

IMF Electrical Industry Activities— Conclusions and Implications

The IMF has thus established the union organizational framework for bargaining on a multinational basis in the electrical machinery industry as it has in automobiles. It has made what it regards as the initial step toward bargaining— limited contact between its multinational union committees and major companies. Will these admittedly "symbolic" meetings grow into something more substantial? Perhaps, but it does not appear that any such developments are on the near horizon.

There is, first of all, no inclination among electrical machinery concerns which have been the target of IMF ambitions to accede to a multinational bargaining arrangement. Besides the rea-

---

[65] *IMF News*, No. 30, September 1970, p. 2.

[66] Letter to one of the authors from Dr. G. Bütikofer, Director, Brown Boveri & Cie, October 23, 1973.

[67] Letter to one of the authors, October 23, 1973.

[68] *IMF News*, No. 211, December 1970, p. 1.

[69] Charles Levinson, *International Trade Unionism*, Ruskin House Series in Trade Union Studies (London: George Allen & Unwin Ltd, 1972), pp. 320–21.

sons for opposing such arrangements discussed in the previous analysis of the automobile industry situation, electrical concerns lack the integrated production which might encourage broader bargaining boundaries. Such companies produce a wide variety of products in various facilities. Although there is some plant interdependence, a strike in one does not have the same impact that a shutdown of an auto parts facility has on automobile assembly plants. Consequently, electrical machinery companies on the IMF target list see nothing to be gained by acceding to IMF aspirations and much to be lost. They may be expected to continue to oppose multinational bargaining.

There is another basic reason why IMF is not likely to accomplish its objective in the near future. In the European Economic Community, where the climate is most favourable for possible bargaining arrangements, the IMF finds itself in a secondary position. There the dynamics of the movement have been seized by the regional organization, the European Metalworkers' Federation in the Community (EMF). As our discussion below demonstrates, it is EMF that has moved closest to the union goal.

THE EMF AND MULTINATIONAL BARGAINING

In 1963, unions in the various metals industries located in the European Economic Community countries formed the Metal Committee of the European Confederation of Free Trade Unions in the Community (ECFTU). The Metal Committee thus maintained a relationship with the International Confederation of Free Trade Unions (ICFTU) through the ECFTU, but no direct affiliation with the IMF, although the latter apparently supported the organization of the committee.[70]

In 1973, unions in the expanded EEC formed the European Trade Union Confederation (ETUC) as a replacement for the European Confederation of Free Trade Unions. The ETUC specifically rejected affiliation or any formal relationship either with the secretariats or with the ICFTU, and equally specifically rejected efforts to place the word "free" in its name. ETUC has

since been in the forefront of the union confederation amalgamation movement in the EEC, which has brought the now deconfessionalized Christian and free union confederations close to amalgamation and initiated discussions with the Communist ones as well. Most free and Christian unions in the EEC are now ETUC affiliates as well as the Communist Italian CGIL.[71] (In Italy, Communist and free unions are working together and their merger is a possibility. Thus the ETUC represents a strong movement toward regional unity but international separatism.) There is speculation that the French Communist CGT will join ETUC in 1975.

In that framework, the Metal Committee, now known as the European Metalworkers' Federation in the Community, affiliated with ETUC despite IMF efforts to bring it into its fold.

The establishment of the EMF and its affiliation to the ETUC led to questions pertaining to such actions and their potential impact on the IMF. While it appeared at first that the IMF–EMF relationship would be strained, IMF president Eugen Loderer made the following points at the Stockholm Congress in July 1974: "While on the subject of regional offices Loderer made it clear that the tension with the EMF—European Metalworkers' Federation—was now overcome and that the Central Committee [of the IMF] had stated its agreement with the EMF in principle, as it was not a rival organization, and would have European contacts only."[72] IMF will continue to operate the auto councils and it remains to be seen what kind of co-ordination of other activities will occur.

The move to create the EMF, and its affiliation to ETUC, is significant for multinational bargaining because, since 1967, EMF has been quite persistent in its avowed aim of pushing key European multinational concerns toward multibargaining arrangements. Among these are Philips and Fokker-VFW.

Philips

No company has had more detailed experience in multinational union discussions than Philips, the giant multinational electrical manufacturer headquartered in Eindhoven, Netherlands. The third largest industrial concern outside

---

[70] Other secretariat officials in conversations with the authors have been highly critical of the IMF for not insisting upon an affiliation arrangement with the Metal Committee. These other secretariats have striven to establish industry groups in the EEC that are directly affiliated with the appropriate secretariat. Nevertheless, there is much regional separatist sentiment among such groups, which is a cause of concern for several secretariats.

[71] See, e.g., Selig S. Harrison, "Labor's Ties Abroad Wearing Thin," *Washington Post*, April 8, 1974, pp. A-1–A-4; and *Industrial Relations—Europe Newsletter*, No. 21, Vol. 11, p. 1.

[72] *IMF News*, No. 23, July 1974, p. 2.

of the United States,[73] Philips in July 1973 employed 390,000 persons in 20 countries, of whom 250,000 were located in the EEC.[74] Philips' management has long prided itself on leadership in providing superior wages, benefits, and working conditions for its employees.[75] The company operates on a decentralized management principle (referred to as a Federal organizational structure in Europe) with a great deal of autonomy vested in the national groups. "This particularly holds true for personnel and industrial relations policies, which have to follow national legislation in the field of labour and social security and have to fit in the national labour market situation, industrial relations structure, and climate and take into account national characteristics and preference."[76]

Philips' contacts with European trade unions began in 1967 when it received a "request to hold informative discussions with representatives of European trade unions in the metal and engineering industries" belonging to the EMF and other bodies.[77] The company complied with this request believing that it was consistent with its support of the EEC and economic integration. It was thought in 1967 that the EEC would be able to move Europe toward economic unity and that economic harmonization should be accompanied by some form of social harmonization. Furthermore, the company expected that mutual gains would be made by itself and the unions if each clearly understood its respective objectives, policies, and plans in the social field. Philips further thought that an informal meeting with the unions would give its representatives an opportunity to explain the company concept of "federal organization" and national autonomy in decision-making.

Four meetings between Philips and the EMF have occurred since 1967:

The first was largely concerned with the subject of Philips production policy in EEC countries and with the Philips decision making process. Philips officials with the help of relevant data were able to prove that union fears about unequal distribution by

a "power centre in Eindhoven" of the then prevailing redundancy in Philips plants were not justified. The echo in trade union circles was positive as this was the first time the management of an international firm was prepared to meet and amply to inform European union representatives.

In *the second* meeting (1969) in connection with the unions' concern for workers affected by transfer of production between EEC countries the company promised that—should there be substantial moves within that area—the European union representatives would be informed.

In *the third* meeting (1970) a union paper regarding social consequences of rationalisation and restructuring of production was discussed.

During *the fourth* meeting (1972) the accent was on information provided as to the economic situation and prospects, personnel planning and policy, whilst at the request of the unions the social consequences for workers in case of shorter working hours and redundancies were discussed.[78]

The foregoing meetings were obviously intended by the company to be solely for orientation and information pertaining to matters of mutual interest to it and to employees and the unions. Equally obvious, however, the EMF saw the opportunity to consummate an international collective bargaining agreement with Philips. According to the *London Times*:

Herr Günter Köpke, West German secretary of the European Metal Unions Committee, told a news conference in Brussels . . . (in September 1970) . . . that it was the intention of his 15-man labour delegation to sign an international collective bargaining agreement with Philips. Eeventually, he said, such a contract would cover conditions of labour, including wages and hours.

Herr Köpke made it clear that at first he would expect to sign an accord concerned only with general principles. He could not say how long it would take to get a full agreement. "But we are not prepared to wait for years," he added.[79]

In response to Köpke's remarks, P. L. Dronkers, Director of Personnel and Industrial Relations at Philips, reacted as follows:

First he made it absolutely clear that the company has no intention of signing an international collective bargaining accord of the kind outlined by Herr Köpke. The group intends to continue its current practice of negotiating individual agreements in separate countries where it operates, with individual trade unions and employers associations, except in Holland where Philips bargains with the unions collectively.

[73] "Philips: A Multinational Copes with Profitless Growth," *Business Week*, January 13, 1973, p. 64.

[74] P. L. Dronkers, "A Multinational Organization and Industrial Relations: The Philips Case," address before the International Industrial Relations Association, 3d World Congress, London, September 1973, p. 1. Interview with P. L. Dronkers, July 15, 1974.

[75] See, e.g., John P. Windmuller, *Labor Relations in the Netherlands* (Ithaca, N.Y.: Cornell University Press, 1969), pp. 235, 310, 372–74.

[76] Dronkers, "A Multinational Organization," p. 1.

[77] Ibid.

[78] Ibid., p. 2.

[79] Anthony Rowley, "After the Talks with Philips . . . A Step to Cross-Border Unions?" *London Times Business Supplement*, October 21, 1970.

Secondly . . . the three meetings which Philips' Board of Management have had with European trade union organizations had been of an "informal and informative" nature only and had not discussed anything as specific as an international collective bargaining agreement.[80]

The EMF sought to make multinational collective bargaining the major thrust for the proposed fifth meeting of the parties which was scheduled for May 1973. It proposed that the company should be prepared to discuss, in terms of all Philips employees in Europe, 100 percent wages in case of shorter working hours, and the same redundancy rules in the case of such events as mergers and reorganizations. In addition, the EMF suggested that an IMF representative would appear at the meeting as an observer.

These proposals were rejected by Philips executives, who repeated "their point of view that they were not able nor prepared to conclude national agreements on an EEC level. Not able because of the autonomy of the national Philips organizations."[81] The company further explained that a multinational labour agreement might be in conflict in the EEC vis-à-vis national and government policy. In regard to IMF participation, Philips took the position that this violated earlier agreements with the EMF to deal only with EEC matters.

The Philips position was reiterated by Dronkers in his IIRA address in September 1973. In response to a letter from one of the authors, Köpke agreed that the Dronkers paper "is from the company point of view in the most important points correct," but he emphasized the EMF belief "that despite the actual position of Philips we will come to multinational collective bargaining." He further stated that "our reason to insist on" IMF participation "is that the Philips activities around the world should be considered by an IMF representative when the EMF has meetings on European level with Philips."[82]

At this writing, no further meetings between the parties have been held. It is apparent that the EMF feels that the time is ripe to insist upon a bargaining relationship. It is equally clear that Philips approached these meetings with the idea that it could satisfy the unions with a good faith demonstration of its willingness to provide information, its openness, and the fairness of its wage and personnel policies. This, of course, ignores the drive by unions, whether local or international, to achieve parity of decisionmaking with management and to develop an organization and a framework of operations that require consultation and mutual consent *before* policies are determined and actions taken, rather than after the fact. The dynamics of union policy see value in informational meetings only as a stepping-stone to what is regarded as a necessary bargaining relationship between parties of at least equal stature.

Thus the Philips-EMF relationship is stalled at the crossroads. In any effort to arrange future meetings, the company will insist on a formal agenda and formal minutes of the proceedings. The EMF has accomplished its first objective of securing meetings on a multinational basis and now desires to accomplish its prime objective. Managements considering an invitation to meet with a multinational union group should understand clearly that the Philips type of meeting is, from the union point of view, a transitory phase only.

Fokker-VFW

The experience of Fokker-VFW with the EMF provides a further illustration of how unions seek informational meetings as a prelude to bargaining relationships. Fokker-VFW is an international aerospace company created by a merger in January 1970 of Germany's Vereinigte Flugtechnische Werke (VFW) and the Royal Netherlands Aircraft Factories Fokker. The company, which has its central office in Dusseldorf, Germany, employs approximately 24,000 workers in eight Dutch and nine German plants. Fokker-VFW also jointly controls the Belgian firm SABCA with the French aircraft company Dassault.[83]

There have been five meetings between Fokker-VFW and EMF since 1970. In contrast to the Philips case, the IMF has been represented at two of these meetings, and in addition, a representative of the European metalworkers' organization of the World Confederation of Labor attended the last session on October 17, 1973.[84] The company did not refuse to meet with IMF representatives present but it did question the propriety thereof.

---

[80] Ibid.

[81] Dronkers, "A Multinational Organization," p. 71.

[82] Letter from Günter Köpke to one of the authors, October 4, 1973.

[83] Philip Siekman, "Europe's Love Affair with Bigness," *Fortune*, Vol. 81, No. 3, March 1970, p. 168; also *IMF News*, No. 41, December 1970, p. 2, and No. 46, December 1973, p. 3. See also "Racing to Build Fighter Planes Worth $20 Billion," *Business Week*, August 10, 1974, p. 156.

[84] *IMF News*, No. 16, April 1973, p. 1, and No. 46, December 1973, p. 3. The World Confederation of Labor is the organization of the former Christian unions, which is now talking merger with ICFTU.

Meetings with Fokker-VFW have considered a variety of matters, such as medium-term investment plans and personnel planning, but major emphasis by the union in all sessions has been on the harmonization of working conditions between the Dutch and German plants and the regularization of a contract structure between multinational management and worker representatives. Neither of these latter two union claims has been resolved by the parties.[85] On the matter of harmonization which was raised at the fourth meeting on April 13, 1973, the IMF states: "This was rejected outright by management on various grounds, a particularly interesting one being that they saw no reason for so much international concern when the workers affected had not been creating any serious problems in the shop over this matter in the first place."[86] In regard to regularizing meetings and recognizing "a permanent trade union committee representing the workers of all Fokker-VFW plants," the company replied "that it was considering its own plan for improved communications and hoped to have it ready in 'a few months.' "[87] The company again rejected harmonization at the fifth meeting on October 17, 1973, but agreed to have better communications between national unions in Germany (Gesamtbetriebsrat) and in the Netherlands (Centrale Ondernemingsraad).

That there will be no more meetings between EMF-led committees and the Fokker-VFW management seems certain. Given the complex and varying collective bargaining and legal arrangements in Holland and Germany, where the company operates, and the lack of an effective EEC measure on harmonization, future meetings between EMF and Fokker-VFW will concentrate on such matters as general information on civilian and military projects, forecasting about what they mean for employment, and anticipated workloads. The company has insisted that bargaining relationships should be between national unions and company managements in various countries and that if for no other reason existing national legal systems make multinational bargaining neither possible nor desirable.[88] Nevertheless, the company's dependence on government and the relationships of the unions with various European governments and political parties at least raise the question whether the company can fend off the obvious EMF push for a formal bargaining relationship. There appears, moreover, a strong possibility that the EMF will now see the necessity, in terms of its credibility with its constituents, to move ahead to the next step of seeking firm agreement with the company on specific working conditions.

CONCLUDING REMARKS

Multinational bargaining in the metals and electrical industries appears to be difficult to accomplish. Both the IMF and EMF have been successful in arranging meetings with multinational companies, but such meetings have centred almost entirely on an exchange of information and not on bargaining. In general, the international unions have seen information sessions as a step toward the broader objective of multinational bargaining. On the other hand, the companies have recognized the meetings with the unions as a basis for informal talks about matters of mutual concern.

An IMF representative describes the union steps in pursuing multinational bargaining as follows:

1. Contact: This may be a casual communication between the union and some level of the company; it may occur between a union leader and a corporate head above industrial relations.
2. Consultation: This goes a bit beyond the contact; the union and management representatives might sit down and consult a bit about various matters; this may be just a general discussion on a host of items.
3. Negotiation: This limits the consultation to discussion on specific items where there is some hope for joint agreement.
4. Agreement: Negotiation leads to a written agreement that can be enforced.[89]

The first two steps of the above process have been carried out in several instances as described herein. The unions are now pushing for negotiation and agreement where they have achieved stage two. This, of course, leads to stalemates between the parties since the companies, in the cases we have studied, make it clear that multinational bargaining has not been their intention and that it would be impractical and legally impossible to accomplish.

It appears clear that the EMF is in a much better position to accomplish its objectives than is IMF. The latter is likely to continue to operate, as it has for most of the 20th century, as an effective information gathering and disseminating

---

[85] *IMF News*, note 75 above.

[86] Ibid., No. 16, April 1973, p. 1.

[87] Ibid.

[88] Letter to one of the authors from VFW-Fokker, January 23, 1974.

[89] Interview, IMF, Geneva, April 15, 1972.

organization while giving assistance to new labour organizations in underdeveloped areas of the world. The IMF will undoubtedly seek, as it has in the past, to interject itself into collective bargaining arrangements, but again, as in the past, its success in becoming a direct participant appears to be limited.

The EMF is more singly directed and located where success is more likely. It will attempt to carry out Herr Köpke's charge to seek bargaining arrangements despite all obstacles. If industry in the EEC moves toward harmonization, the unions will continue to demand harmonization of wages, working conditions, and legal frameworks. This will not be achieved lightly. For one thing, national unions must be convinced that they should cede power and authority to a multinational confederation. If the unions do so, they will then have to agree on priorities, on what issues should remain in national and local negotiations, and on where workers' councils, shop stewards, and/or local unions fit into the scheme of things.

Another reason why the EMF is better positioned to push multinational bargaining than is the IMF is that the latter must by its coverage and size cater to much more divergent interests. The sudden espousal of the American UAW of restrictions on imports is illustrative of IMF's problem. The representation of IMF of many unions from underdeveloped countries further complicates its attempts at a united front since these unions have interests that are even more different than those in the advanced countries.

Of course, all is not serene and united even in the EEC. In April 1974, the Italian Government restricted imports over the objections of its EEC partners. Economic stress has always strained precarious union solidarity and can be expected to do so in the future. But the EEC does provide a hospitable framework for EMF's aspirations. Besides its meetings with Philips and Fokker-VFW, EMF is also consulting with EEC officials and managements about "harmonization" in the shipbuilding, maritime, and aerospace industries, and it has met with the European management of Continental Can. EMF is literally on the ground floor, ready and waiting to grasp opportunity as it arises.

It would thus be a mistake to conclude that the obstacles to multinational bargaining will not be overcome. The contacts between multinational companies and multinational union groups have not resulted from the application of force by the unions. This could mean that, despite much protestation, a few multinational company managements are not completely negative concerning a possible formal multinational union bargaining relationship. Then too, the unions have accomplished a public relations coup by inducing the press, the business journals, and many academicians to accept highly exaggerated accounts of the importance of discussions with multinational companies.[90] This tends to influence both public opinion and perhaps even some companies to believe that multinational bargaining is either more accepted or closer at hand than realistic analysis would concede—and by so doing may bring it closer at hand.

The next few years could be decisive in determining whether multinational bargaining will develop. Given the framework of the EEC, this is obviously where the unions will find their greatest opportunity. And for those who are concerned about multinational bargaining, it seems obvious that the EMF is the organization that deserves immediate attention.

[90] For an analysis of successful promulgation of the most exaggerated accounts, see the authors' articles cited in note 1 above.

part seven

Public Policy and Labor Relations
Development and Impact of Legislative Controls

Federal and state legislation have a considerable impact on industrial relations in this country. The Taft-Hartley Act, public employee laws, and the Civil Rights Act, among other laws, have specified certain rules of conduct for labor and management in their involvements with one another.

The first article in this section presents parts of the Taft-Hartley Act as they relate to particular issues or problems: rights of employees, unfair labor practices, representatives and elections, section 14–b (right-to-work), and the procedures for handling national emergency situations. Excerpts from Taft-Hartley are presented here since many texts do not reproduce the laws, and it is advantageous to students and faculty members to have them available when discussing labor policy.

Several articles are included that provide insight into the development and impact of legislative controls in regard to women and Negro workers. Title VII of the Civil Rights Act of 1964 offers protection to women and Negroes in industry. Raymond Munts and David Rice explore the question of protection or equality for women workers, while the last article discusses Title VII in regard to blacks and seniority discrimination. The *Harvard Law Review* article develops the very important "rightful place" doctrine that has been generally accepted by the courts in employment discrimination cases.

The concluding two articles present various facets of manpower programs. Decentralization of manpower programs under the Comprehensive Employment and Training Act (CETA) is discussed by the U.S. Department of Labor and Iacobelli explains the administration of a particular program in the Cleveland, Ohio area.

51. The Taft-Hartley Act: Findings and Policies, Rights of Employees, Unfair Labor Practices, Representatives and Elections, and Section 14(b)*

The following presents certain sections from the Text of Labor Management Relations Act, 1947, as Amended by Public Law 86–257, 1959[1] (Public Law 101—80th Congress).

AN ACT

To amend the National Labor Relations Act, to provide additional facilities for the mediation of labor disputes affecting commerce, to equalize legal responsibilities of labor organizations and employers, and for other purposes.

Be it enacted by the Senate and House of Representatives of the United States of America in Congress assembled,

Short Title and Declaration of Policy

SECTION 1.

(a) This Act may be cited as the "Labor Management Relations Act, 1947."

(b) Industrial strife which interferes with the normal flow of commerce and with the full

production of articles and commodities for commerce, can be avoided or substantially minimized if employers, employees, and labor organizations each recognize under law one another's legitimate rights in their relations with each other, and above all recognize under law that neither party has any right in its relations with any other to engage in acts or practices which jeopardize the public health, safety, or interest.

It is the purpose and policy of this Act, in order to promote the full flow of commerce, to prescribe the legitimate rights of both employees and employers in their relations affecting commerce, to provide orderly and peaceful procedures for preventing the interference by either with the legitimate rights of the other, to protect the rights of individual employees in their relations with labor organizations whose activities affect commerce, to define and proscribe practices on the part of labor and management which affect commerce and are inimical to the general welfare, and to protect the rights of the public in connection with labor disputes affecting commerce.

TITLE I—AMENDMENT OF NATIONAL LABOR RELATIONS ACT

SECTION 101.

The National Labor Relations Act is hereby amended to read as follows:

Findings and Policies

SECTION 1.

The denial by some employers of the right of employees to organize and the refusal by some employers to accept the procedure of collective bargaining lead to strikes and other forms of

---

* This article presents a selected part of the Taft-Hartley Act of 1947 (Labor Management Relations Act of 1947, as Amended by Public Law 86–257, 1959).

[1] Section 201(d) and (e) of the Labor-Management Reporting and Disclosure Act of 1959 which repealed Section 9(f), (g), and (h) of the Labor Management Relations Act, 1947, and Section 505 amending Section 302(a), (b), and (c) of the Labor Management Relations Act, 1947, took effect upon enactment of Public Law 86–257, September 14, 1959. As to the other amendments of the Labor Management Relations Act, 1947, Section 707 of the Labor-Management Reporting and Disclosure Act provides:

The amendments made by this title shall take effect 60 days after the date of the enactment of this Act and no provision of this title shall be deemed to make an unfair labor practice, any act which is performed prior to such effective date which did not constitute an unfair labor practice prior thereto.

industrial strife or unrest, which have the intent or the necessary effect of burdening or obstructing commerce by (a) impairing the efficiency, safety, or operation of the instrumentalities of commerce; (b) occurring in the current of commerce; (c) materially affecting, restraining, or controlling the flow of raw materials or manufactured or processed goods from or into the channels of commerce, or the prices of such materials or goods in commerce; or (d) causing diminution of employment and wages in such volume as substantially to impair or disrupt the market for goods flowing from or into the channels of commerce.

The inequality of bargaining power between employees who do not possess full freedom of association or actual liberty of contract, and employers who are organized in the corporate or other forms of ownership association substantially burdens and affects the flow of commerce, and tends to aggravate recurrent business depressions, by depressing wage rates and the purchasing power of wage earners in industry and by preventing the stabilization of competitive wage rates and working conditions within and between industries.

Experience has proved that protection by law of the right of employees to organize and bargain collectively safeguards commerce from injury, impairment, or interruption, and promotes the flow of commerce by removing certain recognized sources of industrial strife and unrest, by encouraging practices fundamental to the friendly adjustment of industrial disputes arising out of differences as to wages, hours, or other working conditions, and by restoring equality of bargaining power between employers and employees.

Experience has further demonstrated that certain practices by some labor organizations, their officers, and members have the intent or the necessary effect of burdening or obstructing commerce by preventing the free flow of goods in such commerce through strikes and other forms of industrial unrest or through concerted activities which impair the interest of the public in the free flow of such commerce. The elimination of such practices is a necessary condition to the assurance of the rights herein guaranteed.

It is hereby declared to be the policy of the United States to eliminate the causes of certain substantial obstructions to the free flow of commerce and to mitigate and eliminate these obstructions when they have occurred by encouraging the practice and procedure of collective bargaining and by protecting the exercise by workers of full freedom of association, self-organization, and designation of representatives of their own choosing, for the purpose of negotiating the terms and conditions of their employment or other mutual aid or protection.

❋ ❋ ❋ ❋ ❋

National Labor Relations Board

SECTION 3.

(a) The National Labor Relations Board (hereinafter called the "Board") created by this Act prior to its amendment by the Labor Management Relations Act, 1947, is hereby continued as an agency of the United States, except that the Board shall consist of five instead of three members, appointed by the President by and with the advice and consent of the Senate. Of the two additional members so provided for, one shall be appointed for a term of five years and the other for a term of two years. Their successors, and the successors of the other members, shall be appointed for terms of five years each, excepting that any individual chosen to fill a vacancy shall be appointed only for the unexpired term of the member whom he shall succeed. The President shall designate one member to serve as Chairman of the Board. Any member of the Board may be removed by the President, upon notice and hearing, for neglect of duty or malfeasance in office, but for no other cause.

(b) The Board is authorized to delegate to any group of three or more members any or all of the powers which it may itself exercise. The Board is also authorized to delegate to its regional directors its powers under section 9 to determine the unit appropriate for the purpose of collective bargaining, to investigate and provide for hearings, and determine whether a question of representation exists, and to direct an election or take a secret ballot under subsection (c) or (e) of section 9 and certify the results thereof, except that upon the filing of a request therefor with the Board by any interested person, the Board may review any action of a regional director delegated to him under this paragraph, but such a review shall not, unless specifically ordered by the Board, operate as a stay of any action taken by the regional director. A vacancy in the Board shall not impair the right of the remaining members to exercise all of the powers of the Board, and three members of the Board shall, at all times, constitute a quorum of the Board, except that two members shall constitute a quorum of any group designated pursuant to the first sentence hereof. The Board shall have an official seal which shall be judicially noticed.

(c) The Board shall at the close of each fiscal year make a report in writing to Congress and to the President stating in detail the cases it has heard, the decisions it has rendered, the names, salaries, and duties of all employees and officers in the employ or under the supervision of the Board, and an account of all moneys it has disbursed.

(d) There shall be a General Counsel of the Board who shall be appointed by the President, by and with the advice and consent of the Senate, for a term of four years. The General Counsel of the Board shall exercise general supervision over all attorneys employed by the Board (other than trial examiners and legal assistants to Board members) and over the officers and employees in the regional offices. He shall have final authority, on behalf of the Board, in respect of the investigation of charges and issuance of complaints under section 10, and in respect of the prosecution of such complaints before the Board, and shall have such other duties as the Board may prescribe or as may be provided by law. In case of a vacancy in the office of the General Counsel the President is authorized to designate the officer or employee who shall act as General Counsel during such vacancy, but no person or persons so designated shall so act (1) for more than 40 days when the Congress is in session unless a nomination to fill such vacancy shall have been submitted to the Senate, or (2) after the adjournment *sine die* of the session of the Senate in which such nomination was submitted.

SECTION 4.

(a) Each member of the Board and the General Counsel of the Board shall receive a salary of $12,000[2] a year, shall be eligible for reappointment, and shall not engage in any other business, vocation, or employment. The Board shall appoint an executive secretary, and such attorneys, examiners, and regional directors, and such other employees as it may from time to time find necessary for the proper performance of its duties. The Board may not employ any attorneys for the purpose of reviewing transcripts of hearings or preparing drafts of opinions except that any attorney employed for assignment as a legal assistant to any Board member may for

such Board member review such transcripts and prepare such drafts. No trial examiner's report shall be reviewed, either before or after its publication, by any person other than a member of the Board or his legal assistant, and no trial examiner shall advise or consult with the Board with respect to exceptions taken to his findings, rulings, or recommendations. The Board may establish or utilize such regional, local, or other agencies, and utilize such voluntary and uncompensated services, as may from time to time be needed. Attorneys appointed under this section may, at the direction of the Board, appear for and represent the Board in any case in court. Nothing in this Act shall be construed to authorize the Board to appoint individuals for the purpose of conciliation or mediation, or for economic analysis.

(b) All of the expenses of the Board, including all necessary traveling and subsistence expenses outside the District of Columbia incurred by the members of employees of the Board under its orders, shall be allowed and paid on the presentation of itemized vouchers therefor approved by the Board or by any individual it designates for that purpose.

SECTION 5.

The principal office of the Board shall be in the District of Columbia, but it may meet and exercise any or all of its powers at any other place. The Board may, by one or more of its members or by such agents or agencies as it may designate, prosecute any inquiry necessary to its functions in any part of the United States. A member who participates in such an inquiry shall not be disqualified from subsequently participating in a decision of the Board in the same case.

SECTION 6.

The Board shall have authority from time to time to make, amend, and rescind, in the manner prescribed by the Administrative Procedure Act, such rules and regulations as may be necessary to carry out the provisions of this Act.

※　※　※　※　※

Rights of Employees

SECTION 7.

Employees shall have the right to self-organization, to form, join, or assist labor organizations, to bargain collectively through representatives of their own choosing, and to engage in other concerted activities for the purpose of collective bargaining or other mutual aid or protection, *and shall also have the right to refrain from any or all of such activities except to the extent*

---

[2] Pursuant to Public Law 88–426, 88th Congress, 2d Session, Title III, approved August 14, 1964, the salary of the Chairman of the Board shall be $28,500 per year and the salaries of the General Counsel and each Board member shall be $27,000 per year.

that such right may be affected by an agreement requiring membership in a labor organization as a condition of employment as authorized in section 8(a)(3). (Italics notes T–H amendment).

✻ ✻ ✻ ✻ ✻

Unfair Labor Practices

SECTION 8(a).

(a) *It shall be an unfair labor practice for an employer—*

(1) to interfere with, restrain, or coerce employees in the exercise of the rights guaranteed in section 7;

(2) to dominate or interfere with the formation or administration of any labor organization or contribute financial or other support to it: *Provided,* That subject to rules and regulations made and published by the Board pursuant to section 6, an employer shall not be prohibited from permitting employees to confer with him during working hours without loss of time or pay;

(3) by discrimination in regard to hire or tenure of employment or any term or condition of employment to encourage or discourage membership in any labor organization: *Provided,* That nothing in this Act, or in any other statute of the United States, shall preclude an employer from making an agreement with a labor organization (not established, maintained, or assisted by any action defined in section 8(a) of this Act as an unfair labor practice) to require as a condition of employment membership therein on or after the 30th day following the beginning of such employment or the effective date of such agreement, whichever is the later, (i) if such labor organization is the representative of the employees as provided in section 9(a), in the appropriate collective-bargaining unit covered by such agreement when made, and (ii) unless following an election held as provided in section 9(e) within one year preceding the effective date of such agreement, the Board shall have certified that at least a majority of the employees eligible to vote in such election have voted to rescind the authority of such labor organization to make such an agreement: *Provided further,* That no employer shall justify any discrimination against an employee for nonmembership in a labor organization (A) if he has reasonable grounds for believing that such membership was not available to the employee on the same terms and conditions generally applicable to other members, or (B) if he has reasonable grounds for believing that membership was denied or

terminated for reasons other than the failure of the employee to tender the periodic dues and the initiation fees uniformly required as a condition of acquiring or retaining membership;

(4) to discharge or otherwise discriminate against an employee because he has filed charges or given testimony under this Act;

(5) to refuse to bargain collectively with the representatives of his employees, subject to the provisions of section 9(a).

SECTION 8(b).

(b) *It shall be an unfair labor practice for a labor organization or its agents—*

(1) to restrain or coerce (A) employees in the exercise of the rights guaranteed in section 7: *Provided,* That this paragraph shall not impair the right of a labor organization to prescribe its own rules with respect to the acquisition or retention of membership therein; or (B) an employer in the selection of his representatives for the purposes of collective bargaining or the adjustment of grievances;

(2) to cause or attempt to cause an employer to discriminate against an employee in violation of subsection (a)(3) or to discriminate against an employee with respect to whom membership in such organization has been denied or terminated on some ground other than his failure to tender the periodic dues and the initiation fees uniformly required as a condition of acquiring or retaining membership;

(3) to refuse to bargain collectively with an employer, provided it is the representative of his employees subject to the provisions of section 9(a);

(4) (i) to engage in, or to induce or encourage any individual employed by any person engaged in commerce or in an industry affecting commerce to engage in, a strike or a refusal in the course of his employment to use, manufacture, process, transport, or otherwise handle or work on any goods, articles, materials, or commodities or to perform any services; or (ii) to threaten, coerce, or restrain any person engaged in commerce or in an industry affecting commerce, where in either case an object thereof is:

(A)   forcing or requiring any employer or self-employed person to join any labor or employer organization or to enter into any agreement which is prohibited by section 8(e);

(B)   forcing or requiring any person to cease using, selling, handling, transporting, or otherwise dealing in the products of any other producer, processor, or manufacturer, or to cease doing business with any other person, or forcing or requiring any other employer to recognize or bargain with a labor organization as the representative of his employees unless such labor organization has been certified as the representative of such employees under the provisions of section 9: *Provided,* That nothing contained in this clause (B) shall be construed to make unlawful, where not otherwise unlawful, any primary strike or primary picketing;

(C) forcing or requiring any employer to recognize or bargain with a particular labor organization as the representative of his employees if another labor organization has been certified as the representative of such employees under the provisions of section 9;

(D) forcing or requiring any employer to assign particular work to employees in a particular labor organization or in a particular trade, craft, or class rather than to employees in another labor organization or in another trade, craft, or class, unless such employer is failing to conform to an order or certification of the Board determining the bargaining representative for employees performing such work:

Provided, That nothing contained in this subsection (b) shall be construed to make unlawful a refusal by any person to enter upon the premises of any employer (other than his own employer), if the employees of such employer are engaged in a strike ratified or approved by a representative of such employees whom such employer is required to recognize under this Act: *Provided further,* That for the purposes of this paragraph (4) only, nothing contained in such paragraph shall be construed to prohibit publicity, other than picketing, for the purpose of truthfully advising the public, including consumers and members of a labor organization, that a product or products are produced by an employer with whom the labor organization has a primary dispute and are distributed by another employer, as long as such publicity does not have an effect of inducing any individual employed by any person other than the primary employer in the course of his employ-

ment to refuse to pick up, deliver, or transport any goods, or not to perform any services, at the establishment of the employer engaged in such distribution;

(5) to require of employees covered by an agreement authorized under subsection (a)(3) the payment, as a condition precedent to becoming a member of such organization, of a fee in an amount which the Board finds excessive or discriminatory under all the circumstances. In making such a finding, the Board shall consider, among other relevant factors, the practices and customs of labor organizations in the particular industry, and the wages currently paid to the employees affected;

(6) to cause or attempt to cause an employer to pay or deliver or agree to pay or deliver any money or other thing of value, in the nature of an exaction, for services which are not performed or not to be performed; and

(7) to picket or cause to be picketed, or threaten to picket or cause to be picketed, any employer where an object thereof is forcing or requiring an employer to recognize or bargain with a labor organization as the representative of his employees, or forcing or requiring the employees of an employer to accept or select such labor organization as their collective bargaining representative, unless such labor organization is currently certified as the representative of such employees:

(A) where the employer has lawfully recognized in accordance with this Act any other labor organization and a question concerning representation may not appropriately be raised under section 9(c) of this Act,

(B) where within the preceding 12 months a valid election under section 9(c) of this Act has been conducted, or

(C) where such picketing has been conducted without a petition under section 9(c) being filed within a reasonable period of time not to exceed thirty days from the commencement of such picketing: *Provided,* That when such a petition has been filed the Board shall forthwith, without regard to the provisions of section 9(c)(1) or the absence of a showing of a substantial interest on the part of the labor organization, direct an election in such unit as the Board finds to be appropriate and shall certify the results thereof: *Provided further,* That nothing in this subparagraph (C) shall be construed to prohibit any picketing or other publicity for the purpose of truthfully advising the public (including consumers) that an employer does not employ members of, or have a contract with, a labor organization, unless an effect of such picketing is to induce any individual employed by any other person in the course of his employment, not to pick up, deliver or transport any goods or not to perform any services.

Nothing in this paragraph (7) shall be construed to permit any act which would otherwise be an unfair labor practice under this section 8(b).

(c) The expressing of any views, argument, or opinion, or the dissemination thereof, whether in written, printed, graphic, or visual form, shall not constitute or be evidence of an unfair labor practice under any of the provisions of this Act, if such expression contains no threat of reprisal or force or promise of benefit.

(d) For the purposes of this section, to bargain collectively is the performance of the mutual obligation of the employer and the representative of the employees to meet at reasonable times and confer in good faith with respect to wages, hours, and other terms and conditions of employment, or the negotiation of an agreement, or any question arising thereunder, and the execution of a written contract incorporating any agreement reached if requested by either party, but such obligation does not compel either party to agree to a proposal or require the making of a concession: *Provided,* That where there is in effect a collective-bargaining contract covering employees in an industry affecting commerce, the duty to bargain collectively shall also mean that no party to such contract shall terminate or modify such contract, unless the party desiring such termination or modification—

(1) serves a written notice upon the other party to the contract of the proposed termination or modification 60 days prior to the expiration date thereof, or in the event such contract contains no expiration date, 60 days prior to the time it is proposed to make such termination or modification;

(2) offers to meet and confer with the other party for the purpose of negotiating a new contract or a contract containing the proposed modifications;

(3) notifies the Federal Mediation and Conciliation Service within 30 days after such notice of the existence of a dispute, and simultaneously therewith notifies any State or Territorial agency established to mediate and conciliate disputes within the State or Territory where the dispute occurred, provided no agreement has been reached by that time; and

(4) continues in full force and effect, without resorting to strike or lockout, all the terms and conditions of the existing contract for a period of 60 days after such notice is given or until the expiration date of such contract, whichever occurs later:

The duties imposed upon employers, employees, and labor organizations by paragraphs (2), (3), and (4) shall become inapplicable upon an intervening certification of the Board, under which the labor organization or individual, which is a party to the contract, has been superseded as or ceased to be the representative of the employees subject to the provisions of section 9(a), and the duties so imposed shall not be construed as requiring either party to discuss or agree to any modification of the terms and conditions contained in a contract for a fixed period, if such modification is to become effective before such terms and conditions can be reopened under the provisions of the contract. Any employee who engages in a strike within the sixty-day period specified in this subsection shall lose his status as an employee of the employer engaged in the particular labor dispute, for the purposes of sections 8, 9, and 10 of this Act, as amended, but such loss of status for such employee shall terminate if and when he is reemployed by such employer.

(e) It shall be an unfair labor practice for any labor organization and any employer to enter into any contract or agreement, express, or implied, whereby such employer ceases or refrains or agrees to cease or refrain from handling, using, selling, transporting or otherwise dealing in any of the products of any other employer, or to cease doing business with any other person, and any contract or agreement entered into heretofore or hereafter containing such an agreement shall be to such extent unenforceable and void: *Provided,* That nothing in this subsection (e) shall apply to an agreement between a labor organization and an employer in the construction industry relating to the contracting or subcontracting of work to be done at the site of the construction, alteration, painting, or repair of a building, structure, or other work: *Provided further,* That for the purposes of this subsection (e) and section 8(b)(4)(B) the terms "any employer," "any person engaged in commerce or in industry affecting commerce," and "any person" when used in relation to the terms "any other producer, processor, or manufacturer," "any other employer," or "any other person" shall not include persons in the relation of a jobber, manufacturer, contractor, or subcontractor working on the goods or premises of the jobber or manufacturer or performing parts of an integrated process of production in the apparel and clothing industry; *Provided further,* That nothing in this Act shall prohibit the enforcement of any agreement which is within the foregoing exception.

(f) It shall not be an unfair labor practice under subsections (a) and (b) of this section for an employer engaged primarily in the building and construction industry to make an agreement covering employees engaged (or who, upon their employment, will be engaged) in the building and construction industry with a labor organization of which building and construction employees are members (not established, maintained, or assisted by any action defined in section 8(a) of this Act as an unfair labor practice) because (1) the majority status of such labor organization has not been established under the provisions of section 9 of this Act prior to the making of such agreement, or (2) such agreement requires as a condition of employment, membership in such labor organization after the seventh day following the beginning of such employment or the effective date of the agreement, whichever is later, or (3) such agreement requires the employer to notify such labor organization of opportunities for employment with such employer, or gives such labor organization an opportunity to refer qualified applicants for such employment, or (4) such agreement specifies minimum training or experience qualifications for employment or provides for priority in opportunities for employment based upon length of service with such employer, in the industry or in the particular geographical area: *Provided,* That nothing in this subsection shall set aside the final proviso to section 8(a)(3) of this Act: *Provided further,* That any agreement which would be invalid, but for clause (1) of this subsection, shall not be a bar to a petition filed pursuant to section 9(c) or 9(e).[3]

* * * * *

---

[3] Section 8(f) is inserted in the Act by subsection (a) of Section 705 of Public Law 86–257. Section 705(b) provides:

Representatives and Elections

SECTION 9.

(a) Representatives designated or selected for the purposes of collective bargaining by the majority of the employees in a unit appropriate for such purposes, shall be the exclusive representatives of all the employees in such unit for the purposes of collective bargaining in respect to rates of pay, wages, hours of employment, or other conditions of employment: *Provided,* That any individual employee or a group of employees shall have the right at any time to present grievances to their employer and to have such grievances adjusted, without the intervention of the bargaining representative, as long as the adjustment is not inconsistent with the terms of a collective-bargaining contract or agreement then in effect: *Provided further,* That the bargaining representative has been given opportunity to be present at such adjustment.

(b) The Board shall decide in each case whether, in order to assure to employees the fullest freedom in exercising the rights guaranteed by this Act, the unit appropriate for the purposes of collective bargaining shall be the employer unit, craft unit, plant unit, or subdivision thereof: *Provided,* That the Board shall not (1) decide that any unit is appropriate for such purposes if such unit includes both professional employees and employees who are not professional employees unless a majority of such professional employees vote for inclusion in such unit; or (2) decide that any craft unit is inappropriate for such purposes on the ground that a different unit has been established by a prior Board determination, unless a majority of the employees in the proposed craft unit vote against separate representation or (3) decide that any unit is appropriate for such purposes if it includes, together with other employees, any individual employed as a guard to enforce against employees and other persons rules to protect property of the employer or to protect the safety of persons on the employer's premises; but no labor organization shall be certified as the representative of employees in a bargaining unit of guards if such organization admits to membership, or is affiliated directly or indirectly with an organization which admits to membership, employees other than guards.

Nothing contained in the amendment made by subsection (a) shall be construed as authorizing the execution or application of agreements requiring membership in a labor organization as a condition of employment in any State or Territory in which such execution or application is prohibited by State or Territorial law.

(c)(1) Wherever a petition shall have been filed, in accordance with such regulations as may be prescribed by the Board—

(A) by an employee or group of employees or any individual or labor organization acting in their behalf alleging that a substantial number of employees (i) wish to be represented for collective bargaining and that their employer declines to recognize their representative as the representative defined in section 9 (a), or (ii) assert that the individual or labor organization, which has been certified or is being currently recognized by their employer as the bargaining representative, is no longer a representative as defined in section 9(a); or

(B) by an employer, alleging that one or more individuals or labor organizations have presented to him a claim to be recognized as the representative defined in section 9(a);

the Board shall investigate such petition and if it has reasonable cause to believe that a question of representation affecting commerce exists shall provide for an appropriate hearing upon due notice. Such hearing may be conducted by an officer or employee of the regional office, who shall not make any recommendations with respect thereto. If the Board finds upon the record of such hearing that such a question of representation exists, it shall direct an election by secret ballot and shall certify the results thereof.

(2) In determining whether or not a question of representation affecting commerce exists, the same regulations and rules of decision shall apply irrespective of the identity of the persons filing the petition or the kind of relief sought and in no case shall the Board deny a labor organization a place on the ballot by reason of an order with respect to such labor organization or its predecessor not issued in conformity with section 10(c).

(3) No election shall be directed in any bargaining unit or any subdivision within which, in the preceding twelve-month period, a valid election shall have been held. Employees engaged in an economic strike who are not entitled to reinstatement shall be eligible to vote under such regulations as the Board shall find are consistent with the purposes and provisions of this Act in any election conducted within twelve months after the commencement of the strike. In any election where none of the choices on the ballot receives a majority, a run-off shall be conducted, the ballot providing for a selection between the two choices receiving the largest and second largest number of valid votes cast in the election.

(4) Nothing in this section shall be construed to prohibit the waiving of hearings by stipulation for the purpose of a consent election in conformity with regulations and rules of decision of the Board.

(5) In determining whether a unit is appropriate for the purposes specified in subsection (b) the extent to which the employees have organized shall not be controlling.

(d) Whenever an order of the Board made pursuant to section 10(c) is based in whole or in part upon facts certified following an investigation pursuant to subsection (c) of this section and there is a petition for the enforcement or review of such order, such certification and the record of such investigation shall be included in the transcript of the entire record required to be filed under section 10(e) or 10(f), and thereupon the decree of the court enforcing, modifying, or setting aside in whole or in part the order of the Board shall be made and entered upon the pleadings, testimony, and proceedings set forth in such transcript.

(e)(1) Upon the filing with the Board, by 30 per centum or more of the employees in a bargaining unit covered by an agreement between their employer and a labor organization made pursuant to section 8(a)(3), of a petition alleging they desire that such authority be rescinded, the Board shall take a secret ballot of the employees in such unit and certify the results thereof to such labor organization and to the employer.

(2) No election shall be conducted pursuant to this subsection in any bargaining unit or any subdivision within which, in the preceding twelve-month period, a valid election shall have been held.

* * * * *

Limitations—Union Security Issue

SECTION 14.

(b) Nothing in this Act shall be construed as authorizing the execution or application of agreements requiring membership in a labor organization as a condition of employment in any State or Territory in which such execution or application is prohibited by State or Territorial law.

* * * * *

National Emergencies

SECTION 206.

Whenever in the opinion of the President of the United States, a threatened or actual strike or lock-out affecting an entire industry or a substantial part thereof engaged in trade, commerce, transportation, transmission, or communication among the several States or with foreign nations, or engaged in the production of goods for commerce, will, if permitted to occur or to continue, imperil the national health or safety, he may appoint a board of inquiry to inquire into the issues involved in the dispute and to make a written report to him within such time as he shall prescribe. Such report shall include a statement of the facts with respect to the dispute, including each party's statement of its position but shall not contain any recommendations. The President shall file a copy of such report with the Service and shall make its contents available to the public.

SECTION 207.

(a) A board of inquiry shall be composed of a chairman and such other members as the President shall determine, and shall have power to sit and act in any place within the United States and to conduct such hearings either in public or in private, as it may deem necessary or proper, to ascertain the facts with respect to the causes and circumstances of the dispute.

(b) Members of a board of inquiry shall receive compensation at the rate of $50 for each day actually spent by them in the work of the board, together with necessary travel and subsistence expenses.

(c) For the purpose of any hearing or inquiry conducted by any board appointed under this title, the provisions of sections 9 and 10 (relating to the attendance of witnesses and the production of books, papers, and documents) of the Federal Trade Commission Act of September 16, 1914, as amended (U.S.C. 19, title 15, secs. 49 and 50, as amended), are hereby made applicable to the powers and duties of such board.

SECTION 208.

(a) Upon receiving a report from a board of inquiry the President may direct the Attorney General to petition any district court of the United States having jurisdiction of the parties to enjoin such strike or lock-out or the continuing thereof, and if the court finds that such threatened or actual strike or lock-out—

(i) affects an entire industry or a substantial part thereof engaged in trade, commerce, transportation, transmission, or communication among the several States or with foreign nations, or engaged in the production of goods for commerce; and

(ii) if permitted to occur or to continue, will imperil the national health or safety, it shall have jurisdiction to enjoin any such

strike or lock-out, or the continuing thereof, and to make such other orders as may be appropriate.

(b) In any case, the provisions of the Act of March 23, 1932, entitled "An Act to amend the Judicial Code and to define and limit the jurisdiction of courts sitting in equity, and for other purposes," shall not be applicable.

(c) The order or orders of the court shall be subject to review by the appropriate circuit court of appeals and by the Supreme Court upon writ of certiorari or certification as provided in sections 239 and 240 of the Judicial Code, is amended (U.S.C., title 29, secs. 346 and 347).

SECTION 209.

(a) Whenever a district court has issued an order under section 208 enjoining acts or practices which imperil or threaten to imperil the national health or safety, it shall be the duty of the parties to the labor dispute giving rise to such order to make every effort to adjust and settle their differences, with the assistance of the Service created by this Act. Neither party shall be under any duty to accept, in whole or in part, any proposal of settlement made by the Service.

(b) Upon the issuance of such order, the President shall reconvene the board of inquiry which has previously reported with respect to the dispute. At the end of a sixty-day period (unless the dispute has been settled by that time), the board of inquiry shall report to the President the current position of the parties and the efforts which have been made for settlement, and shall include a statement by each party of its position and a statement of the employer's last offer of settlement. The President shall make such report available to the public. The National Labor Relations Board, within the succeeding fifteen days, shall take a secret ballot of the employees of each employer involved in the dispute on the question of whether they wish to accept the final offer of settlement made by their employer as stated by him and shall certify the results thereof to the Attorney General within five days thereafter.

SECTION 210.

Upon the certification of the results of such ballot or upon a settlement being reached, whichever happens sooner, the Attorney General shall move the court to discharge the injunction, which motion shall then be granted and the injunction discharged. When such motion is granted, the President shall submit to the Congress a full and comprehensive report of the proceedings, including the findings of the board of inquiry and the ballot taken by the National Labor Relations Board, together with such recommendations as he may see fit to make for consideration and appropriate action.

Compilation of Collective-Bargaining Agreements, etc.

SECTION 211.

(a) For the guidance and information of interested representatives of employers, employees, and the general public, the Bureau of Labor Statistics of the Department of Labor shall maintain a file of copies of all available collective-bargaining agreements and other available agreements and actions thereunder settling or adjusting labor disputes. Such file shall be open to inspection under appropriate conditions prescribed by the Secretary of Labor, except that no specific information submitted in confidence shall be disclosed.

(b) The Bureau of Labor Statistics in the Department of Labor is authorized to furnish upon request of the Service, or employers, employees, or their representatives, all available data and factual information which may aid in the settlement of any labor dispute, except that no specific information disclosed in confidence shall be disclosed.

Exemption of Railway Labor Act

SECTION 212.

The provisions of this title shall not be applicable with respect to any matter which is subject to the provisions of the Railway Labor Act, as amended from time to time.

52. Women Workers: Protection or Equality?*

Raymond Munts and David C. Rice†

During the reform period of the decade preceding World War I, states began enacting protective laws for workers. This was acclaimed widely as a public victory over unchecked industrialization. Some of these laws apply only to women, regulating their hours of work and conditions of employment. Now legislatures and courts are taking a new look at women's protective law at the urging of those who feel such legislation restricts women's access to certain jobs and places women at a disadvantage in competing with men. The Equal Employment Opportunities Commission claims that Title VII of the Civil Rights Act of 1964 invalidates women's protective law because it prohibits employment discrimination based on sex. This amendment was added to the Civil Rights Act during congressional debate and was regarded, at the time, as a mere maneuver intended to block passage of the Act, but the ultimate fate of female protective law may turn on the primacy of this federal statute.

STATE LAWS REGULATING ASPECTS OF WOMEN'S EMPLOYMENT

With the rapid growth of industry, finance, and commerce at the end of the 19th century, women entered the labor force in substantial numbers. By 1900 the 5 million female employees constituted 18 percent of the labor force. Public attention was directed by the National Consumers' League and others to the long hours, low wages, and miserable conditions of many

working women. Immigration and rapid urbanization had provided an overabundance of female "help." With few skills, low mobility, and no union protection, women were easily exploited. In the reform movement which began about 1900 as a response to unchecked industrial expansion, legislative protection for women and children laborers was a prominent theme.

The reformers argued vigorously for laws limiting the hours of employment for women. By 1913, 27 states had created maximum weekly or daily hours to protect the "health and morals" of women.[1] The constitutionality of using state police power in this way was upheld in *Muller* v. *Oregon* (1908), the case in which Louis Brandeis as counsel for the State of Oregon first introduced the "sociological brief." He built his case almost entirely on the testimony of doctors, sociologists, and economists. Judge Brewer, speaking for the court, acknowledged the "abundant testimony of the medical fraternity" and added,

History discloses the fact that woman has always depended upon man. . . . Though limitations upon personal and contractual rights be removed by legislation, there is that in her disposition and habits of life which will operate against a full assertion of those rights. She will still be where some legislation to protect her seems necessary to secure a real equality of right. . . . Differentiated by these matters from the other sex, she is properly placed in a class by herself, and legislation designed for her protection may be sustained . . . her physical structure and a proper discharge of her maternal functions—having in view not merely her own health, but the well-being of the race—justify legislation to protect her from the greed as well as the passion of man.[2]

* Reprinted from *Industrial and Labor Relations Review*, Vol. 24, No. 1, October 1970. Copyright © 1970 by Cornell University. All rights reserved.

† Raymond Munts is professor of social work and assistant director of the Institute for Research on Poverty, and David C. Rice is a law student, University of Wisconsin.

[1] The most complete account of this activity is still Elizabeth Brandeis' "Women's Hours Law," in John R. Commons et al., *History of Labor in the United States*, Vol. 3 (New York: Macmillan, 1935), pp. 457–500.

[2] *Muller* v. *Oregon*, 208 U.S. 412 (1908).

Although today it has a ring of quaint chivalry, this is still the best statement of principle behind standards governing women's hours of employment. At their peak, in 1967, these laws existed in 46 states, the District of Columbia, and Puerto Rico. Some standards were established by statute; others were the orders of minimum wage or industrial commission boards. The standards apply to maximum daily or weekly hours, days of rest, meal and rest periods, and limitations on night work.

Minimum wage legislation for women has a quite different history. Eight laws were enacted in 1912 and 1913 and eight more in the next ten years, but these efforts came to naught in 1923 when they were declared unconstitutional in *Adkins* v. *Children's Hospital*. The decision in this case provides the best statement of the "equality" argument which always has existed as an antithesis to the "protection" argument. Justice Sutherland's argument in the Adkins case occurred in a climate of significant social change brought by World War I. The end of large-scale immigration and war-time pressures for production had brought higher wages, better conditions, and new jobs for women in both the government and private sectors. In addition to their new economic opportunities, women had won the right to vote.

The Muller decision proceeded upon the theory that the difference between the sexes may justify a different rule respecting hours in the case of women than in the case of men. . . . In view of the great—not to say revolutionary—changes which have taken place since that utterance, in the contractual, political, and civil status of women, culminating in the 19th Amendment, it is not unreasonable to say that these differences have now come almost, if not quite, to the vanishing point . . . *we cannot accept the doctrine that women of mature age, sui juris, require or may be subjected to restrictions upon their liberty of contract which could not be imposed in the case of men under similar circumstances.* To do so would be to ignore all the implications to be drawn from the present-day trend of legislation, as well as that of common thought and usage, by which woman is accorded emancipation from the old doctrine that she must be given special protection or be subjected to special restraint in her contractual and civil relationships.[3]

Thus began a period of 15 years of ambivalence in public policy with one set of legal precedents supporting state laws limiting women's hours and another group denying women minimum wages. The ambivalence was resolved with the crucial one-vote shift on the Supreme Court which followed the 1936 election and the Court "packing" fight. The case involved a hotel chambermaid, Elsie Parrish, who sued for pay due under a hitherto unenforced Washington state minimum-wage law. The argument of the court was an echo of the argument in *Muller* v. *Oregon:* "What can be closer," said Chief Justice Hughes, "to the public interest than the health of women and their protection from unscrupulous and over-reaching employers? . . . how can it be said that the requirement of the payment of a minimum wage fairly fixed in order to meet the very necessities of existence is not an admissible means to that end?"[4] *Adkins* v. *Children's Hospital* was overthrown, and protection of women's wages took its place alongside protection of their hours. As a result of the Parrish decision and the subsequent enactment of the Fair Labor Standards Act, many states adopted minimum-wage laws. In 1970 40 jurisdictions provide minimum wages, of which 7 apply to women (or women and minors) only and 7 others have some provisions applying to women only. Twenty-six of the minimum wage laws have premium-pay-for-overtime provisions, four of which apply to women only; there are other states in which the premium pay for women is found in separate statutes which limit hours of work for women.[5]

In addition to hours and minimum-wage laws, protection for women workers has found expression in statutes governing industrial homework, regulating employment before and after childbirth, prohibiting female workers from entering some occupations, establishing requirements for seating, and imposing restrictions on weight-lifting.[6]

The critics of this legislative history argue that such laws, by making a distinction based on sex, open the door to discrimination. They point out that the Fourteenth Amendment to the U.S. Constitution guarantees equal protection of the laws, but if sex is a valid basis for classification, the meaning of equal protection of the laws for women is defeated.[7]

---

[3] *Adkins* v. *Children's Hospital*, 261 U.S. 525 (1923). (Italics added.)

[4] *West Coast Hotel Company* v. *Parrish*, 300 U.S. 379 (1937).

[5] U.S. Bureau of Labor Standards, *State Minimum Wage Laws, February 1, 1970* (Washington: G.P.O.).

[6] U.S. Department of Labor, *Summary of State Labor Laws for Women* (Washington, D.C., March 1969).

[7] Pauli Murray and Mary O. Eastwood, "Jane Crow and the Law: Sex Discrimination and Title VII," *The George Washington Law Review*, Vol. 34, No. 2 (December 1965), p. 238.

TITLE VII AND THE EQUAL RIGHTS MOVEMENT

The 6-year tradition of protective laws for women is being challenged by Title VII of the Civil Rights Act of 1964. The Civil Rights bill was introduced in the House of Representatives without any mention of "sex." While the bill was before the House Judiciary Committee, Howard Smith of Virginia decided to add an amendment which would assure its defeat—equal rights for women. His strategy backfired—both the amendment and the bill passed—and the law became effective July 2, 1965. It is interesting that no women's group petitioned for or supported the sex amendment to Title VII.[8]

The trivial circumstances leading to enactment of the sex provision of Title VII and the profound changes it eventually may bring appear to qualify as historical accident. Such a conclusion, however, would overlook a tradition of "equal rights" which has long been a counterpoint to the prevailing protectionist policy. Every year since 1923 an "Equal Rights Amendment" has been proposed to the federal Constitution. This amendment covers the ground of Title VII but goes beyond, providing that "Equality of rights under law shall not be denied or abridged by the United States or by any state on account of sex." Its proponents have argued that economic progress has made protective legislation for women obsolete and that the real effect of such law now is to disadvantage women by providing a basis for discrimination under the guise of safety and welfare legislation.

Although the amendment has not been enacted, interest has continued, and in 1961 a Presidential Commission on the Status of Women further investigated these questions. The Commission recommended that minimum-wage and working standards be extended to men as well as women and emphasized premium overtime pay as a way of limiting hours. Until universally ap-

plicable standards could come into being, the Commission urged retention of present laws. It also asked for greater flexibility in regard to weight-lifting restrictions, night work, and occupational limitations.[9]

The Commission endorsed the idea of an equal pay law, an objective long sought by the labor movement, women's groups, and the U.S. Department of Labor. The Equal Pay Act was enacted in 1963. It amended the Fair Labor Standards Act to require that each covered employer pay equal wage rates to men and women doing equal work.[10] At the state level, some dozen states and the District of Columbia now include clauses prohibiting sex discrimination in their fair employment practice statutes (only two of which were enacted prior to the Civil Rights Act), and 29 states have equal pay laws.[11]

However, it is the amended Civil Rights Act of 1964 which is doing most to bring the equal rights philosophy to bear on labor legislation. Coverage of Title VII, which deals with discrimination in employment, is extended to four major groups: (1) employers of 25 or more persons, (2) public and private employment agencies dealing with employers of 25 or more persons, (3) labor unions with 25 or more members or which operate hiring halls, and (4) joint labor-management apprenticeship programs.

The specifications directly applicable to women are those which prohibit any employer, union, or employment agency from discriminating in hiring or firing; wages, terms, conditions, or privileges of employment; classifying, assigning, or promoting employees; extending or assign-

---

[8] The House debate on Smith's amendment turned "ladies afternoon" into a comic discussion. Smith read a letter from a woman constituent decrying the excess of 2 million [sic] more males than females. Congressman Tuten argued that no southern gentleman would support legislation discriminating against women. Congresswoman St. George spoke in support of the amendment, "We outlast you, we outlive you, we nag you to death. So why should we want special privileges? . . . We are entitled to this crumb of equality." This debate suggests the difficulties the courts have since had in discovering the legislative intent behind the sex discrimination provision. See U.S. Equal Employment Opportunity Commission, *Legislative History of Titles VII and XI of the Civil Rights Act of 1964* (Washington: G.P.O., 1968), p. 3213 ff.

[9] President's Commission on the Status of Women, *American Woman* (Washington: G.P.O., 1963), pp. 35–38.

[10] The Equal Pay Act was a major step forward in ending sex discrimination in employment. The most obvious limitation of the act is the fact that a guarantee of equal pay is of little value to a woman who cannot get the job in the first place due to sex discrimination.

[11] Demands for government action for equal pay date back to the Knights of Labor Convention in Philadelphia in 1868, where a resolution was passed urging federal and state governments "to pass laws securing equal salaries for equal work to all women employed under the various departments of government." Public attention was focused on the problem of equal pay for women during World War I when large numbers of women were employed in war industries on the same jobs as men. The National War Labor Board enforced the policy of "no wage discrimination against women on the grounds of sex." In 1919, two states—Michigan and Montana—enacted equal pay legislation. For nearly 25 years, these were the only states with statutes providing for equal pay for women. However, stimulated by the Second World War, ten additional states have passed similar laws. Seventeen others have acted since World War II.

ing use of facilities; and training, retraining, and apprenticeships.

The most important issue in administering the sex discrimination provision of Title VII has been the interpretation of the "bona fide occupation qualification" exception which provides exceptions to Title VII where the employment of members of only one sex is reasonably necessary for the normal operation of a particular business or enterprise. Immediately after passage, this exception assumed great importance as the only meaningful defense to a sex discrimination complaint and it was interpreted by some to be a "saving exception."[12] In fact, however, the Equal Employment Opportunity Commission (EEOC), established by Title VII to interpret and apply its provisions, has construed the bona fide occupational qualification very restrictively. As with the rest of the problems created by Title VII, it ". . . remains for the judiciary to set a final standard for the scope of the exemption, and to pass on the problem of what types of evidence will be relevant in establishing a bona fide occupational qualification."[13]

ENFORCEMENT BY THE EEOC

In an attempt to end some of the confusion arising from the interaction of Title VII and state laws, the EEOC has issued guidelines for compliance with Title VII. These guidelines have gone through several stages. The EEOC began (on December 2, 1965) with a position relative to state protective legislation as follows:

The Commission will not find an unlawful employment practice where an employer's refusal to hire women for certain work is based on a state law which precludes the employment of women for such work: *Provided*, that the employer is acting in good faith and that the effect of the law in question is to protect women rather than subject them to discrimination. However, an employer may not refuse to hire women because state law requires that certain conditions of employment such as minimum wages, overtime pay, rest periods, or physical facilities be provided.[14]

On August 19, 1966 the EEOC changed its position and adopted a new policy stating that it ". . . would not make determinations on the merits in cases which present a conflict between the Act and state protective legislation . . . that in such cases the Commission would advise the charging parties of their right to bring suit. . . ."[15] But in February 1968 the Commission rescinded this policy and reaffirmed the earlier one.[16]

In August 1969 the EEOC went further and declared that state laws prohibiting women from certain occupations or limiting their hours of work "have ceased to be relevant to our technology or the expanding role of the female worker in our economy . . . such laws and regulations do not take into account the capacities, preferences, and abilities of individual females and tend to discriminate rather than protect. . . ." In this, its strongest statement, the Commission asserts that all such laws are in conflict with Title VII "and will not be considered a defense to an otherwise unlawful employment practice or as the basis for the application of the bona fide occupational qualification exemption."[17]

The importance of the EEOC guidelines does not lie in enforcement powers of the Commission but in its role as the administrative agency which interprets the law. It has no power to issue cease-and-desist orders nor to go to court to enforce its recommendations. It can only investigate, recommend, and attempt to conciliate; and when that fails, the original complainant is entitled to go to court. Here the EEOC guidelines become significant: The EEOC may file *amicus curiae* briefs in these cases, and the courts give the Commission's views great weight on the ground that the EEOC has responsibility to interpret and apply the statute.[18]

ACCOMMODATION BY STATES

Since 1965 a pressing question has been how states could reconcile their protective laws with Title VII. A Task Force on Labor Standards was created in the federal government to study the issues. It recommended that states with minimum wage and prescribed rest period laws extend the same privileges to men as well as women, and that states incorporate their statutes pertaining to lunch periods, weight-lifting limits, and occupational hazards into a comprehensive safety and health program applicable to men and women alike. The Task Force urged removal of current restrictions, including prohibition on night work. Lastly, it recommended hour limits be replaced

---

[12] Anthony R. Mansfield, "Sex Discrimination is Employment under Title VII of the Civil Rights Act of 1964," *Vanderbilt Law Review*, Vol. 21, No. 4 (May 1968), p. 495.

[13] Ibid., p. 496.

[14] 21 *Fed. Reg.*, p. 1 (1968).

[15] Ibid.

[16] Ibid.

[17] 34 *Fed. Reg.*, p. 11,367 (1969).

[18] See *Weeks* v. *Southern Bell Telephone and Telegraph Co.*, cited in fn. 30, below.

with overtime provisions when agreed to by employees. The AFL-CIO representative on the Task Force, Ann Draper, dissented on the grounds that past experience showed voluntarism would not work and that the premium pay provisions are insufficient leverage against excessive weekly hours.[19]

There now exists a clear trend in the states toward eliminating and changing women's hours and weight-lifting restrictions.[20] Delaware has repealed all its women's protective laws, and Nebraska repealed its maximum hours law in the 1969 legislative session. Also in 1969, the legislatures of New Mexico, New York, Puerto Rico, Massachusetts, Connecticut, and Maryland amended their hours laws, allowing more flexibility for women to work longer hours or to work at times previously forbidden. Since 1965, nine states have eliminated or diminished restrictions on women's hours where the women workers are subject to the standards of the federal Fair Labor Standards Act. Many states have considered bills which were not enacted. Some proposals have been made to apply hours legislation to men as well as women, but the direction of most bills is toward diminishing or abolishing restrictions on women. More states probably will take such action during the odd-year state legislative sessions of 1971.

Meanwhile, decisions by state law enforcement officials also are undermining the state statutes.[21] In February 1969 the South Dakota attorney general held that a state law limiting the hours of women was superseded by Title VII. The North Dakota attorney general made a similar decision the next month. In December, following the new EEOC guidelines of August, the attorney generals of Michigan and Oklahoma ruled their laws invalid because of conflict with Title VII. In January 1970 the Department of Industrial Relations in Ohio stated it would no longer enforce its law as did the Corporation Council of the District of Columbia in April—both because of Title VII. The Wisconsin attorney general ruled in July that the state hours law is superseded by Title VII with respect to employers covered by the Act.

Intense feelings are generated about the questions involved. These can be found on opposite sides of the issue even within the same organization. An example is the United Automobile Workers union. The general counsel of the UAW has called protective state laws "undesirable relics of the past. . . . Only a square confrontation with these so-called protective state laws can do the job. The point is, very simply, they do not protect women, they injure them."[22] However, when the issue came up in Michigan, an Ad Hoc Committee Against Repeal of Protective Legislation, led by representatives of the Hotel and Restaurant Workers' union, sought to prevent termination of the hours limitations. Among the witnesses were women members of the UAW who worked in a Chrysler plant.[23]

The Michigan experience is of interest because it produced evidence of what can occur in some companies when hours limitations are suspended. The Michigan law limiting hours to 54 a week and 10 a day was repealed in 1967 and almost immediately reinstated; the legislature decided instead of repeal to establish an Occupational Safety Standards Commission which was empowered to make an administrative decision on women's hours limitations. In the confusion created, it appears that a Chrysler plant demanded considerable overtime from its employees. A female employee of Chrysler testified before the Commission that she had to work 69 hours a week—6 days at 10 hours and 9 on Sunday. She further testified that women dropped over from fatigue and exhaustion daily and had to be removed by stretcher. Other Chrysler female employees corroborated her testimony. Another witness from a packing company reported, "My boss ordered us to work 12 hours a day, 7 days a week."[24]

The dangers of too much overtime also were described by telephone operators who were members of the Communications Workers of America. Expert medical testimony was presented, recalling many of the same issues which arose in the *Muller* case of 1908.[25] An Ad Hoc Commit-

[19] Task Force on Labor Standards, Report (Washington: G.P.O., 1968).

[20] Ora G. Mitchell and Clara T. Sorenson, "State Labor Legislation Enacted in 1969," *Monthly Labor Review*, Vol. 93, No. 1 (January 1970), pp. 48–56.

[21] Bureau of National Affairs, *State Labor Law Reporter*, 1.32–1.34, March 16, 1970.

[22] United Automobile Workers Women's Department, *Statement of Stephen Schlossberg, General Counsel, International Union, UAW, to the EEOC at the Public Hearing* (May 2, 1967), Washington, D.C.

[23] Other persons associated with the Ad Hoc Committee came from such groups as the American Federation of State, County, and Municipal Employees, Amalgamated Clothing Workers, Building Service Employees, Council of Catholic Women, Council of Jewish Women, Michigan Credit Union League, YWCA State Council, Musicians Union Local 5, and some 13 other groups.

[24] *Detroit Free Press*, January 21, 1969.

[25] Testimony of Dr. E. R. Tichauer, professor of biomechanics, Institute of Rehabilitation Medicine, New York University Medical Center.

tee Against Repeal of Protective Legislation issued a statement saying:

Exemptions can be made for executive, administrative, and professional women since they frequently
find that limitations on hours adversely effect their
opportunities for employment and advancement. But
the overwhelming majority of the women working in
this state need and demand the freedom from forced
overtime.[26]

The Occupational Safety Standards Commission chose nevertheless to remove any limit on
daily hours. Later, its ruling was successfully
challenged in court by the Chrysler women.[27]
Still later the attorney general of Michigan declared that state's law invalid, as noted above.

The Michigan experience may or may not be
the only instance of a "grass roots" revolt against
repeal of a protective hours law, but it indicates
that long hours on a compulsory basis still can
occur. Since overtime is rarely subject to the controls of collective bargaining, protective law is the
main preventive constraint against excessive work
demands.

REACTION OF THE COURTS

Three separate cases appear, at this writing,
to be headed for eventual resolution by the Supreme Court.

In the *Mengelkoch* case,[28] three female plaintiffs, all heads of families, alleged that the California maximum-hours law conflicts with Title
VII and the Fourteenth Amendment. The defendant corporation admitted the women were
denied overtime and promotions to positions requiring overtime but urged as justification the
state's maximum-hours law, under which no administrative exceptions are available. There is no
suggestion that the health or welfare of the

charging parties would be affected adversely.
The case is now pending in the Court of Appeals.

Another case in the Central District of California, *Rosenfeld* v. *Southern Pacific Company*,[29]
also involved the question of whether a company
discriminated against a woman on the basis of
her sex. The court held that the "bona fide occupational qualification" clause of Title VII could
not be applied in this case. It further held that
the California hours and weights legislation discriminates against women on the basis of sex and
is therefore void because of the supremacy of the
federal law. A summary judgment was granted
ordering the company to consider the employee
for any position sought—without regard to her
sex and without regard to the California law.
This case also has gone to the Court of Appeals.

Perhaps the case most likely to reach the Supreme Court is *Weeks* v. *Southern Bell*.[30] The
District Court had held that Southern Bell had
not violated Title VII of the Civil Rights Act
when it refused to promote Mrs. Weeks to a job
which required lifting 31 pounds. At the time of
this ruling, Georgia had a regulation prohibiting
women from lifting more than 30 pounds. By the
time the case was heard by the Circuit Court of
Appeals, the regulation had been restated more
generally: no weight limit was specified, and
weights were to be limited "so as to avoid strain
or undue fatigue." Furthermore, the regulation
applied equally to men and women.

The Circuit Court of Appeals, therefore, based
its ruling entirely on whether the company
could refuse to assign Mrs. Weeks on the basis
that there was here a "bona fide occupational
qualification" under Title VII. In interpreting this
clause, the court said:

. . . that in order to rely on the bona fide occupational qualification exception, an employer has the
burden of proving that he had reasonable cause to
believe, that is, a factual basis for believing, that all
or substantially all women would be unable to perform safely and efficiently the duties of the job involved.[31]

This goes far toward plugging any major exception.

Understandably, the EEOC is pleased with
the *Rosenfeld* and *Weeks* cases as well as with
the general drift of state legislative and executive
decisions. The embattled posture of the EEOC is

---

[26] "Statement of Policy of the Ad Hoc Committee
against the Repeal of Protective Labor Legislation for
Women Workers in Michigan," mimeo, undated.

[27] This decision was based primarily on the court's
estimate of the powers of the commission. It argued that
the commission did not have the power to rescind the
act, and that furthermore it was an employment safety
body and did not deal with the field of discrimination.
But the decision also ranged over the basic issues of
whether women's health and safety required differential
treatment, and noted that the commission could have,
within its powers, offered some compromise such as "allowance of excess overtime by consent of the woman
worker," an approach, the court noted, that seemed to
find favor among women who testified in the trial.
Stephanie Prociuk v. *Occupational Safety Standards
Commission*. 3d Circuit Court of Michigan. Wayne
County, Michigan, June 20, 1969.

[28] *Mengelkoch et al.* v. *Industrial Welfare Commission of California and North American Aviation, Inc.*
(C.D., California, 1968).

[29] 293 F. Supp. 1219 (C.D., California, 1968).

[30] *Weeks* v. *Southern Bell Telephone and Telegraph
Co.*, 408 F. 2d 228 (C.A. 5, 1969) *reversed* 279 F. Supp.
117 (S.D. Ga., 1967).

[31] Ibid.

impassive, and its effectiveness beyond question. We are assured there is much more to come. In a recent weight case[32] which did not involve a state protective law, the chairman of the EEOC stated that this case

. . . will simplify the law concerning discrimination based on sex, making it easier for employers to understand their obligations under the law, and the court's decision regarding back pay relief should result in substantial encouragement for potential discriminators to obey the law.[33]

COMMENT AND CONCLUSION

In his study of the legal status of women, Leo Kanowitz has concluded that there has been improvement. Some of the common law doctrine that disparages married women relative to their husbands has been abrogated by statutes; unmarried women also have made legal gains. "The legal status of American women," he says, "has risen to the point that it is not now far below that of the American men."[34] But he notes that discrimination continues flagrantly in laws regulating sexual conduct and in the employment area. The authors agree that much needs to be done in the world of work to assure equality of treatment for women. We question whether eliminating all protective legislation for women is either a necessary or proper means to that end.

A suspicion persists that the more ardent advocates of "equal rights" care nothing for protective labor legislation, for either men or women. For example, this language of the court in the *Weeks* case has been cited jubilantly by equal rights advocates:

Moreover, Title VII rejects just this type of romantic paternalism as unduly Victorian and instead vests individual women with the power to decide whether or not to take on unromantic tasks. Men have always had the right to determine whether the incremental increase to remuneration for strenuous, dangerous, obnoxious, boring, or unromantic tasks is worth the candle. The promise of Title VII is that women are now to be on equal footing. . . .[35]

This is exactly the argument which was advanced earlier against workmen's compensation

and other labor legislation. It is a statement of Adam Smith's principle of "equal net advantages," which Smith himself pointed out could function only in the theory of a free market.[36] The notion that any intervention by the state distorts the unfettered interplay of supply and demand factors has been used improperly against labor legislation from the beginning. The recurrence now of such an argument, even in vestigal form, carries the discussion beyond the issue of equal treatment of women to the heart of protective legislation itself. The point that equal rights advocates are overlooking is that under many circumstances employers can and do exercise controls over the labor market, particularly in the lesser skilled factory and service employments.

The origins of protective legislation are rooted in the recurring crises which have characterized the growth of industrialization. What was required was use of state police power to assure degrees of freedom for employees through minimum wages, maximum hours, safety codes, and social insurance.[37]

The idea of balance and mutuality in the employer-employee relationship still remains an important objective. The search for equality among employees—particularly women and racial minorities—should be sought within this framework and not at its expense. Nevertheless, a noteworthy aspect of the current situation is that instead of protectionist legislation being extended to include men, it is being rooted out altogether.

It is possible unwittingly to destroy the foundations of protective legislation. There seems to be little awareness of this risk, probably because the tight labor markets of the last eight years have diminished public sensitivity to the multiplicity of interests operating. The danger of depending solely on economic forces is obscured while the opportunities are emphasized. It is not coincidental that employer groups have encouraged the repeal of women's protective legislation and opposed its extension to men.[38] The issue is now maximum hours; will it be minimum wages next?[39]

[32] *Bowie* v. *Colgate Palmolive Co.,* 408 F. 2d 711 (7th Cir., 1969) *reversed,* 272 F. Supp. 332 (S.D. Ind., 1967).

[33] Bureau of National Affairs, *Labor Relations Reporter,* 72 Analysis 25, October 13, 1969, pp. 227–28.

[34] Leo Kanowitz, *Women and the Law, the Unfinished Revolution* (Albuquerque: University of New Mexico Press, 1969), p. 197.

[35] Cited in fn. 30, above.

[36] Adam Smith, *Wealth of Nations* (New York: Random House, Modern Library, 1937), pp. 99 ff.

[37] See John R. Commons and John B. Andrews, *Principles of Labor Legislation* (New York: Harper, 1927).

[38] In the 1969 session of the Wisconsin legislature, for example, two bills were considered, the one extending hours limitation to men, the other removing hours limitations for female employees. Employers strongly opposed the first and favored the latter.

[39] The recent EEOC guideline abolishes the former specific distinction made between laws which require

The hours question is more complex than equal rights advocates paint it. Overtime work is attractive for men and women alike as a way of solving pressing financial problems, but prolonged compulsory overtime usually brings a reaction as the family, social, and psychic cost becomes clear.[40] When one is exhausted with compulsory overtime, he or she is of course free to quit, but this cannot by itself be an argument against protective legislation. The availability of alternative employment must be a consideration. At this time it is premature indeed to base a policy on the assumption that future labor markets always will be tight. Furthermore, a new phenomenon in recent history is the high cost of hiring, due in part to health and welfare programs and other fringe benefits which are employee-related rather than hours-related.[41] It also has been noted that finding, interviewing, processing, and training people often cost several hundred dollars per employee, and that labor layoffs and downgrading through seniority systems can cost additional amounts in lost time and training.[42] Under these conditions overtime even at premium rates is cheaper for employers than hiring new employees. Employers have a heavy stake in unilateral control of overtime policy.

In the current discussions one is struck by the abstract nature of the arguments and the paucity of information on possible effects of rooting out protectionist law. This is somewhat ironic, since the legal precedent for women's hours law was the *Muller* case in which Brandeis filed the brief which attempted to bring the realities of economic life into the apparatus of legal thought. If the courts have erred in the past in not being sensitive to discriminatory aspects of protectionist law, it is equally dangerous to block one's vision to the dangers of compulsory overtime. It does not appear that enough attention is being directed toward legislation requiring that overtime must be voluntary for *both* men and women. If hours limitations for women are to be repealed rather than extended to men, the only remaining why to achieve both equality and protection is through laws which require the employee's consent in assigning overtime work. However, as a remedy for the all-at-one-blow extirpation of protective hours law by Title VII, the enactment of voluntary overtime law state-by-state is a difficult and therefore unlikely remedy.

Although further research is required in those states where women's protective law has been repealed, the Michigan experience indicates that some women may still fall victim to compulsory overtime. Such women should not be denied hours protection until voluntary overtime statutes are enacted. On the other hand, there are some women who are qualified to perform jobs requiring lifting weight or working hours beyond the statutory limits. These women should not be denied the opportunity to fill such positions in reliance on state protective laws.

Thus, the question is whether state law which protects some women from the hardships of compulsory overtime must fall under Title VII in order to provide equal employment opportunity for other female workers. It is suggested that until voluntary overtime laws are enacted or until protective legislation is extended to cover men equally, protective laws be retained with administrative exemptions for women desiring positions requiring more overtime. In this way, women desiring protection would be covered while women desiring more strenuous positions would not be denied such employment because of their sex.

However, in light of cases currently pending, the Supreme Court may have to determine whether the abolition of female protective legislation is, as the EEOC contends, a *sine qua non* for eliminating discrimination and whether quality for some women must necessarily entail misery for others.

"benefits" for women (such as minimum wages, premium pay for overtime, rest periods, or physical facilities) and laws which "prohibit" the employment of women. There is in the guideline no longer a specific direction that an employer may not refuse to employ or promote in order to avoid providing a "benefit" for a woman as required by law.

[40] This generalization is based on experience of one of the authors (Munts) in the Textile Workers Union of America.

[41] Joseph W. Garbarino, "Fringe Benefits and Overtime as Barriers to Expanding Employment," *Industrial and Labor Relations Review,* Vol. 17, No. 3 (April 1964), pp. 426–30.

[42] Herbert R. Northrup, "Reduction in Hours," in Clyde E. Dankert, Floyd C. Mann, and Herbert R. Northrup, eds., *Hours of Work* (New York: Harper, 1965), chap. 1, p. 14.

53. Title VII, Seniority Discrimination, and the Incumbent Negro.*

Staff of the Harvard Law Review

After a 20-year struggle on the part of civil rights advocates[1] the 88th Congress enacted a fair employment practices law as Title VII of the Civil Rights Act of 1964.[2] Title VII prohibits discrimination on the basis of race, religion, sex, or national origin in hiring and in all aspects of the employment relation. The Equal Employment Opportunity Commission, the agency created to administer Title VII, quickly discovered that difficult legal and practical problems resulted from the long-standing use of discriminatory seniority systems which limited the advancement and job security of Negro workers.[3] As a result of past action taken pursuant to discriminatory systems, wide disparities have developed between the employment situations of Negro workers and those of whites with equal or shorter terms in the service of the same employer.[4] By excluding the senior Negro from promotion to higher paid, skilled jobs, and by rendering him more vulnerable to layoffs, these discriminatory systems have reduced the earnings of Negro workers in the past. So long as the relative subordination of Negroes to whites of equal or shorter tenure continues, economic losses to Negroes attributable to discrimination will continue to accrue in the future. On the other hand, white workers have acquired "seniority rights," or expectations of promotion and job security, which are based on the assumption that the relative competitive standings of whites and Negroes established by these discriminatory systems will remain in force. This Note will focus primarily on the problem of striking an appropriate balance between the protection of these "seniority rights" of white workers and the Title VII's requirement that there be no discrimination on racial grounds.

I. TITLE VII[5]

Following the pattern established by state fair employment practice laws,[6] Title VII makes it an "unlawful employment practice" for any employer covered by the Act:

. . . to fail or refuse to hire or to discharge any individual, or otherwise to discriminate against any individual with respect to his compensation, terms, conditions, or privileges of employment, because of

---

* Reproduced with permission from the *Harvard Law Review*, Vol. 80:1260–1283, 1967. Copyright 1967 by The Harvard Law Review Association.

[1] Bureau of National Affairs, The Civil Rights Act of 1964, at 17–19 (1964); Vaas, *Title VII: Legislative History*, 7 B.C. Ind. & Com. L. Rev. 431 & N. 2 (1966).

[2] Pub. L. No. 88–352, 78 Stat. 241. In addition to Title VII, the Act contains provisions directed against discrimination in voting, public accommodations, public education, and federally assisted programs. See 78 *Harv. L. Rev.* 684 (1965).

[3] Report by Commission Chairman Franklin D. Roosevelt, Jr., on the Commission's "first 100 days," *CCH Emp. Prac. Guide*, ¶ 8024 (1965); see id. ¶ 8046 (1966) (speech by Comm'r Samuel C. Jackson). Although this Note will focus on seniority discrimination against Negroes, its conclusions generally apply to other groups protected by Title VII.

[4] See, e.g., 3 U.S. Commission on Civil Rights, 1961 Report 137.

[5] 42 U.S.C. § § 2000e to 2000e-15 (1964). Title VII is based on H.R. 405, originally reported out by the House Committee on Education and Labor. H.R. Rep. No. 570, 88th Cong., 1st Sess. (1963). The House Committee on the Judiciary incorporated H.R. 405, with some modifications, in H.R. 7152, the Kennedy administration's "omnibus" civil rights bill, the replace a much narrower proposal. H.R. Rep. No. 914, 88th Cong., 1st Sess. (1963).

[6] See, e.g., the first state fair employment practices (FEP) law, N.Y. Executive Law § § 290–301, enacted in 1945. On the state commissions generally, see P. Norgren & S. Hill, *Toward Fair Employment*, 93–148 (1964); M. Sovern, *Legal Restraints on Racial Discrimination in Employment* 19–60 (1966).

such individual's race, color, religion, sex, or national origin; . . ."[7]

Nor may an employer, on such grounds, "limit, segregate, or classify his employees in any way which would deprive or tend to deprive any individual of employment opportunities or otherwise adversely affect his status as an employee. . . ."[8] Labor organizations may not deny membership to a worker or act to deprive him of or limit his employment opportunities or "otherwise adversely affect his status as an employee or as an applicant for employment" because of his race, religion, sex, or national origin.[9] In addition, labor organizations covered by the Act cannot lawfully "cause or attempt to cause an employer to discriminate against an individual" in violation of duties imposed on the employer by Title VII.[10] These prohibitions will extend with some exceptions to all employers "engaged in an industry affecting commerce" who have 25 or more employees,[11] and, in general, to all unions with 25 or more members which represent or seek to represent employees of covered employers.[12]

The title directs the Equal Employment Opportunity Commission to investigate charges of unlawful employment practices filed either by "persons claiming to be aggrieved" or by individual commissioners.[13] If, after investigation, it finds "reasonable cause" to believe the truth of the charge, the Commission must attempt by "informal methods of conference, conciliation, and persuasion" to procure the elimination of the alleged discriminatory practice.[14] Title VII does not preempt the jurisdiction of state or local FEPCs;[15] when conduct alleged in a charge violates both Title VII and a state or local law, the Commission may not investigate the matter until 60 days after proceedings have been commenced before any state or local authority empowered "to grant or seek relief" against the alleged discriminatory practice.[16] Unlike the state and local FEPCs to which it must defer, however, the Commission has no independent enforcement powers. Should its conciliation efforts fail, the Commission may refer the case to the Attorney General, who can seek injunctive relief against persons "engaged in a pattern or practice of resistance to the full enjoyment of any of the rights secured" by Title VII.[17] In any case, an aggrieved individual may seek relief through a private action in a federal district court;[18] if the court finds that the respondent has intentionally engaged in an unlawful employment practice, it may enjoin the offending conduct and order appropriate affirmative action.[19]

Although Title VIII represents, in large part, a response to congressional concern over the depressed economic status of the Negro in American society, that response is limited to outlawing reference to a man's race as a factor in making decisions affecting his employment or union membership.[20] The Act clearly does not oblige employers or unions to take affirmative action, in the form of special training programs or recruitment practices, preferential hiring or otherwise, to improve the employment situation of Negroes or other minority groups;[21] nor does it require an employer to lower or change job qualification

---

[7] § 703(a)(1), 42 U.S.C. § 2000e-2(a)(1) (1964).

[8] § 703(a)(2), 42 U.S.C. 2000e-2(a)(2) (1964).

[9] § § 703(c)(1)–(2), 42 U.S.C. § § 2000e-2(c)(1)–(2) (1964).

[10] § 703(c)(3), 42 U.S.C. § 2000e-2(c)(3) (1964).

[11] § 701(b), 42 U.S.C. § 2000e(b) (1964). See Benewitz, *Coverage under Title VII of the Civil Rights Act*, 17 Lab. L. J. 285 (1966). If Title VII had been fully in force in 1964, see p. 1266 infra, it would have covered employers of approximately 40 percent of the 73,000,000 persons then employed in the United States. M. Sovern, supra note 6, at 65.

[12] § § 701(d)-(e), 42 U.S.C. § § 2000e(d)-(e) (1964). Unions maintaining hiring halls supplying workers to covered employers are also covered regardless of whether they have 25 members.

[13] § 705, 42 U.S.C. § 2000e-4 (1964).

[14] § 706(a), 42 U.S.C. § 2000e-5(a) (1964).

[15] § 708, 42 U.S.C. § 2000e-7 (1964).

[16] § § 706(b)-(c), 42 U.S.C. § § 2000e-5(b)-(c) (1964). Pursuant to this provision, the Commission will refer complaints initially filed with it to 29 state agencies, as well as those of Puerto Rico and the District of Columbia. *CCH Emp. Prac. Guide* ¶ 17,252.34 (1965). After the 60-day waiting period, both the Commission and the state or local agency apparently may proceed in the matter independently, and action taken by one does not appear to preclude inconsistent action taken by the other. See M. Sovern, supra note 6, at 91–98; Purdy, *Title VII: Relationship and Effect on State Action*, 7 B.C. Ind & Com. L. Rev. 525 (1966).

[17] § 707, 42 U.S.C. § 2000e-6 (1964). Although Title VII does not expressly authorize referral of cases to the Attorney General, the Commission has adopted this practice, referring ten cases in its first year of operation. *CCH Emp. Prac. Guide* ¶ 8076 (1966).

[18] § 706(e), 42 U.S.C. § 2000e-5(e) (1964). Legislative history seems to suggest that a complainant may sue even without seeking conciliation. 110 *Cong. Rec.* 13691 (daily ed. June 17, 1964) (remarks of Senator Humphrey). See also Walker, *Title VII: Complaint and Enforcement Procedures and Relief and Remedies*, 7 B.C. Ind. & Com. L. Rev. 495, 496–98 (1966).

[19] § 706(g), 42 U.S.C. § 2000e-5(g) (1964).

[20] See, e.g., 3 U.S. Commission on Civil Rights, supra note 4; *Hearings on S. 773 Before the Subcommittee on Employment and Manpower of the Senate Committee on Labor and Public Welfare*, 88th Cong., 1st Sess. 116–19, 321–74, 433–55 (1963).

[21] Section 703(j), 42 U.S.C. § 2000e-2(j) (1964), states that Title VII does not require preferential treatment for members of any racial, religious, or national group or of either sex merely because it is "under-represented" in a particular plant, union, or training program.

standards, either generally or on a preferential basis, in order to make it easier for members of these groups to qualify for employment or promotion.[22] Thus, while Title VII prohibits the rejection of a man because of his race or because of racial stereotypes which attribute certain characteristics to all members of a racial group, these prohibitions may not benefit particular individuals unless they are capable of competing on equal terms with other applicants.

II. DISCRIMINATORY SENIORITY SYSTEMS

A "seniority system," for the purposes of this Note, may be defined as a set of rules governing job movements, including promotion, transfer, downgrading, and layoff, in an employment unit.[23] The most "senior" man among a group of competing workers is preferred, provided that he is qualified to fill the job in question and that he is eligible to bid for it. Seniority in this sense may be measured by length of service in a whole plant, in a department, in a "line of progression," or even in a particular job. However seniority is measured, its effect largely depends upon the range of jobs for which a man holding a particular position can compete when openings occur and from which he can "bump" a less senior man if he is displaced from his present position. In order to compete successfully for a job, the senior worker must also be qualified to fill it; but the relation between seniority and ability and the rules for determining ability vary considerably from plant to plant. A demonstrably more able junior man, one "head and shoulders" above his competitors, may in some units defeat less able senior workers.[24] In other situations, where jobs in a unit differ only slightly or require short training periods, seniority alone may in fact control job movement.[25] In determining qualifications some companies use "probation periods"

during which an employee learns a job and demonstrates his ability to hold it; others may require him to show himself qualified in advance of an award.

Wherever a fairly well-defined seniority system limits management's power to control job movements, it enables individuals to estimate their competitive status relative to other employees and, to some extent, to assess the security of their present jobs and their chances for advancement. Although the term "seniority rights" is often used to describe employee expectations of future employer action under a seniority system, these employee claims are legal rights only in a limited sense. Unlike rights in a pension plan or other similar "fringe benefits," seniority "rights" do not represent accrued rights to deferred compensation which may, like claims for past wages, "vest" absolutely in particular workers. Seniority rights arise from the establishment of regular procedures for allocating jobs among workers in a particular plant; they therefore remain subject to modification when changes in the economic situation or production methods in the plant lead to changes in the underlying procedures.[26] Ordinarily, seniority rights derive solely from the provisions of collective bargaining agreements, supplemented by local customs in administering the agreement and by the "common law" of the contract as expressed in arbitration awards.[27] Individual workers have no right to participate in framing these provisions, which the contracting parties may modify at any time. The union, however, has broad discretion to bargain for changes in existing seniority arrangements, even though the changes seriously curtail the expectations of some employees,[28] provided only that the union act in good faith and have some reasonable basis for its action.[29] Similarly, the union exercises substantial control over the grievance procedure through which employees must initially prosecute seniority claims. If the union acts in good faith, it may compromise or refuse to proceed with such claims, not only if it considers them without merit, but also where it

---

[22] *Hearings on H.R. 405 before the General Subcommittee on Labor of the House Committee on Education and Labor,* 88th Cong., 1st Sess. 24, 37, 57 (1963); 110 Cong. Rec. 6992 (daily ed. April 8, 1964) (memorandum by Senators Clark and Case); id. at 11463 (daily ed. May 25, 1964) (memorandum by Senator Humphrey).

[23] See generally S. Slichter, J. Healy & E. Livernash, *The Impact of Collective Bargaining on Management* 104–210 (1960). Seniority in this sense, in which it serves to allocate particular privileges among competing workers, is sometimes termed "competitive status seniority" as contrasted with "benefit seniority" which merely grants certain rights, such as pension benefits or extra vacation time, to all workers who have served a specified length of time. Id. at 106.

[24] Id. at 203.

[25] Id. at 205.

[26] See Gould, *Employment Security, Seniority and Race: The Role of Title VII of the Civil Rights Act of 1964,* 13 How. L. J. 1, 5–7 (1967).

[27] Although some nonunion companies have seniority systems, these systems are generally the products of collective bargaining and have been incorporated in the vast majority of collective agreements. See Aaron, "Reflections on the Legal Nature and Enforceability of Seniority Rights." 75 *Harv. L. Rev.* 1532, 1534 (1962).

[28] *Ford Motor Co.* v. *Huffman,* 345 U.S. 330 (1953); *Elder* v. *New York C. R.R.,* 152 F. 2d 361 (6th Cir. 1945).

[29] *Steele* v. *Louisville & N.R.R.,* 323 U.S. 192 (1944); *Syres* v. *Oil Workers Local 23,* 350 U.S. 892 (1955).

determines that pressing the claim, although it might succeed, would lead to an undesirable construction of the agreement or otherwise adversely affect its relations with management.[30]

Probably few, if any, collective bargaining agreements expressly discriminate against Negroes; usually, the discriminatory elements of seniority systems appear in informal understandings supplementing the general terms of the written agreement.[31] Individual seniority systems vary considerably in detail, reflecting peculiarities in each plant's organization and the relative bargaining strength and attitudes of union and management. Discriminatory practices mirror this variety. Nevertheless, certain distinct and recurrent discriminatory patterns may be identified.[32] In the first, separate seniority lists are maintained for white and Negro employees doing the same work, and the rule followed prefers the most junior white to the most senior Negro or employs some other less extreme but nonetheless discriminatory principle.[33] A variant form classifies whites and Negroes who in fact do similar or identical work as holding different jobs, with the Negroes receiving lower wages and organized in a separate seniority district, subordinated to the parallel white district.[34] In these systems, manipulation of either job classifications or the seniority principle itself produces inequalities in earnings and seniority rights between whites and Negroes doing the same work.

The second pattern involves a group of jobs so closely related in terms of the skills they require or in their function within the production process that they would, in normal industrial practice, constitute a single unit or "district" for seniority purposes. In this pattern, Negroes and whites together fill the lowest level jobs in the unit or district, but only whites can bid for promotion to functionally related jobs higher in the unit.[35] A similar effect may be produced by employing only Negroes in the lower level jobs and hiring whites into the unit at a higher level, training them to start at an intermediate point rather than promoting the Negroes. In such cases, the arbitrary line barring Negro advancement beyond a certain point in a group of related jobs constitutes a clear discrimination, which results in holding down Negro wage rates and denying to the Negroes on-the-job training and experience which may be necessary to qualify them for higher level jobs to which their seniority, fairly applied, would entitle them.

In the third and most common pattern, two or more groups of related jobs are organized in separate seniority districts, but each group of jobs considered as a whole has little or no functional relation to the other. Only Negroes are hired for the district encompassing the least desirable jobs and only whites for the others; the seniority system either prohibits transfers between the districts or provides that seniority acquired in one district does not follow a worker who transfers to another.[36] This pattern discloses a clearly discriminatory hiring policy. The organization of jobs into separate seniority districts, however, may be justified by independent nonracial considerations, such as the differences in work content or skill requirements among the districts. In fact, mutually exclusive "departmental" seniority arrangements exist in a good many plants where discrimination does not occur.[37]

Particular seniority systems may combine elements of more than one of these discriminatory patterns. Furthermore, distinguishing between the second and third discriminatory patterns involves an identification of the limiting cases in a continuum of possible situations. Extreme examples of the second pattern, in which no racially neutral basis for the system appears and Negroes are simply classified as "unpromotable," will be rare.[38] Although the principle of promotion from within the bargaining unit, as opposed to hiring from outside, has been so widely accepted that restrictions on promotion out of a Negro unit must initially be suspect, there are no accepted job classification practices which require promotion from one job to another as an

[30] Broomfield, *Grievants' Suits under Labor Agreements*, 3 Harv. Legal Comm. 338 (1966).

[31] See, e.g., *Butler* v. *Celotex Corp.*, 3 Race Rel. L. Rep. 503 (E.D. La. 1958); *Goodyear Tire & Rubber Co.*, 45 Lab. Arb. 240 (1965).

[32] See Doeringer, *Promotion Systems and Equal Employment Opportunity*, in Industrial Relations Research Ass'n, *Proceedings of the 19th Annual Meeting* (1967).

[33] *Daye* v. *Tobacco Workers Int'l Union*, 234 F. Supp. 815 (D.D.C. 1964); Local 12, United Rubber Workers, 150 N.L.R.B. 312 (1964), *enforced*, 368 F. 2d 12 (5th Cir. 1966); Local 1367, Int'l Longshoremen's Ass'n. 148 N.L.R.B. 897 (1964), *enforced per curiam*, 368 F. 2d 1010 (5th Cir. 1966).

[34] See *Richardson* v. *Texas & N.O.R.R.* 242 F. 2d 230 (5th Cir. 1957).

[35] See *Central of Ga. Ry.* v. *Jones*, 229 F. 2d 648 (5th Cir.), *cert. denied*, 352 U.S. 848 (1956).

[36] See *Syres* v. *Oil Workers Local 23*, 223 F. 2d 739 (5th Cir.), *rev'd per curiam*, 350 U.S. 892 (1955); *Whitfield* v. *United Steelworkers Local 2708*, 156 F. Supp. 430 (S.D. Tex. 1957), *aff'd*, 263 F. 2d 546 (5th Cir.), *cert. denied*, 360 U.S. 902 (1959).

[37] M. Sovern, *supra* note 6, at 151.

[38] See *Rolax* v. *Atlantic Coast Line R.R.*, 186 F. 2d 473 (4th Cir. 1951); *Clark* v. *Norfolk & W. Ry.*, 3 Race Rel. L. Rep. 988, 993 (W.D. Va. 1956).

obviously necessary step.[39] In some situations of the second type, an employer might find a racially neutral basis for treating the lowest in a group of closely related jobs as a separate unit in the argument that by placing all undesirable, low-skill jobs in one independent unit, he may hire unskilled labor at a lower wage rate than would be necessary if he hired workers of greater ability who eventually could be promoted to higher level jobs. As the functional relationship between the white and Negro jobs becomes more attenuated and the independent, nonracial grounds for the separation of these jobs into distinct seniority districts become more persuasive, the second discriminatory pattern shades into the third. Ultimately a point is reached where no real relation between the jobs exists, as in the case of an airline with an all-white pilot unit and a Negro terminal maintenance staff and, though hiring discrimination may occur, the mere absence of transfer provisions linking the two units affords no basis for terming the seniority system itself discriminatory.

III. THE SCOPE OF TITLE VII'S PROHIBITIONS

A. Retroactivity and Prior Agreements

The sections of Title VII which define unlawful employment practices and the related conciliation and enforcement procedures did not become applicable until July 2, 1965, one year after the title's enactment.[40] In the year following July 2, 1965, Title VII applied only to employers or unions with 100 or more regular employees or members. This numerical limit dropped to 75 or more workers or members a year later, will drop to 50 or more on July 2, of this year, and will reach its eventual limit of 25-man firms and unions on July 2, 1968.[41] This elaborate transition provision was designed "to enable employers . . . to bring their policies and procedures into line with the requirements of the title and to avoid a multitude of claims arising while such adjustments are being made."[42] Since neither the title's substantive commands nor the related complaint procedures apply to a particular employer or union until the appropriate effective date, it follows that action taken before that date to set

up or administer a discriminatory seniority system does not itself constitute an unlawful employment practice. However, conceding that Title VII's operation "is prospective and not retrospective," the application of this principle to seniority systems raises two important questions.[43] First, does this rule immunize from Title VII proceedings discriminatory action adversely affecting Negro employees taken after the title's effective date but pursuant to a seniority clause agreed to before that date? Second, can the seniority rights or expectations of white employees "acquired" under a discriminatory system prior to the title's effective date be modified in Title VII proceedings in order to eliminate discriminatory disparities in the competitive status of whites and Negroes from the future operation of the system?

The Commission's General Counsel has ruled that Title VII's mandates supersede inconsistent terms of existing collective bargaining agreements.[44] Section 703, in defining unlawful employment practices, literally prohibits all discriminatory action adversely affecting individual workers, regardless of whether it is taken on an ad hoc basis or in compliance with a prior contract and regardless of whether it occurs in the administration or in the negotiation of a collective agreement. Congress has undoubted power under the commerce clause to invalidate the terms of existing private agreements.[45] In addition, the transition period postponing the effective date of application afforded an adequate opportunity for the renegotiation of nonconforming collective agreements. Thus, in the absence of any qualifying language, section 703's standards should apply to all employer or union action occurring after the effective date.

Before it orders remedial action under Title VII, however, a court must determine that the respondent has "intentionally engaged in . . . an unlawful employment practice."[46] It may be

[39] S. Slichter et al., supra note 23, at 189.

[40] Pub. L. No. 88–352, § 716, 78 Stat. 266 (1964).

[41] § § 701(b), (e)(2), 42 U.S.C. § § 2000e(b), (e)(2) (1964).

[42] 110 Cong. Rec. 7022 (daily ed. April 8, 1964) (remarks of Senator Case); see id. at 6343 (daily ed. March 30, 1964) (remarks of Senator Kuchel); id. at 1458 (daily ed. Jan. 31, 1964) (remarks of Representative Celler).

[43] 110 Cong. Rec. 6992 (daily ed. April 8, 1964) (memorandum by Senators Clark and Case).

[44] EEOC General Counsel, Opinion Letter 344–65, CCH Emp. Prac. Guide ¶ 17,251.042 (1965).

[45] Louisville & N.R.R. v. Mottley, 219 U.S. 467, 482–483 (1911); Philadelphia, B.&W.R.R. v. Schubert, 224 U.S. 603, 613–14 (1912).

[46] § 706(g), 42 U.S.C. § 2000e-5(g) (1964). A Senate amendment added the word "intentionally" to § 706(g) as a "clarifying change" to make it clear that the "employer must have intended to discriminate. . . ." 110 Cong. Rec. 12298 (daily ed. June 4, 1964) (remarks of Senator Humphrey); id. at 13838 (daily ed. June 18, 1964) (remarks of Senator Williams). Since § 703 defines unlawful employment practices in terms of adverse action taken "because of . . . race, color, religion, sex, or national origin," and since this could hardly be done inadvertently, the amendment would appear unnecessary.

argued that in acting pursuant to a contract negotiated before Title VII became law, an employer is merely fulfilling his contractual obligations without presently intending to discriminate in the statutory sense against the individual affected; an intention to discriminate may have moved one or both of the parties in negotiating the agreement, but that intention, occurring in the past, cannot now be reached by Title VII. In view of Title VII's short statute of limitations, however, so narrow a reading of intent would mean that discriminatory collective agreements, and action taken in accordance with their terms, could be attacked under Title VIII only at the time the agreements are made or shortly thereafter.[47] Such an interpretation would clearly undercut Title VII's focus on action adversely affecting particular individuals and its complaint procedures which offer a remedy to these individuals when such action occurs. Thus, when an employer has entered into a binding agreement containing seniority provisions designed to discriminate against Negroes, it seems reasonable to impute this discriminatory intent to all subsequent conduct giving effect to the discriminatory plan and to hold such conduct unlawful when it occurs after Title VII's effective date.

B. Established Seniority Rights

When the substantive provisions of Title VII become effective, the title immediately bars any further application of discriminatory seniority rules, such as those which exclude Negroes from particular jobs or those which classify whites and Negroes doing the same work into separate seniority districts. Yet, the past operation of a discriminatory system will have established a particular distribution of jobs among the plant's employees and a fixed competitive standing among them with respect to future job movements. For example, white workers will have acquired seniority rights in the jobs in a "white" unit from which Negroes have been excluded, and so long as these rights remain unchanged even the most junior white will have a seniority status with respect to these jobs superior to that of the most senior man in the Negro unit, when the latter transfers into the formerly white unit.

Three interpretations of Title VII have been advanced to answer the question whether the title, contrary to the employee expectations existing at the time Title VII became effective, should be read as requiring the elimination of differences in competitive standing between white and Negro workers attributable to past discrimination. The first, or "status quo," approach would leave the seniority rights of white workers intact, at least where giving current effect to these rights would not involve the direct application of a racial principle.[48] Under "status quo," positions in the hiearchy already achieved would be preserved; relative to their white contemporaries who had been preferred, Negro incumbents could not improve their status. The second theory, the "rightful place" approach, holds that the continued maintenance of the relative competitive disadvantage imposed on Negroes by the past operation of a discriminatory system violates Title VII, just as the continued use of the discriminatory rules which created the differential would violate it. To eliminate this differential from the future operation of the system, the "rightful place" approach would allow an incumbent Negro to bid for openings in white jobs comparable to those held by whites of equal tenure, on the basis of his full length of service with the employer. If he met the existing ability requirements for such a job, he would be entitled to fill it, without regard to the seniority expectations of junior white employees. The "rightful place" approach requires an adjustment in competitive standing with regard to future job movements arising in the ordinary course of an employer's business. The third approach to Title VII, which might be termed the "freedom now" theory, would go further and argue that maintenance of the distribution of jobs established by a discriminatory system after Title VII became law constitutes an unlawful employment practice. If the adjustment of seniority rights contemplated by the rightful place theory indicates that a senior Negro would have priority over a white worker currently holding a particular job if that job were unfilled, then under "freedom now" the Negro would be immediately entitled to it, even though this would require the displacement of the white incumbent.

The principal argument favoring the "status quo" theory rests on the essentially negative

<hr />

[47] A complaint must "be filed within 90 days after the alleged unlawful employment practice occurred" when filed directly with the Commission, and within 210 days when initially filed with a state or local FEPC. § 706(d), 42 U.S.C. § 2000e-5(d) (1964).

[48] This view of Title VII is often associated with *Whitfield* v. *United Steelworkers Local 2708*. 263 F. 2d 546 (5th Cir.), *cert. denied,* 360 U.S. 902 (1959), where it was held that a union had not violated its duty of fair representation in negotiating a contract which eliminated certain discriminatory seniority practices but did not attempt to rmove the continuing effects of past discrimination. The court felt that it could not "turn back the clock" on such effects, which were a "product of the past." 263 F. 2d at 551.

proposition that any modification of existing seniority rights and job distribution patterns would involve an unauthorized retroactive application of Title VII. It is argued that white workers acquired their present jobs and seniority rights as a result of employer action occurring before Title VII became effective; if this action cannot constitute an unlawful employment practice, then no basis exists for depriving white employees of resulting benefits. This argument appears most persuasive as a refutation of the "freedom now" theory. When a seniority right "matures" in the award of a particular job before Title VII's effective date, the award may plausibly be viewed as a closed transaction, not subject to attack after the title comes into force. Until the need for layoffs or the occasion for promotion or transfer arises, the system entitles the employee to retain the job awarded him. In construing Title VII's statute of limitations, the Commission has ruled that each discriminatory job award constitutes an offense when it occurs, and that the statute runs from that date.[49] The fact that the employee improperly preferred retains the job does not create a continuing violation.[50] The interest in maintaining the stability of an employer's distribution of his work force presumably served by the title's short period of limitation would be wholly undermined if each discriminatory job assignment could be attacked so long as it continued.

It should be pointed out, however, that a seniority right with respect to future job movements stands on a different footing from a job that has already been acquired. To say that a worker has such a right means that under the seniority system currently in force he stands in a determinable competitive relation to other workers with respect to a defined class of possible job movements. Although a worker's past service enters into the determination of his status, its value to him depends on the seniority rules in force at the time when a particular job movement affecting him occurs. These rules remain subject to change by the parties to the collective agreement; thus, the rights which derive from them likewise remain conditional, and the rights of an individual cannot become fixed with respect to a job movement until it happens.[51] Once Title VII becomes effective, it in effect modifies existing seniority rules by operation of law; these rules and action taken pursuant to them must conform to the title's requirements, regardless of white workers' expectations created before the effective date.

The nonretroactive character of a "rightful place" approach is clear in the cases where giving effect to seniority rights "acquired" before the effective date would require the present application of a discriminatory principle. Thus, where whites and Negroes both work on a particular job, but only whites have been eligible for further promotion, the most junior white has an expectation of being promoted before the most senior Negro.[52] To honor this expectation once Title VII becomes law would constitute an unlawful employment practice, since preferring the junior white to the senior Negro could only be explained by reference to a racial criterion.

On the other hand, where discrimination has taken the form of excluding Negroes from a "white" seniority district in which promotion depends on service within the district and where the organization of the district in this fashion could be justified on independent, nonracial grounds, it might be argued that only the rule against Negro entry into the white unit need be abandoned to conform the system to Title VII's requirements. The continued application of the white unit's preexisting seniority rules can be justified on neutral grounds, independent of any racial criterion; therefore, their use does not involve any present discrimination. It is essential to note, however, that Title VII allows differences "pursuant to a bona fide seniority system," only when "such differences are not the result of an intention to discriminate because of race. . . ."[53] Furthermore, racial discrimination need not be the sole motive for these differences; a system adopted with discriminatory intent is not saved from illegality by the fact that other acceptable motives also influenced its creation.[54] All the

---

[49] See note 47 supra.

[50] Opinions of EEOC General Counsel. *CCH Emp. Prac. Guide* ¶ 17,252.304 (1965). The Commission's interpretations of the title's provisions have been held to be entitled to considerable weight before the courts. *International Chemical Workers Union* v. *Planters Mfg. Co.,* 259 F. Supp. 365 (N.D. Miss. 1966). See *Skidmore* v. *Swift & Co.,* 323 U.S. 134, 139–40 (1944).

[51] See p. 1264 supra.

[52] See, e.g., *Central of Ga. Ry.* v. *Jones,* 229 F. 2d 648 (5th Cir.), *cert. denied,* 352 U.S. 848 (1956). In this fair representation case the court affirmed a "freedom now" order. 229 F. 2d at 650 n. 3. It is not clear whether the decree was enforced on this basis. See Herring, *The "Fair Representation Doctrine": An Effective Weapon against Union Racial Discrimination?* 24 Md. L. Rev. 113, 130 (1964).

[53] § 703(h), 42 U.S.C. § 2000e-2(h) (1964). See pp. 1272–73 infra.

[54] This proposition is strengthened by the Senate's rejection of Senator McClellan's amendment which would have limited the title to prohibiting discrimination occurring *"solely* because of . . . race, color, religion, sex, or national origin." 110 Cong. Rec. 13361 (daily ed. June 5, 1964) (emphasis added).

rules of a seniority system operate together to establish the relative competitive standing of all the employees in a particular bargaining unit; when one of these rules is discriminatory, it affects this relative standing and creates differences between whites and Negroes which are "the result of an intention to discriminate." To remove a rule barring Negro entry into a white unit insures that this differential will not be widened but does not remove it. Moreover, a failure to eliminate this difference in the competitive standing of otherwise equal whites and Negroes leads to the present and future subordination of Negro workers on racial grounds. Thus, employer conduct applying such white seniority rights should be held to involve a present violation of Title VII.

Proponents of the "status quo" theory may argue, however, that legislative history reflects a congressional consensus that Title VII would not affect preexisting seniority rights. Throughout the debates, opponents of Title VII asserted that the bill would "destroy seniority"[55] and supporters of the legislation responded with equally general assurances that this would not occur.[56] An authoritative statement of the majority[57] view appears in a memorandum prepared by Senators Clark and Case:

Title VII would have no effect on established seniority rights. Its effect is prospective and not retrospective. Thus, for example, if a business had been discriminating in the past and as a result has an all-white working force, when the title comes into effect the employer's obligation would be simply to fill future vacancies on a nondiscriminatory basis. He would not be obliged—or indeed, permitted—to fire whites in order to hire Negroes, or to prefer Negroes for future vacancies, or, once Negroes are hired, to give them special seniority rights at the expense of the white workers hired earlier.[58]

The memorandum makes it clear that Title VII does not require that incumbent whites be fired so that Negroes may be hired or that their seniority rights be curtailed for the benefit of new Negro employees; such action would clearly involve preferring these Negroes because of their race and would subvert the basic principle of any seniority system, discriminatory or non-discriminatory. However, it does not necessarily follow from this proposition that Title VII may not require a redistribution of jobs currently held by incumbent white and Negro employees or a redetermination of their seniority rights to reflect seniority and ability on a non-discriminatory basis. Congress did not, at any point in the debate or related hearings, directly confront the problem of seniority systems in which discrimination had subordinated Negro workers to whites of equal or lesser tenure. As the Clark-Case memorandum indicates, proponents of Title VII concentrated on refuting charges that the bill authorized "reverse discrimination" and that it would interfere with the normal operation of non-discriminatory seniority systems.[59] The "rightful place" and "freedom now" theories of Title VII should not be seen as falling within the scope of these concerns, however, since they do not accelerate the advancement of Negroes simply because of their race; rather, they prefer them only if they are senior employees who have been denied advancement which, absent discrimination, their length of service would have secured for them.

The version of Title VII passed by the House contained provisions defining unlawful employment practices and determining the title's effective dates substantially similar to those eventually enacted. However, to gain the support of a group of Senators headed by Senator Dirksen against the filibuster conducted by Southern opponents of the Civil Rights Act, the bill's supporters informally negotiated a series of amendments with the Dirksen group.[60] Although notable with regard to Title VII principally as the

[55] E.g., 110 Cong. Rec. 459 (daily ed. Jan. 15, 1964) (remarks of Senator Hill); id. at 6871 (daily ed. April 7, 1964) (remarks of Senator Stennis); id. at 12783 (daily ed. June 10, 1964) (remarks of Senator Russell).

[56] 110 Cong. Rec. 6329 (daily ed. March 30, 1964), id. at 11463 (daily ed. May 25, 1964) (remarks of Senator Humphrey); id. at 6343 (daily ed. April 1, 1964) (remarks of Senator Kuchel); id. at 1455 (daily ed. Jan. 31, 1964) (remarks of Representative Celler).

[57] Senators Clark and Case were the "bi-partisan captains" selected by Senate supporters of the Civil Rights Act to explain and defend the provisions of Title VII. Vaas, supra note 1, at 444–45.

[58] 110 Cong. Rec. 6992 (daily ed. April 8, 1964). Cf. the Justice Department memorandum prepared for Senator Clark which qualified the assertion that "Title VII would have no effect on seniority rights existing at the time it takes effect," by adding, "[o]f course, if the seniority rule itself is discriminatory, it would be unlawful." Id. at 6986.

[59] Compare, however, Senator Clark's response to a question raised earlier by Senator Dirksen:
Q: If an employer is directed to abolish his employment list because of discrimination, what happens to seniority?
A: The bill is not retroactive, and it will not require an employer to change existing seniority lists.
110 Cong. Rec. 6996 (daily ed. April 8, 1964). Depending on what sort of "discrimination" the Senators had in mind, this exchange might be read to suggest that *any* seniority rights existing before Title VII's effective date would be preserved.

[60] Vaas, supra note 1, at 445–56. No records of these negotiatons have been published. Senator Dirksen introduced the revised version of the Civil Rights Act first as Amendment No. 656 on May 25, 110 Cong. Rec. 11537 (daily ed.), and, with further changes, as Amendment No. 1052 on June 10, id. at 12857.

source of its bizarre enforcement procedures, the amendments also added several provisos to section 703. In particular, section 703(h) declares that, notwithstanding other provisions of Title VII:[61]

> . . . it shall not be an unlawful employment practice for an employer to apply different standards of compensation, or different terms, conditions, or privileges of employment pursuant to a bona fide seniority . . . system . . . provided that such differences are not the result of an intention to discriminate because of race. . . .

It has been suggested that this proviso, read in light of the Senate debate, reflects a congressional consensus favoring the protection of all seniority rights existing before Title VII's effective date.[62] Senator Dirksen never explained what his proviso was intended to mean;[63] Senator Humphrey felt that it clarified the "present intent and effect" of Title VII without narrowing its application.[64] But, however one reads the Dirksen proviso, it does not seem possible to interpret it as providing a blanket exemption for all differences in treatment resulting from seniority arrangements set up before Title VII came into force. The proviso does not expressly refer to such preexisting systems, but to all "bona fide" systems. A "bona fide" seniority system appears to be one which can be explained or justified on nonracial grounds.[65] Some seniority systems which are in fact designed to discriminate against Negroes may be justifiable on neutral grounds and would be lawful absent this discriminatory intent. However, even though a discriminatory system of this type might be termed bona fide, certain "differences" in treatment authorized by the system will "result" from the discriminatory intention which entered into its establishment. These differences must, therefore, fall outside the scope of the Dirksen proviso's protection.

On the assumption that Title VII does not interfere with expectations arising from discrim-

inatory seniority systems which did not violate any other legal duty existing before Title VII came into effect, it has been suggested that a "rightful place" remedy under Title VII may nonetheless apply to seniority systems which were unlawful on other grounds.[66] Seniority systems which would now violate Title VII might well have also infringed state or local FEPC laws. Moreover, where a union acting as bargaining representative under federal labor law had sought or acquiesced in racially discriminatory seniority arrangements, its action would have violated the union's duty of fair representation of all members of the bargaining unit.[67] Independent remedies still exist for the breach of such duties, and they may be pursued unaffected by Title VII.[68] Under Title VII, however, conciliation cannot begin until the Commission finds "reasonable cause to believe" that an unlawful employment practice has occurred;[69] judicial relief also requires a finding that such a practice has occurred.[70] Nothing in the statute's definition of unlawful employment practices or in its legislative history suggests that the question whether an unlawful employment practice has occurred can be answered by asking whether the employer or union involved has, in the past, violated an entirely separate duty not imposed by Title VII itself. If it is ever true that the present application of seniority rights based on a discriminatory system antedating Title VII can be lawful under Title VII, then it must be lawful, so far as Title VII is concerned, in all cases.

If a strict concept of retroactivity does not bar its application, the "rightful place" remedy seems best adapted to the achievement of the title's purpose. The title prohibits discrimination in all

---

[61] § 703(h), 42 U.S.C. § 2000e-2(h) (1964).

[62] Rachlin, *Title VII: Limitations and Qualifications*, 7 B.C. Ind. Com. L. Rev. 473, 478 (1966); Note, *The Civil Rights Act of 1964: Racial Discrimination by Labor Unions*, 41 St. John's L. Rev. 58, 78 (1966); see M. Sovern, supra note 6, at 70–73.

[63] Senator Dirksen's own explanatory memorandum concerning the leadership amendments, 110 Cong. Rec. 12381 (daily ed. June 5, 1964), merely paraphrases section 703(h). Id. at 12383.

[64] Id. at 12297 (daily ed. June 4, 1964).

[65] "Bona fide" might be read to require subjective good faith, but in the context of Title VII, this would seem to mean absence of discriminatory intent, and it is impossible to conceive how a system lacking such intent could produce differences in treatment which would be "the result of an intention to discriminate."

[66] Gould, supra, note 26, at 23–27; Walker, supra note 18, at 519.

[67] *Steele* v. *Louisville & N.R.R.*, 323 U.S. 192 (1944) (Ralway Labor Act); *Syres* v. *Oil Workers Local 23*, 350 U.S. 892 (1955) (*per curiam*) (NLRA); see M. Sovern, supra note 6, at 143–75.

[68] With respect to state and local FEPC laws, see pp. 1261–62 supra. No provision of Title VII expressly deals with the relation between it and federal labor legislation. However, a Justice Department memorandum introduced in the debate by Senator Clark, 110 Cong. Rec. 6986 (daily ed. April 8, 1964), states:
Nothing in title VII . . . affects rights and obligations under the NLRA and the Railway Labor Act. The procedures set up in title VII are the exclusive means of relief against . . . unlawful employment practices. . . . Of course, title VII is not intended to and does not deny to any individual, rights, and remedies which he may pursue under other federal and state statutes. The NLRB has adopted this view. Local 12, United Rubber Workers, 150 N.L.R.B. 312, 321 (1964), *enforced*, 368 F. 2d 12, 24 (5th Cir. 1966).

[69] § 706(a), 42 U.S.C. § 2000e-5(a) (1964).

[70] § 706(g), 42 U.S.C. § 2000e-5(g) (1964).

"terms, conditions, or privileges of employment," and thus clearly encompasses discriminatory seniority practices; its language discloses no intention to exclude from its protection the generation of Negroes who have worked under discriminatory systems. Moreover, a desire to eliminate the economic losses to the Negro and to the nation caused by racial discrimination in employment constituted a principal motive underlying the effort to pass Title VII.[71] In the case of the Negro who already has a job, these losses result from discriminatory promotion, layoff, and wage practices. In particular, the continued maintenance of the unequal relative positions of whites and Negroes established in the past will impose future economic losses on the Negro.[72] To tolerate the imposition of such costs on incumbent Negroes would thus undermine a basic statutory policy. On the other hand, the "rightful place" remedy does not deprive white workers of the benefits of discrimination which have accrued to them in the past; they retain their present jobs and the economic gains resulting from past discrimination. All seniority systems in their ordinary operation "discriminate" within the unit in favor of older, long-term employees, and the white workers who stand to gain from this will continue to benefit. The "rightful place" theory would deprive them only of so much of their seniority expectations as depend on the continuation of a competitive differential based on racial considerations.

On the other hand, however, advocates of the "freedom now" approach may also consider the "rightful place" theory inadequate. If all white workers are allowed to hold their present jobs regardless of past discrimination, then, even if the seniority system is modified to allow senior Negroes to bid for vacancies on the basis of their full seniority, they must wait until such vacancies occur and, while waiting, must continue to suffer economic loss resulting from discrimination. In plants where new jobs are not being created or where the employee turnover rate is low, the waiting period may be lengthy and the resulting losses correspondingly great. The "freedom now" approach would avoid imposing these costs on Negro employees, but insofar as it would reverse job awards made before Title VII became law it seems vulnerable to the charge that it is retroactive.[73] Further, although legislative history sheds little light on the question, it seems unlikely that Congress expected Title VII in any circumstances to operate directly to remove a white employee from his job.[74] Finally, by merely modifying white expectations of future job movement, the "rightful place" approach has a built-in quality of "deliberate speed." Where white employees have relied on their seniority expectations in organizing their affairs, they would have some opportunity to adjust these arrangements in the light of the non-discriminatory system. The "freedom now" approach, in contrast, operates immediately and, in the case of particular individuals, may cause drastic reductions in present income. Moreover, it may be noted that, while any view of Title VII which impairs present white expectations will generate opposition, the "freedom now" approach appears so radical and so abrupt as to foreclose any possibility of securing voluntary, if grudging, compliance with the title's requirements.

C. The Ability Factor

The extent to which adoption by the courts of a "rightful place" approach will in a particular situation prove more advantageous to Negro workers than a "status quo" solution and, conversely, the extent to which its application will disturb white expectations will depend upon the Negro workers' qualifications to meet existing ability requirements. Employers may set such requirements at whatever level they consider appropriate, and there appears to be no basis for requiring them to provide special training facilities to enable Negro workers to meet these standards,[75] although, of course, where training

---

[71] H.R. Rep. No. 570, 88th Cong., 1st Sess. 2–4 (1963).

[72] Economists have expressed the effect of racial discrimination in employment in terms of comparisons of the expected lifetime earnings of whites and Negroes of the same age and qualifications. See Hearings on S. 773, supra note 20, at 321–74. Adapting this approach the real economic effect of a discriminatory seniority system may be measured by the amount by which a Negro's earnings in a year fall below those of an actual or hypothetical white worker of equal qualifications and length of service, the total of such losses indicating the full effect of seniority discrimination. Unless a "rightful place" remedy is imposed by Title VII, these losses will continue to accrue and will tend to be greater in amount the longer the Negro has worked under the discriminatory system. Of course, no theory of Title VII will close the gap in lifetime earnings figures, since the economic losses experienced before Title VII became effective cannot be restored.

[73] See p. 1269 supra.

[74] See Clark-Case memorandum, 110 Cong. Rec. 6992 (daily ed. April 8, 1964); id. at 6532 (daily ed. April 1, 1964) (remarks of Senator Moss). See also Gould, supra note 26, at 8–9.

[75] Past exclusion from "white" jobs mght well have deprived Negroes of on-the-job training which would have given them the skills necessary for "rightful place" positions. However, where such training opportunities were lost before the title became effective, they would appear, like past wage losses, to be uncompensable in Title VII proceedings.

programs exist, they must be administered on a non-discriminatory basis.[76] Whether a particular Negro meets the relevant ability standards presents a question of fact which might become the subject of grievance and arbitration proceedings under the collective agreement. It has been suggested that an unsympathetic union could frustrate the application of a "rightful place" remedy by extensive resort to such proceedings and by insisting on a strict interpretation of the "ability clause" of the collective agreement.[77] The courts, however, should be able to meet this problem by requiring inclusion of a fairly detailed statement of the parties' understanding of the degree of ability which must be shown and the methods appropriate for showing it in the final decree or in a supplement to the collective agreement.[78]

One practice on which the courts should look with suspicion consists of attempts by employers to introduce new and more stringent ability requirements at the same time that they are compelled to open formerly "white" jobs to incumbent Negroes. Thus, the settlement in one dispute over discriminatory seniority practices provided "that Negroes with high-school diplomas could move out of the Labor Division into the line of progression for skilled jobs on the basis of a qualifying test. . . ."[79] The introduction of a test might be justified on the ground that the Negroes involved had not been originally hired for skilled work and that the employer should be able to secure some proof of their potential capacity to acquire the abilities needed in the skilled line.[80] However, if the diploma requirement and other standards not closely related to the ability question had not previously been imposed on whites entering the skilled line, and if they excluded a large number of Negro incumbents, they would appear, at least prima facie,

to operate as a continuation of discrimination. Such added requirements should be rejected unless the employer can rebut this presumption by showing that they have some reasonable basis in the present or future skill requirements of his work force.

IV. THE FORM OF REMEDIAL ACTION

Once a court in a "private" Title VII action has determined that an unlawful employment practice has occurred, it has the power to enjoin the offending practice and to "order such affirmative action as may be appropriate, which may include reinstatement or hiring of employees, with or without back pay. . . ."[81] This phrase closely parallels the terms of the enforcement powers given to the National Labor Relations Board by section 10(c) of the Taft-Hartley Act,[82] powers which have been read as conferring a broad discretion, although subject to some limitation.[83] Despite this intended correspondence in language,[84] the policies of the Board and court decisions construing section 10(c) seem unlikely to provide much guidance for the fashioning of Title VII remedies.[85] Until its recent determination that racial discrimination in the negotiation and administration of collective agreements constituted an unfair labor practice, the NLRB had little, if any, occasion to render orders modifying seniority systems in the manner that Title VII requires.[86] Thus, the courts trying Title VII actions will be breaking new ground in determining the shape of "appropriate" remedies for discriminatory seniority practices.

A. Appropriate "Affirmative Action"

Title VII does not outlaw employment practices which may, in particular cases, work to the

---

[76] Section 703(d), 42 U.S.C. § 2000e-2(d) (1964), prohibits discrimination in admission to "on-the-job training programs." Legislative history suggests that Ttile VII bars the use of waiting lists for such programs compiled on a discriminatory basis before the title takes effect. 110 Cong. Rec. 6992 (daily ed. April 8, 1964) (Clark-Case memorandum).

[77] See Doeringer supra note 32.

[78] See p. 1279 infra.

[79] R. Marshall, *The Negro and Organized Labor* 148 (1965).

[80] The title generally sanctions the use of "any professionally developed ability test," provided the test and the manner of its administration and use are not discriminatory. § 703(h), 42 U.S.C. § 2000e-2(h) (1964). It has been suggested that such tests are inherently discriminatory, since they favor the generally greater verbal abilities of whites who have not suffered educational discrimination. See Kovarsky, *The Harlequinesque Motorola Decision and Its Implications*, 7 B.C. Ind. & Com. L. Rev. 535 (1966).

[81] § 706(g), 42 U.S.C. § 2000e-5(g) (1964).

[82] 29 U.S.C. § 160(c) (1964): the NLRB may order a respondent "to take such affirmative action including reinstatement of employees with or without back pay, as will effectuate the policies of this [Act]. . . ."

[83] See, e.g., *Morrison-Knudsen Co.* v. *NLRB*, 275 F. 2d 914, 918 (2d Cir. 1960), *cert. denied*, 366 U.S. 909 (1961). The NLRB's power extends to remedial, but not to "punitive" orders. *Local 60, United Bhd. of Carpenters* v. *NLRB*, 365 U.S. 651, 655 (1961).

[84] 110 Cong. Rec. 6329 (daily ed. March 30, 1964) (remarks of Senator Humphrey); id. at 6993 (daily ed. April 8, 1964) (Clark-Case memorandum).

[85] The EEOC General Counsel has, however, announced that back pay awards under § 706(g) will be sought on principles laid down by the courts and the NLRB under § 10(c). *CCH Emp. Prac. Guide* ¶ 17,304.03 (1966).

[86] Independent Metal Workers Union, 147 N.L.R.B. 1573 (1964), noted in 78 Harv. L. Rev. 679 (1965); see *Vacca* v. *Sipes*, 87 S. Ct. 903 (1967).

disadvantage of Negroes but which were not adopted for that reason. Certain types of seniority systems, such as the "departmental" system which divides a plant into mutually exclusive seniority units, may limit the opportunities of those holding inferior jobs, jobs which may be largely or wholly filled by Negroes; yet, such systems may have a reasonable basis in the firm's organization or the legitimate interest of employee groups. Even where such a system has been adopted with an intent to discriminate, Title VII does not require that it be abandoned permanently in favor of "plant-wide" seniority or some other system which favors workers in low-level jobs. The "rightful place" approach only requires that incumbent Negroes be permitted to use seniority acquired in a "Negro" unit in bidding for jobs in a formerly "white" unit as a device for remedying the subordinate competitive status which discrimination has produced.

In outlining Title VII remedies for particular types of discriminatory seniority, the least difficulty would seem to arise in situations where separate white and Negro seniority lists or job classifications covered employees doing the same work; here, merger of the two lists, measuring Negro seniority on the basis previously accorded whites, would suffice to eliminate any future effects of past discrimination. The strict application of the merged list might require the reallocation of certain jobs within the unit and the recall of senior Negroes who had been laid off while whites junior to them had continued working. However, so long as the "freedom now" rule is not adopted, such Negroes would have to wait for vacancies to occur through normal attrition or expansion of the employer's activities.

In the second type of discriminatory system, where arbitrary limitations have been placed on the promotion of Negroes in a group of functionally related jobs, no exact rule can be stated for calculating the "rightful place" of particular individuals. Since the theory's purpose is to secure present equality of status between whites and Negroes of equal tenure, an approximation might be made by identifying the range of jobs held by whites with similar length of service and permitting the Negro to bid for any vacancy occurring within this range. A senior Negro might find that his white contemporaries occupied positions for which he could not immediately qualify, since he lacked experience which they had gained in intermediate positions. In such circumstances, the Negro would have to take the best job for which he can qualify. Subject to reasonable contract limitations on frequent

job movement, however, he should be permitted to bid for his "rightful place" as soon as he can qualify for it.[87]

The application of the "rightful place" theory to the third discriminatory pattern, typified by the leading case of *Whitfield* v. *United Steelworkers Local 2708,* involves particular difficulties.[88] In *Whitfield,* the employer had established two "lines of progression" in each department, the lines constituting separate seniority districts; each line contained a "logically interrelated" series of jobs in which each individual job required experience and skills acquired in the preceding position on the line. The company hired only whites for the skilled job line in each department and only Negroes for the unskilled line, and no transfers between lines were permitted.[89] In such a situation Title VII would now clearly oblige the employer to abandon his discriminatory hiring policies, but once such policies were abandoned, it would seem that he could continue to treat each line as a separate unit. However, with respect to incumbent Negro employees, who have, at least in part for racial reasons, been limited to the unskilled line, Title VII would appear to require that they be allowed to transfer to the skilled lines on a basis which would not force them to give up job security or income levels attained in the unskilled line. Such employees cannot be treated as equivalent to new applicants for skilled jobs coming in "off the street." They have, in the past, been limited and classified for racial reasons in a manner which deprived them of employment opportunities. As to them, the ban on interline transfers has operated to reinforce a policy of racial discrimination. To eliminate the transfer bar, but to leave in its place economic constraints which make transfers impracticable means that the use of what is, so far as incumbent Negroes are concerned, a racial classification, still tends

---

[87] In order to insure some stability in job assignments, collective agreements might provide that a worker must occupy a job for a specified minimum period before bidding for another.

[88] 156 F. Supp. 430 (S.D. Tex. 1957), aff'd, 263 F. 2d 546 (5th Cir.), *cert. denied,* 360 U.S. 902 (1959). The Fifth Circuit approved as consistent with the union's duty of fair representation a new contract which gave Negroes in the unskilled lines a preferential right to bid for vacancies at the bottom of the skilled lines, provided they had passed a qualifying exam. No carryover of seniority for layoff or promotion purposes was allowed, nor did the contract protect Negroes who were earning higher wages in the unskilled line than they would at the bottom of the skilled line.

[89] A few interdepartmental transfers from one skilled line to another were permitted, but no seniority rights were carried over in these instances. 156 F. Supp. at 436.

to deprive them of opportunities and "adversely affect" their status as employees.[90] The problem that transfers may result in a decrease in job security where seniority rights do not carry over from one line to another can be met by allowing the transferring Negro to "bump back" into his former job if he is laid off from his skilled job. Where this solution disrupts the entire unskilled job line, the employer might prefer to guarantee the Negro a full wage until layoffs in the white line reach men of comparable seniority.[91] The potential earnings loss could be met by "red circling" the Negro's present wage, if higher than the starting wage in the white unit, and paying him at that rate so long as it is greater than the normal rate for the job he is doing.[92]

The remaining problem posed by the *Whitfield* situation concerns the extent to which transferring Negroes can seek their "rightful place" in the skilled line. The "rightful" place approach might appear to require that Negroes be allowed to enter the skilled lines of progression at the point where whites of comparable seniority are found. However, this process would conflict with the rule that promotion to a particular job in a line of progression requires that the worker bidding for the job have already held all the preceding jobs in the line. To the extent that such a rule has a basis in job qualification, so that skills acquired in the earlier jobs are needed for the higher level positions, the courts would have to defer to it in fashioning a remedial order, unless individual Negroes can show that they have in fact filled higher level jobs satisfactorily.[93] On the other hand, where the line of progression techniques has been adopted simply to channel and rationalize job movements in a department, other techniques for demonstrating qualifications, such as testing or the use of "probation periods," could be utilized and the "rightful place" approach applied. Even where transferring Negroes must follow the established *cursus honorum* of the line of progression, a minimum period of occupancy for each job should be defined, so that Negroes who had worked in a job for the designated period could be presumed to have acquired the skills necessary to be eligible for the next vacancy in the following job.

B. General Considerations

When a seniority system has been adjudged unlawful in a particular case, adequate relief for the aggrieved complainant requires more than a negative injunction prohibiting the continued application of the system. To aid future enforcement,[94] the terms of the reformed system should be expressly stated in the final decree.[95] Since discriminatory practices often result from unwritten agreements supplementing the general terms of the collective agreement, a fairly detailed order or one requiring that the seniority system be described in detail in the collective agreement itself seems necessary to reduce the danger of similar evasions in the future. Although some doubt has been expressed about the powers of courts in fair representation cases to order substantive changes in collective agreements, Title VII clearly contemplates that such changes are within the scope of appropriate "affirmative action" under section 706(g).[96] Nonetheless, seniority systems are a central factor in collective agreements, and they affect numerous interests other than the white-Negro conflict emphasized in a Title VII action. Courts may naturally be reluctant to interfere unilaterally with the terms of the collective agreement, especially where arrangements motivated in part by racial considerations also reflect legitimate interests of the employer or the resolution of conflicts between various employee groups. At least where bona fide doubt exists about what Title VII requires, it may be desirable for a court, after determining that an unlawful employment practice has occurred, initially to defer to collective bargaining and to permit the employer and the union[97] to

---

[90] § 703(a)(2), 42 U.S.C. § 2000e–2(a)(2) (1964).

[91] The guarantee might take the form of supplemental unemployment compensation equal to the difference between the employee's regular wage and unemployment insurance payments.

[92] See Conciliation Agreement, Newport News Shipbuilding & Drydock Co., II, § 3(b), *CCH Emp. Prac. Guide* ¶ 8055 (1966).

[93] Individual Negroes in the "labor department" or other low-level job classifications may be temporarily assigned to "white" jobs when regular workers are on sick-leave or vacation, or they may have otherwise acquired the skills necessary for such jobs. See, e.g., Rachlin, supra note 62, at 479.

[94] The Commission may commence proceedings to compel compliance with an outstanding § 706(g) order. § 706(i), 42 U.S.C. § 2000e–5(i) (1964).

[95] *Cf.* Note, *The Need for Creative Orders under Section 10(c) of the National Labor Relations Act,* 112 U. Pa. L. Rev. 69, 79 (1963), emphasizing the need for more precise orders to facilitate contempt proceedings in unfair labor practice cases.

[96] *Central of Ga. Ry.* v. *Jones,* 229 F. 2d 648, 649 (5th Cir. 1956) (Brown, J., dissenting), *cert. denied.* 352 U.S. 848 (1956).

[97] Although the initial charge may not name both the employer and the union as respondents, the involvement of both in conciliation and any subsequent litigation is probably necessary to a binding settlement of claims requiring modification of a seniority system established by a collective agreement. See Walker, supra note 18, at

attempt to work out a satisfactory substitute for the old agreement, with the court retaining jurisdiction to approve the outcome of these negotiations.[98] Such a procedure would recognize the strong federal policy in favor of collective bargaining and would place the problem in the hands of experienced negotiators familiar with the peculiarities of the particular employment situation. On the other hand, it might add further delay in an already lengthy process and would allow reluctant parties to exercise their expertise in the search for a minimally acceptable agreement. The success of such a procedure would depend to a considerable extent on the court's ability to formulate useful guidelines to direct the negotiators' efforts.[99]

A situation which might seem to raise few difficulties in formulating a Title VII remedy would arise if a court found that a collective agreement, although lawful as written, had been administered according to a discriminatory understanding which violates both the title and the contract.[100] In such a case, the court might simply order the parties to follow the contract as written. However, if the "freedom now" approach is rejected, Title VII would not require the displacement of employees from jobs which they presently hold, even though they acquired these positions as a result of discrimination. This limitation could be accommodated by an order similar to the consent decree approved in *Butler* v. *Celotex Corp.*[101] in which individuals who had acquired special benefits from "unwritten seniority were permitted to retain them so long as they held their present positions but could rely only on "contract seniority" when they moved to different jobs. Of course, whether a particular discriminatory understanding actually violates rather than merely supplements the general terms of the collective agreement may not be easy to determine. Thus, under a contract which provided generally that seniority should govern

promotions and layoffs, an arbitrator found that the longstanding practice of maintaining separate seniority lists for white males, Negro males, and women did not violate the contract, since both parties had known of and acquiesced in the practice.[102] To raise a presumption against such a result and thus open the contract's own enforcement procedures for use against discriminatory practices, courts should, as a matter of course, require the inclusion of anti-discrimination clauses in collective agreements modified by Title VII proceedings.[103]

C. Damage Remedies

Because any externally imposed restructuring of a seniority system which upsets white expectations will create tensions and resistance among the white workers, respondent employers or unions, and the Negro workers themselves might find preferable a remedy which substituted an award of prospective damages for the right to bid for a "rightful place" position. This award might take the form of a wage increment, calculated as the difference between the Negro's present rate and what he would earn in his "rightful place," or a lump-sum payment, calculated as the present discounted value of the expected loss to the incumbent Negro resulting from the failure to purge the seniority system of disparities in status caused by past discrimination. A remedy of this sort would maintain existing expectations based on the seniority system, but it would compensate Negro workers for their real economic loss.

A damage remedy, however, would not compensate the Negro for the loss of certain noneconomic benefits, in particular, the dignity attaching to the status of occupying a "white" job, and it would deny him the opportunity to acquire through experience the skills involved in such jobs, thus limiting his ability to compete on the job market. Furthermore, it would be difficult to measure on a hypothetical basis what job constituted an individual's rightful place, particularly with respect to his ability to fill it, and, to the extent that a damage remedy compensated employees who would not in fact have sought or won promotion, it imposes an unnecessary cost

---

512. The practice in most fair representation cases has been to join both the union and the employer as parties defendant, even where one or the other has actually opposed the discrimination in question. See *Mitchell* v. *Gulf, M.&O.R.R.*, 91 F. Supp. 175 (N.D. Ala. 1950), *aff'd as modified sub nom., Brotherhood of Locomotive Firemen* v. *Mitchell*, 190 F. 2d 308 (5th Cir. 1951).

[98] Compare the practice of allowing malapportioned legislatures to attempt to reform themselves. Note, "Reapportionment," 79 *Harv. L. Rev.* 1226, 1267–69 (1966).

[99] See *State Commission for Human Rights* v. *Farrell*, 43 Misc. 2d 958, 252 N.Y.S. 2d 649 (Sup. Ct. 1964), discussed in M. Sovern, *supra* note 6, at 182–83.

[100] E.g., *Butler* v. *Celotex Corp.*, 3 Race Rel. L. Rep. 503 (E.D. La. 1958).

[101] Id.

[102] Goodyear Tire & Rubber Co., 45 Lab. Arb. 240 (1965).

[103] Cf. Local 12, United Rubber Workers, 150 N.L.R.B. 312, 322 (1964), *enforced*, 368 F. 2d 12 (5th Cir. 1966). See generally, Bureau of National Affairs, *supra* note 1, at 71–78; AFL-CIO Dept. of Civil Rights, *Sample Nondiscrimination Clauses in Collective Bargaining Agreements*, in *Hearings on H.R. 405*, *supra* note 22, at 80–82.

on the respondent.[104] Although employers and unions are required by Title VII to eliminate discriminatory practices, they ordinarily do not, at least in the case of seniority systems, derive any direct economic benefit from such practices. Thus, in any situation in which substantial payments would be required, employers and unions would probably resist the prospective damages approach unless they anticipated very great difficulty in persuading white workers to accept a reformed seniority system. Since an award of damages or other alternative remedy may not conform strictly to the requirements of the "rightful place" approach, a court should not impose it over the objections of the complainant or employer-respondent in a Title VII action.[105] However, in the interest of maintaining flexibility in the conciliation process, a court could approve such a remedy where the parties had agreed to it and where it appeared to provide a reasonable equivalent to a "rightful place" award.

V. CONCLUSION

This Note argues that Title VII should be interpreted as requiring a "rightful place" remedy for discriminatory seniority practices. Considerations of prudence might, however, be thought to dictate something less than an uncompromising insistence on "rightful place." The feasibility of equal employment opportunity legislation depends to a great extent on voluntary compliance. The EEOC does not have the facilities to oversee all the employers and unions which come before it and to police their compliance with conciliation agreements or court orders. In addition, the requirement that workers invoking a rightful place remedy meet existing ability standards may make possible obstructive practices by hostile unions and employers which will make the benefits of the remedy difficult to secure. Moreover, the necessity for pursuing a civil remedy in the federal courts when conciliation fails may impose a considerable financial burden and prospect of

delay on complainants.[106] Further, Negro employees must work together with their white colleagues, and where insistence on a "rightful place" remedy generates resentment, white hostility may in practice make the "rightful place" an unpleasant one. Such considerations and, perhaps, an overreaction to charges that FEP laws would interfere excessively with the operations of employers have led some states FEPC's to avoid interfering with white expectations to benefit Negroes.[107] Thus, the New York State Commission does not seek conciliation agreements which adversely affect white seniority rights.[108] The Commission even took the position that where a white has been hired in preference to a Negro for discriminatory reasons, the Negro need not be employed immediately if this would entail firing the white.[109]

Nonetheless, whatever the practical merits of some kind of compromise as the outcome of conciliation in particular cases, it would not be proper for the Commission or the courts to reject the "rightful place" approach in order to avoid the difficulties involved in fashioning and enforcing appropriate remedies or because these difficulties were thought to make the cost of securing a rightful place remedy exceed in many cases the benefit to be derived from it. It should be remembered that the interpretation of Title VII by the courts will itself be a major factor in the calculations of the parties in conciliation. Title VII applies fair employment mandates for the first time to areas of the South in which discriminatory employment practices are firmly entrenched. Where no disposition exists to do more than the law requires, the success of the conciliation process depends largely on the threat of resort to the courts. If the courts determine that Title VII requires an adjustment of seniority

---

[104] See *Clark* v. *Norfolk & W. Ry.*, 3 Race Rel. L. Rep. 988 (W.D. Va. 1958) (fair representation). The court awarded damages for lost income resulting from discriminatory denial of promotion on the ground that the plaintiff had in testifying seemed "alert and very intelligent." Damages were denied two other plaintiffs who had failed a qualifying test for the job administered while the litigation was in progress.

[105] Doeringer, supra note 32, suggests that special training programs could be created for Negro workers as a partial alternative to a "rightful place" order. It would be difficult to determine what amount or types of training would be an adequate substitute for the promotion opportunities surrendered.

[106] In a § 706 proceeding, upon complainant's application "and in such circumstances as the court may deem just, the court may appoint an attorney for such complainant and may authorize the commencement of the action without the payment of fees, costs, or security." § 706(e), 42 U.S.C. § 2000e-5(e) (1964). The court "in its discretion, may allow the prevailing party, other than the Commission or the United States, a reasonable attorney's fee as part of the costs. . . ." in any Title VII proceeding. § 706(k), 42 U.S.C. § 2000e-5(k) (1964). *See* Walker, *supra* note 18, at 501–6.

[107] Hill, "Twenty Years of State Fair Employment Practice Commissions: A Critical Analysis," 14 *Buffalo L. Rev.* 22 (1964).

[108] Spitz, "Tailoring the Techniques to Eliminate and Prevent Employment Discrimination," 14 *Buffalo L. Rev.* 79, 82 (1964).

[109] Carter, "Practical Considerations of Anti-Discrimination Legislation–Experience under the New York Law against Discrimination," 40 *Cornell L. Q.* 40, 48 (1954).

rights to eliminate differences in present competitive status attributable to past employer discrimination, particular complainants will have a firm basis for negotiation of a voluntary agreement acceptable to both sides. If the cost and difficulty of securing and effectively enforcing a "rightful place" remedy appear to be great, some complainants may settle in conciliation for something less satisfactory than or different from the remedy which a "rightful place" approach would require. Even such limited gains would be foreclosed, however, if the courts allow a consciousness of the "practical" difficulties of enforcing a "rightful place" approach to lead to its rejection.

54. Manpower Programs: Moving toward Decentralization*

U.S. Department of Labor

A long step forward on the road to a decentralized and decategorized manpower system was taken in 1973. On December 28 the President signed into law the Comprehensive Employment and Training Act (CETA), greatly advancing the administration's aim of transferring the responsibility and resources for manpower programs to states and localities with minimal federal direction of program design and operation. The transfer promises to reduce the fragmented manpower development efforts in which multiple projects—approximately 10,000 nationwide—are independently aimed at similar problems. Under the new legislation, elected officials will act as prime sponsors of comprehensive manpower programs for target populations in their jurisdictions. The latter may be comprised of a state, a city, a county, or a consortium of jurisdictions.

While the administration took further steps in 1973 toward a decentralized manpower system, the Congress renewed its efforts to achieve comprehensive manpower reform.[1] Near the end of the session, the bipartisan Comprehensive Employment and Training Act of 1973 was passed, ending several years of controversy over the basic design of the nation's manpower efforts on behalf of the disadvantaged and unemployed. The first of the President's proposals for decentralization of major social programs to win congressional assent, the legislation measurably advanced the administration's initiative toward a change in federal-state relationships, which was proposed early in its tenure as the "New Federalism."

COMPREHENSIVE MANPOWER REFORM LEGISLATION

The Department of Labor intends to implement the CETA in as many areas as possible during 1974. However, specific provision is made for a transitional period through fiscal 1974, during which programs financed under other authorities may be continued. The new law calls for making governors and the chief elected officials of major cities and counties responsible for planning and operating manpower programs. Henceforth, they will decide on the mix of manpower services they will make available. Keyed to "economically disadvantaged, unemployed, and underemployed persons," the act authorizes the full range of manpower services, including transitional public service employment. It also provides special funding (under title II) for areas where unemployment is 6½ percent or higher for 3 consecutive months. While the legislation provides an open-ended authorization, it specifies that at least $250 million is to be set aside for title II activities in fiscal 1974 and $350 million in fiscal 1975.

Up to 20 percent of the resources provided are made available to the Secretary of Labor to administer certain national programs (including, specifically, the Job Corps) and to discharge other assigned responsibilities. In determining how these discretionary funds are to be employed, the Secretary is enjoined to take into account the need for continued funding of programs of demonstrated effectiveness. The remainder—after subtraction of the title II funds and the portion needed by the Secretary—are for

---

* From U.S. Department of Labor, *Manpower Report of the President,* April 1974, pp. 38–66.

[1] The Manpower Development and Training Act, which has furnished authorization for federal manpower programs since 1962, expired at the end of fiscal 1973. Thereafter, authority rested in part on a continuing resolution for funding programs and in part on the Economic Opportunity Act.

implementing comprehensive manpower program activities in states and localities (authorized under title I).

Title I funds are to be allocated as follows:

Eighty percent to state and local prime sponsors to enable them to carry out comprehensive programs in their jurisdictions. (One percent of this allocation is to be available to State prime sponsors for staffing and serving State Manpower Services Councils. Councils are to review state and local manpower plans, monitor program operations, and make annual reports to governors.)

Up to 5 percent to encourage combinations of units of general local government as prime sponsors to achieve organization along labor market area rather than strictly political lines. (Such allocations are to be decided upon in consultation with the appropriate governors.)

Five percent to provide grants to governors for needed skill training in areas served by prime sponsors (to be obtained through state vocational agencies).

Four percent to states for flexible manpower activities, e.g., labor market information, technical assistance to prime sponsors, special services in rural areas, and model programs for offenders.

The remainder to be available for the discretionary use of the Secretary of Labor, especially in meeting "hold harmless" funding requirements.

Each state's share of the $2.05 billion requested in the President's budget to implement the CETA in fiscal 1975 is determined on the basis of a weighted three-part formula: (1) its percentage of the previous year's national manpower allotment (weight, 50 percent); (2) its share of national unemployment (weight, 37.5 percent); and (3) the relative number of adults in families with an annual income below the low-income level, defined as $7,000 as of 1969 with subsequent adjustment in accordance with increases in the Consumer Price Index (weight, 12.5 percent). The same factors—previous allotment (the "hold harmless" provision to prevent abrupt and disruptive changes), unemployment, and incidence of low-income adults—will determine the distribution among prime sponsors within states. However, no prime sponsor is to receive more than 150 percent of the previous fiscal year's allotment of funds to the area served. If, as a result of this limitation, the prime sponsor would receive less than 50 percent of the amount determined by the formula for the current year, his allotment would then be raised to the 50-percent level. A further provision would give prime sponsors at least 90 percent of the previous year's allotment, to be achieved by reallocating funds saved by application of the 150-percent maximum. If these are inadequate for the purpose, additional funds are to be drawn from the Secretary's title I discretionary funds.

Manpower services and activities authorized by title I include, but are not limited to, those presently associated with manpower programs, such as outreach; assessment of individual capacities and interests; referral to jobs, training, or other opportunities; orientation; counseling; education and skill training; on-the-job training; training subsidies for employers; supportive services; subsistence and expense allowances for enrollees; programs conducted by community-based organizations (referring, for example, to Opportunities Industrialization Centers, Jobs for Progress—frequently termed "SER," standing for Service, Employment, and Redevelopment—and Community Action agencies); and transitional public service employment programs.[2]

Under title III, the Secretary is authorized to provide manpower services for special groups, including youth, offenders, persons of limited English-speaking ability, older workers, and other persons determined by the Secretary of Labor to have particular disadvantages in the labor market. As a result of Congress findings that Indians and Alaska natives, as well as migrant and seasonal farmworkers, are economically disadvantaged, the Secretary is specifically instructed to conduct programs for them. The Secretary is further directed to consult with the Secretary of Health, Education, and Welfare concerning "arrangements for services of a health, education, or welfare character" and to obtain the approval of the HEW Secretary when he arranges directly for the provision of basic education and vocational training.

The Secretary is also authorized to conduct research and demonstration programs, develop labor market information, evaluate manpower activities to guide policy and program decisions, operate a nationwide computerized job bank and worker-job matching program, and provide technical assistance and staff training to prime sponsors in order to improve program performance.

Newly required are the development of "pre-

---

[2] Prime sponsors may use title II funds for these title I purposes, or conversely, title I funds for public service employment.

liminary data for an annual statistical measure of labor market related economic hardship in the nation" and of "methods to establish and maintain more comprehensive household budget data at different levels of living. . . ." A report to the Congress on labor market information activities and progress in developing economic hardship measures is due by the end of 1974.

All prime sponsors are to establish planning councils as nearly as possible representative of the client community and of community-based organizations, the employment service, education and training agencies, business, labor, and, where appropriate, agriculture. Councils will advise prime sponsors on program plans, goals, policies, and procedures and will help to monitor activities and provide for objective evaluations of programs as well. An annual comprehensive plan must be submitted to the Secretary by each prime sponsor (local plans also go to the governor for his comment); it will be approved when the Secretary determines that it meets statutory requirements. (Subsequently, it can be revoked if he determines that the prime sponsor has failed to meet those requirements in carrying it out.)

An important new feature of the manpower apparatus is a National Commission for Manpower Policy, established to examine national manpower issues and bring correctives to bear on "the lack of a coherent, flexible, national manpower policy." It will be composed of 17 members, of whom the President will appoint 11 who either are broadly representative of labor, industry, commerce, education, and the general public, are state and local elected officials involved with manpower programs, or are persons served by the programs. The remaining six members (serving ex officio) will be the Secretaries of five federal departments—Labor; Health, Education, and Welfare; Defense; Commerce; and Agriculture—and the Administrator of Veterans Affairs. The chairman, appointed by the President from among the public members, will name an executive director, who will have a staff to assist him in serving the Commission as it:

Identifies national manpower goals and needs and assesses the approach of human development programs, including many authorized outside the CETA, to these needs and goals.

Conducts relevant studies, hearings, and research.

Examines the effectiveness of federally assisted manpower development programs, whether or not they are implemented under the CETA.

Evaluates major federal programs aimed at achieving the objectives of manpower and related legislation, especially research and demonstration programs and training programs for occupational guidance, counseling, and placement personnel.

Evaluates and makes recommendations to the Congress on a study of the impact of energy shortages on manpower needs (which the Secretary of Labor is required to submit to Congress by the end of March 1974).

FIRST STEPS IN IMPLEMENTING THE LEGISLATION

The first order of business for the Department of Labor upon passage of the legislation was its translation into operating programs. With the intention of rapidly converting categorical programs to the new design for manpower activities, several priorities were established:

Immediate funding of operational planning grants in preparation for prime sponsorship to more than 100 newly eligible counties. (Such grants had already been awarded to many jurisdictions, as discussed in the following section.)

Determination of areas eligible for title II funding and preparation of regulations governing implementation in the expectation of providing full funding to grantees by April.

Providing funds by early June, using the title I formula, to those prime sponsors who wish to develop summer youth programs. (About $300 million will be made available.)

Preparation of federal regulations and of technical assistance and training materials for Department of Labor regional staffs and prime sponsors staffs to make possible the early startup of comprehenisve manpower programs.

The accomplishment of a great many tasks in the short span of 6 months poses a real challenge. For title I alone, these tasks include: determining eligibility for prime sponsorship; applying the allocation formula; approving proposed federal regulations; approving multijurisdictional agreements; training a great many people at various administrative levels in the new ways of performing manpower functions; and reviewing and approving plans and applications drafted by prime sponsors. If the change had not been anticipated for several years and steps taken to prepare for it, the objective would be even more difficult to achieve.

ADMINISTRATIVE MEASURES TO
SPEED DECENTRALIZED ACTIVITIES

Planning Grants

An early step toward bringing decisionmaking closer to the local areas where jobs and the people who need them are brought together was the funding of manpower planning positions on the staffs of elected officials. Begun in 1970, the process has been extended to 1,200 such positions with governors and mayors by the end of fiscal 1973. Early in the current fiscal year, some $7 million was allotted to planning grants for 34 additional cities and, for the first time, 161 counties with populations exceeding 150,000. These grants have helped the jurisdictions to prepare for the impending program grants by inventorying ongoing programs, establishing relationships with local Cooperative Area Manpower Planning System (CAMPS) councils, exploring possible cooperative arrangements with adjacent jurisdictions, and studying local manpower needs with a view to developing goals and priorities.

CAMPS, which since 1967 has brought together federal departments and agencies for manpower planning purposes, had already been restructured (in fiscal 1972) to make it an advisory unit to governors and mayors and to Assistant Regional Directors for Manpower of the Department of Labor as well as other federal agency officials. The Department of Labor, charged with negotiating and administering contracts for categorical manpower programs, has followed closely the advice of the CAMPS state and local Manpower Planning councils.

Pilot Comprehensive Manpower Programs

During fiscal 1973, the concept of decentralization began to be tested in nine states and areas, where agreements were signed with governors and mayors to conduct pilot Comprehensive Manpower Programs (CMPs). The Departments of Labor and Health, Education, and Welfare and the Office of Economic Opportunity had started developing these projects late in 1971 in order to explore the feasibility of proceeding with manpower revenue sharing under then-existing legislation. Nevertheless, the CMP experience is germane to decentralization and decategorization under the new legislation, even though participating jurisdictions are not necessarily representative of the cities and states which will assume prime sponsor roles.

. . . the pilot projects are widely dispersed

and differ markedly in size and characteristics. In all cases, the initiative for a CMP project came from political leaders and their manpower administrators, with support from regional Manpower Administration staff.

These pilot projects are administering a combination of Manpower Development and Training Act and Economic Opportunity Act funds; grants range from slightly less than $2 million in Omaha to about $12.7 million in South Carolina. Local arrangements are as diverse as the variations in size, geography, and political structures of the areas covered would suggest.

A single example of how a CMP translated concept into reality is the experience of the Albuquerque pilot. The first to be developed, the project rests on a joint powers agreement between the city and Bernalillo County, each of which is governed by a commission. The 18 members of the Manpower Planning Council are jointly appointed by the city and the county to represent the citizenry rather than organizations and agencies. The city is the prime sponsor, with the Office of Manpower Programs carrying the responsibility for operations.

The initial core of the Albuquerque CMP was the Concentrated Employment Program (CEP), transferred from the local Community Action Agency (CAA) to CMP management. (The CAA nominates a third of the Council members.) The Public Employment and Work Incentive programs have since been brought under the CMPs aegis. The Job Opportunities in the Business Sector (JOBS) Program has been incorporated as well, and a major employer has signed an agreement with the CMP that places all his production openings under a JOBS contract, with the CMP paying for supportive services and the employer providing all the training. Training and education for CMP clients may be obtained either through a locally supported vocational-technical school (which has altered its admission and scheduling procedures to accommodate disadvantaged students) or in the MDTA skills center. The local public employment service (ES), the subcontractor for most manpower services, has been decentralized into five neighborhood centers, a step toward unified, one-stop manpower centers readily accessible to manpower program clients.

The Planning Council is organized around five functions: public employment, private employment, adult training, youth training, and labor market analysis. The CMP staff is organized in much the same way, with a staff director for each of the five program areas to direct program operations under the guidance of the Council.

Data for the first 6 months of full operation indicate that the new way of handling manpower programs has produced a dramatic increase in the number of persons served and placed in jobs. Enrollments in the CMP reached more than twice the level recorded for categorical programs during 1972, and job placements nearly doubled. Unquestionably, a high degree of coordination among manpower agenices has been achieved and service to program clients streamlined through the five ES centers. However, the goal of significantly upgrading the jobs in which clients are placed is still to be met.

All nine areas with CMP projects have had experience with PEP (which helped set the stage for the pilots, particularly for the Utah CMP); all have had considerable experience with categorical programs; and six had functioning CEP projects with unified delivery systems at the time the CMP's were initiated. Planners who had been involved in CAMPS played leading roles in preparing CMP proposals.[3] But new planning councils were formed to serve specific political jurisdictions. CAMPS Planning councils, keyed to differently defined areas, were not carried over, although some CAMPS members were included in CMP council memberships, and some CAMPS staff members found themselves in CMP administrative positions.

A review of CMP experience completed by the Department of Labor in December 1973 produced several findings which have implications for the general transition to decentralized and comprehensive programs under the CETA:

Great diversity in state and local legal constraints was encountered, making consultations with legal advisers, governors' offices, and city councils not only advisable but essential.

Some planners tended to overstate the advantages of CMP in order to encourage formation of consortia of jurisdictions, while elected officials in areas with relatively little experience with categorical manpower programs tended to develop unrealistic expectations of future benefits.

The planning process was most helpful when it was extended beyond allocation of resources among program activities to such concerns as determination of total resources available for operating a manpower system and clarification of the roles, relationships, and functions of major participants.

Useful incentives for forming multijurisdictional consortia were found to include: liberal representation of jurisdictions on planning councils and on CMP staffs; assurances of continuation of certain program activities despite consolidation; and, where the state was prime sponsor, agreement in principle to allot major cities their fair share of funds.

Conversion from categorical programs to a comprehensive program proved to be time consuming and, in some cases, arduous. While elected officials generally welcomed decentralization and decategorization, the newness and experimental nature of CMP complicated the process. However, a climate was created in which diverse political jurisdictions were willing to work together to attain common manpower objectives.

NATIONAL PROGRAMS IN THE TRANSITION PERIOD

During fiscal 1974, the process of converting the manpower administrative structure to the new pattern will be far advanced, although it probably cannot be completed until the following year. In planning for the conversion, the Department of Labor recognized (as does the new legislation) that certain manpower needs cannot be appropriately addressed through state and local prime sponsors but can best be served through nationally administered programs. Therefore, prior to passage of the CETA, about a fourth of all program resources were reserved for these purposes[4]—i.e., to meet administration or congressional priorities, respond to national emergencies which disrupt employment patterns, handle the temporary interruptions in manpower services that may occur during the period of putting revenue sharing into operation, and serve special target groups (such as migrants and youth needing a residential program) who are unlikely to be adequately reached by state or local program sponsors.

Thus, the nationally administered Construction Outreach Program, which seeks equal employment opportunity for minority youth in the

---

[3] For a description of the early experience in establishing CMP's, as well as of the evolution of at least a partial consensus on achieving state and local responsibility for planning and carrying out decategorized comprehensive manpower delivery systems, see Howard W. Hallman, *Pilot Comprehensive Manpower Program: Implications of Its Experience for Local and State Manpower Organization* (Washington: Center for Governmental Studies, October 1973).

[4] The WIN Program is, of course, also a nationally administered program with separate authorization and funding.

skilled apprenticeable trades (and includes up-grade training for journeymen), continues with the cooperation and contract services of national labor unions. Special services for migrant and seasonal farmworkers and for veterans (especially disabled veterans) and some activities for offenders also continue under national direction. The JOBS Program, operated in cooperation with the National Alliance of Businessmen (NAB), also remains a nationally run program through fiscal 1974.

Similarly, redevelopment area projects (in areas certified by the Economic Development Administration), certain Operation Mainstream services, and the Job Corps are components of the complex of manpower activities administered from Washington in fiscal 1974. However, both Operation Mainstream and Job Corps are to be increasingly integrated with the decentralized system as it takes shape. Recently, Job Corps has been emphasizing the assignment of recruits to centers as close to their residences as possible. It is hoped that certain centers, serving largely local populations, can in time be operated as part of local comprehensive programs. However, a few centers will probably continue under federal direction to serve multistate areas and to meet specialized training needs. Relocation of some centers to accommodate these new patterns is under consideration.

PROGRAMS IN REVIEW: 1973

Enrollment Trends

A decade-long uptrend in enrollments in manpower programs came to a halt in fiscal 1973. (See Table 1.) New enrollments, which had reached 3.3 million in the previous year, fell to 2.9 million. Volume was lower in most programs administered by the Department of Labor, especially in the NYC in-school and summer programs, while the JOBS and PSC programs and PEP also contributed significantly to the downturn. Increases in some programs—WIN, NYC out-of-school, Operation Mainstream, Veterans Administration manpower programs, and the Department of Health, Education, and Welfare vocational rehabilitation program—were smaller than the decreases, yielding a net loss of 13 percent from 1972 to 1973.

The estimate of new enrollments in the current fiscal year is necessarily tentative because of the changeover from national categorical programs to state and local comprehensive programs under the new manpower legislation. In the first half

TABLE 1 New Enrollments in Federally Assisted Work and Training Programs, Fiscal Years 1972–74 (thousands)*

		Fiscal Year	
Program	1972	1973	1974 (esti-mated)
Total....................	3,300	2,885	2,736
Comprehensive manpower assistance..................	—	—	1,166†
Institutional training under the MDTA..................	151	120	—
JOBS (federally financed).....	83	52	65
Other national OJT‡..........	151	148	—
Neighborhood Youth Corps:			
In-school and summer......	946	554	—
Out-of-school...............	65	75	—
Operation Mainstream........	31	38	—
Public Service Careers........	66	25	—
Concentrated Employment Program....................	85	69	—
Job Corps.....................	49	43	45
Work Incentive Program......	121	239	80
Public Employment Program..	226	178	104
Veterans programs...........	89	107	118
Vocational rehabilitation......	497	503	535
Other programs§..............	740	734	623

Note: Detail may not add to totals because of rounding.

* Generally larger than the number of training or work opportunities programed because turnover or short-term training results in more than one individual in a given enrollment opportunity. Persons served by more than one program are counted only once.

† Estimated enrollments funded by appropriations under the Comprehensive Employment and Training Act of 1973; the JOBS and Job Corps programs are also funded under this legislation but are shown separately since they continue under national administration through fiscal 1974.

‡ Includes MDTA-OJT national contracts; the JOBS-Optional Program; and Construction Outreach, with 72,000 enrollees in fiscal 1973.

§ Includes a variety of programs, of which by far the largest is Social Services Training for public assistance recipients funded under grants to states by the Social Rehabilitation Services Administration in the Department of Health, Education, and Welfare. Others are quite small, e.g., vocational training for Indians, provided by the Department of the Interior, and on-the-job training and work support in the Model Cities Program, run by the Department of Housing and Urban Development.

Sources: Office of Management and Budget, Special Analyses, *Budget of the United States Government*, and U.S. Department of Labor.

of the year, enrollments in categorical programs ran slightly below fiscal 1973, and it seems likely, in the light of a projected sizable decline in other programs as well, that some further overall slippage is in prospect.

For fiscal 1975, however, the administration's budget request of $4.8 billion indicates a significant upturn to more than 3.3 million new entries into federally assisted manpower programs. (See Table 2.) Federal outlays for training, rehabilitation, and work-support programs are estimated at more than $3.3 billion, of which $1.9 billion is for implementing the Comprehensive Employment and Training Act (denoted as "Comprehensive manpower assistance" in the table).

Other substantial outlays for manpower and related activities are projected for job placement assistance and antidiscrimination efforts, including the public employment service ($663 million); for supportive services, including those for individuals in the WIN, AFDC, and vocational rehabilitation ($1.1 billion); and for program direction, research, and support ($150 million).

When enrollment trends are viewed from a point-in-time perspective, the 656,100 individuals on the rolls of programs administered by the Department of Labor at the end of April 1973 were 6 percent fewer than a year earlier, and the seasonal peak of 1 million at the end of July (when youth were enrolled in summer projects) was about a quarter of a million, or 20 percent, lower than the July 1972 level. By late 1973, further declines had occurred in most categorical programs, declines that were only partially compensated for by initial enrollments in pilot Comprehensive Manpower Programs. Falling enrollments in PEP were, of course, related to the expiration of the temporary authorizing legislation. Except for the WIN Program, in which enrollments have advanced steadily since the conclusion of the shakedown period for the revised program near the end of 1972, and Operation Mainstream, other manpower programs reflected accommodations to budgetary uncertainties.[5] The prospect of transition to state and locally run programs also inhibited some program activities.

Having fulfilled their purpose as demonstrations, the Public Service Careers (PSC) Program, Plan B (employment and upgrading of the disadvantaged in federal grant-in-aid programs) and Plan D (in the federal service), began phasing down in fiscal 1973. Plan B terminated in December 1973 and Plan D is scheduled to end in June 1974. Both activities will continue, however—the former as an option in some local comprehensive programs and the latter under the sponsorship of the Civil Service Commission.

Among on-the-job training (OJT) programs, funding for the JOBS Program was revised sharply downward during fiscal 1973. Obligation of these resources, which provide federal support to the training of disadvantaged workers by pri-

---

[5] A freeze on funding and enrollments was imposed in the third quarter of fiscal 1973. Not until late in the year was it clear that there would be no appropriations legislation and that a "continuing resolution" would govern the entire year's activity. The same uncertainties prevailed in the first half of fiscal 1974.

TABLE 2   Estimated Outlays and New Enrollments in Federal Manpower Programs, Fiscal Year 1975

Activity	Expenditures (millions)	New Enrollees (thousands)
All activities	$3,337	3,318
Institutional training	785	958
Comprehensive manpower assistance	633	338
Work incentive program	50	32
Social services training	61	550
Other	41	38
On-the-job training	594	470
Comprehensive manpower assistance	302	386
Work incentive program	45	16
Veterans OJT	241	66
Other	6	2
Vocational rehabilitation	864	572
HEW	770	554
Veterans	94	18
Work support	1,094	1,318
Comprehensive manpower assistance	967	1,235
Work incentive program	29	30
Other	98	53

Source: Office of Management and Budget, *Special Analyses, Budget of the United States Government, Fiscal Year 1975.*

vate employers, has lagged—partly because of high termination rates. The state-administered JOBS-Optional Program (JOP) has had difficulty in contracting for sufficient openings with employers, with marked variations among regions. However, an uptrend has marked enrollments in OJT under nationally administered contracts and the Construction Outreach Program. And Operation Mainstream had higher enrollments in 1973 than in previous years.

At the end of the fiscal year, 76 CEP projects were in operation—down from a peak of 82 in 1969. Four were terminated due to poor performance during the past year (and two were transferred to pilot CMPs). The enrollment decline from fiscal 1972 to fiscal 1973 reflected this reduction, as well as a funding cutback.

Job Corps funding was reduced for fiscal 1974 to $184 million. During 1973, 6 small, high-cost residential support centers were closed, and there was a cut of about 3,000 openings in overall capacity. The cutback is visible in the April–July enrollment decline. Funds to support volunteer activities in recruitment and tutoring were reduced, but resources for the successful union-run training and placement programs were augmented.

While NYC in-school and summer enrollments rose to a seasonal peak of only 340,200 in July

TABLE 3   Characteristics of Enrollees in Federally-Assisted Work and Training Programs, Fiscal Year 1973 (percent of total enrollees)

Program	Women	Blacks*	Spanish-Speaking	Age Under 22 Years	Age 45 Years and Over	Years of School Completed 8 or Less	Years of School Completed 9 through 11	On Public Assistance†
Institutional training under the MDTA	33	30	10	36	8	8	29	13
JOBS (federally financed) and other OJT‡	25	26	15	36	7	11	31	10
Neighborhood Youth Corps:								
In-school and summer	47	48	14	100	—	19	76	37
Out-of-school	54	44	18	98	2	25	75	39
Operation Mainstream	34	20	14	2	52	42	27	20
Public Service Careers§	65	35	16	25	14	8	25	31
Concentrated Employment Program	45	58	16	46	5	12	42	16
Job Corps	26	59	12	100	—	28	63	40
Work Incentive Program	70	45	10	18	8	19	39	100
Public Employment Program	28	26	14	30	9	3‖	26#	14

* Substantially all the remaining enrollees were white, except for 3 to 12 percent in each program who were American Indians, Eskimos, or Orientals.

† The definition of "public assistance" used for these figures varies somewhat among programs (e.g., it may or may not include recipients of food stamps and "in kind" benefits). In the NYC program, it may relate to enrollees' families as well as enrollees themselves.

‡ Includes the MDTA-OJT program, which ended with fiscal 1970 except for national contracts and the JOBS-Optional Program, which began in fiscal 1971; Construction Outreach is not included.

§ Data relate to only three of four program components.

‖ 7 years or less.

8 to 11 years.

1973, well below that of earlier years, summer youth enrollments were buoyed by the use of over $100 million in PEP funds.

Characteristics of Enrollees

New priorities in Department of Labor programs were reflected in the changed proportions of women, blacks, and young people enrolled in fiscal 1973. Overall, the programs enrolled 44 percent women, up from 40 percent the previous year and more nearly in line with the 46 percent of all unemployed workers who were women in 1972. The WIN Program was the most significant factor in the relative increase; women welfare recipients accounted for 70 percent of those served by WIN, compared with 60 percent in fiscal 1972. Young women were also more heavily represented in NYC, rising from 43 to 47 percent of enrollees in the in-school and summer program and from 50 to 54 percent in the out-of-school program. (See Table 3.)

The percentage of blacks enrolled in all programs slipped from 45 to 40 percent between fiscal 1972 and 1973. However, this minority was still enrolled in twice the proportions they constitute of all unemployed workers. Their per-

centages were off modestly in most programs, substantially in JOBS and other OJT, and sharply (from 45 to 35 percent) in the relatively small PCS Program. However, they gained appreciably among WIN participants (up from 36 to 45 percent) and slightly in NYC out-of-school, Operation Mainstream, and PEP.

New enrollments of Spanish-speaking individuals numbered more than 200,000 in fiscal 1973. They were fairly evenly represented among programs, ranging only from 10 percent of the enrollees in institutional training and in WIN to 18 percent among NYC out-of-school participants. Overall, they accounted for 13 in every 100 enrollees as they had in fiscal 1972, considerably above their proportion of all the unemployed.[6]

With smaller enrollment totals posted for NYC and a downturn in Job Corps enrollments, young people under 22 years of age accounted for a much smaller percentage of all program enrollments in fiscal 1973 than during the previous

[6] Unemployment data are not regularly collected for this group. However, they comprise only about 5 percent of the population and, with relatively low labor force participation rates, probably account for an even smaller proportion of total unemployment, despite an above-average unemployment *rate*.

year. Whereas they had been 68 percent of the total, they were only 60 percent—still well above their 38-percent share of total unemployment.

Despite such changing patterns, the programs, for the most part, continued to focus on a poor population, one that is seriously handicapped in finding jobs. In addition to the welfare recipients newly enrolled in WIN, more than a third of NYC enrollees were from welfare families, as were 40 percent of Job Corps enrollees. Only in on-the-job training activities were as few as 1 in 10 enrollees on public assistance. Altogether, 85 percent of all enrollees met Department of Labor criteria characterizing them as "disadvantaged."[7]

Several programs included sizable proportions of enrollees who had only eight or fewer years of schooling (over two-fifths in Operation Mainstream, a fourth or more in NYC out-of-school and Jobs Corps, and nearly a fifth in WIN). High school dropouts accounted for sizable majorities of enrollees in youth programs (NYC out-of-school, 75 percent, and Job Corps, 63 percent) and for proportions varying from 25 to 42 percent in all other programs. On the other hand, programs not targeted exclusively to the disadvantaged—institutional training, on-the-job training, PSC, and PEP—had a majority of high school graduates on their rolls, ranging up to 71 percent in PEP. (However, it is worth noting that repeated testing in research and development projects has shown that academic achievement for disadvantaged manpower program enrollees consistently lags several years behind the number of years of formal schooling completed.)

Postprogram Experience

Partly because of steady expansion in overall employment, fiscal 1973 saw a substantial increase in the job placement rate of persons leaving manpower programs which have the primary purpose of imparting new or improved occupational skills.

The overall proportion of terminees from seven programs who found jobs rose to 62 percent, from 52 percent in the preceding year; the number of both terminations and former enrollees employed decreased, but the former fell sharply, the latter only moderately.

A program which registered strong perform-

[7] For manpower program purposes, a disadvantaged person is a poor person who does not have suitable employment and who is either (1) a school dropout, (2) a member of a minority group, (3) under 22 years of age, (4) 45 years of age or over, or (5) handicapped. Members of families receiving cash welfare payments are deemed poor for purposes of this definition.

ance gains was CEP. As a result of a small decline in terminations and an increase in the number of enrollees who obtained jobs in the posttraining period, the placement rate for fiscal 1973 was 65 percent, 20 percentage points ahead of 1972. With the exception of state and nationally administered OJT under the MDTA, all programs showed some improvement in postprogram employment. The placement rate for JOP remained stable at 55 percent, while the rate in the nationally administered OJT program slipped slightly from 80 to 78 percent—still a rate equaled only by Job Corps .

Data on average hourly earnings in postprogram jobs, available for only four programs for both fiscal 1972 and 1973, show an upward movement. The general rise in wage levels was undoubtedly a factor, and shifts in the occupational composition and geographic distribution of the training courses or in the characteristics of trainees may also have contributed.

Increases in average hourly earnings between the two years ranged from $1.05 for former enrollees in national OJT projects down to only $0.09 for trainees who got jobs after going through CEP and $0.07 for those who had been in PEP. OJT completers were earning $4.21 an hour, while those placed following PEP participation had average hourly earnings of $3.46 and those from CEP, which serves enrollees with multiple job problems, $2.33 per hour. Former classroom trainees, with an intermediate average increase of $0.27 an hour, were earning $2.76 per hour in their posttraining jobs. Data for 1973 show that former enrollees in the upgrade component of JOP were paid an average of $3.15 per hour and those in the entry component, $2.56 per hour in the postprogram period.

Men earned consistently more than women who completed the same program during fiscal 1973. The largest differential was $1.80 an hour, reported for the national OJT program; however, women are present in this program in relatively small numbers. The smallest differential, $0.43, showed up in PEP. Moreover, the earnings range among the programs was narrower for women than for men. There was a $2.00 difference between the average hourly earnings of men completing OJT ($4.54) and of those from CEP ($2.54), while women's earnings ranged only from $3.14 for those who had been in PEP to $2.06 for CEP completers, a difference of $1.08.

Whites tended to earn more than either blacks or Spanish-speaking Americans. Only in CEP did both black and Spanish-speaking trainees secure somewhat higher paying jobs than whites. In fiscal 1973, the Spanish speaking outdistanced blacks but lagged behind whites in both the institutional and the OJT programs. On the other hand, in both components of the JOP program and in PEP, blacks had higher hourly postprogram earnings than Spanish-speaking Americans.

NATIONAL PROGRAMS FOR SPECIAL GROUPS

All manpower programs administered from the national office were reappraised in 1973 in the course of planning for an orderly transition to decentralization. As the new legislation recognizes, nationally designed and administered programs will continue to provide the most appropriate responses to the problems of some special groups. Moreover, a federal capability must be maintained to deal with the occasional disruptions in employment patterns which arise from such natural disasters as 1972's Hurricane Agnes or which may occur in some areas as a result of the current energy shortage. Two ongoing programs, for farm migrants and criminal offenders, are briefly described in this section, and a special effort for unemployed engineers, scientists, and technicians undertaken in 1971–73 is reviewed and evaluated. In addition, wide-ranging activities on behalf of Vietnam-era veterans are discussed.

Migrant and Seasonal Farmworkers

Conducted by the Department of Labor since 1971, the pilot National Migrant Worker Program marshals the resources of a number of agencies to give support services to migratory farmworkers. Individual projects have helped such workers (and their families) who want to leave the migratory stream for more stable, year-round employment. During fiscal 1973, about $6 million was obligated for ongoing projects in Indiana, Utah, Idaho, Wisconsin, and Ohio and for new projects in California, Texas, and Illinois. Projects were also operating in four other states using unexpended funds from the previous year. Over 3,800 persons were enrolled during fiscal 1973.

The Office of Economic Opportunity initiated migrant and seasonal farmworker programs in 1965.[8] With their transfer to the Department of Labor in August 1973, the Department's attempts to relieve the serious poverty and multiple employment problems of seasonal farmworkers assumed new dimensions. A total of $42.5 million

is authorized for the programs in 33 states in the current fiscal year, and a task force is now reassessing the Department's responsibilities to the estimated 4 million people (workers and families)[9] who derive the majority of their income from seasonal agricultural labor.

Under the CETA, the Secretary of Labor will reserve nearly $53 million in fiscal 1975 for programs addressed to the problems of this group, since the Congress found that "chronic seasonal unemployment and underemployment in the agricultural industry . . . constitute a substantial portion of the nation's rural manpower problem and . . . affect the entire national economy." The legislation includes a formula for determining the proportion of CETA resources to be expended on programs for migrant and seasonal farmworkers and directs that the activities may include, but are not limited to, the comprehensive services spelled out in title I.

In the interim, while planning for implementing the new legislation goes forward, the family approach and broad-scale services provided by the former OEO program are being maintained. Those services include day care, high school equivalency instruction, self-help housing, and emergency food, medical, and legal services, in addition to manpower efforts. For the time being, guidelines and regulations formulated by OEO will continue to govern the operations of grantees who provide services in the transferred programs. The majority of these sponsors are private nonprofit agencies controlled by boards comprised mostly of farmworkers. Others are institutions of higher learning and public agencies.

Two evaluation studies in progress (one focusing on the National Migrant Worker Program and one on the former OEO activities) should help in determining future program directions. In seeking a more coordinated and comprehensive approach to the needs of farmworkers, those responsible for mapping plans will observe two guidelines: equitable distribution of available resources according to the geographic locations of farm populations and concentration of resources in the most effective program areas.

Correctional Programs

Since passage of the Manpower Development and Training Act, the Departments of Labor; Health, Education, and Welfare; and Justice have conducted research on the employment problems

---

[8] Funded under title III of the Economic Opportunity Act.

[9] The number of workers in this group is estimated at slightly over 1 million, of whom 180,000 are in the migratory stream.

of the approximately 3 million persons who pass through the criminal justice system in the course of a year. Program models aimed at job rehabilitation have been developed and tested by these agencies, which have then turned them over to state and local sponsorship more and more frequently in recent years—a trend which is likely to be sustained as states and localities gain increased control over manpower resources.[10]

Many of the correctional manpower initiatives developed by the Department of Labor with nationally administered funding are now supported wholly or partly by other resources. For example, experimental models of coordinated job placement services for ex-prisoners have been adopted by Pennsylvania, Oklahoma, Georgia, Massachusetts, and Arizona. The models involve the creation of "correctional desks" in state employment security agencies and in metropolitan area public employment offices to coordinate the efforts of counselors, job developers, and community aides in working with inmates and those recently released.

Pretrial intervention is taking a similar course. Two demonstration projects which pioneered in the area of providing manpower services to young first-time offenders before their trials have been taken over and expanded by local sponsors. Most of the nine additional pretrial intervention projects supported by the Department of Labor also have favorable prospects for local funding.

Many of the skill-training projects for inmates previously funded through the national MDTA account are now receiving full state and local backing. Others are being continued under regional office supervision with funding variously drawn from the MDTA state-apportioned and national accounts. Efforts are also underway to obtain state and local sponsorship for nationally supported special projects involving Spanish-speaking offenders in Colorado and New Mexico.

Fidelity bonding for workers with police records is the most decentralized of the services currently available to offenders. The Federal Bonding Program is now available in each of more than 2,200 local public employment offices. Although the number of people bonded has been small (about 4,300), bonding has been the key to finding a job for them.

Evaluations of previous correctional manpower activities and the imperatives of an era of decentralization have encouraged increased attention

to program coordination in the states and localities. Comprehensive manpower programs for offenders are now functioning in Florida, Illinois, Maryland, Michigan, New Jersey, North Carolina, South Carolina, and Texas under the supervision of the respective governors. These states are in the process of examining the diverse needs of their criminal justice systems and of developing innovative demonstration projects. Although their endeavors vary somewhat, each is attempting to bring together the services of all existing offender programs, whether sponsored by public or private agencies, and to foster institutional change in the criminal justice system itself. Under planning grants from the Department of Labor, the eight states have prepared detailed assessments of the need for manpower and related services by all groups in the offender population. The approach has the potential of achieving better use of state work-training and release laws and modification of state personnel systems to allow hiring of ex-inmates.

Additional efforts to increase the effectiveness of the correctional manpower program in the past year have included the development by the Department of Labor of new program models for special groups of offenders—drug addicts, youth, older workers, the Spanish-speaking, women, and welfare recipients.

Technology Mobilization and Reemployment Program

After substantially meeting its objective, a 2-year special effort to mitigate the employment problems of specialized technical personnel who lost their jobs as a result of the 1971 downturn in the aerospace and other defense-related industries ended in June 1973. At a cost of about $28 million (considerably less than the $42 million initially allotted for the program), the Technology Mobilization and Reemployment Program (TMRP) helped many engineers, scientists, and technicians to become reemployed. During the life of the program, more than 53,000 unemployed individuals registered with state ES agencies for TMRP services, including interviewing, counseling, and referral to jobs. About 34,000 of them were known to be reemployed when the TMRP ended.[11]

---

[10] For a more complete description of these programs, see the *1973 Manpower Report*, pp. 39–40; the *1972 Manpower Report*, pp. 70–72; and the *1971 Manpower Report*, pp. 54–58.

[11] No estimate is available of the dimensions of unemployment among engineers, scientists, and technicians during this period. The unemployment *rate* for engineers alone was back to a characteristically low 0.8 percent early in 1973 after reaching 3.7 percent 2 years earlier. A mid-1971 study by the National Science Foundation had reported an unemployment rate of 6.8 percent for

A majority (59 percent) of the registrants were engineers; 5 percent were scientists, and the remainder technicians. For the most part (75 percent), they were 35 years of age or older, and nearly half (44 percent) were 45 or over. Practically all had some post-high school education or training and three-fourths held at least a bachelor's degree. Most (82 percent) earned $10,000 or more in their aerospace or defense jobs, with about a third at the $15,000 level or higher. As jobseekers, they had both advantages and disadvantages—the advantages of education and experience and the disadvantages of being, in the eyes of many employers, beyond the age preferred for new hires and too likely to be recalled to aerospace employment. Much of the TMRP effort was therefore devoted to combating age discrimination and to increasing the interindustry mobility of aerospace/defense workers. To accomplish this, several approaches were employed.

Job promotion and development units were established in local public employment offices in 23 areas with serious unemployment problems for defense and aerospace workers. (The list of locations includes names long associated with aerospace and defense such as San Diego, Cape Kennedy, Seattle, Wichita, and Huntsville, Ala.) In addition, all states were allotted funds to appoint a specialist to handle requests from local offices for relocation assistance, job search grants, and retraining for TMRP registrants. Job search grants (averaging approximately $190) were provided for 4,900 persons to explore specific job openings away from their home areas, and relocation grants (averaging about $620) given to over 2,000 registrants. These alternatives were especially useful in hard-hit, single industry areas.

Training (both on-the-job and short-term institutional) was used as a means of accelerating reemployment of 4,500 registrants. OJT (at an average cost of $1,165 per participant) influenced employers to hire applicants, especially those in the upper age group, whom they would not otherwise have considered. And many of the short courses which emphasized skill conversion (at an average cost of $1,785 per enrollee) were tailored to industries and occupations offering ready reemployment for engineers. Identification of appropriate training areas was facilitated by a study conducted for the Department of Labor

by the National Society of Professional Engineers (NSPE).

Other components of the program included workshops in job finding conducted by the American Institute of Aeronautics and Astronautics; organized mutual job-finding assistance by unemployed volunteer registrants who used space and equipment supplied by state ES agencies; and the National Registry for Engineers, which predated TMRP and was maintained in California under the direction of the State Department of Human Resources Development with the cooperation of the NSPE. In addition, the National Science Foundation was commissioned to administer 1-year internships in government-sponsored laboratories for young, unemployed scientists and engineers with advanced degrees. Well over 500 of these internships were awarded.

Designed as a response to a temporary emergency, TMRP has provided a valuable experience in handling industry-specific layoffs. The program has demonstrated how a variety of manpower resources can be mobilized and concentrated to address a particular goal, and the benefits resulting from job search and relocation incentives suggest that they should continue to be available as tools for discretionary use. Studies are underway to determine their relative cost in comparison with other forms of assistance (for example, unemployment insurance benefits).

The experience also suggests the feasibility of extending to other occupational categories such TMRP innovations as making extensive use of long-distance telephone calls on behalf of individual jobseekers and supplying materials, facilities, and equipment for the use of local volunteer groups.

Priority Services for Vietnam-Era Veterans

Public agencies have continued to accord top priority in manpower services to Vietnam-era veterans, and a number of nongovernmental organizations have lent their support to the goal of easing the transition of new veterans to civilian life.[12] In a joint undertaking, the publicity campaign conducted by the Advertising Council (a private agency) for Jobs for Veterans (a public/

---

engineers in the aerospace industry. And the National Society of Professional Engineers estimated that in March 1972 there were 92,500 unemployed professional and technical workers in the aerospace/defense industry.

[12] A Vietnam-era veteran is one who served in the Armed Forces after August 4, 1964. For a detailed description of the employment problems faced by returning servicemen and the varied kinds of assistance available to them, see Sar A. Levitan and Karen Cleary, *Old Wars Remain Unfinished: The Veterans Benefit System* (Baltimore: The Johns Hopkins University Press, 1973), pp. 105–61.

private program) was prolonged in 43 areas of 25 states where unemployment rates for this group continue high. The current focus of the effort is on younger veterans and on those who are disabled.

Easing the Adjustment. The crisis of adjustment to the civilian job market appears to have eased appreciably for returning servicemen; in 1973, the 5.2 percent unemployment rate for Vietnam-era veterans approximated that of nonveteran men in the same 20- to 34-year age group. In fact, at the close of 1973 the rate for both veterans and nonveterans had dropped to about 4 percent, the lowest level in more than three years. On the average, 5.3 million Vietnam-era veterans were in the 1973 labor force, 435,000 more than in 1972. All of the increase was in employment, while average unemployment dropped below 300,000, mirroring the strong expansion in the nation's job market.

The jobless rate for younger (20- to 24-year-old) Vietnam veterans continued to outrun not only the rate for older veterans but also that for their nonveteran counterparts. At an average 8.9 percent during 1973, it exceeded the latter by 2.1 percentage points. However, near the end of the year their unemployment rate was down to 7.6 percent, compared with 6.9 percent for nonveterans in the same age group. Their numbers (1.6 million), as well as their proportion of all Vietnam-era veterans (25 percent), have been declining with the slowing of military discharges and the aging of the group in question. Discharges peaked in 1968–71.

The 1973 unemployment rate for veterans who are black or members of other minority races was 8.4 percent, nearly double the rate for white veterans but not materially different from the 8.6 percent characterizing nonveterans of the same ages and racial backgrounds. Disabled Vietnam-era veterans also have serious unemployment problems. According to the Veterans Administration, they number over 350,000, of whom an estimated 300,000 are in the labor force and may have special needs for manpower services.

The fiscal 1973 record of federal assistance to these young men[13] seeking civilian jobs and careers includes new enrollments of 525,900 in education and training under the GI bill. Of these, 270,600 were pursuing college courses and the remainder were in technical and vocational programs or in on-the-job/apprentice training. The public employment service made 395,000

---

[13] Only about 2 percent of Vietnam-era veterans are women.

placements of Vietnam-era veterans (as well as 219,000 placements of veterans of earlier periods of service) aided by the mandatory listing of job vacancies by federal contractors. . . .

Members of the National Alliance of Businessmen found jobs for 232,000 returning servicemen in private industry, and the Civil Service Commission channeled 84,100 Vietnam-era veterans into the federal service. Another 139,900 were enrolled in federally supported manpower programs.

An additional component of the "package" offered to the roughly quarter of a million servicemen who resumed their civilian roles in 1973 was the Transition Program, aimed at preparing men for civilian jobs in advance of their release. This program, which has been sponsored by private industry, the military, the Department of Labor's MDTA training program, and other federal agencies, is phasing out in fiscal 1974. However, in 1973 counseling and/or vocational training were offered to 103,900 servicemen at military installations in the United States, while others received job counseling overseas.

Overseas counseling programs to acquaint soldiers, sailors, and airmen with postdischarge opportunities for education, training, and employment assistance were continued by the Department of Labor in 1973. Counselors met with nearly 135,000 servicemen in the Far East and Europe, mostly in group sessions.

This array of activities makes up the coordinated President's Veterans Program, which was initiated in 1971. The program has been extended into fiscal 1974 with the added goals of making special efforts to help younger veterans and those who are disabled or members of minority groups. In addition, a study of the program has been undertaken by the Department of Labor. Its objective is to determine more specifically the needs of these three groups for manpower services in fiscal 1975 and to suggest appropriate approaches and program mixes for the several agencies involved.

Another program to help veterans find jobs is run by an arm of the AFL-CIO, the Human Resources Development Institute (HRDI), under a $4 million contract with the Department of Labor. For three years, HRDI has been developing jobs for the disadvantaged, serving Vietnam-era veterans (as well as welfare recipients and criminal offenders) who have few skills and little work experience to offer employers. Working through 55 offices throughout the country, the Institute placed more than 2,300 young veterans in 1973, in jobs paying an average of $3.70 an hour. Four-fifths of them were union jobs at an average of $3.79 per hour.

In addition to manpower services, income support in the form of unemployment compensation is available to ex-servicemen during the readjustment period, by virtue of their military service. In fiscal 1973, $234.5 million was paid to 246,000 veterans.

Disabled Veterans. American society feels a special responsibility for its members who were disabled in the course of their military service. Vietnam-era veterans evaluated as having a 30-percent or greater disability and who will be able to hold a job after training are eligible through the Veterans Administration for vocational rehabilitation services with a specific employment goal. Those with less than 30-percent disability may still receive training at the discretion of the VA counselor who assesses need. In fiscal 1973, 9,400 trainees entered the vocational rehabilitation program, bringing the total for the Vietnam war period to 52,000.

Of the 29,500 disabled veterans in the program during the year, 21,000 were in colleges and universities, 6,600 in trade and technical schools and special rehabilitation facilities, and 1,900 in individual on-the-job training and on-the-farm programs. Each service-disabled veteran in need of training is helped through counseling to select a future educational or vocational objective; he is given continuing assistance by a vocational rehabilitation specialist in completing his training program and securing employment.

The VA reaches many men while they are still in military or VA hospitals to begin intensive testing and counseling, as well as individualized programs of therapy and training. Additional numbers are referred by state vocational rehabilitation agencies when their veterans' eligibility is established. While other veterans in school or in training receive only the stipend to which they are entitled, disabled veterans receive full payment of expenses in addition to subsistence allowances. VA rehabilitation specialists use the job placement services of a number of public agencies—particularly the employment service, which must, by law, give top priority to disabled veterans. (In the course of discharging this responsibility, the ES is employing about 150 disabled veterans who are serving their peers under a New Careers manpower program contract.)

This year an intensive effort is being made to provide suitable and rewarding jobs for service-disabled Vietnam-era veterans who need employment assistance through a cooperative venture by the National Alliance of Businessmen, the Department of Labor, and the Veterans Administration. The VA is sending these veterans letters offering job placement and training assistance, in hopes of providing either job referrals or individually developed training plans to respondents.

THE INFORMATION BASE FOR MANPOWER PROGRAMS

Decentralization of manpower planning and program management holds the promise of better quality manpower services, more closely tailored to the clients whom programs are designed to serve. In order for that promise to be realized, the complex process of gathering, processing, and disseminating the information on which decisions are based must be strengthened. This section reviews the shifting emphases anticipated for the management information system and describes developments in the labor market information program, the backbone of state and local planning for manpower activities.

MANAGEMENT INFORMATION IN A DECENTRALIZED SYSTEM

Decentralization poses a dilemma for a management information system attempting to measure actual performance against quantified goals and objectives in order to determine the most effective allocation of resources. If the varying levels of effectiveness achieved by local sponsors are to be compared, then statistics on program activities, outcomes, and expenditures must rest on uniform data elements and definitions. Yet standardized definitions could lead to equally standardized views of target populations and program approaches, and uniform methods for data collection could lead to the imposition of uniform administrative structures. Either of these outcomes would contravene the spirit of manpower reform.

The Department of Labor's approach to management information will therefore accord first priority to local needs. Federal reporting and recordkeeping requirements must allow prime sponsors to use optional methods—while maintaining equivalent measures. Unlike reporting requirements for categorical programs, which were based on the federal "need to know," those for the new era must be accommodated to local information systems.

Because local sponsors will want to know how well programs are meeting planned objectives, and at what cost, they will maintain records on the numbers and kinds of clients enrolled, services given, and program outcomes, along with the cost of project activities. Reports flowing from these records will be submitted for federal review, which will focus on the same criteria as those used by the sponsor, although the federal concern will be with more aggregative measures than those useful for guiding local management.

Historically, the federal government has collected data on the major socioeconomic characteristics of all enrollees in manpower programs, on the services provided them, and on each individual's status when he or she left a program. Not only has this created a heavy processing burden at the national level, but project operations have been hampered by the volume of paperwork. Moreover, the results of this collection of individual records have been mixed, with the statistical reliability of data varying widely among programs. Better results have been achieved where summaries of enrollee characteristics were accepted. One future direction for management reporting thus lies in submission of summary data by prime sponsors. More detailed data would be maintained at the local level by the sponsor, in a format most convenient to him.

LABOR MARKET INFORMATION

Facts of three varieties provide the raw material for a labor market information (LMI) program: the nature and number of current and anticipated job openings; the characteristics and numbers of workers seeking jobs and those potentially available to fill the openings; and how the two come together in the worker-job matching process. Job-seekers need this information, just as employers do. So, too, do such intermediaries in the labor market process as government policymakers and planners, public and private employment services, educators, and unions. All of them have a stake in an orderly flow of accurate labor market information, packaged in a readily usable form. And since production suffers and wages are lost each day a job goes unfilled, the economy and the public at large stand to benefit from an efficient LMI system which facilitates moving individuals into the right jobs.

The kinds of information required comprise a lengthy list, including:

On the demand side: the skills required, wage rates, hiring specifications, hiring channels, and timing and location of job openings.

On the supply side: the personal characteristics, skills and experience, and wage requirements of workers and the sources they use to find jobs.

Measures to describe the labor markets in which the matching process occurs, e.g., size and characteristics of the labor force, employment, by industry and occupation; and unemployment rates.

The techniques employed must be constantly adapted and improved if the business community is to have a sound basis for planning and management decisions, if government personnel at all levels are to make the right choices in programs designed to facilitate the labor market process, and if workers are to locate and obtain jobs making maximum use of their capabilities and offering the greatest rewards.

Moreover, new kinds of information need to be added to that already gathered. For example, the measures of economic hardship and the comprehensive household budget data whose development is mandated by the new manpower legislation will, if they can be satisfactorily obtained, be valuable additions to the statistical tools employed in studying the economic health of the nation.

LMI and Decentralization

The shift to decentralized planning and operation of manpower programs clearly puts a new premium on labor market information related to states, cities, counties, and consortia of jurisdictions that may combine to coincide as nearly as possible with labor market areas. Fortunately, state employment security agencies have had long experience in obtaining and processing state and area data, especially for major areas. This experience has been drawn upon by CAMPS committees and planning councils. But much remains to be done to shape LMI activity to new uses, insure that information flows in the right channels, and refine and improve it for all its intended uses. For example, the need for data on a total community education and skill development system, of which manpower programs are a part, does not originate with local control of the programs. Rather, the opportunity to make good use of such information will be enhanced, if it can be made available to planners of comprehensive programs. In the same way, information on concentrations of demand for manpower services—in ghettos, in correctional institutions—has been useful in the past, but the greater potential for focusing local resources on such problem areas should encourage a stronger effort to obtain comprehensive, reliable local information.

The Manpower Administration has identified four objectives for meeting the data requirements of manpower revenue sharing:

Developing the better data needed for equitable distribution of funds among states and localities.

Developing local information on the number and characteristics of persons in need of manpower services.

Developing long- and short-term projections of occupational demand and supply.

Developing and testing ways for local planners, employers, workers, and intermediaries in the labor market to have access to and make use of data. Complicating the picture is the fact that the jurisdictions administering comprehensive manpower programs will not necessarily coincide with natural labor market areas, which are determined by the locations of jobs and workers' access to them.

OUTLOOK FOR MANPOWER POLICY AND PROGRAMS

In 1974, with the passage of the Comprehensive Employment and Training Act, the nation moves into a second phase of manpower program activity—one that is marked by the attempt to make manpower programs truly responsive to the problem of those they are intended to serve. The new law, developed cooperatively with the Congress on a bipartisan basis, signals a recognition that employment-related problems of low-income persons, the unemployed, and the underemployed can be identified on the national level but that manpower programs seeking to address them are unlikely to succeed if they reflect the assumption that such problems are uniformly present in each local setting.

Some federal programs are not yet amenable to the CETA approach (e.g., WIN because of its direct relation to the federal welfare laws and specific statutory constraints). In other activities, however, the new law brings freedom from over-emphasis on program procedures and the details of project administration. Now federal attention —reinforced by past experience, combined with the creative energies and broader perspectives of responsive elected officials—can be clearly focused on aiding states and localities in the identification of solutions to specific problems. The continuing federal responsibility for achieving improvements in the lives of workers and their families is thereby significantly enhanced.

CETA also encourages another essential element of improved programing: the coordination of program planning and review of non-CETA-financed manpower activity with the activities of program sponsors. It has always been apparent that many diverse groups and institutions had to work together on common problems. CAMPS was a major thrust in this direction. Now CETA greatly extends the possiblity of such cooperation by establishing State Manpower Services councils and prime sponsors planning councils on which relevant groups will be represented. It also encourages common program planning and the development of standards of evaluation that will enable program managers to compare the results of various programs.

55. Training Avoidance: Manpower Waste and Skill Shortages*

John L. Iacobelli†

There currently is much concern about the high rate of unemployment, which is a form of wasted manpower during periods of slack economic activity. A more subtle form of manpower waste affects both employed and unemployed persons who could be more productive if they were given nonuniversity training that would better qualify them for existing jobs. Industry training is a method of increasing productivity that is not given enough attention. The effects of industry training—or its avoidance—on the quality of the labor supply are vital matters for manpower policy.

Significant gaps exist in our knowledge of both the supply and demand sides of the manpower ledger. Most training takes place in private industry, where information about manpower planning, recruiting, and training is most fragmentary. Without this information, it is difficult to formulate successful government-supported manpower programs which involve industry yet do not duplicate its training efforts.[1] This article attempts to fill some of these information gaps by discussing the reactions of employers in both private industry and government to skill shortages and how they attempt to meet their manpower requirements by emphasizing either training or its avoidance.

The article is based on a broad study which was conducted in 1968, and the report was completed in January 1970.[2] In early 1966, unemployment went below 4 percent and remained there until the end of 1969. Skill shortages appeared; some previously unemployed persons obtained jobs; but this period revealed, for the first time, that economic expansion alone was insufficient to employ many disadvantaged persons.[3] This period was an ideal time to test components of our manpower system under stress to see how they responded when operating at close to full capacity while confronting the twin challenge of shortages of skilled workers and surpluses of poorly qualified persons.

The sample of 131 Greater Cleveland employers to be interviewed was selected using stratified random sampling. It closely approximates the national distribution of employers by size and percentage of total employment in major indus-

* Reprinted with permission from *Proceedings of the 24th Annual Meeting of the Industrial Relations Research Association*, pp. 262–72.

This research was supported by the Manpower Administration, U.S. Department of Labor. The interpretation and views expressed are those of the author and do not represent the official position or policy of the Department of Labor.

† John L. Iacobelli is an Associate Professor in the College of Business Administration, Cleveland State University.

[1] U.S. Department of Labor, *Manpower Report of the President*, 1967, pp. 162–63; 1968, 75–76; 1969, 94–96, 155–65; 1970, 61–64, 79–85; 1971, 50–52, 179–84. Although somewhat incomplete, much detailed information on the supply side is available for many government-supported training programs with record-keeping requirements that provide information for the Manpower Report. On the demand side, the Department of Labor began publishing rough job vacancy data in 1970. During its investigation in 1968, the Task Force on Occupational Training in Industry encountered many gaps in information on the extent, cost, and quality of ongoing occupational training.

[2] See John L. Iacobelli, *Training Programs of Private Industry in the Greater Cleveland Area*, PB 191 706 (Springfield, Va.: Clearinghouse, U.S. Department of Commerce, 1970), for a more comprehensive report on employer policies, attitudes, and practices in training regular and disadvantaged labor.

[3] There is no sharp dichotomy between disadvantaged and regular labor. There is an area where the two shade into each other, yet it is necessary to distinguish between them. Employers identify disadvantaged labor as persons who do not meet their minimum requirements for entry level jobs; therefore, this criterion was used as the bench mark.

tries including government.[4] Interviews were conducted at various management levels, ranging from the president of an establishment to the personnel director, using a lengthy structured questionnaire designed to allow ending on any of the detailed questions after the first page.

SKILL SHORTAGES

During this study there were over four establishments experiencing shortages of workers with the necessary skills for every one that was not.[5] Although individual employers experienced their greatest shortages at different skill levels (skilled, semiskilled, or unskilled) and for different types of workers within blue-collar, white-collar, managerial, or technical groups, the most frequent shortages were at the upper level of technical skills and at all levels of blue-collar workers.

Some employers were forced to initiate new training programs in order to overcome skill shortages. Other employers, especially the very large ones or those requiring very specialized skills, stated: "We get along pretty well by training our own,"[6] or "For three years there has been a shortage, but we are only mildly concerned because our company has the ability to train for our needs."[7] There tended to be less concern over skill shortages among employers with long established training programs than among employers who had new training programs or who did very little training.

But an increase in training activities was not the only reaction of employers who were concerned with the future labor supply. Some employers admitted that "we are dragging our feet on doing more training, but we are worried."[8]

Other employers tended to keep a surplus of one to three people on a shift or in a critical skill. In general, very few employers were not concerned about the future labor supply at the time of the study, even those who had not experienced any skill shortages in the past six months.

GOVERNMENT MANPOWER PROGRAMS

Given the great concern expressed by employers about the severe shortages of both skilled and unskilled labor, one would suspect that employers might be anxious to participate in government manpower training programs in an attempt to alleviate some of their manpower shortages, especially for unskilled and semiskilled labor. But the findings showed weak interest or participation in government-supported training programs by employers.

Among the group of employers who responded, 53 percent had been consulted about federal, state, or local training programs. Of those consulted, less than half were participating in any of the area manpower programs. This means that approximately 25 percent of the employers in the area were participating in a government manpower training program. The very large employers have been the main participants in government manpower training programs in the Cleveland area. The small to medium size employers were not actively participating in area manpower training programs even after they had been contacted.

Among employers who were participating in area manpower programs, participation was minimal. Most of it tended to be the hiring of some graduates of a local program. Very few employers were conducting government-related manpower training programs on their premises. Employers were not very enthusiastic about participating in government manpower training programs; they were not using the vast untapped supply of disadvantaged labor to meet their acute manpower shortages.[9]

INDUSTRY TRAINING PROGRAMS
AND RECRUITMENT

Employers also have options concerning the hiring and training of regular labor to meet their manpower needs. One of the 112 respondents admitted that his firm left all training to the union, which had its own extensive program. Training programs which they finance and con-

[4] The industry strata and their percentage of total nonagricultural employment in the Cleveland SMSA are contract construction, 4.0; manufacturing, 38.4; transportation and other public utilities, 6.2; wholesale and retail trade, 20.6; finance, insurance, and real estate, 4.7; service and miscellaneous, 14.0; and government, 11.9. The final sample of 131 employees also was almost equally divided among small, medium, and large establishments (less than 50 employees, 50 to 249, and 250 or more, respectively), in line with national patterns. Firms employing less than six were excluded, and the sample of large firms favored those with more than 350 employees.

[5] In this study, the term "skill" means any physical, mental, or technical abilities that a person must have in order to fill a job vacancy. Since this definition was most widely used by employers in this study, this was the one given to all employers who raised a question about the meaning of skill shortages.

[6] A grinding job shop with medium employment.

[7] A manufacturer of aircraft accessories and parts with large employment.

[8] Establishments with small to large employment in varied industries such as institutional food distributor to manufacturing.

[9] See also John L. Iacobelli, "A Survey of Employer Attitudes toward Training the Disadvantaged," *Monthly Labor Review*, June 1970, pp. 51–55.

duct were classified as "extensive" by 12.5 percent of the 112 respondents, "combined" by 25 percent, and "learning on the job" (LOJ) by 62.5 percent.[10] One of the objectives of this study was to see if, in the prevailing tight labor market, employers reacted to prolonged shortages of trained and qualified employees by attempting to increase their company training programs or by trying to avoid additional training with practices aimed at recruiting experienced workers.

Employers ranked the method or action which took precedence over other activities used to overcome skill shortages. Table 1 shows that employers with the three different types of training programs used quite different approaches to overcome skill shortages. The three methods used most by LOJ employers were increased recruiting through methods (f) help wanted advertising, (b) employment agencies, and (c) by "word of mouth." Method (e) increasing company training programs or activity was the fourth most popular, whereas (h₁) working overtime was the only other method used by as many as 10 percent of the LOJ companies. The 28 employers with combined programs placed greater emphasis on increased company training, although they relied as much on the same three recruiting methods as did LOJ employers. Employers with extensive programs behaved quite differently than those with the other two types of programs by concentrating on (e) increased company training and (d) recruiting through high schools, colleges, or private schools. The three recruiting methods prevalent among employers with LOJ and combined programs were not popular among employers with extensive programs, who also were most likely to use area manpower training programs.

The recruiting activities of employers with extensive programs focused on people with limited or no work experience with their newly acquired skills, whereas employers with combined and LOJ programs were recruiting from sources that emphasized experienced and currently employed workers.

Employers with extensive programs were hiring the people with the greatest potential for the future of their individual company; they were

skimming off the cream of the labor supply. By recruiting the most desirable graduates of schools and colleges, they are able to attract people with proven ability to learn who can be further developed in the company's own training program. Although most employers attempt to hire people with the greatest potential, employers with extensive programs are most likely to succeed for two reasons. First, they often pay the highest wages in the industry, either at entry levels or at upper levels for successful graduates of their training programs who stay with the company. The other reason is that they enjoy great prestige in the area because their large size and extensive training programs give the impression that talented employees can rise as high as their abilities and aspirations allow. Little is known, however, about the actual linkage between an extensive training program and a company policy of promotion from within by upgrading employees through training.

Having extensive training programs seems to influence the employer's choice of other methods to overcome manpower shortages. Items (a) through (g) suggest that employers with extensive programs tend to overcome manpower shortages by using methods that indicate a leaning toward a policy of giving training, while employers with combined and LOJ programs use methods that indicate a policy of avoiding training. In order to further test this, all methods were classified according to whether they tended toward a policy of avoiding training, giving training, or had no strong tendency toward either (mostly neutral). Table 2 shows that among the 70 employers with informal LOJ programs, training-avoidance policies outnumbered training-giving policies by almost 4 to 1; and among the 28 employers with combined programs, the ratio was almost 2 to 1. In sharp contrast, the 14 companies with extensive training programs had a reversed ratio of 1 to 2. Hence, although all three groups of employers use some training-avoidance policies, employers with extensive training programs use them much less than either of the other two groups that rely on them. Instead, they place a disproportionate emphasis upon various training-giving policies. This becomes more apparent when the use of training-giving policies by the three groups of employers is compared after adjusting for different size samples. Employers with extensive programs used training-giving policies 5 times as much as employers with LOJ programs (105 to 23) and almost twice as often as employers with combined programs (105 to 55).

---

[10] The three different types of training programs are defined as follows: (1) extensive, for very extensive training programs having formal training programs for a very wide range of positions or for most positions in the establishment, ranging from entry level jobs up to top management; (2) combined, for programs having formal training combined with learning on the job; (3) LOJ, for programs where learning informally on the job was the only type of training conducted.

TABLE 1   Ranking of Methods of Overcoming Skill Shortages, by Type of Employer Training Program

70 Employers with Informal LOJ Training

	Method	Total Number in All Ranks*	Percent† In All Ranks	Ranked Precedence of Action First	Second	Third
a	Lower job requirements	4	5.7	4.3	1.4	—
b	Actively recruit through employment agencies	20	28.6	7.1	14.3	7.1
c	Actively recruit by "word of mouth"	16	22.9	2.9	12.9	7.1
d	Actively recruit through high schools, colleges, or private schools	4	5.7	4.3	1.4	—
e	Increase company training activity	14	20.0	14.3	4.3	1.4
f	Increase "help wanted" advertising	28	40.0	27.1	5.7	7.1
g	Use area manpower programs	2	2.9	1.4	—	1.4
h_i	Contact Ohio Bureau of Employment Services	4	5.7	2.9	1.4	1.4
h_j	Work overtime	8	11.4	7.1	1.4	2.9
h_k	Display sign outside or walk-ins	4	5.7	1.4	4.3	—
h_l	Increase hours of supervisors without extra pay	3	4.3	2.9	1.4	—
h_m	Make deliberate decrease in business	1	1.4	1.4	—	—
h_n	Increase pay scale	2	2.9	2.9	—	—
h_o	Use or apply for government or civil service register	1	1.4	1.4	—	—
h_p	Pirate or recruit from other employers	2	2.9	1.4	1.4	—
h_q	Support private education for employees	2	2.9	1.4	—	1.4
h_r	Use own agency, state training center graduates, intra-company, or contact union	2	2.9	2.9	—	—
h_s	Hire for short term, use "moonlighters" for part time, or subcontract work	4	5.7	2.9	1.4	1.4
h_t	Hire at lower level and train, hire married women, or contact Bureau of Apprenticeship and Training	1	1.4	1.4	—	—
h_u	Install computer or redesign jobs	2	2.9	—	2.9	—

28 Employers with Combined Formal and LOJ Training

	Method	Total Number in All Ranks*	Percent† In All Ranks	Ranked Precedence of Action First	Second	Third
a	Lower job requirements	1	3.6	—	—	3.6
b	Actively recruit through employment agencies	9	32.1	10.7	7.1	14.3
c	Actively recruit by "word of mouth"	8	28.6	7.1	7.1	14.3
d	Actively recruit through high schools, colleges, or private schools	5	17.9	3.6	7.1	7.1
e	Increase company training activity	14	50.0	28.6	10.7	10.7
f	Increase "help wanted" advertising	11	39.3	17.9	10.7	10.7
g	Use area manpower programs	0	—	—	—	—
h_i	Contact Ohio Bureau of Employment Services	3	10.7	—	7.1	3.6
h_j	Work overtime	3	10.7	3.6	3.6	3.6
h_k	Display sign outside or walk-ins	1	3.6	3.6	—	—
h_l	Increase hours of supervisors without extra pay	1	3.6	3.6	—	—
h_m	Make deliberate decrease in business	1	3.6	3.6	—	—
h_n	Increase pay scale	2	7.1	7.1	—	—
h_o	Use or apply for government or civil service register	2	7.1	3.6	3.6	—
h_p	Pirate or recruit from other employers	1	3.6	—	—	3.6
h_q	Support private education for employees	1	3.6	—	3.6	—
h_r	Use own agency, state training center graduates, intra-company, or contact union	2	7.1	3.6	3.6	—
h_s	Hire for short term, use "moonlighters" for part time, or subcontract work	0	—	—	—	—
h_t	Hire at lower level and train, hire married women, or contact Bureau of Apprenticeship and Training	2	7.1	3.6	—	3.6
h_u	Install computer or redesign jobs	0	—	—	—	—

TABLE 1   (continued)

		14 Employers with Extensive Training			
		Total Number in All Ranks*	Percent†		
			In All Ranks	Ranked Precedence of Action		
	Method			First	Second	Third
a	Lower job requirements	1	7.1	—	—	7.1
b	Actively recruit through employment agencies	2	14.3	—	14.3	—
c	Actively recruit by "word of mouth"	1	7.1	—	7.1	—
d	Actively recruit through high schools, colleges, or private schools	7	50.0	14.3	28.6	7.1
e	Increase company training activity	12	85.7	64.3	14.3	7.1
f	Increase "help wanted" advertising	2	14.3	—	14.3	—
g	Use area manpower programs	2	14.3	—	7.1	7.1
h_i	Contact Ohio Bureau of Employment Services	1	7.1	—	7.1	—
h_j	Work overtime	2	14.3	14.3	—	—
h_k	Display sign outside or walk-ins	0	—	—	—	—
h_l	Increase hours of supervisors without extra pay	0	—	—	—	—
h_m	Make deliberate decrease in business	1	7.1	—	7.1	—
h_n	Increase pay scale	0	—	—	—	—
h_o	Use or apply for government or civil service register	1	7.1	7.1	—	—
h_p	Pirate or recruit from other employers	1	7.1	—	—	7.1
h_q	Support private education for employees	0	—	—	—	—
h_r	Use own agency, state training center graduates, intra-company, or contact union	1	7.1	7.1	—	—
h_s	Hire for short term, use "moonlighters" for part time, or subcontract work	1	7.1	—	7.1	—
h_t	Hire at lower level and train, hire married women, or contact Bureau of Apprenticeship and Training	0	—	—	—	—
h_u	Install computer or redesign jobs	0	—	—	—	—

* Number of responses exceeds number of employers because each employer could mention and rank more than one action.

† Number of responses divided by number of employers in group, not total number of responses.

Almost all of these establishments with extensive programs are very large employers. Except for one company, each had at least 1,700 employees. Included were some of the most successful companies in the United States. This group of 14 employers is not restricted to any 1 industry: 3 are highly diversified establishments, 1 is in construction, 4 in manufacturing, 3 in transportation and public utilities, 2 in government, and 1 in wholesale and retail trade. This

TABLE 2   Employer Reliance on Training-Avoidance Policies or Training-Giving Policies to Overcome Skill Shortages, by Type of Employer Training Program

| | Number of Responses* Indicating— | | | |
| | Training-Avoidance Policies† | | Training-Giving Policies‡ | |
Type of Training Program and Total Number of Employers	Actual Number	Adjusted Number§	Actual Number	Adjusted Number§
70 employers with informal LOJ training	89	89	23	23
28 employers with combined formal & LOJ training	39	97.5	22	55
14 employers with extensive training	11	55	21	105

* Number of responses exceeds number of employers, since employers could mention more than one policy.

† Policies tending mostly toward avoiding training, especially the hiring of experienced people. Includes items b, c, f, j, k, l, m, n, o, p, and s from Table 1.

‡ Policies tending mostly toward giving additional company training, especially to new entrants into the labor force. Includes items d, e, g, q, and t from Table 1.

§ Adjusted for different size of sample in each group: The actual number of responses for the 28-employer group was multiplied by 2.5 and those for the 14-employer group by 5 in order to make the totals comparable with those for the group of 70 employers.

group included less than half of the large employers, so training is not just a function of company size. It depends on other factors, especially employer attitudes about manpower.

In addition to having extensive training programs, these employers also consider manpower as a resource worthy of long term specific planning which, as was shown in another part of this manpower systems study, focuses upon individuals as the planning period lengthens.[11] Twelve of the 14 employers in this group made manpower projections for 1 to 10 years, with 9 of them doing it for 5 to 10 years. This consideration of manpower as a precious resource worthy of company development—as shown by both the planning and training practices of employers with extensive programs—is the opposite of manpower considerations by most other employers, who showed less concern about the path by which individuals acquire skills and who acted as though they could always recruit a sufficient supply of qualified labor instead of having to train workers for their company's specific job demands.

The correlation between successful establishments, extensive training programs, and manpower planning was not apparent until the research had been completed and summarized. The topic needs further research beyond the scope of this study to determine if there is a causal relationship and, if so, whether training causes success or vice-versa. However, this study does show clearly that (a) training avoidance is widespread even in a tight labor market, and (b) training is emphasized by only a small group of large employers who operate the most prestigious, exclusive, and successful business establishments.

MANPOWER POLICY RECOMMENDATIONS

The above findings are invaluable insights for improving national manpower policy. Since training avoidance is so widespread except for the few companies with extensive training programs, one component of federal manpower policy should focus on recruiting these companies to participate in government manpower programs and an industry-government training system. The JOBS program is a partial step in this direction, but a much broader approach is necessary. The federal government should maintain full employment because an extended tight labor market causes some employers to increase their training activities to overcome prolonged skill shortages. Federal financial assistance should also be available for some establishments in private industry to train regular labor because the firms with extensive training programs already do a disproportionate share of the non-university training. This federal assistance should be tied to a commitment from the employer to train an equal number of disadvantaged workers (possibly with greater financial assistance). These firms might thus be induced to become trainers for a larger share of private industry or to increase the quality of the labor force and the total supply of well-trained manpower. Better training of the regular labor force could be an easy way to increase productivity, lower labor costs, and stimulate economic growth for the American economy by making our goods and services more competitive in world markets.

Federal manpower policy must also consider periods of high unemployment over the business cycle, which require different policy measures. Job creation through federally funded public service jobs will not necessarily absorb all the unemployed nor provide sufficient training or experience for lasting employment. Therefore, federal funds should be diverted toward increased occupational training by government manpower programs in close cooperation with private industry, because the economic opportunity costs are low when workers are unemployed. This requires more precise forecasting of three- to eight-year occupational and industry trends to identify long-term growth occupations requiring training as opposed to declining occupations where training should be curtailed to minimize surpluses. These efforts need to be coordinated between private industry and all levels of government. To do this, the federal government should establish a Human Resources Commission to (1) coordinate both long-term and short-term industry-occupational forecasting and planning, and (2) to expand one of our greatest competitive advantages: a highly trained work force.

[11] See U.S. Department of Labor, *Training in Private Industry: Policies, Attitudes, and Practices of Employers in Greater Cleveland*, Manpower Research Monograph No. 22 by John L. Iacobelli, 1971. See also Herbert G. Heneman, Jr., et al., *Manpower Planning and Forecasting in the Firm: An Exploratory Probe*, PB 179 078 (Springfield, Va.: Clearinghouse, U.S. Department of Commerce, 1968).